Continental Aesthetics

BLACKWELL PHILOSOPHY ANTHOLOGIES

Each volume in this outstanding series provides an authoritative and comprehensive collection of the essential primary readings from philosophy's main fields of study. Designed to complement the *Blackwell Companions to Philosophy* series, each volume represents an unparalleled resource in its own right, and will provide the ideal platform for course use.

Continental Aesthetics
Romanticism to Postmodernism
An Anthology

Edited by

Richard Kearney and *David Rasmussen*

BLACKWELL
Publishers

Copyright © Blackwell Publishers Ltd 2001

First published 2001

2 4 6 8 10 9 7 5 3 1

Blackwell Publishers Inc.
350 Main Street
Malden, Massachusetts 02148
USA

Blackwell Publishers Ltd
108 Cowley Road
Oxford OX4 1JF
UK

Library of Congress Cataloging-in-Publication Data

Continental aesthetics: romanticism to postmodernism: an anthology / edited by Richard Kearney and David Rasmussen.
     p.   cm. — (Blackwell philosophy anthologies; 12)
  Includes bibliographical references and index.
  ISBN 0–631–21610–3 (hardcover: alk. paper) — ISBN 0–631–21611–1 (pbk.: alk. paper)
  1. Aesthetics, European. 2. Aesthetics, Modern. I. Kearney, Richard. II. Rasmussen, David M. III. Series.

BH221.E853 C66 2001
111′.85′094—dc21

                                    00–060799

British Library Cataloguing in Publication Data
A CIP catalogue record for this book is available from the British Library.

Typeset in 9 on 11 pt Ehrhardt
by Kolam Information Services Pvt Ltd, Pondicherry, India

This book is printed on acid-free paper.

Contents

Contents

Preface

An anthology of continental aesthetics is long overdue. Questions about art, beauty, the sublime, and aesthetic judgment have been an essential and abiding concern of major thinkers from Kant to the present. One of the signal features of continental thinking has been a willingness to cross boundaries and mix disciplines; hence the wide interest in continental theories of art and culture (both high and popular) in such varied disciplines as sociology, literature, romance languages, cultural studies, psychoanalysis, women's studies, psychology, music, art criticism, politics, linguistics, film studies, anthropology, and, of course, philosophy itself. The range of interdisciplinary interest does not, however, diminish the rigor and coherence of philosophical aesthetics as a discourse. An additional reason for the growing interest in aesthetics in modern times is the fact that, with the breakdown of tradition, art began to provide a context in which citizens of the new secular society could explore fundamental questions of meaning and value.

Our story begins with Kant and his monumental separation of aesthetics from morality and science. In his famous *Critique of Judgement* he established aesthetics as an independent discipline worthy of conceptual investigation in its own right. Reflective judgment became the emblematic mode of a new kind of thinking, to be distinguished from both the determinate mode of scientific reflection and the imperative demands of moral reasoning. Kant was not a romantic but he made the philosophy of romanticism possible.

Indeed, as a reading of this anthology will illustrate, Kant's formative influence extends well beyond romanticism to both modernism and postmodernism.

The term "continental" is used here in as inclusive a sense as possible. While the term sometimes assumes a sectarian guise, focusing on twentieth-century German and French thinkers, we have made a deliberate point of including several thinkers who might normally be considered ineligible – Wittgenstein, Coleridge, Bakhtin, and Freud, for example. Some may prefer the term "European," but that, in our view, would be appropriate only if this anthology also featured the major contributions to aesthetics made by a number of very significant thinkers in the Anglo-Saxon tradition. Since this volume will be followed by a companion anthology devoted to analytic theories of aesthetics, we thought it wiser and more representative of our selections to focus on the range of possibilities offered by the term "continental."

The anthology is divided into three sections: *romanticism*, from Kant and the German Idealists to Coleridge and Nietzsche; *modernism*, from Benjamin and Heidegger to the contemporary theories of Habermas and Ricoeur; and *postmodernism*, from Barthes and Lyotard to Derrida and Kristeva. Where possible we have sought to respect the integral nature of our selections, publishing full essays and chapters of individual authors. In several instances, however, it has been necessary to edit or excerpt texts in the interests of accessibility and coherence.

Special thanks are owed to Fiona Sewell and Julia Legas (sine qua non) whose profound patience, expert skill, and good humor have been essential to this project from beginning to end. We are also grateful to Jonathan Harmon, Joseph Tanke, Elizabeth Southerland, and Robert Clewis, who assisted in our initial research. A special debt of gratitude is owed to colleagues who made helpful suggestions and comments regarding the selection of texts: Steven Houlgate, Jacques Taminiaux, Robin Lindenberg, Christoph Menke, Allesandro Ferrara, Vanessa Rumble, William Richardson, Brian O'Connor, Timothy Mooney, Mark Dooley, and Simon Critchley. Finally, to the editors at Blackwell, Jeff Dean and Beth Remmes, we offer our thanks for their unfailing support.

2001

Acknowledgments

The publisher and editors wish to thank the following for permission to reprint copyright material in this book:

Adorno, Theodor, "Aesthetic Theory," from *Aesthetic Theory*, trans. C. Lenhardt, eds Gretel Adorno and Rolf Tidermann. Routledge & Kegan Paul, London, 1984. Copyright © Surhkamp Verlag, Frankfurt a. M.

Bakhtin, M. M., "Discourse in the Novel," from *The Dialogic Imagination: Four Essays*, ed. Michael Holquist, trans. Caryl Emerson and Michael Holquist. Copyright © 1981. By permission of the University of Texas Press.

Barthes, Roland, "The Death of the Author," from *Image, Music, Text*, trans. and ed. Stephen Heath. HarperCollins Publishers Ltd, London, 1977: Farrar, Straus and Giroux, LLC, New York, 1977.

Baudrillard, Jean, "Simulations," from *Simulations*, trans. Paul Foss, Paul Patton, and Philip Beitchman. Semiotext Inc., New York, 1983.

Benjamin, Walter, "The Work of Art in the Age of Mechanical Reproduction," from *Illuminations* by Walter Benjamin. Copyright © 1955 Suhrkamp Verlag, Frankfurt a. M. English translation by Harry Zohn copyright © 1968 and renewed 1996 by Harcourt, Inc. Reprinted by permission of Harcourt, Inc.

Blanchot, Maurice, "Literature One More Time," from *The Infinite Conversation*, trans. Susan Hanson. University of Minnesota Press, 1993.

Cixous, Hélène, "The Laugh of the Medusa," from *New French Feminisms*, eds Marks and de Courtivron. University of Massachusetts Press, Amherst, 1981. Originally published in *Signs*. University of Chicago Press, Chicago.

Coleridge, Samuel Taylor, "Biographia Literaria," from *Biographia Literaria* (2 vols). Menston, Yorkshire, 1971, Scholar Press.

Croce, Benedetto, "Taste and the Reproduction of Art," from *Aesthetic: As Science of Expression and General Linguistics*, trans. Douglas Ainslie. Noonday Press, 1909.

Derrida, Jacques, "Economimesis," from *Diacritics* 11 (1981), pp. 57–93. © The Johns Hopkins University Press, Baltimore.

Eco, Umberto, "Travels in Hyperreality," from *Travels in Hyperreality* by Umberto Eco. Copyright © 1983, 1976, 1973 by Gruppo Editoriale Fabbri-Bompiani, Sonzogno, Etas S.p.A. English translation by William Weaver, copyright © 1986 by Harcourt, Inc. Reprinted by permission of Harcourt, Inc.

Foucault, Michel, "This Is Not a Pipe," from *This Is Not a Pipe*, trans. and ed. James Harkness.

University of California Press, Berkeley. Copyright © 1983.

Freud, Sigmund, "Leonardo da Vinci," from *The Standard Edition of the Complete Psychological Works of Sigmund Freud*, trans. and ed. James Strachey. Hogarth Press and the Institute of Psychoanalysis, London, 1910/1968.

Gadamer, Hans-Georg, "Truth and Method," from *Truth and Method* (2nd edn, rev.). Crossroad Publishing, New York, 1989.

Habermas, Jürgen, "On Leveling the Genre Distinction between Philosophy and Literature," from *Philosophical Discourse of Modernity: Twelve Lectures*, trans. Frederick Lawrence. MIT Press, Cambridge, 1987, and Polity Press, Cambridge.

Hegel, G. W. F., "Lectures on Aesthetics," from *Lectures on Fine Art*, trans. T. M. Knox. Oxford University Press, Oxford and New York, 1975.

Heidegger, Martin, "The Origin of the Work of Art," from *Poetry, Language, Thought*. Copyright © 1971 by Martin Heidegger. Reprinted by permission of HarperCollins Publishers, Inc.

Kant, Immanuel, "The Critique of Judgement," from *The Critique of Judgement*, trans. James Creed. Clarendon Press, Oxford, 1952.

Kristeva, Julia, "The Malady of Grief: Duras," from *Black Sun* by Julia Kristeva. © 1989 Columbia University Press. Reprinted by permission of the publisher.

Lukács, György, "The Ideology of Modernism," from *The Theory of the Novel*. MIT Press, Cambridge, 1971, and Merlin Press, Woodbridge.

Lyotard, Jean-François, "Note on the Meaning of the Word 'Post' and Answering the Question 'What is Postmodernism?'," from *Innovation/ Renovation*, ed. Hassan. University of Wisconsin Press, 1983.

Marcuse, Herbert, "The Aesthetic Dimension," from *The Aesthetic Dimension*. Beacon Press, Boston, 1978.

Merleau-Ponty, Maurice, "Eye and Mind," from *The Primacy of Perception*, ed. James Edie. Northwestern University Press, 1964.

Nietzsche, Friedrich, "The Birth of Tragedy," from *The Birth of Tragedy: Out of the Spirit of Music*, trans. Shaun Whiteside. Penguin Classics, 1993. Translation copyright © Shaun Whiteside 1993.

Ricoeur, Paul, "Metaphor and the Problem of Hermeneutics," from *Hermeneutics and the Human Sciences: Essays on Language, Action and Interpretation*, trans. John Brookshire Thompson. Cambridge University Press, 1981.

Sartre, Jean-Paul, "What is Literature?," from *What is Literature and Other Essays*. Harvard University Press, Cambridge, 1988.

Schelling, Friedrich Wilhelm Joseph von, "The Philosophy of Art," from *The Philosophy of Art*, trans. Douglas W. Scott. University of Minnesota Press, 1989.

Schiller, Friedrich, "Letter of an Aesthetic Education of Man," from *On the Aesthetic Education of Man*, ed. and trans. Elizabeth M. Wilkinson and L. A. Willoughby. Clarendon Press, Oxford, 1967.

Schoepenhauer, Arthur, "The World as Will and Representation," from *The World as Will and Representation*, trans. E. F. J. Payne. Dover Publications Inc., New York, no date given.

Wittgenstein, Ludwig, "Lectures on Aesthetics," from *Lectures and Conversations on Aesthetics, Psychology, and Religious Belief*, trans. and ed. Cyril Barrett. University of California Press, Berkeley, 1966. Copyright © Basil Blackwell, Oxford, 1966.

Part I

Romanticism

Introduction

Kant's *Critique of Judgement* begins our section on romanticism. Although Kant was an Enlightenment thinker, his famous "Third Critique" made romanticism possible by separating the aesthetic from the moral and the scientific. The result was that the "Third Critique" was used to support romanticism's claim that the aesthetic was an autonomous form liberated from the scrutiny of science and the principles of morality. This selection focuses upon the most distinctive and influential part of the "Third Critique," namely the "Analytic of the Beautiful," including the four moments of the judgment of taste and elements of the "Analytic of the Sublime," which includes Kant's notion of the *sensus communis* and the concept of genius.

Schiller transforms Kant's account of aesthetic experience into an anthropological insight into human nature, conceiving beauty as "our second creatress," which offers us the "possibility of becoming human beings." Schopenhauer, influenced by both Kant and Plato, conceives of art in relationship to human will; he associates the aesthetic with both the Kantian notion of genius and the Platonic conception of ideas. Most importantly, he provides a link between Kant's appropriation of aesthetic experience as unique and Nietzsche's use of aesthetics as the basis of a critique of modern culture.

Hegel differs from Kant, Schiller, and Schopenhauer by subordinating art to the history of philosophy and culture. He simply claims that art, as both object and experience, must be understood from the perspective of history. Hence, Hegel would focus as much on the content of art as on its ideal expression. Art would vary according to the period in which it was created. Classical art would differ from romantic art because the historical experience of the ancient Greeks was essentially different from that of the modern Europeans. For Hegel, it would follow that if art was a product of human "spirit" as it developed in history, art could come to an end in modern culture, which was capable of expressing that experience in other ways.

Schelling, in contrast to Hegel, claims that art has an intimate relation to philosophy as its "other side." The philosophy of art is, he declares, "a necessary goal of the philosopher, who in art views the inner essence of his own discipline as if in a magic and symbolic mirror." Since art expresses symbolically what the philosopher approaches systematically, an approach to aesthetics would be essential for any understanding of philosophy. This was particularly the case for Schelling, who also considered himself a philosopher of religion and myth, where symbols play an equally central role.

Coleridge was to develop many of the most revolutionary insights of Schelling and the German Idealists into a fully fledged theory of literary romanticism. His *Biographia Literaria*, published in 1814, was to become the Bible of the nineteenth-century romantic movement in the English-speaking world, its influence extending well beyond Britain and Europe to include North America and many overseas colonies in Africa and Australasia. Indeed, Coleridge's canonical distinction between primary and secondary imagination was to achieve classic status, establishing the human power of creativity as a quasi-divine property of near limitless application. The primary imagination, as he puts it, is nothing less than the "repetition in the finite mind of the eternal act of creation in the infinite I AM." After Coleridge, one could say of the romantic imagination that nothing human or superhuman was alien to it.

Nietzsche's *The Birth of Tragedy* shows him as both the product of attempts to establish aesthetics as an independent phenomenon and heir to the historical contextualization of art identified with a distinctive moment in Western culture. He argued that the bringing together of the Dionysian and the Apollonian in fifth-century BCE Attic tragedy was a unique and overwhelming moment in Western history, raising "aesthetics" to a supreme status as privileged medium for the disclosure of truth. Nietzsche's discussion of the historical form in which tragedy was presented, namely the tragic chorus, linked him with an earlier claim made by Kant about the transcendental and, at the same time, allowed him to show how his predecessors were wrong (particularly Hegel) to identify romanticism with the end of aesthetics.

The Critique of Judgement

Immanuel Kant

Part I
Critique of Aesthetic Judgement

First Section
Analytic of Aesthetic Judgement

First Book
Analytic of the Beautiful

First Moment of the Judgement of Taste:[1] Moment of Quality

§ 1
The judgement of taste is aesthetic

If we wish to discern whether anything is beautiful or not, we do not refer the representation of it to the Object by means of understanding with a view to cognition, but by means of the imagination (acting perhaps in conjunction with understanding) we refer the representation to the Subject and its feeling of pleasure or displeasure. The judgement of taste, therefore, is not a cognitive judgement, and so not logical, but is aesthetic – which means that it is one whose determining ground *cannot be other than subjective*. Every reference of representations is capable of being objective, even that of sensations (in which case it signifies the real in an empirical representation). The one exception to this is the feeling of pleasure or displeasure. This denotes nothing in the object, but is a feeling which the Subject has of itself and of the manner in which it is affected by the representation.

To apprehend a regular and appropriate building with one's cognitive faculties, be the mode of representation clear or confused, is quite a different thing from being conscious of this representation with an accompanying sensation of delight. Here the representation is referred wholly to the Subject, and what is more to its feeling of life – under the name of the feeling of pleasure or displeasure – and this forms the basis of a quite separate faculty of discriminating and estimating, that contributes nothing to knowledge. All it does is to compare the given representation in the Subject with the entire faculty of representations of which the mind is conscious in the feeling of its state. Given representations in a judgement may be empirical, and so aesthetic; but the judgement which is pronounced by their means is logical, provided it refers them to the Object. Conversely, be the given representations even rational, but referred in a judgement solely to the

Subject (to its feeling), they are always to that extent aesthetic.

§ 2
The delight which determines the judgement of taste is independent of all interest.

The delight which we connect with the representation of the real existence of an object is called interest. Such a delight, therefore, always involves a reference to the faculty of desire, either as its determining ground, or else as necessarily implicated with its determining ground. Now, where the question is whether something is beautiful, we do not want to know, whether we, or any one else, are, or even could be, concerned in the real existence of the thing, but rather what estimate we form of it on mere contemplation (intuition or reflection). If any one asks me whether I consider that the palace I see before me is beautiful, I may, perhaps, reply that I do not care for things of that sort that are merely made to be gaped at. Or I may reply in the same strain as that Iroquois *sachem* who said that nothing in Paris pleased him better than the eating-houses. I may even go a step further and inveigh with the vigour of a *Rousseau* against the vanity of the great who spend the sweat of the people on such superfluous things. Or, in fine, I may quite easily persuade myself that if I found myself on an uninhabited island, without hope of ever again coming among men, and could conjure such a palace into existence by a mere wish, I should still not trouble to do so, so long as I had a hut there that was comfortable enough for me. All this may be admitted and approved; only it is not the point now at issue. All one wants to know is whether the mere representation of the object is to my liking, no matter how indifferent I may be to the real existence of the object of this representation. It is quite plain that in order to say that the object *is beautiful*, and to show that I have taste, everything turns on the meaning which I can give to this representation, and not on any factor which makes me dependent on the real existence of the object. Every one must allow that a judgement on the beautiful which is tinged with the slightest interest, is very partial and not a pure judgement of taste. One must not be in the least prepossessed in favour of the real existence of the thing, but must preserve complete indifference in this respect, in order to play the part of judge in matters of taste.

This proposition, which is of the utmost importance, cannot be better explained than by contrasting the pure disinterested[2] delight which appears in the judgement of taste with that allied to an interest – especially if we can also assure ourselves that there are no other kinds of interest beyond those presently to be mentioned.

§ 3
Delight IN THE AGREEABLE *is coupled with interest.*

That is AGREEABLE *which the senses find pleasing in sensation.* This at once affords a convenient opportunity for condemning and directing particular attention to a prevalent confusion of the double meaning of which the word 'sensation' is capable. All delight (as is said or thought) is itself sensation (of a pleasure). Consequently everything that pleases, and for the very reason that it pleases, is agreeable – and according to its different degrees, or its relations to other agreeable sensations, is attractive, charming, delicious, enjoyable, &c. But if this is conceded, then impressions of sense, which determine inclination, or principles of reason, which determine the will, or mere contemplated forms of intuition, which determine judgement, are all on a par in everything relevant to their effect upon the feeling of pleasure, for this would be agreeableness in the sensation of one's state; and since, in the last resort, all the elaborate work of our faculties must issue in and unite in the practical as its goal, we could credit our faculties with no other appreciation of things and the worth of things, than that consisting in the gratification which they promise. How this is attained is in the end immaterial; and, as the choice of the means is here the only thing that can make a difference, men might indeed blame one another for folly or imprudence, but never for baseness or wickedness; for they are all, each according to his own way of looking at things, pursuing one goal, which for each is the gratification in question.

When a modification of the feeling of pleasure or displeasure is termed sensation, this expression is given quite a different meaning to that which it bears when I call the representation of a thing (through sense as a receptivity pertaining to the faculty of knowledge) sensation. For in the latter case the representation is referred to the Object, but in the former it is referred solely to the Subject and is not available for any cognition, not even for that by which the Subject *cognizes* itself.

Now in the above definition the word sensation is used to denote an objective representation of sense; and, to avoid continually running the risk of misinterpretation, we shall call that which must always remain purely subjective, and is absolutely incapable of forming a representation of an object, by the familiar name of feeling. The green colour of the meadows belongs to *objective* sensation, as the perception of an object of sense; but its agreeableness to *subjective* sensation, by which no object is represented: i.e. to feeling, through which the object is regarded as an Object of delight (which involves no cognition of the object).

Now, that a judgement on an object by which its agreeableness is affirmed, expresses an interest in it, is evident from the fact that through sensation it provokes a desire for similar objects, consequently the delight presupposes, not the simple judgement about it, but the bearing its real existence has upon my state so far as affected by such an Object. Hence we do not merely say of the agreeable that it *pleases*, but that it *gratifies*. I do not accord it a simple approval, but inclination is aroused by it, and where agreeableness is of the liveliest type a judgement on the character of the Object is so entirely out of place, that those who are always intent only on enjoyment (for that is the word used to denote intensity of gratification) would fain dispense with all judgement.

§ 4
Delight IN THE GOOD *is coupled with interest*

That is *good* which by means of reason commends itself by its mere concept. We call that *good for something* (useful) which only pleases as a means; but that which pleases on its own account we call *good in itself*. In both cases the concept of an end is implied, and consequently the relation of reason to (at least possible) willing, and thus a delight in the *existence* of an Object or action, i.e. some interest or other.

To deem something good, I must always know what sort of a thing the object is intended to be, i.e. I must have a concept of it. That is not necessary to enable me to see beauty in a thing. Flowers, free patterns, lines aimlessly intertwining – technically termed foliage, – have no signification, depend upon no definite concept, and yet please. Delight in the beautiful must depend upon the reflection on an object precursory to some (not definitely determined) concept. It is thus also differentiated

from the agreeable, which rests entirely upon sensation.

In many cases, no doubt, the agreeable and the good seem convertible terms. Thus it is commonly said that all (especially lasting) gratification is of itself good; which is almost equivalent to saying that to be permanently agreeable and to be good are identical. But it is readily apparent that this is merely a vicious confusion of words, for the concepts appropriate to these expressions are far from interchangeable. The agreeable, which, as such, represents the object solely in relation to sense, must in the first instance be brought under principles of reason through the concept of an end, to be, as an object of will, called good. But that the reference to delight is wholly different where what gratifies is at the same time called *good*, is evident from the fact that with the good the question always is whether it is mediately or immediately good, i.e. useful or good in itself; whereas with the agreeable this point can never arise, since the word always means what pleases immediately – and it is just the same with what I call beautiful.

Even in everyday parlance a distinction is drawn between the agreeable and the good. We do not scruple to say of a dish that stimulates the palate with spices and other condiments that it is agreeable – owning all the while that it is not good: because, while it immediately *satisfies* the senses, it is mediately displeasing, i.e. in the eye of reason that looks ahead to the consequences. Even in our estimate of health this same distinction may be traced. To all that possess it, it is immediately agreeable – at least negatively, i.e. as remoteness of all bodily pains. But, if we are to say that it is good, we must further apply to reason to direct it to ends, that is, we must regard it as a state that puts us in a congenial mood for all we have to do. Finally, in respect of happiness every one believes that the greatest aggregate of the pleasures of life, taking duration as well as number into account, merits the name of a true, nay even of the highest, good. But reason sets its face against this too. Agreeableness is enjoyment. But if this is all that we are bent on, it would be foolish to be scrupulous about the means that procure it for us – whether it be obtained passively by the bounty of nature or actively and by the work of our own hands. But that there is any intrinsic worth in the real existence of a man who merely lives for *enjoyment*, however busy he may be in this respect, even when in so doing he serves others – all equally with himself intent only on enjoyment – as an excellent means to that one end, and does so, moreover, because through sympathy he shares all their gratifications, – this is a view to which reason will never let itself be brought round. Only by what a man does heedless of enjoyment, in complete freedom and independently of what he can procure passively from the hand of nature, does he give to his existence, as the real existence of a person, an absolute worth. Happiness, with all its plethora of pleasures, is far from being an unconditioned good.[3]

But, despite all this difference between the agreeable and the good, they both agree in being invariably coupled with an interest in their object. This is true, not alone of the agreeable, § 3, and of the mediately good, i.e. the useful, which pleases as a means to some pleasure, but also of that which is good absolutely and from every point of view, namely the moral good which carries with it the highest interest. For the good is the Object of will, i.e. of a rationally determined faculty of desire. But to will something, and to take a delight in its existence, i.e. to take an interest in it, are identical.

§ 5
Comparison of the three specifically different kinds of delight.

Both the Agreeable and the Good involve a reference to the faculty of desire, and are thus attended, the former with a delight pathologically conditioned (by stimuli), the latter with a pure practical delight. Such delight is determined not merely by the representation of the object, but also by the represented bond of connexion between the Subject and the real existence of the object. It is not merely the object, but also its real existence, that pleases. On the other hand the judgement of taste is simply *contemplative*, i.e. it is a judgement which is indifferent as to the existence of an object, and only decides how its character stands with the feeling of pleasure and displeasure. But not even is this contemplation itself directed to concepts; for the judgement of taste is not a cognitive judgement (neither a theoretical one nor a practical), and hence, also, is not *grounded* on concepts, nor yet *intentionally directed* to them.

The agreeable, the beautiful, and the good thus denote three different relations of representations to the feeling of pleasure and displeasure, as a feeling in respect of which we distinguish different objects or modes of representation. Also, the corresponding expressions which indicate our satisfaction in them are different. The *agreeable* is what GRATIFIES a man; the *beautiful* what simply PLEASES him; the *good* what is ESTEEMED (*approved*), i.e. that on which he sets an objective worth. Agreeableness is a significant factor even with irrational animals; beauty has purport and significance only for human beings, i.e. for beings at once animal and rational (but not merely for them as rational – intelligent beings – but only for them as at once animal and rational); whereas the good is good for every rational being in general; – a proposition which can only receive its complete justification and explanation in the sequel. Of all these three kinds of delight, that of taste in the beautiful may be said to be the one and only disinterested and *free* delight; for, with it, no interest, whether of sense or reason, extorts approval. And so we may say that delight, in the three cases mentioned, is related to *inclination*, to *favour*, or to *respect*. For FAVOUR is the only free liking. An object of inclination, and one which a law of reason imposes upon our desire, leaves us no freedom to turn anything into an object of pleasure. All interest presupposes a want, or calls one forth; and, being a ground determining approval, deprives the judgement on the object of its freedom.

So far as the interest of inclination in the case of the agreeable goes, every one says: Hunger is the best sauce; and people with a healthy appetite relish everything, so long as it is something they can eat. Such delight, consequently, gives no indication of taste having anything to say to the choice. Only when men have got all they want can we tell who among the crowd has taste or not. Similarly there may be correct habits (conduct) without virtue, politeness without good-will, propriety without honour, &c. For where the moral law dictates, there is, objectively, no room left for free choice as to what one has to do; and to show taste in the way one carries out these dictates, or in estimating the way others do so, is a totally different matter from displaying the moral frame of one's mind. For the latter involves a command and produces a need of something, whereas moral taste only plays with the objects of delight without devoting itself sincerely to any.

Definition of the beautiful derived from the first moment

Taste is the faculty of estimating an object or a mode of representation by means of a delight or aversion *apart from any interest*. The object of such a delight is called *beautiful*.

Second Moment of the Judgement of Taste: Moment of Quantity

§6

The beautiful is that which, apart from concepts, is represented as the Object of a UNIVERSAL *delight.*

This definition of the beautiful is deducible from the foregoing definition of it as an object of delight apart from any interest. For where any one is conscious that his delight in an object is with him independent of interest, it is inevitable that he should look on the object as one containing a ground of delight for all men. For, since the delight is not based on any inclination of the Subject (or on any other deliberate interest), but the Subject feels himself completely *free* in respect of the liking which he accords to the object, he can find as reason for his delight no personal conditions to which his own subjective self might alone be party. Hence he must regard it as resting on what he may also presuppose in every other person; and therefore he must believe that he has reason for demanding a similar delight from every one. Accordingly he will speak of the beautiful as if beauty were a quality of the object and the judgement logical (forming a cognition of the Object by concepts of it); although it is only aesthetic, and contains merely a reference of the representation of the object to the Subject; – because it still bears this resemblance to the logical judgement, that it may be presupposed to be valid for all men. But this universality cannot spring from concepts. For from concepts there is no transition to the feeling of pleasure or displeasure (save in the case of pure practical laws, which, however, carry an interest with them; and such an interest does not attach to the pure judgement of taste). The result is that the judgement of taste, with its attendant consciousness of detachment from all interest, must involve a claim to validity for all men, and must do so apart from universality attached to Objects, i.e. there must be coupled with it a claim to subjective universality.

§7

Comparison of the beautiful with the agreeable and the good by means of the above characteristic.

As regards the *agreeable* every one concedes that his judgement, which he bases on a private feeling, and in which he declares that an object pleases him, is restricted merely to himself personally. Thus he does not take it amiss if, when he says that Canary-wine is agreeable, another corrects the expression and reminds him that he ought to say: It is agreeable *to me.* This applies not only to the taste of the tongue, the palate, and the throat, but to what may with any one be agreeable to eye or ear. A violet colour is to one soft and lovely: to another dull and faded. One man likes the tone of wind instruments, another prefers that of string instruments. To quarrel over such points with the idea of condemning another's judgement as incorrect when it differs from our own, as if the opposition between the two judgements were logical, would be folly. With the agreeable, therefore, the axiom holds good: *Every one has his own taste* (that of sense).

The beautiful stands on quite a different footing. It would, on the contrary, be ridiculous if any one who plumed himself on his taste were to think of justifying himself by saying: This object (the building we see, the dress that person has on, the concert we hear, the poem submitted to our criticism) is beautiful *for me.* For if it merely pleases *him,* he must not call it *beautiful.* Many things may for him possess charm and agreeableness – no one cares about that; but when he puts a thing on a pedestal and calls it beautiful, he demands the same delight from others. He judges not merely for himself, but for all men, and then speaks of beauty as if it were a property of things. Thus he says the *thing* is beautiful; and it is not as if he counted on others agreeing in his judgement of liking owing to his having found them in such agreement on a number of occasions, but he *demands* this agreement of them. He blames them if they judge differently, and denies them taste, which he still requires of them as something they ought to have; and to this extent it is not open to men to say: Every one has his own taste. This would be equivalent to saying that there is no such thing at all as taste, i.e. no aesthetic judgement capable of making a rightful claim upon the assent of all men.

Yet even in the case of the agreeable we find that the estimates men form do betray a prevalent agreement among them, which leads to our crediting some with taste and denying it to others, and that, too, not as an organic sense but as a critical faculty in respect of the agreeable generally. So of one who knows how to entertain his guests with pleasures (of enjoyment through all the senses) in such a way that one and all are pleased, we say that he has taste. But the universality here is only understood in a comparative sense; and the rules that apply are, like all empirical rules, *general* only, not *universal*, – the latter being what the judgement of taste upon the beautiful deals or claims to deal in. It is a judgement in respect of sociability so far as resting on empirical rules. In respect of the good it is true that judgements also rightly assert a claim to validity for every one; but the good is only represented as an Object of universal delight *by means of a concept*, which is the case neither with the agreeable nor the beautiful.

§8
In a judgement of taste the universality of delight is only represented as subjective.

This particular form of the universality of an aesthetic judgement, which is to be met with in a judgement of taste, is a significant feature, not for the logician certainly, but for the transcendental philosopher. It calls for no small effort on his part to discover its origin, but in return it brings to light a property of our cognitive faculty which, without this analysis, would have remained unknown.

First, one must get firmly into one's mind that by the judgement of taste (upon the beautiful) the delight in an object is imputed to *every one*, yet without being founded on a concept (for then it would be the good), and that this claim to universality is such an essential factor of a judgement by which we describe anything as *beautiful*, that were it not for its being present to the mind it would never enter into any one's head to use this expression, but everything that pleased without a concept would be ranked as agreeable. For in respect of the agreeable every one is allowed to have his own opinion, and no one insists upon others agreeing with his judgement of taste, which is what is invariably done in the judgement of taste about beauty. The first of these I may call the taste of sense, the second, the taste of reflection: the first laying down judgements merely private, the second, on the other hand, judgements ostensibly of general validity (public), but both alike being aesthetic (not practical) judgements about an object merely in respect of the bearings of its representation on the feeling of pleasure or displeasure. Now it does seem strange that while with the taste of sense it is not alone experience that shows that its judgement (of pleasure or displeasure in something) is not universally valid, but every one willingly refrains from imputing this agreement to others (despite the frequent actual prevalence of a considerable consensus of general opinion even in these judgements), the taste of reflection, which, as experience teaches, has often enough to put up with a rude dismissal of its claims to universal validity of its judgement (upon the beautiful), can (as it actually does) find it possible for all that, to formulate judgements capable of demanding this agreement in its universality. Such agreement it does in fact require from every one for each of its judgements of taste, – the persons who pass these judgements not quarrelling over the possibility of such a claim, but only failing in particular cases to come to terms as to the correct application of this faculty.

First of all we have here to note that a universality which does not rest upon concepts of the Object (even though these are only empirical) is in no way logical, but aesthetic, i.e. does not involve any objective quantity of the judgement, but only one that is subjective. For this universality I use the expression *general validity*, which denotes the validity of the reference of a representation, not to the cognitive faculties, but to the feeling of pleasure or displeasure for every Subject. (The same expression, however, may also be employed for the logical quantity of the judgement, provided we add *objective* universal validity, to distinguish it from the merely subjective validity which is always aesthetic.)

Now a judgement that has *objective universal validity* has always got the subjective also, i.e. if the judgement is valid for everything which is contained under a given concept, it is valid also for all who represent an object by means of this concept. But from a *subjective universal validity*, i.e. the aesthetic, that does not rest on any concept, no conclusion can be drawn to the logical; because judgements of that kind have no bearing upon the Object. But for this very reason the aesthetic universality attributed to a judgement must also be of a special kind, seeing that it does not join the predicate of beauty to the concept of the *Object* taken in its entire logical sphere, and yet does extend this predicate over the whole sphere of *judging Subjects*.

In their logical quantity all judgements of taste are *singular* judgements. For, since I must present the object immediately to my feeling of pleasure or displeasure, and that, too, without the aid of concepts, such judgements cannot have the quantity of judgements with objective general validity. Yet by taking the singular representation of the Object of the judgement of taste, and by comparison converting it into a concept according to the conditions determining that judgement, we can arrive at a logically universal judgement. For instance, by a judgement of taste I describe the rose at which I am looking as beautiful. The judgement, on the other hand, resulting from the comparison of a number of singular representations: Roses in general are beautiful, is no longer pronounced as a purely aesthetic judgement, but as a logical judgement founded on one that is aesthetic. Now the judgement, 'The rose is agreeable' (to smell) is also, no doubt, an aesthetic and singular judgement, but then it is not one of taste but of sense. For it has this point of difference from a judgement of taste, that the latter imports an *aesthetic quantity* of universality, i.e. of validity for every one which is not to be met with in a judgement upon the agreeable. It is only judgements upon the good which, while also determining the delight in an object, possess logical and not mere aesthetic universality; for it is as involving a cognition of the Object that they are valid of it, and on that account valid for every one.

In forming an estimate of Objects merely from concepts, all representation of beauty goes by the board. There can, therefore, be no rule according to which any one is to be compelled to recognize anything as beautiful. Whether a dress, a house, or a flower is beautiful is a matter upon which one declines to allow one's judgement to be swayed by any reasons or principles. We want to get a look at the Object with our own eyes, just as if our delight depended on sensation. And yet, if upon so doing, we call the object beautiful, we believe ourselves to be speaking with a universal voice, and lay claim to the concurrence of every one, whereas no private sensation would be decisive except for the observer alone and *his* liking.

Here, now, we may perceive that nothing is postulated in the judgement of taste but such a *universal voice* in respect of delight that is not mediated by concepts; consequently, only the *possibility* of an aesthetic judgement capable of being at the same time deemed valid for every one. The judgement of taste itself does not *postulate* the agreement of every one (for it is only competent for a logically universal judgement to do this, in that it is able to bring forward reasons); it only *imputes* this agreement to every one, as an instance of the rule in respect of which it looks for confirmation, not from concepts, but from the concurrence of others. The universal voice is, therefore, only an idea – resting upon grounds the investigation of which is here postponed. It may be a matter of uncertainty whether a person who thinks he is laying down a judgement of taste is, in fact, judging in conformity with that idea; but that this idea is what is contemplated in his judgement, and that, consequently, it is meant to be a judgement of taste, is proclaimed by his use of the expression 'beauty'. For himself he can be certain on the point from his mere consciousness of the separation of everything belonging to the agreeable and the good from the delight remaining to him; and this is all for which he promises himself the agreement of every one – a claim which, under these conditions, he would also be warranted in making, were it not that he frequently sinned against them, and thus passed an erroneous judgement of taste.

§ 9

Investigation of the question of the relative priority in a judgement of taste of the feeling of pleasure and the estimating of the object.

The solution of this problem is the key to the Critique of taste, and so is worthy of all attention.

Were the pleasure in a given object to be the antecedent, and were the universal communicability of this pleasure to be all that the judgement of taste is meant to allow to the representation of the object, such a sequence would be self-contradictory. For a pleasure of that kind would be nothing but the feeling of mere agreeableness to the senses, and so, from its very nature, would possess no more than private validity, seeing that it would be immediately dependent on the representation through which the object *is given*.

Hence it is the universal capacity for being communicated incident to the mental state in the given representation which, as the subjective condition of the judgement of taste, must be fundamental, with the pleasure in the object as its consequent. Nothing, however, is capable of being universally communicated but cognition and representation so far as appurtenant to cognition. For it is only as thus appurtenant that the representation is objective, and it is this alone that gives it a universal point of reference with which the power of representation of every one is obliged to harmonize. If, then, the determining ground of the judgement as to this universal communicability of the representation is to be merely subjective, that is to say, is to be conceived independently of any concept of the object, it can be nothing else than the mental state that presents itself in the mutual relation of the powers of representation so far as they refer a given representation *to cognition in general.*

The cognitive powers brought into play by this representation are here engaged in a free play, since no definite concept restricts them to a particular rule of cognition. Hence the mental state in this representation must be one of a feeling of the free play of the powers of representation in a given representation for a cognition in general. Now a representation, whereby an object is given, involves, in order that it may become a source of cognition at all, *imagination* for bringing together the manifold of intuition, and *understanding* for the unity of the concept uniting the representations. This state of *free play* of the cognitive faculties attending a representation by which an object is given must admit of universal communication: because cognition, as a definition of the Object with which given representations (in any Subject whatever) are to accord, is the one and only representation which is valid for every one.

As the subjective universal communicability of the mode of representation in a judgement of taste is to subsist apart from the presupposition of any definite concept, it can be nothing else than the mental state present in the free play of imagination and understanding (so far as these are in mutual accord, as is requisite for *cognition in general*): for we are conscious that this subjective relation suitable for a cognition in general must be just as valid for every one, and consequently as universally communicable, as is any determinate cognition, which always rests upon that relation as its subjective condition.

Now this purely subjective (aesthetic) estimating of the object, or of the representation through which it is given, is antecedent to the pleasure in it, and is the basis of this pleasure in the harmony of the cognitive faculties. Again, the above-described universality of the subjective conditions of estimating objects forms the sole foundation of this universal subjective validity of the delight which we connect with the representation of the object that we call beautiful.

That an ability to communicate one's mental state, even though it be only in respect of our cognitive faculties, is attended with a pleasure, is a fact which might easily be demonstrated from the natural propensity of mankind to social life, i.e.

empirically and psychologically. But what we have here in view calls for something more than this. In a judgement of taste the pleasure felt by us is exacted from every one else as necessary, just as if, when we call something beautiful, beauty was to be regarded as a quality of the object forming part of its inherent determination according to concepts; although beauty is for itself, apart from any reference to the feeling of the Subject, nothing. But the discussion of this question must be reserved until we have answered the further one of whether, and how, aesthetic judgements are possible *a priori*.

At present we are exercised with the lesser question of the way in which we become conscious, in a judgement of taste, of a reciprocal subjective common accord of the powers of cognition. Is it aesthetically by sensation and our mere internal sense? Or is it intellectually by consciousness of our intentional activity in bringing these powers into play?

Now if the given representation occasioning the judgement of taste were a concept which united understanding and imagination in the estimate of the object so as to give a cognition of the Object, the consciousness of this relation would be intellectual (as in the objective schematism of judgement dealt with in the Critique). But, then, in that case the judgement would not be laid down with respect to pleasure and displeasure, and so would not be a judgement of taste. But, now, the judgement of taste determines the Object, independently of concepts, in respect of delight and of the predicate of beauty. There is, therefore, no other way for the subjective unity of the relation in question to make itself known than by sensation. The quickening of both faculties (imagination and understanding) to an indefinite, but yet, thanks to the given representation, harmonious activity, such as belongs to cognition generally, is the sensation whose universal communicability is postulated by the judgement of taste. An objective relation can, of course, only be thought, yet in so far as, in respect of its conditions, it is subjective, it may be felt in its effect upon the mind, and, in the case of a relation (like that of the powers of representation to a faculty of cognition generally) which does not rest on any concept, no other consciousness of it is possible beyond that through sensation of its effect upon the mind – an effect consisting in the more facile play of both mental powers (imagination and understanding) as quickened by their mutual accord. A representation which is singular and independent of comparison with other representations, and, being such, yet accords with the conditions of the universality that is the general concern of understanding, is one that brings the cognitive faculties into that proportionate accord which we require for all cognition and which we therefore deem valid for every one who is so constituted as to judge by means of understanding and sense conjointly (i.e. for every man).

Definition of the beautiful drawn from the second moment

The *beautiful* is that which, apart from a concept, pleases universally.

Third Moment of Judgements of Taste: Moment of the *Relation* of the Ends Brought Under Review in Such Judgements

§ 10
Finality in general.

Let us define the meaning of 'an end' in transcendental terms (i.e. without presupposing anything empirical, such as the feeling of pleasure). An end is the object of a concept so far as this concept is regarded as the cause of the object (the real ground of its possibility); and the causality of a *concept* in respect of its *Object* is finality (*forma finalis*). Where, then, not the cognition of an object merely, but the object itself (its form or real existence) as an effect, is thought to be possible only through a concept of it, there we imagine an end. The representation of the effect is here the determining ground of its cause and takes the lead of it. The consciousness of the causality of a representation in respect of the state of the Subject as one tending *to preserve a continuance* of that state, may here be said to denote in a general way what is called pleasure; whereas displeasure is that representation which contains the ground for converting the state of the representations into their opposite (for hindering or removing them).

The faculty of desire, so far as determinable only through concepts, i.e. so as to act in conformity with the representation of an end, would be the will. But an Object, or state of mind, or even an action may, although its possibility does not necessarily presuppose the representation of an end, be called final simply on account of its possibility being only explicable and intelligible for us by virtue of an assumption on our part of a fundamental causality according to ends, i.e. a will that would have so ordained it according to a certain represented rule. Finality, therefore, may exist apart from an end, in so far as we do not locate the causes of this form in a will, but yet are able to render the explanation of its possibility intelligible to ourselves only by deriving it from a will. Now we are not always obliged to look with the eye of reason into what we observe (i.e. to consider it in its possibility). So we may at least observe a finality of form, and trace it in objects – though by reflection only – without resting it on an end (as the material of the *nexus finalis*).

§ 11
The sole foundation of the judgement of taste is the FORM *of* FINALITY *of an object (or mode of representing it).*

Whenever an end is regarded as a source of delight it always imports an interest as determining ground of the judgement on the object of pleasure. Hence the judgement of taste cannot rest on any subjective end as its ground. But neither can any representation of an objective end, i.e. of the possibility of the object itself on principles of final connexion, determine the judgement of taste, and, consequently, neither can any concept of the good. For the judgement of taste is an aesthetic and not a cognitive judgement, and so does not deal with any *concept* of the nature or of the internal or external possibility, by this or that cause, of the object, but simply with the relative bearing of the representative powers so far as determined by a representation.

Now this relation, present when an object is characterized as beautiful, is coupled with the feeling of pleasure. This pleasure is by the judgement of taste pronounced valid for every one; hence an agreeableness attending the representation is just as incapable of containing the determining ground of the judgement as the representation of the perfection of the object or the concept of the good. We are thus left with the subjective finality in the representation of an object, exclusive of any end (objective or subjective) – consequently the bare form of finality in the representation whereby an object is *given* to us, so far as we are conscious of it – as that which is alone capable of constituting the delight which, apart from any concept, we estimate as universally communicable, and so of forming the determining ground of the judgement of taste.

§ 12
The judgement of taste rests upon a priori *grounds.*

To determine *a priori* the connexion of the feeling of pleasure or displeasure as an effect, with some representation or other (sensation or concept) as its cause, is utterly impossible; for that would be a causal relation which, (with objects of experience,) is always one that can only be cognized *a posteriori* and with the help of experience. True, in the Critique of Practical Reason we did actually derive *a priori* from universal moral concepts the feeling of respect (as a particular and peculiar modification of this feeling which does not strictly answer either to the pleasure or displeasure which we receive from empirical objects). But there we were further able to cross the border of experience and call in aid a causality resting on a supersensible attribute of the Subject, namely that of freedom. But even there it was not this *feeling* exactly that we deduced from the idea of the moral as cause, but from this was derived simply the determination of the will. But the mental state present in the determination of the will by any means is at once in itself a feeling of pleasure and identical with it, and so does not issue from it as an effect. Such an effect must only be assumed where the concept of the moral as a good precedes the determination of the will by the law; for in that case it would be futile to derive the pleasure combined with the concept from this concept as a mere cognition.

Now the pleasure in aesthetic judgements stands on a similar footing: only that here it is merely contemplative and does not bring about an interest in the Object; whereas in the moral judgement it is practical. The consciousness of mere formal finality in the play of the cognitive faculties of the Subject attending a representation whereby an object is given, is the pleasure itself, because it involves a determining ground of the Subject's activity in respect of the quickening of its cognitive powers, and thus an internal causality (which is final) in respect of cognition generally, but without being limited to a definite cognition, and consequently a mere form of the subjective finality of a representation in an aesthetic judgement. This pleasure is also in no way practical, neither resembling that from the pathological ground of agreeableness nor that from the intellectual ground of the represented good. But still it

involves an inherent causality, that, namely, of *preserving a continuance* of the state of the representation itself and the active engagement of the cognitive powers without ulterior aim. We *dwell* on the contemplation of the beautiful because this contemplation strengthens and reproduces itself. The case is analogous (but analogous only) to the way we linger on a charm in the representation of an object which keeps arresting the attention, the mind all the while remaining passive.

§ 13
The pure judgement of taste is independent of charm and emotion.

Every interest vitiates the judgement of taste and robs it of its impartiality. This is especially so where instead of, like the interest of reason, making finality take the lead of the feeling of pleasure, it grounds it upon this feeling – which is what always happens in aesthetic judgements upon anything so far as it gratifies or pains. Hence judgements so influenced can either lay no claim at all to a universally valid delight, or else must abate their claim in proportion as sensations of the kind in question enter into the determining grounds of taste. Taste that requires an added element of *charm* and *emotion* for its delight, not to speak of adopting this as the measure of its approval, has not yet emerged from barbarism.

And yet charms are frequently not alone ranked with beauty (which ought properly to be a question merely of the form) as supplementary to the aesthetic universal delight, but they have been accredited as intrinsic beauties, and consequently the matter of delight passed off for the form. This is a misconception which, like many others that have still an underlying element of truth, may be removed by a careful definition of these concepts.

A judgement of taste which is uninfluenced by charm or emotion, (though these may be associated with the delight in the beautiful,) and whose determining ground, therefore, is simply finality of form, is *a pure judgement of taste.*

§ 14
Exemplification.

Aesthetic, just like theoretical (logical) judgements, are divisible into empirical and pure. The first are those by which agreeableness or disagreeableness, the second those by which beauty, is predicated of an object or its mode of representation. The former are judgements of sense (material aesthetic judgements), the latter (as formal) alone judgements of taste proper.

A judgement of taste, therefore, is only pure so far as its determining ground is tainted with no merely empirical delight. But such a taint is always present where charm or emotion have a share in the judgement by which something is to be described as beautiful.

Here now there is a recrudescence of a number of specious pleas that go the length of putting forward the case that charm is not merely a necessary ingredient of beauty, but is even of itself sufficient to merit the name of beautiful. A mere colour, such as the green of a plot of grass, or a mere tone (as distinguished from sound or noise), like that of a violin, is described by most people as in itself beautiful, notwithstanding the fact that both seem to depend merely on the matter of the representations – in other words, simply on sensation, which only entitles them to be called agreeable. But it will at the same time be observed that sensations of colour as well as of tone are only entitled to be immediately regarded as beautiful where, in either case, they are *pure*. This is a determination which at once goes to their form, and it is the only one which these representations possess that admits with certainty of being universally communicated. For it is not to be assumed that even the quality of the sensations agrees in all Subjects, and we can hardly take it for granted that the agreeableness of a colour, or of the tone of a musical instrument, which we judge to be preferable to that of another, is given a like preference in the estimate of every one.

Assuming with *Euler* that colours are isochronous vibrations (*pulsus*) of the aether, as tones are of the air set in vibration by sound, and, what is most important, that the mind not alone perceives by sense their effect in stimulating the organs, but also, by reflection, the regular play of the impressions, (and consequently the form in which different representations are united,) – which I, still, in no way doubt – then colour and tone would not be mere sensations. They would be nothing short of formal determinations of the unity of a manifold of sensations, and in that case could even be ranked as intrinsic beauties.

But the purity of a simple mode of sensation means that its uniformity is not disturbed or broken by any foreign sensation. It belongs merely to the form; for abstraction may there be made

from the quality of the mode of such sensation (what colour or tone, if any, it represents). For this reason all simple colours are regarded as beautiful so far as pure. Composite colours have not this advantage, because, not being simple, there is no standard for estimating whether they should be called pure or impure.

But as for the beauty ascribed to the object on account of its form, and the supposition that it is capable of being enhanced by charm, this is a common error and one very prejudicial to genuine, uncorrupted, sincere taste. Nevertheless charms may be added to beauty to lend to the mind, beyond a bare delight, an adventitious interest in the representation of the object, and thus to advocate taste and its cultivation. This applies especially where taste is as yet crude and untrained. But they are positively subversive of the judgement of taste, if allowed to obtrude themselves as grounds of estimating beauty. For so far are they from contributing to beauty, that it is only where taste is still weak and untrained, that, like aliens, they are admitted as a favour, and only on terms that they do not violate that beautiful form.

In painting, sculpture, and in fact in all the formative arts, in architecture and horticulture, so far as fine arts, the *design* is what is essential. Here it is not what gratifies in sensation but merely what pleases by its form, that is the fundamental prerequisite for taste. The colours which give brilliancy to the sketch are part of the charm. They may no doubt, in their own way, enliven the object for sensation, but make it really worth looking at and beautiful they cannot. Indeed, more often than not the requirements of the beautiful form restrict them to a very narrow compass, and, even where charm is admitted, it is only this form that gives them a place of honour.

All form of objects of sense (both of external and also, mediately, of internal sense) is either *figure* or *play*. In the latter case it is either play of figures (in space: mimic and dance), or mere play of sensations (in time). The *charm* of colours, or of the agreeable tones of instruments, may be added: but the *design* in the former and the *composition* in the latter constitute the proper object of the pure judgement of taste. To say that the purity alike of colours and of tones, or their variety and contrast, seem to contribute to beauty, is by no means to imply that, because in themselves agreeable, they therefore yield an addition to the delight in the form and one on a par with it. The real meaning rather is that they make this form more clearly,

15

definitely, and completely intuitable, and besides stimulate the representation by their charm, as they excite and sustain the attention directed to the object itself.

Even what is called *ornamentation* (*parerga*), i.e. what is only an adjunct, and not an intrinsic constituent in the complete representation of the object, in augmenting the delight of taste does so only by means of its form. Thus it is with the frames of pictures or the drapery on statues, or the colonnades of palaces. But if the ornamentation does not itself enter into the composition of the beautiful form – if it is introduced like a gold frame merely to win approval for the picture by means of its charm – it is then called *finery* and takes away from the genuine beauty.

Emotion – a sensation where an agreeable feeling is produced merely by means of a momentary check followed by a more powerful outpouring of the vital force – is quite foreign to beauty. Sublimity (with which the feeling of emotion is connected) requires, however, a different standard of estimation from that relied upon by taste. A pure judgement of taste has, then, for its determining ground neither charm nor emotion, in a word, no sensation as matter of the aesthetic judgement.

§ 15

The judgement of taste is entirely independent of the concept of perfection.

Objective finality can only be cognized by means of a reference of the manifold to a definite end, and hence only through a concept. This alone makes it clear that the beautiful, which is estimated on the ground of a mere formal finality, i.e. a finality apart from an end, is wholly independent of the representation of the good. For the latter presupposes an objective finality, i.e. the reference of the object to a definite end.

Objective finality is either external, i.e. the *utility*, or internal, i.e. the *perfection*, of the object. That the delight in an object on account of which we call it beautiful is incapable of resting on the representation of its utility, is abundantly evident from the two preceding articles; for in that case, it would not be an immediate delight in the object, which latter is the essential condition of the judgement upon beauty. But in an objective, internal finality, i.e. perfection, we have what is more akin to the predicate of beauty, and so this has been held even by philosophers of reputation to be convertible with beauty, though subject to the

qualification: *where it is thought in a confused way*. In a Critique of taste it is of the utmost importance to decide whether beauty is really reducible to the concept of perfection.

For estimating objective finality we always require the concept of an end, and, where such finality has to be, not an external one (utility), but an internal one, the concept of an internal end containing the ground of the internal possibility of the object. Now an end is in general that, the *concept* of which may be regarded as the ground of the possibility of the object itself. So in order to represent an objective finality in a thing we must first have a concept of *what sort of a thing it is to be*. The agreement of the manifold in a thing with this concept (which supplies the rule of its synthesis) is the *qualitative perfection* of the thing. *Quantitative* perfection is entirely distinct from this. It consists in the completeness of anything after its kind, and is a mere concept of quantity (of totality). In its case the question of *what the thing is to be* is regarded as definitely disposed of, and we only ask whether it is possessed of *all* the requisites that go to make it such. What is formal in the representation of a thing, i.e. the agreement of its manifold with a unity (i.e. irrespective of what it is to be) does not, of itself, afford us any cognition whatsoever of objective finality. For since abstraction is made from this unity as *end* (what the thing is to be) nothing is left but the subjective finality of the representations in the mind of the Subject intuiting. This gives a certain finality of the representative state of the Subject, in which the Subject feels itself quite at home in its effort to grasp a given form in the imagination, but no perfection of any Object, the latter not being here thought through any concept. For instance, if in a forest I light upon a plot of grass, round which trees stand in a circle, and if I do not then form any representation of an end, as that it is meant to be used, say, for country dances, then not the least hint of a concept of perfection is given by the mere form. To suppose a formal *objective* finality that is yet devoid of an end, i.e. the mere form of a *perfection* (apart from any matter or *concept* of that to which the agreement relates, even though there was the mere general idea of a conformity to law) is a veritable contradiction.

Now the judgement of taste is an aesthetic judgement, i.e. one resting on subjective grounds. No concept can be its determining ground, and hence not one of a definite end. Beauty, therefore, as a formal subjective finality, involves no thought whatsoever of a perfection of the object, as a would-be formal finality which yet, for all that, is objective: and the distinction between the concepts of the beautiful and the good, which represents both as differing only in their logical form, the first being merely a confused, the second a clearly defined, concept of perfection, while otherwise alike in content and origin, all goes for nothing; for then there would be no *specific* difference between them, but the judgement of taste would be just as much a cognitive judgement as one by which something is described as good – just as the man in the street, when he says that deceit is wrong, bases his judgement on confused, but the philosopher on clear grounds, while both appeal in reality to identical principles of reason. But I have already stated that an aesthetic judgement is quite unique, and affords absolutely no, (not even a confused,) knowledge of the Object. It is only through a logical judgement that we get knowledge. The aesthetic judgement, on the other hand, refers the representation, by which an Object is given, solely to the Subject, and brings to our notice no quality of the object, but only the final form in the determination of the powers of representation engaged upon it. The judgement is called aesthetic for the very reason that its determining ground cannot be a concept, but is rather the feeling (of the internal sense) of the concept in the play of the mental powers as a thing only capable of being felt. If, on the other hand, confused concepts, and the objective judgement based on them, are going to be called aesthetic, we shall find ourselves with an understanding judging by sense, or a sense representing its objects by concepts – a mere choice of contradictions. The faculty of concepts, be they confused or be they clear, is understanding; and although understanding has (as in all judgements) its rôle in the judgement of taste, as an aesthetic judgement, its rôle there is not that of a faculty for cognizing an object, but of a faculty for determining that judgement and its representation (without a concept) according to its relation to the Subject and its internal feeling, and for doing so in so far as that judgement is possible according to a universal rule.

§ 16

A judgement of taste by which an object is described as beautiful under the condition of a definite concept is not pure.

There are two kinds of beauty: free beauty (*pulchritudo vaga*), or beauty which is merely depen-

dent (*pulchritudo adhaerens*). The first presupposes no concept of what the object should be; the second does presuppose such a concept and, with it, an answering perfection of the object. Those of the first kind are said to be (self-subsisting) beauties of this thing or that thing; the other kind of beauty, being attached to a concept (conditioned beauty), is ascribed to Objects which come under the concept of a particular end.

Flowers are free beauties of nature. Hardly any one but a botanist knows the true nature of a flower, and even he, while recognizing in the flower the reproductive organ of the plant, pays no attention to this natural end when using his taste to judge of its beauty. Hence no perfection of any kind – no internal finality, as something to which the arrangement of the manifold is related – underlies this judgement. Many birds (the parrot, the humming-bird, the bird of paradise), and a number of crustacea, are self-subsisting beauties which are not appurtenant to any object defined with respect to its end, but please freely and on their own account. So designs *à la grecque*, foliage for framework or on wall-papers, &c., have no intrinsic meaning; they represent nothing – no Object under a definite concept – and are free beauties. We may also rank in the same class what in music are called fantasias (without a theme), and, indeed, all music that is not set to words.

In the estimate of a free beauty (according to mere form) we have the pure judgement of taste. No concept is here presupposed of any end for which the manifold should serve the given Object, and which the latter, therefore, should represent – an incumbrance which would only restrict the freedom of the imagination that, as it were, is at play in the contemplation of the outward form.

But the beauty of man (including under this head that of a man, woman, or child), the beauty of a horse, or of a building (such as a church, palace, arsenal, or summer-house), presupposes a concept of the end that defines what the thing has to be, and consequently a concept of its perfection; and is therefore merely appendant beauty. Now, just as it is a clog on the purity of the judgement of taste to have the agreeable (of sensation) joined with beauty to which properly only the form is relevant, so to combine the good with beauty, (the good, namely, of the manifold to the thing itself according to its end,) mars its purity.

Much might be added to a building that would immediately please the eye, were it not intended for a church. A figure might be beautified with all manner of flourishes and light but regular lines, as is done by the New Zealanders with their tattooing, were we dealing with anything but the figure of a human being. And here is one whose rugged features might be softened and given a more pleasing aspect, only he has got to be a man, or is, perhaps, a warrior that has to have a warlike appearance.

Now the delight in the manifold of a thing, in reference to the internal end that determines its possibility, is a delight based on a concept, whereas delight in the beautiful is such as does not presuppose any concept, but is immediately coupled with the representation through which the object is given (not through which it is thought). If, now, the judgement of taste in respect of the latter delight is made dependent upon the end involved in the former delight as a judgement of reason, and is thus placed under a restriction, then it is no longer a free and pure judgement of taste.

Taste, it is true, stands to gain by this combination of intellectual delight with the aesthetic. For it becomes fixed, and, while not universal, it enables rules to be prescribed for it in respect of certain definite final Objects. But these rules are then not rules of taste, but merely rules for establishing a union of taste with reason, i.e. of the beautiful with the good – rules by which the former becomes available as an intentional instrument in respect of the latter, for the purpose of bringing that temper of the mind which is self-sustaining and of subjective universal validity to the support and maintenance of that mode of thought which, while possessing objective universal validity, can only be preserved by a resolute effort. But, strictly speaking, perfection neither gains by beauty, nor beauty by perfection. The truth is rather this, when we compare the representation through which an object is given to us with the Object (in respect of what it is meant to be) by means of a concept, we cannot help reviewing it also in respect of the sensation in the Subject. Hence there results a gain to the *entire faculty* of our representative power when harmony prevails between both states of mind.

In respect of an object with a definite internal end, a judgement of taste would only be pure where the person judging either has no concept of this end, or else makes abstraction from it in his judgement. But in cases like this, although such a person should lay down a correct judgement of taste, since he would be estimating the object as a free beauty, he would still be found fault with by another who saw nothing in its beauty but a dependent quality (i.e. who looked to the end of the object) and would be accused by him of false taste, though both would, in their own way, be judging correctly: the one according to what he had present to his senses, the other according to what was present in his thoughts. This distinction enables us to settle many disputes about beauty on the part of critics; for we may show them how one side is dealing with free beauty, and the other with that which is dependent: the former passing a pure judgement of taste, the latter one that is applied intentionally.

§ 17
The Ideal of beauty.

There can be no objective rule of taste by which what is beautiful may be defined by means of concepts. For every judgement from that source is aesthetic, i.e. its determining ground is the feeling of the Subject, and not any concept of an Object. It is only throwing away labour to look for a principle of taste that affords a universal criterion of the beautiful by definite concepts; because what is sought is a thing impossible and inherently contradictory. But in the universal communicability of the sensation (of delight or aversion) – a communicability, too, that exists apart from any concept – in the accord, so far as possible, of all ages and nations as to this feeling in the representation of certain objects, we have the empirical criterion, weak indeed and scarce sufficient to raise a presumption, of the derivation of a taste, thus confirmed by examples, from grounds deep-seated and shared alike by all men, underlying their agreement in estimating the forms under which objects are given to them.

For this reason some products of taste are looked on as *exemplary* – not meaning thereby that by imitating others taste may be acquired. For taste must be an original faculty; whereas one who imitates a model, while showing skill commensurate with his success, only displays taste as himself a critic of this model.[4] Hence it follows that the highest model, the archetype of taste, is a mere idea, which each person must beget in his own consciousness, and according to which he must form his estimate of everything that is an Object of taste, or that is an example of critical taste, and even of universal taste itself. Properly speaking, an *idea* signifies a concept of reason, and an *ideal* the representation of an individual existence as adequate to an idea. Hence this archetype of taste – which rests, indeed, upon reason's indeterminate idea of a maximum, but is not, however, capable of being represented by means of concepts, but only in an individual presentation – may more appropriately be called the ideal of the beautiful. While not having this ideal in our possession, we still strive to beget it within us. But it is bound to be merely an ideal of the imagination, seeing that it rests, not upon concepts, but upon the presentation – the faculty of presentation being the imagination. – Now, how do we arrive at such an ideal of beauty? Is it *a priori* or empirically? Further, what species of the beautiful admits of an ideal?

First of all, we do well to observe that the beauty for which an ideal has to be sought cannot be a beauty that is *free and at large*, but must be one *fixed* by a concept of objective finality. Hence it cannot belong to the Object of an altogether pure judgement of taste, but must attach to one that is partly intellectual. In other words, where an ideal is to have place among the grounds upon which any estimate is formed, then beneath grounds of that kind there must lie some idea of reason according to determinate concepts, by which the end underlying the internal possibility of the object is determined *a priori*. An ideal of beautiful flowers, of a beautiful suite of furniture, or of a beautiful view, is unthinkable. But, it may also be impossible to represent an ideal of a beauty dependent on definite ends, e.g. a beautiful residence, a beautiful tree, a beautiful garden, &c., presumably because their ends are not sufficiently defined and fixed by their concept, with the result that their finality is nearly as free as with beauty that is quite *at large*. Only what has in itself the end of its real existence – only *man* that is able himself to determine his ends by reason, or, where he has to derive them from external perception, can still compare them with essential and universal ends, and then further pronounce aesthetically upon their accord with such ends, only he, among all objects in the world, admits, therefore, of an ideal of *beauty*, just as humanity in his person, as intelligence, alone admits of the ideal of *perfection*.

Two factors are here involved. *First*, there is the aesthetic *normal idea*, which is an individual intuition (of the imagination). This represents the norm by which we judge of a man as a member of a particular animal species. *Secondly*, there is the *rational idea*. This deals with the ends of humanity so far as capable of sensuous representation, and

converts them into a principle for estimating his outward form, through which these ends are revealed in their phenomenal effect. The normal idea must draw from experience the constituents which it requires for the form of an animal of a particular kind. But the greatest finality in the construction of this form – that which would serve as a universal norm for forming an estimate of each individual of the species in question – the image that, as it were, forms an intentional basis underlying the technic of nature, to which no separate individual, but only the race as a whole, is adequate, has its seat merely in the idea of the judging Subject. Yet it is, with all its proportions, an aesthetic idea, and, as such, capable of being fully presented *in concreto* in a model image. Now, how is this effected? In order to render the process to some extent intelligible (for who can wrest nature's whole secret from her?), let us attempt a psychological explanation.

It is of note that the imagination, in a manner quite incomprehensible to us, is able on occasion, even after a long lapse of time, not alone to recall the signs for concepts, but also to reproduce the image and shape of an object out of a countless number of others of a different, or even of the very same, kind. And, further, if the mind is engaged upon comparisons, we may well suppose that it can in actual fact, though the process is unconscious, superimpose as it were one image upon another, and from the coincidence of a number of the same kind arrive at a mean contour which serves as a common standard for all. Say, for instance, a person has seen a thousand full-grown men. Now if he wishes to judge normal size determined upon a comparative estimate, then imagination (to my mind) allows a great number of these images (perhaps the whole thousand) to fall one upon the other, and, if I may be allowed to extend to the case the analogy of optical presentation, in the space where they come most together, and within the contour where the place is illuminated by the greatest concentration of colour, one gets a perception of the *average size*, which alike in height and breadth is equally removed from the extreme limits of the greatest and smallest statures; and this is the stature of a beautiful man. (The same result could be obtained in a mechanical way, by taking the measures of all the thousand, and adding together their heights, and their breadths (and thicknesses), and dividing the sum in each case by a thousand.) But the power of imagination does all this by means of a dynamical effect upon the organ of internal sense, arising from the frequent apprehension of such forms. If, again, for our average man we seek on similar lines for the average head, and for this the average nose, and so on, then we get the figure that underlies the normal idea of a beautiful man in the country where the comparison is instituted. For this reason a negro must necessarily (under these empirical conditions) have a different normal idea of the beauty of forms from what a white man has, and the Chinaman one different from the European. And the process would be just the same with the *model* of a beautiful horse or dog (of a particular breed). – This *normal idea* is not derived from proportions taken from experience *as definite rules*: rather is it according to this idea that rules for forming estimates first become possible. It is an intermediate between all singular intuitions of individuals, with their manifold variations – a floating image for the whole genus, which nature has set as an archetype underlying those of her products that belong to the same species, but which in no single case she seems to have completely attained. But the normal idea is far from giving the complete *archetype* of *beauty* in the genus. It only gives the form that constitutes the indispensable condition of all beauty, and, consequently, only *correctness* in the presentation of the genus. It is, as the famous *Doryphorus* of *Polycletus* was called, the *rule* (and *Myron's* Cow might be similarly employed for its kind). It cannot, for that very reason, contain anything specifically characteristic; for otherwise it would not be the *normal idea* for the genus. Further, it is not by beauty that its presentation pleases, but merely because it does not contradict any of the conditions under which alone a thing belonging to this genus can be beautiful. The presentation is merely academically correct.[5]

But the *ideal* of the beautiful is still something different from its *normal idea*. For reasons already stated it is only to be sought in the *human figure*. Here the ideal consists in the expression of the *moral*, apart from which the object would not please at once universally and positively (not merely negatively in a presentation academically correct). The visible expression of moral ideas that govern men inwardly can, of course, only be drawn from experience; but their combination with all that our reason connects with the morally good in the idea of the highest finality – benevolence, purity, strength, or equanimity, &c. – may be made, as it were, visible in bodily manifestation (as effect of what is internal), and this embodiment

involves a union of pure ideas of reason and great imaginative power, in one who would even form an estimate of it, not to speak of being the author of its presentation. The correctness of such an ideal of beauty is evidenced by its not permitting any sensuous charm to mingle with the delight in its Object, in which it still allows us to take a great interest. This fact in turn shows that an estimate formed according to such a standard can never be purely aesthetic, and that one formed according to an ideal of beauty cannot be a simple judgement of taste.

Definition of the beautiful derived from this third moment

Beauty is the form of *finality* in an object, so far as perceived in it *apart from the representation of an end*.[6]

Fourth Moment of the Judgement of Taste: Moment of the Modality of the Delight in the Object

§ 18
Nature of the modality in a judgement of taste.

I may assert in the case of every representation that the synthesis of a pleasure with the representation (as a cognition) is at least *possible*. Of what I call *agreeable* I assert that it *actually* causes pleasure in me. But what we have in mind in the case of the *beautiful* is a *necessary* reference on its part to delight. However, this necessity is of a special kind. It is not a theoretical objective necessity – such as would let us cognize *a priori* that every one *will feel* this delight in the object that is called beautiful by me. Nor yet is it a practical necessity, in which case, thanks to concepts of a pure rational will in which free agents are supplied with a rule, this delight is the necessary consequence of an objective law, and simply means that one ought absolutely (without ulterior object) to act in a certain way. Rather, being such a necessity as is thought in an aesthetic judgement, it can only be termed *exemplary*. In other words it is a necessity of the assent of *all* to a judgement regarded as exemplifying a universal rule incapable of formulation. Since an aesthetic judgement is not an objective or cognitive judgement, this necessity is not derivable from definite concepts, and so is not apodictic. Much less is it inferable from universality of experience (of a thorough-going agreement of judgements about the beauty of a certain object). For, apart from the fact that experience would hardly furnish evidences sufficiently numerous for this purpose, empirical judgements do not afford any foundation for a concept of the necessity of these judgements.

§ 19
The subjective necessity attributed to a judgement of taste is conditioned.

The judgement of taste exacts agreement from every one; and a person who describes something as beautiful insists that every one *ought* to give the object in question his approval and follow suit in describing it as beautiful. The *ought* in aesthetic judgements, therefore, despite an accordance with all the requisite data for passing judgement, is still only pronounced conditionally. We are suitors for agreement from every one else, because we are fortified with a ground common to all. Further, we would be able to count on this agreement, provided we were always assured of the correct subsumption of the case under that ground as the rule of approval.

§ 20
The condition of the necessity advanced by a judgement of taste is the idea of a common sense.

Were judgements of taste (like cognitive judgements) in possession of a definite objective principle, then one who in his judgement followed such a principle would claim unconditioned necessity for it. Again, were they devoid of any principle, as are those of the mere taste of sense, then no thought of any necessity on their part would enter one's head. Therefore they must have a subjective principle, and one which determines what pleases or displeases, by means of feeling only and not through concepts, but yet with universal validity. Such a principle, however, could only be regarded as a *common sense*. This differs essentially from common understanding, which is also sometimes called common sense (*sensus communis*): for the judgement of the latter is not one by feeling, but always one by concepts, though usually only in the shape of obscurely represented principles.

The judgement of taste, therefore, depends on our presupposing the existence of a common sense

(But this is not to be taken to mean some external sense, but the effect arising from the free play of our powers of cognition.) Only under the presupposition, I repeat, of such a common sense, are we able to lay down a judgement of taste.

§ 21
Have we reason for presupposing a common sense?

Cognitions and judgements must, together with their attendant conviction, admit of being universally communicated; for otherwise a correspondence with the Object would not be due to them. They would be a conglomerate constituting a mere subjective play of the powers of representation, just as scepticism would have it. But if cognitions are to admit of communication, then our mental state, i.e. the way the cognitive powers are attuned for cognition generally, and, in fact, the relative proportion suitable for a representation (by which an object is given to us) from which cognition is to result, must also admit of being universally communicated, as, without this, which is the subjective condition of the act of knowing, knowledge, as an effect, would not arise. And this is always what actually happens where a given object, through the intervention of sense, sets the imagination at work in arranging the manifold, and the imagination, in turn, the understanding in giving to this arrangement the unity of concepts. But this disposition of the cognitive powers has a relative proportion differing with the diversity of the Objects that are given. However, there must be one in which this internal ratio suitable for quickening (one faculty by the other) is best adapted for both mental powers in respect of cognition (of given objects) generally; and this disposition can only be determined through feeling (and not by concepts). Since, now, this disposition itself must admit of being universally communicated, and hence also the feeling of it (in the case of a given representation), while again, the universal communicability of a feeling presupposes a common sense: it follows that our assumption of it is well founded. And here, too, we do not have to take our stand on psychological observations, but we assume a common sense as the necessary condition of the universal communicability of our knowledge, which is presupposed in every logic and every principle of knowledge that is not one of scepticism.

§ 22

The necessity of the universal assent that is thought in a judgement of taste, is a subjective necessity which, under the presupposition of a common sense, is represented as objective.

In all judgements by which we describe anything as beautiful we tolerate no one else being of a different opinion, and in taking up this position we do not rest our judgement upon concepts, but only on our feeling. Accordingly we introduce this fundamental feeling not as a private feeling, but as a public sense. Now, for this purpose, experience cannot be made the ground of this common sense, for the latter is invoked to justify judgements containing an 'ought'. The assertion is not that every one *will* fall in with our judgement, but rather that every one *ought* to agree with it. Here I put forward my judgement of taste as an example of the judgement of common sense, and attribute to it on that account *exemplary* validity. Hence common sense is a mere ideal norm. With this as presupposition, a judgement that accords with it, as well as the delight in an Object expressed in that judgement, is rightly converted into a rule for every one. For the principle, while it is only subjective, being yet assumed as subjectively universal (a necessary idea for every one), could, in what concerns the consensus of different judging Subjects, demand universal assent like an objective principle, provided we were assured of our subsumption under it being correct.

This indeterminate norm of a common sense is, as a matter of fact, presupposed by us; as is shown by our presuming to lay down judgements of taste. But does such a common sense in fact exist as a constitutive principle of the possibility of experience, or is it formed for us as a regulative principle by a still higher principle of reason, that for higher ends first seeks to beget in us a common sense? Is taste, in other words, a natural and original faculty, or is it only the idea of one that is artificial and to be acquired by us, so that a judgement of taste, with its demand for universal assent, is but a requirement of reason for generating such a con*sensus*, and does the 'ought', i.e. the objective necessity of the coincidence of the feeling of all with the particular feeling of each, only betoken the possibility of arriving at some sort of unanimity in these matters, and the judgement of taste only adduce an example of the application of this principle? These are questions which as yet we are

neither willing nor in a position to investigate. For the present we have only to resolve the faculty of taste into its elements, and to unite these ultimately in the idea of a common sense.

Definition of the beautiful drawn from the fourth moment

The beautiful is that which, apart from a concept, is cognized as object of a *necessary* delight.

General remark on the first section of the Analytic

The result to be extracted from the foregoing analysis is in effect this: that everything runs up into the concept of taste as a critical faculty by which an object is estimated in reference to the *free conformity to law* of the imagination. If, now, imagination must in the judgement of taste be regarded in its freedom, then, to begin with, it is not taken as reproductive, as in its subjection to the laws of association, but as productive and exerting an activity of its own (as originator of arbitrary forms of possible intuitions). And although in the apprehension of a given object of sense it is tied down to a definite form of this Object and, to that extent, does not enjoy free play, (as it does in poetry,) still it is easy to conceive that the object may supply ready-made to the imagination just such a form of the arrangement of the manifold, as the imagination, if it were left to itself, would freely project in harmony with the general *conformity to law of the understanding*. But that the *imagination* should be both *free* and *of itself conformable to law*, i.e. carry autonomy with it, is a contradiction. The understanding alone gives the law. Where, however, the imagination is compelled to follow a course laid down by a definite law, then what the form of the product is to be is determined by concepts; but, in that case, as already shown, the delight is not delight in the beautiful, but in the good, (in perfection, though it be no more than formal perfection), and the judgement is not one due to taste. Hence it is only a conformity to law without a law, and a subjective harmonizing of the imagination and the understanding without an objective one – which latter would mean that the representation was referred to a definite concept of the object – that can consist with the free conformity to law of the understanding (which has also been called finality apart from an end) and with the specific character of a judgement of taste.

Now geometrically regular figures, a circle, a square, a cube, and the like, are commonly brought forward by critics of taste as the most simple and unquestionable examples of beauty. And yet the very reason why they are called regular, is because the only way of representing them is by looking on them as mere presentations of a determinate concept by which the figure has its rule (according to which alone it is possible) prescribed for it. One or other of these two views must, therefore, be wrong: either the verdict of the critics that attributes beauty to such figures, or else our own, which makes finality apart from any concept necessary for beauty.

One would scarce think it necessary for a man to have taste to take more delight in a circle than in a scrawled outline, in an equilateral and equiangular quadrilateral than in one that is all lob-sided, and, as it were, deformed. The requirements of common understanding ensure such a preference without the least demand upon taste. Where some purpose is perceived, as, for instance, that of forming an estimate of the area of a plot of land, or rendering intelligible the relation of divided parts to one another and to the whole, then regular figures, and those of the simplest kind, are needed; and the delight does not rest immediately upon the way the figure strikes the eye, but upon its serviceability for all manner of possible purposes. A room with the walls making oblique angles, a plot laid out in a garden in a similar way, even any violation of symmetry, as well in the figure of animals (e.g. being one-eyed) as in that of buildings, or of flower-beds, is displeasing because of its perversity of form, not alone in a practical way in respect of some definite use to which the thing may be put, but for an estimate that looks to all manner of possible purposes. With the judgement of taste the case is different. For, when it is pure, it combines delight or aversion immediately with the bare *contemplation* of the object irrespective of its use or of any end.

The regularity that conduces to the concept of an object is, in fact, the indispensable condition (*condition sine qua non*) of grasping the object as a single representation and giving to the manifold its determinate form. This determination is an end in respect of knowledge; and in this connexion it is invariably coupled with delight (such as attends the accomplishment of any, even problematical, purpose). Here, however, we have merely the value set upon the solution that satisfies the problem, and not a free and indeterminately final entertainment of the mental powers with what is called beautiful. In the latter case understanding is at the service of imagination, in the former this relation is reversed.

With a thing that owes its possibility to a purpose, a building, or even an animal, its regularity, which consists in symmetry, must express the unity of the intuition accompanying the concept of its end, and belongs with it to cognition. But where all that is intended is the maintenance of a free play of the powers of representation (subject, however, to the condition that there is to be nothing for understanding to take exception to), in ornamental gardens, in the decoration of rooms, in all kinds of furniture that shows good taste, &c., regularity in the shape of constraint is to be avoided as far as possible. Thus English taste in gardens, and fantastic taste in furniture, push the freedom of imagination to the verge of what is grotesque – the idea being that in this divorce from all constraint of rules the precise instance is being afforded where taste can exhibit its perfection in projects of the imagination to the fullest extent.

All stiff regularity (such as borders on mathematical regularity) is inherently repugnant to taste, in that the contemplation of it affords us no lasting entertainment. Indeed, where it has neither cognition nor some definite practical end expressly in view, we get heartily tired of it. On the other hand, anything that gives the imagination scope for unstudied and final play is always fresh to us. We do not grow to hate the very sight of it. *Marsden* in his description of Sumatra observes that the free beauties of nature so surround the beholder on all sides that they cease to have much attraction for him. On the other hand he found a pepper garden full of charm, on coming across it in mid-forest with its rows of parallel stakes on which the plant twines itself. From all this he infers that wild, and in its appearance quite irregular beauty, is only pleasing as a change to one whose eyes have become surfeited with regular beauty. But he need only have made the experiment of passing one day in his pepper garden to realize that once the regularity has enabled the understanding to put itself in accord with the order that is its constant requirement, instead of the object diverting him any longer, it imposes an irksome constraint upon the imagination: whereas nature subject to no constraint of artificial rules, and lavish, as it there is, in its luxuriant variety can supply constant food for his taste. – Even a bird's song, which we can reduce to no musical rule, seems to have more freedom in it, and thus to be richer for taste, than the human voice singing in accordance with all the rules that the art of music prescribes; for we grow tired much sooner of frequent and lengthy repetitions of the latter. Yet here most likely our sympathy with the mirth of a dear little creature is confused with the beauty of its song, for if exactly imitated by man (as has been sometimes done with the notes of the nightingale) it would strike our ear as wholly destitute of taste.

Further, beautiful objects have to be distinguished from beautiful views of objects (where the distance often prevents a clear perception). In the latter case taste appears to fasten, not so much on what the imagination *grasps* in this field, as on the incentive it receives to indulge in poetic fiction, i.e. in the peculiar fancies with which the mind entertains itself as it is being continually stirred by the variety that strikes the eye. It is just as when we watch the changing shapes of the fire or of a rippling brook: neither of which are things of beauty, but they convey a charm to the imagination, because they sustain its free play.

Second Book
Analytic of the Sublime

§ 23
Transition from the faculty of estimating the beautiful to that of estimating the sublime.

The beautiful and the sublime agree on the point of pleasing on their own account. Further they agree in not presupposing either a judgement of sense or one logically determinant, but one of reflection. Hence it follows that the delight does not depend upon a sensation, as with the agreeable, nor upon a definite concept, as does the delight in the good, although it has, for all that, an indeterminate reference to concepts. Consequently the delight is connected with the mere presentation or faculty of presentation, and is thus taken to express the accord, in a given intuition, of the faculty of presentation, or the imagination, with the *faculty of concepts* that belongs to understanding or reason, in the sense of the former assisting the latter. Hence both kinds of judgements are *singular*, and yet such as profess to be universally valid in respect of every Subject, despite the fact that their claims are directed merely to the feeling of pleasure and not to any knowledge of the object.

There are, however, also important and striking differences between the two. The beautiful in nature is a question of the form of the object, and this consists in limitation, whereas the sublime is to be found in an object even devoid of form, so far as it immediately involves, or else by its presence provokes, a representation of *limitlessness*, yet with a super-added thought of its totality. Accordingly the beautiful seems to be regarded as a presentation of an indeterminate concept of understanding, the sublime as a presentation of an indeterminate concept of reason. Hence the delight is in the former case coupled with the representation of *Quality*, but in this case with that of *Quantity*. Moreover, the former delight is very different from the latter in kind. For the beautiful is directly attended with a feeling of the furtherance of life, and is thus compatible with charms and a playful imagination. On the other hand, the feeling of the sublime is a pleasure that only arises indirectly, being brought about by the feeling of a momentary check to the vital forces followed at once by a discharge all the more powerful, and so it is an emotion that seems to be no sport, but dead earnest in the affairs of the imagination. Hence charms are repugnant to it; and, since the mind is not simply attracted by the object, but is also alternately repelled thereby, the delight in the sublime does not so much involve positive pleasure as admiration or respect, i.e. merits the name of a negative pleasure.

But the most important and vital distinction between the sublime and the beautiful is certainly this: that if, as is allowable, we here confine our attention in the first instance to the sublime in Objects of nature, (that of art being always restricted by the conditions of an agreement with nature,) we observe that whereas natural beauty (such as is self-subsisting) conveys a finality in its form making the object appear, as it were, pre-adapted to our power of judgement, so that it thus forms of itself an object of our delight, that which, without our indulging in any refinements of thought, but, simply in our apprehension of it, excites the feeling of the sublime, may appear, indeed, in point of form to contravene the ends of our power of judgement, to be ill-adapted to our faculty of presentation, and to be, as it were, an outrage on the imagination, and yet it is judged all the more sublime on that account.

From this it may be seen at once that we express ourselves on the whole inaccurately if we term any *Object of nature* sublime, although we may with perfect propriety call many such objects beautiful. For how can that which is apprehended as inherently contra-final be noted with an expression of approval? All that we can say is that the object lends itself to the presentation of a sublimity discoverable in the mind. For the sublime, in the strict sense of the word, cannot be contained in any sensuous form, but rather concerns ideas of reason, which, although no adequate presentation of them is possible, may be excited and called into the mind by that very inadequacy itself which does admit of sensuous presentation. Thus the broad ocean agitated by storms cannot be called sublime. Its aspect is horrible, and one must have stored one's mind in advance with a rich stock of ideas, if such an intuition is to raise it to the pitch of a feeling which is itself sublime – sublime because the mind has been incited to abandon sensibility, and employ itself upon ideas involving higher finality.

Self-subsisting natural beauty reveals to us a technic of nature which shows it in the light of a system ordered in accordance with laws the principle of which is not to be found within the range of our entire faculty of understanding. This principle is that of a finality relative to the employment of judgement in respect of phenomena which have thus to be assigned, not merely to nature regarded as aimless mechanism, but also to nature regarded after the analogy of art. Hence it gives a veritable extension, not, of course, to our knowledge of Objects of nature, but to our conception of nature itself – nature as mere mechanism being enlarged to the conception of nature as art – an extension inviting profound inquiries as to the possibility of such a form. But in what we are wont to call sublime in nature there is such an absence of anything leading to particular objective principles and corresponding forms of nature, that it is rather in its chaos, or in its wildest and most irregular disorder and desolation, provided it gives signs of magnitude and power, that nature chiefly excites the ideas of the sublime. Hence we see that the concept of the sublime in nature is far less important and rich in consequences than that of its beauty. It gives on the whole no indication of anything final in nature itself, but only in the possible *employment* of our intuitions of it in inducing a feeling in our own selves of a finality quite independent of nature. For the beautiful in nature we must seek a ground external to ourselves, but

for the sublime one merely in ourselves and the attitude of mind that introduces sublimity into the representation of nature. This is a very needful preliminary remark. It entirely separates the ideas of the sublime from that of a finality of *nature*, and makes the theory of the sublime a mere appendage to the aesthetic estimate of the finality of nature, because it does not give a representation of any particular form in nature, but involves no more than the development of a final employment by the imagination of its own representation.

[...]

B. The Dynamically Sublime in Nature

§ 28
Nature as Might.

Might is a power which is superior to great hindrances. It is termed *dominion* if it is also superior to the resistance of that which itself possesses might. Nature considered in an aesthetic judgement as might that has no dominion over us, is *dynamically sublime*.

If we are to estimate nature as dynamically sublime, it must be represented as a source of fear (though the converse, that every object that is a source of fear is, in our aesthetic judgement, sublime, does not hold). For in forming an aesthetic estimate (no concept being present) the superiority to the hindrances can only be estimated according to the greatness of the resistance. Now that which we strive to resist is an evil, and, if we do not find our powers commensurate to the task, an object of fear. Hence the aesthetic judgement can only deem nature a might, and so dynamically sublime, in so far as it is looked upon as an object of fear.

But we may look upon an object as *fearful*, and yet not be afraid *of* it, if, that is, our estimate takes the form of our simply *picturing to ourselves* the case of our wishing to offer some resistance to it, and recognizing that all such resistance would be quite futile. So the righteous man fears God without being afraid of Him, because he regards the case of his wishing to resist God and His commandments as one which need cause *him* no anxiety. But in every such case, regarded by him as not intrinsically impossible, he cognizes Him as One to be feared.

One who is in a state of fear can no more play the part of a judge of the sublime of nature than one captivated by inclination and appetite can of the beautiful. He flees from the sight of an object filling him with dread; and it is impossible to take delight in terror that is seriously entertained. Hence the agreeableness arising from the cessation of an uneasiness is *a state of joy*. But this, depending upon deliverance from a danger, is a rejoicing accompanied with a resolve never again to put oneself in the way of the danger: in fact we do not like bringing back to mind how we felt on that occasion – not to speak of going in search of an opportunity for experiencing it again.

Bold, overhanging, and, as it were, threatening rocks, thunder-clouds piled up the vault of heaven, borne along with flashes and peals, volcanoes in all their violence of destruction, hurricanes leaving desolation in their track, the boundless ocean rising with rebellious force, the high waterfall of some mighty river, and the like, make our power of resistance of trifling moment in comparison with their might. But, provided our own position is secure, their aspect is all the more attractive for its fearfulness; and we readily call these objects sublime, because they raise the forces of the soul above the height of vulgar commonplace, and discover within us a power of resistance of quite another kind, which gives us courage to be able to measure ourselves against the seeming omnipotence of nature.

In the immeasurableness of nature and the incompetence of our faculty for adopting a standard proportionate to the aesthetic estimation of the magnitude of its *realm*, we found our own limitation. But with this we also found in our rational faculty another non-sensuous standard, one which has that infinity itself under it as unit, and in comparison with which everything in nature is small, and so found in our minds a preeminence over nature even in its immeasurability. Now in just the same way the irresistibility of the might of nature forces upon us the recognition of our physical helplessness as beings of nature, but at the same time reveals a faculty of estimating ourselves as independent of nature, and discovers a pre-eminence above nature that is the foundation of a self-preservation of quite another kind from that which may be assailed and brought into danger by external nature. This saves humanity in our own person from humiliation, even though as mortal men we have to submit to external violence. In this way external nature is not estimated in our aesthetic judgement as sublime so far as exciting fear, but rather because it challenges our power (one not of nature) to regard as small those things

of which we are wont to be solicitous (worldly goods, health, and life), and hence to regard its might (to which in these matters we are no doubt subject) as exercising over us and our personality no such rude dominion that we should bow down before it, once the question becomes one of our highest principles and of our asserting or forsaking them. Therefore nature is here called sublime merely because it raises the imagination to a presentation of those cases in which the mind can make itself sensible of the appropriate sublimity of the sphere of its own being, even above nature.

This estimation of ourselves loses nothing by the fact that we must see ourselves safe in order to feel this soul-stirring delight – a fact from which it might be plausibly argued that, as there is no seriousness in the danger, so there is just as little seriousness in the sublimity of our faculty of soul. For here the delight only concerns the *province* of our faculty disclosed in such a case, so far as this faculty has its root in our nature; notwithstanding that its development and exercise is left to ourselves and remains an obligation. Here indeed there is truth – no matter how conscious a man, when he stretches his reflection so far abroad, may be of his actual present helplessness.

This principle has, doubtless, the appearance of being too far-fetched and subtle, and so of lying beyond the reach of an aesthetic judgement. But observation of men proves the reverse, and that it may be the foundation of the commonest judgements, although one is not always conscious of its presence. For what is it that, even to the savage, is the object of the greatest admiration? It is a man who is undaunted, who knows no fear, and who, therefore, does not give way to danger, but sets manfully to work with full deliberation. Even where civilization has reached a high pitch there remains this special reverence for the soldier; only that there is then further required of him that he should also exhibit all the virtues of peace – gentleness, sympathy and even becoming thought for his own person; and for the reason that in this we recognize that his mind is above the threats of danger. And so, comparing the statesman and the general, men may argue as they please as to the pre-eminent respect which is due to either above the other; but the verdict of the aesthetic judgement is for the latter. War itself, provided it is conducted with order and a sacred respect for the rights of civilians, has something sublime about it, and gives nations that carry it on in such a manner a stamp of mind only the more sublime the more numerous the dangers to which they are exposed, and which they are able to meet with fortitude. On the other hand, a prolonged peace favours the predominance of a mere commercial spirit, and with it a debasing self-interest, cowardice, and effeminacy, and tends to degrade the character of the nation.

So far as sublimity is predicated of might, this solution of the concept of it appears at variance with the fact that we are wont to represent God in the tempest, the storm, the earthquake, and the like, as presenting Himself in His wrath, but at the same time also in His sublimity, and yet here it would be alike folly and presumption to imagine a pre-eminence of our minds over the operations and, as it appears, even over the direction of such might. Here, instead of a feeling of the sublimity of our own nature, submission, prostration, and a feeling of utter helplessness seem more to constitute the attitude of mind befitting the manifestation of such an object, and to be that also more customarily associated with the idea of it on the occasion of a natural phenomenon of this kind. In religion, as a rule, prostration, adoration with bowed head, coupled with contrite, timorous posture and voice, seems to be the only becoming demeanour in presence of the Godhead, and accordingly most nations have assumed and still observe it. Yet this cast of mind is far from being intrinsically and necessarily involved in the idea of the *sublimity* of a religion and of its object. The man that is actually in a state of fear, finding in himself good reason to be so, because he is conscious of offending with his evil disposition against a might directed by a will at once irresistible and just, is far from being in the frame of mind for admiring divine greatness, for which a temper of calm reflection and a quite free judgement are required. Only when he becomes conscious of having a disposition that is upright and acceptable to God, do those operations of might serve to stir within him the idea of the sublimity of this Being, so far as he recognizes the existence in himself of a sublimity of disposition consonant with His will, and is thus raised above the dread of such operations of nature, in which he no longer sees God pouring forth the vials of the wrath. Even humility, taking the form of an uncompromising judgement upon his shortcomings, which, with the consciousness of good intentions, might readily be glossed over on the ground of the frailty of human nature, is a sublime temper of the mind voluntarily to undergo the pain of remorse as a means of more and more effectually

eradicating its cause. In this way religion is intrinsically distinguished from superstition, which latter rears in the mind, not reverence for the sublime, but dread and apprehension of the all-powerful Being to whose will terror-stricken man sees himself subjected, yet without according Him due honour. From this nothing can arise but grace-begging and vain adulation, instead of a religion consisting in a good life.

Sublimity, therefore, does not reside in any of the things of nature, but only in our own mind, in so far as we may become conscious of our superiority over nature within, and thus also over nature without us (as exerting influence upon us). Everything that provokes this feeling in us, including the *might* of nature which challenges our strength, is then, though improperly, called sublime, and it is only under presupposition of this idea within us, and in relation to it, that we are capable of attaining to the idea of the sublimity of that Being which inspires deep respect in us, not by the mere display of its might in nature, but more by the faculty which is planted in us of estimating that might without fear, and of regarding our estate as exalted above it.

[...]

§ 39
The communicability of a sensation.

Sensation, as the real in perception, where referred to knowledge, is called organic sensation and its specific Quality may be represented as completely communicable to others in a like mode, provided we assume that every one has a like sense to our own. This, however, is an absolutely inadmissible presupposition in the case of an organic sensation. Thus a person who is without a sense of smell cannot have a sensation of this kind communicated to him, and, even if he does not suffer from this deficiency, we still cannot be certain that he gets precisely the same sensation from a flower that we get from it. But still more divergent must we consider men to be in respect of the *agreeableness* or *disagreeableness* derived from the sensation of one and the same object of sense, and it is absolutely out of the question to require that pleasure in such objects should be acknowledged by every one. Pleasure of this kind, since it enters into the mind through sense – our rôle, therefore, being a passive one – may be called the pleasure of *enjoyment*.

On the other hand delight in an action on the score of its moral character is not a pleasure of enjoyment, but one of self-asserting activity and in this coming up to the idea of what it is meant to be. But this feeling, which is called the moral feeling, requires concepts, and is the presentation of a finality, not free, but according to law. It, therefore, admits of communication only through the instrumentality of reason and, if the pleasure is to be of the same kind for every one, by means of very determinate practical concepts of reason.

The pleasure in the sublime in nature, as one of rationalizing contemplation, lays claim also to universal participation, but still it presupposes another feeling, that, namely, of our supersensible sphere, which feeling, however obscure it may be, has a moral foundation. But there is absolutely no authority for my presupposing that others will pay attention to this, and take a delight in beholding the uncouth dimensions of nature, (one that in truth cannot be ascribed to its aspect, which is terrifying rather than otherwise). Nevertheless, having regard to the fact that attention ought to be paid upon every appropriate occasion to this moral birthright, we may still demand that delight from every one; but we can do so only through the moral law, which, in its turn, rests upon concepts of reason.

The pleasure in the beautiful is, on the other hand, neither a pleasure of enjoyment nor of an activity according to law, nor yet one of a rationalizing contemplation according to ideas, but rather of mere reflection. Without any guiding-line of end or principle this pleasure attends the ordinary apprehension of an object by means of the imagination, as the faculty of intuition, but with a reference to the understanding as faculty of concepts, and through the operation of a process of judgement which has also to be invoked in order to obtain the commonest experience. In the latter case, however, its functions are directed to perceiving an empirical objective concept, whereas in the former (in the aesthetic mode of estimating) merely to perceiving the adequacy of the representation for engaging both faculties of knowledge in their freedom in an harmonious (subjectively-final) employment, i.e. to feeling with pleasure the subjective bearings of the representation. This pleasure must of necessity depend for every one upon the same conditions, seeing that they are the subjective conditions of the possibility of a cognition in general, and the proportion of these cognitive faculties which is requisite for taste is requisite also for ordinary sound understanding, the presence of which we are entitled to presup-

pose in every one. And, for this reason also, one who judges with taste, (provided he does not make a mistake as to this consciousness, and does not take the matter for the form, or charm for beauty,) can impute the subjective finality, i.e. his delight in the Object, to every one else, and suppose his feeling universally communicable, and that, too, without the mediation of concepts.

§ 40
Taste as a kind of sensus communis.

The name of sense is often given to judgement where what attracts attention is not so much its reflective act as merely its result. So we speak of a sense of truth, of a sense of propriety, or of justice, &c. And yet, of course, we know, or at least ought well enough to know, that a sense cannot be the true abode of these concepts, not to speak of its being competent, even in the slightest degree, to pronounce universal rules. On the contrary, we recognize that a representation of this kind, be it of truth, propriety, beauty, or justice, could never enter our thoughts were we not able to raise ourselves above the level of the senses to that of higher faculties of cognition. *Common human understanding* which, as mere sound (not yet cultivated) understanding, is looked upon as the least we can expect from any one claiming the name of man, has therefore the doubtful honour of having the name of common sense (*sensus communis*) bestowed upon it; and bestowed, too, in an acceptation of the word *common* (not merely in our own language, where it actually has a double meaning, but also in many others) which makes it amount to what is *vulgar* – what is everywhere to be met with – a quality which by no means confers credit or distinction upon its possessor.

However, by the name *sensus communis* is to be understood the idea of a *public* sense, i.e. a critical faculty which in its reflective act takes account (*a priori*) of the mode of representation of every one else, in order, *as it were*, to weigh its judgement with the collective reason of mankind, and thereby avoid the illusion arising from subjective and personal conditions which could readily be taken for objective, an illusion that would exert a prejudicial influence upon its judgement. This is accomplished by weighing the judgement, not so much with actual, as rather with the merely possible, judgements of others, and by putting ourselves in the position of every one else, as the result of a mere abstraction from the limitations which contingently affect our own estimate. This, in turn, is effected by so far as possible letting go the element of matter, i.e. sensation, in our general state of representative activity, and confining attention to the formal peculiarities of our representation or general state of representative activity. Now it may seem that this operation of reflection is too artificial to be attributed to the faculty which we call *common* sense. But this is an appearance due only to its expression in abstract formulae. In itself nothing is more natural than to abstract from charm and emotion where one is looking for a judgement intended to serve as a universal rule.

While the following maxims of common human understanding do not properly come in here as constituent parts of the Critique of Taste, they may still serve to elucidate its fundamental propositions. They are these: (1) to think for oneself; (2) to think from the standpoint of every one else; (3) always to think consistently. The first is the maxim of *unprejudiced* thought, the second that of *enlarged* thought, the third that of *consistent* thought. The first is the maxim of a never-*passive* reason. To be given to such passivity, consequently to heteronomy of reason, is called *prejudice*; and the greatest of all prejudices is that of fancying nature not to be subject to rules which the understanding by virtue of its own essential law lays at its basis, i.e. *superstition*. Emancipation from superstition is called *enlightenment*;[7] for although this term applies also to emancipation from prejudices generally, still superstition deserves pre-eminently (*in sensu eminenti*) to be called a prejudice. For the condition of blindness into which superstition puts one, which it as much as demands from one as an obligation, makes the need of being led by others, and consequently the passive state of the reason, pre-eminently conspicuous. As to the second maxim belonging to our habits of thought, we have quite got into the way of calling a man narrow (*narrow*, as opposed to being *of enlarged mind*) whose talents fall short of what is required for employment upon work of any magnitude (especially that involving intensity). But the question here is not one of the faculty of cognition, but of the *mental habit* of making a final use of it. This, however small the range and degree to which a man's natural endowments extend, still indicates a man of *enlarged mind*: if he detaches himself from the subjective personal conditions of his judgement, which cramp the minds of so many others, and reflects upon his own judgement from a *universal standpoint* (which he can only determine by shifting his

ground to the standpoint of others). The third maxim – that, namely, of *consistent* thought – is the hardest of attainment, and is only attainable by the union of both the former, and after constant attention to them has made one at home in their observance. We may say: the first of these is the maxim of understanding, the second that of judgement, the third that of reason.

I resume the thread of the discussion interrupted by the above digression, and I say that taste can with more justice be called a *sensus communis* than can sound understanding; and that the aesthetic, rather than the intellectual, judgement can bear the name of a public sense,[8] i.e. taking it that we are prepared to use the word 'sense' of an effect that mere reflection has upon the mind; for then by sense we mean the feeling of pleasure. We might even define taste as the faculty of estimating what makes our feeling in a given representation *universally communicable* without the mediation of a concept.

The aptitude of men for communicating their thoughts requires, also, a relation between the imagination and the understanding, in order to connect intuitions with concepts, and concepts, in turn, with intuitions, which both unite in cognition. But there the agreement of both mental powers is *according to law*, and under the constraint of definite concepts. Only when the imagination in its freedom stirs the understanding, and the understanding apart from concepts puts the imagination into regular play, does the representation communicate itself not as thought, but as an internal feeling of a final state of the mind.

Taste is, therefore, the faculty of forming an *a priori* estimate of the communicability of the feelings that, without the mediation of a concept, are connected with a given representation.

Supposing, now, that we could assume that the mere universal communicability of our feeling must of itself carry with it an interest for us (an assumption, however, which we are not entitled to draw as a conclusion from the character of a merely reflective judgement), we should then be in a position to explain how the feeling in the judgement of taste comes to be exacted from every one as a sort of duty.

§ 41
The empirical interest in the beautiful.

Abundant proof has been given above to show that the judgement of taste by which something is declared beautiful must have no interest *as its determining ground*. But it does not follow from this that after it has once been posited as a pure aesthetic judgement, an interest cannot then enter into combination with it. This combination, however, can never be anything but indirect. Taste must, that is to say, first of all be represented in conjunction with something else, if the delight attending the mere reflection upon an object is to admit of having further conjoined with it *a pleasure in the real existence* of the object (as that wherein all interest consists). For the saying, *a posse ad esse non valet consequentia*, which is applied to cognitive judgements, holds good here in the case of aesthetic judgements. Now this 'something else' may be something empirical, such as an inclination proper to the nature of human beings, or it may be something intellectual, as a property of the will whereby it admits of rational determination *a priori*. Both of these involve a delight in the existence of the Object, and so can lay the foundation for an interest in what has already pleased of itself and without regard to any interest whatsoever.

The empirical interest in the beautiful exists only in *society*. And if we admit that the impulse to society is natural to mankind, and that the suitability for and the propensity towards it, i.e. *sociability*, is a property essential to the requirements of man as a creature intended for society, and one, therefore, that belongs to *humanity*, it is inevitable that we should also look upon taste in the light of a faculty for estimating whatever enables us to communicate even our *feeling* to every one else, and hence as a means of promoting that upon which the natural inclination of every one is set.

With no one to take into account but himself a man abandoned on a desert island would not adorn either himself or his hut, nor would he look for flowers, and still less plant them, with the object of providing himself with personal adornments. Only in society does it occur to him to be not merely a man, but a man refined after the manner of his kind (the beginning of civilization) – for that is the estimate formed of one who has the bent and turn for communicating his pleasure to others, and who is not quite satisfied with an Object unless his feeling of delight in it can be shared in communion with others. Further, a regard to universal communicability is a thing which every one expects and requires from every one else, just as if it were part of an original compact dictated by humanity itself. And thus, no doubt, at first only charms,

e.g. colours for painting oneself (roucou among the Caribs and cinnabar among the Iroquois), or flowers, sea-shells, beautifully coloured feathers, then, in the course of time, also beautiful forms (as in canoes, wearing-apparel, &c.) which convey no gratification, i.e. delight of enjoyment, become of moment in society and attract a considerable interest. Eventually, when civilization has reached its height it makes this work of communication almost the main business of refined inclination, and the entire value of sensations is placed in the degree to which they permit of universal communication. At this stage, then, even where the pleasure which each one has in an object is but insignificant and possesses of itself no conspicuous interest, still the idea of its universal communicability almost indefinitely augments its value.

This interest, indirectly attached to the beautiful by the inclination towards society, and, consequently, empirical, is, however, of no importance for us here. For that to which we have alone to look is what can have a bearing *a priori*, even though indirect, upon the judgement of taste. For, if even in this form an associated interest should betray itself, taste would then reveal a transition on the part of our critical faculty from the enjoyment of sense to the moral feeling. This would not merely mean that we should be supplied with a more effectual guide for the final employment of taste, but taste would further be presented as a link in the chain of the human faculties *a priori* upon which all legislation must depend. This much may certainly be said of the empirical interest in objects of taste, and in taste itself, that as taste thus pays homage to inclination, however refined, such interest will nevertheless readily fuse also with all inclinations and passions, which in society attain to their greatest variety and highest degree, and the interest in the beautiful, if this is made its ground, can but afford a very ambiguous transition from the agreeable to the good. We have reason, however, to inquire whether this transition may not still in some way be furthered by means of taste when taken in its purity.

§ 42

The intellectual interest in the beautiful.

It has been with the best intentions that those who love to see in the ultimate end of humanity, namely the morally good, the goal of all activities to which men are impelled by the inner bent of their nature, have regarded it as a mark of a good moral character to take an interest in the beautiful generally. But they have, not without reason, been contradicted by others who appeal to the fact of experience, that *virtuosi* in matters of taste, being not alone often, but one might say as a general rule, vain, capricious, and addicted to injurious passions, could perhaps more rarely than others lay claim to any pre-eminent attachment to moral principles. And so it would seem, not only that the feeling for the beautiful is specifically different from the moral feeling (which as a matter of fact is the case), but also that the interest which we may combine with it, will hardly consort with the moral, and certainly not on grounds of inner affinity.

Now I willingly admit that the interest in the *beautiful of art* (including under this heading the artificial use of natural beauties for personal adornment, and so from vanity) gives no evidence at all of a habit of mind attached to the morally good, or even inclined that way. But, on the other hand, I do maintain that to take an *immediate interest* in the beauty of *nature* (not merely to have taste in estimating it) is always a mark of a good soul; and that, where this interest is habitual, it is at least indicative of a temper of mind favourable to the moral feeling that it should readily associate itself with the *contemplation of nature*. It must, however, be borne in mind that I mean to refer strictly to the beautiful *forms* of nature, and to put to one side the *charms* which she is wont so lavishly to combine with them; because, though the interest in these is no doubt immediate, it is nevertheless empirical.

One who alone (and without any intention of communicating his observations to others) regards the beautiful form of a wild flower, a bird, an insect, or the like, out of admiration and love of them, and being loath to let them escape him in nature, even at the risk of some misadventure to himself – so far from there being any prospect of advantage to him – such a one takes an immediate, and in fact intellectual, interest in the beauty of nature. This means that he is not alone pleased with nature's product in respect of its form, but is also pleased at its existence, and is so without any charm of sense having a share in the matter, or without his associating with it any end whatsoever.

In this connexion, however, it is of note that were we to play a trick on our lover of the beautiful, and plant in the ground artificial flowers (which can be made so as to look just like natural ones), and perch artfully carved birds on the branches of trees, and he were to find out how he

had been taken in, the immediate interest which these things previously had for him would at once vanish – though, perhaps, a different interest might intervene in its stead, that, namely, of vanity in decorating his room with them for the eyes of others. The fact is that our intuition and reflection must have as their concomitant the thought that the beauty in question is nature's handiwork; and this is the sole basis of the immediate interest that is taken in it. Failing this we are either left with a bare judgement of taste void of all interest whatever, or else only with one that is combined with an interest that is mediate, involving, namely, a reference to society; which latter affords no reliable indication of morally good habits of thought.

The superiority which natural beauty has over that of art, even where it is excelled by the latter in point of form, in yet being alone able to awaken an immediate interest, accords with the refined and well-grounded habits of thought of all men who have cultivated their moral feeling. If a man with taste enough to judge of works of fine art with the greatest correctness and refinement readily quits the room in which he meets with those beauties that minister to vanity or, at least, social joys, and betakes himself to the beautiful in nature, so that he may there find as it were a feast for his soul in a train of thought which he can never completely evolve, we will then regard this his choice even with veneration, and give him credit for a beautiful soul, to which no connoisseur or art collector can lay claim on the score of the interest which his objects have for him. – Here, now, are two kinds of Objects which in the judgement of mere taste could scarcely contend with one another for a superiority. What then, is the distinction that makes us hold them in such different esteem?

We have a faculty of judgement which is merely aesthetic – a faculty of judging of forms without the aid of concepts, and of finding, in the mere estimate of them, a delight that we at the same time make into a rule for every one, without this judgement being founded on an interest, or yet producing one. – On the other hand we have also a faculty of intellectual judgement for the mere forms of practical maxims, (so far as they are of themselves qualified for universal legislation,) – a faculty of determining an *a priori* delight, which we make into a law for every one, without our judgement being founded on any interest, *though here it produces one*. The pleasure or displeasure in the former judgement is called that of taste; the latter is called that of the moral feeling.

But, now, reason is further interested in ideas (for which in our moral feeling it brings about an immediate interest,) having also objective reality. That is to say, it is of interest to reason that nature should at least show a trace or give a hint that it contains in itself some ground or other for assuming a uniform accordance of its products with our wholly disinterested delight (a delight which we cognize *a priori* as a law for every one without being able to ground it upon proofs). That being so, reason must take an interest in every manifestation on the part of nature of some such accordance. Hence the mind cannot reflect on the beauty of *nature* without at the same time finding its interest engaged. But this interest is akin to the moral. One, then, who takes such an interest in the beautiful in nature can only do so in so far as he has previously set his interest deep in the foundations of the morally good. On these grounds we have reason for presuming the presence of at least the germ of a good moral disposition in the case of a man to whom the beauty of nature is a matter of immediate interest.

It will be said that this interpretation of aesthetic judgements on the basis of kinship with our moral feeling has far too studied an appearance to be accepted as the true construction of the cypher in which nature speaks to us figuratively in its beautiful forms. But, first of all, this immediate interest in the beauty of nature is not in fact common. It is peculiar to those whose habits of thought are already trained to the good or else are eminently susceptible of such training; and under these circumstances the analogy in which the pure judgement of taste that, without relying upon any interest, gives us a feeling of delight, and at the same time represents it *a priori* as proper to mankind in general, stands to the moral judgement that does just the same from concepts, is one which, without any clear, subtle, and deliberate reflection, conduces to a like immediate interest being taken in the objects of the former judgement as in those of the latter – with this one difference, that the interest in the first case is free, while in the latter it is one founded on objective laws. In addition to this there is our admiration of nature which in her beautiful products displays herself as art, not as mere matter of chance, but, as it were, designedly, according to a law-directed arrangement, and as finality apart from any end. As we never meet with such an end outside ourselves, we naturally look for it in ourselves, and, in fact, in that which constitutes the ultimate

end of our existence – the moral side of our being. [...]

The fact that the delight in beautiful art does not, in the pure judgement of taste, involve an immediate interest, as does that in beautiful nature, may be readily explained. For the former is either such an imitation of the latter as goes the length of deceiving us, in which case it acts upon us in the character of a natural beauty, which we take it to be; or else it is an intentional art obviously directed to our delight. In the latter case, however, the delight in the product would, it is true, be brought about immediately by taste, but there would be nothing but a mediate interest in the cause that lay beneath – an interest, namely, in an art only capable of interesting by its end, and never in itself. It will, perhaps, be said that this is also the case where an Object of nature only interests by its beauty so far as a moral idea is brought into partnership therewith. But it is not the object that is of immediate interest, but rather the inherent character of the beauty qualifying it for such a partnership – a character, therefore, that belongs to the very essence of beauty.

The charms in natural beauty, which are to be found blended, as it were, so frequently with beauty of form, belong either to the modifications of light (in colouring) or of sound (in tones). For these are the only sensations which permit not merely of a feeling of the senses, but also of reflection upon the form of these modifications of sense, and so embody as it were a language in which nature speaks to us and which has the semblance of a higher meaning. Thus the white colour of the lily seems to dispose the mind to ideas of innocence, and the other seven colours, following the series from the red to the violet, similarly to ideas of (1) sublimity, (2) courage, (3) candour, (4) amiability, (5) modesty, (6) constancy, (7) tenderness. The bird's song tells of joyousness and contentment with its existence. At least so we interpret nature – whether such be its purpose or not. But it is the indispensable requisite of the interest which we here take in beauty, that the beauty should be that of nature, and it vanishes completely as soon as we are conscious of having been deceived, and that it is only the work of art – so completely that even taste can then no longer find in it anything beautiful nor sight anything attractive. What do poets set more store on than the nightingale's bewitching and beautiful note, in a lonely thicket on a still summer evening by the soft light of the moon? And yet we have instances of how, where no such songster was to be found, a jovial host has played a trick on the guests with him on a visit to enjoy the country air, and has done so to their huge satisfaction, by hiding in a thicket a rogue of a youth who (with a reed or rush in his mouth) knew how to reproduce this note so as to hit off nature to perfection. But the instant one realizes that it is all a fraud no one will long endure listening to this song that before was regarded as so attractive. And it is just the same with the song of any other bird. It must be nature, or be mistaken by us for nature, to enable us to take an immediate *interest* in the beautiful as such; and this is all the more so if we may even call upon others to take a similar interest. And such a demand we do in fact make, since we regard as coarse and low the habits of thought of those who have no *feeling* for beautiful nature (for this is the word we use for susceptibility to an interest in the contemplation of beautiful nature), and who devote themselves to the mere enjoyments of sense found in eating and drinking.

§ 43
Art in general.

(1.) *Art* is distinguished from *nature* as making (*facere*) is from acting or operating in general (*agere*), and the product or the result of the former is distinguished from that of the latter as *work* (*opus*) from operation (*effectus*).

By right it is only production through freedom, i.e. through an act of will that places reason at the basis of its action, that should be termed art. For, although we are pleased to call what bees produce (their regularly constructed cells) a work of art, we only do so on the strength of an analogy with art; that is to say, as soon as we call to mind that no rational deliberation forms the basis of their labour, we say at once that it is a product of their nature (of instinct), and it is only to their Creator that we ascribe it as art.

If, as sometimes happens, in a search through a bog, we light on a piece of hewn wood, we do not say it is a product of nature but of art. Its producing cause had an end in view to which the object owes its form. Apart from such cases, we recognize an art in everything formed in such a way that its actuality must have been preceded by a representation of the thing in its cause (as even in the case of the bees), although the effect could not have been *thought* by the cause. But where anything is called absolutely a work of art, to distinguish it from a

natural product, then some work of man is always understood.

(2.) *Art*, as human skill, is distinguished also from *science* (as *ability* from *knowledge*), as a practical from a theoretical faculty, as technic from theory (as the art of surveying from geometry). For this reason, also, what one *can* do the moment one only *knows* what is to be done, hence without anything more than sufficient knowledge of the desired result, is not called art. To art that alone belongs for which the possession of the most complete knowledge does not involve one's having then and there the skill to do it. *Camper* describes very exactly how the best shoe must be made, but he, doubtless, was not able to turn one out himself.[9]

(3.) *Art* is further distinguished from *handicraft*. The first is called *free*, the other may be called *industrial art*. We look on the former as something which could only prove final (be a success) as play, i.e. an occupation which is agreeable on its own account; but on the second as labour, i.e. a business, which on its own account is disagreeable (drudgery), and is only attractive by means of what it results in (e.g. the pay), and which is consequently capable of being a compulsory imposition. Whether in the list of arts and crafts we are to rank watchmakers as artists, and smiths on the contrary as craftsmen, requires a standpoint different from that here adopted – one, that is to say, taking account of the proportion of the talents which the business undertaken in either case must necessarily involve. Whether, also, among the so-called seven free arts some may not have been included which should be reckoned as sciences, and many, too, that resemble handicraft, is a matter I will not discuss here. It is not amiss, however, to remind the reader of this: that in all free arts something of a compulsory character is still required, or, as it is called, a *mechanism*, without which the *soul*, which in art must be *free*, and which alone gives life to the work, would be bodyless and evanescent (e.g. in the poetic art there must be correctness and wealth of language, likewise prosody and metre). For not a few leaders of a newer school believe that the best way to promote a free art is to sweep away all restraint, and convert it from labour into mere play.

§ 44
Fine art.

There is no science of the beautiful, but only a Critique. Nor, again, is there an elegant (*schöne*) science, but only a fine (*schöne*) art. For a science of the beautiful would have to determine scientifically, i.e. by means of proofs, whether a thing was to be considered beautiful or not; and the judgement upon beauty, consequently, would, if belonging to science, fail to be a judgement of taste. As for a beautiful science – a science which, as such, is to be beautiful, is a nonentity. For if, treating it as a science, we were to ask for reasons and proofs, we would be put off with elegant phrases (*bons mots*). What has given rise to the current expression *elegant sciences* is, doubtless, no more than this, that common observation has, quite accurately, noted the fact that for fine art, in the fulness of its perfection, a large store of science is required, as, for example, knowledge of ancient languages, acquaintance with classical authors, history, antiquarian learning, &c. Hence these historical sciences, owing to the fact that they form the necessary preparation and groundwork for fine art, and partly also owing to the fact that they are taken to comprise even the knowledge of the products of fine art (rhetoric and poetry), have by a confusion of words, actually got the name of elegant sciences.

Where art, merely seeking to actualize a possible object to the *cognition* of which it is adequate, does whatever acts are required for that purpose, then it is *mechanical*. But should the feeling of pleasure be what it has immediately in view it is then termed *aesthetic* art. As such it may be either *agreeable* or *fine* art. The description 'agreeable art' applies where the end of the art is that the pleasure should accompany the representations considered as mere *sensations*, the description 'fine art' where it is to accompany them considered as *modes of cognition*.

Agreeable arts are those which have mere enjoyment for their object. Such are all the charms that can gratify a dinner party: entertaining narrative, the art of starting the whole table in unrestrained and sprightly conversation, or with jest and laughter inducing a certain air of gaiety. Here, as the saying goes, there may be much loose talk over the glasses, without a person wishing to be brought to book for all he utters, because it is only given out for the entertainment of the moment, and not as a lasting matter to be made the subject of reflection or repetition. (Of the same sort is also the art of arranging the table for enjoyment, or, at large banquets, the music of the orchestra – a quaint idea intended to act on the mind merely as an agreeable noise fostering a genial spirit, which, without any one paying the smallest attention to the composition, promotes the free flow of conversation between guest and guest.) In addition must be included play of every kind which is attended with no further interest than that of making the time pass by unheeded.

Fine art, on the other hand, is a mode of representation which is intrinsically final, and which, although devoid of an end, has the effect of advancing the culture of the mental powers in the interests of social communication.

The universal communicability of a pleasure involves in its very concept that the pleasure is not one of enjoyment arising out of mere sensation, but must be one of reflection. Hence aesthetic art, as art which is beautiful, is one having for its standard the reflective judgement and not organic sensation.

§ 45
Fine art is an art, so far as it has at the same time the appearance of being nature.

A product of fine art must be recognized to be art and not nature. Nevertheless the finality in its form must appear just as free from the constraint of arbitrary rules as if it were a product of mere nature. Upon this feeling of freedom in the play of our cognitive faculties – which play has at the same time to be final – rests that pleasure which alone is universally communicable without being based on concepts. Nature proved beautiful when it wore the appearance of art; and art can only be termed beautiful, where we are conscious of its being art, while yet it has the appearance of nature.

For, whether we are dealing with beauty of nature or beauty of art, we may make the universal statement: *that is beautiful which pleases in the mere estimate of it* (not in sensation or by means of a concept). Now art has always got a definite intention of producing something. Were this 'something', however, to be mere sensation (something merely subjective), intended to be accompanied with pleasure, then such product would, in our estimation of it, only please through the agency of the feeling of the senses. On the other hand, were the intention one directed to the production of a definite object, then, supposing this were attained by art, the object would only please by means of a concept. But in both cases the art would please, not in *the mere estimate of it*, i.e. not as fine art, but rather as mechanical art.

Hence the finality in the product of fine art, intentional though it be, must not have the appearance of being intentional; i.e. fine art must be clothed *with the aspect* of nature, although we recognize it to be art. But the way in which a product of art seems like nature, is by the presence of perfect *exactness* in the agreement with rules prescribing how alone the product can be what it is intended to be, but with an absence of *laboured effect*, (without academic form betraying itself,) i.e. without a trace appearing of the artist having always had the rule present to him and of its having fettered his mental powers.

§ 46
Fine art is the art of genius.

Genius is the talent (natural endowment) which gives the rule to art. Since talent, as an innate productive faculty of the artist, belongs itself to nature, we may put it this way: *Genius* is the innate mental aptitude (*ingenium*) *through which* nature gives the rule to art.

Whatever may be the merits of this definition, and whether it is merely arbitrary, or whether it is adequate or not to the concept usually associated with the word *genius* (a point which the following sections have to clear up), it may still be shown at the outset that, according to this acceptation of the word, fine arts must necessarily be regarded as arts of *genius*.

For every art presupposes rules which are laid down as the foundation which first enables a product, if it is to be called one of art, to be represented as possible. The concept of fine art, however, does not permit of the judgement upon the beauty of its product being derived from any rule that has a *concept* for its determining ground, and that depends, consequently, on a concept of the way in which the product is possible. Consequently fine art cannot of its own self excogitate the rule according to which it is to effectuate its product. But since, for all that, a product can never be called art unless there is a preceding rule, it follows that nature in the individual (and by virtue of the harmony of his faculties) must give the rule to art, i.e. fine art is only possible as a product of genius.

From this it may be seen that genius (1) is a *talent* for producing that for which no definite rule can be given: and not an aptitude in the way of cleverness for what can be learned according to some rule; and that consequently *originality* must be its primary property. (2) Since there may also be original nonsense, its products must at the same

time be models, i.e. be *exemplary*; and, consequently, though not themselves derived from imitation, they must serve that purpose for others, i.e. as a standard or rule of estimating. (3) It cannot indicate scientifically how it brings about its product, but rather gives the rule as *nature*. Hence, where an author owes a product to his genius, he does not himself know how the *ideas* for it have entered into his head, nor has he it in his power to invent the like at pleasure, or methodically, and communicate the same to others in such precepts as would put them in a position to produce similar products. (Hence, presumably, our word *Genie* is derived from *genius*, as the peculiar guardian and guiding spirit given to a man at his birth, by the inspiration of which those original ideas were obtained.) (4) Nature prescribes the rule through genius not to science but to art, and this also only in so far as it is to be fine art.

§ 47
Elucidation and confirmation of the above explanation of genius.

Every one is agreed on the point of the complete opposition between genius and the *spirit of imitation*. Now since learning is nothing but imitation, the greatest ability, or aptness as a pupil (capacity), is still, as such, not equivalent to genius. Even though a man weaves his own thoughts or fancies, instead of merely taking in what others have thought, and even though he go so far as to bring fresh gains to art and science, this does not afford a valid reason for calling such a man of *brains*, and often great brains, a *genius*, in contradistinction to one who goes by the name of *shallow-pate*, because he can never do more than merely learn and follow a lead. For what is accomplished in this way is something that *could* have been learned. Hence it all lies in the natural path of investigation and reflection according to rules, and so is not specifically distinguishable from what may be acquired as the result of industry backed up by imitation. So all that *Newton* has set forth in his immortal work on the Principles of Natural Philosophy may well be learned, however great a mind it took to find it all out, but we cannot learn to write in a true poetic vein, no matter how complete all the precepts of the poetic art may be, or however excellent its models. The reason is that all the steps that Newton had to take from the first elements of geometry to his greatest and most profound discoveries were such as he could make intuitively evident and plain to follow, not only for himself but for every one else. On the other hand no *Homer* or *Wieland* can show how his ideas, so rich at once in fancy and in thought, enter and assemble themselves in his brain, for the good reason that he does not himself know, and so cannot teach others. In matters of science, therefore, the greatest inventor differs only in degree from the most laborious imitator and apprentice, whereas he differs specifically from one endowed by nature for fine art. No disparagement, however, of those great men, to whom the human race is so deeply indebted, is involved in this comparison of them with those who on the score of their talent for fine art are the elect of nature. The talent for science is formed for the continued advances of greater perfection in knowledge, with all its dependent practical advantages, as also for imparting the same to others. Hence scientists can boast a ground of considerable superiority over those who merit the honour of being called geniuses, since genius reaches a point at which art must make a halt, as there is a limit imposed upon it which it cannot transcend. This limit has in all probability been long since attained. In addition, such skill cannot be communicated, but requires to be bestowed directly from the hand of nature upon each individual, and so with him it dies, awaiting the day when nature once again endows another in the same way – one who needs no more than an example to set the talent of which he is conscious at work on similar lines.

Seeing, then, that the natural endowment of art (as fine art) must furnish the rule, what kind of rule must this be? It cannot be one set down in a formula and serving as a precept – for then the judgement upon the beautiful would be determinable according to concepts. Rather must the rule be gathered from the performance, i.e. from the product, which others may use to put their own talent to the test, so as to let it serve as a model, not for *imitation*, but for *following*. The possibility of this is difficult to explain. The artist's ideas arouse like ideas on the part of his pupil, presuming nature to have visited him with a like proportion of the mental powers. For this reason the models of fine art are the only means of handing down this art to posterity. This is something which cannot be done by mere descriptions (especially not in the line of the arts of speech), and in these arts, furthermore, only those models can become classical of which the ancient, dead languages, preserved as learned, are the medium.

Despite the marked difference that distinguishes mechanical art, as an art merely depending upon industry and learning, from fine art, as that of genius, there is still no fine art in which something mechanical, capable of being at once comprehended and followed in obedience to rules, and consequently something *academic* does not constitute the essential condition of the art. For the thought of something as end must be present, or else its product would not be ascribed to an art at all, but would be a mere product of chance. But the effectuation of an end necessitates determinate rules which we cannot venture to dispense with. Now, seeing that originality of talent is one (though not the sole) essential factor that goes to make up the character of genius, shallow minds fancy that the best evidence they can give of their being full-blown geniuses is by emancipating themselves from all academic constraint of rules, in the belief that one cuts a finer figure on the back of an ill-tempered than of a trained horse. Genius can do no more than furnish rich *material* for products of fine art; its elaboration and its *form* require a talent academically trained, so that it may be employed in such a way as to stand the test of judgement. But, for a person to hold forth and pass sentence like a genius in matters that fall to the province of the most patient rational investigation, is ridiculous in the extreme. One is at a loss to know whether to laugh more at the impostor who envelops himself in such a cloud – in which we are given fuller scope to our imagination at the expense of all use of our critical faculty, – or at the simple-minded public which imagines that its inability clearly to cognize and comprehend this masterpiece of penetration is due to its being invaded by new truths *en masse*, in comparison with which, detail, due to carefully weighed exposition and an academic examination of rootprinciples, seems to it only the work of a tyro.

§ 48
The relation of genius to taste.

For *estimating* beautiful objects, as such, what is required is *taste*; but for fine art, i.e. the *production* of such objects, one needs *genius*.

If we consider genius as the talent for fine art (which the proper signification of the word imports), and if we would analyse it from this point of view into the faculties which must concur to constitute such a talent, it is imperative at the outset accurately to determine the difference between beauty of nature, which it only requires taste to estimate, and beauty of art, which requires genius for its possibility (a possibility to which regard must also be paid in estimating such an object).

A beauty of nature is a *beautiful thing*; beauty of art is a *beautiful representation* of a thing.

To enable me to estimate a beauty of nature, as such, I do not need to be previously possessed of a concept of what sort of a thing the object is intended to be, i.e. I am not obliged to know its material finality (the end), but, rather, in forming an estimate of it apart from any knowledge of the end, the mere form pleases on its own account. If, however, the object is presented as a product of art, and is as such to be declared beautiful, then, seeing that art always presupposes an end in the cause (and its causality), a concept of what the thing is intended to be must first of all be laid at its basis. And, since the agreement of the manifold in a thing with an inner character belonging to it as its end constitutes the perfection of the thing, it follows that in estimating beauty of art the perfection of the thing must be also taken into account – a matter which in estimating a beauty of nature, as beautiful, is quite irrelevant. – It is true that in forming an estimate, especially of animate objects of nature, e.g. of a man or a horse, objective finality is also commonly taken into account with a view to judgement upon their beauty; but then the judgement also ceases to be purely aesthetic, i.e. a mere judgement of taste. Nature is no longer estimated as it appears like art, but rather in so far as it actually *is* art, though superhuman art; and the teleological judgement serves as basis and condition of the aesthetic, and one which the latter must regard. In such a case, where one says, for example, 'that is a beautiful woman,' what one in fact thinks is only this, that in her form nature excellently portrays the ends present in the female figure. For one has to extend one's view beyond the mere form to a concept, to enable the object to be thought in such manner by means of an aesthetic judgement logically conditioned.

Where fine art evidences its superiority is in the beautiful descriptions it gives of things that in nature would be ugly or displeasing. The Furies, diseases, devastations of war, and the like, can (as evils) be very beautifully described, nay even represented in pictures. One kind of ugliness alone is incapable of being represented conformably to nature without destroying all aesthetic delight, and consequently artistic beauty, namely,

that which excites *disgust*. For, as in this strange sensation, which depends purely on the imagination, the object is represented as insisting, as it were, upon our enjoying it, while we still set our face against it, the artificial representation of the object is no longer distinguishable from the nature of the object itself in our sensation, and so it cannot possibly be regarded as beautiful. The art of sculpture, again, since in its products art is almost confused with nature, has excluded from its creations the direct representation of ugly objects, and, instead, only sanctions, for example, the representation of death (in a beautiful genius), or of the warlike spirit (in Mars), by means of an allegory, or attributes which wear a pleasant guise, and so only indirectly, through an interpretation on the part of reason, and not for the pure aesthetic judgement.

So much for the beautiful representation of an object, which is properly only the form of the presentation of a concept, and the means by which the latter is universally communicated. To give this form, however, to the product of fine art, taste merely is required. By this the artist, having practised and corrected his taste by a variety of examples from nature or art, controls his work and, after many, and often laborious, attempts to satisfy taste, finds the form which commends itself to him. Hence this form is not, as it were, a matter of inspiration, or of a free swing of the mental powers, but rather of a slow and even painful process of improvement, directed to making the form adequate to his thought without prejudice to the freedom in the play of those powers.

Taste is, however, merely a critical, not a productive faculty; and what conforms to it is not, merely on that account, a work of fine art. It may belong to useful and mechanical art, or even to science, as a product following definite rules which are capable of being learned and which must be closely followed. But the pleasing form imparted to the work is only the vehicle of communication and a mode, as it were, of execution, in respect of which one remains to a certain extent free, notwithstanding being otherwise tied down to a definite end. So we demand that table appointments, or even a moral dissertation, and, indeed, a sermon, must bear this form of fine art, yet without its appearing *studied*. But one would not call them on this account works of fine art. A poem, a musical composition, a picture-gallery, and so forth, would, however, be placed under this head; and so in a would-be work of fine art we may frequently recognize genius without taste, and in another taste without genius.

§ 49
The faculties of the mind which constitute genius.

Of certain products which are expected, partly at least, to stand on the footing of fine art, we say they are *soul*less; and this, although we find nothing to censure in them as far as taste goes. A poem may be very pretty and elegant, but is soulless. A narrative has precision and method, but is soulless. A speech on some festive occasion may be good in substance and ornate withal, but may be soulless. Conversation frequently is not devoid of entertainment, but yet soulless. Even of a woman we may well say, she is pretty, affable, and refined, but soulless. Now what do we here mean by 'soul'?

'*Soul*' (*Geist*) in an aesthetical sense, signifies the animating principle in the mind. But that whereby this principle animates the psychic substance (*Seele*) – the material which it employs for that purpose – is that which sets the mental powers into a swing that is final, i.e. into a play which is self-maintaining and which strengthens those powers for such activity.

Now my proposition is that this principle is nothing else than the faculty of presenting *aesthetic ideas*. But, by an aesthetic idea I mean that representation of the imagination which induces much thought, yet without the possibility of any definite thought whatever, i.e. *concept*, being adequate to it, and which language, consequently, can never get quite on level terms with or render completely intelligible. – It is easily seen, that an aesthetic idea is the counterpart (pendant) of a *rational idea*, which, conversely, is a concept, to which no *intuition* (representation of the imagination) can be adequate.

The imagination (as a productive faculty of cognition) is a powerful agent for creating, as it were, a second nature out of the material supplied to it by actual nature. It affords us entertainment where experience proves too commonplace; and we even use it to remodel experience, always following, no doubt, laws that are based on analogy, but still also following principles which have a higher seat in reason (and which are every whit as natural to us as those followed by the understanding in laying hold of empirical nature). By this means we get a sense of our freedom from the law of association (which attaches to the empirical employment of the imagination), with the result that the material can be borrowed by us from nature in accordance with that law, but be worked up by us into something else – namely, what surpasses nature.

Such representations of the imagination may be termed *ideas*. This is partly because they at least strain after something lying out beyond the confines of experience, and so seek to approximate to a presentation of rational concepts (i.e. intellectual ideas), thus giving to these concepts the semblance of an objective reality. But, on the other hand, there is this most important reason, that no concept can be wholly adequate to them as internal intuitions. The poet essays the task of interpreting to sense the rational ideas of invisible beings, the kingdom of the blessed, hell, eternity, creation, &c. Or, again, as to things of which examples occur in experience, e.g. death, envy, and all vices, as also love, fame, and the like, transgressing the limits of experience he attempts with the aid of an imagination which emulates the display of reason in its attainment of a maximum, to body them forth to sense with a completeness of which nature affords no parallel; and it is in fact precisely in the poetic art that the faculty of aesthetic ideas can show itself to full advantage. This faculty, however, regarded solely on its own account, is properly no more than a talent (of the imagination).

If, now, we attach to a concept a representation of the imagination belonging to its presentation, but inducing solely on its own account such a wealth of thought as would never admit of comprehension in a definite concept, and, as a consequence, giving aesthetically an unbounded expansion to the concept itself, then the imagination here displays a creative activity, and it puts the faculty of intellectual ideas (reason) into motion – a motion, at the instance of a representation, towards an extension of thought, that, while germane, no doubt, to the concept of the object, exceeds what can be laid hold of in that representation or clearly expressed.

Those forms which do not constitute the presentation of a given concept itself, but which, as secondary representations of the imagination, express the derivatives connected with it, and its kinship with other concepts, are called (aesthetic) *attributes* of an object, the concept of which, as an idea of reason, cannot be adequately presented. In this way Jupiter's eagle, with the lightning in its claws, is an attribute of the mighty king of heaven, and the peacock of its stately queen. They do not, like *logical attributes*, represent what lies in our concepts of the sublimity and majesty of creation, but rather something else – something that gives the imagination an incentive to spread its flight over a whole host of kindred representations that provoke more thought than admits of expression in a concept determined by words. They furnish an *aesthetic idea*, which serves the above rational idea as a substitute for logical presentation, but with the proper function, however, of animating the mind by opening out for it a prospect into a field of kindred representations stretching beyond its ken. But it is not alone in the arts of painting or sculpture, where the name of attribute is customarily employed, that fine art acts in this way; poetry and rhetoric also derive the soul that animates their works wholly from the aesthetic attributes of the objects – attributes which go hand in hand with the logical, and give the imagination an impetus to bring more thought into play in the matter, though in an undeveloped manner, than allows of being brought within the embrace of a concept, or, therefore, of being definitely formulated in language. – For the sake of brevity I must confine myself to a few examples only. When the great king expresses himself in one of his poems by saying:

Oui, finissons sans trouble, et mourons sans regrets,
En laissant l'Univers comblé de nos bienfaits.
Ainsi l'Astre du jour, au bout de sa carrière,
Répand sur l'horizon une douce lumière,
Et les derniers rayons qu'il darde dans les airs
Sont les derniers soupirs qu'il donne à l'Univers;

he kindles in this way his rational idea of a cosmopolitan sentiment even at the close of life, with the help of an attribute which the imagination (in remembering all the pleasures of a fair summer's day that is over and gone – a memory of which pleasures is suggested by a serene evening) annexes to that representation, and which stirs up a crowd of sensations and secondary representations for which no expression can be found. On the other hand, even an intellectual concept may serve, conversely, as attribute for a representation of sense, and so animate the latter with the idea of the supersensible; but only by the aesthetic factor subjectively attaching to the consciousness of the supersensible being employed for the purpose. So, for example, a certain poet says in his description of a beautiful morning: 'The sun arose, as out of virtue rises peace.' The consciousness of virtue, even where we put ourselves only in thought in the position of a virtuous man, diffuses in the mind a multitude of sublime and tranquillizing feelings, and gives a boundless outlook into a happy future, such as no expression within the compass of a definite concept completely attains.[10]

In a word, the aesthetic idea is a representation of the imagination, annexed to a given concept, with which, in the free employment of imagination, such a multiplicity of partial representations are bound up, that no expression indicating a definite concept can be found for it – one which on that account allows a concept to be supplemented in thought by much that is indefinable in words, and the feeling of which quickens the cognitive faculties, and with language, as a mere thing of the letter, binds up the spirit (soul) also.

The mental powers whose union in a certain relation constitutes *genius* are imagination and understanding. Now, since the imagination, in its employment on behalf of cognition, is subjected to the constraint of the understanding and the restriction of having to be conformable to the concept belonging thereto, whereas aesthetically it is free to furnish of its own accord, over and above that agreement with the concept, a wealth of undeveloped material for the understanding, to which the latter paid no regard in its concept, but which it can make use of, not so much objectively for cognition, as subjectively for quickening the cognitive faculties, and hence also indirectly for cognitions, it may be seen that genius properly consists in the happy relation, which science cannot teach nor industry learn, enabling one to find out ideas for a given concept, and, besides, to hit upon the *expression* for them – the expression by means of which the subjective mental condition induced by the ideas as the concomitant of a concept may be communicated to others. This latter talent is properly that which is termed soul. For to get an expression for what is indefinable in the mental state accompanying a particular representation and to make it universally communicable – be the expression in language or painting or statuary – is a thing requiring a faculty for laying hold of the rapid and transient play of the imagination, and for unifying it in a concept (which for that very reason is original, and reveals a new rule which could not have been inferred from any preceding principles or examples) that admits of communication without any constraint of rules.

If, after this analysis, we cast a glance back upon the above definition of what is called *genius*, we find: *First*, that it is a talent for art – not one for science, in which clearly known rules must take the lead and determine the procedure. *Secondly*, being a talent in the line of art, it presupposes a definite concept of the product – as its end. Hence it presupposes understanding, but, in addition, a representation, indefinite though it be, of the material, i.e. of the intuition, required for the presentation of that concept, and so a relation of the imagination to the understanding. *Thirdly*, it displays itself, not so much in the working out of the projected end in the presentation of a definite *concept*, as rather in the portrayal, or expression of *aesthetic ideas* containing a wealth of material for effecting that intention. Consequently the imagination is represented by it in its freedom from all guidance of rules, but still as final for the presentation of the given concept. *Fourthly*, and lastly, the unsought and undesigned subjective finality in the free harmonizing of the imagination with the understanding's conformity to law presupposes a proportion and accord between these faculties such as cannot be brought about by any observance of rules, whether of science or mechanical imitation, but can only be produced by the nature of the individual.

Genius, according to these presuppositions, is the exemplary originality of the natural endowments of an individual in the *free* employment of his cognitive faculties. On this showing, the product of a genius (in respect of so much in this product as is attributable to genius, and not to possible learning or academic instruction,) is an example, not for imitation (for that would mean the loss of the element of genius, and just the very soul of the work), but to be followed by another genius – one whom it arouses to a sense of his own originality in putting freedom from the constraint of rules so into force in his art, that for art itself a new rule is won – which is what shows a talent to be exemplary. Yet, since the genius is one of nature's elect – a type that must be regarded as but a rare phenomenon – for other clever minds his example gives rise to a school, that is to say a methodical instruction according to rules, collected, so far as the circumstances admit, from such products of genius and their peculiarities. And, to that extent, fine art is for such persons a matter of imitation, for which nature, through the medium of a genius, gave the rule.

But this imitation becomes *aping* when the pupil *copies* everything down to the deformities which the genius only of necessity suffered to remain,

because they could hardly be removed without loss of force to the idea. This courage has merit only in the case of a genius. A certain *boldness* of expression, and, in general, many a deviation from the common rule becomes him well, but in no sense is it a thing worthy of imitation. On the contrary it remains all through intrinsically a blemish, which one is bound to try to remove, but for which the genius is, as it were, allowed to plead a privilege, on the ground that a scrupulous carefulness would spoil what is inimitable in the impetuous ardour of his soul. *Mannerism* is another kind of aping – an aping of *peculiarity* (originality) in general, for the sake of removing oneself as far as possible from imitators, while the talent requisite to enable one to be at the same time *exemplary* is absent. – There are, in fact, two modes (*modi*) in general of arranging one's thoughts for utterance. The one is called a *manner* (*modus aestheticus*), the other a *method* (*modus logicus*). The distinction between them is this: the former possesses no standard other than the *feeling* of unity in the presentation, whereas the latter here follows definite *principles*. As a consequence the former is alone admissible for fine art. It is only, however, where the manner of carrying the idea into execution in a product of art is *aimed at* singularity instead of being made appropriate to the idea, that *mannerism* is properly ascribed to such a product. The ostentatious (*précieux*), forced, and affected styles, intended to mark one out from the common herd (though soul is wanting), resemble the behaviour of a man who, as we say, hears himself talk, or who stands and moves about as if he were on a stage to be gaped at – action which invariably betrays a tyro.

§ 50
The combination of taste and genius in products of fine art.

To ask whether more stress should be laid in matters of fine art upon the presence of genius or upon that of taste, is equivalent to asking whether more turns upon imagination or upon judgement. Now, imagination rather entitles an art to be called an *inspired* (*geistreiche*) than a *fine* art. It is only in respect of judgement that the name of fine art is deserved. Hence it follows that judgement, being the indispensable condition (*conditio sine qua non*), is at least what one must look to as of capital importance in forming an estimate of art as fine art. So far as beauty is concerned, to be fertile and

original in ideas is not such an imperative requirement as it is that the imagination in its freedom
should be in accordance with the understanding's
conformity to law. For in lawless freedom imagination, with all its wealth, produces nothing but
nonsense; the power of judgement, on the other
hand, is the faculty that makes it consonant with
understanding.

Taste, like judgement in general, is the discipline (or corrective) of genius. It severely clips its
wings, and makes it orderly or polished; but at the
same time it gives it guidance, directing and controlling its flight, so that it may preserve its character of finality. It introduces a clearness and order

into the plenitude of thought, and in so doing gives
stability to the ideas, and qualifies them at once for
permanent and universal approval, for being followed by others, and for a continually progressive
culture. And so, where the interests of both these
qualities clash in a product, and there has to be a
sacrifice of something, then it should rather be on
the side of genius; and judgement, which in matters of fine art bases its decision on its own proper
principles, will more readily endure an abatement
of the freedom and wealth of the imagination, than
that the understanding should be compromised.

The requisites for fine art are, therefore, *imagination, understanding, soul*, and *taste*.[11]

Notes

1   The definition of taste here relied upon is that it is
the faculty of estimating the beautiful. But the discovery of what is required for calling an object beautiful must be reserved for the analysis of judgements
of taste. In my search for the moments to which
attention is paid by this judgement in its reflection,
I have followed the guidance of the logical functions
of judging (for a judgement of taste always involves a
reference to understanding). I have brought the
moment of quality first under review, because this
is what the aesthetic judgement on the beautiful looks
to in the first instance.

2   A judgement upon an object of our delight may be
wholly *disinterested* but withal very *interesting*, i.e. it
relies on no interest, but it produces one. Of this kind
are all pure moral judgements. But, of themselves,
judgements of taste do not even set up any interest
whatsoever. Only in society is it *interesting* to have
taste – a point which will be explained in the sequel.

3   An obligation to enjoyment is a patent absurdity. And
the same, then, must also be said of a supposed
obligation to actions that have merely enjoyment for
their aim, no matter how spiritually this enjoyment
may be refined in thought (or embellished), and even
if it be a mystical, so-called heavenly, enjoyment.

4   Models of taste with respect to the arts of speech
must be composed in a dead and learned language;
the first, to prevent their having to suffer the changes
that inevitably overtake living ones, making dignified
expressions become degraded, common ones antiquated, and ones newly coined after a short currency
obsolete; the second to ensure its having a grammar
that is not subject to the caprices of fashion, but has
fixed rules of its own.

5   It will be found that a perfectly regular face – one that
a painter might fix his eye on for a model – ordinarily
conveys nothing. This is because it is devoid of anything characteristic, and so the idea of the race is

expressed in it rather than the specific qualities of a
person. The exaggeration of what is characteristic in
this way, i.e. exaggeration violating the normal idea
(the finality of the race), is called *caricature*. Also
experience shows that these quite regular faces indicate as a rule internally only a mediocre type of man;
presumably – if one may assume that nature in its
external form expresses the proportions of the internal – because, where none of the mental qualities
exceed the proportion requisite to constitute a man
free from faults, nothing can be expected in the way
of what is called *genius*, in which nature seems to
make a departure from its wonted relations of the
mental powers in favour of some special one.

6   As telling against this explanation, the instance may
be adduced, that there are things in which we see a
form suggesting adaptation to an end, without any
end being cognized in them – as, for example, the
stone implements frequently obtained from sepul-
chral tumuli and supplied with a hole, as if for
[inserting] a handle; and although these by their
shape manifestly indicate a finality, the end of
which is unknown, they are not on that account
described as beautiful. But the very fact of their
being regarded as art-products involves an immediate
recognition that their shape is attributed to some
purpose or other and to a definite end. For this
reason there is no immediate delight whatever in
their contemplation. A flower, on the other hand,
such as a tulip, is regarded as beautiful, because we
meet with a certain finality in its perception, which,
in our estimate of it, is not referred to any end
whatever.

7   We readily see that enlightenment, while easy, no
doubt, *in thesi, in hypothesi* is difficult and slow of
realization. For not to be passive with one's reason,
but always to be self legislative is doubtless quite an
easy matter for a man who only desires to be adapted

to his essential end, and does not seek to know what is beyond his understanding. But as the tendency in the latter direction is hardly avoidable, and others are always coming and promising with full assurance that they are able to satisfy one's curiosity, it must be very difficult to preserve or restore in the mind (and particularly in the public mind) that merely negative attitude (which constitutes enlightenment proper).

8   Taste may be designated a *sensus communis aestheticus*, common human understanding a *sensus communis logicus*.

9   In my part of the country, if you set a common man a problem like that of Columbus and his egg, he says, 'There is no art in that, it is only science': i.e. you *can* do it if you know *how*; and he says just the same of all the would-be arts of jugglers. To that of the tight-rope dancer, on the other hand, he has not the least compunction in giving the name of art.

10   Perhaps there has never been a more sublime utterance, or a thought more sublimely expressed, than the well-known inscription upon the Temple of *Isis* (Mother *Nature*): 'I am all that is, and that was, and that shall be, and no mortal hath raised the veil from before my face.' *Segner* made use of this idea in a suggestive vignette on the frontispiece of his Natural Philosophy, in order to inspire his pupil at the threshold of that temple into which he was about to lead him, with such a holy awe as would dispose his mind to serious attention.

11   The first three faculties are first *brought into union* by means of the fourth. *Hume*, in his history, informs the English that although they are second in their works to no other people in the world in respect of the evidences they afford of the three first qualities *separately* considered, still in what unites them they must yield to their neighbours, the French.

2

Letter of an Aesthetic Education of Man

Friedrich Schiller

Twentieth Letter

1. That freedom cannot be affected by anything whatsoever follows from our very notion of freedom. But that freedom is itself an effect of Nature (this word taken in its widest sense) and not the work of Man, that it can, therefore, also be furthered or thwarted by natural means, follows no less inevitably [...] It arises only when man is a complete being, when both his fundamental drives [for form and matter] are fully developed; it will, therefore, be lacking as long as he is incomplete, as long as one of the two drives is excluded, and it should be capable of being restored by anything which gives him back his completeness.

2. Now we can, in fact, in the species as a whole as well as in the individual human being, point to a moment in which man is not yet complete, and in which one of his two drives is exclusively active within him. We know that he begins by being nothing but life, in order to end by becoming form; that he is an Individual before he is a Person, and that he proceeds from limitation to infinity. The sensuous drive, therefore, comes into operation earlier than the rational, because sensation precedes consciousness, and it is this priority of the sensuous drive which provides the clue to the whole history of human freedom.

3. For there is, after all, a moment in which the life-impulse, just because the form-impulse is not yet running counter to it, operates as nature and as necessity; a moment in which the life of sense is a power because man has not yet begun to be a human being; for in the human being proper there cannot exist any power other than the will. But in the state of reflection into which he is now to pass, it will be precisely the opposite: Reason is to be a power, and a logical or moral necessity to take the place of that physical necessity. Hence sensation as a power must first be destroyed before law can be enthroned as such. It is, therefore, not simply a matter of something beginning which was not there before; something which was there must first cease to be. Man cannot pass directly from feeling to thought; he must first take one step backwards, since only through one determination being annulled again can a contrary determination take its place. In order to exchange passivity for autonomy, a passive determination for an active one, man must therefore be momentarily free of all determination whatsoever, and pass through a state of pure determinability. He must consequently, in a certain sense, return to that negative state of complete absence of determination in which he found himself before anything at all had made an impression upon his senses. But that former condition was completely devoid of content; and now it is a question of combining such sheer absence of determination, and an equally unlimited determinability, with the greatest possible content, since directly from this condition something positive is to result. The determination he has received through sensation must therefore be preserved, because there must be no loss of reality; but at the same time it must, inasmuch as it is limitation, be annulled, since an unlimited determinability is to come into existence. The problem is, therefore, at one and the

same time to destroy and to maintain the determination of the condition – and this is possible in one way only: by confronting it with another determination. The scales of the balance stand level when they are empty; but they also stand level when they contain equal weights.

4. Our psyche passes, then, from sensation to thought *via* a middle disposition in which sense and reason are both active at the same time. Precisely for this reason, however, they cancel each other out as determining forces, and bring about a negation by means of an opposition. This middle disposition, in which the psyche is subject neither to physical nor to moral constraint, and yet is active in both these ways, pre-eminently deserves to be called a free disposition; and if we are to call the condition of sensuous determination the physical, and the condition of rational determination the logical or moral, then we must call this condition of real and active determinability the aesthetic. (*[Author's note:]* For readers not altogether familiar with the precise meaning of this word, which is so much abused through ignorance, the following may serve as an explanation. Every thing which is capable of phenomenal manifestation may be thought of under four different aspects. A thing can relate directly to our sensual condition (to our being and well-being): that is its physical character. Or it can relate to our intellect, and afford us knowledge: that is its logical character. Or it can relate to our will, and be considered as an object of choice for a rational being: that is its moral character. Or, finally, it can relate to the totality of our various functions without being a definite object for any single one of them: that is its aesthetic character. A man can please us through his readiness to oblige; he can, through his discourse, give us food for thought; he can, through his character, fill us with respect; but finally he can also, independently of all this, and without our taking into consideration in judging him any law or any purpose, please us simply as we contemplate him and by the sheer manner of his being. Under this last-named quality of being we are judging him aesthetically. Thus there is an education to health, an education to understanding, an education to morality, an education to taste and beauty. This last has as its aim the development of the whole complex of our sensual and spiritual powers in the greatest possible harmony. Because, however, misled by false notions of taste and confirmed still further in this error by false reasoning, people are inclined to include in the notion of the aesthetic the notion of the arbitrary too, I add here the superfluous comment (despite the fact that these Letters on Aesthetic Education are concerned with virtually nothing else but the refutation of that very error) that our psyche in the aesthetic state does indeed act freely, is in the highest degree free from all compulsion, but is in no wise free from laws; and that this aesthetic freedom is distinguishable from logical necessity in thinking, or moral necessity in willing, only by the fact that the laws according to which the psyche then behaves do not become apparent as such, and since they encounter no resistance, never appear as a constraint.)

Twenty-first Letter

1. There is, as I observed at the beginning of the last Letter, a twofold condition of determinability and a twofold condition of determination. I can now clarify this statement.

2. The psyche may be said to be determinable simply because it is not determined at all; but it is also determinable inasmuch as it is determined in a way which does not exclude anything, i.e., when the determination it undergoes is of a kind which does not involve limitation. The former is mere indetermination (it is without limits, because it is without reality); the latter is aesthetic determinability (it has no limits, because it embraces all reality).

3. And the psyche may be said to be determined inasmuch as it is limited at all; but it is also determined inasmuch as it limits itself, by virtue of its own absolute power. It finds itself in the first of these two states whenever it feels; in the second, whenever it thinks. What thought is in respect of determination, therefore, the aesthetic disposition is in respect of determinability; the former is limitation by virtue of the infinite force within it, the latter is negation by virtue of the infinite abundance within it. Even as sensation and thought have one single point of contact – viz., that in both states the psyche is determined, and man is something, either individual or person, to the exclusion of all else – but in all other respects are poles apart: so, in like manner, aesthetic determinability has one single point of contact with mere indetermination – viz., that both exclude any determinate mode of existence – while in all other respects they are to each other as nothing is to everything, hence, utterly and entirely different.

If, therefore, the latter – indetermination through sheer absence of determination – was thought of as an empty infinity, then aesthetic freedom of determination, which is its counterpart in reality, must be regarded as an infinity filled with content: an idea which accords completely with the results of the foregoing inquiry.

4. In the aesthetic state, then, man is Nought, if we are thinking of any particular result rather than of the totality of his powers, and considering the absence in him of any specific determination. Hence we must allow that those people are entirely right who declare beauty, and the mood it induces in us, to be completely indifferent and unfruitful as regards either knowledge or character. They are entirely right; for beauty produces no particular result whatsoever, neither for the understanding nor for the will. It accomplishes no particular purpose, neither intellectual nor moral; it discovers no individual truth, helps us to perform no individual duty and is, in short, as unfitted to provide a firm basis for character as to enlighten the understanding. By means of aesthetic culture, therefore, the personal worth of a man, or his dignity, inasmuch as this can depend solely upon himself, remains completely indeterminate; and nothing more is achieved by it than that he is henceforth enabled by the grace of Nature to make of himself what he will – that the freedom to be what he ought to be is completely restored to him.

5. But precisely thereby something Infinite is achieved. For as soon as we recall that it was precisely of this freedom that he was deprived by the one-sided constraint of nature in the field of sensation and by the exclusive authority of reason in the realm of thought, then we are bound to consider the power which is restored to him in the aesthetic mode as the highest of all bounties, as the gift of humanity itself. True, he possesses this humanity *in potentia* before every determinate condition into which he can conceivably enter. But he loses it in practice with every determinate condition into which he does enter. And if he is to pass into a condition of an opposite nature, this humanity must be restored to him each time anew through the life of the aesthetic. ([*Author's note:*] Admittedly the rapidity with which certain types pass from sensation to thought or decision scarcely – if indeed at all – allows them to become aware of the aesthetic mode through which they must in that time necessarily pass. Such natures cannot for any length of time tolerate the state of indetermination, but press impatiently for some result which in the state of aesthetic limitlessness they cannot find. In others, by contrast, who find enjoyment more in the feeling of total capacity than in any single action, the aesthetic state tends to spread itself over a much wider area. Much as the former dread emptiness, just as little are the latter capable of tolerating limitation. I need scarcely say that the former are born for detail and subordinate occupations, the latter, provided they combine this capacity with a sense of reality, destined for wholeness and for great roles.)

6. It is, then, not just poetic licence but philosophical truth when we call beauty our second creatress. For although it only offers us the possibility of becoming human beings, and for the rest leaves it to our own free will to decide how far we wish to make this a reality, it does in this resemble our first creatress, Nature, which likewise conferred upon us nothing more than the power of becoming human, leaving the use and practice of that power to our own free will and decision.

3

The World as Will and Representation

Arthur Schopenhauer

§ 30.

In the first book the world was shown to be mere *representation*, object for a subject. In the second book, we considered it from its other side, and found that this is *will*, which proved to be simply what this world is besides being representation. In accordance with this knowledge, we called the world as representation, both as a whole and in its parts, the *objectivity of the will*, which accordingly means the will become object, i.e., representation. Now we recall further that such objectification of the will had many but definite grades, at which, with gradually increasing distinctness and completeness, the inner nature of the will appeared in the representation, in other words, presented itself as object. In these grades we recognized the Platonic Ideas once more, namely in so far as such grades are just the definite species, or the original unchanging forms and properties of all natural bodies, whether organic or inorganic, as well as the universal forces that reveal themselves according to natural laws. Therefore these Ideas as a whole present themselves in innumerable individuals and in isolated details, and are related to them as the archetype is to its copies. The plurality of such individuals can be conceived only through time and space, their arising and passing away through causality. In all these forms we recognize only the different aspects of the principle of sufficient reason that is the ultimate principle of all finiteness, of all individuation, and the universal form of the representation as it comes to the knowledge of the individual as

such. On the other hand, the Idea does not enter into that principle; hence neither plurality nor change belongs to it. While the individuals in which it expresses itself are innumerable and are incessantly coming into existence and passing away, it remains unchanged as one and the same, and the principle of sufficient reason has no meaning for it. But now, as this principle is the form under which all knowledge of the subject comes, in so far as the subject knows as an *individual*, the Ideas will also lie quite outside the sphere of its knowledge as such. Therefore, if the Ideas are to become object of knowledge, this can happen only by abolishing individuality in the knowing subject. The more definite and detailed explanation of this is what will now first concern us.

§ 31.

First of all, however, the following very essential remark. I hope that in the preceding book I have succeeded in producing the conviction that what in the Kantian philosophy is called the *thing-in-itself*, and appears therein as so significant but obscure and paradoxical a doctrine, is, if reached by the entirely different path we have taken, nothing but the *will* in the sphere of this concept, widened and defined in the way I have stated. It appears obscure and paradoxical in Kant especially through the way in which he introduced it, namely by inference from what is grounded to what is the ground, and it was considered to be a stumbling-block, in fact the weak side of his philosophy.

Further, I hope that, after what has been said, there will be no hesitation in recognizing again in the definite grades of the objectification of that will, which forms the in-itself of the world, what Plato called the *eternal Ideas* or unchangeable forms (ειδη). Acknowledged to be the principal, but at the same time the most obscure and paradoxical, dogma of his teaching, these Ideas have been a subject of reflection and controversy, of ridicule and reverence, for many and very differently endowed minds in the course of centuries.

Now if for us the will is the *thing-in-itself*, and the *Idea* is the immediate objectivity of that will at a definite grade, then we find Kant's thing-in-itself and Plato's Idea, for him the only ὄντως ὄν[1] – those two great and obscure paradoxes of the two greatest philosophers of the West – to be, not exactly identical, but yet very closely related, and distinguished by only a single modification. The two great paradoxes, just because, in spite of all inner harmony and relationship, they sound so very different by reason of the extraordinarily different individualities of their authors, are even the best commentary on each other, for they are like two entirely different paths leading to one goal. This can be made clear in a few words. What Kant says is in essence as follows: "Time, space, and causality are not determinations of the thing-in-itself, but belong only to its phenomenon, since they are nothing but forms of our knowledge. Now as all plurality and all arising and passing away are possible only through time, space, and causality, it follows that they too adhere only to the phenomenon, and by no means to the thing-in-itself. But since our knowledge is conditioned by these forms, the whole of experience is only knowledge of the phenomenon, not of the thing-in-itself; hence also its laws cannot be made valid for the thing-in-itself. What has been said extends even to our own ego, and we know that only as phenomenon, not according to what it may be in itself." This is the meaning and content of Kant's teaching in the important respect we have considered. Now Plato says: "The things of this world, perceived by our senses, have no true being at all; *they are always becoming, but they never are*. They have only a relative being; they are together only in and through their relation to one another; hence their whole existence can just as well be called a non-being. Consequently, they are likewise not objects of a real knowledge (ἐπιστήμη), for there can be such a knowledge only of what exists in and for

itself, and always in the same way. On the contrary, they are only the object of an opinion or way of thinking, brought about by sensation (δόξα μετ᾽ αἰσθήσεως ἀλόγου).[2] As long as we are confined to their perception, we are like persons sitting in a dark cave, and bound so fast that they cannot even turn their heads. They see nothing but the shadowy outlines of actual things that are led between them and a fire which burns behind them; and by the light of this fire these shadows appear on the wall in front of them. Even of themselves and of one another they see only the shadows on this wall. Their wisdom would consist in predicting the sequence of those shadows learned from experience. On the other hand, only the real archetypes of those shadowy outlines, the eternal Ideas, the original forms of all things, can be described as truly existing (ὄντως ὄν), since they *always are but never become and never pass away. No plurality* belongs to them; for each by its nature is only one, since it is the archetype itself, of which all the particular, transitory things of the same kind and name are copies or shadows. Also *no coming into existence and no passing away* belong to them, for they are truly being or existing, but are never becoming or vanishing like their fleeting copies. (But in these two negative definitions there is necessarily contained the presupposition that time, space, and causality have no significance or validity for these Ideas, and do not exist in them.) Thus only of them can there be a knowledge in the proper sense, for the object of such a knowledge can be only that which always and in every respect (and hence in-itself) is, not that which is and then again is not, according as we look at it." This is Plato's teaching. It is obvious, and needs no further demonstration, that the inner meaning of both doctrines is wholly the same; that both declare the visible world to be a phenomenon which in itself is void and empty, and which has meaning and borrowed reality only through the thing that expresses itself in it (the thing-in-itself in the one case, the Idea in the other). To this latter, however, which truly is, all the forms of that phenomenon, even the most universal and essential, are, in the light of both doctrines, entirely foreign. In order to deny these forms, Kant has directly expressed them even in abstract terms, and has definitely deprived the thing-in-itself of time, space, and causality, as being mere forms of the phenomenon. On the other hand, Plato did not reach the highest expression, and only indirectly did he deprive his Ideas of those forms, in that he denied of the Ideas what is possible only through those forms, namely plurality of the homogeneous, origination and disappearance. Though it is superfluous, I wish to make this remarkable and important agreement clear by an example. Let us suppose an animal standing before us in the full activity of its life. Plato will say: "This animal has no true existence, but only an apparent one, a constant becoming, a relative existence that can just as well be called non-being as being. Only the Idea which is depicted in that animal is truly 'being' or the animal-in-itself (αὐτὸ τὸ θηρίον), which is dependent on nothing, but which is in and by itself (χαθ' ἑαυτό, ἀεὶ ὡσαύτως);[3] it has not become, it is not passing away, but always is in the same way (ἀεὶ ὄν, χαὶ μηδέποτε οὔτε γιγνόμενον, οὔτε ἀπολλύμενον).[4] Now, in so far as we recognize in this animal its Idea, it is all one and of no importance whether we now have before us this animal or its progenitor of a thousand years ago; also whether it is here or in a distant country; whether it presents itself in this manner, posture, or action, or in that; finally, whether it is this or any other individual of its species. All this is void and unreal, and concerns only the phenomenon; the Idea of the animal alone has true being, and is the object of real knowledge." Thus Plato. Kant would say something like this: "This animal is a phenomenon in time, space, and causality, which are collectively the conditions *a priori* of the possibility of experience residing in our faculty of knowledge, not determinations of the thing-in-itself. Therefore this animal, as we perceive it at this particular time, in this given place, as an individual that has come into existence and will just as necessarily pass away in the connexion of experience, in other words, in the chain of causes and effects, is not a thing-in-itself, but a phenomenon, valid only in reference to our knowledge. In order to know it according to what it may be in itself, and so independently of all determinations residing in time, space, and causality, a different kind of knowledge from that which is alone possible to us through the senses and understanding would be required."

In order to bring Kant's expression even closer to Plato's, we might also say that time, space, and causality are that arrangement of our intellect by virtue of which the *one* being of each kind that alone really exists, manifests itself to us as a plurality of homogeneous beings, always being originated anew and passing away in endless succession. The apprehension of things by means

of and in accordance with this arrangement is *immanent*; on the other hand, that which is conscious of the true state of things is *transcendental*. We obtain this *in abstracto* through the *Critique of Pure Reason*, but in exceptional cases it can also appear intuitively. This last point is my own addition, which I am endeavouring to explain in the present third book.

If Kant's teaching, and, since Kant's time, that of Plato, had ever been properly understood and grasped; if men had truly and earnestly reflected on the inner meaning and content of the teachings of the two great masters, instead of lavishly using the technical expressions of the one and parodying the style of the other, they could not have failed long ago to discover how much the two great sages agree, and that the true significance, the aim, of both teachings is absolutely the same. Not only would they have refrained from constantly comparing Plato with Leibniz, on whom his spirit certainly did not rest, or even with a well-known gentleman still living,[5] as if they wanted to mock at the manes of the great thinker of antiquity, but in general they would have gone much farther than they did, or rather would not have fallen behind so shamefully as they have done in the last forty years. They would not have allowed themselves to be led by the nose, today by one braggart tomorrow by another, and would not have opened with philosophical farces the nineteenth century that announced itself so importantly in Germany. These were performed over Kant's grave (just as was done sometimes by the ancients at the funeral rites of their dead), and occasioned the well-merited ridicule of other nations, for such things least suit the serious and even solid German. But so small is the real public of genuine philosophers, that even followers who understand are brought to them only sparingly by the centuries. Εἰσὶ δὴ ναρθηχοφόροι μὲν πολλοί, βάκχοι δέγε παῦροι. (*Thyrsigeri quidem multi, Bacchi vero pauci.*) Ἡ ἀτιμία φιλοσοφία διὰ ταῦτα προσπέπτωχεν, ὅτι οὐ χατ' ἀξίαν αὐτῆς ἄπτονται οὐ γὰρ νόθους ἔδει ἄπτεσθαι, ἀλλὰ γνησίους. (*Eam ob rem philosophia in infamiam incidit, quod non pro dignitate ipsam attingunt; neque enim a spuriis, sed a legitimis erat attrectanda,*) Plato [*Republic*, 535 C].[6]

Men followed words, such words as "representations *a priori*," "forms of perceiving and thinking known independently of experience," "primary concepts of the pure understanding," and so on. They now asked whether Plato's Ideas, which were also primary concepts and which, moreover, were supposed to be reminiscences from a prenatal perception of truly existing things, were in some way the same thing as Kant's forms of intuition and thought, residing *a priori* in our consciousness. As there was a slight resemblance in the expression of these two entirely different doctrines, the Kantian doctrine of forms, limiting the knowledge of the individual to the phenomenon, and the Platonic doctrine of Ideas, the knowledge of which expressly denies those very forms, these doctrines, in this respect diametrically opposite, were carefully compared, and men deliberated and disputed over their identity. Ultimately, they found that they were not the same, and concluded that Plato's doctrine of Ideas and Kant's critique of reason had no agreement at all. But enough of this.[7]

§ 32.

It follows from our observations so far that, in spite of all the inner agreement between Kant and Plato, and of the identity of the aim that was in the mind of each, or of the world-view that inspired and led them to philosophize, Idea and thing-in-itself are not for us absolutely one and the same. On the contrary, for us the Idea is only the immediate, and therefore adequate, objectivity of the thing-in-itself, which itself, however, is the *will* – the will in so far as it is not yet objectified, has not yet become representation. For, precisely according to Kant, the thing-in-itself is supposed to be free from all the forms that adhere to knowledge as such. It is merely an error of Kant [. . .] that he did not reckon among these forms, before all others, that of being-object-for-a-subject; for this very form is the first and most universal of all phenomenon, i.e., of all representation. He should therefore have expressly denied being-object to his thing-in-itself, for this would have protected him from that great inconsistency which was soon discovered. On the other hand, the Platonic Idea is necessarily object, something known, a representation, and precisely, but only, in this respect is it different from the thing-in-itself. It has laid aside merely the subordinate forms of the phenomenon, all of which we include under the principle of sufficient reason; or rather it has not yet entered into them. But it has retained the first and most universal form, namely that of the representation in general, that of being object for a

subject. It is the forms subordinate to this (the general expression of which is the principle of sufficient reason) which multiply the Idea in particular and fleeting individuals, whose number in respect of the Idea is a matter of complete indifference. Therefore the principle of sufficient reason is again the form into which the Idea enters, since the Idea comes into the knowledge of the subject as individual. The particular thing, appearing in accordance with the principle of sufficient reason, is therefore only an indirect objectification of the thing-in-itself (which is the will). Between it and the thing-in-itself the Idea still stands as the only direct objectivity of the will, since it has not assumed any other form peculiar to knowledge as such, except that of the representation in general, i.e., that of being object for a subject. Therefore, it alone is the most *adequate objectivity* possible of the will or of the thing-in-itself; indeed it is even the whole thing-in-itself, only under the form of the representation. Here lies the ground of the great agreement between Plato and Kant, although in strict accuracy that of which they both speak is not the same. The particular things, however, are not an entirely adequate objectivity of the will, but this is obscured in them by those forms, whose common expression is the principle of sufficient reason, but which are the condition of knowledge such as is possible to the individual as such. If it is permitted to infer from an impossible presupposition, we should in fact no longer know particular things, or events, or change, or plurality, but apprehend only Ideas, only the grades of objectification of that one will, of the true thing-in-itself, in pure unclouded knowledge. Consequently, our world would be a *nunc stans*,[8] if we were not, as subject of knowledge, at the same time individuals, in other words, if our perception did not come about through the medium of a body, from whose affections it starts. This body itself is only concrete willing, objectivity of will; hence it is an object among objects, and as such comes into the knowing consciousness in the only way it can, namely in the forms of the principle of sufficient reason. Consequently, it presupposes and thus introduces time and all the other forms expressed by that principle. Time is merely the spread-out and piecemeal view that an individual being has of the Ideas. These are outside time, and consequently *eternal*. Therefore Plato says that time is the moving image of eternity: αἰῶνος εἰχὼν χινητὴ ὁ χρόνος. [*Timaeus*, 37 D . . .]

§ 33.

Now since as individuals we have no other knowledge than that which is subject to the principle of sufficient reason, this form, however, excluding knowledge of the Ideas, it is certain that, if it is possible for us to raise ourselves from knowledge of particular things to that of the Ideas, this can happen only by a change taking place in the subject. Such a change is analogous and corresponds to that great change of the whole nature of the object, and by virtue of it the subject, in so far as it knows an Idea, is no longer individual.

[K]nowledge in general itself belongs to the objectification of the will at its higher grades. Sensibility, nerves, brain, just like other parts of the organic being, are only an expression of the will at this grade of its objectivity; hence the representation that arises through them is also destined to serve the will as a means (μηχανή) for the attainment of its now complicated (πολυτελέστερα) ends, for the maintenance of a being with many different needs. Thus, originally and by its nature, knowledge is completely the servant of the will, and, like the immediate object which, by the application of the law of causality, becomes the starting-point of knowledge, is only objectified will. And so all knowledge which follows the principle of sufficient reason remains in a nearer or remoter relation to the will. For the individual finds his body as an object among objects, to all of which it has many different relations and connexions according to the principle of sufficient reason. Hence a consideration of these always leads back, by a shorter or longer path, to his body, and thus to his will. As it is the principle of sufficient reason that places the objects in this relation to the body and so to the will, the sole endeavour of knowledge, serving this will, will be to get to know concerning objects just those relations that are laid down by the principle of sufficient reason, and thus to follow their many different connexions in space, time, and causality. For only through these is the object *interesting* to the individual, in other words, has it a relation to the will. Therefore, knowledge that serves the will really knows nothing more about objects than their relations, knows the objects only in so far as they exist at such a time, in such a place, in such and such circumstances, from such and such causes, and in such and such effects – in a word, as particular things. If all these relations were eliminated, the objects also would have disappeared for knowledge, just because it did not recog-

nize in them anything else. We must also not conceal the fact that what the sciences consider in things is also essentially nothing more than all this, namely their relations, the connexions of time and space, the causes of natural changes, the comparison of forms, the motives of events, and thus merely relations. What distinguishes science from ordinary knowledge is merely its form, the systematic, the facilitating of knowledge by summarizing everything particular in the universal by means of the subordination of concepts, and the completeness of knowledge thus attained. All relation has itself only a relative existence; for example, all being in time is also a non-being, for time is just that by which opposite determinations can belong to the same thing. Therefore every phenomenon in time again is not, for what separates its beginning from its end is simply time, essentially an evanescent, unstable, and relative thing, here called duration. But time is the most universal form of all objects of this knowledge that is in the service of the will, and is the prototype of the remaining forms of such knowledge.

Now as a rule, knowledge remains subordinate to the service of the will, as indeed it came into being for this service; in fact, it sprang from the will, so to speak, as the head from the trunk. With the animals, this subjection of knowledge to the will can never be eliminated. With human beings, such elimination appears only as an exception, as will shortly be considered in more detail. This distinction between man and animal is outwardly expressed by the difference in the relation of head to trunk. In the lower animals both are still deformed; in all, the head is directed to the ground, where the objects of the will lie. Even in the higher animals, head and trunk are still far more one than in man, whose head seems freely set on to the body, only carried by the body and not serving it. This human superiority is exhibited in the highest degree by the Apollo Belvedere. The head of the god of the Muses, with eyes looking far afield, stands so freely on the shoulders that it seems to be wholly delivered from the body, and no longer subject to its cares.

§ 34.

As we have said, the transition that is possible, but to be regarded only as an exception, from the common knowledge of particular things to knowledge of the Idea takes place suddenly, since knowledge tears itself free from the service of the will precisely by the subject's ceasing to be merely individual, and being now a pure will-less subject of knowledge. Such a subject of knowledge no longer follows relations in accordance with the principle of sufficient reason; on the contrary, it rests in fixed contemplation of the object presented to it out of its connexion with any other, and rises into this.

To be made clear, this needs a detailed discussion, and the reader must suspend his surprise at it for a while, until it has vanished automatically after he has grasped the whole thought to be expressed in this work.

Raised up by the power of the mind, we relinquish the ordinary way of considering things, and cease to follow under the guidance of the forms of the principle of sufficient reason merely their relations to one another, whose final goal is always the relation to our own will. Thus we no longer consider the where, the when, the why, and the whither in things, but simply and solely the *what*. Further, we do not let abstract thought, the concepts of reason, take possession of our consciousness, but, instead of all this, devote the whole power of our mind to perception, sink ourselves completely therein, and let our whole consciousness be filled by the calm contemplation of the natural object actually present, whether it be a landscape, a tree, a rock, a crag, a building, or anything else. We *lose* ourselves entirely in this object, to use a pregnant expression; in other words, we forget our individuality, our will, and continue to exist only as pure subject, as clear mirror of the object, so that it is as though the object alone existed without anyone to perceive it, and thus we are no longer able to separate the perceiver from the perception, but the two have become one, since the entire consciousness is filled and occupied by a single image of perception. If, therefore, the object has to such an extent passed out of all relation to something outside it, and the subject has passed out of all relation to the will, what is thus known is no longer the individual thing as such, but the *Idea*, the eternal form, the immediate objectivity of the will at this grade. Thus at the same time, the person who is involved in this perception is no longer an individual, for in such perception the individual has lost himself; he is *pure* will-less, painless, timeless *subject of knowledge*. This, which for the moment is so remarkable (which I well know confirms the saying, attributed to Thomas Paine, that *du*

sublime au ridicule il n'y a qu'un pas),[9] will gradually become clearer and less surprising through what follows. It was this that was in Spinoza's mind when he wrote: *Mens aeterna est, quatenus res sub aeternitatis specie concipit* (*Ethics*, V, prop. 31, schol.).[10] Now in such contemplation, the particular thing at one stroke becomes the *Idea* of its species, and the perceiving individual becomes the *pure subject of knowing*. The individual, as such knows only particular things; the pure subject of knowledge knows only Ideas. For the individual is the subject of knowledge in its relation to a definite particular phenomenon of will and in subjection thereto. This particular phenomenon of will is, as such, subordinate to the principle of sufficient reason in all its forms; therefore all knowledge which relates itself to this, also follows the principle of sufficient reason, and no other knowledge than this is fit to be of any use to the will; it always has only relations to the object. The knowing individual as such and the particular thing known by him are always in a particular place, at a particular time, and are links in the chain of causes and effects. The pure subject of knowledge and its correlative, the Idea, have passed out of all these forms of the principle of sufficient reason. Time, place, the individual that knows, and the individual that is known, have no meaning for them. First of all, a knowing individual raises himself in the manner described to the pure subject of knowing, and at the same time raises the contemplated object to the Idea; the *world as representation* then stands out whole and pure, and the complete objectification of the will takes place, for only the Idea is the *adequate objectivity* of the will. In itself, the Idea includes object and subject in like manner, for these are its sole form. In it, however, both are of entirely equal weight; and as the object also is here nothing but the representation of the subject, so the subject, by passing entirely into the perceived object, has also become that object itself, since the entire consciousness is nothing more than its most distinct image. This consciousness really constitutes the whole *world as representation*, since we picture to ourselves the whole of the Ideas, or grades of the will's objectivity, passing through it successively. The particular things of all particular times and spaces are nothing but the Ideas multiplied through the principle of sufficient reason (the form of knowledge of the individuals as such), and thus obscured in their pure objectivity. When the Idea appears, subject and object can no longer be distinguished in it, because the Idea, the adequate objectivity of the will, the real world as representation, arises only when subject and object reciprocally fill and penetrate each other completely. In just the same way the knowing and the known individual, as things-in-themselves, are likewise not different. For if we look entirely away from that true *world as representation*, there is nothing left but the *world as will*. The will is the "in-itself" of the Idea that completely objectifies it; it is also the "in-itself" of the particular thing and of the individual that knows it, and these two objectify it incompletely. As will, outside the representation and all its forms, it is one and the same in the contemplated object and in the individual who soars aloft in this contemplation, who becomes conscious of himself as pure subject. Therefore in themselves these two are not different; for in themselves they are the will that here knows itself. Plurality and difference exist only as the way in which this knowledge comes to the will, that is to say, only in the phenomenon, by virtue of its form, the principle of sufficient reason. Without the object, without the representation, I am not knowing subject, but mere, blind will; in just the same way, without me as subject of knowledge, the thing known is not object, but mere will, blind impulse. In itself, that is to say outside the representation, this will is one and the same with mine; only in the world as representation, the form of which is always at least subject and object, are we separated out as known and knowing individual. As soon as knowledge, the world as representation, is abolished, nothing in general is left but mere will, blind impulse. That it should obtain objectivity, should become representation, immediately supposes subject as well as object; but that this objectivity should be pure, complete, adequate objectivity of the will, supposes the object as Idea, free from the forms of the principle of sufficient reason, and the subject as pure subject of knowledge, free from individuality and from servitude to the will.

Now whoever has, in the manner stated, become so absorbed and lost in the perception of nature that he exists only as purely knowing subject, becomes in this way immediately aware that, as such, he is the condition, and hence the supporter, of the world and of all objective existence, for this now shows itself as dependent on his existence. He therefore draws nature into himself, so that he feels it to be only an accident of his own being. In this sense Byron says:

Are not the mountains, waves and skies, a part
Of me and of my soul, as I of them?[11]

But how could the person who feels this regard himself as absolutely perishable in contrast to imperishable nature? Rather will he be moved by the consciousness of what the Upanishad of the Veda expresses: *Hae omnes creaturae in totum ego sum, et praeter me aliud (ens) non est.* (*Oupnek'hat* [ed. Anquetil Duperron, 2 vols., Paris, 1801–2], I, 122.)[12]

§ 35.

In order to reach a deeper insight into the nature of the world, it is absolutely necessary for us to learn to distinguish the will as thing-in-itself from its adequate objectivity, and then to distinguish the different grades at which this objectivity appears more distinctly and fully, i.e., the Ideas themselves, from the mere phenomenon of the Ideas in the forms of the principle of sufficient reason, the restricted method of knowledge of individuals. We shall then agree with Plato, when he attributes actual being to the Ideas alone, and only an apparent, dreamlike existence to the things in space and time, to this world that is real for the individual. We shall then see how one and the same Idea reveals itself in so many phenomena, and presents its nature to knowing individuals only piecemeal, one side after another. Then we shall also distinguish the Idea itself from the way in which its phenomenon comes into the observation of the individual, and shall recognize the former as essential, and the latter as inessential. We intend to consider this by way of example on the smallest scale, and then on the largest. When clouds move, the figures they form are not essential, but indifferent to them. But that as elastic vapour they are pressed together, driven off, spread out, and torn apart by the force of the wind, this is their nature, this is the essence of the forces that are objectified in them, this is the Idea. The figures in each case are only for the individual observer. To the brook which rolls downwards over the stones, the eddies, waves, and foam-forms exhibited by it are indifferent and inessential; but that it follows gravity, and behaves as an inelastic, perfectly mobile, formless, and transparent fluid, this is its essential nature, this, *if known through perception*, is the Idea. Those foam-forms exist only for us so long as we know as individuals. The ice on the windowpane is formed into crystals according to the laws of crystallization, which reveal the essence of the natural force here appearing, which exhibit the Idea. But the trees and flowers formed by the ice on the window-pane are inessential, and exist only for us. What appears in clouds, brook, and crystal is the feeblest echo of that will which appears more completely in the plant, still more completely in the animal, and most completely in man. But only the *essential* in all these grades of the will's object-ification constitutes the *Idea*; on the other hand, its unfolding or development, because drawn apart in the forms of the principle of sufficient reason into a multiplicity of many-sided phenomena, is inessential to the Idea; it lies merely in the individ-ual's mode of cognition, and has reality only for that individual. Now the same thing necessarily holds good of the unfolding of that Idea which is the most complete objectivity of the will. Conse-quently, the history of the human race, the throng of events, the change of times, the many varying forms of human life in different countries and centuries, all this is only the accidental form of the phenomenon of the Idea. All this does not belong to the Idea itself, in which alone lies the adequate objectivity of the will, but only to the phenomenon. The phenomenon comes into the knowledge of the individual, and is just as foreign, inessential, and indifferent to the Idea itself as the figures they depict are to the clouds, the shape of its eddies and foam-forms to the brook, and the trees and flowers to the ice.

To the man who has properly grasped this, and is able to distinguish the will from the Idea, and the Idea from its phenomenon, the events of the world will have significance only in so far as they are the letters from which the Idea of man can be read, and not in and by themselves. He will not believe with the general public that time may produce something actually new and significant; that through it or in it something positively real may attain to existence, or indeed that time itself as a whole has beginning and end, plan and develop-ment, and in some way has for its final goal the highest perfection (according to their conceptions) of the latest generation that lives for thirty years. Therefore just as little will he, with Homer, set up a whole Olympus full of gods to guide the events of time, as he will, with Ossian, regard the figures of the clouds as individual beings. For, as we have said, both have just as much significance with regard to the Idea appearing in them. In the many different forms and aspects of human life,

and in the interminable change of events, he will consider only the Idea as the abiding and essential, in which the will-to-live has its most perfect object-ivity, and which shows its different sides in the qualities, passions, errors, and excellences of the human race, in selfishness, hatred, love, fear, boldness, frivolity, stupidity, slyness, wit, genius, and so on. All of these, running and congealing together into a thousand different forms and shapes (individuals), continually produce the his-tory of the great and the small worlds, where in itself it is immaterial whether they are set in motion by nuts or by crowns. Finally, he will find that in the world it is the same as in the dramas of Gozzi, in all of which the same persons always appear with the same purpose and the same fate. The motives and incidents certainly are dif-ferent in each piece, but the spirit of the incidents is the same. The persons of one piece know noth-ing of the events of another, in which, of course, they themselves performed. Therefore, after all the experiences of the earlier pieces, Pantaloon has become no more agile or generous, Tartaglia no more conscientious, Brighella no more cour-ageous, and Columbine no more modest.

Suppose we were permitted for once to have a clear glance into the realm of possibility, and over all the chains of causes and effects, then the earth-spirit would appear and show us in a picture the most eminent individuals, world-enlighteners, and heroes, destroyed by chance before they were ripe for their work. We should then be shown the great events that would have altered the history of the world, and brought about periods of the highest culture and enlightenment, but which the blindest chance, the most insignificant accident, prevented at their beginning. Finally, we should see the splendid powers of great individuals who would have enriched whole world-epochs, but who, mis-led through error or passion, or compelled by necessity, squandered them uselessly on unworthy or unprofitable objects, or even dissipated them in play. If we saw all this, we should shudder and lament at the thought of the lost treasures of whole periods of the world. But the earth-spirit would smile and say: "The source from which the indi-viduals and their powers flow is inexhaustible, and is as boundless as are time and space; for, just like these forms of every phenomenon, they too are only phenomenon, visibility of the will. No finite measure can exhaust that infinite source; therefore undiminished infinity is still always open for the return of any event or work that was nipped in the bud. In this world of the phenomenon, true loss is as little possible as is true gain. The will alone is; it is the thing-in-itself, the source of all those phenomena. Its self-knowledge and its affirmation or denial that is then decided on, is the only event in-itself."[13]

§ 36.

History follows the thread of events; it is pragmatic in so far as it deduces them according to the law of motivation, a law that determines the appearing will where that will is illuminated by knowledge. At the lower grades of its objectivity, where it still acts without knowledge, natural science as etiology considers the laws of the changes of its phenomena, and as morphology considers what is permanent in them. This almost endless theme is facilitated by the aid of concepts that comprehend the general, in order to deduce from it the particular. Finally, mathematics considers the mere forms, that is, time and space, in which the Ideas appear drawn apart into plurality for the knowledge of the subject as individual. All these, the common name of which is science, therefore follow the principle of sufficient reason in its different forms, and their theme remains the phenomenon, its laws, connexion, and the relations resulting from these. But now, what kind of knowledge is it that considers what continues to exist outside and independently of all relations, but which alone is really essential to the world, the true content of its phenomena, that which is subject to no change, and is therefore known with equal truth for all time, in a word, the *Ideas* that are the immediate and adequate objectivity of the thing-in-itself, of the will? It is *art*, the work of genius. It repeats the eternal Ideas apprehended through pure contemplation, the essential and abiding element in all the phenomena of the world. According to the material in which it repeats, it is sculpture, painting, poetry, or music. Its only source is knowledge of the Ideas; its sole aim is communication of this knowledge. Whilst science, following the restless and unstable stream of the fourfold forms of reasons or grounds and consequents, is with every end it attains again and again directed farther, and can never find an ultimate goal or complete satisfaction, any more than by running we can reach the point where the clouds touch the horizon; art, on the contrary, is everywhere at its goal. For it plucks the object of

its contemplation from the stream of the world's course, and holds it isolated before it. This particular thing, which in that stream was an infinitesimal part, becomes for art a representative of the whole, an equivalent of the infinitely many in space and time. It therefore pauses at this particular thing; it stops the wheel of time; for it the relations vanish; its object is only the essential, the Idea. We can therefore define it accurately as *the way of considering things independently of the principle of sufficient reason*, in contrast to the way of considering them which proceeds in exact accordance with this principle, and is the way of science and experience. This latter method of consideration can be compared to an endless line running horizontally, and the former to a vertical line cutting the horizontal at any point. The method of consideration that follows the principle of sufficient reason is the rational method, and it alone is valid and useful in practical life and in science. The method of consideration that looks away from the content of this principle is the method of genius, which is valid and useful in art alone. The first is Aristotle's method; the second is, on the whole, Plato's. The first is like the mighty storm, rushing along without beginning or aim, bending, agitating, and carrying everything away with it; the second is like the silent sunbeam, cutting through the path of the storm, and quite unmoved by it. The first is like the innumerable violently agitated drops of the waterfall, constantly changing and never for a moment at rest; the second is like the rainbow silently resting on this raging torrent. Only through the pure contemplation described above, which becomes absorbed entirely in the object, are the Ideas comprehended; and the nature of *genius* consists precisely in the preeminent ability for such contemplation. Now as this demands a complete forgetting of our own person and of its relations and connexions, the *gift of genius* is nothing but the most complete *objectivity*, i.e., the objective tendency of the mind, as opposed to the subjective directed to our own person, i.e., to the will. Accordingly, genius is the capacity to remain in a state of pure perception, to lose oneself in perception, to remove from the service of the will the knowledge which originally existed only for this service. In other words, genius is the ability to leave entirely out of sight our own interest, our willing, and our aims, and consequently to discard entirely our own personality for a time, in order to remain *pure knowing subject*, the clear eye of the world;

and this not merely for moments, but with the necessary continuity and conscious thought to enable us to repeat by deliberate art what has been apprehended, and "what in wavering apparition gleams fix in its place with thoughts that stand for ever!"[14] For genius to appear in an individual, it is as if a measure of the power of knowledge must have fallen to his lot far exceeding that required for the service of an individual will; and this superfluity of knowledge having become free, now becomes the subject purified of will, the clear mirror of the inner nature of the world. This explains the animation, amounting to disquietude, in men of genius, since the present can seldom satisfy them, because it does not fill their consciousness. This gives them that restless zealous nature, that constant search for new objects worthy of contemplation, and also that longing, hardly ever satisfied, for men of like nature and stature to whom they may open their hearts. The common mortal, on the other hand, entirely filled and satisfied by the common present, is absorbed in it, and, finding everywhere his like, has that special ease and comfort in daily life which are denied to the man of genius. Imagination has been rightly recognized as an essential element of genius; indeed, it has sometimes been regarded as identical with genius, but this is not correct. The objects of genius as such are the eternal Ideas, the persistent, essential forms of the world and of all its phenomena; but knowledge of the Idea is necessarily knowledge through perception, and is not abstract. Thus the knowledge of the genius would be restricted to the Ideas of objects actually present to his own person, and would be dependent on the concatenation of circumstances that brought them to him, did not imagination extend his horizon far beyond the reality of his personal experience, and enable him to construct all the rest out of the little that has come into his own actual apperception, and thus to let almost all the possible scenes of life pass by within himself. Moreover, the actual objects are almost always only very imperfect copies of the Idea that manifests itself in them. Therefore the man of genius requires imagination, in order to see in things not what nature has actually formed, but what she endeavoured to form, yet did not bring about, because of the conflict of her forms with one another [...]. We shall return to this later, when considering sculpture. Thus imagination extends the mental horizon of the genius beyond the objects that actually present themselves to his person, as regards both quality and quantity. For this reason, unusual strength of imagination is a companion, indeed a condition, of genius. But the converse is not the case, for strength of imagination is not evidence of genius; on the contrary, even men with little or no touch of genius may have much imagination. For we can consider an actual object in two opposite ways, purely objectively, the way of genius grasping the Idea of the object, or in the common way, merely in its relations to other objects according to the principle of sufficient reason, and in its relations to our own will. In a similar manner, we can also perceive an imaginary object in these two ways. Considered in the first way, it is a means to knowledge of the Idea, the communication of which is the work of art. In the second case, the imaginary object is used to build castles in the air, congenial to selfishness and to one's own whim, which for the moment delude and delight; thus only the relations of the phantasms so connected are really ever known. The man who indulges in this game is a dreamer; he will easily mingle with reality the pictures that delight his solitude, and will thus become unfit for real life. Perhaps he will write down the delusions of his imagination, and these will give us the ordinary novels of all kinds which entertain those like him and the public at large, since the readers fancy themselves in the position of the hero, and then find the description very "nice."[15]

As we have said, the common, ordinary man, that manufactured article of nature which she daily produces in thousands, is not capable, at any rate continuously, of a consideration of things wholly disinterested in every sense, such as is contemplation proper. He can direct his attention to things only in so far as they have some relation to his will, although that relation may be only very indirect. As in this reference that always demands only knowledge of the relations, the abstract concept of the thing is sufficient and often even more appropriate, the ordinary man does not linger long over the mere perception, does not fix his eye on an object for long, but, in everything that presents itself to him, quickly looks merely for the concept under which it is to be brought, just as the lazy man looks for a chair, which then no longer interests him. Therefore he is very soon finished with everything, with works of art, with beautiful natural objects, and with that contemplation of life in all its scenes which is really of significance everywhere. He does not linger; he seeks only his way in life, or at most all that might at any time become his way. Thus he makes topographical notes in the widest sense, but on the consideration of life itself as such he wastes no time. On the other hand, the man of genius, whose power of knowledge is, through its excess, withdrawn for a part of his time from the service of his will, dwells on the consideration of life itself, strives to grasp the Idea of each thing, not its relations to other things. In doing this, he frequently neglects a consideration of his own path in life, and therefore often pursues this with insufficient skill. Whereas to the ordinary man his faculty of knowledge is a lamp that lights his path, to the man of genius it is the sun that reveals the world. This great difference in their way of looking at life soon becomes visible even in the outward appearance of them both. The glance of the man in whom genius lives and works readily distinguishes him; it is both vivid and firm and bears the character of thoughtfulness, of contemplation. We can see this in the portraits of the few men of genius which nature has produced here and there among countless millions. On the other hand, the real opposite of contemplation, namely spying or prying, can be readily seen in the glance of others, if indeed it is not dull and vacant, as is often the case. Consequently a face's "expression of genius" consists in the fact that a decided predominance of knowing over willing is visible in it, and hence that there is manifested in it a knowledge without any relation to a will, in other words, a *pure knowing*. On the other hand, in the case of faces that follow the rule, the expression of the will predominates, and we see that knowledge comes into activity only on the impulse of the will, and so is directed only to motives.

As the knowledge of the genius, or knowledge of the Idea, is that which does not follow the principle of sufficient reason, so, on the other hand, the knowledge that does follow this principle gives us prudence and rationality in life, and brings about the sciences. Thus individuals of genius will be affected with the defects entailed in the neglect of the latter kind of knowledge. Here, however, a limitation must be observed, that what I shall state in this regard concerns them only in so far as, and while, they are actually engaged with the kind of knowledge peculiar to the genius. Now this is by no means the case at every moment of their lives, for the great though spontaneous exertion required for the will-free comprehension of the Ideas necessarily relaxes again, and there are long intervals during which men of genius stand in very

much the same position as ordinary persons, both as regards merits and defects. On this account, the action of genius has always been regarded as an inspiration, as indeed the name itself indicates, as the action of a superhuman being different from the individual himself, which takes possession of him only periodically. The disinclination of men of genius to direct their attention to the content of the principle of sufficient reason will show itself first in regard to the ground of being, as a disinclination for mathematics. The consideration of mathematics proceeds on the most universal forms of the phenomenon, space and time, which are themselves only modes or aspects of the principle of sufficient reason; and it is therefore the very opposite of that consideration that seeks only the content of the phenomenon, namely the Idea expressing itself in the phenomenon apart from all relations. Moreover, the logical procedure of mathematics will be repugnant to genius, for it obscures real insight and does not satisfy it; it presents a mere concatenation of conclusions according to the principle of the ground of knowing. Of all the mental powers, it makes the greatest claim on memory, so that one may have before oneself all the earlier propositions to which reference is made. Experience has also confirmed that men of great artistic genius have no aptitude for mathematics; no man was ever very distinguished in both at the same time. Alfieri relates that he was never able to understand even the fourth proposition of Euclid. Goethe was reproached enough with his want of mathematical knowledge by the ignorant opponents of his colour theory. Here, where it was naturally not a question of calculation and measurement according to hypothetical data, but one of direct knowledge by understanding cause and effect, this reproach was so utterly absurd and out of place, that they revealed their total lack of judgement just as much by such a reproach as by the rest of their Midas-utterances. The fact that even today, nearly half a century after the appearance of Goethe's colour theory, the Newtonian fallacies still remain in undisturbed possession of the professorial chair even in Germany, and that people continue to talk quite seriously about the seven homogeneous rays of light and their differing refrangibility, will one day be numbered among the great intellectual peculiarities of mankind in general, and of the Germans in particular. From the same above-mentioned cause may be explained the equally well-known fact that, conversely, distinguished mathematicians have little susceptibility to works of fine art. This is expressed with particular naïvety in the well-known anecdote of that French mathematician who, after reading Racine's *Iphigenia*, shrugged his shoulders and asked: *Qu'est-ce que cela prouve?*[16] Further, as keen comprehension of relations according to the laws of causality and motivation really constitutes prudence or sagacity, whereas the knowledge of genius is not directed to relations, a prudent man will not be a genius insofar as and while he is prudent, and a genius will not be prudent insofar as and while he is a genius. Finally, knowledge of perception generally, in the province of which the Idea entirely lies, is directly opposed to rational or abstract knowledge which is guided by the principle of the ground of knowing. It is also well known that we seldom find great genius united with preeminent reasonableness; on the contrary, men of genius are often subject to violent emotions and irrational passions. But the cause of this is not weakness of the faculty of reason, but partly unusual energy of that whole phenomenon of will, the individual genius. This phenomenon manifests itself through vehemence of all his acts of will. The cause is also partly a preponderance of knowledge from perception through the senses and the understanding over abstract knowledge, in other words, a decided tendency to the perceptive. In such men the extremely energetic impression of the perceptive outshines the colourless concepts so much that conduct is no longer guided by the latter, but by the former, and on this very account becomes irrational. Accordingly, the impression of the present moment on them is very strong, and carries them away into thoughtless actions, into emotion and passion. Moreover, since their knowledge has generally been withdrawn in part from the service of the will, they will not in conversation think so much of the person with whom they are speaking as of the thing they are speaking about, which is vividly present in their minds. Therefore they will judge or narrate too objectively for their own interests; they will not conceal what it would be more prudent to keep concealed, and so on. Finally, they are inclined to soliloquize, and in general may exhibit several weaknesses that actually are closely akin to madness. It is often remarked that genius and madness have a side where they touch and even pass over into each other, and even poetic inspiration has been called a kind of madness; *amabilis insania*, as Horace calls it (*Odes*, iii, 4); and in the introduction to *Oberon*

Wieland speaks of "amiable madness." Even Aristotle, as quoted by Seneca (*De Tranquillitate Animi*, xv, 16 [xvii, 10]), is supposed to have said: *Nullum magnum ingenium sine mixtura dementiae fuit.*[17] Plato expresses it in the above mentioned myth of the dark cave (*Republic*, Bk. 7) by saying that those who outside the cave have seen the true sunlight and the things that actually are (the Ideas), cannot afterwards see within the cave any more, because their eyes have grown unaccustomed to the darkness; they no longer recognize the shadow-forms correctly. They are therefore ridiculed for their mistakes by those others who have never left that cave and those shadow-forms. Also in the *Phaedrus* (245 A), he distinctly says that without a certain madness there can be no genuine poet, in fact (249 D) that everyone appears mad who recognizes the eternal Ideas in fleeting things. Cicero also states: *Negat enim sine furore Democritus quemquam poetam magnum esse posse; quod idem dicit Plato* (*De Divinatione*, i, 37).[18] And finally, Pope says:

Great wits to madness sure are near allied,
And thin partitions do their bounds divide.[19]

Particularly instructive in this respect is Goethe's *Torquato Tasso*, in which he brings before our eyes not only suffering, the essential martyrdom of genius as such, but also its constant transition into madness. Finally, the fact of direct contact between genius and madness is established partly by the biographies of great men of genius, such as Rousseau, Byron, and Alfieri, and by anecdotes from the lives of others. On the other hand, I must mention having found, in frequent visits to lunatic asylums, individual subjects endowed with unmistakably great gifts. Their genius appeared distinctly through their madness which had completely gained the upper hand. Now this cannot be ascribed to chance, for on the one hand the number of mad persons is relatively very small, while on the other a man of genius is a phenomenon rare beyond all ordinary estimation, and appearing in nature only as the greatest exception. We may be convinced of this from the mere fact that we can compare the number of the really great men of genius produced by the whole of civilized Europe in ancient and modern times, with the two hundred and fifty millions who are always living in Europe and renew themselves every thirty years. Among men of genius, however, can be reckoned only those who have furnished works that have retained through all time an enduring value for mankind. Indeed, I will not refrain from mentioning that I have known some men of decided, though not remarkable, mental superiority who at the same time betrayed a slight touch of insanity. Accordingly, it might appear that every advance of the intellect beyond the usual amount, as an abnormality, already disposes to madness. Meanwhile, however, I will give as briefly as possible my opinion about the purely intellectual ground of the kinship between genius and madness, for this discussion will certainly contribute to the explanation of the real nature of genius, in other words, of that quality of the mind which is alone capable of producing genuine works of art. But this necessitates a brief discussion of madness itself. [...].

A clear and complete insight into the nature of madness, a correct and distinct conception of what really distinguishes the sane from the insane, has, so far as I know, never yet been found. Neither the faculty of reason nor understanding can be denied to the mad, for they talk and understand, and often draw very accurate conclusions. They also, as a rule, perceive quite correctly what is present, and see the connexion between cause and effect. Visions, like the fancies of an overwrought brain, are no ordinary symptom of madness; delirium falsifies perception, madness the thoughts. For the most part, mad people do not generally err in the knowledge of what is immediately *present;* but their mad talk relates always to what is *absent* and *past*, and only through these to its connexion with what is present. Therefore, it seems to me that their malady specially concerns the *memory*. It is not, indeed, a case of memory failing them entirely, for many of them know a great deal by heart, and sometimes recognize persons whom they have not seen for a long time. Rather is it a case of the thread of memory being broken, its continuous connexion being abolished, and of the impossibility of a uniformly coherent recollection of the past. Individual scenes of the past stand out correctly, just like the individual present; but there are gaps in their recollection that they fill up with fictions. These are either always the same, and so become fixed ideas; it is then a fixed mania or melancholy; or they are different each time, momentary fancies; it is then called folly, *fatuitas*. This is the reason why it is so difficult to question a mad person about his previous life-history when he enters an asylum. In his memory the true is for ever mixed up with the false. Although the immediate present is correctly known, it is falsified through a fictitious connexion with an imaginary past. Mad people therefore consider themselves and others as identical with persons who live merely in their fictitious past. Many acquaintances they do not recognize at all, and, in spite of a correct representation or mental picture of the individual actually present, they have only false relations of this to what is absent. If the madness reaches a high degree, the result is a complete absence of memory; the mad person is then wholly incapable of any reference to what is absent or past, but is determined solely by the whim of the moment in combination with fictions that in his head fill up the past. In such a case, we are then not safe for one moment from ill-treatment or murder, unless we constantly and visibly remind the insane person of superior force. The mad person's knowledge has in common with the animal's the fact that both are restricted to the present; but what distinguishes them is that the animal has really no notion at all of the past as such, although the past acts on it through the medium of custom. Thus, for instance, the dog recognizes his former master even after years, that is to say, it receives the accustomed impression at the sight of him; but the dog has no recollection of the time that has since elapsed. On the other hand, the madman always carries about in his faculty of reason a past in the abstract, but it is a false past that exists for him alone, and that either all the time or merely for the moment. The influence of this false past then prevents the use of the correctly known present which the animal makes. The fact that violent mental suffering or unexpected and terrible events are frequently the cause of madness, I explain as follows. Every such suffering is as an actual event always confined to the present; hence it is only transitory, and to that extent is never excessively heavy. It becomes insufferably great only in so far as it is a lasting pain, but as such it is again only a thought, and therefore resides in the *memory*. Now if such a sorrow, such painful knowledge or reflection, is so harrowing that it becomes positively unbearable, and the individual would succumb to it, then nature, alarmed in this way, seizes on *madness* as the last means of saving life. The mind, tormented so greatly, destroys, as it were, the thread of its memory, fills up the gaps with fictions, and thus seeks refuge in madness from the mental suffering that exceeds its strength, just as a limb affected by mortification is cut off and replaced with a wooden one. As examples, we may consider the raving Ajax, King Lear, and Ophelia; for the creations of the genuine genius, to which alone we can here refer, as being generally known, are equal in truth to real persons; moreover, frequent actual experience in this respect shows the same thing. A faint analogy of this kind of transition from pain to madness is to be found in the way in which we all frequently try, as it were mechanically, to banish a tormenting memory that suddenly occurs to us by some loud exclamation or movement, to turn ourselves from it, to distract ourselves by force.

Now, from what we have stated, we see that the madman correctly knows the individual present as well as many particulars of the past, but that he fails to recognize the connexion, the relations, and therefore goes astray and talks nonsense. Just this is his point of contact with the genius; for he too leaves out of sight knowledge of the connexion of things, as he neglects that knowledge of relations which is knowledge according to the principle of sufficient reason, in order to see in things only their Ideas, and to try to grasp their real inner nature which expresses itself to perception, in regard to which *one* thing represents its whole species, and hence, as Goethe says, one case is valid for a thousand. The individual object of his contemplation, or the present which he apprehends with excessive vividness, appears in so strong a light that the remaining links of the chain, so to speak, to which they belong, withdraw into obscurity, and this gives us phenomena that have long been recognized as akin to those of madness. That which exists in the actual individual thing, only imperfectly and weakened by modifications, is enhanced to perfection, to the Idea of it, by the method of contemplation used by the genius. Therefore he everywhere sees extremes, and on this account his own actions tend to extremes. He does not know how to strike the mean; he lacks cool-headedness, and the result is as we have said. He knows the Ideas perfectly, but not the individuals. Therefore it has been observed that a poet may know *man* profoundly and thoroughly, but *men* very badly; he is easily duped, and is a plaything in the hands of the cunning and crafty. [. . .]

§ 37.

Now according to our explanation, genius consists in the ability to know, independently of the principle of sufficient reason, not individual things which have their existence only in the relation, but the Ideas of such things, and in the ability to be, in face of these, the correlative of the Idea, and hence no longer individual, but pure subject of knowing. Yet this ability must be inherent in all men in a lesser and different degree, as otherwise they would be just as incapable of enjoying works of art as of producing them. Generally they would have no susceptibility at all to the beautiful and to the sublime; indeed, these words could have no meaning for them. We must therefore assume as existing in all men that power of recognizing in things their Ideas, of divesting themselves for a moment of their personality, unless indeed there are some who are not capable of any aesthetic pleasure at all. The man of genius excels them only in the far higher degree and more continuous duration of this kind of knowledge. These enable him to retain that thoughtful contemplation necessary for him to repeat what is thus known in a voluntary and international work, such repetition being the work of art. Through this he communicates to others the Idea he has grasped. Therefore this Idea remains unchanged and the same, and hence aesthetic pleasure is essentially one and the same, whether it be called forth by a work of art, or directly by the contemplation of nature and of life. The work of art is merely a means of facilitating that knowledge in which this pleasure consists. That the Idea comes to us more easily from the work of art than directly from nature and from reality, arises solely from the fact that the artist, who knew only the Idea and not reality, clearly repeated in his work only the Idea, separated it out from reality, and omitted all disturbing contingencies. The artist lets us peer into the world through his eyes. That he has these eyes, that he knows the essential in things which lies outside all relations, is the gift of genius and is inborn; but that he is able to lend us this gift, to let us see with his eyes, is acquired, and is the technical side of art. Therefore, after the account I have given in the foregoing remarks of the inner essence of the aesthetic way of knowing in its most general outline, the following more detailed philosophical consideration of the beautiful and the sublime will explain both simultaneously, in nature and in art, without separating them further. We shall first consider what takes place in a man when he is affected by the beautiful and the sublime. Whether he draws this emotion directly from nature, from life, or partakes of it only through the medium of art, makes no essential difference, but only an outward one.

§ 38.

In the aesthetic method of consideration we found *two inseparable constituent parts*: namely, knowledge of the object not as individual thing, but as Platonic *Idea*, in other words, as persistent form of this whole species of things; and the self-consciousness of the knower, not as individual, but as *pure, will-less subject of knowledge*. The condition under which the two constituent parts appear always united was the abandonment of the method of knowledge that is bound to the principle of sufficient reason, a knowledge that, on the contrary, is the only appropriate kind for serving the will and also for science. Moreover, we shall see that the *pleasure* produced by contemplation of the beautiful arises from those two constituent parts, sometimes more from the one than from the other, according to what the object of aesthetic contemplation may be.

All *willing* springs from lack, from deficiency, and thus from suffering. Fulfilment brings this to an end; yet for one wish that is fulfilled there remain at least ten that are denied. Further, desiring lasts a long time, demands and requests go on to infinity; fulfilment is short and meted out sparingly. But even the final satisfaction itself is only apparent; the wish fulfilled at once makes way for a new one; the former is a known delusion, the latter a delusion not as yet known. No attained object of willing can give a satisfaction that lasts and no longer declines; but it is always like the alms thrown to a beggar, which reprieves him today so that his misery may be prolonged till tomorrow. Therefore, so long as our consciousness is filled by our will, so long as we are given up to the throng of desires with its constant hopes and fears, so long as we are the subject of willing, we never obtain lasting happiness or peace. Essentially, it is all the same whether we pursue or flee, fear harm or aspire to enjoyment; care for the constantly demanding will, no matter in what form, continually fills and moves consciousness; but without peace and calm, true well-being is absolutely impossible. Thus the subject of willing is constantly lying on the revolving wheel of Ixion, is always drawing water in the sieve of the Danaids, and is the eternally thirsting Tantalus.

When, however, an external cause or inward disposition suddenly raises us out of the endless stream of willing, and snatches knowledge from the thraldom of the will, the attention is now no longer directed to the motives of willing, but comprehends things free from their relation to the will. Thus it considers things without interest, without subjectivity, purely objectively; it is entirely given up to them in so far as they are merely representations, and not motives. Then all at once the peace, always sought but always escaping us on that first path of willing, comes to us of its own accord, and all is well with us. It is the painless state, prized by Epicurus as the highest good and as the state of the gods; for that moment we are delivered from the miserable pressure of the will. We celebrate the Sabbath of the penal servitude of willing; the wheel of Ixion stands still.

But this is just the state that I described above as necessary for knowledge of the Idea, as pure contemplation, absorption in perception, being lost in the object, forgetting all individuality, abolishing the kind of knowledge which follows the principle of sufficient reason, and comprehends only relations. It is the state where, simultaneously and inseparably, the perceived individual thing is raised to the Idea of its species, and the knowing individual to the pure subject of will-less knowing, and now the two, as such, no longer stand in the stream of time and of all other relations. It is then all the same whether we see the setting sun from a prison or from a palace.

Inward disposition, predominance of knowing over willing, can bring about this state in any environment. This is shown by those admirable Dutchmen who directed such purely objective perception to the most insignificant objects, and set up a lasting monument of their objectivity and spiritual peace in paintings of *still life*. The aesthetic beholder does not contemplate this without emotion, for it graphically describes to him the calm, tranquil, will-free frame of mind of the artist which was necessary for contemplating such insignificant things so objectively, considering them so attentively, and repeating this perception with such thought. Since the picture invites the beholder to participate in this state, his emotion is often enhanced by the contrast between it and his own restless state of mind, disturbed by vehement willing, in which he happens to be. In the same spirit landscape painters, especially Ruysdael, have often painted extremely insignificant landscape objects, and have thus produced the same effect even more delightfully.

So much is achieved simply and solely by the inner force of an artistic disposition; but that purely objective frame of mind is facilitated and favoured from without by accommodating objects, by the abundance of natural beauty that invites contemplation, and even presses itself on us. Whenever it presents itself to our gaze all at once, it almost always succeeds in snatching us, although only for a few moments, from subjectivity, from the thraldom of the will, and transferring us into the state of pure knowledge. This is why the man tormented by passions, want, or care, is so suddenly revived, cheered, and comforted by a single, free glance into nature. The storm of passions, the pressure of desire and fear, and all the miseries of willing are then at once calmed and appeased in a marvellous way. For at the moment when, torn from the will, we have given ourselves up to pure, will-less knowing, we have stepped into another world, so to speak, where everything that moves our will, and thus violently agitates us, no longer exists. This liberation of knowledge lifts us as wholly and completely above all this as do sleep and dreams. Happiness and unhappiness have vanished; we are no longer the individual; that is forgotten; we are only pure subject of knowledge. We are only that *one* eye of the world which looks out from all knowing creatures, but which in man alone can be wholly free from serving the will. In this way, all difference of individuality disappears so completely that it is all the same whether the perceiving eye belongs to a mighty monarch or to a stricken beggar; for beyond that boundary neither happiness nor misery is taken with us. There always lies so near to us a realm in which we have escaped entirely from all our affliction; but who has the strength to remain in it for long? As soon as any relation to our will, to our person, even of those objects of pure contemplation, again enters consciousness, the magic is at an end. We fall back into knowledge governed by the principle of sufficient reason; we now no longer know the Idea, but the individual thing, the link of a chain to which we also belong, and we are again abandoned to all our woe. Most men are almost always at this standpoint, because they entirely lack objectivity, i.e., genius. Therefore they do not like to be alone with nature; they need company, or at any rate a book, for their knowledge remains subject to the will. Therefore in objects they seek only some relation to their will, and with everything that

has not such a relation there sounds within them, as it were like a ground-bass, the constant, inconsolable lament, "It is of no use to me." Thus in solitude even the most beautiful surroundings have for them a desolate, dark, strange, and hostile appearance.

Finally, it is also that blessedness of will-less perception which spreads so wonderful a charm over the past and the distant, and by a self-deception presents them to us in so flattering a light. For by our conjuring up in our minds days long past spent in a distant place, it is only the objects recalled by our imagination, not the subject of will, that carried around its incurable sorrows with it just as much then as it does now. But these are forgotten, because since then they have frequently made way for others. Now in what is remembered, objective perception is just as effective as it would be in what is present, if we allowed it to have influence over us, if, free from will, we surrendered ourselves to it. Hence it happens that, especially when we are more than usually disturbed by some want, the sudden recollection of past and distant scenes flits across our minds like a lost paradise. The imagination recalls merely what was objective, not what was individually subjective, and we imagine that that something objective stood before us then just as pure and undisturbed by any relation to the will as its image now stands in the imagination; but the relation of objects to our will caused us just as much affliction then as it does now. We can withdraw from all suffering just as well through present as through distant objects, whenever we raise ourselves to a purely objective contemplation of them, and are thus able to produce the illusion that only those objects are present, not we ourselves. Then, as pure subject of knowing, delivered from the miserable self, we become entirely one with those objects, and foreign as our want is to them, it is at such moments just as foreign to us. Then the world as representation alone remains; the world as will has disappeared.

In all these remarks, I have sought to make clear the nature and extent of the share which the subjective condition has in aesthetic pleasure, namely the deliverance of knowledge from the service of the will, the forgetting of oneself as individual, and the enhancement of consciousness to the pure, will-less, timeless subject of knowing that is independent of all relations. With this subjective side of aesthetic contemplation there always appears at the same time as necessary correlative its objective side, the intuitive apprehension of the Platonic Idea. But before we turn to a closer consideration of this and to the achievements of art in reference to it, it is better to stop for a while at the subjective side of aesthetic pleasure, in order to complete our consideration of this by discussing the impression of the *sublime*, which depends solely on it, and arises through a modification of it. After this, our investigation of aesthetic pleasure will be completed by a consideration of its objective side.

But first of all, the following remarks appertain to what has so far been said. Light is most pleasant and delightful; it has become the symbol of all that is good and salutary. In all religions it indicates eternal salvation, while darkness symbolizes damnation. Ormuzd dwells in the purest light, Ahriman in eternal night. Dante's Paradise looks somewhat like Vauxhall in London, since all the blessed spirits appear there as points of light that arrange themselves in regular figures. The absence of light immediately makes us sad, and its return makes us feel happy. Colours directly excite a keen delight, which reaches its highest degree when they are translucent. All this is due to the fact that light is the correlative and condition of the most perfect kind of knowledge through perception, of the only knowledge that in no way directly affects the will. For sight, unlike the affections of the other senses, is in itself, directly, and by its sensuous effect, quite incapable of pleasantness or unpleasantness of *sensation* in the organ; in other words, it has no direct connexion with the will. Only perception arising in the understanding can have such a connexion, which then lies in the relation of the object to the will. In the case of hearing, this is different; tones can excite pain immediately, and can also be directly agreeable sensuously without reference to harmony or melody. Touch, as being one with the feeling of the whole body, is still more subject to this direct influence on the will; and yet there is a touch devoid of pain and pleasure. Odours, however, are always pleasant or unpleasant, and tastes even more so. Thus the last two senses are most closely related to the will, and hence are always the most ignoble, and have been called by Kant the subjective senses. Therefore the pleasure from light is in fact the pleasure from the objective possibility of the purest and most perfect kind of knowledge from perception. As such it can be deduced from the fact that pure knowing, freed and delivered from all willing, is extremely gratifying, and, as

such, has a large share in aesthetic enjoyment. Again, the incredible beauty that we associate with the reflection of objects in water can be deduced from this view of light. That lightest, quickest, and finest species of the effect of bodies on one another, that to which we owe also by far the most perfect and pure of our perceptions, namely the impression by means of reflected light-rays, is here brought before our eyes quite distinctly, clearly, and completely, in cause and effect, and indeed on a large scale. Hence our aesthetic delight from it, which in the main is entirely rooted in the subjective ground of aesthetic pleasure, and is delight from pure knowledge and its ways. [. . .]

§ 39.

All these considerations are intended to stress the subjective part of aesthetic pleasure, namely, that pleasure in so far as it is delight in the mere knowledge of perception as such, in contrast to the will. Now directly connected with all this is the following explanation of that frame of mind which has been called the feeling of the *sublime*.

It has already been observed that transition into the state of pure perception occurs most easily when the objects accommodate themselves to it, in other words, when by their manifold and at the same time definite and distinct form they easily become representatives of their Ideas, in which beauty, in the objective sense, consists. Above all, natural beauty has this quality, and even the most stolid and apathetic person obtains therefrom at least a fleeting, aesthetic pleasure. Indeed, it is remarkable how the plant world in particular invites one to aesthetic contemplation, and, as it were, obtrudes itself thereon. It might be said that such accommodation was connected with the fact that these organic beings themselves, unlike animal bodies, are not immediate objects of knowledge. They therefore need the foreign intelligent individual in order to come from the world of blind willing into the world of the representation. Thus they yearn for this entrance, so to speak, in order to attain at any rate indirectly what directly is denied to them. For the rest, I leave entirely undecided this bold and venturesome idea that perhaps borders on the visionary, for only a very intimate and devoted contemplation of nature can excite or justify it.[20] Now so long as it is this accommodation of nature, the significance and distinctness of its forms, from which the Ideas individualized in them readily speak to us; so long as it is this which moves us from knowledge of mere relations serving the will into aesthetic contemplation, and thus raises us to the will-free subject of knowing, so long is it merely the *beautiful* that affects us, and the feeling of beauty that is excited. But these very objects, whose significant forms invite us to a pure contemplation of them, may have a hostile relation to the human will in general, as manifested in its objectivity, the human body. They may be opposed to it; they may threaten it by their might that eliminates all resistance, or their immeasurable greatness may reduce it to nought. Nevertheless, the beholder may not direct his attention to this relation to his will which is so pressing and hostile, but, although he perceives and acknowledges it, he may consciously turn away from it, forcibly tear himself from his will and its relations, and, giving himself up entirely to knowledge, may quietly contemplate, as pure, will-less subject of knowing, those very objects so terrible to the will. He may comprehend only their Idea that is foreign to all relation, gladly linger over its contemplation, and consequently be elevated precisely in this way above himself, his person, his willing, and all willing. In that case, he is then filled with the feeling of the *sublime*; he is in the state of exaltation, and therefore the object that causes such a state is called *sublime*. Thus what distinguishes the feeling of the sublime from that of the beautiful is that, with the beautiful, pure knowledge has gained the upper hand without a struggle, since the beauty of the object, in other words that quality of it which facilitates knowledge of its Idea, has removed from consciousness, without resistance and hence imperceptibly, the will and knowledge of relations that slavishly serve this will. What is then left is pure subject of knowing, and not even a recollection of the will remains. On the other hand, with the sublime, that state of pure knowing is obtained first of all by a conscious and violent tearing away from the relations of the same object to the will which are recognized as unfavourable, by a free exaltation, accompanied by consciousness, beyond the will and the knowledge related to it. This exaltation must not only be won with consciousness, but also be maintained, and it is therefore accompanied by a constant recollection of the will, yet not of a single individual willing, such as fear or desire, but of human willing in general, in so far as it is expressed universally through its

objectivity, the human body. If a single, real act of will were to enter consciousness through actual personal affliction and danger from the object, the individual will, thus actually affected, would at once gain the upper hand. The peace of contemplation would become impossible, the impression of the sublime would be lost, because it had yielded to anxiety, in which the effort of the individual to save himself supplanted every other thought. A few examples will contribute a great deal to making clear this theory of the aesthetically sublime, and removing any doubt about it. At the same time they will show the difference in the degrees of this feeling of the sublime. For in the main it is identical with the feeling of the beautiful, with pure will-less knowing, and with the knowledge, which necessarily appears therewith, of the Ideas out of all relation that is determined by the principle of sufficient reason. The feeling of the sublime is distinguished from that of the beautiful only by the addition, namely the exaltation beyond the known hostile relation of the contemplated object to the will in general. Thus there result several degrees of the sublime, in fact transitions from the beautiful to the sublime, according as this addition is strong, clamorous, urgent, and near, or only feeble, remote, and merely suggested. I regard it as more appropriate to the discussion to adduce first of all in examples these transitions, and generally the weaker degrees of the impression of the sublime, although those whose aesthetic susceptibility in general is not very great, and whose imagination is not vivid, will understand only the examples, given later, of the higher and more distinct degrees of that impression. They should therefore confine themselves to these, and should ignore the examples of the very weak degree of the above-mentioned impression, which are to be spoken of first.

Just as man is simultaneously impetuous and dark impulse of willing (indicated by the pole of the genitals as its focal point), and eternal, free, serene subject of pure knowing (indicated by the pole of the brain), so, in keeping with this antithesis, the sun is simultaneously the source of *light*, the condition for the most perfect kind of knowledge, and therefore of the most delightful of things; and the source of *heat*, the first condition of all life, in other words, of every phenomenon of the will at its higher grades. Therefore what heat is for the will, light is for knowledge. For this reason, light is the largest diamond in the crown of beauty, and has the most decided influence on the knowledge of every beautiful object. Its presence generally is an indispensable condition; its favourable arrangement enhances even the beauty of the beautiful. But above all else, the beautiful in architecture is enhanced by the favour of light, and through it even the most insignificant thing becomes a beautiful object. Now if in the depth of winter, when the whole of nature is frozen and stiff, we see the rays of the setting sun reflected by masses of stone, where they illuminate without warming, and are thus favourable only to the purest kind of knowledge, not to the will, then contemplation of the beautiful effect of light on these masses moves us into the state of pure knowing, as all beauty does. Yet here, through the faint recollection of the lack of warmth from those rays, in other words, of the absence of the principle of life, a certain transcending of the interest of the will is required. There is a slight challenge to abide in pure knowledge, to turn away from all willing, and precisely in this way we have a transition from the feeling of the beautiful to that of the sublime. It is the faintest trace of the sublime in the beautiful, and beauty itself appears here only in a slight degree. The following is an example almost as weak.

Let us transport ourselves to a very lonely region of boundless horizons, under a perfectly cloudless sky, trees and plants in the perfectly motionless air, no animals, no human beings, no moving masses of water, the profoundest silence. Such surroundings are as it were a summons to seriousness, to contemplation, with complete emancipation from all willing and its cravings; but it is just this that gives to such a scene of mere solitude and profound peace a touch of the sublime. For, since it affords no objects, either favourable or unfavourable, to the will that is always in need of strife and attainment, there is left only the state of pure contemplation, and whoever is incapable of this is abandoned with shameful ignominy to the emptiness of unoccupied will, to the torture and misery of boredom. To this extent it affords us a measure of our own intellectual worth, and for this generally the degree of our ability to endure solitude, or our love of it, is a good criterion. The surroundings just described, therefore, give us an instance of the sublime in a low degree, for in them with the state of pure knowing in its peace and all-sufficiency there is mingled, as a contrast, a recollection of the dependence and wretchedness of the will in need of constant activity. This is the species of the sublime

for which the sight of the boundless prairies of the interior of North America is renowned.

Now let us imagine such a region denuded of plants and showing only bare rocks; the will is at once filled with alarm through the total absence of that which is organic and necessary for our subsistence. The desert takes on a fearful character; our mood becomes more tragic. The exaltation to pure knowledge comes about with a more decided emancipation from the interest of the will, and by our persisting in the state of pure knowledge, the feeling of the sublime distinctly appears.

The following environment can cause this in an even higher degree. Nature in turbulent and tempestuous motion; semi-darkness through threatening black thunder-clouds; immense, bare, overhanging cliffs shutting out the view by their interlacing; rushing, foaming masses of water; complete desert; the wail of the wind sweeping through the ravines. Our dependence, our struggle with hostile nature, our will that is broken in this, now appear clearly before our eyes. Yet as long as personal affliction does not gain the upper hand, but we remain in aesthetic contemplation, the pure subject of knowing gazes through this struggle of nature, through this picture of the broken will, and comprehends calmly, unshaken and unconcerned, the Ideas in those very objects that are threatening and terrible to the will. In this contrast is to be found the feeling of the sublime.

But the impression becomes even stronger, when we have before our eyes the struggle of the agitated forces of nature on a large scale, when in these surroundings the roaring of a falling stream deprives us of the possibility of hearing our own voices. Or when we are abroad in the storm of tempestuous seas; mountainous waves rise and fall, are dashed violently against steep cliffs, and shoot their spray high into the air. The storm howls, the sea roars, the lightning flashes from black clouds, and thunder-claps drown the noise of storm and sea. Then in the unmoved beholder of this scene the twofold nature of his consciousness reaches the highest distinctness. Simultaneously, he feels himself as individual, as the feeble phenomenon of will, which the slightest touch of these forces can annihilate, helpless against powerful nature, dependent, abandoned to chance, a vanishing nothing in face of stupendous forces; and he also feels himself as the eternal, serene subject of knowing, who as the condition of every object is the supporter of this whole world, the fearful struggle of nature being only his mental picture or representation; he himself is free from, and foreign to, all willing and all needs, in the quiet comprehension of the Ideas. This is the full impression of the sublime. Here it is caused by the sight of a power beyond all comparison superior to the individual, and threatening him with annihilation.

The impression of the sublime can arise in quite a different way by our imagining a mere magnitude in space and time, whose immensity reduces the individual to nought. By retaining Kant's terms and his correct division, we can call the first kind the dynamically sublime, and the second the mathematically sublime, although we differ from him entirely in the explanation of the inner nature of that impression, and can concede no share in this either to moral reflections or to hypostases from scholastic philosophy.

If we lose ourselves in contemplation of the infinite greatness of the universe in space and time, meditate on the past millennia and on those to come; or if the heavens at night actually bring innumerable worlds before our eyes, and so impress on our consciousness the immensity of the universe, we feel ourselves reduced to nothing; we feel ourselves as individuals, as living bodies, as transient phenomena of will, like drops in the ocean, dwindling and dissolving into nothing. But against such a ghost of our own nothingness, against such a lying impossibility, there arises the immediate consciousness that all these worlds exist only in our representation, only as modifications of the eternal subject of pure knowing. This we find ourselves to be, as soon as we forget individuality; it is the necessary, conditional supporter of all worlds and of all periods of time. The vastness of the world, which previously disturbed our peace of mind, now rests within us; our dependence on it is now annulled by its dependence on us. All this, however, does not come into reflection at once, but shows itself as a consciousness, merely felt, that in some sense or other (made clear only by philosophy) we are one with the world, and are therefore not oppressed but exalted by its immensity. It is the felt consciousness of what the Upanishads of the Vedas express repeatedly in so many different ways, but most admirably in the saying already quoted: *Hae omnes creaturae in totum ego sum, et praeter me aliud (ens) non est (Oupnek'hat,* Vol. I, p. 122).[21] It is an exaltation beyond our own individuality, a feeling of the sublime.

We receive this impression of the mathematically sublime in quite a direct way through a space which is small indeed as compared with the universe, but which, by becoming directly and wholly perceptible to us, affects us with its whole magnitude in all three dimensions, and is sufficient to render the size of our own body almost infinitely small. This can never be done by a space that is empty for perception, and therefore never by an open space, but only by one that is directly perceivable in all its dimensions through delimitation, and so by a very high and large dome, like that of St. Peter's in Rome or of St. Paul's in London. The feeling of the sublime arises here through our being aware of the vanishing nothingness of our own body in the presence of a greatness which itself, on the other hand, resides only in our representation, and of which we, as knowing subject, are the supporter. Therefore, here as everywhere, it arises through the contrast between the insignificance and dependence of ourselves as individuals, as phenomena of will, and the consciousness of ourselves as pure subject of knowing. Even the vault of the starry heavens, if contemplated without reflection, has only the same effect as that vault of stone, and acts not with its true, but only with its apparent, greatness. Many objects of our perception excite the impression of the sublime; by virtue both of their spatial magnitude and of their great antiquity, and therefore of their duration in time, we feel ourselves reduced to nought in their presence, and yet revel in the pleasure of beholding them. Of this kind are very high mountains, the Egyptian pyramids, and colossal ruins of great antiquity.

Our explanation of the sublime can indeed be extended to cover the ethical, namely what is described as the sublime character. Such a character springs from the fact that the will is not excited here by objects certainly well calculated to excite it, but that knowledge retains the upper hand. Such a character will accordingly consider men in a purely objective way, and not according to the relations they might have to his will. For example, he will observe their faults, and even their hatred and injustice to himself, without being thereby stirred to hatred on his own part. He will contemplate their happiness without feeling envy, recognize their good qualities without desiring closer association with them, perceive the beauty of women without hankering after them. His personal happiness or unhappiness will not violently affect him; he will be rather as Hamlet describes Horatio:

for thou hast been
As one, in suffering all, that suffers nothing;
A man, that fortune's buffets and rewards
Hast ta'en with equal thanks, *etc.*

(Act III, Sc. 2.)

For, in the course of his own life and in its misfortunes, he will look less at his own individual lot than at the lot of mankind as a whole, and accordingly will conduct himself in this respect rather as a knower than as a sufferer.

§ 40.

Since opposites throw light on each other, it may here be in place to remark that the real opposite of the sublime is something that is not at first sight recognized as such, namely the *charming or attractive*. By this I understand that which excites the will by directly presenting to it satisfaction, fulfilment. The feeling of the sublime arose from the fact that something positively unfavourable to the will becomes object of pure contemplation. This contemplation is then maintained only by a constant turning away from the will and exaltation above its interests; and this constitutes the sublimity of the disposition. On the other hand, the charming or attractive draws the beholder down from pure contemplation, demanded by every apprehension of the beautiful, since it necessarily stirs his will by objects that directly appeal to it. Thus the beholder no longer remains pure subject of knowing, but becomes the needy and dependent subject of willing. That every beautiful thing of a cheering nature is usually called charming or attractive is due to a concept too widely comprehended through want of correct discrimination, and I must put it entirely on one side, and even object to it. But in the sense already stated and explained, I find in the province of art only two species of the charming, and both are unworthy of it. The one species, a very low one, is found in the still life painting of the Dutch, when they err by depicting edible objects. By their deceptive appearance these necessarily excite the appetite, and this is just a stimulation of the will which puts an end to any aesthetic contemplation of the object. Painted fruit, however, is, admissible, for it exhibits itself as a further development of the flower, and as a beautiful product of nature through form and colour, without our being positively forced to think of its edibility. But unfortu-nately we often find, depicted with deceptive naturalness, prepared and served-up dishes, oysters, herrings, crabs, bread and butter, beer, wine, and so on, all of which is wholly objectionable. In historical painting and in sculpture the charming consists in nude figures, the position, semi-drapery, and whole treatment of which are calculated to excite lustful feeling in the beholder. Purely aesthetic contemplation is at once abolished, and the purpose of art thus defeated. This mistake is wholly in keeping with what was just censured when speaking of the Dutch. In the case of all beauty and complete nakedness of form, the ancients are almost always free from this fault, since the artist himself created them with a purely objective spirit filled with ideal beauty, not in the spirit of subjective, base sensuality. The charming, therefore, is everywhere to be avoided in art.

There is also a negatively charming, even more objectionable than the positively charming just discussed, and that is the disgusting or offensive. Just like the charming in the proper sense, it rouses the will of the beholder, and therefore disturbs purely aesthetic contemplation. But it is a violent non-willing, a repugnance, that it excites; it rouses the will by holding before it objects that are abhorrent. It has therefore always been recognized as absolutely inadmissible in art, where even the ugly can be tolerated in its proper place so long as it is not disgusting, as we shall see later.

§ 41.

The course of our remarks has made it necessary to insert here a discussion of the sublime, when the treatment of the beautiful has been only half completed, merely from one side, the subjective. For it is only a special modification of this subjective side which distinguishes the sublime from the beautiful. The difference between the beautiful and the sublime depends on whether the state of pure, will-less knowing, presupposed and demanded by any aesthetic contemplation, appears of itself, without opposition, by the mere disappearance of the will from consciousness, since the object invites and attracts us to it; or whether this state is reached only by free, conscious exaltation above the will, to which the contemplated object itself has an unfavourable, hostile relation, a relation that would do away with contemplation if we gave ourselves up to it. This is the distinction between the beautiful and the sublime. In the object the two are not essentially different, for in every case the object of aesthetic contemplation is not the individual thing, but the Idea in it striving for revelation, in other words, the adequate objectivity of the will at a definite grade. Its necessary correlative, withdrawn like itself from the principle of sufficient reason, is the pure subject of knowing, just as the correlative of the particular thing is the knowing individual, both of which lie within the province of the principle of sufficient reason.

By calling an object *beautiful*, we thereby assert that it is an object of our aesthetic contemplation, and this implies two different things. On the one hand, the sight of the thing makes us *objective*, that is to say, in contemplating it we are no longer conscious of ourselves as individuals, but as pure, will-less subjects of knowing. On the other hand, we recognize in the object not the individual thing, but an Idea; and this can happen only in so far as our contemplation of the object is not given up to the principle of sufficient reason, does not follow the relation of the object to something outside it (which is ultimately always connected with relations to our own willing), but rests on the object itself. For the Idea and the pure subject of knowing always appear simultaneously in consciousness as necessary correlatives, and with this appearance all distinction of time at once vanishes, as both are wholly foreign to the principle of sufficient reason in all its forms. Both lie outside the relations laid down by this principle; they can be compared to the rainbow and the sun that take no part in the constant movement and succession of the falling drops. Therefore if, for example, I contemplate a tree aesthetically, i.e., with artistic eyes, and thus recognize not it but its Idea, it is immediately of no importance whether it is this tree or its ancestor that flourished a thousand years ago, and whether the contemplator is this individual, or any other living anywhere and at any time. The particular thing and the knowing individual are abolished with the principle of sufficient reason, and nothing remains but the Idea and the pure subject of knowing, which together constitute the adequate objectivity of the will at this grade. And the Idea is released not only from time but also from space; for the Idea is not really this spatial form which floats before me, but its expression, its pure significance, its innermost being, disclosing itself and appealing to me; and it can be wholly the same, in spite of great difference in the spatial relations of the form.

Now since, on the one hand, every existing thing can be observed purely objectively and outside all relation, and, on the other, the will appears in everything at some grade of its objectivity, and this thing is accordingly the expression of an Idea, everything is also *beautiful*. That even the most insignificant thing admits of purely objective and will-less contemplation and thus proves itself to be beautiful, is testified by the still life paintings of the Dutch, already mentioned in this connexion in para. 38. But one thing is more beautiful than another because it facilitates this purely objective contemplation, goes out to meet it, and, so to speak, even compels it, and then we call the thing very beautiful. This is the case partly because, as individual thing, it expresses purely the Idea of its species through the very distinct, clearly defined, and thoroughly significant relation of its parts. It also completely reveals that Idea through the completeness, united in it, of all the manifestations possible to its species, so that it greatly facilitates for the beholder the transition from the individual thing to the Idea, and thus also the state of pure contemplation. Sometimes that eminent quality of special beauty in an object is to be found in the fact that the Idea itself, appealing to us from the object, is a high grade of the will's objectivity, and is therefore most significant and suggestive. For this reason, man is more beautiful than all other objects, and the revelation of his inner nature is the highest aim of art. Human form and human expression are the most important object of plastic art, just as human conduct is the most important object of poetry. Yet each thing has its own characteristic beauty, not only everything organic that manifests itself in the unity of an individuality, but also everything inorganic and formless, and even every manufactured article. For all these reveal the Ideas through which the will objectifies itself at the lowest grades; they sound, as it were, the deepest, lingering bass-notes of nature. Gravity, rigidity, fluidity, light, and so on, are the Ideas that express themselves in rocks, buildings, and masses of water. Landscape-gardening and architecture can do no more than help them to unfold their qualities distinctly, perfectly, and comprehensively. They give them the opportunity to express themselves clearly, and in this way invite and facilitate aesthetic contemplation. On the other hand, this is achieved in a slight degree, or not at all, by inferior buildings and localities neglected by nature or spoiled by art. Yet these universal basic Ideas of nature do not entirely disappear even from them.

Here too they address themselves to the observer who looks for them, and even bad buildings and the like are still capable of being aesthetically contemplated; the Ideas of the most universal properties of their material are still recognizable in them. The artificial form given to them, however, is a means not of facilitating, but rather of hindering, aesthetic contemplation. Manufactured articles also help the expression of Ideas, though here it is not the Idea of the manufactured articles that speaks from them, but the Idea of the material to which this artificial form has been given. In the language of the scholastics this can be very conveniently expressed in two words; thus in the manufactured article is expressed the Idea of its *forma substantialis*, not that of its *forma accidentalis*; the latter leads to no Idea, but only to a human conception from which it has come. It goes without saying that by manufactured article we expressly do not mean any work of plastic art. Moreover, by *forma substantialis* the scholastics in fact understood what I call the grade of the will's objectification in a thing. We shall return once more to the Idea of the material when we consider architecture. Consequently, from our point of view, we cannot agree with Plato when he asserts (*Republic*, X [596 ff.] [...], and *Parmenides* [130 ff.], p. 79, *ed. Bip.*) that table and chair express the Ideas of table and chair, but we say that they express the Ideas already expressed in their mere material as such. However, according to Aristotle (*Metaphysics*, xii, chap. 3), Plato himself would have allowed Ideas only of natural beings and entities: ὁ Πλάτων ἔφη, ὅτι εἴδη ἐστὶν ὁπόσα φύσει (*Plato dixit, quod ideae eorum sunt, quae natura sunt*),[22] and in chapter 5 it is said that, according to the Platonists, there are no Ideas of house and ring. In any case, Plato's earliest disciples, as Alcinous informs us (*Introductio in Platonicam philosophiam*, chap. 9), denied that there were Ideas of manufactured articles. Thus he says: Ὁρίζονται δὲ τὴν ἰδέαν, παράδειγμα τῶν κατὰ φύσιν αἰώνιον. Οὔτε γὰρ τοῖς πλείστοις τῶν ἀπὸ Πλάτωνος ἀρέσκει, τῶν τεκνικῶν εἶναι ἰδέας, οἷον ἀσπιδος ἤ λύρας, οὔτε μὴν τῶν παρὰ φύσιν, οἷον πυρετοῦ καὶ χολέρας, οὔτε τῶν κατὰ μέρος, οἷον Σωκράτους καὶ Πλάτωνος, ἀλλ' οὔτε τῶν εὐτελῶν τινός, οἷον ῥύπου καὶ κάρφους, οὔτε τῶν πρός τι, οἷον μείζονος καὶ ὑπερέχοντος· εἶναι γὰρ τὰς ἰδέας νοήσεις θεοῦ αἰωνίους τε καὶ αὐτοτελεῖς – (*Definiunt autem IDEAM exemplar aeternum eorum quae secundum naturam existunt. Nam pluri-*

mis ex iis, qui Platonem secuti sunt, minime placuit, arte factorum ideas esse, ut clypei atque lyrae; neque rursus eorum, quae praeter naturam, ut febris et cholerae; neque particularium, ceu Socratis et Platonis; neque etiam rerum vilium, veluti sordium et festucae; neque relationum, ut majoris et excedentis: esse namque ideas intellectiones dei aeternas, ac seipsis perfectas.)[23] We may take this opportunity to mention yet another point in which our theory of Ideas differs widely from that of Plato. Thus he teaches (*Republic*, X [601] [...]) that the object which art aims at expressing, the prototype of painting and poetry, is not the Idea, but the individual thing. The whole of our discussion so far maintains the very opposite, and Plato's opinion is the less likely to lead us astray, as it is the source of one of the greatest and best known errors of that great man, namely of his disdain and rejection of art, especially of poetry. His false judgement of this is directly associated with the passage quoted.

§ 42.

I return to our discussion of the aesthetic impression. Knowledge of the beautiful always supposes, simultaneously and inseparably, a purely knowing subject and a known Idea as object. But yet the source of aesthetic enjoyment will lie sometimes rather in the apprehension of the known Idea, sometimes rather in the bliss and peace of mind of pure knowledge free from all willing, and thus from all individuality and the pain that results therefrom. And in fact, this predominance of the one or the other constituent element of aesthetic enjoyment will depend on whether the intuitively grasped Idea is a higher or a lower grade of the will's objectivity. Thus with aesthetic contemplation (in real life or through the medium of art) of natural beauty in the inorganic and vegetable kingdoms and of the works of architecture, the enjoyment of pure, will-less knowing will predominate, because the Ideas here apprehended are only low grades of the will's objectivity, and therefore are not phenomena of deep significance and suggestive content. On the other hand, if animals and human beings are the object of aesthetic contemplation or presentation, the enjoyment will consist rather in the objective apprehension of these Ideas that are the most distinct revelations of the will. For these exhibit the greatest variety of forms, a wealth and deep significance of phenomena; they reveal to us most completely the essence of the will, whether in its violence, its terribleness, its satisfaction, or its being broken (this last in tragic situations), finally even in its change or self-surrender, which is the particular theme of Christian painting. Historical painting and the drama generally have as object the Idea of the will enlightened by full knowledge. We will now go over the arts one by one, and in this way the theory of the beautiful that we put forward will gain in completeness and distinctness.

§ 43.

Matter as such cannot be the expression of an Idea. For, as we found in the first book, it is causality through and through; its being is simply its acting. But causality is a form of the principle of sufficient reason; knowledge of the Idea, on the other hand, essentially excludes the content of this principle. In the second book we also found matter to be the common substratum of all individual phenomena of the Ideas, and consequently the connecting link between the Idea and the phenomenon or the individual thing. Therefore, for both these reasons, matter cannot by itself express an Idea. This is confirmed *a posteriori* by the fact that of matter as such absolutely no representation from perception is possible, but only an abstract concept. In the representation of perception are exhibited only the forms and qualities, the supporter of which is matter, and in all of which Ideas reveal themselves. This is also in keeping with the fact that causality (the whole essence of matter) cannot by itself be exhibited in perception, but only a definite causal connexion. On the other hand, every *phenomenon* of an Idea, because, as such, it has entered into the form of the principle of sufficient reason, or the *principium individuationis*, must exhibit itself in matter as a quality thereof. Therefore, as we have said, matter is to this extent the connecting link between the Idea and the *principium individuationis*, which is the individual's form of knowledge, or the principle of sufficient reason. Therefore Plato was quite right, for after the Idea and its phenomenon, namely the individual thing, both of which include generally all the things of the world, he put forward matter only as a third thing different from these two (*Timaeus* [48–9] [...]). The individual, as phenomenon of the Idea, is always matter. Every quality of matter is also always phenomenon of an Idea, and as such is also susceptible of aesthetic contemplation, i.e., of

knowledge of the Idea that expresses itself in it. Now this holds good even of the most universal qualities of matter, without which it never exists, and the Ideas of which are the weakest objectivity of the will. Such are gravity, cohesion, rigidity, fluidity, reaction to light, and so on.

Now if we consider *architecture* merely as a fine art and apart from its provision for useful purposes, in which it serves the will and not pure knowledge, and thus is no longer art in our sense, we can assign it no purpose other than that of bringing to clearer perceptiveness some of those Ideas that are the lowest grades of the will's objectivity. Such Ideas are gravity, cohesion, rigidity, hardness, those universal qualities of stone, those first, simplest, and dullest visibilities of the will, the fundamental bass-notes of nature; and along with these, light, which is in many respects their opposite. Even at this low stage of the will's objectivity, we see its inner nature revealing itself in discord; for, properly speaking, the conflict between gravity and rigidity is the sole aesthetic material of architecture; its problem is to make this conflict appear with perfect distinctness in many different ways. It solves this problem by depriving these indestructible forces of the shortest path to their satisfaction, and keeping them in suspense through a circuitous path; the conflict is thus prolonged, and the inexhaustible efforts of the two forces become visible in many different ways. The whole mass of the building, if left to its original tendency, would exhibit a mere heap or lump, bound to the earth as firmly as possible, to which gravity, the form in which the will here appears, presses incessantly, whereas rigidity, also objectivity of the will, resists. But this very tendency, this effort, is thwarted in its immediate satisfaction by architecture, and only an indirect satisfaction by roundabout ways is granted to it. The joists and beams, for example, can press the earth only by means of the column; the arch must support itself, and only through the medium of the pillars can it satisfy its tendency towards the earth, and so on. By just these enforced digressions, by these very hindrances, those forces inherent in the crude mass of stone unfold themselves in the most distinct and varied manner; and the purely aesthetic purpose of architecture can go no farther. Therefore the beauty of a building is certainly to be found in the evident and obvious suitability of every part, not to the outward arbitrary purpose of man (to this extent the work belongs to practical architecture), but directly to the stability of the whole. The position, size, and form of every part must have so necessary a relation to this stability that if it were possible to remove some part, the whole would inevitably collapse. For only by each part bearing as much as it conveniently can, and each being supported exactly where it ought to be and to exactly the necessary extent, does this play of opposition, this conflict between rigidity and gravity, that constitutes the life of the stone and the manifestations of its will, unfold itself in the most complete visibility. These lowest grades of the will's objectivity distinctly reveal themselves. In just the same way, the form of each part must be determined not arbitrarily, but by its purpose and its relation to the whole. The column is the simplest form of support, determined merely by the purpose or intention. The twisted column is tasteless; the four-cornered pillar is in fact less simple than the round column, though it happens to be more easily made. Also the forms of frieze, joist, arch, vault, dome are determined entirely by their immediate purpose, and are self-explanatory therefrom. Ornamental work on capitals, etc., belongs to sculpture and not to architecture, and is merely tolerated as an additional embellishment, which might be dispensed with. From what has been said, it is absolutely necessary for an understanding and aesthetic enjoyment of a work of architecture to have direct knowledge through perception of its matter as regards its weight, rigidity, and cohesion. Our pleasure in such a work would suddenly be greatly diminished by the disclosure that the building material was pumice-stone, for then it would strike us as a kind of sham building. We should be affected in almost the same way if we were told that it was only of wood, when we had assumed it to be stone, just because this alters and shifts the relation between rigidity and gravity, and thus the significance and necessity of all the parts; for those natural forces reveal themselves much more feebly in a wooden building. Therefore, no architectural work as fine art can really be made of timber, however many forms this may assume; this can be explained simply and solely by our theory. If we were told clearly that the building, the sight of which pleased us, consisted of entirely different materials of very unequal weight and consistency, but not distinguishable by the eye, the whole building would become as incapable of affording us pleasure as would a poem in an unknown language. All this proves that architecture affects us not only mathematically, but dynamically, and that what speaks to us

through it is not mere form and symmetry, but rather those fundamental forces of nature, those primary Ideas, those lowest grades of the will's objectivity. The regularity of the building and its parts is produced to some extent by the direct adaptation of each member to the stability of the whole; to some extent it serves to facilitate a survey and comprehension of the whole. Finally regular figures contribute to the beauty by revealing the conformity to law of space as such. All this, however, is only of subordinate value and necessity, and is by no means the principal thing, for symmetry is not invariably demanded, as even ruins are still beautiful.

Now architectural works have a quite special relation to light; in full sunshine with the blue sky as a background they gain a twofold beauty; and by moonlight again they reveal quite a different effect. Therefore when a fine work of architecture is erected, special consideration is always given to the effects of light and to the climate. The reason for all this is to be found principally in the fact that only a bright, strong illumination makes all the parts and their relations clearly visible. Moreover, I am of the opinion that architecture is destined to reveal not only gravity and rigidity, but at the same time the nature of light, which is their very opposite. The light is intercepted, impeded, and reflected by the large, opaque, sharply contoured and variously formed masses of stone, and thus unfolds its nature and qualities in the purest and clearest way, to the great delight of the beholder; for light is the most agreeable of things as the condition and objective correlative of the most perfect kind of knowledge through perception.

Now since the Ideas, brought to clear perception by architecture, are the lowest grades of the will's objectivity, and since, in consequence, the objective significance of what architecture reveals to us is relatively small, the aesthetic pleasure of looking at a fine and favourably illuminated building will lie not so much in the apprehension of the Idea as in the subjective correlative thereof which accompanies this apprehension. Hence this pleasure will consist preeminently in the fact that, at the sight of this building, the beholder is emancipated from the kind of knowledge possessed by the individual, which serves the will and follows the principle of sufficient reason, and is raised to that of the pure, will-free subject of knowing. Thus it will consist in pure contemplation itself, freed from all the suffering of will and of individuality.

In this respect, the opposite of architecture, and the other extreme in the series of fine arts, is the drama, which brings to knowledge the most significant of all the Ideas; hence in the aesthetic enjoyment of it the objective side is predominant throughout.

Architecture is distinguished from the plastic arts and poetry by the fact that it gives us not a copy, but the thing itself. Unlike those arts, it does not repeat the known Idea, whereby the artist lends his eyes to the beholder. But in it the artist simply presents the object to the beholder, and makes the apprehension of the Idea easy for him by bringing the actual individual object to a clear and complete expression of its nature.

Unlike the works of the other fine arts, those of architecture are very rarely executed for purely aesthetic purposes. On the contrary, they are subordinated to other, practical ends that are foreign to art itself. Thus the great merit of the architect consists in his achieving and attaining purely aesthetic ends, in spite of their subordination to other ends foreign to them. This he does by skilfully adapting them in many different ways to the arbitrary ends in each case, and by correctly judging what aesthetically architectural beauty is consistent and compatible with a temple, a palace, a prison, and so on. The more a harsh climate increases those demands of necessity and utility, definitely determines them, and inevitably prescribes them, the less scope is there for the beautiful in architecture. In the mild climate of India, Egypt, Greece, and Rome, where the demands of necessity were fewer and less definite, architecture was able to pursue its aesthetic ends with the greatest freedom. Under a northern sky these are greatly curtailed for architecture; here, where the requirements were coffers, pointed roofs, and towers, it could unfold its beauty only within very narrow limits, and had to make amends all the more by making use of embellishments borrowed from sculpture, as can be seen in Gothic architecture.

In this way architecture is bound to suffer great restrictions through the demands of necessity and utility. On the other hand, it has in these a very powerful support, for with the range and expense of its works and with the narrow sphere of its aesthetic effect, it certainly could not maintain itself merely as a fine art unless it had at the same time, as a useful and necessary profession, a firm and honourable place among men's occupations. It is the lack of this that prevents another art from standing beside architecture as a sister art, although, in an aesthetic respect, this can be quite properly coordinated with architecture as its companion; I am referring to the artistic arrangement of water. For what architecture achieves for the Idea of gravity where this appears associated with rigidity, is the same as what this other art achieves for the same Idea where this Idea is associated with fluidity, in other words, with formlessness, maximum mobility, and transparency. Waterfalls tumbling, dashing, and foaming over rocks, cataracts softly dispersed into spray, springs gushing up as high columns of water, and clear reflecting lakes reveal the Ideas of fluid heavy matter in exactly the same way as the works of architecture unfold the Ideas of rigid matter. Hydraulics as a fine art finds no support in practical hydraulics, for as a rule the ends of the one cannot be combined with those of the other. Only by way of an exception does this come about, for example, in the *Cascata di Trevi* in Rome.[...]

§ 44.

What the two arts just mentioned achieve for these lowest grades of the will's objectivity is achieved to a certain extent for the higher grade of vegetable nature by artistic horticulture. The landscape-beauty of a spot depends for the most part on the multiplicity of the natural objects found together in it, and on the fact that they are clearly separated, appear distinctly, and yet exhibit themselves in fitting association and succession. It is these two conditions that are assisted by artistic horticulture; yet this art is not nearly such a master of its material as architecture is of its, and so its effect is limited. The beauty displayed by it belongs almost entirely to nature; the art itself does little for it. On the other hand, this art can also do very little against the inclemency of nature, and where nature works not for but against it, its achievements are insignificant.

Therefore, in so far as the plant world, which offers itself to aesthetic enjoyment everywhere without the medium of art, is an object of art, it belongs principally to landscape-painting, and in the province of this is to be found along with it all the rest of nature-devoid-of-knowledge. In paintings of still life and of mere architecture, ruins, church interiors, and so on, the subjective side of aesthetic pleasure is predominant, in other words, our delight does not reside mainly in the immediate apprehension of the manifested Ideas, but rather in the subjective correlative of this apprehension, in pure will-less knowing. For since the painter lets us see the things through his eyes, we here obtain at the same time a sympathetic and reflected feeling of the profound spiritual peace and the complete silence of the will, which were necessary for plunging knowledge so deeply into those inanimate objects, and for comprehending them with such affection, in other words with such a degree of objectivity. Now the effect of landscape-painting proper is on the whole also of this kind; but because the Ideas manifested, as higher grades of the will's objectivity, are more significant and suggestive, the objective side of aesthetic pleasure comes more to the front, and balances the subjective. Pure knowing as such is no longer entirely the main thing, but the known Idea, the world as representation at an important grade of the will's objectification, operates with equal force.

But an even much higher grade is revealed by animal painting and animal sculpture. Of the latter we have important antique remains, for example, the horses in Venice, on Monte Cavallo, in the Elgin Marbles, also in Florence in bronze and marble; in the same place the ancient wild boar, the howling wolves; also the lions in the Venice Arsenal; in the Vatican there is a whole hall almost filled with ancient animals and other objects. In these presentations the objective side of aesthetic pleasure obtains a decided predominance over the subjective. The peace of the subject who knows these Ideas, who has silenced his own will, is present, as indeed it is in any aesthetic contemplation, but its effect is not felt, for we are occupied with the restlessness and impetuosity of the depicted will. It is that willing, which also constitutes our own inner nature, that here appears before us in forms and figures. In these the phenomenon of will is not, as in us, controlled and tempered by thoughtfulness, but is exhibited in stronger traits and with a distinctness verging on the grotesque and monstrous. On the other hand, this phenomenon manifests itself without dissimulation, naïvely and openly, freely and evidently, and precisely on this rests our interest in animals. The characteristic of the species already appeared in the presentation of plants, yet it showed itself only in the forms; here it becomes much more significant, and expresses itself not only in the form, but in the action, position, and deportment, though always

only as the character of the species, not of the individual. This knowledge of the Ideas at higher grades, which we receive in painting through the agency of another person, can also be directly shared by us through the purely contemplative perception of plants, and by the observation of animals, and indeed of the latter in their free, natural, and easy state. The objective contemplation of their many different and marvellous forms, and of their actions and behaviour, is an instructive lesson from the great book of nature; it is the deciphering of the true *signatura rerum*.[24] We see in it the manifold grades and modes of manifestation of the will that is one and the same in all beings and everywhere wills the same thing. This will objectifies itself as life, as existence, in such endless succession and variety, in such different forms, all of which are accommodations to the various external conditions, and can be compared to many variations on the same theme. But if we had to convey to the beholder, for reflection and in a word, the explanation and information about their inner nature, it would be best for us to use the Sanskrit formula which occurs so often in the sacred books of the Hindus, and is called *Mahavakya*, i.e., the great word: "*Tat tvam asi*," which means "This living thing art thou."

§ 45.

Finally, the great problem of historical painting and of sculpture is to present, immediately and for perception, the Idea in which the will reaches the highest degree of its objectification. The objective side of pleasure in the beautiful is here wholly predominant, and the subjective is now in the background. Further, it is to be observed that at the next grade below this, in other words, in animal painting, the characteristic is wholly one with the beautiful; the most characteristic lion, wolf, horse, sheep, or ox is always the most beautiful. The reason for this is that animals have only the character of the species, not an individual character. But in the manifestation of man the character of the species is separated from the character of the individual. The former is now called beauty (wholly in the objective sense), but the latter retains the name of character or expression, and the new difficulty arises of completely presenting both at the same time in the same individual.

Human beauty is an objective expression that denotes the will's most complete objectification at the highest grade at which this is knowable, namely the Idea of man in general, completely and fully expressed in the perceived form. But however much the objective side of the beautiful appears here, the subjective still always remains its constant companion. No object transports us so rapidly into purely aesthetic contemplation as the most beautiful human countenance and form, at the sight of which we are instantly seized by an inexpressible satisfaction and lifted above ourselves and all that torments us. This is possible only because of the fact that this most distinct and purest perceptibility of the will raises us most easily and rapidly into the state of pure knowing in which our personality, our willing with its constant pain, disappears, as long as the purely aesthetic pleasure lasts. Therefore, Goethe says that "Whoever beholds human beauty cannot be infected with evil; he feels in harmony with himself and the world." Now, that nature succeeds in producing a beautiful human form must be explained by saying that the will at this highest grade objectifies itself in an individual, and thus, through fortunate circumstances and by its own power, completely overcomes all the obstacles and opposition presented to it by phenomena of the lower grades. Such are the forces of nature from which the will must always wrest and win back the matter that belongs to them all. Further, the phenomenon of the will at the higher grades always has multiplicity in its form. The tree is only a systematic aggregate of innumerably repeated sprouting fibres. This combination increases more and more the higher we go, and the human body is a highly complex system of quite different parts, each of which has its *vita propria*, a life subordinate to the whole, yet characteristic. That all these parts are precisely and appropriately subordinated to the whole and coordinated with one another; that they conspire harmoniously to the presentation of the whole, and there is nothing excessive or stunted; all these are the rare conditions, the result of which is beauty, the completely impressed character of the species. Thus nature: but how is it with art? It is imagined that this is done by imitating nature. But how is the artist to recognize the perfect work to be imitated, and how is he to discover it from among the failures, unless he anticipates the beautiful *prior to experience*? Moreover, has nature ever produced a human being perfectly beautiful in all his parts? It has been supposed that the artist must gather the beautiful parts separately distributed among many human beings, and construct a beautiful whole from them; an absurd and meaningless opinion. Once again, it is asked, how is he to know that just these forms and not others are beautiful? We also see how far the old German painters arrived at beauty by imitating nature. Let us consider their nude figures. No knowledge of the beautiful is at all possible purely *a posteriori* and from mere experience. It is always, at least partly, *a priori*, though of quite a different kind from the forms of the principle of sufficient reason, of which we are *a priori* conscious. These concern the universal form of the phenomenon as such, as it establishes the possibility of knowledge in general, the universal *how* of appearance without exception, and from this knowledge proceed mathematics and pure natural science. On the other hand, that other kind of knowledge *a priori*, which makes it possible to present the beautiful, concerns the content of phenomena instead of the form, the *what* of the appearance instead of the *how*. We all recognize human beauty when we see it, but in the genuine artist this takes place with such clearness that he shows it as he has never seen it, and in his presentation he surpasses nature. Now this is possible only because *we ourselves* are the will, whose adequate objectification at its highest grade is here to be judged and discovered. In fact, only in this way have we an anticipation of what nature (which is in fact just the will constituting our own inner being) endeavours to present. In the true genius this anticipation is accompanied by a high degree of thoughtful intelligence, so that, by recognizing in the individual thing its *Idea*, he, so to speak, *understands nature's half-spoken words*. He expresses clearly what she merely stammers. He impresses on the hard marble the beauty of the form which nature failed to achieve in a thousand attempts, and he places it before her, exclaiming as it were, "This is what you desired to say!" And from the man who knows comes the echoing reply, "Yes, that is it!" Only in this way was the Greek genius able to discover the prototype of the human form, and to set it up as the canon for the school of sculpture. Only by virtue of such an anticipation also is it possible for all of us to recognize the beautiful where nature has actually succeeded in the particular case. This anticipation is the *Ideal*; it is the *Idea* in so far as it is known *a priori*, or at any rate half-known; and it becomes practical for art by accommodating and supplementing as such what is given *a posteriori* through nature. The possibility of such anticipation of the beautiful *a priori* in the artist, as well as of its recognition *a posteriori* by the connoisseur, is to be found in the fact that artist and connoisseur are themselves the "in-itself" of nature, the will objectifying itself. For, as Empedocles said, like can be recognized only by like; only nature can understand herself; only nature will fathom herself; but also only by the mind is the mind comprehended.[25]

The opinion is absurd, although expressed by Xenophon's Socrates (Stobaeus, *Florilegium*, ii [...]), that the Greeks discovered the established ideal of human beauty wholly empirically by collecting separate beautiful parts, uncovering and noting here a knee, and there an arm. It has its exact parallel in regard to the art of poetry, namely the assumption that Shakespeare, for example, noted, and then reproduced from his own experience of life, the innumerable and varied characters in his dramas, so true, so sustained, so thoroughly and profoundly worked out. The impossibility and absurdity of such an assumption need not be discussed. It is obvious that the man of genius produces the works of poetic art only by an anticipation of what is characteristic just as he produces the works of plastic and pictorial art only by a prophetic anticipation of the beautiful, though both require experience as a schema or model. In this alone is that something of which they are dimly aware *a priori*, called into distinctness, and the possibility of thoughtful and intelligent presentation appears.

Human beauty was declared above to be the most complete objectification of the will at the highest grade of its knowability. It expresses itself through the form, and this resides in space alone, and has no necessary connexion with time, as movement for example has. To this extent we can say that the adequate objectification of the will through a merely spatial phenomenon is beauty, in the objective sense. The plant is nothing but such a merely spatial phenomenon of the will; for no movement, and consequently no relation to time (apart from its development), belong to the expression of its nature. Its mere form expresses and openly displays its whole inner being. Animal and man, however, still need for the complete revelation of the will appearing in them a series of actions, and thus that phenomenon in them obtains a direct relation to time. All this [...] is connected with our present remarks in the following way. As the merely spatial phenomenon of the will can objectify that will perfectly or imperfectly at each definite grade – and it is just this that

constitutes beauty or ugliness – so also can the temporal objectification of the will, i.e., the action, and indeed the direct action, and hence the movement, correspond purely and perfectly to the will which objectifies itself in it, without foreign admixture, without superfluity, without deficiency, expressing only the exact act of will determined in each case; or the converse of all this may occur. In the first case, the movement occurs with *grace*; in the second, without it. Thus as beauty is the adequate and suitable manifestation of the will in general, through its merely spatial phenomenon, so *grace* is the adequate manifestation of the will through its temporal phenomenon, in other words, the perfectly correct and appropriate expression of each act of will through the movement and position that objectifies it. As movement and position presuppose the body, Winckelmann's expression is very true and to the point when he says: "Grace is the peculiar relation of the acting person to the action." (*Werke*, Vol. I [...]) It follows automatically that beauty can be attributed to plants, but not grace, unless in a figurative sense; to animals and human beings, both beauty and grace. In accordance with what has been said, grace consists in every movement being performed and every position taken up in the easiest, most appropriate, and most convenient way, and consequently in being the purely adequate expression of its intention or of the act of will, without any superfluity that shows itself as unsuitable meaningless bustle or absurd posture; without any deficiency that shows itself as wooden stiffness. Grace presupposes a correct proportion in all the limbs, a symmetrical, harmonious structure of the body, as only by means of these are perfect ease and evident appropriateness in all postures and movements possible. Therefore grace is never without a certain degree of beauty of the body. The two, complete and united, are the most distinct phenomenon of the will at the highest grade of its objectification.

As mentioned above, it is one of the distinguishing features of mankind that therein the character of the species and that of the individual are separated so that [...] each person exhibits to a certain extent an Idea that is wholly characteristic of him. Therefore the arts, aiming at a presentation of the Idea of mankind, have as their problem both beauty as the character of the species, and the character of the individual, which is called *character par excellence*. Again, they have this only in so far as this character is to be regarded not as something accidental and quite peculiar to the man as a single individual, but as a side of the Idea of mankind, specially appearing in this particular individual; and thus the presentation of this individual serves to reveal this Idea. Therefore the character, although individual as such, must be comprehended and expressed ideally in other words, with emphasis on its significance in regard to the Idea of mankind in general (to the objectifying of which it contributes in its own way). Moreover, the presentation is a portrait, a repetition of the individual as such, with all his accidental qualities. And as Winckelmann says, even the portrait should be the ideal of the individual.

That *character*, to be comprehended ideally, which is the emphasis of a particular and peculiar side of the Idea of mankind, now manifests itself visibly, partly through permanent physiognomy and bodily form, partly through fleeting emotion and passion, the reciprocal modification of knowing and willing through each other; and all this is expressed in mien and movement. The individual always belongs to humanity; on the other hand, humanity always reveals itself in the individual, and that with the peculiar ideal significance of this individual; therefore beauty cannot be abolished by character, or character by beauty. For the abolition of the character of the species by that of the individual would give us caricature, and the abolition of the character of the individual by that of the species would result in meaninglessness. Therefore, the presentation that aims at beauty, as is done mainly by sculpture, will always modify this (i.e., the character of the species) in some respect by the individual character, and will always express the Idea of mankind in a definite individual way, emphasizing a particular side of it. For the human individual as such has, to a certain extent, the dignity of an Idea of his own; and it is essential to the Idea of mankind that it manifest itself in individuals of characteristic significance. Therefore we find in the works of the ancients that the beauty distinctly apprehended by them is expressed not by a single form, but by many forms bearing various characters. It is always grasped, so to speak, from a different side, and is accordingly presented in one manner in Apollo, in another in Bacchus, in another in Hercules, and in yet another in Antinous. In fact, the characteristic can limit the beautiful, and finally can appear even as ugliness, in the drunken Silenus, in the Faun, and so on. But if the characteristic goes so far as actually to abolish the character of the species, that is, if it extends to the unnatural, it becomes caricature. But far less than beauty can grace be interfered with by what is characteristic, for the expression of the character also demands graceful position and movement; yet it must be achieved in a way that is most fitting, appropriate, and easy for the person. This will be observed not only by the sculptor and painter, but also by every good actor, otherwise caricature appears here also as grimace or distortion.

In sculpture beauty and grace remain the principal matter. The real character of the mind, appearing in emotion, passion, alternations of knowing and willing, which can be depicted only by the expression of the face and countenance, is preeminently the province of *painting*. For although eyes and colour, lying outside the sphere of sculpture, contribute a great deal to beauty, they are far more essential for the character. Further, beauty unfolds itself more completely to contemplation from several points of view; on the other hand, the expression, the character, can be completely apprehended from a single viewpoint.

Since beauty is obviously the chief aim of sculpture, Lessing tried to explain the fact that the Laocoön *does not cry out* by saying that crying out is incompatible with beauty. This subject became for Lessing the theme, or at any rate the starting-point, of a book of his own, and a great deal has been written on the subject both before and after him. I may therefore be permitted incidentally to express my opinion about it here, although such a special discussion does not really belong to the sequence of our argument, which throughout is directed to what is general.

§ 46.

It is obvious that, in the famous group, Laocoön is not crying out, and the universal and ever-recurring surprise at this must be attributable to the fact that we should all cry out in his place. Nature also demands this; for in the case of the most acute physical pain and the sudden appearance of the greatest bodily fear, all reflection that might induce silent endurance is entirely expelled from consciousness, and nature relieves itself by crying out, thus expressing pain and fear at the same time, summoning the deliverer and terrifying the assailant. Therefore Winckelmann regretted the absence of the expression of crying out; but as he tried to justify the artist, he really made Laocoön into a Stoic who considered it beneath his dignity to cry out *secundum naturam*,[26] but added to his pain the useless constraint of stifling its expression. Winckelmann therefore sees in him "the tried spirit of a great man writhing in agony, and trying to suppress the expression of feeling and to lock it up in himself. He does not break out into a loud shriek, as in Virgil, but only anxious sighs escape him," and so on. (*Werke*, Vol. vii, p. 98; the same in more detail in Vol. vi, pp. 104 *seq.*) This opinion of Winckelmann was criticized by Lessing in his Laocoön, and improved by him in the way mentioned above. In place of the psychological reason, he gave the purely aesthetic one that beauty, the principle of ancient art, does not admit the expression of crying out. Another argument he gives is that a wholly fleeting state, incapable of any duration, should not be depicted in a motionless work of art. This has against it a hundred examples of excellent figures that are fixed in wholly fleeting movements, dancing, wrestling, catching, and so on. Indeed, Goethe, in the essay on the Laocoön which opens the *Propyläen* [. . .,] considers the choice of such a wholly fleeting moment to be absolutely necessary. In our day, Hirt (*Horae*, 1797, tenth St.), reducing everything to the highest truth of the expression, decided the matter by saying that Laocoön does not cry out because he is no longer able to, as he is on the point of dying from suffocation. Finally, Fernow (*Römische Studien*, Vol. I [. . .]) weighed and discussed all these three opinions; he did not, however, add a new one of his own, but reconciled and amalgamated all three.

I cannot help being surprised that such thoughtful and acute men laboriously bring in far-fetched and inadequate reasons, and resort to psychological and even physiological arguments, in order to explain a matter the reason of which is quite near at hand, and to the unprejudiced is immediately obvious. I am particularly surprised that Lessing, who came so near to the correct explanation, completely missed the point.

Before all psychological and physiological investigation as to whether Laocoön in his position would cry out or not (and I affirm that he certainly would), it has to be decided as regards the group that crying out ought not to be expressed in it, for the simple reason that the presentation of this lies entirely outside the province of sculpture. A shrieking Laocoön could not be produced in marble, but only one with the mouth wide open fruitlessly endeavouring to shriek, a Laocoön whose voice was stuck in his throat, *vox faucibus haesit*.[27]

The essence of shrieking, and consequently its effect on the onlooker, lies entirely in the sound, not in the gaping mouth. This latter phenomenon that necessarily accompanies the shriek must be motivated and justified first through the sound produced by it; it is then permissible and indeed necessary, as characteristic of the action, although it is detrimental to beauty. But in plastic art, to which the presentation of shrieking is quite foreign and impossible, it would be really foolish to exhibit the violent medium of shrieking, namely the gaping mouth, which disturbs all the features and the rest of the expression, since we should then have before us the means, which moreover demands many sacrifices, whilst its end, the shrieking itself together with its effect on our feelings, would fail to appear. Moreover there would be produced each time the ridiculous spectacle of a permanent exertion without effect. This could actually be compared to the wag who, for a joke, stopped up with wax the horn of the sleeping night watchman, and then woke him up with the cry of fire, and amused himself watching the man's fruitless efforts to blow. On the other hand, where the expression of shrieking lies in the province of dramatic art, it is quite admissible, because it serves truth, in other words, the complete expression of the Idea. So in poetry, which claims for perceptive presentation the imagination of the reader. Therefore in Virgil Laocoön cries out like an ox that has broken loose after being struck by an axe. Homer (*Iliad*, xx, 48–53) represents Ares and Athene as shrieking horribly without detracting from their divine dignity or beauty. In just the same way with acting; on the stage Laocoön would certainly have to cry out. Sophocles also represents Philoctetes as shrieking, and on the ancient stage he would certainly have done so. In quite a similar case, I remember having seen in London the famous actor Kemble in a piece called *Pizarro*, translated from the German. He played the part of the American, a half-savage, but of very noble character. Yet when he was wounded, he cried out loudly and violently, and this was of great and admirable effect, since it was highly characteristic and contributed a great deal to the truth. On the other hand, a painted or voiceless shrieker in stone would be much more ridiculous than the painted music that is censured in Goethe's *Propyläen*. For shrieking is much more detrimental to the rest of the expression and to beauty than music is; for at most this concerns only hands and arms, and is to be looked upon as an action characterizing the person. Indeed, to this extent it can be quite rightly painted, so long as it does not require any violent movement of the body or distortion of the mouth; thus for example, St. Cecilia at the organ, Raphael's violinist in the Sciarra Gallery in Rome, and many others. Now since, on account of the limitations of the art, the pain of Laocoön could not be expressed by shrieking, the artist had to set in motion every other expression of pain. This he achieved to perfection, as is ably described by Winckelmann (*Werke*, Vol. vi, pp. 104 *seq.*), whose admirable account therefore retains its full value and truth as soon as we abstract from the stoical sentiment underlying it.[. . .]

§ 47.

Because beauty with grace is the principal subject of sculpture, it likes the nude, and tolerates clothing only in so far as this does not conceal the form. It makes use of drapery, not as a covering, but as an indirect presentation of the form. This method of presentation greatly engrosses the understanding, since the understanding reaches the perception of the cause, namely the form of the body, only through the one directly given effect, that is to say, the arrangement of the drapery. Therefore in sculpture drapery is to some extent what foreshortening is in painting. Both are suggestions, yet not symbolical, but such that, if they succeed, they force the understanding immediately to perceive what is suggested, just as if it were actually given.

Here I may be permitted in passing to insert a comparison relating to the rhetorical arts. Just as the beautiful bodily form can be seen to the best advantage with the lightest clothing, or even no clothing at all, and thus a very handsome man, if at the same time he had taste and could follow it, would prefer to walk about almost naked, clothed only after the manner of the ancients; so will every fine mind rich in ideas express itself always in the most natural, candid, and simple way, concerned if it be possible to communicate its thoughts to others, and thus to relieve the loneliness that one is bound to feel in a world such as this. Conversely, poverty of mind, confusion and perversity of thought will clothe themselves in the most far-fetched expressions and obscure forms of speech, in order to cloak in difficult and pompous phrases small, trifling, insipid, or commonplace ideas. It is like the man who lacks the majesty of beauty, and wishes to make up for this deficiency by clothing;

he attempts to cover up the insignificance or ugliness of his person under barbaric finery, tinsel, feathers, ruffles, cuffs, and mantles. Thus many an author, if compelled to translate his pompous and obscure book into its little clear content, would be as embarrassed as that man would be if he were to go about naked.

§ 48.

Historical painting has, besides beauty and grace, character as its principal object; by character is to be understood in general the manifestation of the will at the highest grade of its objectification. Here the individual, as emphasizing a particular side of the Idea of mankind, has peculiar significance, and makes this known not by mere form alone; on the contrary, he renders it visible in mien and countenance by action of every kind, and by the modifications of knowing and willing which occasion and accompany it. Since the Idea of mankind is to be exhibited in this sphere, the unfolding of its many-sidedness must be brought before our eyes in significant individuals, and these again can be made visible in their significance only through many different scenes, events, and actions. Now this endless problem is solved by historical painting, for it brings before our eyes scenes from life of every kind, of great or trifling significance. No individual and no action can be without significance; in all and through all, the Idea of mankind unfolds itself more and more. Therefore no event in the life of man can possibly be excluded from painting. Consequently, a great injustice is done to the eminent painters of the Dutch school, when their technical skill alone is esteemed, and in other respects they are looked down on with disdain, because they generally depict objects from everyday life, whereas only events from world or biblical history are regarded as significant. We should first of all bear in mind that the inward significance of an action is quite different from the outward, and that the two often proceed in separation from each other. The outward significance is the importance of an action in relation to its consequences for and in the actual world, and hence according to the principle of sufficient reason. The inward significance is the depth of insight into the Idea of mankind which it discloses, in that it brings to light sides of that Idea which rarely appear. This it does by causing individualities, expressing themselves distinctly and decidedly, to unfold their peculiar characteristics by means of appropriately arranged circumstances. In art only the inward significance is of importance; in history the outward. The two are wholly independent of each other; they can appear together, but they can also appear alone. An action of the highest significance for history can in its inner significance be very common and ordinary. Conversely, a scene from everyday life can be of great inward significance, if human individuals and the innermost recesses of human action and will appear in it in a clear and distinct light. Even in spite of very different outward significance, the inward can be the same; thus, for example, it is all the same as regards inward significance whether ministers dispute about countries and nations over a map, or boors in a beer-house choose to wrangle over cards and dice; just as it is all the same whether we play chess with pieces of gold or of wood. Moreover, the scenes and events that make up the life of so many millions of human beings, their actions, their sorrows, and their joys, are on that account important enough to be the object of art, and by their rich variety must afford material enough to unfold the many-sided Idea of mankind. Even the fleeting nature of the moment, which art has fixed in such a picture (nowadays called *genre painting*), excites a slight, peculiar feeling of emotion. For to fix the fleeting world, which is for ever transforming itself, in the enduring picture of particular events that nevertheless represent the whole, is an achievement of the art of painting by which it appears to bring time itself to a standstill, since it raises the individual to the Idea of its species. Finally, the historical and outwardly significant subjects of painting often have the disadvantage that the very thing that is significant in them cannot be presented in perception, but must be added in thought. In this respect the nominal significance of the picture must generally be distinguished from the real. The former is the outward significance, to be added, however, only as concept; the latter is that side of the Idea of mankind which becomes evident for perception through the picture. For example, Moses found by the Egyptian princess may be the nominal significance of a picture, an extremely important moment for history; on the other hand, the real significance, that which is actually given to perception, is a foundling rescued from its floating cradle by a great lady, an incident that may have happened more than once. The costume alone can here make known to the cultured person the defin-

ite historical case; but the costume is of importance only for the nominal significance; for the real significance it is a matter of indifference, for the latter knows only the human being as such, not the arbitrary forms. Subjects taken from history have no advantage over those which are taken from mere possibility, and are thus to be called not individual, but only general. For what is really significant in the former is not the individual, not the particular event as such, but the universal in it, the side of the Idea of mankind that is expressed through it. On the other hand, definite historical subjects are not on any account to be rejected; only the really artistic view of such subjects, both in the painter and in the beholder, concerns never the individual particulars in them, which properly constitute the historical, but the universal that is expressed in them, namely the Idea. Only those historical subjects are to be chosen in which the main thing can actually be shown, and has not to be merely added in thought; otherwise the nominal significance is too remote from the real. What is merely thought in connexion with the picture becomes of the greatest importance, and interferes with what is perceived. If, even on the stage, it is not right for the main incident to take place behind the scenes (as in French tragedy), it is obviously a far greater fault in the picture. Historical subjects have a decidedly detrimental effect only when they restrict the painter to a field chosen arbitrarily, and not for artistic but for other purposes. This is particularly the case when this field is poor in picturesque and significant objects, when, for example, it is the history of a small, isolated, capricious, hierarchical (i.e., ruled by false notions), obscure people, like the Jews, despised by the great contemporary nations of the East and of the West. Since the great migration of peoples lies between us and all the ancient nations, just as between the present surface of the earth and the surface whose organisms appear only as fossil remains there lies the former change of the bed of the ocean, it is to be regarded generally as a great misfortune that the people whose former culture was to serve mainly as the basis of our own were not, say, the Indians or the Greeks, or even the Romans, but just these Jews. But it was a particularly unlucky star for the Italian painters of genius in the fifteenth and sixteenth centuries that, in the narrow sphere to which they were arbitrarily referred for the choice of subjects, they had to resort to miserable wretches of every kind. For the New Testament, as regards its historical part, is almost more unfavourable to painting than is the Old, and the subsequent history of martyrs and doctors of the Church is a very unfortunate subject. Yet we have to distinguish very carefully between those pictures whose subject is the historical or mythological one of Judaism and Christianity, and those in which the real, i.e., the ethical, spirit of Christianity is revealed for perception by the presentation of persons full of this spirit. These presentations are in fact the highest and most admirable achievements of the art of painting, and only the greatest masters of this art succeeded in producing them, in particular Raphael and Correggio, the latter especially in his earlier pictures. Paintings of this kind are really not to be numbered among the historical, for often they do not depict any event or action, but are mere groups of saints with the Saviour himself, often still as a child with his mother, angels, and so on. In their countenances, especially in their eyes, we see the expression, the reflection, of the most perfect knowledge, that knowledge namely which is not directed to particular things, but which has fully grasped the Ideas, and hence the whole inner nature of the world and of life. This knowledge in them, reacting on the will, does not, like that other knowledge, furnish *motives* for the will, but on the contrary has become a *quieter* of all willing. From this has resulted perfect resignation, which is the innermost spirit of Christianity as of Indian wisdom, the giving up of all willing, turning back, abolition of the will and with it of the whole inner being of this world, and hence salvation. Therefore, those eternally praiseworthy masters of art expressed the highest wisdom perceptibly in their works. Here is the summit of all art that has followed the will in its adequate objectivity, namely in the Ideas, through all the grades, from the lowest where it is affected, and its nature is unfolded, by causes, then where it is similarly affected by stimuli, and finally by motives. And now art ends by presenting the free self-abolition of the will through the one great quieter that dawns on it from the most perfect knowledge of its own nature.[28]

§ 49.

The truth which lies at the foundation of all the remarks we have so far made on art is that the object of art, the depiction of which is the aim of the artist, and the knowledge of which must con-sequently precede his work as its germ and source, is an *Idea* in Plato's sense, and absolutely nothing else; not the particular thing, the object of common apprehension, and not the concept, the object of rational thought and of science. Although Idea and concept have something in common, in that both as unities represent a plurality of actual things, the great difference between the two will have become sufficiently clear and evident from what was said in the first book about the concept, and what has been said in the present book about the Idea. I certainly do not mean to assert that Plato grasped this difference clearly; indeed many of his examples of Ideas and his discussions of them are applicable only to concepts. However, we leave this aside, and go our way, glad whenever we come across traces of a great and noble mind, yet pursuing not his footsteps, but our own aim. The *concept* is abstract, discursive, wholly undetermined within its sphere, determined only by its limits, attainable and intelligible only to him who has the faculty of reason, communicable by words without further assistance, entirely exhausted by its definition. The *Idea*, on the other hand, definable perhaps as the adequate representative of the concept, is absolutely perceptive, and, although representing an infinite number of individual things, is yet thoroughly definite. It is never known by the individual as such, but only by him who has raised himself above all willing and all individuality to the pure subject of knowing. Thus it is attainable only by the man of genius, and by him who, mostly with the assistance of works of genius, has raised his power of pure knowledge, and is now in the frame of mind of the genius. Therefore it is communicable not absolutely, but only conditionally, since the Idea, apprehended and repeated in the work of art, appeals to everyone only according to the measure of his own intellectual worth. For this reason the most excellent works of any art, the noblest productions of genius, must eternally remain sealed books to the dull majority of men, and are inaccessible to them. They are separated from them by a wide gulf, just as the society of princes is inaccessible to the common people. It is true that even the dullest of them accept on authority works which are acknowledged to be great, in order not to betray their own weakness. But they always remain in silence, ready to express their condemnation the moment they are allowed to hope that they can do so without running the risk of exposure. Then their long-restrained hatred of all that is great and beautiful and of the authors thereof readily relieves itself; for such things never appealed to them, and so humiliated them. For in order to acknowledge, and freely and willingly to admit, the worth of another, a man must generally have some worth of his own. On this is based the necessity for modesty in spite of all merit, as also for the disproportionately loud praise of this virtue, which alone of all its sisters is always included in the eulogy of anyone who ventures to praise a man distinguished in some way, in order to conciliate and appease the wrath of worthlessness. For what is modesty but hypocritical humility, by means of which, in a world swelling with vile envy, a man seeks to beg pardon for his excellences and merits from those who have none? For whoever attributes no merits to himself because he really has none, is not modest, but merely honest.

The *Idea* is the unity that has fallen into plurality by virtue of the temporal and spatial form of our intuitive apprehension. The *concept*, on the other hand, is the unity once more produced out of plurality by means of abstraction through our faculty of reason; the latter can be described as *unitas post rem*, and the former as *unitas ante rem*. Finally, we can express the distinction between concept and Idea figuratively, by saying that the *concept* is like a dead receptacle in which whatever has been put actually lies side by side, but from which no more can be taken out (by analytical judgements) than has been put in (by synthetical reflection). The *Idea*, on the other hand, develops in him who has grasped it representations that are new as regards the concept of the same name; it is like a living organism, developing itself and endowed with generative force, which brings forth that which was not previously put into it.

Now it follows from all that has been said that the concept, useful as it is in life, serviceable, necessary, and productive as it is in science, is eternally barren and unproductive in art. The apprehended Idea, on the contrary, is the true and only source of every genuine work of art. In its powerful originality it is drawn only from life itself, from nature, from the world, and only by the genuine genius, or by him whose momentary inspiration reaches the point of genius. Genuine works bearing immortal life arise only from such immediate apprehension. Just because the Idea is and remains perceptive, the artist is not conscious *in abstracto* of the intention and aim of his work. Not a concept but an Idea is present in his mind; hence he cannot give an account of his actions. He

works, as people say, from mere feeling and unconsciously, indeed instinctively. On the other hand, imitators, mannerists, *imitatores, servum pecus*,[29] in art start from the concept. They note what pleases and affects in genuine works, make this clear to themselves, fix it in the concept, and hence in the abstract, and then imitate it, openly or in disguise, with skill and intention. Like parasitic plants, they suck their nourishment from the works of others; and like polyps, take on the colour of their nourishment. Indeed, we could even carry the comparison farther, and assert that they are like machines which mince very fine and mix up what is put into them, but can never digest it, so that the constituent elements of others can always be found again, and picked out and separated from the mixture. Only the genius, on the other hand, is like the organic body that assimilates, transforms, and produces. For he is, indeed, educated and cultured by his predecessors and their works; but only by life and the world itself is he made directly productive through the impression of what is perceived; therefore the highest culture never interferes with his originality. All imitators, all mannerists apprehend in the concept the essential nature of the exemplary achievements of others; but they can never impart inner life to a work. The generation, in other words the dull multitude of any time, itself knows only concepts and sticks to them; it therefore accepts mannered works with ready and loud applause. After a few years, however, these works become unpalatable, because the spirit of the times, in other words the prevailing concepts, in which alone those works could take root, has changed. Only the genuine works that are drawn directly from nature and life remain eternally young and strong, like nature and life itself. For they belong to no age, but to mankind; and for this reason they are received with indifference by their own age to which they disdained to conform; and because they indirectly and negatively exposed the errors of the age, they were recognized tardily and reluctantly. On the other hand, they do not grow old, but even down to the latest times always make an ever new and fresh appeal to us. They are then no longer exposed to neglect and misunderstanding; for they now stand crowned and sanctioned by the approbation of the few minds capable of judging. These appear singly and sparingly in the course of centuries,[30] and cast their votes, the slowly increasing number of which establishes the authority, the only judgement-seat that is meant when an appeal is made to posterity.

It is these successively appearing individuals alone; for the mass and multitude of posterity will always be and remain just as perverse and dull as the mass and multitude of contemporaries always were and always are. Let us read the complaints of the great minds of every century about their contemporaries; they always sound as if they were of today, since the human race is always the same. In every age and in every art affectation takes the place of the spirit, which always is only the property of individuals. Affectation, however, is the old, cast-off garment of the phenomenon of the spirit which last existed and was recognized. In view of all this, the approbation of posterity is earned as a rule only at the expense of the approbation of one's contemporaries, and *vice versa*. [...]

§ 50.

Now, if the purpose of all art is the communication of the apprehended Idea, and this Idea is then grasped by the man of weaker susceptibility and no productive capacity through the medium of the artist's mind, in which it appears isolated and purged of everything foreign; further, if starting from the concept is objectionable in art, then we shall not be able to approve, when a work of art is intentionally and avowedly chosen to express a concept; this is the case in *allegory*. An allegory is a work of art signifying something different from what it depicts. But that which is perceptive, and consequently the Idea as well, expresses itself immediately and completely, and does not require the medium of another thing through which it is outlined or suggested. Therefore that which is suggested and represented in this way by something quite different is always a concept, because it cannot itself be brought before perception. Hence through the allegory a concept is always to be signified, and consequently the mind of the beholder has to be turned aside from the depicted representation of perception to one that is quite different, abstract, and not perceptive, and lies entirely outside the work of art. Here, therefore, the picture or statue is supposed to achieve what a written work achieves far more perfectly. Now what we declare to be the aim of art, namely presentation of the Idea to be apprehended only through perception, is not the aim here. But certainly no great perfection in the work of art is demanded for what is here intended; on the contrary, it is enough if we see what the thing is

supposed to be; for as soon as this is found, the end is reached, and the mind is then led on to quite a different kind of representation, to an abstract concept which was the end in view. Allegories in plastic and pictorial art are consequently nothing but hieroglyphics; the artistic value they may have as expressions of perception does not belong to them as allegories, but otherwise. That the *Night* of Correggio, the *Genius of Fame* of Annibale Carracci, and the *Goddesses of the Seasons* of Poussin are very beautiful pictures is to be kept quite apart from the fact that they are allegories. As allegories, they do not achieve more than an inscription, in fact rather less. Here we are again reminded of the above-mentioned distinction between the real and the nominal significance of a picture. Here the nominal is just the allegorical as such, for example, the *Genius of Fame*. The real is what is actually depicted, namely a beautiful winged youth with beautiful boys flying round him; this expresses an Idea. This real significance, however, is effective only so long as we forget the nominal, allegorical significance. If we think of the latter, we forsake perception, and an abstract concept occupies the mind; but the transition from the Idea to the concept is always a descent. In fact, that nominal significance, that allegorical intention, often detracts from the real significance, from the truth of perception. For example, the unnatural light in Correggio's *Night*, which, although beautifully executed, has yet a merely allegorical motive and is in reality impossible. When, therefore, an allegorical picture has also artistic value, that is quite separate from and independent of what it achieves as allegory. Such a work of art serves two purposes simultaneously, namely the expression of a concept and the expression of an Idea. Only the latter can be an aim of art; the other is a foreign aim, namely the trifling amusement of causing a picture to serve at the same time as an inscription, as a hieroglyphic, invented for the benefit of those to whom the real nature of art can never appeal. It is the same as when a work of art is at the same time a useful implement, where it also serves two purposes; for example, a statue that is at the same time a candelabrum or a caryatid; or a bas-relief that is at the same time the shield of Achilles. Pure lovers of art will not approve either the one or the other. It is true that an allegorical picture can in just this quality produce a vivid impression on the mind and feelings; but under the same circumstances even an inscription would have the same effect. For instance, if the desire for fame is firmly and permanently rooted in a man's mind, since he regards fame as his rightful possession, withheld from him only so long as he has not yet produced the documents of its ownership; and if he now stands before the *Genius of Fame* with its laurel crowns, then his whole mind is thus excited, and his powers are called into activity. But the same thing would also happen if he suddenly saw the word "fame" in large clear letters on the wall. Or if a person has proclaimed a truth that is important either as a maxim for practical life or as an insight for science, but has not met with any belief in it, then an allegorical picture depicting time as it lifts the veil and reveals the naked truth will affect him powerfully. But the same thing would be achieved by the motto "*Le temps découvre la vérité.*"[31] For what really produces the effect in this case is always only the abstract thought, not what is perceived.

If, then, in accordance with the foregoing, allegory in plastic and pictorial art is a mistaken effort, serving a purpose entirely foreign to art, it becomes wholly intolerable when it leads one so far astray that the depicting of forced and violently far-fetched subtleties degenerates into the silly and absurd. Such, for example, is a tortoise to suggest feminine seclusion; the downward glance of Nemesis into the drapery of her bosom, indicating that she sees what is hidden; Bellori's explanation that Annibale Carracci clothed voluptuousness in a yellow robe because he wished to indicate that her pleasures soon fade and become as yellow as straw. Now, if there is absolutely no connexion between what is depicted and the concept indicated by it, a connexion based on subsumption under that concept or on association of Ideas, but the sign and the thing signified are connected quite conventionally by positive fixed rule casually introduced, I call this degenerate kind of allegory *symbolism*. Thus the rose is the symbol of secrecy, the laurel the symbol of fame, the palm the symbol of victory, the mussel-shell the symbol of pilgrimage, the cross the symbol of the Christian religion. To this class also belong all indications through mere colours, such as yellow as the colour of falseness and blue the colour of fidelity. Symbols of this kind may often be of use in life, but their value is foreign to art. They are to be regarded entirely as hieroglyphics, or like Chinese calligraphy, and are really in the same class as armorial bearings, the bush that indicates a tavern, the key by which chamberlains are recognized, or the leather signifying mountaineers. Finally, if certain

historical or mythical persons or personified conceptions are made known by symbols fixed on once for all, these are properly called *emblems*. Such are the animals of the Evangelists, the owl of Minerva, the apple of Paris, the anchor of hope, and so on. But by emblems we often understand those symbolical, simple presentations elucidated by a motto which are supposed to illustrate a moral truth, of which there are large collections by J. Camerarius, Alciati, and others. They form the transition to poetical allegory, of which we shall speak later. Greek sculpture appeals to perception, and is therefore *aesthetic*; Indian sculpture appeals to the concept, and is therefore *symbolical*.

This opinion of allegory, based on our consideration of the inner nature of art and quite consistent with it, is directly opposed to Winckelmann's view. Far from explaining allegory, as we do, as something quite foreign to the aim of art and often interfering with it, he speaks everywhere in favour of it; indeed (*Werke*, Vol. i, pp. 55 *seq.*), he places art's highest aim in the "presentation of universal concepts and non-sensuous things." It is left to everyone to assent either to one view or to the other. With these and similar views of Winckelmann concerning the real metaphysics of the beautiful, the truth became very clear to me that a man can have the greatest susceptibility to artistic beauty and the most correct opinion with regard to it, without his being in a position to give an abstract and really philosophical account of the nature of the beautiful and of art. In the same way, a man can be very noble and virtuous, and can have a very tender conscience that weighs decisions accurately in particular cases, without being on that account in a position to ascertain philosophically, and explain in the abstract, the ethical significance of actions.

But allegory has an entirely different relation to *poetry* from that which it has to plastic and pictorial art; and although it is objectionable in the latter, it is quite admissible and very effective in the former. For in plastic and pictorial art allegory leads away from what is given in perception, from the real object of all art, to abstract thoughts; but in poetry the relation is reversed. Here the concept is what is directly given in words, and the first aim is to lead from this to the perceptive, the depiction of which must be undertaken by the imagination of the hearer. If in plastic and pictorial art we are led from what is immediately given to something else, this must always be a concept, because here only the abstract cannot be immediately given. But a concept can never be the source, and its communication can never be the aim, of a work of art. On the other hand, in poetry the concept is the material, the immediately given, and we can therefore very well leave it, in order to bring about something perceptive which is entirely different, and in which the end is attained. Many a concept or abstract thought may be indispensable in the sequence and connexion of a poem, while in itself and immediately it is quite incapable of being perceived. It is then often brought to perception by some example to be subsumed under it. This occurs in every figurative expression, in every metaphor, simile, parable, and allegory, all of which differ only by the length and completeness of their expression. Therefore similes and allegories are of striking effect in the rhetorical arts. How beautifully Cervantes says of sleep, in order to express that it withdraws us from all bodily and mental suffering: "It is the mantle that covers the whole person." How beautifully Kleist expresses allegorically the thought that philosophers and men of science enlighten the human race, in the verse [Der Frühling]:

Those whose nocturnal lamp illumines all the
   globe.

How strongly and graphically Homer describes the fatal and pernicious Ate, when he says: "She has tender feet, for she walks not on the hard ground, but only on the heads of men." (Iliad, xix, 91.) How very effective the fable of Menenius Agrippa about the stomach and limbs was when it was addressed to the Roman people who had quitted their country! How beautifully is a highly abstract philosophical dogma expressed by Plato's allegory of the cave at the beginning of the seventh book of the Republic, which we have already mentioned. The fable of Persephone is also to be regarded as a profound allegory of philosophical tendency, for she falls into the underworld through tasting a pomegranate. This becomes particularly illuminating in the treatment of this fable which Goethe introduced as an episode in the Triumph der Empfindsamkeit, which is beyond all praise. Three fairly long allegorical works are known to me; one open and avowed, is the incomparable Criticón of Balthasar Gracián. It consists of a great rich web of connected and highly ingenious allegories, serving here as bright clothing for moral truths, and to these he thus imparts the greatest perceptiveness,

and astonishes us with the wealth of his inventions. Two, however, are concealed allegories, Don Quixote and Gulliver's Travels. The first is an allegory of the life of every man who, unlike others, will not be careful merely for his own personal welfare, but pursues an objective, ideal end that has taken possession of his thinking and willing; and then, of course, in this world he looks queer and odd. In the case of Gulliver, we need only take everything physical as spiritual or intellectual, in order to observe what the "satirical rogue," as Hamlet would have called him, meant by it. Therefore, since the concept is always what is given in the poetical allegory, and tries to make this perceptive through a picture, it may sometimes be expressed or supported by a painted picture. Such a picture is not for this reason regarded as a work of pictorial art, but only as an expressive hieroglyph, and it makes no claims to pictorial, but only to poetic, worth. Of such a kind is that beautiful allegorical vignette of Lavater, which must have so heartening an effect on every champion of truth: a hand holding a light is stung by a wasp, while in the flame above, gnats are being burnt; underneath is the motto:

And though it singes the wing of the gnat,
Destroys its skull and scatters all its little brains;
   Light remains light!
And although I am stung by the angriest of
   wasps,
   I will not let it go.

To this class belongs also the gravestone with the blown-out, smoking candle and the encircling inscription:

When it is out, it becomes clear
Whether the candle be tallow or wax.

Finally, of this kind is an old German genealogical tree on which the last descendant of a very ancient family expressed the determination to live his life to the end in complete continence and chastity, and thus to let his race die out. This he did by depicting himself at the root of the tree of many branches, clipping it above himself with a pair of shears. In general, the above-mentioned symbols, usually called emblems, which might also be described as short painted fables with an expressed moral, belong to this class. Allegories of this kind are always to be reckoned among the poetical and not the pictorial, and as being justified in precisely this way. Here the pictorial execution also is always a matter of secondary importance, and no more is demanded of it than that it depict the thing conspicuously. But in poetry, as in plastic and pictorial art, the allegory passes over into the symbol, if there is none but an arbitrary connexion between what is presented in perception and what is expressed by this in the abstract. Since everything symbolical rests at bottom on a stipulated agreement, the symbol has this disadvantage among others, that its significance is forgotten in the course of time, and it then becomes dumb. Indeed, who would guess why the fish is the symbol of Christianity, if he did not know? Only a Champollion, for it is a phonetic hieroglyphic through and through. Therefore as a poetical allegory the *Revelation* of John stands roughly in the same position as the reliefs with *Magnus Deus sol Mithra*, which are still always being explained. [. . .]

§ 51.

If with the foregoing observations on art in general we turn from the plastic and pictorial arts to *poetry*, we shall have no doubt that its aim is also to reveal the Ideas, the grades of the will's objectification, and to communicate them to the hearer with that distinctness and vividness in which they were apprehended by the poetical mind. Ideas are essentially perceptive; therefore, if in poetry only abstract concepts are directly communicated by words, yet it is obviously the intention to let the hearer perceive the Ideas of life in the representatives of these concepts; and this can take place only by the assistance of his own imagination. But in order to set this imagination in motion in accordance with the end in view, the abstract concepts that are the direct material of poetry, as of the driest prose, must be so arranged that their spheres intersect one another, so that none can continue in its abstract universality, but instead of it a perceptive representative appears before the imagination, and this is then modified further and further by the words of the poet according to his intention. Just as the chemist obtains solid precipitates by combining perfectly clear and transparent fluids, so does the poet know how to precipitate, as it were, the concrete, the individual, the representation of perception, out of the abstract, transparent universality of the concepts by the way in which he combines them. For the Idea can be known only

through perception, but knowledge of the Idea is the aim of all art. The skill of a master in poetry as in chemistry enables one always to obtain the precise precipitate that was intended. The many epithets in poetry serve this purpose, and through them the universality of every concept is restricted more and more till perceptibility is reached. To almost every noun Homer adds an adjective, the concept of which cuts, and at once considerably diminishes, the sphere of the first concept, whereby it is brought so very much nearer to perception; for example:

Ἐν δ'ἔπεσ' Ὠκεανῷ λαμπρὸν φάος ἠελίοιο,
"Ἕλκον νύκτα μέλαιναν ἐπὶ ζείδωρον
ἄρουραν.

(*Occidit vero in Oceanum splendidum lumen solis,
Trahens noctem nigram super almam terram.*)[32]

And

Where gentle breezes from the blue heavens
   sigh,
There stands the myrtle still, the laurel high,
                    [Goethe, *Mignon*]

precipitates from a few concepts before the imagination the delight of the southern climate.

Rhythm and rhyme are quite special aids to poetry. I can give no other explanation of their incredibly powerful effect than that our powers of representation have received from time, to which they are essentially bound, some special characteristic, by virtue of which we inwardly follow and, as it were, consent to each regularly recurring sound. In this way rhythm and rhyme become a means partly of holding our attention, since we more willingly follow the poem when read; and partly through them there arises in us a blind consent to what is read, prior to any judgement, and this gives the poem a certain emphatic power of conviction, independent of all reason or argument.

In virtue of the universality of the material, and hence of the concepts of which poetry makes use to communicate the Ideas, the range of its province is very great. The whole of nature, the Ideas of all grades, can be expressed by it, since it proceeds, according to the Idea to be communicated, to express these sometimes in a descriptive, sometimes in a narrative, and sometimes in a directly dramatic way. But if, in the presentation of the lower grades of the will's objectivity, plastic and pictorial art often surpasses poetry, because inanimate, and also merely animal, nature reveals almost the whole of its inner being in a single well-conceived moment; man, on the other hand, in so far as he expresses himself not through the mere form and expression of his features and countenance, but through a chain of actions and of the accompanying thoughts and emotions, is the principal subject of poetry. In this respect no other art can compete with poetry, for it has the benefit of progress and movement which the plastic and pictorial arts lack.

Revelation of that Idea which is the highest grade of the will's objectivity, namely the presentation of man in the connected series of his efforts and actions, is thus the great subject of poetry. It is true that experience and history teach us to know man, yet more often *men* rather than *man*; in other words, they give us empirical notes about the behaviour of men towards one another. From these we obtain rules for our own conduct rather than a deep insight into the inner nature of man. This latter, however, is by no means ruled out; yet, whenever the inner nature of mankind itself is disclosed to us in history or in our own experience, we have apprehended this experience poetically, and the historian has apprehended history with artistic eyes, in other words, according to the Idea, not to the phenomenon; according to its inner nature, not to the relations. Our own experience is the indispensable condition for understanding poetry as well as history, for it is, so to speak, the dictionary of the language spoken by both. But history is related to poetry as portrait-painting to historical painting; the former gives us the true in the individual, the latter the true in the universal; the former has the truth of the phenomenon and can verify it therefrom; the latter has the truth of the Idea, to be found in no particular phenomenon, yet speaking from them all. The poet from deliberate choice presents us with significant characters in significant situations; the historian takes both as they come. In fact, he has to regard and select the events and persons not according to their inner genuine significance expressing the Idea, but according to the outward, apparent, and relatively important significance in reference to the connexion and to the consequences. He cannot consider anything in and by itself according to its essential character and expression, but must look at everything according to its relation, its concatenation, its influence on what follows, and especially on its

own times. Therefore he will not pass over a king's action, in itself quite common and of little significance, for it has consequences and influence. On the other hand, extremely significant actions of very distinguished individuals are not to be mentioned by him if they have no consequences and no influence. For his considerations proceed in accordance with the principle of sufficient reason, and apprehend the phenomenon of which this principle is the form. The poet, however, apprehends the Idea, the inner being of mankind outside all relation and all time, the adequate objectivity of the thing-in-itself at its highest grade. Even in that method of treatment necessary to the historian, the inner nature, the significance of phenomena, the kernel of all those shells, can never be entirely lost, and can still be found and recognized by the person who looks for it. Yet that which is significant in itself, not in the relation, namely the real unfolding of the Idea, is found to be far more accurate and clear in poetry than in history; therefore, paradoxical as it may sound, far more real, genuine, inner truth is to be attributed to poetry than to history. For the historian should accurately follow the individual event according to life as this event is developed in time in the manifold tortuous and complicated chains of reasons or grounds and consequents. But he cannot possibly possess all the data for this; he cannot have seen all and ascertained everything. At every moment he is forsaken by the original of his picture, or a false picture is substituted for it; and this happens so frequently, that I think I can assume that in all history the false outweighs the true. On the other hand, the poet has apprehended the Idea of mankind from some definite side to be described; thus it is the nature of his own self that is objectified in it for him. His knowledge, as was said above in connexion with sculpture, is half *a priori*; his ideal is before his mind, firm, clear, brightly illuminated, and it cannot forsake him. He therefore shows us in the mirror of his mind the Idea purely and distinctly, and his description down to the last detail is as true as life itself.[33] The great ancient historians are therefore poets in the particulars where data forsake them, e.g., in the speeches of their heroes; indeed, the whole way in which they handle their material approaches the epic. But this gives their presentations unity, and enables them to retain inner truth, even where outer truth was not accessible to them, or was in fact falsified. If just now we compared history to portrait-painting, in contrast to poetry that corresponded to historical painting, we find Winckelmann's maxim, that the portrait should be the ideal of the individual, also followed by the ancient historians, for they depict the individual in such a way that the side of the Idea of mankind expressed in it makes its appearance. On the other hand, modern historians, with few exceptions, generally give us only "an offal-barrel and a lumber-garret, or at the best a Punch-and-Judy play."[34] Therefore, he who seeks to know mankind according to its inner nature which is identical in all its phenomena and developments, and thus according to its Idea, will find that the works of the great, immortal poets present him with a much truer and clearer picture than the historians can ever give. For even the best of them are as poets far from being the first, and also their hands are not free. In this respect we can illustrate the relation between historian and poet by the following comparison. The mere, pure historian, working only according to data, is like a man who, without any knowledge of mathematics, investigates by measurement the proportions of figures previously found by accident, and therefore the statement of these measurements found empirically is subject to all the errors of the figure as drawn. The poet, on the contrary, is like the mathematician who constructs these ratios *a priori* in pure intuition or perception, and expresses them not as they actually are in the drawn figure, but as they are in the Idea that the drawing is supposed to render perceptible. Therefore Schiller [*An die Freunde*] says:

What has never anywhere come to pass,
That alone never grows old.

In regard to knowledge of the inner nature of mankind, I must concede a greater value to biographies, and particularly to autobiographies, than to history proper, at any rate to history as it is usually treated. This is partly because, in the former, the data can be brought together more accurately and completely than in the latter; partly because, in history proper, it is not so much men that act as nations and armies, and the individuals who do appear seem to be so far off, surrounded by such pomp and circumstance, clothed in the stiff robes of State, or in heavy and inflexible armour, that it is really very difficult to recognize human movement through it all. On the other hand, the truly depicted life of the individual in a narrow sphere shows the conduct of men in all its nuances and forms, the excellence, the virtue, and even the holiness of individuals, the perversity, meanness, and malice of most, the profligacy of many. Indeed, from the point of view we are here considering, namely in regard to the inner significance of what appears, it is quite immaterial whether the objects on which the action hinges are, relatively considered, trifling or important, farmhouses or kingdoms. For all these things are without significance in themselves, and obtain it only in so far as the will is moved by them. The motive has significance merely through its relation to the will; on the other hand, the relation that it has as a thing to other such things does not concern us at all. Just as a circle of one inch in diameter and one of forty million miles in diameter have absolutely the same geometrical properties, so the events and the history of a village and of a kingdom are essentially the same; and we can study and learn to know mankind just as well in the one as in the other. It is also wrong to suppose that autobiographies are full of deceit and dissimulation; on the contrary, lying, though possible everywhere, is perhaps more difficult there than anywhere else. Dissimulation is easiest in mere conversation; indeed, paradoxical as it may sound, it is fundamentally more difficult in a letter, since here a man, left to his own devices, looks into himself and not outwards. The strange and remote are with difficulty brought near to him, and he does not have before his eyes the measure of the impression made on another. The other person, on the contrary, peruses the letter calmly, in a mood that is foreign to the writer, reads it repeatedly and at different times, and thus easily finds out the concealed intention. We also get to know an author as a man most easily from his book, since all those conditions have there an even stronger and more lasting effect; and in an autobiography it is so difficult to dissimulate, that there is perhaps not a single one that is not on the whole truer than any history ever written. The man who records his life surveys it as a whole; the individual thing becomes small, the near becomes distant, the distant again becomes near, motives shrink and contract. He is sitting at the confessional, and is doing so of his own free will. Here the spirit of lying does not seize him so readily, for there is to be found in every man an inclination to truth which has first to be overcome in the case of every lie, and has here taken up an unusually strong position. The relation between biography and the history of nations can be made clear to perception by the following comparison. History shows us mankind just as a view from a high mountain shows us nature. We see a great deal at a time, wide stretches, great masses, but nothing is distinct or recognizable according to the whole of its real nature. On the other hand, the depicted life of the individual shows us the person, just as we know nature when we walk about among her trees, plants, rocks, and stretches of water. Through landscape-painting, in which the artist lets us see nature through his eyes, the knowledge of her Ideas and the condition of pure, will-less knowing required for this are made easy for us. In the same way, poetry is far superior to history and biography for expressing the Ideas that we are able to seek in both. For here also genius holds up before us the illuminating glass in which everything essential and significant is gathered together and placed in the brightest light; but everything accidental and foreign is eliminated. [...]

The expression of the Idea of mankind, which devolves on the poet, can now be carried out in such a way that the depicted is also at the same time the depicter. This occurs in lyric poetry, in the song proper, where the poet vividly perceives and describes only his own state; hence through the object, a certain subjectivity is essential to poetry of this kind. Or again, the depicter is entirely different from what is to be depicted, as is the case with all other kinds of poetry. Here the depicter more or less conceals himself behind what is depicted, and finally altogether disappears. In the ballad the depicter still expresses to some extent his own state through the tone and proportion of the whole; therefore, though much more objective than the song, it still has something subjective in it. This fades away more in the idyll, still more in the romance, almost entirely in the epic proper, and finally to the last vestige in the drama, which is the most objective, and in more than one respect the most complete, and also the most difficult, form of poetry. The lyric form is therefore the easiest, and if in other respects art belongs only to the true genius who is so rare, even the man who is on the whole not very eminent can produce a beautiful song, when in fact, through strong excitement from outside, some inspiration enhances his mental powers. For this needs only a vivid perception of his own state at the moment of excitement. This is proved by many single songs written by individuals who have otherwise remained unknown, in particular by the German national songs, of which we have an excellent collection in the *Wunderhorn*, and also by innumer-

able love-songs and other popular songs in all languages. For to seize the mood of the moment, and embody it in the song, is the whole achievement of poetry of this kind. Yet in the lyrics of genuine poets is reflected the inner nature of the whole of mankind; and all that millions of past, present, and future human beings have found and will find in the same constantly recurring situations, finds in them its corresponding expression. Since these situations, by constant recurrence, exist as permanently as humanity itself, and always call up the same sensations, the lyrical productions of genuine poets remain true, effective, and fresh for thousands of years. If, however, the poet is the universal man, then all that has ever moved a human heart, and all that human nature produces from itself in any situation, all that dwells and broods in any human breast – all these are his theme and material, and with these all the rest of nature as well. Therefore the poet can just as well sing of voluptuousness as of mysticism, be Anacreon or Angelus Silesius, write tragedies or comedies, express the sublime or the common sentiment, according to his mood and disposition. Accordingly, no one can prescribe to the poet that he should be noble and sublime, moral, pious, Christian, or anything else, still less reproach him for being this and not that. He is the mirror of mankind, and brings to its consciousness what it feels and does.

Now if we consider more closely the nature of the lyric proper, and take as examples exquisite and at the same time pure models, not those in any way approximating to another kind of poetry, such as the ballad, the elegy, the hymn, the epigram, and so on, we shall find that the characteristic nature of the song in the narrowest sense is as follows. It is the subject of the will, in other words, the singer's own willing, that fills his consciousness, often as a released and satisfied willing (joy), but even more often as an impeded willing (sorrow), always as emotion, passion, an agitated state of mind. Besides this, however, and simultaneously with it, the singer, through the sight of surrounding nature, becomes conscious of himself as the subject of pure, will-less knowing, whose unshakable, blissful peace now appears in contrast to the stress of willing that is always restricted and needy. The feeling of this contrast, this alternate play, is really what is expressed in the whole of the song, and what in general constitutes the lyrical state. In this state pure knowing comes to us, so to speak, in order to deliver us from willing and its stress. We follow, yet only for a few moments; willing, desire, the recollection of our own personal aims, always tears us anew from peaceful contemplation; but yet again and again the next beautiful environment, in which pure, will-less knowledge presents itself to us, entices us away from willing. Therefore in the song and in the lyrical mood, willing (the personal interest of the aims) and pure perception of the environment that presents itself are wonderfully blended with each other. Relations between the two are sought and imagined; the subjective disposition, the affection of the will, imparts its hue to the perceived environment, and this environment again imparts in the reflex its colour to that disposition. The genuine song is the expression or copy of the whole of this mingled and divided state of mind. In order to make clear in examples this abstract analysis of a state that is very far from all abstraction, we can take up any of the immortal songs of Goethe. As specially marked out for this purpose I will recommend only a few; *The Shepherd's Lament, Welcome and Farewell, To the Moon, On the Lake, Autumnal Feelings*; further the real songs in the *Wunderhorn* are excellent examples, especially the one that begins: "O Bremen, I must leave you now." As a comical and really striking parody of the lyric character, a song by Voss strikes me as remarkable. In it he describes the feelings of a drunken plumber, falling from a tower, who in passing observes that the clock on the tower is at half past eleven, a remark quite foreign to his condition, and hence belonging to will-free knowledge. Whoever shares with me the view expressed of the lyrical state of mind will also admit that this is really the perceptive and poetical knowledge of that principle, which I advanced in my essay *On the Principle of Sufficient Reason*, and which I have also mentioned in this work, namely that the identity of the subject of knowing with the subject of willing can be called the miracle $\kappa\alpha\tau$' $\dot{\epsilon}\xi o\chi\acute{\eta}\nu$,[35] so that the poetical effect of the song really rests ultimately on the truth of that principle. In the course of life, these two subjects, or in popular language head and heart, grow more and more apart; men are always separating more and more their subjective feeling from their objective knowledge. In the child the two are still fully blended; it hardly knows how to distinguish itself from its surroundings; it is merged into them. In the youth all perception in the first place affects feeling and mood, and even mingles with these, as is very beautifully expressed by Byron:

> I live not in myself, but I become
> Portion of that around me; and to me
> High mountains are a feeling.
> [*Childe Harold's Pilgrimage*, III, lxxii.]

This is why the youth clings so much to the perceptive and outward side of things; this is why he is fit only for lyrical poetry, and only the mature man for dramatic poetry. We can think of the old man as at most an epic poet, like Ossian or Homer, for narration is characteristic of the old.

In the more objective kinds of poetry, especially in the romance, the epic, and the drama, the end, the revelation of the Idea of mankind, is attained especially by two means, namely by true and profound presentation of significant characters, and by the invention of pregnant situations in which they disclose themselves. For it is incumbent on the chemist not only to exhibit purely and genuinely the simple elements and their principal compounds, but also to expose them to the influence of those reagents in which their peculiar properties become clearly and strikingly visible. In just the same way, it is incumbent on the poet not only to present to us significant characters as truly and faithfully as does nature herself, but, so that we may get to know them, he must place them in those situations in which their peculiar qualities are completely unfolded, and in which they are presented distinctly in sharp outline; in situations that are therefore called significant. In real life and in history, situations of this nature are only rarely brought about by chance; they exist there alone, lost and hidden in the mass of insignificant detail. The universal significance of the situations should distinguish the romance, the epic, and the drama from real life just as much as do the arrangement and selection of the significant characters. In both, however, the strictest truth is an indispensable condition of their effect, and want of unity in the characters, contradiction of themselves or of the essential nature of mankind in general, as well as impossibility of the events or improbability amounting almost to impossibility, even though it is only in minor circumstances, offend just as much in poetry as do badly drawn figures, false perspective, or defective lighting in painting. For in both poetry and painting we demand a faithful mirror of life, of mankind, of the world, only rendered clear by the presentation, and made significant by the arrangement. As the purpose of all the arts is merely the expression and presentation of the Ideas, and as their essential difference lies only in what grade of the will's objectification the Idea is that we are to express, by which again the material of expression is determined, even those arts that are most widely separated can by comparison throw light on one another. For example, to grasp completely the Ideas expressing themselves in water, it is not sufficient to see it in the quiet pond or in the evenly-flowing stream, but those Ideas completely unfold themselves only when the water appears under all circumstances and obstacles. The effect of these on it causes it to manifest completely all its properties. We therefore find it beautiful when it rushes down, roars, and foams, or leaps into the air, or falls in a cataract of spray, or finally, when artificially forced, it springs up as a fountain. Thus, exhibiting itself differently in different circumstances, it always asserts its character faithfully; it is just as natural for it to spirt upwards as to lie in glassy stillness; it is as ready for the one as for the other, as soon as the circumstances appear. Now what the hydraulic engineer achieves in the fluid matter of water, the architect achieves in the rigid matter of stone; and this is just what is achieved by the epic or dramatic poet in the Idea of mankind. The common aim of all the arts is the unfolding and elucidation of the Idea expressing itself in the object of every art, of the will objectifying itself at each grade. The life of man, as often seen in the world of reality, is like the water as seen often in pond and river; but in the epic, the romance, and the tragedy, selected characters are placed in those circumstances in which all their characteristics are unfolded, the depths of the human mind are revealed and become visible in extraordinary and significant actions. Thus poetry objectifies the Idea of man, an Idea which has the peculiarity of expressing itself in highly individual characters.

Tragedy is to be regarded, and is recognized, as the summit of poetic art, both as regards the greatness of the effect and the difficulty of the achievement. For the whole of our discussion, it is very significant and worth noting that the purpose of this highest poetical achievement is the description of the terrible side of life. The unspeakable pain, the wretchedness and misery of mankind, the triumph of wickedness, the scornful mastery of chance, and the irretrievable fall of the just and the innocent are all here presented to us; and here is to be found a significant hint as to the nature of the world and of existence. It is the antagonism of the will with itself which is here most completely unfolded at the highest grade of its objectivity, and which comes into fearful prominence. It becomes visible in the suffering of mankind which is produced partly by chance and error; and these stand forth as the rulers of the world, personified as fate through their insidiousness which appears almost like purpose and intention. In part it proceeds from mankind itself through the self-mortifying efforts of will on the part of individuals, through the wickedness and perversity of most. It is one and the same will, living and appearing in them all, whose phenomena fight with one another and tear one another to pieces. In one individual it appears powerfully, in another more feebly. Here and there it reaches thoughtfulness and is softened more or less by the light of knowledge, until at last in the individual case this knowledge is purified and enhanced by suffering itself. It then reaches the point where the phenomenon, the veil of Maya, no longer deceives it. It sees through the form of the phenomenon, the *principium individuationis*; the egoism resting on this expires with it. The *motives* that were previously so powerful now lose their force, and instead of them, the complete knowledge of the real nature of the world, acting as a *quieter* of the will, produces resignation, the giving up not merely of life, but of the whole will-to-live itself. Thus we see in tragedy the noblest men, after a long conflict and suffering, finally renounce for ever all the pleasures of life and the aims till then pursued so keenly, or cheerfully and willingly give up life itself. Thus the steadfast prince of Calderón, Gretchen in *Faust*, Hamlet whom his friend Horatio would gladly follow, but who enjoins him to remain for a while in this harsh world and to breathe in pain in order to throw light on Hamlet's fate and clear his memory; also the *Maid of Orleans*, the *Bride of Messina*. They all die purified by suffering, in other words after the will-to-live has already expired in them. In Voltaire's *Mohammed* this is actually expressed in the concluding words addressed to Mohammed by the dying Palmira: "The world is for tyrants: live!" On the other hand, the demand for so-called poetic justice rests on an entire misconception of the nature of tragedy, indeed of the nature of the world. It boldly appears in all its dullness in the criticisms that Dr. Samuel Johnson made of individual plays of Shakespeare, since he very naïvely laments the complete disregard of it; and this disregard certainly exists, for what wrong have the Ophelias, the Desdemonas, and the Cordelias done? But only a dull, insipid, optimistic, Protestant-rationalistic, or really Jewish view of the world will make the demand for poetic justice, and find its own satisfaction in that of the demand. The true sense of the tragedy is the deeper insight that what the hero atones for is not his own particular sins, but original sin, in other words, the guilt of existence itself:

> *Pues el delito mayor*
> *Del hombre es haber nacido.*

> (For man's greatest offence
> Is that he has been born,)

as Calderón [*La Vida es Sueño*] frankly expresses it.

I will allow myself only one observation more closely concerning the treatment of tragedy. The presentation of a great misfortune is alone essential to tragedy. But the many different ways in which it is produced by the poet can be brought under three typical characteristics. It can be done through the extraordinary wickedness of a character, touching the extreme bounds of possibility, who becomes the author of the misfortune. Examples of this kind are *Richard III*, Iago in *Othello*, Shylock in *The Merchant of Venice*, Franz Moor, the *Phaedra* of Euripides, Creon in the *Antigone*, and others. Again, it can happen through blind fate, i.e., chance or error; a true model of this kind is the *King Oedipus* of Sophocles, also the *Trachiniae;* and in general most of the tragedies of the ancients belong to this class. Examples among modern tragedies are *Romeo and Juliet*, Voltaire's *Tancred*, and *The Bride of Messina*. Finally, the misfortune can be brought about also by the mere attitude of the persons to one another through their relations. Thus there is no need either of a colossal error, or of an unheard-of accident, or even of a character reaching the bounds of human possibility in wickedness, but characters as they usually are in a moral regard in circumstances that frequently occur, are so situated with regard to one another that their position forces them, knowingly and with their eyes open, to do one another the greatest injury, without any one of them being entirely in the wrong. This last kind of tragedy seems to me far preferable to the other two; for it shows us the greatest misfortune not as an exception, not as something brought about by rare circumstances or by monstrous characters, but as something that arises easily and spontaneously out of the actions and characters of

men, as something almost essential to them, and in this way it is brought terribly near to us. In the other two kinds of tragedy, we look on the prodigious fate and the frightful wickedness as terrible powers threatening us only from a distance, from which we ourselves might well escape without taking refuge in renunciation. The last kind of tragedy, however, shows us those powers that destroy happiness and life, and in such a way that the path to them is at any moment open even to us. We see the greatest suffering brought about by entanglements whose essence could be assumed even by our own fate, and by actions that perhaps even we might be capable of committing, and so we cannot complain of injustice. Then, shuddering, we feel ourselves already in the midst of hell. In this last kind of tragedy the working out is of the greatest difficulty; for the greatest effect has to be produced in it with the least use of means and occasions for movement, merely by their position and distribution. Therefore even in many of the best tragedies this difficulty is evaded. One play, however, can be mentioned as a perfect model of this kind, a tragedy that in other respects is far surpassed by several others of the same great master; it is *Clavigo*. To a certain extent *Hamlet* belongs to this class, if, that is to say, we look merely at his relation to Laërtes and to Ophelia. *Wallenstein* also has this merit. *Faust* is entirely of this kind, if we consider merely the event connected with Gretchen and her brother as the main action; also the *Cid* of Corneille, only that this lacks the tragic conclusion, while, on the other hand, the analogous relation of Max to Thecla has it. [. . .]

§ 52.

We have now considered all the fine arts in the general way suitable to our point of view. We began with architecture, whose aim as such is to elucidate the objectification of the will at the lowest grade of its visibility, where it shows itself as the dumb striving of the mass, devoid of knowledge and conforming to law; yet it already reveals discord with itself and conflict, namely that between gravity and rigidity. Our observations ended with tragedy, which presents to us in terrible magnitude and distinctness at the highest grade of the will's objectification that very conflict of the will with itself. After this, we find that there is yet another fine art that remains excluded, and was bound to be excluded, from our consideration, for in the systematic connexion of our discussion there was no fitting place for it; this art is *music*. It stands quite apart from all the others. In it we do not recognize the copy, the repetition, of any Idea of the inner nature of the world. Yet it is such a great and exceedingly fine art, its effect on man's innermost nature is so powerful, and it is so completely and profoundly understood by him in his innermost being as an entirely universal language, whose distinctness surpasses even that of the world of perception itself, that in it we certainly have to look for more than that *exercitium arithmeticae occultum nescientis se numerare animi* which Leibniz took it to be.[36] Yet he was quite right, in so far as he considered only its immediate and outward significance, its exterior. But if it were nothing more, the satisfaction afforded by it would inevitably be similar to that which we feel when a sum in arithmetic comes out right, and could not be that profound pleasure with which we see the deepest recesses of our nature find expression. Therefore, from our standpoint, where the aesthetic effect is the thing we have in mind, we must attribute to music a far more serious and profound significance that refers to the innermost being of the world and of our own self. In this regard the numerical ratios into which it can be resolved are related not as the thing signified, but only as the sign. That in some sense music must be related to the world as the depiction to the thing depicted, as the copy to the original, we can infer from the analogy with the remaining arts, to all of which this character is peculiar; from their effect on us, it can be inferred that of music is on the whole of the same nature, only stronger, more rapid, more necessary and infallible. Further, its imitative reference to the world must be very profound, infinitely true, and really striking, since it is instantly understood by everyone, and presents a certain infallibility by the fact that its form can be reduced to quite definite rules expressible in numbers, from which it cannot possibly depart without entirely ceasing to be music. Yet the point of comparison between music and the world, the regard in which it stands to the world in the relation of a copy or a repetition, is very obscure. Men have practised music at all times without being able to give an account of this; content to understand it immediately, they renounce any abstract conception of this direct understanding itself.

I have devoted my mind entirely to the impression of music in its many different forms; and then I have returned again to reflection and to the train of my thought expounded in the present work, and have arrived at an explanation of the inner essence of music, and the nature of its imitative relation to the world, necessarily to be presupposed from analogy. This explanation is quite sufficient for me, and satisfactory for my investigation, and will be just as illuminating also to the man who has followed me thus far, and has agreed with my view of the world. I recognize, however, that it is essentially impossible to demonstrate this explanation, for it assumes and establishes a relation of music as a representation to that which of its essence can never be representation, and claims to regard music as the copy of an original that can itself never be directly represented. Therefore, I can do no more than state here at the end of this third book, devoted mainly to a consideration of the arts, this explanation of the wonderful art of tones which is sufficient for me. I must leave the acceptance or denial of my view to the effect that both music and the whole thought communicated in this work have on each reader. Moreover, I regard it as necessary, in order that a man may assent with genuine conviction to the explanation of the significance of music here to be given, that he should often listen to music with constant reflection on this; and this again requires that he should be already very familiar with the whole thought which I expound.

The (Platonic) Ideas are the adequate objectification of the will. To stimulate the knowledge of these by depicting individual things (for works of art are themselves always such) is the aim of all the other arts (and is possible with a corresponding change in the knowing subject). Hence all of them objectify the will only indirectly, in other words, by means of the Ideas. As our world is nothing but the phenomenon or appearance of the Ideas in plurality through entrance into the *principium individuationis* (the form of knowledge possible to the individual as such), music, since it passes over the Ideas, is also quite independent of the phenomenal world, positively ignores it, and, to a certain extent, could still exist even if there were no world at all, which cannot be said of the other arts. Thus music is as *immediate* an objectification and copy of the whole *will* as the world itself is, indeed as the Ideas are, the multiplied phenomenon of which constitutes the world of individual things. Therefore music is by no means like the other arts, namely a copy of the Ideas, but a *copy of the will itself*, the objectivity of which is the Ideas. For this reason the effect of music is so very much more powerful and penetrating than is that of the other arts, for these others speak only of the shadow, but music of the essence. However, as it is the same will that objectifies itself both in the Ideas and in music, though in quite a different way in each, there must be, not indeed an absolutely direct likeness, but yet a parallel, an analogy, between music and the Ideas, the phenomenon of which in plurality and in incompleteness is the visible world. The demonstration of this analogy will make easier, as an illustration, an understanding of this explanation, which is difficult because of the obscurity of the subject.

I recognize in the deepest tones of harmony, in the ground-bass, the lowest grades of the will's objectification, inorganic nature, the mass of the planet. It is well known that all the high notes, light, tremulous, and dying away more rapidly, may be regarded as resulting from the simultaneous vibrations of the deep bass-note. With the sounding of the low note, the high notes always sound faintly at the same time, and it is a law of harmony that a bass-note may be accompanied only by those high notes that actually sound automatically and simultaneously with it (its *sons harmoniques*)[37] through the accompanying vibrations. Now this is analogous to the fact that all the bodies and organizations of nature must be regarded as having come into existence through gradual development out of the mass of the planet. This is both their supporter and their source, and the high notes have the same relation to the ground-bass. There is a limit to the depth, beyond which no sound is any longer audible. This corresponds to the fact that no matter is perceivable without form and quality, in other words, without the manifestation of a force incapable of further explanation, in which an Idea expresses itself, and, more generally, that no matter can be entirely without will. Therefore, just as a certain degree of pitch is inseparable from the tone as such, so a certain grade of the will's manifestation is inseparable from matter. Therefore, for us the ground-bass is in harmony what inorganic nature, the crudest mass on which everything rests and from which everything originates and develops, is in the world. Further, in the whole of the ripienos that produce the harmony, between the bass and the leading voice singing the melody, I recognize the whole gradation of the Ideas in which the will objectifies itself. Those

nearer to the bass are the lower of those grades, namely the still inorganic bodies manifesting themselves, however, in many ways. Those that are higher represent to me the plant and animal worlds. The definite intervals of the scale are parallel to the definite grades of the will's objectification, the definite species in nature. The departure from the arithmetical correctness of the intervals through some temperament, or produced by the selected key, is analogous to the departure of the individual from the type of the species. In fact, the impure discords, giving no definite interval, can be compared to the monstrous abortions between two species of animals, or between man and animal. But all these bass-notes and ripienos that constitute the *harmony*, lack that sequence and continuity of progress which belong only to the upper voice that sings the *melody*. This voice alone moves rapidly and lightly in modulations and runs, while all the others have only a slower movement without a connexion existing in each by itself. The deep bass moves most ponderously, the representative of the crudest mass; its rising and falling occur only in large intervals, in thirds, fourths, fifths, never by *one* tone, unless it be a bass transposed by double counterpoint. This slow movement is also physically essential to it; a quick run or trill in the low notes cannot even be imagined. The higher ripienos, running parallel to the animal world, move more rapidly, yet without melodious connexion and significant progress. The disconnected course of the ripienos and their determination by laws are analogous to the fact that in the whole irrational world, from the crystal to the most perfect animal, no being has a really connected consciousness that would make its life into a significant whole. No being experiences a succession of mental developments, none perfects itself by training or instruction, but at any time everything exists uniformly according to its nature, determined by a fixed law. Finally, in the *melody*, in the high, singing, principal voice, leading the whole and progressing with unrestrained freedom, in the uninterrupted significant connexion of *one* thought from beginning to end, and expressing a whole, I recognize the highest grade of the will's objectification, the intellectual life and endeavour of man. He alone, because endowed with the faculty of reason, is always looking before and after on the path of his actual life and of its innumerable possibilities, and so achieves a course of life that is intellectual, and is thus connected as a whole. In keeping with this, *melody* alone has significant and intentional connexion from beginning to end. Consequently, it relates the story of the intellectually enlightened will, the copy or impression whereof in actual life is the series of its deeds. Melody, however, says more; it relates the most secret history of the intellectually enlightened will, portrays every agitation, every effort, every movement of the will, everything which the faculty of reason summarizes under the wide and negative concept of feeling, and which cannot be further taken up into the abstractions of reason. Hence it has always been said that music is the language of feeling and of passion, just as words are the language of reason. Plato explains it as ἡ τῶν μελῶν κίνησις μεμιμημένη, ἐν τοῖς παθήμασιν ὅταν ψυχὴ γίνηται (*melodiarum motus, animi affectus imitans*),[38] *Laws*, VIII [812c]; and Aristotle also says: διὰ τί οἱ ῥυθμοὶ καὶ τὰ μέλη, φωνὴ οὖσα, ἤθεσιν ἔοικε; (*Cur numeri musici et modi, qui voces sunt, moribus similes sese exhibent?*), *Problemata*, c. 19.[39]

Now the nature of man consists in the fact that his will strives, is satisfied, strives anew, and so on and on; in fact his happiness and well-being consist only in the transition from desire to satisfaction, and from this to a fresh desire, such transition going forward rapidly. For the non-appearance of satisfaction is suffering; the empty longing for a new desire is languor, boredom. Thus, corresponding to this, the nature of melody is a constant digression and deviation from the keynote in a thousand ways, not only to the harmonious intervals, the third and dominant, but to every tone, to the dissonant seventh, and to the extreme intervals; yet there always follows a final return to the keynote. In all these ways, melody expresses the many different forms of the will's efforts, but also its satisfaction by ultimately finding again a harmonious interval, and still more the keynote. The invention of melody, the disclosure in it of all the deepest secrets of human willing and feeling, is the work of genius, whose effect is more apparent here than anywhere else, is far removed from all reflection and conscious intention, and might be called an inspiration. Here, as everywhere in art, the concept is unproductive. The composer reveals the innermost nature of the world, and expresses the profoundest wisdom in a language that his reasoning faculty does not understand, just as a magnetic somnambulist gives information about things of which she has no conception when she is awake. Therefore in the composer, more than in any other artist, the man is entirely separate and distinct from the artist. Even in the explanation of this wonderful art, the concept shows its inadequacy and its limits; however, I will try to carry out our analogy. Now, as rapid transition from wish to satisfaction and from this to a new wish are happiness and well-being, so rapid melodies without great deviations are cheerful. Slow melodies that strike painful discords and wind back to the keynote only through many bars, are sad, on the analogy of delayed and hard-won satisfaction. Delay in the new excitement of the will, namely languor, could have no other expression than the sustained keynote, the effect of which would soon be intolerable; very monotonous and meaningless melodies approximate to this. The short, intelligible phrases of rapid dance music seem to speak only of ordinary happiness which is easy of attainment. On the other hand, the *allegro maestoso* in great phrases, long passages, and wide deviations expresses a greater, nobler effort towards a distant goal, and its final attainment. The *adagio* speaks of the suffering of a great and noble endeavour that disdains all trifling happiness. But how marvellous is the effect of *minor* and *major*! How astonishing that the change of half a tone, the entrance of a minor third instead of a major, at once and inevitably forces on us an anxious and painful feeling, from which we are again delivered just as instantaneously by the major! The *adagio* in the minor key reaches the expression of the keenest pain, and becomes the most convulsive lament. Dance music in the minor key seems to express the failure of the trifling happiness that we ought rather to disdain; it appears to speak of the attainment of a low end with toil and trouble. The inexhaustibleness of possible melodies corresponds to the inexhaustibleness of nature in the difference of individuals, physiognomies, and courses of life. The transition from one key into quite a different one, since it entirely abolishes the connexion with what went before, is like death inasmuch as the individual ends in it. Yet the will that appeared in this individual lives on just the same as before, appearing in other individuals, whose consciousness, however, has no connexion with that of the first.

But we must never forget when referring to all these analogies I have brought forward, that music has no direct relation to them, but only an indirect one; for it never expresses the phenomenon, but only the inner nature, the in-itself, of every phenomenon, the will itself. Therefore music does not express this or that particular and definite pleasure, this or that affliction, pain, sorrow, horror, gaiety, merriment, or peace of mind, but joy, pain, sorrow, horror, gaiety, merriment, peace of mind *themselves*, to a certain extent in the abstract, their essential nature, without any accessories, and so also without the motives for them. Nevertheless, we understand them perfectly in this extracted quintessence. Hence it arises that our imagination is so easily stirred by music, and tries to shape that invisible, yet vividly aroused, spirit-world that speaks to us directly, to clothe it with flesh and bone, and thus to embody it in an analogous example. This is the origin of the song with words, and finally of the opera. For this reason they should never forsake that subordinate position in order to make themselves the chief thing, and the music a mere means of expressing the song, since this is a great misconception and an utter absurdity. Everywhere music expresses only the quintessence of life and of its events, never these themselves, and therefore their differences do not always influence it. It is just this universality that belongs uniquely to music, together with the most precise distinctness, that gives it that high value as the panacea of all our sorrows. Therefore, if music tries to stick too closely to the words, and to mould itself according to the events, it is endeavouring to speak a language not its own. No one has kept so free from this mistake as Rossini; hence his music speaks its *own* language so distinctly and purely that it requires no words at all, and therefore produces its full effect even when rendered by instruments alone.

As a result of all this, we can regard the phenomenal world, or nature, and music as two different expressions of the same thing; and this thing itself is therefore the only medium of their analogy, a knowledge of which is required if we are to understand that analogy. Accordingly, music, if regarded as an expression of the world, is in the highest degree a universal language that is related to the universality of concepts much as these are related to the particular things. Yet its universality is by no means that empty universality of abstraction, but is of quite a different kind; it is united with thorough and unmistakable distinctness. In this respect it is like geometrical figures and numbers, which are the universal forms of all possible objects of experience and are *a priori* applicable to them all, and yet are not abstract, but perceptible and thoroughly definite. All possible efforts, stirrings, and manifestations of the will, all the events that occur within man himself and are included by the reasoning faculty in the wide, negative concept

of feeling, can be expressed by the infinite number of possible melodies, but always in the universality of mere form without the material, always only according to the in-itself, not to the phenomenon, as it were the innermost soul of the phenomenon without the body. This close relation that music has to the true nature of all things can also explain the fact that, when music suitable to any scene, action, event, or environment is played, it seems to disclose to us its most secret meaning, and appears to be the most accurate and distinct commentary on it. Moreover, to the man who gives himself up entirely to the impression of a symphony, it is as if he saw all the possible events of life and of the world passing by within himself. Yet if he reflects, he cannot assert any likeness between that piece of music and the things that passed through his mind. For, as we have said, music differs from all the other arts by the fact that it is not a copy of the phenomenon, or, more exactly, of the will's adequate objectivity, but is directly a copy of the will itself, and therefore expresses the metaphysical to everything physical in the world, the thing-in-itself to every phenomenon. Accordingly, we could just as well call the world embodied music as embodied will; this is the reason why music makes every picture, indeed every scene from real life and from the world, at once appear in enhanced significance, and this is, of course, all the greater, the more analogous its melody is to the inner spirit of the given phenomenon. It is due to this that we are able to set a poem to music as a song, or a perceptive presentation as a pantomime, or both as an opera. Such individual pictures of human life, set to the universal language of music, are never bound to it or correspond to it with absolute necessity, but stand to it only in the relation of an example, chosen at random, to a universal concept. They express in the distinctness of reality what music asserts in the universality of mere form. For, to a certain extent, melodies are, like universal concepts, an abstraction from reality. This reality, and hence the world of particular things, furnishes what is perceptive, special, and individual, the particular case, both to the universality of the concepts and to that of the melodies. These two universalities, however, are in a certain respect opposed to each other, since the concepts contain only the forms, first of all abstracted from perception, so to speak the stripped-off outer shell of things; hence they are quite properly *abstracta*. Music, on the other hand, gives the innermost kernel preceding all form, or the heart of things.

This relation could very well be expressed in the language of the scholastics by saying that the concepts are the *universalia post rem*, but music gives the *universalia ante rem*, and reality the *universalia in re*. Even other examples, just as arbitrarily chosen, of the universal expressed in a poem could correspond in the same degree to the general significance of the melody assigned to this poem; and so the same composition is suitable to many verses; hence also the *vaudeville*. But that generally a relation between a composition and a perceptive expression is possible is due, as we have said, to the fact that the two are simply quite different expressions of the same inner nature of the world. Now when in the particular case such a relation actually exists, thus when the composer has known how to express in the universal language of music the stirrings of will that constitute the kernel of an event, then the melody of the song, the music of the opera, is expressive. But the analogy discovered by the composer between these two must have come from the immediate knowledge of the inner nature of the world unknown to his faculty of reason; it cannot be an imitation brought about with conscious intention by means of concepts, otherwise the music does not express the inner nature of the will itself, but merely imitates its phenomenon inadequately. All really imitative music does this; for example, *The Seasons* by Haydn, also many passages of his *Creation*, where phenomena of the world of perception are directly imitated; also in all battle pieces. All this is to be entirely rejected.

The inexpressible depth of all music, by virtue of which it floats past us as a paradise quite familiar and yet eternally remote, and is so easy to understand and yet so inexplicable, is due to the fact that it reproduces all the emotions of our innermost being, but entirely without reality and remote from its pain. In the same way, the seriousness essential to it and wholly excluding the ludicrous from its direct and peculiar province is to be explained from the fact that its object is not the representation, in regard to which deception and ridiculousness alone are possible, but that this object is directly the will; and this is essentially the most serious of all things, as being that on which all depends. How full of meaning and significance the language of music is we see from the repetition signs, as well as from the *Da capo* which would be intolerable in the case of works composed in the language of words. In music, however, they are very appropriate and

beneficial; for to comprehend it fully, we must hear it twice.

In the whole of this discussion on music I have been trying to make it clear that music expresses in an exceedingly universal language, in a homogeneous material, that is, in mere tones, and with the greatest distinctness and truth, the inner being, the in-itself, of the world, which we think of under the concept of will, according to its most distinct manifestation. Further, according to my view and contention, philosophy is nothing but a complete and accurate repetition and expression of the inner nature of the world in very general concepts, for only in these is it possible to obtain a view of that entire inner nature which is everywhere adequate and applicable. Thus whoever has followed me and has entered into my way of thinking will not find it so very paradoxical when I say that, supposing we succeeded in giving a perfectly accurate and complete explanation of music which goes into detail, and thus a detailed repetition in concepts of what it expresses, this would also be at once a sufficient repetition and explanation of the world in concepts, or one wholly corresponding thereto, and hence the true philosophy. Consequently, we can parody in the following way the above-mentioned saying of Leibniz, in the sense of our higher view of music, for it is quite correct from a lower point of view: *Musica est exercitium metaphysices occultum nescientis se philosophari animi.*[40] For *scire*, to know, always means to have couched in abstract concepts. But further, in virtue of the truth of the saying of Leibniz, corroborated in many ways, music, apart from its aesthetic or inner significance, and considered merely externally and purely empirically, is nothing but the means of grasping, immediately and in the concrete, larger numbers and more complex numerical ratios that we can otherwise know only indirectly by comprehension in concepts. Therefore, by the union of these two very different yet correct views of music, we can now arrive at a conception of the possibility of a philosophy of numbers, like that of Pythagoras and of the Chinese in the *I Ching*, and then interpret in this sense that saying of the Pythagoreans quoted by Sextus Empiricus (*Adversus Mathematicos*, Bk. vii [§ 94]): τῷ ἀριθμῷ δὲ τὰ πάντ' ἐπέοικεν (*numero cuncta assimilantur*).[41] And if, finally, we apply this view to our above-mentioned interpretation of harmony and melody, we shall find a mere moral philosophy without an explanation of nature, such as Socrates tried to introduce, to be wholly analogous to a melody without harmony, desired exclusively by

Rousseau; and in contrast to this, mere physics and metaphysics without ethics will correspond to mere harmony without melody. Allow me to add to these occasional observations a few more remarks concerning the analogy of music with the phenomenal world. We found in the previous book that the highest grade of the will's objectification, namely man, could not appear alone and isolated, but that this presupposed the grades under him, and these again presupposed lower and lower grades. Now music, which, like the world, immediately objectifies the will, is also perfect only in complete harmony. In order to produce its full impression, the high leading voice of melody requires the accompaniment of all the other voices down to the lowest bass which is to be regarded as the origin of all. The melody itself intervenes as an integral part in the harmony, as the harmony does in the melody, and only thus, in the full-toned whole, does music express what it intends to express. Thus the one will outside time finds its complete objectification only in the complete union of all the grades that reveal its inner nature in the innumerable degrees of enhanced distinctness. The following analogy is also remarkable. In the previous book we saw that, notwithstanding the self-adaptation of all the phenomena of the will to one another as regards the species, which gives rise to the teleological view, there yet remains an unending conflict between those phenomena as individuals. It is visible at all grades of individuals, and makes the world a permanent battle-field of all those phenomena of one and the same will; and in this way the will's inner contradiction with itself becomes visible. In music there is also something corresponding to this; thus a perfectly pure harmonious system of tones is impossible not only physically, but even arithmetically. The numbers themselves, by which the tones can be expressed, have insoluble irrationalities. No scale can ever be computed within which every fifth would be related to the keynote as 2 to 3, every major third as 4 to 5, every minor third as 5 to 6, and so on. For if the tones are correctly related to the keynote, they no longer are so to one another, because, for example, the fifth would have to be the minor third to the third, and so on. For the notes of the scale can be compared to actors, who have to play now one part, now another. Therefore a perfectly correct music cannot even be conceived, much less worked out; and for this reason all possible music deviates from perfect purity. It can merely conceal the discords essential to it by dividing these among all the notes, i.e., by temperament.

On this see Chladni's *Akustik*, § 30, and his *Kurze Übersicht der Schall- und Klanglehre* [. . .]

I might still have much to add on the way in which music is perceived, namely in and through time alone, with absolute exclusion of space, even without the influence of the knowledge of causality, and thus of the understanding. For the tones make the aesthetic impression as effect, and this without our going back to their causes, as in the case of perception. But I do not wish to make these remarks still more lengthy, as I have perhaps already gone too much into detail with regard to many things in this third book, or have dwelt too much on particulars. However, my aim made it necessary, and will be the less disapproved of, if the importance and high value of art, seldom sufficiently recognized, are realized. According to our view, the whole of the visible world is only the objectification, the mirror, of the will, accompanying it to knowledge of itself, and indeed, as we shall soon see, to the possibility of its salvation. At the same time, the world as representation, if we consider it in isolation, by tearing ourselves from willing, and letting it alone take possession of our consciousness, is the most delightful, and the only innocent, side of life. We have to regard art as the greater enhancement, the more perfect development, of all this; for essentially it achieves just the same thing as is achieved by the visible world itself, only with greater concentration, perfection, intention, and intelligence; and therefore, in the full sense of the world, it may be called the flower of life. If the whole world as representation is only the visibility of the will, then art is the elucidation of this visibility, the *camera obscura* which shows the objects more purely, and enables us to survey and comprehend them better. It is the play within the play, the stage on the stage in *Hamlet*.

The pleasure of everything beautiful, the consolation afforded by art, the enthusiasm of the artist which enables him to forget the cares of life, this one advantage of the genius over other men alone compensating him for the suffering that is heightened in proportion to the clearness of consciousness, and for the desert loneliness among a different race of men, all this is due to the fact that, as we shall see later on, the in-itself of life, the will, existence itself, is a constant suffering, and is partly woeful, partly fearful. The same thing, on the other hand, as representation alone, purely contemplated, or repeated through art, free from pain, presents us with a significant spectacle.

This purely knowable side of the world and its repetition in any art is the element of the artist. He is captivated by a consideration of the spectacle of the will's objectification. He sticks to this, and does not get tired of contemplating it, and of repeating it in his descriptions. Meanwhile, he himself bears the cost of producing that play; in other words, he himself is the will objectifying itself and remaining in constant suffering. That pure, true, and profound knowledge of the inner nature of the world now becomes for him an end in itself; at it he stops. Therefore it does not become for him a quieter of the will [...]; it does not deliver him from life for ever, but only for a few moments. For him it is not the way out of life, but only an occasional consolation in it, until his power, enhanced by this contemplation, finally becomes tired of the spectacle, and seizes the serious side of things. The St. Cecilia of Raphael can be regarded as a symbol of this transition.

Notes

1 "Truly being." [Tr.]

2 "A mere thinking by means of irrational sense perception." [Tr.]

3 "In itself always in the same way." [Tr.]

4 "Always being, and never either arising or passing away." [Tr.]

5 F. H. Jacobi.

6 "Many are rod-bearers, yet few become Bacchantes." [Tr.] "Philosophy has fallen into contempt, because people are not engaged in it to the extent that it merits; for not spurious, but genuine, philosophers should devote themselves to it." [Tr.]

7 See, for example, *Immanuel Kant, ein Denkmal*, by Fr. Bouterweck, p. 49; and Buhle's *Geschichte der Philosophie*, Vol. 6, pp. 802–15, and 823.

8 "Persisting in the present." [Tr.]

9 "From the sublime to the ridiculous is but a step." [Tr.]

10 "The mind is eternal in so far as it conceives things from the standpoint of eternity." [Tr.]
I also recommend what he says *ibid.*, 1. II, prop. 40, schol. 2, and 1. V, prop. 25–38, about the *cognitio tertii generis, sive intuitiva*, in illustration of the method of cognition we are here considering, and most particularly prop. 29, schol.; prop. 36, schol.; and prop. 38 demonstr. et schol.

11 [*Childe Harold's Pilgrimage*, III, lxxv. – Tr.]

12 "I am all this creation collectively, and besides me there exists no other being." [Tr. ...]

13 This last sentence cannot be understood without some acquaintance with the following book.

14 Goethe's *Faust*, Bayard Taylor's translation. [Tr.]

15 The word used by Schopenhauer is "*gemütlich*." [Tr.]

16 "What does all that prove?" [Tr.]

17 "There has been no great mind without an admixture of madness." [Tr.]

18 "For Democritus asserts that there can be no great poet without madness; and Plato says the same thing." [Tr.]

19 From Dryden's *Absalom and Achitophel*, I, 163; not from Pope as attributed by Schopenhauer. [Tr.]

20 I am now all the more delighted and surprised, forty years after advancing this thought so timidly and hesitatingly, to discover that St. Augustine had already expressed it: *Arbusta formas suas varias, quibus mundi hujus visibilis structura formosa est, sentiendas sensibus praebent; ut, pro eo quod NOSSE non possunt, quasi INNOTESCERE velle videantur.* (*De Civitate Dei*, xi, 27.) "The trees offer to the senses for perception the many different forms by which the structure of this visible world is adorned, so that, because they are unable to *know*, they may appear, as it were, to want to *be known*." [Tr.]

21 "I am all this creation collectively, and besides me there exists no other being." [Tr.]

22 "Plato taught that there are as many Ideas as there are natural things." [Tr.]

23 "But they define *Idea* as a timeless prototype of natural things. For most of Plato's followers do not admit that there are Ideas of products of art, e.g., of shields or lyres, or of things opposed to nature like fever or cholera, or even of individuals like Socrates and Plato, or even of trifling things like bits and chips, or of relations such as being greater or being taller; for the Ideas are the eternal thoughts of God which are in themselves complete." [Tr.]

24 Jacob Böhme in his book *De Signatura Rerum*, chap. I, §§ 15, 16, 17, says: "And there is no thing in nature that does not reveal its inner form outwardly as well; for the internal continually works towards revelation ... Each thing has its mouth for revelation. And this is the language of nature in which each thing speaks out of its own property, and always reveals and manifests itself ... For each thing reveals its mother, who therefore gives the *essence and the will* to the form."

25 The last sentence is the translation of *il n'y a que l'esprit qui sente l'esprit* of Helvetius. There was no need to mention this in the first edition. But since then, the times have become so degraded and crude through the stupefying influence of Hegel's sham wisdom, that many might well imagine here an

allusion to the antithesis between "spirit and nature." I am therefore compelled to guard myself expressly against the interpolation of such vulgar philosophemes.

26 "In accordance with nature." [Tr.]

27 Virgil, *Aeneid*, xii, 868. [Tr.]

28 This passage presupposes for its comprehension the whole of the following book.

29 "Imitators, the slavish mob." [Tr.]

30 *Apparent rari, nantes in gurgite vasto.* ("Singly they appear, swimming by in the vast waste of waves." Virgil, *Aeneid*, i, 118. [Tr.])

31 "Time discloses the truth." [Tr.]

32 "Into the ocean sank the sun's glittering orb, drawing dark night over the bountiful earth." *Iliad*, viii, 485–6 [Tr.]

33 It goes without saying that everywhere I speak exclusively of the great and genuine poet, who is so rare. I mean no one else; least of all that dull and shallow race of mediocre poets, rhymesters, and devisers of fables which flourishes so luxuriantly, especially in Germany at the present time; but we ought to shout incessantly in their ears from all sides:

*Mediocribus esse poetis
Non homines, non Di, non concessere columnae.*

["Neither gods, nor men, nor even advertising pillars permit the poet to be a mediocrity." Horace, *Ars Poetica*, 372–3. Tr.] It is worth serious consideration how great an amount of time – their own and other people's – and of paper is wasted by this swarm of mediocre poets, and how injurious their influence is. For the public always seizes on what is new, and shows even more inclination to what is perverse and dull, as being akin to its own nature. These works of the mediocre, therefore, draw the public away and hold it back from genuine masterpieces, and from the education they afford. Thus they work directly against the benign influence of genius, ruin taste more and more, and so arrest the progress of the age. Therefore criticism and satire should scourge mediocre poets without pity or sympathy, until they are induced for their own good to apply their muse rather to read what is good than to write what is bad. For if the bungling of the meddlers put even the god of the Muses in such a rage that he could flay Marsyas, I do not see on what mediocre poetry would base its claims to tolerance.

34 From Goethe's *Faust*, Bayard Taylor's translation. [Tr.]

35 "*Par excellence.*" [Tr.]

36 Leibniz' *Letters*, Kortholt's edition, *ep.* 154. "An unconscious exercise in arithmetic in which the mind does not know it is counting." [Tr.]

37 "Harmonics." [Tr.]

38 "The movement of the melody which it imitates, when the soul is stirred by passions." [Tr.]

39 "How is it that rhythms and melodies, although only sound, resemble states of the soul?" [Tr.]

40 "Music is an unconscious exercise in metaphysics in which the mind does not know it is philosophizing." [Tr.]

41 "All things are similar to number." [Tr.]

4

Lectures on Aesthetics

G. W. F. Hegel

[4] Scientific Ways of Treating Beauty and Art

If we now ask about the *kind* of scientific treatment [of art] we meet here again two opposed ways of treating the subject; each appears to exclude the other and not to let us reach any true result.

On the one hand we see the science of art only busying itself with actual works of art from the outside, arranging them into a history of art, setting up discussions about existing works or outlining theories which are to yield general considerations for both criticizing and producing works of art.

On the other hand, we see science abandoning itself on its own account to reflections on the beautiful and producing only something universal, irrelevant to the work of art in its peculiarity, in short, an abstract philosophy of the beautiful.

(1) As for the first mode of treatment, which has the *empirical* for its starting-point, it is the indispensable route for anyone who thinks of becoming a *scholar* in the field of art. And just as, at the present day, everyone, even if not a devotee of physics, still likes to be equipped with the most essential physical facts, so it has been more or less necessary for a cultured man to have some acquaintance with art, and the pretension of proving oneself a dilettante and a connoisseur of art is almost universal.

(*a*) But if acquaintance of this sort with art is to be recognized as real scholarship, it must be of many kinds and of wide range. For the first requirement is a precise acquaintance with the immeasurable realm of individual works of art, ancient and modern, some of which (α) have already perished in reality, or (β) belong to distant lands or continents and which the unkindness of fate has withdrawn from our own inspection. Further, every work of art belongs to its own time, its own people, its own environment, and depends on particular historical and other ideas and purposes; consequently, scholarship in the field of art demands a vast wealth of historical, and indeed very detailed, facts, since the individual nature of the work of art is related to something individual and necessarily requires detailed knowledge for its understanding and explanation. Finally, scholarship demands here not only, as in other fields, a memory of the facts, but also a keen imagination to retain pictures of artistic forms in all their varied details, and especially to have them present to the mind for comparison with other works of art.

(*b*) Within this primarily historical treatment there arise at once different considerations which must not be lost sight of if we are to derive judgements from them. Now these considerations, as in other sciences which have an empirical basis, form, when extracted and assembled, general criteria and propositions, and, by still further generalization, *theories* of the arts. This is not the place to go through the literature of this kind, and it must therefore be enough to cite just a few works in the most general way. Thus, for example (α) Aristotle's *Poetics* – its theory of tragedy is even now of interest, and (β) more particularly, Horace's *Ars Poetica* and Longinus *On the Sublime* provide, among the classics, a general idea of the manner in which this theorizing has been handled. The general characteristics abstracted by these authors were supposed to count in particular as prescriptions and rules in accordance with which works of art had to be produced, especially in times when poetry and art had deteriorated. Yet the prescriptions which these art-doctors wrote to cure art were even less reliable than those of ordinary doctors for restoring human health.

On these theories of art I will only mention that, although in *single* instances they contain much that is instructive, still their remarks were drawn from a very restricted range of works of art which happened to be accounted genuinely beautiful [at the time] yet which always constituted only a small extent of the sphere of art. On the other hand, such characteristics are in part very trivial reflections which in their *universality* make no advance towards establishing the *particular*, which is principally what is at issue; for example, the Horatian *Epistle* that I have mentioned is full of such reflections and therefore is a book for everybody, but for that reason contains much that is vapid: *omne tulit punctum*, etc.[1] This is just like so many proverbial instructions: 'Dwell in the land and thou shalt be fed',[2] which are right enough thus generally expressed, but which lack the concrete specifications necessary for action.

Another kind of interest consisted not in the express aim of producing genuine works of art directly but in the intention of developing through such theories a judgement on works of art, in short, of developing *taste*. As examples, Home's *Elements of Criticism*,[3] the works of Batteux, and Ramler's *Einleitung in die schönen Wissenschaften*[4] were books much read in their day. Taste in this sense concerns the arrangement and treatment, the aptness and perfection of what belongs to the external appearance of a work of art. Moreover they drew into the principles of taste views which were taken from the old psychology and had been derived from empirical observations of mental capacities and activities, passions and their probable intensification, sequence, etc. But it remains ever the case that every man apprehends works of art or characters, actions, and events according to the measure of his insight and his feelings; and since the development of taste only touched on what was external and meagre, and besides took its prescriptions likewise from only a narrow range of works of art and a limited training of the intellect and the feelings, its scope was unsatisfactory

and incapable of grasping the inner [meaning] and truth [of art] and sharpening the eye for detecting these things.

In general, such theories proceed in the same kind of way as the other non-philosophical sciences. What they take as their subject matter is derived from our perception as something really *there*; [but] now a further question arises about the character of this perception, since we need closer specifications which are likewise found in our perception and, drawn thence, are settled in definitions. But thus we find ourselves at once on uncertain and disputed ground. For at first it might seem that the beautiful was a quite simple idea. But it is soon obvious that several sides may be found in it, and so one author emphasizes one and another author another, or, if the same considerations are kept in view, a dispute arises about the question which side is now to be treated as the essential one.

In this regard it is a part of scientific completeness to cite and criticize the different definitions of the beautiful. We will not do this either in historical completeness in order to get to know all the various subtleties of definition, or for the sake of *historical* interest; we will only pick out as an example some of the more recent and more interesting ways of looking at beauty which are aimed more precisely at what is in fact implied in the Idea of the beautiful. To this end we must give pride of place to Goethe's[5] account of the beautiful which [J. H.] Meyer [1760–1832] has embodied in his *Geschichte der bildenden Künste in Griechenland*[6] where without naming Hirt he quotes his view too.

[A. L.] Hirt, one of the greatest genuine connoisseurs in our time, wrote an essay on the beauty of art in *Die Horen*,[7] 1797, pt. 7, in which, after writing about the beautiful in the different arts, he sums up in conclusion that the basis for a just criticism of beauty in art and for the formation of taste is the concept of the *characteristic*; i.e. he lays it down that the beautiful is 'the perfect which is or can be an object of eye, ear, or imagination'. He then further defines the perfect as 'what corresponds with its aim, what nature or art intended to produce in the formation of the object within its genus and species'. It follows then that, in order to form our judgement of beauty, we must direct our observation so far as possible to the individual marks which constitute the essence of a thing [*ein Wesen*], since it is just these marks which constitute its characteristic. By 'character' as a law of art Hirt understands 'that specific individuality whereby forms, movement and gesture, mien and expression, local colour, light and shade, *chiaroscuro*, and bearing are distinguished, and indeed, as the previously envisaged object demands'. This formulation is already more significant than other definitions, for if we go on to ask what 'the characteristic' is, we see at once that it involves (i) a content, as, for example, a specific feeling, situation, occurrence, action, individual, and (ii) the mode and manner in which this content is presented. It is on this manner of presentation that the artistic law of 'the characteristic' depends, since it demands that everything particular in the mode of expression shall serve towards the specific designation of its content and be a link in the expression of that content. The abstract category of 'the characteristic' thus refers to the degree of appropriateness with which the particular detail of the artistic form sets in relief the content it is meant to present. If we wish to explain this conception in a quite popular way, the following is the limitation which it involves. In a dramatic work, for example, an action constitutes the content; the drama is to display how this action happens. Now people do all sorts of things; they join in talk, eat occasionally, sleep, put on their clothes, say this and that, and so on. But whatever of all this does not stand immediately in relation to that specific action (which is the content proper) should be excluded, so that, in that content, nothing remains without significance. In the same way, in a picture, which seizes on only one phase of that action, there could be included – such are the wide ramifications of the external world – a mass of circumstances, persons, situations, and other incidents which have no relation to the specific action in that phase and contribute nothing to its distinctive character. But according to the principle of 'the characteristic', nothing is to enter the work of art except what belongs to the appearance and essentially to the expression of this content alone; nothing is to be otiose or superfluous.

This is a very important principle which may be justified in certain respects. Yet Meyer in the book mentioned above thinks that this view has been superseded without trace and, as he maintains, to the benefit of art, on the ground that this idea would probably have led to something like caricature. This judgement immediately implies the perversity of supposing that such a definition of the beautiful would have to do with *leading* to something. The philosophy of art has no concern with prescriptions for artists; on the contrary, it has to determine what the beautiful is as such, and how it has displayed itself in reality, in works of art, without wishing to provide rules for their production. Now, apart from this, in respect to this criticism, it is of course true that Hirt's definition does cover caricature and the like too, for after all what is caricatured may be a characteristic; only one must say at once on the other side that in caricature the specific character is exaggerated and is, as it were, a superfluity of the characteristic. But the superfluity is no longer what is strictly required for the characteristic, but a troublesome repetition whereby the 'characteristic' itself may be made unnatural. Moreover, caricature and the like may also be the characterizing of the ugly, which is certainly a distortion. Ugliness for its part is closely related to the subject-matter, so that it may be said that the principle of the characteristic involves as a fundamental feature an acceptance of the ugly and its presentation. On what is to be 'characterized' in the beauty of art, and what is not, on the content of the beautiful, Hirt's definition of course gives us no more precise information. In this respect he provides only a purely formal prescription which yet contains something true, even if in an abstract way.

But now the further question arises of what Meyer opposes to Hirt's artistic principle. What does he prefer? In the first place he deals only with the principle in the works of art of antiquity, which must however contain the definition of the beautiful as such. In this connection he comes to speak of Mengs' and Winckelmann's[8] definition of [beauty as] the ideal and says that he neither rejects this law of beauty nor wholly accepts it; on the other hand he has no hesitation in agreeing with the opinion of an enlightened judge of art (Goethe) since it is definitive and seems to be nearer solving the riddle. Goethe says: 'The supreme principle of antiquity was the *significant*, but the supreme result of a successful *treatment* was the *beautiful*.'[9] If we look more closely at what this expression implies, we again find in it two things: (i) the content, the thing, and (ii) the manner and mode of presentation. In a work of art we begin with what is immediately presented to us and only then ask what its meaning or content is. The former, the external appearance, has no immediate value for us; we assume behind it something inward, a meaning whereby the external appearance is endowed with the spirit. It is to this, its soul, that the external points. For an appearance that means something does not present *itself* to our minds, or what it is *as* external, but something else. Consider, for example, a symbol, and, still more obviously, a fable the meaning of which is constituted by its moral and message. Indeed any word hints at a meaning and counts for nothing in itself. Similarly the spirit and the soul shine through the human eye, through a man's face, flesh, skin, through his whole figure, and here the meaning is always something wider than what shows itself in the immediate appearance. It is in this way that the work of art is to be significant and not appear exhausted by these lines, curves, surfaces, carvings, hollowings in the stone, these colours, notes, word-sounds, or whatever other material is used; on the contrary, it should disclose an inner life, feeling, soul, a content and spirit, which is just what we call the significance of a work of art.

With this demand for meaningfulness in a work of art, therefore, little is said that goes beyond or is different from Hirt's principle of the 'characteristic'.

According to this view, to sum up, we have characterized as the elements of the beautiful something inward, a content, and something outward which signifies that content; the inner shines in the outer and makes itself known through the outer, since the outer points away from itself to the inner. But we cannot go further into detail.

(*c*) This earlier manner of theorizing has after all been already violently cast aside in Germany, along with those practical rules, principally owing to the appearance of genuinely living poetry. The right of genius, its works and their effects, have been made to prevail against the presumptions of those legalisms and the watery wastes of theories. From this foundation of a genuine spiritual art, and the sympathy it has received and its widespread influence, there has sprung a receptivity for and freedom to enjoy and recognize great works of art which have long been available, whether those of the modern world or the Middle Ages, or even of wholly foreign peoples in the past, e.g. the Indian. These works, because of their age or foreign nationality, have of course something strange about them for us, but they have a content which outsoars their foreignness and is common to all mankind, and only by the prejudice of theory could they be stamped as products of a barbarous bad taste. This general recognition of works of art which lie outside the circle and forms which were the principal basis for the abstractions of theory has in the first place led to the recognition of a special kind of art – Romantic Art, and it has

become necessary to grasp the Concept and nature of the beautiful in a deeper way than was possible for those theories. Bound up with this at the same time is the fact that the Concept, aware of itself as the thinking spirit, has now recognized itself on its side, more deeply, in philosophy, and this has thereby immediately provided an inducement for taking up the essence of art too in a profounder way.

Thus then, simply following the phases of this more general development, the mode of reflecting on art, the theorizing we have been considering, has become out of date, alike in its principles and its achievements. Only the *scholarship* of the history of art has retained its abiding value, and must do so all the more, the more the growth of spiritual receptivity, which I mentioned, has extended people's intellectual horizons in every direction. Its task and vocation consists in the aesthetic appreciation of individual works of art and in a knowledge of the historical circumstances which condition the work of art externally; it is only an appreciation, made with sense and spirit, and supported by the historical facts, which can penetrate into the entire individuality of a work of art. Goethe, for example, has written a great deal in this way about art and works of art. This mode of treating the subject does not aim at theorizing in the strict sense, although it may indeed often concern itself with abstract principles and categories, and may fall into them unintentionally, but if anyone does not let this hinder him but keeps before his eyes only those concrete presentations, it does provide a philosophy of art with tangible examples and authentications, into the historical particular details of which philosophy cannot enter.

This is then the first mode of treating art, the one that starts from particular and existent [works].

(2) From this it is essential to distinguish the opposite side, namely the purely theoretical reflection which labours at understanding the beautiful as such out of itself and fathoming its *Idea*.

We all know that Plato, in a deeper way, began to demand of philosophical inquiry that its objects should be understood not in their particularity, but in their universality, in their genus, in their essential reality, because he maintained that it was not single good actions, true opinions, beautiful human beings or works of art, that were the truth, but goodness, beauty, and truth themselves. Now if in fact the beautiful is to be understood in its essence and its Concept, this is possible only through the conceptual thinking whereby the logico-metaphysical nature of the *Idea in general*, as well as of the particular *Idea of the beautiful*, enters conscious reflection. But this treatment of the beautiful by itself in its Idea may itself turn again into an abstract metaphysics. Even if Plato in this connection be taken as foundation and guide, still the Platonic abstraction, even for the logical Idea of the beautiful, can satisfy us no longer. We must grasp this Idea more concretely, more profoundly, since the emptiness, which clings to the Platonic Idea, no longer satisfies the richer philosophical needs of our spirit today. It is indeed the case that we too must begin, in the philosophy of art, with the Idea of the beautiful, but we ought not to be in the position of clinging simply to Platonic Ideas, to that abstract mode with which philosophizing about art first began.

(3) The philosophical Concept of the beautiful, to indicate its true nature at least in a preliminary way, must contain, reconciled within itself, both the extremes which have been mentioned, because it unites metaphysical universality with the precision of real particularity. Only so is it grasped absolutely in its truth: for, on the one hand, over against the sterility of one-sided reflection, it is in that case fertile, since, in accordance with its own Concept, it has to develop into a totality of specifications, and it itself, like its exposition, contains the necessity of its particularizations and of their progress and transition one into another; on the other hand, the particularizations, to which a transition has been made, carry in themselves the universality and essentiality of the Concept, as the proper particularizations whereof they appear. The previously mentioned modes of treating the subject lack both these characteristics,[10] and for this reason it is only this full Concept which leads to substantial, necessary, and complete principles.

[5] Concept of the Beauty of Art

After these preliminary remarks, we now come closer to our proper subject, the philosophy of the beauty of art, and, since we are undertaking to treat it scientifically, we have to make a beginning with its Concept. Only when we have established this Concept can we lay down the division, and therefore the plan, of the whole of this science. For a division, if not undertaken in a purely external manner, as it is in a non-philosophical inquiry, must find its principle in the Concept of the subject-matter itself.

Confronted with such a requirement, we are at once met with the question 'whence do we derive this Concept?' If we start with the Concept itself of the beauty of art, it at once becomes a *presupposition* and a mere assumption; mere assumptions, however, philosophical method does not allow; on the contrary, what is to pass muster has to have its truth proved, i.e. has to be shown to be necessary.

About this difficulty, which affects the introduction to every philosophical discipline considered independently and by itself, we will come to an understanding in a short space.

In the case of the object of every science, two things come at once into consideration: (i) that there *is* such an object, and (ii) *what* it is.

On the first point little difficulty usually arises in the ordinary [i.e. physical] sciences. Why, it would at once be ridiculous to require astronomy and physics to prove that there are a sun, stars, magnetic phenomena, etc.! In these sciences which have to do with what is present to sensation, the objects are taken from experience of the external world, and instead of *proving* them, it is thought sufficient to *point* to them. Yet even within the non-philosophical disciplines, doubts may arise about the existence of their objects, as, for example, in psychology, the science of mind, there may be a doubt whether there *is* a soul, a spirit, i.e. an explicitly independent subjective entity distinct from what is material; or in theology, a doubt whether there is a God. If, moreover, the objects are of a subjective sort, i.e. present only in the mind and not as things externally perceptible, we know that in mind there is only what its own activity has produced. Hence there arises at once the chance that men may or may not have produced this inner idea or intuition in themselves, and, even if the former is really the case, that they have not made such an idea vanish again, or at least degraded it to a purely subjective idea whose content has no independent reality of its own. Thus, for example, the beautiful has often been regarded as not being absolutely necessary in our ideas but as a purely subjective pleasure, or a merely accidental sense. Our intuitions, observations, and perceptions of the external world are often deceptive and erroneous, but this is even more true of our inner ideas, even if they have in themselves the greatest vividness and could carry us away into passion irresistibly.

Now the doubt whether an object of our inner ideas and general outlook *is* or is *not*, like the question whether subjective consciousness has generated it in itself and whether the manner and mode in which it has brought it before itself was also in correspondence with the object in its essential nature, is precisely what arouses in men the higher scientific need which demands that, even if we have a notion that an object *is* or that there is such an object, nevertheless the object must be exhibited or proved in accordance with its *necessity*.

With this proof, provided it be developed really scientifically, the other question of *what* an object is, is sufficiently answered at the same time. However, to expound this fully would take us too far afield at this point, and only the following indications can be given.

If the necessity of our subject, the beauty of art, is to be exhibited, we would have to prove that art or the beautiful was a result of an antecedent which, considered according to its true Concept, was such as to lead on with scientific necessity to the Concept of fine art. But since we begin with art and wish to treat of *its* Concept and the realization thereof, not of its antecedent in its essential character (the antecedent pursuant to its own Concept), art has for us, as a particular scientific subject-matter, a presupposition which lies outside our consideration and, handled scientifically as a different subject-matter, belongs to a different philosophical discipline. Thus the only course left to us is to take up the Concept of art *lemmatically*,[11] so to say, and this is the case with all particular philosophical sciences if they are to be treated *seriatim*. For it is only the *whole* of philosophy which is knowledge of the universe as in itself that *one* organic totality which develops itself out of its own Concept and which, in its self-relating necessity, withdrawing into itself to form a whole, closes with itself to form *one* world of truth. In the circlet of this scientific necessity each single part is on the one hand a circle returning into itself, while on the other hand it has at the same time a necessary connection with other parts. It has a backward whence it is itself derived, and a forward to which it ever presses itself on, in so far as it is fertile, engendering an 'other' out of itself once more, and issuing it for scientific knowledge. Thus it is not our present aim, but the task of an encyclopedic development of the whole of philosophy and its particular disciplines, to prove the Idea of the beautiful with which we began, i.e. to

derive it necessarily from the presuppositions which antecede it in philosophy and out of the womb of which it is born. For us the Concept of the beautiful and art is a presupposition given by the system of philosophy. But since we cannot here expound this system and the connection of art with it, we have not yet got the Concept of the beautiful before us scientifically. What *is* before us is only elements and aspects of it as they occur already in the different ideas of the beautiful and art held by ordinary people, or have formerly been accepted by them. From this point we intend to pass on to a deeper consideration of these views in order to gain the advantage, in the first place, of acquiring a general idea of our subject, as well as, by a brief critique, a preliminary acquaintance with the higher determinations with which we will have to do in the sequel. In this way our final introductory treatment of the subject will present, as it were, an overture to the lectures on the matter at issue and will tend [to provide] a general collection and direction [of our thoughts] to our proper subject.

[6] Common Ideas of Art

What we are acquainted with at the start, as a familiar idea of the work of art, falls under the three following heads:

(i) The work of art is no natural product; it is brought about by human activity;

(ii) it is essentially made for man's apprehension, and in particular is drawn more or less from the sensuous field for apprehension by the senses;

(iii) it has an end and aim in itself.

(i) The Work of Art as a Product of Human Activity

(a) As for the first point, that a work of art is a product of human activity, this view has given rise to the thought that this activity, being the *conscious* production of an external object, can also be *known* and expounded, and learnt and pursued by others. For what one man makes, another, it may seem, could make or imitate too, if only he were first acquainted with the manner of proceeding; so that, granted universal acquaintance with the rules of artistic production, it would only be a matter of everyone's pleasure to carry out the procedure in the same manner and produce works of art. It is in this way that the rule-providing theories, mentioned above [p. 99], with their prescriptions calculated for practical application, have arisen. But what can be carried out on such directions can only be something formally regular and mechanical. For the mechanical alone is of so external a kind that only a purely empty exercise of will and dexterity is required for receiving it into our ideas and activating it; this exercise does not require to be supplemented by anything concrete, or by anything not prescribed in universal rules. This comes out most vividly when such prescriptions do not limit themselves to the purely external and mechanical, but extend to the significant and spiritual activity of the artist. In this sphere the rules contain only vague generalities, for example that 'the theme should be interesting, every character should speak according to his standing, age, sex, and situation'. But if rules are to satisfy here, then their prescriptions should have been drawn up at the same time with such precision that they could be observed just as they are expressed, without any further spiritual activity of the artist's. Being abstract in content, however, such rules reveal themselves, in their pretence of adequacy to fill the consciousness of the artist, as wholly inadequate, since artistic production is not a formal activity in accordance with given specifications. On the contrary, as spiritual activity it is bound to work from its own resources and bring before the mind's eye a quite other and richer content and more comprehensive individual creations [than formulae can provide]. Therefore, in so far as such rules do actually contain something specific and therefore of practical utility, they may apply in case of need, but still can afford no more than specifications for purely external circumstances.

(*b*) Thus, as it turns out, the tendency just indicated has been altogether abandoned, and instead of it the opposite one has been adopted to the same extent. For the work of art was no longer regarded as a product of *general* human activity, but as a work of an entirely *specially gifted* spirit which now, however, is supposed to give free play simply and *only* to its own particular gift, as if to a specific natural force; it is to cut itself altogether loose from attention to universally valid laws and from a conscious reflection interfering with its own instinctive-like productive activity. Indeed it is supposed to be protected from such reflection, since its productions could only be contaminated and spoiled by such awareness. From this point of view the work of art has been claimed as a product of *talent* and *genius*, and the natural element in talent and genius has been especially emphasized. In a way, rightly, since talent is specific and genius universal capability, which man has not the power to give to himself purely and simply through his own self-conscious activity. On this topic we shall speak at greater length later [. . .].

Here we have only to mention the false aspect of this view, namely that in artistic production all consciousness of the artist's own activity is regarded as not merely superfluous but even deleterious. In that case production by talent and genius appears as only a *state* and, in particular, a state of *inspiration*. To such a state, it is said, genius is excited in part by an object, and in part can transpose itself into it by its own caprice, a process in which, after all, the good services of the champagne bottle are not forgotten. In Germany this notion became prominent at the time of the so-called *Period of Genius* which was introduced by Goethe's first poetical productions and then sustained by Schiller's. In their earliest works [. . .] these poets began afresh, setting aside all the rules then fabricated; they worked deliberately against these rules and thereby surpassed all other writers. However, I will not go further into the confusions which have been prevalent about the concept of inspiration and genius, and which prevail even today about the omnicompetence of inspiration as such. All that is essential is to state the view that, even if the talent and genius of the artist has in it a natural element, yet this element essentially requires development by thought, reflection on the mode of its productivity, and practice and skill in producing. For, apart from anything else, a main feature of artistic production is external workmanship, since the work of art has a purely technical side which extends into handicraft, especially in architecture and sculpture, less so in painting and music, least of all in poetry. Skill in technique is not helped by any inspiration, but only by reflection, industry, and practice. But such skill the artist is compelled to have in order to master his external material and not be thwarted by its intractability.

Now further, the higher the standing of the artist, the more profoundly should he display the depths of the heart and the spirit; these are not known directly but are to be fathomed only by the direction of the artist's own spirit on the inner and outer world. So, once again, it is study whereby the artist brings this content into his consciousness and wins the stuff and content of his conceptions.

Of course, in this respect, one art needs more than another the consciousness and knowledge of such content. Music, for example, which is concerned only with the completely indeterminate movement of the inner spirit and with sounds as if they were feeling without thought, needs to have little or no spiritual material present in consciousness. Therefore musical talent announces itself in most cases very early in youth,[12] when the head is empty and the heart little moved, and it may sometimes attain a very considerable height before spirit and life have experience of themselves. Often enough, after all, we have seen very great virtuosity in musical composition and performance accompanied by remarkable barrenness of spirit and character.

In poetry, on the other hand, it is quite different. In it all depends on the presentation, full of content and thought, of man, of his deeper interests, and of the powers that move him; and therefore the spirit and heart must be richly and deeply educated by life, experience, and reflection before genius can bring into being anything mature, of sterling worth, and complete in itself. The first productions of Goethe and Schiller are of an immaturity, yes even of a crudity and barbarity, that can be terrifying. It is this phenomenon, that in most of these attempts there is an overwhelming mass of elements through and through prosaic, partly cold and flat, which principally tells against the common opinion that inspiration is bound up with the fire and time of youth. It was only in their manhood that these two geniuses, our national poets, the first, we may say, to give poetical works to our country, endowed us with works deep, substantial, the product of true inspiration, and no less perfectly finished in form; just as it was only in old age that Homer was inspired and produced his ever undying songs.

(c) A third view concerning the idea of the work of art as a product of human activity refers to the placing of the work of art in relation to the external phenomena of nature. Here the ordinary way of looking at things took easily to the notion that the human art-product ranked below the product of nature; for the work of art has no feeling in itself and is not through and through enlivened, but, regarded as an external object, is dead; but we are accustomed to value the living higher than the dead. That the work of art has no life and movement in itself is readily granted. What is alive in nature is, within and without, an organism purposefully elaborated into all its tiniest parts,

while the work of art attains the appearance of life only on its surface; inside it is ordinary stone, or wood and canvas, or, as in poetry, an idea expressed in speech and letters. But this aspect – external existence – is not what makes a work into a product of fine art; a work of art is such only because, originating from the spirit, it now belongs to the territory of the spirit; it has received the baptism of the spiritual and sets forth only what has been formed in harmony with the spirit. Human interest, the spiritual value possessed by an event, an individual character, an action in its complexity and outcome, is grasped in the work of art and blazoned more purely and more transparently than is possible on the ground of other non-artistic things. Therefore the work of art stands higher than any natural product which has not made this journey through the spirit. For example, owing to the feeling and insight whereby a landscape has been represented in a painting, this work of the spirit acquires a higher rank than the mere natural landscape. For everything spiritual is better than any product of nature. Besides, no natural being is able, as art is, to present the divine Ideal.

Now on what the spirit draws from its own inner resources in works of art it confers permanence in their external existence too; on the other hand, the individual living thing in nature is transient, vanishing, changeable in outward appearance, while the work of art persists, even if it is not mere permanence which constitutes its genuine pre-eminence over natural reality, but its having made spiritual inspiration conspicuous.

But nevertheless this higher standing of the work of art is questioned by another idea commonly entertained. For nature and its products, it is said, are a work of God, created by his goodness and wisdom, whereas the art-product is a purely human work, made by human hands according to human insight. In this contrast between natural production as a divine creation and human activity as something merely finite there lies directly the misunderstanding that God does not work in and through men at all, but restricts the sphere of his activity to nature alone. This false opinion must be completely rejected if we are to penetrate to the true nature of art. Indeed, over against this view we must cling to the opposite one, namely that God is more honoured by what the spirit makes than by the productions and formations of nature. For not only is there something divine in man, but it is active in him in a form appropriate to the being of God in a totally different and higher manner than it is in nature. God is spirit, and in man alone does the medium, through which the Divine passes, have the form of conscious and actively self-productive spirit; but in nature this medium is the unconscious, the sensuous, and the external, which stands far below consciousness in worth. Now in art-production God is just as operative as he is in the phenomena of nature; but the Divine, as it discloses itself in the work of art, has been generated out of the spirit, and thus has won a suitable thoroughfare for its existence, whereas just being *there* in the unconscious sensuousness of nature is not a mode of appearance appropriate to the Divine.

(*d*) Now granted that the work of art is made by man as the creation of his spirit, a final question arises, in order to derive a deeper result from the foregoing [discussion], namely, what is man's *need* to produce works of art? On the one hand, this production may be regarded as a mere play of chance and fancies which might just as well be left alone as pursued; for it might be held that there are other and even better means of achieving what art aims at and that man has still higher and more important interests than art has the ability to satisfy. On the other hand, however, art seems to proceed from a higher impulse and to satisfy higher needs, – at times the highest and absolute needs since it is bound up with the most universal views of life and the religious interests of whole epochs and peoples. – This question about the non-contingent but absolute need for art, we cannot yet answer completely, because it is more concrete than an answer could turn out to be at this stage. Therefore we must content ourselves in the meantime with making only the following points.

The universal and absolute need from which art (on its formal side) springs has its origin in the fact that man is a *thinking* consciousness, i.e. that man draws out of himself and puts *before himself* what he is and whatever else is. Things in nature are only *immediate* and *single*, while man as spirit *duplicates* himself, in that (i) he *is* as things in nature are, but (ii) he is just as much *for* himself; he sees himself, represents himself to himself, thinks, and only on the strength of this active placing himself before himself is he spirit. This consciousness of himself man acquires in a twofold way: *first, theoretically*, in so far as inwardly he must bring himself into his own consciousness, along with whatever moves, stirs, and presses in

the human breast; and in general he must see himself, represent himself to himself, fix before himself what thinking finds as his essence, and recognize himself alone alike in what is summoned out of himself and in what is accepted from without. *Secondly*, man brings himself before himself by *practical* activity, since he has the impulse, in whatever is directly given to him, in what is present to him externally, to produce himself and therein equally to recognize himself. This aim he achieves by altering external things whereon he impresses the seal of his inner being and in which he now finds again his own characteristics. Man does this in order, as a free subject, to strip the external world of its inflexible foreignness and to enjoy in the shape of things only an external realization of himself. Even a child's first impulse involves this practical alteration of external things; a boy throws stones into the river and now marvels at the circles drawn in the water as an effect in which he gains an intuition of something that is his own doing. This need runs through the most diversiform phenomena up to that mode of self-production in external things which is present in the work of art. And it is not only with external things that man proceeds in this way, but no less with himself, with his own natural figure which he does not leave as he finds it but deliberately alters. This is the cause of all dressing up and adornment, even if it be barbaric, tasteless, completely disfiguring, or even pernicious like crushing the feet of Chinese ladies, or slitting the ears and lips. For it is only among civilized people that alteration of figure, behaviour, and every sort and mode of external expression proceeds from spiritual development.

The universal need for art, that is to say, is man's rational need to lift the inner and outer world into his spiritual consciousness as an object in which he recognizes again his own self. The need for this spiritual freedom he satisfies, on the one hand, within by making what is within him explicit to himself, but correspondingly by giving outward reality to this his explicit self, and thus in this duplication of himself by bringing what is in him into sight and knowledge for himself and others. This is the free rationality of man in which all acting and knowing, as well as art too, have their basis and necessary origin. The specific need of art, however, in distinction from other action, political and moral, from religious portrayal and scientific knowledge, we shall see later [...].

(ii) The Work of Art, as being for Apprehension by Man's Senses, is drawn from the Sensuous Sphere

So far we have considered in the work of art the aspect in which it is made by man. We have now to pass on to its second characteristic, namely that it is produced for apprehension by man's *senses* and therefore is more or less derived from the sensuous sphere.

(*a*) This reflection has given rise to the consideration that fine art is meant to arouse feeling, in particular the feeling that suits us, pleasant feeling. In this regard, the investigation of fine art has been made into an investigation of the feelings, and the question has been raised, 'what feelings should be aroused by art, fear, for example, and pity? But how can these be agreeable, how can the treatment of misfortune afford satisfaction?' Reflection on these lines dates especially from Moses Mendelssohn's times[13] and many such discussions can be found in his writings. Yet such investigation did not get far, because feeling is the indefinite dull region of the spirit; what is felt remains enveloped in the form of the most abstract individual subjectivity, and therefore differences between feelings are also completely abstract, not differences in the thing itself. For example, fear, anxiety, alarm, terror are of course further modifications of one and the same sort of feeling, but in part they are only quantitative intensifications, in part just forms not affecting their content, but indifferent to it. In the case of fear, for example, something is present in which the subject has an interest, but at the same time he sees the approach of the negative which threatens to destroy what he is interested in, and now he finds directly in himself the interest and the negative, both as contradictory affections of his subjectivity. But such fear cannot by itself condition any content; on the contrary, it is capable of receiving into itself the most varied and opposite contents.[14] Feeling as such is an entirely empty form of subjective affection. Of course this form may be manifold in itself, as hope, grief, joy, pleasure; and, again, in this variety it may encompass different contents, as there is a feeling for justice, moral feeling, sublime religious feeling, and so on. But the fact that such content [e.g. justice] is present in different forms of feeling [e.g. hope or grief] is not enough to bring to light its essential and specific nature. Feeling remains a purely subjective emotional state of mind in which the concrete thing vanishes, contracted into a cir-

cle of the greatest abstraction.[15] Consequently the investigation of the feelings which art evokes, or is supposed to evoke, does not get beyond vagueness; it is a study which precisely abstracts from the content proper and its concrete essence and concept. For reflection on *feeling* is satisfied with observing subjective emotional reaction in its particular character, instead of immersing itself in the thing at issue i.e. in the work of art, plumbing its depths, and in addition relinquishing mere subjectivity and its states. But in the case of feeling it is precisely this empty subjectivity which is not only retained but is the chief thing, and this is why men are so fond of having feelings. But this too is why a study of this kind becomes wearisome on account of its indefiniteness and emptiness, and disagreeable by its concentration on tiny subjective peculiarities.

(*b*) But since the work of art is not, as may be supposed, meant merely in general to arouse feelings (for in that case it would have this aim in common, without any specific difference, with oratory, historical writing, religious edification, etc.), but to do so only in so far as it is beautiful, reflection on the beautiful hit upon the idea of looking for a peculiar *feeling* of the beautiful, and finding a specific *sense* of beauty. In this quest it soon appeared that such a sense is no blind instinct, made firmly definite by nature, capable from the start in and by itself of distinguishing beauty. Hence education was demanded for this sense, and the educated sense of beauty was called *taste* which, although an educated appreciation and discovery of beauty, was supposed to remain still in the guise of immediate feeling. We have already [p. 100] touched on how abstract theories undertook to educate such a sense of taste and how it itself remained external and one-sided. Criticism at the time of these views was on the one hand deficient in universal principles; on the other hand, as the particular criticism of individual works of art, it aimed less at grounding a more definite judgement – the implements for making one being not yet available – than at advancing rather the education of taste in general. Thus this education likewise got no further than what was rather vague, and it laboured only, by reflection, so to equip feeling, as a sense of beauty, that now it could find beauty wherever and however it existed. Yet the depths of the thing remained a sealed book to taste, since these depths require not only sensing and abstract reflections, but the entirety of reason and the solidity of the spirit, while taste was directed only to the external surface on which feelings play and where one-sided principles may pass as valid. Consequently, however, so-called 'good taste' takes fright at all the deeper effects [of art] and is silent when the thing at issue comes in question and externalities and incidentals vanish. For when great passions and the movements of a profound soul are revealed, there is no longer any question of the finer distinctions of taste and its pedantic preoccupation with individual details. It feels genius striding over such ground, and, retreating before its power, finds the place too hot for itself and knows not what to do with itself.

(c) For this reason the study of works of art has given up keeping in view merely the education of taste and proposing only to exhibit taste. The *connoisseur* has taken the place of the man of taste or the judge of artistic taste. The positive side of connoisseurship, in so far as it concerns a thorough acquaintance with the whole sweep of the individual character of a work of art, we have already [pp. 99ff.] described as necessary for the study of art. For, on account of its nature, at once material and individual, the work of art issues essentially from particular conditions of the most varied sort, amongst them especially the time and place of its origin, then the specific individuality of the artist, and above all the technical development of his art. Attention to all these aspects is indispensable for a distinct and thorough insight into, and acquaintance with, a work of art, and indeed for the enjoyment of it; with them connoisseurship is principally preoccupied, and what it achieves in its way is to be accepted with gratitude. Now while such scholarship is justly counted as something essential, it still may not be taken as the single and supreme element in the relation which the spirit adopts to a work of art and to art in general. For connoisseurship, and this is its defective side, may stick at acquaintance with purely external aspects, the technical, historical, etc., and perhaps have little notion of the true nature of the work of art, or even know nothing of it at all; indeed it can even disesteem the value of deeper studies in comparison with purely positive, technical, and historical information. Yet connoisseurship, if it be of a genuine kind, does itself strive at least for specific grounds and information, and for an intelligent judgement with which after all is bound up a more precise discrimination of the different, even if partly external, aspects of a work of art and the evaluation of these.

(d) After these remarks on the modes of study occasioned by that aspect of the work of art which,

as itself a sensuous object, gave it an essential relation to men as sensuous beings, we propose now to treat this aspect in its more essential bearing on art itself, namely (α) in regard to the work of art as an object, and (β) in regard to the subjectivity of the artist, his genius, talent, etc., yet without our entering upon what in this connection can proceed only from the knowledge of art in its universal essence. For here we are not yet really on scientific ground and territory; we are still only in the province of external reflections.

(α) Of course the work of art presents itself to sensuous apprehension. It is there for sensuous feeling, external or internal, for sensuous intuition and ideas, just as nature is, whether the external nature that surrounds us, or our own sensitive nature within. After all, a speech, for example, may be addressed to sensuous ideas and feelings. But nevertheless the work of art, as a sensuous object, is not merely for *sensuous* apprehension; its standing is of such a kind that, though sensuous, it is essentially at the same time for *spiritual* apprehension; the spirit is meant to be affected by it and to find some satisfaction in it.

Now the fact that this is what the work of art is meant to be explains at once how it can in no way be a natural product or have in its natural aspect a natural vitality, whether a natural product is supposed to have a higher or a lower value than a *mere* work of art, as a work of art is often called in a depreciatory sense.

For the sensuous element in a work of art should be there only in so far as it exists for the human spirit, regardless of its existing independently as a sensuous object.

If we examine more closely in what way the sensuous is *there* for man, we find that what is sensuous can be related in various ways to the spirit.

(αα) The poorest mode of apprehension, the least adequate to spirit, is purely sensuous apprehension. It consists, in the first place, of merely looking on, hearing, feeling, etc., just as in hours of spiritual fatigue (indeed for many people at any time) it may be an amusement to wander about without thinking, just to listen here and look round there, and so on. Spirit does not stop at the mere apprehension of the external world by sight and hearing; it makes it into an object for its inner being which then is itself driven, once again in the form of sensuousness, to realize itself in things, and relates itself to them as *desire*. In this appetitive relation to the external world, man, as a sensuous individual, confronts things as being individuals; likewise he does not turn his mind to them as a thinker with universal categories; instead, in accord with individual impulses and interests, he relates himself to the objects, individuals themselves, and maintains himself in them by using and consuming them, and by sacrificing them works his own self-satisfaction. In this negative relation, desire requires for itself not merely the superficial appearance of external things, but the things themselves in their concrete physical existence. With mere pictures of the wood that it might use, or of the animals it might want to eat, desire is not served. Neither can desire let the object persist in its freedom, for its impulse drives it just to cancel this independence and freedom of external things, and to show that they are only there to be destroyed and consumed. But at the same time the person too, caught up in the individual, restricted, and nugatory interests of his desire, is neither free in himself, since he is not determined by the essential universality and rationality of his will, nor free in respect of the external world, for desire remains essentially determined by external things and related to them.

Now this relation of desire is not the one in which man stands to the work of art. He leaves it free as an object to exist on its own account; he relates himself to it without desire, as to an object which is for the contemplative side of spirit alone. Consequently the work of art, though it has sensuous existence, does not require in this respect a sensuously concrete being and a natural life; indeed it ought not to remain on this level, seeing that it is meant to satisfy purely spiritual interests and exclude all desire from itself. Hence it is true that practical desire rates organic and inorganic individual things in nature, which can serve its purpose, higher than works of art which show themselves useless to serve it and are enjoyable only by other forms of the spirit.

(ββ) A second way in which what is externally present can be *for* the spirit is, in contrast to individual sense-perception and practical desire, the purely theoretical relation to *intelligence*. The theoretical study of things is not interested in consuming them in their individuality and satisfying itself and maintaining itself sensuously by means of them, but in coming to know them in their *universality*, finding their inner essence and law, and conceiving them in accordance with their Concept. Therefore theoretical interest lets individual things alone and retreats from them as

sensuous individualities, since this sensuous individualism is not what intelligence tries to study. For the rational intelligence does not belong to the individual person as such in the way that desires do, but to him as at the same time inherently universal. Inasmuch as man relates himself to things in accordance with his universality, it is his universal reason which strives to find itself in nature and thereby to re-establish that inner essence of things which sensuous existence, though that essence is its basis, cannot immediately display. This theoretical interest, the satisfaction of which is the work of science, art does not share, however, in this scientific form, nor does it make common cause with the impulses of purely practical desires. Of course science can start from the sensuous in its individuality and possess an idea of how this individual thing comes to be there in its individual colour, shape, size, etc. Yet in that case this isolated sensuous thing has as such no further bearing on the spirit, inasmuch as intelligence goes straight for the universal, the law, the thought and concept of the object; on this account not only does it turn its back on the object in its immediate individuality, but transforms it within; out of something sensuously concrete it makes an abstraction, something thought, and so something essentially other than what that same object was in its sensuous appearance. This the artistic interest, in distinction from science, does not do. Just as the work of art proclaims itself *qua* external object in its sensuous individuality and immediate determinateness in respect of colour, shape, sound, or *qua* a single insight, etc., so the consideration of art accepts it like this too, without going so far beyond the immediate object confronting it as to endeavour to grasp, as science does, the concept of this object as a universal concept.

From the practical interest of desire, the interest of art is distinguished by the fact that it lets its object persist freely and on its own account, while desire converts it to its own use by destroying it. On the other hand, the consideration of art differs in an opposite way from theoretical consideration by scientific intelligence, since it cherishes an interest in the object in its individual existence and does not struggle to change it into its universal thought and concept.

(γγ) Now it follows from this that the sensuous must indeed be present in the work of art, but should appear only as the surface and as a pure appearance of the sensuous. For in the sensuous aspect of a work of art the spirit seeks neither the concrete material stuff, the empirical inner completeness and development of the organism which desire demands, nor the universal and purely ideal thought. What it wants is sensuous presence which indeed should remain sensuous, but liberated from the scaffolding of its purely material nature. Thereby the sensuous aspect of a work of art, in comparison with the immediate existence of things in nature, is elevated to a pure appearance, and the work of art stands in the *middle* between immediate sensuousness and ideal thought. It is *not yet* pure thought, but, despite its sensuousness, is *no longer* a purely material existent either, like stones, plants, and organic life; on the contrary, the sensuous in the work of art is itself something ideal, but which, not being ideal as thought is ideal, is still at the same time there externally as a thing. If spirit leaves the objects free yet without descending into their essential inner being (for if it did so they would altogether cease to exist for it externally as individuals), then this pure appearance of the sensuous presents itself to spirit from without as the shape, the appearance, or the sonority of things. Consequently the sensuous aspect of art is related only to the two theoretical senses of sight and hearing, while smell, taste, and touch remain excluded from the enjoyment of art. For smell, taste, and touch have to do with matter as such and its immediately sensible qualities – smell with material volatility in air, taste with the material liquefaction of objects, touch with warmth, cold, smoothness, etc. For this reason these senses cannot have to do with artistic objects, which are meant to maintain themselves in their real independence and allow of no *purely* sensuous relationship. What is agreeable for these senses is not the beauty of art. Thus art on its sensuous side deliberately produces only a shadow-world of shapes, sounds, and sights; and it is quite out of the question to maintain that, in calling works of art into existence, it is from mere impotence and because of his limitations that man produces no more than a surface of the sensuous, mere *schemata*. These sensuous shapes and sounds appear in art not merely for the sake of themselves and their immediate shape, but with the aim, in this shape, of affording satisfaction to higher spiritual interests, since they have the power to call forth from all the depths of consciousness a sound and an echo in the spirit. In this way the sensuous aspect of art is *spiritualized*, since the spirit appears in art as made *sensuous*.

(β) But precisely for this reason an art-product is only there in so far as it has taken its passage through the spirit and has arisen from spiritual productive activity. This leads on to the other question which we have to answer, namely in what way the necessary sensuous side of art is operative in the artist as his subjective productive activity. – This sort and manner of production contains in itself, as subjective activity, just the same characteristics which we found objectively present in the work of art; it must be a spiritual activity which yet contains at the same time the element of sensuousness and immediacy. Still, it is neither, on the one hand, purely mechanical work, a purely unconscious skill in sensuous manipulation or a formal activity according to fixed rules to be learnt by heart, nor, on the other hand, is it a scientific production which passes over from the sensuous to abstract ideas and thoughts or is active entirely in the element of pure thinking. In artistic production the spiritual and the sensuous aspects must be as one. For example, someone might propose to proceed in poetic composition by first apprehending the proposed theme as a prosaic thought and then putting it into poetical images, rhyme, and so forth, so that now the image would simply be hung on to the abstract reflections as an ornament and decoration. But such a procedure could only produce bad poetry, because in it there would be operative as *separate* activities what in artistic production has validity only as an undivided unity. This genuine mode of production constitutes the activity of artistic imagination.

This activity is the rational element which exists as spirit only in so far as it actively drives itself forth into consciousness, yet what it bears within itself it places before itself only in sensuous form. Thus this activity has a spiritual content which yet it configurates sensuously because only in this sensuous guise can it gain knowledge of the content. This can be compared with the characteristic mentality of a man experienced in life, or even of a man of quick wit and ingenuity, who, although he knows perfectly well what matters in life, what in substance holds men together, what moves them, what power dominates them, nevertheless has neither himself grasped this knowledge in general rules nor expounded it to others in general reflections. What fills his mind he just makes clear to himself and others in particular cases always, real or invented, in adequate examples, and so forth; for in his ideas anything and everything is shaped into concrete pictures, determined in time and space, to which there may not be wanting names and all sorts of other external circumstances. Yet such a kind of imagination rests rather on the recollection of situations lived through, of experiences enjoyed, instead of being creative itself. Recollection preserves and renews the individuality and the external fashion of the occurrence of such experiences, with all their accompanying circumstances, but does not allow the universal to emerge on its own account. But the productive fancy of an artist is the fancy of a great spirit and heart, the apprehension and creation of ideas and shapes, and indeed the exhibition of the profoundest and most universal human interests in pictorial and completely definite sensuous form.

Now from this it follows at once that, on one side, imagination rests of course on natural gifts and talent in general, because its productive activity requires sensuousness [as a medium]. We do indeed speak of 'scientific' talent too, but the sciences presuppose only the universal capacity for thinking, and thinking, instead of proceeding in a natural way, like imagination, precisely abstracts from all natural activity, and so we are righter to say that there is no specifically scientific talent, in the sense of a *merely* natural gift. On the other hand, imagination has at the same time a sort of instinct-like productiveness, in that the essential figurativeness and sensuousness of the work of art must be present in the artist as a natural gift and natural impulse, and, as an unconscious operation, must belong to the natural side of man too. Of course natural capacity is not the *whole* of talent and genius, since the production of art is also of a spiritual, self-conscious kind, yet its spirituality must somehow have in itself an element of natural picturing and shaping. Consequently almost anyone can get up to a certain point in an art, but to get beyond this point, where art proper only now begins, an inborn, higher talent for art is indispensable.

As a natural gift, this talent declares itself after all in most cases in early youth,[16] and it shows itself in the driving restlessness to shape a specific sensuous material at once in a lively and active way and to seize this mode of expression and communication as the only one, or as the most important and appropriate one. And after all an early technical facility, which up to a certain point is effortless, is a sign of inborn talent. For a sculptor everything turns into shapes, and from early years he lays hold of clay in order to model it. In short, whatever ideas such talented men have,

whatever rouses and moves them inwardly, turns at once into figure, drawing, melody, or poem.

(γ) Thirdly, and lastly, the subject-matter of art is in a certain respect also drawn from the sensuous, from nature; or, in any case, even if the subject is of a spiritual kind, it can still only be grasped by displaying spiritual things, like human relationships, in the shape of phenomena possessed of external reality.

(iii) The Aim of Art

Now the question arises of what interest or *end* man sets before himself when he produces such subject-matter in the form of works of art. This was the third point which we adduced [p. 104] with regard to the work of art, and its closer discussion will lead us on at last to the true concept of art itself.

If in this matter we cast a glance at what is commonly thought, one of the most prevalent ideas which may occur to us is

(a) the principle of the imitation of nature. According to this view, imitation, as facility in copying natural forms just as they are, in a way that corresponds to them completely, is supposed to constitute the essential end and aim of art, and the success of this portrayal in correspondence with nature is supposed to afford complete satisfaction.

(α) This definition contains, prima facie, only the purely formal aim that whatever exists already in the external world, and the manner in which it exists there, is now to be made over again as a copy, as well as a man can do with the means at his disposal. But this repetition can be seen at once to be

(αα) a *superfluous* labour, since what pictures, theatrical productions, etc., display imitatively – animals, natural scenes, human affairs – we already possess otherwise in our gardens or in our own houses or in matters within our narrower or wider circle of acquaintance. And, looked at more closely, this superfluous labour may even be regarded as a presumptuous game

(ββ) which falls far short of nature. For art is restricted in its means of portrayal, and can only produce one-sided deceptions, for example a pure appearance of reality for *one* sense only, and, in fact, if it abides by the formal aim of *mere* imitation, it provides not the reality of life but only a pretence of life. After all, the Turks, as Mahommedans, do not, as is well known, tolerate any pictures or copies of men, etc. James Bruce in his journey to Abyssinia[17] showed paintings of a fish to a Turk; at first the Turk was astonished, but quickly enough he found an answer: 'If this fish shall rise up against you on the last day and say: "You have indeed given me a body but no living soul", how will you then justify yourself against this accusation?' The prophet too, as is recorded in the Sunna,[18] said to the two women, Ommi Habiba and Ommi Selma, who had told him about pictures in Ethiopian churches: 'These pictures will accuse their authors on the day of judgment.'

Even so, there are doubtless examples of completely deceptive copying. The grapes painted by Zeuxis have from antiquity onward been styled a triumph of art and also of the principle of the imitation of nature, because living doves are supposed to have pecked at them. To this ancient example we could add the modern one of Büttner's monkey[19] which ate away a painting of a cockchafer in Rösel's *Insektbelustigungen* [Amusements of Insects] and was pardoned by his master because it had proved the excellence of the pictures in this book, although it had thus destroyed the most beautiful copy of this expensive work. But in such examples and others it must at least occur to us at once that, instead of praising works of art because they have deceived *even* doves and monkeys, we should just precisely censure those who think of exalting a work of art by predicating so miserable an effect as this as its highest and supreme quality. In sum, however, it must be said that, by mere imitation, art cannot stand in competition with nature, and, if it tries, it looks like a worm trying to crawl after an elephant.

($\gamma\gamma$) If we have regard to the continual, though comparative, failure of the copy compared with the original in nature, then there remains over as an aim nothing but taking pleasure in the conjuring trick of producing something *like* nature. And of course a man may enjoy himself in now producing over again by his own work, skill, and assiduity what otherwise is there already. But this enjoyment and admiration become in themselves the more frigid and cold, the more the copy is like the natural original, or they may even be perverted into tedium and repugnance. There are portraits which, as has been wittily said, are 'disgustingly like', and Kant,[20] in relation to this pleasure in imitation as such, cites another example, namely that we soon get tired of a man who can imitate to perfection the warbling of the nightingale (and

there are such men); as soon as it is discovered that it is a man who is producing the notes, we are at once weary of the song. We then recognize in it nothing but a trick, neither the free production of nature, nor a work of art, since from the free productive power of man we expect something quite different from such music which interests us only when, as is the case with the nightingale's warbling, it gushes forth purposeless from the bird's own life, like the voice of human feeling. In general this delight in imitative skill can always be but restricted, and it befits man better to take delight in what he produces out of himself. In this sense the discovery of any insignificant technical product has higher value, and man can be prouder of having invented the hammer, the nail, etc., than of manufacturing tricks of imitation. For this enthusiasm for copying merely as copying is to be respected as little as the trick of the man who had learnt to throw lentils through a small opening without missing. He displayed this dexterity before Alexander, but Alexander gave him a bushel of lentils as a reward for this useless and worthless art.[21]

(β) Now further, since the principle of imitation is purely formal, *objective beauty* itself disappears when this principle is made the end of art. For if it is, then there is no longer a question of the character of *what* is supposed to be imitated, but only of the correctness of the imitation. The object and content of the beautiful is regarded as a matter of complete indifference. Even if, apart from this, we speak of a difference between beauty and ugliness in relation to animals, men, localities, actions, or characters, yet according to that principle this remains a difference which does not properly belong to art, to which we have left nothing but imitation pure and simple. So that the above-mentioned lack of a criterion for the endless forms of nature leaves us, so far as the choice of objects and their beauty and ugliness are concerned, with mere subjective taste as the last word, and such taste will not be bound by rules, and is not open to dispute. And indeed if, in choosing objects for representation, we start from what people find beautiful or ugly and therefore worthy of artistic representation, i.e. from their taste, then all spheres of natural objects stand open to us, and none of them is likely to lack an admirer. For among us, e.g., it may not be every husband who finds his wife beautiful but he did before they were married, to the exclusion of all others too, and the fact that the subjective taste for this beauty has no fixed rule may be considered a good thing for both parties. If finally we look beyond single individuals and their capricious taste to the taste of *nations*, this too is of the greatest variety and contrariety. How often do we hear it said that a European beauty would not please a Chinese, or a Hottentot either, since the Chinese has inherently a totally different conception of beauty from the negro's, and his again from a European's, and so on. Indeed, if we examine the works of art of these non-European peoples, their images of the gods, for example, which have sprung from their fancy as sublime and worthy of veneration, they may present themselves to us as the most hideous idols; and while their music may sound in our ears as the most detestable noise, they on their side will regard our sculptures, pictures, and music, as meaningless or ugly.

(γ) But even if we abstract from an objective principle for art, and if beauty is to be based on subjective and individual taste, we soon nevertheless find on the side of art itself that the imitation of nature, which indeed appeared to be a universal principle and one confirmed by high authority, is not to be adopted, at least in this general and wholly abstract form. For if we look at the different arts, it will be granted at once that, even if painting and sculpture portray objects that appear to be like natural ones or whose type is essentially drawn from nature, on the other hand works of architecture, which is also one of the fine arts, can as little be called imitations of nature as poetical works can, in so far as the latter are not confined, e.g., to mere description. In any case, if we still wanted to uphold this principle in relation to these latter arts, we would at least find ourselves compelled to take a long circuitous route, because we would have to attach various conditions to the proposition and reduce the so-called 'truth' of imitation to probability at least. But with probability we would again encounter a great difficulty, namely in setting what is probable and what is not, and, apart from this, we would not wish or be able to exclude from poetry all purely arbitrary and completely fanciful inventions.

The aim of art must therefore lie in something still other than the purely mechanical imitation of what is there, which in every case can bring to birth only technical *tricks*, not *works*, of art. It is true that it is an essential element in a work of art to have a natural shape as its basis because what it portrays it displays in the form of an external and therefore also natural phenomenon. In painting, e.g., it is an important study to get to know and copy with precision the colours in their relation to one another, the effects of light, reflections, etc., as well as the forms and shapes of objects down to the last detail. It is in this respect, after all, that chiefly in recent times the principle of the imitation of nature, and of naturalism generally, has raised its head again in order to bring back to the vigour and distinctness of nature an art which had relapsed into feebleness and nebulosity; or, on the other hand, to assert the regular, immediate, and explicitly fixed sequences of nature against the manufactured and purely arbitrary conventionalism, really just as inartistic as unnatural, into which art had strayed. But whatever is right enough from one point of view in this endeavour, still the naturalism demanded is as such not the substantial and primary basis of art, and, even if external appearance in its naturalness constitutes one essential characteristic of art, still neither is the given natural world the *rule* nor is the mere imitation of external phenomena, as external, the *aim* of art.

(b) Therefore the further question arises: what, then, is the *content* of art, and why is this content to be portrayed? In this matter our consciousness confronts us with the common opinion that the task and aim of art is to bring home to our sense, our feeling, and our inspiration everything which has a place in the human spirit. That familiar saying 'nihil humani a me alienum puto'[22] art is supposed to make real in us.

Its aim therefore is supposed to consist in awakening and vivifying our slumbering feelings, inclinations, and passions of every kind, in filling the heart, in forcing the human being, educated or not, to go through the whole gamut of feelings which the human heart in its inmost and secret recesses can bear, experience, and produce, through what can move and stir the human breast in its depths and manifold possibilities and aspects, and to deliver to feeling and contemplation for its enjoyment whatever the spirit possesses of the essential and lofty in its thinking and in the Idea – the splendour of the noble, eternal, and true: moreover to make misfortune and misery, evil and guilt intelligible, to make men intimately acquainted with all that is horrible and shocking, as well as with all that is pleasurable and felicitous; and, finally, to let fancy loose in the idle plays of imagination and plunge it into the seductive magic of sensuously bewitching visions and feelings. According to this view, this universal wealth of subject-matter art is, on the one hand, to embrace in order to complete the natural experience of our external existence, and, on the other hand, to arouse those passions in general so that the experiences of life do not leave us unmoved and so that we might now acquire a receptivity for all phenomena. But [on this view] such a stimulus is not given in this field by actual experience itself, but only through the pure appearance of it, since art deceptively substitutes its productions for reality. The possibility of this deception through the pure appearance of art rests on the fact that, for man, all reality must come through the medium of perception and ideas, and only through this medium does it penetrate the heart and the will. Now here it is a matter of indifference whether a man's attention is claimed by immediate external reality or whether this happens in another way, namely through pictures, symbols, and ideas containing in themselves and portraying the material of reality. We can envisage things which are not real as if they *were* real. Therefore it remains all the same for our feelings whether it is external reality, or only the appearance of it, whereby a situation, a relation, or, in general, a circumstance of life, is brought home to us, in order to make us respond appropriately to the essence of such a matter, whether by grief or rejoicing, whether by being touched or agitated, or whether by making us go through the gamut of the feelings and passions of wrath, hatred, pity, anxiety, fear, love, reverence and admiration, honour and fame.

This arousing of all feelings in us, this drawing of the heart through all the circumstances of life, this actualizing of all these inner movements by means of a purely deceptive externally presented object is above all what is regarded, on the view we have been considering, as the proper and supreme power of art.

But now since, on this view, art is supposed to have the vocation of imposing on the heart and the imagination good and bad alike, strengthening man to the noblest ideals and yet enervating him to the most sensuous and selfish feelings of pleasure, art is given a purely formal task; and without any explicitly fixed aim would thus provide only the empty form for every possible kind of content and worth.

(*c*) In fact art does have also this formal side, namely its ability to adorn and bring before perception and feeling every possible material, just as the thinking of ratiocination can work on every possible object and mode of action and equip them with reasons and justifications. But confronted by such a multiple variety of content, we are at once forced to notice that the different feelings and ideas, which art is supposed to arouse or confirm, counteract one another, contradict and reciprocally cancel one another. Indeed, in this respect, the more art inspires to contradictory [emotions] the more it increases the contradictory character of feelings and passions and makes us stagger about like Bacchantes or even goes on, like ratiocination, to sophistry and scepticism. This variety of material itself compels us, therefore, not to stop at so formal a definition [of the aim of art], since rationality penetrates this jumbled diversity and demands to see, and know to be attained, even out of elements so contradictory, a higher and inherently more universal end. It is claimed indeed similarly that the final end of the state and the social life of men is that *all* human capacities and *all* individual powers be developed and given expression in every way and in every direction. But against so formal a view the question arises soon enough: into what *unity* are these manifold formations to be brought together, what *single* aim must they have as their fundamental concept and final end? As with the Concept of the state, so too with the Concept of art there arises the need (*a*) for a *common* end for its particular aspects, but (*b*) also for a higher *substantial* end. As such a substantial end, the first thing that occurs to reflection is the view that art has the capacity and the vocation to mitigate the ferocity of desires.

(α) In respect of this first idea, we have only to discover in what feature peculiar to art there lies the capacity to cancel rudeness and to bridle and educate impulses, inclinations, and passions. Rudeness in general is grounded in a direct selfishness of the impulses which make straight away precisely and exclusively for the satisfaction of their concupiscence. But desire is all the ruder and imperious the more, as single and restricted, it engrosses the *whole man*, so that he loses the power to tear himself free, as a universal being, from this determinateness and become aware of himself as universal. And if the man says in such a case, as may be supposed, 'The passion is stronger than *I*', then for consciousness the abstract 'I' *is* separated from the particular passion, but only in a purely formal way, since all that is pronounced with this cleavage is that, in face of the power of the passion, the 'I' as a universal is of no account whatever. Thus the ferocity of passion consists in the unity of the 'I' as universal with the restricted object of his desire, so that the man has no longer any will beyond this single passion. Now such rudeness and untamed force of passion is *prima facie* mitigated by art, in that it gives a man an idea of what he feels and achieves in such a situation. And even if art restricts itself to setting up pictures of passions for contemplation, even if indeed it were to flatter them, still there is here already a power of mitigation, since thereby a man is at least made *aware* of what otherwise he only immediately *is*. For then the man contemplates his impulses and inclinations, and while previously they carried him reflectionless away, he now sees them outside himself and already begins to be free from them because they confront him as something objective.

For this reason it may often be the case with an artist that, overtaken by grief, he mitigates and weakens for himself the intensity of his own feeling by representing it in art. Tears, even, provide some comfort; at first entirely sunk and concentrated in grief, a man may then in this direct way utter this purely inward feeling. But still more of an alleviation is the expression of one's inner state in words, pictures, sounds, and shapes. For this reason it was a good old custom at deaths and funerals to appoint wailing women in order that by its expression grief might be contemplated. Even by expressions of condolence the burden of a man's misfortune is brought before his mind; if it is much spoken about he has to reflect on it, and this alleviates his grief. And so to cry one's eyes out and to speak out has ever been regarded as a means of freeing oneself from the oppressive burden of care or at least of relieving the heart. The mitigation of the power of passions therefore has its universal ground in the fact that man is released from his immediate imprisonment in a feeling and becomes conscious of it as something external to him, to which he must now relate himself in an ideal way. Art by means of its representations, while remaining within the sensuous sphere, liberates man at the same time from the power of sensuousness. Of course we may often hear favourite phraseology about man's duty to remain in immediate unity with nature; but such unity, in its abstraction, is purely and simply rudeness and ferocity, and by dissolving this unity for man, art lifts him with gentle hands out of and above imprisonment in nature. For man's preoccupation with artistic objects remains purely contemplative, and thereby it educates, even if at first only an attention to artistic portrayals in general, later on an attention to their meaning and to a comparison with other subjects, and it opens the mind to a general consideration of them and the points of view therein involved.

(β) Now on this there follows quite logically the second characteristic that has been attributed to art as its essential aim, namely the *purification* of the passions, instruction, and *moral* improvement. For the theory that art was to curb rudeness and educate the passions, remained quite formal and general, so that it has become again a matter of what *specific* sort of education this is and what is its essential aim.

(αα) It is true that the doctrine of the purification of passion still suffers the same deficiency as the previous doctrine of the mitigation of desires, yet it does at least emphasize more closely the fact that artistic representations needed a criterion for assessing their worth or unworthiness. This criterion [on this view] is just their effectiveness in separating pure from impure in the passions. This effectiveness therefore requires a content which can exercise this purifying force, and, in so far as producing such an effect is supposed to constitute the substantial aim of art, the purifying content will have to be brought into consciousness in accordance with its *universality* and *essentiality*.

(ββ) From this latter point of view, the aim of art has been pronounced to be that it should *instruct*. On this view, on the one hand, the special character of art consists in the movement of feelings and in the satisfaction lying in this movement, lying even in fear, in pity, in grievous emotion and agitation, i.e. in the satisfying enlistment of feelings and passions, and to that extent in a gusto, a pleasure, and delight in artistic subjects, in their representation and effect. But, on the other hand, this aim of art is supposed to have its higher criterion only in its instructiveness, in *fabula docet*,[. . .] and so in the useful influence which the work of art may exert on the individual. In this respect the Horatian aphorism *Et prodesse volunt et delectare poetae*[23] contains, concentrated in a few words, what later has been elaborated in an infinite degree, diluted, and made into a view of art reduced to the uttermost extreme of shallowness. – Now in connection with such instruction we must ask at once whether it is supposed to be contained in the work of art directly or indirectly, explicitly or implicitly. If, in general, what is at issue is a universal and non-contingent aim, then this end and aim, in view of the essentially spiritual nature of art, can itself only be a spiritual one, and moreover one which is not contingent but absolute. This aim in relation to teaching could only consist in bringing into consciousness, by means of the work of art, an absolutely essential spiritual content. From this point of view we must assert that the more highly art is ranked the more it has to adopt such a content into itself and find only in the essence of that content the criterion of whether what is expressed is appropriate or not. Art has in fact been the first *instructress* of peoples.

If, however, the aim of instruction is treated as an aim in such a way that the universal nature of the content represented is supposed to emerge and be explained directly and explicitly as an abstract proposition, prosaic reflection, or general doctrine, and not to be contained implicitly and only indirectly in the concrete form of a work of art, then by this separation the sensuous pictorial form, which is precisely what alone makes a work of art a work of art, becomes a useless appendage, a veil and a pure appearance, expressly pronounced to be a mere veil and a mere pure appearance. But thereby the nature of the work of art itself is distorted. For the work of art should put before our eyes a content, not in its universality as such, but one whose universality has been absolutely individualized and sensuously particularized. If the work of art does not proceed from this principle but emphasizes the universality with the aim of [providing] abstract instruction, then the pictorial and sensuous element is only an external and superfluous adornment, and the work of art is broken up internally, form and content no longer appear as coalesced. In that event the sensuously individual and the spiritually universal have become external to one another.

Now, further, if the aim of art is restricted to this usefulness for instruction, the other side, pleasure, entertainment, and delight, is pronounced explicitly to be inessential, and ought to have its substance only in the utility of the doctrine on which it is attendant. But what is implied here at the same time is that art does not carry its vocation, end, and aim in itself, but that its essence lies in something else to which it serves as a means. In that event art is only one amongst several means which are proved useful for and applied to the end of instruction. But this brings us to the boundary at which art is supposed to cease to be an end in itself, because it is reduced either to a mere entertaining game or a mere means of instruction.

(γγ) This boundary is most sharply marked if in turn a question is raised about a supreme aim and end for the sake of which passions are to be purified and men instructed. As this aim, *moral* betterment has often been adduced in recent times, and the end of art has been placed in the function of preparing inclinations and impulses for moral perfection and of leading them to this final end. This idea unites instruction with purification, inasmuch as art, by affording an insight into genuinely moral goodness and so by instruction, at the same time incites to purification and only so is to accomplish the betterment of mankind as its utility and its highest aim.

Now as regards art in relation to moral betterment, the same must be said, in the first place, about the aim of art as instruction. It is readily granted that art may not take immorality and the intention of promoting it as its principle. But it is one thing to make immorality the express aim of the presentation, and another not to take morality as that aim. From every genuine work of art a good moral may be drawn, yet of course all depends on interpretation and on *who* draws the moral.[24] We can hear the most immoral presentations defended on the ground that one must be acquainted with evil and sins in order to act morally; conversely, it has been said that the portrayal of Mary Magdalene, the beautiful sinner who afterwards repented, has seduced many into sin, because art makes repentance look so beautiful, and sinning must come before repentance. But the doctrine of moral betterment, carried through logically, is not content with holding that a moral may be pointed from a work of art; on the contrary, it would want the moral instruction to shine forth clearly as the substantial aim of the work of art, and indeed would expressly permit the presentation of none but moral subjects, moral characters, actions, and events. For art can choose its subjects, and is thus distinct from history or the sciences, which have their material given to them.

In order, in this aspect of the matter, to be able to form a thorough estimate of the view that the aim of art is moral, we must first ask what specific standpoint of morality this view professes. If we keep more clearly in view the standpoint of the 'moral' as we have to take it in the best sense of the word today, it is soon obvious that its concept does not immediately coincide with what apart from it we generally call virtue, conventional life, respectability, etc. From this point of view a conventionally virtuous man is not *ipso facto moral*, because to be moral needs *reflection*, the specific consciousness of what accords with duty, and action on this preceding consciousness. Duty itself is the law of the will, a law which man nevertheless freely lays

down out of himself, and then he ought to determine himself to this duty for the sake of duty and
its fulfilment, by doing good solely from the conviction he has won that it is the good.[...] But this
law, the duty chosen for duty's sake as a guide out
of free conviction and inner conscience, and then
carried out, is by itself the abstract universal of the
will and this has its direct opposite in nature, in
sensuous impulses, selfish interests, passions, and
everything grouped together under the name of
feeling and emotion. In this opposition one side
is regarded as *cancelling* the other, and since both
are present in the subject as opposites, he has a
choice, since his decision is made from within,
between following either the one or the other.
But such a decision is a *moral* one, from the standpoint we are considering, and so is the action
carried out in accordance with it, but only if it is
done, on the one hand, from a free conviction of
duty, and, on the other hand, by the conquest not
only of the particular will, natural impulses, inclinations, passions, etc., but also of noble feelings and
higher impulses. For the modern moralistic view
starts from the fixed opposition between the will in
its spiritual universality and the will in its sensuous
natural particularity; and it consists not in the
complete reconciliation of these opposed sides,
but in their reciprocal battle against one another,
which involves the demand that impulses in their
conflict with duty must give way to it.[...]

Now this opposition does not arise for consciousness in the restricted sphere of moral action
alone; it emerges in a thoroughgoing cleavage and
opposition between what is *absolute* and what is
external reality and existence. Taken quite
abstractly, it is the opposition of universal and
particular, when each is fixed over against the
other on its own account in the same way; more
concretely, it appears in nature as the opposition of
the abstract law to the abundance of individual
phenomena, each explicitly with its own character;
in the spirit it appears as the contrast between the
sensuous and the spiritual in man, as the battle of
spirit against flesh, of duty for duty's sake, of the
cold command against particular interest, warmth
of heart, sensuous inclinations and impulses,
against the individual disposition in general; as
the harsh opposition between inner freedom and
the necessity of external nature, further as the
contradiction between the dead inherently empty
concept, and the full concreteness of life, between
theory or subjective thinking, and objective existence and experience.

These are oppositions which have not been
invented at all by the subtlety of reflection or the
pedantry of philosophy; in numerous forms they
have always preoccupied and troubled the human
consciousness, even if it is modern culture that has
first worked them out most sharply and driven
them up to the peak of harshest contradiction.
Spiritual culture, the modern intellect, produces
this opposition in man which makes him an amphi-
bious animal, because he now has to live in two
worlds which contradict one another. The result is
that now consciousness wanders about in this contradiction, and, driven from one side to the other,
cannot find satisfaction for itself in either the one
or the other. For on the one side we see man
imprisoned in the common world of reality and
earthly temporality, borne down by need and poverty, hard pressed by nature, enmeshed in matter,
sensuous ends and their enjoyment, mastered and
carried away by natural impulses and passions. On
the other side, he lifts himself to eternal ideas, to a
realm of thought and freedom, gives to himself, as
will, universal laws and prescriptions, strips the
world of its enlivened and flowering reality and
dissolves it into abstractions, since the spirit now
upholds its right and dignity only by mishandling
nature and denying its right, and so retaliates on
nature the distress and violence which it has suffered from it itself. But for modern culture and its
intellect this discordance in life and consciousness
involves the demand that such a contradiction be
resolved. Yet the intellect cannot cut itself free
from the rigidity of these oppositions; therefore
the solution remains for consciousness a mere
ought, and the present and reality move only in
the unrest of a hither and thither which seeks a
reconciliation without finding one. Thus the question then arises whether such a universal and thoroughgoing opposition, which cannot get beyond a
mere ought and a postulated solution, is in general
the absolute truth and supreme end. If general
culture has run into such a contradiction, it
becomes the task of philosophy to supersede the
oppositions, i.e. to show that neither the one alternative in its abstraction, nor the other in the like
one-sidedness, possesses truth, but that they are
both self-dissolving; that truth lies only in the
reconciliation and mediation of both, and that this
mediation is no mere demand, but what is absolutely accomplished and is ever self-accomplishing.
This insight coincides immediately with the ingenuous faith and will which does have precisely this
dissolved opposition steadily present to its view,

and in action makes it its end and achieves it. Philosophy affords a reflective insight into the essence of the opposition only in so far as it shows how truth is just the dissolving of opposition and, at that, not in the sense, as may be supposed, that the opposition and its two sides *do not exist at all*, but that they exist reconciled.

Now since the ultimate end, moral betterment, has pointed to a higher standpoint, we will have to vindicate this higher standpoint for art too. Thereby the false position, already noticed, is at once abandoned, the position, namely, that art has to serve as a means to moral purposes, and the moral end of the world in general, by instructing and improving, and thus has its substantial aim, not in itself, but in something else. If on this account we now continue to speak of a final end and aim, we must in the first place get rid of the perverse idea which, in the question about an end, clings to the accessory meaning of the question, namely that it is one about utility. The perversity lies here in this, that in that case the work of art is supposed to have a bearing on something else which is set before our minds as the essential thing or as what ought to be, so that then the work of art would have validity only as a useful tool for realizing this end which is independently valid on its own account outside the sphere of art. Against this we must maintain that art's vocation is to unveil the *truth* in the form of sensuous artistic configuration, to set forth the reconciled opposition just mentioned, and so to have its end and aim in itself, in this very setting forth and unveiling. For other ends, like instruction, purification, bettering, financial gain, struggling for fame and honour, have nothing to do with the work of art as such, and do not determine its nature.

[. . .]

Part II
Development of the Ideal into the Particular Forms of Art

Introduction

What up to this point we have dealt with, in Part I, concerned the actuality of the Idea of the beautiful as the Ideal of art, but [no matter] under how many aspects we also developed the Concept of the ideal

work of art, still all our distinctions bore only on the ideal work of art in *general*. But, like the Idea, the Idea of the beautiful is a totality of essential differences which must issue as such and be actualized. Their actualization we may call on the whole the *particular forms* of art, as the development of what is implicit in the Concept of the Ideal and comes into existence through art. Yet if we speak of these art forms as different species of the Ideal, we may not take 'species' in the ordinary sense of the word, as if here the particular forms came from without to the Idea as their universal genus and had become modifications of it: on the contrary, 'species' should mean nothing here but the distinctive and therefore more concrete determinations of the Idea of the beautiful and the Ideal of art itself. The general character of [artistic] representation, i.e., is here made determinate not from without but in itself through its own Concept, so that it is this Concept which is spread out into a totality of particular modes of artistic formation.

Now, in more detail, the forms of art, as the actualizing and unfolding of the beautiful, find their origin in the Idea itself, in the sense that through them the Idea presses on to representation and reality, and whenever it is explicit to itself either only in its abstract determinacy or else in its concrete totality, it also brings itself into appearance in another real formation. This is because the Idea as such is only truly Idea as developing itself explicitly by its own activity; and since as Ideal it is immediate appearance, and indeed with its appearance is the identical Idea of the beautiful, so also at every particular stage on which the Ideal treads the road of its unfolding there is immediately linked with every *inner* determinacy another *real* configuration. It is therefore all one whether we regard the advance in this development as an inner advance of the Idea in itself or of the shape in which it gives itself existence. Each of these two sides is immediately bound up with the other. The consummation of the Idea as content appears therefore simultaneously as also the consummation of form; and conversely the deficiencies of the artistic shape correspondingly prove to be a deficiency of the Idea which constitutes the inner meaning of the external appearance and in that appearance becomes real to itself. Thus if in this Part we encounter art-forms at first which are still inadequate in comparison with the true Ideal, this is not the sort of case in which people ordinarily speak of unsuccessful works of art which either express nothing or lack the capacity to achieve what they are supposed to represent; on the contrary, the specific shape which every content of the Idea gives to itself in the particular forms of art is always adequate to that content, and the deficiency or consummation lies only in the relatively untrue or true determinateness in which and as which the Idea is explicit to itself. This is because the content must be true and concrete in itself before it can find its truly beautiful shape.

In this connection, as we saw already in the general division of the subject [. . .], we have three chief art-forms to consider:

(i) The *Symbolic*. In this the Idea still *seeks* its genuine expression in art, because in itself it is still abstract and indeterminate and therefore does not have its adequate manifestation on and in itself, but finds itself confronted by what is external to itself, external things in nature and human affairs. Now since it has only an immediate inkling of its own abstractions in this objective world or drives itself with its undetermined universals into a concrete existence, it corrupts and falsifies the shapes that it finds confronting it. This is because it can grasp them only arbitrarily, and therefore, instead of coming to a complete identification, it comes only to an accord, and even to a still abstract harmony, between meaning and shape; in this neither completed nor to be completed mutual formation, meaning and shape present, equally with their affinity, their mutual externality, foreignness, and incompatibility.

(ii) But, secondly, the Idea, in accordance with its essential nature, does not stop at the abstraction and indeterminacy of universal thoughts but is in itself free infinite subjectivity and apprehends this in its actuality as spirit. Now spirit, as free subject, is determined through and by itself, and in this self-determination, and also in its own nature, has that external shape, adequate to itself, with which it can close as with its absolutely due reality. On this entirely harmonious unity of content and form, the second art-form, the *classical*, is based. Yet if the consummation of this unity is to become actual, spirit, in so far as it is made a topic for art, must not yet be the purely absolute spirit which finds its adequate existence only in spirituality and inwardness, but the spirit which is still particular and therefore burdened with an abstraction. That is to say, the free subject, which classical art configurates outwardly, appears indeed as essentially universal and therefore freed from all the accident

and mere particularity of the inner life and the outer world, but at the same time as filled solely with a universality particularized within itself. This is because the external shape is, as such, an external determinate particular shape, and for complete fusion [with a content] it can only present again in itself a specific and therefore restricted content, while too it is only the inwardly particular spirit which can appear perfectly in an external manifestation and be bound up with that in an inseparable unity.

Here art has reached its own essential nature by bringing the Idea, as spiritual individuality, directly into harmony with its bodily reality in such a perfect way that external existence now for the first time no longer preserves any independence in contrast with the meaning which it is to express, while conversely the inner [meaning], in its shape worked out for our vision, shows there only itself and in it is related to itself affirmatively.[25]

(iii) But, thirdly, when the Idea of the beautiful is comprehended as absolute spirit, and therefore as the spirit which is free in its own eyes, it is no longer completely realized in the external world, since its true determinate being it has only in itself as spirit. It therefore dissolves that classical unification of inwardness and external manifestation and takes flight out of externality back into itself. This provides the fundamental typification of the *romantic* art-form; the content of this form, on account of its free spirituality, demands more than what representation in the external world and the bodily can supply; in romantic art the shape is externally more or less indifferent, and thus that art reintroduces, in an opposite way from the symbolic, the separation of content and form.

In this way, symbolic art *seeks* that perfect unity of inner meaning and external shape which classical art *finds* in the presentation of substantial individuality to sensuous contemplation, and which romantic art *transcends* in its superior spirituality.

[. . .]

(c) The End of the Romantic Form of Art

Art, as it has been under our consideration hitherto, had as its basis the unity of meaning and shape and so the unity of the artist's subjective activity with his topic and work. Looked at more closely, it was the specific kind of this unification [at each stage] which provided, for the content and its corresponding portrayal, the substantial norm penetrating all artistic productions.

In this matter we found at the beginning of art, in the East, that the spirit was not yet itself explicitly free; it still sought for its Absolute in nature and therefore interpreted nature as in itself divine. Later on, the vision of classical art represented the Greek gods as naïve and inspired, yet even so essentially as individuals burdened with the natural human form as with an *affirmative* feature. Romantic art for the first time deepened the spirit in its own inwardness, in contrast to which the flesh, external reality, and the world in general was at first posited as *negative*, even though the spirit and the Absolute had to appear in this element alone; yet at last this element could be given validity for itself again in a more and more positive way.

(α) These ways of viewing the world constitute religion, the substantial spirit of peoples and ages, and are woven into, not art alone, but all the other spheres of the living present at all periods. Now just as every man is a child of his time in every activity, whether political, religious, or scientific, and just as he has the task of bringing out the essential content and the therefore necessary form of that time, so it is the vocation of art to find for the spirit of a people the artistic expression corresponding to it. Now so long as the artist is bound up with the specific character of such a world-view and religion, in immediate identity with it and with firm faith in it, so long is he genuinely in earnest with this material and its representation; i.e. this material remains for him the infinite and true element in his own consciousness – a material with which he lives in an original unity as part of his inmost self, while the form in which he exhibits it is for him as artist the final, necessary, and supreme manner of bringing before our contemplation the Absolute and the soul of objects in general. By the substance of his material, a substance immanent in himself, he is tied down to the specific mode of its exposition. For in that case the material, and therefore the form belonging to it, the artist carries immediately in himself as the proper essence of his existence which he does not imagine for himself but which he *is*; and therefore he only has the task of making this truly essential element objective to himself, to present and develop it in a living way out of his own resources. Only in that event is the artist completely inspired by his material and its presentation; and his inventions are no product of caprice, they originate in him, out of him, out of this substantial

ground, this stock, the content of which is not at rest until through the artist it acquires an individual shape adequate to its inner essence. If, on the other hand, we nowadays propose to make the subject of a statue or a painting a Greek god, or, Protestants as we are today, the Virgin Mary, we are not seriously in earnest with this material. It is the innermost faith which we lack here, even if the artist in days when faith was still unimpaired did not exactly need to be what is generally called a pious man, for after all in every age artists have not as a rule been the most pious of men! The requirement is only this, that for the artist the content [of his work] shall constitute the substance, the inmost truth, of his consciousness and make his chosen mode of presentation necessary. For the artist in his production is at the same time a creature of nature, his skill is a *natural* talent; his work is not the pure activity of comprehension which confronts its material entirely and unites itself with it in free thoughts, in pure thinking; on the contrary, the artist, not yet released from his *natural* side, is united *directly* with the subject-matter, believes in it, and is identical with it in accordance with his very own self. The result is then that the artist is entirely absorbed in the object; the work of art proceeds entirely out of the undivided inwardness and force of genius; the production is firm and unwavering, and in it the full intensity [of creation] is preserved. This is the fundamental condition of art's being present in its integrity.

(β) On the other hand, in the position we have been forced to assign to art in the course of its development, the whole situation has altogether altered. This, however, we must not regard as a mere accidental misfortune suffered by art from without owing to the distress of the times, the sense for the prosaic, lack of interest, etc.; on the contrary, it is the effect and the progress of art itself which, by bringing before our vision as an object its own indwelling material, at every step along this road makes its own contribution to freeing art from the content represented. What through art or thinking we have before our physical or spiritual eye as an object has lost all absolute interest for us if it has been put before us so completely that the content is exhausted, that everything is revealed, and nothing obscure or inward is left over any more. For interest is to be found only in the case of lively activity [of mind]. The spirit only occupies itself with objects so long as there is something secret, not revealed, in them. This is the case so long as the material is identical with the substance of our own being. But if the essential world-views implicit in the concept of art, and the range of the content belonging to these, are in every respect revealed by art, then art has got rid of this content which on every occasion was determinate for a particular people, a particular age, and the true need to resume it again is awakened only with the need to turn *against* the content that was alone valid hitherto; thus in Greece Aristophanes rose up against his present world, and Lucian against the whole of the Greek past, and in Italy and Spain, when the Middle Ages were closing, Ariosto and Cervantes began to turn against chivalry.

Now contrasted with the time in which the artist owing to his nationality and his period stands with the substance of his being within a specific world-view and its content and forms of portrayal, we find an altogether opposed view which in its complete development is of importance only in most recent times. In our day, in the case of almost all peoples, criticism, the cultivation of reflection, and, in our German case, freedom of thought have mastered the artists too, and have made them, so to say, a *tabula rasa* in respect of the material and the form of their productions, after the necessary particular stages of the romantic art-form have been traversed. Bondage to a particular subject-matter and a mode of portrayal suitable for this material alone are for artists today something past, and art therefore has become a free instrument which the artist can wield in proportion to his subjective skill in relation to any material of whatever kind. The artist thus stands above specific consecrated forms and configurations and moves freely on his own account, independent of the subject-matter and mode of conception in which the holy and eternal was previously made visible to human apprehension. No content, no form, is any longer immediately identical with the inwardness, the nature, the unconscious substantial essence of the artist; every material may be indifferent to him if only it does not contradict the formal law of being simply beautiful and capable of artistic treatment. Today there is no material which stands in and for itself above this relativity, and even if one matter be raised above it, still there is at least no absolute need for its representation by *art*. Therefore the artist's attitude to his topic is on the whole much the same as the dramatist's who brings on the scene and delineates different characters who are strangers to him. The artist does still put his genius into them, he weaves his web

out of his own resources but only out of what is purely universal or quite accidental there, whereas its more detailed individualization is not his. For this purpose he needs his supply of pictures, modes of configuration, earlier forms of art which, taken in themselves, are indifferent to him and only become important if they seem to him to be those most suitable for precisely this or that material. Moreover, in most arts, especially the visual arts, the topic comes to the artist from the outside; he works to a commission, and in the case of sacred or profane stories, or scenes, portraits, ecclesiastical buildings, etc., he has only to see what he can make of his commission. For, however much he puts his heart into the given topic, that topic yet always remains to him a material which is not in itself directly the substance of his own consciousness. It is therefore no help to him to adopt again, as that substance, so to say, past world-views, i.e. to propose to root himself firmly in one of these ways of looking at things, e.g. to turn Roman Catholic as in recent times many have done for art's sake in order to give stability to their mind and to give the character of something absolute to the specifically limited character of their artistic product in itself. The artist need not be forced first to settle his accounts with his mind or to worry about the salvation of his own soul. From the very beginning, before he embarks on production, his great and free soul must know and possess its own ground, must be sure of itself and confident in itself. The great artist today needs in particular the free development of the spirit; in that development all superstition, and all faith which remains restricted to determinate forms of vision and presentation, is degraded into mere aspects and features. These the free spirit has mastered because he sees in them no absolutely sacrosanct conditions for his exposition and mode of configuration, but ascribes value to them only on the strength of the higher content which in the course of his re-creation he puts into them as adequate to them.

In this way every form and every material is now at the service and command of the artist whose talent and genius is explicitly freed from the earlier limitation to one specific art-form.

(γ) But if in conclusion we ask about the content and the forms which can be considered as *peculiar* to this stage of our inquiry in virtue of its general standpoint, the answer is as follows.

The universal forms of art had a bearing above all on the absolute truth which art attains, and they had the origin of their particular differences in the specific interpretation of what counted for consciousness as absolute and carried in itself the principle for its mode of configuration. In this matter we have seen in symbolic art natural meanings appearing as the *content*, natural things and human personifications as the *form* of the representation; in classical art spiritual individuality, but as a corporeal, not inwardized, present over which there stood the abstract necessity of fate; in romantic art spirituality with the subjectivity immanent therein, for the inwardness of which the external shape remained accidental. In this final art-form too, as in the earlier ones, the Divine is the absolute subject-matter of art. But the Divine had to objectify itself, determine itself, and therefore proceed out of itself into the secular content of subjective personality. At first the infinity of personality lay in honour, love, and fidelity, and then later in particular individuality, in the specific character which coalesced with the particular content of human existence. Finally this cohesion with such a specific limitation of subject-matter was cancelled by humour which could make every determinacy waver and dissolve and therefore made it possible for art to transcend itself. Yet in this self-transcendence art is nevertheless a withdrawal of man into himself, a descent into his own breast, whereby art strips away from itself all fixed restriction to a specific range of content and treatment, and makes *Humanus* its new holy of holies: i.e. the depths and heights of the human heart as such, mankind in its joys and sorrows, its strivings, deeds, and fates. Herewith the artist acquires his subject-matter in himself and is the human spirit actually self-determining and considering, meditating, and expressing the infinity of its feelings and situations: nothing that can be living in the human breast is alien to that spirit any more.[26] This is a subject-matter which does not remain determined artistically in itself and on its own account; on the contrary, the specific character of the topic and its outward formation is left to capricious invention, yet no interest is excluded – for art does not need any longer to represent only what is absolutely at home at one of its specific stages, but everything in which man as such is capable of being at home.

In face of this breadth and variety of material we must above all make the demand that the actual presence of the spirit today shall be displayed at the same time throughout the mode of treating this material. The modern artist, it is true, may associ-

ate himself with the classical age and with still more ancient times; to be a follower of Homer, even if the last one, is fine, and productions reflecting the medieval veering to romantic art will have their merits too; but the universal validity, depth, and special idiom of some material is one thing, its mode of treatment another. No Homer, Sophocles, etc., no Dante, Ariosto, or Shakespeare can appear in our day; what was so magnificently sung, what so freely expressed, has been expressed; these are materials, ways of looking at them and treating them which have been sung once and for all. Only the present is fresh, the rest is paler and paler.

The French must be reproached on historical grounds, and criticized on the score of beauty, for presenting Greek and Roman heroes, Chinese, and Peruvians, as French princes and princesses and for ascribing to them the motives and views of the time of Louis XIV and XV; yet, if only these motives and views had been deeper and finer in themselves, drawing them into present-day works of art would not be exactly bad. On the contrary, all materials, whatever they be and from whatever period and nation they come, acquire their artistic truth only when imbued with living and contemporary interest. It is in this interest that artistic truth fills man's breast, provides his own mirror-image, and brings truth home to our feelings and imagination. It is the appearance and activity of imperishable humanity in its many-sided significance and endless all-round development which in this reservoir of human situations and feelings can now constitute the absolute content of our art.

If after thus determining in a general way the subject-matter peculiar to this stage, we now look back at what we have considered in conclusion as the forms of the dissolution of romantic art, we have stressed principally how art falls to pieces, on the one hand, into the imitation of external objectivity in all its contingent shapes; on the other hand, however, into the liberation of subjectivity, in accordance with its inner contingency, in humour. Now, finally, still within the material indicated above, we may draw attention to a coalescence of these extremes of romantic art. In other words, just as in the advance from symbolic to classical art we considered the transitional forms of image, simile, epigram, etc., so here in romantic art we have to make mention of a similar transitional form. In those earlier modes of treatment the chief thing was that inner meaning and external shape fell apart from one another, a cleavage partly superseded by the subjective activity of the artist and converted, particularly in epigram, so far as possible into an identification. Now romantic art was from the beginning the deeper disunion of the inwardness which was finding its satisfaction in itself and which, since objectivity does not completely correspond with the spirit's inward being, remained broken or indifferent to the objective world. In the course of romantic art this opposition developed up to the point at which we had to arrive at an exclusive interest, either in contingent externality or in equally contingent subjectivity. But if this satisfaction in externality or in the subjective portrayal is intensified, according to the principle of romantic art, into the heart's deeper immersion in the object, and if, on the other hand, what matters to humour is the object and its configuration within its subjective reflex, then we acquire thereby a growing intimacy with the object, a sort of *objective* humour. Yet such an intimacy can only be partial and can perhaps be expressed only within the compass of a song or only as part of a greater whole. For if it were extended and carried through within objectivity, it would necessarily become action and event and an objective presentation of these. But what we may regard as necessary here is rather a sensitive abandonment of the heart in the object, which is indeed unfolded but remains a *subjective* spirited movement of imagination and the heart – a fugitive notion, but one which is not purely accidental and capricious but an inner movement of the spirit devoted entirely to its object and retaining it as its content and interest.

In this connection we may contrast such final blossomings of art with the old Greek epigram in which this form appeared in its first and simplest shape. The form meant here displays itself only when to talk of the object is not just to name it, not an inscription or epigraph which merely says in general terms what the object is, but only when there are added a deep feeling, a felicitous witticism, an ingenious reflection, and an intelligent movement of imagination which vivify and expand the smallest detail through the way that poetry treats it. But such poems to or about something, a tree, a mill-lade, the spring, etc., about things animate or inanimate, may be of quite endless variety and arise in any nation, yet they remain of a subordinate kind and, in general, readily become lame. For especially when reflection and speech have been developed, anyone may be struck in connection with most objects and circumstances by some

fancy or other which he now has skill enough to express, just as anyone is good at writing a letter. With such a general sing-song, often repeated even if with new nuances, we soon become bored. Therefore at this stage what is especially at stake is that the heart, with its depth of feeling, and the spirit and a rich consciousness shall be entirely absorbed in the circumstances, situation, etc., tarry there, and so make out of the object something new, beautiful, and intrinsically valuable.

A brilliant example of this, even for the present and for the subjective spiritual depth of today, is afforded especially by the Persians and Arabs in the eastern splendour of their images, in the free bliss of their imagination which deals with its objects entirely contemplatively. The Spaniards and Italians too have done excellent work of this kind. Klopstock does say[27] of Petrarch: 'Petrarch sang songs of his Laura, beautiful to their admirer, but to the lover – nothing.' Yet Klopstock's love-poems are full only of moral reflections, pitiable longing, and strained passion for the happiness of immortality – whereas in Petrarch we admire the freedom of the inherently ennobled feeling which, however much it expresses desire for the beloved, is still satisfied in itself. For the desire, the passion, cannot be missing in the sphere of these subjects, provided it be confined to wine and love, the tavern and the glass, just as, after all, the Persian pictures are of extreme voluptuousness. But in its subjective interest imagination here removes the object altogether from the scope of practical desire; it has an interest only in this imaginative occupation, which is satisfied in the freest way with its hundreds of changing turns of phrase and conceits, and plays in the most ingenious manner with joy and sorrow alike. Amongst modern poets those chiefly possessed of this equally ingenious freedom of imagination, but also of its subjectively more heartfelt depth, are Rückert, and Goethe in his *West-östliche Divan*. Goethe's poems in the *Divan* are particularly and essentially different from his earlier ones. In *Wilkommen und Abschied* [Welcome and Farewell], e.g., the language and the depiction are beautiful indeed, and the feeling is heartfelt, but otherwise the situation is quite ordinary, the conclusion trivial, and imagination and its freedom has added nothing further. Totally different is the poem called *Wiederfinden* [Meeting again] in the *Divan*. Here love is transferred wholly into the imagination, its movement, happiness, and bliss. In general, in similar productions of this kind we have before us no subjective longing, no being in love, no desire, but a pure delight in the topics, an inexhaustible self-yielding of imagination, a harmless play, a freedom in toying alike with rhyme and ingenious metres – and, with all this, a depth of feeling and a cheerfulness of the inwardly self-moving heart which through the serenity of the outward shape lift the soul high above all painful entanglement in the restrictions of the real world.

With this we may close our consideration of the particular forms into which the ideal of art has been spread in the course of its development. I have made these forms the subject of a rather extensive investigation in order to exhibit the content out of which too their mode of portrayal has been derived. For it is the content which, as in all human work, so also in art is decisive. In accordance with its essential nature, art has nothing else for its function but to set forth in an adequate sensuous present what is itself inherently rich in content, and the philosophy of art must make it its chief task to comprehend in thought what this fullness of content and its beautiful mode of appearance are.

Notes

1   *Ars Poetica*, 343: 'He gets all applause who has mingled the useful with the pleasant' etc.
2   Ps. 37:3.
3   1762. By Henry Home, Lord Kames, 1698–1782.
4   Charles Batteux (1713–80) was a prolific writer, mostly about classical authors. But Hegel is doubtless referring to *Les Beaux Arts réduits à un même principe* (1746). See also K. W. Ramler, 1725–98. His *Introduction to the Beaux Arts* is his translation of part of Batteux's *Cours de belles-lettres*, amplified and annotated by himself (1762).
5   Since this is the first of Hegel's many mentions of Goethe in these lectures, it may be as well to recall that Goethe (1749–1832) was Hegel's senior by eleven years and outlived him by a year. Hegel knew him well and often visited him in Weimar. Goethe thought highly of Hegel but wished that he could express himself more clearly. Others have had a similar wish.
6   1824–36 – History of the *bildenden* arts in Greece. Bosanquet [...], p. 67, tentatively suggests 'formative' as a translation of *bildenden*. But all the arts are 'formative' in one way or another. Hegel refers often to the *bildenden* arts, and he means by them architecture, sculpture, and painting, as distinct from music and poetry. These three arts are collectively referred to in English as the 'visual' arts, and I have therefore used this word to render *bildenden*. E. Panofsky, *Meaning in the Visual Arts* (Peregrine Books, 1970), does not mention Hegel, but the book contains a good deal of material which illuminates Hegel's discussion of these arts.
7   A periodical conducted by Schiller, 1795–8. Hirt (1759–1839) [...] was a professor of archaeology in Berlin, and Hegel was friendly with him.
8   A. R. Mengs, 1728–79. J. J. Winckelmann, 1717–68, frequently mentioned below.
9   The usual works of reference give no clue to the source of this quotation. Probably it comes from Meyer's book (see p. 100 above).
10 i.e. finding particulars in the universal, and the universal diversified in the particulars.
11 i.e. assume that it has been demonstrated.
12 Hegel may be thinking of Mozart. But see below, p. 112. He could have mentioned Mendelssohn but he was blind to contemporary composers as others have been and perhaps are.
13 1729–86. *Über die Empfindungen* (1755) or *Beirachtungen über das Erhabene u.s.w.* (1757).
14 'You can be afraid of all sorts of things, but being afraid does not determine what you are afraid of' (Bosanquet's note [...], p. 98).
15 This is obscure, but the meaning would seem to be that morality, justice, etc., vanish when contracted into the circle of my private feeling which is abstract or ill defined in comparison with their concreteness.
16 Hegel either changed his mind on this subject or did not make himself clear. See p. 106 [...].
17 *Travels to Discover the Source of the Nile* (3rd edn., London, 1813, vol. vi, pp. 526–7). Hegel quotes from memory, and usually inaccurately, but here he has given the gist of the story accurately enough for his purpose.
18 The Sunna is a body of traditions incorporating the history of Mahomet's life and so is a sort of supplement to the Koran.
19 For Zeuxis see, e.g., Pliny, *Natural History*, xxxv. 36. (J. F.) Blumenbach (1752–1840) told a story of an old fellow-student of Linnaeus (1707–78) called Büttner [? C. W., 1716–1801, professor in Göttingen] who put all his money into books and acquired a copy of Rösel's book with coloured plates, 'the most beautiful thing he had ever seen' etc. (Lasson, p. 30). A. J. Rösel, 1705–59, published his book in parts, 1746–55.
20 *Critique of Judgment*, part i, § 42.
21 The source of this story I have been unable to trace.
22 Terence: *Heauton Timorumenos*, I. i. 25: 'I count nothing human indifferent to me.' As usual, Hegel quotes inaccurately.

23 *Ars Poetica*, 333: 'Poets wish alike to benefit and to please.'

24 e.g., for one reader the moral of Goethe's *Elective Affinities* is approval of marriage, while for another reader it is disapproval (G. H. Lewes, *Life of Goethe*, bk. VII, ch. iv). In a work of art, as in life, the greater a man's character the more are different interpretations put on it by different people.

25 The translation of this paragraph rests on accepting Hotho's text, and rejecting Bassenge's emendation of it.

26 Hegel is obviously alluding to the familiar line of Terence. See [n. 22].

27 In *Die künftige Geliebte* (The Future Sweetheart), 1747.

5

The Philosophy of Art

Friedrich Wilhelm Joseph von Schelling

Introduction

The methodical study or science of art can first of all mean the historical construction of art.[1] In this sense it requires as its necessary external condition the direct evaluation of extant monuments and examples. Since such evaluation is generally possible with regard to literary works, such science in this regard, as philology, is expressly included among the objects of academic discussion. In spite of this, nothing is taught less often at universities than philology in this sense, though this cannot surprise us, since philology is just as much an art as is poesy, and the philologist no less than the poet must be born, not made.

The idea of a historical construction of the works of the formative arts is even rarer in universities, since it is robbed of any direct observation of such works. Even where such lectures are attempted for the sake of honor and with the support of a rich library, they automatically restrict themselves to merely scholarly knowledge of art history.

Since universities are not art schools, the science of art in a practical or technical sense can be taught there with even less justification.

Thus only the completely speculative science is left, one not directed toward the cultivation of the empirical intuition of art, but rather of its intellectual intuition. Yet just this constitutes the prerequisite for a philosophical construction of art, one against which significant doubts can be raised from the side of both philosophy and art.

In the first place, should the philosopher, whose intellectual intuition should be directed only toward that particular truth that is concealed to sensual eyes, unattainable and accessible only to the spirit itself – should that philosopher concern himself with the science of art? For the latter intends only the production of beautiful appearances, and either shows merely the deceiving, reflected images of the same or is totally sensual. This is how the majority of people understand art, viewing it as sensual stimulation, as recreation, as relaxation for a spirit fatigued by more serious matters and as a pleasant stimulant, one with the advantage of occurring through a more delicate medium. For the judgment of the philosopher, however, who in addition must view it as an effect of sensual impulse or desire, it thereby acquires the even more objectionable imprint of corruption and civilization. According to this view, only through absolute condemnation might philosophy distinguish itself from the flaccid sensuality art tolerates in this respect.

I am speaking of a more sacred art, one that in the words of antiquity is a tool of the gods, a proclaimer of divine mysteries, the unveiler of the ideas; I am speaking of that unborn beauty whose undesecrated radiance only dwells in and illuminates purer souls, and whose form is just as concealed and inaccessible to the sensual eye as is the truth corresponding to it. Nothing of that which a baser sensibility calls art can concern the philosopher. For him it is a necessary phenomenon emanating directly from the absolute, and only to the extent it can be presented and proved as such does it possess reality for him.

But did not even the divine Plato condemn imitative art in his *Republic*, and ban poets from his state of reason not only as useless members but as pernicious as well, and can any authority be more persuasive for the incompatibility of poesy and philosophy than this judgment of the king of philosophers?

It is essential that we recognize the particular standpoint from which Plato speaks this judgment on poets. If any philosopher observed the careful distinction between points of view, he did, and as is the case everywhere, without such differentiation it would be impossible, especially here, to comprehend all the ramifications of his meaning or to unite the contradictions in his works concerning the same topic. We must first resolve to understand the higher philosophy, and that of Plato in particular, as the decisive opposing factor within Greek culture with respect not only to the sensual concepts of religion but also to the objective and thoroughly real forms of the state. An answer to the question of whether in a completely ideal and, in a sense, inner state such as the Platonic one there might be other ways of speaking about poesy, and whether that restriction he imposes might not be a necessary one – this answer would lead us too far astray here. That particular opposition of all public institutions against philosophy necessarily had to elicit a similar opposition of the latter toward the former, and Plato is neither the earliest nor the only example of this. From Pythagoras onward, and even further back, down to Plato, philosophy perceived itself as an exotic plant in Greek soil, and this feeling expressed itself among other places in the universal impulse leading those initiated into higher teachings – either through the wisdom of earlier philosophers or through the mysteries – back to the birthplace of the ideas, namely, the Orient.

Yet aside from this merely historical, not philosophical, opposition, an opposition philosophers readily admit, what is Plato's rejection of the poetic arts – compared particularly with what he says in other works in praise of enthusiastic poesy – other than a polemic against poetic realism, a foreboding of that later inclination of the spirit in general and of poesy in particular? That judgment could be applied least of all to Christian poesy, which on the whole just as decisively displays the character of the infinite as the poesy of antiquity as a whole displays that of the finite. We owe it to the experience of subsequent ages that we can determine the limits of the latter more exactly than could Plato, who was not acquainted with its opposite. For just that reason we are able to elevate

ourselves to a more comprehensive understanding and construction of poesy than he. That which he saw as the objectionable element in the poesy of his age we refer to only as its beautiful limitations, and we see it as the fulfillment of what Plato foresaw but did not experience. The Christian religion, and with it a sensibility directed toward the intellectual and ideal – a sensibility that in the poesy of antiquity could find neither its full satisfaction nor even the means for portrayal – created its own poesy and art in which such sensibility could find satisfaction. This creates the conditions for a complete and totally objective view of art, including that of antiquity.

This shows clearly that the construction of that art is a worthy object not only of the philosopher as such but of the Christian philosopher in particular, who should make it his concern to measure and present the universe of that art.

Viewing things from the other side, we must ask whether the philosopher for his own part is suited to penetrate the essence of art and to portray it with truth.

Who can, I already hear being asked, speak worthily of that divine principle driving the artist, and of that spiritual breath animating his works, other than he who is himself possessed by this sacred flame? Can one really attempt to subject to construction that which is just as incomprehensible in its origin as it is miraculous in its effects? Can one claim to subsume and to determine according to laws that whose essence is precisely to recognize no law other than itself? Or cannot genius be comprehended by concepts just as little as it can be created through methodical principles? Who dares to claim actual insights into that which is obviously the most free and absolute element in the entire universe? Or to claim an expansion of his own mental horizon beyond the ultimate boundaries in order to establish yet newer boundaries there?

Such could speak a certain enthusiasm that had comprehended art only in its effects, and which was genuinely acquainted neither with art itself nor with the position given to philosophy in the universe. Even assuming that art is not comprehensible from any higher perspective, that law of the universe which decrees that everything encompassed by it have its prototype of reflex in something else is so pervasive and so omnipotent, and the form of the universal juxtaposition of the real and the ideal is so absolute, that even at the ultimate boundaries of the infinite and the finite, where the contradictions of phenomenal appearance disappear into the purest absoluteness, the same relationship asserts its rights and recurs in the final potence. This is the relationship between philosophy and art.

The ultimate, albeit completely absolute, and perfect informing into unity of the real and the ideal is itself related to philosophy as the real to the ideal. In the latter the final contradiction of knowledge resolves itself into pure identity, and nonetheless it too, in its antithesis to art, always remains only ideal. Hence, both encounter one another on the final pinnacle, and precisely by virtue of that common absoluteness are for one another both prototype and reflex. This is the reason no sensibility can penetrate scientifically more deeply into the interior of art than that of philosophy; indeed, this is why the philosopher possesses better vision within the essence of art than does the artist himself. Insofar as the ideal is always a higher reflex of the real, the philosopher necessarily possesses an even higher ideal reflex of that which in the artist is real. This indicates not only in a larger sense that art can become the object of knowledge in philosophy, but more specifically that outside of philosophy and other than through philosophy, nothing can be known about art in an absolute fashion.

Since in the artist the same principle is objective that in the philosopher reflects itself subjectively, he thus does not relate to that principle subjectively or consciously – though he, too, could become conscious of it through a higher reflex. He is not, however, conscious of it in the quality of being an artist. As such he is driven by that principle and for just that reason does not himself possess it. When he does achieve the standpoint of the ideal reflex with regards to that principle, he thereby elevates himself as an artist to a higher potence, yet as an artist still always relates to it *objectively*. The subjective element within him passes over again to the objective element, just as in the philosopher the objective element is constantly taken up into the subjective one. For this reason philosophy, notwithstanding its inner identity with art, is nonetheless always and necessarily science, that is, ideal, whereas art is always and necessarily art, that is, real.

Hence, the way in which the philosopher is thus able to pursue art even into its secret primal source and into the first workshop of its production is incomprehensible only from the purely objective standpoint, or from that of a philosophy that does not achieve the same heights within the ideal as does art within the real. The particular rules that genius is able to cast off are only those that a merely mechanical understanding may prescribe. Genius is autonomous, yet it escapes only external determination by laws, not determination by its own laws, since it is only genius insofar as it actually constitutes the highest law-governed qualities. Yet it is precisely this absolute legislation that philosophy recognizes in it. It is not only itself autonomous but also penetrates through to the principle of all autonomy. Thus in all ages it has been evident that the true artists are self-contained, simple, great, and necessary in their own fashion, just as is nature. That enthusiasm that sees in them nothing but genius unfettered by rules itself emerges first only through reflection, which recognizes only the negative side of genius. It is a derivative enthusiasm, not that which inspires the artist and which in its godlike freedom is simultaneously the purest and highest necessity.

Yet even if the philosopher is best suited for presenting the unfathomable quality of art, and for recognizing the absolute within it, will he be just as skilled at comprehending that which really is comprehensible within it and in determining it according to laws? I mean the technical side of art: will philosophy be able to lower itself to the empirical sphere of execution and of the medium itself and the conditions for execution?

Philosophy, which concerns itself only with ideas, must present only the general laws of phenomenal appearance as regards the empirical side of art, and must present these only in the form of ideas, for the forms of art are the essential forms of things as they are in the archetypes. Hence, to the extent that these can be comprehended universally and from the perspective of the universe in and for itself, their presentation is a necessary part of the philosophy of art, not, however, to the extent that they encompass rules for the execution and the practice of art. Philosophy of art in the larger sense is the presentation of the absolute world in the form of art. Only theory concerns itself directly with the particular or with a goal, and only according to theory can a project be executed empirically. In contrast, philosophy is totally unconditioned and without external purpose. Even if one were to object that the technical side of art is that whereby it acquires the appearance of truth, the concern for which might then fall to the philosopher, this truth is nonetheless merely empirical. That which the philosopher must recognize and present in it is of a higher sort, and is one and the same with absolute beauty: the truth of the ideas.

The situation of contradiction and dissension, even concerning the primary concepts, in which artistic judgment must necessarily find itself in an age that wishes to reopen the exhausted sources of art, makes it doubly desirable that the absolute view of art be carried through in a methodical, scientific fashion also as regards the forms in which art expresses itself, from the first principles onward. As long as this has not been done, a limited, one-sided, and capricious view will persist both in judgment and in demands, alongside what is already base and vulgar in and of itself.

The construction of art in each of its specific forms all the way into the concrete leads of itself to the determination of art through temporal conditions, and thus passes over into historical construction. One can doubt neither the possibility of such a construction nor its expansion to include the entire history of art; that is, such doubt is removed when the pervasive dualism of the universe in the antithesis between ancient and modern art has been presented in this area as well and has been thoroughly validated partly through the organ of poesy itself, partly through criticism. Since construction as such is the suspension of antitheses, and since those that obtain regarding art through its temporal dependency must, like time itself, be nonessential and merely formal, then scientific construction will consist in the presentation of the common unity from which these features have emanated, and thus will elevate itself above them to a more comprehensive viewpoint.

Such a construction of art can by no means be compared with anything that has existed up to the present under the name of aesthetics, theory of the fine arts and sciences, or any other designation. In the most general principles of the first founder of that designation there still inhered at least the trace of the idea of the beautiful as that archetypal element appearing in the concrete and reflected world. Since then this designation has acquired an ever more definite dependency on the moral and useful, just as in psychological theories certain phenomena have been explained away more or less like ghost stories or similar superstitions, until Kantian formalism, following upon all this, bore a new and higher view, though also a host of artistically empty doctrines of art.

The seeds of a genuine methodical presentation or science of art that excellent spirits have sown since then have not yet structured themselves into a scientific whole – something they do, however, lead us to expect.[2] The philosophy of art is a necessary goal of the philosopher, who in art views the inner essence of his own discipline as if in a magic and symbolic mirror.[3] As a science it is important to him in and for itself, just as is, for example, the philosophy of nature, as the construction of the most remarkable of all products and phenomenal appearances, or as the construction of a world as self-enclosed and as perfect as nature itself. Through such philosophy the inspired natural scientist learns to recognize symbolically or emblematically the true archetypes of forms in works of art, archetypes he finds expressed only in a confused fashion in nature:[4] through such works of art themselves he learns to recognize symbolically the way sensual things emerge from those archetypes.

The inner bond uniting art and religion – the total impossibility on the one hand of giving the former any other poetic world than within and through religion, and the impossibility on the other hand of bringing the latter to any true objective manifestation other than through art – makes the scientific knowledge of art in this respect a necessity for the genuinely religious person.[5]

Finally, it is shameful for anyone either directly or indirectly involved in state government to have neither receptivity for art nor any true knowledge of it. Just as nothing is more honorable for princes and those in power than to value and appreciate the arts, to respect artistic works, and to elicit them through encouragement, nothing, in contrast, is more grievous and disgraceful than for those who have the means to promote art to its highest fruition to squander such means on tastelessness, barbarianism, or ingratiating baseness. Even if not everyone can comprehend that art is a necessary and integral part of a state constitution conceived according to ideas, at least antiquity should remind us of this fact, for the universal festivals of antiquity, its immortalizing monuments and plays, as well as all the actions of public life were merely the different branches of *one* universal, objective, and living work of art.

During the following lectures, I would like for you constantly to keep in mind their purely scientific intentions. Just as in the case of all other scientific or methodical investigations, so also is the science of art interesting *in itself* and without any external purpose. So many unimportant objects attract the attention of our desire for knowledge and even the attention of scientific investigation – how utterly peculiar if art itself were not able to do so, this *one* object that almost by itself encompasses the loftiest objects of our admiration.

That person is still lagging far behind for whom art has not yet appeared just as unified, organic, and in all its parts necessary a whole as does nature. If we feel perpetually moved to view the inner essence of nature and to discover that fertile source that generates so many great phenomena with eternal consistency of form and regularity, how much more must it interest us to penetrate the organism of art, which generates the highest unity and regularity and reveals to us far more directly than does nature the miracles of our own spirit? If we are interested in tracing as far as possible the structure, inner disposition, relationships, and intricacies of a plant or of an organic being in general, how much more alluring must it be for us to recognize the same intricacies and relationships in the much more highly organized and complex growths that we call works of art?

Most people have the same experience with art as Molière's Monsieur Jourdain[6] had with prose: he was astonished to find he had spoken prose his whole life without even knowing it. Very few people realize that even the language in which they express themselves is the most perfect work of art. How many people have stood before a theater without asking themselves even once just how many conditions are necessary to ensure even a relatively successful theatrical production? How many have enjoyed the noble effect of beautiful architecture without ever being tempted to retrace the source of the harmony therein that addresses them? How many have been affected by a poem or by a sublime dramatic piece, have been moved by it, enchanted, or stirred without ever looking to see by what means the artist has succeeded in dominating their disposition, cleansing their soul, and exciting their innermost being – without ever thinking of transforming this completely passive and to that extent rather lowly pleasure into the much more sublime pleasure of active perception and reconstruction of the work of art by the understanding!

We consider crude and uncultured any person who does not *everywhere* allow art to flow over and affect him. It is, however, while perhaps not to the same degree, nonetheless in the same spirit just as crude if the merely sensual feelings, responses, and pleasure elicited by works of art are taken to be the effects of art as such.

All effects of art are merely effects of nature for the person who has not attained a perception of art that is free, that is, one that is both passive and active, both swept away and reflective. Such a person behaves merely as a creature of nature and has never really experienced and appreciated art as art. What moves him are perhaps individual moments of beauty, while in the true work of art there is no individualized beauty; only the whole is beautiful. The person who has not yet elevated himself to the idea of the *whole* is totally incapable of evaluating a work of art. Yet in spite of this indifference, the majority of those who consider themselves cultured are most prone to display their judgment in matters of art and to play the connoisseur; rarely is a negative judgment more painful for them than the accusation that they have no taste at all. Those who sense a weakness in their own judgment would rather withhold judgment entirely – regardless of how decisively a work of art affects them or how original their view of it may well be – than expose that weakness. Others, those who are less modest, make fools of themselves with their judgment or annoy those who do understand. It is therefore an integral part of one's general social education – since there is in any case no realm of study that is more social than that of art[7] – to acquire a methodical and well-founded knowledge of art, to cultivate the ability to comprehend the *idea* or the whole as well as the mutual relationships between the various parts and between those parts and the whole. Yet this is possible only through *science*, and specifically through philosophy. The more strictly one construes the idea both of art and of the work of art, the more strictly can one provide a corrective both for the laxity of judgement and for those thoughtless attempts made in art or poesy usually undertaken without any idea of what art actually is.

In what follows I want to indicate briefly just how necessary precisely this kind of strictly methodical view of art is for the cultivation of the intellectual intuition of a work of art as well as for the cultivation of artistic judgement itself.

Very often, particularly nowadays, one finds that even artists themselves disagree in their judgement; indeed they often hold completely opposite opinions in matters of art. This phenomenon can be easily explained. In periods in which art flourishes, the necessity of the generally dominant spirit of the time, fortunate circumstances, and what one might call the springtime of the age generate more or less a common, fundamental agreement among the great masters. As the history of art shows, this causes the great works of art to arise and mature virtually on one another's heels, almost simultaneously, as if animated by a common breath of life beneath a common sun: Albrecht Dürer simultaneous with Raphael, Cervantes and Calderón simultaneous with Shakespeare. When such a fortunate age of pure production has passed, reflection enters, and with it an element of estrangement. What was earlier living spirit is now transmitted theory.

The inclination of the artists of antiquity proceeded from the center out toward the periphery. Later artists take the externally extracted form and seek to imitate it, retaining the shadow without the body. Each forms his own particular point of view regarding art and employs it to evaluate even existing art. Those who notice the emptiness of form without content preach the return to substantiality by means of imitation of nature. Those who cannot elevate themselves above that empty and vacant external extraction of form preach the ideal, the imitation of what has already been formed. None, however, returns to the true primal sources of art from which form and substance issue together as one. This is more or less the present situation of art and of artistic judgment. As multifarious as art is within itself, so also are the various viewpoints of artistic evaluation multifarious and full of nuances. None of the disputants understands the others. The one judges according to the standard of truth, the other according to that of beauty; yet neither knows what truth or beauty is. With few exceptions, one can learn very little about the essence of art from those who actually practice art in such an age, since as a rule they have no guide concerning the actual idea of art and of beauty. Precisely this dominant disagreement even among those who practice art is a compelling reason for seeking the true idea and principles of art itself by means of science.

A serious study of art based on ideas is even more necessary in this age of literary peasant wars, wars conducted against all that is sublime, great, or ideal, indeed against beauty itself in poesy and art, an age in which the frivolous, the sensually provocative, or nobly base are the idols to which the greatest reverence is paid.

Only philosophy can reopen the primal sources of art for reflection, sources that for the most part no longer nourish production. Only through philosophy can we hope to attain a true science of art. Philosophy cannot lend meaning to art; only a god can do that. It cannot bestow artistic sensibility on someone to whom nature has already denied such sensibility. Philosophy can, however, express immutably in ideas that which true artistic sensibility actually intuits in the concrete work of art, and can disclose those factors determining genuine artistic judgement.

I think it is appropriate that I also indicate which *specific* factors have prompted me not only to study this science but also to give these lectures.

Above all I request that you not confuse this science of art with anything previously presented under this or any other title as aesthetics or as a theory of the fine arts and sciences.[8] There does not yet exist anywhere a scientific and philosophical doctrine of art. At most only fragments of such a doctrine exist, and even these are little understood and can be comprehended only within the context of the whole.

All pre-Kantian doctrines of art in Germany were merely children of Baumgarten's *Aesthetica*, since the latter was the first to employ the term aesthetics.[9] It suffices merely to point out that this aesthetics was in its own turn an offspring of Wolffian philosophy. In the period immediately preceding Kant, a period in which shallow popularity and philosophical empiricism held sway, various well-known theories of the fine arts and sciences were proposed, theories whose foundations were the psychological principles of the English and the French. One tried to explain beauty using empirical psychology, and in general treated the miracles of art the same way one treated ghost stories and other superstitions: by enlightening us and explaining them away. We still encounter fragments of this empiricism even in later writings, writings that at least in part have been conceived according to a much more sophisticated point of view.

Other aesthetics are virtual recipes or cookbooks in which the recipe for a tragedy reads approximately as follows: a great deal of fright, but not too much; as much sympathy as possible, and tears without end.

Kant's *Critique of Judgment* experienced the same fate as his other writings. From the Kantians themselves one could naturally expect the most extreme tastelessness, just as one could expect complete sterility of spirit in their philosophy. A multitude of people learned the *Critique of Judgment* by heart and then presented it both from the lectern and in writing as aesthetics.

After Kant a few excellent minds provided us with some admirable points of departure for the idea of a genuine philosophical science of art and even with various contributions to such a science. No one, however, has yet brought forth a scientifically constructed whole or even the *absolute* principles themselves, principles that would be universally valid and presented in a consistent, strict form. Furthermore, many of these people have not yet rigorously separated empiricism from philosophy, a separation absolutely necessary for true scientific investigation.

The system of the philosophy of art that I intend to present here will thus differentiate itself fundamentally from the previous systems, and will do so as regards both form and content; I will retrace even the principles themselves further back than has hitherto been the case. The method by which, if I am not mistaken, my philosophy of nature has been able to unravel the intricately entwined web of nature to a certain extent and to order the chaos of its phenomena – this same method will guide us through the even more labyrinthine entwinements of the world of art and will illuminate anew the objects of that world.

I can be less sure of satisfying my own demands regarding the *historical* side of art, a side that as I will explain later, is an essential element of any construction. I recognize too well how difficult it is in this most infinite of all areas to acquire even the most general knowledge of each part, not to speak of acquiring the most pointed and specific knowledge about all of those parts. The only thing I can claim for myself is that I have long been engaged in serious study of both ancient and contemporary works of poesy, and that I have made it my most earnest business to acquire some acquaintance and views regarding works of the plastic arts. I have spent time with actual practicing artists, and must admit that I have in part become acquainted only with their own disagreement and lack of understanding of the matter at hand; yet I have also spent time with those who besides having been successful in their artistic endeavors have also considered their art philosophically. From all these I have acquired at least a part of the historical background I consider necessary for my present purpose.[10]

For those already acquainted with my system of philosophy, the philosophy of art will be merely the repetition of that same philosophy in the highest potence. For those not yet acquainted with it, its method as I employ it in the present context will be perhaps even more obvious and clear.

The construction will encompass not merely generalities, but will also extend to those individuals who represent an entire genre. I will construe both them and the world of their poesy. For now I will mention only Homer, Dante, and Shakespeare. In the discussion of the formative or plastic arts the personalities of the greatest masters will be discussed in a general sense. In the discussion of poesy and poetic genres I will even progress as far as a characterization of individual works of the most preeminent poets, for example, Shakespeare, Cervantes, and Goethe, so as to provide the contemporary view of those poets that is as yet still lacking.

In general philosophy we are fortunate to view the stern countenance of truth in and for itself. In the particular sphere of philosophy circumscribing the philosophy of art we attain to an intuition of eternal beauty and of the archetypes of all that is beautiful.[11]

Philosophy is the basis of everything, encompasses everything, and extends its constructions to all potences and objects of knowledge. Only through it does one have access to the highest. By means of the doctrine of art an even smaller circle is formed within philosophy itself, one in which we view more immediately the eternal in a visible form, as it were. Hence, the doctrine of art, properly understood, is in complete agreement with philosophy.

A hint at what the philosophy of art actually is has in part already been suggested in our discussion. It is necessary, however, that I now explain myself more specifically in this regard. I will pose the question in the most general terms: *how is the philosophy of art possible?* (Proof of possibility as regards science is also proof of its reality.)

Anyone can see that the concept of a philosophy of art combines antithetical elements. Art is real and objective, philosophy ideal and subjective. We might thus define in advance the task of the philosophy of art as *the presentation in the ideal medium of the real element inherent in art*. Of course, the question is then precisely what it means to present *something real in the ideal*; before we know this, we have not yet sufficiently clarified our concept of the philosophy of art. Hence, we must address the investigation on an even deeper level. Since presentation within an ideal medium in general = construction, and hence also the philosophy of art should = construction of art, this investigation will of necessity simultaneously have to penetrate more deeply into the nature of construction itself.

[...]

In the philosophy of art I accordingly intend to construe first of all not art *as* art, as this *particular*, but rather *the universe in the form of art*, and the philosophy of art is *the science of the All in the form or potence of art*. Not until we have taken this step do we elevate ourselves regarding this science to the level of an absolute science of art.

The assertion that the philosophy of art is the presentation of the universe in the form of art does not yet, however, give us any complete idea of this science; we must specify more closely the *mode* of construction necessary for a philosophy of art.

An object of construction and thereby of philosophy is essentially only that which is capable as a particular of taking up the infinite into itself. Therefore, art, in order to be the object of philosophy, must as such either genuinely represent the infinite within itself as the particular, or must be capable of doing so. Not only does this actually take place as regards art, but it also stands as a representation of the infinite on the same level with philosophy; just as philosophy presents the absolute in the *archetype* so also does art present the absolute in a *reflex* or *reflected image*.[12]

Since art exactly corresponds to philosophy and is merely the latter's complete objective reflex, it must also proceed through all the potences within the real as does philosophy in the ideal. This one fact suffices to remove all doubt regarding the necessary method of our science.

Philosophy does not present real things, but rather only their archetypes; the same holds true for art. The same archetypes that according to philosophy are merely reproduced imperfectly by these (the real things) are those that become objective in art itself – as archetypes and accordingly in their perfection. They thus represent the intellectual world in the reflected world. As examples we might take *music*, which is nothing other than the primal rhythm of nature and of the universe itself, which by means of this art breaks through into the world of representation. The complete forms generated by the *plastic* arts are the objectively portrayed archetypes of organic nature itself. The Homeric epic is identity itself as this identity lies at the base of history within the absolute. Every painting discloses the intellectual world.

Given these assertions, in the philosophy of art we will have all those problems to solve regarding art that we also must solve in general philosophy regarding the universe.

(1) In the philosophy of art, no principle other than that of the infinite can serve as our point of departure; hence, we must present the infinite as the unconditioned principle of art. Just as for philosophy in general the absolute is the archetype of truth, so also for art is it the archetype of *beauty*. We must therefore show that truth and beauty are merely two different ways of viewing the one absolute.[13]

(2) The second question, both as regards philosophy as such as well as the philosophy of art, will be just how this principle, a principle that is in and for itself absolutely one and simple, can pass over into multiplicity and differentiation, and thus how individual beautiful things can issue from universal and absolute beauty.[14] Philosophy answers this question with the doctrine of the ideas or archetypes.[15] The absolute is absolutely one; viewed absolutely in particular forms, however, such that the absolute is thereby not suspended, this one = idea. The same holds true for art. It, too, views or intuits primal beauty only in ideas as particular forms, each of which, however, is divine and absolute for itself. Whereas philosophy intuits these ideas as they are *in themselves*, art intuits them *objectively*. The *ideas*, to the extent that they are intuited objectively, are therefore the substance and as it were the universal and absolute material of art from which all particular works of art emerge as mature entities. These *real* or *objective*, living and existing ideas are the gods. The universal symbolism or universal *representation* of the *ideas* as real is thus given in mythology, and the solution to the second aforementioned task consists in the construction of mythology. Indeed, the gods of any mythology are nothing other than the ideas of philosophy intuited objectively or concretely.

This still does not answer the question of how a *real*, individual work of art comes to be. Just as the absolute or unreal is always characterized by the condition of identity, so also is the real always characterized by the nonidentity of the universal and the particular, by disjunction, such that either the particular or universal predominates. An antithesis thus arises here, one between plastic or formative art on the one hand, and verbal art on the other. Formative and verbal art = the real and ideal series of philosophy. The former is characterized by that unity in which the infinite is taken up into the finite, and the construction of this series corresponds to the *philosophy of nature*. The latter is characterized by the other unity, the one in which the finite is formed into the infinite, and the construction of this series corresponds to *idealism* in the general system of philosophy. I will call the first unity the real unity, the second the ideal unity; that which encompasses both I will call indifference.

If we now concentrate on each of these unities individually, then, since each is absolute for itself, the same unities must recur in each; hence, the real unity, the ideal unity, and that in which both are one must all recur in the real unity itself. The same holds true for the ideal unity.

A particular form of art corresponds to each of these forms to the extent that they are encompassed within the real or ideal unity. *Music* corresponds to the real form within the real series. *Painting* corresponds to the ideal form within the real series. The *plastic arts* correspond to that form within the real series that represents the confluence of the previous two unities.

The same holds true as regards the ideal unity, which in its own turn encompasses within itself the three forms of lyric, epic, and dramatic poetry. Lyric poetry = the informing of the infinite into the finite = the particular. The epic = the representation (subsumption) of the finite within the infinite = the universal. Drama = the synthesis of the universal and the particular. Hence, the entire world of art is to be construed according to these basic forms both in its real and ideal manifestation.

By tracing art in each of its particular forms all the way into the concrete, we also arrive at a determination of art within the conditions of time. Just as art is inherently eternal and necessary, so also is there no fortuitousness in its temporal manifestation, but rather only absolute necessity. In this respect, too, it is the object of possible knowledge, and the elements of this construction are given in the antitheses manifested in art in its temporal appearance. Any antitheses posited as regards art in its temporal dependence, however, are, as is time itself, necessarily nonessential and merely formal antitheses; hence, they are completely different from those *real* antitheses grounded in the essence or in the idea of art itself. This universal, formal antithesis extending through all branches of art is that of *ancient* and *modern* art.

It would be an essential weakness of our construction if we were to neglect the consideration of this antithesis in our discussion of each individual form of art. Since, however, we consider this antithesis to be a merely formal one, its construction necessarily consists in negation or suspension. By considering this antithesis, we will simultaneously present the *historical* dimension of art; only by this means can we hope to bring our construction in the larger sense to its final completion.

According to my entire understanding here, art is itself an emanation of the absolute. The history of art will show us most revealingly its immediate connections to the conditions of the universe and thereby to that absolute identity in which art is preordained. Only in the history of art does the essential and inner unity of all works of art reveal itself, a unity showing that all poetry is of the same spirit, a spirit that even in the antitheses of ancient and modern art is merely showing us two different faces.

Notes

1 The initial pages of this introduction were reprinted in Schelling's lecture series entitled *On University Studies*, fourteenth lecture, under the title "On the Science of Art in Relation to Academic Study."

2 Among many others, Schelling may be thinking here of Karl Philipp Moritz (1756–93), who after 1789 held a position at the Academy of Arts in Berlin. Schelling, as will be seen, thought especially highly of Moritz's views on the mythology of antiquity. Kant, in the *Critique of Judgement*, book 2, "The Analytic of the Sublime," had also offered a system for ordering the various art forms. Kant, *Critique of Judgement*, trans. James Creed Meredith (Oxford: Clarendon, 1964).

3 Schelling is underscoring the relationship between philosophy and art he first discussed in the concluding section to the *System of Transcendental Idealism* (1800), though now – particularly after the reflections of the essay *Bruno* (1802) – the relationship is more equitable. In the *System of Transcendental Idealism* Schelling had written the following (p. 233):

Take away objectivity from art, one might say, and it ceases to be what it is, and becomes philosophy; grant objectivity to philosophy, and it ceases to be philosophy and becomes art. Philosophy attains, indeed, to the highest, but it brings to this summit only, so to say, the fraction of a man. Art brings *the whole man*, as he is, to that point, namely to the knowledge of the highest, and this is what underlies the eternal difference and the marvel of art.

In *Bruno; or, On the Divine and Natural Principle of Things*, philosophy has risen in stature as regards what it is able to disclose of that absolute identity; *intellectual intuition* (in philosophy) becomes the equal of *aesthetic intuition* (in art). Art portrays *objectively* what philosophy portrays *subjectively*. Schelling will make this point several times during the present lectures.

4 This passage illustrates well Schelling's proximity to the thought of Goethe (1749–1832). At Goethe's first meeting with Schiller (1759–1805) in 1794, he and Schiller had engaged in a conversation concerning the "dissecting manner of dealing with Nature." Goethe remarked that "perhaps there was still the possibility of another method, one which would not tackle Nature by merely dissecting and particularizing, but show her at work and alive, *manifesting herself in her wholeness in every single part of her being*." As we shall see, this concept will be fulcral in Schelling's own estimation of art and its metaphysical implications. Schiller insisted in that conversation that such insights actually emerge from experience itself. Goethe continues: "I explained to him with great vivacity the Metamorphosis of Plants [Goethe's theory of plant morphology] and, with a few characteristic strokes of the pen, conjured up before his eyes a symbolical plant [that is, a prototypical plant or 'plant as such,' an approximation of the archetype or idea 'plant']. He listened, and looked at it all with great interest and intelligence; but when I had ended, he shook his head saying: This has nothing to do with *experience*, it is an *idea* ... Well, so much the better [Goethe counters]; it means that I have ideas without knowing it, and can even *see them with my eyes*." "How," Schiller asks, "can one ever equate experience with ideas? For an idea is characterized precisely by the fact that experience can never be fully congruous to it" [...]. Goethe draws the conclusion later that if "he [Schiller] takes for an idea what to me is experience, then there must, after all, prevail some mediation, some relationship between the two." Indeed, this is precisely Schelling's point, one he will work out in more detail in the present lectures; just as Goethe *intuits* in a particular, concrete plant the idea "plant," so also, according to Schelling, can aesthetic intuition *intuit* the ideas of philosophy in a particular, concrete work of art. For a discussion of this complex regarding Goethe, see Erich Heller, "Goethe and the Idea of Scientific Truth," in *The Disinherited Mind: Essays in Modern German Literature and Thought*, 3rd ed. (London: Bowes & Bowes, 1971).

5 Since [...] art reveals in actuality (in concrete, individual works of art) a reflection of that absolute identity lying as the absolute behind all things, it possesses religious (revelatory) significance. Her-

mann August Korff, in his survey of this period of German literary history, cites the "religion of art" as one of the three main movements during the period (*Geist der Goethezeit*, 4 vols., 1923ff.). The early Romantic circle in general was enamored of the idea of the religious significance of art, and we shall encounter several reflections of this in these lectures.

Perhaps the most influential piece in this regard during the period was *Outpourings of an Art-Loving Friar* by Wilhelm Heinrich Wackenroder (1773–98) and Ludwig Tieck (1773–1853). In this work as in no other, the religious implications of both art and nature are extolled on virtually every page. "Art must come before love in his [the artist's] heart, for art is of heavenly provenance. Only religion may be dearer to him. Art must become a sacred love or a loved religion, if I may express myself in such terms" (p. 27). Although Wackenroder and Tieck were particularly concerned with art, the references to nature clearly show the kind of parallel thinking characterizing Schelling's lectures, that is, the assertion that ultimately the realms of nature, intellect, and art reveal one and the same divinity. In the essay "Of Two Wonderful Languages and Their Mysterious Power," Wackenroder and Tieck sound remarkably Schellingian:

> Yet I know of two wonderful languages through which the Creator has granted man the means of grasping and comprehending the Divine in all its force, at least (not to appear presumptuous) insofar as that is at all possible for poor mortals. These languages speak to our inner selves, but not in words; suddenly and in wondrous fashion they invade our whole being, permeating every nerve and every drop of blood in our veins. One of these wonderful languages is spoken by God alone; the other is spoken only by a few chosen men whom He has anointed as His favorites. They are: Nature and Art. (p. 59).

One even finds in this work the suggestion of a dialectic of the spirit through both nature and art of the kind both Schelling and Hegel will speak: "In every work of art, in every zone of the earth, He sees the trace of that divine spark which, issuing from Him, passed through the souls of men and into their little creations, which reflect it back to the great Creator again" (pp. 45–46).

Similarly, Friedrich Schlegel (1772–1829), brother of August Wilhelm Schlegel (1767–1845) and a member of the early Romantic circles in Berlin and Jena, extolled the same view concerning the proximity of art, religion, and philosophy as Schelling does in this paragraph: "He who has religion will speak poetry." "Poetry and philosophy are, according to how you take them, different spheres, different forms, or factors of religion. Try to really combine both, and you will have nothing but religion." From Friedrich Schlegel, *Dialogue on Poetry and Literary Aphorisms*, pp. 152 and 154 ("Selected Ideas," aphorisms 34 and 46).

6   Monsieur Jourdain is the principal character in Molière's play *Le Bourgeois Gentilhomme* (1670), act II, scene 4. A. W. Schlegel makes the same point with the same example in his lecture series *Schöne Literatur und Kunst*, I, p. 264.

7   [T]he Romantics were keen on the social or communal nature of much of their work (sympoetry, symphilosophy). From Friedrich Schlegel we have the account of such an encounter in his *Dialogue on Poetry*; from August Wilhelm Schlegel we have an account of a visit to the Dresden Art Gallery: "Die Gemählde: Ein Gespräch" (The paintings: a dialogue), in *Athenaeum* II, 1. In that dialogue, Louise complains to her artist friend that art galleries are not there primarily to instruct artists in their own craft. "No, my friend, mutual participation and social contact is the main purpose... For all arts, no matter which ones, language is, after all, the universal organ of communication... the common currency wherein all spiritual goods can be exchanged. Hence, one must talk and communicate, communicate!" (pp. 49–59).

8   Schelling may be thinking here of several writers: Johann Georg Sulzer (1720–79), *Allgemeine Theorie der schönen Künste und Wissenschaften* (General theory of the fine arts and sciences) (1771–74, 1792–94); Johann Augustus Eberhard (1739–1809), *Theorie der schönen Künste und Wissenschaften &c* (Theory of the fine arts and sciences) (1783; 3rd ed., 1790) and *Handbuch der Ästhetik* (1803–5); Johann Joachim Eschenburg (1743–1820), *Entwurf einer Theorie und Literatur der schönen Wissenschaften* (Outline of a theory and literature of the science of the fine arts) (1783). In *Schöne Literatur und Kunst*, August Wilhelm Schlegel took a similarly strident attitude toward traditional aesthetics, and also avoided the word, suggesting instead *Kunstlehre* (doctrine of the arts) or *Poetik* (from the Greek root, meaning to make or create). He, too, was concerned with replacing the traditional views with a philosophical theory of art, which would determine the goal or essence of art (the "what"), whereas a technical theory of art would determine the means (the "how") to realize that goal. See Schlegel, *Schöne Literatur und Kunst*, I, pp. 1–5.

9   Immanuel Kant, *The Critique of Judgement* (1790). Alexander Gottlieb Baumgarten (1714–62), professor of philosophy at Frankfurt an der Oder and a follower of Christian Wolff (1679–1754, the leading rationalist philosopher in the early years of the Enlightenment), is generally recognized as the founder of aesthetics as a systematic discipline and part of philosophy; he published the first two volumes of his *Aesthetica* between 1750 and 1758 (his death prevented the completion of the work). A. W. Schlegel similarly rejects the designation *aesthetics*, and wishes rather

that we understand it based on its etymology, as the study of sensory perception, and refers to Kant's use of the term in his "Transcendental Aesthetic."

10 This, of course, was what prompted Schelling to request a copy of Schlegel's *Schöne Literatur und Kunst* [...]

11 Schelling again underscores the equal access both art and philosophy have to the ideas or archetypes; see the illuminating introduction to the archetypes and their relationship to the ideas given by Michael G. Vater in the introduction to his translation of *Bruno*.

12 In *Bruno* Schelling expressed this in yet another fashion, asserting that philosophy was esoteric, whereas art was exoteric (p. 231):

> But tell me what you think, should we not call every sort of cognition that displays ideas only in things, not in themselves, "exoteric"? And, on the other hand, should we not call those kinds of cognition that exhibit the archetypes of things in and for themselves "esoteric"?
>
> That seems quite appropriate to me.
>
> Then the artistic creator will never exhibit beauty in and for itself; he will depict beautiful things instead.
>
> So we have said.
>
> Then the mark of his artistry will not consist in the presence of the idea of beauty itself. It will instead be his ability to produce so many things that are possibly similar to beauty.
>
> Of course.
>
> Necessarily, then, his art is exoteric.
>
> That is obvious.
>
> But the philosopher strives to recognize truth and beauty in and for themselves, not the particular truth and the particular beauty.
>
> That is the case.
>
> He thus employs, but in an inward way, the same God-given faculty that the artist uses externally and unknowingly.

13 The discussion of this point is of fulcral significance in the essay *Bruno*, pp. 224ff., as well as in these lectures.

14 The problem of the derivation of finite content from the absolute plagued Schelling during the entire period of his philosophy of identity. It has been argued that dissatisfaction with his own treatment of the problem prompted him, ultimately, to abandon the philosophy of identity in this form and move on to a different treatment of metaphysical problems. See especially Alan White, *Schelling: An Introduction to the System of Freedom*, pp. 37ff., 76ff., and passim.

15 German: *Ideen oder Urbilder*. I have translated *Urbild* as *archetype* for several reasons. The first is that Schelling is very much a Platonist in his use of

certain terminology, and in this instance is recalling the Platonic use of *idea* (which German renders as *Idee*), and *eidos*, which German renders in this context as *Idee* or *Urbild*. Etymologically, *archetype* closely approximates that meaning here. Schelling often uses the terms interchangeably, as this passage suggests, or in close proximity. The use of the term by C. G. Jung in depth psychology is somewhat removed from the Platonic (and here Schellingian) use, and the reader is advised against associating that usage too freely here. Furthermore, my translation of *Urbild* as *archetype* follows Michael Vater's translation of the term in *Bruno* [...]; the reader can thus cross-reference the two works with a certain degree of confidence.

6

Biographia Literaria

Samuel Taylor Coleridge

Chapters XIII–XIV
On the imagination, or esemplastic power.

Des Cartes, speaking as a naturalist, and in imitation of Archimedes, said, give me matter and motion and I will construct you the universe. We must of course understand him to have meant; I will render the construction of the universe intelligible. In the same sense the transcendental philosopher says; grant me a nature having two contrary forces, the one of which tends to expand infinitely, while the other strives to apprehend or *find* itself in this infinity, and I will cause the world of intelligences with the whole system of their representations to rise up before you. Every other science pre-supposes intelligence as already existing and complete: the philosopher contemplates it in its growth, and as it were represents its history to the mind from its birth to its maturity.

The venerable Sage of Koenigsberg has preceded the march of this master-thought as an effective pioneer in his essay on the introduction of negative quantities into philosophy, published 1763. In this he has shown, that instead of assailing the science of mathematics by metaphysics, as Berkley did in his Analyst, or of sophisticating it, as Wolff did, by the vain attempt of deducing the first principles of geometry from supposed deeper grounds of ontology, it behoved the metaphysician rather to examine whether the only province of knowledge, which man has succeeded in erecting into a pure science, might not furnish materials or at least hints for establishing and pacifying the unsettled, warring, and embroiled domain of philosophy. An imitation of the mathematical *method* had indeed been attempted with no better success than attended the essay of David to wear the armour of Saul. Another use however is possible and of far greater promise, namely, the actual application of the positions which had so wonderfully enlarged the discoveries of geometry, mutatis mutandis, to philosophical subjects. Kant having briefly illustrated the utility of such an attempt in the questions of space, motion, and infinitely small quantities, as employed by the mathematician, proceeds to the idea of negative quantities and the transfer of them to metaphysical investigation. Opposites, he well observes, are of two kinds, either logical, i.e. such as are absolutely incompatible; or real without being contradictory. The former he denominates Nihil negativum irrepræsentabile, the connexion of which produces nonsense. A body in motion is something – Aliquid cogitabile; but a body, at one and the same time in motion and not in motion, is nothing, or at most, air articulated into nonsense. But a motory force of a body in one direction, and an equal force of the same body in an opposite direction is not incompatible, and the result, namely rest, is real and representable. For the purposes of mathematical calculus it is indifferent which force we term negative, and which positive, and consequently we appropriate the latter to that, which happens to be the principal object in our thoughts. Thus if a man's capital be ten and his debts eight, the subtraction will be the same, whether we call the capital negative debt, or the debt negative capital.

But in as much as the latter stands practically in reference to the former, we of course represent the sum as $10 - 8$. It is equally clear that two equal forces acting in opposite directions, both being finite and each distinguished from the other by its direction only, must neutralize or reduce each other to inaction. Now the transcendental philosophy demands; first, that two forces should be conceived which counteract each other by their essential nature; not only not in consequence of the accidental direction of each, but as prior to all direction, nay, as the primary forces from which the conditions of all possible directions are derivative and deducible: secondly, that these forces should be assumed to be both alike infinite, both alike indestructible. The problem will then be to discover the result or product of two such forces, as distinguished from the result of those forces which are finite, and derive their difference solely from the circumstance of their direction. When we have formed a scheme or outline of these two different kinds of force, and of their different results by the process of discursive reasoning, it will then remain for us to elevate the Thesis from notional to actual, by contemplating intuitively this one power with its two inherent indestructible yet counteracting forces, and the results or generations to which their inter-penetration gives existence, in the living principle and in the process of our own self-consciousness. By what instrument this is possible the solution itself will discover, at the same time that it will reveal, to and for whom it is possible. Non omnia possumes omnes. There is a philosophic, no less than a poetic genius, which is differenced from the highest perfection of talent, not by degree but by kind.

The counteraction then of the two assumed forces does not depend on their meeting from opposite directions; the power which acts in them is indestructible; it is therefore inexhaustibly re-ebullient; and as something must be the result of these two forces, both alike infinite, and both alike indestructible; and as rest or neutralization cannot be this result; no other conception is possible, but that the product must be a tertium aliquid, or finite generation. Consequently this conception is necessary. Now this tertium aliquid can be no other than an inter-penetration of the counteracting powers, partaking of both

* * *

Thus far had the work been transcribed for the press, when I received the following letter from a friend, whose practical judgement I have had ample reason to estimate and revere, and whose taste and sensibility preclude all the excuses which my self-love might possibly have prompted me to set up in plea against the decision of advisers of equal good sense, but with less tact and feeling.

Dear C.

You ask my opinion concerning your Chapter on the Imagination, both as to the impressions it made on myself, and as to those which I think it will make on the PUBLIC, i.e. that part of the public, who from the title of the work and from its forming a sort of introduction to a volume of poems, are likely to constitute the great majority of your readers.

As to myself, and stating in the first place the effect on my *understanding*, your opinions and method of argument were not only so *new* to me, but so directly the reverse of all I had ever been accustomed to consider as truth, that even if I had comprehended your premises sufficiently to have admitted them, and had seen the necessity of your conclusions, I should still have been in that state of mind, which in your note, p. 75, 76, you have so ingeniously evolved, as the antithesis to that in which a man is, when he makes a *bull*. In your own words, I should have felt as if I had been standing on my head.

The effect on my *feelings*, on the other hand, I cannot better represent, than by supposing myself to have known only our light airy modern chapels of ease, and then for the first time to have been placed, and left alone, in one of our largest Gothic cathedrals in a gusty moonlight night of autumn. "Now in glimmer, and now in gloom," often in palpable darkness not without a chilly sensation of terror; then suddenly emerging into broad yet visionary lights with coloured shadows, of fantastic shapes yet all decked with holy insignia and mystic symbols; and ever and anon coming out full upon pictures and stone-work images of great men, with whose *names* I was familiar, but which looked upon me with countenances and an expression, the most dissimilar to all I had been in the habit of connecting with those names. Those whom I had been taught to venerate as almost super-human in magnitude of intellect, I found perched in little fret-work niches, as grotesque dwarfs; while the grotesques, in my hitherto belief, stood guarding the high altar with all the characters of Apotheosis. In short, what I had supposed substances were thinned away into shadows, while every where shadows were deepened into substances:

If substance may be call'd what shadow seem'd,
For each seem'd either!

MILTON.

Yet after all, I could not but repeat the lines which you had quoted from a MS. poem of your own in the FRIEND, and applied to a work of Mr. Wordsworth's though with a few of the words altered:

—— An orphic tale indeed,
A tale *obscure* of high and passionate thoughts
To *a strange* music chaunted!

Be assured, however, that I look forward anxiously to your great book on the CONSTRUCTIVE PHILOSOPHY, which you have promised and announced: and that I will do my best to understand it. Only I will not promise to descend into the dark cave of Trophonius with you, there to rub my own eyes, in order to *make* the sparks and figured flashes, which I am required to see.

So much for myself. But as for the PUBLIC, I do not hesitate a moment in advising and urging you to withdraw the Chapter from the present work, and to reserve it for your announced treatises on the Logos or communicative intellect in Man and Deity. First, because imperfectly as I understand the present Chapter, I see clearly that you have done too much, and yet not enough. You have been obliged to omit so many links, from the necessity of compression, that what remains, looks (if I may recur to my former illustration) like the fragments of the winding steps of an old ruined tower. Secondly, a still stronger argument (at least one that I am sure will be more forcible with you) is, that your readers will have both right and reason to complain of you. This Chapter, which cannot, when it is printed, amount to so little as an hundred pages, will of necessity greatly increase the expense of the work; and every reader who, like myself, is neither prepared or perhaps calculated for the study of so abstruse a subject so abstrusely treated, will, as I have before hinted, be almost entitled to accuse you of a sort of imposition on him. For who, he might truly observe, could from your title-page, viz. "My Literary Life and Opinions," published too as introductory to a volume of miscellaneous poems, have anticipated, or even conjectured, a long treatise on ideal Realism, which holds the same relation in abstruseness to Plotinus, as Plotinus does to Plato. It will be well, if already you have not too much of metaphysical disquisition in your work, though as the larger part of the disquisition is historical, it will doubtless be both interesting and instructive to many to whose *unprepared* minds your speculations on the esemplastic power would be utterly unintelligible. Be assured, if you do publish this Chapter in the present work, you will be reminded of Bishop Berkley's Siris, announced as an Essay on Tar-water, which beginning with Tar ends with the Trinity, the omne scibile forming the interspace. I say in the *present* work. In that greater work to which you have devoted so many years, and study so intense and various, it will be in its proper place. Your prospectus will have described and announced both its contents and their nature; and if any persons purchase it, who feel no interest in the subjects of which it treats, they will have themselves only to blame.

I could add to these arguments one derived from pecuniary motives, and particularly from the probable effects on the *sale* of your present publication; but they would weigh little with you compared with the preceding. Besides, I have long observed, that arguments drawn from your own personal interests more often act on you as narcotics than as stimulants, and that in money concerns you have some small portion of pig-nature in your moral idiosyncracy, and like these amiable creatures, must occasionally be pulled backward from the boat in order to make you enter it. All success attend you, for if hard thinking and hard reading are merits, you have deserved it.

Your affectionate, &c.

In consequence of this very judicious letter, which produced complete conviction on my mind, I shall content myself for the present with stating the main result of the Chapter, which I have reserved for that future publication, a detailed prospectus of which the reader will find at the close of the second volume.

The IMAGINATION then I consider either as primary, or secondary. The primary IMAGINATION I hold to be the living Power and prime Agent of all human Perception, and as a repetition in the finite mind of the eternal act of creation in the infinite I AM. The secondary I consider as an echo of the former, co-existing with the conscious will, yet still as identical with the primary in the *kind* of its agency, and differing only in *degree*, and in the *mode* of its operation. It dissolves, diffuses, dissipates, in order to re-create; or where this process is rendered impossible, yet still at all events it struggles to idealize and to unify. It is essentially *vital*, even as all objects (*as* objects) are essentially fixed and dead.

FANCY, on the contrary, has no other counters to play with, but fixities and definites. The Fancy is indeed no other than a mode of Memory emancipated from the order of time and space; and blended with, and modified by that empirical phenomenon of the will, which we express by the word CHOICE. But equally with the ordinary memory it must receive all its materials ready made from the law of association.

Whatever more than this, I shall think it fit to declare concerning the powers and privileges of the imagination in the present work, will be found in the critical essay on the uses of the Supernatural in poetry and the principles that regulate its introduction: which the reader will find prefixed to the poem of The Ancient Mariner.

[. . .]

The Birth of Tragedy

Friedrich Nietzsche

4

The dream analogy may tell us something about this naïve artist [Homer]. Let us recall the dreamer and the way, in the midst of the illusion of the dream world and without disturbing it, he calls out to himself: 'It is a dream! I want to dream on!' If we must conclude from this a deep inner delight in the contemplation of dreams, or if, on the other hand, before we can dream with that inner delight in contemplation we must first completely erase the day and its terrible intrusiveness, we may interpret all these phenomena more or less as follows, guided by Apollo, the interpreter of dreams. Although of life's two halves – waking and sleeping – the former is held to be preferable, more important, more considerable and more worth living, indeed the only one that *is* lived, I should still, paradoxical as it may sound, like to maintain the opposite valuation of the dream in relation to the mysterious foundation of our being, whose phenomena we are. The more aware I become of those omnipotent art impulses in nature, and find in them an ardent longing for illusion and for redemption by illusion, the more I feel compelled to make the metaphysical assumption that the truly existent, the primal Oneness, eternally suffering and contradictory, also needs the delightful vision, the pleasurable illusion for its constant redemption: an illusion that we, utterly caught up in it and consisting of it – as a continuous becoming in time, space and causality, in other words – are required to see as empirical reality. If we look away from our own 'reality',

then, for a moment, if we see our empirical existence, like that of the world in general, as an idea of the primal Oneness created in a moment, then we must see the dream as the *illusion of illusion*, [...] and hence as an even higher satisfaction of the original desire for illusion. It is for the same reason that the innermost core of nature takes such unutterable delight in the naïve artist and the naïve work of art, which is likewise only 'the illusion of illusion'. *Raphael*, himself one of those immortal naïves, in one of his allegorical paintings depicted that reduction of illusion to mere illusion, the original act of the naïve artist and also of Apolline culture. In his *Transfiguration*, the lower half of the painting, with the possessed boy, his despairing bearers, the dismayed and terrified disciples, reveals the reflection of eternal, primal suffering, the sole foundation of the world: 'illusion' here is the reflection of the eternal contradiction, of the father of all things. From this illusion there now arises, like an ambrosial vapour, a new and visionary world of illusion of which those caught up in the first illusion see nothing – a radiant floating in the purest bliss and painless contemplation beaming from wide-open eyes. Here, in the highest artistic symbolism, we behold that Apolline world of beauty and its substratum, the terrible wisdom of Silenus, and we intuitively understand their reciprocal necessity. Apollo, however, appears to us once again as the apotheosis of the *principium individuationis*. [principle of individuation]. Only through him does the perpetually attained goal of primal Oneness, redemption through illusion, reach consummation. With sublime gestures he reveals to us how the whole world of torment is necessary so that the individual can create the redeeming vision, and then, immersed in contemplation of it, sit peacefully in his tossing boat amid the waves.

If it can be seen as at all imperative and prescriptive, this deification of individuation knows but a single law, the individual; that is, the maintenance of the boundaries of the individual, *moderation* in the Hellenic sense. Apollo, as an ethical deity, demands moderation from his followers and, in order to maintain it, self-knowledge. And thus the admonitions 'Know thyself' and 'Nothing to excess!' coexist with the aesthetic necessity of beauty, while hubris and excess are considered the truly hostile spirits of the non-Apolline realm, and hence qualities of the pre-Apolline age, the age of the Titans, and the world beyond the Apolline, the world of the barbarians. It was for his Titanic love of man that Prometheus had to be torn apart by vultures; for his excessive wisdom in solving the riddle of the Sphinx that Oedipus had to be cast into a bewildering vortex of crimes: thus did the Delphic god interpret the Greek past.

The Apolline Greeks also saw the effect of the *Dionysiac* as 'Titanic' and 'barbaric', unable to conceal from themselves the fact that they themselves were also inwardly akin to those fallen Titans and heroes. Indeed, they were forced to feel even more than that: their entire existence, with all its beauty and moderation, was based on a veiled substratum of suffering and knowledge, revealed to them once again by the Dionysiac. And behold! Apollo could not live without Dionysus! The 'Titanic' and the 'barbaric' were, in the end, just as necessary as the Apolline! And let us now imagine how the ecstatic sound of the Dionysiac revels echoed ever more enticingly around this world, built on illusion and *moderation*, and artificially restrained – how their clamour voiced all the *excess* of nature in delight, suffering and knowledge, and even in the most piercing cry: imagine what the psalmodizing Apolline artist, with his phantom harp–notes, could have meant compared to this daemonic folk song! The muses of the arts of 'illusion' blanched before an art that voiced the truth in its intoxication – the wisdom of Silenus cried 'Woe! Woe!' to the cheerful Olympians. The individual, with all his restraints and moderations, was submerged in the self-oblivion of the Dionysiac state and forgot the Apolline dictates. *Excess* was revealed as truth, contradiction; the bliss born of pain spoke from the heart of nature. And

consequently, wherever the Dionysiac invasion was successful, the Apollonian was negated and destroyed. But just as certain is it that where the first onslaught was successfully withstood, the esteem and majesty of the Delphic god was expressed more rigidly and more threateningly than ever. In fact, I can explain the *Doric* state and Doric art only as a continued encampment of the Apolline; only unstinting resistance to the Titanic and barbaric essence of the Dionysiac could explain the long-term survival of such a scornfully remote art, so enclosed in bulwarks, such a warlike and severe training, such a cruel and ruthless state.

I have up until this point expanded on the observation I made at the beginning: how the Dionysiac and the Apolline, in a sequence of renewed births, mutually intensifying one another, dominated the nature of Greece: how the Homeric world developed out of the 'bronze age', with its Titanic battles and its stern popular philosophy, under the constraints of the Apolline impulse to beauty; how this naïve magnificence was engulfed once more by the encroaching Dionysiac flood, and how, in the face of this new power, the Apolline rose to the rigid majesty of Doric art and the Doric view of the world. If the older Greek history falls into four major artistic stages in the battle between these two hostile principles, we must inquire into the final goal of this process of development, lest we see the final period reached, the period of Doric art, as the summit and goal of those artistic impulses. And now we can see the sublime and esteemed work of art that is *Attic tragedy* and the dramatic dithyramb as the common goal of the two impulses, whose mysterious marriage, after a long period of early strife, was finally blessed with such a child, at once Antigone and Cassandra.

5

We are now approaching the true goal of our inquiry: that of understanding the Dionysiac-Apolline genius and its works of art, or at least gaining a sense of the mystery of that union. Now we shall first of all ask ourselves: where in the Hellenic world did that seed first appear which later grew into tragedy and the dramatic dithyramb? The ancient world itself gives us a pictorial answer, presenting the forefathers and torchbearers of Greek poetry, *Homer* and *Archilochus*, side by side on sculptures, gemstones and so on, in the certain belief that these two alone were worthy of respect, both of them completely and equally original, from whom there issued a stream of fire that flowed over the whole of the later Greek world. Homer, the aged, self-absorbed dreamer, the prototype of the Apolline naïve artist, is now astonished to behold the passionate head of the warlike votary of the muses, driven wildly through life; and the new aesthetic has been able to contribute only the interpretation that here the 'objective' artist stood face to face with the first 'subjective' artist. This interpretation is of little use to us, because we know the subjective artist only as a bad artist, and throughout the whole of art we demand above all else the conquest of the subjective, release from the 'self', and the silencing of all individual will and craving; indeed we cannot imagine a truly artistic creation, however unimportant, without objectivity, without a pure and disinterested contemplation. [. . .] For this reason our aesthetic must first resolve the problem of how it is possible to consider the 'lyric poet' as an artist: he who, in the experience of all ages, always says 'I' and sings us through the full chromatic scale of his passions and desires. It is this Archilochus who frightens us, as he stands next to Homer, with the cry of his hate and scorn, the drunken outpourings of his desire; is he, the first artist to be termed 'subjective', not consequently the true non-artist? How, then, did he win the honour bestowed upon him by the Delphic oracle, the home of 'objective' art, in a number of highly remarkable sayings?

Schiller cast some light on the process of writing his poetry in a psychological observation that he himself found inexplicable but which did not give him pause. In the state prior to the act of writing, he does not claim to have had before or within him an ordered causality of ideas, but rather a *musical mood*. ('For me, feeling does not at first have a clearly defined object. This is only formed later on. A certain musical atmosphere of moods precedes it, and the poetic idea only comes afterwards.') If we add to that the most important phenomenon in the whole of ancient poetry, the unification, or indeed the identity – which they assumed to be quite natural – of the *lyric poet with the musician*, compared to which our more modern lyric poetry appears as the headless statue of a god, we can now use the artist's metaphysics described above to explain the lyric poet as follows. First of all, as a Dionysiac artist, he has been thoroughly united with the primal Oneness, its pain and con-

tradiction, and produces the copy of that primal Oneness as music, if we can rightly call music a repetition and recast of the world; but now, under the Apolline dream influence, this music is revealed to him as an *allegorical dream-image*. That reflection of primal pain in music, free of images and concepts, redeemed by illusion, now creates a second mirror image as a single allegory or example. The artist has already abandoned his subjectivity in the Dionysiac process: the image that now reveals to him his unity with the heart of the world is a dream scene symbolizing the primal contradiction and primal suffering, as well as the primal delight in illusion. The 'I' of the lyric poet therefore sounds from the very depths of being: his 'subjectivity' in the sense used by modern aestheticians is a falsehood. When Archilochus, the first lyric poet among the Greeks, proclaims his raging love and at the same time his contempt for the daughters of Lycambes, it is not his passion that dances before us in orgiastic frenzy: we see Dionysus and the Maenads, we see the intoxicated reveller Archilochus sunk in sleep – as Euripides describes it in the *Bacchae*, asleep in a high mountain pasture in the midday sun – and now Apollo comes up to him and touches him with the laurel. The Dionysiac musical enchantment of the sleeping man now sends out sparks of images, lyric poems which, at the peak of their evolution, will bear the name of tragedies and dramatic dithyrambs.

The sculptor, like his close kin the epic poet, has lost himself in pure contemplation of images. Without a single image, the Dionysiac musician is himself nothing but primal suffering and its primal resonance. The lyric genius is aware of a world of images and symbols growing out of this mystical state of self-expression and unity, one that is utterly different in colouring, causality and tempo from the world of the sculptor and epic poet. While the latter lives with joyful ease within these images and only within them, and never tires of lovingly contemplating them down to the minutest detail; while he sees even the image of the raging Achilles as a mere illusion whose raging expression he enjoys with that dreaming delight in illusion, so that this mirror of illusion guards him against becoming as one and fusing with his figures; the lyric poet's images are nothing but the poet himself, and only different objectifications of himself, which is why, as the moving centre of that world, he is able to say 'I': this self is not that of the waking, empirically real man, however, but rather the sole, truly existing and eternal self that dwells at the basis of being, through whose depictions the lyric genius sees right through to the very basis of being. Let us now consider how, amongst these depictions, he also sees *himself* as a non-genius, as his 'subject', the whole horde of subjective passions and stirrings of the will directed at a particular object that seems real to him; if it now appears that the lyric genius and the non-genius connected to him are one, and that the former is using that little word 'I' to refer to himself, this illusion will no longer have the power of seducing us, as it has certainly seduced those who have described the lyric poet as the subjective poet. In fact Archilochus the man, consumed with passion, loving and hating, is only a vision of the genius who has already ceased to be Archilochus and instead becomes the world-genius, and who symbolically expresses his primal pain in that symbol of the man Archilochus: while that subjectively craving and desiring man Archilochus can never, ever be a poet. But it is not at all necessary for the lyric poet to see only the phenomenon of the man Archilochus before him as the reflection of eternal being; and tragedy proves how remote the visionary world of the lyric poet can be from that most immediate phenomenon.

Schopenhauer, who did not conceal from himself the difficulty presented by the lyric poet when it comes to the philosophical consideration of art, believes that he has found an escape route along which I cannot follow him. He alone, in his profound metaphysics of music, has been given the means to achieve a solution. I hope that I have here resolved those same difficulties according to his spirit and his honour. However, he described the singular essence of song as follows:

> It is the subject of the will, that is, his own willing, that fills the singer's consciousness, often as an unbound and satisfied willing (joy), but even more often as a hampered willing (sorrow), always as emotion, passion, an agitated state of mind. Beside this, however, and simultaneously with it, the singer, through the sight of surrounding nature, becomes aware of himself as the subject of pure, will-less knowing, whose unshakeable, blissful peace now appears in contrast to the pressure of willing, always restricted and needy. The feeling of this contrast, this alternate play, is really what is being expressed in the whole of the song, and what constitutes the lyrical state in general. In this

state pure knowing comes to us, as it were, in order to deliver us from willing and its pressure. We follow, but only for a few moments; willing, desire, the recollection of our own personal aims, always tears us away again from peaceful contemplation; but again and again the next beautiful surroundings, in which pure, will-less knowledge presents itself to us, entice us away from willing. Therefore in the song and in the lyrical mood, willing (the personal interest of our aims) and pure perception of the surroundings that present themselves are wonderfully blended with each other. Relations between the two are sought and imagined; the subjective mood, the affection of the will, imparts its colour to the perceived environment, and the environment imparts its own to the mood. The genuine song is the copy or impression of the whole of this mingled and divided state of mind. (*The World as Will and Representation*, I [...])

Who could fail to understand that in this description lyric poetry is being characterized as an incompletely achieved art that seldom reaches its goal, and then only by means of a leap – a half-art, whose *essence* lies in the miraculous fusing of willing and pure contemplation, the non-aesthetic and the aesthetic states? We insist, instead, that the opposition of the subjective and the objective, which Schopenhauer employs as a yardstick in his classification of the arts, has no place in aesthetics, since the subject, the individual who wills and furthers his own egoistic purposes, can be considered only the adversary and not the origin of art. But in so far as the subject is an artist, he is already liberated from his individual will and has become a medium through which the only truly existent subject celebrates his redemption through illusion. For this above all must be plain to us, to our humiliation *and* our enhancement, that the whole comedy of art is not at all performed for us, for our improvement or edification, any more than we are the actual creators of that art world: but we can indeed assume for our own part that we are images and artistic projections for the true creator of that world, and that our highest dignity lies in the meaning of works of art – for it is only as *an aesthetic phenomenon* that existence and the world are eternally *justified* [...] – while of course our awareness of our meaning differs hardly at all from the awareness that warriors painted on canvas have of the battle portrayed. Thus all of our knowledge of art is utterly illusory, because we, as knowing subjects, are not identical with that being which, as sole creator and spectator of that comedy of art, prepares an eternal enjoyment for itself. Only in so far as the genius is fused with the primal artist of the world in the act of artistic creation does he know anything of the eternal essence of art; for in that state he is wonderfully similar to the weird fairy-tale image of the creature than can turn its eyes around and look at itself; now he is at once subject and object, at once poet, actor and audience.

6

As regards Archilochus, learned research has revealed that he introduced the *folk song* into literature, and that for this deed he was accorded his unique place beside Homer in the universal estimation of the Greeks. But what is the folk song as distinct from the utterly Apolline epos? What is it but the *perpetuum vestigium* [continuous track] of a unification of the Apolline and the Dionysiac? Its tremendously wide dissemination amongst all peoples, intensified in constantly new manifestations, tells us of the strength of nature's dual artistic impulse, which leaves its trace in the folk song just as the orgiastic movements of a people are immortalized in its music. Indeed, it must also be historically demonstrable that any period richly productive of folk songs has also been most intensely stimulated by Dionysiac currents, which we must always see as the substratum and precondition for the folk song.

But first of all we must see the folk song as a musical mirror to the world, the original melody, which now seeks a parallel manifestation in dream and expresses it in poetry. *Melody, then, is both primary and universal*, which is why it can therefore bear various objectifications in various texts. It is also more important and necessary by far in the naïve estimation of the people. Melody gives birth to poetry, over and over again; this is precisely what *the strophic form of the folk song* tells us: a phenomenon that always astonished me, until I finally hit upon this explanation. If we consider a collection of folk songs such as *Des Knaben Wunderborn* [...] in the light of this theory, we shall find countless examples of constantly generating melody emitting sparks of images which, in their brilliance, their sudden transitions, their headlong rush, reveal a power that is utterly alien to epic illusion and its peaceful flow. From the point of view of the epic this uneven and irregular world of images in lyric poetry is simply to be condemned: and certainly the solemn epic rhapsodies of Apolline festivals in the age of Terpander did just that.

In the poetry of the folk song, then, we see language doing its utmost *to imitate music*: hence, with Archilochus, we see the beginning of a new world of poetry that most profoundly contradicts the Homeric world. Thus we have described the only possible relationship between poetry and music, word and sound: now imbued with music's power, the word, the image and the concept seek an expression analogous to music. In this sense we can distinguish two main currents in the linguistic history of the Greek people, in which language imitated either the world of images and phenomena or the world of music. We need only consider the linguistic differences in colour, syntactical construction and phraseology in Homer and Pindar to understand the meaning of this opposition; it becomes immediately obvious that between Homer and Pindar the *orgiastic flute melodies of Olympus* must have sounded – even in the age of Aristotle, in the midst of an infinitely more highly developed music, this music must have inspired a drunken enthusiasm, and certainly in its original effect have stirred the people of the day to imitate it with every available means of expression. I am here recalling a familiar phenomenon of our own time, one which is repellent to our aesthetic. Again and again, we hear individual listeners impelled by a Beethoven symphony to speak of it in images, even if any comparison of the various image worlds thus conjured up by a piece of music shows them to be fantastically diverse or even contradictory. Turning their feeble wits to such comparisons, and ignoring the phenomenon that truly demands explanation, is very much a part of that aesthetic. Indeed, even if the composer has discussed a composition in terms of images – if, for example, he has called a symphony 'Pastoral' and described one movement as 'Stream Scene', or another as 'Merry Gathering of Peasant Folk' – these are but symbols, ideas born from the music, and not the imitated objects of the music. They are ideas that have nothing to teach us about the *Dionysiac* content of the music, and have no distinctive value as images. We must now transfer this process of the discharge of music in images to a youthful people, fresh and linguistically creative, before we can have any idea of how the strophic folk song came about, and how the linguistic faculty as a whole was stimulated by the new principle of the imitation of music.

If we can therefore see lyric poetry as the imitative effulgence of music in images and concepts, we may now ask: 'How does music *appear* in the mirror of imagery and concepts?' *It appears as will* in Schopenhauer's sense of the word, as an opposite of the aesthetic, purely contemplative will-less state. We should here distinguish as sharply as possible between the concepts of essence and appearance: it is by its essence impossible for music to be will, since as such it would be entirely excluded from the realm of art, given that the will is precisely that which is not aesthetic; yet it is manifest as will. For in order to express its appearance in images, the lyric poet needs all the stirrings of passion, from the whisper of affection to the roar of madness; impelled to speak of music in Apolline symbols, he sees the whole of nature, and himself within it, as eternally willing, desiring, yearning. But in so far as he interprets music in images, he himself lies amidst the peaceful waves of Apolline contemplation, though all that he considers through the medium of music may be in urgent, driven motion. Indeed, if he glimpses himself through the same medium, he sees his own image in the state of unappeased emotion: his own desire, his yearning, his moans and his jubilation become a symbol with which he interprets music to himself. This is the phenomenon of the lyric poet: as an Apolline genius he interprets music through the image of the will, while he himself, completely delivered of the greed of the will, is the pure and undimmed eye of the sun.

Throughout this discussion I have relied on the idea that lyric poetry is dependent on the spirit of music to the same extent as music itself, in its absolute sovereignty, does not *require* images or concepts but can *tolerate* both. Lyric poetry can express nothing that was not already most universally present, with the most universal validity, within the music that compelled the lyric poet to use the language of images. For this very reason, the world-symbolism of music cannot be exhaustively interpreted through language, because it symbolically refers to the primal contradiction and the primal suffering within the primal Oneness, and thus symbolizes a sphere beyond and prior to all phenomena. In comparison with this, all phenomena are mere symbols: hence *language*, as the organ and symbol of phenomena, can never uncover the innermost core of music but, once it attempts to imitate music, always remains in superficial contact with it, and no amount of lyrical eloquence can bring its deepest meaning a step closer.

7

We must now call upon all the aesthetic principles we have so far discussed in order to find our way around the labyrinth, which is how we must refer to the *origin of Greek tragedy*. I do not think I am making an extravagant claim when I say that the problem of this origin has not yet even been seriously tackled, however many times the tattered rags of the classical tradition have been sewn together in their various combinations, and ripped apart again. This tradition tell us quite categorically *that tragedy arose from the tragic chorus*, and was originally only chorus and nothing else. This is what obliges us to penetrate to the core of this tragic chorus as the true primal drama, disregarding the usual aesthetic clichés: that it is the ideal viewer, or that it represents the populace as against the noble realm of the drama proper. This latter interpretation, edifying as certain politicians may find it – suggesting that the immutable moral law of the democratic Athenians was represented in the popular chorus, always correct in its appraisal of the passionate misdeeds and extravagances of the kings – may indeed have been suggested by a phrase of Aristotle's: it can have had no influence on the original formation of tragedy, whose purely religious beginnings rule out the very idea of contrasting the populace with the nobility, as indeed they exclude the whole area of political and social concerns; but with reference to the classical form of the chorus as we know it from Aeschylus and Sophocles, we should also consider it blasphemous to speak of the idea of a presentiment of the 'constitutional representation of the people', though others have not shrunk from such sacrilege. Constitutional representation of the people was unknown to the classical polities, and it is to be hoped that the ancient tragedies had no such 'presentiment' of it.

Much more celebrated than this political explanation of the chorus is the idea put forward by A. W. Schlegel, [...] who proposes that we should see the chorus as being to some degree the epitome and concentration of the mass of spectators, the 'ideal spectator'. This view, when seen alongside the historically traditional idea that the tragedy was originally only the chorus, reveals itself in its true colours, a crude and unscientific yet brilliant statement, but one whose brilliance has been preserved only through the concentrated form of its expression, the truly Germanic predilection for everything that is called 'ideal', and our momentary astonishment. We will be truly astonished once we compare the theatre audience – one which we know very well – with that chorus, and ask ourselves whether it is indeed possible to idealize from that audience anything resembling the tragic chorus. We inwardly deny this, and are just as amazed by the boldness of Schlegel's claim as by the totally different nature of the German audience. We had actually always believed that the true spectator, whoever he might be, must always remain aware that he is watching a work of art and not an empirical reality, while the tragic chorus of the Greeks is required to grant the figures on the stage a physical existence. The chorus of the Oceanides really believes that it is seeing the Titan Prometheus, and thinks itself just as real as the stage god. And is that supposed to be the highest and purest kind of spectator, one who, like the Oceanides, believes that he sees Prometheus real and present in the flesh? And would it be a sign of the ideal spectator to run on to the stage and free the god from his tormentors? We had previously believed in an aesthetic audience, and seen the individual viewer as being all the more skilful the more capable he was of seeing the work of art as art, in an aesthetic way; and now Schlegel's pronouncement tells us that the perfect ideal viewer allows the world on stage to affect him not in an aesthetic way, but in a physically empirical way. 'Oh, those Greeks!' we sighed. 'They are turning our aesthetic on its head!' But once we had become accustomed to it, we repeated Schlegel's dictum every time the chorus was mentioned.

But the very emphatic tradition I mentioned before refutes Schlegel in this instance: the chorus as such, without the stage – the primitive form of tragedy, then – and the chorus of ideal spectators are incompatible. What sort of artistic genre would it be that took as its foundation the concept of the spectator, and whose actual form was 'the spectator as such'? The idea of the spectator without a play is an absurd one. I fear that the birth of tragedy may no more be explained with reference to respect for the moral intelligence of the masses than with reference to the concept of the spectator without a play, and I consider this problem too profound even to be touched on by such shallow interpretations.

An infinitely more valuable insight into the meaning of the chorus was put forward by Schiller in the famous preface to the *Bride of Messina*, in which he sees the chorus as a living wall that tragedy pulls around itself to close itself off entirely from the real world and maintain its ideal ground and its poetic freedom.

Schiller uses this as his chief weapon in his fight against the commonplace concept of naturalism, against the illusionism commonly demanded from dramatic poetry. While, for Schiller, in the theatre the daylight itself is merely artificial, the architecture is merely symbolic and the metrical language is idealized, delusions still predominate; it is not enough, for Schiller, that we should only tolerate as a poetic liberty what is in fact the essence of all poetry. The introduction of the chorus is the crucial step towards the open and honest declaration of war on all naturalism in art. This is the kind of interpretation, it seems to me, for which our own age, convinced of its superiority, uses the dismissive catch-word 'pseudo-idealism'. I fear, on the other hand, that in our idolization of the natural and the real we have arrived at the opposite pole from our idealism – the realm of the wax museums. These too are without art, like certain popular novels of the present day: I only ask that I should not be troubled with the claim that in this art Schiller's and Goethe's 'pseudo-idealism' has been vanquished.

It is certainly the case, as Schiller rightly saw, that the ground walked upon by the Greek satyr chorus, the chorus of the original tragedy, is an 'ideal' ground, a ground lifted high above the real paths of mortal men. For this chorus the Greeks built the floating scaffold of an invented *natural state*, and placed upon it *natural beings* invented especially for it. It was on this foundation that tragedy arose, and it was indeed for this reason that it was excused from the start from precise depiction of reality. Yet this is not a world randomly imagined to fit in between heaven and earth; rather it is a world of equal reality and credibility, as Olympus with its inhabitants was for the Hellenes. The satyr, the Dionysiac chorist, lives in a world granted existence under the religious sanction of myth and ritual. That tragedy begins with him, that the Dionysiac wisdom of tragedy speaks through him, is for us a phenomenon just as surprising as the very origin of tragedy out of the chorus. Perhaps we shall find a point of departure for our reflections in the claim that the satyr, the invented natural being, relates to cultural humanity as Dionysiac music relates to civilization. Of the latter, Richard Wagner says that it is annulled by music as lamplight is annulled by the light of day. In the same way, I believe, the Greek man of culture felt himself annulled in the face of the satyr chorus, and the immediate effect of Dionysiac tragedy is that state and society, the gulfs separating man from man, make way for an overwhelming sense of unity that goes back to the very heart of nature. The metaphysical consolation (with which, as I wish to point out, every true tragedy leaves us), that whatever superficial changes may occur, life is at bottom indestructibly powerful and joyful, is given concrete form as a satyr chorus, a chorus of natural beings, living ineradicably behind all civilization, as it were, remaining the same for ever, regardless of the changing generations and the path of history.

This chorus was a consolation to the Hellene, thoughtful and uniquely susceptible as he was to the tenderest and deepest suffering, whose piercing gaze has seen to the core of the terrible destructions of world history and nature's cruelty; and who runs the risk of longing for a Buddha-like denial of the will. He is saved by art, and through art life has saved him for itself.

The ecstasy of the Dionysiac state, abolishing the habitual barriers and boundaries of existence, actually contains, for its duration, a lethargic element into which all past personal experience is plunged. Thus, through this gulf of oblivion, the worlds of everyday and Dionysiac reality become separated. But when one once more becomes aware of this everyday reality, it becomes repellent; this leads to a mood of asceticism, of denial of the will. This is something that Dionysiac man shares with Hamlet: both have truly seen to the essence of things, they have *understood*, and action repels them; for their action can change nothing in the eternal essence of things, they consider it ludicrous or shameful that they should be expected to restore order to the chaotic world. Understanding kills action, action depends on a veil of illusion – this is what Hamlet teaches us, not the stock interpretation of Hamlet as a John-a-dreams who, from too much reflection, from an excess of possibilities, so to speak, fails to act. Not reflection, not that! – True understanding, insight into the terrible truth, outweighs every motive for action, for Hamlet and Dionysiac man alike. No consolation will be of any use from now on, longing passes over the world towards death, beyond the gods themselves; existence, radiantly reflected in the gods or in an immortal 'Beyond', is denied. Aware of truth from a single glimpse of it, all man can now see is the horror and absurdity of existence; now he understands the symbolism of Ophelia's fate, now he understands the wisdom of Silenus, the god of the woods: it repels him.

Here, in this supreme menace to the will, there approaches a redeeming, healing enchantress – *art*. She alone can turn these thoughts of repulsion at the horror and absurdity of existence into ideas compatible with life: these are the *sublime* – the taming of horror through art; and *comedy* – the artistic release from the repellence of the absurd. The satyr chorus of the dithyramb is the salvation of Greek art; the frenzies described above were exhausted in the middle world of these Dionysiac attendants.

8

The satyr, like the idyllic shepherd of our own more recent age, is the product of a longing for the primal and the natural; but how firmly and fearlessly did the Greeks hold on to this man of the woods, and how effeminately and timidly has modern man dallied with the flattering image of a dainty, flute-playing, sentimental shepherd! Nature, still unaffected by knowledge, the bolts of culture still unforced – that is what the Greeks saw in their satyr, and for that reason they did not conflate him with the apes. On the contrary – he was the archetype of man, the expression of his highest and most intense emotions, an inspired reveller enraptured by the closeness of his god, a sympathetic companion in whom god's suffering is repeated, the harbinger of wisdom from the very breast of nature, a symbol of nature's sexual omnipotence, which the Greeks were accustomed to considering with respectful astonishment. The satyr was something divine and sublime; he must have seemed particularly so to the painfully broken gaze of Dionysiac man. He would have been insulted by the dressed-up, meretricious shepherd: his eye rested in sublime satisfaction on the undisguised, untroubled and wondrous traits of nature; here, the illusion of culture had been erased from the archetype of man – it was here that the true man revealed himself, the bearded satyr celebrating his god. Before him, the man of culture shrivelled up into a mendacious caricature. Schiller was right in his appraisal of these origins of tragic art: the chorus is a living wall against encroaching reality because it – the satyr chorus – depicts existence more truly, more authentically, more completely than the man of culture who sees himself as the sole reality. The realm of poetry does not lie outside the world, a fantastic impossibility, the product of a poet's mind; it wishes to be precisely the opposite of this, the unadorned expression of truth, and must for that very reason cast off the mendacious finery of the supposed reality of the man of culture. The contrast between this authentic, natural truth and the lie of culture masquerading as the sole reality is like the contrast between the eternal core of things, the thing in itself, and the entire world of phenomena; and just as tragedy, with its metaphysical consolation, points to the eternal life of that core and the constant destruction of phenomena, the symbolism of the satyr chorus analogously expresses the primal relationship between the thing in itself and the world of appearances. Modern man's idyllic shepherd is nothing but a counterfeit of the sum of cultural illusions that he takes to be nature; the Dionysiac Greek wanted truth and nature at the summit of their power – and saw himself transformed into a satyr.

The ecstatic horde of Dionysiac votaries celebrated under the influence of such moods and insights, whose power was so transformed before their very eyes that they imagined they saw themselves as reconstituted geniuses of nature, as satyrs. The later constitution of the tragic chorus is the artistic imitation of this natural phenomenon, which required a separation between Dionysiac spectators and Dionysiac votaries who are under the god's spell. But we must never forget that the audience of the Attic tragedy discovered itself in the chorus of the orchestra, and that there was no fundamental opposition between the audience and the chorus: for everything was simply a great, sublime chorus of dancing, singing satyrs, or of those whom the satyrs represented. Schlegel's phrase must take on a different sense in this context. The chorus is the 'ideal spectator' in so far as it is the only *viewer*, the viewer of the visionary world on the stage. The audience of spectators as we know it was unknown to the Greeks: in their theatres anyone in the terraces, rising in concentric arcs, was able to *overlook* the whole of the surrounding cultural world, and, in satisfied contemplation, to imagine themselves members of the chorus. Thus we may call the chorus, at this primitive stage of the original tragedy, a reflection of Dionysiac man for his own contemplation. We can

imagine this phenomenon most clearly if we think of an actor who, such is his talent, can see the role that he is to perform hovering palpably before his eyes. The satyr chorus is primarily a vision of the Dionysiac mass, just as the world on the stage is a vision of this satyr chorus: the power of this vision is strong enough to make the gaze dull and unresponsive to the impression of 'reality', to the men of culture in the seats all around. The shape of the Greek theatre recalls a lonely mountain valley: the stage architecture appears as a luminous cloud formation seen by the Bacchae, as they swarm down from the mountains, as the wonderful frame in the middle of which the image of Dionysus is revealed to them.

To our scholarly view of the elemental artistic processes, this primal aesthetic phenomenon, evoked as a way of explaining the tragic chorus, is almost repellent; while nothing could be clearer than that the poet becomes a poet only by seeing himself surrounded by characters living and acting before him, and allowing him to see into their innermost natures. A particularly modern weakness inclines us to see the primal aesthetic phenomenon in too complicated and abstract a way. For the true poet the metaphor is not a rhetorical figure but a representative image that really hovers before him in place of a concept. For him, the character is not a whole laboriously assembled from individual traits, but a person, insistently living before his eyes, distinguished from the otherwise identical vision of the painter by his continuous life and action. How is it that Homer describes things so much more visually than any other poet? Because he looks so much more clearly. We talk of poetry in such an abstract way because most of us are bad poets. The aesthetic phenomenon is fundamentally a simple one: grant someone only the ability continually to see a living play, to live constantly surrounded by hordes of spirits, and he will be a poet. If one feels the desire to transform oneself and to speak from other bodies and souls, one is a dramatist.

Dionysiac excitement is capable of communicating to a whole crowd of people the artistic gift of seeing itself surrounded by a host of spirits with which it knows itself to be profoundly united. This process is the primal dramatic phenomenon in the tragic chorus: seeing oneself transformed and acting as though one had truly entered another body, another character. This process is the start of the evolution of the drama. This is a different matter from the rhapsodist who does not fuse with his images but rather, like the painter, sees them out-side himself with a contemplative eye; it is an abandonment of individuality by entering another character. And this phenomenon appears with epidemic frequency: a whole host of people can be cast under this spell. For this reason the dithyramb is significantly different from all other forms of choric song. The virgins who solemnly enter the temple of Apollo, laurel branches in their hands, singing a processional song, remain who they are and keep their names as citizens: the dithyrambic chorus is a chorus of people transformed, whose civic past and social status are completely forgotten: they have become the timeless worshippers of their god, beyond all social contingencies. All the other choral lyrics of the Greeks are merely a tremendous intensification of the individual Apolline singer, while in the dithyramb a community of unconscious actors stands before us, seeing themselves as transformed.

Enchantment is the precondition of all dramatic art. In this enchantment the Dionysiac reveller sees himself as a satyr, *and it is as a satyr that he looks upon the god*: in his transformation he sees a new vision outside himself, the Apolline complement of his state. With this new vision the drama is complete.

In the light of this insight, we must see Greek tragedy as the Dionysiac chorus, continuously discharging itself in an Apolline world of images. Those choric sections which recur throughout the tragedy are therefore, so to speak, the womb of what is called the dialogue, the entire on-stage world, the drama proper. In several successive discharges this primal ground of tragedy radiates that vision of the drama which is entirely a dream phenomenon and thus epic in nature, but on the other hand, as the objectification of a Dionysiac state, it is not Apolline redemption through illusion but rather a representation of the fragmentation of the individual and his unification with primal being. Thus the drama is the Apolline symbol of Dionysiac knowledge and Dionysiac effects, and consequently separated from the epic as by a tremendous chasm.

This interpretation perfectly explains the *chorus* in Greek tragedy, the symbol of the crowd in a Dionysiac state. Accustomed as we are to the function of a chorus on the modern stage, and the operatic chorus in particular, we are unable to understand that the tragic chorus of the Greeks is older, more primordial, indeed more important than the 'action' itself – as tradition has so clearly

told us. Given that traditionally great importance and originality, we cannot discern why it should have been made up exclusively of humble votaries, at first only of goat-like satyrs, and the orchestra in front of the stage was always a puzzle to us. But we now know that the stage, and the action, were fundamentally and originally conceived only as a *vision*, that the sole 'reality' is the chorus, which generates the vision from within itself, and speaks of it with all the symbolism of dance, sound and words. In its vision this chorus beholds its lord and master, Dionysus, and hence it is always a chorus of *votaries*: it sees how he, the god, suffers and is exalted, and it therefore does not *act* itself. In this function of complete devotion to the god, it is the supreme, Dionysiac expression of *nature*, and therefore, like nature, it speaks under the spell of wise and oracular sayings. *Sharing his suffering*, it is also *wise*, heralding the truth from the very heart of the world. This is the origin of that fantastic, apparently repellent figure of the wise and inspired satyr, which is also the 'simple man' in contrast to the god: the image of nature and nature's strongest impulses, the symbol of those impulses and also the herald of its wisdom and art – musician, poet, dancer and clairvoyant in a single person.

At first *Dionysus*, the true stage hero and the focus of the vision, is, in the light of this insight and according to tradition, not really present in the very oldest period of tragedy, but is only imagined to be present: tragedy, that is, is originally 'chorus' and not 'drama'. Later, the attempt is made to show the god as real, and to represent the visionary form as well as its transfiguring frame in a form visible to all eyes: this is the beginning of the 'drama' in the narrower sense. Now the dithyrambic chorus is given the task of stimulating the mood of the audience in such a Dionysiac way that when the tragic hero appears on the stage they do not see, for example, the awkwardly masked man, but rather a visionary form born, so to speak, out of their own rapt vision. If we consider Admetus lost in contemplation, recalling his recently departed wife Alcestis and completely consumed by his imaginary vision of her – and suddenly a woman with a similar form and gait is led towards him in disguise; if we imagine his sudden tremor of unease, his impetuous comparison, his instinctive conviction – then we have an analogy to the emotion that the spectator felt when, in a state of Dionysiac excitement, he saw the god, with whose suffering he had already identified, walking on to the stage. He involuntarily translated the entire image of the god that was trembling before his soul to that masked figure, and dissolved its reality into a ghostly unreality. This is the Apolline dream state, in which the daylight world is veiled and a new world, more distinct, comprehensible and affecting than the other and yet more shadowy, is constantly reborn before our eyes. Accordingly, we can see a radical contrast of styles in tragedy: the language, colour, mobility and dynamic of speech become completely separate spheres of expression in the Dionysiac lyric of the chorus and the Apolline dream world of the stage. The Apolline phenomena in which Dionysus is objectified are no longer 'a boundless sea, a changing weft, a glowing life', like the music of the chorus; they are not only those powers that the inspired worshipper of Dionysus merely feels and does not condense into an image, in which he feels the closeness of the god. Now, the clarity and solidity of the epic form speak to him from the stage. Dionysus no longer speaks through powers, but as an epic hero, almost with the language of Homer.

9

Everything that comes to the surface in the Apolline part of Greek tragedy, the dialogue, looks simple, transparent and beautiful. In this sense the dialogue is an image of the Hellene, whose nature is revealed in dance, because in dance the greatest strength is only potential, but is betrayed in the suppleness and luxuriance of movement. Thus the language of Sophoclean heroes surprises us with its Apolline precision and lucidity, so that we immediately imagine we can see into the innermost core of their being, somewhat astonished that the way to that core is such a short one. But if we leave aside the characteristics of the hero – who is basically merely a light-image cast on a dark screen, *appearance* through and through – that come to the surface and attain visibility; if we instead penetrate the myth projected in these bright reflections, we suddenly experience something that is the opposite of a familiar optical phenomenon. If we make a concerned effort to stare into the sun and turn away blinded, we have dark-coloured patches before our eyes as what we might call remedies. The light-image manifestations of the Sophoclean hero – the Apolline mask, in short – are the inevitable products of a glance into the terrible depths of nature: light-patches, we might say, to heal the gaze seared by

terrible night. Only in this sense can we imagine that we correctly understand the serious and meaningful concept of 'Greek cheerfulness' – while today, of course, we constantly encounter this concept of cheerfulness wrongly understood as a state of untroubled contentment.

Sophocles saw the most suffering character on the Greek stage, the unhappy Oedipus, as the noble man who is predestined for error and misery despite his wisdom, but who finally, through his terrible suffering, exerts a magical and beneficial power that continues to prevail after his death. The noble man does not sin, the profound poet wishes to tell us: through his actions every law, every natural order, the whole moral world can be destroyed, and through these actions a higher magic circle of effects is drawn, founding a new world on the ruins of the old, now destroyed. This is what the poet, in so far as he is also a religious thinker, wishes to say to us: as a poet, he first presents us with a wonderfully intricate legal knot which the judge slowly unravels, piece by piece, to his own ruin; such is the truly Hellenic delight in this dialectical unravelment that it casts a sense of triumphant cheerfulness over the whole work, and takes the sting from all the terrible premises of the plot. In *Oedipus at Colonus* we encounter this same cheerfulness, but elevated in a process of infinite transfiguration. The aged man, afflicted by an excess of misery, abandoned to every misfortune that comes his way as a passively *suffering* man, is confronted by a super-terrestrial cheerfulness that descends from the gods, which suggests to us that the hero, through his passivity, has found his supreme activity, the effects of which will resonate far beyond his own life, while his conscious strivings in his former life led him only to passivity. Thus the legal knot of the Oedipus fable, which mortal eyes could not disentangle, is slowly unravelled – and the most profound human delight overcomes us at the sight of this divine counterpart of the dialectic.

If this explanation does justice to the poet, we may still ask whether it has exhausted the content of the myth: and here it becomes apparent that the whole vision of the poet is nothing but that light-image that healing nature holds up to us after we have glimpsed the abyss. Oedipus his father's murderer, his mother's husband, Oedipus who solved the riddle of the Sphinx! What can we learn from the cryptic trinity of these fateful deeds? There is an ancient folk belief, particularly prevalent in Persia, that a wise magus can be born only from incest: our immediate interpretation of this, with reference to Oedipus the riddle-solver and suitor of his own mother, is that for clairvoyant and magical powers to have broken the spell of the present and the future, the rigid law of individuation and the true magic of nature itself, the cause must have been a monstrous crime against nature – incest in this case; for how could nature be forced to offer up her secrets if not by being triumphantly resisted – by unnatural acts? I see this insight as quite clearly present in the terrible trinity that shapes Oedipus' fate: the man who solves the riddle of nature – of the dual-natured Sphinx – must also, as his father's murderer and his mother's lover, transgress the sacred codes of nature. Indeed, what the myth seems to whisper to us is that wisdom, and Dionysiac wisdom in particular, is an abominable crime against nature; that anyone who, through his knowledge, casts nature into the abyss of destruction, must himself experience the dissolution of nature. 'The blade of wisdom is turned against the wise; wisdom is a crime against nature': such are the awful sentences that the myth cries out to us. But like a beam of sunlight the Hellenic poet touches the sublime and terrible Memnon's Column of the myth, which suddenly begins to resound in Sophoclean melodies!

I shall now contrast the glory of passivity with the glory of activity that illuminates Aeschylus' *Prometheus*. What the thinker Aeschylus had to say, but what as a poet he only hinted at with his symbolic image, the young Goethe revealed in the bold words of his Prometheus:

> Hier sitz' ich, forme Menschen
> Nach meinem Bilde,
> Ein Geschlecht, das mir gleich sei,
> Zu leiden, zu weinen,
> Zu genießen und zu freuen sich,
> Und dein nicht zu achten,
> Wie ich!

> (Here I sit, making men
> In my image,
> A race which shall be like me,
> To suffer, to weep,
> To enjoy and be glad,
> And to ignore you,
> As I do!)

Man, rising to Titanic stature, fights for his own culture and compels allegiance from the gods, because in his very own wisdom he has their exist-

ence and their limitations under his command. But the most wonderful thing about the Prometheus poem, which is, by virtue of its fundamental idea, a true hymn of impiety, is its profound Aeschylean longing for *justice*: the immeasurable suffering of the bold 'individual' on the one hand and the divine tribulation, the intimation of a twilight of the gods, on the other; the power of both suffering worlds compelling reconciliation, metaphysical unity, insistently recalls the core and the chief premise of Aeschylus' view of the world, which sees the Moira enthroned as eternal justice above gods and men. Given the astounding boldness with which Aeschylus places the Olympian world on his scales of justice, we must not forget that the profound Greek had an unshakeable substratum of metaphysical thought in his mysteries, and was able to discharge all his feelings of scepticism on to the Olympian gods. The Greek artist in particular felt an obscure sense of reciprocal dependency with these gods – and this feeling is symbolized in the Prometheus of Aeschylus. The Titanic artist found within himself the defiant belief that he was enabled to create men and at least to destroy Olympian gods by his superior wisdom, for which he was, of course, compelled to atone with eternal suffering. The glorious 'ability' of the great genius, for which even eternal suffering is not recompense enough, the austere pride of the *artist*, is the very essence of Aeschylean poetry, while in his *Oedipus* Sophocles intones, as a prelude, [a] song of triumph to the *saint*.

But even Aeschylus' interpretation of the myth does not plumb the full depths of its terrors: the artist's desire for development, the cheerfulness of artistic creation in its defiance of all misfortune, is merely a bright image of clouds and sky reflected on a black lake of sorrow. The story of Prometheus is the indigenous property of all Aryan peoples, and a testament to their talent for profundity and tragedy – indeed it may well be that this myth has precisely the same characteristic meaning for the Aryan spirit as does the myth of the Fall for the Semitic, and that the two myths are as siblings to one another. But the premise for the Prometheus myth is the supreme value that primitive man places on *fire* as the true palladium of any rising culture: but the idea that man has complete control of fire, and does not only receive it as a gift from heaven, as a kindling bolt of lightning or a warming sunbeam, struck those contemplative primitive men as a sacrilege, a plundering of divine nature. And thus the first philosophical problem created a painful and insoluble contradiction between man and the gods, and placed it like a boulder at the gates of every culture. The best and highest blessing that mankind can attain was won by an act of sacrilege, and man must now take the consequences – the tide of suffering and troubles with which the offended divinities punish the nobly ambitious human race: a severe idea, which by the *dignity* that it confers on sacrilege contrasts oddly with the Semitic myth of the Fall, in which curiosity, mendacious deception, susceptibility, lasciviousness – a whole series of predominantly feminine attributes – were seen as the origin of evil. What distinguishes the Aryan version is the sublime idea of *active sin* as the truly Promethean virtue: this provides both the ethical background to pessimistic tragedy and the justification of human evil, and hence of human guilt as well as the suffering it brings. Misfortune the essence of things – which the contemplative Aryan was not inclined to quibble away – the contradiction at the heart of the world was revealed to him as a confusion of different worlds, a divine and a human world, for example, both individually in the right, but each merely one individual beside another, suffering from its individuation. In the individual's heroic effort to achieve universality, in the attempt to escape the spell of individuation, to become the only being in the world, he encounters the hidden primal contradiction – he commits sacrilege, that is, and he suffers. Thus the Aryans saw sacrilege as a man, while the Semites saw sin as a woman, just as the primal sacrilege was committed by man, the primal sin by woman. As the witches' chorus has it, incidentally:

Wir nehmen das nicht so genau:
Mit tausend Schritten macht's die Frau;
Doch wie sie auch sich eilen kann,
Mit einem Sprunge macht's der Mann. [...]

(That's not exactly what we'd say:
A thousand steps is woman's way;
But however fast she covers ground
Man does it in a single bound.)

Once we understand the innermost core of the Prometheus myth – the necessity of sacrilege that confronts the Titanically striving individual – we must also immediately perceive the non-Apolline qualities of this pessimistic idea. For Apollo seeks to pacify individuals by drawing boundaries between them, and by repeatedly calling them to mind as the most sacred universal laws in his demands for self-knowledge and moderation. But lest the Apolline tendency should freeze all form into an Egyptian rigidity and coldness, lest the effort to prescribe the course and compass of the individual wave should still the motion of the lake, from time to time the Dionysiac flood-tide destroyed all the little circles with which the one-sided Apolline 'will' sought to captivate Hellenism. The sudden rise of the Dionysiac tide then takes upon its back the little individual wavelets, just as Prometheus' brother, the Titan Atlas, took the world on his. This Titanic impulse to become the Atlas of all individuals, and on one's broad back to bear them ever higher, ever further, is the bond that unites the Promethean and the Dionysiac. In this respect the Aeschylean Prometheus is a Dionysiac mask, while in the profound longing for justice that I have already mentioned, Aeschylus reveals his paternal descent from Apollo, the god of individuation and of just boundaries, the god of understanding. And the two-faced nature of the Aeschylean Prometheus, at once Apolline and Promethean, might be expressed in this conceptual formula: 'All that exists is just and unjust and equally justified in both.'

Your world, this! So that's a world! [...]

10

It is an uncontested tradition that Greek tragedy in its oldest form dealt only with the sufferings of Dionysus, and that for a long time Dionysus was the only theatrical hero. But we may claim with equal certainty that, until Euripides, Dionysus never ceased to be the tragic hero, and that all the celebrated characters of the Greek stage – Prometheus, Oedipus and so on – are merely masks of that original hero, Dionysus. The fact that a divinity lurks behind all these masks is the major reason for the typical 'ideality' of those celebrated characters that has so often aroused astonishment. Someone, I do not know who, claims that all individuals, as individuals, are comic and consequently untragic: from which we can deduce that the Greeks were actually *unable* to bear individuals on the tragic stage. And they do seem to have felt that way, just as the Platonic distinguishing valuation of the 'idea' as against the 'idol' lies deep within the Hellenic spirit. But to use Plato's terminology, we might speak of the tragic figures of the Hellenic stage rather as follows: the one real Dionysus appears in a multiplicity of figures, in the mask of a warrior hero and, we might say, entangled in the net of the individual will. As the god on stage speaks and acts, he resembles an erring, striving, suffering individual: and the fact that he *appears* with this precision and clarity is the effect of Apollo, the interpreter of dreams, who shows the chorus its Dionysiac state through this symbolic appearance. In fact, however, this hero is the suffering Dionysus of the mysteries, the god who himself experiences the suffering of individuation, of whom marvellous myths relate that he was dismembered by the Titans and that, in this condition, he is worshipped as Zagreus. This suggests that dismemberment, the true Dionysiac *suffering*, amounts to a transformation into air, water, earth and fire, and that we should therefore see the condition of individuation as the source and origin of all suffering and hence as something reprehensible. From the smile of this Dionysus were born the Olympian gods, from his tears mankind. In his existence as a dismembered god Dionysus had the dual nature of a cruel, savage daemon and a mild, gentle ruler. But the hope of the epopts [Dionysiac initiates] was the rebirth of Dionysus, which we can now interpret, with some foreboding, as the end of individuation: the roaring hymn of joy of the epopts celebrated the coming of this third Dionysus. This hope alone casts a ray of joy across the face of the world, torn and fragmented into individuals, mythically symbolized by Demeter, sunk in eternal grief, who *rejoices* once more only when told that she can give birth to Dionysus *again*. In these ideas we already have all the component parts of a profound and pessimistic view of the world, and at the same time the *mystery doctrine of tragedy*: the basic understanding of the unity of all things, individuation seen as the primal source of evil, art as the joyful hope that the spell of individuation can be broken, as a presentiment of a restored oneness.

We suggested earlier that the Homeric epic is the poetry of Olympian culture, its own song of triumph about the terrors of the battle with the Titans. Now, under the overwhelming influence of tragic poetry, the Homeric myths are reborn in a different form, and in this metempsychosis show that Olympian culture too has been vanquished by an even deeper vision of the world. The defiant Titan Prometheus informed his Olympian tormentor that his supremacy was in the greatest danger if he delayed too long in joining forces with him. In Aeschylus we see Zeus, terrified and fearful of his end, forging an alliance with the Titan. Thus the former age of the Titans is belatedly brought back from Tartarus into the light of day. The philosophy of wild and naked nature sees the myths of the Homeric world dancing by, with the frank and honest gaze of truth: they blanch, they tremble under the flashing eye of this goddess – until the mighty fist of the Dionysiac artist compels them to worship this new deity. Dionysiac truth takes over the whole sphere of myth as a symbolic expression of its own insights, and gives it voice partly in the public cult of tragedy and partly in the secret rites of the dramatic mysteries, but always in the old mythic trappings. What was this force that freed Prometheus from his vultures and made myth the vehicle of Dionysiac wisdom? It was the Herculean force of music – which, supremely manifested in tragedy, was able to interpret myth with a new and most profound eloquence. This, as we have already shown, is music's most powerful capacity. For it is the lot of all myths to creep gradually into the confines of a supposedly historical reality, and to be treated by some later age as unique fact with claims to historical truth; and the Greeks, cleverly and capriciously, were already well on the way to recasting the whole of their youthful mythic dream as a pragmatic *youthful history*. For this is how religions tend to die: the mythic premises of a religion are systematized, beneath the stern and intelligent eyes of an orthodox dogmatism, into a fixed sum of historical events; one begins nervously defending the veracity of myths, at the same time resisting their continuing life and growth. The feeling for myth dies and is replaced by religious claims to foundations in history. This dying myth was now seized by the new-born genius of Dionysiac music; and in the hand of that music it blossomed anew, with colours such as it had never shown before, with a fragrance that hinted wistfully at the existence of a metaphysical world. After this last florescence it decays, its leaves wither, and soon the mocking Lucians of antiquity are clutching at the faded, ravaged blossoms as they are carried away by the four winds. It is through tragedy that myth attains its most profound content, its most expressive form; it rises up once more, like a wounded hero, and all the surplus energy, together with the sagacious calm of the dying man, burns in its eyes with a last, powerful glow.

What was your wish, sacrilegious Euripides, when you tried to force that dying myth into your service once more? [. . .] It died beneath your violent hands: and then you needed a counterfeit, masked myth which, like Heracles' monkey, could only deck itself out in the old finery. And as myth died for you, so the genius of music died as well: though you greedily plundered all the gardens of music, all you could manage was a counterfeit, masked music. And because you abandoned Dionysus, Apollo in his turn abandoned you; though you rouse all the passions from their beds and bewitch them into your circle, though you whet and hone a sophistical dialectic for the speeches of your heroes, they too will have only counterfeit, masked passions, and speak only counterfeit, masked speeches.

II

Greek tragedy met her death in a different way from all the older sister arts: she died tragically by her own hand, after irresolvable conflicts, while the others died happy and peaceful at an advanced age. If a painless death, leaving behind beautiful progeny, is the sign of a happy natural state, then the endings of the other arts show us the example of just such a happy natural state: they sink slowly, and with their dying eyes they behold their fairer offspring, who lift up their heads in bold impatience. The death of Greek tragedy, on the other hand, left a great void whose effects were felt profoundly, far and wide; as once Greek sailors in Tiberius' time heard the distressing cry 'the god Pan is dead' issuing from a lonely island, now, throughout the Hellenic world, this cry resounded like an agonized lament: 'Tragedy is dead! Poetry itself died with it! Away, away with you, puny, stunted imitators! Away with you to Hades, and eat your fill of the old masters' crumbs!'

But when a new artistic genre did spring into life, honouring tragedy as its predecessor and its master, it was frighteningly apparent that although it bore its mother's features they were the features she had borne during her long death-struggle. It was *Euripides* who fought tragedy's death-struggle; the later genre is known as the *New Attic Comedy*. It was in comedy that the degenerate figure of tragedy lived on, a monument to its miserable and violent death.

This context enables us to understand the passionate affection in which the poets of the New Comedy held Euripides; so that we are no longer startled by the desire of Philemon, who wished to be hanged at once so that he might meet Euripides in the underworld, as long as he could be sure that the deceased was still in full possession of his senses. But if we wished, quite briefly and without claiming to be exhaustive, to identify the bonds that linked Euripides with Menander and Philemon, and so say what they found exciting and exemplary in him, we need say only that Euripides brought the *spectator* on to the stage. Once we have recognized the stuff of which the pre-Euripidean Promethean dramatists shaped their heroes, and understood how little concerned they were to bring on to the stage an accurate mask of reality, we shall also understand the quite opposite tendency in Euripides. Through him, everyday man pushed his way through the auditorium on to the stage, and the mirror in which only great and bold features had hitherto found expression now showed the painful fidelity that also reflected the blemished lines of nature. Odysseus, the typical Hellene of the older art, now sank, beneath the hands of the new poets, into the figure of the Graeculus, who from this point onwards occupied centre-stage as a good-natured, cunning slave. What Euripides, in the *Frogs* of Aristophanes, accounts a merit in himself – that he has, with his nostrum, rid tragic art of its pompous obesity – is particularly apparent in his tragic heroes. In essence, the spectator now saw and heard his double on the Euripidean stage, and was overjoyed by his eloquence. But joy was not all: Euripides taught the people to speak for themselves, as he boasts in his competition with Aeschylus – how he taught the people to observe, to act and to think logically, artfully and with the cleverest sophistries. In this transformation of ordinary language he paved the way for the new comedy. For from that point on, it was no longer a mystery how to represent everyday life on the stage, and which maxims to use. The bourgeois mediocrity on which Euripides staked all his political hopes now had its chance to speak, where previously its dramatic language had been defined in tragedy by the demigod, and in comedy by the drunken satyr, the half-human. And Aristophanes' Euripides was able to pride himself on having portrayed mundane, commonplace, everyday life, which anyone was in a position to judge. If the populace was now philosophizing, conducting its business and pleading its legal cases with a hitherto unknown shrewdness, this was his doing, the product of the wisdom he had inculcated in the people.

It was to such a primed and enlightened populace that the new comedy was now able to address itself, with Euripides as a kind of chorus-master – although this time the chorus of spectators needed some rehearsing. Once this chorus was practised at singing in the Euripidean key, there came to the fore the dramatic genre that is like a game of chess, the New Comedy, with its perpetual triumphs of cunning and guile. But Euripides – the chorus-master – was the object of untiring praise: indeed, there were some who would have killed themselves to learn more from him, had they not known that the tragic poet was just as dead as tragedy itself. But along with tragedy the Hellene had relinquished belief in his immortality, belief not only in an ideal past, but also in an ideal future. The celebrated epitaph, 'frivolous and whimsical in old age', applies equally well to the senescent phase of Hellenism. The pleasure of the moment, wit, whimsy and caprice were its supreme deities; the fifth estate, the slaves, now came into its own, at least in attitude: and if we may still speak at all of 'Greek cheerfulness', we mean the cheerfulness of the slave, who has no serious responsibilities and nothing great to strive for, and who values nothing, past or future, more highly than the present. It was this illusion of 'Greek cheerfulness' that so enraged the profound and formidable minds of the first four centuries after Christ: they considered this womanish flight from seriousness and terror, this craven acquiescence in cosy enjoyment, not only contemptible but the very opposite of the Christian attitude. And it is due to their influence that the vision of Greek antiquity that survived for centuries, with almost unconquerable resilience, retained the rosy hues of cheerfulness – as though there had never been a sixth century, with its birth of tragedy, its mysteries, its Pythagoras and Heraclitus; as though the works of art from that great age simply did not exist. Yet none of those works could have grown from the soil of such a senescent, slavish cheerfulness and pleasure in life, and they point to a completely different vision of the world as the basis for their existence.

In asserting as I have done that Euripides brought the spectator on to the stage in order to render the spectator competent to judge the drama, I may have given the impression that the older tragic art had always had a poor relationship with the spectator; and one might be tempted to praise Euripides' radical intentions, aiming for an appropriate relationship between the work and the audience, as marking an advance over the work of Sophocles. But 'audience' is merely a word, and not a constant, immutable standard. Why should the artist feel obliged to accommodate himself to a force whose strength lies purely in its numbers? And if he feels superior, in talent and aspiration, to every single spectator, how could he feel greater respect for the collective expression of all those subordinate capacities than for that individual spectator who is, in relative terms, the most gifted among them? In truth, no Greek artist treated his audience with greater audacity and self-sufficiency throughout a whole lifetime than did Euripides: he who, even when the populace threw itself at his feet, publicly and with sublime defiance renounced his own intentions, those same intentions that had established his victory over the populace. Had this genius had the slightest reverence for the pandemonium that was his audience, he would have collapsed beneath the bludgeons of his failures long before the mid-course of his life. We now come to realize that our formula: 'Euripides brought the spectator on to the stage to render the spectator capable of judgement', was merely provisional, and that we must look further for a deeper understanding of his intentions. On the other hand, everyone knows that Aeschylus and Sophocles were held in the highest popular favour in their lifetimes and long afterwards, so we cannot speak of poor relationships between the work and the audience. What was it that drove the richly talented, tirelessly creative artist so violently away from a path illumined by the sun of the greatest poets and the clear sky of popular favour? What strange consideration for the spectator led him towards the spectator? How did an excessive respect for his audience lead him to treat his audience with disrespect?

As a poet, Euripides felt – and this is the answer to the riddle that we have just expressed – superior to the populace, but not to two of his spectators: he brought the populace on to the stage, but revered those two spectators as the sole judges and masters competent to judge his art as a whole; following their directives and exhortations he translated the whole world of emotions, passions and experiences, hitherto present in the ranks of spectators, into the souls of his stage heroes, deferring to them in his quest for a new language, a new music for these new characters. In their voices alone he heard both conclusive verdicts on his work and the encouragement that promised victory when the judgement of the audience once more held him in disfavour.

One of these two spectators is Euripides himself: Euripides the *thinker*, not the poet. It might be said that the extraordinary richness of his critical talent, like that of Lessing, while it might not have generated a supplementary productive impetus to his art, at least gave it constant sustenance. With this talent, this critical brilliance and agility, Euripides had sat in the theatre striving to rediscover in the masterworks of his great predecessors feature after feature, line after line, which time had darkened as it darkens old paintings. And in doing so he had discovered what anyone initiated into the deep secrets of Aeschylean tragedy might have expected: in every feature, every line, he found something incommensurable, a certain deceptive precision and at the same time an enigmatic depth, an infinite background. The clearest character still had a comet's tail attached to it, which seemed to point to uncertainty, to something that could not be illuminated. The same twilight shrouded the structure of the play, particularly the meaning of the chorus. And how dubious the solution of the ethical problems remained to him! How questionable the treatment of myth! How irregular the distribution of fortune and misfortune! Even in the language of the older tragedies he found much that was repellent, or puzzling at the very least. In particular, he found too much pomp for simple relationships, too many tropes and monstrosities for such plain characters. He sat there in the theatre, brooding restlessly, and he, as a spectator, confessed that he did not understand his great predecessors. But given his belief that reason was the true source of all enjoyment and creativity, he was obliged to wonder whether no one else thought as he did and admitted the existence of this incommensurability. But the multitude, and its finest individuals, answered him only with a suspicious smile; yet no one could tell him why, despite his doubts and misgivings, the great masters were right. And in this tormented state he came upon *the second spectator*, who did not understand tragedy and therefore chose to ignore it. Having joined forces with him, he was able, from his isolated position, to launch his tremendous battle against the works of Aeschylus and Sophocles – not by means of polemics, but as a dramatic poet, confronting traditional conceptions of tragedy with his own.

Introduction

We can find grounds for the transition of aesthetics from romanticism to modernism in Walter Benjamin's bold thesis about mechanical reproduction in relation to art. According to Benjamin, what is distinctive about modern art is not its uniqueness or "authenticity" but its ability to reproduce any image at any time *ad infinitum*. With this claim goes another: "that which withers in the age of mechanical reproduction is the aura of the work of art." Benjamin meant by this that with modernism the techniques of mass replication remove the art object from the domain of tradition. Benjamin reads this claim about the emancipation of art from tradition optimistically, stating that for the first time in history, mechanical reproduction emancipates the aesthetic work from its parasitical dependence on ritual. But he also expresses some nostalgia about what is lost in the process.

In contrast to Benjamin, Heidegger attempts to reclaim the relationship of art and tradition, but with the acknowledgement that modernity has separated us from the originary experience of great art. He begins with a simple question, "what is art?" In answer, Heidegger does not put forth a thesis, but performs an interrogation, which is circular. "What art is should be inferable from the work. What the work of art is we can come to know only from the nature of art. Anyone can easily see that we are moving in a circle." As the circle expands from the interrogation of the thing to the manifestation of the work of art as art, Heidegger takes his readers through a confrontation with the logocentric prejudice of Western thought and at the same time brings us back to

an originary perception of art in its unconcealedness. His inaugural question regarding art brings us in the end to an experience of art as revealing itself as truth.

Wittgenstein was equally concerned with the relations between art and truth, but with a difference. Where Benjamin focused on the sociopolitical implications of this relationship, and Heidegger on the ontological, Wittgenstein was to initiate quite another method of interrogating aesthetic questions – as epistemological conundrums of language. This linguistic approach to art was of course to prove of seminal importance for the entire "analytic" tradition of modern aesthetics (covered in a forthcoming Blackwell volume), but its impact on a number of important "continental" thinkers – notably Ricoeur, Habermas, and Lyotard – cannot be overestimated. Our inclusion of Wittgenstein in this current volume also signals our distaste for over-hasty divisions into rival theoretical camps. Wittgenstein's argument, in our selection from his *Lectures on Aesthetics*, is that art is a specific mode of experience irreducible to the standard norms of causal explanation.

Freud presents a reflection on aesthetics and the unconscious. Leonardo da Vinci's famous *Mona Lisa* becomes for Freud a basis for a psychoanalytic interrogation of its creator. He surmises that Mona Lisa's intriguing smile was a "free creation" of Leonardo's fantasy, probably an "old memory" to which he was continuously forced to give "new expression." The memory, which had been repressed, was that of his mother. For Freud this thesis is further elaborated in Leonardo's *St Anne with Two Others*, which presents a similar smile. Freud elaborates his theory by suggesting that in the latter painting we can discover the "synthesis of the history" of Leonardo's childhood. Although this text remains controversial, it provides a powerful case for the link between psychoanalysis and art.

Lukács, together with Benjamin, represents the formative impact of Hegelian-Marxist dialectics on much modern thinking about art. Opting for a "humanist" reading of dialectical materialism, based on the early Marx, Lukács exerted an enormous influence on several generations of radical aesthetic theorists determined to expose the hidden connections between works of art and the predominant power structures of social ideologies and class interests. The selection here, "The Ideology of Modernism," is a pointed and polemical text in which Lukács challenges some of the most revered premises of modernist literature.

Marcuse, a founding figure of the Frankfurt School of critical theory, challenges the Marxist reduction of art to ideological critique. Instead he argues for a specifically "aesthetic dimension" which signals qualities of innovation, transcendence, and strangeness. The main target of his essay, written toward the end of his philosophical career in 1978, is the orthodox doctrine of "social realism," which construes works of art and literature as little more than mirror reflections of existing material conditions (Lukács being the most sophisticated exponent of this view). What this reductive doctrine neglects, in Marcuse's view, is the most revolutionary aspect of all aesthetic creation: imagination's basic challenge to the status quo. Genuine aesthetic experience carries a utopian demand that things as they are must change.

Adorno, a second key exponent of the critical theory approach, explores a less utopian critique on the dialectical rapport between aesthetics and politics. In the opening chapter of his monumental *Aesthetic Theory* (1970), entitled "Art, Society, Aesthetics," he announces that everything about art has become problematic today – its relation to its inner life, to its original creator, and to the material world in which it emerges. Against the neo-Kantian and romantic idealists who claim the aesthetic bears no relation to society, Adorno retorts that even the most "sublime" work takes up a definite position vis-à-vis reality by stepping outside of current reality's sway in very concrete ways. But this does not prevent art from, in turn,

inscribing critical and alternative modes of cognizing the world. Within the dialectical school of criticism, Adorno might be said to occupy something of a middle position between Lukács's sociological critique and Marcuse's utopianism.

Bakhtin contributes yet another original, one might even say idiosyncratic, voice to the controversy about the social impact of art. For Bakhtin two main characteristics, the carnivalesque and heteroglossia, distinguish the great works of modern literature. In "Discourse in the Novel," he relates literary texts to their historical circumstances, endorsing the view that "prose art" carries a revolutionary charge capable of transforming the existing structures of society by introducing a radical multiplicity of voices. Where poetry indulges in rarefied language, the art of prose evinces "a deliberate feeling for the historical and social concreteness of living discourse." All great modern novels are, for Bakhtin, "still warm from [the social] struggle" of their times. Somewhat marginalized in his native Russia and isolated from the main aesthetic debates taking place elsewhere in Europe, Bakhtin adds a singular and arresting perspective to the contemporary literature–politics debate.

Croce, one of the founding fathers of Italian idealism, construes art as a *sui generis* act of creation independent of all predetermining influences. The short selection included here from his classic *Theory of Aesthetic* features the argument that the original act of artistic production ("genius") is identical to the reproductive act of critical judgment (what he calls "taste"). Promoting a radical method of "historical interpretation" – which was to greatly inform theorists such as Gentile in Italy, Collingwood in Britain, and White in America – Croce argues that genuine aesthetic judgment enables us to live in dialogical "communication with other men of the present and of the past."

Sartre and Merleau-Ponty represent the hugely influential movement of existentialism. The existential approach to art focuses on the way in which creative works express a specific life-project of the artist. For these thinkers, an aesthetic image or text epitomizes the way in which a human subject relates to his or her concrete lived experience. In *What is Literature?*, Sartre contends that authentic writing should express the *commitment* of its creator to change his or her society. "Words are loaded pistols," he argues, and the important thing is to aim in the right direction at the right goal. From this point of view, prose writers are preferred to poets, for while the former express their project in a clear and transparent language, the latter mesmerize us with images that pacify our minds and distract us from action on the world. This sense of urgency to transform our existence was intensified by Sartre's first-hand experience of the disasters occasioned by World War II. Sartre responded to the Nazi invasion of Europe, and of his native France, with a defiant plea to all artists to make their work politically engaged in the cause of revolutionary change and justice.

Merleau-Ponty gives a different twist to the existential dimension of art in *Eye and Mind* (1961), written some fourteen years after Sartre's *What is Literature?* Concentrating on painting rather than literature, Merleau-Ponty outlines a more ontological (and less ideological) approach to art as disclosure of the "invisible genesis of things." Where Sartre stressed the voluntary and activist aspects of creative imagination, Merleau-Ponty emphasizes the artist's immersion in the very being of the world he or she is trying to bring to visible expression. "There is no break at all in this circuit," he remarks, "it is impossible to say that nature ends here and that man or expression starts there." At times it appears that art, for Merleau-Ponty, possesses an almost mystical vision of things.

Habermas, the leading current Frankfurt school theorist, is not known for his writings on art; however, his reflections on the genre distinction between philosophy and literature add a valuable contribution to contemporary aesthetics. Informed by his position on communicative reason, Habermas defends the traditional distinction between logic and rhetoric, through a separation between the normal use of language for communicative purposes and the uses of language for mimetic purposes. A literary work releases illocutionary speech acts from their "binding force," associated with ordinary "communicative practice," opening them to the possibility of the "playful creation of new worlds" with the force of "innovative linguistic expressions." Against the position which takes the literary text to be autonomous – meaning that philosophy can be reduced to literary analysis – this view holds that there is a fundamental relation between ordinary language (and the philosophical analysis thereof) and literary expression, which in some sense may be viewed as a world-disclosing reconstruction of ordinary language.

Gadamer, whose outstanding work, *Truth and Method*, begins with a consideration of aesthetics, provides us with an ontological reflection on the nature of the work of art. Against Kant, and with Nietzsche and Heidegger, he associates the claims of art with those of truth. By elaborating the notion of aesthetics through a consideration of the concept of play, Gadamer provides us with a key to the structure of a work of art as dynamic, conveyed through temporal presentation as exemplified by the festival: "The festival exists only in its being celebrated." So it is with any work of art. In this sense, the very being of the work of art is through its temporal representation. Hence, he can claim that the specific temporality of art has "its being in the process of being represented, becomes existent in reproduction as a separate independent phenomenon."

Finally, Ricoeur adds a further inflection to the hermeneutic understanding of art and literature by foregrounding the crucial role played by "writing" and "metaphor." Whereas speech presents us with an actual world, writing transforms words into a "text" which represents a quasi-world. This metaphorizing power of texts eclipses our circumstantial environment and opens up new horizons of possible meaning – what Ricoeur calls a textual "aura" or "surplus." The metaphorical character of a work thus marks a specific "autonomy" vis-à-vis the intention of the author, the situation of the work, and the original reader. Declaring its independence from all three ties, metaphorical discourse calls for a new and deeper understanding of reference and interpretation. It reveals the curious phenomenon, central to all genuine aesthetic experience, of "semantic innovation."

The Work of Art in the Age of Mechanical Reproduction

Walter Benjamin

Our fine arts were developed, their types and uses were established, in times very different from the present, by men whose power of action upon things was insignificant in comparison with ours. But the amazing growth of our techniques, the adaptability and precision they have attained, the ideas and habits they are creating, make it a certainty that profound changes are impending in the ancient craft of the Beautiful. In all the arts there is a physical component which can no longer be considered or treated as it used to be, which cannot remain un-affected by our modern knowledge and power. For the last twenty years neither matter nor space nor time has been what it was from time immemorial. We must expect great innovations to transform the entire technique of the arts, thereby affecting artistic invention itself and perhaps even bringing about an amazing change in our very notion of art.[1]

—Paul Valéry, *Pièces sur l'art,*
"La Conquète de l'ubiquité," Paris.

Preface

When Marx undertook his critique of the capital-istic mode of production, this mode was in its infancy. Marx directed his efforts in such a way as to give them prognostic value. He went back to the basic conditions underlying capitalistic pro-duction and through his presentation showed what could be expected of capitalism in the future. The result was that one could expect it not only to exploit the proletariat with increasing intensity, but ultimately to create conditions which would make it possible to abolish capitalism itself.

The transformation of the superstructure, which takes place far more slowly than that of the substructure, has taken more than half a cen-tury to manifest in all areas of culture the change in the conditions of production. Only today can it be indicated what form this has taken. Certain prognostic requirements should be met by these statements. However, theses about the art of the proletariat after its assumption of power or about the art of a classless society would have less bearing on these demands than theses about the develop-mental tendencies of art under present conditions of production. Their dialectic is no less noticeable in the superstructure than in the economy. It would therefore be wrong to underestimate the value of such theses as a weapon. They brush aside a number of outmoded concepts, such as creativity and genius, eternal value and mystery – concepts whose uncontrolled (and at present almost uncontrollable) application would lead to a processing of data in the Fascist sense. The con-cepts which are introduced into the theory of art in what follows differ from the more familiar terms in that they are completely useless for the purposes of Fascism. They are, on the other hand, useful for the formulation of revolutionary demands in the politics of art.

I

In principle a work of art has always been repro-ducible. Manmade artifacts could always be imi-tated by men. Replicas were made by pupils in practice of their craft, by masters for diffusing their works, and, finally, by third parties in the pursuit of gain. Mechanical reproduction of a work of art, however, represents something new. Historically, it advanced intermittently and in leaps at long intervals, but with accelerated intensity. The Greeks knew only two procedures of technically reproducing works of art: founding and stamping. Bronzes, terra cottas, and coins were the only art works which they could produce in quantity. All others were unique and could not be mechanically reproduced. With the woodcut graphic art became mechanically reproducible for the first time, long before script became reproducible by print. The enormous changes which printing, the mechanical reproduction of writing, has brought about in literature are a familiar story. However, within the phenomenon which we are here examining from the perspective of world history, print is merely a special, though particularly important, case. During the Middle Ages engraving and etching were added to the woodcut; at the beginning of the nineteenth century lithography made its appearance.

With lithography the technique of reproduction reached an essentially new stage. This much more direct process was distinguished by the tracing of the design on a stone rather than its incision on a block of wood or its etching on a copperplate and permitted graphic art for the first time to put its products on the market, not only in large numbers as hitherto, but also in daily changing forms. Lithography enabled graphic art to illustrate everyday life, and it began to keep pace with printing. But only a few decades after its invention, lithography was surpassed by photography. For the first time in the process of pictorial reproduction, photography freed the hand of the most important artistic functions which henceforth devolved only upon the eye looking into a lens. Since the eye perceives more swiftly than the hand can draw, the process of pictorial reproduction was accelerated so enormously that it could keep pace with speech. A film operator shooting a scene in the studio captures the images at the speed of an actor's speech. Just as lithography virtually implied the illustrated newspaper, so did photography foreshadow the sound film. The technical reproduction of sound was tackled at the end of the last century. These convergent endeavors made predictable a situation which Paul Valéry pointed up in this sentence: "Just as water, gas, and electricity are brought into our houses from far off to satisfy our needs in response to a minimal effort, so we shall be supplied with visual or auditory images, which will appear and disappear at a simple movement of the hand, hardly more than a sign" (["The Conquest of Ubiquity,"] p. 226). Around 1900 technical reproduction had reached a standard that not only permitted it to reproduce all transmitted works of art and thus to cause the most profound change in their impact upon the public; it also had captured a place of its own among the artistic processes. For the study of this standard nothing is more revealing than the nature of the repercussions that these two different manifestations – the reproduction of works of art and the art of the film – have had on art in its traditional form.

II

Even the most perfect reproduction of a work of art is lacking in one element: its presence in time and space, its unique existence at the place where it happens to be. This unique existence of the work of art determined the history to which it was subject throughout the time of its existence. This includes the changes which it may have suffered in physical condition over the years as well as the various changes in its ownership.[2] The traces of the first can be revealed only by chemical or physical analyses which it is impossible to perform on a reproduction; changes of ownership are subject to a tradition which must be traced from the situation of the original.

The presence of the original is the prerequisite to the concept of authenticity. Chemical analyses of the patina of a bronze can help to establish this, as does the proof that a given manuscript of the Middle Ages stems from an archive of the fifteenth century. The whole sphere of authenticity is outside technical – and, of course, not only technical – reproducibility.[3] Confronted with its manual reproduction, which was usually branded as a forgery, the original preserved all its authority; not so vis à vis technical reproduction. The reason is twofold. First, process reproduction is more independent of the original than manual reproduction. For example, in photography, process reproduction can bring out those aspects of the original that are unattainable to the naked eye yet accessible to the lens, which is adjustable and chooses its angle at will. And photographic reproduction, with the aid of certain processes, such as enlargement or slow motion, can capture images which escape natural vision. Secondly, technical reproduction can put the copy of the original into situations which would be out of reach for the original itself. Above all, it enables the original to meet the beholder halfway, be it in the form of a photograph or a phonograph record. The cathedral leaves its locale to be received in the studio of a lover of art; the choral production, performed in an auditorium or in the open air, resounds in the drawing room.

The situations into which the product of mechanical reproduction can be brought may not touch the actual work of art, yet the quality of its presence is always depreciated. This holds not only for the art work but also, for instance, for a landscape which passes in review before the spectator in a movie. In the case of the art object, a most sensitive nucleus – namely, its authenticity – is interfered with whereas no natural object is vulnerable on that score. The authenticity of a thing is the essence of all that is transmissible from its beginning, ranging from its substantive duration to its testimony to the history which it has experienced. Since the historical testimony rests on the authenticity, the former, too, is jeopardized by reproduction when substantive duration ceases to matter. And what is really jeopardized when the historical testimony is affected is the authority of the object.[4]

One might subsume the eliminated element in the term "aura" and go on to say: that which withers in the age of mechanical reproduction is the aura of the work of art. This is a symptomatic process whose significance points beyond the realm of art. One might generalize by saying: the technique of reproduction detaches the reproduced object from the domain of tradition. By making many reproductions it substitutes a plurality of copies for a unique existence. And in permitting the reproduction to meet the beholder or listener in his own particular situation, it reactivates the object reproduced. These two processes lead to a tremendous shattering of tradition which is the obverse of the contemporary crisis and renewal of mankind. Both processes are intimately connected with the contemporary mass movements. Their most powerful agent is the film. Its social significance, particularly in its most positive form, is inconceivable without its destructive, cathartic aspect, that is, the liquidation of the traditional value of the cultural heritage. This phenomenon is most palpable in the great historical films. It extends to ever new positions. In 1927

Abel Gance exclaimed enthusiastically: "Shakespeare, Rembrandt, Beethoven will make films ...all legends, all mythologies and all myths, all founders of religion, and the very religions... await their exposed resurrection, and the heroes crowd each other at the gate."[5] Presumably without intending it, he issued an invitation to a far-reaching liquidation.

III

During long periods of history, the mode of human sense perception changes with humanity's entire mode of existence. The manner in which human sense perception is organized, the medium in which it is accomplished, is determined not only by nature but by historical circumstances as well. The fifth century, with its great shifts of population, saw the birth of the late Roman art industry and the Vienna Genesis, and there developed not only an art different from that of antiquity but also a new kind of perception. The scholars of the Viennese school, Riegl and Wickhoff, who resisted the weight of classical tradition under which these later art forms had been buried, were the first to draw conclusions from them concerning the organization of perception at the time. However far-reaching their insight, these scholars limited themselves to showing the significant, formal hallmark which characterized perception in late Roman times. They did not attempt – and, perhaps, saw no way – to show the social transformations expressed by these changes of perception. The conditions for an analogous insight are more favorable in the present. And if changes in the medium of contemporary perception can be comprehended as decay of the aura, it is possible to show its social causes.

The concept of aura which was proposed above with reference to historical objects may usefully be illustrated with reference to the aura of natural ones. We define the aura of the latter as the unique phenomenon of a distance, however close it may be. If, while resting on a summer afternoon, you follow with your eyes a mountain range on the horizon or a branch which casts its shadow over you, you experience the aura of those mountains, of that branch. This image makes it easy to comprehend the social bases of the contemporary decay of the aura. It rests on two circumstances, both of which are related to the increasing significance of the masses in contemporary life. Namely, the desire of contemporary masses to bring things "closer" spatially and humanly, which is just as ardent as their bent toward overcoming the uniqueness of every reality by accepting its reproduction.[6] Every day the urge grows stronger to get hold of an object at very close range by way of its likeness, its reproduction. Unmistakably, reproduction as offered by picture magazines and newsreels differs from the image seen by the unarmed eye. Uniqueness and permanence are as closely linked in the latter as are transitoriness and reproducibility in the former. To pry an object from its shell, to destroy its aura, is the mark of a perception whose "sense of the universal equality of things" has increased to such a degree that it extracts it even from a unique object by means of reproduction. Thus is manifested in the field of perception what in the theoretical sphere is noticeable in the increasing importance of statistics. The adjustment of reality to the masses and of the masses to reality is a process of unlimited scope, as much for thinking as for perception.

IV

The uniqueness of a work of art is inseparable from its being imbedded in the fabric of tradition. This tradition itself is thoroughly alive and extremely changeable. An ancient statue of Venus, for example, stood in a different traditional context with the Greeks, who made it an object of veneration, than with the clerics of the Middle Ages, who viewed it as an ominous idol. Both of them, however, were equally confronted with its uniqueness, that is, its aura. Originally the contextual integration of art in tradition found its expression in the cult. We know that the earliest art works originated in the service of a ritual – first the magical, then the religious kind. It is significant that the existence of the work of art with reference to its aura is never entirely separated from its ritual function.[7] In other words, the unique value of the "authentic" work of art has its basis in ritual, the location of its original use value. This ritualistic basis, however remote, is still recognizable as secularized ritual even in the most profane forms of the cult of beauty.[8] The secular cult of beauty, developed during the Renaissance and prevailing for three centuries, clearly showed that ritualistic basis in its decline and the first deep crisis which befell it. With the advent of the first truly revolutionary means of reproduction, photography,

simultaneously with the rise of socialism, art sensed the approaching crisis which has become evident a century later. At the time, art reacted with the doctrine of *L'art pour L'art*, that is, with a theology of art. This gave rise to what might be called a negative theology in the form of the idea of "pure" art, which not only denied any social function of art but also any categorizing by subject matter. (In poetry, Mallarmé was the first to take this position.)

An analysis of art in the age of mechanical reproduction must do justice to these relationships, for they lead us to an all-important insight: for the first time in world history, mechanical reproduction emancipates the work of art from its parasitical dependence on ritual. To an ever greater degree the work of art reproduced becomes the work of art designed for reproducibility.[9] From a photographic negative, for example, one can make any number of prints; to ask for the "authentic" print makes no sense. But the instant the criterion of authenticity ceases to be applicable to artistic production, the total function of art is reversed. Instead of being based on ritual, it begins to be based on another practice – politics.

V

Works of art are received and valued on different planes. Two polar types stand out: with one, the accent is on the cult value; with the other, on the exhibition value of the work.[10] Artistic production begins with ceremonial objects destined to serve in a cult. One may assume that what mattered was their existence, not their being on view. The elk portrayed by the man of the Stone Age on the walls of his cave was an instrument of magic. He did expose it to his fellow men, but in the main it was meant for the spirits. Today the cult value would seem to demand that the work of art remain hidden. Certain statues of gods are accessible only to the priest in the cella; certain Madonnas remain covered nearly all year round; certain sculptures on medieval cathedrals are invisible to the spectator on ground level. With the emancipation of the various art practices from ritual go increasing opportunities for the exhibition of their products. It is easier to exhibit a portrait bust that can be sent here and there than to exhibit the statue of a divinity that has its fixed place in the interior of a temple. The same holds for the painting as against the mosaic or fresco that preceded it. And even though the public presentability of a mass originally may have been just as great as that of a symphony, the latter originated at the moment when its public presentability promised to surpass that of the mass.

With the different methods of technical reproduction of a work of art, its fitness for exhibition increased to such an extent that the quantitative shift between its two poles turned into a qualitative transformation of its nature. This is comparable to the situation of the work of art in prehistoric times when, by the absolute emphasis on its cult value, it was, first and foremost, an instrument of magic. Only later did it come to be recognized as a work of art. In the same way today, by the absolute emphasis on its exhibition value the work of art becomes a creation with entirely new functions, among which the one we are conscious of, the artistic function, later may be recognized as incidental.[11] This much is certain: today photography and the film are the most serviceable exemplifications of this new function.

VI

In photography, exhibition value begins to displace cult value all along the line. But cult value does not give way without resistance. It retires into an ultimate retrenchment: the human countenance. It is no accident that the portrait was the focal point of early photography. The cult of remembrance of loved ones, absent or dead, offers a last refuge for the cult value of the picture. For the last time the aura emanates from the early photographs in the fleeting expression of a human face. This is what constitutes their melancholy, incomparable beauty. But as man withdraws from the photographic image, the exhibition value for the first time shows its superiority to the ritual value. To have pinpointed this new stage constitutes the incomparable significance of Atget, who, around 1900, took photographs of deserted Paris streets. It has quite justly been said of him that he photographed them like scenes of crime. The scene of a crime, too, is deserted; it is photographed for the purpose of establishing evidence. With Atget, photographs become standard evidence for historical occurrences, and acquire a hidden political significance. They demand a specific kind of approach; free-floating contemplation is not appropriate to them. They stir the viewer; he feels challenged by them in a new way. At the same time picture magazines begin to put up signposts for him, right ones or wrong ones, no matter. For the first time, captions have become obligatory. And it is clear that they have an altogether different character than the title of a painting. The directives which the captions give to those looking at pictures in illustrated magazines soon become even more explicit and more imperative in the film where the meaning of each single picture appears to be prescribed by the sequence of all preceding ones.

VII

The nineteenth-century dispute as to the artistic value of painting versus photography today seems devious and confused. This does not diminish its importance, however; if anything, it underlines it. The dispute was in fact the symptom of a historical transformation the universal impact of which was not realized by either of the rivals. When the age of mechanical reproduction separated art from its basis in cult, the semblance of its autonomy disappeared forever. The resulting change in the function of art transcended the perspective of the century; for a long time it even escaped that of the twentieth century, which experienced the development of the film.

Earlier much futile thought had been devoted to the question of whether photography is an art. The primary question – whether the very invention of photography had not transformed the entire nature of art – was not raised. Soon the film theoreticians asked the same ill-considered question with regard to the film. But the difficulties which photography caused traditional aesthetics were mere child's play as compared to those raised by the film. Whence the insensitive and forced character of early theories of the film. Abel Gance, for instance, compares the film with hieroglyphs: "Here, by a remarkable regression, we have come back to the level of expression of the Egyptians.... Pictorial language has not yet matured because our eyes have not yet adjusted to it. There is as yet insufficient respect for, insufficient cult of, what it expresses."[12] Or, in the words of Séverin-Mars: "What art has been granted a dream more poetical and more real at the same time! Approached in this fashion the film might represent an incomparable means of expression. Only the most high-minded persons, in the most perfect and mysterious moments of their lives, should be allowed to enter its ambience."[13] Alexandre Arnoux concludes his fantasy about the silent film with the question: "Do not all the bold descriptions we have given amount to the definition of prayer?"[14] It is instructive to note how their desire to class the film among the "arts" forces these theoreticians to read ritual elements into it – with a striking lack of discretion. Yet when these speculations were published, films like *L'Opinion publique* and *The Gold Rush* had already appeared. This, however, did not keep Abel Gance from adducing hieroglyphs for purposes of comparison, nor Séverin-Mars from speaking of the film as one might speak of paintings by Fra Angelico. Characteristically, even today ultrareactionary authors give the film a similar contextual significance – if not an outright sacred one, then at least a supernatural one. Commenting on Max Reinhardt's film version of *A Midsummer Night's Dream*, Werfel states that undoubtedly it was the sterile copying of the exterior world with its streets, interiors, railroad stations, restaurants, motorcars, and beaches which until now had obstructed the elevation of the film to the realm of art. "The film has not yet realized its true meaning, its real possibilities . . . these consist in its unique faculty to express by natural means and with incomparable persuasiveness all that is fairylike, marvelous, supernatural."[15]

VIII

The artistic performance of a stage actor is definitely presented to the public by the actor in person; that of the screen actor, however, is presented by a camera, with a twofold consequence. The camera that presents the performance of the film actor to the public need not respect the performance as an integral whole. Guided by the cameraman, the camera continually changes its position with respect to the performance. The sequence of positional views which the editor composes from the material supplied him constitutes the completed film. It comprises certain factors of movement which are in reality those of the camera, not to mention special camera angles, close-ups, etc. Hence, the performance of the actor is subjected to a series of optical tests. This is the first consequence of the fact that the actor's performance is presented by means of a camera. Also, the film actor lacks the opportunity of the stage actor to adjust to the audience during his performance, since he does not present his performance to the

audience in person. This permits the audience to take the position of a critic, without experiencing any personal contact with the actor. The audience's identification with the actor is really an identification with the camera. Consequently the audience takes the position of the camera; its approach is that of testing.[16] This is not the approach to which cult values may be exposed.

IX

For the film, what matters primarily is that the actor represents himself to the public before the camera, rather than representing someone else. One of the first to sense the actor's metamorphosis by this form of testing was Pirandello. Though his remarks on the subject in his novel *Si Gira* were limited to the negative aspects of the question and to the silent film only, this hardly impairs their validity. For in this respect, the sound film did not change anything essential. What matters is that the part is acted not for an audience but for a mechanical contrivance – in the case of the sound film, for two of them. "The film actor," wrote Pirandello, "feels as if in exile – exiled not only from the stage but also from himself. With a vague sense of discomfort he feels inexplicable emptiness: his body loses its corporeality, it evaporates, it is deprived of reality, life, voice, and the noises caused by his moving about, in order to be changed into a mute image, flickering an instant on the screen, then vanishing into silence. . . . The projector will play with his shadow before the public, and he himself must be content to play before the camera."[17] This situation might also be characterized as follows: for the first time – and this is the effect of the film – man has to operate with his whole living person, yet forgoing its aura. For aura is tied to his presence; there can be no replica of it. The aura which, on the stage, emanates from Macbeth, cannot be separated for the spectators from that of the actor. However, the singularity of the shot in the studio is that the camera is substituted for the public. Consequently, the aura that envelops the actor vanishes, and with it the aura of the figure he portrays.

It is not surprising that it should be a dramatist such as Pirandello who, in characterizing the film, inadvertently touches on the very crisis in which we see the theater. Any thorough study proves that there is indeed no greater contrast than that of the stage play to a work of art that is completely subject to or, like the film, founded in, mechanical reproduction. Experts have long recognized that in the film "the greatest effects are almost always obtained by 'acting' as little as possible. . . ." In 1932 Rudolf Arnheim saw "the latest trend . . . in treating the actor as a stage prop chosen for its characteristics and . . . inserted at the proper place."[18] With this idea something else is closely connected. The stage actor identifies himself with the character of his role. The film actor very often is denied this opportunity. His creation is by no means all of a piece; it is composed of many separate performances. Besides certain fortuitous considerations, such as cost of studio, availability of fellow players, décor, etc., there are elementary necessities of equipment that split the actor's work into a series of mountable episodes. In particular, lighting and its installation require the presentation of an event that, on the screen, unfolds as a rapid and unified scene, in a sequence of separate shootings which may take hours at the studio; not to mention more obvious montage. Thus a jump from the window can be shot in the studio as a jump from a scaffold, and the ensuing flight, if need be, can be shot weeks later when outdoor scenes are taken. Far more paradoxical cases can easily be construed. Let us assume that an actor is supposed to be startled by a knock at the door. If his reaction is not satisfactory, the director can resort to an expedient: when the actor happens to be at the studio again he has a shot fired behind him without his being forewarned of it. The frightened reaction can be shot now and be cut into the screen version. Nothing more strikingly shows that art has left the realm of the "beautiful semblance" which, so far, had been taken to be the only sphere where art could thrive.

X

The feeling of strangeness that overcomes the actor before the camera, as Pirandello describes it, is basically of the same kind as the estrangement felt before one's own image in the mirror. But now the reflected image has become separable, transportable. And where is it transported? Before the public.[19] Never for a moment does the screen actor cease to be conscious of this fact. While facing the camera he knows that ultimately he will face the public, the consumers who constitute the market. This market, where he offers not only his labor but also his whole self, his heart and soul, is beyond his reach. During the shooting he has as little contact with it as any article made in a factory. This may contribute to that oppression, that new anxiety which, according to Pirandello, grips the actor before the camera. The film responds to the shrivelling of the aura with an artificial build-up of the "personality" outside the studio. The cult of the movie star, fostered by the money of the film industry, preserves not the unique aura of the person but the "spell of the personality," the phony spell of a commodity. So long as the moviemakers' capital sets the fashion, as a rule no other revolutionary merit can be accredited to today's film than the promotion of a revolutionary criticism of traditional concepts of art. We do not deny that in some cases today's films can also promote revolutionary criticism of social conditions, even of the distribution of property. However, our present study is no more specifically concerned with this than is the film production of Western Europe.

It is inherent in the technique of the film as well as that of sports that everybody who witnesses its accomplishments is somewhat of an expert. This is obvious to anyone listening to a group of newspaper boys leaning on their bicycles and discussing the outcome of a bicycle race. It is not for nothing that newspaper publishers arrange races for their delivery boys. These arouse great interest among the participants, for the victor has an opportunity to rise from delivery boy to professional racer. Similarly, the newsreel offers everyone the opportunity to rise from passer-by to movie extra. In this way any man might even find himself part of a work of art, as witness Vertoff's *Three Songs About Lenin* or Ivens' *Borinage*. Any man today can lay claim to being filmed. This claim can best be elucidated by a comparative look at the historical situation of contemporary literature.

For centuries a small number of writers were confronted by many thousands of readers. This changed toward the end of the last century. With the increasing extension of the press, which kept placing new political, religious, scientific, professional, and local organs before the readers, an increasing number of readers became writers – at first, occasional ones. It began with the daily press opening to its readers space for "letters to the editor." And today there is hardly a gainfully employed European who could not, in principle, find an opportunity to publish somewhere or other comments on his work, grievances, documentary reports, or that sort of thing. Thus, the distinction between author and public is about to lose its basic character. The difference becomes merely functional; it may vary from case to case. At any moment the reader is ready to turn into a writer. As expert, which he had to become willy-nilly in an extremely specialized work process, even if only in some minor respect, the reader gains access to authorship. In the Soviet Union work itself is given a voice. To present it verbally is part of a man's ability to perform the work. Literary license is now founded on polytechnic rather than specialized training and thus becomes common property.[20]

All this can easily be applied to the film, where transitions that in literature took centuries have come about in a decade. In cinematic practice, particularly in Russia, this change-over has partially become established reality. Some of the players whom we meet in Russian films are not actors in our sense but people who portray *themselves* – and primarily in their own work process. In Western Europe the capitalistic exploitation of the film denies consideration to modern man's legitimate claim to being reproduced. Under these circumstances the film industry is trying hard to spur the interest of the masses through illusion-promoting spectacles and dubious speculations.

XI

The shooting of a film, especially of a sound film, affords a spectacle unimaginable anywhere at any time before this. It presents a process in which it is impossible to assign to a spectator a viewpoint which would exclude from the actual scene such extraneous accessories as camera equipment, lighting machinery, staff assistants, etc. – unless his eye were on a line parallel with the lens. This circumstance, more than any other, renders superficial and insignificant any possible similarity between a scene in the studio and one on the stage. In the theater one is well aware of the place from which the play cannot immediately be detected as illusionary. There is no such place for the movie scene that is being shot. Its illusionary nature is that of the second degree, the result of cutting. That is to say, in the studio the mechanical equipment has penetrated so deeply into reality that its pure aspect freed from the foreign substance of equipment is the result of a special procedure, namely, the shooting by the specially adjusted camera and the mounting of the shot together with other similar ones. The equipment-free aspect of reality here has become the height of artifice; the sight of

immediate reality has become an orchid in the land of technology.

Even more revealing is the comparison of these circumstances, which differ so much from those of the theater, with the situation in painting. Here the question is: How does the cameraman compare with the painter? To answer this we take recourse to an analogy with a surgical operation. The surgeon represents the polar opposite of the magician. The magician heals a sick person by the laying on of hands; the surgeon cuts into the patient's body. The magician maintains the natural distance between the patient and himself; though he reduces it very slightly by the laying on of hands, he greatly increases it by virtue of his authority. The surgeon does exactly the reverse; he greatly diminishes the distance between himself and the patient by penetrating into the patient's body, and increases it but little by the caution with which his hand moves among the organs. In short, in contrast to the magician – who is still hidden in the medical practitioner – the surgeon at the decisive moment abstains from facing the patient man to man; rather, it is through the operation that he penetrates into him.

Magician and surgeon compare to painter and cameraman. The painter maintains in his work a natural distance from reality, the cameraman penetrates deeply into its web.[21] There is a tremendous difference between the pictures they obtain. That of the painter is a total one, that of the cameraman consists of multiple fragments which are assembled under a new law. Thus, for contemporary man the representation of reality by the film is incomparably more significant than that of the painter, since it offers, precisely because of the thoroughgoing permeation of reality with mechanical equipment, an aspect of reality which is free of all equipment. And that is what one is entitled to ask from a work of art.

XII

Mechanical reproduction of art changes the reaction of the masses toward art. The reactionary attitude toward a Picasso painting changes into the progressive reaction toward a Chaplin movie. The progressive reaction is characterized by the direct, intimate fusion of visual and emotional enjoyment with the orientation of the expert. Such fusion is of great social significance. The greater the decrease in the social significance of an art form, the sharper the distinction between criticism and enjoyment by the public. The conventional is uncritically enjoyed, and the truly new is criticized with aversion. With regard to the screen, the critical and the receptive attitudes of the public coincide. The decisive reason for this is that individual reactions are predetermined by the mass audience response they are about to produce, and this is nowhere more pronounced than in the film. The moment these responses become manifest they control each other. Again, the comparison with painting is fruitful. A painting has always had an excellent chance to be viewed by one person or by a few. The simultaneous contemplation of paintings by a large public, such as developed in the nineteenth century, is an early symptom of the crisis of painting, a crisis which was by no means occasioned exclusively by photography but rather in a relatively independent manner by the appeal of art works to the masses.

Painting simply is in no position to present an object for simultaneous collective experience, as it was possible for architecture at all times, for the epic poem in the past, and for the movie today. Although this circumstance in itself should not lead one to conclusions about the social role of painting, it does constitute a serious threat as soon as painting, under special conditions and, as it were, against its nature, is confronted directly by the masses. In the churches and monasteries of the Middle Ages and at the princely courts up to the end of the eighteenth century, a collective reception of paintings did not occur simultaneously, but by graduated and hierarchized mediation. The change that has come about is an expression of the particular conflict in which painting was implicated by the mechanical reproducibility of paintings. Although paintings began to be publicly exhibited in galleries and salons, there was no way for the masses to organize and control themselves in their reception.[22] Thus the same public which responds in a progressive manner toward a grotesque film is bound to respond in a reactionary manner to surrealism.

XIII

The characteristics of the film lie not only in the manner in which man presents himself to mechanical equipment but also in the manner in which, by means of this apparatus, man can represent his environment. A glance at occupational psychology illustrates the testing capacity of the equipment. Psychoanalysis illustrates it in a different perspective. The film has enriched our field of perception with methods which can be illustrated by those of Freudian theory. Fifty years ago, a slip of the tongue passed more or less unnoticed. Only exceptionally may such a slip have revealed dimensions of depth in a conversation which had seemed to be taking its course on the surface. Since the *Psychopathology of Everyday Life* things have changed. This book isolated and made analyzable things which had heretofore floated along unnoticed in the broad stream of perception. For the entire spectrum of optical, and now also acoustical, perception the film has brought about a similar deepening of apperception. It is only an obverse of this fact that behavior items shown in a movie can be analyzed much more precisely and from more points of view than those presented on paintings or on the stage. As compared with painting, filmed behavior lends itself more readily to analysis because of its incomparably more precise statements of the situation. In comparison with the stage scene, the filmed behavior item lends itself more readily to analysis because it can be isolated more easily. This circumstance derives its chief importance from its tendency to promote the mutual penetration of art and science. Actually, of a screened behavior item which is neatly brought out in a certain situation, like a muscle of a body, it is difficult to say which is more fascinating, its artistic value or its value for science. To demonstrate the identity of the artistic and scientific uses of photography which heretofore usually were separated will be one of the revolutionary functions of the film.[23]

By close-ups of the things around us, by focusing on hidden details of familiar objects, by exploring commonplace milieus under the ingenious guidance of the camera, the film, on the one hand, extends our comprehension of the necessities which rule our lives; on the other hand, it manages to assure us of an immense and unexpected field of action. Our taverns and our metropolitan streets, our offices and furnished rooms, our railroad stations and our factories appeared to have us locked up hopelessly. Then came the film and burst this prison-world asunder by the dynamite of the tenth of a second, so that now, in the midst of its far-flung ruins and debris, we calmly and adventurously go traveling. With the close-up, space expands; with slow motion, movement is extended. The enlargement of a snapshot does not simply render more precise what in any case was visible, though unclear: it reveals entirely new structural formations of the subject. So, too, slow motion not only presents familiar qualities of movement but reveals in them entirely unknown ones "which, far from looking like retarded rapid movements, give the effect of singularly gliding, floating, supernatural motions."[24] Evidently a different nature opens itself to the camera than opens to the naked eye – if only because an unconsciously penetrated space is substituted for a space consciously explored by man. Even if one has a general knowledge of the way people walk, one knows nothing of a person's posture during the fractional second of a stride. The act of reaching for a lighter or a spoon is familiar routine, yet we hardly know what really goes on between hand and metal, not to mention how this fluctuates with our moods. Here the camera intervenes with the resources of its lowerings and liftings, its interruptions and isolations, its extensions and accelerations, its enlargements and reductions. The camera introduces us to unconscious optics as does psychoanalysis to unconscious impulses.

XIV

One of the foremost tasks of art has always been the creation of a demand which could be fully satisfied only later.[25] The history of every art form shows critical epochs in which a certain art form aspires to effects which could be fully obtained only with a changed technical standard, that is to say, in a new art form. The extravagances and crudities of art which thus appear, particularly in the so-called decadent epochs, actually arise from the nucleus of its richest historical energies. In recent years, such barbarisms were abundant in Dadaism. It is only now that its impulse becomes discernible: Dadaism attempted to create by pictorial – and literary – means the effects which the public today seeks in the film.

Every fundamentally new, pioneering creation of demands will carry beyond its goal. Dadaism did so to the extent that it sacrificed the market values which are so characteristic of the film in favor of higher ambitions – though of course it was not conscious of such intentions as here described. The Dadaists attached much less importance to the sales value of their work than to its uselessness for contemplative immersion. The studied degradation of their material was not the least of their means to achieve this uselessness. Their poems are "word salad" containing obscenities and every imaginable waste product of language. The same is true of their paintings, on which they mounted buttons and tickets. What they intended and achieved was a relentless destruction of the aura of their creations, which they branded as reproductions with the very means of production. Before a painting of Arp's or a poem by August Stramm it is impossible to take time for contemplation and evaluation as one would before a canvas of Derain's or a poem by Rilke. In the decline of middle-class society, contemplation became a school for asocial behavior; it was countered by distraction as a variant of social conduct.[26] Dadaistic activities actually assured a rather vehement distraction by making works of art the center of scandal. One requirement was foremost: to outrage the public.

From an alluring appearance or persuasive structure of sound the work of art of the Dadaists became an instrument of ballistics. It hit the spectator like a bullet, it happened to him, thus acquiring a tactile quality. It promoted a demand for the film, the distracting element of which is also primarily tactile, being based on changes of place and focus which periodically assail the spectator. Let us compare the screen on which a film unfolds with the canvas of a painting. The painting invites the spectator to contemplation; before it the spectator can abandon himself to his associations. Before the movie frame he cannot do so. No sooner has his eye grasped a scene than it is already changed. It cannot be arrested. Duhamel, who detests the film and knows nothing of its significance, though something of its structure, notes this circumstance as follows: "I can no longer think what I want to think. My thoughts have been replaced by moving images."[27] The spectator's process of association in view of these images is indeed interrupted by their constant, sudden change. This constitutes the shock effect of the film, which, like all shocks, should be cushioned by heightened presence of mind.[28] By means of its technical structure, the film has taken the physical shock effect out of the wrappers in which Dadaism had, as it were, kept it inside the moral shock effect.[29]

XV

The mass is a matrix from which all traditional behavior toward works of art issues today in a new form. Quantity has been transmuted into quality.

The greatly increased mass of participants has produced a change in the mode of participation. The fact that the new mode of participation first appeared in a disreputable form must not confuse the spectator. Yet some people have launched spirited attacks against precisely this superficial aspect. Among these, Duhamel has expressed himself in the most radical manner. What he objects to most is the kind of participation which the movie elicits from the masses. Duhamel calls the movie "a pastime for helots, a diversion for uneducated, wretched, worn-out creatures who are consumed by their worries..., a spectacle which requires no concentration and presupposes no intelligence..., which kindles no light in the heart and awakens no hope other than the ridiculous one of someday becoming a 'star' in Los Angeles."[30] Clearly, this is at bottom the same ancient lament that the masses seek distraction whereas art demands concentration from the spectator. That is a commonplace. The question remains whether it provides a platform for the analysis of the film. A closer look is needed here. Distraction and concentration form polar opposites which may be stated as follows: A man who concentrates before a work of art is absorbed by it. He enters into this work of art the way legend tells of the Chinese painter when he viewed his finished painting. In contrast, the distracted mass absorbs the work of art. This is most obvious with regard to buildings. Architecture has always represented the prototype of a work of art the reception of which is consummated by a collectivity in a state of distraction. The laws of its reception are most instructive.

Buildings have been man's companions since primeval times. Many art forms have developed and perished. Tragedy begins with the Greeks, is extinguished with them, and after centuries its "rules" only are revived. The epic poem, which had its origin in the youth of nations, expires in Europe at the end of the Renaissance. Panel painting is a creation of the Middle Ages, and nothing guarantees its uninterrupted existence. But the human need for shelter is lasting. Architecture has never been idle. Its history is more ancient than that of any other art, and its claim to being a living force has significance in every attempt to comprehend the relationship of the masses to art. Buildings are appropriated in a twofold manner: by use and by perception – or rather, by touch and sight. Such appropriation cannot be understood in terms of the attentive concentration of a tourist before a famous building. On the tactile side there is no counterpart to contemplation on the optical side. Tactile appropriation is accomplished not so much by attention as by habit. As regards architecture, habit determines to a large extent even optical reception. The latter, too, occurs much less through rapt attention than by noticing the object in incidental fashion. This mode of appropriation, developed with reference to architecture, in certain circumstances acquires canonical value. For the tasks which face the human apparatus of perception at the turning points of history cannot be solved by optical means, that is, by contemplation, alone. They are mastered gradually by habit, under the guidance of tactile appropriation.

The distracted person, too, can form habits. More, the ability to master certain tasks in a state of distraction proves that their solution has become a matter of habit. Distraction as provided by art presents a covert control of the extent to which new tasks have become soluble by apperception. Since, moreover, individuals are tempted to avoid such tasks, art will tackle the most difficult and most important one where it is able to mobilize the masses. Today it does so in the film. Reception in a state of distraction, which is increasing noticeably in all fields of art and is symptomatic of profound changes in apperception, finds in the film its true means of exercise. The film with its shock effect meets this mode of reception halfway. The film makes the cult value recede into the background not only by putting the public in the position of the critic, but also by the fact that at the movies this position requires no attention. The public is an examiner, but an absent-minded one.

Epilogue

The growing proletarianization of modern man and the increasing formation of masses are two aspects of the same process. Fascism attempts to organize the newly created proletarian masses without affecting the property structure which the masses strive to eliminate. Fascism sees its salvation in giving these masses not their right, but instead a chance to express themselves.[31] The masses have a right to change property relations; Fascism seeks to give them an expression while preserving property. The logical result of Fascism is the introduction of aesthetics into political life. The violation of the masses, whom Fascism, with its *Führer* cult, forces to their knees, has its counterpart in the violation of an apparatus which is pressed into the production of ritual values.

All efforts to render politics aesthetic culminate in one thing: war. War and war only can set a goal for mass movements on the largest scale while respecting the traditional property system. This is the political formula for the situation. The technological formula may be stated as follows: Only war makes it possible to mobilize all of today's technical resources while maintaining the property system. It goes without saying that the Fascist apotheosis of war does not employ such arguments. Still, Marinetti says in his manifesto on the Ethiopian colonial war: "For twenty-seven years we Futurists have rebelled against the branding of war as antiaesthetic.... Accordingly we state:... War is beautiful because it establishes man's dominion over the subjugated machinery by means of gas masks, terrifying megaphones, flame throwers, and small tanks. War is beautiful because it initiates the dreamt-of metalization of the human body. War is beautiful because it enriches a flowering meadow with the fiery orchids of machine guns. War is beautiful because it combines the gunfire, the cannonades, the cease-fire, the scents, and the stench of putrefaction into a symphony. War is beautiful because it creates new architecture, like that of the big tanks, the geometrical formation flights, the smoke spirals from burning villages, and many others.... Poets and artists of Futurism!... remember these principles of an aesthetics of war so that your struggle for a new literature and a new graphic art...may be illuminated by them!"

This manifesto has the virtue of clarity. Its formulations deserve to be accepted by dialectic-ians. To the latter, the aesthetics of today's war appears as follows: If the natural utilization of productive forces is impeded by the property system, the increase in technical devices, in speed, and in the sources of energy will press for an unnatural utilization, and this is found in war. The destructiveness of war furnishes proof that society has not been mature enough to incorporate technology as its organ, that technology has not been sufficiently developed to cope with the elemental forces of society. The horrible features of imperialistic warfare are attributable to the discrepancy between the tremendous means of production and their inadequate utilization in the process of production – in other words, to unemployment and the lack of markets. Imperialistic war is a rebellion of technology which collects, in the form of "human material," the claims to which society has denied its natural material. Instead of draining rivers, society directs a human stream into a bed of trenches; instead of dropping seeds from airplanes, it drops incendiary bombs over cities; and through gas warfare the aura is abolished in a new way.

"*Fiat ars – pereat mundus*," says Fascism, and, as Marinetti admits, expects war to supply the artistic gratification of a sense perception that has been changed by technology. This is evidently the consummation of "*l'art pour l'art*." Mankind, which in Homer's time was an object of contemplation for the Olympian gods, now is one for itself. Its self-alienation has reached such a degree that it can experience its own destruction as an aesthetic pleasure of the first order. This is the situation of politics which Fascism is rendering aesthetic. Communism responds by politicizing art.

Notes

1 Quoted from Paul Valéry, *Aesthetics*, "The Conquest of Ubiquity," translated by Ralph Manheim, p. 225. Pantheon Books, Bollingen Series, New York, 1964.

2 Of course, the history of a work of art encompasses more than this. The history of the "Mona Lisa," for instance, encompasses the kind and number of its copies made in the 17th, 18th, and 19th centuries.

3 Precisely because authenticity is not reproducible, the intensive penetration of certain (mechanical) processes of reproduction was instrumental in differentiating and grading authenticity. To develop such differentiations was an important function of the trade in works of art. The invention of the woodcut may be said to have struck at the root of the quality of authenticity even before its late flowering. To be sure, at the time of its origin a medieval picture of the Madonna could not yet be said to be "authentic." It became "authentic" only during the succeeding centuries and perhaps most strikingly so during the last one.

4 The poorest provincial staging of *Faust* is superior to a Faust film in that, ideally, it competes with the first performance at Weimar. Before the screen it is unprofitable to remember traditional contents which might come to mind before the stage – for instance, that Goethe's friend Johann Heinrich Merck is hidden in Mephisto, and the like.

5   Abel Gance, "Le Temps de l'image est venu," *L'Art cinématographique*, Vol. 2, pp. 94 f, Paris, 1927.

6   To satisfy the human interest of the masses may mean to have one's social function removed from the field of vision. Nothing guarantees that a portraitist of today, when painting a famous surgeon at the breakfast table in the midst of his family, depicts his social function more precisely than a painter of the 17th century who portrayed his medical doctors as representing this profession, like Rembrandt in his "Anatomy Lesson."

7   The definition of the aura as a "unique phenomenon of a distance however close it may be" represents nothing but the formulation of the cult value of the work of art in categories of space and time perception. Distance is the opposite of closeness. The essentially distant object is the unapproachable one. Unapproachability is indeed a major quality of the cult image. True to its nature, it remains "distant, however close it may be." The closeness which one may gain from its subject matter does not impair the distance which it retains in its appearance.

8   To the extent to which the cult value of the painting is secularized the ideas of its fundamental uniqueness lose distinctness. In the imagination of the beholder the uniqueness of the phenomena which hold sway in the cult image is more and more displaced by the empirical uniqueness of the creator or of his creative achievement. To be sure, never completely so; the concept of authenticity always transcends mere genuineness. (This is particularly apparent in the collector who always retains some traces of the fetishist and who, by owning the work of art, shares in its ritual power.) Nevertheless, the function of the concept of authenticity remains determinate in the evaluation of art; with the secularization of art, authenticity displaces the cult value of the work.

9   In the case of films, mechanical reproduction is not, as with literature and painting, an external condition for mass distribution. Mechanical reproduction is inherent in the very technique of film production. This technique not only permits in the most direct way but virtually causes mass distribution. It enforces distribution because the production of a film is so expensive that an individual who, for instance, might afford to buy a painting no longer can afford to buy a film. In 1927 it was calculated that a major film, in order to pay its way, had to reach an audience of nine million. With the sound film, to be sure, a setback in its international distribution occurred at first: audiences became limited by language barriers. This coincided with the Fascist emphasis on national interests. It is more important to focus on this connection with Fascism than on this setback, which was soon minimized by synchronization. The simultaneity of both phenomena is attributable to the depression. The same disturbances which, on a larger scale, led to an attempt to maintain the existing property structure

by sheer force led the endangered film capital to speed up the development of the sound film. The introduction of the sound film brought about a temporary relief, not only because it again brought the masses into the theaters but also because it merged new capital from the electrical industry with that of the film industry. Thus, viewed from the outside, the sound film promoted national interests, but seen from the inside it helped to internationalize film production even more than previously.

10 This polarity cannot come into its own in the aesthetics of Idealism. Its idea of beauty comprises these polar opposites without differentiating between them and consequently excludes their polarity. Yet in Hegel this polarity announces itself as clearly as possible within the limits of Idealism. We quote from his *Philosophy of History*:

> Images were known of old. Piety at an early time required them for worship, but it could do without *beautiful* images. These might even be disturbing. In every beautiful painting there is also something nonspiritual, merely external, but its spirit speaks to man through its beauty. Worshipping, conversely, is concerned with the work as an object, for it is but a spiritless stupor of the soul.... Fine art has arisen... in the church..., although it has already gone beyond its principle as art.

Likewise, the following passage from *The Philosophy of Fine Art* indicates that Hegel sensed a problem here.

> We are beyond the stage of reverence for works of art as divine and objects deserving our worship. The impression they produce is one of a more reflective kind, and the emotions they arouse require a higher test...." – G. W. F. Hegel, *The Philosophy of Fine Art*, trans., with notes, by F. P. B. Osmaston, Vol. I, p. 12, London, 1920.

The transition from the first kind of artistic reception to the second characterizes the history of artistic reception in general. Apart from that, a certain oscillation between these two polar modes of reception can be demonstrated for each work of art. Take the Sistine Madonna. Since Hubert Grimme's research it has been known that the Madonna originally was painted for the purpose of exhibition. Grimme's research was inspired by the question: What is the purpose of the molding in the foreground of the painting which the two cupids lean upon? How, Grimme asked further, did Raphael come to furnish the sky with two draperies? Research proved that the Madonna had been commissioned for the public lying-in-state of Pope Sixtus. The Popes lay in state in a certain side chapel of

St. Peter's. On that occasion Raphael's picture had been fastened in a nichelike background of the chapel, supported by the coffin. In this picture Raphael portrays the Madonna approaching the papal coffin in clouds from the background of the niche, which was demarcated by green drapes. At the obsequies of Sixtus a pre-eminent exhibition value of Raphael's picture was taken advantage of. Some time later it was placed on the high altar in the church of the Black Friars at Piacenza. The reason for this exile is to be found in the Roman rites which forbid the use of paintings exhibited at obsequies as cult objects on the high altar. This regulation devalued Raphael's picture to some degree. In order to obtain an adequate price nevertheless, the Papal See resolved to add to the bargain the tacit toleration of the picture above the high altar. To avoid attention the picture was given to the monks of the far-off provincial town.

11 Bertolt Brecht, on a different level, engaged in analogous reflections: "If the concept of 'work of art' can no longer be applied to the thing that emerges once the work is transformed into a commodity, we have to eliminate this concept with cautious care but without fear, lest we liquidate the function of the very thing as well. For it has to go through this phase without mental reservation, and not as noncommittal deviation from the straight path; rather, what happens here with the work of art will change it fundamentally and erase its past to such an extent that should the old concept be taken up again – and it will, why not? – it will no longer stir any memory of the thing it once designated."

12 Abel Gance, ["Le Temps de l'image,"] pp. 100–1.

13 Séverin-Mars, quoted by Abel Gance, ["Le Temps de l'image,"] p. 100.

14 Alexandre Arnoux, Cinéma pris, 1929, p. 28.

15 Franz Werfel, "Ein Sommernachtstraum, Ein Film von Shakespeare und Reinhardt," Neues Wiener Journal, cited in Lu 15, November, 1935.

16 "The film . . . provides – or could provide – useful insight into the details of human actions. . . . Character is never used as a source of motivation; the inner life of the persons never supplies the principal cause of the plot and seldom is its main result." (Bertolt Brecht, Versuche, "Der Dreigroschenprozess," p. 268.) The expansion of the field of the testable which mechanical equipment brings about for the actor corresponds to the extraordinary expansion of the field of the testable brought about for the individual through economic conditions. Thus, vocational aptitude tests become constantly more important. What matters in these tests are segmental performances of the individual. The film shot and the vocational aptitude test are taken before a committee of experts. The camera director in the studio occupies a place identical with that of the examiner during aptitude tests.

17 Luigi Pirandello, Si Gira, quoted by Léon Pierre-Quint, "Signification du cinéma," L'Art cinématographique, vol. 2, pp. 14–15.

18 Rudolf Arnheim, Film als Kunst, Berlin, 1932, pp. 176f. In this context certain seemingly unimportant details in which the film director deviates from stage practices gain in interest. Such is the attempt to let the actor play without make-up, as made among others by Dreyer in his Jeanne d'Arc. Dreyer spent months seeking the forty actors who constitute the Inquisitors' tribunal. The search for these actors resembled that for stage properties that are hard to come by. Dreyer made every effort to avoid resemblances of age, build, and physiognomy. If the actor thus becomes a stage property, this latter, on the other hand, frequently functions as actor. At least it is not unusual for the film to assign a role to the stage property. Instead of choosing at random from a great wealth of examples, let us concentrate on a particularly convincing one. A clock that is working will always be a disturbance on the stage. There it cannot be permitted its function of measuring time. Even in a naturalistic play, astronomical time would clash with theatrical time. Under these circumstances it is highly revealing that the film can, whenever appropriate, use time as measured by a clock. From this more than from many other touches it may clearly be recognized that under certain circumstances each and every prop in a film may assume important functions. From here it is but one step to Pudovkin's statement that "the playing of an actor which is connected with an object and is built around it . . . is always one of the strongest methods of cinematic construction." (W. Pudovkin, Filmregie und Filmmanuskript, Berlin, 1928, p. 126.) The film is the first art form capable of demonstrating how matter plays tricks on man. Hence, films can be an excellent means of materialistic representation.

19 The change noted here in the method of exhibition caused by mechanical reproduction applies to politics as well. The present crisis of the bourgeois democracies comprises a crisis of the conditions which determine the public presentation of the rulers. Democracies exhibit a member of government directly and personally before the nation's representatives. Parliament is his public. Since the innovations of camera and recording equipment make it possible for the orator to become audible and visible to an unlimited number of persons, the presentation of the man of politics before camera and recording equipment becomes paramount. Parliaments, as much as theaters, are deserted. Radio and film not only affect the function of the professional actor but likewise the function of those who also exhibit themselves before this mechanical equipment, those who govern. Though their tasks may be different, the change affects equally the actor

and the ruler. The trend is toward establishing controllable and transferrable skills under certain social conditions. This results in a new selection, a selection before the equipment from which the star and the dictator emerge victorious.

20 The privileged character of the respective techniques is lost. Aldous Huxley writes:

> Advances in technology have led...to vulgarity.... Process reproduction and the rotary press have made possible the indefinite multiplication of writing and pictures. Universal education and relatively high wages have created an enormous public who know how to read and can afford to buy reading and pictorial matter. A great industry has been called into existence in order to supply these commodities. Now, artistic talent is a very rare phenomenon; whence it follows...that, at every epoch and in all countries, most art has been bad. But the proportion of trash in the total artistic output is greater now than at any other period. That it must be so is a matter of simple arithmetic. The population of Western Europe has a little more than doubled during the last century. But the amount of reading – and seeing – matter has increased, I should imagine, at least twenty and possibly fifty or even a hundred times. If there were n men of talent in a population of x millions, there will presumably be 2n men of talent among 2x millions. The situation may be summed up thus. For every page of print and pictures published a century ago, twenty or perhaps even a hundred pages are published today. But for every man of talent then living, there are now only two men of talent. It may be of course that, thanks to universal education, many potential talents which in the past would have been still-born are now enabled to realize themselves. Let us assume, then, that there are now three or even four men of talent to every one of earlier times. It still remains true to say that the consumption of reading – and seeing – matter has far outstripped the natural production of gifted writers and draughtsmen. It is the same with hearing-matter. Prosperity, the gramophone and the radio have created an audience of hearers who consume an amount of hearing-matter that has increased out of all proportion to the increase of population and the consequent natural increase of talented musicians. It follows from all this that in all the arts the output of trash is both absolutely and relatively greater than it was in the past; and that it must remain greater for just so long as the world continues to consume the present inordinate quantities of reading-matter, seeing-matter, and hearing-matter." – Aldous Huxley, *Beyond the Mexique Bay. A Traveller's Journal*, London, 1949, pp. 274 ff. First published in 1934.

This mode of observation is obviously not progressive. –

21 The boldness of the cameraman is indeed comparable to that of the surgeon. Luc Durtain lists among specific technical sleights of hand those "which are required in surgery in the case of certain difficult operations. I choose as an example a case from otorhino-laryngology;...the so-called endonasal perspective procedure; or I refer to the acrobatic tricks of larynx surgery which have to be performed following the reversed picture in the laryngoscope. I might also speak of ear surgery which suggests the precision work of watchmakers. What range of the most subtle muscular acrobatics is required from the man who wants to repair or save the human body! We have only to think of the couching of a cataract where there is virtually a debate of steel with nearly fluid tissue, or of the major abdominal operations (laparotomy)." – Luc Durtain [...].

22 This mode of observation may seem crude, but as the great theoretician Leonardo has shown, crude modes of observation may at times be usefully adduced. Leonardo compares painting and music as follows: "Painting is superior to music because, unlike unfortunate music, it does not have to die as soon as it is born.... Music which is consumed in the very act of its birth is inferior to painting which the use of varnish has rendered eternal." (Trattato I, 29.)

23 Renaissance painting offers a revealing analogy to this situation. The incomparable development of this art and its significance rested not least on the integration of a number of new sciences, or at least of new scientific data. Renaissance painting made use of anatomy and perspective, of mathematics, meteorology, and chromatology. Valéry writes: "What could be further from us than the strange claim of a Leonardo to whom painting was a supreme goal and the ultimate demonstration of knowledge? Leonardo was convinced that painting demanded universal knowledge, and he did not even shrink from a theoretical analysis which to us is stunning because of its very depth and precision...." – Paul Valéry, *Pièces sur l'art*, "Autour de Corot," Paris, p. 191.

24 Rudolf Arnheim, *Film als Kunst*, p. 138.

25 "The work of art," says André Breton, "is valuable only in so far as it is vibrated by the reflexes of the future." Indeed, every developed art form intersects three lines of development. Technology works toward a certain form of art. Before the advent of the film there were photo booklets with pictures which flitted by the onlooker upon pressure of the thumb, thus portraying a boxing bout or a tennis match. Then there were the slot machines in bazaars; their picture sequences were produced by the turning of a crank.

Secondly, the traditional art forms in certain phases of their development strenuously work toward effects which later are effortlessly attained by the new ones. Before the rise of the movie the Dadaists' performances tried to create an audience reaction which Chaplin later evoked in a more natural way.

Thirdly, unspectacular social changes often promote a change in receptivity which will benefit the new art form. Before the movie had begun to create its public, pictures that were no longer immobile captivated an assembled audience in the so-called *Kaiserpanorama*. Here the public assembled before a screen into which stereoscopes were mounted, one to each beholder. By a mechanical process individual pictures appeared briefly before the stereoscopes, then made way for others. Edison still had to use similar devices in presenting the first movie strip before the film screen and projection were known. This strip was presented to a small public which stared into the apparatus in which the succession of pictures was reeling off. Incidentally, the institution of the *Kaiserpanorama* shows very clearly a dialectic of the development. Shortly before the movie turned the reception of pictures into a collective one, the individual viewing of pictures in these swiftly outmoded establishments came into play once more with an intensity comparable to that of the ancient priest beholding the statue of a divinity in the cella.

26 The theological archetype of this contemplation is the awareness of being alone with one's God. Such awareness, in the heyday of the bourgeoisie, went to strengthen the freedom to shake off clerical tutelage. During the decline of the bourgeoisie this awareness had to take into account the hidden tendency to withdraw from public affairs those forces which the individual draws upon in his communion with God.

27 Georges Duhamel, *Scènes de la vie future*, Paris, 1930, p. 52.

28 The film is the art form that is in keeping with the increased threat to his life which modern man has to face. Man's need to expose himself to shock effects is his adjustment to the dangers threatening him. The film corresponds to profound changes in the apperceptive apparatus – changes that are experienced on an individual scale by the man in the street in big-city traffic, on a historical scale by every present-day citizen.

29 As for Dadaism, insights important for Cubism and Futurism are to be gained from the movie. Both appear as deficient attempts of art to accommodate the pervasion of reality by the apparatus. In contrast to the film, these schools did not try to use the apparatus as such for the artistic presentation of reality, but aimed at some sort of alloy in the joint presentation of reality and apparatus. In Cubism, the premonition that this apparatus will be structurally based on optics plays a dominant part; in Futurism, it is the premonition of the effects of this apparatus which are brought out by the rapid sequence of the film strip.

30 Duhamel, *Scènes de la vie future*, p. 58.

31 One technical feature is significant here, especially with regard to newsreels, the propagandist importance of which can hardly be overestimated. Mass reproduction is aided especially by the reproduction of masses. In big parades and monster rallies, in sports events, and in war, all of which nowadays are captured by camera and sound recording, the masses are brought face to face with themselves. This process, whose significance need not be stressed, is intimately connected with the development of the techniques of reproduction and photography. Mass movements are usually discerned more clearly by a camera than by the naked eye. A bird's-eye view best captures gatherings of hundreds of thousands. And even though such a view may be as accessible to the human eye as it is to the camera, the image received by the eye cannot be enlarged the way a negative is enlarged. This means that mass movements, including war, constitute a form of human behavior which particularly favors mechanical equipment.

9

The Origin of the Work of Art

Martin Heidegger

Origin here means that from and by which something is what it is and as it is. What something is, as it is, we call its essence or nature. The origin of something is the source of its nature. The question concerning the origin of the work of art asks about the source of its nature. On the usual view, the work arises out of and by means of the activity of the artist. But by what and whence is the artist what he is? By the work; for to say that the work does credit to the master means that it is the work that first lets the artist emerge as a master of his art. The artist is the origin of the work. The work is the origin of the artist. Neither is without the other. Nevertheless, neither is the sole support of the other. In themselves and in their interrelations artist and work *are* each of them by virtue of a third thing which is prior to both, namely that which also gives artist and work of art their names – art.

As necessarily as the artist is the origin of the work in a different way than the work is the origin of the artist, so it is equally certain that, in a still different way, art is the origin of both artist and work. But can art be an origin at all? Where and how does art occur? Art – this is nothing more than a word to which nothing real any longer corresponds. It may pass for a collective idea under which we find a place for that which alone is real in art: works and artists. Even if the word art were taken to signify more than a collective notion, what is meant by the word could exist only on the basis of the actuality of works and artists. Or is the converse the case? Do works and artists exist only because art exists as their origin?

Whatever the decision may be, the question of the origin of the work of art becomes a question about the nature of art. Since the question whether and how art in general exists must still remain open, we shall attempt to discover the nature of art in the place where art undoubtedly prevails in a real way. Art is present in the art work. But what and how is a work of art?

What art is should be inferable from the work. What the work of art is we can come to know only from the nature of art. Anyone can easily see that we are moving in a circle. Ordinary understanding demands that this circle be avoided because it violates logic. What art is can be gathered from a comparative examination of actual art works. But how are we to be certain that we are indeed basing such an examination on art works if we do not know beforehand what art is? And the nature of art can no more be arrived at by a derivation from higher concepts than by a collection of characteristics of actual art works. For such a derivation, too, already has in view the characteristics that must suffice to establish that what we take in advance to be an art work is one in fact. But selecting works from among given objects, and deriving concepts from principles, are equally impossible here, and where these procedures are practiced they are a self-deception.

Thus we are compelled to follow the circle. This is neither a makeshift nor a defect. To enter upon this path is the strength of thought, to continue on it is the feast of thought, assuming that thinking is a craft. Not only is the main step from work to art a circle like the step from art to work, but every separate step that we attempt circles in this circle.

In order to discover the nature of the art that really prevails in the work, let us go to the actual work and ask the work what and how it is.

Works of art are familiar to everyone. Architectural and sculptural works can be seen installed in public places, in churches, and in dwellings. Art works of the most diverse periods and peoples are housed in collections and exhibitions. If we consider the works in their untouched actuality and do not deceive ourselves, the result is that the works are as naturally present as are things. The picture hangs on the wall like a rifle or a hat. A painting, e.g., the one by Van Gogh that represents a pair of peasant shoes, travels from one exhibition to another. Works of art are shipped like coal from the Ruhr and logs from the Black Forest. During the First World War Hölderlin's hymns were packed in the soldier's knapsack together with cleaning gear. Beethoven's quartets lie in the storerooms of the publishing house like potatoes in a cellar.

All works have this thingly character. What would they be without it? But perhaps this rather crude and external view of the work is objectionable to us. Shippers or charwomen in museums may operate with such conceptions of the work of art. We, however, have to take works as they are encountered by those who experience and enjoy them. But even the much-vaunted aesthetic experience cannot get around the thingly aspect of the art work. There is something stony in a work of architecture, wooden in a carving, colored in a painting, spoken in a linguistic work, sonorous in a musical composition. The thingly element is so irremovably present in the art work that we are compelled rather to say conversely that the architectural work is in stone, the carving is in wood, the painting in color, the linguistic work in speech, the musical composition in sound. "Obviously," it will be replied. No doubt. But what is this self-evident thingly element in the work of art?

Presumably it becomes superfluous and confusing to inquire into this feature, since the art work is something else over and above the thingly element. This something else in the work constitutes its artistic nature. The art work is, to be sure, a thing that is made, but it says something other than the mere thing itself is, *allo agoreuei* [it says something else]. The work makes public something other than itself; it manifests something other; it is an allegory. In the work of art something other is brought together with the thing that is made. To bring together is, in Greek, *sumballein*. The work is a symbol.

Allegory and symbol provide the conceptual frame within whose channel of vision the art work has for a long time been characterized. But this one element in a work that manifests another, this one element that joins with another, is the thingly feature in the art work. It seems almost as though the thingly element in the art work is like the substructure into and upon which the other, authentic element is built. And is it not this thingly feature in the work that the artist really makes by his handicraft?

Our aim is to arrive at the immediate and full reality of the work of art, for only in this way shall we discover real art also within it. Hence we must first bring to view the thingly element of the work. To this end it is necessary that we should know with sufficient clarity what a thing is. Only then can we say whether the art work is a thing, but a thing to which something else adheres; only then can we decide whether the work is at bottom something else and not a thing at all.

Thing and Work

What in truth is the thing, so far as it is a thing? When we inquire in this way, our aim is to come to know the thing-being (thingness) of the thing. The point is to discover the thingly character of the thing. To this end we have to be acquainted with the sphere to which all those entities belong which we have long called by the name of thing.

The stone in the road is a thing, as is the clod in the field. A jug is a thing, as is the well beside the road. But what about the milk in the jug and the water in the well? These too are things if the cloud in the sky and the thistle in the field, the leaf in the autumn breeze and the hawk over the wood, are rightly called by the name of thing. All these must indeed be called things, if the name is applied even to that which does not, like those just enumerated, show itself, i.e., that which does not appear. According to Kant, the whole of the world, for example, and even God himself, is a thing of this sort, a thing that does not itself appear, namely, a "thing-in-itself." In the language of philosophy both things-in-themselves and things that appear, all beings that in any way are, are called things.

Airplanes and radio sets are nowadays among the things closest to us, but when we have ultimate things in mind we think of something altogether different. Death and judgment – these are ultimate things. On the whole the word "thing" here designates whatever is not simply nothing. In this sense the work of art is also a thing, so far as it is not simply nothing. Yet this concept is of no use to us, at least immediately, in our attempt to delimit entities that have the mode of being of a thing, as against those having the mode of being of a work. And besides, we hesitate to call God a thing. In the same way we hesitate to consider the peasant in the field, the stoker at the boiler, the teacher in the school as things. A man is not a thing. It is true that we speak of a young girl who is faced with a task too difficult for her as being a young thing, still too young for it, but only because we feel that being human is in a certain way missing here and think that instead we have to do here with the factor that constitutes the thingly character of things. We hesitate even to call the deer in the forest clearing, the beetle in the grass, the blade of grass a thing. We would sooner think of a hammer as a thing, or a shoe, or an ax, or a clock. But even these are not mere things. Only a stone, a clod of earth, a piece of wood are for us such mere things. Lifeless beings of nature and objects of use. Natural things and utensils are the things commonly so called.

We thus see ourselves brought back from the widest domain, within which everything is a thing (thing = res = ens = an entity), including even the highest and last things, to the narrow precinct of mere things. "Mere" here means, first, the pure thing, which is simply a thing and nothing more; but then, at the same time, it means that which is only a thing, in an almost pejorative sense. It is mere things, excluding even use-objects, that count as things in the strict sense. What does the thingly character of these things, then, consist in? It is in reference to these that the thingness of things must be determinable. This determination enables us to characterize what it is that is thingly as such. Thus prepared, we are able to characterize the almost palpable reality of works, in which something else inheres.

Now it passes for a known fact that as far back as antiquity, no sooner was the question raised as to what entities are in general, than things in their thingness thrust themselves into prominence again and again as the standard type of beings. Consequently we are bound to meet with the definition of the thingness of things already in the traditional interpretations of beings. We thus need only to ascertain explicitly this traditional knowledge of the thing, to be relieved of the tedious labor of making our own search for the thingly character of the thing. The answers to the question "What is the thing?" are so familiar that we no longer sense anything questionable behind them.

The interpretations of the thingness of the thing which, predominant in the course of Western thought, have long become self-evident and are now in everyday use, may be reduced to three.

This block of granite, for example, is a mere thing. It is hard, heavy, extended, bulky, shapeless, rough, colored, partly dull, partly shiny. We can take note of all these features in the stone. Thus we acknowledge its characteristics. But still, the traits signify something proper to the stone itself. They are its properties. The thing has them. The thing? What are we thinking of when we now have the thing in mind? Obviously a thing is not merely an aggregate of traits, nor an accumulation of properties by which that aggregate arises. A thing, as everyone thinks he knows, is that around which the properties have assembled. We speak in this connection of the core of things. The Greeks are supposed to have called it *to hupokeimenon*. For them, this core of the thing was something lying at the ground of the thing, something always already there. The characteristics, however, are called *ta sumbebekota*, that which has always turned up already along with the given core and occurs along with it.

These designations are no arbitrary names. Something that lies beyond the purview of this essay speaks in them, the basic Greek experience of the Being of beings in the sense of presence. It is by these determinations, however, that the interpretation of the thingness of the thing is established which henceforth becomes standard, and the Western interpretation of the Being of beings stabilized. The process begins with the appropriation of Greek words by Roman-Latin thought. *Hupokeimenon* becomes *subiectum*; *hupostasis* becomes *substantia*; *sumbebekos* becomes *accidens*. However, this translation of Greek names into Latin is in no way the innocent process it is considered to this day. Beneath the seemingly literal and thus faithful translation there is concealed, rather, a *trans*lation of Greek experience into a different way of thinking. *Roman thought takes over the Greek words without a corresponding, equally authentic experience of what they say, without the Greek word*. The rootlessness of Western thought begins with this translation.

According to current opinion, this definition of the thingness of the thing as the substance with its accidents seems to correspond to our natural outlook on things. No wonder that the current attitude toward things – our way of addressing ourselves to things and speaking about them – has adapted itself to this common view of the thing. A simple propositional statement consists of the subject, which is the Latin translation, hence already a reinterpretation, of *hupokeimenon* and the predicate, in which the thing's traits are stated of it. Who would have the temerity to assail these simple fundamental relations between thing and statement, between sentence structure and thing-structure? Nevertheless we must ask: Is the structure of a simple propositional statement (the combination of subject and predicate) the mirror image of the structure of the thing (of the union of substance with accidents)? Or could it be that even the structure of the thing as thus envisaged is a projection of the framework of the sentence?

What could be more obvious than that man transposes his propositional way of understanding things into the structure of the thing itself? Yet this view, seemingly critical yet actually rash and ill-considered, would have to explain first how such a transposition of propositional structure into the thing is supposed to be possible without the thing having already become visible. The question which comes first and functions as the standard, proposition structure or thing-structure remains to this hour undecided. It even remains doubtful whether in this form the question is at all decidable.

Actually, the sentence structure does not provide the standard for the pattern of thing-structure, nor is the latter simply mirrored in the former. Both sentence and thing-structure derive, in their typical form and their possible mutual relationship, from a common and more original source. In any case this first interpretation of the thingness of the thing, the thing as bearer of its characteristic traits, despite its currency, is not as natural as it appears to be. What seems natural to us is probably just something familiar in a long tradition that has forgotten the unfamiliar source from which it arose. And yet this unfamiliar source once struck man as strange and caused him to think and to wonder.

Our reliance on the current interpretation of the thing is only seemingly well founded. But in addition this thing-concept (the thing as bearer of its characteristics) holds not only of the mere thing in its strict sense, but also of any being whatsoever. Hence it cannot be used to set apart thingly beings from non-thingly beings. Yet even before all reflection, attentive dwelling within the sphere of things already tells us that this thing-concept does not hit upon the thingly element of the thing, its independent and self-contained character. Occasionally we still have the feeling that violence has long been done to the thingly element of things and that thought has played a part in this violence, for which reason people disavow thought instead of taking pains to make it more thoughtful. But in defining the nature of the thing, what is the use of a feeling, however certain, if thought alone has the right to speak here? Perhaps however what we call feeling or mood, here and in similar instances, is more reasonable – that is, more intelligently perceptive – because more open to Being than all that reason which, having meanwhile become *ratio*, was misinterpreted as being rational. The hankering after the irrational, as abortive offspring of the unthought rational, therewith performed a curious service. To be sure, the current thing-concept always fits each thing. Nevertheless it does not lay hold of the thing as it is in its own being, but makes an assault upon it.

Can such an assault perhaps be avoided – and how? Only, certainly, by granting the thing, as it were, a free field to display its thingly character directly. Everything that might interpose itself between the thing and us in apprehending and talking about it must first be set aside. Only then do we yield ourselves to the undisguised presence of the thing. But we do not need first to call or arrange for this situation in which we let things encounter us without mediation. The situation always prevails. In what the senses of sight, hearing, and touch convey, in the sensations of color, sound, roughness, hardness, things move us bodily, in the literal meaning of the word. The thing is the *aistheton*, that which is perceptible by sensations in the senses belonging to sensibility. Hence the concept later becomes a commonplace according to which a thing is nothing but the unity of a manifold of what is given in the senses. Whether this unity is conceived as sum or as totality or as form alters nothing in the standard character of this thing-concept.

Now this interpretation of the thingness of the thing is as correct and demonstrable in every case as the previous one. This already suffices to cast doubt on its truth. If we consider moreover what we are searching for, the thingly character of the thing, then this thing-concept again leaves us at a loss. We never really first perceive a throng of sensations, e.g., tones and noises, in the appearance of things – as this thing-concept alleges; rather we hear the storm whistling in the chimney, we hear the three-motored plane, we hear the Mercedes in immediate distinction from the Volkswagen. Much closer to us than all sensations are the things themselves. We hear the door shut in the house and never hear acoustical sensations or even mere sounds. In order to hear a bare sound we have to listen away from things, divert our ear from them, i.e., listen abstractly.

In the thing-concept just mentioned there is not so much an assault upon the thing as rather an inordinate attempt to bring it into the greatest possible proximity to us. But a thing never reaches that position as long as we assign as its thingly feature what is perceived by the senses. Whereas the first interpretation keeps the thing at arm's length from us, as it were, and sets it too far off, the second makes it press too hard upon us. In both interpretations the thing vanishes. It is therefore necessary to avoid the exaggerations of both. The thing itself must be allowed to remain in its self-containment. It must be accepted in its own constancy. This the third interpretation seems to do, which is just as old as the first two.

That which gives things their constancy and pith but is also at the same time the source of their particular mode of sensuous pressure – colored, resonant, hard, massive – is the matter in things. In this analysis of the thing as matter (*hule*), form (*morphe*) is already coposited. What is constant in a thing, its consistency, lies in the fact that matter stands together with a form. The thing is formed matter. This interpretation appeals to the immediate view with which the thing solicits us by its looks (*eidos*). In this synthesis of matter and form a thing-concept has finally been found which applies equally to things of nature and to use-objects.

This concept puts us in a position to answer the question concerning the thingly element in the work of art. The thingly element is manifestly the matter of which it consists. Matter is the substrate and field for the artist's formative action. But we could have advanced this obvious and well-known definition of the thingly element at the very outset. Why do we make a detour through other current thing-concepts? Because we also mistrust this concept of the thing, which represents it as formed matter.

But is not precisely this pair of concepts, matter–form, usually employed in the domain in which we are supposed to be moving? To be sure. The distinction of matter and form is *the conceptual schema which is used, in the greatest variety of ways, quite generally for all art theory and aesthetics*. This incontestable fact, however, proves neither that the distinction of matter and form is adequately founded, nor that it belongs originally to the domain of art and the art work. Moreover, the range of application of this pair of concepts has long extended far beyond the field of aesthetics. Form and content are the most hackneyed concepts under which anything and everything may be subsumed. And if form is correlated with the rational and matter with the irrational; if the rational is taken to be the logical and the irrational the alogical; if in addition the subject–object relation is coupled with the conceptual pair form–matter; then representation has at its command a conceptual machinery that nothing is capable of withstanding.

If, however, it is thus with the distinction between matter and form, how then shall we make use of it to lay hold of the particular domain of mere things by contrast with all other entities? But perhaps this characterization in terms of matter and form would recover its defining power if only we reversed the process of expanding and emptying these concepts. Certainly, but this presupposes that we know in what sphere of beings they realize their true defining power. That this is the domain of mere things is so far only an assumption. Reference to the copious use made of this conceptual framework in aesthetics might sooner lead to the idea that matter and form are specifications stemming from the nature of the art work and were in the first place transferred from it back to the thing. Where does the matter–form structure have its origin – in the thingly character of the thing or in the workly character of the art work?

The self-contained block of granite is something material in a definite if unshapely form. Form means here the distribution and arrangement of the material parts in spatial locations, resulting in a particular shape, namely that of a block. But a jug, an ax, a shoe are also matter occurring in a form. Form as shape is not the consequence here of a prior distribution of the matter. The form, on the contrary, determines the arrangement of the matter. Even more, it prescribes in each case the kind and selection of the matter – impermeable for a jug, sufficiently hard for an ax, firm yet flexible for shoes. The interfusion of form and matter prevailing here is, moreover, controlled beforehand by the purposes served by jug, ax, shoes. Such usefulness is never assigned or added on afterward to a being of the type of a jug, ax, or pair of shoes. But neither is it something that floats somewhere above it as an end.

Usefulness is the basic feature from which this entity regards us, that is, flashes at us and thereby is present and thus is this entity. Both the formative act and the choice of material – a choice given with the act – and therewith the dominance of the conjunction of matter and form, are all grounded in such usefulness. A being that falls under usefulness is always the product of a process of making. It is made as a piece of equipment for something. As determinations of beings, accordingly, matter and form have their proper place in the essential nature of equipment. This name designates what is produced expressly for employment and use. Matter and form are in no case original determinations of the thingness of the mere thing.

A piece of equipment, a pair of shoes for instance, when finished, is also self-contained like the mere thing, but it does not have the character of having taken shape by itself like the granite boulder. On the other hand, equipment displays an affinity with the art work insofar as it is something produced by the human hand. However, by its self-sufficient presence the work of art is similar rather to the mere thing which has taken shape by itself and is self-contained. Nevertheless we do not count such works among mere things. As a rule it is the use-objects around us that are the nearest and authentic things. Thus the piece of equipment is half thing, because characterized by thingliness, and yet it is something more; at the same time it is half art work and yet something less, because lacking the self-sufficiency of the art work. Equipment has a peculiar position intermediate between thing and work, assuming that such a calculated ordering of them is permissible.

The matter–form structure, however, by which the being of a piece of equipment is first determined, readily presents itself as the immediately intelligible constitution of every entity, because here man himself as maker participates in the way in which the piece of equipment comes into being. Because equipment takes an intermediate place between mere thing and work, the suggestion is that nonequipmental beings – things and works and ultimately everything that is – are to be comprehended with the help of the being of equipment (the matter–form structure).

The inclination to treat the matter–form structure as *the* constitution of every entity receives a yet additional impulse from the fact that on the basis of a religious faith, namely, the biblical faith, the totality of all beings is represented in advance as something created, which here means made. The philosophy of this faith can of course assure us that all of God's creative work is to be thought of as different from the action of a craftsman. Nevertheless, if at the same time or even beforehand, in accordance with a presumed predetermination of Thomistic philosophy for interpreting the Bible, the *ens creatum* is conceived as a unity of *materia* and *forma*, then faith is expounded by way of a philosophy whose truth lies in an unconcealedness of beings which differs in kind from the world believed in by faith.

The idea of creation, grounded in faith, can lose its guiding power of knowledge of beings as a whole. But the theological interpretation of all beings, the view of the world in terms of matter and form borrowed from an alien philosophy, having once been instituted, can still remain a force. This happens in the transition from the Middle Ages to modern times. The metaphysics of the modern period rests on the form–matter structure devised in the medieval period, which itself merely recalls in its words the buried natures of *eidos* and *hule*. Thus the interpretation of "thing" by means of matter and form, whether it remains medieval or becomes Kantian-transcendental, has become current and self-evident. But for that reason, no less than the other interpretations mentioned of the thingness of the thing, it is an encroachment upon the thing-being of the thing.

The situation stands revealed as soon as we speak of things in the strict sense as mere things. The "mere," after all, means the removal of the character of usefulness and of being made. The mere thing is a sort of equipment, albeit equipment denuded of its equipmental being. Thingbeing consists in what is then left over. But this remnant is not actually defined in its ontological character. It remains doubtful whether the thingly character comes to view at all in the process of stripping off everything equipmental. Thus the third mode of interpretation of the thing, that which follows the lead of the matter–form structure, also turns out to be an assault upon the thing.

These three modes of defining thingness conceive of the thing as a bearer of traits, as the unity of a manifold of sensations, as formed matter. In the course of the history of truth about beings, the interpretations mentioned have also entered into combinations, a matter we may now pass over. In such combination they have further strengthened their innate tendency to expand so as to apply in similar ways to thing, to equipment, and to work. Thus they give rise to a mode of thought by which we think not only about thing, equipment, and work but about all beings in general. This long-familiar mode of thought preconceives all immediate experience of beings. The preconception shackles reflection on the being of any given entity. Thus it comes about that prevailing thing-concepts obstruct the way toward the thingly character of the thing as well as toward the equipmental character of equipment, and all the more toward the workly character of the work.

This fact is the reason why it is necessary to know about these thing-concepts, in order thereby to take heed of their derivation and their boundless presumption, but also of their semblance of self-evidence. This knowledge becomes all the more necessary when we risk the attempt to bring to view and express in words the thingly character of the thing, the equipmental character of equipment, and the workly character of the work. To this end, however, only one element is needful: to keep at a distance all the preconceptions and assaults of the above modes of thought, to leave the thing to rest in its own self, for instance, in its thing-being. What seems easier than to let a being be just the being that it is? Or does this turn out to be the most difficult of tasks, particularly if such an intention – to let a being be as it is – represents the opposite of the indifference that simply turns its back upon the being itself in favor of an unexamined concept of being? We ought to turn toward the being, think about it in regard to its being, but by means of this thinking at the same time let it rest upon itself in its very own being.

This exertion of thought seems to meet with its greatest resistance in defining the thingness of the thing; for where else could the cause lie of the failure of the efforts mentioned? The unpretentious thing evades thought most stubbornly. Or can it be that this self-refusal of the mere thing, this self-contained independence, belongs precisely to the nature of the thing? Must not this strange and uncommunicative feature of the nature of the thing become intimately familiar to thought that tries to think the thing? If so, then we should not force our way to its thingly character.

That the thingness of the thing is particularly difficult to express and only seldom expressible is infallibly documented by the history of its interpretation indicated above. This history coincides with the destiny in accordance with which Western thought has hitherto thought the Being of beings. However, not only do we now establish this point; at the same time we discover a clue in this history. Is it an accident that in the interpretation of the thing the view that takes matter and form as guide attains to special dominance? This definition of the thing derives from an interpretation of the equipmental being of equipment. And equipment, having come into being through human making, is particularly familiar to human thinking. At the same time, this familiar being has a peculiar intermediate position between thing and work. We shall follow this clue and search first for the equipmental character of equipment. Perhaps this will suggest something to us about the thingly character of the thing and the workly character of the work. We must only avoid making thing and work prematurely into subspecies of equipment. We are disregarding the possibility, however, that differences relating to the history of Being may yet also be present in the way equipment *is*.

But what path leads to the equipmental quality of equipment? How shall we discover what a piece of equipment truly is? The procedure necessary at present must plainly avoid any attempts that again immediately entail the encroachments of the usual interpretations. We are most easily insured against this if we simply describe some equipment without any philosophical theory.

We choose as example a common sort of equipment – a pair of peasant shoes. We do not even need to exhibit actual pieces of this sort of useful article in order to describe them. Everyone is acquainted with them. But since it is a matter here of direct description, it may be well to facilitate the visual realization of them. For this purpose a pictorial representation suffices. We shall choose a well-known painting by Van Gogh, who painted such shoes several times. But what is there to see here? Everyone knows what shoes consist of. If they are not wooden or bast shoes, there will be leather soles and uppers, joined together by thread and nails. Such gear serves to clothe the feet. Depending on the use to which the shoes are to be put, whether for work in the field or for dancing, matter and form will differ.

Such statements, no doubt correct, only explicate what we already know. The equipmental quality of equipment consists in its usefulness. But what about this usefulness itself? In conceiving it, do we already conceive along with it the equipmental character of equipment? In order to succeed in doing this, must we not look out for useful equipment in its use? The peasant woman wears her shoes in the field. Only here are they what they are. They are all the more genuinely so, the less the peasant woman thinks about the shoes while she is at work, or looks at them at all, or is even aware of them. She stands and walks in them. That is how shoes actually serve. It is in this process of the use of equipment that we must actually encounter the character of equipment.

As long as we only imagine a pair of shoes in general, or simply look at the empty, unused shoes as they merely stand there in the picture, we shall never discover what the equipmental being of the equipment in truth is. From Van Gogh's painting we cannot even tell where these shoes stand. There is nothing surrounding this pair of peasant shoes in or to which they might belong – only an undefined space. There are not even clods of soil from the field or the field-path sticking to them, which would at least hint at their use. A pair of peasant shoes and nothing more. And yet –

From the dark opening of the worn insides of the shoes the toilsome tread of the worker stares forth. In the stiffly rugged heaviness of the shoes there is the accumulated tenacity of her slow trudge through the far-spreading and ever-uniform furrows of the field swept by a raw wind. On the leather lie the dampness and richness of the soil. Under the soles slides the loneliness of the field-path as evening falls. In the shoes vibrates the silent call of the earth, its quiet gift of the ripening grain and its unexplained self-refusal in the fallow desolation of the wintry field. This equipment is pervaded by uncomplaining anxiety as to the certainty of bread, the wordless joy of having once more withstood want, the trembling before the impending childbed and shivering at the surrounding menace of death. This equipment belongs to the *earth*, and it is protected in the *world* of the peasant woman. From out of this protected belonging the equipment itself rises to its resting-within-itself.

But perhaps it is only in the picture that we notice all this about the shoes. The peasant woman, on the other hand, simply wears them. If only this simple wearing were so simple. When she takes off her shoes late in the evening, in deep but healthy fatigue, and reaches out for them again in the still dim dawn, or passes them by on the day of rest, she knows all this without noticing or reflecting. The equipmental quality of the equipment consists indeed in its usefulness. But this usefulness itself rests in the abundance of an essential being of the equipment. We call it reliability. By virtue of this reliability the peasant woman is made privy to the silent call of the earth; by virtue of the reliability of the equipment she is sure of her world. World and earth exist for her, and for those who are with her in her mode of being, only thus – in the equipment. We say "only" and therewith fall into error; for the reliability of the equipment first gives to the simple world its security and assures to the earth the freedom of its steady thrust.

The equipmental being of equipment, reliability, keeps gathered within itself all things according to their manner and extent. The usefulness of equipment is nevertheless only the essential consequence of reliability. The former vibrates in the latter and would be nothing without it. A single piece of equipment is worn out and used up; but at the same time the use itself also falls into disuse, wears away, and becomes usual. Thus equipmentality wastes away, sinks into mere stuff. In such wasting, reliability vanishes. This dwindling, however, to which use-things owe their boringly obtrusive usualness, is only one more testimony to the original nature of equipmental being. The worn-out usualness of the equipment then obtrudes itself as the sole mode of being, apparently peculiar to it exclusively. Only blank usefulness now remains visible. It awakens the impression that the origin of equipment lies in a mere fabricating that impresses a form upon some matter. Nevertheless, in its genuinely equipmental being, equipment stems from a more distant source. Matter and form and their distinction have a deeper origin.

The repose of equipment resting within itself consists in its reliability. Only in this reliability do we discern what equipment in truth is. But we still know nothing of what we first sought: the thing's thingly character. And we know nothing at all of what we really and solely seek: the workly character of the work in the sense of the work of art.

Or have we already learned something unwittingly, in passing so to speak, about the work-being of the work?

The equipmental quality of equipment was discovered. But how? Not by a description and explanation of a pair of shoes actually present; not by a report about the process of making shoes; and also not by the observation of the actual use of shoes occurring here and there; but only by bringing ourselves before Van Gogh's painting. This painting spoke. In the vicinity of the work we were suddenly somewhere else than we usually tend to be.

The art work let us know what shoes are in truth. It would be the worst self-deception to think that our description, as a subjective action, had first depicted everything thus and then projected it into the painting. If anything is questionable here, it is rather that we experienced too little in the neighborhood of the work and that we expressed the experience too crudely and too literally. But above all, the work did not, as it might seem at first, serve merely for a better visualizing of what a piece of equipment is. Rather, the equipmentality of equipment first genuinely arrives at its appearance through the work and only in the work.

What happens here? What is at work in the work? Van Gogh's painting is the disclosure of what the equipment, the pair of peasant shoes, *is* in truth. This entity emerges into the unconcealedness of its being. The Greeks called the unconcealedness of beings *aletheia*. We say "truth" and think little enough in using this word. If there occurs in the work a disclosure of a particular being, disclosing what and how it is, then there is here an occurring, a happening of truth at work.

In the work of art the truth of an entity has set itself to work. "To set" means here: to bring to a stand. Some particular entity, a pair of peasant shoes, comes in the work to stand in the light of its being. The being of the being comes into the steadiness of its shining.

The nature of art would then be this: the truth of beings setting itself to work. But until now art presumably has had to do with the beautiful and beauty, and not with truth. The arts that produce such works are called the beautiful or fine arts, in contrast with the applied or industrial arts that manufacture equipment. In fine art the art itself is not beautiful, but is called so because it produces the beautiful. Truth, in contrast, belongs to logic. Beauty, however, is reserved for aesthetics.

But perhaps the proposition that art is truth setting itself to work intends to revive the fortunately obsolete view that art is an imitation and depiction of reality? The reproduction of what exists requires, to be sure, agreement with the actual being, adaptation to it; the Middle Ages called it *adaequatio*; Aristotle already spoke of *homoiosis*. Agreement with what *is* has long been taken to be the essence of truth. But then, is it our opinion that this painting by Van Gogh depicts a pair of actually existing peasant shoes, and is a work of art because it does so successfully? Is it our opinion that the painting draws a likeness from something actual and transposes it into a product of artistic – production? By no means.

The work, therefore, is not the reproduction of some particular entity that happens to be present at any given time; it is, on the contrary, the reproduction of the thing's general essence. But then where and how is this general essence, so that art works are able to agree with it? With what nature of what thing should a Greek temple agree? Who could maintain the impossible view that the Idea of Temple is represented in the building? And yet, truth is set to work in such a work, if it is a work. Or let us think of Hölderlin's hymn, "The Rhine." What is pregiven to the poet, and how is it given, so that it can then be regiven in the poem? And if in the case of this hymn and similar poems the idea of a copy-relation between something already actual and the art work clearly fails, the view that the work is a copy is confirmed in the best possible way by a work of the kind presented in C. F. Meyer's poem "Roman Fountain."

Roman Fountain

The jet ascends and falling fills
The marble basin circling round;
This, veiling itself over, spills
Into a second basin's ground.
The second in such plenty lives,
Its bubbling flood a third invests,
And each at once receives and gives
And streams and rests.

This is neither a poetic painting of a fountain actually present nor a reproduction of the general essence of a Roman fountain. Yet truth is put into the work. What truth is happening in the work? Can truth happen at all and thus be historical? Yet truth, people say, is something timeless and supertemporal.

We seek the reality of the art work in order to find there the art prevailing within it. The thingly substructure is what proved to be the most immediate reality in the work. But to comprehend this thingly feature the traditional thing-concepts are not adequate; for they themselves fail to grasp the nature of the thing. The currently predominant thing-concept, thing as formed matter, is not even derived from the nature of the thing but from the nature of equipment. It also turned out that equipmental being generally has long since occupied a peculiar preeminence in the interpretation of beings. This preeminence of equipmentality, which however did not actually come to mind, suggested that we pose the question of equipment anew while avoiding the current interpretations.

We allowed a work to tell us what equipment is. By this means, almost clandestinely, it came to light what is at work in the work: the disclosure of the particular being in its being, the happening of truth. If, however, the reality of the work can be defined solely by means of what is at work in the work, then what about our intention to seek out the real art work in its reality? As long as we supposed that the reality of the work lay primarily in its thingly substructure we were going astray. We are now confronted by a remarkable result of our considerations – if it still deserves to be called a result at all. Two points become clear:

First: the dominant thing-concepts are inadequate as means of grasping the thingly aspect of the work.

Second: what we tried to treat as the most immediate reality of the work, its thingly substructure, does not belong to the work in that way at all.

As soon as we look for such a thingly substructure in the work, we have unwittingly taken the work as equipment, to which we then also ascribe a superstructure supposed to contain its artistic quality. But the work is not a piece of equipment that is fitted out in addition with an aesthetic value that adheres to it. The work is no more anything of the kind than the bare thing is a piece of equipment that merely lacks the specific equipmental characteristics of usefulness and being made.

Our formulation of the question of the work has been shaken because we asked, not about the work but half about a thing and half about equipment. Still, this formulation of the question was not first developed by us. It is the formulation native to aesthetics. The way in which aesthetics views the art work from the outset is dominated by the traditional interpretation of all beings. But the shaking of this accustomed formulation is not the essential point. What matters is a first opening of our vision to the fact that what is workly in the work, equipmental in equipment, and thingly in

the thing comes closer to us only when we think the Being of beings. To this end it is necessary beforehand that the barriers of our preconceptions fall away and that the current pseudo concepts be set aside. That is why we had to take this detour. But it brings us directly to a road that may lead to a determination of the thingly feature in the work. The thingly feature in the work should not be denied; but if it belongs admittedly to the work-being of the work, it must be conceived by way of the work's workly nature. If this is so, then the road toward the determination of the thingly reality of the work leads not from thing to work but from work to thing.

The art work opens up in its own way the Being of beings. This opening up, i.e., this deconcealing, i.e., the truth of beings, happens in the work. In the art work, the truth of what is has set itself to work. Art is truth setting itself to work. What is truth itself, that it sometimes comes to pass as art? What is this setting-itself-to-work?

The Work and Truth

The origin of the art work is art. But what is art? Art is real in the art work. Hence we first seek the reality of the work. In what does it consist? Art works universally display a thingly character, albeit in a wholly distinct way. The attempt to interpret this thing-character of the work with the aid of the usual thing-concepts failed – not only because these concepts do not lay hold of the thingly feature, but because, in raising the question of its thingly substructure, we force the work into a preconceived framework by which we obstruct our own access to the work-being of the work. Nothing can be discovered about the thingly aspect of the work so long as the pure self-subsistence of the work has not distinctly displayed itself.

Yet is the work ever in itself accessible? To gain access to the work, it would be necessary to remove it from all relations to something other than itself, in order to let it stand on its own for itself alone. But the artist's most peculiar intention already aims in this direction. The work is to be released by him to its pure self-subsistence. It is precisely in great art – and only such art is under consideration here – that the artist remains inconsequential as compared with the work, almost like a passageway that destroys itself in the creative process for the work to emerge.

Well, then, the works themselves stand and hang in collections and exhibitions. But are they here in themselves as the works they themselves are, or are they not rather here as objects of the art industry? Works are made available for public and private art appreciation. Official agencies assume the care and maintenance of works. Connoisseurs and critics busy themselves with them. Art dealers supply the market. Art-historical study makes the works the objects of a science. Yet in all this busy activity do we encounter the work itself?

The Aegina sculptures in the Munich collection, Sophocles' *Antigone* in the best critical edition, are, as the works they are, torn out of their own native sphere. However high their quality and power of impression, however good their state of preservation, however certain their interpretation, placing them in a collection has withdrawn them from their own world. But even when we make an effort to cancel or avoid such displacement of works – when, for instance, we visit the temple in Paestum at its own site or the Bamberg cathedral on its own square – the world of the work that stands there has perished.

World-withdrawal and world-decay can never be undone. The works are no longer the same as they once were. It is they themselves, to be sure, that we encounter there, but they themselves are gone by. As bygone works they stand over against us in the realm of tradition and conservation. Henceforth they remain merely such objects. Their standing before us is still indeed a consequence of, but no longer the same as, their former self-subsistence. This self-subsistence has fled from them. The whole art industry, even if carried to the extreme and exercised in every way for the sake of works themselves, extends only to the object-being of the works. But this does not constitute their work-being.

But does the work still remain a work if it stands outside all relations? Is it not essential for the work to stand in relations? Yes, of course – except that it remains to ask in what relations it stands.

Where does a work belong? The work belongs, as work, uniquely within the realm that is opened up by itself. For the work-being of the work is present in, and only in, such opening up. We said that in the work there was a happening of truth at work. The reference to Van Gogh's picture tried to point to this happening. With regard to it there arose the question as to what truth is and how truth can happen.

We now ask the question of truth with a view to the work. But in order to become more familiar with what the question involves, it is necessary to make visible once more the happening of truth in the work. For this attempt let us deliberately select a work that cannot be ranked as representational art.

A building, a Greek temple, portrays nothing. It simply stands there in the middle of the rock-cleft valley. The building encloses the figure of the god, and in this concealment lets it stand out into the holy precinct through the open portico. By means of the temple, the god is present in the temple. This presence of the god is in itself the extension and delimitation of the precinct as a holy precinct. The temple and its precinct, however, do not fade away into the indefinite. It is the temple-work that first fits together and at the same time gathers around itself the unity of those paths and relations in which birth and death, disaster and blessing, victory and disgrace, endurance and decline acquire the shape of destiny for human being. The all-governing expanse of this open relational context is the world of this historical people. Only from and in this expanse does the nation first return to itself for the fulfillment of its vocation.

Standing there, the building rests on the rocky ground. This resting of the work draws up out of the rock the mystery of that rock's clumsy yet spontaneous support. Standing there, the building holds its ground against the storm raging above it and so first makes the storm itself manifest in its violence. The luster and gleam of the stone, though itself apparently glowing only by the grace of the sun, yet first brings to light the light of the day, the breadth of the sky, the darkness of the night. The temple's firm towering makes visible the invisible space of air. The steadfastness of the work contrasts with the surge of the surf, and its own repose brings out the raging of the sea. Tree and grass, eagle and bull, snake and cricket first enter into their distinctive shapes and thus come to appear as what they are. The Greeks early called this emerging and rising in itself and in all things *phusis*. It clears and illuminates, also, that on which and in which man bases his dwelling. We call this ground the *earth*. What this word says is not to be associated with the idea of a mass of matter deposited somewhere, or with the merely astronomical idea of a planet. Earth is that whence the arising brings back and shelters everything that arises without violation. In the things that arise, earth is present as the sheltering agent.

The temple-work, standing there, opens up a world and at the same time sets this world back again on earth, which itself only thus emerges as native ground. But men and animals, plants and things, are never present and familiar as unchangeable objects, only to represent incidentally also a fitting environment for the temple, which one fine day is added to what is already there. We shall get closer to what *is*, rather, if we think of all this in reverse order, assuming of course that we have, to begin with, an eye for how differently everything then faces us. Mere reversing, done for its own sake, reveals nothing.

The temple, in its standing there, first gives to things their look and to men their outlook on themselves. This view remains open as long as the work is a work, as long as the god has not fled from it. It is the same with the sculpture of the god, votive offering of the victor in the athletic games. It is not a portrait whose purpose is to make it easier to realize how the god looks; rather, it is a work that lets the god himself be present and thus *is* the god himself. The same holds for the linguistic work. In the tragedy nothing is staged or displayed theatrically, but the battle of the new gods against the old is being fought. The linguistic work, originating in the speech of the people, does not refer to this battle; it transforms the people's saying so that now every living word fights the battle and puts up for decision what is holy and what unholy, what great and what small, what brave and what cowardly, what lofty and what flighty, what master and what slave (cf. Heraclitus, Fragment 53).

In what, then, does the work-being of the work consist? Keeping steadily in view the points just crudely enough indicated, two essential features of the work may for the moment be brought out more distinctly. We set out here, from the long familiar foreground of the work's being, the thingly character which gives support to our customary attitude toward the work.

When a work is brought into a collection or placed in an exhibition we say also that it is "set up." But this setting up differs essentially from setting up in the sense of erecting a building, raising a statue, presenting a tragedy at a holy festival. Such setting up is erecting in the sense of dedication and praise. Here "setting up" no longer means a bare placing. To dedicate means to consecrate, in the sense that in setting up the work the holy is opened up as holy and the god is invoked into the openness of his presence. Praise

belongs to dedication as doing honor to the dignity and splendor of the god. Dignity and splendor are not properties beside and behind which the god, too, stands as something distinct, but it is rather in the dignity, in the splendor that the god is present. In the reflected glory of this splendor there glows, i.e., there lightens itself, what we called the word. To e-rect means: to open the right in the sense of a guiding measure, a form in which what belongs to the nature of being gives guidance. But why is the setting up of a work an erecting that consecrates and praises? Because the work, in its work-being, demands it. How is it that the work comes to demand such a setting up? Because it itself, in its own work-being, is something that sets up. What does the work, as work, set up? Towering up within itself, the work opens up a *world* and keeps it abidingly in force.

To be a work means to set up a world. But what is it to be a world? The answer was hinted at when we referred to the temple. On the path we must follow here, the nature of world can only be indicated. What is more, this indication limits itself to warding off anything that might at first distort our view of the world's nature.

The world is not the mere collection of the countable or uncountable, familiar and unfamiliar things that are just there. But neither is it a merely imagined framework added by our representation to the sum of such given things. The *world worlds*, and is more fully in being than the tangible and perceptible realm in which we believe ourselves to be at home. World is never an object that stands before us and can be seen. World is the ever-nonobjective to which we are subject as long as the paths of birth and death, blessing and curse keep us transported into Being. Wherever those decisions of our history that relate to our very being are made, are taken up and abandoned by us, go unrecognized and are rediscovered by new inquiry, there the world worlds. A stone is worldless. Plant and animal likewise have no world; but they belong to the covert throng of a surrounding into which they are linked. The peasant woman, on the other hand, has a world because she dwells in the overtness of beings, of the things that are. Her equipment, in its reliability, gives to this world a necessity and nearness of its own. By the opening up of a world, all things gain their lingering and hastening, their remoteness and nearness, their scope and limits. In a world's worlding is gathered that spaciousness out of which the protective grace of the gods is granted or withheld.

Even this doom of the god remaining absent is a way in which world worlds.

A work, by being a work, makes space for that spaciousness. "To make space for" means here especially to liberate the Open and to establish it in its structure. This in-stalling occurs through the erecting mentioned earlier. The work as work sets up a world. The work holds open the Open of the world. But the setting up of a world is only the first essential feature in the work-being of a work to be referred to here. Starting again from the foreground of the work, we shall attempt to make clear in the same way the second essential feature that belongs with the first.

When a work is created, brought forth out of this or that work-material – stone, wood, metal, color, language, tone – we say also that it is made, set forth out of it. But just as the work requires a setting up in the sense of a consecrating-praising erection, because the work's work-being consists in the setting up of a world, so a setting forth is needed because the work-being of the work itself has the character of setting forth. The work as work, in its presencing, is a setting forth, a making. But what does the work set forth? We come to know about this only when we explore what comes to the fore and is customarily spoken of as the making or production of works.

To work-being there belongs the setting up of a world. Thinking of it within this perspective, what is the nature of that in the work which is usually called the work material? Because it is determined by usefulness and serviceability, equipment takes into its service that of which it consists: the matter. In fabricating equipment – e.g., an ax – stone is used, and used up. It disappears into usefulness. The material is all the better and more suitable the less it resists perishing in the equipmental being of the equipment. By contrast the temple-work, in setting up a world, does not cause the material to disappear, but rather causes it to come forth for the very first time and to come into the Open of the work's world. The rock comes to bear and rest and so first becomes rock; metals come to glitter and shimmer, colors to glow, tones to sing, the word to speak. All this comes forth as the work sets itself back into the massiveness and heaviness of stone, into the firmness and pliancy of wood, into the hardness and luster of metal, into the lighting and darkening of color, into the clang of tone, and into the naming power of the word.

That into which the work sets itself back and which it causes to come forth in this setting back of

itself we called the earth. Earth is that which comes forth and shelters. Earth, self-dependent, is effortless and untiring. Upon the earth and in it, historical man grounds his dwelling in the world. In setting up a world, the work sets forth the earth. This setting forth must be thought here in the strict sense of the word. The work moves the earth itself into the Open of a world and keeps it there. *The work lets the earth be an earth.*

But why must this setting forth of the earth happen in such a way that the work sets itself back into it? What is the earth that it attains to the unconcealed in just such a manner? A stone presses downward and manifests its heaviness. But while this heaviness exerts an opposing pressure upon us it denies us any penetration into it. If we attempt such a penetration by breaking open the rock, it still does not display in its fragments anything inward that has been disclosed. The stone has instantly withdrawn again into the same dull pressure and bulk of its fragments. If we try to lay hold of the stone's heaviness in another way, by placing the stone on a balance, we merely bring the heaviness into the form of a calculated weight. This perhaps very precise determination of the stone remains a number, but the weight's burden has escaped us. Color shines and wants only to shine. When we analyze it in rational terms by measuring its wavelengths, it is gone. It shows itself only when it remains undisclosed and unexplained. Earth thus shatters every attempt to penetrate into it. It causes every merely calculating importunity upon it to turn into a destruction. This destruction may herald itself under the appearance of mastery and of progress in the form of the technical-scientific objectivation of nature, but this mastery nevertheless remains an impotence of will. The earth appears openly cleared as itself only when it is perceived and preserved as that which is by nature undisclosable, that which shrinks from every disclosure and constantly keeps itself closed up. All things of earth, and the earth itself as a whole, flow together into a reciprocal accord. But this confluence is not a blurring of their outlines. Here there flows the stream, restful within itself, of the setting of bounds, which delimits everything present within its presence. Thus in each of the self-secluding things there is the same not-knowing-of-one-another. The earth is essentially self-secluding. To set forth the earth means to bring it into the Open as the self-secluding.

This setting forth of the earth is achieved by the work as it sets itself back into the earth. The self-seclusion of earth, however, is not a uniform, inflexible staying under cover, but unfolds itself in an inexhaustible variety of simple modes and shapes. To be sure, the sculptor uses stone just as the mason uses it, in his own way. But he does not use it up. That happens in a certain way only where the work miscarries. To be sure, the painter also uses pigment, but in such a way that color is not used up but rather only now comes to shine forth. To be sure, the poet also uses the word – not, however, like ordinary speakers and writers who have to use them up, but rather in such a way that the word only now becomes and remains truly a word.

Nowhere in the work is there any trace of a work-material. It even remains doubtful whether, in the essential definition of equipment, what the equipment consists of is properly described in its equipmental nature as matter.

The setting up of a world and the setting forth of earth are two essential features in the work-being of the work. They belong together, however, in the unity of work-being. This is the unity we seek when we ponder the self-subsistence of the work and try to express in words this closed, unitary repose of self-support.

But in the essential features just mentioned, if our account has any validity at all, we have indicated in the work rather a happening and in no sense a repose, for what is rest if not the opposite of motion? It is at any rate not an opposite that excludes motion from itself, but rather includes it. Only what is in motion can rest. The mode of rest varies with the kind of motion. In motion as the mere displacement of a body, rest is, to be sure, only the limiting case of motion. Where rest includes motion, there can exist a repose which is an inner concentration of motion, hence a highest state of agitation, assuming that the mode of motion requires such a rest. Now the repose of the work that rests in itself is of this sort. We shall therefore come nearer to this repose if we can succeed in grasping the state of movement of the happening in work-being in its full unity. We ask: What relation do the setting up of a world and the setting forth of the earth exhibit in the work itself?

The world is the self-disclosing openness of the broad paths of the simple and essential decisions in the destiny of an historical people. The earth is the spontaneous forthcoming of that which is continually self-secluding and to that extent sheltering and concealing. World and earth are essentially different from one another and yet are never separated. The world grounds itself on the earth, and earth juts through world. But the relation between world and earth does not wither away into the empty unity of opposites unconcerned with one another. The world, in resting upon the earth, strives to surmount it. As self-opening it cannot endure anything closed. The earth, however, as sheltering and concealing, tends always to draw the world into itself and keep it there.

The opposition of world and earth is a striving. But we would surely all too easily falsify its nature if we were to confound striving with discord and dispute, and thus see it only as disorder and destruction. In essential striving, rather, the opponents raise each other into the self-assertion of their natures. Self-assertion of nature, however, is never a rigid insistence upon some contingent state, but surrender to the concealed originality of the source of one's own being. In the struggle, each opponent carries the other beyond itself. Thus the striving becomes ever more intense as striving, and more authentically what it is. The more the struggle overdoes itself on its own part, the more inflexibly do the opponents let themselves go into the intimacy of simple belonging to one another. The earth cannot dispense with the Open of the world if it itself is to appear as earth in the liberated surge of its self-seclusion. The world, again, cannot soar out of the earth's sight if, as the governing breadth and path of all essential destiny, it is to ground itself on a resolute foundation.

In setting up a world and setting forth the earth, the work is an instigating of this striving. This does not happen so that the work should at the same time settle and put an end to the conflict in an insipid agreement, but so that the strife may remain a strife. Setting up a world and setting forth the earth, the work accomplishes this striving. The work-being of the work consists in the fighting of the battle between world and earth. It is because the struggle arrives at its high point in the simplicity of intimacy that the unity of the work comes about in the fighting of the battle. The fighting of the battle is the continually self-over-reaching gathering of the work's agitation. The repose of the work that rests in itself thus has its presencing in the intimacy of striving.

From this repose of the work we can now first see what is at work in the work. Until now it was a merely provisional assertion that in an art work the truth is set to work. In what way does truth happen in the work-being of the work, i.e., now, how does truth happen in the fighting of the battle between world and earth? What is truth?

How slight and stunted our knowledge of the nature of truth is, is shown by the laxity we permit ourselves in using this basic word. By truth is usually meant this or that particular truth. That means: something true. A cognition articulated in a proposition can be of this sort. However, we call not only a proposition true, but also a thing, true gold in contrast with sham gold. True here means genuine, real gold. What does the expression "real" mean here? To us it is what is in truth. The true is what corresponds to the real, and the real is what is in truth. The circle has closed again.

What does "in truth" mean? Truth is the essence of the true. What do we have in mind when speaking of essence? Usually it is thought to be those features held in common by everything that is true. The essence is discovered in the generic and universal concept, which represents the one feature that holds indifferently for many things. This indifferent essence (essentiality in the sense of *essentia*) is, however, only the inessential essence. What does the essential essence of something consist in? Presumably it lies in what the entity *is* in truth. The true essential nature of a thing is determined by way of its true being, by way of the truth of the given being. But we are now seeking not the truth of essential nature but the essential nature of truth. There thus appears a curious tangle. Is it only a curiosity or even merely the empty sophistry of a conceptual game, or is it – an abyss?

Truth means the nature of the true. We think this nature in recollecting the Greek word *aletheia*, the unconcealedness of beings. But is this enough to define the nature of truth? Are we not passing off a mere change of word usage – unconcealedness instead of truth – as a characterization of fact? Certainly we do not get beyond an interchange of names as long as we do not come to know what must have happened in order to be compelled to tell the *nature* of truth in the word "unconcealedness."

Does this require a revival of Greek philosophy? Not at all. A revival, even if such an impossibility were possible, would be of no help to us; for the hidden history of Greek philosophy consists from its beginning in this, that it does not remain in conformity with the nature of truth that flashes out in the word *aletheia*, and has to misdirect its knowing and its speaking about the nature of truth more

and more into the discussion of a derivative nature of truth. The nature of truth as *aletheia* was not thought out in the thinking of the Greeks nor since then, and least of all in the philosophy that followed after. Unconcealedness is, for thought, the most concealed thing in Greek existence, although from early times it determines the presence of everything present.

Yet why should we not be satisfied with the nature of truth that has by now been familiar to us for centuries? Truth means today and has long meant the agreement or conformity of knowledge with fact. However, the fact must show itself to be fact if knowledge and the proposition that forms and expresses knowledge are to be able to conform to the fact; otherwise the fact cannot become binding on the proposition. How can fact show itself if it cannot itself stand forth out of concealedness, if it does not itself stand in the unconcealed? A proposition is true by conforming to the unconcealed, to what is true. Propositional truth is always, and always exclusively, this correctness. The critical concepts of truth which, since Descartes, start out from truth as certainty, are merely variations of the definition of truth as correctness. This nature of truth which is familiar to us – correctness in representation – stands and falls with truth as unconcealedness of beings.

If here and elsewhere we conceive of truth as unconcealedness, we are not merely taking refuge in a more literal translation of a Greek word. We are reminding ourselves of what, unexperienced and unthought, underlies our familiar and therefore outworn nature of truth in the sense of correctness. We do, of course, occasionally take the trouble to concede that naturally, in order to understand and verify the correctness (truth) of a proposition one really should go back to something that is already evident, and that this presupposition is indeed unavoidable. As long as we talk and believe in this way, we always understand truth merely as correctness, which of course still requires a further presupposition, that we ourselves just happen to make, heaven knows how or why.

But it is not we who presuppose the unconcealedness of beings; rather, the unconcealedness of beings (Being) puts us into such a condition of being that in our representation we always remain installed within and in attendance upon unconcealedness. Not only must that in *conformity* with which a cognition orders itself be already in some way unconcealed. The entire *realm* in which this "conforming to something" goes on must already occur as a whole in the unconcealed; and this holds equally of that *for* which the conformity of a proposition to fact becomes manifest. With all our correct representations we would get nowhere, we could not even presuppose that there already is manifest something to which we can conform ourselves, unless the unconcealedness of beings had already exposed us to, placed us in that lighted realm in which every being stands for us and from which it withdraws.

But how does this take place? How does truth happen as this unconcealedness? First, however, we must say more clearly what this unconcealedness itself is.

Things are, and human beings, gifts, and sacrifices are, animals and plants are, equipment and works are. That which is, the particular being, stands in Being. Through Being there passes a veiled destiny that is ordained between the godly and the countergodly. There is much in being that man cannot master. There is but little that comes to be known. What is known remains inexact, what is mastered insecure. What is, is never of our making or even merely the product of our minds, as it might all too easily seem. When we contemplate this whole as one, then we apprehend, so it appears, all that is – though we grasp it crudely enough.

And yet – beyond what is, not away from it but before it, there is still something else that happens. In the midst of beings as a whole an open place occurs. There is a clearing, a lighting. Thought of in reference to what is, to beings, this clearing is in a greater degree than are beings. This open center is therefore not surrounded by what is; rather, the lighting center itself encircles all that is, like the Nothing which we scarcely know.

That which is can only be, as a being, if it stands within and stands out within what is lighted in this clearing. Only this clearing grants and guarantees to us humans a passage to those beings that we ourselves are not, and access to the being that we ourselves are. Thanks to this clearing, beings are unconcealed in certain changing degrees. And yet a being can be *concealed*, too, only within the sphere of what is lighted. Each being we encounter and which encounters us keeps to this curious opposition of presence in that it always withholds itself at the same time in a concealedness. The clearing in which beings stand is in itself at the same time concealment. Concealment, however, prevails in the midst of beings in a twofold way.

Beings refuse themselves to us down to that one and seemingly least feature which we touch upon most readily when we can say no more of beings than that they are. Concealment as refusal is not simply and only the limit of knowledge in any given circumstance, but the beginning of the clearing of what is lighted. But concealment, though of another sort, to be sure, at the same time also occurs within what is lighted. One being places itself in front of another being, the one helps to hide the other, the former obscures the latter, a few obstruct many, one denies all. Here concealment is not simple refusal. Rather, a being appears, but it presents itself as other than it is.

This concealment is dissembling. If one being did not simulate another, we could not make mistakes or act mistakenly in regard to beings; we could not go astray and transgress, and especially could never overreach ourselves. That a being should be able to deceive as semblance is the condition for our being able to be deceived, not conversely.

Concealment can be a refusal or merely a dissembling. We are never fully certain whether it is the one or the other. Concealment conceals and dissembles itself. This means: the open place in the midst of beings, the clearing, is never a rigid stage with a permanently raised curtain on which the play of beings runs its course. Rather, the clearing happens only as this double concealment. The unconcealedness of beings – this is never a merely existent state, but a happening. Unconcealedness (truth) is neither an attribute of factual things in the sense of beings, nor one of propositions.

We believe we are at home in the immediate circle of beings. That which is, is familiar, reliable, ordinary. Nevertheless, the clearing is pervaded by a constant concealment in the double form of refusal and dissembling. At bottom, the ordinary is not ordinary; it is extra-ordinary, uncanny. The nature of truth, that is, of unconcealedness, is dominated throughout by a denial. Yet this denial is not a defect or a fault, as though truth were an unalloyed unconcealedness that has rid itself of everything concealed. If truth could accomplish this, it would no longer be itself. *This denial, in the form of a double concealment, belongs to the nature of truth as unconcealedness.* Truth, in its nature, is un-truth. We put the matter this way in order to serve notice, with a possibly surprising trenchancy, that denial in the manner of concealment belongs to unconcealedness as clearing. The proposition, "the nature of truth is untruth," is not, however, intended to state that truth is at bottom falsehood. Nor does it mean that truth is never itself but, viewed dialectically, is always also its opposite.

Truth occurs precisely as itself in that the concealing denial, as refusal, provides its constant source to all clearing, and yet, as dissembling, it metes out to all clearing the indefeasible severity of error. Concealing denial is intended to denote that opposition in the nature of truth which subsists between clearing, or lighting, and concealing. It is the opposition of the primal conflict. The nature of truth is, in itself, the primal conflict in which that open center is won within which what is, stands, and from which it sets itself back into itself.

This Open happens in the midst of beings. It exhibits an essential feature which we have already mentioned. To the Open there belong a world and the earth. But the world is not simply the Open that corresponds to clearing, and the earth is not simply the Closed that corresponds to concealment. Rather, the world is the clearing of the paths of the essential guiding directions with which all decision complies. Every decision, however, bases itself on something not mastered, something concealed, confusing; else it would never be a decision. The earth is not simply the Closed but rather that which rises up as self-closing. World and earth are always intrinsically and essentially in conflict, belligerent by nature. Only as such do they enter into the conflict of clearing and concealing.

Earth juts through the world and world grounds itself on the earth only so far as truth happens as the primal conflict between clearing and concealing. But how does truth happen? We answer: it happens in a few essential ways. One of these ways in which truth happens is the work-being of the work. Setting up a world and setting forth the earth, the work is the fighting of the battle in which the unconcealedness of beings as a whole, or truth, is won.

Truth happens in the temple's standing where it is. This does not mean that something is correctly represented and rendered here, but that what is as a whole is brought into unconcealedness and held therein. To hold (*halten*) originally means to tend, keep, take care (*hüten*). Truth happens in Van Gogh's painting. This does not mean that something is correctly portrayed, but rather that in the revelation of the equipmental being of the shoes, that which is as a whole – world and earth in their counterplay – attains to unconcealedness.

Thus in the work it is truth, not only something true, that is at work. The picture that shows the peasant shoes, the poem that says the Roman fountain, do not just make manifest what this isolated being as such is – if indeed they manifest anything at all; rather, they make unconcealedness as such happen in regard to what is as a whole. The more simply and authentically the shoes are engrossed in their nature, the more plainly and purely the fountain is engrossed in its nature – the more directly and engagingly do all beings attain to a greater degree of being along with them. That is how self-concealing being is illuminated. Light of this kind joins its shining to and into the work. This shining, joined in the work, is the beautiful. *Beauty is one way in which truth occurs as unconcealedness.*

We now, indeed, grasp the nature of truth more clearly in certain respects. What is at work in the work may accordingly have become more clear. But the work's now visible work-being still does not tell us anything about the work's closest and most obtrusive reality, about the thingly aspect of the work. Indeed it almost seems as though, in pursuing the exclusive aim of grasping the work's independence as purely as possible, we had completely overlooked the one thing, that a work is always a work, which means that it is something worked out, brought about, effected. If there is anything that distinguishes the work as work, it is that the work has been created. Since the work is created, and creation requires a medium out of which and in which it creates, the thingly element, too, enters into the work. This is incontestable. Still the question remains: how does being created belong to the work? This can be elucidated only if two points are cleared up:

1. What do being created and creation mean here in distinction from making and being made?

2. What is the inmost nature of the work itself, from which alone can be gauged how far createdness belongs to the work and how far it determines the work-being of the work?

Creation is here always thought of in reference to the work. To the nature of the work there belongs the happening of truth. From the outset we define the nature of creating by its relation to the nature of truth as the unconcealedness of beings. The pertinence of createdness to the work can be elucidated only by way of a more fundamental clarification of the nature of truth. The question of truth and its nature returns again.

We must raise that question once more, if the proposition that truth is at work in the work is not to remain a mere assertion.

We must now first ask in a more essential way: how does the impulse toward such a thing as a work lie in the nature of truth? Of what nature is truth, that it can be set into work, or even under certain conditions must be set into work, in order to be *as* truth? But we defined the setting-into-a-work of truth as the nature of art. Hence our last question becomes:

What is truth, that it can happen as, or even must happen as, art? How is it that art exists at all?

Truth and Art

Art is the origin of the art work and of the artist. Origin is the source of the nature in which the being of an entity is present. What is art? We seek its nature in the actual work. The actual reality of the work has been defined by that which is at work in the work, by the happening of truth. This happening we think of as the fighting of the conflict between world and earth. Repose occurs in the concentrated agitation of this conflict. The independence or self-composure of the work is grounded here.

In the work, the happening of truth is at work. But what is thus at work, is so *in* the work. This means that the actual work is here already presupposed as the bearer of this happening. At once the problem of the thingly feature of the given work confronts us again. One thing thus finally becomes clear: however zealously we inquire into the work's self-sufficiency, we shall still fail to find its actuality as long as we do not also agree to take the work as something worked, effected. To take it thus lies closest at hand, for in the word "work" we hear what is worked. The workly character of the work consists in its having been created by the artist. It may seem curious that this most obvious and all-clarifying definition of the work is mentioned only now.

The work's createdness, however, can obviously be grasped only in terms of the process of creation. Thus, constrained by the facts, we must consent after all to go into the activity of the artist in order to arrive at the origin of the work of art. The attempt to define the work-being of the work purely in terms of the work itself proves to be unfeasible.

In turning away now from the work to examine the nature of the creative process, we should like nevertheless to keep in mind what was said first of the picture of the peasant shoes and later of the Greek temple.

We think of creation as a bringing forth. But the making of equipment, too, is a bringing forth. Handicraft – a remarkable play of language – does not, to be sure, create works, not even when we contrast, as we must, the handmade with the factory product. But what is it that distinguishes bringing forth as creation from bringing forth in the mode of making? It is as difficult to track down the essential features of the creation of works and the making of equipment as it is easy to distinguish verbally between the two modes of bringing forth. Going along with first appearances we find the same procedure in the activity of potter and sculptor, of joiner and painter. The creation of a work requires craftsmanship. Great artists prize craftsmanship most highly. They are the first to call for its painstaking cultivation, based on complete mastery. They above all others constantly strive to educate themselves ever anew in thorough craftsmanship. It has often enough been pointed out that the Greeks, who knew quite a bit about works of art, use the same word *techne* for craft and art and call the craftsman and the artist by the same name: *technites*.

It thus seems advisable to define the nature of creative work in terms of its craft aspect. But reference to the linguistic usage of the Greeks, with their experience of the facts, must give us pause. However usual and convincing the reference may be to the Greek practice of naming craft and art by the same name, *techne*, it nevertheless remains oblique and superficial; for *techne* signifies neither craft nor art, and not at all the technical in our present-day sense; it never means a kind of practical performance.

The word *techne* denotes rather a mode of knowing. To know means to have seen, in the widest sense of seeing, which means to apprehend what is present, as such. For Greek thought the nature of knowing consists in *aletheia*, that is, in the uncovering of beings. It supports and guides all comportment toward beings. *Techne*, as knowledge experienced in the Greek manner, is a bringing forth of beings in that it *brings forth* present beings as such beings *out of* concealedness and specifically *into* the unconcealedness of their appearance; *techne* never signifies the action of making.

The artist is a *technites* not because he is also a craftsman, but because both the setting forth of works and the setting forth of equipment occur in a bringing forth and presenting that causes beings in the first place to come forward and be present in assuming an appearance. Yet all this happens in the midst of the being that grows out of its own accord, *phusis*. Calling art *techne* does not at all imply that the artist's action is seen in the light of craft. What looks like craft in the creation of a work is of a different sort. This doing is determined and pervaded by the nature of creation, and indeed remains contained within that creating.

What then, if not craft, is to guide our thinking about the nature of creation? What else than a view of what is to be created: the work? Although it becomes actual only as the creative act is performed, and thus depends for its reality upon this act, the nature of creation is determined by the nature of the work. Even though the work's createdness has a relation to creation, nevertheless both createdness and creation must be defined in terms of the work-being of the work. And now it can no longer seem strange that we first and at length dealt with the work alone, to bring its createdness into view only at the end. If createdness belongs to the work as essentially as the word "work" makes it sound, then we must try to understand even more essentially what so far could be defined as the work-being of the work.

In the light of the definition of the work we have reached at this point, according to which the happening of truth is at work in the work, we are able to characterize creation as follows: to create is to cause something to emerge as a thing that has been brought forth. The work's becoming a work is a way in which truth becomes and happens. It all rests on the nature of truth. But what is truth, that it has to happen in such a thing as something created? How does truth have an impulse toward a work grounded in its very nature? Is this intelligible in terms of the nature of truth as thus far elucidated?

Truth is un-truth, insofar as there belongs to it the reservoir of the not-yet-uncovered, the un-uncovered, in the sense of concealment. In unconcealedness, as truth, there occurs also the other "un-" of a double restraint or refusal. Truth occurs as such in the opposition of clearing and double concealing. Truth is the primal conflict in which, always in some particular way, the Open is won within which everything stands and from which everything withholds itself that shows itself and withdraws itself as a being. Whenever and however this conflict breaks out and happens, the opponents, lighting or clearing and concealing, move apart because of it. Thus the Open of the place of conflict is won. The openness of this Open, that is, truth, can be what it is, namely, *this* openness, only if and as long as it establishes itself within its Open. Hence there must always be some being in this Open, something that is, in which the openness takes its stand and attains its constancy. In taking possession thus of the Open, the openness holds open the Open and sustains it. Setting and taking possession are here everywhere drawn from the Greek sense of *thesis*, which means a setting up in the unconcealed.

In referring to this self-establishing of openness in the Open, thinking touches on a sphere that cannot yet be explicated here. Only this much should be noted, that if the nature of the unconcealedness of beings belongs in any way to Being itself (cf. *Being and Time*, § 44),[1] then Being, by way of its own nature, lets the place of openness (the lighting-clearing of the There) happen, and introduces it as a place of the sort in which each being emerges or arises in its own way.

Truth happens only by establishing itself in the conflict and sphere opened up by truth itself. Because truth is the opposition of clearing and concealing, there belongs to it what is here to be called establishing. But truth does not exist in itself beforehand, somewhere among the stars, only later to descend elsewhere among beings. This is impossible for the reason alone that it is after all only the openness of beings that first affords the possibility of a somewhere and of a place filled by present beings. Clearing of openness and establishment in the Open belong together. They are the same single nature of the happening of truth. This happening is historical in many ways.

One essential way in which truth establishes itself in the beings it has opened up is truth setting itself into work. Another way in which truth occurs is the act that founds a political state. Still another way in which truth comes to shine forth is the nearness of that which is not simply a being, but the being that is most of all. Still another way in which truth grounds itself is the essential sacrifice. Still another way in which truth becomes is the thinker's questioning, which, as the thinking of Being, names Being in its question-worthiness. By contrast, science is not an original happening of truth, but always the cultivation of a domain of truth already opened, specifically by apprehending and confirming that which shows itself to be possibly and necessarily correct within that field. When and insofar as a science passes beyond correctness and goes on to a truth, which means that it arrives at the essential disclosure of what is as such, it is philosophy.

Because it is in the nature of truth to establish itself within that which is, in order thus first to become truth, therefore the impulse toward the work lies in the nature of truth as one of truth's distinctive possibilities by which it can itself occur as being in the midst of beings.

The establishing of truth in the work is the bringing forth of a being such as never was before and will never come to be again. The bringing forth places this being in the Open in such a way that what is to be brought forth first clears the openness of the Open into which it comes forth. Where this bringing forth expressly brings the openness of beings, or truth, that which is brought forth is a work. Creation is such a bringing forth. As such a bringing, it is rather a receiving and an incorporating of a relation to unconcealedness. What, accordingly, does the createdness consist in? It may be elucidated by two essential determinations.

Truth establishes itself in the work. Truth is present only as the conflict between lighting and concealing in the opposition of world and earth. Truth wills to be established in the work as this conflict of world and earth. The conflict is not to be resolved in a being brought forth for the purpose, nor is it to be merely housed there; the conflict, on the contrary, is started by it. This being must therefore contain within itself the essential traits of the conflict. In the strife the unity of world and earth is won. As a world opens itself, it submits to the decision of an historical humanity the question of victory and defeat, blessing and curse, mastery and slavery. The dawning world brings out what is as yet undecided and measureless, and thus discloses the hidden necessity of measure and decisiveness.

But as a world opens itself the earth comes to rise up. It stands forth as that which bears all, as that which is sheltered in its own law and always wrapped up in itself. World demands its decisiveness and its measure and lets beings attain to the Open of their paths. Earth, bearing and jutting, strives to keep itself closed and to entrust everything to its law. The conflict is not a rift (*Riss*) as a mere cleft is ripped open; rather, it is the intimacy with which opponents belong to each other. This rift carries the opponents into the source of their unity by virtue of their common ground. It is a basic design, an outline sketch, that draws the basic features of the rise of the lighting of beings. This rift does not let the opponents break apart; it brings the opposition of measure and boundary into their common outline.

Truth establishes itself as a strife within a being that is to be brought forth only in such a way that the conflict opens up in this being, that is, this being is itself brought into the rift-design. The rift-design is the drawing together, into a unity, of sketch and basic design, breach and outline. Truth establishes itself in a being in such a way, indeed, that this being itself occupies the Open of truth. This occupying, however, can happen only if what is to be brought forth, the rift, entrusts itself to the self-secluding factor that juts up in the Open. The rift must set itself back into the heavy weight of stone, the dumb hardness of wood, the dark glow of colors. As the earth takes the rift back into itself, the rift is first set forth into the Open and thus placed, that is, set, within that which towers up into the Open as self-closing and sheltering.

The strife that is brought into the rift and thus set back into the earth and thus fixed in place is *figure, shape, Gestalt*. Createdness of the work means: truth's being fixed in place in the figure. Figure is the structure in whose shape the rift composes and submits itself. This composed rift is the fitting or joining of the shining of truth. What is here called figure, *Gestalt*, is always to be thought in terms of the particular placing (*Stellen*) and framing or framework (*Ge-Stell*) as which the work occurs when it sets itself up and sets itself forth.

In the creation of a work, the conflict, as rift, must be set back into the earth, and the earth itself must be set forth and used as the self-closing factor. This use, however, does not use up or misuse the earth as matter, but rather sets it free to be nothing but itself. This use of the earth is a working with it that, to be sure, looks like the employment of matter in handicraft. Hence the appearance that artistic creation is also an activity of handicraft. It never is. But it is at all times a use of the earth in the fixing in place of truth in the figure. In contrast, the making of equipment is never directly the effecting of the happening of truth. The production of equipment is finished when a material has been so formed as to be ready for use. For equipment to be ready means that it is dismissed beyond itself, to be used up in serviceability.

Not so when a work is created. This becomes clear in the light of the second characteristic, which may be introduced here.

The readiness of equipment and the createdness of the work agree in this, that in each case something is produced. But in contrast to all other modes of production, the work is distinguished by being created so that its createdness is part of the created work. But does not this hold true for everything brought forth, indeed for anything that has in any way come to be? Everything brought forth surely has this endowment of having been brought forth, if it has any endowment at all. Certainly. But in the work, createdness is expressly created into the created being, so that it stands out from it, from the being thus brought forth, in an expressly particular way. If this is how matters stand, then we must also be able to discover and experience the createdness explicitly in the work.

The emergence of createdness from the work does not mean that the work is to give the impression of having been made by a great artist. The point is not that the created being be certified as the performance of a capable person, so that the producer is thereby brought to public notice. It is not the "N. N. fecit" that is to be made known. Rather, the simple "factum est" is to be held forth into the Open by the work: namely this, that unconcealedness of what is has happened here, and that as this happening it happens here for the first time; or, that such a work *is* at all rather than is not. The thrust that the work as this work is, and the uninterruptedness of this plain thrust, constitute the steadfastness of the work's self-subsistence. Precisely where the artist and the process and the circumstances of the genesis of the work remain unknown, this thrust, this "*that it is*" of createdness, emerges into view most purely from the work.

To be sure, "that" it is made is a property also of all equipment that is available and in use. But this "that" does not become prominent in the equipment; it disappears in usefulness. The more handy a piece of equipment is, the more inconspicuous it remains that, for example, such a hammer is and the more exclusively does the equipment keep itself in its equipmentality. In general, of everything present to us, we can note that it *is*; but this also, if it is noted at all, is noted only soon to fall into oblivion, as is the wont of everything commonplace. And what is more commonplace than this, that a being is? In a work, by contrast, this fact, that it *is* as a work, is just what is unusual. The event of its being created does not simply reverberate through the work; rather, the work casts before itself the eventful fact that the work is as this work, and it has constantly this fact about itself. The more essentially the work opens itself, the more luminous becomes the uniqueness of the fact that it is rather than is not. The more essentially this thrust comes into the Open, the stronger and more solitary the work becomes. In the bringing forth of the work there lies this offering "that it be."

The question of the work's createdness ought to have brought us nearer to its workly character and therewith to its reality. Createdness revealed itself as the conflict's being fixed in place in the figure by means of the rift. Createdness here is itself expressly created into the work and stands as the silent thrust into the Open of the "that." But the work's reality does not exhaust itself even in createdness. However, this view of the nature of the work's createdness now enables us to take the step toward which everything thus far said tends.

The more solitarily the work, fixed in the figure, stands on its own and the more cleanly it seems to cut all ties to human beings, the more simply does the thrust come into the Open that such a work *is*, and the more essentially is the extraordinary thrust to the surface and the long-familiar thrust down. But this multiple thrusting is nothing violent, for the more purely the work is itself transported into the openness of beings – an openness opened by itself – the more simply does it transport us into this openness and thus at the same time transport us out of the realm of the ordinary. To submit to this displacement means: to transform our accustomed ties to world and to earth and henceforth to restrain all usual doing and prizing, knowing and looking, in order to stay within the truth that is happening in the work. Only the restraint of this staying lets what is created be the work that it is. This letting the work be a work we call the preserving of the work. It is only for such preserving that the work yields itself in its createdness as actual, i.e., now: present in the manner of a work.

Just as a work cannot be without being created but is essentially in need of creators, so what is created cannot itself come into being without those who preserve it.

However, if a work does not find preservers, does not at once find them such as respond to the truth happening in the work, this does not at all mean that the work may also be a work without preservers. Being a work, it always remains tied to preservers, even and particularly when it is still only waiting for preservers and only pleads and waits for them to enter into its truth. Even the oblivion into which the work can sink is not nothing; it is still a preservation. It feeds on the work. Preserving the work means: standing within the openness of beings that happens in the work. This "standing-within" of preservation, however, is a knowing. Yet knowing does not consist in mere information and notions about something. He who truly knows what is, knows what he wills to do in the midst of what is.

The willing here referred to, which neither merely applies knowledge nor decides beforehand, is thought of in terms of the basic experience of thinking in *Being and Time*. Knowing that remains a willing, and willing that remains a knowing, is the existing human being's entrance into and compliance with the unconcealedness of Being. The resoluteness intended in *Being and Time* is not the deliberate action of a subject, but the opening up of human being, out of its captivity in that which is, to the openness of Being.[2] However, in existence, man does not proceed from some inside to some outside; rather, the nature of *Existenz* is outstanding standing-within the essential sunderance of the clearing of beings. Neither in the creation mentioned before nor in the willing mentioned now do we think of the performance or act of a subject striving toward himself as his self-set goal.

Willing is the sober resolution of that existential self-transcendence which exposes itself to the openness of beings as it is set into the work. In this way, standing-within is brought under law. Preserving the work, as knowing, is a sober standing-within the extraordinary awesomeness of the truth that is happening in the work.

This knowledge, which as a willing makes its home in the work's truth and only thus remains a knowing, does not deprive the work of its independence, does not drag it into the sphere of mere experience, and does not degrade it to the role of a stimulator of experience. Preserving the work does not reduce people to their private experiences, but brings them into affiliation with the truth happening in the work. Thus it grounds being for and with one another as the historical standing-out of human existence in reference to unconcealedness. Most of all, knowledge in the manner of preserving is far removed from that merely aestheticizing connoisseurship of the work's formal aspects, its qualities and charms. Knowing as having seen is a

being resolved; it is standing within the conflict that the work has fitted into the rift.

The proper way to preserve the work is cocreated and prescribed only and exclusively by the work. Preserving occurs at different levels of knowledge, with always differing degrees of scope, constancy, and lucidity. When works are offered for merely artistic enjoyment, this does not yet prove that they stand in preservation as works.

As soon as the thrust into the extraordinary is parried and captured by the sphere of familiarity and connoisseurship, the art business has begun. Even a painstaking handing on of works to posterity, all scientific efforts to regain them, no longer reach the work's own being, but only a recollection of it. But even this recollection may still offer to the work a place from which it joins in shaping history. The work's own peculiar reality, on the other hand, is brought to bear only where the work is preserved in the truth that happens by the work itself.

The work's reality is determined in its basic features by the nature of the work's being. We can now return to our opening question: how do matters stand with the work's thingly feature that is to guarantee its immediate reality? They stand so that now we no longer raise this question about the work's thingly element; for as long as we ask it, we take the work directly and as a foregone conclusion, as an object that is simply there. In that way we never question in terms of the work, but in our own terms – we, who then do not let the work be a work but view it as an object that is supposed to produce this or that state of mind in us.

But what looks like the thingly element, in the sense of our usual thing-concepts, in the work taken as object, is, seen from the perspective of the work, its earthy character. The earth juts up within the work because the work exists as something in which truth is at work and because truth occurs only by installing itself within a particular being. In the earth, however, as essentially self-closing, the openness of the Open finds the greatest resistance (to the Open) and thereby the site of the Open's constant stand, where the figure must be fixed in place.

Was it then superfluous, after all, to enter into the question of the thingly character of the thing? By no means. To be sure, the work's work-character cannot be defined in terms of its thingly character, but as against that the question about the thing's thingly character can be brought into the right course by way of a knowledge of the work's work–character. This is no small matter, if we recollect that those ancient, traditional modes of thought attack the thing's thingly character and make it subject to an interpretation of what is as a whole, which remains unfit to apprehend the nature of equipment and of the work, and which makes us equally blind to the original nature of truth.

To determine the thing's thingness neither consideration of the bearer of properties is adequate, nor that of the manifold of sense data in their unity, and least of all that of the matter–form structure regarded by itself, which is derived from equipment. Anticipating a meaningful and weighty interpretation of the thingly character of things, we must aim at the thing's belonging to the earth. The nature of the earth, in its free and unhurried bearing and self-closure, reveals itself, however, only in the earth's jutting into a world, in the opposition of the two. This conflict is fixed in place in the figure of the work and becomes manifest by it. What holds true of equipment – namely that we come to know its equipmental character specifically only through the work itself – also holds of the thingly character of the thing. The fact that we never know thingness directly, and if we know it at all, then only vaguely and thus require the work – this fact proves indirectly that in the work's work-being the happening of truth, the opening up or disclosure of what is, is at work.

But, we might finally object, if the work is indeed to bring thingness cogently into the Open, must it not then itself – and indeed before its own creation and for the sake of its creation – have been brought into a relation with the things of earth, with nature? Someone who was bound to know what he was talking about, Albrecht Dürer, did after all make the well-known remark: "For in truth, art lies hidden within nature; he who can wrest it from her, has it." "Wrest" here means to draw out the rift and to draw the design with the drawing-pen on the drawing-board.[3] But we at once raise the counterquestion: how can the rift-design be drawn out if it is not brought into the Open by the creative sketch as a rift, which is to say, brought out beforehand as a conflict of measure and unmeasure? True, there lies hidden in nature a rift-design, a measure and a boundary and, tied to it, a capacity for bringing forth – that is, art. But it is equally certain that this art hidden in nature becomes manifest only through the work, because it lies originally in the work.

The trouble we are taking over the reality of the work is intended as spadework for discovering art and the nature of art in the actual work. The question concerning the nature of art, the way toward knowledge of it, is first to be placed on a firm ground again. The answer to the question, like every genuine answer, is only the final result of the last step in a long series of questions. Each answer remains in force as an answer only as long as it is rooted in questioning.

The reality of the work has become not only clearer for us in the light of its work-being, but also essentially richer. The preservers of a work belong to its createdness with an essentiality equal to that of the creators. But it is the work that makes the creators possible in their nature, and that by its own nature is in need of preservers. If art is the origin of the work, this means that art lets those who naturally belong together at work, the creator and the preserver, originate, each in his own nature. What, however, is art itself that we call it rightly an origin?

In the work, the happening of truth is at work and, indeed, at work according to the manner of a work. Accordingly the nature of art was defined to begin with as the setting-into-work of truth. Yet this definition is intentionally ambiguous. It says on the one hand: art is the fixing in place of a self-establishing truth in the figure. This happens in creation as the bringing forth of the unconcealed-ness of what is. Setting-into-work, however, also means: the bringing of work-being into movement and happening. This happens as preservation. Thus art is: the creative preserving of truth in the work. *Art then is the becoming and happening of truth.* Does truth, then, arise out of nothing? It does indeed if by nothing is meant the mere not of that which is, and if we here think of that which is as an object present in the ordinary way, which thereafter comes to light and is challenged by the existence of the work as only presumptively a true being. Truth is never gathered from objects that are present and ordinary. Rather, the opening up of the Open, and the clearing of what is, happens only as the openness is projected, sketched out, that makes its advent in thrownness.[4]

Truth, as the clearing and concealing of what is, happens in being composed, as a poet composes a poem. *All art*, as the letting happen of the advent of the truth of what is, is, as such, *essentially poetry*. The nature of art, on which both the art work and the artist depend, is the setting-itself-into-work of truth. It is due to art's poetic nature that, in the midst of what is, art breaks open an open place, in whose openness everything is other than usual. By virtue of the projected sketch set into the work of the unconcealedness of what is, which casts itself toward us, everything ordinary and hitherto existing becomes an unbeing. This unbeing has lost the capacity to give and keep being as measure. The curious fact here is that the work in no way affects hitherto existing entities by causal connections. The working of the work does not consist in the taking effect of a cause. It lies in a change, happening from out of the work, of the unconcealedness of what is, and this means, of Being.

Poetry, however, is not an aimless imagining of whimsicalities and not a flight of mere notions and fancies into the realm of the unreal. What poetry, as illuminating projection, unfolds of unconcealedness and projects ahead into the design of the figure, is the Open which poetry lets happen, and indeed in such a way that only now, in the midst of beings, the Open brings beings to shine and ring out. If we fix our vision on the nature of the work and its connection with the happening of the truth of what is, it becomes questionable whether the nature of poetry, and this means at the same time the nature of projection, can be adequately thought of in terms of the power of imagination.

The nature of poetry, which has now been ascertained very broadly – but not on that account vaguely, may here be kept firmly in mind as something worthy of questioning, something that still has to be thought through.

If all art is in essence poetry, then the arts of architecture, painting, sculpture, and music must be traced back to poesy. That is pure arbitrariness. It certainly is, as long as we mean that those arts are varieties of the art of language, if it is permissible to characterize poesy by that easily misinterpretable title. But poesy is only one mode of the lighting projection of truth, i.e., of poetic composition in this wider sense. Nevertheless, the linguistic work, the poem in the narrower sense, has a privileged position in the domain of the arts.

To see this, only the right concept of language is needed. In the current view, language is held to be a kind of communication. It serves for verbal exchange and agreement, and in general for communicating. But language is not only and not primarily an audible and written expression of what is to be communicated. It not only puts forth in words and statements what is overtly or covertly intended to be communicated; language alone brings what is, as something that is, into the Open for the first time. Where there is no language, as in the being of stone, plant, and animal, there is also no openness of what is, and consequently no openness either of that which is not and of the empty.

Language, by naming beings for the first time, first brings beings to word and to appearance. Only this naming nominates beings *to* their being *from out of* their being. Such saying is a projecting of the clearing, in which announcement is made of what it is that beings come into the Open *as*. Projecting is the release of a throw by which unconcealedness submits and infuses itself into what is as such. This projective announcement forthwith becomes a renunciation of all the dim confusion in which what is veils and withdraws itself.

Projective saying is poetry: the saying of world and earth, the saying of the arena of their conflict and thus of the place of all nearness and remoteness of the gods. Poetry is the saying of the unconcealedness of what is. Actual language at any given moment is the happening of this saying, in which a people's world historically arises for it and the earth is preserved as that which remains closed. Projective saying is saying which, in preparing the sayable, simultaneously brings the unsayable as such into a world. In such saying, the concepts of an historical people's nature, i.e., of its belonging to world history, are formed for that folk, before it.

Poetry is thought of here in so broad a sense and at the same time in such intimate unity of being with language and word, that we must leave open whether art, in all its modes from architecture to poesy, exhausts the nature of poetry.

Language itself is poetry in the essential sense. But since language is the happening in which for man beings first disclose themselves to him each time as beings, poesy – or poetry in the narrower sense – is the most original form of poetry in the essential sense. Language is not poetry because it is the primal poesy; rather, poesy takes place in language because language preserves the original nature of poetry. Building and plastic creation, on the other hand, always happen already, and happen only, in the Open of saying and naming. It is the Open that pervades and guides them. But for this very reason they remain their own ways and modes in which truth orders itself into work. They are an ever special poetizing within the clearing of what is, which has already happened unnoticed in language.

Art, as the setting-into-work of truth, is poetry. Not only the creation of the work is poetic, but equally poetic, though in its own way, is the preserving of the work; for a work is in actual effect as a work only when we remove ourselves from our commonplace routine and move into what is disclosed by the work, so as to bring our own nature itself to take a stand in the truth of what is.

The nature of art is poetry. The nature of poetry, in turn, is the founding of truth. We understand founding here in a triple sense: founding as bestowing, founding as grounding, and founding as beginning. Founding, however, is actual only in preserving. Thus to each mode of founding there corresponds a mode of preserving. We can do no more now than to present this structure of the nature of art in a few strokes, and even this only to the extent that the earlier characterization of the nature of the work offers an initial hint.

The setting-into-work of truth thrusts up the unfamiliar and extraordinary and at the same time thrusts down the ordinary and what we believe to be such. The truth that discloses itself in the work can never be proved or derived from what went before. What went before is refuted in its exclusive reality by the work. What art founds can therefore never be compensated and made up for by what is already present and available. Founding is an overflow, an endowing, a bestowal.

The poetic projection of truth that sets itself into work as figure is also never carried out in the direction of an indeterminate void. Rather, in the work, truth is thrown toward the coming preservers, that is, toward an historical group of men. What is thus cast forth is, however, never an arbitrary demand. Genuinely poetic projection is the opening up or disclosure of that into which human being as historical is already cast. This is the earth and, for an historical people, its earth, the self-closing ground on which it rests together with everything that it already is, though still hidden from itself. It is, however, its world, which prevails in virtue of the relation of human being to the unconcealedness of Being. For this reason, everything with which man is endowed must, in the projection, be drawn up from the closed ground and expressly set upon this ground. In this way the ground is first grounded as the bearing ground.

All creation, because it is such a drawing-up, is a drawing, as of water from a spring. Modern subjectivism, to be sure, immediately misinterprets creation, taking it as the self-sovereign subject's performance of genius. The founding of truth is a founding not only in the sense of free bestowal, but at the same time foundation in the sense of this ground-laying grounding. Poetic projection comes from Nothing in this respect, that it never takes its gift from the ordinary and traditional. But it never comes from Nothing in that what is projected by it is only the withheld vocation of the historical being of man itself.

Bestowing and grounding have in themselves the unmediated character of what we call a beginning. Yet this unmediated character of a beginning, the peculiarity of a leap out of the unmediable, does not exclude but rather includes the fact that the beginning prepares itself for the longest time and wholly inconspicuously. A genuine beginning, as a leap, is always a head start, in which everything to come is already leaped over, even if as something disguised. The beginning already contains the end latent within itself. A genuine beginning, however, has nothing of the neophyte character of the primitive. The primitive, because it lacks the bestowing, grounding leap and head start, is always futureless. It is not capable of releasing anything more from itself because it contains nothing more than that in which it is caught.

A beginning, on the contrary, always contains the undisclosed abundance of the unfamiliar and extraordinary, which means that it also contains strife with the familiar and ordinary. Art as poetry is founding, in the third sense of instigation of the strife of truth: founding as beginning. Always when that which is as a whole demands, as what is, itself, a grounding in openness, art attains to its historical nature as foundation. This foundation happened in the West for the first time in Greece. What was in the future to be called Being was set into work, setting the standard. The realm of beings thus opened up was then transformed into a being in the sense of God's creation. This happened in the Middle Ages. This kind of being was again transformed at the beginning and in the course of the modern age. Beings became objects that could be controlled and seen through by calculation. At each time a new and essential world arose. At each time the openness of what is had to be established in beings themselves, by the fixing in place of truth in figure. At each time there happened unconcealedness of what is. Unconcealedness sets itself into work, a setting which is accomplished by art.

Whenever art happens – that is, whenever there is a beginning – a thrust enters history, either begins or starts over again. History means here not a sequence in time of events of whatever sort, however important. History is the transporting of a people into its appointed task as entrance into that people's endowment.

Art is the setting-into-work of truth. In this proposition an essential ambiguity is hidden, in which truth is at once the subject and the object of the setting. But subject and object are unsuitable names here. They keep us from thinking precisely this ambiguous nature, a task that no longer belongs to this consideration. Art is historical, and as historical it is the creative preserving of truth in the work. Art happens as poetry. Poetry is founding in the triple sense of bestowing, grounding, and beginning. Art, as founding, is essentially historical. This means not only that art has a history in the external sense that in the course of time it, too, appears along with many other things, and in the process changes and passes away and offers changing aspects for historiology. Art is history in the essential sense that it grounds history.

Art lets truth originate. Art, founding preserving, is the spring that leaps to the truth of what is, in the work. To originate something by a leap, to bring something into being from out of the source of its nature in a founding leap – this is what the word origin (German *Ursprung*, literally, primal leap) means.

The origin of the work of art – that is, the origin of both the creators and the preservers, which is to say of a people's historical existence, is art. This is so because art is by nature an origin: a distinctive way in which truth comes into being, that is, becomes historical.

We inquire into the nature of art. Why do we inquire in this way? We inquire in this way in order to be able to ask more truly whether art is or is not an origin in our historical existence, whether and under what conditions it can and must be an origin.

Such reflection cannot force art and its coming-to-be. But this reflective knowledge is the preliminary and therefore indispensable preparation for the becoming of art. Only such knowledge prepares its space for art, their way for the creators, their location for the preservers.

In such knowledge, which can only grow slowly, the question is decided whether art can be an origin and then must be a head start, or whether it is to remain a mere appendix and then can only be carried along as a routine cultural phenomenon.

Are we in our existence historically at the origin? Do we know, which means do we give heed to, the nature of the origin? Or, in our relation to art, do we still merely make appeal to a cultivated acquaintance with the past?

For this either-or and its decision there is an infallible sign. Hölderlin, the poet – whose work still confronts the Germans as a test to be stood – named it in saying:

> Schwer verlässt
> was nahe dem Ursprung wohnet, den Ort.

> Reluctantly
> that which dwells near its origin departs.
> – "The Journey," verses 18–19

Epilogue

The foregoing reflections are concerned with the riddle of art, the riddle that art itself is. They are far from claiming to solve the riddle. The task is to see the riddle.

Almost from the time when specialized thinking about art and the artist began, this thought was called aesthetic. Aesthetics takes the work of art as an object, the object of *aisthesis*, of sensuous apprehension in the wide sense. Today we call this apprehension experience. The way in which man experiences art is supposed to give information about its nature. Experience is the source that is standard not only for art appreciation and enjoyment, but also for artistic creation. Everything is an experience. Yet perhaps experience is the element in which art dies. The dying occurs so slowly that it takes a few centuries.

To be sure, people speak of immortal works of art and of art as an eternal value. Speaking this way means using that language which does not trouble with precision in all essential matters, for fear that in the end to be precise would call for – thinking. And is there any greater fear today than that of thinking? Does this talk about immortal works and the eternal value of art have any content or substance? Or are these merely the half-baked clichés of an age when great art, together with its nature, has departed from among men?

In the most comprehensive reflection on the nature of art that the West possesses – comprehensive because it stems from metaphysics – namely Hegel's *Vorlesungen über die Ästhetik*, the following propositions occur:

Art no longer counts for us as the highest manner in which truth obtains existence for itself.

One may well hope that art will continue to advance and perfect itself, but its form has ceased to be the highest need of the spirit.

In all these relationships art is and remains for us, on the side of its highest vocation, something past.[5]

The judgment that Hegel passes in these statements cannot be evaded by pointing out that since Hegel's lectures in aesthetics were given for the last time during the winter of 1828–29 at the University of Berlin, we have seen the rise of many new art works and new art movements. Hegel never meant to deny this possibility. But the question remains: is art still an essential and necessary way in which that truth happens which is decisive for our historical existence, or is art no longer of this character? If, however, it is such no longer, then there remains the question why this is so. The truth of Hegel's judgment has not yet been decided; for behind this verdict there stands Western thought since the Greeks, which thought corresponds to a truth of beings that has already happened. Decision upon the judgment will be made, when it is made, from and about this truth of what is. Until then the judgment remains in force. But for that very reason the question is necessary whether the truth that the judgment declares is final and conclusive and what follows if it is.

Such questions, which solicit us more or less definitely, can be asked only after we have first taken into consideration the nature of art. We attempt to take a few steps by posing the question of the origin of the art work. The problem is to bring to view the work-character of the work. What the word "origin" here means is thought by way of the nature of truth.

The truth of which we have spoken does not coincide with that which is generally recognized under the name and assigned to cognition and science as a quality in order to distinguish from it the beautiful and the good, which function as names for the values of nontheoretical activities.

Truth is the unconcealedness of that which is as something that is. Truth is the truth of Being. Beauty does not occur alongside and apart from this truth. When truth sets itself into the work, it appears. Appearance – as this being of truth in the work and as work – is beauty. Thus the beautiful belongs to the advent of truth, truth's taking of its

place. It does not exist merely relative to pleasure and purely as its object. The beautiful does lie in form, but only because the *forma* once took its light from Being as the isness of what is. Being at that time made its advent as *eidos*. The *idea* fits itself into the *morphe*. The *sunolon*, the unitary whole of *morphe* and *hule*, namely the *ergon*, *is* in the manner of *energeia*. This mode of presence becomes the *actualitas* of the *ens actu*. The *actualitas* becomes reality. Reality becomes objectivity. Objectivity becomes experience. In the way in which, for the world determined by the West, that which is, is as the real, there is concealed a peculiar confluence of beauty with truth. The history of the nature of Western art corresponds to the change of the nature of truth. This is no more intelligible in terms of beauty taken for itself than it is in terms of experience, supposing that the metaphysical concept of art reaches to art's nature.

Addendum

On pages 201 and 204 a real difficulty will force itself on the attentive reader: it looks as if the remarks about the "fixing in place of truth" and the "letting happen of the advent of truth" could never be brought into accord. For "fixing in place" implies a willing which blocks and thus prevents the advent of truth. In *letting*-happen on the other hand, there is manifested a compliance and thus, as it were, a nonwilling, which clears the way for the advent of truth.

The difficulty is resolved if we understand fixing in place in the sense intended throughout the entire text of the essay, above all in the key specification "setting-into-work." Also correlated with "to place" and "to set" is "to lay"; all three meanings are still intended jointly by the Latin *ponere*.

We must think of "to place" in the sense of *thesis*. Thus on page 200 the statement is made, "Setting and taking possession are here everywhere (!) drawn from the Greek sense of *thesis*, which means a setting up in the unconcealed." The Greek "setting" means placing, as for instance, letting a statue be set up. It means laying, laying down an oblation. Placing and laying have the sense of bringing *here* into the unconcealed, bringing *forth* into what is present, that is, letting or causing to lie forth. Setting and placing here never mean the modern concept of the summoning of things to be placed over against the self (the ego-subject). The standing of the statue (i.e., the presence of the radiance facing us) is different from the standing of what stands over against us in the sense of the object. "Standing" – (cf. p. 190)—is the constancy of the showing or shining. By contrast, thesis, antithesis, and synthesis in the dialectic of Kant and German idealism mean a placing or putting within the sphere of subjectivity of consciousness. Accordingly, Hegel – correctly in terms of his position – interpreted the Greek *thesis* in the sense of the immediate positing of the object. Setting in this sense, therefore, is for him still untrue, because it is not yet mediated by antithesis and synthesis. (Cf. "Hegel und die Griechen" in the *Festschrift* for H. G. Gadamer, 1960.)

But if, in the context of our essay on the work of art, we keep in mind the Greek sense of *thesis* – to let lie forth in its radiance and presence – then the "fix" in "fix in place" can never have the sense of rigid, motionless, and secure.

"Fixed" means outlined, admitted into the boundary (*peras*), brought into the outline – (cf. p. 201). The boundary in the Greek sense does not block off; rather, being itself brought forth, it first brings to its radiance what is present. Boundary sets free into the unconcealed; by its contour in the Greek light the mountain stands in its towering and repose. The boundary that fixes and consolidates is in this repose – repose in the fullness of motion – all this holds of the work in the Greek sense of *ergon*; this work's "being" is *energeia*, which gathers infinitely more movement within itself than do the modern "energies."

Thus the "fixing in place" of truth, rightly understood, can never run counter to the "letting happen." For one thing, this "letting" is nothing passive but a doing in the highest degree (cf. "Wissenschaft und Besinnung" in *Vorträge und Aufsätze*, p. 49)[6] in the sense of *thesis*, a "working" and "willing" which in the present essay – (p. 203) is characterized as the "existing human being's entrance into and compliance with the unconcealedness of Being." For another thing, the "happen" in the letting happen of truth is the movement that prevails in the clearing *and* concealing or more precisely in their union, that is to say, the movement of the lighting of self-concealment as such, from which again all self-lighting stems. What is more, this "movement" even requires a fixing in place in the sense of a bringing forth, where the bringing is to be understood in the sense given it on page 201, in that the creative bringing forth "is rather a receiving and an incorporating of a relation to unconcealedness."

In accordance with what has so far been explained, the meaning of the noun "*Ge-Stell*," frame, framing, framework, used on page 201, is thus defined: the gathering of the bringing-forth, of the letting-come-forth-here into the rift-design as bounding outline (*peras*). The Greek sense of *morphe* as figure, *Gestalt*, is made clear by "*Ge-Stell*," "framing," so understood. Now the word "Ge-Stell," frame, which we used in later writings as the explicit key expression for the nature of modern technology, was indeed conceived in reference to that sense of frame (*not* in reference to such other senses as bookshelf or montage, which it also has). That context is essential, because related to the destiny of Being. Framing, as the nature of modern technology, derives from the Greek way of experiencing letting-lie-forth, *logos*, from the Greek *poiesis* and *thesis*. In setting up the frame, the framework – which now means in commandeering everything into assured availability – there sounds the claim of the *ratio reddenda*, i.e., of the *logon didonai*, but in such a way that today this claim that is made in framing takes control of the absolute, and the process of representation – of *Vor-stellen* or putting forth – takes form, on the basis of the Greek perception, as making secure, fixing in place.

When we hear the words "fix in place" and "framing" or "framework" in "The Origin of the Work of Art," we must, on the one hand, put out of mind the modern meaning of placing or framing, and yet at the same time we must not fail to note that, and in what way, the Being that defines the modern period – Being as framing, framework – stems from the Western destiny of Being and has not been thought *up* by philosophers but rather thought to thinking men (cf. *Vorträge und Aufsätze*, pp. 28 and 49).[7]

It is still our burden to discuss the specifications given briefly on pages 200 f. about the "establishing" and "self-establishing of truth in that which is, in beings." Here again we must avoid understanding "establish" in the modern sense and in the manner of the lecture on technology as "organize" and "finish or complete." Rather, "establishing" recalls the "impulse of truth toward the work," mentioned on page 201, the impulse that, in the midst of beings, truth should itself be in the manner of work, should itself occur as being.

If we recollect how truth as unconcealedness of beings means nothing but the presence of beings as such, that is, *Being* – see page 205 – then talk about the self-establishing of truth, that is, of Being, in all that is, touches on the problem of the ontological difference.[8] For this reason there is the note of caution on page 200 of "The Origin of the Work of Art": "In referring to this self-establishing of openness in the Open, thinking touches on a sphere that cannot yet be explicated here." The whole essay, "The Origin of the Work of Art," deliberately yet tacitly moves on the path of the question of the nature of Being. Reflection on what *art* may be is completely and decidedly determined only in regard to the question of *Being*. Art is considered neither an area of cultural achievement nor an appearance of spirit; it belongs to the *disclosure of appropriation* by way of which the "meaning of Being" (cf. *Being and Time*) can alone be defined. What art may be is one of the questions to which no answers are given in the essay. What gives the impression of such an answer [is] directions for questioning. (Cf. the first sentences of the Epilogue.)

Among these directions there are two *important hints*, on pages 204 and 207. In both places mention is made of an "ambiguity." On page 207 an "essential ambiguity" is noted in regard to the definition of art as "the setting-into-work of truth." In this ambiguity, truth is "subject" on the one hand and "object" on the other. *Both* descriptions remain "unsuitable." If truth is the "subject," then the definition "the setting-into-work of truth" means: "truth's setting itself into work" – compare pages 204 and 190. Art is then conceived in terms of disclosive appropriation. Being, however, is a call to man and is not without man. Accordingly, art is at the same time defined as the setting-into-work of truth, where truth *now* is "object" and art is human creating and preserving.

Within the *human* relation to art there results the second ambiguity of the setting-into-work of truth, which on page 204 was called creation and preservation. According to pages 204 and 199 f. the art *work* and the art*ist* rest "especially" in what goes on in art. In the heading "the setting-into-work of truth," in which it remains undecided but decid*able* who does the setting or in what way it occurs, there is concealed *the relation of Being and human being*, a relation which is unsuitably conceived even in this version – a distressing difficulty, which has been clear to me since *Being and Time* and has since been expressed in a variety of versions (cf., finally, "Zur Seinsfrage" and the present essay, p. 200, "Only this much should be noted, that . . . ").

The problematic context that prevails here then comes together at the proper place in the discussion, where the nature of language and of poetry is touched on, all this again only in regard to the belonging together of Being and Saying.

There is an unavoidable necessity for the reader, who naturally comes to the essay from without, to refrain at first and for a long time from perceiving and interpreting the facts of the case in terms of the reticent domain that is the source of what has to be thought. For the author himself, however, there remains the pressing need of speaking each time in the language most opportune for each of the various stations on his way.

Notes

1 Martin Heidegger, *Being and Time*, translated by John Macquarrie and Edward Robinson, New York: Harper & Row, 1962 – Tʀ.

2 The word for resoluteness, *Entschlossenheit*, if taken literally, would mean "unclosedness." – Tʀ.

3 "Reissen heisst hier Herausholen des Risses und den Riss reissen mit der Reissfeder auf dem Reissbrett."

4 Thrownness, *Geworfenheit*, is understood in *Being and Time* as an existential characteristic of *Dasein*, human being, its thatness, its "that it is," and it refers to the facticity of human being's being handed over to itself, its being on its own responsibility; as long as human being is what it is, it is thrown, cast, "im Wurf." Projection, *Entwurf*, on the other hand, is a second existential character of human being, referring to its driving forward toward its own possibility of being. It takes the form of understanding, which the author speaks of as the mode of being of human being in which human being *is* in its possibilities *as* possibilities. It is not the mere having of a preconceived plan, but is the projecting of possibility in human being that occurs antecedently to all plans and makes planning possible. Human being is both thrown and projected; it is thrown project, factical directedness toward possibilities of being. – Tʀ.

5 In the original pagination of the *Vorlesungen*, which is repeated in the Jubiläum edition edited by H. Glockner (Stuttgart, 1953), these passages occur at X, 1, 134; 135; 16. All are in vol. 12 of this edition. – Tʀ.

6 The reference is to a discussion of the German *Tun*, doing, which points to the core of its meaning as a

laying forth, placing here, bringing here and bringing forth – "working," in the sense either of something bringing itself forth out of itself into presence or of man performing the bringing here and bringing forth of something. Both are a way in which something that is present presences. – Tr.

7   The reference to page 49 is to the conception of doing, as given in the previous note. The passage on page 28 of *Vorträge und Aufsätze* appears in the essay "*Die Frage nach der Technik.*" The "*-Stell*" in "*Ge-Stell*" comes from the German "stellen," a transitive verb meaning to place, put, set, stand, arrange. "*Ge-Stell*," if taken literally, would then be the collective name for all sorts of placing, putting, setting, arranging, ordering, or in general, putting in place. Heidegger pushes this collective reading further, in the light of his interpretation of early Greek language and thought, his general concept of truth and the history of Being, and his view of the work of Being in summoning and gathering men to their destiny. The gathering agent today is the call that challenges men to put everything that discloses itself into the position of stock, resource, material for technological processing. For this call, this gathering power, Heidegger makes use of this collective word which expresses the gathering of all forms of ordering things as resources – *das Ge-Stell*, the collective unity of all the putting, placing, setting, standing, arraying, arranging that goes into modern technology and the life oriented to it. The "*stellen,*" the setting, placing, in the word, derives from an older mode, that of *poiesis*, which lets what is present come forth into unconcealedness, as in the setting up of a statue in the temple precinct; yet both the modern technological setting up of things as resources and this ancient poetic setting up of them as bearing their world are modes of unconcealing, of truth as *aletheia*. They are not mere inventions of men or mere doings of men, but are phases in the history of the destiny of Being and of man in his historical situation in relation to Being. Contemporary man's technological "things" bear his technological "world" in their own distorted way – distorting man's earth, his heaven, his divinities, and, in the end, himself and his mortality. – Tr.

8   Cf. *Identität und Differenz* (1957), pp. 37 ff.; English *Identity and Difference*, trans. by Joan Stambaugh (New York: Harper & Row, 1969), pp. 50 ff., 116 ff.

10

Lectures on Aesthetics

Ludwig Wittgenstein

II

1. One interesting thing is the idea that people have of a kind of science of Aesthetics. I would almost like to talk of what could be meant by Aesthetics.

2. You might think Aesthetics is a science telling us what's beautiful – almost too ridiculous for words. I suppose it ought to include also what sort of coffee tastes well.[1]

3. I see roughly this – there is a realm of utterance of delight, when you taste pleasant food or smell a pleasant smell, etc., then there is the realm of Art which is quite different, though often you may make the same face when you hear a piece of music as when you taste good food. (Though you may cry at something you like very much.)

4. Supposing you meet someone in the street and he tells you he has lost his greatest friend, in a voice extremely expressive of his emotion.[2] You might say: "It was extraordinarily beautiful, the way he expressed himself." Supposing you then asked: "What similarity has my admiring this person with my eating vanilla ice and liking it?" To compare them seems almost disgusting. (But you can connect them by intermediate cases.) Suppose someone said: "But this is a quite different kind of delight." But did you learn two meanings of 'delight'? You use the same word on both occasions.[3] There is some connection between these delights. Although in the first case the emotion of delight would in our judgement hardly count.[4]

5. It is like saying: "I classify works of Art in this way: at some I look up and at some I look down." This way of classifying might be interesting.[5] We might discover all sorts of connections between looking up or down at works of Art and looking up or down at other things. If we found, perhaps, that eating vanilla ice made us look up, we might not attach great importance to looking up. There may be a realm, a small realm of experiences which may make me look up or down where I can infer a lot from the fact that I looked up or down; another realm of experiences where nothing can be inferred from my looking up or down.[6] Cf wearing blue or green trousers may in a certain society mean a lot, but in another society it may not mean anything.

6. What are expressions of liking something? Is it only what we say or interjections we use or faces we make? Obviously not. It is, often, how often I read something or how often I wear a suit. Perhaps I won't even say: "It's fine", but wear it often and look at it.[7]

7. Suppose we build houses and we give doors and windows certain dimensions. Does the fact that we *like* these dimensions necessarily show in anything we say? Is what we like necessarily shown by an expression of *liking*?[8] [For instance – R] suppose our children draw windows and when they draw them in the wrong way we punish them. Or when someone builds a certain house we refuse to live in it or run away.

8. Take the case of fashions. How does a fashion come about? Say, we wear lapels broader than last year. Does this mean that the tailors like them better broader? No, not necessarily. He cuts it like this and this year he makes it broader. Perhaps this

year he finds it too narrow and makes it wider. Perhaps no expression [of delight – R] is used at all.[9]

9. You design a door and look at it and say: "Higher, higher, higher...oh, all right."[10] (Gesture) What is this? Is it an expression of content?

10. Perhaps the most important thing in connection with aesthetics is what may be called aesthetic reactions, e.g. discontent, disgust, discomfort. The expression of discontent is not the same as the expression of discomfort. The expression of discontent says: "Make it higher... too low!... do something to this."

11. Is what I call an expression of discontent something like an expression of discomfort *plus* knowing the cause of the discomfort and asking for it to be removed? If I say: "This door is too low. Make it higher", should we say I know the cause of my discomfort?

12. 'Cause' is used in very many different ways, e.g.

(1) "What is the cause of unemployment?" "What is the cause of this expression?"
(2) "What was the cause of your jumping?" "That noise."
(3) "What was the cause of that wheel going round?" You trace a mechanism.[11]

13. [*Redpath*: "Making the door higher removes your discontent."]

Wittgenstein asked: "Why is this a bad way of putting it?" It is in the wrong form because it presupposes ' – removes – '.

14. Saying you know the cause of your discomfort could mean two things.

(1) I predict correctly that if you lower the door, I will be satisfied.
(2) But that when in fact I say: "Too high!" 'Too high!' is in this case not conjecture. Is 'Too high' comparable with 'I think I had too many tomatoes today'?

15. If I ask: "If I make it lower will your discomfort cease?", you may say: "I'm *sure* it will." The important thing is that I say: "Too high!" It is a reaction analogous to my taking my hand away from a hot plate – which may not relieve my discomfort. The reaction peculiar to this discomfort is saying 'Too high' or whatever it is.

16. To say: "I feel discomfort and know the cause", is entirely misleading because 'know

the cause' normally means something quite different. How misleading it is depends on whether when you said: "I know the cause", you meant it to be an explanation or not. 'I feel discomfort and know the cause' makes it sound as if there were two things going on in my soul – discomfort and knowing the cause.

17. In these cases the word 'cause' is hardly ever used at all. You use 'why?' and 'because', but not 'cause'.[12]

18. We have here a kind of discomfort which you may call 'directed', e.g. if I am afraid of you, my discomfort is directed.[13] Saying 'I know the cause' brings in mind the case of statistics or tracing a mechanism. If I say: "I know the cause", it looks as if I had analysed the feelings (as I analyse the feeling of hearing my own voice and, at the same time, rubbing my hands) which, of course, I haven't done. We have given, as it were, a *grammatical* explanation [in saying, the feeling is 'directed'].

19. There is a 'Why?' to aesthetic discomfort not a 'cause' to it. The expression of discomfort takes the form of a criticism and not 'My mind is not at rest' or something. It might take the form of looking at a picture and saying: "What's wrong with it?"[14]

20. It's all very well to say: "Can't we get rid of this analogy?" Well, we cannot. If we think of discomfort – cause, pain – cause of pain naturally suggests itself.

21. The cause, in the sense of the object it is directed to is also the cause in other senses. When you remove it, the discomfort ceases and what not.

22. If one says: "Can we be immediately aware of the cause?", the first thing that comes into our mind is not statistics [(as in 'the cause of the rise in unemployment') – R], but tracing a mechanism. It has so very often been said that if something has been caused by something else this is only a matter of concomitance. Isn't this very queer? Very queer. 'It's only concomitance' shows you think it can be something else.[15] It could be an experiential proposition, but then I don't know what it would be. Saying this shows you know of something different, i.e. connection. What are they denying when they say: "There is no necessary connection"?

23. You say constantly in philosophy things like: "People say there is a super-mechanism, but there isn't." But no one knows what a super-mechanism is.

24. (The idea of a super-mechanism doesn't really come in here. What comes in is the idea of a mechanism.)

25. We have the idea of a super-mechanism when we talk of logical necessity, e.g. physics tried as an ideal to reduce things to mechanisms or something hitting something else.[16]

26. We say that people condemn a man to death and then we say the Law condemns him to death. "Although the Jury can pardon [acquit?] him, the Law can't." (This *may* mean the Law can't take bribes, etc.) The idea of something super-strict, something stricter than any Judge can be,[17] super-rigidity. The point being, you are inclined to ask: "Do we have a picture of something more rigorous?" Hardly. But we are inclined to express ourselves in the form of a superlative.

27.

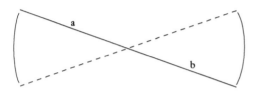

Cf. a lever-fulcrum. The idea of a super-hardness. "The geometrical lever is harder than any lever can be. It can't bend." Here you have the case of logical necessity. "Logic is a mechanism made of an infinitely hard material. Logic cannot bend."[18] (Well, no more it can.) This is the way we arrive at a super-something. This is the way certain superlatives come about, how they are used, e.g. the infinite.

28. People would say that even in the case of tracing a mechanism there is also concomitance. But need there be? I just follow the string to the person at the other end.

29. Suppose there was a super-mechanism in the sense that there was a mechanism inside the string. Even if there was such a mechanism, it would do no good. You do recognize tracing the mechanism as tracing a peculiar kind of causal reaction.

30. You wish to get rid of the idea of connection altogether. "This is also only concomitance." Then there is nothing more to be said.[19] You would have to specify what is a case you wouldn't call concomitance. "Tracing a mechanism is only finding concomitance. In the end it can all be reduced to concomitance." It might be proved that people never traced a mechanism unless they had had a lot of experience of a certain sort. This could be put in the way: "It all reduces to concomitance."

31. Cf. "Physics doesn't explain anything. It just describes cases of concomitance."

32. You could mean by 'There is no super-mechanism', 'Don't imagine mechanisms between the atoms in the case of a lever. There aren't any mechanisms there'.[20] (You are taking for granted the atomistic picture.[21] What does this come to? We are so used to this picture that it's as though we had all seen atoms. Every educated eight-year old child knows that things are made of atoms. We would think it lack of education if a person didn't think of a rod as being made of atoms.)

33. (You can look on the mechanism as a set of concomitant causal phenomena. You don't, of course.) You say: "Well, this moves this, this this, this this, and so on."

34. Tracing a mechanism is one way of finding the cause; we speak of 'the cause' in this case. But if cases of wheels made of butter and looking like steel were frequent we might say: "This ('this wheel') is not the only cause at all. This may only look like a mechanism."[22]

35. People often say that aesthetics is a branch of psychology. The idea is that once we are more advanced, everything – all the mysteries of Art – will be understood by psychological experiments. Exceedingly stupid as the idea is, this is roughly it.

36. Aesthetic questions have nothing to do with psychological experiments, but are answered in an entirely different way.[23]

Notes

1 It is hard to find boundaries. – R.
2 Someone...who tells you he has lost his friend, in a restrained way. – R.
3 But notice that you use the same word and not in the same chance way you use the same word 'bank' for two things [like 'river bank' and 'money bank' – R.] – T.

4 Although in the first case the gesture or expression of delight may be most unimportant in a way. – T.
5 You might discover further characters of things which make us look up. – R.
6 Some one might exaggerate the importance of the type of indication. – T.

7   If I like a suit I may buy it, or wear it often – without interjections or making faces. – R. I may never smile at it. – T.

8   Our preferring these shows itself in all sorts of ways. – T.

9   But the tailor does not say: 'This is nice.' He is a good cutter. He is just contented. – R. If you mean 'this year he cuts it broader' then you can say this. This way we are contented, the other not. – T.

10 '... *there*: thank God.' – R. '... yes, that's right.' – T.

11 Cause: (1) Experiment and statistics.
        (2) Reason.
        (3) Mechanism. – T.

12 Why are you disgusted? Because it is too high. – R.

13 What is the advantage of 'My feeling of fear is directed' as opposed to 'I know the cause'? – R.

14 If I look at a picture and say: 'What's wrong with this?', then it is better to say that my feeling has direction, and not that my feeling has a cause and I don't know what it is. Otherwise we suggest an analogy with 'pain' and 'cause of pain' – i.e. what you have eaten. This is wrong or misleading, because, although we do use the word 'cause' in the sense of 'what it is directed to' ('What made you jump?' – 'Seeing him appear in the doorway'), we often use it in other senses also. – R.

15 If you say: 'To speak of the cause of some development is only to speak of the concomitants' – 'cause is only a question of concomitants' – then if you put 'only', you are admitting that it *could* be something else. It means that you know of something entirely different. – R.

16 You want to say: 'Surely there is a connection.' But what is a connection? Well, levers, chains, cogwheels. These are connections, and here we have them, but here what we ought to explain is 'super'. – R.

17 Something that cannot be swayed. – R.

18 Suppose that we treat of kinematics. Give the distance of the lever from the point, and calculate the distance of the arc.

    But then we say: 'If the lever is made of metal, however hard, it will bend a little, and the point will not come just there.' And so we have the idea of a super-rigidity: the idea of a *geometrical* lever which *cannot* bend. Here we have the idea of logical necessity: a mechanism of infinitely hard material. – R.

    If someone says: 'You mustn't think that logic is made of an infinitely hard material', you must ask: 'What mustn't I think?' – T.

19 What we call '*explanation*' is a form of *connection*. And we wish to get rid of connection altogether. We wish to get rid of the notion of mechanism, and say: 'It's all concomitants.' Why 'all'? – R.

20 You reduce the actual mechanism to a more complicated atomic mechanism, but don't go on. – T.

21 We might have a primitive mechanism. Then we have the picture of its all being formed of particles – atoms, etc. And we might then want to say: 'Don't go on to think of atoms between these atoms.' Here we take for granted the atomic picture – which is a queer business. If we had to say what a super-mechanism was, we might say it was one which did not consist of atoms: bits of the mechanism were just solid – R.

22 We are constantly inclined to reduce things to other things. So excited by finding that it's sometimes concomitance, we wish to say it's all *really* concomitance. – T.

23 I wish to make it clear that the important problems in aesthetics are not settled by psychological research. – T.

    These problems are answered in a different way – more in the form 'What is in my mind when I say so and so?' – R.

11

Leonardo da Vinci

Sigmund Freud

IV

We have not yet done with Leonardo's vulture phantasy. In words which only too plainly recall a description of a sexual act ('and struck me many times with its tail against [...] my lips'), Leonardo stresses the intensity of the erotic relations between mother and child. From this linking of his mother's (the vulture's) activity with the prominence of the mouth zone it is not difficult to guess that a second memory is contained in the phantasy. This may be translated: 'My mother pressed innumerable passionate kisses on my mouth.' The phantasy is compounded from the memory of being suckled and being kissed by his mother.

Kindly nature has given the artist the ability to express his most secret mental impulses, which are hidden even from himself, by means of the works that he creates; and these works have a powerful effect on others who are strangers to the artist, and who are themselves unaware of the source of their emotion. Can it be that there is nothing in Leonardo's life work to bear witness to what his memory preserved as the strongest impression of his childhood? One would certainly expect there to be something. Yet if one considers the profound transformations through which an impression in an artist's life has to pass before it is allowed to make its contribution to a work of art, one will be bound to keep any claim to certainty in one's demonstration within very modest limits; and this is especially so in Leonardo's case.

Anyone who thinks of Leonardo's paintings will be reminded of a remarkable smile, at once fascinating and puzzling, which he conjured up on the lips of his female subjects. It is an unchanging smile, on long, curved lips; it has become a mark of his style and the name 'Leonardesque' has been chosen for it.[1] In the strangely beautiful face of the Florentine Mona Lisa del Giocondo it has produced the most powerful and confusing effect on whoever looks at it. [...] This smile has called for an interpretation, and it has met with many of the most varied kinds, none of which has been satisfactory. 'Voilà quatre siècles bientôt que Monna Lisa fait perdre la tête à tous ceux qui parlent d'elle, après l'avoir longtemps regardée.'[2]

Muther (1909, 1, 314) writes: 'What especially casts a spell on the spectator is the daemonic magic of this smile. Hundreds of poets and authors have written about this woman who now appears to smile on us so seductively, and now to stare coldly and without soul into space; and no one has solved the riddle of her smile, no one has read the meaning of her thoughts. Everything, even the landscape, is mysteriously dream-like, and seems to be trembling in a kind of sultry sensuality.'

The idea that two distinct elements are combined in Mona Lisa's smile is one that has struck several critics. They accordingly find in the beautiful Florentine's expression the most perfect representation of the contrasts which dominate the erotic life of women; the contrast between reserve and seduction, and between the most devoted tenderness and a sensuality that is ruthlessly demanding – consuming men as if they were alien beings. [...]

Leonardo spent four years painting at this picture, perhaps from 1503 to 1507, during his second period of residence in Florence, when he was over fifty. According to Vasari he employed the most elaborate artifices to keep the lady amused during the sittings and to retain the famous smile on her features. In its present condition the picture has preserved but little of all the delicate details which his brush reproduced on the canvas at that time; while it was being painted it was considered to be the highest that art could achieve, but it is certain that Leonardo himself was not satisfied with it, declaring it to be incomplete, and did not deliver it to the person who had commissioned it, but took it to France with him, where his patron, Francis I, acquired it from him for the Louvre.

Let us leave unsolved the riddle of the expression on Mona Lisa's face, and note the indisputable fact that her smile exercised no less powerful a fascination on the artist than on all who have looked at it for the last four hundred years. From that date the captivating smile reappears in all his pictures and in those of his pupils. As Leonardo's Mona Lisa is a portrait, we cannot assume that he added on his own account such an expressive feature to her face – a feature that she did not herself possess. The conclusion seems hardly to be avoided that he found this smile in his model and fell so strongly under its spell that from then on he bestowed it on the free creations of his phantasy. This interpretation, which cannot be called far-fetched, is put forward, for example, by Konstantinowa (1907, 44):

'During the long period in which the artist was occupied with the portrait of Mona Lisa del Giocondo, he had entered into the subtle details of the features on this lady's face with such sympathetic feeling that he transferred its traits – in particular the mysterious smile and the strange gaze – to all the faces that he painted or drew afterwards. The Gioconda's peculiar facial expression can even be perceived in the picture of John the Baptist in the Louvre; but above all it may be clearly recognized in the expression on Mary's face in the "Madonna and Child with St. Anne".'[3] [. . .]

Yet this situation may also have come about in another way. The need for a deeper reason behind the attraction of La Gioconda's smile, which so moved the artist that he was never again free from it, has been felt by more than one of his biographers. Walter Pater, who sees in the picture of Mona Lisa a 'presence . . . expressive of what in the ways of a thousand years men had come to desire'

[1873, 118], and who writes very sensitively of 'the unfathomable smile, always with a touch of something sinister in it, which plays over all Leonardo's work' [ibid., 117], leads us to another clue when he declares (loc. cit.):

'Besides, the picture is a portrait. From childhood we see this image defining itself on the fabric of his dreams; and but for express historical testimony, we might fancy that this was but his ideal lady, embodied and beheld at last . . .'

Marie Herzfeld (1906, 88) has no doubt something very similar in mind when she declares that in the Mona Lisa Leonardo encountered his own self and for this reason was able to put so much of his own nature into the picture 'whose features had lain all along in mysterious sympathy within Leonardo's mind'.

Let us attempt to clarify what is suggested here. It may very well have been that Leonardo was fascinated by Mona Lisa's smile for the reason that it awoke something in him which had for long lain dormant in his mind – probably an old memory. This memory was of sufficient importance for him never to get free of it when it had once been aroused; he was continually forced to give it new expression. Pater's confident assertion that we can see, from childhood, a face like Mona Lisa's defining itself on the fabric of his dreams, seems convincing and deserves to be taken literally.

Vasari mentions that 'teste di femmine, che ridono'[4] formed the subject of Leonardo's first artistic endeavours. The passage – which, since it is not intended to prove anything, is quite beyond suspicion – runs more fully according to Schorn's translation (1843, 3, 6): 'In his youth he made some heads of laughing women out of clay, which were reproduced in plaster, and some children's heads which were as beautiful as if they had been modelled by the hand of a master . . .'

Thus we learn that he began his artistic career by portraying two kinds of objects; and these cannot fail to remind us of the two kinds of sexual objects that we have inferred from the analysis of his vulture-phantasy. If the beautiful children's heads were reproductions of his own person as it was in his childhood, then the smiling women are nothing other than repetitions of his mother Caterina, and we begin to suspect the possibility that it was his mother who possessed the mysterious smile – the smile that he had lost and that fascinated him so much when he found it again in the Florentine lady.[5]

The painting of Leonardo's which stands nearest to the Mona Lisa in point of time is the so-called 'St. Anne with Two Others', St. Anne with the Madonna and child. [. . .] In it the Leonardesque smile is most beautifully and markedly portrayed on both the women's faces. It is not possible to discover how long before or after the painting of the Mona Lisa Leonardo began to paint this picture. As both works extended over years, it may, I think, be assumed that the artist was engaged on them at the same time. It would best agree with our expectations if it was the intensity of Leonardo's preoccupation with the features of Mona Lisa which stimulated him to create the composition of St. Anne out of his phantasy. For if the Gioconda's smile called up in his mind the memory of his mother, it is easy to understand how it drove him at once to create a glorification of motherhood, and to give back to his mother the smile he had found in the noble lady. We may therefore permit our interest to pass from Mona Lisa's portrait to this other picture – one which is hardly less beautiful, and which to-day also hangs in the Louvre.

St. Anne with her daughter and her grandchild is a subject that is rarely handled in Italian painting. At all events Leonardo's treatment of it differs widely from all other known versions. Muther (1909, 1, 309) writes:

'Some artists, like Hans Fries, the elder Holbein and Girolamo dai Libri, made Anne sit beside Mary and put the child between them. Others, like Jakob Cornelisz in his Berlin picture, painted what was truly a "St. Anne with Two Others";[6] in other words, they represented her as holding in her arms the small figure of Mary upon which the still smaller figure of the child Christ is sitting.' In Leonardo's picture Mary is sitting on her mother's lap, leaning forward, and is stretching out both arms towards the boy, who is playing with a young lamb and perhaps treating it a little unkindly. The grandmother rests on her hip the arm that is not concealed and gazes down on the pair with a blissful smile. The grouping is certainly not entirely unconstrained. But although the smile that plays on the lips of the two women is unmistakably the same as that in the picture of Mona Lisa, it has lost its uncanny and mysterious character; what it expresses is inward feeling and quiet blissfulness.[7]

After we have studied this picture for some time, it suddenly dawns on us that only Leonardo could have painted it, just as only he could have created the phantasy of the vulture. The picture contains the synthesis of the history of his childhood: its details are to be explained by reference to the most personal impressions in Leonardo's life. In his father's house he found not only his kind stepmother, Donna Albiera, but also his grandmother, his father's mother, Monna Lucia, who – so we will assume – was no less tender to him than grandmothers usually are. These circumstances might well suggest to him a picture representing childhood watched over by mother and grandmother. Another striking feature of the picture assumes even greater significance. St. Anne, Mary's mother and the boy's grandmother, who must have been a matron, is here portrayed as being perhaps a little more mature and serious than the Virgin Mary, but as still being a young woman of unfaded beauty. In point of fact Leonardo has given the boy two mothers, one who stretches her arms out to him, and another in the background; and both are endowed with the blissful smile of the joy of motherhood. This peculiarity of the picture has not failed to surprise those who have written about it: Muther, for example, is of the opinion that Leonardo could not bring himself to paint old age, lines and wrinkles, and for this reason made Anne too into a woman of radiant beauty. But can we be satisfied with this explanation? Others have had recourse to denying that there is any similarity in age between the mother and daughter.[8] But Muther's attempt at an explanation is surely enough to prove that the impression that St. Anne has been made more youthful derives from the picture and is not an invention for an ulterior purpose.

Leonardo's childhood was remarkable in precisely the same way as this picture. He had had two mothers: first, his true mother Caterina, from whom he was torn away when he was between three and five, and then a young and tender stepmother, his father's wife, Donna Albiera. By his combining this fact about his childhood with the one mentioned above (the presence of his mother and grandmother)[9] and by his condensing them into a composite unity, the design of 'St. Anne with Two Others' took shape for him. The maternal figure that is further away from the boy – the grandmother – corresponds to the earlier and true mother, Caterina, in its appearance and in its special relation to the boy. The artist seems to have used the blissful smile of St. Anne to disavow and to cloak the envy which the unfortunate woman felt when she was forced to give up her son to her better-born rival, as she had once given up his father as well.[10]

We thus find a confirmation in another of Leonardo's works of our suspicion that the smile of Mona Lisa del Giocondo had awakened in him as a grown man the memory of the mother of his earliest childhood. From that time onward, madonnas and aristocratic ladies were depicted in Italian painting humbly bowing their heads and smiling the strange, blissful smile of Caterina, the poor peasant girl who had brought into the world the splendid son who was destined to paint, to search and to suffer.

If Leonardo was successful in reproducing on Mona Lisa's face the double meaning which this smile contained, the promise of unbounded tenderness and at the same time sinister menace (to quote Pater's phrase [above, p. 217]), then here too he had remained true to the content of his earliest memory. For his mother's tenderness was fateful for him; it determined his destiny and the privations that were in store for him. The violence of the caresses, to which his phantasy of the vulture points, was only too natural. In her love for her child the poor forsaken mother had to give vent to all her memories of the caresses she had enjoyed as well as her longing for new ones; and she was forced to do so not only to compensate herself for having no husband, but also to compensate her child for having no father to fondle him. So, like all unsatisfied mothers, she took her little son in place of her husband, and by the too early maturing of his erotism robbed him of a part of his masculinity. A mother's love for the infant she suckles and cares for is something far more profound than her later affection for the growing child. It is in the nature of a completely satisfying love-relation, which not only fulfils every mental wish but also every physical need; and if it represents one of the forms of attainable human happiness, that is in no little measure due to the possibility it offers of satisfying, without reproach, wishful impulses which have long been repressed and which must be called perverse.[11] In the happiest young marriage the father is aware that the baby, especially if he is a baby son, has become his rival, and this is the starting-point of an antagonism towards the favourite which is deeply rooted in the unconscious.

When, in the prime of life, Leonardo once more encountered the smile of bliss and rapture which had once played on his mother's lips as she fondled him, he had for long been under the dominance of an inhibition which forbade him ever again to desire such caresses from the lips of women. But he had become a painter, and therefore he strove to reproduce the smile with his brush, giving it to all his pictures (whether he in fact executed them himself or had them done by his pupils under his direction) – to Leda, to John the Baptist and to Bacchus. The last two are variants of the same type. 'Leonardo has turned the locust-eater of the Bible', says Muther [1909, 1, 314], 'into a Bacchus, a young Apollo, who, with a mysterious smile on his lips, and with his smooth legs crossed, gazes at us with eyes that intoxicate the senses.' These pictures breathe a mystical air into whose secret one dares not penetrate; at the very most one can attempt to establish their connection with Leonardo's earlier creations. The figures are still androgynous, but no longer in the sense of the vulture-phantasy. They are beautiful youths of feminine delicacy and with effeminate forms; they do not cast their eyes down, but gaze in mysterious triumph, as if they knew of a great achievement of happiness, about which silence must be kept. The familiar smile of fascination leads one to guess that it is a secret of love. It is possible that in these figures Leonardo has denied the unhappiness of his erotic life and has triumphed over it in his art, by representing the wishes of the boy, infatuated with his mother, as fulfilled in this blissful union of the male and female natures.

Notes

1 [*Footnote added* 1919:] The connoisseur of art will think here of the peculiar fixed smile found in archaic Greek sculptures – in those, for example, from Aegina; he will perhaps also discover something similar in the figures of Leonardo's teacher Verrocchio and therefore have some misgivings in accepting the arguments that follow.

2 ['For almost four centuries now Mona Lisa has caused all who talk of her, after having gazed on her for long, to lose their heads.'] The words are Gruyer's quoted by von Seidlitz (1909, 2, 280).

3 [The title of this subject in German is '*heilige Anna Selbdritt*', literally 'St. Anne with Two Others', a point which is referred to below, p. 218.]

4 ['Heads of laughing women.'] Quoted by Scogna-miglio (1900, 32).

5 The same assumption is made by Merezhkovsky. But the history of Leonardo's childhood as he imagines it departs at the essential points from the conclusions we have drawn from the phantasy of the vulture. Yet if the smile had been that of Leonardo himself [as Merezhkovsky also assumes] tradition would hardly have failed to inform us of the coincidence.

6 [I.e., St Anne was the most prominent figure in the picture. See [n.3] above.]

7 Konstantinowa (1907, [44]): 'Mary gazes down full of inward feeling on her darling, with a smile that recalls the mysterious expression of La Gioconda.' In another passage [ibid., 52] she says of Mary: 'The Gioconda's smile hovers on her features.'

8 Von Seidlitz (1909, **2**, 274), notes.

9 [The words in parentheses were added in 1923.]

10 [*Footnote added* 1919:] If an attempt is made to separate the figures of Anne and Mary in this picture and to trace the outline of each, it will not be found altogether easy. One is inclined to say that they are fused with each other like badly condensed dream-figures, so that in some places it is hard to say where Anne ends and where Mary begins. But what appears to a critic's eye [in 1919 only: 'to an artist's eye'] as a fault, as a defect in composition, is vindicated in the eyes of analysis by reference to its secret meaning. It seems that for the artist the two mothers of his childhood were melted into a single form.

[*Added* 1923:] It is especially tempting to compare the 'St. Anne with Two Others' of the Louvre with the celebrated London cartoon, where the same material is used to form a different composition. [. . .] Here the forms of the two mothers are fused even more closely and their separate outlines are even harder to make out, so that critics, far removed from any attempt to offer an interpretation, have been forced to say that it seems 'as if two heads were growing from a single body'.

Most authorities are in agreement in pronouncing the London cartoon to be the earlier work and in assigning its origin to Leonardo's first period in Milan (before 1500). Adolf Rosenberg (1898), on the other hand, sees the composition of the cartoon as a later – and more successful – version of the same theme, and follows Anton Springer in dating it even after the Mona Lisa. It would fit in excellently with our arguments if the cartoon were to be much the earlier work. It is also not hard to imagine how the picture in the Louvre arose out of the cartoon, while the reverse course of events would make no sense. If we take the composition shown in the cartoon as our starting point, we can see how Leonardo may have felt the need to undo the dream-like fusion of the two women – a fusion corresponding to his childhood memory – and to separate the two heads in space. This came about as follows: From the group formed by the mothers he detached Mary's head and the upper part of her body and bent them downwards. To provide a reason for this displacement the child Christ had to come down from her lap on to the ground. There was then no room for the little St. John, who was replaced by the lamb.

[*Added* 1919:] A remarkable discovery has been made in the Louvre picture by Oskar Pfister, which is of undeniable interest, even if one may not feel inclined to accept it without reserve. In Mary's curiously arranged and rather confusing drapery he has discovered the *outline of a vulture* and he interprets it as an *unconscious picture-puzzle*: –

'In the picture that represents the artist's mother *the vulture, the symbol of motherhood*, is perfectly clearly visible.

'In the length of blue cloth, which is visible around the hip of the woman in front and which extends in the direction of her lap and her right knee, one can see the vulture's extremely characteristic head, its neck and the sharp curve where its body begins. Hardly any observer whom I have confronted with my little find has been able to resist the evidence of this picture-puzzle.' (Pfister 1913, 147.)

At this point the reader will not, I feel sure, grudge the effort of looking at the accompanying illustration, to see if he can find in it the outlines of the vulture seen by Pfister. The piece of blue cloth, whose border marks the edges of the picture-puzzle, stands out in the reproduction as a light grey field against the darker ground of the rest of the drapery. [. . .]

Pfister continues: 'The important question however is: How far does the picture-puzzle extend? If we follow the length of cloth, which stands out so sharply from its surroundings, starting at the middle of the wing and continuing from there, we notice that one part of it runs down to the woman's foot, while the other part extends in an upward direction and rests on her shoulder and on the child. The former of these parts might more or less represent the vulture's wing and tail, as it is in nature; the latter might be a pointed belly and – especially when we notice the radiating lines which resemble the outlines of feathers – a bird's outspread tail, whose right-hand end, *exactly as in Leonardo's fateful childhood dream* [sic], *leads to the mouth of the child, i.e. of Leonardo himself.*'

The author goes on to examine the interpretation in greater detail, and discusses the difficulties to which it gives rise.

11 See my *Three Essays on the Theory of Sexuality* (1905), [*Standard Ed.*, 7, 223].

Bibliography

Freud, S. (1905) *Drei Abhandlungen zur Sexualtheorie,* Vienna. *Gesammelte Schriften* (12 vols.), Vienna, 1924–34, 5, 3; *Gesammelte Werke* (18 vols.), London, from 1940, 5, 29. (42, 43, 100, 101, 117, 136, 178, 189, 215, 216) [*Trans.: Three Essays on the Theory of Sexuality,* London, 1949; *Standard Ed.,* 7, 125.]

Herzfeld, M. (1906) *Leonardo da Vinci: Der Denker, Forscher und Poet: Nach den veröffentlichten Handschriften* (2nd ed.), Jena. (61, 70, 76, 82, 102, 103, 110, 124, 125, 128, 137)

Konstantinowa, A. (1907) *Die Entwickelung des Madonnentypus bei Leonardo da Vinci,* Strasbourg. (*Zur Kunstgeschichte des Auslandes,* Heft 54.) (63, 109–10, 112)

Muther, R. (1909) *Geschichte der Malerei* (3 vols.), Leipzig. (108, 112, 113, 117, 124)

Pater, W. (1873) *Studies in the History of the Renaissance,* London, (68, 110, 111, 115)

Pfister, O. (1913) 'Kryptolalie, Kryptographie und unbewusstes Vexierbild bei Normalen', *Jb. psychoan. psychopath. Forsch.,* 5, 115. (60, 61, 115–16)

Rosenberg, A. (1898) *Leonardo da Vinci,* Leipzig. (115)

Scognamiglio, N. (1900). See Smiraglia Scognamiglio, N. (1900)

Seidlitz, W. von (1909) *Leonardo da Vinci, der Wendepunkt der Renaissance* (2 vols.), Berlin. (67, 68, 108, 113, 122, 133)

Smiraglia Scognamiglio, N. (1900) *Ricerche e Documenti sulla Giovinezza di Leonardo da Vinci (1452–1482),* Naples. (60, 67, 72, 81, 82, 111)

Vasari, G. (1550) *Le vite de' più eccellenti Architetti, Pittori et Scultori Italiani,* Florence; (2nd ed., 1568; ed. Poggi, Florence, 1919). (64, 109, 111, 121, 124, 127, 128, 133) [*German Trans.: Leben der ausgezeichnetsten Maler, Bildhauer und Baumeister* (trans. L. Schorn), Stuttgart, 1843.]

12

The Ideology of Modernism

György Lukács

It is in no way surprising that the most influential contemporary school of writing should be committed to the dogmas of "modernist" antirealism. It is here that we must begin our investigation if we are to chart the possibilities of a bourgeois realism. We must compare the two main trends in contemporary bourgeois literature and look at the answers they give to the major ideological and artistic questions of our time.

We shall concentrate on the underlying ideological basis of these trends (ideological in the above-defined, not in the strictly philosophical, sense). What must be avoided at all costs is the approach generally adopted by bourgeois-modernist critics themselves: that exaggerated concern with formal criteria, with questions of style and literary technique. This approach may appear to distinguish sharply between "modern" and "traditional" writing (i.e., contemporary writers who adhere to the styles of the last century). In fact it fails to locate the decisive formal problems and turns a blind eye to their inherent dialectic. We are presented with a false polarization which, by exaggerating the importance of stylistic differences, conceals the opposing principles actually underlying and determining contrasting styles.

To take an example: the *monologue intérieur*. Compare, for instance, Bloom's monologue in the lavatory or Molly's monologue in bed, at the beginning and at the end of *Ulysses*, with Goethe's early-morning monologue as conceived by Thomas Mann in his *Lotte in Weimar*. Plainly, the same stylistic technique is being employed. And certain of Thomas Mann's remarks

about Joyce and his methods would appear to confirm this.

Yet it is not easy to think of any two novels more basically dissimilar than *Ulysses* and *Lotte in Weimar*. This is true even of the superficially rather similar scenes I have indicated. I am not referring to the – to my mind – striking difference in intellectual quality. I refer to the fact that with Joyce the stream-of-consciousness technique is no mere stylistic device; it is itself the formative principle governing the narrative pattern and the presentation of character. Technique here is something absolute; it is part and parcel of the esthetic ambition informing *Ulysses*. With Thomas Mann, on the other hand, the *monologue intérieur* is simply a technical device, allowing the author to explore aspects of Goethe's world which would not have been otherwise available. Goethe's experience is not presented as confined to momentary sense impressions. The artist reaches down to the core of Goethe's personality, to the complexity of his relations with his own past, present and even future experience. The stream of association is only apparently free. The monologue is composed with the utmost artistic rigor: it is a carefully plotted sequence gradually piercing to the core of Goethe's personality. Every person or event, emerging momentarily from the stream and vanishing again, is given a specific weight, a definite position, in the pattern of the whole. However unconventional the presentation, the compositional principle is that of the traditional epic; in the way the pace is controlled and the transitions and climaxes are organized, the ancient rules of epic narration are faithfully observed.

It would be absurd, in view of Joyce's artistic ambitions and his manifest abilities, to qualify the exaggerated attention he gives to the detailed recording of sense data and his comparative neglect of ideas and emotions as artistic failure. All this was in conformity with Joyce's artistic intentions; and, by use of such techniques, he may be said to have achieved them satisfactorily. But between Joyce's intentions and those of Thomas Mann there is a total opposition. The perpetually oscillating patterns of sense- and memory-data, their powerfully charged – but aimless and directionless – fields of force, give rise to an epic structure which is *static*, reflecting a belief in the basically static character of events.

These opposed views of the world – dynamic and developmental on the one hand, static and sensational on the other – are of crucial importance in examining the two schools of literature I have mentioned. I shall return to the opposition later. Here, I want only to point out that an exclusive emphasis on formal matters can lead to serious misunderstanding of the character of an artist's work.

What determines the style of a given work of art? How does the intention determine the form? (We are concerned here, of course, with the intention realized in the work; it need not coincide with the writer's conscious intention.) The distinctions that concern us are not those between stylistic "techniques" in the formalistic sense. It is the view of the world, the ideology or *Weltanschauung* underlying a writer's work, that counts. And it is the writer's attempt to reproduce this view of the world which constitutes his "intention" and is the formative principle underlying the style of a given piece of writing. Looked at in this way, style ceases to be a formalistic category. Rather, it is rooted in content; it is the specific form of a specific content.

Content determines form. But there is no content of which man himself is not the focal point. However various the *données* of literature (a particular experience, a didactic purpose), the basic question is, and will remain: what is man?

Here is a point of division: if we put the question in abstract, philosophical terms, leaving aside all formal considerations, we arrive – for the realist school – at the traditional Aristotelean dictum (which was also reached by other than purely esthetic considerations): Man is *zoon politikon*, a social animal. The Aristotelean dictum is applicable to all great realistic literature. Achilles and

Werther, Oedipus and Tom Jones, Antigone and Anna Karenina: their individual existence – their *Sein an sich*, in the Hegelian terminology; their "ontological being," as a more fashionable terminology has it – cannot be distinguished from their social and historical environment. Their human significance, their specific individuality, cannot be separated from the context in which they were created.

The ontological view governing the image of man in the work of leading modernist writers is the exact opposite of this. Man, for these writers, is by nature solitary, asocial, unable to enter into relationships with other human beings. Thomas Wolfe once wrote: "My view of the world is based on the firm conviction that solitariness is by no means a rare condition, something peculiar to myself or to a few specially solitary human beings, but the inescapable, central fact of human existence." Man, thus imagined, may establish contact with other individuals, but only in a superficial, accidental manner; only, ontologically speaking, by retrospective reflection. For "the others," too, are basically solitary, beyond significant human relationship.

This basic solitariness of man must not be confused with that individual solitariness to be found in the literature of traditional realism. In the latter case, we are dealing with a particular situation in which a human being may be placed, due either to his character or to the circumstances of his life. Solitariness may be objectively conditioned, as with Sophocles' Philoctetes, put ashore on the bleak island of Lemnos. Or it may be subjective, the product of inner necessity, as with Tolstoy's Ivan Ilyitch or Flaubert's Frédéric Moreau in the *Education Sentimentale*. But it is always merely a fragment, a phase, a climax or anticlimax, in the life of the community as a whole. The fate of such individuals is characteristic of certain human types in specific social or historical circumstances. Beside and beyond their solitariness, the common life, the strife and togetherness of other human beings, goes on as before. In a word, their solitariness is a specific social fate, not a universal *condition humaine*.

The latter, of course, is characteristic of the theory and practice of modernism. I would like, in the present study, to spare the reader tedious excursions into philosophy. But I cannot refrain from drawing the reader's attention to Heidegger's description of human existence as a "thrownness-into-being" (*Geworfenheit ins Dasein*). A more graphic evocation of the ontological solitariness of the individual would be hard to imagine. Man is "thrown-into-being." This implies, not merely that man is constitutionally unable to establish relationships with things or persons outside himself; but also that it is impossible to determine theoretically the origin and goal of human existence.

Man, thus conceived, is an ahistorical being. (The fact that Heidegger does admit a form of "authentic" historicity in his system is not really relevant. I have [written of] elsewhere that Heidegger tends to belittle historicity as "vulgar"; and his "authentic" historicity is not distinguishable from ahistoricity.) This negation of history takes two different forms in modernist literature. First, the hero is strictly confined within the limits of his own experience. There is not for him – and apparently not for his creator – any preexistent reality beyond his own self, acting upon him or being acted upon by him. Secondly, the hero himself is without personal history. He is "thrown-into-the-world": meaninglessly, unfathomably. He does not develop through contact with the world; he neither forms nor is formed by it. The only "development" in this literature is the gradual revelation of the human condition. Man is now what he has always been and always will be. The narrator, the examining subject, is in motion; the examined reality is static.

Of course, dogmas of this kind are only really viable in philosophical abstraction, and then only with a measure of sophistry. A gifted writer, however extreme his theoretical modernism, will in practice have to compromise with the demands of historicity and of social environment. Joyce uses Dublin, Kafka and Musil the Hapsburg monarchy, as the locus of their masterpieces. But the locus they lovingly depict is little more than a backcloth; it is not basic to their artistic intention.

This view of human existence has specific literary consequences. Particularly in one category, of primary theoretical and practical importance, to which we must now give our attention: that of *potentiality*. Philosophy distinguishes between *abstract* and *concrete* (in Hegel, "real") *potentiality*. These two categories, their interrelation and opposition, are rooted in life itself. *Potentiality* – seen abstractly or subjectively – is richer than actual life. Innumerable possibilities for man's development are imaginable, only a small percentage of which will be realized. Modern subjectivism, taking these imagined possibilities for actual complexity of life, oscillates between melancholy and fascination. When the world declines to realize these possibilities, this melancholy becomes tinged with contempt. Hofmannsthal's Sobeide expressed the reaction of the generation first exposed to this experience:

> The burden of those endlessly pored-over
> And now forever perished possibilities...

How far were those possibilities even concrete or "real"? Plainly, they existed only in the imagination of the subject, as dreams or daydreams. Faulkner, in whose work this subjective potentiality plays an important part, was evidently aware that reality must thereby be subjectivized and made to appear arbitrary. Consider this comment of his: "They were all talking simultaneously, getting flushed and excited, quarreling, making the unreal into a possibility, then into a probability, then into an irrefutable fact, as human beings do when they put their wishes into words." The possibilities in a man's mind, the particular pattern, intensity and suggestiveness they assume, will of course be characteristic of that individual. In practice, their number will border on the infinite, even with the most unimaginative individual. It is thus a hopeless undertaking to define the contours of individuality, let alone to come to grips with a man's actual fate, by means of potentiality. The *abstract* character of potentiality is clear from the fact that it cannot determine development – subjective mental states, however permanent or profound, cannot here be decisive. Rather, the development of personality is determined by inherited gifts and qualities; by the factors, external or internal, which further or inhibit their growth.

But in life potentiality can, of course, become reality. Situations arise in which a man is confronted with a choice; and in the act of choice a man's character may reveal itself in a light that surprises even himself. In literature – and particularly in dramatic literature – the denouement often consists in the realization of just such a potentiality, which circumstances have kept from coming to the fore. These potentialities are, then, "real" or concrete potentialities. The fate of the character depends upon the potentiality in question, even if it should condemn him to a tragic end. In advance, while still a subjective potentiality in the character's mind, there is no way of distinguishing it from the innumerable abstract potentialities in his mind. It may even be buried away so completely that, before the moment of decision, it has never entered his mind even as an abstract potentiality. The subject, after taking his decision, may be unconscious of his own motives. Thus Richard Dudgeon, Shaw's Devil's Disciple, having sacrificed himself as Pastor Andersen, confesses: "I have often asked myself for the motive, but I find no good reason to explain why I acted as I did."

Yet it is a decision which has altered the direction of his life. Of course, this is an extreme case. But the qualitative leap of the denouement, canceling and at the same time renewing the continuity of individual consciousness, can never be predicted. The concrete potentiality cannot be isolated from the myriad abstract potentialities. Only actual decision reveals the distinction.

The literature of realism, aiming at a truthful reflection of reality, must demonstrate both the concrete and abstract potentialities of human beings in extreme situations of this kind. A character's concrete potentiality once revealed, his abstract potentialities will appear essentially inauthentic. Moravia, for instance, in his novel *The Indifferent Ones*, describes the young son of a decadent bourgeois family, Michel, who makes up his mind to kill his sister's seducer. While Michel, having made his decision, is planning the murder, a large number of abstract – but highly suggestive – possibilities are laid before us. Unfortunately for Michel the murder is actually carried out; and, from the sordid details of the action, Michel's character emerges as what it is – representative of that background from which, in subjective fantasy, he had imagined he could escape.

Abstract potentiality belongs wholly to the realm of subjectivity; whereas concrete potentiality is concerned with the dialectic between the individual's subjectivity and objective reality. The literary presentation of the latter thus implies a description of actual persons inhabiting a palpable, identifiable world. Only in the interaction of character and environment can the concrete potentiality of a particular individual be singled out from the "bad infinity" of purely abstract potentialities, and emerge as the determining potentiality of just this individual at just this phase of his development. This principle alone enables the artist to distinguish concrete potentiality from a myriad of abstractions.

But the ontology on which the image of man in modernist literature is based invalidates this principle. If the "human condition" – man as a solitary being, incapable of meaningful relationships – is identified with reality itself, the distinction between abstract and concrete potentiality becomes null and void. The categories tend to merge. Thus Cesare Pavese notes with John Dos Passos, and his German contemporary, Alfred Döblin, a sharp oscillation between "superficial *verisme*" and "abstract expressionist schematism." Criticizing Dos Passos, Pavese writes that fictional characters "ought to be created by deliberate selection and description of individual features" – implying that Dos Passos' characterizations are transferable from one individual to another. He describes the artistic consequences: by exalting man's subjectivity, at the expense of the objective reality of his environment, man's subjectivity itself is impoverished.

The problem, once again, is ideological. This is not to say that the ideology underlying modernist writings is identical in all cases. On the contrary: the ideology exists in extremely various, even contradictory forms. The rejection of narrative objectivity, the surrender to subjectivity, may take the form of Joyce's stream of consciousness, or of Musil's "active passivity," his "existence without quality," or of Gide's "*action gratuite*," where abstract potentiality achieves pseudorealization. As individual character manifests itself in life's moments of decision, so too in literature. If the distinction between abstract and concrete potentiality vanishes, if man's inwardness is identified with an abstract subjectivity, human personality must necessarily disintegrate.

T. S. Eliot described this phenomenon, this mode of portraying human personality, as

Shape without form, shade without colour,
Paralysed force, gesture without motion.

The disintegration of personality is matched by a disintegration of the outer world. In one sense, this is simply a further consequence of our argument. For the identification of abstract and concrete human potentiality rests on the assumption that the objective world is inherently inexplicable. Certain leading modernist writers, attempting a theoretical apology, have admitted this quite frankly. Often this theoretical impossibility of understanding reality is the point of departure, rather than the exaltation of subjectivity. But in any case the connection between the two is plain. The German poet Gottfried Benn, for instance, informs us that "there is no outer reality, there is only human consciousness, constantly building, modifying, rebuilding new worlds out of its own creativity." Musil, as always, gives a moral twist to this line of thought. Ulrich, the hero of his *The Man without Qualities*, when asked what he would do if he were in God's place, replies: "I should be compelled to abolish reality." Subjective existence "without qualities" is the complement of the negation of outward reality.

The negation of outward reality is not always demanded with such theoretical rigor. But it is present in almost all modernist literature. In conversation, Musil once gave as the period of his great novel, "between 1912 and 1914." But he was quick to modify this statement by adding: "I have not, I must insist, written a historical novel. I am not concerned with actual events. ...Events, anyhow, are interchangeable. I am interested in what is typical, in what one might call the ghostly aspect of reality." The word "ghostly" is interesting. It points to a major tendency in modernist literature: the attenuation of actuality. In Kafka, the descriptive detail is of an extraordinary immediacy and authenticity. But Kafka's artistic ingenuity is really directed towards substituting his *angst*-ridden vision of the world for objective reality. The realistic detail is the expression of a ghostly unreality, of a nightmare world, whose function is to evoke *angst*. The same phenomenon can be seen in writers who attempt to combine Kafka's techniques with a critique of society – like the German writer, Wolfgang Koeppen, in his satirical novel about Bonn, *Das Treibhaus*. A similar attenuation of reality underlies Joyce's stream of consciousness. It is, of course, intensified where the stream of consciousness is itself the medium through which reality is presented. And it is carried *ad absurdum* where the stream of consciousness is that of an abnormal subject or of an idiot – consider the first part of Faulkner's *The Sound and the Fury* or, a still more extreme case, Beckett's *Molloy*.

Attenuation of reality and dissolution of personality are thus interdependent: the stronger the one, the stronger the other. Underlying both is the lack of a consistent view of human nature. Man is reduced to a sequence of unrelated experiential fragments; he is as inexplicable to others as to himself. In Eliot's *The Cocktail Party* the psychiatrist, who voices the opinions of the author, describes the phenomenon:

Ah, but we die to each other daily.
What we know of other people
Is only our memory of the moments
During which we knew them. And they have
    changed since then.
To pretend that they and we are the same
Is a useful and convenient social convention
Which must sometimes be broken. We must
    also remember
That at every meeting we are meeting a
    stranger.

The dissolution of personality, originally the unconscious product of the identification of concrete and abstract potentiality, is elevated to a deliberate principle in the light of consciousness. It is no accident that Gottfried Benn called one of his theoretical tracts "*Doppelleben*." For Benn, this dissolution of personality took the form of a schizophrenic dichotomy. According to him, there was in man's personality no coherent pattern of motivation or behavior. Man's animal nature is opposed to his denaturized, sublimated thought processes. The unity of thought and action is "backward philosophy"; thought and being are "quite separate entities." Man must be either a moral or a thinking being – he cannot be both at once.

These are not, I think, purely private, eccentric speculations. Of course, they are derived from Benn's specific experience. But there is an inner connection between these ideas and a certain tradition of bourgeois thought. It is more than a hundred years since Kierkegaard first attacked the Hegelian view that the inner and outer world form an objective dialectical unity, that they are indissolubly married in spite of their apparent opposition. Kierkegaard denied any such unity. According to Kierkegaard, the individual exists within an opaque, impenetrable "incognito."

This philosophy attained remarkable popularity after the second world war – proof that even the most abstruse theories may reflect social reality. Men like Martin Heidegger, Ernst Jünger, the lawyer Carl Schmitt, Gottfried Benn and others passionately embraced this doctrine of the eternal incognito which implies that a man's external deeds are no guide to his motives. In this case, the deeds obscured behind the mysterious incognito were, needless to say, these intellectuals' participation in Nazism: Heidegger, as rector of Freiburg University, had glorified Hitler's seizure of power at his inauguration; Carl Schmitt had put his great legal gifts at Hitler's disposal. The facts were too well-known to be simply denied. But, if this impenetrable incognito were the true "*condi-*

tion humaine," might not – concealed within their incognito – Heidegger or Schmitt have been secret opponents of Hitler all the time, only supporting him in the world of appearances? Ernst von Salomon's cynical frankness about his opportunism in *The Questionnaire* (keeping his reservations to himself or declaring them only in the presence of intimate friends) may be read as an ironic commentary on this ideology of the incognito as we find it, say, in the writings of Ernst Jünger.

This digression may serve to show, taking an extreme example, what the social implications of such an ontology may be. In the literary field, this particular ideology was of cardinal importance; by destroying the complex tissue of man's relations with his environment, it furthered the dissolution of personality. For it is just the opposition between a man and his environment that determines the development of his personality. There is no great hero of fiction – from Homer's Achilles to Mann's Adrian Leverkühn or Sholokhov's Grigory Melyekov – whose personality is not the product of such an opposition. I have shown how disastrous the denial of the distinction between abstract and concrete potentiality must be for the presentation of character. The destruction of the complex tissue of man's interaction with his environment likewise saps the vitality of this opposition. Certainly, some writers who adhere to this ideology have attempted, not unsuccessfully, to portray this opposition in concrete terms. But the underlying ideology deprives these contradictions of their dynamic, developmental significance. The contradictions coexist, unresolved, contributing to the further dissolution of the personality in question.

It is to the credit of Robert Musil that he was quite conscious of the implications of his method. Of his hero Ulrich he remarked: "One is faced with a simple choice: either one must run with the pack (when in Rome, do as the Romans do); or one becomes a neurotic." Musil here introduces the problem, central to all modernist literature, of the significance of psychopathology.

This problem was first widely discussed in the naturalist period. More than fifty years ago, that doyen of Berlin dramatic critics, Alfred Kerr, was writing: "Morbidity is the legitimate poetry of naturalism. For what is poetic in everyday life? Neurotic aberration, escape from life's dreary routine. Only in this way can a character be translated to a rarer clime and yet retain an air of reality." Interesting, here, is the notion that the poetic necessity of the pathological derives from the pro-

saic quality of life under capitalism. I would maintain – we shall return to this point – that in modern writing there is a continuity from naturalism to the modernism of our day – a continuity restricted, admittedly, to underlying ideological principles. What at first was no more than dim anticipation of approaching catastrophe developed, after 1914, into an all-pervading obsession. And I would suggest that the ever-increasing part played by psychopathology was one of the main features of the continuity. At each period – depending on the prevailing social and historical conditions – psychopathology was given a new emphasis, a different significance and artistic function. Kerr's description suggests that in naturalism the interest in psychopathology sprang from an esthetic need; it was an attempt to escape from the dreariness of life under capitalism. The quotation from Musil shows that some years later the opposition acquired a moral slant. The obsession with morbidity had ceased to have a merely decorative function, bringing color into the grayness of reality, and become a moral protest against capitalism.

With Musil – and with many other modernist writers – psychopathology became the goal, the *terminus ad quem*, of their artistic intention. But there is a double difficulty inherent in their intention, which follows from its underlying ideology. There is, first, a lack of definition. The protest expressed by this flight into psychopathology is an abstract gesture; its rejection of reality is wholesale and summary, containing no concrete criticism. It is a gesture, moreover, that is destined to lead nowhere; it is an escape into nothingness. Thus the propagators of this ideology are mistaken in thinking that such a protest could ever be fruitful in literature. In any protest against particular social conditions, these conditions themselves must have the central place. The bourgeois protest against feudal society, the proletarian against bourgeois society, made their point of departure a criticism of the old order. In both cases the protest – reaching out beyond the point of departure – was based on a concrete *terminus ad quem*: the establishment of a new order. However indefinite the structure and content of this new order, the will toward its more exact definition was not lacking.

How different the protest of writers like Musil! The *terminus a quo* (the corrupt society of our time) is inevitably the main source of energy, since the *terminus ad quem* (the escape into psychopathology) is a mere abstraction. The rejection of modern reality is purely subjective. Considered in terms of man's relation with his environment, it lacks both content and direction. And this lack is exaggerated still further by the character of the *terminus ad quem*. For the protest is an empty gesture, expressing nausea or discomfort or longing. Its content – or rather lack of content – derives from the fact that such a view of life cannot impart a sense of direction. These writers are not wholly wrong in believing that psychopathology is their surest refuge; it is the ideological complement of their historical position.

This obsession with the pathological is not only to be found in literature. Freudian psychoanalysis is its most obvious expression. The treatment of the subject is only superficially different from that in modern literature. As everybody knows, Freud's starting point was "everyday life." In order to explain "slips" and daydreams, however, he had to have recourse to psychopathology. In his lectures, speaking of resistance and repression, he says: "Our interest in the general psychology of symptom-formation increases as we understand to what extent the study of pathological conditions can shed light on the workings of the normal mind." Freud believed he had found the key to the understanding of the normal personality in the psychology of the abnormal. This belief is still more evident in the typology of Kretschmer, which also assumes that psychological abnormalities can explain normal psychology. It is only when we compare Freud's psychology with that of Pavlov, who takes the Hippocratic view that mental abnormality is a deviation from a norm, that we see it in its true light.

Clearly, this is not strictly a scientific or literary-critical problem. It is an ideological problem, deriving from the ontological dogma of the solitariness of man. The literature of realism, based on the Aristotelean concept of man as *zoon politikon*, is entitled to develop a new typology for each new phase in the evolution of a society. It displays the contradictions within society and within the individual in the context of a dialectical unity. Here, individuals embodying violent and extraordinary passions are still within the range of a socially normal typology (Shakespeare, Balzac, Stendhal). For, in this literature, the average man is simply a dimmer reflection of the contradictions always existing in man and society; eccentricity is a socially conditioned distortion. Obviously, the passions of the great heroes must not be confused with "eccentricity" in the colloquial sense: Christian Buddenbrook is an "eccentric"; Adrian Leverkühn is not.

The ontology of *Geworfenheit* makes a true typology impossible; it is replaced by an abstract polarity of the eccentric and the socially average. We have seen why this polarity – which in traditional realism serves to increase our understanding of social normality – leads in modernism to a fascination with morbid eccentricity. Eccentricity becomes the necessary complement of the average; and this polarity is held to exhaust human potentiality. The implications of this ideology are shown in another remark of Musil's: "If humanity dreamt collectively, it would dream Moosbrugger." Moosbrugger, you will remember, was a mentally retarded sexual pervert with homicidal tendencies.

What served, with Musil, as the ideological basis of a new typology – escape into neurosis as a protest against the evils of society – becomes with other modernist writers an immutable *condition humaine*. Musil's statement loses its conditional "if" and becomes a simple description of reality. Lack of objectivity in the description of the outer world finds its complement in the reduction of reality to a nightmare. Beckett's *Molloy* is perhaps the *ne plus ultra* of this development, although Joyce's vision of reality as an incoherent stream of consciousness had already assumed in Faulkner a nightmare quality. In Beckett's novel we have the same vision twice over. He presents us with an image of the utmost human degradation – an idiot's vegetative existence. Then, as help is imminent from a mysterious unspecified source, the rescuer himself sinks into idiocy. The story is told through the parallel streams of consciousness of the idiot and of his rescuer.

Along with the adoption of perversity and idiocy as types of the *condition humaine*, we find what amounts to frank glorification. Take Montherlant's *Pasiphae*, where sexual perversity – the heroine's infatuation with a bull – is presented as a triumphant return to nature, as the liberation of impulse from the slavery of convention. The chorus – i.e., the author – puts the following question (which, though rhetorical, clearly expects an affirmative reply): "*Si l'absence de pensée et l'absence de morale ne contribuent pas beaucoup à la dignité des bêtes, des plantes et des eaux...?*" ["Whether the absence of thought and the absence of morality do not contribute a lot to the dignity of animals, plants and waters...?"] Montherlant expresses as plainly as Musil, though with different moral and emotional emphasis, the hidden – one might say repressed – social character of the protest underlying this obsession with psychopathology, its perverted Rousseauism, its anarchism. There are many illustrations of this in modernist writing. A poem of Benn's will serve to make the point:

O that we were our primal ancestors,
Small lumps of plasma in hot, sultry swamps;
Life, death, conception, parturition
Emerging from those juices soundlessly.

A frond of seaweed or a dune of sand,
Formed by the wind and heavy at the base;
A dragonfly or gull's wing – already, these
Would signify excessive suffering.

This is not overtly perverse in the manner of Beckett or Montherlant. Yet, in his primitivism, Benn is at one with them. The opposition of man as animal to man as social being (for instance, Heidegger's devaluation of the social as *"das Man,"* Klages' assertion of the incompatibility of *Geist* and *Seele*, or Rosenberg's racial mythology) leads straight to a glorification of the abnormal and to an undisguised antihumanism.

A typology limited in this way to the *homme moyen sensuel* and the idiot also opens the door to "experimental" stylistic distortion. Distortion becomes as inseparable a part of the portrayal of reality as the recourse to the pathological. But literature must have a concept of the normal if it is to "place" distortion correctly; that is to say, to see it *as* distortion. With such a typology this placing is impossible, since the normal is no longer a proper object of literary interest. Life under capitalism is, often rightly, presented as a distortion (a petrification or paralysis) of the human substance. But to present psychopathology as a way of escape from this distortion is itself a distortion. We are invited to measure one type of distortion against another and arrive, necessarily, at universal distortion. There is no principle to set against the general pattern, no standard by which the petty-bourgeois and the pathological can be seen in their social context. And these tendencies, far from being relativized with time, become ever more absolute. Distortion becomes the normal condition of human existence; the proper study, the formative principle, of art and literature.

I have demonstrated some of the literary implications of this ideology. Let us now pursue the argument further. It is clear, I think, that modernism must deprive literature of a sense of *perspec-*

tive. This would not be surprising; rigorous modernists such as Kafka, Benn and Musil have always indignantly refused to provide their readers with any such thing. I will return to the ideological implications of the idea of perspective later. Let me say here that, in any work of art, perspective is of overriding importance. It determines the course and content; it draws together the threads of the narration; it enables the artist to choose between the important and the superficial, the crucial and the episodic. The direction in which characters develop is determined by perspective, only those features being described which are material to their development. The more lucid the perspective – as in Molière or the Greeks – the more economical and striking the selection.

Modernism drops this selective principle. It asserts that it can dispense with it, or can replace it with its dogma of the *condition humaine*. A naturalistic style is bound to be the result. This state of affairs – which to my mind characterizes all modernist art of the past fifty years – is disguised by critics who systematically glorify the modernist movement. By concentrating on formal criteria, by isolating technique from content and exaggerating its importance, these critics refrain from judgment on the social or artistic significance of subject matter. They are unable, in consequence, to make the aesthetic distinction between *realism* and *naturalism*. This distinction depends on the presence or absence in a work of art of a "hierarchy of significance" in the situations and characters presented. Compared with this, formal categories are of secondary importance. That is why it is possible to speak of the basically *naturalistic* character of modernist literature – and to see here the literary expression of an ideological continuity. This is not to deny that variations in style reflect changes in society. But the particular form this principle of naturalistic arbitrariness, this lack of hierarchic structure, may take is not decisive. We encounter it in the all-determining "social conditions" of naturalism, in symbolism's impressionist methods and its cultivation of the exotic, in the fragmentation of objective reality in futurism and constructivism and the German *Neue Sachlichkeit*, or, again, in surrealism's stream of consciousness.

These schools have in common a basically static approach to reality. This is closely related to their lack of perspective. Characteristically, Gottfried Benn actually incorporated this in his artistic programme. One of his volumes bears the title, *Static Poems*. The denial of history, of development and thus of perspective, becomes the mark of true insight into the nature of reality.

> The wise man is ignorant
> of change and development
> his children and children's children
> are no part of his world.

The rejection of any concept of the future is for Benn the criterion of wisdom. But even those modernist writers who are less extreme in their rejection of history tend to present social and historical phenomena as static. It is, then, of small importance whether this condition is "eternal," or only a transitional stage punctuated by sudden catastrophes (even in early naturalism the static presentation was often broken up by these catastrophes, without altering its basic character). Musil, for instance, writes in his essay, *The Writer in our Age*: "One knows just as little about the present. Partly, this is because we are, as always, too close to the present. But it is also because the present into which we were plunged some two decades ago is of a particularly all-embracing and inescapable character." Whether or not Musil knew of Heidegger's philosophy, the idea of *Geworfenheit* is clearly at work here. And the following reveals plainly how, for Musil, this static state was upset by the catastrophe of 1914: "All of a sudden, the world was full of violence. . . . In European civilization, there was a sudden rift. . . ." In short: this static apprehension of reality in modernist literature is no passing fashion; it is rooted in the ideology of modernism.

To establish the basic distinction between modernism and that realism which, from Homer to Thomas Mann and Gorky, has assumed change and development to be the proper subject of literature, we must go deeper into the underlying ideological problem. In *The House of the Dead* Dostoevsky gave an interesting account of the convict's attitude to work. He described how the prisoners, in spite of brutal discipline, loafed about, working badly or merely going through the motions of work until a new overseer arrived and allotted them a new project, after which they were allowed to go home. "The work was hard," Dostoevsky continues, "but, Christ, with what energy they threw themselves into it! Gone was all their former indolence and pretended incompetence." Later in the book Dostoevsky sums up his experiences: "If a man loses hope and has no aim in view, sheer boredom can turn him into a

beast. . . ." I have said that the problem of perspective in literature is directly related to the principle of selection. Let me go further: underlying the problem is a profound ethical complex, reflected in the composition of the work itself. Every human action is based on a presupposition of its inherent meaningfulness, at least to the subject. Absence of meaning makes a mockery of action and reduces art to naturalistic description.

Clearly, there can be no literature without at least the appearance of change or development. This conclusion should not be interpreted in a narrowly metaphysical sense. We have already diagnosed the obsession with psychopathology in modernist literature as a desire to escape from the reality of capitalism. But this implies the absolute primacy of the *terminus a quo*, the condition from which it is desired to escape. Any movement toward a *terminus ad quem* is condemned to impotence. As the ideology of most modernist writers asserts the unalterability of outward reality (even if this is reduced to a mere state of consciousness) human activity is, *a priori*, rendered impotent and robbed of meaning.

The apprehension of reality to which this leads is most consistently and convincingly realized in the work of Kafka. Kafka remarks of Josef K., as he is being led to execution: "He thought of flies, their tiny limbs breaking as they struggle away from the fly-paper." This mood of total impotence, of paralysis in the face of the unintelligible power of circumstances, informs all his work. Though the action of *The Castle* takes a different, even an opposite, direction to that of *The Trial*, this view of the world, from the perspective of a trapped and struggling fly, is all-pervasive. This experience, this vision of a world dominated by *angst* and of man at the mercy of incomprehensible terrors, makes Kafka's work the very prototype of modernist art. Techniques, elsewhere of merely formal significance, are used here to evoke a primitive awe in the presence of an utterly strange and hostile reality. Kafka's *angst* is the experience *par excellence* of modernism.

Two instances from musical criticism – which can afford to be both franker and more theoretical than literary criticism – show that it is indeed a universal experience with which we are dealing. The composer, Hanns Eisler, says of Schönberg: "Long before the invention of the bomber, he expressed what people were to feel in the air raid shelters." Even more characteristic – though seen from a modernist point of view – is Theodor W.

Adorno's analysis (in *The Aging of Modern Music*) of symptoms of decadence in modernist music: "The sounds are still the same. But the experience of *angst*, which made their originals great, has vanished." Modernist music, he continues, has lost touch with the truth that was its *raison d'être*. Composers are no longer equal to the emotional presuppositions of their modernism. And that is why modernist music has failed. The diminution of the original *angst*-obsessed vision of life (whether due, as Adorno thinks, to inability to respond to the magnitude of the horror or, as I believe, to the fact that this obsession with *angst* among bourgeois intellectuals has already begun to recede) has brought about a loss of substance in modern music and destroyed its authenticity as a modernist art-form.

This is a shrewd analysis of the paradoxical situation of the modernist artist, particularly where he is trying to express deep and genuine experience. The deeper the experience, the greater the damage to the artistic whole. But this tendency toward disintegration, this loss of artistic unity, cannot be written off as a mere fashion, the product of experimental gimmicks. Modern philosophy, after all, encountered these problems long before modern literature, painting or music. A case in point is the problem of *time*. Subjective idealism had already separated time, abstractly conceived, from historical change and particularity of place. As if this separation were insufficient for the new age of imperialism, Bergson widened it further. Experienced time, subjective time, now became identical with real time; the rift between this time and that of the objective world was complete. Bergson and other philosophers who took up and varied this theme claimed that their concept of time alone afforded insight into authentic, i.e., subjective, reality. The same tendency soon made its appearance in literature.

The German left-wing critic and essayist of the twenties, Walter Benjamin, has well described Proust's vision and the techniques he uses to present it in his great novel: "We all know that Proust does not describe a man's life as it actually happens, but as it is remembered by a man who has lived through it. Yet this puts it far too crudely. For it is not actual experience that is important, but the texture of reminiscence, the Penelope's tapestry of a man's memory." The connection with Bergson's theories of time is obvious. But whereas with Bergson, in the abstraction of philosophy, the unity of perception is preserved, Ben-

jamin shows that with Proust, as a result of the radical disintegration of the time sequence, objectivity is eliminated: "A lived event is finite, concluded at least on the level of experience. But a remembered event is infinite, a possible key to everything that preceded it and to everything that will follow it."

It is the distinction between a philosophical and an artistic vision of the world. However hard philosophy, under the influence of idealism, tries to liberate the concepts of space and time from temporal and spatial particularity, literature continues to assume their unity. The fact that, nevertheless, the concept of subjective time cropped up in literature only shows how deeply subjectivism is rooted in the experience of the modern bourgeois intellectual. The individual, retreating into himself in despair at the cruelty of the age, may experience an intoxicated fascination with his forlorn condition. But then a new horror breaks through. If reality cannot be understood (or no effort is made to understand it), then the individual's subjectivity – alone in the universe, reflecting only itself – takes on an equally incomprehensible and horrific character. Hugo von Hofmannsthal was to experience this condition very early in his poetic career:

It is a thing that no man cares to think on,
And far too terrible for mere complaint,
That all things slip from us and pass away,

And that my ego, bound by no outward force –
Once a small child's before it became mine –
Should now be strange to me, like a strange dog.

By separating time from the outer world of objective reality, the inner world of the subject is transformed into a sinister, inexplicable flux and acquires – paradoxically, as it may seem – a static character.

On literature this tendency toward disintegration, of course, will have an even greater impact than on philosophy. When time is isolated in this way, the artist's world disintegrates into a multiplicity of partial worlds. The static view of the world, now combined with diminished objectivity, here rules unchallenged. The world of man – the only subject matter of literature – is shattered if a single component is removed. I have shown the consequences of isolating time and reducing it to a subjective category. But time is by no means the only component whose removal can lead to such disintegration. Here, again, Hofmannsthal antici-

231

pated later developments. His imaginary "Lord Chandos" reflects: "I have lost the ability to concentrate my thoughts or set them out coherently." The result is a condition of apathy, punctuated by manic fits. The development toward a definitely pathological protest is here anticipated – admittedly in glamorous, romantic guise. But it is the same distintegration that is at work.

Previous realistic literature, however violent its criticism of reality, had always assumed the unity of the world it described and seen it as a living whole inseparable from man himself. But the major realists of our time deliberately introduce elements of disintegration into their work – for instance, the subjectivizing of time – and use them to portray the contemporary world more exactly. In this way, the once natural unity becomes a conscious, constructed unity (I have [written] elsewhere that the device of the two temporal planes in Thomas Mann's *Doctor Faustus* serves to emphasize its historicity). But in modernist literature the disintegration of the world of man – and consequently the disintegration of personality – coincides with the ideological intention. Thus *angst*, this basic modern experience, this by-product of *Geworfenheit*, has its emotional origin in the experience of a disintegrating society. But it attains its effects by evoking the disintegration of the world of man.

To complete our examination of modernist literature, we must consider for a moment the question of allegory. Allegory is that esthetic genre which lends itself par excellence to a description of man's alienation from objective reality. Allegory is a problematic genre because it rejects that assumption of an immanent meaning to human existence which – however unconscious, however combined with religious concepts of transcendence – is the basis of traditional art. Thus in medieval art we observe a new secularity (in spite of the continued use of religious subjects) triumphing more and more, from the time of Giotto, over the allegorizing of an earlier period.

Certain reservations should be made at this point. First, we must distinguish between literature and the visual arts. In the latter, the limitations of allegory can be the more easily overcome in that transcendental, allegorical subjects can be clothed in an esthetic immanence (even if of a merely decorative kind) and the rift in reality in some sense be eliminated – we have only to think of Byzantine mosaic art. This decorative element has no real equivalent in literature; it exists only in

a figurative sense, and then only as a secondary component. Allegorical art of the quality of Byzantine mosaic is only rarely possible in literature. Secondly, we must bear in mind in examining allegory – and this is of great importance for our argument – a historical distinction: does the concept of transcendence in question contain within itself tendencies toward immanence (as in Byzantine art or Giotto), or is it the product precisely of a rejection of these tendencies?

Allegory, in modernist literature, is clearly of the latter kind. Transcendence implies here, more or less consciously, the negation of any meaning immanent in the world or the life of man. We have already examined the underlying ideological basis of this view and its stylistic consequences. To conclude our analysis, and to establish the allegorical character of modernist literature, I must refer again to the work of one of the finest theoreticians of modernism – to Walter Benjamin. Benjamin's examination of allegory was a product of his researches into German Baroque drama. Benjamin made his analysis of these relatively minor plays the occasion for a general discussion of the esthetics of allegory. He was asking, in effect, why it is that transcendence, which is the essence of allegory, cannot but destroy esthetics itself.

Benjamin gives a very contemporary definition of allegory. He does not labor the analogies between modern art and the Baroque (such analogies are tenuous at best, and were much overdone by the fashionable criticism of the time). Rather, he uses the Baroque drama to criticize modernism, imputing the characteristics of the latter to the former. In so doing, Benjamin became the first critic to attempt a philosophical analysis of the esthetic paradox underlying modernist art. He writes:

> In allegory, the *facies hippocratica* of history looks to the observer like a petrified primeval landscape. History, all the suffering and failure it contains, finds expression in the human face – or, rather, in the human skull. No sense of freedom, no classical proportion, no human emotion lives in its features – not only human existence in general, but the fate of every individual human being is symbolized in this most palpable token of mortality. This is the core of the allegorical vision, of the Baroque idea of history as the passion of the world; history is significant only in the stations of its corruption. Signifi-

cance is a function of mortality – because it is death that marks the passage from corruptibility to meaningfulness.

Benjamin returns again and again to this link between allegory and the annihilation of history:

In the light of this vision history appears, not as the gradual realization of the eternal, but as a process of inevitable decay. Allegory thus goes beyond beauty. What ruins are in the physical world, allegories are in the world of the mind.

Benjamin points here to the esthetic consequences of modernism – though projected into the Baroque drama – more shrewdly and consistently than any of his contemporaries. He sees that the notion of objective time is essential to any understanding of history and that the notion of subjective time is a product of a period of decline. "A thorough knowledge of the problematic nature of art" thus becomes for him – correctly, from his point of view – one of the hallmarks of allegory in Baroque drama. It is problematic, on the one hand, because it is an art intent on expressing absolute transcendence that fails to do so because of the means at its disposal. It is also problematic because it is an art reflecting the corruption of the world and bringing about its own dissolution in the process. Benjamin discovers "an immense, antiesthetic subjectivity" in Baroque literature, associated with "a theologically-determined subjectivity." (We shall presently show – a point I have [written of] elsewhere in relation to Heidegger's philosophy – how in literature a "religious atheism" of this kind can acquire a theological character.) Romantic – and, on a higher plane, Baroque – writers were well aware of this problem, and gave their understanding, not only theoretical, but artistic – that is to say allegorical – expression. "The image," Benjamin remarks, "becomes a rune in the sphere of allegorical intuition. When touched by the light of theology, its symbolic beauty is gone. The false appearance of totality vanishes. The image dies; the parable no longer holds true: the world it once contained disappears."

The consequences for art are far-reaching, and Benjamin does not hesitate to point them out: "Every person, every object, every relationship can stand for something else. This transferability constitutes a devastating, though just, judgment on the profane world – which is thereby branded as a world where such things are of small import-

ance." Benjamin knows, of course, that although details are "transferable," and thus insignificant, they are not banished from art altogether. On the contrary. Precisely in modern art, with which he is ultimately concerned, descriptive detail is often of an extraordinary sensuous, suggestive power – we think again of Kafka. But this, as we showed in the case of Musil (a writer who does not consciously aim at allegory) does not prevent the materiality of the world from undergoing permanent alteration, from becoming transferable and arbitrary. Just this, modernist writers maintain, is typical of their own apprehension of reality. Yet presented in this way, the world becomes, as Benjamin puts it, "exalted and depreciated at the same time." For the conviction that phenomena are *not* ultimately transferable is rooted in a belief in the world's rationality and in man's ability to penetrate its secrets. In realistic literature each descriptive detail is both *individual* and *typical*. Modern allegory and modernist ideology however, deny the *typical*. By destroying the coherence of the world, they reduce detail to the level of mere particularity (once again, the connection between modernism and naturalism is plain). Detail, in its allegorical transferability, though brought into a direct, if paradoxical connection with transcendence, becomes an abstract function of the transcendence to which it points. Modernist literature thus replaces concrete typicality with abstract particularity.

We are here applying Benjamin's paradox directly to aesthetics and criticism, and particularly to the aesthetics of modernism. And, though we have reversed his scale of values, we have not deviated from the course of his argument. Elsewhere, he speaks out even more plainly – as though the Baroque mask had fallen, revealing the modernist skull underneath:

Allegory is left empty-handed. The forces of evil, lurking in its depths, owe their very existence to allegory. Evil is, precisely, the nonexistence of that which allegory purports to represent.

The paradox Benjamin arrives at – his investigation of the esthetics of Baroque tragedy has culminated in a negation of esthetics – sheds a good deal of light on modernist literature, and particularly on Kafka. In interpreting his writings allegorically I am not, of course, following Max Brod, who finds a specifically religious allegory in

Kafka's works. Kafka refuted any such interpretation in a remark he is said to have made to Brod himself: "We are nihilistic figments, all of us; suicidal notions forming in God's mind." Kafka rejected, too, the gnostic concept of God as an evil demiurge: "The world is a cruel whim of God, an evil day's work." When Brod attempted to give this an optimistic slant, Kafka shrugged off the attempt ironically: "Oh, hope enough, hope without end – but not, alas, for us." These remarks, quoted by Benjamin in his brilliant essay on Kafka, point to the general spiritual climate of his work: "His profoundest experience is of the hopelessness, the utter meaninglessness of man's world, and particularly that of present-day bourgeois man." Kafka, whether he says so openly or not, is an atheist. An atheist, though, of that modern species who regard God's removal from the scene not as a liberation – as did Epicurus and the Encyclopedists – but as a token of the "God-forsakenness" of the world, its utter desolation and futility. Jacobsen's *Niels Lyhne* was the first novel to describe this state of mind of the atheistic bourgeois intelligentsia. Modern religious atheism is characterized, on the one hand, by the fact that unbelief has lost its revolutionary *élan* – the empty heavens are the projection of a world beyond hope of redemption. On the other hand, religious atheism shows that the desire for salvation lives on with undiminished force in a world without God, worshipping the void created by God's absence.

The supreme judges in *The Trial*, the castle administration in *The Castle*, represent transcendence in Kafka's allegories: the transcendence of nothingness. Everything points to them, and they could give meaning to everything. Everybody believes in their existence and omnipotence; but nobody knows them, nobody knows how they can be reached. If there is a God here, it can only be the God of religious atheism: *atheos absconditus*. We become acquainted with a repellent host of subordinate authorities; brutal, corrupt, pedantic – and, at the same time, unreliable and irresponsible. It is a portrait of the bourgeois society Kafka knew, with a dash of Prague local coloring. But it is also allegorical in that the doings of this bureaucracy and of those dependent on it, its impotent victims, are not concrete and realistic, but a reflection of that nothingness which governs existence. The hidden, nonexistent God of Kafka's world derives his spectral character from the fact that his own nonexistence is the ground of all existence; and the portrayed reality, uncannily accurate as it

is, is spectral in the shadow of that dependence. The only purpose of transcendence – the intangible *nichtendes Nichts* – is to reveal the *facies hippocratica* of the world.

That abstract particularity which we saw to be the esthetic consequence of allegory reaches its high mark in Kafka. He is a marvelous observer; the spectral character of reality affects him so deeply that the simplest episodes have an oppressive, nightmarish immediacy. As an artist, he is not content to evoke the surface of life. He is aware that individual detail must point to general significance. But how does he go about the business of abstraction? He has emptied everyday life of meaning by using the allegorical method; he has allowed detail to be annihilated by his transcendental nothingness. This allegorical transcendence bars Kafka's way to realism, prevents him from investing observed detail with typical significance. Kafka is not able, in spite of his extraordinarily evocative power, in spite of his unique sensibility, to achieve that fusion of the particular and the general which is the essence of realistic art. His aim is to raise the individual detail in its immediate particularity (without generalizing its content) to the level of abstraction. Kafka's method is typical, here, of modernism's allegorical approach. Specific subject matter and stylistic variation do not matter; what matters is the basic ideological determination of form and content. The particularity we find in Beckett and Joyce, in Musil and Benn, various as the treatment of it may be, is essentially of the same kind.

If we combine what we have up to now discussed separately we arrive at a consistent pattern. We see that modernism leads not only to the destruction of traditional literary forms; it leads to the destruction of literature as such. And this is true not only of Joyce, or of the literature of expressionism and surrealism. It was not André Gide's ambition, for instance, to bring about a revolution in literary style; it was his philosophy that compelled him to abandon conventional forms. He planned his *Counterfeiters* as a novel. But its structure suffered from a characteristically modernist schizophrenia: it was supposed to be written by the man who was also the hero of the novel. And, in practice, Gide was forced to admit that no novel, no work of literature, could be constructed in that way. We have here a practical demonstration that – as Benjamin showed in another context – modernism means not the enrichment but the negation of art.

13

The Aesthetic Dimension

Herbert Marcuse

I

In a situation where the miserable reality can be changed only through radical political praxis, the concern with aesthetics demands justification. It would be senseless to deny the element of despair inherent in this concern: the retreat into a world of fiction where existing conditions are changed and overcome only in the realm of the imagination. However, this purely ideological conception of art is being questioned with increasing intensity. It seems that art as art expresses a truth, an experience, a necessity which, although not in the domain of radical praxis, are nevertheless essential components of revolution. With this insight, the basic conception of Marxist aesthetics, that is its treatment of art as ideology, and the emphasis on the class character of art, become again the topic of critical reexamination.[1]

This discussion is directed to the following theses of Marxist aesthetics:

1 There is a definite connection between art and the material base, between art and the totality of the relations of production. With the change in production relations, art itself is transformed as part of the superstructure, although, like other ideologies, it can lag behind or anticipate social change.

2 There is a definite connection between art and social class. The only authentic, true, progressive art is the art of an ascending class. It expresses the consciousness of this class.

3 Consequently, the political and the aesthetic, the revolutionary content and the artistic quality tend to coincide.

4 The writer has an obligation to articulate and express the interests and needs of the ascending class. (In capitalism, this would be the proletariat.)

5 A declining class or its representatives are unable to produce anything but "decadent" art.

6 Realism (in various senses) is considered as the art form which corresponds most adequately to the social relationships, and thus is the "correct" art form.

Each of these theses implies that the social relations of production must be represented in the literary work – not imposed upon the work externally, but a part of its inner logic and the logic of the material.

This aesthetic imperative follows from the base–superstructure conception. In contrast to the rather dialectical formulations of Marx and Engels, the conception has been made into a rigid schema, a schematization that has had devastating consequences for aesthetics. The schema implies a normative notion of the material base as the true reality and a political devaluation of nonmaterial forces particularly of the individual consciousness and subconscious and their political function. This function can be either regressive or emancipatory. In both cases, it can become a material force. If historical materialism does not account for this role of subjectivity, it takes on the coloring of vulgar materialism.

Ideology becomes mere ideology, in spite of Engels's emphatic qualifications, and a devaluation of the entire realm of subjectivity takes place, a devaluation not only of the subject as *ego cogito*, the rational subject, but also of inwardness, emotions, and imagination. The subjectivity of individuals, their own consciousness and unconscious tends to be dissolved into class consciousness. Thereby, a major prerequisite of revolution is minimized, namely, the fact that the need for radical change must be rooted in the subjectivity of individuals themselves, in their intelligence and their passions, their drives and their goals. Marxist theory succumbed to that very reification which it had exposed and combated in society as a whole. Subjectivity became an atom of objectivity; even in its rebellious form it was surrendered to a collective consciousness. The deterministic component of Marxist theory does not lie in its concept of the relationship between social existence and consciousness, but in the reductionistic concept of consciousness which brackets the particular content of individual consciousness and, with it, the subjective potential for revolution.

This development was furthered by the interpretation of subjectivity as a "bourgeois" notion. Historically, this is questionable.[2] But even in bourgeois society, insistence on the truth and right of inwardness is not really a bourgeois value. With the affirmation of the inwardness of subjectivity, the individual steps out of the network of exchange relationships and exchange values, withdraws from the reality of bourgeois society, and enters another dimension of existence. Indeed, this escape from reality led to an experience which could (and did) become a powerful force in *invalidating* the actually prevailing bourgeois values, namely, by shifting the locus of the individual's realization from the domain of the performance principle and the profit motive to that of the inner resources of the human being: passion, imagination, conscience. Moreover, withdrawal and retreat were not the last position. Subjectivity strove to break out of its inwardness into the material and intellectual culture. And today, in the totalitarian period, it has become a political value as a counterforce against aggressive and exploitative socialization.

Liberating subjectivity constitutes itself in the inner history of the individuals – their own history, which is not identical with their social existence. It is the particular history of their encounters, their passions, joys, and sorrows –

experiences which are not necessarily grounded in their class situation, and which are not even comprehensible from this perspective. To be sure, the actual manifestations of their history are determined by their class situation, but this situation is not the ground of their fate – of that which happens to them. Especially in its nonmaterial aspects it explodes the class framework. It is all too easy to relegate love and hate, joy and sorrow, hope and despair to the domain of psychology, thereby removing them from the concerns of radical praxis. Indeed, in terms of political economy they may not be "forces of production," but for every human being they are decisive, they constitute reality.

Even in its most distinguished representatives. Marxist aesthetics has shared in the devaluation of subjectivity. Hence the preference for realism as the model of progressive art; the denigration of romanticism as simply reactionary; the denunciation of "decadent" art – in general, the embarrassment when confronted with the task of evaluating the aesthetic qualities of a work in terms other than class ideologies.

I shall submit the following thesis: the radical qualities of art, that is to say, its indictment of the established reality and its invocation of the beautiful image (*schöner Schein*) of liberation are grounded precisely in the dimensions where art *transcends* its social determination and emancipates itself from the given universe of discourse and behavior while preserving its overwhelming presence. Thereby art creates the realm in which the subversion of experience proper to art becomes possible: the world formed by art is recognized as a reality which is suppressed and distorted in the given reality. This experience culminates in extreme situations (of love and death, guilt and failure, but also joy, happiness, and fulfillment) which explode the given reality in the name of a truth normally denied or even unheard. The inner logic of the work of art terminates in the emergence of another reason, another sensibility, which defy the rationality and sensibility incorporated in the dominant social institutions.

Under the law of the aesthetic form, the given reality is necessarily *sublimated*: the immediate content is stylized, the "data" are reshaped and reordered in accordance with the demands of the art form, which requires that even the representation of death and destruction invoke the need for hope – a need rooted in the new consciousness embodied in the work of art.

Aesthetic sublimation makes for the affirmative, reconciling component of art, [...] though it is at the same time a vehicle for the critical, negating function of art. The transcendence of immediate reality shatters the reified objectivity of established social relations and opens a new dimension of experience: rebirth of the rebellious subjectivity. Thus, on the basis of aesthetic sublimation, a *desublimation* takes place in the perception of individuals – in their feelings, judgments, thoughts; an invalidation of dominant norms, needs, and values. With all its affirmative-ideological features, art remains a dissenting force.

We can tentatively define "aesthetic form" as the result of the transformation of a given content (actual or historical, personal or social fact) into a self-contained whole: a poem, play, novel, etc.[3] The work is thus "taken out" of the constant process of reality and assumes a significance and truth of its own. The aesthetic transformation is achieved through a reshaping of language, perception, and understanding so that they reveal the essence of reality in its appearance: the repressed potentialities of man and nature. The work of art thus re-presents reality while accusing it.[4]

The critical function of art, its contribution to the struggle for liberation, resides in the aesthetic form. A work of art is authentic or true not by virtue of its content (i.e., the "correct" representation of social conditions), nor by its "pure" form, but by the content having become form.

True, the aesthetic form removes art from the actuality of the class struggle – from actuality pure and simple. The aesthetic form constitutes the autonomy of art vis à vis "the given." However, this dissociation does not produce "false consciousness" or mere illusion but rather a counter-consciousness: negation of the realistic-conformist mind.

Aesthetic form, autonomy, and truth are interrelated. Each is a socio-historical phenomenon, and each *transcends* the socio-historical arena. While the latter limits the autonomy of art it does so without invalidating the *trans*historical truths expressed in the work. The truth of art lies in its power to break the monopoly of established reality (i.e., of those who established it) to *define* what is *real*. In this rupture, which is the achievement of the aesthetic form, the fictitious world of art appears as true reality.

Art is committed to that perception of the world which alienates individuals from their functional existence and performance in society – it is committed to an emancipation of sensibility, imagination, and reason in all spheres of subjectivity and objectivity. The aesthetic transformation becomes a vehicle of recognition and indictment. But this achievement presupposes a degree of autonomy which withdraws art from the mystifying power of the given and frees it for the expression of its own truth. Inasmuch as man and nature are constituted by an unfree society, their repressed and distorted potentialities can be represented only in an *estranging* form. The world of art is that of another *Reality Principle*, of estrangement – and only as estrangement does art fulfill a *cognitive* function: it communicates truths not communicable in any other language; *it contradicts*.

However, the strong affirmative tendencies toward reconciliation with the established reality coexist with the rebellious ones. I shall try to show that they are not due to the specific class determination of art but rather to the redeeming character of the *catharsis*. The catharsis itself is grounded in the power of aesthetic form to call fate by its name, to demystify its force, to give the word to the victims – the power of recognition which gives the individual a modicum of freedom and fulfillment in the realm of unfreedom. The interplay between the affirmation and the indictment of that which is, between ideology and truth, pertains to the very structure of art.[5] But in the authentic works, the affirmation does not cancel the indictment: reconciliation and hope still preserve the memory of things past.

The affirmative character of art has yet another source: it is in the commitment of art to Eros, the deep affirmation of the Life Instincts in their fight against instinctual and social oppression. The permanence of art, its historical immortality throughout the millennia of destruction, bears witness to this commitment.

Art stands under the law of the given, while transgressing this law. The concept of art as an essentially autonomous and negating productive force contradicts the notion which sees art as performing an essentially dependent, affirmative-ideological function, that is to say, glorifying and absolving the existing society.[6] Even the militant bourgeois literature of the eighteenth century remains ideological: the struggle of the ascending class with the nobility is primarily over issues of bourgeois morality. The lower classes play only a marginal role, if any. With a few notable exceptions, this literature is not one of class struggle. According to this point of view, the ideological character of art can be remedied today only by grounding art in revolutionary praxis and in the *Weltanschauung* of the proletariat.

It has often been pointed out that this interpretation of art does not do justice to the views of Marx and Engels.[7] To be sure, even this interpretation admits that art aims at representing the essence of a given reality and not merely its appearance. Reality is taken to be the totality of social relations and its essence is defined as the laws determining these relations in the "complex of social causality."[8] This view demands that the protagonists in a work of art represent individuals as "types" who in turn exemplify "objective tendencies of social development, indeed of humanity as a whole."[9]

Such formulations provoke the question whether literature is not hereby assigned a function which could only be fulfilled in the medium of theory. The representation of the social totality requires a conceptual analysis, which can hardly be transposed into the medium of sensibility. During the great debate on Marxist aesthetics in the early thirties, Lu Märten suggested that Marxist theory possesses a theoretical form of its own which militates against any attempt to give it an aesthetic form.[10]

But if the work of art cannot be comprehended in terms of social theory, neither can it be comprehended in terms of philosophy. In his discussion with Adorno, Lucien Goldmann rejects Adorno's claim that in order to understand a literary work "one has to transcend it towards philosophy, philosophical culture and critical knowledge." Against Adorno, Goldmann insists on the concreteness immanent in the work which makes it into an (aesthetic) totality in its own right: "The work of art is a universe of colors, sounds and words, and concrete characters. There is no death, there is only Phaedra dying."[11]

The reification of Marxist aesthetics depreciates and distorts the truth expressed in this universe – it minimizes the cognitive function of art as ideology. For the radical potential of art lies precisely in its ideological character, in its transcendent relation to the "basis." Ideology is not always *mere* ideology, false consciousness. The consciousness and the representation of truths which appear as abstract in relation to the established process of production are also ideological functions. Art presents one of these truths. As ideology, it opposes the given society. The autonomy of art contains the categorical imperative: "things must change."

If the liberation of human beings and nature is to be possible at all, then the social nexus of destruction and submission must be broken. This does not mean that the revolution becomes thematic; on the contrary, in the aesthetically most perfect works, it does not. It seems that in these works the necessity of revolution is presupposed, as the *a priori* of art. But the revolution is also as it were surpassed and questioned as to how far it responds to the anguish of the human being, as to how far it achieves a rupture with the past.

Compared with the often one-dimensional optimism of propaganda, art is permeated with pessimism, not seldom intertwined with comedy. Its "liberating laughter" recalls the danger and the evil that have passed – this time! But the pessimism of art is not counterrevolutionary. It serves to warn against the "happy consciousness" of radical praxis: as if all of that which art invokes and indicts could be settled through the class struggle. Such pessimism permeates even the literature in which the revolution itself is affirmed, and becomes thematic; Büchner's play *The Death of Danton* is a classic example.

Marxist aesthetics assumes that all art is *somehow* conditioned by the relations of production, class position, and so on. Its first task (but only its first) is the specific analysis of this "somehow," that is to say, of the limits and modes of this conditioning. The question as to whether there are qualities of art which transcend specific social conditions and how these qualities are related to the particular social conditions remains open. Marxist aesthetics has yet to ask: What are the qualities of art which transcend the specific social content and form and give art its universality? Marxist aesthetics must explain why Greek tragedy and the medieval epic, for example, can still be experienced today as "great," "authentic" literature, even though they pertain to ancient slave society and feudalism respectively. Marx's remark at the end of *The Introduction to the Critique of Political Economy* is hardly persuasive; one simply cannot explain the attraction of Greek art for us today as our rejoicing in the unfolding of the social "childhood of humanity."

However correctly one has analyzed a poem, play, or novel in terms of its social content, the questions as to whether the particular work is good, beautiful, and true are still unanswered. But the answers to these questions cannot again be given in terms of the specific relations of production which constitute the historical context of the respective work. The circularity of this method is obvious. In addition it falls victim to an easy relativism which is contradicted clearly enough by the permanence of certain qualities of art through all changes of style and historical periods (transcendence, estrangement, aesthetic order, manifestations of the beautiful).

The fact that a work truly represents the interests or the outlook of the proletariat or of the bourgeoisie does not yet make it an authentic work of art. This "material" quality may facilitate its reception, may lend it greater concreteness, but it is in no way constitutive. The universality of art cannot be grounded in the world and world outlook of a particular class, for art envisions a concrete universal, humanity (*Menschlichkeit*), which no particular class can incorporate, not even the proletariat, Marx's "universal class." The inexorable entanglement of joy and sorrow, celebration and despair, Eros and Thanatos cannot be dissolved into problems of class struggle. History is also grounded in nature. And Marxist theory has the least justification to ignore the metabolism between the human being and nature, and to denounce the insistence on this natural soil of society as a regressive ideological conception.

The emergence of human beings as "species beings" – men and women capable of living in that community of freedom which is the potential of the species – this is the subjective basis of a classless society. Its realization presupposes a radical transformation of the drives and needs of the individuals: an organic development within the socio-historical. Solidarity would be on weak grounds were it not rooted in the instinctual structure of individuals. In this dimension, men and women are confronted with psycho-physical forces which they have to make their own without being able to overcome the naturalness of these forces. This is the domain of the primary drives: of libidinal and destructive energy. Solidarity and community have their basis in the subordination of destructive and aggressive energy to the social emancipation of the life instincts.

Marxism has too long neglected the radical political potential of this dimension, though the revolutionizing of the instinctual structure is a prerequisite for a change in the system of needs, the mark of a socialist society as qualitative difference. Class society knows only the appearance, the image of the qualitative difference; this image, divorced from praxis, has been preserved in the realm of art. In the aesthetic form, the autonomy

of art constitutes itself. It was forced upon art through the separation of mental and material labor, as a result of the prevailing relations of domination. Dissociation from the process of production became a refuge and a vantage point from which to denounce the reality established through domination.

Nevertheless society remains present in the autonomous realm of art in several ways: first of all as the "stuff" for the aesthetic representation which, past and present, is transformed in this representation. This is the historicity of the conceptual, linguistic, and imaginable material which the tradition transmits to the artists and with or against which they have to work; secondly, as the scope of the actually available possibilities of struggle and liberation; thirdly as the specific position of art in the social division of labor, especially in the separation of intellectual and manual labor through which artistic activity, and to a great extent also its reception, become the privilege of an "elite" removed from the material process of production.

The class character of art consists only in these objective limitations of its autonomy. The fact that the artist belongs to a privileged group negates neither the truth nor the aesthetic quality of his work. What is true of "the classics of socialism" is true also of the great artists: they break through the class limitations of their family, background, environment. Marxist theory is not family research. The progressive character of art, its contribution to the struggle for liberation cannot be measured by the artists' origins nor by the ideological horizon of their class. Neither can it be determined by the presence (or absence) of the oppressed class in their works. The criteria for the progressive character of art are given only in the work itself as a whole: in what it says and how it says it.

In this sense art is "art for art's sake" inasmuch as the aesthetic form reveals tabooed and repressed dimensions of reality: aspects of liberation. The poetry of Mallarmé is an extreme example; his poems conjure up modes of perception, imagination, gestures – a feast of sensuousness which shatters everyday experience and anticipates a different reality principle.

The degree to which the distance and estrangement from praxis constitute the emancipatory value of art becomes particularly clear in those works of literature which seem to close themselves rigidly against such praxis. Walter Benjamin has traced this in the works of Poe, Baudelaire, Proust, and Valéry. They express a "consciousness of crisis" (*Krisenbewusstsein*): a pleasure in decay, in destruction, in the beauty of evil; a celebration of the asocial, of the anomic – the secret rebellion of the bourgeois against his own class. Benjamin writes about Baudelaire:

> It seems of little value to give his work a position on the most advanced ramparts of the human struggle for liberation. From the beginning, it appears much more promising to follow him in his machinations where he is without doubt at home: in the enemy camp. These machinations are a blessing for the enemy only in the rarest cases. Baudelaire was a secret agent, an agent of the secret discontent of his class with its own rule. One who confronts Baudelaire with this class gets more out of him than one who rejects him as uninteresting from a proletarian standpoint.[12]

The "secret" protest of this esoteric literature lies in the ingression of the primary erotic-destructive forces which explode the normal universe of communication and behavior. They are asocial in their very nature, a subterranean rebellion against the social order. Inasmuch as this literature reveals the dominion of Eros and Thanatos beyond all social control, it invokes needs and gratifications which are essentially destructive. In terms of political praxis, this literature remains elitist and decadent. It does nothing in the struggle for liberation – except to open the tabooed zones of nature and society in which even death and the devil are enlisted as allies in the refusal to abide by the law and order of repression. This literature is one of the historical forms of critical aesthetic transcendence. Art cannot abolish the social division of labor which makes for its esoteric character, but neither can art "popularize" itself without weakening its emancipatory impact.

Notes

1 Especially among the authors of the periodicals *Kursbuch* (Frankfurt: Suhrkamp, later Rotbuch Verlag), *Argument* (Berlin), *Literaturmagazin* (Reinbek: Rowohlt). In the center of this discussion is the idea of an autonomous art in confrontation with the capitalist art industry on the one hand, and the radical propaganda art on the other. See especially the excellent articles by Nicolas Born, H. C. Buch, Wolfgang Harich, Hermann Peter Piwitt, and Michael Schneider in volumes I and II of the *Literaturmagazin*, the volume *Autonomie der Kunst* (Frankfurt: Suhrkamp, 1972) and Peter Bürger, *Theorie der Avant-garde* (Frankfurt: Suhrkamp, 1974).

2 See Erich Köhler, *Ideal und Wirklichkeit in der Höfischen Epik* (Tübingen: Niemeyer, 1956; second edition 1970), especially chapter V, for a discussion of this in relation to the courtly epic.

3 See my *Counterrevolution and Revolt* (Boston: Beacon Press, 1972), p. 81.

4 Ernst Fischer in *Auf den Spuren der Wirklichkeit; sechs Essays* (Reinbek: Rowohlt, 1968) recognizes in the "will to form" (*Wille zur Gestalt*) the will to transcend the actual: negation of that which is, and presentiment (*Ahnung*) of a freer and purer existence. In this sense, art is the "irreconcilable, the resistance of the human being to its vanishing in the [established] order and systems" (p. 67).

5 "Two antagonistic attitudes toward the powers that be are prevalent in literature: *resistance* and *submission*. Literature is certainly not mere ideology and does not merely express a social consciousness that invokes the illusion of harmony, assuring the individuals that everything is as it ought to be, and that nobody has the right to expect fate to give him more than he receives. To be sure, literature has time and again justified established social relationships; nevertheless, it has always kept alive that human yearning which cannot find gratification in the existing society. Grief and sorrow are essential elements of bourgeois literature" (Leo Lowenthal, *Das Bild des Menschen in der Literatur* [Neuwied: Luchterhand, 1966] pp. 14f.). (Published in English as *Literature and the Image of Man* [Boston: Beacon Press 1957].)

6 See my essay "The Affirmative Character of Culture" in *Negations* (Boston: Beacon Press, 1968).

7 In his book *Marxistische Ideologie und allgemeine Kunsttheorie* (Tübingen: Mohr, 1970), Hans-Dietrich Sander presents a thorough analysis of Marx's and Engels' contribution to a theory of art. The provocative conclusion: most of Marxist aesthetics is not only a gross vulgarization – Marx's and Engels' views are also turned into their opposite! He writes: Marx and Engels saw "the essence of a work of art precisely not in its political or social relevance" (p. 174). They are closer to Kant, Fichte, and Schelling than to Hegel (p. 171). Sander's documentation for this thesis may well be too selective and minimize statements by Marx and Engels which contradict Sander's interpretation. However, his analysis does show

clearly the difficulty of Marxist aesthetics in coming to grips with the problems of the theory of art.

8   Bertolt Brecht, "Volkstümlichkeit und Realismus," in *Gesammelte Werke* (Frankfurt: Suhrkamp, 1967), volume VIII, p. 323.

9   Georg Lukács, "Es geht um den Realismus," in *Marxismus und Literatur*, edited by Fritz J. Raddatz (Reinbek: Rowohlt, 1969), volume II, p. 77.

10   In *Die Linkskurve* III, 5 (Berlin: May 1931, reprinted 1970), p. 17.

11   *Colloque international sur la sociologie de la littérature* (Bruxelles: Institut de la Sociologie, 1974), p. 40.

12   Walter Benjamin, "Fragment über Methodenfrage einer Marxistischen Literatur-Analyse," in *Kursbuch* 20 (Frankfurt: Suhrkamp, 1970), p. 3.

14

Aesthetic Theory

Theodor Adorno

Art, Society, Aesthetics

1 Loss of certainty

Today it goes without saying that nothing concerning art goes without saying, much less without thinking. Everything about art has become problematic: its inner life, its relation to society, even its right to exist. One would have thought that the loss of an intuitive and naive approach to art would be offset by a tendency to increased reflection which seizes upon the chance to fill the void of infinite possibilities. This has not happened. What looked at first like an expansion of art turned out to be its contraction. The great expanse of the unforeseen which revolutionary artistic movements began to explore around 1910 did not live up to the promise of happiness and adventure it had held out. What has happened instead is that the process begun at that time came to corrode the very same categories which were its own reason for being. An ever-increasing number of things artistic were drawn into an eddy of new taboos, and rather than enjoy their newly won freedom, artists everywhere were quick to look for some presumed foundation for what they were doing. This flight into a new order, however flimsy, is a reflection of the fact that absolute freedom in art – which is a particular – contradicts the abiding unfreedom of the social whole. That is why the place and function of art in society have become uncertain. To put it another way, the autonomy art gained after having freed itself from its earlier cult function and its derivatives

depended on the idea of humanity. As society grew less humane, art became less autonomous. Those constituent elements of art that were suffused with the ideal of humanity have lost their force.

All the same, autonomy is an irrevocable aspect of art. There is no point in trying to allay the self-doubts of art – doubts, incidentally, which find expression in art itself – by restoring to her a social role. Such attempts are in vain. Today, however, autonomous art shows signs of being blind. A trait of art from time immemorial, blindness in the age of emancipation has become the dominant characteristic despite, and because of, the fact that, as Hegel realized, art can no longer afford to be naive art. Nowadays artistic sophistication amalgamates itself with a *naïveté* of a different and stronger kind, which is the uncertainty about the purpose of art and the conditions for its continued existence. Did art not lose its foundation when it gained complete freedom from external purposes? Questions like this touch on the intrinsically historical nature of aesthetics.

Works of art, it is said, leave the real empirical world behind, producing a counter-realm of their own, a realm which is an existent like the empirical world. This claim is false; it implies an *a priori* affirmation of that which is, no matter how 'tragic' the content of the work of art may be. Those clichés about art casting a glow of happiness and harmony over an unhappy and divided real world are loathsome because they make a mockery of any emphatic concept of art by looking only at perverse bourgeois practices such as the employment of art as a dispenser of solace. These clichés also point to the wound of art itself. Having dissociated itself from religion and its redemptive truths, art was able to flourish. Once secularized, however, art was condemned, for lack of any hope for a real alternative, to offer to the existing world a kind of solace that reinforced the fetters autonomous art had wanted to shake off. There is a sense in which the principle of autonomy is itself solace of this kind, for in claiming to be able to posit a well-rounded totality entirely on its own, the principle of artistic autonomy willy-nilly creates the false impression that the world outside is such a rounded whole, too. By rejecting reality – and this is not a form of escapism but an inherent quality of art – art vindicates reality.

Helmut Kuhn's thesis[1] that every work of art is a paean would be true if it were critical in spirit, which it is not. Given the abnormities of real life today, the affirmative essence of art, while an integral part of art, has become insufferable. True art challenges its own essence, thereby heightening the sense of uncertainty that dwells in the artist.

It would be wrong, too, to try to dispose of art through abstract negation. Art undergoes qualitative change when it attacks its traditional foundations. Thus art becomes a qualitatively different entity by virtue of its opposition, at the level of artistic form, to the existing world and also by virtue of its readiness to aid and shape that world. Neither the concept of solace nor its opposite, refusal, captures the meaning of art.

2 Origins – a false question

The concept of art balks at being defined, for it is a historically changing constellation of moments. Nor can the nature of art be ascertained by going back to the origin of art in order to find some fundamental and primary layer that supports everything else. The late romantics believed in the supremacy and purity of archaic art. This view is no more persuasive than the opposite argument, put forth by classicists, that the earliest works of art are impure and muddy, inasmuch as they were inseparable from magic, from historical records and from practical aims, like wanting to communicate over long distances by means of calling and blowing sounds. There is no way of deciding the issue because historical facts are hard to come by.

Similarly, any attempt to subsume the historical genesis of art ontologically under some supreme principle would necessarily get lost in a mass of detail. The only theoretically relevant insight that might be obtained is the negative one that, for the plurality of what are called 'the arts', there does not even seem to exist a universal concept of art able to accommodate them all.[2] Studies devoted to prehistoric art tend to present raw empirical material side by side with wild speculation. Johann Jakob Bachofen is the best-known example here.

Philosophers are used to distinguishing conceptually between two types of problems of origin, one belonging to metaphysics, the other to primal history. Upholding this distinction too rigidly leads however to a distortion of the literal meaning of the concept of origin.[3] The definition of art does indeed depend on what art once was, but it must also take into account what has become of art and what might possibly become of it in the future. Art, we said, is different from empirical reality. Now this difference itself does not stay the same; it changes because art changes. History, for example, has transformed certain cult objects into art long after they were first produced. Or, to give another example, at a certain moment in time particular art objects have ceased to be viewed as art. In this connection, the abstractly posed question of whether a phenomenon like the film is art or something else is instructive, although it leads nowhere. As we saw, art has a changing scope and it may be just as well not to try to define sharply what's inside and what's outside of it.

What are called questions of aesthetic constitution are demarcated by the tension between the motive force of art and art as past history. It is through its dynamic laws, not through some invariable principle, that art can be understood. It is defined by its relation to what is different from art. This other makes it possible for us to arrive at a substantive understanding of the specifically artistic in art. It is this approach to art that alone meets the criteria of a materialist and dialectical aesthetic, which evolves by segregating itself from its own matrix. Its law of motion and its law of form are one and the same.

Central to contemporary aesthetics is the assumption that even a product of historical becoming may be true. It was Nietzsche who developed this notion in reference to traditional philosophy. Rephrasing and putting a point to Nietzsche's insight, I think truth exists only as a product of historical becoming. As far as art is concerned, this is true throughout: works of art became what they are by negating their origin. It was only fairly recently, namely after art had become thoroughly secular and subject to a process of technological evolution and after secularization had firmly taken hold, that art acquired another important feature: an inner logic of development. Art should not be blamed for its one-time ignominious relation to magical abracadabra, human servitude and entertainment, for it has after all annihilated these dependencies along with the memory of its fall from grace. Moreover, it is an over-simplification to think that dinner music, for example, could never achieve the heights of autonomous music just because it was dinner music. Conversely, it is also fallacious to argue that dinner music, because it represented a service to mankind, has the edge on autonomous music with its haughty refusal to be serviceable to anything or to anybody. Let us remember, too, that the greatest part of what passes for musical art today is an echo of the contemptuous clatter of dinner music. Unfortunately, this fact does nothing to make the quality of early eighteenth-century dinner music any better.

3 Truth, life and death of art

The Hegelian notion of a possible withering away of art is consistent with the historical essence of art as a product of becoming. This seemingly paradoxical fact, that Hegel conceived of art as something mortal while at the same time treating it as a moment of absolute spirit, is fully in line with the dual character of his system. His view however implies a conclusion he would never have drawn himself, namely that the content of art – its absolute aspect, according to Hegel – is not identical with the dimension of life and death. It is conceivable that that content might precisely be art's mortality. Music is a case in point. A latecomer among the arts, great music may well turn out to be an art form that was possible only during a limited period of human history. The revolt of art which programmatically defined itself in terms of a new stance towards the objective, historical world has become a revolt against art. Whether art will survive these developments is anybody's guess. Nobody however should ignore the fact that for once reactionary cultural pessimism and a critical theory of culture see eye to eye on the following proposition: art may, as Hegel speculated it would, soon enter the age of its demise. A century ago Rimbaud's dictum intuitively anticipated the history of modern art; later

his silence and his being co-opted on becoming an employee anticipated the decline of art.

Aesthetics today is powerless to avert its becoming a necrologue of art. What it can and must avoid is making graveside speeches, soothsaying the end of everything, savouring past achievements and jumping on the bandwagon of barbarism – which barbarism is no better and no worse than the culture that rallies to its side, with the two fully deserving each other. Assuming art is abolished, abolishes itself, vanishes or barely hangs on to a precarious existence – all this does not mean that the content of past art will necessarily go down the drain, too. Art could well be survived by its past content in a new and different society, rid of its barbarous culture.

What [have] already died are not only aesthetic forms but also many substantive motifs. To mention only one example, the literature about adultery, which had its efflorescence during the Victorian period and into the early twentieth century, is difficult to appreciate today, what with the dissolution of the bourgeois nuclear family and the loosening up of monogamy. A popular version of that kind of literature today has found a new but miserable home: illustrated magazines. The authentic element in *Madame Bovary*, at one time an integral part of the subject matter of the novel, has long since outlived both that content and its demise – a statement that is not at all meant to lure anybody into the optimistic belief in the invincibility of the spirit. There are of course many instances where the death of the content of a work of art has in fact entailed the perdition of the higher authentic moment as well. What makes art and its products mortal – and this includes heteronomous and autonomous art, with the latter vindicating the social division of labour and the special position held therein by the intellect – what makes art mortal is the fact that it is not only art but something other than, and opposed to, art. Admixed to the concept of art is the germ that will dialectically supersede art.

4 On the relation between art and society

Aesthetic refraction is as incomplete without the refracted object as imagination is without the imagined object. This has special significance for the problem of the inherent functionality of art. Tied to the real world, art adopts the principle of self-preservation of that world, turning it into the ideal of self-identical art, the essence of which Schönberg once summed up in the statement that the painter paints a picture rather than what it represents. Implied here is the idea that every work of art spontaneously aims at being identical with itself, just as in the world outside a fake identity is everywhere forcibly imposed on objects by the insatiable subject. Aesthetic identity is different, however, in one important respect: it is meant to assist the non-identical in its struggle against the repressive identification compulsion that rules the outside world. It is by virtue of its separation from empirical reality that the work of art can become a being of a higher order, fashioning the relation between the whole and its parts in accordance with its own needs. Works of art are after-images or replicas of empirical life, inasmuch as they proffer to the latter what in the outside world is being denied them. In the process they slough off a repressive, external–empirical mode of experiencing the world. Whereas the line separating art from real life should not be fudged, least of all by glorifying the artist, it must be kept in mind that works of art are alive, have a life *sui generis*. Their life is more than just an outward fate. Over time, great works reveal new faces of themselves, they age, they become rigid, and they die. Being human artefacts, they do not 'live' in the same sense as human beings. Of course not. To put the accent on the artefactual aspect in works of art seems to imply that the way in which they came to be is important. It is not. The emphasis must be on their inner constitution. They have life because they speak in ways nature and man cannot. They talk because there is communication between their individual constituents, which cannot be said of things that exist in a state of mere diffusion.

As artefacts, works of art communicate not only internally but also with the external reality which they try to get away from and which none the less is the substratum of their content. Art negates the conceptualization foisted on the real world and yet harbours in its own substance elements of the empirically existent. Assuming that one has to differentiate form and content before grasping their mediation, we can say that art's opposition to the real world is in the realm of form; but this occurs, generally speaking, in a mediated way such that aesthetic form is a sedimentation of content. What seem like pure forms in art, namely those of traditional music, do in all respects, and all the way down to details of musical idiom, derive from external content such as dance. Similarly, ornaments in the visual arts originally tended to be cult symbols. Members of the Warburg Institute were following this lead, studying the derivability of aesthetic forms from contents in the context of classical antiquity and its influence on later periods. This kind of work needs to be undertaken on a larger scale.

The manner in which art communicates with the outside world is in fact also a lack of communication, because art seeks, blissfully or unhappily, to seclude itself from the world. This non-communication points to the fractured nature of art. It is natural to think that art's autonomous domain has no more in common with the outside world than a few borrowed elements undergoing radical change in the context of art. But there is more to it than that. There is some truth to the historical cliché which states that the developments of artistic methods, usually lumped together under the term 'style', correspond to social development. Even the most sublime work of art takes up a definite position *vis-à-vis* reality by stepping outside of reality's spell, not abstractly once and for all, but occasionally and in concrete ways, when it unconsciously and tacitly polemicizes against the condition of society at a particular point in time.

How can works of art be like windowless monads, representing something which is other than they? There is only one way to explain this, which is to view them as being subject to a dynamic or immanent historicity and a dialectical tension between nature and domination of nature, a dialectic that seems to be of the same kind as the dialectic of society. Or to put it more cautiously, the dialectic of art resembles the social dialectic without consciously imitating it. The productive force of useful labour and that of art are the same. They both have the same teleology. And what might be termed aesthetic relations of production – defined as everything that provides an outlet for the productive forces of art or everything in which these forces become embedded – are sedimentations of social relations of production bearing the imprint of the latter. Thus in all dimensions of its productive process art has a twofold essence, being both an autonomous entity and a social fact in the Durkheimian sense of the term.

It is through this relationship to the empirical that works of art salvage, albeit in neutralized fashion, something that once upon a time was literally a shared experience of all mankind and which enlightenment has since expelled. Art, too, partakes of enlightenment, but in a different way: works of art do not lie; what they say is literally true. Their reality however lies in the fact that they are answers to questions brought before them from outside. The tension in art therefore has meaning only in relation to the tension outside. The fundamental layers of artistic experience are akin to the objective world from which art recoils.

The unresolved antagonisms of reality reappear in art in the guise of immanent problems of artistic form. This, and not the deliberate injection of objective moments or social content, defines art's relation to society. The aesthetic tensions manifesting themselves in works of art express the essence of reality in and through their emancipation from the factual façade of exteriority. Art's simultaneous dissociation from and secret connection with empirical being confirms the strength of Hegel's analysis of the nature of a conceptual barrier (*Schranke*): the intellect, argues Hegel against Kant, no sooner posits a barrier than it has to go beyond it, absorbing into itself that against which the barrier was set up.[4] We have here, among other things, a basis for a non-moralistic critique of the idea of *l'art pour l'art* with its abstract negation of the empirical and with its monomaniac separatism in aesthetic theory.

Freedom, the presupposition of art and the self-glorifying conception art has of itself, is the cunning of art's reason. Blissfully soaring above the real world, art is still chained by each of its elements to the empirical other, into which it may even sink back altogether at every instant. In their relation to empirical reality works of art recall the theologumenon that in a state of redemption everything will be just as it is and yet wholly different. There is an unmistakable similarity in all this with the development of the profane. The profane secularizes the sacred realm to the point where the latter is the only secular thing left. The sacred realm is thus objectified, staked out as it were, because its moment of untruth awaits secularization as much as it tries to avert it through incantation.

It follows that art is not defined once and for all by the scope of an immutable concept. Rather, the concept of art is a fragile balance attained now and then, quite similar to the psychological equilibrium between id and ego. Disturbances continually upset the balance, keeping the process in motion. Every work of art is an instant; every great work of art is a stoppage of the process, a momentary standing still, whereas a persistent eye sees only the process. While it is true that works of art provide answers to their own questions, it is

equally true that in so doing they become questions for themselves. Take a look at the widespread inclination (which to this day has not been mitigated by education) to perceive art in terms of extra-aesthetic or pre-aesthetic criteria. This tendency is, on the one hand, a mark of atrocious backwardness or of the regressive consciousness of many people. On the other hand, there is no denying that that tendency is promoted by something in art itself. If art is perceived strictly in aesthetic terms, then it cannot be properly perceived in aesthetic terms. The artist must feel the presence of the empirical other in the foreground of his own experience in order to be able to sublimate that experience, thus freeing himself from his confinement to content while at the same time saving the being-for-itself of art from slipping into outright indifference toward the world.

Art is and is not being-for-itself. Without a heterogeneous moment, art cannot achieve autonomy. Great epics that survive their own oblivion were originally shot through with historical and geographical reporting. Valéry, for one, was aware of the degree to which the Homeric, pagan-germanic and Christian epics contained raw materials that had never been melted down and recast by the laws of form, noting that this did not diminish their rank in comparison with 'pure' works of art. Similarly, tragedy, the likely origin of the abstract idea of aesthetic autonomy, was also an after-image of pragmatically oriented cult acts. At no point in its history of progressive emancipation was art able to stamp out that moment. And the reason is not that the bonds were simply too strong. Long before socialist realism rationally planned its debasement, the realistic novel, which was at its height as a literary form in the nineteenth century, bears the marks of reportage, anticipating what was later to become the task of social science surveys. Conversely, the fanatic thoroughness of linguistic integration that characterizes *Madame Bovary*, for instance, is probably the result of the contrary moment. The continued relevance of this work is due to the unity of both.

In art, the criterion of success is twofold: first, works of art must be able to integrate materials and details into their immanent law of form; and, second, they must not try to erase the fractures left by the process of integration, preserving instead in the aesthetic whole the traces of those elements which resisted integration. Integration as such does not guarantee quality. There is no privileged single category, not even the aesthetically central one of form, that defines the essence of art and suffices to judge its product. In short, art has defining characteristics that go against the grain of what philosophy of art ordinarily conceives as art. Hegel is the exception. His aesthetics of content recognized the moment of otherness inherent in art, thus superseding the old aesthetic of form. The latter seems to be operating with too pure a concept of art, even though it has at least one advantage, which is that it does not, unlike Hegel's (and Kierkegaard's) substantive aesthetics, place obstacles in the way of certain historical developments such as abstract painting. This is one weakness of Hegel's aesthetic. The other is that, by conceiving form in terms of content, Hegel's theory of art regresses to a position that can only be called 'pre-aesthetic' and crude. Hegel mistakes the replicatory (*abbildende*) or discursive treatment of content for the kind of otherness that is constitutive of art. He sins, as it were, against his own dialectical concept of aesthetics, with results that he could not foresee. He in effect helped prepare the way for the banausic tendency to transform art into an ideology of repression.

The moment of unreality and non–existence in art is not independent of the existent, as though it were posited or invented by some arbitrary will. Rather, that moment of unreality is a structure resulting from quantitative relations between elements of being, relations which are in turn a response to, and an echo of, the imperfections of real conditions, their constraints, their contradictions, and their potentialities. Art is related to its other like a magnet to a field of iron filings. The elements of art as well as their constellation, or what is commonly thought to be the spiritual essence of art, point back to the real other. The identity of the works of art with existent reality also accounts for the centripetal force that enables them to gather unto themselves the traces and *membra disiecta*[5] of real life. Their affinity with the world lies in a principle that is conceived to be a contrast to that world but is in fact no different from the principle whereby spirit has dominated the world. Synthesis is not some process of imposing order on the elements of a work of art. It is important, rather, that the elements interact with each other; hence there is a sense in which synthesis is a mere repetition of the pre-established interdependence among elements, which interdependence is a product of otherness, of non–art. Synthesis, therefore, is firmly grounded in the material aspects of works of art.

There is a link between the aesthetic moment of form and non-violence. In its difference from the existent, art of necessity constitutes itself in terms of that which is not a work of art yet is indispensable for its being. The emphasis on non-intentionality in art, noticeable first in the sympathy for popular art in Apollinaire, early Cubism and Wedekind (who derided what he called 'art-artists'), indicates that art became aware, however dimly, that it interacted with its opposite. This new self-conception of art gave rise to a critical turn signalling an end to the illusory equation of art with pure spirituality.

5 Critique of the psychoanalytic theory of art

Art is the social antithesis of society. The constitution of the domain of art resembles the constitution of an inner space of ideas in the individual. Both areas intersect in the concept of sublimation. Hence it is natural and promising to attempt to conceptualize art in terms of some theory of psychic life.

A comparison between an anthropological theory of human constants and a psychoanalytic one would seem to favour the latter. But caution is in order: psychoanalysis is better suited to explain purely psychic phenomena than aesthetic ones. According to psychoanalytic theory, works of art are essentially projections of the unconscious. Psychoanalysis thus puts the emphasis on the individual producer of art and the interpretation of aesthetic content as psychic content, to the detriment of the categories of form. What psychoanalysis does when it turns to the analysis of art is to transfer the banausic sensitivity of the therapist to such unlikely objects as Leonardo and Baudelaire. It is important to debunk such studies, which are frequently offshoots of the biographical genre, in no uncertain terms; for despite their stress on sex they are hopelessly philistine in conception, dismissing as neurotics men of art who in fact merely objectified in their work the negativity of life. The book by Laforgue, for instance, seriously accuses Baudelaire of having suffered from a mother complex.[6] The author does not even touch on the problem of whether Baudelaire could have written the *Fleurs du mal* had he been healthy, let alone whether, because of the neurosis, the poems turned out worse than they might otherwise have been. Psychic normalcy is raised to a criterion of judgment even in the case of someone like Baudelaire, whose greatness was so unequivocally tied up with the absence of a *mens sana*. The tenor of psychoanalytic monographs on artists conveys the sense of an implicit ought: that art should deal affirmatively with the negativity of experience. To the psychoanalytic authors, the negative moment is just a mark of the process of repression finding its way into the work of art.

From the point of view of psychoanalysis, art is day-dreaming. It is a view that, on the one hand, mistakes works of art for documents, lodged in the dreaming person's head. On the other hand, as a kind of trade-off for having first excised the extra-mental sphere, it reduces art to content, in strange opposition incidentally to Freud, who after all had already emphasized the importance of dream *work*. With their assumption of an analogy between dreaming and artistic creation, psychoanalysts, like all positivists, vastly overrate the moment of fiction in art. The projection that occurs in the creative process is not at all the decisive moment in works of art; equally important are idiom, material and, above all, the product itself, the latter being virtually ignored by psychoanalysts. For example, the psychoanalytic thesis that music is a defence mechanism against impending paranoia, while it may well be clinically correct, is useless for an appreciation of the quality and substance of a single musical composition.

Compared with the idealist theory of art, the psychoanalytic one has the advantage of bringing to light those elements in art that are not art-like. In so doing, psychoanalysis helps to free art from its enthralment to absolute spirit. Its opposition against vulgar idealism, which gives to art a sanctuary in some allegedly higher sphere and avidly protects it against all insights into its own essence and above all into the connection it has with instinct – this opposition is part of the spirit of enlightenment. To the extent to which psychoanalysis decodes the social character of a work and its author, it is able to furnish concrete, mediating links between the structure of works of art and that of society. On the other hand, psychoanalysis, not unlike idealism, is spreading its own kind of enthralment by reducing art to an absolutely subjective system of signs denoting drive states of the subject. Given this tendency, psychoanalysis is able to decipher phenomena but not the phenomenon of art itself. To psychoanalysis works of art are factual. It neglects to consider their real objectivity, their inner consistency, the level of form, their critical impulses, their relation to non-psychic reality and, last but not least, their truth content.

A woman painter, in the spirit of sincerity that governs a pact between analyst and patient, once complained in the doctor's office that she was appalled at the poor quality of the engravings he had hung up to decorate his walls, whereupon he explained to her that she was merely showing her aggression . . . Works of art are much less replicas and properties of the artist than a physician likes to think who knows artists only as persons lying on a couch. Only a dilettante will even try to reduce everything about art to the unconscious, reiterating one hackneyed psychoanalytic cliché after another. In the process of artistic production, unconscious drives are one impetus among many. They become integrated with the work of art through the law of form. The real human being who created the work is no more a part of that work than a real horse is a part of a painted one.

Works of art are not some kind of thematic apperception tests, either. In so far as psychoanalysis implies that they are, it reveals another seamy side of its anti-aestheticism. Part of the blame for this ignorance of what art is all about lies, incidentally, in the pre-eminence psychoanalysis gives to the reality principle. Adaptation to reality has the status of a *summum bonum*, whereas any deviation from the reality principle is immediately branded as an escape. The experience of reality is such that it provides all kinds of legitimate grounds for wanting to escape. This exposes the harmonistic ideology behind the psychoanalytic indignation about people's escape mechanisms. Even at the level of psychology, the need for art can be given a better justification than it has so far got from psychoanalysis. It is true, there is an element of escape in imagination, but the two are not synonymous.

Art transcends the reality principle in the direction both of something higher and of something even more mundane. There is no reason to point a taunting finger at that. The image of the artist as a neurotic, tolerated by and integrated into the social division of labour, is a distortion. In artists of the highest calibre like Beethoven and Rembrandt, the keenest awareness of reality was joined to an equally acute sense of alienation from reality. It is phenomena like this which would be truly appropriate subjects for a psychology of art. Its task would be to decode the work of art as something that is identical with the artist and yet different from him, inasmuch as it represents labour spent upon a resistant other. And if art has one psychoanalytically relevant root, it has got to be that of omnipotence fantasy. But again, what shines forth in these fantasies beneath the raw psychological need for power is the desire to bring about a better world. This sets free the entire dialectic of art and society. By contrast, the psychological view of the art work in terms of a purely subjective language of the unconscious does not even come close to a dialectical understanding.

6 Kant and Freud on art

Freud's theory of art as wish-fulfilment has its antithesis in the theory of Kant. Kant states at the start of the 'Analytic of the Beautiful' that the first moment of a judgment of taste is disinterested satisfaction,[7] where interest is defined as 'the satisfaction which we combine with the representation of the existence of an object'.[8] Right away there is an ambiguity. It is impossible to tell whether Kant means, by representation of the existence of an object, the empirical object dealt with in a work of art, in other words its subject matter or content, or whether he means the work of art itself. Is he referring to the pretty nude model or to the sweetly pleasing sound of a piece of music (which, incidentally, can be pure artistic trash or an integral part of artistic quality)? Kant's stress on representation flows directly from his subjectivist approach, which locates the aesthetic quality in the effect a work of art has upon the viewer. This is in accord with the rationalist tradition, notably Moses Mendelssohn. While staying in the old tradition of an aesthetic that emphasizes effect (*Wirkungsaesthetik*), the *Critique of Judgment* is none the less a radical immanent critique of then contemporary rationalist aesthetics. Let us remember that the significance of Kantian subjectivism as a whole lies in its objective intention, its attempt to salvage objectivity by means of an analysis of subjective moments.

It is through the concept of disinterestedness that Kant breaks up the supremacy of pleasure in aesthetics. Satisfaction is meant to preserve effect but disinterestedness draws away from it. Bereft of what Kant calls interest, satisfaction and pleasure become wholly indeterminate, losing the capacity to define the beautiful. All the same, the doctrine of disinterested satisfaction is impoverished in view of the richness of aesthetic phenomena. It reduces them either to the formally beautiful – a questionable entity when viewed in isolation – or in the case of natural objects to the sublime. The reduction of art to absolute form misses the point about the why and wherefore of art. Kant's murky

footnote,[9] which says that a judgment about an object of satisfaction is disinterested, i.e. not based on interest, even though it may be 'interesting', i.e. capable of evoking an interest, testifies honestly, if indirectly, to the fact that he was aware of a difficulty. Kant separates aesthetic feeling – and therefore, according to his own understanding, virtually the whole of art – from the faculty of desire at which the 'representation of the existence of an object' is aimed. Or, as he puts it, satisfaction in such a representation 'always has reference to the faculty of desire'.[10] Kant was the first to have gained an insight that was never to be forgotten since: namely, that aesthetic conduct is free of immediate desire. Thus he rescued art from the greedy clutches of a kind of insensitivity that forever wants to touch and savour it.

Comparing Kant and Freud, it is interesting to note that the Kantian motif is not entirely foreign to the Freudian theory. Even for Freud, works of art, far from being direct wish-fulfilment, transform repressed libido into socially productive accomplishments. What is, of course, uncritically presupposed in this theory is the social value of art, whose quality as art simply rests on public reputation. By putting the difference between art, on the one hand, and the faculty of desire and empirical reality, on the other, into much sharper relief than Freud, Kant does more than simply idealize art. Isolating the aesthetic from the empirical sphere, he constitutes art. He then, however, proceeds to arrest this process of constitution in the framework of his transcendental philosophy, simplistically equating constitution with the essence of art and ignoring the fact that the subjective instinctual components of art crop up, in different form, even in the most mature manifestations of art.

In his theory of sublimation, on the other hand, Freud was more clearly aware of the dynamic nature of art. The price he paid was no smaller than Kant's. For Freud, the spiritual essence of art remains hidden. For Kant, it does emerge from the distinctions between aesthetic, practical and appetitive behaviour, Kant's preference for sensuous intuition notwithstanding. In the Freudian view works of art, although products of sublimation, are little more than plenipotentiaries of sensuous impulses made unrecognizable to some degree by a kind of dream-work.

A comparison between two thinkers as different as Kant and Freud – Kant, for example, not only rejected philosophical psychologism but with age also became hostile to psychology as such – is justified by the presence of a common denominator that outweighs the differences between the Kantian construction of the transcendental subject and the Freudian focus on the empirical subject. Where they differ is in their positive and negative approaches, respectively, to the faculty of desire. What they have in common, however, is the underlying subjective orientation. For both, the work of art exists only in relation to the individual who contemplates or produces it. There is a mechanism in Kant's thought that forces him, both in moral and in aesthetic philosophy, to consider the ontic, empirical individual to a larger extent than seems warranted by the notion of the transcendental subject. In aesthetics this implies that there can be no pleasure without a living being to whom an object is pleasing. Without explicit recognition, Kant devotes the entire *Critique of Judgment* to an analysis of *constituta*. Therefore, despite the programmatic idea of building a bridge between theoretical and practical pure reason, the faculty of judgment turns out to be *sui generis* in relation to both forms of reason.

Perhaps the most important taboo in art is the one that prohibits an animal-like attitude toward the object, say, a desire to devour it or otherwise to subjugate it to one's body. Now, the strength of such a taboo is matched by the strength of the repressed urge. Hence, all art contains in itself a negative moment from which it tries to get away. If Kant's disinterestedness is to be more than a synonym for indifference, it has to have a trace of untamed interest somewhere. Indeed, there is much to be said for the thesis that the dignity of works of art depends on the magnitude of the interest from which they were wrested. Kant denies this in order to protect his concept of freedom from spurious heteronomies that he saw lurking everywhere. In this regard, his theory of art is tainted by an insufficiency of his theory of practical reason. In the context of Kant's philosophy, the idea of a beautiful object possessing a kind of independence from the sovereign ego must seem like a digression into intelligible worlds. The source from which art antithetically originates, as well as the content of art, are of no concern to Kant, who instead posits something as formal as aesthetic satisfaction as the defining characteristic of art. His aesthetics presents the paradox of a castrated hedonism, of a theory of pleasure without pleasure. This position fails to do justice either to artistic experience wherein satisfaction is a subordinate moment in a larger whole, or to the material–corporeal interest, i.e. repressed and unsatisfied needs that resonate in their aesthetic negations – the works of art – turning them into something more than empty patterns.

Aesthetic disinterestedness has moved interest beyond particularity. Objectively, the interest in constituting an aesthetic totality entailed an interest in the proper arrangement of the social whole. In the last analysis aesthetic interest aimed not at some particular fulfilment, but at the fulfilment of infinite possibilities, which in turn cannot be thought without fulfilment of the particular.

A corresponding weakness can be noticed in Freud's theory of art, which is a good deal more idealistic than Freud had thought it was. By placing works of art squarely into a realm of psychic immanence, Freud's theory loses sight of their antithetical relation to the non-subjective, which thus remains unmolested, as it were, by the thorns pointed toward it by works of art. As a result, psychic processes like instinctual denial and adaptation are left as the only relevant aspects of art. Psychologistic interpretations of art are in league with the philistine view that art is a conciliatory force capable of smoothing over differences, or that it is the dream of a better life, never mind the fact that such dreams should recall the negativity from which they were forcibly extracted. Psychoanalysis in conformist fashion simply takes over the prevalent view of art as some sort of beneficent cultural heritage. To this corresponds the aesthetic hedonism which has psychoanalysis banish all negativity from art *qua* result, pushing the analysis of that negativity back to the level of instinctual conflict. Once successful sublimation and integration become the be-all and end-all of a work of art, it loses the power to transcend mere existence. However, as soon as we conceive of the work of art in terms of its ability to keep a hold on the negativity of the real and to enter into a definite relation to it, we have to change the concept of disinterestedness as well. In contrast to the Kantian and Freudian views on the matter, works of art necessarily evolve in a dialectic of interests and disinterestedness.

There is a grain of validity even in a contemplative attitude towards art, inasmuch as it underscores the important posture of art's turning away from immediate praxis and refusing to play the worldly game. This has long been a component of artistic behaviour. We see here, incidentally, that works of art are tied up with specific modes of behaviour; indeed, that they *are* modes of behaviour. Now it is only those works of art that manifest themselves as modes of behaviour which have a reason for being. Art is like a plenipotentiary of a type of praxis that is better than the prevailing praxis of society, dominated as it is by brutal self-interest. This is what art criticizes. It gives the lie to the notion that production for production's sake is necessary, by opting for a mode of praxis beyond labour. Art's *promesse du bonheur*, then, has an even more emphatically critical meaning: it not only expresses the idea that current praxis denies happiness, but also carries the connotation that happiness is something beyond praxis. The chasm between praxis and happiness is surveyed and measured by the power of negativity of the work of art.

Surely a writer like Kafka does anything but appeal to our faculty of desire. Prose writings such as *Metamorphosis* and *Penal Colony*, on the contrary, seem to call forth in us responses like real anxiety, a violent drawing back, an almost physical revulsion. They seem to be the opposite of desire. Yet these phenomena of psychic defence and rejection have more in common with desire than with the old Kantian disinterestedness. Kafka and the literature that followed his example have swept away the notion of disinterestedness. In relation to Kafka's works, disinterestedness is a completely inadequate concept of interpretation. In the last analysis the postulate of disinterestedness debases all art, turning it into a pleasant or useful plaything, in accord with Horace's *ars poetica*. Idealist aesthetics and its contemporaneous art products have emancipated themselves from this misconception. The precondition for the autonomy of artistic experience is the abandonment of the attitude of tasting and savouring. The trajectory leading to aesthetic autonomy passes through the stage of disinterestedness; and well it should, for it was during this stage that art emancipated itself from cuisine and pornography, an emancipation that has become irrevocable. However, art does not come to rest in disinterestedness. It moves on. And in so doing it reproduces, in different form, the interest inherent in disinterestedness. In a false world all *hedone* is false. This goes for artistic pleasure, too. Art renounces happiness for the sake of happiness, thus enabling desire to survive in art.

7 Enjoyment of art

In Kant, we saw that enjoyment comes in the guise of disinterestedness, a guise that makes enjoyment unrecognizable. What ordinary language and conformist aesthetics have termed enjoyment of art, on analogy with real enjoyment, has probably never existed and will probably never exist. The individual has a limited share in artistic experience as such. This share varies with the quality of a work of art: the better the work, the smaller the subjective component in it. To fetishize the enjoyment of art is to be a crude and insensitive person, who tends to give himself away by describing something as a 'feast for the eye'.

Let us acknowledge a limitation of this critique, though: if the last trace of enjoyment were expunged from art, we would face the embarrassing question of what works of art are for. Still, it remains a fact that people enjoy works of art the less, the more they know about them, and vice versa. If we must discuss attitudes to art works at all, it is probably correct to say that the traditional attitude was one not of enjoyment, but of admiration – admiration for what those works are in themselves, regardless of their relation to the viewer. What the viewer noticed in them and what enraptured him was their truth (again, Kafka is a good example of art as truth). They were not some kind of higher type of means of enjoyment. The relation between the viewer and work had nothing to do with the incorporation of art by the viewer. On the contrary, the viewer seemed to vanish in the work of art. This holds *a fortiori* for the products of modern art that come at the viewer sometimes like train engines in a film.

If you ask a musician if he enjoys playing his instrument, he will probably reply: 'I hate it', just like the grimacing cellist in the American joke. People who have a genuine relation to art would rather immerse themselves in art than reduce art to an object. They cannot live without art, but its individual manifestations are not so many sources of pleasure for them. It goes without saying that nobody would concern himself with art if he did not get something out of it. But this does not mean that people should actually draw up balance sheets, entering such items as 'Heard Ninth Symphony tonight, enjoyed myself so and so much'. Unfortunately, such feeble-minded thinking has by now almost become the commonsensical rule. The bourgeois wants his art luxurious, his life ascetic. It would make more sense if it were the other way around.

Having deprived people of real gratification in the sphere of immediate sense experience, reified consciousness is feeding them a substitute in the

Theodor Adorno

form of sensuously dressed-up art, assigning to art a place that is beneath its dignity. On the surface, the strategy seems to move the works of art closer to the consumer by stressing their sensuous attraction. At a deeper level, what happens is that he becomes alienated from them, as he begins to treat them like a commodity belonging to him and yet expropriable at any moment. This raises fears in him. In short, the false attitude towards art is intimately related to anxieties about loss of property; for the fetishistic notion of art as a good which can be owned and, through reflection, destroyed corresponds neatly with the idea of a piece of property in the psychic household.

Like art as a whole, the classification of art as one among the means of enjoyment is a product of historical development. Granted, the magical and animistic predecessors of works of art were components of ritual practices and hence devoid of aesthetic autonomy. But they were certainly not to be enjoyed, for they were sacred. It was only after art had become thoroughly spiritualized that those who did not understand it began to clamour resentfully for a new species of consumer art that would be able to give them something to enjoy. Conversely, the artists, full of aversion against these demands, were forced to find ever more ingenious ways to spiritualize art even further. No nude Greek sculpture was a pin-up. This explains in part why there is such a friendly attitude in modernism towards the distant past and towards primitive exotic places: modern artists are pleased to find examples there of an art that abstracts from natural objects and their desirability. Hegel, too, in his analysis of what he called symbolic art saw the non-sensuous moment in archaic art. Protesting against the universal mediation of life through commodities, the element of pleasure in art is mediable in its own way, in that he who vanished in a work of art is *ipso facto* exempted from the penury of life. Such pleasure can take on inebriating proportions. At this point one cannot help realizing just how meagre the concept of aesthetic enjoyment really is when we compare it with drunkenness – so meagre, in fact, that what it stands for does not even seem worth going after. Strangely enough, the aesthetic theory

that has singled out subjective feeling as the ground of the beautiful has never seriously analysed that feeling. What descriptions there are of it appear, all and sundry, to be lacking in depth. The subjectivist approach to art simply fails to understand that the subjective experience of art in itself is meaningless, and that in order to grasp the importance of art one has to zero in on the artistic object rather than on the fun of the art lover.

The concept of aesthetic enjoyment was a bad compromise between the social essence of art and the critical tendencies inherent in it. Underlying this compromise is a bourgeois mentality which, after sternly noting how useless art is for the business of self-preservation, grudgingly concedes to art a place in society, provided it offers at least a kind of use-value modelled on the phenomenon of sensuous pleasure. This expectation perverts the nature of art as well as the nature of real sensuous pleasure, for art is unable to provide it. There is no denying that an individual who cannot differentiate sensually between a beautiful sound and a dissonant one, between brilliant colours and dull ones, lacks the ability for artistic experience. But this ability ought not to be hypostatized. To be sure, artistic experience requires a considerable capacity for sensual differentiation as a medium of creativity, but in true art the pleasure component is not given free rein; depending on the time, it is more or less narrowly circumscribed. In periods following an age of asceticism, pleasure became an emancipatory force. This is true of the Renaissance in its relation to the Middle Ages. It is also true of impressionism in its relation to the Victorian age. At other times, the metaphysical content of human sadness manifested itself in art when erotic stimuli were allowed to permeate artistic form. However strong historically the tendency towards a recurrence of pleasure may be, pleasure remains infantile when it asserts itself directly and without mediation. Art absorbs pleasure as remembrance and longing; it does not copy it, does not seek to produce pleasure as an immediate effect. Aversion against the crudely sensuous in art may have been the undoing of impressionism, which had gone too far in the hedonistic direction.

Notes

1 H. Kuhn, *Schriften zur Ästhetik* (Munich 1966), pp. 236ff.

2 Cf. T. W. Adorno, *Ohne Leitbild. Parva Aesthetica*, 2nd ed. (Frankfurt 1968), pp. 168ff.

3   Presumably, Adorno is alluding here to the dynamic connotation of *Ursprung* (origin) as a 'primal leap'. – Tr.

4   Cf. G. W. F. Hegel, *Science of Logic*, 1, section 1, ch. 2 – Tr.

5   Scattered parts. – Tr.

6   René Laforgue, *The Defeat of Baudelaire; a Psycho-analytical Study of the Neurosis of Charles Baudelaire* (London 1932). – Tr.

7   I. Kant, *Critique of Judgment*, trans. J. H. Bernard (New York 1951), p. 39.

8   Ibid., p. 38.

9   Ibid., p. 39.

10 Ibid., p. 38.

15

Discourse in the Novel

Mikhail Bakhtin

Heteroglossia in the Novel

The compositional forms for appropriating and organizing heteroglossia in the novel, worked out during the long course of the genre's historical development, are extremely heterogeneous in their variety of generic types. Each such compositional form is connected with particular stylistic possibilities, and demands particular forms for the artistic treatment of the heteroglot "languages" introduced into it. We will pause here only on the most basic forms that are typical for the majority of novel types.

The so-called comic novel makes available a form for appropriating and organizing heteroglossia that is both externally very vivid and at the same time historically profound: its classic representatives in England were Fielding, Smollett, Sterne, Dickens, Thackeray and others, and in Germany Hippel and Jean Paul.

In the English comic novel we find a comic-parodic re-processing of almost all the levels of literary language, both conversational and written, that were current at the time. Almost every novel we mentioned above as being a classic representative of this generic type is an encyclopedia of all strata and forms of literary language: depending on the subject being represented, the story-line parodically reproduces first the forms of parliamentary eloquence, then the eloquence of the court, or particular forms of parliamentary protocol, or court protocol, or forms used by reporters in newspaper articles, or the dry business language of the City, or the dealings of speculators, or the pedantic speech of scholars, or the high epic style, or Biblical style, or the style of the hypocritical moral sermon or finally the way one or another concrete and socially determined personality, the subject of the story, happens to speak.

This usually parodic stylization of generic, professional and other strata of language is sometimes interrupted by the direct authorial word (usually as an expression of pathos, of Sentimental or idyllic sensibility), which directly embodies (without any refracting) semantic and axiological intentions of the author. But the primary source of language usage in the comic novel is a highly specific treatment of "common language." This "common language" – usually the average norm of spoken and written language for a given social group – is taken by the author precisely as the *common view*, as the verbal approach to people and things normal for a given sphere of society, as the *going point of view* and the going *value*. To one degree or another, the author distances himself from this common language, he steps back and objectifies it, forcing his own intentions to refract and diffuse themselves through the medium of this common view that has become embodied in language (a view that is always superficial and frequently hypocritical).

The relationship of the author to a language conceived as the common view is not static – it is always found in a state of movement and oscillation that is more or less alive (this sometimes is a rhythmic oscillation): the author exaggerates, now strongly, now weakly, one or another aspect of the "common language," sometimes abruptly exposing its inadequacy to its object and sometimes, on the contrary, becoming one with it, maintaining an almost imperceptible distance, sometimes even directly forcing it to reverberate with his own "truth," which occurs when the author completely merges his own voice with the common view. As a consequence of such a merger, the aspects of common language, which in the given situation had been parodically exaggerated or had been treated as mere things, undergo change. The comic style demands of the author a lively to-and-fro movement in his relation to language, it demands a continual shifting of the distance between author and language, so that first some, then other aspects of language are thrown into relief. If such were not the case, the style would be monotonous or would require a greater individualization of the narrator – would, in any case, require a quite different means for introducing and organizing heteroglossia.

Against this same backdrop of the "common language," of the impersonal, going opinion, one can also isolate in the comic novel those parodic stylizations of generic, professional and other languages we have mentioned, as well as compact masses of direct authorial discourse – pathos-filled, moral-didactic, sentimental-elegiac or idyllic. In the comic novel the direct authorial word is thus realized in direct, unqualified stylizations of poetic genres (idyllic, elegiac, etc.) or stylizations of rhetorical genres (the pathetic, the moral-didactic). Shifts from common language to parodying of generic and other languages and shifts to the direct authorial word may be gradual, or may be on the contrary quite abrupt. Thus does the system of language work in the comic novel.

We will pause for analysis on several examples from Dickens, from his novel *Little Dorrit*.

(1) The conference was held at four or five o'clock in the afternoon, when all the region of Harley Street, Cavendish Square, was resonant of carriage-wheels and double-knocks. It had reached this point when Mr. Merdle came home *from his daily occupation of causing the British name to be more and more respected in all parts of the civilized globe capable of appreciation of worldwide commercial enterprise and gigantic combinations of skill and capital*. For, though nobody knew with the least precision what Mr. Merdle's business was, except that it was to coin money, these were the terms in which everybody defined it on all ceremonious occasions, and which it was the last

new polite reading of the parable of the camel and the needle's eye to accept without inquiry. [book I, ch. 33]

The italicized portion represents a parodic stylization of the language of ceremonial speeches (in parliaments and at banquets). The shift into this style is prepared for by the sentence's construction, which from the very beginning is kept within bounds by a somewhat ceremonious epic tone. Further on – and already in the language of the author (and consequently in a different style) – the parodic meaning of the ceremoniousness of Merdle's labors becomes apparent: such a characterization turns out to be "another's speech," to be taken only in quotation marks ("these were the terms in which everybody defined it on all ceremonious occasions").

Thus the speech of another is introduced into the author's discourse (the story) in *concealed form*, that is, without any of the *formal* markers usually accompanying such speech, whether direct or indirect. But this is not just another's speech in the same "language" – it is another's utterance in a language that is itself "other" to the author as well, in the archaicized language of oratorical genres associated with hypocritical official celebrations.

(2) In a day or two it was announced to all the town, that Edmund Sparkler, Esquire, son-in-law of the eminent Mr. Merdle of world-wide renown, was made one of the Lords of the Circumlocution Office; and proclamation was issued, to all true believers, that this admirable *appointment was to be hailed as a graceful and gracious mark of homage, rendered by the graceful and gracious Decimus, to that commercial interest which must ever in a great commercial country – and all the rest of it, with blast of trumpet*. So, bolstered by this mark of Government homage, the *wonderful* Bank and all the other *wonderful* undertakings went on and went up; and gapers came to Harley Street, Cavendish Square, only to look at the house where the golden wonder lived. [book 2, ch. 12]

Here, in the italicized portion, another's speech in another's (official-ceremonial) language is openly introduced as indirect discourse. But it is surrounded by the hidden, diffused speech of another (in the same official-ceremonial language) that clears the way for the introduction of a form more easily perceived *as* another's speech and that can reverberate more fully as such. The clearing of the way comes with the word "Esquire," characteristic of official speech, added to Sparkler's name; the final confirmation that this is another's speech comes with the epithet "wonderful." This epithet does not of course belong to the author but to that same "general opinion" that had created the commotion around Merdle's inflated enterprises.

> (3) It was a dinner to provoke an appetite, though he had not had one. The rarest dishes, sumptuously cooked and sumptuously served; the choicest fruits, the most exquisite wines; marvels of workmanship in gold and silver, china and glass; innumerable things delicious to the senses of taste, smell, and sight, were insinuated into its composition. *O, what a wonderful man this Merdle, what a great man, what a master man, how blessedly and enviably endowed* – in one word, what a rich man! [book 2, ch. 12]

The beginning is a parodic stylization of high epic style. What follows is an enthusiastic glorification of Merdle, a chorus of his admirers in the form of the concealed speech of another (the italicized portion). The whole point here is to expose the real basis for such glorification, which is to unmask the chorus' hypocrisy: "wonderful," "great," "master," "endowed" can all be replaced by the single word "rich." This act of authorial unmasking, which is openly accomplished within the boundaries of a single simple sentence, merges with the unmasking of another's speech. The ceremonial emphasis on glorification is complicated by a second emphasis that is indignant, ironic, and this is the one that ultimately predominates in the final unmasking words of the sentence.

We have before us a typical double-accented, double-styled *hybrid construction*.

What we are calling a hybrid construction is an utterance that belongs, by its grammatical (syntactic) and compositional markers, to a single speaker, but that actually contains mixed within it two utterances, two speech manners, two styles, two "languages," two semantic and axiological belief systems. We repeat, there is no formal – compositional and syntactic – boundary between these utterances, styles, languages, belief systems; the division of voices and languages takes place within the limits of a single syntactic whole, often within

the limits of a simple sentence. It frequently happens that even one and the same word will belong simultaneously to two languages, two belief systems that intersect in a hybrid construction – and, consequently, the word has two contradictory meanings, two accents (examples below). As we shall see, hybrid constructions are of enormous significance in novel style. [. . .]

> (4) But Mr. Tite Barnacle was a buttoned-up man, and *consequently* a weighty one. [book 2, ch. 12]

The above sentence is an example of *pseudo-objective motivation*, one of the forms for concealing another's speech – in this example, the speech of "current opinion." If judged by the formal markers above, the logic motivating the sentence seems to belong to the author, i.e., he is formally at one with it; but in actual fact, the motivation lies within the subjective belief system of his characters, or of general opinion.

Pseudo-objective motivation is generally characteristic of novel style,[1] since it is one of the manifold forms for concealing another's speech in hybrid constructions. Subordinate conjunctions and link words ("thus," "because," "for the reason that," "in spite of" and so forth), as well as words used to maintain a logical sequence ("therefore," "consequently," etc.) lose their direct authorial intention, take on the flavor of someone else's language, become refracted or even completely reified.

Such motivation is especially characteristic of comic style, in which someone else's speech is dominant (the speech of concrete persons, or, more often, a collective voice).[2]

> (5) As a vast fire will fill the air to a great distance with its roar, so the sacred flame which the mighty Barnacles had fanned caused the air to resound more and more with the name of Merdle. It was deposited on every lip, and carried into every ear. There never was, there never had been, there never again should be, such a man as Mr. Merdle. Nobody, as aforesaid, knew what he had done; but *everybody knew him to be the greatest that had appeared.* [book 2, ch. 13]

Here we have an epic, "Homeric" introduction (parodic, of course) into whose frame the crowd's glorification of Merdle has been inserted (concealed speech of another in another's language). We then get direct authorial discourse; however, the author gives an objective tone to this "aside" by suggesting that "everybody knew" (the italicized portion). It is as if even the author himself did not doubt the fact.

> (6) That illustrious man and great national ornament, Mr. Merdle, continued his shining course. It began to be widely understood that one who had done society the admirable service *of making so much money out of it,* could not be suffered to remain a commoner. A baronetcy was spoken of with confidence; a peerage was frequently mentioned. [book 2, ch. 24]

We have here the same fictive solidarity with the hypocritically ceremonial general opinion of Merdle. All the epithets referring to Merdle in the first sentences derive from general opinion, that is, they are the concealed speech of another. The second sentence – "it began to be widely understood," etc. – is kept within the bounds of an emphatically objective style, representing not subjective opinion but the admission of an objective and completely indisputable fact. The epithet "who had done society the admirable service" is completely at the level of common opinion, repeating its official glorification, but the subordinate clause attached to that glorification ("of making so much money out of it") are the words of the author himself (as if put in parentheses in the quotation). The main sentence then picks up again at the level of common opinion. We have here a typical hybrid construction, where the subordinate clause is in direct authorial speech and the main clause in someone else's speech. The main and subordinate clauses are constructed in different semantic and axiological conceptual systems.

The whole of this portion of the novel's action, which centers around Merdle and the persons associated with him, is depicted in the language (or more accurately, the languages) of hypocritically ceremonial common opinion about Merdle, and at the same time there is a parodic stylization of that everyday language of banal society gossip, or of the ceremonial language of official pronouncements and banquet speeches, or the high epic style or Biblical style. This atmosphere around Merdle, the common opinion about him and his enterprises, infects the positive heroes of the novel as well, in particular the sober Pancks, and forces him to invest his entire estate – his own, and Little Dorrit's – in Merdle's hollow enterprises.

> (7) Physician had engaged to break the intelligence in Harley Street. Bar could not at once return to his inveiglements of the most enlightened and remarkable jury he had ever seen in that box, with whom, he could tell his learned friend, no shallow sophistry would go down, and no unhappily abused professional tact and skill prevail (this was the way he meant to begin with them); so he said he would go too, and would loiter to and fro near the house while his friend was inside. [book 2, ch. 25, mistakenly given as ch. 15 in Russian text, tr.]

Here we have a clear example of hybrid construction where within the frame of authorial speech (informative speech – the beginning of a speech prepared by the lawyer has been inserted, "Bar could not at once return to his inveiglements . . . of the jury . . . so he said he would go too. . . ." etc. – while this speech is simultaneously a fully developed epithet attached to the subject of the author's speech, that is, "jury." The word "jury" enters into the context of informative authorial speech (in the capacity of a necessary object to the word "inveiglements") as well as into the context of the parodic-stylized speech of the lawyer. The author's word "inveiglement" itself emphasizes the parodic nature of the re-processing of the lawyer's speech, the hypocritical meaning of which consists precisely in the fact that it would be impossible to inveigle such a remarkable jury.

> (8) It followed that Mrs. Merdle, as a woman of fashion and good breeding *who had been sacrificed to the wiles of a vulgar barbarian* (for Mr. Merdle was found out from the crown of his head to the sole of his foot, the moment he was found out in his pocket), must be actively championed by her order for her order's sake. [book 2, ch. 33]

This is an analogous hybrid construction, in which the definition provided by the general opinion of society – "a sacrifice to the wiles of a vulgar barbarian" – merges with authorial speech, exposing the hypocrisy and greed of common opinion.

So it is throughout Dickens' whole novel. His entire text is, in fact, everywhere dotted with quotation marks that serve to separate out little islands of scattered direct speech and purely authorial speech, washed by heteroglot waves from all sides. But it would have been impossible actually to insert such marks, since, as we have seen, one and the same word often figures both as the speech of the author and as the speech of another – and at the same time.

Another's speech – whether as storytelling, as mimicking, as the display of a thing in light of a particular point of view, as a speech deployed first in compact masses, then loosely scattered, a speech that is in most cases impersonal ("common opinion," professional and generic languages) – is at none of these points clearly separated from authorial speech: the boundaries are deliberately flexible and ambiguous, often passing through a single syntactic whole, often through a simple sentence, and sometimes even dividing up the main parts of a sentence. This varied *play with the boundaries of speech types*, languages and belief systems is one of the most fundamental aspects of comic style.

Comic style (of the English sort) is based, therefore, on the stratification of common language and on the possibilities available for isolating from these strata, to one degree or another, one's own intentions, without ever completely merging with them. *It is precisely the diversity of speech, and not the unity of a normative shared language, that is the ground of style.* It is true that such speech diversity does not exceed the boundaries of literary language conceived as a linguistic whole (that is, language defined by abstract linguistic markers), does not pass into an authentic heteroglossia and is based on an abstract notion of language as unitary (that is, it does not require knowledge of various dialects or languages). However a mere concern for language is but the abstract side of the concrete and active (i.e., dialogically engaged) understanding of the living heteroglossia that has been introduced into the novel and artistically organized within it.

In Dickens' predecessors, Fielding, Smollett and Sterne, the men who founded the English comic novel, we find the same parodic stylization of various levels and genres of literary language, but the distance between these levels and genres is greater than it is in Dickens and the exaggeration is stronger (especially in Sterne). The parodic and objectivized incorporation into their work of various types of literary language (especially in Sterne) penetrates the deepest levels of literary

and ideological thought itself, resulting in a parody of the logical and expressive structure of any ideological discourse as such (scholarly, moral and rhetorical, poetic) that is almost as radical as the parody we find in Rabelais.

Literary parody understood in the narrow sense plays a fundamental role in the way language is structured in Fielding, Smollett and Sterne (the Richardsonian novel is parodied by the first two, and almost all contemporary novel-types are parodied by Sterne). Literary parody serves to distance the author still further from language, to complicate still further his relationship to the literary language of his time, especially in the novel's own territory. The novelistic discourse dominating a given epoch is itself turned into an object and itself becomes a means for refracting new authorial intentions.

Literary parody of dominant novel-types plays a large role in the history of the European novel. One could even say that the most important novelistic models and novel-types arose precisely during this parodic destruction of preceding novelistic worlds. This is true of the work of Cervantes, Mendoza, Grimmelshausen, Rabelais, Lesage and many others.

In Rabelais, whose influence on all novelistic prose (and in particular the comic novel) was very great, a parodic attitude toward almost all forms of ideological discourse – philosophical, moral, scholarly, rhetorical, poetic and in particular the pathos-charged forms of discourse (in Rabelais, pathos almost always is equivalent to lie) – was intensified to the point where it became a parody of the very act of conceptualizing anything in language. We might add that Rabelais taunts the deceptive human word by a parodic destruction of syntactic structures, thereby reducing to absurdity some of the logical and expressively accented aspects of words (for example, predication, explanations and so forth). Turning away from language (by means of language, of course), discrediting any direct or unmediated intentionality and expressive excess (any "weighty" seriousness) that might adhere in ideological discourse, presuming that all language is conventional and false, maliciously inadequate to reality – all this achieves in Rabelais almost the maximum purity possible in prose. But the truth that might oppose such falsity receives almost no direct intentional and verbal expression in Rabelais, it does not receive its *own* word – it reverberates only in the parodic and unmasking accents in which the lie is present. Truth is restored by reducing the lie to an absurdity, but truth itself does not seek words; she is afraid to entangle herself in the word, to soil herself in verbal pathos.

Rabelais' "philosophy of the word" – a philosophy expressed not as much in direct utterances as in stylistic practice – has had enormous influence on all consequent novel prose and in particular on the great representative forms of the comic novel; with that in mind we bring forward the purely Rabelaisian formulation of Sterne's Yorick, which might serve as an epigraph to the history of the most important stylistic lines of development in the European novel:

> For aught I know there might be some mixture of unlucky wit at the bottom of such Fracas: – For, to speak the truth, Yorick had an invincible dislike and opposition in his nature to gravity; – not to gravity as such; – for where gravity was wanted, he would be the most grave or serious of mortal men for days and weeks together; – but he was an enemy to the affectation of it, and declared open war against it, only as it appeared a cloak for ignorance, or for folly; and then, whenever it fell his way, however sheltered and protected, he seldom gave it much quarter.
>
> Sometimes, in his wild way of talking, he would say, That gravity was an errant scoundrel; and he would add, – of the most dangerous kind too, – because a sly one; and that, he verily believed, more honest, well-meaning people were bubbled out of their goods and money by it in one twelve-month, than by pocket-picking and shop-lifting in seven. In the naked temper which a merry heart discovered, he would say, There was no danger, – but to itself: – whereas the very essence of gravity was design, and consequently deceit; – 'twas a taught trick to gain credit of the world for more sense and knowledge than a man was worth; and that, with all its pretensions, – it was no better, but often worse, than what a French wit had long ago defined it, – viz. A mysterious carriage of the body to cover the defects of the mind; – which definition of gravity, Yorick, with great imprudence, would say, deserved to be wrote in letters of gold. [Bakhtin does not locate citation; it is from *Tristram Shandy*, vol. I, ch. II, tr.]

Close to Rabelais, but in certain respects even exceeding him in the decisive influence he had on all of novelistic prose, is Cervantes. The English comic novel is permeated through and through with the spirit of Cervantes. It is no accident that this same Yorick, on his deathbed, quotes the words of Sancho Panza.

While the attitude toward language and toward its stratification (generic, professional and otherwise) among the German comic writers, in Hippel and especially in Jean Paul, is basically of the Sternean type, it is raised – as it is in Sterne himself – to the level of a purely philosophical problem, the very possibility of literary and ideological speech as such. The philosophical and ideological element in an author's attitude toward his own language forces into the background the play between intention and the concrete, primarily generic and ideological levels of literary language (cf. the reflection of just this in the aesthetic theories of Jean Paul).[3]

Thus the stratification of literary language, its speech diversity, is an indispensable prerequisite for comic style, whose elements are projected onto different linguistic planes while at the same time the intention of the author, refracted as it passes through these planes, does not wholly give itself up to any of them. It is as if the author has no language of his own, but does possess his own style, his own organic and unitary law governing the way he plays with languages and the way his own real semantic and expressive intentions are refracted within them. Of course this play with languages (and frequently the complete absence of a direct discourse of his own) in no sense degrades the general, deep-seated intentionality, the overarching ideological conceptualization of the work as a whole.

In the comic novel, the incorporation of heteroglossia and its stylistic utilization is characterized by two distinctive features:

(1) Incorporated into the novel are a multiplicity of "language" and verbal-ideological belief systems – generic, professional, class-and-interest-group (the language of the nobleman, the farmer, the merchant, the peasant); tendentious, everyday (the languages of rumour, of society chatter, servants' language) and so forth, but these languages are, it is true, kept primarily within the limits of the literary written and conversational language; at the same time these languages are not, in most cases, consolidated into fixed persons (heroes, storytellers) but rather are incorporated in an impersonal form "from the author," alternating (while ignoring precise formal boundaries) with direct authorial discourse.

(2) The incorporated languages and socio-ideological belief systems, while of course utilized to refract the author's intentions, are unmasked and destroyed as something false, hypocritical, greedy, limited, narrowly rationalistic, inadequate to reality. In most cases these languages – already fully formed, officially recognized, reigning languages that are authoritative and reactionary – are (in real life) doomed to death and displacement. Therefore what predominate [. . .] in the novel are various forms and degrees of *parodic stylization* of incorporated languages, a stylization that, in the most radical, most Rabelaisian[4] representatives of this novel-type (Sterne and Jean Paul), verges on a rejection of any straightforward and unmediated seriousness (true seriousness is the destruction of all false seriousness, not only in its pathos-charged expression but in its Sentimental one as well);[5] that is, it limits itself to a principled criticism of the word as such.

There is a fundamental difference between this comic form for incorporating and organizing heteroglossia in the novel and other forms that are defined by their use of a personified and concretely posited author (written speech) or teller (oral speech).

Play with a posited author is also characteristic of the comic novel (Sterne, Hippel, Jean Paul), a heritage from *Don Quixote*. But in these examples such play is purely a compositional device, which strengthens the general trend toward relativity, objectification and the parodying of literary forms and genres.

The posited author and teller assume a completely different significance where they are incorporated as carriers of a particular verbal-ideological linguistic belief system, with a particular point of view on the world and its events, with particular value judgments and intonations – "particular" both as regards the author, his real direct discourse, and also as regards "normal" literary narrative and language.

This particularity, this distancing of the posited author or teller from the real author and from conventional literary expectations, may occur in differing degrees and may vary in its nature. But in every case a particular belief system belonging to someone else, a particular point of view on the world belonging to someone else, is used by the author because it is highly productive, that is, it is able on the one hand to show the object of representation in a new light (to reveal new sides or dimensions in it) and on the other hand to illumin-

ate in a new way the "expected" literary horizon, that horizon against which the particularities of the teller's tale are perceivable.

For example: Belkin was chosen (or better, created) by Pushkin because of his particular "unpoetic" point of view on objects and plots that are traditionally poetic (the highly characteristic and calculated use of the *Romeo and Juliet* plot in "Mistress into Maid" or the romantic "Dances of Death" in "The Coffinmaker"). Belkin, who is on the same level with those narrators-at-third-remove out of whose mouths he has taken his stories, is a "prosaic" man, a man without a drop of poetic pathos. The successful "prosaic" resolutions of the plots and the very means of the story's telling destroy any expectation of traditional poetic effects. The fruitfulness of the prosaic quality in Belkin's point of view consists in just this failure to understand poetic pathos.

Maxim Maximych in *A Hero of Our Time*, Rudy Panko, the narrators of "Nose" and "Overcoat," Dostoevsky's chroniclers, folkloric narrators and storytellers who are themselves characters in Melnikov-Pechersky and Mamin-Sibiryak, the folkloric and down-to-earth storytellers in Leskov, the character-narrators in populist literature and finally the narrators in Symbolist and post-Symbolist prose (in Remizov, Zamyatin and others) – with all their widely differing forms of narration (oral and written), with all their differing narrative languages (literary, professional, social-and-special-interest-group language, everyday, slang, dialects and others) – everywhere, they recommend themselves as specific and limited verbal ideological points of view, belief systems, opposed to the literary expectations and points of view that constitute the background needed to perceive them; but these narrators are productive precisely *because* of this very limitedness and specificity.

The speech of such narrators is always *another's speech* (as regards the real or potential direct discourse of the author) and in *another's language* (i.e., insofar as it is a particular variant of the literary language that clashes with the language of the narrator).

Thus we have in this case "nondirect speaking" – not *in* language but *through* language, through the linguistic medium of another – and consequently through a refraction of authorial intentions.

The author manifests himself and his point of view not only in his effect on the narrator, on his speech and his language (which are to one or another extent objectivized, objects of display) but also in his effect on the subject of the story – as a point of view that differs from the point of view of the narrator. Behind the narrator's story we read a second story, the author's story; he is the one who tells us how the narrator tells stories, and also tells us about the narrator himself. We acutely sense two levels at each moment in the story; one, the level of the narrator, a belief system filled with his objects, meanings and emotional expressions, and the other, the level of the author, who speaks (albeit in a refracted way) by means of this story and through this story. The narrator himself, with *his* own discourse, enters into this authorial belief system along with what is actually being told. We puzzle out the author's emphases that overlie the subject of the story, while we puzzle out the story itself and the figure of the narrator as he is revealed in the process of telling his tale. If one fails to sense this second level, the intentions and accents of the author himself, then one has failed to understand the work.

As we have said above, the narrator's story or the story of the posited author is structured against the background of normal literary language, the expected literary horizon. Every moment of the story has a conscious relationship with this normal language and its belief system, is in fact set against them, and set against them *dialogically*: one point of view opposed to another, one evaluation opposed to another, one accent opposed to another (i.e., they are not contrasted as two abstractly linguistic phenomena). This interaction, this dia- logic tension between two languages and two belief systems, permits authorial intentions to be realized in such a way that we can acutely sense their presence at every point in the work. The author is not to be found in the language of the narrator, not in the normal literary language to which the story opposes itself (although a given story may be closer to a given language) – but rather, the author utilizes now one language, now another, in order to avoid giving himself up wholly to either of them; he makes use of this verbal give-and-take, this dialogue of languages at every point in his work, in order that he himself might remain as it were neutral with regard to language, a third party in a quarrel between two people (although he might be a *biased* third party).

All forms involving a narrator or a posited author signify to one degree or another by their presence the author's freedom from a unitary and singular language, a freedom connected with the relativity of literary and language systems; such forms open up the possibility of never having to define oneself in language, the possibility of trans- lating one's own intentions from one linguistic system to another, of fusing "the language of truth" with "the language of the everyday," of saying "I am me" in someone else's language, and in my own language, "I am other."

Such a refracting of authorial intentions takes place in all these forms (the narrator's tale, the tale of a posited author or that of one of the characters); it is therefore possible to have in them, as in the comic novel, a variety of different distances between distinct aspects of the narrator's language and the author's language: the refraction may be at times greater, at times lesser, and in some aspects of language there may be an almost complete fusion of voices.

The next form for incorporating and organizing heteroglossia in the novel – a form that every novel without exception utilizes – is the language used by characters.

The language used by characters in the novel, how they speak, is verbally and semantically autonomous; each character's speech possesses its own belief system, since each is the speech of another in another's language; thus it may also refract authorial intentions and consequently may to a certain degree constitute a second language for the author. Moreover, the character speech almost always influences authorial speech (and sometimes powerfully so), sprinkling it with another's words (that is, the speech of a character perceived as the concealed speech of another) and in this way introducing into it stratification and speech diversity.

Thus even where there is no comic element, no parody, no irony and so forth, where there is no narrator, no posited author or narrating character, speech diversity and language stratification still serve as the basis for style in the novel. Even in those places where the author's voice seems at first glance to be unitary and consistent, direct and unmediatedly intentional, beneath that smooth single-languaged surface we can nevertheless uncover prose's three-dimensionality, its profound speech diversity, which enters the project of style and is its determining factor.

Thus the language and style of Turgenev's novels have the appearance of being single- languaged and pure. Even in Turgenev, however, this unitary language is very far from poetic abso- lutism. Substantial masses of this language are drawn into the battle between points of view, value judgments and emphases that the characters introduce into it; they are infected by mutually contradictory intentions and stratifications, words, sayings, expressions, definitions and epithets are scattered throughout it, infected with others' intentions with which the author is to some extent at odds, and through which his own personal intentions are refracted. We sense acutely the various distances between the author and various aspects of his language, which smack of the social universes and belief systems of others. We acutely sense in various aspects of his language varying degrees of the presence of the author and of his *most recent semantic instantiation.* In Turgenev, heteroglossia and language stratification serve as the most fundamental factors of style, and orchestrate an authorial truth of their own; the author's linguistic consciousness, his consciousness as a writer of prose, is thereby relativized.

In Turgenev, social heteroglossia enters the novel primarily in the direct speeches of his characters, in dialogues. But this heteroglossia, as we have said, is also diffused throughout the authorial speech that surrounds the characters, creating highly particularized *character zones* [*zony geroev*]. These zones are formed from the fragments of character speech [*polureč'*], from various forms for hidden transmission of someone else's word, from scattered words and sayings belonging to someone else's speech, from those invasions into authorial speech of others' expressive indicators (ellipsis, questions, exclamations). Such a character zone is the field of action for a character's voice, encroaching in one way or another upon the author's voice.

However – we repeat – in Turgenev, the novelistic orchestration of the theme is concentrated in direct dialogues; the characters do not create around themselves their own extensive or densely saturated zones, and in Turgenev fully developed, complex stylistic hybrids are relatively rare.

We pause here on several examples of diffuse heteroglossia in Turgenev.[6]

(1) His name is Nikolai Petrovich Kirsanov. Some ten miles from the coaching-inn stands a respectable little property of his consisting of a couple of hundred serfs – or five thousand acres, as he expresses it now that he has divided up his land and let it to the peasants, and started a "farm." [*Fathers and Sons*, ch. I]

Here the new expressions, characteristic of the era and in the style of the liberals, are put in quotation marks or otherwise "qualified."

(2) He was secretly beginning to feel irritated. Bazarov's complete indifference exasperated his aristocratic nature. *This son of a medico was not only self-assured: he actually returned abrupt and reluctant answers, and there was a churlish, almost insolant [sic] note in his voice.* [*Fathers and Sons*, ch. 4]

The third sentence of this paragraph, while being a part of the author's speech if judged by its formal syntactic markers, is at the same time in its choice of expressions ("this son of a medico") and in its emotional and expressive structure the hidden speech of someone else (Pavel Petrovich).

(3) Pavel Petrovich sat down at the table. He was wearing an elegant suit cut in the English fashion, and a gay little fez graced his head. The fez and the carelessly knotted cravat carried a suggestion of the more free life in the country but the stiff collar of his shirt – not white, it is true, but striped *as is correct for morning wear* – stood up as inexorably as ever against his well-shaven chin. [*Fathers and Sons*, ch. 5]

This ironic characterization of Pavel Petrovich's morning attire is consistent with the tone of a gentleman, precisely in the style of Pavel Petrovich. The statement "as is correct for morning wear" is not, of course, a simple authorial statement, but rather the norm of Pavel Petrovich's gentlemanly circle, conveyed ironically. One might with some justice put it in quotation marks. This is an example of a pseudo–objective underpinning.

(4) *Matvei Ilyich's suavity of demeanour was equalled only by his stately manner.* He had a gracious word for everyone – with an added shade of disgust in some cases and deference in others; he was gallant, "un vrai chevalier français," to all the ladies, and was continually bursting into hearty resounding laughter, in which no one else took part, as befits a high official. [*Fathers and Sons*, ch. 14]

Here we have an analogous case of an ironic characterization given from the point of view of the high official himself. Such is the nature of this form of pseudo-objective underpinning: "as befits a high official."

(5) The following morning Nezhdanov betook himself to Sipyagin's town residence, and there, in a magnificent study, filled with furniture of a severe style, *in full harmony with the dignity of a liberal politician and modern gentleman.... [Virgin Soil, ch. 4]*

This is an analogous pseudo-objective construction.

(6) Semyon Petrovich was in the ministry of the Court, he had the title of a *kammeryunker. He was prevented by his patriotism from join-ing the diplomatic service,* for which he seemed destined by everything, his educa-tion, his knowledge of the world, his popu-larity with women, and his very appearance.... [*Virgin Soil*, ch. 5][7]

The motivation for refusing a diplomatic career is pseudo-objective. The entire characterization is consistent in tone and given from the point of view of Kallomyetsev himself, fused with his direct speech, being – at least judging by its syntactic markers – a subordinate clause attached to author-ial speech ("for which he seemed destined by everything...mais quitter la Russie!" and so forth).

(7) Kallomyetsev had come to S——Province on a two months' leave to look after his property, that is to say, "to scare some and squeeze others." *Of course, there's no doing anything without that.* [*Virgin Soil*, ch. 5]

The conclusion of the paragraph is a character-istic example of a pseudo-objective statement. Pre-cisely in order to give it the appearance of an objective authorial judgment, it is not put in quo-tation marks, as are the preceding words of Kallo-myetsev himself; it is incorporated into authorial speech and deliberately placed directly after Kal-lomyetsev's own words.

(8) But Kallomyetsev deliberately stuck his round eyeglass between his nose and his eyebrow, and stared at the [snit of a] *student who dared not share* his "apprehensions." [*Virgin Soil*, ch. 7]

This is a typical hybrid construction. Not only the subordinate clause but also the direct object ("the [snit of a] student") of the main authorial sentence is rendered in Kallomyetsev's tone. The choice of words ("snit of a student," "dared not share") are determined by Kallomyetsev's irritated intonation, and at the same time, in the context of authorial speech, these words are permeated with the ironic intonation of the author; therefore the construction has two accents (the author's ironic transmission, and a mimicking of the irritation of the character).

Finally, we adduce examples of an intrusion of the emotional aspects of someone else's speech into the syntactic system of authorial speech (ellipsis, questions, exclamations).

(9) Strange was the state of his mind. In the last two days so many new sensations, new faces.... For the first time in his life he had come close to a girl, whom, in all prob-ability, he loved; he was present at the beginning of the thing to which, in all prob-ability, all his energies were conse-crated.... Well? was he rejoicing? No. Was he wavering, afraid, confused? Oh, certainly not. Was he at least, feeling that tension of his whole being, that impulse forward into the front ranks of the battle, to be expected as the struggle grew near? No again. Did he believe, then, in this cause? Did he believe in his own love? "Oh, damned artistic tem-perament! sceptic!" his lips murmured inaudibly. Why this weariness, this disinclin-ation to speak even, without shrieking and raving? What inner voice did he want to stifle with those ravings? [*Virgin Soil*, ch. 18]

Here we have, in essence, a form of a character's quasi-direct discourse [*nesobstvenno-prjamaja reč*]. Judging by its syntactic markers, it is authorial speech, but its entire emotional structure belongs to Nezhdanov. This is his inner speech, but trans-mitted in a way regulated by the author, *with provocative questions from the author and with ironic-ally debunking reservations* ("in all probability"), although Nezhdanov's emotional overtones are preserved.

Such a form for transmitting inner speech is common in Turgenev (and is generally one of the most widespread forms for transmitting inner speech in the novel). This form introduces order and stylistic symmetry into the disorderly and impetuous flow of a character's internal speech (a disorder and impetuosity would otherwise have to be re-processed into direct speech) and, moreover, through its syntactic (third-person) and basic stylistic markers (lexicological and other), such a form permits another's inner speech to merge, in an organic and structured way, with a context belonging to the author. But at the same time it is precisely this form that permits us to preserve the expressive structure of the character's inner speech, its inability to exhaust itself in words, its flexibility, which would be absolutely impossible within the dry and logical form of indirect discourse [*kosvennaja reč'*]. Precisely these features make this form the most convenient for transmitting the inner speech of characters. It is of course a hybrid form, for the author's voice may be present in varying degrees of activity and may introduce into the transmitted speech a second accent of its own (ironic, irritated and so on).

The same hybridization, mixing of accents and erasing of boundaries between authorial speech and the speech of others is also present in other forms for transmitting characters' speech. With only three templates for speech transcription (direct speech [*prjamaja reč'*], indirect speech [*kosvennaja reč'*] and quasi-direct speech [*nesobstvenno-prjamaja reč'*]) a great diversity is nevertheless made possible in the treatment of character speech – i.e., the way characters overlap and infect each other – the main thing being how the authorial context succeeds in exploiting the various means for replicating frames and re-stratifying them.

The examples we have offered from Turgenev provide a typical picture of the character's role in stratifying the language of the novel and incorporating heteroglossia into it. A character in a novel always has, as we have said, a zone of his own, his own sphere of influence on the authorial context surrounding him, a sphere that extends – and often quite far – beyond the boundaries of the direct discourse allotted to him. The area occupied by an important character's voice must in any event be broader than his direct and "actual" words. This zone surrounding the important characters of the novel is stylistically profoundly idiosyncratic: the most varied hybrid constructions hold sway in it, and it is always, to one degree or another, dialogized; inside this area a dialogue is played out between the author and his characters – not a dramatic dialogue broken up into statement-and-response, but that special type of novelistic dialogue that realizes itself within the boundaries

of constructions that externally resemble monologues. The potential for such dialogue is one of the most fundamental privileges of novelistic prose, a privilege available neither to dramatic nor to purely poetic genres.

Character zones are a most interesting object of study for stylistic and linguistic analysis: in them one encounters constructions that cast a completely new light on problems of syntax and stylistics.

Let us pause finally on one of the most basic and fundamental forms for incorporating and organizing heteroglossia in the novel – "incorporated genres."

The novel permits the incorporation of various genres, both artistic (inserted short stories, lyrical songs, poems, dramatic scenes, etc.) and extra-artistic (everyday, rhetorical, scholarly, religious genres and others). In principle, any genre could be included in the construction of the novel, and in fact it is difficult to find any genres that have not at some point been incorporated into a novel by someone. Such incorporated genres usually preserve within the novel their own structural integrity and independence, as well as their own linguistic and stylistic peculiarities.

There exists in addition a special group of genres that play an especially significant role in structuring novels, sometimes by themselves even directly determining the structure of a novel as a whole – thus creating novel-types named after such genres. Examples of such genres would be the confession, the diary, travel notes, biography, the personal letter and several others. All these genres may not only enter the novel as one of its essential structural components, but may also determine the form of the novel as a whole (the novel-confession, the novel-diary, the novel-in-letters, etc.). Each of these genres possesses its own verbal and semantic forms for assimilating various aspects of reality. The novel, indeed, utilizes these genres precisely because of their capacity, as well-worked-out forms, to assimilate reality in words.

So great is the role played by these genres that are incorporated into novels that it might seem as if the novel is denied any primary means for verbally appropriating reality, that it has no approach of its own, and therefore requires the help of other genres to re-process reality; the novel itself has the appearance of being merely a secondary syncretic unification of other seemingly primary verbal genres.

All these genres, as they enter the novel, bring into it their own languages, and therefore stratify the linguistic unity of the novel and further intensify its speech diversity in fresh ways. It often happens that the language of a nonartistic genre (say, the epistolary), when introduced into the novel, takes on a significance that creates a chapter not only in the history of the novel, but in the history of literary language as well.

The languages thus introduced into a novel may be either directly intentional or treated completely as objects, that is, deprived of any authorial intentions – not as a word that has been spoken, but as a word to be displayed, like a thing. But more often than not, these languages do refract, to one degree or another, authorial intentions – although separate aspects of them may in various ways *not* coincide with the semantic operation of the work that immediately precedes their appearance.

Thus poetic genres of verse (the lyrical genres, for example) when introduced into the novel may have the direct intentionality, the full semantic charge, of poetry. Such, for example, are the verses Goethe introduced into *Wilhelm Meister*. In such a way did the Romantics incorporate their own verses into their prose – and, as is well known, the Romantics considered the presence of verses in the novel (verses taken as directly intentional expressions of the author) one of its constitutive features. In other examples, incorporated verses refract authorial intentions; for example, Lensky's poem in *Evgenij Onegin*, "Where, o where have you gone...." Although the verses from *Wilhelm Meister* may be directly attributed to Goethe (which is actually done), then "Where, o where have you gone...." can in no way be attributed to Pushkin, or if so, only as a poem belonging to a special group comprising "parodic stylizations" (where we must also locate Grinev's poem in *The Captain's Daughter*). Finally, poems incorporated into a novel can also be completely objectified, as are, for example, Captain Lebyadkin's verses in Dostoevsky's *The Possessed*.

A similar situation is the novel's incorporation of every possible kind of maxim and aphorism; they too may oscillate between the purely objective (the "word on display") and the directly intentional, that is, the fully conceptualized philosophical dicta of the author himself (unconditional discourse spoken with no qualifications or distancing). Thus we find, in the novels of Jean Paul – which are so rich in aphorisms – a broad scale of gradations between the various aphorisms, from purely objective to directly intentional, with the

author's intentions refracted in varying degrees in each case.

In *Evgenij Onegin* aphorisms and maxims are present either on the plane of parody or of irony – that is, authorial intentions in these dicta are to a greater or lesser extent refracted. For example, the maxim

> He who has lived and thought can never
> Look on mankind without disdain;
> He who has felt is haunted ever
> By days that will not come again;
> No more for him enchantments semblance,
> On him the serpent of remembrance
> Feeds, and remorse corrodes his heart.[8]

is given us on a lighthearted, parodic plane, although one can still feel throughout a close proximity, almost a fusion with authorial intentions. And yet the lines that immediately follow:

> All this is likely to impart
> An added charm to conversation

(a conversation of the posited author with Onegin) strengthen the parodic-ironic emphasis, make the maxim more of an inert thing. We sense that the maxim is constructed in a field of activity dominated by Onegin's voice, in his – Onegin's – belief system, with his – Onegin's – emphases.

But this refraction of authorial intentions, in the field that resounds with Onegin's voice, in Onegin's zone – is different than the refraction in, say, Lensky's zone (cf. the almost objective parody on his poems).

This example may also serve to illustrate the influence of a character's language on authorial speech, something discussed by us above: the aphorism in question here is permeated with Onegin's (fashionably Byronic) intentions, therefore the author maintains a certain distance and does not completely merge with him.

The question of incorporating those genres fundamental to the novel's development (the confession, the diary and others) is much more complicated. Such genres also introduce into the novel their own languages, of course, but these languages are primarily significant for making available points of view that are generative in a material sense, since they exist outside literary conventionality and thus have the capacity to broaden the horizon of language available to literature, helping to win for literature new worlds of verbal perception, worlds that had been already sought and partially subdued in other – extraliterary – spheres of linguistic life.

A comic playing with languages, a story "not from the author" (but from a narrator, posited author or character), character speech, character zones and lastly various introductory or framing genres are the basic forms for incorporating and organizing heteroglossia in the novel. All these forms permit languages to be used in ways that are indirect, conditional, distanced. They all signify a relativizing of linguistic consciousness in the perception of language borders – borders created by history and society, and even the most fundamental borders (i.e., those between languages as such) – and permit expression of a feeling for the materiality of language that defines such a relativized consciousness. This relativizing of linguistic consciousness in no way requires a corresponding relativizing in the semantic intentions themselves: even within a prose linguistic consciousness, intentions themselves can be unconditional. But because the idea of a singular language (a sacrosanct, unconditional language) is foreign to prose, prosaic consciousness must orchestrate its *own* – even though unconditional – semantic intentions. Prose consciousness feels cramped when it is confined to only *one* out of a multitude of heteroglot languages, for one linguistic timbre is inadequate to it.

We have touched upon only those major forms typical of the most important variants of the European novel, but in themselves they do not, of course, exhaust all the possible means for incorporating and organizing heteroglossia in the novel. A combination of all these forms in separate given novels, and consequently in various generic types generated by these novels, is also possible. Of such a sort is the classic and purest model of the novel as genre – Cervantes' *Don Quixote*, which realizes in itself, in extraordinary depth and breadth, all the artistic possibilities of heteroglot and internally dialogized novelistic discourse.

Heteroglossia, once incorporated into the novel (whatever the forms for its incorporation), is *another's speech in another's language*, serving to express authorial intentions but in a refracted way. Such speech constitutes a special type of *double-voiced discourse*. It serves two speakers at the same time and expresses simultaneously two different intentions: the direct intention of the character who is speaking, and the refracted intention of the author. In such discourse there are two

voices, two meanings and two expressions. And all the while these two voices are dialogically interrelated, they – as it were – know about each other (just as two exchanges in a dialogue know of each other and are structured in this mutual knowledge of each other); it is as if they actually hold a conversation with each other. Double-voiced discourse is always internally dialogized. Examples of this would be comic, ironic or parodic discourse, the refracting discourse of a narrator, refracting discourse in the language of a character and finally the discourse of a whole incorporated genre – all these discourses are double-voiced and internally dialogized. A potential dialogue is embedded in them, one as yet unfolded, a concentrated dialogue of two voices, two world views, two languages.

Double-voiced, internally dialogized discourse is also possible, of course, in a language system that is hermetic, pure and unitary, a system alien to the linguistic relativism of prose consciousness; it follows that such discourse is also possible in the purely poetic genres. But in those systems there is no soil to nourish the development of such discourse in the slightest meaningful or essential way. Double-voiced discourse is very widespread in rhetorical genres, but even there – remaining as it does within the boundaries of a single language system – it is not fertilized by a deep-rooted connection with the forces of historical becoming that serve to stratify language, and therefore rhetorical genres are at best merely a distanced echo of this becoming, narrowed down to an individual polemic.

Such poetic and rhetorical double-voicedness, cut off from any process of linguistic stratification, may be adequately unfolded into an individual dialogue, into individual argument and conversation between two persons, even while the exchanges in the dialogue are immanent to a single unitary language: they may not be in agreement, they may even be opposed, but they are diverse neither in their speech nor in their language. Such double-voicing, remaining within the boundaries of a single hermetic and unitary language system, without any underlying fundamental socio-linguistic orchestration, may be only a stylistically secondary accompaniment to the dialogue and forms of polemic.[9] The internal bifurcation (double-voicing) of discourse, sufficient to a single and unitary language and to a consistently monologic style, can never be a fundamental form of discourse: it is merely a game, a tempest in a teapot.

The double-voicedness one finds in prose is of another sort altogether. There – on the rich soil of novelistic prose – double-voicedness draws its energy, its dialogized ambiguity, not from *individual* dissonances, misunderstandings or contradictions (however tragic, however firmly grounded in individual destinies);[10] in the novel, this double-voicedness sinks its roots deep into a fundamental, socio-linguistic speech diversity and multi-languagedness. True, even in the novel heteroglossia is by and large always personified, incarnated in individual human figures, with disagreements and oppositions individualized. But such oppositions of individual wills and minds are submerged in *social* heteroglossia, they are reconceptualized through it. Oppositions between individuals are only surface upheavals of the untamed elements in social heteroglossia, surface manifestations of those elements that play *on* such individual oppositions, make them contradictory, saturate their consciousness and discourses with a more fundamental speech diversity.

Therefore the internal dialogism of double-voiced prose discourse can never be exhausted thematically (just as the metaphoric energy of language can never be exhausted thematically); it can never be developed into the motivation or subject for a manifest dialogue, such as might fully embody, with no residue, the internally dialogic potential embedded in linguistic heteroglossia. The internal dialogism of authentic prose discourse, which grows organically out of a stratified and heteroglot language, cannot fundamentally be dramatized or dramatically resolved (brought to an authentic end); it cannot ultimately be fitted into the frame of any manifest dialogue, into the frame of a mere conversation between persons; it is not ultimately divisible into verbal exchanges possessing precisely marked boundaries.[11] This double-voicedness in prose is prefigured in language itself (in authentic metaphors, as well as in myth), in language as a social phenomenon that is becoming in history, socially stratified and weathered in this process of becoming.

The relativizing of linguistic consciousness, its crucial participation in the social multi- and vari-languagedness of evolving languages, the various wanderings of semantic and expressive intentions and the trajectory of this consciousness through various languages (languages that are all equally well conceptualized and equally objective), the inevitable necessity for such a consciousness to speak indirectly, conditionally, in a refracted way – these are all indispensable prerequisites for an authentic double-voiced prose discourse. This double-voicedness makes its presence felt by the novelist in the living heteroglossia of language, and in the multi-languagedness surrounding and nourishing his own consciousness; it is not invented in superficial, isolated rhetorical polemics with another person.

If the novelist loses touch with this linguistic ground of prose style, if he is unable to attain the heights of a relativized, Galilean linguistic consciousness, if he is deaf to organic double-voicedness and to the internal dialogization of living and evolving discourse, then he will never comprehend, or even realize, the actual possibilities and tasks of the novel as a genre. He may, of course, create an artistic work that compositionally and thematically will be similar to a novel, will be "made" exactly as a novel is made, but he will not thereby have created a novel. The style will always give him away. We will recognize the naively self-confident or obtusely stubborn unity of a smooth, pure single-voiced language (perhaps accompanied by a primitive, artificial, worked-up double-voicedness). We quickly sense that such an author finds it easy to purge his work of speech diversity: he simply does not listen to the fundamental heteroglossia inherent in actual language; he mistakes social overtones, which create the timbres of words, for irritating noises that it is his task to eliminate. The novel, when torn out of authentic linguistic speech diversity, emerges in most cases as a "closet drama," with detailed, fully developed and "artistically worked out" stage directions (it is, of course, bad drama). In such a novel, divested of its language diversity, authorial language inevitably ends up in the awkward and absurd position of the language of stage directions in plays.[12]

The double-voiced prose word has a double meaning. But the poetic word, in the narrow sense, also has a double, even a multiple, meaning. It is this that basically distinguishes it from the word as concept, or the word as term. The poetic word is a trope, requiring a precise feeling for the two meanings contained in it.

But no matter how one understands the interrelationship of meanings in a poetic symbol (a trope), this interrelationship is never of the dialogic sort; it is impossible under any conditions or at any time to imagine a trope (say, a metaphor) being unfolded into the two exchanges of a dialogue, that is, two meanings parceled out between two separate voices. For this reason the dual meaning (or multiple meaning) of the symbol never brings in its wake dual accents. On the contrary, one voice, a single-accent system, is fully sufficient to express poetic ambiguity. It is possible to interpret the interrelationships of different meanings in a symbol logically (as the relationship of a part or an individual to the whole, as for example a proper noun that has become a symbol, or the relationship of the concrete to the abstract and so on); one may grasp this relationship philosophically and ontologically, as a special kind of representational relationship, or as a relationship between essence and appearance and so forth, or one may shift into the foreground the emotional and evaluative dimension of such relationship – but all these types of relationships between various meanings do not and cannot go beyond the boundaries of the relationship between a word and its object, or the boundaries of various aspects in the object. The entire event is played out between the word and its object; all of the play of the poetic symbol is in that space. A symbol cannot presuppose any fundamental relationship to another's word, to another's voice. The polysemy of the poetic symbol presupposes the unity of a voice with which it is identical, and it presupposes that such a voice is completely alone within its own discourse. As soon as another's voice, another's accent, the possibility of another's point of view breaks through this play of the symbol, the poetic plane is destroyed and the symbol is translated onto the plane of prose.

To understand the difference between ambiguity in poetry and double-voicedness in prose, it is sufficient to take any symbol and give it an ironic accent (in a correspondingly appropriate context, of course), that is, to introduce into it one's own voice, to refract within it one's own fresh intention.[13] In this process the poetic symbol – while remaining, of course, a symbol – is at one and the same time translated onto the plane of prose and becomes a double-voiced word: in the space between the word and its object another's word, another's accent intrudes, a mantle of materiality is cast over the symbol (an operation of this sort would naturally result in a rather simple and primitive double-voiced structure).

An example of this simplest type of prosification of the poetic symbol in *Evgenij Onegin* is the stanza on Lensky:

Of love he [Lensky] sang, love's service choosing,
And timid was his simple tune
As ever artless maiden's musing,
As babes aslumber, as the moon....[...]

The poetic symbols of this stanza are organized simultaneously at two levels: the level of Lensky's lyrics themselves – in the semantic and expressive system of the "Göttigen Geist" – and on the level of Pushkin's speech, for whom the "Göttigen Geist" with its language and its poetics is merely an instantiation of the literary heteroglossia of the epoch, but one that is already becoming typical: a fresh tone, a fresh voice amid the multiple voices of literary language, literary world views and the life these world views regulate. Some other voices in this heteroglossia – of literature and of the real life contemporaneous with it – would be Onegin's Byronic-Chateaubriandesque language, the Richardsonian language and world of the provincial Tatiana, the down-to-earth rustic language spoken at the Larins' estate, the language and the world of Tatiana in Petersburg and other languages as well – including the indirect languages of the author – which undergo change in the course of the work. The whole of this heteroglossia (*Evgenij Onegin* is an encyclopedia of the styles and languages of the epoch) orchestrates the intentions of the author and is responsible for the authentically novelistic style of this work.

Thus the images in the above-cited stanza, being ambiguous (metaphorical) poetic symbols serving Lensky's intentions in Lensky's belief system, become double-voiced prose symbols in the system of Pushkin's speech. These are, of course, authentic prose symbols, arising from the heteroglossia inherent in the epoch's evolving literary language, not a superficial, rhetorical parody or irony.

Such is the distinction between true double-voicedness in fictive practice, and the *single-voiced* double or multiple meaning that finds expression in the purely poetic symbol. The ambiguity of double-voiced discourse is internally dialogized, fraught with dialogue, and may in fact even give birth to dialogues comprised of truly separate voices (but such dialogues are not dramatic; they are, rather, interminable prose dialogues). What is more, double-voicedness is never exhausted in these dialogues, it cannot be extracted fully from the discourse – not by a rational, logical counting of the individual parts, nor by drawing distinctions between the various parts of a monologic unit of discourse (as happens in rhetoric), nor by a definite cut-off between the verbal exchanges of a finite dialogue, such as occurs in the theater. Authentic double-voicedness, although it generates novelistic prose dialogues, is not exhausted in these dialogues and remains in the discourse, in language, like a spring of dialogism that never runs dry – for the internal dialogism of discourse is something that inevitably accompanies the social, contradictory historical becoming of language.

If the central problem in poetic theory is the problem of the poetic symbol, then the central problem in prose theory is the problem of the double-voiced, internally dialogized word, in all its diverse types and variants.

For the novelist working in prose, the object is always entangled in someone else's discourse about it, it is already present with qualifications, an object of dispute that is conceptualized and evaluated variously, inseparable from the heteroglot social apperception of it. The novelist speaks of this "already qualified world" in a language that is heteroglot and internally dialogized. Thus both object and language are revealed to the novelist in their historical dimension, in the process of social and heteroglot becoming. For the novelist, there is no world outside his socio-heteroglot perception – and there is no language outside the heteroglot intentions that stratify that world. Therefore it is possible to have, even in the novel, that profound but unique unity of a language (or more precisely, of languages) with its own object, with its own world, unity of the sort one finds in poetry. Just as the poetic image seems to have been born out of language itself, to have sprung organically from it, to have been pre-formed in it, so also novelistic images seem to be grafted organically on to their own double-voiced language, pre-formed, as it were, within it, in the innards of the distinctive multi-speechedness organic to that language. In the novel, the "already bespoke quality" [ogovor-ennost'] of the world is woven together with the "already uttered" quality [peregovorennost'] of language, into the unitary event of the world's hetero-glot becoming, in both social consciousness and language.

Even the poetic word (in the narrow sense) must break through to its object, penetrate the alien word in which the object is entangled; it also encounters heteroglot language and must break through in order to create a unity and a pure intentionality (which is neither given nor ready-made). But the trajectory of the poetic word toward its own object and toward the unity of language is a path along which the poetic word is continually encountering someone else's word, and each takes new bearings from the other; the records of the passage remain in the slag of the creative process, which is then cleared away (as scaffolding is cleared away once construction is finished), so that the finished work may rise as unitary speech, one co-extensive with its object, as if it were speech about an "Edenic" world. This single-voiced purity and unqualified directness that intentions possess in poetic discourse so crafted is purchased at the price of a certain con-ventionality in poetic language.

If the art of poetry, as a utopian philosophy of genres, gives rise to the conception of a purely poetic, extrahistorical language, a language far removed from the petty rounds of everyday life, a language of the gods – then it must be said that the art of prose is close to a conception of lan-guages as historically concrete and living things. The prose art presumes a deliberate feeling for the historical and social concreteness of living dis-course, as well as its relativity, a feeling for its participation in historical becoming and in social struggle; it deals with discourse that is still warm from that struggle and hostility, as yet unresolved and still fraught with hostile intentions and accents; prose art finds discourse in this state and subjects it to the dynamic-unity of its own style.

Notes

1 Such a device is unthinkable in the epic.
2 Cf. the grotesque pseudo-objective motivations in Gogol.
3 Intellect as embodied in the forms and the methods of verbal and ideological thought (i.e., the linguistic horizon of normal human intellectual activity) becomes in Jean Paul something infinitely petty and ludicrous when seen in the light of "reason." His humor results from play with intellectual activity and its forms.

4 It is of course impossible in the strict sense to include Rabelais himself – either chronologically or in terms of his essential character – among the representatives of comic novelists.
5 Nevertheless sentimentality and "high serious-ness" is not completely eliminated (especially in Jean Paul).
6 Citations from *Fathers and Sons* are from: Ivan Tur-genev, *Fathers and Sons*, tr. Rosemary Edmonds (London: Penguin, 1965).

7 Citations from *Virgin Soil* are from: Ivan Turgenev, *Virgin Soil*, tr. Constance Garnett (New York: Grove Press, n.d.).

8 Citations from *Eugene Onegin* are from the Walter Arndt translation (New York: Dutton, 1963), slightly modified to correspond with Bakhtin's remarks about particulars.

9 In neoclassicism, this double-voicing becomes crucial only in the low genres, especially in satire.

10 Within the limits of the world of poetry and a unitary language, everything important in such disagreements and contradictions can and must be laid out in a direct and pure dramatic dialogue.

11 The more consistent and unitary the language, the more acute, dramatic and "finished" such exchanges generally are.

12 In his well-known works on the theory and technique of the novel, Spielhagen focuses on precisely such unnovelistic novels, and ignores precisely the kind of potential specific to the novel as a genre. As a theoretician Spielhagen was deaf to heteroglot language and to that which it specifically generates: double-voiced discourse.

13 Alexei Alexandrovich Karenin had the habit of avoiding certain words, and expressions connected with them. He made up double-voiced constructions outside any context, exclusively on the intonational plane: "'Well, yes, as you see, your devoted husband, as devoted as in the first year of marriage, is burning with impatience to see you,' he said in his slow high-pitched voice and in the tone in which he almost always addressed her, a tone of derision for anyone who could really talk like that" (*Anna Karenina* [New York: Signet, 1961] part I, ch. 30; translation by David Magarshack).

16

Taste and the Reproduction of Art

Benedetto Croce

When the entire aesthetic and externalizing process has been completed, when a beautiful expression has been produced and it has been fixed in a definite physical material, what is meant by *judging it? To reproduce it in oneself*, answer the critics of art, almost with one voice. Very good. Let us try thoroughly to understand this fact, and with that object in view, let us represent it schematically.

The individual A is seeking the expression of an impression which he feels or anticipates, but has not yet expressed. See him trying various words and phrases which may give the sought-for expression, that expression which must exist, but which he does not possess. He tries the combination *m*, but rejects it as unsuitable, inexpressive, incomplete, ugly: he tries the combination *n*, with a like result. *He does not see at all, or does not see clearly.* The expression still eludes him. After other vain attempts, during which he sometimes approaches, sometimes retreats from the mark at which he aims, all of a sudden (almost as though formed spontaneously of itself) he forms the sought-for expression, and *lux facta est*. He enjoys for an instant aesthetic pleasure or the pleasure of the beautiful. The ugly, with its correlative displeasure, was the aesthetic activity which had not succeeded in conquering the obstacle; the beautiful is the expressive activity which now displays itself triumphant.

We have taken this example from the domain of speech, as being nearer and more accessible, and because we all talk, though we do not all draw or paint. Now if another individual, whom we shall call B, is to judge that expression and decide whether it be beautiful or ugly, he *must of necessity place himself at A's point of view*, and go through the whole process again, with the help of the physical sign supplied to him by A. If A has seen clearly, then B (who has placed himself at A's point of view) will also see clearly and will see this expression as beautiful. If A has not seen clearly, then B also will not see clearly, and will find the expression more or less ugly, *just as A did*.

It may be observed that we have not taken into consideration two other cases: that of A having a clear and B an obscure vision; and that of A having an obscure and B a clear vision. Strictly speaking, these two cases are *impossible*.

Expressive activity, just because it is activity, is not caprice, but spiritual necessity; it cannot solve a definite aesthetic problem save in one way, which is the right way. It will be objected to this plain statement that works which seem beautiful to the artists are afterwards found to be ugly by the critics; while other works with which the artists were discontented and held to be imperfect or failures are, on the contrary, held to be beautiful and perfect by the critics. But in this case, one of the two is wrong: either the critics or the artists, sometimes the artists, at other times the critics. Indeed, the producer of an expression does not always fully realize what is happening in his soul. Haste, vanity, want of reflexion, theoretic prejudices, make people say, and others sometimes almost believe, that works of ours are beautiful, which, if we really looked into ourselves, we should see to be ugly, as they are in reality. Thus poor Don Quixote, when he had reattached to his helmet as well as he could the vizor of cardboard – the vizor that had showed itself to possess but the feeblest force of resistance at the first encounter, – took good care not to test it again with a well-delivered sword-thrust, but simply declared and maintained it to be (says the author) *por celada finisima de encaxe*. And in other cases, the same reasons, or opposite but analogous ones, trouble the consciousness of the artist, and cause him to value badly what he has successfully produced, or to strive to undo and do again for the worse what he has done well in artistic spontaneity. An instance of this is Tasso and his passage from the *Gerusalemme liberata* to the *Gerusalemme conquistata*. In the same way, haste, laziness, want of reflexion, theoretic prejudices, personal sympathies or animosities, and other motives of a similar sort, sometimes cause the critics to proclaim ugly what is beautiful, and beautiful what is ugly. Were they to eliminate such disturbing elements, they would feel the work of art as it really is, and would not leave it to posterity, that more diligent and more dispassionate judge, to award the palm, or to do that justice which they have refused.

It is clear from the preceding theorem that the activity of judgement which criticizes and recognizes the beautiful is identical with what produces it. The only difference lies in the diversity of circumstances, since in the one case it is a question of aesthetic production, in the other of reproduction. The activity which judges is called *taste*; the productive activity is called *genius*: genius and taste are therefore substantially *identical*.

The common remark that the critic should possess something of the genius of the artist and that the artist should possess taste, gives a glimpse of this identity; or the remark that there exists an active (productive) and a passive (reproductive) taste. But it is also negated in other equally common remarks, as when people speak of taste without genius, or of genius without taste. These last observations are meaningless, unless they allude to quantitative or psychological differences, those being called geniuses without taste who produce works of art, inspired in their chief parts and neglected or defective in their secondary parts, and men of taste without genius, those who, while they succeed in obtaining certain isolated or secondary merits, do not possess sufficient power for a great artistic synthesis. Analogous explanations can easily be given of other similar expressions. But to posit a substantial difference between genius and taste, between artistic produc-

tion and reproduction, would render both communication and judgement alike inconceivable. How could we judge what remained external to us? How could that which is produced by a given activity be judged by a *different* activity? The critic may be a small genius, the artist a great one; the former may have the strength of ten, the latter of a hundred; the former, in order to reach a certain height, will have need of the assistance of the other; but the nature of both must remain the same. To judge Dante, we must raise ourselves to his level: let it be well understood that empirically we are not Dante, nor Dante we; but in that moment of contemplation and judgement, our spirit is one with that of the poet, and in that moment we and he are one thing. In this identity alone resides the possibility that our little souls can echo great souls, and grow great with them in the universality of the spirit.

Let us remark in passing that what has been said of the aesthetic judgement holds good equally for every other activity and for every other judgement; and that scientific, economic, and ethical criticism is effected in a like manner. To limit ourselves to this last, only if we place ourselves ideally in the same conditions in which he found himself who took a given resolution, can we form a judgement as to whether his decision were moral or immoral. An action would otherwise remain incomprehensible and therefore impossible to judge. A homicide may be a rascal or a hero: if this be, within limits, indifferent as regards the defence of society, which condemns both to the same punishment, it is not indifferent to one who wishes to distinguish and judge from the moral point of view, and we therefore cannot dispense with reconstructing the individual psychology of the homicide, in order to determine the true nature of his deed, not merely in its legal, but also in its moral aspect. In Ethics, a moral taste or tact is sometimes mentioned, answering to what is generally called the moral consciousness, that is to say, to the activity of the good will itself.

The explanation above given of aesthetic judgement or reproduction both agrees with and condemns the absolutists and relativists, those who affirm and those who deny the absoluteness of taste.

In affirming that the beautiful can be judged, the absolutists are right; but the theory on which they found their affirmation is not tenable, because they conceive of the beautiful, that is, aesthetic value, as something placed outside the aesthetic activity, as a concept or a model which an artist realizes in his work, and of which the critic avails himself afterwards in judging the work itself. These concepts and models have no existence in art, for when proclaiming that every art can be judged only in itself and that it has its model in itself, they implicitly denied the existence of objective models of beauty, whether these are intellectual concepts, or ideas suspended in a metaphysical heaven.

In proclaiming this, their adversaries, the relativists, are perfectly right, and effect an advance upon them. However, the initial rationality of their thesis in its turn becomes converted into a false theory. Repeating the ancient adage that there is no accounting for tastes, they believe that aesthetic expression is of the same nature as the pleasant and the unpleasant, which every one feels in his own way, and about which there is no dispute. But we know that the pleasant and the unpleasant are utilitarian, practical facts. Thus the relativists deny the specific character of the aesthetic fact, and again confound expression with impression, the theoretic with the practical.

The true solution lies in rejecting alike relativism or psychologism and false absolutism; and in recognizing that the criterion of taste is absolute, but absolute in a different way from that of the intellect, which expresses itself in ratiocination. The criterion of taste is absolute, with the intuitive absoluteness of the imagination. Thus any act of expressive activity, which is so really, is to be recognized as beautiful, and any fact as ugly in which expressive activity and passivity are found engaged with one another in an unfinished struggle.

Between absolutists and relativists is a third class, which may be called that of the relative relativists. These affirm the existence of absolute values in other fields, such as Logic and Ethic, but deny it in the field of Aesthetic. To dispute about science or morals seems to them to be rational and justifiable, because science depends upon the universal, common to all men, and morality upon duty, which is also a law of human nature; but how dispute about art, which depends upon imagination? Not only, however, is the imaginative activity universal and no less inherent in human nature than the logical concept and practical duty; but there is a preliminary objection to the thesis in question. If the absoluteness of the imagination be denied, we must also deny intellectual or conceptual truth and implicitly morality. Does not morality presuppose logical distinctions? How could

these be known, otherwise than in expressions and words, that is to say, in imaginative form? If the absoluteness of the imagination were removed, the life of the spirit would tremble to its foundations. One individual would no longer understand another, nor indeed his own self of a moment before, which is already another individual considered a moment after.

Nevertheless, variety of judgements is an indubitable fact. Men disagree as to logical, ethical, and economical valuations; and they disagree equally or even more as to the aesthetic. If certain reasons recorded by us above, such as haste, prejudices, passions, etc., may lessen the importance of this disagreement, they do not on that account annul it. When speaking of the stimuli of reproduction we have added a caution, for we said that reproduction takes place, *if all the other conditions remain equal.* Do they remain equal? Does the hypothesis correspond to reality?

It would appear not. In order to reproduce an impression several times by means of a suitable physical stimulus it is necessary that this stimulus be not changed, and that the organism remain in the same psychical conditions as those in which was experienced the impression that it is desired to reproduce. Now it is a fact that the physical stimulus is continually changing, and in like manner the psychological conditions.

Oil-paintings grow dark, frescoes fade, statues lose noses, hands and legs, architecture becomes totally or partially a ruin, the tradition of the execution of a piece of music is lost, the text of a poem is corrupted by bad copyists or bad printing. These are obvious instances of the changes which daily occur in objects or physical stimuli. As regards psychological conditions, we will not dwell upon the cases of deafness or blindness, that is to say, upon the loss of entire orders of psychical impressions; these cases are secondary and of less importance compared with the fundamental, daily, inevitable and perpetual changes of the society around us and of the internal conditions of our individual life. The phonetic manifestations or words and verses of Dante's *Commedia* must produce a very different impression on an Italian citizen engaged in the politics of the third Rome, from that experienced by a well-informed and intimate contemporary of the poet. The Madonna of Cimabue is still in the Church of Santa Maria Novella; but does she speak to the visitor of to-day as to the Florentines of the thirteenth century? Even though she were not also darkened by time, must we not suppose that the impression which she now produces is altogether different from that of former times? And even in the case of the same individual poet, will a poem composed by him in youth make the same impression upon him when he re-reads it in his old age, with psychic conditions altogether changed?

It is true that certain aestheticians have attempted a distinction between stimuli and stimuli, between *natural* and *conventional* signs. The former are held to have a constant effect upon all; the latter only upon a limited circle. In their belief, signs employed in painting are natural, those used in poetry conventional. But the difference between them is at the most only one of degree. It has often been said that painting is a language understood by all, while with poetry it is otherwise. Here, for example, Leonardo found one of the prerogatives of his art, "which hath not need of interpreters of different tongues as have letters," and it pleases man and beast. He relates the anecdote of that portrait of the father of a family "which the little grandchildren were wont to caress while they were still in swaddling-clothes, and the dogs and cats of the house in like manner." But other anecdotes, such as those of the savages who took the portrait of a soldier for a boat, or considered the portrait of a man on horseback to be furnished with only one leg, are apt to shake one's faith in the understanding of painting by sucklings, dogs and cats. Fortunately, no arduous researches are necessary to convince oneself that pictures, poetry and all works of art only produce effects upon souls prepared to receive them. Natural signs do not exist; because all are equally conventional, or, to speak with greater exactness, *historically conditioned*.

Granting this, how are we to succeed in causing the expression to be reproduced by means of the physical object? How obtain the same effect, when the conditions are no longer the same? Would it not, rather, seem necessary to conclude that expressions cannot be reproduced, despite the physical instruments made for the purpose, and that what is called reproduction consists in ever new expressions? Such would indeed be the conclusion if the varieties of physical and psychical conditions were intrinsically insurmountable. But since the insuperability has none of the characteristics of necessity we must on the contrary conclude that reproduction always occurs when we can replace ourselves in the conditions in which the stimulus (physical beauty) was produced.

Not only can we replace ourselves in these conditions as an abstract possibility, but as a matter of fact we do so continually. Individual life, which is communion with ourselves (with our past), and social life, which is communion with our like, would not otherwise be possible.

As regards the physical object, palaeographers and philologists, who *restore* to texts their original physiognomy, *restorers* of pictures and of statues and other industrious toilers strive precisely to preserve or to restore to the physical object all its primitive energy. These efforts are certainly not always successful, or are not completely successful, for it is never or hardly ever possible to obtain a restoration complete in its smallest details. But the insurmountable is here only present accidentally and must not lead us to overlook the successes which actually are achieved.

Historical interpretation labours for its part to reintegrate in us the psychological conditions which have changed in the course of history. It revives the dead, completes the fragmentary, and enables us to see a work of art (a physical object) as its author saw it in the moment of production.

A condition of this historical labour is tradition, with the help of which it is possible to collect the scattered rays and concentrate them in one focus. With the help of memory we surround the physical stimulus with all the facts among which it arose; and thus we enable it to act upon us as it acted upon him who produced it.

Where the tradition is broken, interpretation is arrested; in this case, the products of the past remain silent for us. Thus the expressions contained in the Etruscan or Mexican inscriptions are unattainable; thus we still hear discussions among ethnographers as to whether certain products of the art of savages are pictures or writings; thus archaeologists and prehistorians are not always able to establish with certainty whether the figures found on the pottery of a certain region, and on other instruments employed, are of a religious or profane nature. But the arrest of interpretation, as that of restoration, is never a definitely insurmountable barrier; and the daily discoveries of new historical sources and of new methods of better exploiting the old, which we may hope to see ever improving, link up again broken traditions.

We do not wish to deny that erroneous historical interpretation sometimes produces what may be called *palimpsests*, new expressions imposed upon the ancient, artistic fancies instead of historical reproductions. The so-called "fascination of the past" depends in part upon these expressions of ours, which we weave upon the historical. Thus has been discovered in Greek plastic art the calm and serene intuition of life of those peoples, who nevertheless felt the universal sorrow so poignantly; thus "the terror of the year 1000" has recently been discerned on the faces of the Byzantine saints, a terror which is a misunderstanding, or an artificial legend invented later by men of learning. But *historical criticism* tends precisely to circumscribe fancies and to establish exactly the point of view from which we must look.

By means of the above process we live in communication with other men of the present and of the past; and we must not conclude because we sometimes, and indeed often, meet with an unknown or an ill-known, that therefore, when we believe we are engaged in a dialogue, we are always speaking a monologue; or that we are unable even to repeat the monologue which we formerly held with ourselves.

17

What is Literature?

Jean-Paul Sartre

'If you want to commit yourself,' writes a young imbecile, 'what are you waiting for? Join the Communist Party.' A great writer who committed himself often and then cried off still more often, but who has forgotten, said to me, 'The worst artists are the most committed. Look at the Soviet painters.' An old critic gently complained, 'You want to murder literature. Contempt for belles-lettres is spread out insolently all through your review.' A petty mind calls me pigheaded, which for him is evidently the highest insult. An author who barely crawled from one war to the other and whose name sometimes awakens languishing memories in old men accuses me of not being concerned with immortality; he knows, thank God, any number of people whose chief hope it is. In the eyes of an American hack-journalist the trouble with me is that I have not read Bergson or Freud; as for Flaubert, who did not commit himself, it seems that he haunts me like remorse. Smart-alecks wink at me, 'And poetry? And painting? And music? You want to commit them, too?' And some martial spirits demand, 'What's it all about? Commitment in literature? Well, it's the old socialist realism, unless it's a revival of populism, only more aggressive.'

What nonsense. They read quickly, badly, and pass judgement before they have understood. So let's begin all over again. This doesn't amuse anyone, neither you nor me. But we have to hit the nail on the head. And since critics condemn me in the name of literature without ever saying what they mean by that, the best answer to give them is to examine the art of writing without prejudice.

What is writing? Why does one write? For whom? The fact is, it seems that nobody has ever asked himself these questions.

What Is Writing?

No, we do not want to 'commit' painting, sculpture, and music 'too', or at least not in the same way. And why would we want to? When a writer of past centuries expressed an opinion about his craft, was he immediately asked to apply it to the other arts? But today it's the thing to 'talk painting' in the jargon of the musician or the literary man and to 'talk literature' in the jargon of the painter, as if at bottom there were only one art which expressed itself indifferently in one or the other of these languages, like the Spinozistic substance which is adequately reflected by each of its attributes.

Doubtless, one could find at the origin of every artistic calling a certain undifferentiated choice which circumstances, education, and contact with the world particularized only later. Besides, there is no doubt that the arts of a period mutually influence each other and are conditioned by the same social factors. But those who want to expose the absurdity of a literary theory by showing that it is inapplicable to music must first prove that the arts are parallel.

Now, there is no such parallelism. Here, as everywhere, it is not only the form which differentiates, but the matter as well. And it is one thing to work with colour and sound, and another to express oneself by means of words. Notes, colours, and forms are not signs. They refer to nothing exterior to themselves. To be sure, it is quite impossible to reduce them strictly to themselves, and the idea of a pure sound, for example, is an abstraction. As Merleau-Ponty has pointed out in *The Phenomenology of Perception*, there is no quality of sensation so bare that it is not penetrated with significance. But the dim little meaning which dwells within it, a light joy, a timid sadness, remains immanent or trembles about it like a heat mist; it *is* colour or sound. Who can distinguish the green apple from its tart gaiety? And aren't we already saying too much in naming 'the tart gaiety of the green apple'? There is green, there is red, and that is all. They are things, they exist by themselves.

It is true that one might, by convention, confer the value of signs upon them. Thus, we talk of the language of flowers. But if, after the agreement, white roses signify 'fidelity' to me, the fact is that I have stopped seeing them as roses. My attention cuts through them to aim beyond them at this abstract virtue. I forget them. I no longer pay attention to their mossy abundance, to their sweet stagnant odour. I have not even perceived them. That means that I have not behaved like an artist. For the artist, the colour, the bouquet, the tinkling of the spoon on the saucer, are *things*, in the highest degree. He stops at the quality of the sound or the form. He returns to it constantly and is enchanted with it. It is this colour–object that he is going to transfer to his canvas, and the only modification he will make it undergo is that he will transform it into an *imaginary* object. He is therefore as far as he can be from considering colours and signs as a *language*.[1]

What is valid for the elements of artistic creation is also valid for their combinations. The painter does not want to draw signs on his canvas, he wants to create a thing.[2] And if he puts together red, yellow, and green, there is no reason why this collection of colours should have a definable significance, that is, should refer particularly to another object. Doubtless the composition is also inhabited by a soul, and since there must have been motives, even hidden ones, for the painter to have chosen yellow rather than violet, it may be asserted that the objects thus created reflect his deepest tendencies. However, they never express his anger, his anguish, or his joy as do words or the expression of the face; they are impregnated with these emotions; and in order for them to have crept into these colours, which by themselves already

had something like a meaning, his emotions get mixed up and grow obscure. Nobody can quite recognize them there.

Tintoretto did not choose that yellow rift in the sky above Golgotha to *signify* anguish or to *provoke* it. It is anguish and yellow sky at the same time. Not sky of anguish or anguished sky; it is an anguish become thing, an anguish which has turned into yellow rift of sky, and which thereby is submerged and impasted by the qualities peculiar to things, by their impermeability, their extension, their blind permanence, their externality, and that infinity of relations which they maintain with other things. That is, it is no longer *readable*. It is like an immense and vain effort, forever arrested half-way between sky and earth, to express what their nature keeps them from expressing.

Similarly, the significance of a melody – if one can still speak of significance – is nothing outside the melody itself, unlike ideas, which can be adequately rendered in several ways. Call it joyous or sad. It will always be over and above anything you can say about it. Not because its passions, which are perhaps at the origin of the invented theme, have, by being incorporated into notes, undergone a transubstantiation and a transmutation. A cry of grief is a sign of the grief which provokes it, but a song of grief is both grief itself and something other than grief. Or, if one wishes to adopt the existentialist vocabulary, it is a grief which does not *exist* any more, which *is*. But, you will say, suppose the painter portrays houses? That's just it. He *makes* them, that is, he creates an imaginary house on the canvas and not a sign of a house. And the house which thus appears preserves all the ambiguity of real houses.

The writer can guide you and, if he describes a hovel, make it seem the symbol of social injustice and provoke your indignation. The painter is mute. He presents you with *a* hovel, that's all. You are free to see in it what you like. That attic window will never be the symbol of misery; for that, it would have to be a sign, whereas it is a thing. The bad painter looks for the type. He paints the Arab, the Child, the Woman; the good one knows that neither the Arab nor the proletarian exists either in reality or on his canvas. He offers a workman, a certain workman. And what are we to think about a workman? An infinity of contradictory things. All thoughts and all feelings are there, adhering to the canvas in a state of profound undifferentiation. It is up to you to choose. Sometimes, high-minded artists try to move us. They paint long lines of workmen waiting in the snow to be hired, the emaciated faces of the unemployed, battlefields. They affect us no more than does Greuze with his 'Prodigal Son'. And that masterpiece, 'The Massacre of Guernica', does anyone think that it won over a single heart to the Spanish cause? And yet something is said that can never quite be heard and that would take an infinity of words to express. And Picasso's long harlequins, ambiguous and eternal, haunted with inexplicable meaning, inseparable from their stooping leanness and their pale diamond-shaped tights, are emotion become flesh, emotion which the flesh has absorbed as the blotter absorbs ink, and emotion which is unrecognizable, lost, strange to itself, scattered to the four corners of space and yet present to itself.

I have no doubt that charity or anger can produce other objects, but they will likewise be swallowed up; they will lose their name; there will remain only things haunted by a mysterious soul. One does not paint meanings; one does not put them to music. Under these conditions, who would dare require that the painter or musician commit himself?

On the other hand, the writer deals with meanings. Still, a distinction must be made. The empire of signs is prose; poetry is on the side of painting, sculpture, and music. I am accused of detesting it; the proof, so they say, is that *Les Temps Modernes*[3] publishes very few poems. On the contrary, this is proof that we like it. To be convinced, all one need do is take a look at contemporary production. 'At least,' critics say triumphantly, 'you can't even dream of committing it.' Indeed. But why should I want to? Because it uses words as does prose? But it does not use them in the same way, and it does not even *use* them at all. I should rather say that it serves them. Poets are men who refuse to *utilize* language. Now, since the quest for truth takes place in and by language conceived as a certain kind of instrument, it is unnecessary to imagine that they aim to discern or expound the true. Nor do they dream of *naming* the world, and, this being the case, they name nothing at all, for naming implies a perpetual sacrifice of the name to the object named, or, as Hegel would say, the name is revealed as the inessential in the face of the thing which is essential. They do not speak, neither do they keep silent; it is something different. It has been said that they wanted to destroy the 'word' by monstrous couplings, but this is false. For then they would have to be thrown into the midst of utilitarian language and would have had to try to retrieve words from it in odd little groups, as for example 'horse' and 'butter' by writing 'horses of butter'.[4]

Besides the fact that such an enterprise would require infinite time, it is not conceivable that one can keep oneself on the plane of the utilitarian project, consider words as instruments, and at the same time contemplate taking their instrumentality away from them. In fact, the poet has withdrawn from language-instrument in a single movement. Once and for all he has chosen the poetic attitude which considers words as things and not as signs. For the ambiguity of the sign implies that one can penetrate it at will like a pane of glass and pursue the thing signified, or turn one's gaze towards its *reality* and consider it as an object. The man who talks is beyond words and near the object, whereas the poet is on this side of them. For the former, they are domesticated; for the latter they are in the wild state. For the former, they are useful conventions, tools which gradually wear out and which one throws away when they are no longer serviceable; for the latter, they are natural things which sprout naturally upon the earth like grass and trees.

But if the poet dwells upon words, as does the painter with colours and the musician with sounds, that does not mean that they have lost all meaning in his eyes. Indeed, it is meaning alone which can give words their verbal unity. Without it they are frittered away into sounds and strokes of the pen. Only, it too becomes natural. It is no longer the goal which is always out of reach and which human transcendence is always aiming at, but a property of each term, analogous to the expression of a face, to the little sad or gay meaning of sounds and colours. Having flowed into the word, having been absorbed by its sonority or visual aspect, having been thickened and defaced, it too is a thing, uncreated and eternal.

For the poet, language is a structure of the external world. The speaker is *in a situation* in language; he is invested by words. They are prolongations of his senses, his pincers, his antennae, his spectacles. He manoeuvres them from within; he feels them as if they were his body; he is surrounded by a verbal body which he is hardly conscious of and which extends his action upon the world. The poet is outside language. He sees the reverse side of words, as if he did not share the human condition and as if he were first meeting the word as a barrier as he comes towards men.

Instead of first knowing things by their name, it seems that first he has a silent contact with them, since, turning towards that other species of thing which for him is the word, touching words, testing them, fingering them, he discovers in them a slight luminosity of their own and particular affinities with the earth, the sky, the water, and all created things.

Not knowing how to use them as a *sign* of an aspect of the world, he sees in the word the *image* of one of these aspects. And the verbal image he chooses for its resemblance to the willow tree or the ash tree is not necessarily the word which we use to designate these objects. As he is already on the outside, he considers words as a trap to catch a fleeing reality rather than as indicators which throw him out of himself into the midst of things. In short, all language is for him the mirror of the world. As a result, important changes take place in the internal economy of the word. Its sonority, its length, its masculine or feminine endings, its visual aspect, compose for him a face of flesh which *represents* rather than expresses meaning. Inversely, as the meaning is *realized*, the physical aspect of the word is reflected within it, and it, in its turn, functions as an image of the verbal body. Like its sign, too, for it has lost its pre-eminence; since words, like things, are given, the poet does not decide whether the former exist for the latter or vice versa.

Thus, between the word and the thing signified, there is established a double reciprocal relation of magical resemblance and meaning. And the poet does not *utilize* the word, he does not choose between different senses given to it; each of them, instead of appearing to him as an autonomous function, is given to him as a material quality which merges before his eyes with the other accepted meanings.

Thus, in each word he realizes, solely by the effect of the poetic *attitude*, the metaphors which Picasso dreamed of when he wanted to do a matchbox which was completely a bat without ceasing to be a matchbox. Florence is city, flower, and woman. It is city-flower, city-woman, and girl-flower all at the same time. And the strange object which thus appears has the liquidity of the *river*, the soft, tawny ardency of *gold*, and finally gives itself up with *propriety* and, by the continuous diminution of the silent *e*, prolongs indefinitely its modest blossoming.[5] To that is added the insidious effect of biography. For me, Florence is also a certain woman, an American actress who played in the silent films of my childhood, and about whom I have forgotten everything except that she was as long as a long evening glove and always a bit weary and always chaste and always married and misunderstood and whom I loved and whose name was Florence.

For the word, which tears the writer of prose away from himself and throws him out into the world, sends back to the poet his own image, like a mirror. This is what justifies the double undertaking of Leiris who, on the one hand, in his *Glossary*, tries to give certain words a *poetic definition*, that is, one which is by itself a synthesis of reciprocal implications between the sonorous body and the verbal soul, and, on the other hand, in a still unpublished work, goes in quest of remembrance of things past, taking as guides a few words which for him are particularly charged with feeling. Thus, the poetic word is a microcosm.

The crisis of language which broke out at the beginning of this century is a poetic crisis. Whatever the social and historical factors, it showed itself in an attack of depersonalization when the writer was confronted by words. He no longer knew how to use them, and, in Bergson's famous formula, he only half recognized them. He approached them with a completely fruitful feeling of strangeness. They were no longer his; they were no longer he; but in those strange mirrors, the sky, the earth, and his own life were reflected. And, finally, they became things themselves, or rather the black heart of things. And when the poet joins several of these microcosms together the case is like that of painters when they assemble their colours on the canvas. One might think that he is composing a sentence, but this is only what it appears to be. He is creating an object. The words-things are grouped by magical associations of fitness and incongruity, like colours and sounds. They attract, repel, and '*burn*' one another, and their association composes the veritable poetic unity which is the *phrase-object*.

More often the poet first has the scheme of the sentence in his mind, and the words follow. But this scheme has nothing in common with what one ordinarily calls a verbal scheme. It does not govern the construction of a meaning. Rather, it is comparable to the creative project by which Picasso, even before touching his brush, prefigures in space the *thing* which will become a buffoon or a harlequin.

Fuir, là-bas fuir, je sens que des oiseaux sont
   ivres
Mais ô mon coeur entends le chant des matelots.

[Flying, flying down there, I sense that the birds
   are drunk
But oh my heart listen to the sailors' song.]

This 'but' which rises like a monolith at the
threshold of the sentence does not tie the second
line to the preceding one. It colours it with a
certain reserved nuance, with 'private associations'
which penetrate it completely. In the same way,
certain poems begin with 'and'. This conjunction
no longer indicates to the mind an operation which
is to be carried out; it extends throughout the
paragraph to give it the absolute quality of a *sequel*.
For the poet, the sentence has a tonality, a taste; by
means of it he tastes for their own sake the irritating flavours of objection, of reserve, of disjunction.
He carries them to the absolute. He makes them
real properties of the sentence, which becomes an
utter objection without being an objection *to* anything precise. He finds here those relations of
reciprocal implication which we pointed out a
short time ago between the poetic word and its
meaning; the unit made up of the words chosen
functions as an *image* of the interrogative or
restrictive nuance, and vice versa, the interrogation
is an image of the verbal unit which it delimits.

As in the following admirable lines:

        O saisons! O châteaux!
        Quelle âme est sans défaut?

        Oh seasons! Oh castles!
        Which soul is without flaw?

Nobody is questioned; nobody is questioning;
the poet is absent. And the question involves no
answer, or rather it is its own answer. Is it therefore a false question? But it would be absurd to
believe that Rimbaud 'meant' that everybody has
his faults. As Breton said of Saint-Pol Roux, 'If he
had meant it, he would have said it.' Nor did he
mean to say something else. He asked an absolute
question. He conferred upon the beautiful word
'âme' an interrogative existence. The interrogation
has become a thing as the anguish of Tintoretto
became a yellow sky. It is no longer a meaning, but
a substance. It is seen from the outside, and Rimbaud invites us to see it from the outside with him.
Its strangeness arises from the fact that, in order to

consider it, we place ourselves on the other side of
the human condition, on the side of God.

If this is the case, one easily understands how
foolish it would be to require a poetic commitment. Doubtless, emotion, even passion – and
why not anger, social indignation, and political
hatred? – are at the origin of the poem. But they
are not *expressed* there, as in a pamphlet or in a
confession. In so far as the writer of prose exhibits
feelings, he illustrates them; whereas, if the poet
injects his feelings into his poem, he ceases to
recognize them; the words take hold of them,
penetrate them, and metamorphose them; they
do not signify them, even in his eyes. Emotion
has become thing; it now has the opacity of things;
it is compounded by the ambiguous properties of
the words in which it has been enclosed. And
above all, there is always much more in each
phrase, in each verse, as there is more than simple
anguish in the yellow sky over Golgotha. The
word, the phrase-thing, inexhaustible as things,
everywhere overflow the feeling which has produced them. How can one hope to provoke the
indignation or the political enthusiasm of the
reader when the very thing one does is to withdraw
him from the human condition and invite him to
consider with the eyes of God a language that has
been turned inside out? Someone may say, 'You're
forgetting the poets of the Resistance. You're forgetting Pierre Emmanuel.' Not a bit! They're the
very ones I was going to give as examples.[6]

But even if the poet is forbidden to commit
himself, is that a reason for exempting the writer
of prose? What do they have in common? It is true
that the prose-writer and the poet both write. But
there is nothing in common between these two acts
of writing except the movement of the hand which
traces the letters. Otherwise, their universes are
incommunicable, and what is good for one is not
good for the other. Prose is, in essence, utilitarian.
I would readily define the prose-writer as a man
who *makes use* of words. M. Jourdan made prose so
that he could ask for his slippers, and Hitler, so that
he could declare war on Poland. The writer is a
speaker; he designates, demonstrates, orders,
refuses, interpolates, begs, insults, persuades, in-
sinuates. If he does so without any effect, he does
not therefore become a poet; he is a writer who
is talking and saying nothing. We have seen
enough of language's reverse; it is now time to
look at its right side.[7]

The art of prose is employed in discourse; its
substance is by nature significative – that is, the

words are first of all not objects but designations for objects. It is not first of all a matter of knowing whether they please or displease in themselves; it is a matter of knowing whether they correctly indicate a certain thing or a certain notion. Thus, it often happens that we find ourselves possessing a certain idea that someone has taught us by means of words without being able to recall a single one of the words which have transmitted it to us.

Prose is first of all an attitude of mind. As Valéry would say, there is prose when the word passes across our gaze as the glass across the sun. When one is in danger or in difficulty one grabs any instrument. When the danger is past, one does not even remember whether it was a hammer or a stick; moreover, one never knew; all one needed was a prolongation of one's body, a means of extending one's hand to the highest branch. It was a sixth finger, a third leg, in short, a pure function which one assimilated. Thus, regarding language, it is our shell and our antennae; it protects us against others and informs us about them; it is a prolongation of our senses, a third eye which is going to look into our neighbour's heart. We are within language as within our body. We *feel* it spontaneously while going beyond it towards other ends, as we feel our hands and our feet; we perceive it when it is someone else who is using it, as we perceive the limbs of others. There is the word which is lived and the word which is met. But in both cases it is in the course of an undertaking, either of me acting upon others, or the others upon me. The word is a certain particular moment of action and has no meaning outside it. In certain cases of aphasia the possibilities of acting, of understanding situations, and of having normal relations with the other sex, are lost.

At the heart of this apraxia the destruction of language appears only as the collapse of one of the structures, the finest and the most apparent. And if prose is never anything but the privileged instrument of a certain undertaking, if it is only the poet's business to contemplate words in a disinterested fashion, then one has the right to ask the prose-writer from the very start, 'What is your aim in writing? What undertaking are you engaged in, and why does it require you to have recourse to writing?' In any case this undertaking cannot have pure contemplation as an end. For, intuition is silence, and the end of language is to communicate. One can doubtless *pin down* the results of intuition, but in this case a few words hastily scrawled on paper will suffice; it will always be enough for the author to recognize what he had in mind. If the words are assembled into sentences, with a concern for clarity, a decision foreign to the intuition, to the language itself, must intervene, the decision of confiding to others the results obtained. In each case one must ask how this decision can be justified. And the good sense which our pedants too readily forget never stops repeating it. Are we not in the habit of putting this basic question to young people who are thinking of writing: 'Do you have anything to say?' Which means: something which is worth the trouble of being communicated. But what do we mean by something which is 'worth the trouble' if it is not by recourse to a system of transcendent values?

Moreover, to consider only this secondary structure of the undertaking, which is what the *verbal moment* is, the serious error of pure stylists is to think that the word is a gentle breeze which plays lightly over the surface of things, grazing them without altering them, and that the speaker is a pure *witness* who sums up with a word his harmless contemplation. To speak is to act; anything which one names is already no longer quite the same; it has lost its innocence.

If you name the behaviour of an individual, you reveal it to him; he sees himself. And since you are at the same time naming it to all others, he knows that he is *seen* at the moment he *sees* himself. The furtive gesture, which he forgot while making it, begins to exist enormously, to exist for everybody; it is integrated into the objective mind; it takes on new dimensions; it is retrieved. After that, how can you expect him to act in the same way? Either he will persist in his behaviour out of obstinacy and with full knowledge of what he is doing, or he will give it up. Thus, by speaking, I reveal the situation by my very intention of changing it; I reveal it to myself and to others *in order* to change it. I strike at its very heart, I transfix it, and I display it in full view; at present I dispose of it; with every word I utter, I involve myself a little more in the world, and by the same token I emerge from it a little more, since I go beyond it towards the future.

Thus, the prose-writer is a man who has chosen a certain method of secondary action which we may call action by disclosure. It is therefore permissible to ask him this second question: 'What aspect of the world do you want to disclose? What change do you want to bring into the world by this disclosure?' The 'committed' writer knows that words are action. He knows that to reveal is to change and that one can reveal only by planning to change. He has given up the impossible dream of giving an impartial picture of Society and the human condition. Man is the being towards whom no being can be impartial, not even God. For God, if He existed, would be, as certain mystics have seen Him, in a *situation* in relationship to man. And He is also the being Who cannot even see a situation without changing it, for His gaze congeals, destroys, or sculpts, or, as does eternity, changes the object in itself. It is in love, in hate, in anger, in fear, in joy, in indignation, in admiration, in hope, in despair, that man and the world reveal themselves *in their truth*. Doubtless, the committed writer can be mediocre; he can even be conscious of being so; but as one cannot write without the intention of succeeding perfectly, the modesty with which he envisages his work should not divert him from constructing it *as if* it were to have the greatest celebrity. He should never say to himself, 'Bah! I'll be lucky if I have three thousand readers,' but rather, 'What would happen if everybody read what I wrote?' He remembers what Mosca said beside the coach which carried Fabrice and Sanseverina away: 'If the word Love comes up between them, I'm lost.' He knows that he is the man who names what has not yet been named or what dares not tell its name. He knows that he makes the word 'love' and the word 'hate' *surge up* and with them love and hate between men who had not yet decided upon their feelings. He knows that words, as Brice Parain says, are 'loaded pistols'. If he speaks, he fires. He may be silent, but since he has chosen to fire, he must do it like a man, by aiming at targets, and not like a child, at random, by shutting his eyes and firing merely for the pleasure of hearing the shot go off.

Later on we shall try to determine what the goal of literature may be. But from this point on we may conclude that the writer has chosen to reveal the world and particularly to reveal man to other men so that the latter may assume full responsibility before the object which has been thus laid bare. It is assumed that no one is ignorant of the law because there is a code and because the law is written down; thereafter, you are free to violate it, but you know the risks you run. Similarly, the function of the writer is to act in such a way that nobody can be ignorant of the world and that nobody may say that he is innocent of what it's all about. And since he has once committed himself in the universe of language, he can never again pretend that he cannot speak. Once you enter the universe of meanings, there is nothing you can do to get out of it. Let words organize themselves freely and they will make sentences, and each sentence contains language in its entirety and refers back to the whole universe. Silence itself is defined in relationship to words, as the pause in music receives its meaning from the group of notes round it. This silence is a moment of language; being silent is not being dumb; it is to refuse to speak, and therefore to keep on speaking. Thus, if a writer has chosen to remain silent on any aspect whatever of the world, or, according to an expression which says just what it means, to *pass over* it in silence, one has the right to ask him a third question: 'Why have you spoken of this rather than that, and — since you speak in order to bring about change — why do you want to change this rather than that?'

All this does not prevent there being a manner of writing. One is not a writer for having chosen to say certain things, but for having chosen to say them in a certain way. And, to be sure, the style makes the value of the prose. But it should pass unnoticed. Since words are transparent and since the gaze looks through them, it would be absurd to slip in among them some panes of rough glass. Beauty is in this case only a gentle and imperceptible force. In a painting it shines forth at the very first sight; in a book it hides itself; it acts by persuasion like the charm of a voice or a face. It does not coerce; it inclines a person without his suspecting it, and he thinks that he is yielding to arguments when he is really being solicited by a charm that he does not see. The ceremonial of the Mass is not faith; it disposes. The harmony of words, their beauty, the balance of the phrases, *dispose* the passions of the reader without his being aware and order them like the Mass, like music, like the dance. If he happens to consider them by themselves, he loses the meaning; there remains only a boring seesaw of phrases.

In prose the aesthetic pleasure is pure only if it is thrown in into the bargain. I blush at recalling such simple ideas, but it seems that today they have been forgotten. If that were not the case, would we be told that we are planning the murder of literature, or, more simply, that commitment is harmful to the art of writing? If the contamination of a certain kind of prose by poetry had not confused the ideas of our critics, would they dream of attacking us on the matter of form, when we have never spoken of anything but the content? There is nothing to be said about form in advance, and we have said nothing. Everyone invents his own, and one judges it afterwards. It is true that the subjects suggest the style, but they do not order it. There are no styles ranged *a priori* outside the literary art. What is more 'committed', what is more boring, than the idea of attacking the Jesuits? Yet, out of this Pascal made his *Provincial Letters*. In short, it is a matter of knowing what one wants to write about, whether butterflies or the condition of the Jews. And when one knows, then it remains to decide how one will write about it.

Often the two choices are only one, but among good writers the second choice never precedes the first. I know that Giraudoux has said that 'the only concern is finding one's style; the idea comes afterwards'; but he was wrong. The idea did not come. On the contrary, if one considers subjects as problems which are always open, as solicitations, as expectations, it will be easily understood that art loses nothing by being committed. On the contrary, just as physics submits to mathematicians new problems which require them to produce a new symbolism, in like manner the always new requirements of the social and the metaphysical involve the artist in finding a new language and new techniques. If we no longer write as they did in the eighteenth century, it is because the language of Racine and Saint-Evremond does not lend itself to talking about locomotives or the proletariat. After that, the purists will perhaps forbid us to write about locomotives. But art has never been on the side of the purists.

If that is the principle of commitment, what objection can one have to it? And above all *what objection has been made to it?* It has seemed to me that my opponents have not had their hearts in their work very much and that their articles contain nothing more than a long scandalized sigh which drags on over two or three columns. I should have liked to know *in the name of what*, with what conception of literature, they condemned commitment. But they have not said; they themselves have not known. The most reasonable thing would have been to support their condemnation on the old theory of art for art's sake. But none of them can accept it. That is also disturbing. We know very well that pure art and empty art are the same thing and that aesthetic purism was a brilliant manoeuvre of the bourgeois of the last century who preferred to see themselves denounced as philistines rather than as exploiters. Therefore, they themselves admitted that the writer had to speak about something. But about what? I believe that their embarrassment would have

been extreme if Fernandez had not found for them, after the other war, the notion of the *message*. The writer of today, they say, should in no case occupy himself with temporal affairs. Neither should he set up lines without meaning, or seek only beauty of phrase and of imagery. His function is to deliver messages to his readers. Well, what is a message?

It must be borne in mind that most critics are men who have not had much luck and who, just about the time they were growing desperate, found quiet little jobs as cemetery watchmen. God knows whether cemeteries are peaceful; none of them are more cheerful than a library. The dead are there; the only thing they have done is write. They have long since been washed clean of the sin of living, and besides, their lives are known only through other books which other dead men have written about them. Rimbaud is dead. So are Paterne Berrichon and Isabelle Rimbaud. The trouble makers have disappeared; all that remains are the little coffins that are stacked on shelves along the walls like urns in a columbarium. The critic lives badly; his wife does not appreciate him as she ought to; his children are ungrateful; the first of the month is hard on him. But it is always possible for him to enter his library, take down a book from the shelf, and open it. It gives off a slight odour of the cellar, and a strange operation begins which he has decided to call reading. From one point of view it is a possession; he lends his body to the dead in order that they may come back to life. And from another point of view it is a contact with the beyond. Indeed, the book is by no means an object; neither is it an act, or even a thought. Written by a dead man about dead things, it no longer has any place on this earth; it speaks of nothing which interests us directly. Left to itself, it falls back and collapses; there remain only ink spots on musty paper. And when the critic reanimates these spots, when he makes letters and words of them, they speak to him of passions which he does not feel, of bursts of anger without objects, of dead fears and hopes. It is a whole disembodied world which surrounds him, where human feelings, because they are no longer affecting, have passed on to the status of exemplary feelings and, in short, of *values*. So he persuades himself that he has entered into relations with an intelligible world which is like the truth of his daily sufferings. And their reason for being. He thinks that nature imitates art, as for Plato the world of the senses imitates that of the archetypes. And during the time he is reading, his everyday life becomes an appearance. His nagging wife, his hunchbacked son, they too are appearances. And he will put up with them because Xenophon has drawn the portrait of Xantippe, and Shakespeare that of Richard the Third.

It is a holiday for him when contemporary authors do him the favour of dying. Their books, too raw, too living, too urgent, pass on to the other shore; they become less and less affecting and more and more beautiful. After a short stay in Purgatory they go on to people the intelligible heaven with new values. Bergotte, Swann, Siegfried and Bella, and M. Teste are recent acquisitions. He is waiting for Nathanaël and Ménalque. As for the writers who persist in living, he asks them only not to move about too much, and to make an effort to resemble from now on the dead men they will be. Valéry, who for twenty-five years had been publishing posthumous books, managed the matter very nicely. That is why, like some highly exceptional saints, he was canonized during his lifetime. But Malraux is scandalous.

Our critics are Catharists. They don't want to have anything to do with the real world except eat and drink in it, and since it is absolutely necessary to have relations with our fellow-creatures, they have chosen to have them with the defunct. They get excited only about classified matters, closed quarrels, stories whose ends are known. They never bet on uncertain issues, and since history has decided for them, since the objects which terrified or angered the authors they read have disappeared, since bloody disputes seem futile at a distance of two centuries, they can be charmed with balanced periods, and everything happens for them as if all literature were only a vast tautology and as if every new prose-writer had invented a new way of speaking only for the purpose of saying nothing.

To speak of archetypes and 'human nature' – is that speaking in order to say nothing? All the conceptions of our critics oscillate from one idea to the other. And, of course, both of them are false. Our great writers wanted to destroy, to edify, to demonstrate. But we no longer retain the proofs which they have advanced because we have no concern with what they mean to prove. The abuses which they denounced are no longer those of our time. There are others which rouse us which they did not suspect. History has given the lie to some of their predictions, and those which have been fulfilled became true so long ago that we have

forgotten that at first they were flashes of their genius. Some of their thoughts are utterly dead, and there are others which the whole human race has taken up to its advantage and which we now regard as commonplace. It follows that the best arguments of these writers have lost their effectiveness. We admire only their order and rigour. Their most compact composition is in our eyes only an ornament, an elegant architecture of exposition, with no more practical application than such architectures as the fugues of Bach and the arabesques of the Alhambra.

We are still moved by the passion of these impassioned geometries when the geometry no longer convinces us. Or rather, by the representation of the passion. In the course of centuries the ideas have turned flat, but they remain the little personal objectives of a man who was once flesh and bone; behind the reasons of reason, which wither, we perceive the reasons of the heart, the virtues, the vices, and that great pain that men have in living. Sade does his best to win us over, but we hardly find him scandalous. He is no longer anything but a soul eaten by a beautiful disease, a pearl-oyster. The *Letter on the Theatre* no longer keeps anyone from going to the theatre, but we find it piquant that Rousseau detested the art of the drama. If we are a bit versed in psychoanalysis, our pleasure is perfect. We shall explain the *Social Contract* by the Oedipus complex and *The Spirit of the Laws* by the inferiority complex. That is, we shall fully enjoy the well-known superiority of live dogs to dead lions. Thus, when a book presents befuddled thoughts which have only the appearance of being reasons before melting under our scrutiny and dwindling into the beatings of a heart, when the teaching that one can draw from it is radically different from what its author intended, the book is called a message. Rousseau, the father of the French Revolution, and Gobineau, the father of racism, both sent us messages. And the critic considers them with equal sympathy. If they were alive, he would have to choose between the two, to love one and hate the other. But what brings them together, above all, is that they are both profoundly and deliciously wrong, and in the same way: they are dead.

Thus, contemporary writers should be advised to deliver messages, that is, voluntarily to limit their writing to the involuntary expression of their souls. I say involuntary because the dead, from Montaigne to Rimbaud, have portrayed themselves completely, but without having meant to – it is something they have simply thrown into the bargain. The surplus which they have given us unintentionally should be the primary and professed goal of living writers. They are not to be forced to give us confessions without any affectation, nor are they to abandon themselves to the too-naked lyricism of the romantics. But since we find pleasure in foiling the ruses of Chateaubriand or Rousseau, in surprising them in the secret places of their being at the moment they are playing at being the public man, in distinguishing the private motives from their most universal assertions, we shall ask newcomers to procure us this pleasure deliberately. So let them reason, assert, deny, refute, and prove; but the cause they are defending must be only the apparent aim of their discourse; the deeper goal is to yield themselves without seeming to do so. They must first disarm themselves of their arguments as time has done for those of the classic writers; they must bring them to bear upon subjects which interest no one or on truths so general that readers are convinced in advance. As for their ideas, they must give them an air of profundity, but with an effect of emptiness, and they must shape them in such a way that they are obviously explained by an unhappy childhood, a class hatred, or an incestuous love. Let them not presume to think in earnest; thought conceals the man, and it is the man alone who interests us. A bare tear is not lovely. It offends. A good argument also offends, as Stendhal well observed. But an argument that masks a tear – that's what we're after. The argument removes the obscenity from the tears; the tears, by revealing their origin in the passions, remove the aggressiveness from the argument. We shall be neither too deeply touched nor at all convinced, and we shall be able to yield ourselves safely to that moderate pleasure which, as everyone knows, we derive from the contemplation of works of art. Thus, this is 'true', 'pure' literature, a subjective thing which reveals itself under the aspect of the objective, a discourse so curiously contrived that it is equivalent to silence, a thought which debates with itself, a reason which is only the mask of madness, an Eternal which lets it be understood that it is only a moment of History, a historical moment which, by the hidden side which it reveals, suddenly sends back a perpetual lesson to the eternal man, but which is produced against the express wishes of those who do the teaching.

When all is said and done, the message is a soul which is made object. A soul, and what is to be done with a soul? One contemplates it at a respectful distance. It is not customary to show one's soul in society without a powerful motive. But, with certain reservations, convention permits some individuals to put theirs into commerce, and all adults may procure it for themselves. For many people today, works of the mind are thus little wandering souls which one acquires at a modest price; there is good old Montaigne's, dear La Fontaine's, and that of Jean-Jacques and of Jean-Paul and of delicious Gérard. What is called literary art is the sum of the treatments which make them inoffensive. Tanned, refined, chemically treated, they provide their acquirers with the opportunity of devoting some moments of a life completely turned outwards to the cultivation of subjectivity. Custom guarantees it to be without risk. Montaigne's scepticism? Who can take it seriously since the author of the *Essays* got frightened when the plague ravaged Bordeaux? Or Rousseau's humanitarianism, since 'Jean-Jacques' put his children into an orphanage? And the strange revelations of *Sylvie*, since Gérard de Nerval was mad? At the very most, the professional critic will set up infernal dialogues between them and will inform us that French thought is a perpetual colloquy between Pascal and Montaigne. In so doing he has no intention of making Pascal and Montaigne more alive, but of making Malraux and Gide more dead. Finally, when the internal contradictions of the life and the work have made both of them useless, when the message, in its imponderable depth, has taught us these capital truths, 'that man is neither good nor bad', 'that there is a great deal of suffering in human life', 'that genius is only great patience', this dismal bungling will have achieved its ultimate purpose, and the reader, as he lays down the book, will be able to cry out with a tranquil soul, 'All this is only literature.'

But since, for us, writing is an enterprise; since writers are alive before being dead; since we think that we must try to be as right as we can in our books; and since, even if afterwards the centuries show us to be in the wrong, this is no reason why they should prove us wrong in advance; since we think that the writer should commit himself completely in his works, and not in an abjectly passive rôle by putting forward his vices, his misfortunes, and his weaknesses, but as a resolute will and as a choice, as this total enterprise of living that each one of us is, it is then proper that we take up this problem at its beginning and that we, in our turn, ask ourselves: '*Why* does one write?'

Notes

1 At least in general. The greatness and error of Klee lie in his attempt to make a painting both sign and object.

2 I say 'create', not 'imitate', which is enough to squelch the bombast of M. Charles Estienne, who has obviously not understood a word of my argument and who is dead set on tilting at shadows.

3 A periodical edited by M. Sartre. – TRANSLATOR.

4 This is the example cited by Bataille in *Expérience intérieure*.

5 This sentence is not fully intelligible in translation as the author is here associating the component sounds of the word Florence with the meaning of the French words they evoke. Thus: FL-OR-ENCE, *fleuve, or,* and *décence*. The latter part of the sentence refers to the practice in French poetry of giving, in certain circumstances, a syllabic value to the otherwise silent terminal *e*. – TRANSLATOR.

6 If you wish to know the origin of this attitude towards language, the following are a few brief indications.

Originally, poetry creates the *myth*, while the prose-writer draws its *portrait*. In reality, the human act, governed by needs and urged on by the useful, is, in a sense, a *means*. It passes unnoticed, and it is the result which counts. When I extend my hand *in order* to take up my pen, I have only a fleeting and obscure consciousness of my gesture; it is the pen which I see. Thus, man is alienated by his ends. Poetry reverses the relationship: the world and things become inessential, become a pretext for the act which becomes its own end. The vase is there so that the girl may perform the graceful act of filling it; the Trojan War, so that Hector and Achilles may engage in that heroic combat. The action, detached from its goals, which become blurred, becomes an act of prowess or a dance. Nevertheless, however indifferent he might have been to the success of the enterprise, the poet, before the nineteenth century, remained in harmony with society as a whole. He did not use language for the end which prose seeks, but he had the same confidence in it as the prose-writer.

With the coming of bourgeois society, the poet puts up a common front with the prose-writer to declare it unliveable. His job is always to create the myth of man, but he passes from white magic to black magic. Man is always presented as the absolute end, but by the success of his enterprise he is sucked into a utilitarian collectivity. The thing that is in the background of his act and that will allow transition to the myth is thus no longer success, but defeat. By stopping the infinite series of his projects like a screen, defeat alone returns him to himself in his purity. The world remains the inessential, but it is now there as a pretext for defeat. The finality of the thing is to send man back to himself by blocking the route. Moreover, it is not a matter of arbitrarily introducing defeat and ruin into the course of the world, but rather of having no eyes for anything but that. Human enterprise has two aspects: it is both success and failure. The dialectical scheme is inadequate for reflecting upon it. We must make our vocabulary and the frames of our reason more supple. Some day I am going to try to describe that strange reality, History, which is neither objective, nor ever quite subjective, in which the dialectic is contested, penetrated, and corroded by a kind of antidialectic, but which is still a dialectic. But that is the philosopher's affair. One does not ordinarily consider the two faces of Janus; the man of action sees one and the poet sees the other. When the instruments are broken and unusable, when plans are blasted and effort is useless, the world appears with a childlike and terrible freshness, without supports, without paths. It has the maximum reality because it is crushing for man, and as action, in any case, generalizes, defeat restores to things their individual reality. But, by an expected reversal, the defeat, considered as a final end, is both a contesting and an appropriation of this universe. A contesting, because man *is worth more* than that which crushes; he no longer contests things in their 'little bit of reality', like the engineer or the captain, but, on the contrary, in their 'too full of reality', by his very existence as a vanquished person; he is the remorse of the world. An appropriation, because the world, by ceasing to be the tool of success, becomes the instrument of failure. So there it is, traversed by an obscure finality; it is its coefficient of adversity which serves, the more human in so far as it is more hostile to man. The defeat itself turns into salvation. Not that it makes us yield to some 'beyond', but by itself it shifts and is metamorphosed. For example, poetic language rises out of the ruins of prose. If it is true that the word is a betrayal and that communication is impossible, then each word by itself recovers its individuality and becomes an instrument of our defeat and a receiver of the incommunicable. It is not that there is *another thing* to communicate; but the communication of prose having miscarried, it is the very meaning of the word which becomes the pure incommunicable. Thus, the failure of communication becomes a suggestion of the incommunicable, and the thwarted project of utilizing words is succeeded by the pure disinterested intuition of the word. Thus, we again meet with the description which we attempted earlier in this study, but in the more general perspective of the absolute valorization of the defeat, which seems to me the original attitude of contemporary poetry. Note also that this choice confers upon the poet a very precise function in the collectivity: in a highly integrated or religious society, the defeat is masked by the State or redeemed by Religion; in a less integrated and secular society, such as our democracies, it is up to poetry to redeem them.

Poetry is a case of the loser winning. And the genuine poet chooses to lose, even if he has to go so far as to die, in order to win. I repeat that I am talking of contemporary poetry. History presents other forms of poetry. It is not my concern to show their connection with ours. Thus, if one absolutely wishes to speak of the commitment of the poet, let us say that he is the man who commits himself to lose. This is the deeper meaning of that tough-luck, of that curse with which he always claims kinship and which he always attributes to an intervention from without; whereas it is his deepest choice, the source and not the consequence of his poetry. He is certain of the total defeat of the human enterprise and arranges to fail in his own life in order to bear witness, by his individual defeat, to human defeat in general. Thus, he challenges, as we shall see, which is what the prose-writer does too. But the challenge of prose is carried on in the name of a greater success; and that of poetry, in the name of the hidden defeat which every victory conceals.

7 It goes without saying that in all poetry a certain form of prose, that is, of success, is present; and, vice versa, the driest prose always contains a bit of poetry, that is, a certain form of defeat; no prose-writer is *quite* capable of expressing what he wants to say; he says too much or not enough; each phrase is a wager, a risk assumed; the more cautious one is, the more attention the word attracts; as Valéry has shown, no one can understand a word to its very bottom. Thus, each word is used simultaneously for its clear and social meaning and for certain obscure resonances – let me say, almost for its physiognomy. The reader, too, is sensitive to this. At once we are no longer on the level of concerted communication, but on that of grace and chance; the silences of prose are poetic because they mark its limits, and it is for the purpose of greater clarity that I have been considering the extreme cases of pure prose and pure poetry. However, it need not be concluded that we can pass from poetry to prose by a continuous series of intermediate forms. If the prose-writer is too eager to fondle his words, the *eidos* of 'prose' is shattered and we fall into highfalutin nonsense. If the poet relates, explains, or teaches, the poetry complex becomes *prosaic*; he has lost the game. It is a matter of structures – impure, but well-defined.

18

Eye and Mind[1]

Maurice Merleau-Ponty

*What I am trying to translate to you is more myster-
ious; it is entwined in the very roots of being, in the
impalpable source of sensations.*

J. Gasquet, *Cézanne*

I

Science manipulates things and gives up living in
them. It makes its own limited models of things;
operating upon these indices or variables to effect
whatever transformations are permitted by their
definition, it comes face to face with the real
world only at rare intervals. Science is and always
has been that admirably active, ingenious, and bold
way of thinking whose fundamental bias is to treat
everything as though it were an object-in-general –
as though it meant nothing to us and yet was
predestined for our own use.

But classical science clung to a feeling for the
opaqueness of the world, and it expected through
its constructions to get back into the world. For
this reason classical science felt obliged to seek a
transcendent or transcendental foundation for its
operations. Today we find – not in science but in a
widely prevalent philosophy of the sciences – an
entirely new approach. Constructive scientific
activities see themselves and represent themselves
to be autonomous, and their thinking deliberately
reduces itself to a set of data-collecting techniques
which it has invented. To think is thus to test out,
to operate, to transform – on the condition that
this activity is regulated by an experimental control that admits only the most "worked-out" phe-

nomena, more likely produced by the apparatus
than recorded by it. From this state of affairs
arise all sorts of vagabond endeavors.

Today more than ever, science is sensitive to
intellectual fads and fashions. When a model has
succeeded in one order of problems, it is tried out
everywhere else. At the present time, for example,
our embryology and biology are full of "gradi-
ents." Just how these differ from what tradition
called "order" or "totality" is not at all clear. This
question, however, is not raised; it is not even
permitted. The gradient is a net we throw out to
sea, without knowing what we will haul back in it.
Or again, it is the slender twig upon which unforeseeable crystallizations will form. Certainly this
freedom of operation will serve well to overcome
many a pointless dilemma – provided only that we
ask from time to time why the apparatus works in
one place and fails in others. For all its fluency,
science must nevertheless understand itself; it
must see itself as a construction based on a brute,
existent world and not claim for its blind operations that constituting value which "concepts of
nature" were able to have in an idealist philosophy.
To say that the world is, by nominal definition, the
object x of our operations is to treat the scientist's
knowledge as if it were absolute, as if everything
that is and has been was meant only to enter the
laboratory. Thinking "operationally" has become a
sort of absolute artificialism, such as we see in the
ideology of cybernetics, where human creations are
derived from a natural information process, itself
conceived on the model of human machines. If this
kind of thinking were to extend its reign to man

and history; if, pretending to ignore what we know of them through our own situations, it were to set out to construct man and history on the basis of a few abstract indices (as a decadent psychoanalysis and a decadent culturalism have done in the United States) – then, since man really becomes the *manipulandum* (thing to be manipulated) he takes himself to be, we enter into a cultural regimen where there is neither truth nor falsity concerning man and history, into a sleep, or a nightmare, from which there is no awakening.

Scientific thinking, a thinking which looks on from above, and thinks of the object-in-general, must return to the "there is" which underlies it; to the site, the soil of the sensible and opened world such as it is in our life and for our body – not that possible body which we may legitimately think of as an information machine but that actual body I call mine, this sentinel standing quietly at the command of my words and my acts. Further, *associated bodies* must be brought forward along with my body – the "others," not merely as my congeners, as the zoologist says, but the others who haunt me and whom I haunt; the "others" along *with* whom I haunt a single, present, and actual Being as no animal ever haunted those beings of his own species, locale, or habitat. In this primordial historicity, science's agile and improvisatory thought will learn to ground itself upon things themselves and upon itself, and will once more become philosophy . . . .

But art, especially painting, draws upon this fabric of brute meaning which activism [or operationalism – *Trans.*] would prefer to ignore. Art and only art does so in full innocence. From the writer and the philosopher, in contrast, we want opinions and advice. We will not allow them to hold the world suspended. We want them to take a stand; they cannot waive the responsibilities of men who speak. Music, at the other extreme, is too far beyond the world and the designatable to depict anything but certain outlines of Being – its ebb and flow, its growth, its upheavals, its turbulence.

Only the painter is entitled to look at everything without being obliged to appraise what he sees. For the painter, we might say, the watchwords of knowledge and action lose their meaning and force. Political regimes which denounce "degenerate" painting rarely destroy paintings. They hide them, and one senses here an element of "one never knows" amounting almost to a recognition. The reproach of escapism is seldom aimed at the painter; we do not hold it against Cézanne that he lived hidden away at Estaque during the war of 1870. And we recall with respect his "C'est effrayant, la vie," even when the lowliest student, ever since Nietzsche, would flatly reject philosophy if it did not teach how to live fully [*à être de grands vivants*]. It is as if in the painter's calling there were some urgency above all other claims on him. Strong or frail in life, he is incontestably sovereign in his own rumination of the world. With no other technique than what his eyes and hands discover in seeing and painting, he persists in drawing from this world, with its din of history's glories and scandals, *canvases* which will hardly add to the angers or the hopes of man – and no one complains.[2]

What, then, is this secret science which he has or which he seeks? That dimension which lets Van Gogh say he must go "further on"? What is this fundamental of painting, perhaps of all culture?

2

The painter "takes his body with him," says Valéry. Indeed we cannot imagine how a *mind* could paint. It is by lending his body to the world that the artist changes the world into paintings. To understand these transubstantiations we must go back to the working, actual body – not the body as a chunk of space or a bundle of functions but that body which is an intertwining of vision and movement.

I have only to see something to know how to reach it and deal with it, even if I do not know how this happens in the nervous machine. My mobile body makes a difference in the visible world, being a part of it; that is why I can steer it through the visible. Conversely, it is just as true that vision is attached to movement. We see only what we look at. What would vision be without eye movement? And how could the movement of the eyes bring things together if the movement were blind? If it were only a reflex? If it did not have its antennae, its clairvoyance? If vision were not prefigured in it?

In principle all my changes of place figure in a corner of my landscape; they are recorded on the map of the visible. Everything I see is in principle within my reach, at least within reach of my sight, and is marked upon the map of the "I can." Each of the two maps is complete. The visible world and the world of my motor projects are each total parts of the same Being.

This extraordinary overlapping, which we never think about sufficiently, forbids us to conceive of vision as an operation of thought that would set up before the mind a picture or a representation of the world, a world of immanence and of ideality. Immersed in the visible by his body, itself visible, the see-er does not appropriate what he sees; he merely approaches it by looking, he opens himself to the world. And on its side, this world of which he is a part is not *in itself*, or matter. My movement is not a decision made by the mind, an absolute doing which would decree, from the depths of a subjective retreat, some change of place miraculously executed in extended space. It is the natural consequence and the maturation of my vision. I say of a thing that it is moved; but my body moves itself, my movement deploys itself. It is not ignorant of itself; it is not blind for itself; it radiates from a self....

The enigma is that my body simultaneously sees and is seen. That which looks at all things can also look at itself and recognize, in what it sees, the "other side" of its power of looking. It sees itself seeing; it touches itself touching; it is visible and sensitive for itself. It is not a self through transparence, like thought, which only thinks its object by assimilating it, by constituting it, by transforming it into thought. It is a self through confusion, narcissism, through inherence of the one who sees in that which he sees, and through inherence of sensing in the sensed – a self, therefore, that is caught up in things, that has a front and a back, a past and a future....

This initial paradox cannot but produce others. Visible and mobile, my body is a thing among things; it is caught in the fabric of the world, and its cohesion is that of a thing. But because it moves itself and sees, it holds things in a circle around itself.[3] Things are an annex or prolongation of itself; they are incrusted into its flesh, they are part of its full definition; the world is made of the same stuff as the body. This way of turning things around [*ces renversements*], these antinomies,[4] are different ways of saying that vision happens among, or is caught in, things – in that place where something visible undertakes to see, becomes visible for itself by virtue of the sight of things; in that place where there persists, like the mother water in crystal, the undividedness [*l'indivision*] of the sensing and the sensed.

This interiority no more precedes the material arrangement of the human body than it results from it. What if our eyes were made in such a way as to prevent our seeing any part of our body, or if some baneful arrangement of the body were to let us move our hands over things, while preventing us from touching our own body? Or what if, like certain animals, we had lateral eyes with no cross blending of visual fields? Such a body would not reflect itself; it would be an almost adamantine body, not really flesh, not really the body of a human being. There would be no humanity.

But humanity is not produced as the effect of our articulations or by the way our eyes are implanted in us (still less by the existence of mirrors which could make our entire body visible to us). These contingencies and others like them, without which mankind would not exist, do not by simple summation bring it about that there *is* a single man.

The body's animation is not the assemblage or juxtaposition of its parts. Nor is it a question of a mind or spirit coming down from somewhere else into an automaton; this would still suppose that the body itself is without an inside and without a "self." There is a human body when, between the seeing and the seen, between touching and the touched, between one eye and the other, between hand and hand, a blending of some sort takes place – when the spark is lit between sensing and sensible, lighting the fire that will not stop burning until some accident of the body will undo what no accident would have sufficed to do....

Once this strange system of exchanges is given, we find before us all the problems of painting. These exchanges illustrate the enigma of the body, and this enigma justifies them. Since things and my body are made of the same stuff, vision must somehow take place in them; their manifest visibility must be repeated in the body by a secret visibility. "Nature is on the inside," says Cézanne. Quality, light, color, depth, which are there before us, are there only because they awaken an echo in our body and because the body welcomes them.

Things have an internal equivalent in me; they arouse in me a carnal formula of their presence. Why shouldn't these [correspondences] in their turn give rise to some [external] visible shape in which anyone else would recognize those motifs which support his own inspection of the world?[5] Thus there appears a "visible" of the second power, a carnal essence or icon of the first. It is not a faded copy, a *trompe-l'oeil*, or another *thing*. The animals painted on the walls of Lascaux are not there in the same way as the fissures and limestone formations. But they are not *elsewhere*.

Pushed forward here, held back there, held up by the wall's mass they use so adroitly, they spread around the wall without ever breaking from their elusive moorings in it. I would be at great pains to say *where* is the painting I am looking at. For I do not look at it as I do at a thing; I do not fix it in its place. My gaze wanders in it as in the halos of Being. It is more accurate to say that I see according to it, or with it, than that I *see it*.

The word "image" is in bad repute because we have thoughtlessly believed that a design was a tracing, a copy, a second thing, and that the mental image was such a design, belonging among our private bric-a-brac. But if in fact it is nothing of the kind, then neither the design nor the painting belongs to the in-itself any more than the image does. They are the inside of the outside and the outside of the inside, which the duplicity of feeling [*le sentir*] makes possible and without which we would never understand the quasi presence and imminent visibility which make up the whole problem of the imaginary. The picture and the actor's mimicry are not devices to be borrowed from the real world in order to signify prosaic things which are absent. For the imaginary is much nearer to, and much farther away from, the actual – nearer because it is in my body as a diagram of the life of the actual, with all its pulp and carnal obverse [*son envers charnel*] exposed to view for the first time. In this sense, Giacometti[6] says energetically, "What interests me in all paintings is resemblance – that is, what is resemblance for me: something which makes me discover more of the world." And the imaginary is much farther away from the actual because the painting is an analogue or likeness only according to the body; because it does *not* present the *mind* with an occasion to rethink the constitutive relations of things; because, rather, it offers to our *sight* [*regard*], so that it might join with them, the inward traces of vision, and because it offers to vision its inward tapestries, the imaginary texture of the real.[7]

Shall we say, then, that we look out from the inside, that there is a third eye which sees the paintings and even the mental images, as we used to speak of a third ear which grasped messages from the outside through the noises they caused inside us? But how would this help us when the real problem is to understand how it happens that our fleshly eyes are already much more than receptors for light rays, colors, and lines? They are computers of the world, which have the gift of the visible as it was once said that the inspired man had the gift of tongues. Of course this gift is earned by exercise; it is not in a few months, or in solitude, that a painter comes into full possession of his vision. But that is not the question; precocious or belated, spontaneous or cultivated in museums, his vision in any event learns only by seeing and learns only from itself. The eye sees the world, sees what inadequacies [*manques*] keep the world from being a painting, sees what keeps a painting from being itself, sees – on the palette – the colors awaited by the painting, and sees, once it is done, the painting that answers to all these inadequacies just as it sees the paintings of others as other answers to other inadequacies.

It is no more possible to make a restrictive inventory of the visible than it is to catalogue the possible usages of a language or even its vocabulary and devices. The eye is an instrument that moves itself, a means which invents its own ends; it is *that which* has been moved by some impact of the world, which it then restores to the visible through the offices of an agile hand.

In whatever civilization it is born, from whatever beliefs, motives, or thoughts, no matter what ceremonies surround it – and even when it appears devoted to something else – from Lascaux to our time, pure or impure, figurative or not, painting celebrates no other enigma but that of visibility.

What we have just said amounts to a truism. The painter's world is a visible world, nothing but visible: a world almost demented because it is complete when it is yet only partial. Painting awakens and carries to its highest pitch a delirium which is vision itself, for to see is *to have at a distance*; painting spreads this strange possession to all aspects of Being, which must in some fashion become visible in order to enter into the work of art. When, apropos of Italian painting, the young Berenson spoke of an evocation of tactile values, he could hardly have been more mistaken; painting evokes nothing, least of all the tactile. What it does is much different, almost the inverse. It gives visible existence to what profane vision believes to be invisible; thanks to it we do not need a "muscular sense" in order to possess the voluminosity of the world. This voracious vision, reaching beyond the "visual givens," opens upon a texture of Being of which the discrete sensorial messages are only the punctuations or the caesurae. The eye lives in this texture as a man lives in his house.

Let us remain within the visible in the narrow and prosaic sense. The painter, whatever he is, *while he is painting* practices a magical theory of vision. He is obliged to admit that objects before him pass into him or else that, according to Malebranche's sarcastic dilemma, the mind goes out through the eyes to wander among objects; for the painter never ceases adjusting his clairvoyance to them. (It makes no difference if he does not paint from "nature"; he paints, in any case, because he has seen, because the world has at least once emblazoned in him the ciphers of the visible.) He must affirm, as one philosopher has said, that vision is a mirror or concentration of the universe or that, in another's words, the *idios kosmos* [one's own world] opens by virtue of vision upon a *koinos kosmos* [public world]; in short, that the same thing is both out there in the world and here in the heart of vision – the same or, if one prefers, a *similar* thing, but according to an efficacious similarity which is the parent, the genesis, the metamorphosis of Being in his vision. It is the mountain itself which from out there makes itself seen by the painter; it is the mountain that he interrogates with his gaze.

What exactly does he ask of it? To unveil the means, visible and not otherwise, by which it makes itself a mountain before our eyes. Light, lighting, shadows, reflections, color, all the objects of his quest are not altogether real objects; like ghosts, they have only visual existence. In fact they exist only at the threshold of profane vision; they are not seen by everyone. The painter's gaze asks them what they do to suddenly cause something to be and to be *this* thing, what they do to compose this worldly talisman and to make us see the visible.

We see that the hand pointing to us in *The Nightwatch* is truly there only when we see that its shadow on the captain's body presents it simultaneously in profile. The spatiality of the captain lies at the meeting place of two lines of sight which are incompossible and yet together. Everyone with eyes has at some time or other witnessed this play of shadows, or something like it, and has been made by it to see a space and the things included therein. But it works in us without us; it hides itself in making the object visible. To see the object, it is necessary *not* to see the play of shadows and light around it. The visible in the profane sense forgets its premises; it rests upon a total visibility which is to be re-created and which liberates the phantoms captive in it. The moderns, as we know, have liberated many others; they have added many a blank note [*note sourde*] to the official gamut of our means of seeing. But the interrogation of painting in any case looks toward this secret and feverish genesis of things in our body.

And so it is not a question asked of someone who doesn't know by someone who does – the schoolmaster's question. The question comes from one who does not know, and it is addressed to a vision, a seeing, which knows everything and which we do not make, for it makes itself in us. Max Ernst (with the surrealists) says rightly, "Just as the role of the poet since [Rimbaud's] famous *Lettre du voyant* consists in writing under the dictation of what is being thought, of what articulates itself in him, the role of the painter is to grasp and project what is seen in him."[8] The painter lives in fascination. The actions most proper to him – those gestures, those paths which he alone can trace and which will be revelations to others (because the others do not lack what he lacks or in the same way) – to him they seem to emanate from the things themselves, like the patterns of the constellations.

Inevitably the roles between him and the visible are reversed. That is why so many painters have said that things look at them. As André Marchand says, after Klee: "In a forest, I have felt many times over that it was not I who looked at the forest. Some days I felt that the trees were looking at me, were speaking to me.... I was there, listening.... I think that the painter must be penetrated by the universe and not want to penetrate it.... I expect to be inwardly submerged, buried. Perhaps I paint to break out."[9]

We speak of "inspiration," and the word should be taken literally. There really is inspiration and expiration of Being, action and passion so slightly discernible that it becomes impossible to distinguish between what sees and what is seen, what paints and what is painted.

It can be said that a human is born at the instant when something that was only virtually visible, inside the mother's body, becomes at one and the same time visible for itself and for us. The painter's vision is a continued birth.

In paintings themselves we could seek a figured philosophy[10] of vision – its iconography, perhaps. It is no accident, for example, that frequently in Dutch paintings (as in many others) an empty interior is "digested" by the "round eye of the mirror."[11] This prehuman way of seeing things is the painter's way. More completely than lights, shadows, and reflections, the mirror image anticipates, within things, the labor of vision. Like all other technical objects, such as signs and tools, the mirror arises upon the open circuit [that goes] from seeing body to visible body. Every technique is a "technique of the body." A technique outlines and amplifies the metaphysical structure of our flesh. The mirror appears because I am seeing-visible [*voyant-visible*], because there is a reflexivity of the sensible; the mirror translates and reproduces that reflexivity. My outside completes itself in and through the sensible. Everything I have that is most secret goes into this *visage*, this face, this flat and closed entity about which my reflection in the water has already made me puzzle. Schilder[12] observes that, smoking a pipe before a mirror, I feel the sleek, burning surface of the wood not only where my fingers are but also in those ghostlike fingers, those merely visible fingers inside the mirror. The mirror's ghost lies outside my body, and by the same token my own body's "invisibility" can invest the other bodies I see.[13] Hence my body can assume segments derived from the body of another, just as my substance passes into them; man is mirror for man. The mirror itself is the instrument of a universal magic that changes things into a spectacle, spectacles into things, myself into another, and another into myself. Artists have often mused upon mirrors because beneath this "mechanical trick," they recognized, just as they did in the case of the trick of perspective,[14] the metamorphosis of seeing and seen which defines both our flesh and the painter's vocation. This explains why they have so often liked to draw themselves in the act of painting (they still do – witness Matisse's drawings), adding to what *they* saw then, what *things* saw of them. It is as if they were claiming that there is a total or absolute vision, outside of which there is nothing and which closes itself over them. Where in the realm of the understanding can we place these occult operations, together with the potions and idols they concoct? What can we call them? Consider, as Sartre did in *Nausea*, the smile of a long-dead king which continues to exist and to reproduce itself [*de se produire et de se reproduire*] on the surface of a canvas. It is too little to say that it is there as an image or essence; it is there as itself, as that which was always most alive about it, even now as I look at the painting. The "world's instant" that Cézanne wanted to paint, an instant long since passed away, is still thrown at us by his paintings.[15] His Mount Saint Victor is made and remade from one end of the world to the other in a way that is different from, but no less energetic than, that of the hard rock above Aix. Essence and existence,

imaginary and real, visible and invisible – a painting mixes up all our categories in laying out its oneiric universe of carnal essences, of effective likenesses, of mute meanings.

3

How crystal clear everything would be in our philosophy if only we could exorcise these specters, make illusions or object-less perceptions out of them, keep them on the edge of a world that doesn't equivocate!

Descartes' *Dioptric* is an attempt to do just that. It is the breviary of a thought that wants no longer to abide in the visible and so decides to construct the visible according to a model-in-thought. It is worthwhile to remember this attempt and its failure.

Here there is no concern to cling to vision. The problem is to know "how it happens," but only so far as it is necessary to invent, whenever the need arises, certain "artificial organs"[16] which correct it. We are to reason not so much upon the light we see as upon the light which, from outside, enters our eyes and commands our vision. And for that we are to rely upon "two or three comparisons which help us to conceive it [light]" in such a way as to explain its known properties and to deduce others.[17] The question being so formulated, it is best to think of light as an action by contact – not unlike the action of things upon the blind man's cane. The blind, says Descartes, "see with their hands."[18] The Cartesian concept of vision is modeled after the sense of touch.

At one swoop, then, he removes action at a distance and relieves us of that ubiquity which is the whole problem of vision (as well as its peculiar virtue). Why should we henceforth puzzle over reflections and mirrors? These unreal duplications are a class of things; they are real effects like a ball's bouncing. If the reflection resembles the thing itself, it is because this reflection acts upon the eyes more or less as a thing would. It deceives the eye by engendering a perception which has no object but which does not affect our idea of the world. In the world there is the thing itself, and outside this thing itself there is that other thing which is only reflected light rays and which happens to have an ordered correspondence with the real thing; there are two individuals, then, bound together externally by causality. As far as the thing and its mirror image are concerned, their resemblance is only an external denomination; the resemblance belongs to thought. [What for us is] the "cross-eyed" [*louche*] relationship of resemblance is – in the things – a clear relationship of projection.

A Cartesian does not see *himself* in the mirror; he sees a dummy, an "outside," which, he has every reason to believe, other people see in the very same way but which, no more for himself than for others, is not a body in the flesh. His "image" in the mirror is an effect of the mechanics of things. If he recognizes himself in it, if he thinks it "looks like him," it is his thought that weaves this connection. The mirror image is nothing that belongs to him.

Icons lose their powers.[19] As vividly as an etching "represents" forests, towns, men, battles, storms, it does not resemble them. It is only a bit of ink put down here and there on the paper. A figure flattened down onto a plane surface scarcely retains the forms of things; it is a deformed figure that *ought* to be deformed – the square becomes a lozenge, the circle an oval – in order to represent the object. It is an image only as long as it does not resemble its object. If not through resemblance, how, then, does it act? It "excites our thought" to "conceive," as do signs and words "which in no way resemble the things they signify."[20] The etching gives us sufficient indices, unequivocal means for forming an idea of the thing represented that does not come from the icon itself; rather, it arises in us as it is "occasioned." The magic of intentional species – the old idea of effective resemblance as suggested by mirrors and paintings – loses its final argument if the entire potency of a painting is that of a text to be read, a text totally free of promiscuity between the seeing and the seen. We need no longer understand how a painting of things in the body could make them felt in the soul – an impossible task, since the very resemblance between this painting and those things would have to be seen in turn, since we would "have to have other eyes in our head with which to apperceive it,"[21] and since the problem of vision remains whole even when we have given ourselves these likenesses which wander between us and the real things. What the light designs upon our eyes, and thence upon our brain, does not resemble the visible world any more than etchings do. There is nothing more going on between the things and the eyes, and the eyes and vision, than between the things and the blind man's hands, and between his hands and thoughts.

Vision is not the metamorphosis of things themselves into the sight of them; it is not a matter of things' belonging simultaneously to the huge, real world and the small, private world. It is a thinking that deciphers strictly the signs given within the body. Resemblance is the result of perception, not its mainspring. More surely still, the mental image, the clairvoyance which renders present to us what is absent, is nothing like an insight penetrating into the heart of Being. It is still a thought relying upon bodily indices, this time insufficient, which are made to say more than they mean. Nothing is left of the oneiric world of analogy....

What interests us in these famous analyses is that they make us aware of the fact that any theory of painting is a metaphysics. Descartes does not say much about painting, and one might think it unfair on our part to make an issue out of a few pages on copper engravings. And yet even if he speaks of them only in passing, that in itself is significant. Painting for him is not a central operation contributing to the definition of our access to Being; it is a mode or a variant of thinking, where thinking is canonically defined according to intellectual possession and evidence. It is this option that is expressed within the little he does say, and a closer study of painting would lead to another philosophy. It is significant too that when he speaks of "pictures" he takes line drawings as typical. We shall see that all painting is present in each of its modes of expression; one drawing, even a single line, can embrace all its bold potential.

But what Descartes likes most in copper engravings is that they preserve the forms of objects, or at least give us sufficient signs of their forms. They present the object by its outside, or its envelope. If he had examined that other, deeper opening upon things given us by secondary qualities, especially color, then – since there is no ordered or projective relationship between them and the true properties of things and since we understand their message all the same – he would have found himself faced with the problem of a conceptless universality and a conceptless opening upon things. He would have been obliged to find out how the indecisive murmur of colors can present us with things, forests, storms – in short the world, obliged, perhaps, to integrate perspective, as a particular case, with a more ample ontological power. But for him it goes without saying that color is an ornament, mere coloring [*coloriage*], and that the real power of painting lies in design, whose power in turn rests upon the ordered relationship existing between it and space-in-itself as taught to us by perspective-projection. Pascal is remembered for speaking of the frivolity of paintings which attach us to images whose originals would not touch us; this is a Cartesian opinion. For Descartes it is unarguably evident that one can paint only existing things, that their existence consists in being extended, and that design, or line drawing, alone makes painting possible by making the representation of extension possible. Thus painting is only an artifice which presents to our eyes a projection similar to that which the things themselves in ordinary perception would and do inscribe in our eyes. A painting makes us see in the same way in which we actually see the thing itself, even though the thing is absent. Especially it makes us see a *space* where there is none.[22]

The picture is a flat thing contriving to give us what we would see in the [actual] presence of "diversely contoured" things, by offering sufficient diacritical signs of the missing dimension, according to height and width.[23] Depth is a *third dimension* derived from the other two.

It will pay us to dwell for a moment upon this third dimension. It has, first of all, something paradoxical about it. I see objects which hide each other and which consequently I do not see; each one stands behind the other. I see it [the third dimension] and it is not visible, since it goes toward things from, as starting point, this body to which I myself am fastened. But the mystery here is a false one. I don't really see it [the third dimension], or if I do, it is only another *size* [measured by height and width]. On the line which lies between my eyes and the horizon, the first [vertical] plane forever hides all the others, and if from side to side I think I see things spread out in order before me, it is because they do not completely hide each other. Thus I see each thing to be outside the others, according to some measure otherwise reckoned [*autrement compté*].[24] We are always on this side of space or beyond it entirely. It is never the case that things really *are* one behind the other. The fact that things overlap or are hidden does not enter into their definition, and expresses only my incomprehensible solidarity with one of them – my body. And whatever might be positive in these facts, they are only thoughts that I formulate and not attributes of the things. I know that at this very moment another man, situated elsewhere – or better, God, who is everywhere – could penetrate their "hiding place" and see them openly deployed. Either what I call depth is nothing, or else it is my participation in a Being without restriction, a participation primarily in the being of space beyond every [particular] point of view. Things encroach upon one another *because each is outside of the others*. The proof of this is that I can see depth in a painting which everyone agrees has none and which organizes for me an illusion of an illusion....This two-dimensional being,[25] which makes me see another [dimension], is a being that is opened up [*troué*] – as the men of the Renaissance said, a window....

But in the last analysis the window opens only upon those *partes extra partes* [parts outside parts], upon height and width seen merely from another angle – upon the absolute positivity of Being.

It is this identity of Being, or this space without hiding places which in each of its points is only what it is, neither more nor less, that underlies the analysis of copper engravings. Space is in-itself; rather, it is the in-itself *par excellence*. Its definition is *to be* in itself. Every point of space is and is thought to be right where it is – one here, another there; space is the evidence of the "where." Orientation, polarity, envelopment are, in space, derived phenomena inextricably bound to my presence. *Space* remains absolutely in itself, everywhere equal to itself, homogeneous; its dimensions, for example, are interchangeable.

Like all classical ontologies, this one builds certain properties of beings into a structure of Being. Reversing Leibniz's remark, we might say that in doing this, it is true and false: true in what it denies and false in what it affirms. Descartes' space is true over against a too empirical thought which dares not construct. It was necessary first to idealize space, to conceive of that being – perfect in its genus, clear, manageable, and homogeneous – which our thinking glides over without a vantage point of its own: a being which thought reports entirely in terms of three rectangular dimensions. This done, we were enabled eventually to find the limits of construction, to understand that space does not have three dimensions or more or fewer, as an animal has either four or two feet, and to understand that the three dimensions are taken by different systems of measurement from a single dimensionality, a polymorphous Being, which justifies all without being fully expressed by any. Descartes was right in setting space free. His mistake was to erect it into a positive being, outside all points of view, beyond all latency and all depth, having no true thickness [*épaisseur*].

He was right also in taking his inspiration from the perspectival techniques of the Renaissance; they encouraged painting to freely produce experiences of depth and, in general, presentations of Being. These techniques were false only in so far as they pretended to bring an end to painting's quest and history, to found once and for all an exact and infallible art of painting. As Panofsky has shown concerning the men of the Renaissance,[26] this enthusiasm was not without bad faith. The theoreticians tried to forget the spherical visual field of the ancients, their angular perspective which relates the apparent size not to distance but to the angle from which we see the object. They wanted to forget what they disdainfully called the *perspectiva naturalis*, or *communis* [natural or common perspective], in favor of a *perspectiva artificialis* [artificial perspective] capable in principle of founding an exact construction. To accredit this myth, they went so far as to expurgate Euclid, omitting from their translations that eighth theorem which bothered them so much. But the painters, on the other hand, knew from experience that no technique of perspective is an exact solution and that there is no projection of the existing world which respects it in all aspects and deserves to become the fundamental law of painting. They knew too that linear perspective was so far from being an ultimate breakthrough that, on the contrary, it opens several pathways for painting. For example, the Italians took the way of representing the object, but the northern painters discovered and worked out the formal technique of *Hochraum*, *Nahraum*, and *Schrägraum*. Thus plane projection does not always provoke our thought to reach the true form of things, as Descartes believed. Beyond a certain degree of deformation, it refers back, on the contrary, to our own vantage point. And the painted objects are left to retreat into a remoteness out of reach of all thought. Something in space escapes our attempts to look at it from "above."

The truth is that no means of expression, once mastered, resolves the problems of painting or transforms it into a technique. For no symbolic form ever functions as a stimulus. Wherever it has been put to work and has acted, has *gone* to work, it has been put to work and has acted with the entire context of the *oeuvre*, and not in the slightest by means of a *trompe-l'oeil*. The *Stilmoment* never gets rid of the *Wermoment*.[27] The language of painting is never "instituted by nature"; it is to be made and remade over and over again. The perspective of the Renaissance is no infallible "gimmick." It is

only a particular case, a date, a moment in a poetic information of the world which continues after it.

Yet Descartes would not have been Descartes if he had thought to *eliminate* the enigma of vision. There is no vision without thought. But *it is not enough* to think in order to see. Vision is a conditioned thought; it is born "as occasioned" by what happens in the body; it is "incited" to think by the body. It does not *choose* either to be or not to be or to think this thing or that. It has to carry in its heart that heaviness, that dependence which cannot come to it by some intrusion from outside. Such bodily events are "instituted by nature" in order to bring us to see this thing or that. The thinking that belongs to vision functions according to a program and a law which it has not given itself. It does not possess its own premises; it is not a thought altogether present and actual; there is in its center a mystery of passivity.

As things stand, then, everything we say and think of vision has to make a *thought* of it. When, for example, we wish to understand how we see the way objects are situated, we have no other recourse than to suppose the soul to be capable, knowing where the parts of its body are, of "transferring its attention from there" to all the points of space that lie in the prolongation of [i.e., beyond] the bodily members.[28] But so far this is only a "model" of the event. For the question is, how does the soul know this space, its own body's, which it extends toward things, this primary *here* from which all the *there's* will come? This space is not, like them, just another mode or specimen of the extended; it is the place of the body the soul calls "mine," a place the soul inhabits. The body it animates is not, for it, an object among objects, and it does not derive from the body all the rest of space as an implied premise. The soul thinks with reference to the body, not with reference to itself, and space, or exterior distance, is stipulated as well within the natural pact that unites them. If for a certain degree of accommodation and eye convergence the soul takes note of a certain distance, the thought which draws the second relationship from the first is as if immemorially enrolled in our internal "works" [*fabrique*]. "Usually this comes about without our reflecting upon it – just as, when we clasp a body with our hand, we conform the hand to the size and shape of the body and thereby sense the body, without having need to think of those movements of the hand."[29] For the soul, the body is both natal space and matrix of every other existing space. Thus vision divides itself. There is the vision upon which I reflect; I cannot think it except *as* thought, the mind's inspection, judgment, a reading of signs. And then there is the vision that really takes place, an honorary or instituted thought, squeezed into a body – its own body, of which we can have no idea except in the exercise of it and which introduces, between space and thought, the autonomous order of the compound of soul and body. The enigma of vision is not done away with; it is relegated from the "thought of seeing" to vision in act.

Still this *de facto* vision and the "there is" which it contains do not upset Descartes' philosophy. Being thought united with a body, it cannot, by definition, really be thought [conceived]. One can practice it, exercise it, and, so to speak, exist it; yet one can draw nothing from it which deserves to be called true. If, like Queen Elizabeth,[30] we want at all costs to think *something* about it, all we can do is go back to Aristotle and scholasticism, to conceive thought as a corporeal something which cannot be conceived but which is the only way to formulate, for our understanding, the union of soul and body. The truth is that it is absurd to submit to pure understanding the mixture of understanding and body. These would-be thoughts are the hallmarks of "ordinary usage," mere verbalizations of this union, and can be allowed only if they are not taken to be thoughts. They are indices of an order of existence – of man and world as existing – about which we do not have to think. For this order there is no *terra incognita* on our map of Being. It does not confine the reach of our thoughts, because it, just as much as they, is sustained by a truth which grounds its obscurity as well as our own lights.[31]

We have to push Descartes this far to find in him something like a metaphysics of depth [*de la profondeur*]. For we do not attend the birth of this truth; God's being for us is an abyss. An anxious trembling quickly mastered; for Descartes it is just as vain to plumb that abyss as it is to think the space of the soul and the depth of the visible. Our very position, he would say, disqualifies us from looking into such things. Here is the Cartesian secret of equilibrium: a metaphysics which gives us decisive reasons to be no longer involved with metaphysics, which validates our evidences while limiting them, which opens up our thinking without rending it.

The secret has been lost for good, it seems. If we ever again find a balance between science and philosophy, between our models and the obscurity

of the "there is," it must be of a new kind. Our science has rejected the justifications as well as the restrictions which Descartes assigned to its domain. It no longer pretends to deduce its invented models from the attributes of God. The depth of the existing world and that of the unfathomable God come no longer to stand over against the platitudes [and flatness] of "technicized" thinking. Science gets along without the excursion into metaphysics which Descartes had to make at least once in his life; it takes off from the point he ultimately reached. Operational thought claims for itself, in the name of psychology, that domain of contact with oneself and with the world which Descartes reserved for a blind but irreducible experience. It is fundamentally hostile to philosophy as thought-in-contact, and if operational thought rediscovers the sense of philosophy it will be through the very excess of its ingenuousness [*sa désinvolture*]. It will happen when, having introduced all sorts of notions which for Descartes would have arisen from confused thought – quality, scalar structures, solidarity of observer and observed – it will suddenly become aware that one cannot summarily speak of all these beings as *constructs*. As we await this moment, philosophy maintains itself against such thinking, entrenching itself in that dimension of the compound of soul and body, that dimension of the existent world, of the abyssal Being that Descartes opened up and so quickly closed again. Our science and our philosophy are two faithful and unfaithful consequences of Cartesianism, two monsters born from its dismemberment.

Nothing is left for our philosophy but to set out toward the prospection of the actual world. We *are* the compound of soul and body, and so there must be a thought of it. To this knowledge of position or situation Descartes owes what he himself says of it [this compound] or what he says sometimes of the presence of the body "against the soul," or the exterior world "at the end" of our hands. Here the body is not the means of vision and touch but their depository.

Our organs are no longer instruments; on the contrary, our instruments are detachable organs. Space is no longer what it was in the *Dioptric*, a network of relations between objects such as would be seen by a witness to my vision or by a geometer looking over it and reconstructing it from outside. It is, rather, a space reckoned starting from me as the zero point or degree zero of spatiality. I do not see it according to its exterior envelope; I live in it from the inside; I am immersed in it. After all, the world is all around me, not in front of me. Light is viewed once more as action at a distance. It is no longer reduced to the action of contact or, in other words, conceived as it might be by those who do not see in it.[32] Vision reassumes its fundamental power of showing forth more than itself. And since we are told that a bit of ink suffices to make us see forests and storms, light must have its *imaginaire*. Light's transcendence is not delegated to a reading mind which deciphers the impacts of the light-thing upon the brain and which could do this quite as well if it had never lived in a body. No more is it a question of speaking of space and light; the question is to make space and light, which are *there*, speak to us. There is no end to this question, since the vision to which it addresses itself is itself a question. The inquiries we believed closed have been reopened.

What is depth, what is light, τί τὸ ὄν [what is this being]? What are they – not for the mind that cuts itself off from the body but for the mind Descartes says is suffused throughout the body? And what are they, finally, not only for the mind but for themselves, since they pass through us and surround us?

Yet this philosophy still to be done is that which animates the painter – not when he expresses his opinions about the world but in that instant when his vision becomes gesture, when, in Cézanne's words, he "thinks in painting."[33]

4

The entire modern history of painting, with its efforts to detach itself from illusionism and to acquire its own dimensions, has a metaphysical significance. This is not something to be demonstrated. Not for reasons drawn from the limits of objectivity in history and from the inevitable plurality of interpretations, which would prevent the linking of a philosophy and an event; the metaphysics we have in mind is not a body of detached ideas [*idées séparées*] for which inductive justifications could be sought in the experiential realm. There are, in the flesh of contingency, a structure of the event and a virtue peculiar to the scenario. These do not prevent the plurality of interpretations but in fact are the deepest reasons for this plurality. They make the event into a durable theme of historical life and have a right to philosophical status. In a sense everything that could have been said and that will be said about the French Revolution has always been and is henceforth within it, in that wave which arched itself out of a roil of discrete facts, with its froth of the past and its crest of the future. And it is always by looking more deeply into *how it came about* that we give and will go on giving new representations of it. As for the history of art works, if they are great, the sense we give to them later on has issued from them. It is the work itself that has opened the field from which it appears in another light. It changes *itself* and *becomes* what follows; the interminable reinterpretations to which it is *legitimately* susceptible change it only in itself. And if the historian unearths beneath its manifest content the surplus and thickness of meaning, the texture which held the promise of a long history, this active manner of being, then, this possibility he unveils in the work, this monogram he finds there – all are grounds for a philosophical meditation. But such a labor demands a long familiarity with history. We lack everything for its execution, both the competence and the place. Just the same, since the power or the fecundity of art works exceeds every positive causal or filial relation, there is nothing wrong with letting a layman, speaking from his memory of a few paintings and books, tell us how painting enters into his reflections; how painting deposits in him a feeling of profound discordance, a feeling of mutation within the relations of man and Being. Such feelings arise in him when he holds a universe of classical thought, en bloc, up against the explorations [*recherches*] of modern painting. This is a sort of history by contact, perhaps, never extending beyond the limits of one person, owing everything nevertheless to his frequentation of others. . . .

"I believe Cézanne was seeking depth all his life," says Giacometti.[34] Says Robert Delaunay, "Depth is the new inspiration."[35] Four centuries after the "solutions" of the Renaissance and three centuries after Descartes, depth is still new, and it insists on being sought, not "once in a lifetime" but all through life. It cannot be merely a question of an unmysterious interval, as seen from an airplane, between these trees nearby and those farther away. Nor is it a matter of the way things are conjured away, one by another, as we see happen so vividly in a perspective drawing. These two views are very explicit and raise no problems. The enigma, though, lies in their bond, in what is between them. The enigma consists in the fact that I see things, each one in its place, precisely because they eclipse one another, and that they are rivals before my sight precisely because each one is in its own place. Their exteriority is known in their envelopment and their mutual dependence in their autonomy. Once depth is understood in this way, we can no longer call it a third dimension. In the first place, if it were a dimension, it would be the *first* one; there are forms and definite planes only if it is stipulated how far from me their different parts are. But a *first* dimension that contains all the others is no longer a dimension, at least in the ordinary sense of a *certain relationship* according to which we make measurements. Depth thus understood is, rather, the experience of the reversibility of dimensions, of a global "locality" – everything in the same place at the same time, a locality from which height, width, and depth are abstracted, of a voluminosity we express in a word when we say that a thing is *there*. In search of depth Cézanne seeks this deflagration of Being, and it is all in the modes of space, in form as much as anything. Cézanne knows already what cubism will repeat: that the external form, the envelope, is secondary and derived, that it is not that which causes a thing to take form, that this shell of space must be shattered, this fruit bowl broken – and what is there to paint, then? Cubes, spheres, and cones (as he said once)? Pure forms which have the solidity of what could be defined by an internal law of construction, forms which all together, as traces or slices of the thing, let it appear between them like a face in the reeds? This would be to put Being's solidity on one side and its variety on the other. Cézanne made an experiment of this kind in his middle period. He opted for the solid, for space – and came to find that inside this space, a box or container too large for them, the things began to move, color against color; they began to modulate in instability.[36] Thus we must seek space and its content *as* together. The problem is generalized; it is no longer that of distance, of line, of form; it is also, and equally, the problem of color.

Color is the "place where our brain and the universe meet," he says in that admirable idiom of the artisan of Being which Klee liked to cite.[37] It is for the benefit of color that we must break up the form-spectacle. Thus the question is not of colors, "simulacra of the colors of nature."[38] The question, rather, concerns the dimension of color, that dimension which creates identities, differences, a texture, a materiality, a something – creates them from itself, for itself....

Yet (and this must be emphasized) there is no one master key of the visible, and color alone is no closer to being such a key than space is. The return to color has the merit of getting somewhat nearer to "the heart of things,"[39] but this heart is beyond the color envelope just as it is beyond the space envelope. The *Portrait of Vallier* sets white spaces between the colors which take on the function of giving shape to, and setting off, a being more general than the yellow-being or green-being or blue-being. Also in the water colors of Cézanne's last years, for example, space (which had been taken to be evidence itself and of which it was believed that the question of *where* was not to be asked) radiates around planes that cannot be assigned to any place at all: "a superimposing of transparent surfaces," "a flowing movement of planes of color which overlap, which advance and retreat."[40]

Obviously it is not a matter of adding one more dimension to those of the flat canvas, of organizing an illusion or an objectless perception whose perfection consists in simulating an empirical vision to the maximum degree. Pictorial depth (as well as painted height and width) comes "I know not whence" to alight upon, and take root in, the sustaining support. The painter's vision is not a view upon the *outside*, a merely "physical-optical"[41] relation with the world. The world no longer stands before him through representation; rather, it is the painter to whom the things of the world give birth by a sort of concentration or coming-to-itself of the visible. Ultimately the painting relates to nothing at all among experienced things unless it is first of all "autofigurative."[42] It is a spectacle of something only by being a spectacle of nothing,"[43] by breaking the "skin of things"[44] to show how the things become things, how the world becomes world. Apollinaire said that in a poem there are phrases which do not appear to have been *created*, which seem to have *formed themselves*. And Henri Michaux said that sometimes Klee's colors seem to have been born slowly upon the canvas, to have emanated from some primordial ground, "exhaled at the right place"[45] like a patina or a mold. Art is not construction, artifice, meticulous relationship to a space and a world existing outside. It is truly the "inarticulate cry," as Hermes Trismegistus said, "which seemed to be the voice of the light." And once it is present it awakens powers dormant in ordinary vision, a secret of preexistence. When through the water's thickness I see the tiling at the bottom of a pool, I do not see it *despite* the water and the reflections there; I see it through them and because of them. If there were no distortions, no ripples of sunlight, if it were without this flesh that I saw the geometry of the tiles, then I would cease to see it *as* it is and where it is – which is to say, beyond any identical, specific place. I cannot say that the water itself – the aqueous power, the sirupy and shimmering element – is *in* space; all this is not somewhere else either, but it is not in the pool. It inhabits it, it materializes itself there, yet it is not contained there; and if I raise my eyes toward the screen of cypresses where the web of reflections is playing, I cannot gainsay the fact that the water visits it, too, or at least sends into it, upon it, its active and living essence. This internal animation, this radiation of the visible is what the painter seeks under the name of depth, of space, of color.

Anyone who thinks about the matter finds it astonishing that very often a good painter can also make good drawings or good sculpture. Since neither the means of expression nor the creative gestures are comparable, this fact [of competence in several media] is proof that there is a system of equivalences, a Logos of lines, of lighting, of colors, of reliefs, of masses – a conceptless presentation of universal Being. The effort of modern painting has been directed not so much toward choosing between line and color, or even between the figuration of things and the creation of signs, as it has been toward multiplying the systems of equivalences, toward severing their adherence to the envelope of things. This effort might force us to create new materials or new means of expression, but it could well be realized at times by the re-examination and reinvestment of those which existed already.

There has been, for example, a prosaic conception of the line as a positive attribute and a property of the object in itself. Thus, it is the outer contour of the apple or the border between the plowed field and the meadow, considered as present in the world, such that, guided by points taken from the real world, the pencil or brush would only have to pass over them. But this line has been contested by all modern painting, and probably by all painting, as we are led to think by da Vinci's comment in his *Treatise on Painting*: "The secret of the art of drawing is to discover in each object the particular way in which a certain flexuous line, which is, so to speak, its generating axis, is directed through its whole extent..."[46] Both Ravaisson and Bergson sensed something

important in this, without daring to decipher the oracle all the way. Bergson scarcely looked for the "sinuous outline" [*serpentement*] outside living beings, and he rather timidly advanced the idea that the undulating line "could be no one of the visible lines of the figure," that it is "no more here than there," and yet "gives the key to the whole."[47] He was on the threshold of that gripping discovery, already familiar to the painters, that there are no lines visible in themselves, that neither the contour of the apple nor the border between field and meadow is in *this* place or that, that they are always on the near or the far side of the point we look at. They are always between or behind whatever we fix our eyes upon; they are indicated, implicated, and even very imperiously demanded by the things, but they themselves are not things. They were supposed to circumscribe the apple or the meadow, but the apple and the meadow "form themselves" from themselves, and come into the visible as if they had come from a pre-spatial world behind the scenes.

Yet this contestation of the prosaic line is far from ruling out all lines in painting, as the impressionists may have thought. It is simply a matter of freeing the line, of revivifying its constituting power; and we are not faced with a contradiction when we see it reappear and triumph in painters like Klee or Matisse, who more than anyone believed in color. For henceforth, as Klee said, the line no longer imitates the visible; it "renders visible"; it is the blueprint of a genesis of things. Perhaps no one before Klee had "let a line muse."[48] The beginning of the line's path establishes or installs a certain level or mode of the linear, a certain manner for the line to be and to make itself a line, "to go line."[49] Relative to it, every subsequent inflection will have a diacritical value, will be another aspect of the line's relationship to itself, will form an adventure, a history, a meaning of the line – all this according as it slants more or less, more or less rapidly, more or less subtly. Making its way in space, it nevertheless corrodes prosaic space and the *partes extra partes*; it develops a way of extending itself actively into that space which sub-tends the spatiality of a thing quite as much as that of a man or an apple tree. This is so simply because, as Klee said, to give the generating axis of a man the painter "would have to have a network of lines so entangled that it could no longer be a question of a truly elementary representation."[50]

In view of this situation two alternatives are open, and it makes little difference which one is chosen. First, the painter may, like Klee, decide to hold rigorously to the principle of the genesis of the visible, the principle of fundamental, indirect, or – as Klee used to say – absolute painting, and then leave it up to the *title* to designate by its prosaic name the entity thus constituted, in order to leave the painting free to function more purely as a painting. Or alternatively he may choose with Matisse (in his drawings) to put into a single line both the prosaic definition [*signalement*] of the entity and the hidden [*sourde*] operation which composes in it such softness or inertia and such force as are required to constitute it as *nude*, as *face*, as *flower*.

There is a painting by Klee of two holly leaves, done in the most figurative manner. At first glance the leaves are thoroughly indecipherable, and they remain to the end monstrous, unbelievable, ghostly, *on account of their exactness* [*à force d'ex-actitude*]. And Matisse's women (let us keep in mind his contemporaries' sarcasm) were not immediately women; they became women. It is Matisse who taught us to see their contours not in a "physical-optical" way but rather as structural filaments [*des nervures*], as the axes of a corporeal system of activity and passivity. Figurative or not, the line is no longer a thing or an imitation of a thing. It is a certain disequilibrium kept up within the indifference of the white paper; it is a certain process of gouging within the in-itself, a certain constitutive emptiness – an emptiness which, as Moore's statues show decisively, upholds the pretended positivity of the things. The line is no longer the apparition of an entity upon a vacant background, as it was in classical geometry. It is, as in modern geometries, the restriction, segregation, or modulation of a pre-given spatiality.

Just as it has created the latent line, painting has made itself a movement without displacement, a movement by vibration or radiation. And well it should, since, as we say, painting is an art of space and since it comes about upon a canvas or sheet of paper and so lacks the wherewithal to devise things that actually move. But the immobile canvas could suggest a change of place in the same way that a shooting star's track on my retina suggests a transition, a motion not contained in it. The painting itself would offer to my eyes almost the same thing offered them by real movements: a series of appropriately mixed, instantaneous glimpses along with, if a living thing is involved, attitudes unstably suspended between a before and an after – in short, the outsides of a change of place which the spectator would read from the imprint it leaves. Here Rodin's well-known remark reveals its full weight: the instantaneous glimpses, the unstable attitudes, petrify the movement, as is shown by so many photographs in which an athlete-in-motion is forever frozen. We could not thaw him out by multiplying the glimpses. Marey's photographs, the cubists' analyses, Duchamp's *La Mariée* do not move; they give a Zenonian reverie on movement. We see a rigid body as if it were a piece of armor going through its motions; it is here and it is there, magically, but it does not *go* from here to there. Cinema portrays movement, but *how*? Is it, as we are inclined to believe, by copying more closely the changes of place? We may presume not, since slow-motion shows a body floating among objects like an alga but not moving *itself*.

Movement is given, says Rodin,[51] by an image in which the arms, the legs, the trunk, and the head are each taken at a different instant, an image which therefore portrays the body in an attitude which it never at any instant really held and which imposes fictive linkages between the parts, as if this mutual confrontation of incompossibles could, and could alone, cause transition and duration to arise in bronze and on canvas. The only successful instantaneous glimpses of movement are those which approach this paradoxical arrangement – when, for example, a walking man is taken at the moment when both his feet are touching the ground; for then we almost have the temporal ubiquity of the body which brings it about that the man *bestrides* space. The picture makes movement visible by its internal discordance. Each member's position, precisely by virtue of its incompatibility with the others' (according to the body's logic), is otherwise dated or is not "in time" with the others; and since all of them remain visibly within the unity of a body, it is the body which comes to bestride time [*la durée*]. Its movement is something premeditated between legs, trunk, arms, and head in some virtual "control center," and it breaks forth only with a subsequent change of place. When a horse is photographed at that instant when he is completely off the ground, with his legs almost folded under him – an instant, therefore, when he must be moving – why does he look as if he were leaping in place? Then why do Géricault's horses really *run* on canvas, in a posture impossible for a real horse at the gallop? It is just that the horses in *Epsom Derby* bring me to see the body's grip upon the soil and that, according to a logic of body and world I know well, these "grips" upon space are also ways of taking hold of time [*la durée*]. Rodin said very wisely, "It is the artist who is truthful, while the photograph is mendacious; for, in reality, time never stops cold."[52] The photograph keeps open the instants which the onrush of time closes up forthwith; it destroys the overtaking, the overlapping, the "metamorphosis" [Rodin] of time. But this is what painting, in contrast, makes visible, because the horses have in them that "leaving here, going there,"[53] because they have a foot in each instant. Painting searches not for the outside of movement but for its secret ciphers, of which there are some still more subtle than those of which Rodin spoke. All flesh, and even that of the world, radiates beyond itself. But whether or not one is, depending on the times and the "school," attached more to manifest movement or to the monumental, the art of painting is never altogether outside time, because it is always within the carnal [*dans le charnel*].

Now perhaps we have a better sense of what is meant by that little verb "to see." Vision is not a certain mode of thought or presence to self; it is the means given me for being absent from myself, for being present at the fission of Being from the inside – the fission at whose termination, and not before, I come back to myself.

Painters always knew this. Da Vinci[54] invoked a "pictorial science" which does not speak with words (and still less with numbers) but with *oeuvres* which exist in the visible just as natural things do and which nevertheless communicate through those things "to all the generations of the universe." This silent science, says Rilke (apropos of Rodin), brings into the *oeuvre* the forms of things "whose seal has not been broken";[55] it comes from the eye and addresses itself to the eye. We must understand the eye as the "window of the soul." "The eye...through which the beauty of the universe is revealed to our contemplation is of such excellence that whoever should resign himself to losing it would deprive himself of the knowledge of all the works of nature, the sight of which makes the soul live happily in its body's prison, thanks to the eyes which show him the infinite variety of creation: whoever loses them abandons his soul in a dark prison where all hope of once more seeing the sun, the light of the universe, must vanish." The eye accomplishes the prodigious work of opening the soul to what

is not soul – the joyous realm of things and their god, the sun.

A Cartesian can believe that the existing world is not visible, that the only light is that of the mind, and that all vision takes place in God. A painter cannot grant that our openness to the world is illusory or indirect, that what we see is not the world itself, or that the mind has to do only with its thoughts or with another mind. He accepts with all its difficulties the myth of the windows of the soul; it must be that what has no place is subjected to a body – even more, that what has no place be initiated *by* the body to all the others and to nature. We must take literally what vision teaches us: namely, that through it we come in contact with the sun and the stars, that we are everywhere all at once, and that even our power to imagine ourselves elsewhere – "I am in Petersburg in my bed, in Paris, my eyes see the sun" – or to intend [*viser*] real beings wherever they are, borrows from vision and employs means we owe to it. Vision alone makes us learn that beings that are different, "exterior," foreign to one another, are yet absolutely *together*, are "simultaneity"; this is a mystery psychologists handle the way a child handles explosives. Robert Delaunay says succinctly, "The railroad track is the image of succession which comes closest to the parallel: the parity of the rails." The rails converge and do not converge; they converge *in order* to remain equidistant down below. The world is in accordance with my perspective *in order* to be independent of me, is for me in *order to be* without me, and to be the world. The "visual quale"[56] gives me, and alone gives me, the presence of what is not me, of what *is* simply and fully. It does so because, like texture, it is the concretion of a universal visibility, of a unique space which separates and reunites, which sustains every cohesion (and even that of past and future, since there would be no such cohesion if they were not essentially relevant to the same space). Every visual something, as individual as it is, functions also as a dimension, because it gives itself as the result of a dehiscence of Being. What this ultimately means is that the proper essence [*le propre*] of the visible is to have a layer [*doublure*] of invisibility in the strict sense, which it makes present as a certain absence. "In their time, our bygone antipodes, the impressionists, were perfectly right in making their abode with the castaways and the undergrowth of daily life. As for us, our heart throbs to bring us closer to the depths.... These oddities will become...realities...because instead of being held to the diversely intense restoration of the visible, they will annex to it the proper share [la part] of the invisible, occultly apperceived."[57] There is that which reaches the eye directly [de face], the frontal properties of the visible; but there is also that which reaches it from below – the profound postural latency where the body raises itself to see – and that which reaches vision from above like the phenomena of flight, of swimming, of movement, where it participates no longer in the heaviness of origins but in free accomplishments.[58] Through it, then, the painter touches the two extremities. In the immemorial depth of the visible, something moved, caught fire, and engulfed his body; everything he paints is in answer to this incitement, and his hand is "nothing but the instrument of a distant will." Vision encounters, as at a crossroads, all the aspects of Being. "[A] certain fire pretends to be alive; it awakens. Working its way along the hand as conductor, it reaches the support and engulfs it; then a leaping spark closes the circle it was to trace, coming back to the eye, and beyond."[59]

There is no break at all in this circuit; it is impossible to say that nature ends here and that man or expression starts here. It is, therefore, mute Being which itself comes to show forth its own meaning. Herein lies the reason why the dilemma between figurative and nonfigurative art is badly posed; it is true and uncontradictory that no grape was ever what it is in the most figurative painting and that no painting, no matter how abstract, can get away from Being, that even Caravaggio's grape is the grape itself.[60] This precession of what is upon what one sees and makes seen, of what one sees and makes seen upon what is – this is vision itself. And to give the ontological formula of painting we hardly need to force the painter's own words, Klee's words written at the age of thirty-seven and ultimately inscribed on his tomb: "I cannot be caught in immanence."[61]

5

Because depth, color, form, line, movement, contour, physiognomy are all branches of Being and because each one can sway all the rest, there are no separated, distinct "problems" in painting, no really opposed paths, no partial "solutions," no cumulative progress, no irretrievable options. There is nothing to prevent a painter from going back to one of the devices he has shied away from –

making it, of course, speak differently. Rouault's contours are not those of Ingres. Light is the "old sultana," says Georges Limbour, "whose charms withered away at the beginning of this century."[62] Expelled first by the painters of materials [les peintres de le matière], it reappears finally in Dubuffet as a certain texture of matter. One is never immune to this kind of turning back or to the least expected convergences; some of Rodin's fragments are almost statues by Germain Richier because they were both sculptors – that is to say, enmeshed in a single, identical network of Being. For the same reason nothing is ever finally acquired and possessed for good.

In "working over" a favorite problem, even if it is just the problem of velvet or wool, the true painter unknowingly upsets the givens of all the other problems. His quest is total even where it looks partial. Just when he has reached proficiency in some area, he finds that he has reopened another one where everything he said before must be said again in a different way. The upshot is that what he has found he does not yet have. It remains to be sought out; the discovery itself calls forth still further quests. The idea of a universal painting, of a totalization of painting, of a fully and definitively achieved painting is an idea bereft of sense. For painters the world will always be yet to be painted, even if it lasts millions of years . . . it will end without having been conquered in painting.

Panofsky shows that the "problems" of painting which magnetize its history are often solved obliquely, not in the course of inquiries instigated to solve them but, on the contrary, at some point when the painters, having reached an impasse, apparently forget those problems and permit themselves to be attracted by other things. Then suddenly, altogether off guard, they turn up the old problems and surmount the obstacle. This unhearing [sourde] historicity, advancing through the labyrinth by detours, transgression, slow encroachments and sudden drives, does not imply that the painter does not know what he wants. It does imply that what he wants is beyond the means and goals at hand and commands from afar all our useful activity.

We are so fascinated by the classical idea of intellectual adequation that painting's mute "thinking" sometimes leaves us with the impression of a vain swirl of significations, a paralyzed or miscarried utterance. Suppose, then, that one answers that no thought ever detaches itself completely from a sustaining support; that the only privilege of speaking-thought is to have rendered its own support manageable; that the figurations of literature and philosophy are no more settled than those of painting and are no more capable of being accumulated into a stable treasure; that even science learns to recognize a zone of the "fundamental," peopled with dense, open, rent [déchirés] beings of which an exhaustive treatment is out of the question – like the cyberneticians' "aesthetic information" or mathematical-physical "groups of operations"; that, in the end, we are never in a position to take stock of everything objectively or to think of progress in itself; and that the whole of human history is, in a certain sense, stationary. *What*, says the understanding, like [Stendhal's] Lamiel, *is it only that?*

Is this the highest point of reason, to realize that the soil beneath our feet is shifting, to pompously name "interrogation" what is only a persistent state of stupor, to call "research" or "quest" what is only trudging in a circle, to call "Being" that which never fully *is?*

But this disappointment issues from that spurious fantasy[63] which claims for itself a positivity capable of making up for its own emptiness. It is the regret of not being everything, and a rather groundless regret at that. For if we cannot establish a hierarchy of civilizations or speak of progress – neither in painting nor in anything else that matters – it is not because some fate holds us back; it is, rather, because the very first painting in some sense went to the farthest reach of the future. If no painting comes to be *the* painting, if no work is ever absolutely completed and done with, still each creation changes, alters, enlightens, deepens, confirms, exalts, re-creates, or creates in advance all the others. If creations are not a possession, it is not only that, like all things, they pass away; it is also that they have almost all their life still before them.

Le Tholonet, July–August 1960

Notes

1 "L'Oeil et l'esprit" was the last work Merleau-Ponty saw published. It appeared in the inaugural issue of *Art de France*, vol. I, no. 1 (January, 1961). After his death it was reprinted in *Les Temps Modernes*, no. 184–85, along with seven articles devoted to him. It has now been published, in book form, by Editions Gallimard (1964). Both the *Art de France* article and the book contain illustrations chosen by Merleau-Ponty. According to Professor Claude Lefort, "L'Oeil et l'esprit" is a preliminary statement of ideas that were to be developed in the second part of the book Merleau-Ponty was writing at the time of his death – *Le visible et l'invisible* (part of which was published posthumously by Gallimard in February, 1964). [...] – *Trans.*

2 Il est là, fort ou faible dans la vie, mais souverain sans conteste dans sa rumination du monde, sans autre "technique" que celle que ses yeux et ses mains se donnent à force de voir, à force de peindre, acharné à tirer de ce monde où sonnent les scandales et les gloires de l'histoire des *toiles* qui n'ajouteront guère aux colères ni aux espoirs des hommes, et personne ne murmure.

3 Cf. *Le visible et l'invisible* (Paris, 1964), pp. 273, 308–11. – *Trans.*

4 See *Signes* (Paris, 1960), pp. 210, 222–23, especially the footnotes, for a clarification of the "circularity" at issue here – *Trans.*

5 Cet équivalent interne, cette formule charnelle de leur présence que les choses suscitent en moi, pourquoi à leur tour ne susciteraient-ils pas un tracé, visible encore, où tout autre regard retrouvera les motifs qui soutiennent son inspection du monde?

6 G. Charbonnier, *Le monologue du peintre* (Paris, 1959), p. 172.

7 Beaucoup plus loin, puisque le tableau n'est un analogue que selon le corps, qu'il n'offre pas à l'esprit une occasion de repenser les rapports constitutifs des choses, mais au regard, pour qu'il les épouse, les traces de la vision du dedans, à la vision ce qui la tapisse intérieurement, la texture imaginaire du réel.

8 Charbonnier, [*Le monologue du peintre*], p. 34.

9 *Ibid.*, pp. 143–45.

10 "...une philosophie figurée..." Cf. Bergson (Ravaisson), note 46 below. – *Trans.*

11 P. Claudel, *Introduction à la peinture hollandaise* (Paris, 1935).

12 P. Schilder, *The Image and Appearance of the Human Body* (London, 1935; New York, 1950), pp. 223–24. ["...the body-image is not confined to the borderlines of one's own body. It transgresses them in the mirror. There is a body-image outside ourselves, and it is remarkable that primitive peoples even ascribe a substantial existence to the picture in the mirror" (p. 278). Schilder's earlier, shorter study, *Das Körperschema* (Berlin, 1923), is cited several

times in *The Structure of Behavior* and in *Phenomenology of Perception*. Schilder's later work is of especial interest with regard to Merleau-Ponty's own elaborations of the meaning of the human body; it is worth examining for that reason, as well as for the chance it provides to discern some fundamental coincidences between Merleau-Ponty and certain American pragmatists.]

13 Cf. Schilder, *Image*, pp. 281–82. – *Trans.*

14 Robert Delaunay, *Du cubisme à l'art abstrait* (Paris, 1957).

15 "A minute in the world's life passes! to paint it in its reality! and forget everything for that. To become that minute, be the sensitive plate, . . . give the image of what we see, forgetting everything that has appeared before our time. . . . " Cézanne, quoted in B. Dorival, *Paul Cézanne*, trans. H. H. A. Thackthwaite (London, 1948), p. 101. – *Trans.*

16 Descartes, *La Dioptrique*, Discours VII [conclusion], Edition Adam et Tannery, VI, p. 165.

17 *Ibid.*, Discours I. Adam et Tannery, p. 83. [*Oeuvres et lettres de Descartes*, ed. André Bridoux, Edition Pléiade, p. 181. Page references from the Bridoux selections have been added in the belief that this volume is more widely accessible today than the Adam and Tannery complete edition.]

18 *Ibid.*, Adam et Tannery, p. 84. [Bridoux, p. 182.]

19 This paragraph continues the exposition of the *Dioptric*. – *Trans.*

20 *Ibid.*, Discours IV. Adam et Tannery, pp. 112–14. [Bridoux, pp. 203–4; in English, *Descartes: Philosophical Writings*, ed. and trans. N. Kemp Smith, Modern Library Edition, pp. 145–47.]

21 *Ibid.*, p. 130. [Bridoux, p. 217; Smith, p. 148.]

22 The system of means by which painting makes us see is a scientific matter. Why, then, do we not methodically produce perfect images of the world, arriving at a universal art purged of personal art, just as the universal language would free us of all the confused relationships that lurk in existent languages?

23 *Dioptrique*, Discours IV [Note 20 above].

24 Discours V of the *Dioptrique*, especially Descartes' diagrams, helps considerably to clarify this compressed passage. – *Trans.*

25 That is, the painting, – *Trans.*

26 E. Panofsky, *Die Perspektive als symbolische Form*, in *Vorträge der Bibliothek Warburg*, IV (1924–25).

27 *Ibid.*

28 Descartes, [*Dioptrique*], Adam et Tannery, VI, p. 135 [Bridoux, p. 220; Smith, p. 154. Here is Smith's translation of the passage under discussion: "Our knowledge of it (the situation of an object) does not depend on any image or action which comes to us from the object, but solely on the situation of the small parts of the brain whence the nerves take their origin. For this situation – a situation which changes with every change however small in the points at which these nerve-fibers are located – is instituted by nature in order to secure, not only that the mind be aware of the location of each part of the body which it animates, relatively to all the others, but also that it be able to transfer its attention to all the positions contained in the straight line that can be imaged as drawn from the extremity of each of these parts, and as prolonged to infinity."]

29 *Ibid.*, Adam et Tannery, p. 137. [Bridoux, p. 222; Smith, p. 155. Smith's translation is given here.]

30 No doubt Merleau-Ponty is speaking of Princess Elizabeth, Descartes' correspondent. Cf. *Phénoménologie de la perception*, pp. 230–32 (C. Smith translation, pp. 198–99), and Descartes' letter to Elizabeth of June 28, 1643 (Bridoux, pp. 1157–61). – *Trans.*

31 That is, the obscurity of the "existential" order is just as necessary, just as grounded in God, as is the clarity of true thoughts ("nos lumières"). – *Trans.*

32 "those who do not see in it," i.e., the blind (note 18, above). – *Trans.*

33 B. Dorival, *Paul Cézanne* (Paris, 1948), p. 103 *et seq.* [*trans.* Thackthwaite, [. . .] pp. 101–3].

34 Charbonnier, [*Le monologue du peintre*], p. 176.

35 Delaunay, [*Du cubisme à l'art abstrait*], p. 109.

36 F. Novotny, *Cézanne und das Ende der wissenschaftlichen Perspective* (Vienna, 1938).

37 W. Grohmann, *Paul Klee* (Paris, 1954), p. 141 [New York, 1956].

38 Delaunay, [*Du cubisme à l'art abstrait*], p. 118.

39 Klee, *Journal . . .*, French trans. P. Klossowski (Paris, 1959).

40 George Schmidt, *Les aquarelles de Cézanne*, p. 21. [*The Watercolors of Cézanne* (New York, 1953).]

41 Klee, [*Journal*].

42 "The spectacle is first of all a spectacle of itself before it is a spectacle of something outside of it." – *Translator's note from Merleau-Ponty's 1961 lectures.*

43 C. P. Bru, *Esthétique de l'abstraction* (Paris, 1959), pp. 99, 86.

44 Henri Michaux, *Aventures de lignes*.

45 *Ibid.*

46 Ravaisson, cited by Bergson, "La vie et l'oeuvre de Ravaisson," in *La pensée et le mouvant* (Paris, 1934), pp. 264–65. [The passage quoted here is from M. L. Andison's translation of that work, *The Creative Mind* (New York, 1946), p. 229. It remains moot whether these are Ravaisson's or da Vinci's words.]

47 Bergson, *ibid.*

48 Michaux, [*Aventures de lignes*: "laissé rêver une ligne"]

49 *Ibid.* ["d'aller ligne"]

50 Grohmann, [*Paul Klee*], p. 192.

51 Rodin, *L'art*. Interviews collected by Paul Gsell (Paris, 1911).

52 *Ibid.*, p. 86.

53 Michaux, [*Aventures de lignes*].

54 Cited by Delaunay, [*Du cubisme à l'art abstrait*], p. 175.

55 Rilke, *Auguste Rodin*, French translation by Maurice Betz (Paris, 1928), p. 150. [English translation by Jessie Lamont and Hans Trausil (New York, 1919; republished 1945).]

56 Delaunay, [*Du cubisme à l'art abstrait*], pp. 115, 110.

57 Klee, *Conférence d'Iena* (1924), according to Grohmann, [*Paul Klee*], p. 365.

58 Klee, *Wege des Naturstudiums* (1923), as found in G. di San Lazzaro, *Klee* [: *A Study of his Life and Work* (New York, 1957)].

59 Klee, cited by Grohmann, [*Paul Klee*], p. 99.

60 A. Berne-Joffroy, *Le dossier Caravage* (Paris, 1959), and Michel Butor, "La Corbeille de l'Ambrosienne," *Nouvelle Revue Française*, 1959, pp. 969–89.

61 Klee, *Journal*, [. . . "Je suis insaissable dans l'immanence."]

62 G. Limbour, *Tableau bon levain à vous de cuire la pâte: l'art brut de Jean Dubuffet* (Paris, 1953), pp. 54–55.

63 "Mais cette deception est celle du faux imaginaire, qui . . ."

19

On Leveling the Genre Distinction between Philosophy and Literature

Jürgen Habermas

I

Adorno's "negative dialectics" and Derrida's "deconstruction" can be seen as different answers to the same problem. The totalizing self-critique of reason gets caught in a performative contradiction since subject-centered reason can be convicted of being authoritarian in nature only by having recourse to its own tools. The tools of thought, which miss the "dimension of nonidentity" and are imbued with the "metaphysics of presence," are nevertheless the only available means for uncovering their own insufficiency. Heidegger flees from this paradox to the luminous heights of an esoteric, special discourse, which absolves itself of the restrictions of discursive speech generally and is immunized by vagueness against any specific objections. He makes use of metaphysical concepts for purposes of a critique of metaphysics, as a ladder he casts away once he has mounted the rungs. Once on the heights, however, the late Heidegger does not, as did the early Wittgenstein, withdraw into the mystic's silent intuition; instead, with the gestures of the seer and an abundance of words, he lays claim to the authority of the initiate.

Adorno operates differently. He does not slip out of the paradoxes of the self-referential critique of reason; he makes the performative contradiction within which this line of thought has moved since Nietzsche, and which he acknowledges to be unavoidable, into the organizational form of indirect communication. Identity thinking turned against itself becomes pressed into continual self-denial and allows the wounds it inflicts on itself and its

objects to be seen. This exercise quite rightly bears the name negative dialectics because Adorno practices determinate negation unremittingly, even though it has lost any foothold in the categorial network of Hegelian Logic – as a fetishism of demystification, so to speak. This fastening upon a critical procedure that can no longer be sure of its foundations is explained by the fact that Adorno (in contrast to Heidegger) bears no elitist contempt for discursive thought. Like exiles, we wander about lost in the discursive zone; and yet it is only the insistent force of a groundless reflection turned against itself that preserves our connection with the utopia of a long since lost, uncoerced and intuitive knowledge belonging to the primal past.[1] Discursive thought cannot identify itself as the decadent form of this knowledge by means of its own resources; for this purpose, the aesthetic experience gained in contact with avant-garde art is needed. The promise for which the surviving philosophic tradition is no longer a match has withdrawn into the mirror-writing of the esoteric work of art and requires a negativistic deciphering. From this labor of deciphering, philosophy sucks the residue of that paradoxical trust in reason with which negative dialectics executes (in the double sense of this word) its performative contradiction.

Derrida cannot share Adorno's aesthetically certified, residual faith in a de-ranged reason that has been expelled from the domains of philosophy and become, literally, utopian [having no place]. He is just as little convinced that Heidegger actually escaped the conceptual constraints of the philosophy of the subject by using metaphysical concepts in order to "cancel them out." Derrida does, to be sure, want to advance the already forged path of the critique of metaphysics; he, too, would just as soon break out of the paradox as broodingly encircle it. But like Adorno, he guards against the gestures of profundity that Heidegger unhesitatingly imitates from his opposite number, the philosophy of origins. And so there are also parallels between Derrida and Adorno.

This affinity in regard to their thought gestures calls for a more precise analysis. Adorno and Derrida are sensitized in the same way against definitive, totalizing, all-incorporating models, especially against the organic dimension in works of art. Thus, both stress the primacy of the allegorical over the symbolic, of metonymy over metaphor, of the Romantic over the Classical. Both use the fragment as an expository form: they place any system under suspicion. Both are abundantly insightful in decoding the normal case from the point of view of its limit cases; they meet in a negative extremism, finding the essential in the marginal and incidental, the right on the side of the subversive and the outcast, and the truth in the peripheral and the inauthentic. A distrust of everything direct and substantial goes along with an intransigent tracing of mediations, of hidden presuppositions and dependencies. The critique of origins, of anything original, of first principles, goes together with a certain fanaticism about showing what is merely produced, imitated, and secondary in everything. What pervades Adorno's work as a materialist motif – his unmasking of idealist positings, his reversal of false constitutive connections, his thesis about the primacy of the object – even for this there is a parallel in Derrida's logic of the supplement. The rebellious labor of deconstruction aims indeed at dismantling smuggled-in basic conceptual hierarchies, at overthrowing foundational relationships and conceptual relations of domination, such as those between speech and writing, the intelligible and the sensible, nature and culture, inner and outer, mind and matter, male and female. Logic and rhetoric constitute one of these conceptual pairs. Derrida is particularly interested in standing the primacy of logic over rhetoric, canonized since Aristotle, on its head.

It is not as though Derrida concerned himself with these controversial questions in terms of viewpoints familiar from the history of philosophy. If he had done so, he would have had to relativize the status of his own project in relation to the tradition

that was shaped from Dante to Vico, and kept alive through Hamann, Humboldt, and Droysen, down to Dilthey and Gadamer. For the protest against the Platonic-Aristotelian primacy of the logical over the rhetorical that is raised anew by Derrida was articulated in this tradition. Derrida wants to expand the sovereignty of rhetoric over the realm of the logical in order to solve the problem confronting the totalizing critique of reason. As I have indicated, he is satisfied neither with Adorno's negative dialectics nor with Heidegger's critique of metaphysics – the one remaining tied to the rational bliss of the dialectic, the other to the elevation of origins proper to metaphysics, all protestations to the contrary notwithstanding. Heidegger only escapes the paradoxes of a self-referential critique of reason by claiming a special status for *Andenken*, that is, its release from discursive obligations. He remains completely silent about the privileged access to truth. Derrida strives to arrive at the same esoteric access to truth, but he does not want to admit it as a privilege – no matter for what or for whom. He does not place himself in lordly fashion above the objection of pragmatic inconsistency, but renders it *objectless*.

There can only be talk about "contradiction" in the light of consistency requirements, which lose their authority or are at least subordinated to other demands – of an aesthetic nature, for example – if logic loses its conventional primacy over rhetoric. Then the deconstructionist can deal with the works of philosophy as works of literature and adapt the critique of metaphysics to the standards of a literary criticism that does not misunderstand itself in a scientistic way. As soon as we take the *literary* character of Nietzsche's writings seriously, the suitableness of his critique of reason has to be assessed in accord with the standards of rhetorical success and not those of logical consistency. Such a critique (which is more adequate to its object) is not immediately directed toward the network of discursive relationships of which arguments are built, but toward the figures that shape style and are decisive for the literary and rhetorical power of a text. A literary criticism that in a certain sense merely *continues* the literary process of its objects cannot end up in science. Similarly, the deconstruction of great philosophical texts, carried out as literary criticism in this broader sense, is not subject to the criteria of problem-solving, purely cognitive undertakings.

Hence, Derrida *undercuts* the very problem that Adorno acknowledged as unavoidable and turned into the starting point of his reflectively self-transcending identity-thinking. For Derrida, this problem has no object since the deconstructive enterprise cannot be pinned down to the discursive obligations of philosophy and science. He calls his procedure deconstruction because it is supposed to *clear away* the ontological *scaffolding* erected by philosophy in the course of its subject-centered history of reason. However, in his business of deconstruction, Derrida does not proceed analytically, in the sense of identifying hidden presuppositions or implications. This is just the way in which each successive generation has critically reviewed the works of the preceding ones. Instead, Derrida proceeds by a critique of style, in that he finds something like indirect communications, by which the text itself denies its manifest content, in the rhetorical surplus of meaning inherent in the literary strata of texts that present themselves as nonliterary. In this way, he compels texts by Husserl, Saussure, or Rousseau to confess their guilt, against the explicit interpretations of their authors. Thanks to their rhetorical content, texts combed against the grain contradict what they state, such as the explicitly asserted primacy of signification over the sign, of the voice in relation to writing, of the intuitively given and immediately present over the representative and the postponed-postponing. In a philosophical text, the blind spot cannot be identified on the level of manifest content any more than it can in a literary text. "Blindness and insight" are rhetorically interwoven with one another. Thus, the constraints constitutive for knowledge of a philosophical text only become accessible when the text is handled as what it would not like to be – as a literary text.

If, however, the philosophical (or scholarly) text were thereby only *extraneously turned* into an apparently literary one, deconstruction would still be an arbitrary act. Derrida can only attain Heidegger's goal of bursting metaphysical thought-forms from the inside by means of his essentially rhetorical procedure if the philosophical text is *in truth* a literary one – if one can *demonstrate* that the genre distinction between philosophy and literature dissolves upon closer examination. This demonstration is supposed to be carried out by way of deconstruction itself; in every single case we see anew the impossibility of so specializing the language of philosophy and science for cognitive purposes that they are cleansed of everything metaphorical and merely rhetorical, and kept free of literary admixtures. The frailty of the genre

distinction between philosophy and literature is evidenced in the practice of deconstruction; in the end, *all* genre distinctions are submerged in one comprehensive, all-embracing context of texts – Derrida talks in a hypostatizing manner about a "universal text." What remains is self-inscribing writing as the medium in which each text is woven together with everything else. Even before it makes its appearance, every text and every particular genre has already lost its autonomy to an all-devouring context and an uncontrollable happening of spontaneous text production. This is the ground of the primacy of rhetoric, which is concerned with the qualities of texts in general, over logic, as a system of rules to which only certain types of discourse are subjected in an exclusive manner – those bound to argumentation.

II

This – at first glance inconspicuous – transformation of the "destruction" into the "deconstruction" of the philosophical tradition transposes the radical critique of reason into the domain of rhetoric and thereby shows it a way out of the aporia of self-referentiality: Anyone who still wanted to attribute paradoxes to the critique of metaphysics after this transformation would have misunderstood it in a scientistic manner. This argument holds good only if the following propositions are true:

1 Literary criticism is not primarily a scientific (or scholarly: *wissenschaftliches*) enterprise but observes the same rhetorical criteria as its literary objects.
2 Far from there being a genre distinction between philosophy and literature, philosophical texts can be rendered accessible in their essential contents by literary criticism.
3 The primacy of rhetoric over logic means the overall responsibility of rhetoric for the general qualities of an all-embracing context of texts, within which all genre distinctions are ultimately dissolved; philosophy and science no more constitute their own proper universes than art and literature constitute a realm of fiction that could assert its autonomy vis-à-vis the universal text.

Proposition 3 explicates propositions 2 and 1 by despecializing the meaning of "literary criticism."

Literary criticism does serve as a model that clarifies itself through a long tradition; but it is considered precisely as a model case of something more universal, namely, a criticism suited to the rhetorical qualities of everyday discourse as well as of discourse outside the everyday. The procedure of deconstruction deploys this generalized criticism to bring to light the suppressed surpluses of rhetorical meaning in philosophical and scientific texts – against their manifest sense. Derrida's claim that "deconstruction" is an instrument for bringing Nietzsche's radical critique of reason out of the dead end of its paradoxical self-referentiality therefore stands – or falls – along with thesis number 3.

Just this thesis has been the centerpoint of the lively reception Derrida's work has enjoyed in the literature faculties of prominent American universities.[2] In the United States, literary criticism has for a long time been institutionalized as an academic discipline, that is, within the scholarly-scientific enterprise. From the very start, the self-tormenting question about the scholarly-scientific character of literary criticism was institutionalized along with it. This endemic self-doubt forms the background for the reception of Derrida, along with the dissolution of the decades-long domination of the New Criticism, which was convinced of the autonomy of the literary work of art and drew nourishment from the scientific pathos of structuralism. The idea of "deconstruction" could catch on in this constellation because it opened up to literary criticism a task of undoubted significance, under exactly the opposite premises: Derrida disputes the autonomy of the linguistic work of art and the independent meaning of the aesthetic illusion no less energetically than he does the possibility of criticism's ever being able to attain scientific status. At the same time, literary criticism serves him as the model for a procedure that takes on an almost world-historical mission with its overcoming of the thinking of the metaphysics of presence and of the age of logocentrism.

The leveling of the genre distinction between literary criticism and literature frees the critical enterprise from the unfortunate compulsion to submit to pseudo-scientific standards; it simultaneously lifts it above science to the level of creative activity. Criticism does not need to consider itself as something secondary; it gains literary status. In the texts of Hillis Miller, Geoffrey Hartman, and Paul de Man we can find the new self-awareness: "that critics are no more parasites than the texts they interpret, since both inhabit a host-text of pre-existing language which itself parasitically feeds on their host-like willingness to receive it." Deconstructionists break with the traditional Arnoldian conception of criticism's function as a mere servant: "Criticism is now crossing over into literature, rejecting its subservient, Arnoldian stance and taking on the freedom of interpretive style with a matchless gusto."[3] Thus, in perhaps his most brilliant book, Paul de Man deals with critical texts by Lukács, Barthes, Blanchot, and Jakobson with a method and finesse that are usually reserved only for literary texts: "Since they are not scientific, critical texts have to be read with the same awareness of ambivalence that is brought to the study of non-critical literary texts."[4]

Just as important as the equation of literary criticism with creative literary production is the increase in significance enjoyed by literary criticism as sharing in the business of the critique of metaphysics. This upgrading to the critique of metaphysics requires a counterbalancing supplement to Derrida's interpretation of the leveling of the genre distinction between philosophy and literature. Jonathan Culler recalls the strategic meaning of Derrida's treatment of philosophical texts through literary criticism in order to suggest that, in turn, literary criticism treat literary texts also as philosophical texts. Simultaneously maintaining and relativizing the distinction between the two genres "is essential to the demonstration that the most truly philosophical reading of a philosophical text . . . is one that treats the work as literature, as a fictive, rhetorical construct whose elements and order are determined by various textual exigencies." Then he continues: "Conversely, the most powerful and opposite readings of literary works may be those that treat them as philosophical gestures by teasing out the implications of their dealings with the philosophical oppositions that support them."[5] Proposition 2 is thus varied in the following sense:

2′ Far from there being a genre distinction between philosophy and literature, literary texts can be rendered accessible in their essential contents by a critique of metaphysics.

Of course, the two propositions, 2 and 2′, point in the direction of the primacy of rhetoric over logic, which is asserted in proposition 3. Consequently, American literary critics are concerned to develop a concept of *general* literature, equal in overall scope to rhetoric, which would correspond to Derrida's "universal text." The notion of literature as confined to the realm of the fictive is deconstructed at the same time as the conventional notion of philosophy that denies the metaphorical basis of philosophical thought: "The notion of literature or literary discourse is involved in several of the hierarchical oppositions on which deconstruction has focussed: serious/non-serious, literal/metaphorical, truth/fiction.... Deconstruction's demonstration that these hierarchies are undone by the working of the texts that propose them alters the standing of literary language." There now follows, in the form of a conditional statement, the thesis on which everything depends – both the self-understanding of a literary criticism upgraded to the critique of metaphysics and the deconstructionist dissolution of the performative contradiction of a self-referential critique of reason: "If serious language is a special case of non-serious, if truths are fictions whose fictionality has been forgotten, then literature is not a deviant, parasitical instance of language. On the contrary, other discourses can be seen as cases of a generalized literature, or archi-literature."[6] Since Derrida does not belong to those philosophers who like to argue, it is expedient to take a closer look at his disciples in literary criticism within the Anglo-Saxon climate of argument in order to see whether this thesis really can be held.

Jonathan Culler reconstructs in a very clear way the somewhat impenetrable discussion between Derrida and Searle in order to show by the example of Austin's speech-act theory that any attempt to demarcate the ordinary domain of normal speech from an "unusual" use of language, "deviating" from the standard cases, is doomed to failure. Culler's thesis is expanded and indirectly confirmed in a study of speech-act theory by Mary Louise Pratt, who wants to prove, by the example of the structuralist theory of poetics, that even the attempt to delimit the extraordinary domain of fictive discourse from everyday discourse fails (see section III below). But first let us take a look at the debate between Derrida and Searle.[7]

From this complex discussion, Culler selects as the central issue the question of whether Austin does in fact, as it seems he does, make a totally unprejudiced, provisory, and purely methodical move. Austin wants to analyze the rules intuitively mastered by competent speakers, in accordance

with which typical speech acts can be successfully executed. He undertakes this analysis with respect to sentences from *normal* everyday practice that are uttered *seriously* and used as *simply* and *literally* as possible. Thus, the unit of analysis, the standard speech act, is the result of certain abstractions. The theoretician of speech acts directs his attention to a sample of normal linguistic utterances from which all complex, derivative, parasitic, and deviant cases have been filtered out. A concept of "usual" or normal linguistic practice underpins this isolation, a concept of "ordinary language" whose harmlessness and consistency Derrida puts in doubt. Austin's intention is clear: He wants to analyze the universal properties of "promises," for example, with respect to cases in which the utterance of corresponding sentences actually *functions* as a promise. Now there are contexts in which the same sentences lose the illocutionary force of a promise. Spoken by an actor on the stage, as part of a poem, or even in a monologue, a promise, according to Austin, becomes "null and void in a unique manner." The same holds true for a promise that comes up in a quotation, or one merely mentioned. In these contexts, there is no *serious* or *binding* use, and sometimes not even a *literal* use, of the respective performative sentence, but a derivative or parasitic use instead. As Searle constantly repeats, these fictive or simulated or indirect modes of use are "parasitic" in the sense that logically they presuppose the possibility of a serious, literal, and binding use of sentences grammatically appropriate for making promises. Culler extracts what are in essence three objections from Derrida's texts; they point toward the impossibility of such an operation and are meant to show that the common distinctions between serious and simulated, literal and metaphorical, everyday and fictional, usual and parasitic modes of speech break down.

(a) In his initial argument, Derrida posits a not very clear link between quotability and repeatability on the one hand, and fictionality on the other. The quotation of a promise is only apparently something secondary in comparison to the directly made promise, for the indirect rendition of a performative utterance in a quote is a form of repetition, and as quotability presupposes the possibility of repetition in accord with a rule, that is, conventionality, it belongs to the nature of any conventionally generated utterance (including performative ones) that it can be quoted – and fictively imitated, in a broader sense: "If it were not possible for a character in a play to make a promise, there could be no promise in real life, for what makes it possible to promise, as Austin tells us, is the existence of a conventional procedure, of formulas one can repeat. For me to be able to make a promise in real life, there must be iterable procedures or formulas such as are used on stage. Serious behavior is a case of role-playing."[8]

In this argument, Derrida obviously already presupposes what he wants to prove: that any convention which permits the repetition of exemplary actions possesses from the outset not only a symbolic, but also a fictional character. But it must first be shown that the conventions of a game are ultimately indistinguishable from norms of action. Austin introduces the quotation of a promise as an example of a derivative or parasitic form because the illocutionary force is removed from the quoted promise by the form of indirect rendition; it is thereby taken out of the context in which it "functions," that is, in which it coordinates the actions of the different participants in interaction and has consequences relevant to action. Only the actually performed speech act is *effective as action*; the promise mentioned or reported in a quote depends grammatically upon this. A setting that deprives it of its illocutionary force constitutes the bridge between quotation and fictional representation. Even action on the stage rests on a basis of everyday action (on the part of the actors, director, stage-workers, and theater people); and in the context of this framework, promises can function *in another mode* than they do "on stage," that is, with obligations and consequences relevant for action. Derrida makes no attempt to "deconstruct" this distinctive functional mode of ordinary speech within communicative action. In the illocutionary binding force of linguistic utterances Austin discovered a mechanism for coordinating action that places normal speech, as part of everyday practice, under constraints different from those of fictional discourse, simulation, and interior monologue. The constraints under which illocutionary acts develop a force for coordinating action and have consequences relevant to action define the domain of "normal" language. They can be analyzed as the kinds of idealizing suppositions we have to make in communicative action.

(b) The second argument brought forward by Culler, with Derrida, against Austin and Searle relates to just such idealizations. Any generalizing analysis of speech acts has to be able to specify general contextual conditions for the illocutionary success of standardized speech acts. Searle has

been especially occupied with this task.[9] Linguistic expressions, however, change their meanings depending on shifting contexts; moreover, contexts are so constituted as to be open to ever wider-reaching specification. It is one of the peculiarities of our language that we can separate utterances from their original contexts and transplant them into different ones – Derrida speaks of "grafting." In this manner, we can think of a speech act, such as a "marriage vow," in ever new and more improbable contexts; the specification of universal contextual conditions does not run into any natural limits: "Suppose that the requirements for a marriage ceremony were met but that one of the parties were under hypnosis, or that the ceremony were impeccable in all respects but had been called a 'rehearsal,' or finally, that while the speaker was a minister licensed to perform weddings and the couple had obtained a license, that three of them were on this occasion acting in a play that, coincidentally, included a wedding ceremony."[10] These variations of context that change meaning cannot in principle be arrested or controlled, because contexts cannot be exhausted, that is, they cannot be theoretically mastered once and for all. Culler shows clearly that Austin cannot escape this difficulty by taking refuge in the intentions of speakers and listeners. It is not the thoughts of bride, bridegroom, or priest that decide the validity of the ceremony, but their actions and the circumstances under which they are carried out: "What counts is the plausibility of the description: whether or not the features of the context adduced create a frame that alters the illocutionary force of the utterances."[11]

Searle reacted to this difficulty by introducing a qualification to the effect that the literal meaning of a sentence does not completely fix the validity conditions of the speech act in which it is employed; it depends, rather, on tacit supplementation by a system of background assumptions regarding the normality of general world conditions. These parareflective background certainties have a holistic nature; they cannot be exhausted by a countably finite set of specifications. Meanings of sentences, however well analyzed, are thus valid only relative to a shared background knowledge that is constitutive of the lifeworld of a linguistic community. But Searle makes clear that the addition of this relational moment does not bring with it the relativism of meaning that Derrida is after. As long as language games are functioning and the preunderstanding constitutive of the lifeworld has not broken down, participants rightly count on world conditions being what is understood in their linguistic community as "normal." And in cases where individual background convictions do become problematic, they assume that they could reach a rationally motivated agreement. Both are strong, that is to say idealizing, suppositions; but these idealizations are not arbitrary, logocentric acts brought to bear by theoreticians on unmanageable contexts in order to give the illusion of mastery; rather, they are presuppositions that the participants themselves have to make if communicative action is to be at all possible.

(c) The role of idealizing suppositions can also be clarified in connection with some other consequences of this same state of affairs. Because contexts are changeable and can be expanded in any desired direction, the same text can be open to different readings: it is the text itself that makes possible its uncontrollable effective history. Still, Derrida's purposely paradoxical statement that any interpretation is inevitably a false interpretation, and any understanding a misunderstanding, does not follow from this venerable hermeneutic insight. Culler justifies the statement "Every reading is a misreading" as follows: "If a text can be understood, it can in principle be understood repeatedly, by different readers in different circumstances. These acts of reading or understanding are not, of course, identical. They involve modifications and differences, but differences which are deemed not to matter. We can thus say that understanding is a special case of misunderstanding, a particular deviation or determination of misunderstanding. It is a misunderstanding whose misses do not matter."[12] Yet Culler leaves one thing out of consideration. The productivity of the process of understanding remains unproblematic only so long as all participants stick to the reference point of possibly achieving a mutual understanding in which the *same* utterances are assigned the same meaning. As Gadamer has shown, the hermeneutic effort that would bridge over temporal and cultural distances remains oriented toward the idea of a possible consensus being brought about in the present.

Under the pressure for decisions proper to the communicative practice of everyday life, participants are dependent upon agreements that coordinate their actions. The more removed interpretations are from the "seriousness of this type of situation," the more they can prescind from the idealizing supposition of an achievable consensus.

But they can never be wholly absolved of the idea that wrong interpretations must in principle be criticizable in terms of consensus to be aimed for ideally. The interpreter does not impose this idea on his object; rather, with the performative attitude of a participant observer, he takes it over from the direct participants, *who can act communicatively only under the presupposition of intersubjectively identical ascriptions of meaning.* I do not mean to marshal a Wittgensteinian positivism of language games against Derrida's thesis. It is not habitual linguistic practice that determines just what meaning is attributed to a text or an utterance.[13] Rather, language games only work because they presuppose idealizations that transcend any particular language game; as a necessary condition of possibly reaching understanding, these idealizations give rise to the perspective of an agreement that is open to criticism on the basis of validity claims. A language operating under these kinds of constraints is subject to an ongoing test. Everyday communicative practice, in which agents have to reach an understanding about something in the world, stands under the need to prove its worth, and it is the idealizing suppositions that make such testing possible in the first place. It is in relation to this need for standing the test within ordinary practice that one may distinguish, with Austin and Searle, between "usual" and "parasitic" uses of language.

III

Up to this point, I have criticized Derrida's third and fundamental assumption only to the extent that (against Culler's reconstruction of Derrida's arguments) I have defended the possibility of demarcating normal speech from *derivative* forms. I have not yet shown how fictional discourse can be separated from the normal (everyday) use of language. This aspect is the most important for Derrida. If "literature" and "writing" constitute the model for a universal context of texts, which cannot be surpassed and within which all genre distinctions are ultimately dissolved, they cannot be separated from other discourses as an autonomous realm of fiction. For the literary critics who follow Derrida in the United States, the thesis of the autonomy of the linguistic work of art is, as I mentioned, also unacceptable, because they want to set themselves off from the formalism of the New Criticism and from structuralist aesthetics.

The Prague Structuralists originally tried to distinguish poetic from ordinary language in view of their relations to extralinguistic reality. Insofar as language occurs in *communicative functions*, it has to produce relations between linguistic expression and speaker, hearer, and the state of affairs represented. Bühler articulated this in his semiotic scheme as the sign-functions of expression, appeal, and representation.[14] However, when language fulfills a poetic function, it does so in virtue of a reflexive relation of the linguistic expression to itself. Consequently, reference to an object, informational content, and truth-value – conditions of validity in general – are extrinsic to poetic speech; an utterance can be poetic to the extent that it is directed to the linguistic medium itself, to its own linguistic form. Roman Jakobson integrated this characterization into an expanded scheme of functions; in addition to the basic functions – expressing the speaker's intentions, establishing interpersonal relations, and representing states of affairs – which go back to Bühler, and two more functions related to making contact and to the code, he ascribes to linguistic utterances a poetic function, which directs our attention to "the message as such."[15] We are less concerned here with a closer characterization of the poetic function (in accord with which the principle of equivalence is projected from the axis of selection to the axis of combination) than with an interesting consequence that is important for our problem of delimiting normal from other instances of speech: "Any attempt to reduce the sphere of the poetic function would be a deceptive oversimplification. The poetic function is not the only function of verbal artistry, merely a *predominant* and *structurally determinative* one, whereas in all other linguistic activities it plays a subordinate and supplementary role. In as much as it *directs our attention to the sign's perceptibility*, this function deepens the fundamental dichotomy between signs and objects. For this reason, linguistics should not, when it studies the poetic function, restrict itself solely to the field of poetry."[16] Poetic speech, therefore, is to be distinguished only in virtue of the primacy and structure-forming force of a certain function that is always fulfilled together with other linguistic functions.

Richard Ohmann makes use of Austin's approach to specify poetic language in this sense. For him, the phenomenon in need of clarification is the fictionality of the linguistic work of art, that is, the generation of aesthetic illusion by which a second, specifically de-realized arena is opened up on the basis of a continued everyday practice. What distinguishes poetic language is its "world-generating" capacity: "A literary work creates a world...by providing the reader with *impaired* and incomplete speech acts which he completes by supplying the appropriate circumstances."[17] The unique *impairment* of speech acts that generates fictions arises when they are robbed of their illocutionary force, or maintain their illocutionary meanings only as in the refraction of indirect repetition or quotation: "A literary work is a discourse whose sentences lack the illocutionary forces that would normally attach to them. Its illocutionary force is mimetic.... Specifically, a literary work purportedly imitates a series of speech acts, which in fact have no other existence. By doing so, it leads the reader to imagine a speaker, a situation, a set of ancillary events, and so on."[18] The bracketing of illocutionary force virtualizes the relations to the world in which the speech acts are involved due to their illocutionary force, and releases the participants in interaction from reaching agreement about something in the world on the basis of idealizing understandings in such a way that they coordinate their plans of action and thus enter into obligations relevant to the outcomes of action: "Since the quasi-speech acts of literature are not *carrying on the world's business –* describing, urging, contracting, etc. – the reader may well attend to them in a non-pragmatic way."[19] Neutralizing their binding force releases the disempowered illocutionary acts from the pressure to decide proper to everyday communicative practice, removes them from the sphere of usual discourse, and thereby empowers them for the playful creation of new worlds – or, rather, for the pure demonstration of the world-disclosing force of innovative linguistic expressions. This specialization in the world-disclosive function of speech explains the unique self-reflexivity of poetic language to which Jakobson refers and which leads Geoffrey Hartman to pose the rhetorical question: "Is not literary language the name we give to a diction whose frame of reference is such that the words stand out as words (even as sounds) rather than being, at once, assimilable meanings?"[20]

Mary L. Pratt makes use of Ohmann's studies[21] to refute, by means of speech-act theory, the thesis of the independence of the literary work of art in Derrida's sense. She does not consider fictionality, the bracketing of illocutionary force, and the disengagement of poetic language from everyday communicative practice to be adequate selective criteria, because fictional speech elements such as jokes, irony, wish-fantasies, stories, and parables pervade our everyday discourse and by no means constitute an autonomous universe apart from "the world's business." Conversely, nonfiction works, memoirs, travel reports, historical romances, even *romans à clef* or thrillers that, like Truman Capote's *In Cold Blood*, adapt a factually documented case, by no means create an unambiguously fictional world, even though we often relegate these productions, for the most part at least, to "literature." Pratt uses the results of studies in sociolinguistics by W. Labov[22] to prove that natural narratives, that is, the "stories" told spontaneously or upon request in everyday life, follow the same rhetorical laws of construction as and exhibit structural characteristics similar to literary narratives: "Labov's data make it necessary to account for narrative rhetoric in terms that are not exclusively literary; the fact that fictive or mimetically organized utterances can occur in almost any realm of extraliterary discourse requires that we do the same for fictivity or mimesis. In other words, the relation between a work's fictivity and its literariness is indirect."[23]

Nonetheless, the fact that normal language is permeated with fictional, narrative, metaphorical, and, in general, with rhetorical elements does not yet speak against the attempt to explain the autonomy of the linguistic work of art by the bracketing of illocutionary forces, for, according to Jakobson, the mark of fictionality is suited for demarcating literature from everyday discourses only to the degree that the world-disclosing function of language predominates over the other linguistic functions and determines the structure of the linguistic artifact. In a certain respect, it is the refraction and partial elimination of illocutionary validity claims that distinguishes the story from the statement of the eyewitness, teasing from insulting, being ironic from misleading, the hypothesis from the assertion, wish-fantasy from perception, a training maneuver from an act of warfare, and a scenario from a report of an actual catastrophe. But in none of these cases do the illocutionary acts lose their binding force for coordinating action. Even in the cases adduced for the sake of comparison, the communicative functions of the speech acts remain intact insofar as the fictive elements cannot be separated from contexts of life practice. The world-disclosing function of language does not

gain independence over against the expressive, regulative, and informative functions. By contrast, in Truman Capote's literary elaboration of a notorious and carefully researched incident, precisely this may be the case. That is to say, what grounds the *primacy* and the structuring force of the poetic function is not the deviation of a fictional representation from the documentary report of an incident, but the exemplary elaboration that takes the case out of its context and makes it the occasion for an innovative, world-disclosive, and eye-opening representation in which the rhetorical means of representation depart from communicative routines and take on a life of their own.

It is interesting to see how Pratt is compelled to work out this poetic function against her will. Her sociolinguistic counterproposal begins with the analysis of a speech situation that poetic discourse shares with other discourses – the kind of arrangement in which a narrator or lecturer turns to a public and calls its attention to a text. The text undergoes certain procedures of preparation and selection before it is ready for delivery. Before a text can lay claim to the patience and discretion of the audience, it has also to satisfy certain criteria of relevance: it *has to be worth telling*. The tellability is to be assessed in terms of the manifestation of some significant exemplary experience. In its content, a tellable text reaches beyond the local context of the immediate speech situation and is open to further elaboration: "As might be expected, these two features – contextual detachability and susceptibility to elaboration – are equally important characteristics of literature." Of course, literary texts share these characteristics with "display texts" in general. The latter are characterized by their special communicative functions: "They are designed to serve a purpose I have described as that of verbally representing states of affairs and experiences which are held to be *unusual* or *problematic* in such a way that the addressee will respond affectively in the intended way, adopt the intended evaluation and interpretation, take pleasure in doing so, and *generally find the whole undertaking worth it*."[24] One sees how the pragmatic linguistic analyst creeps up on literary texts from outside, as it were. The latter have still to satisfy a final condition; in the case of literary texts, tellability must gain a preponderance over other functional characteristics: "In the end, tellability can take precedence over assertability itself."[25] Only in this case do the functional demands and structural constraints of everyday communicative practice (which Pratt defines by means of Grice's conversation postulates) lose their force. The concern to give one's contribution an informative shape, to say what is relevant, to be straightforward and to avoid obscure, ambiguous, and prolix utterances are idealizing presuppositions of the communicative action *of normal speech*, but not of poetic discourse: "Our tolerance, indeed propensity, for elaboration when dealing with the tellable suggests that, in Gricean terms, the standards of quantity, quality and manner for display texts differ from those Grice suggests for declarative speech in his maxims."

In the end, the analysis leads to a confirmation of the thesis it would like to refute. To the degree that the poetic, world-disclosing function of language gains primacy and structuring force, language escapes the structural constraints and communicative functions of everyday life. The space of fiction that is opened up when linguistic forms of expression become reflexive results from suspending illocutionary binding forces and those idealizations that make possible a use of language oriented toward mutual understanding – and hence make possible a coordination of plans of action that operates via the intersubjective recognition of criticizable validity claims. One can read Derrida's debate with Austin also as a denial of this independently structured domain of everyday communicative practice; it corresponds to the denial of an autonomous realm of fiction.

IV

Because Derrida denies both, he can analyze any given discourse in accord with the model of poetic language, and do so as if language generally were determined by the poetic use of language specialized in world-disclosure. From this viewpoint, language as such converges with literature or indeed with "writing." This *aestheticizing of language, which is purchased with the twofold denial of the proper senses of normal and poetic discourse*, also explains Derrida's insensitivity toward the tension-filled polarity between the poetic-world-disclosive function of language and its prosaic, innerworldly functions, which a modified version of Bühler's functional scheme takes into consideration.[26]

Linguistically mediated processes such as the acquisition of knowledge, the transmission of culture, the formation of personal identity, and social-

ization and social integration involve mastering problems posed by the world; the independence of learning processes that Derrida cannot acknowledge is due to the independent logics of these problems and the linguistic medium tailored to deal with them. For Derrida, linguistically mediated processes within the world are embedded in a *world-constituting* context that prejudices everything; they are fatalistically delivered up to the unmanageable happening of text production, overwhelmed by the poetic-creative transformation of a background designed by archewriting, and condemned to be provincial. An aesthetic contextualism blinds him to the fact that everyday communicative practice makes learning processes possible (thanks to built-in idealizations) in relation to which the world-disclosive force of interpreting language has in turn to prove its worth. These learning processes unfold an independent logic that transcends all local constraints, because experiences and judgments are formed only in the light of criticizable validity claims. Derrida neglects the potential for negation inherent in the validity basis of action oriented toward reaching understanding; he permits the capacity to solve problems to disappear behind the world-creating capacity of language; the former capacity is possessed by language as the medium through which those acting communicatively get involved in relations to the world whenever they agree with one another about something in the objective world, in their common social world, or in the subjective worlds to which each has privileged access.

Richard Rorty proposes a similar leveling; unlike Derrida, however, he does not remain idealistically fixated upon the history of metaphysics as a transcendent happening that determines everything intramundane. According to Rorty, science and morality, economics and politics, are delivered up to a process of language-creating protuberances *in just the same way* as art and philosophy. Like Kuhnian history of science, the flux of interpretations beats rhythmically between revolutions and normalizations of language. He observes this back-and-forth between two situations in all fields of cultural life: "One is the sort of situation encountered when people pretty much agree on what is wanted, and are talking about how best to get it. In such a situation there is no need to say anything terribly unfamiliar, for argument is typically about the truth of assertions rather than about the utility of vocabularies. The contrasting situation is one in which everything is up for grabs at once – in which the motives and terms of discussions are a central subject of argument. . . . In such periods people begin to toss around old words in new senses, to throw in the occasional neologism, and thus to hammer out a new idiom which initially attracts attention to itself and only later gets put to work."[27] One notices how the Nietzschean pathos of a *Lebensphilosophie* that has made the linguistic turn beclouds the sober insights of pragmatism; in the picture painted by Rorty, the renovative process of linguistic world-disclosure no longer has a *counterpoise* in the testing processes of intramundane practice. The "Yes" and "No" of communicatively acting agents is so prejudiced and rhetorically overdetermined by their linguistic contexts that the anomalies that start to arise during the phases of exhaustion are taken to represent only symptoms of waning vitality, or aging processes analogous to processes of nature – and are not seen as the result of *deficient* solutions to problems and *invalid* answers.

Intramundane linguistic practice draws its power of negation from validity claims that go beyond the horizons of any currently given context. But the contextualist concept of language, laden as it is with *Lebensphilosophie*, is impervious to the very real force of the counterfactual, which makes itself felt in the idealizing presuppositions of communicative action. Hence Derrida and Rorty are also mistaken about the unique status of discourses differentiated from ordinary communication and tailored to a single validity dimension (truth or normative rightness), or to a single complex of problems (questions of truth or justice). In modern societies, the spheres of science, morality, and law have crystallized around these forms of argumentation. The corresponding cultural systems of action administer *problem-solving capacities* in a way similar to that in which the enterprises of art and literature administer *capacities for world-disclosure*. Because Derrida overgeneralizes this one linguistic function – namely, the poetic – he can no longer see the complex relationship of the ordinary practice of normal speech to the two extraordinary spheres, differentiated, as it were, in opposite directions. The polar tension between world-disclosure and problem-solving is held together within the functional matrix of ordinary language; but art and literature on the one side, and science, morality, and law on the other, are specialized for experiences and modes of knowledge that can be shaped and worked out within the compass of *one* linguistic function and *one*

dimension of validity at a time. Derrida holistically levels these complicated relationships in order to equate philosophy with literature and criticism. He fails to recognize the special status that both philosophy and literary criticism, each in its own way, assume as mediators between expert cultures and the everyday world.

Literary criticism, institutionalized in Europe since the eighteenth century, has contributed to the differentiation of art. It has responded to the increasing autonomy of linguistic works of art by means of a discourse specialized for questions of taste. In it, the claims with which literary texts appear are submitted to examination – claims to "artistic truth," aesthetic harmony, exemplary validity, innovative force, and authenticity. In this respect, aesthetic criticism is similar to argumentative forms specialized for propositional truth and the rightness of norms, that is, to theoretical and practical discourse. It is, however, not merely an esoteric component of expert culture but, beyond this, has the job of mediating between expert culture and everyday world.

This *bridging function* of art criticism is more obvious in the cases of music and the plastic arts than in that of literary works, which are already formulated in the medium of language, even if it is a poetic, self-referential language. From this second, exoteric standpoint, criticism performs a translating activity of a unique kind. It brings the experiential content of the work of art into normal language; the innovative potential of art and literature for the lifeworlds and life histories that reproduce themselves through everyday communicative practice can only be unleashed in this maieutic way. This is then deposited in the changed configuration of the evaluative vocabulary, in a renovation of value orientations and need interpretations, which alters the color of modes of life by way of altering modes of perception.

Philosophy also occupies a position with two fronts similar to that of literary criticism – or at least this is true of modern philosophy, which no longer promises to redeem the claims of religion in the name of theory. On the one hand, it directs its interest to the foundations of science, morality, and law and attaches theoretical claims to its statements. Characterized by universalist problematics and strong theoretical strategies, it maintains an intimate relationship with the sciences. And yet philosophy is not simply an esoteric component of an expert culture. It maintains just as intimate a relationship with the totality of the lifeworld and with sound common sense, even if in a subversive way it relentlessly shakes up the certainties of everyday practice. Philosophical thinking represents the lifeworld's interest in the whole complex of functions and structures connected and combined in communicative action, and it does so in the face of knowledge systems differentiated out in accord with particular dimensions of validity. Of course, it maintains this relationship to totality with a reflectiveness lacking in the intuitively present background proper to the lifeworld.

If one takes into consideration the two-front position of criticism and philosophy that I have only sketched here – toward the everyday world on the one side, and on the other toward the specialized cultures of art and literature, science and morality – it becomes clear what the leveling of the genre distinction between philosophy and literature, and the assimilation of philosophy to literature and of literature to philosophy, as affirmed in propositions 2 and 2', mean. This leveling and this assimilation confusedly jumble the constellations in which the rhetorical elements of language assume *entirely different* roles. The rhetorical element occurs in its *pure form* only in the self-referentiality of the poetic expression, that is, in the language of fiction specialized for world-disclosure. Even the normal language of everyday life is ineradicably rhetorical; but within the matrix of different linguistic functions, the rhetorical elements recede here. The world-disclosive linguistic framework is almost at a standstill in the routines of everyday practice. The same holds true of the specialized languages of science and technology, law and morality, economics, political science, etc. They, too, live off of the illuminating power of metaphorical tropes; but the rhetorical elements, which are by no means expunged, are tamed, as it were, and enlisted for special purposes of problem-solving.

The rhetorical dimension plays a different and far more important role in the language of literary criticism and philosophy. They are both faced with tasks that are paradoxical in similar ways. They are supposed to feed the contents of expert cultures, in which knowledge is accumulated under one aspect of validity at a time, into an everyday practice in which all linguistic functions and aspects of validity are intermeshed to form one syndrome. And yet literary criticism and philosophy are supposed to accomplish this task of mediation with means of expression taken from languages specialized in questions of taste or of truth. They can only resolve this paradox by rhetorically expanding and enriching their special languages to the extent that is required to link up indirect communications with the manifest contents of statements, and to do so in a deliberate way. That explains the strong rhetorical strain characteristic of studies by literary critics and philosophers alike. Significant critics and great philosophers are also noted writers. Literary criticism and philosophy have a family resemblance to literature – and to this extent to one another as well – in their rhetorical achievements. But their family relationship stops right there, for in each of these enterprises the tools of rhetoric are subordinated to the discipline of a *distinct* form of argumentation.

If, following Derrida's recommendation, philosophical thinking were to be relieved of the duty of solving problems and shifted over to the function of literary criticism, it would be robbed not merely of its seriousness, but of its productivity. Conversely, the literary-critical power of judgment loses its potency when, as is happening among Derrida's disciples in literature departments, it gets displaced from appropriating aesthetic experiential contents into the critique of metaphysics. The false assimilation of one enterprise to the other robs both of their substance. And so we return to the issue with which we started. Whoever transposes the radical critique of reason into the domain of rhetoric in order to blunt the paradox of self-referentiality, also dulls the sword of the critique of reason itself. The false pretense of eliminating the genre distinction between philosophy and literature cannot lead us out of this aporia.[28]

Notes

1 H. Schnädelbach, "Dialektik als Vernunftkritik," in L. von Friedeburg and J. Habermas, eds., *Adorno-Konferenz 1983* (Frankfurt, 1983), pp. 66 ff.

2 This is especially true of the Yale Critics, Paul de Man, Geoffrey Hartman, J. Hillis Miller, and Harold Bloom. See J. Arac, W. Godzich, and W. Martin, eds., *The Yale Critics: Deconstruction in America* (Minneapolis, 1983). In addition to Yale, important centers of deconstructionism are located at Johns Hopkins and Cornell universities.

3 Christopher Norris, *Deconstruction: Theory and Practice* (New York and London, 1982), pp. 93, 98.

4 Paul de Man, *Blindness and Insight*, 2d ed. (Minneapolis, 1983), p. 110.

5 Jonathan Culler, *On Deconstruction* (London, 1983), p. 150.

6 Ibid., p. 181.

7 In his essay "Signature Event Context," in *Margins of Philosophy* (Chicago, 1982), pp. 307–330, Derrida devotes the last section to a discussion of Austin's theory. Searle refers to this in "Reiterating the Differences: A Reply to Derrida," *Glyph* 1(1977):198 ff. Derrida's response appeared in *Glyph* 12(1977):202 ff. under the title "Limited, Inc."

8 Culler, *On Deconstruction*, p. 119.

9 John Searle, *Speech Acts* (Cambridge, 1969) and *Expression and Meaning* (Cambridge, 1979).

10 Culler, *On Deconstruction*, pp. 121 ff.

11 Ibid., p. 123.

12 Ibid., p. 176.

13 Compare ibid., pp. 130 ff.

14 Karl Bühler, *Semiotic Foundations of Language Theory* (New York, 1982).

15 Roman Jakobson, "Linguistics and Poetics," in Thomas A. Sebeok, editor, *Style in Language* (Cambridge, MA, 1960), pp. 350–358.

16 Ibid.

17 R. Ohmann, "Speech-Acts and the Definition of Literature," *Philosophy and Rhetoric* 4(1971):17.

18 Ibid., p. 14.

19 Ibid., p. 17.

20 Geoffrey Hartman, *Saving the Text* (Baltimore, 1981), p. xxi.

21 See also "Speech, Literature, and the Space between," *New Literary History* 5(1974):34 ff.

22 William Labov, *Language in the Inner City* (Philadelphia, 1972).

23 Mary Louise Pratt, *A Speech-Act Theory of Literary Discourse* (Bloomington, 1977), p. 92; I am grateful to Jonathan Culler for his reference to this interesting book.

24 Ibid., p. 148.

25 Ibid., p. 147.

26 See Jürgen Habermas, *Theory of Communicative Action*, volume 1 (Boston, 1984), pp. 273 ff.

27 Richard Rorty, "Deconstruction and Circumvention" (manuscript, 1983); and *Consequences of Pragmatism* (Minneapolis, 1982), especially the introduction and chapters 6, 7 and 9.

28 Our reflections have brought us to a point from which we can see why Heidegger, Adorno, and Derrida get into this aporia at all. They all still defend themselves as if they were living in the shadow of the "last" philosopher, as did the first generation of Hegelian disciples. They are still battling against the "strong" concepts of theory, truth, and system that have actually belonged to the past
for over a century and a half. They still think they have to arouse philosophy from what Derrida calls "the dream of its heart." They believe they have to tear philosophy away from the madness of expounding a theory that has the last word. Such a comprehensive, closed, and definitive system of propositions would have to be formulated in a language that is self-explanatory, that neither needs nor permits commentary, and thus that brings to a standstill the effective history in which interpretations are heaped upon interpretations without end. In this connection, Rorty speaks about the demand for a language "which can receive no gloss, requires no interpretation, cannot be distanced, cannot be sneered at by later generations. It is the hope for a vocabulary which is intrinsically and self-evidently final, not only the most comprehensive and fruitful vocabulary we have come up with so far" (Rorty, *Consequences of Pragmatism*, pp. 93 ff.).

If reason were bound, under penalty of demise, to hold on to these goals of metaphysics classically pursued from Parmenides to Hegel, if reason as such (even after Hegel) stood before the alternative of either maintaining the strong concepts of theory, truth, and system that were common in the great tradition or of throwing in the sponge, then an *adequate* critique of reason would really have to grasp the roots at such a depth that it could scarcely avoid the paradoxes of self-referentiality. Nietzsche viewed the matter in this way. And, unfortunately, Heidegger, Adorno, and Derrida all still seem to confuse the universalist *problematics still maintained* in philosophy with the long since *abandoned status claims* that philosophy once alleged its answers to have. Today, however, it is clear that the scope of universalist questions – for instance, questions of the necessary conditions for the rationality of utterances, or of the universal pragmatic presuppositions of communicative action and argumentation – does indeed have to be reflected in the grammatical form of universal propositions – but not in any unconditional validity or "ultimate foundations" claimed for themselves or their theoretical framework. The fallibilist consciousness of the sciences caught up with philosophy, too, a long time ago.

With this kind of fallibilism, we, philosophers and nonphilosophers alike, do not by any means eschew truth claims. Such claims cannot be raised in the performative attitude of the first person other than as transcending space and time – precisely as claims. But we are also aware that there is no zero-context for truth claims. They are raised here and now and are open to criticism. Hence we reckon upon the trivial *possibility* that they will be revised tomorrow or someplace else. Just as it always has, philosophy understands itself as the defender of rationality in the sense of the claim of reason endogenous to our form of life. In its work, however, it prefers a combination of strong propositions with weak status claims; so little is this totalitarian, that there is no call for a totalizing critique of reason against it. On this point, see my "Die Philosophie als Platzhalter und Interpret," in *Moralbewusstsein und kommunikatives Handeln* (Frankfurt, 1983), pp. 7 ff. (English translation forthcoming).

20

Truth and Method

Hans-Georg Gadamer

The Ontology of the Work of Art and its Hermeneutical Significance

1 Play as the Clue to Ontological Explanation

(A) The concept of play

I select as my starting-point a notion that has played a major role in aesthetics: the concept of play. I wish to free this concept from the subjective meaning which it has in Kant and Schiller and which dominates the whole of modern aesthetics and philosophy of man. If, in connection with the experience of art, we speak of play, this refers neither to the attitude nor even to the state of mind of the creator or of those enjoying the work of art, nor to the freedom of a subjectivity expressed in play, but to the mode of being of the work of art itself. In analysing aesthetic consciousness we recognised that the concept of aesthetic consciousness confronted with an object does not correspond to the real situation. This is why the concept of play is important in my exposition.

We can certainly distinguish between play and the attitude of the player, which, as such, belongs with the other attitudes of subjectivity. Thus it can be said that for the player play is not serious: that is why he plays. We can try to define the concept of play from this point of view. What is merely play is not serious. Play has its own relation to what is serious. It is not only that the latter gives it its 'purpose': we play 'for the sake of recreation', as Aristotle says.[1] It is more important that play itself contains its own, even sacred, seriousness. Yet, in the attitude of play, all those purposive relations which determine active and caring existence have not simply disappeared, but in a curious way acquire a different quality. The player himself knows that play is only play and exists in a world which is determined by the seriousness of purposes. But he does not know this in such a way that, as a player, he actually intends this relation to seriousness. Play fulfils its purpose only if the player loses himself in his play. It is not that relation to seriousness which directs us away from play, but only seriousness in playing makes the play wholly play. One who doesn't take the game seriously is a spoilsport. The mode of being of play does not allow the player to behave towards play as if it were an object. The player knows very well what play is, and that what he is doing is 'only a game'; but he does not know what exactly he 'knows' in knowing that.

Our question concerning the nature of play itself cannot, therefore, find an answer if we look to the subjective reflection of the player to provide it.[2] Instead, we are enquiring into the mode of being of play as such. We have seen that it is not the aesthetic consciousness, but the experience of art and thus the question of the mode of being of the work of art that must form the object of our examination. But this was precisely the experience of the work of art which I maintained in opposition to the levelling process of the aesthetic consciousness: namely, that the work of art is not an object that stands over against a subject for itself. Instead the work of art has its true being in the fact that it becomes an experience changing the person experiencing it. The 'subject' of the experience of art, that which remains and endures, is not the subjectivity of the person who experiences it, but the work itself. This is the point at which the mode of being of play becomes significant. For play has its own essence, independent of the consciousness of those who play. Play also exists – indeed, exists properly – when the thematic horizon is not limited by any being-for-itself of subjectivity, and where there are no subjects who are behaving 'playfully'.

The players are not the subjects of play; instead play merely reaches presentation through the players. We can see this first from the use of the word, especially from its multiple metaphorical applications, which Buytendijk in particular has noted.[3]

The metaphorical usage has here, as always, a methodological priority. If a word is applied to a sphere to which it did not originally belong, the actual 'original' meaning emerges quite clearly. Language has performed in advance a work of abstraction which is, as such, the task of conceptual analysis. Now thinking needs only to make use of this advance achievement.

The same is also true of etymologies. They are far less reliable because they are abstractions which are not performed by language, but by linguistic science, which can never be wholly verified by language itself: that is, by their actual usage. Hence even when they are right, they are not proofs, but advance achievements of conceptual analysis, and only in this obtain a firm foundation.[4]

If we examine how the word 'play' is used and concentrate on its so-called transferred meanings we find talk of the play of light, the play of the waves, the play of a component in a bearing-case, the inter-play of limbs, the play of forces, the play of gnats, even a play on words. In each case what is intended is the to-and-fro movement which is not tied to any goal which would bring it to an end. This accords with the original meaning of the word spiel as 'dance', which is still found in many word forms (eg in Spielmann, jongleur).[5] The movement which is play has no goal which brings it to an end; rather it renews itself in constant repetition. The movement backwards and forwards is obviously so central for the definition of a game that it is not important who or what

performs this movement. The movement of play as such has, as it were, no substrate. It is the game that is played – it is irrelevant whether or not there is a subject who plays. The play is the performance of the movement as such. Thus we speak of the play of colours and do not mean only that there is one colour, that plays against another, but that there is one process or sight, in which one can see a changing variety of colours.

Hence the mode of being of play is not such that there must be a subject who takes up a playing attitude in order that the game may be played. Rather, the most original sense of playing is the medial one. Thus we say that something is 'playing' somewhere or at some time, that something is going on (sich abspielt, im Spiele ist).[6]

This linguistic observation seems to me to be an indirect indication that play is not to be understood as a kind of activity. As far as language is concerned, the actual subject of play is obviously not the subjectivity of an individual who among other activities also plays, but instead the play itself. Only we are so used to relating a phenomenon such as playing to the sphere of subjectivity and its attitudes that we remain closed to these indications from the spirit of language.

However, modern research has conceived the nature of play so widely that it is led more or less to the verge of that attitude to it that is based on subjectivity. Huizinga has investigated the element of play in all cultures and above all worked out the connection of children's and animal play with the 'sacred plays of the religious cult'. That led him to recognise the curious lack of decisiveness in the playing consciousness, which makes it absolutely impossible to decide between belief and non-belief. 'The savage himself knows no conceptional distinction between being and playing; he knows of no identity, image or symbol. And that is why it may be asked whether one does not get closest to the mental condition of the savage in his sacred actions by holding on to the primary idea of play. In our idea of play the difference between faith and pretence is dissolved'.[7]

Here the primacy of play over the consciousness of the player is fundamentally acknowledged and, in fact, even the experiences of play that the psychologist and anthropologist have to describe are illuminated afresh if one starts from the medial sense of the word spielen. Play obviously represents an order in which the to-and-fro motion of play follows of itself. It is part of play that the movement is not only without goal or purpose but also without effort. It happens, as it were, by itself. The ease of play, which naturally does not mean that there is any real absence of effort, but phenomenologically refers only to the absence of strain,[8] is experienced subjectively as relaxation. The structure of play absorbs the player into itself, and thus takes from him the burden of the initiative, which constitutes the actual strain of existence. This is seen also in the spontaneous tendency to repetition that emerges in the player and in the constant self-renewal of play, which influences its form (eg the refrain).

The fact that the mode of being of play is so close to the mobile form of nature permits us to make an important methodological conclusion. It is obviously not correct to say that animals too play and that we can even say metaphorically that water and light play. Rather, on the contrary, we can say that man too plays. His playing is a natural process. The meaning of his play, precisely because – and insofar as – he is part of nature, is a pure self-presentation. Thus it becomes finally meaningless to distinguish in this sphere between literal and metaphorical usage.

But above all there comes from this medial sense of play the connection with the being of the work of art. Nature, inasmuch as it is without purpose or intention, as it is, without exertion, a constantly self-renewing play, can appear as a model for art. Thus Friedrich Schlegel writes: 'All the sacred games of art are only remote imitations of the infinite play of the world, the eternally self-creating work of art'.[9]

Another question that Huizinga discusses is also clarified as a result of the fundamental role of the to-and-fro movement of play, namely the playful character of the contest. It is true that it does not appear to the contestant that he is playing. But there arises through the contest the tense movement to-and-fro from which the victor emerges, thus showing the whole to be a game. The movement to-and-fro obviously belongs so essentially to the game that there is an ultimate sense in which you cannot have a game by yourself. In order for there to be a game, there always has to be, not necessarily literally another player, but something else with which the player plays and which automatically responds to his move with a countermove. Thus the cat at play chooses the ball of wool because it responds to play, and ball games will be with us forever because the ball is freely mobile in every direction, appearing to do surprising things of its own accord.

The primacy of the game over the players engaged in it is experienced by the players themselves in a special way, where it is a question of human subjectivity that adopts an attitude of play. Once more it is the improper uses of the word that offer the most information about its proper essence. Thus we say of someone that he plays with possibilities or with plans. What we mean is clear. He still has not committed himself to the possibilities as to serious aims. He still has the freedom to decide one way or the other, for one or the other possibility. On the other hand this freedom is not without danger. Rather the game itself is a risk for the player. One can only play with serious possibilities. This means obviously that one may become so engrossed in them that they, as it were, outplay one and prevail over one. The attraction of the game, which it exercises on the player, lies in this risk. One enjoys a freedom of decision, which at the same time is endangered and irrevocably limited. One has only to think of jig-saw puzzles, games of patience etc. But the same is true in serious matters. If someone, for the sake of enjoying his own freedom of decision, avoids making pressing decisions or plays with possibilities that he is not seriously envisaging and which, therefore, offer no risk that he will choose them and thereby limit himself, we say he is only 'playing with life' (verspielt).

This suggests a general characteristic of the way in which the nature of play is reflected in an attitude of play: all playing is a being-played. The attraction of a game, the fascination it exerts, consists precisely in the fact that the game tends to master the players. Even when it is a case of games in which one seeks to accomplish tasks that one has set oneself, there is a risk whether or not it will 'work', 'succeed', and 'succeed again', which is the attraction of the game. Whoever 'tries' is in fact the one who is tried. The real subject of the game (this is shown in precisely those experiences in which there is only a single player) is not the player, but instead the game itself. The game is what holds the player in its spell, draws him into play, and keeps him there.

This is shown also by the fact that games have their own proper spirit.[10] But even this does not refer to the mood or the mental state of those who play the game. Rather, this difference of mental attitude in the playing of different games and in the desire to play them is a result and not the cause of the difference of the games themselves. Games themselves differ from one another by their spirit.

The reason for this is that the to-and-fro movement, which is what constitutes the game, is differently arranged. The particular nature of a game lies in the rules and structures which prescribe the way that the area of the game is filled. This is true universally, whenever there is a game. It is true, for example, of the play of fountains and of playing animals. The area in which the game is played is, as it were, set by the nature of the game itself and is defined far more by the structure that determines the movement of the game than by what it comes up against, ie the boundaries of the free area, which limits movement from outside.

Apart from these general determining factors, it seems to me characteristic of human play that it plays something. That means that the structure of movement to which it submits has a definite quality which the player 'chooses'. He first of all expressly separates off his playing behaviour from his other behaviour by wanting to play. But even within his readiness to play he makes a choice. He chooses this game and not that. It accords with this that the movement of the game is not simply the free area in which one 'plays oneself out', but is one that is specially marked out and reserved for the movement of the game. The human game requires its playing field. The setting apart of the playing field – just like that of sacred precincts, as Huizinga rightly points out[11] – sets the sphere of play as a closed world without transition and mediation over against the world of aims. That all play is a playing of something is true here, where the ordered to-and-fro movement of the game is determined as an attitude and marks itself off from other attitudes. The playing man is, even in his play, still someone who takes up an attitude, even if the proper essence of the game consists in his getting rid of the tension which he feels in his attitude to his aims. This determines more exactly why playing is always a playing of something. Every game presents the man who plays it with a task. He cannot enjoy the freedom of playing himself out except by transforming the aims of his behaviour into mere tasks of the game. Thus the child gives itself a task in playing with the ball, and such tasks are playful ones, because the purpose of the game is not really the solution of the task, but the ordering and shaping of the movement of the game itself.

Obviously the characteristic lightness and sense of relief which we find in the attitude of play depends on the particular character of the task set by the game, and comes from solving it.

One can say that to perform a task successfully 'represents it'. One can say this all the more when it is a question of a game, for here the fulfilment of the task does not point to any purposive context. Play is really limited to representing itself. Thus its mode of being is self-representation. But self-representation is a universal aspect of the being of nature. We know today how inadequate biological conceptions of purpose are when it comes to understanding the form of living things.[12] It is likewise true of play that to ask what its life-function is and its biological purpose is is an inadequate approach. It is, pre-eminently, self-representation.

The self-representation of human play depends, as we have seen, on behaviour which is tied to the make-believe goals of the game, but the 'meaning' of the latter does not in fact depend on achieving these goals. Rather, in spending oneself on the task of the game, one is, in fact, playing oneself out. The self-representation of the game involves the player's achieving, as it were, his own self-representation by playing, ie representing something. Only because play is always representation is human play able to find the task of the game in representation itself. Thus there are games which must be called representation games, either in that, by the use of meaningful allusion, they have something about them of representation (say 'Tinker, Tailor, Soldier, Sailor') or in that the game itself consists in representing something (eg when children play motor-cars).

All representation is potentially representative for someone. That this possibility is intended is the characteristic feature of the playful nature of art. The closed world of play lets down as it were, one of its walls.[13] A religious rite and a play in a theatre obviously do not represent in the same sense as the playing child. Their being is not exhausted by the fact that they represent; at the same time they point beyond themselves to the audience which is sharing in them. Play here is no longer the mere self-representation of an ordered movement, nor mere representation, in which the playing child is totally absorbed, but it is 'representing for someone'. This assignment in all representation comes to the fore here and is constitutive of the being of art.

In general, games, however much they are in essence representations and however much the players represent themselves in them, are not represented for anyone, ie they are not aimed at an audience. Children play for themselves, even when they represent. And not even those games, eg sports, which are played before spectators are aimed at them. Indeed, they threaten to lose their real play character as a contest precisely by becoming a show. A procession as part of a religious rite is more than a demonstration, since its real meaning is to embrace the whole religious community. And yet the religious act is a genuine representation for the community, and equally a theatrical drama is a playful act that, of its nature, calls for an audience. The representation of a god in a religious rite, the representation of a myth in a play, are play not only in the sense that the participating players are wholly absorbed in the representative play and find in it their heightened self-representation, but also in that the players represent a meaningful whole for an audience. Thus it is not really the absence of a fourth wall that turned the play into a show. Rather, openness towards the spectator is part of the closedness of the play. The audience only completes what the play as such is.[14]

This is the point which shows the importance of the medial nature of the play process. We have seen that play does not have its being in the consciousness or the attitude of the player, but on the contrary draws the latter into its area and fills him with its spirit. The player experiences the game as a reality that surpasses him. This is more than ever the case where it itself is 'intended' as such a reality – for instance the play which appears as representation for an audience.

Even a theatrical drama remains a game, ie it has the structure of a game, which is that of a closed world. But the religious or profane drama, however much it represents a world that is wholly closed within itself, is as if open toward the side of the spectator, in whom it achieves its whole significance. The players play their roles as in any game, and thus the play is represented, but the play itself is the whole, comprising players and spectators. In fact, it is experienced properly by, and presents itself as what is 'meant' to, one who is not acting in the play, but is watching. In him the game is raised, as it were, to its perfection.

For the players this means that they do not simply fulfil their roles as in any game – rather, they play their roles, they represent them for the audience. Their mode of participation in the game is no longer determined by the fact that they are completely absorbed in it, but by their playing their role in relation and regard to the whole of the play, in which not they, but the audience is to

become absorbed. When a play activity becomes a play in the theatre a total switch takes place. It puts the spectator in the place of the player. He – and not the player – is the person for and in whom the play takes place. Of course this does not mean that the player is not able to experience the significance of the whole, in which he plays his representing role. The spectator has only methodological precedence. In that the play is presented for him, it becomes apparent that it bears within itself a meaning that must be understood and that can therefore be detached from the behaviour of the player. Basically the difference between the player and the spectator is removed here. The requirement that the play itself be intended in its meaningfulness is the same for both.

This is still the case even when the play community is sealed off against all spectators, either because it opposes the social institutionalisation of artistic life, as in so-called chamber music, which seeks to be music-making in a fuller sense, because it is performed for the players themselves and not for an audience. If someone performs music in this way, he is also in fact trying to make the music 'sound well', but that means that it would be properly there for any listener. Artistic presentation, by its nature, exists for someone, even if there is no one there who listens or watches only.

(B) Transformation into structure and total mediation

I call this development, in which human play finds its true perfection in being art, 'the transformation into structure'. Only through this development does play acquire its ideality, so that it can be intended and understood as play. Only now does it emerge as detached from the representing activity of the players and consist in the pure appearance of what they are playing. As such the play – even the unforeseen elements of improvisation – is fundamentally repeatable and hence permanent. It has the character of a work, of an ergon and not only of energeia.[15] In this sense I call it a structure.

What can be separated in this way from the representing activity of the player still remains dependent on representation. This dependence does not mean that it is only through the particular persons representing it that the play acquires its definite meaning, not even through him who as the originator of the work is its real creator, the artist. Rather, the play has, in relation to them all, an absolute autonomy, and that is what is suggested by the idea of transformation.

The implications for the definition of the nature of art emerge when one takes the sense of transformation seriously. Transformation is not change, even a change that is especially far-reaching. A change always means that what is changed also remains the same and is held on to. However totally it may change, something changes in it. In terms of categories, all change (alloiosis) belongs in the sphere of quality, ie of an accident of substance. But transformation means that something is suddenly and as a whole something else, that this other transformed thing that it has become is its true being, in comparison with which its earlier being is nothing. When we find someone transformed we mean precisely this, that he has become, as it were, another person. There cannot here be any transition of gradual change leading from one to the other, since the one is the denial of the other. Thus the transformation into a structure means that what existed previously no longer exists. But also that what now exists, what represents itself in the play of art, is what is lasting and true.

It is clear here that to start from subjectivity is to miss the point. What no longer exists is the players – with the poet or the composer being considered as one of the players. None of them has his own existence for himself, which he retains so that his acting would mean that he 'only acts'. If we describe from the point of view of the actor what his acting is, then obviously it is not transformation, but disguise. A man who is disguised does not want to be recognised, but instead to appear as someone else and be taken for him. In the eyes of others he no longer wants to be himself, but to be taken for someone else. Thus he does not want to be discovered or recognised. He plays another person, but in the way that we play something in our daily intercourse with other people, ie that we merely pretend, act a part and create an impression. A person who plays such a game denies, to all appearances, continuity with himself. But in truth that means that he holds on to this continuity with himself for himself and only keeps it from those before whom he is acting.

According to all that we have observed concerning the nature of play, this subjective distinction between oneself and the play, which is what acting a part is, is not the true nature of play. Play itself is, rather, transformation of such a kind that the identity of the player does not continue to exist for

anybody. Everybody asks instead what it is supposed to be, what is 'meant'. The players (or poets) no longer exist, but only what of theirs is played.

But, above all, what no longer exists is the world, in which we live as our own. Transformation into a structure is not simply transposition into another world. Certainly it is another, closed world in which play takes place. But inasmuch as it is a structure, it has, so to speak, found its measure in itself and measures itself by nothing outside it. Thus the action of a drama – in this it still entirely resembles the religious act – exists absolutely as something that rests within itself. It no longer permits of any comparison with reality as the secret measure of all copied similarity. It is raised above all such comparisons – and hence also above the question whether it is all real – because a superior truth speaks from it. Even Plato, the most radical critic of the high estimation of art in the history of philosophy, speaks sometimes, without differentiating between them, of the comedy and tragedy of life and of the stage.[16] For this difference disappears if one knows how to see the meaning of the game that unfolds before one. The pleasure offered in the spectacle is the same in both cases: it is the joy of knowledge.

This gives the full meaning to what we called transformation into a structure. The transformation is a transformation into the true. It is not enchantment in the sense of a bewitchment that waits for the redeeming word that will transform things to what they were, but it is itself redemption and transformation back into true being. In the representation of play, what is emerges. In it is produced and brought to the light what otherwise is constantly hidden and withdrawn. If someone knows how to perceive the comedy and tragedy of life, he is able to resist the suggestiveness of purposes which conceal the game that is played with us.

'Reality' always stands in a horizon of the future of observed and feared or, at any rate, still undecided possibilities. Hence it is always the case that mutually exclusive expectations are aroused, not all of which can be fulfilled. The undecidedness of the future is what permits such a superfluity of expectations that reality necessarily falls behind them. If, now, in a particular case, a meaningful whole completes and fulfils itself in reality, such that no lines of meaning scatter in the void, then this reality is itself like a drama. Equally, someone who is able to see the whole of reality as a closed circle of meaning, in which everything is fulfilled, will speak of the comedy and tragedy of life. In these cases, in which reality is understood as a play, there emerges what the reality of play is, which we call the play of art. The being of all play is always realisation, sheer fulfilment, energeia which has its telos within itself. The world of the work of art, in which play expresses itself fully in the unity of its course, is in fact a wholly transformed world. By means of it everyone recognises that that is how things are.

Thus the concept of transformation characterises the independent and superior mode of being of what we called structures. From this viewpoint 'reality' is defined as what is untransformed, and art as the raising up of this reality into its truth. Also the classical theory of art, which bases all art on the idea of mimesis, imitation, has obviously started from play which, in the form of dancing, is the representation of the divine.[17]

But the concept of imitation can only describe the play of art if one retains the element of knowledge contained in imitation. What is represented is there – this is the original imitative situation. If a person imitates something, he produces what he knows and in the way that he knows it. A child begins to play by imitation, doing what he knows and affirming his own being in the process. Also, children's delight in dressing-up, to which Aristotle refers, does not seek to be a hiding of themselves, a pretence, in order to be discovered and recognised behind it but, on the contrary, a representation of such a kind that only what is represented exists. The child does not want at any cost to be discovered behind his disguise. He intends that what he represents should exist, and if something is to be guessed, then this is it. What it 'is' should be recognised.[18]

We have established that the element of knowledge in imitation is recognition. But what is recognition? A more exact analysis of the phenomenon will make quite clear to us the nature of representation, which is what we are concerned with. As we know, Aristotle emphasises that artistic representation even makes the unpleasant appear as pleasant,[19] and Kant for this reason defined art as the beautiful representation of something, because it is even able to make the ugly appear beautiful.[20] But this obviously does not refer to artificiality and artistic technique. One does not, as with a circus performer, admire the art with which something is done. This has only secondary interest. What one experiences in a work of art and what one is directed towards is rather how true it is, ie to what extent one knows and recognises something and oneself.

But we do not understand what recognition is in its profoundest nature, if we only see that something that we know already is known again, ie that what is familiar is recognised again. The joy of recognition is rather that more becomes known than is already known. In recognition what we know emerges, as if through an illumination, from all the chance and variable circumstances that condition it and is grasped in its essence. It is known as something.

This is the central motif of Platonism. In his theory of anamnesis Plato combined the mythical idea of remembrance with his dialectic, which sought in the logos, ie the ideality of language, the truth of being.[21] In fact this kind of idealism of being is already suggested in the phenomenon of recognition. The 'known' enters into its true being and manifests itself as what it is only when it is recognised. As recognised it is grasped in its essence, detached from its accidental aspects. This is wholly true of the kind of recognition that takes place in relation to what is represented in a play. This kind of representation leaves behind it everything that is accidental and unessential, eg the private particular being of the actor. He disappears entirely in the recognition of what he is representing. But even that which is represented, a well-known event of mythological tradition, is raised by its representation, as it were, to its own validity and truth. With regard to the recognition of the true, the being of representation is superior to the being of the material represented, the Achilles of Homer more than the original Achilles.

Thus the basic mimic situation that we are discussing not only involves what is represented being there, but also that it has in this way come to exist more fully. Imitation and representation are not merely a second version, a copy, but a recognition of the essence. Because they are not merely repetition, but a 'bringing forth', the spectator is also involved in them. They contain the essential relation to everyone for whom the representation exists.

Indeed, one can say even more: the presentation of the essence, far from being a mere imitation, is necessarily revelatory. When someone makes an imitation, he has to leave out and to heighten. Because he is pointing to something, he has to exaggerate, whether he likes it or not. Hence there exists an unbridgeable gulf between the one thing, that is a likeness, and the other that it seeks to resemble. As we know, Plato insisted on this ontological gulf, on the greater or lesser distance between the copy and the original, and for this reason considered imitation and representation in the play of art, as an imitation of an imitation, in the third rank.[22] Nevertheless, in the representation of art, recognition is operative, which has the character of genuine knowledge of essence, and since Plato considers all knowledge of being to be recognition, this is the ground of Aristotle's remark that poetry is more philosophical than history.[23]

Thus imitation, as representation, has a clear cognitive function. Therefore the idea of imitation was able to continue in the theory of art for as long as the significance of art as knowledge was unquestioned. But that is valid only while it is held that knowledge of the true is knowledge of the essence,[24] for art supports this kind of knowledge in a convincing way. For the nominalism of modern science, however, and its idea of reality, from which Kant drew the conclusion that aesthetics has nothing to do with knowledge, the concept of mimesis has lost its aesthetic force.

Having seen the difficulties of this subjective development in aesthetics, we are forced to return to the older tradition. If art is not the variety of changing experiences whose object is each time filled subjectively with meaning like an empty mould, representation must be recognised as the mode of being of the work of art. This was prepared for by the idea of representation being derived from the idea of play, in that self-representation is the true nature of play – and hence of the work of art also. The playing of the play is what speaks to the spectator, through its representation, and this in such a way that the spectator, despite the distance between it and himself, still belongs to it.

This is seen most clearly in the type of representation that is a religious rite. Here the relation to the community is obvious. An aesthetic consciousness, however reflective, can no longer consider that only the aesthetic differentiation, which sees the aesthetic object in its own right, discovers the true meaning of the religious picture or the religious rite. No one will be able to hold that the performance of the ritual act is unessential to religious truth.

This is equally true for drama, and what it is as a piece of literature. The performance of a play, likewise, cannot be simply detached from the play itself, as if it were something that is not part

of its essential being, but is as subjective and fluid as the aesthetic experiences in which it is experienced. Rather, in the performance, and only in it – as we see most clearly in the case of music – do we encounter the work itself, as the divine is encountered in the religious rite. Here the methodological advantage of starting from the idea of play becomes clear. The work of art cannot be simply isolated from the 'contingency' of the chance conditions in which it appears, and where there is this kind of isolation, the result is an abstraction which reduces the actual being of the work. It itself belongs to the world to which it represents itself. A drama exists really only when it is played, and certainly music must resound.

My thesis, then, is that the being of art cannot be determined as an object of an aesthetic awareness because, on the contrary, the aesthetic attitude is more than it knows of itself. It is a part of the essential process of representation and is an essential part of play as play.

What are the ontological consequences of this? If we start in this way from the play character of play, what emerges for the closer definition of the nature of aesthetic being? This much is clear: drama and the work of art understood in its own terms is not a mere schema of rules or prescriptions of attitudes, within which play can freely realise itself. The playing of the drama does not ask to be understood as the satisfying of a need to play, but as the coming into existence of the work of literature itself. And so there arises the question of the being proper to a poetic work that comes to be only in performance and in theatrical representation, although it is still its own proper being that is there represented.

Let us recall the phrase used above of the 'transformation into a structure'. Play is structure – this means that despite its dependence on being played it is a meaningful whole which can be repeatedly represented as such and the significance of which can be understood. But the structure is also play, because – despite this theoretical unity – it achieves its full being only each time it is played. It is the complementary nature of the two sides of the one thing that we seek to underline, as against the abstraction of aesthetic differentiation.

We may now formulate this by opposing to aesthetic differentiation, the properly constitutive element of aesthetic consciousness, 'aesthetic non-differentiation'. It has become clear that what is imitated in imitation, what is formed by the poet, represented by the actor, recognised by the spectator is to such an extent what is meant – that in which the significance of the representation lies – that the poetic formation or the achievement involved in the representation are not distinguished from it. When a distinction is made, it is between the material and the forming, between the poem and the 'conception'. But these distinctions are of a secondary nature. What the actor plays and the spectator recognises are the forms and the action itself, as they are intended by the poet. Thus we have here a double mimesis: the writer represents and the actor represents. But even this double mimesis is one: it is the same thing that comes to existence in each case.

More exactly, one can say that the mimic representation of the performance brings into being-there what the written play actually requires. The double distinction between a drama and its subject matter and a drama and performance corresponds to a double non-distinction as the unity of the truth which one recognises in the play of art. It is to move out of the actual experience of a piece of literature if one investigates the origin of the plot on which it is based, and equally it is to move out of the actual experience of the drama if the spectator reflects about the conception behind a performance or about the proficiency of the actors. This kind of reflection already contains the aesthetic differentiation of the work itself from its representation. But for the meaningfulness of the experience as such it is, as we have seen, not even important whether the tragic or comic scene which is played before one takes place on the stage or in life – if one is only a spectator. What we have called a structure is one insofar as it presents itself as a meaningful whole. It does not exist in itself, nor is it experienced in a communication accidental to it, but it gains, through being communicated, its proper being.

No matter how much the variety of the performances or realisations of such a structure goes back to the conception of the players – it also does not remain enclosed in the subjectivity of what they think, but it is embodied there. Thus it is not at all a question of a mere subjective variety of conceptions, but of the possibilities of being that the work itself possesses, which lays itself out in the variety of its aspects.

This is not to deny that here there is a possible starting-point for aesthetic reflection. In different performances of the same play, say, one can distinguish between one kind of mediation and another, just as one can conceive the conditions of access to works of art of a different kind in various ways, eg when one looks at a building from the point of view of how it would look on its own or how its surroundings ought to look. Or when one is faced with the question of the restoration of a painting. In all these cases the work itself is distinguished from its 'representation'.[25] But one fails to appreciate the compelling quality of the work of art if one regards the variations possible in the representation as free and optional. In fact they are all subject to the supreme criterion of the 'right' representation.[26]

We know this in the modern theatre as the tradition that stems from a production, the creation of a role, or the practice of a musical performance. Here there is no random succession, a mere variety of conceptions, but rather from the constant following of models and from a productive and changing development there is cultivated a tradition with which every new attempt must come to terms. The interpretative artist too has a sure consciousness of this. The way that he approaches a work or a role is always related in some way to models which did the same. But it has nothing to do with blind imitation. Although the tradition that is created by a great actor, producer or musician remains effective as a model, it is not a brake on free creation, but has become so one with the work that the concern with this model stimulates the creative interpretative powers of an artist no less than the concern with the work itself. The reproductive arts have this special quality that the works with which they are concerned are explicitly left open to this kind of re-creation and thus have visibly opened the identity and continuity of the work of art towards its future.[27]

Perhaps the criterion that determines here whether something is 'a correct representation' is a highly mobile and relative one. But the compelling quality of the representation is not lessened by the fact that it cannot have any fixed criterion. Thus we do not allow the interpretation of a piece of music or a drama the freedom to take the fixed 'text' as a basis for a lot of ad-lib effects, and yet we would regard the canonisation of a particular interpretation, eg in a gramophone recording conducted by the composer, or the detailed notes on performance which come from the canonised first performance, as a failure to understand the actual task of interpretation. A 'correctness', striven for in this way, would not do justice to the true binding nature of the work, which imposes itself on every interpreter in a special and immediate way and does not allow him to make things easy for himself by simply imitating a model.

It is also, as we know, wrong to limit the 'freedom' of interpretative choice to externals or marginal phenomena and not rather to think of the whole of an interpretation in a way that is both bound and free. Interpretation is probably, in a certain sense, re-creation, but this re-creation does not follow the process of the creative act, but the lines of the created work which has to be brought to representation in accord with the meaning the interpreter finds in it. Thus, for example, performances of music played on old instruments are not as faithful as they seem. Rather, they are an imitation of an imitation and in danger 'of standing at a third remove from the truth' (Plato).

In view of the finite nature of our historical existence there is, it would seem, something absurd about the whole idea of a uniquely correct interpretation. We shall come back to this in another context. Here the obvious fact, that every interpretation seeks to be correct, serves only to confirm that the non-differentiation of the interpretation from the work itself is the actual experience of the work. This accords with the fact that the aesthetic consciousness is generally able to make the aesthetic distinction between the work and its interpretation only in a critical way, ie where the interpretation breaks down. The communication of the work is, in principle, a total one.

Total communication means that the communicating element cancels itself out. In other words, reproduction (in the case of drama and music, but also with the recitation of stories or poetry) does not become, as such, thematic, but the work presents itself through it and in it. We shall see that the same is true of the character of approach and encounter in which buildings and statues present themselves. Here also the approach is not, as such, thematic, but neither is it true that one would have to abstract from life-references in order to grasp the work itself. Rather, it exists within them. The fact that works come out of a past from which they stretch into the present as permanent monuments, still does not make their being into an object of aesthetic or historical consciousness. As long as they still fulfil their function, they are contemporaneous with every age. Even if their place is only in museums as works of art, they are not entirely alienated from themselves. Not only does a work of art never completely lose the trace of its original function which enables an expert to recon-

struct it, but the work of art that has its place next to others in a gallery is still its own origin. It affirms itself, and the way in which it does that – by 'killing' other things or using them profitably to complement itself – is still part of itself.

We ask what this identity is that presents itself so differently in the changing course of ages and circumstances. It does not disintegrate into the changing aspects of itself so that it would lose all identity, but it is there in them all. They all belong to it. They are all contemporaneous with it. Thus we have the task of giving an interpretation of the work of art in terms of time.

(C) The temporality of the aesthetic

What kind of contemporaneity is this? What kind of temporality belongs to aesthetic being? This contemporaneity and presentness of aesthetic being is called, in general, its timelessness. But this timelessness has to be thought of together with the temporality to which it essentially belongs. Timelessness is primarily only a dialectical feature which arises out of temporality and in contrast with it. Even if one speaks of two kinds of temporality, a historical and a supra-historical one, as does Sedlmayr, for example, following Baader and with reference to Bollnow, in an effort to determine the temporality of the work of art,[28] one cannot move beyond a dialectical tension between the two. The supra-historical 'sacred' time, in which the 'present' is not the fleeting movement but the fullness of time, is described from the point of view of existential temporality. The inadequacy of this kind of antithesis emerges when one inevitably discovers that 'true time' projects into historical-existential 'appearance time'. This kind of projection would obviously have the character of an epiphany, but this means that for the experiencing consciousness it is without continuity.

This involves again all the difficulties of the aesthetic awareness, which we pointed out above. For it is precisely continuity that every understanding of time has to achieve, even when it is a question of the temporality of a work of art. Here the misunderstanding of Heidegger's ontological exposition of the time horizon avenges itself. Instead of holding on to the methodological significance of the existential analytic of There-being, people treat this existential, historical temporality of There-being, determined by care and the movement towards death, ie radical finiteness, as one among many possible ways of understanding existence, and it is forgotten that it is the mode of being of understanding itself which is here revealed as temporality. The withdrawal of the proper temporality of the work of art as 'sacred time' from transient historical time remains, in fact, a mere mirroring of the human and finite experience of art. Only a biblical theology of time, starting not from the standpoint of human self-understanding, but from divine revelation, would be able to speak of a 'sacred time' and theologically justify the analogy between the timelessness of the work of art and this 'sacred time'. Without this kind of theological justification, to speak of 'sacred time' obscures the real problem, which does not lie in the atemporality of the work of art but in its temporality. Thus we take up our question again: what kind of temporality is this?[29]

We started from the position that the work of art is play, ie that its actual being cannot be detached from its representation and that in the representation the unity and identity of a structure emerge. To be dependent on self-representation is part of its nature. This means that however much it may be changed and distorted in the representation, it still remains itself. This constitutes the validity of every representation, that it contains a relation to the structure itself and submits itself to the criterion of its correctness. Even the extreme of a wholly distorting representation confirms this. It becomes known as a distortion inasmuch as the representation is intended and appreciated as the representation of the structure. The representation has, in an indissoluble, indelible way the character of the repetition. Repetition does not mean here that something is repeated in the literal sense, ie can be reduced to something original. Rather, every repetition is equally an original of the work.

We know this kind of highly puzzling time structure from festivals.[30] It is in the nature, at least of periodic festivals, to be repeated. We call that the return of the festival. But the returning festival is neither another, nor the mere remembrance of the one that was originally celebrated. The originally sacral character of all festivals obviously excludes the kind of distinction that we know in the time-experience of the present; memory and expectation. The time-experience of the festival is rather its celebration, a present time sui generis.

The temporal character of celebration is difficult to grasp on the basis of the customary chronological experience of succession. If the return of the festival is related to the usual experience of time and its dimensions, it appears as historical temporality. The festival changes from one time to the next. For there are always other things going on at the same time. Nevertheless it would still remain, under this historical aspect, one and the same festival that undergoes this kind of change. It was originally of a certain nature and was celebrated in this way, then different, and then different again.

However, this aspect does not cover the time character of the festival that comes from its being celebrated. For the essence of the festival its historical connections are secondary. As a festival it is not an identity, in the manner of an historical event, but neither is it determined by its origin so that there was once the 'real' festival – as distinct from the way in which it came later to be celebrated. From the start it belonged to it that it should be regularly celebrated. Thus it is its own original essence always to be something different (even when celebrated in exactly the same way). An entity that exists only by always being something different is temporal in a more radical sense than everything that belongs to history. It has its being only in becoming and in return.[31]

A festival exists only in being celebrated. This is not to say that it is of a subjective character and has its being only in the subjectivity of those celebrating it. Rather the festival is celebrated because it is there. The same is true of drama – it must be represented for the spectator, and yet its being is by no means just the point of intersection of the experiences that the spectators have. Rather the contrary is true, that the being of the spectator is determined by his being there present. To be present does not mean simply to be in the presence of something else that is there at the same time. To be present means to share. If someone was present at something, he knows all about how it really was. It is only in a derived sense that presence at something means also a kind of subjective attitude, that of attention to something. Thus to watch something is a genuine mode of sharing. Perhaps we may remind the reader of the idea of sacral communion which lies behind the original Greek idea of theoria. Theoros means someone who takes part in a mission to a festival. Such a person has no other qualification and function than to be there. Thus the theoros is a spectator in the literal sense of the word, who shares in the solemn act through his presence at it and in this way acquires his sacred quality: for example, of inviolability.

In the same way, Greek metaphysics still conceives the nature of theoria and of nous as pure presence to what is truly real,[32] and also the capacity to be able to act theoretically is defined for us by the fact that in attending to something it is possible to forget one's own purposes.[33] But theoria is not to be conceived primarily as an attitude of subjectivity, as a self-determination of the subjective consciousness, but in terms of what it is contemplating. Theoria is a true sharing, not something active, but something passive (pathos), namely being totally involved in and carried away by what one sees. It is from this point that people have tried recently to explain the religious background of the Greek idea of reason.[34]

We started by saying that the true being of the spectator, who is part of the play of art, cannot be adequately understood in terms of subjectivity, as an attitude of the aesthetic consciousness. But this does not mean that the nature of the spectator cannot be described in terms of being present at something, in the way that we pointed out. To be present, as a subjective act of a human attitude, has the character of being outside oneself. Even Plato, in his *Phaedrus*, makes the mistake of judging the ecstasy of being outside oneself from the point of view of rational reasonableness and of seeing it as the mere negation of being within oneself, ie as a kind of madness. In fact, being outside oneself is the positive possibility of being wholly with something else. This kind of being present is a self-forgetfulness, and it is the nature of the spectator to give himself in self-forgetfulness to what he is watching. Self-forgetfulness here is anything but a primitive condition, for it arises from the attention to the object, which is the positive act of the spectator.[35]

Obviously there is an important difference between a spectator who gives himself entirely to the play of art, and someone who merely gapes at something out of curiosity. It is also characteristic of curiosity that it is as if drawn away by what it looks at, that it forgets itself entirely in it, and cannot tear itself away from it. But the important thing about an object of curiosity is that it is basically of no concern to the spectator, it has no meaning for him. There is nothing in it which he would really be able to come back to and which would focus his attention. For it is the formal quality of novelty, ie abstract difference, which makes up the charm of what one looks at. This is seen in the fact that its dialectical complement is becoming bored and jaded. Whereas that which

presents itself to the spectator as the play of art does not simply exhaust itself in the ecstatic emotion of the moment, but has a claim to permanence and the permanence of a claim.

The word 'claim' does not occur here by accident. In the type of theological reflection which started with Kierkegaard and which we call 'dialectical theology' this idea has made possible a theological explanation of what is meant by Kierkegaard's notion of simultaneity. A claim is something lasting. Its justification (or pretended justification) is the first thing. Because a claim continues, it can be affirmed at any time. A claim exists against someone and must therefore be asserted against him; but the concept of a claim also contains the idea that it is not itself a fixed demand, the fulfilment of which is agreed by both sides, but is, rather, the ground for such. A claim is the legal basis for an unspecified demand. If it is to be answered in such a way as to be settled, then it must first take the form of a demand when it is made. It belongs to the permanence of a claim that it is concretised into a demand.

The application to lutheran theology is that the claim of the call to faith persists since the proclamation of the gospel and is made afresh in preaching. The words of the sermon perform this total mediation which otherwise is the work of the religious rite, say, of the mass. We shall see that the word is called also in other ways to mediate contemporaneity, and that therefore in the problem of hermeneutics it has the chief place.

At any rate 'contemporaneity' forms part of the being of the work of art. It constitutes the nature of 'being present'. It is not the simultaneity of the aesthetic consciousness, for that simultaneity refers to the coexistence and the equal validity of different aesthetic objects of experience in the one consciousness. Contemporaneity, however, here means that a single thing that presents itself to us achieves in its presentation full presentness, however remote its origin may be. Thus contemporaneity is not a mode of givenness in consciousness, but a task for consciousness and an achievement that is required of it. It consists in holding on to the object in such a way that it becomes contemporaneous, but this means that all mediation is dissolved in total presentness.

This idea of contemporaneity comes, as we know, from Kierkegaard, who gave to it a particular theological emphasis.[36] Contemporaneity, for Kierkegaard, does not mean existing at the same time, but is a formulation of the believer's task of so totally combining one's own presence and the redeeming act of Christ, that the latter is experienced as something present (not as something in the past) and is taken seriously as such. Against this the simultaneity of the aesthetic consciousness depends on the concealment of the task that contemporaneity sets.

Hence contemporaneity is something that is found especially in the religious act, and in the sermon. The sense of being present is here the genuine sharing in the redemptive action itself. No one can doubt that the aesthetic differentiation, eg of a 'beautiful' ceremony or of a 'good' sermon is, in view of the appeal that is made to us, misplaced. Now I maintain that the same thing is basically true for the experience of art. Here also mediation must be conceived as total. Neither the separate life of the creating artist – his biography – nor that of the performer who acts a work, nor that of the spectator who is watching the play, has any separate legitimacy in the face of the being of the work of art.

What unfolds before one is for every one so lifted out of the continuing progression of the world and so self-enclosed as to make an independent circle of meaning that no one is motivated to go beyond it to another future and reality. The spectator is set at an absolute distance which makes any practical, purposive share in it impossible. But the distance is, in the literal sense, aesthetic distance, for it is the distance from seeing that makes possible the proper and comprehensive sharing in what is represented before one. Thus to the ecstatic self-forgetfulness of the spectator there corresponds his continuity with himself. Precisely that in which he loses himself as a spectator requires his own continuity. It is the truth of his own world, the religious and moral world in which he lives, which presents itself to him and in which he recognises himself. Just as the parousia, absolute presence, describes the ontological mode of aesthetic being, and a work of art is the same wherever it becomes such a presence, so the absolute moment in which a spectator stands is at once self-forgetfulness and reconciliation with self. That which detaches him from everything also gives him back the whole of his being.

The dependence of aesthetic being on representation does not mean any deficiency, any lack of autonomous determination of meaning. It belongs to its essence. The spectator is an essential element of the kind of play that we call aesthetic. Let us remember here the famous definition of tragedy which we find in Aristotle's *Poetics*. There the attitude of the spectator is expressly included in the definition.

(D) The example of the tragic

The Aristotelian theory of tragedy may serve as an example for the structure of aesthetic being as a whole. It exists in the content of a poetics and seems to be valid only for dramatic poetry. However, the tragic is a basic phenomenon, a meaningful structure which does not exist only in tragedy, the tragic work of art in the narrower sense, but can have its place also in other artistic genres, especially epic. Indeed, it is not even a specifically artistic phenomenon, inasmuch as it is found also in life. For this reason, the tragic is seen by modern scholars (Richard Hamann, Max Scheler[37]) as something extra-aesthetic. It is an ethical and metaphysical phenomenon that enters into the sphere of aesthetic problems only from outside. But after we have seen how questionable the idea of the aesthetic is, we must now raise the contrary issue, namely, whether the tragic is not, rather, a basic aesthetic phenomenon. The nature of the aesthetic has emerged for us as play and representation. Thus we may also consult the theory of the tragic play, the poetics of tragedy, as to the essence of the tragic.

What we find reflected in thought about the tragic, from Aristotle down to the present, is by no means of an unchangeable nature. There is no doubt that the essence of tragedy is presented in Attic tragedy in a unique way; and differently for Aristotle, for whom Euripides was the 'most tragic',[38] differently again for someone to whom Aeschylus reveals the truth of the tragic phenomenon, and very differently for someone who thinks of Shakespeare. But this change does not simply mean that the question of the unified nature of the tragic would be without an object, but rather, on the contrary, that the phenomenon presents itself in an outline given by a historical unity. The reflection of classical tragedy in modern tragedy of which Kierkegaard speaks is constantly present in all modern thinking on the tragic. If we start with Aristotle, we shall see the whole scope of the tragic phenomenon. In his famous definition of tragedy Aristotle made a point that had a great influence on the problem of the aesthetic: he included in the definition of tragedy the effect on the spectator.

I cannot hope to treat his famous and much discussed definition fully here. But the mere fact that the spectator is taken into the definition makes clear what was said above concerning the essential part that the spectator plays in a drama. The way in which the spectator is part of it makes apparent the meaningfulness of the figure of play. Thus the distance that the spectator retains from the drama is not an optional attitude, but the essential relation whose ground lies in the meaningful unity of the play. Tragedy is the unity of a tragic succession of events that is experienced as such. But what is experienced as a tragic succession of events, even if it is not a play that is shown on the stage, but a tragedy in 'life', is a closed circle of meaning that resists, of itself, all penetration and influence. What is understood as tragic must simply be accepted. Hence it is, in fact, a basic 'aesthetic' phenomenon.

We learn from Aristotle that the representation of the tragic action has a specific effect on the spectator. The representation works through eleos and phobos. The traditional translation of these emotions by 'pity' and 'terror' gives them a far too subjective tinge. Aristotle is not at all concerned with pity or with the evaluation of pity as it has changed through the centuries,[39] and fear is similarly not to be understood as an inner emotion. Rather both are events that overwhelm man and sweep him away. Eleos is the distress that comes over us in the face of what we call distressing. Thus the fate of Oedipus is distressing (the example that Aristotle always returns to). The English word 'distress' is a good equivalent because it too refers not merely to an inner state, but likewise to its manifestation. Accordingly, phobos is not just a state of mind but, as Aristotle says, a cold shudder[40] that makes one's blood run cold, that makes one shiver. In the particular sense in which, in this definition of tragedy, phobos is combined with eleos, phobos means the shivers of apprehension which come over us for someone whom we see rushing to his destruction and for whom we fear. Distress and apprehension are modes of ecstasis, being outside oneself, which testify to the power of what is taking place before us.

Now Aristotle says of these emotions that they are what the play uses in order to purify us of them. As is well-known, this translation is doubtful, especially the sense of the genitive.[41] But what Aristotle means seems to me to be quite independent of this, and this must ultimately show why two conceptions so different grammatically can continue to be held so firmly. It seems clear to me that Aristotle is thinking of the tragic pensiveness that comes over the spectator at a tragedy. But pensiveness is a kind of relief and resolution, in

which pain and pleasure are variously mixed. How can Aristotle call this condition a purification? What is the impure element in feeling, and how is this removed in the tragic emotion? The answer seems to me the following: being overcome by distress and horror involves a painful division. There is a disjunction with what is happening, a refusal to accept, that rebels against the agonising events. But it is precisely the effect of the tragic catastrophe that this disjunction with what exists is removed. The heart is freed from constraint. We are freed not only from the spell in which the painful and horrifying nature of the tragic destiny had held us, but at the same time we are free from everything that divides us from what is.

Thus tragic pensiveness reflects a kind of affirmation, a return to ourselves, and if, as is often the case in modern tragedy, the hero is affected in his own consciousness by the emotion, he himself shares a little in this affirmation, in that he accepts his fate.

But what is the real object of this affirmation? What is affirmed? Certainly not the justice of a moral world order. The notorious tragic theory of guilt that scarcely retains any importance for Aristotle is not a suitable explanation for modern tragedy. For tragedy does not exist where guilt and expiation correspond to each other in the right measure, where a moral bill of guilt is paid in full. Nor in modern tragedy can and must there be a full subjectivisation of guilt and of fate. Rather the excess of tragic consequences is typical of the nature of the tragic. Despite all the subjectivisation of guilt in modern tragedy it still retains an element of that classical sense of the power of destiny that, in the very disproportion between guilt and fate, reveals itself as the same for all. Hebbel seems to stand on the borderline of what can still be called tragedy, so exactly is subjective guilt fitted into the course of the tragic action. For the same reason the idea of christian tragedy presents a special problem, since in the light of divine salvation history the values of happiness and misfortune that are constitutive of the tragic action no longer determine human destiny. Even Kierkegaard's[42] brilliant contrast of the classical suffering that followed from a curse laid on a family, with the suffering that rends the consciousness that is not at one with itself, but involved in conflict, only reaches the bounds of the tragic. His rewritten *Antigone*[43] would no longer be a tragedy.

So we must repeat the question: what is affirmed here of the spectator? Obviously it is the disproportionate, terrible immensity of the consequences that flow from a guilty deed which is the real claim made on the spectator. The tragic affirmation is the fulfilment of this claim. It has the character of a genuine communion. It is something truly common which is experienced in such an excess of tragic suffering. The spectator recognises himself and his own finiteness in the face of the power of fate. What happens to the great ones of the earth has an exemplary significance. The tragic emotion is not a response to the tragic course of events as such or to the justice of the fate that overtakes the hero, but to the metaphysical order of being that is true for all. To see that 'this is how it is' is a kind of self-knowledge for the spectator, who emerges with new insight from the illusions in which he lives. The tragic affirmation is an insight which the spectator has by virtue of the continuity of significance in which he places himself.

It follows from this analysis of the tragic not only that it is a basic aesthetic idea, inasmuch as the distance of the spectator is part of the essence of the tragic but, more importantly, that the distance of the spectator, which determines the nature of the aesthetic, does not include the 'aesthetic differentiation' which we recognised as a feature of 'aesthetic consciousness'. The spectator does not hold himself aloof at a distance of aesthetic consciousness enjoying the art of representation,[44] but in the communion of being present. The real emphasis of the tragic phenomenon lies ultimately on what is represented and recognised and to share in it is not a question of choice. However much the tragic play that is performed solemnly in the theatre represents an exceptional situation in the life of everyone, it is not an experience of an adventure producing a temporary intoxication from which one re-awakens to one's true being, but the emotion that seizes the spectator deepens in fact his continuity with himself. The tragic emotion flows from the self-knowledge that the spectator acquires. He finds himself in the tragic action, because it is his own world, familiar to him from religious or historical tradition, that he encounters, and even if this tradition is no longer binding for a later consciousness – as was already the case with Aristotle, and was certainly true of Seneca or Corneille – there is more in the continuing effect of such tragic works and themes than merely the continuing validity of a literary model. It is not only assumed that the spectator is still familiar with the legend, but it is also necessary that its language still really reaches him. Only then can the encounter with the tragic theme and tragic work become an encounter with self.

What is true here of the tragic, however, is true in a far wider context. For the writer, free invention is always only one side of a communication which is conditioned by what is pre-given as valid. He does not freely invent his plot, however much he imagines that he does. Rather there remains up to the present day some of the old basis of the mimesis theory. The free invention of the writer is the presentation of a common truth that is binding on the writer also.

It is the same with the other arts, especially the plastic arts. The aesthetic myth of freely creative imagination that transforms experience into literature proves only that in the nineteenth century the store of mythical and historical tradition was no longer a self-evident possession. But even then the aesthetic myth of imagination and of the invention of genius is an exaggeration that does not stand up to reality. The choice of material and the formation of it still does not proceed from the free discretion of the artist and is not the mere expression of his inner life. Rather does the artist address people whose minds are prepared and chooses what he expects will have an effect on them. He himself stands in the same tradition as the public that he is aiming at and which he gathers around him. In this sense it is true that he does not need to know explicitly as an individual, a thinking consciousness, what he is doing and what his work says. It is never simply a strange world of magic, of intoxication, of dream to which the play, sculptor or viewer is swept away, but it is always his own world to which he comes to belong more fully by recognising himself more profoundly in it. There remains a continuity of meaning which links the work of art with the world of real existence and from which even the alienated consciousness of a cultured society never quite detaches itself.

Let us sum up. What is aesthetic being? We have sought to show something general in the idea of play and of the transformation into a structure, which is characteristic of the play of art: namely, that the presentation or performance of a work of literature or of music is something essential, and not incidental, for in this is merely completed what the works of art already are: the being there of what is represented in them. The specific temporality of aesthetic being, of having its being in the process of being represented, becomes existent in reproduction as a separate, independent phenomenon.

Notes

1 Aristotle, *Pol* VIII, 3 1337 b 39 and elsewhere Cf *Eth Nic* x, 6, 1176 b 33: *paizein hopos spoudaze kat' anacharsin orthos echein dokei*

2 Kurt Riezler, in his brilliant *Traktat vom Schönen*, has started with the subjectivity of the player and hence preserved the antithesis of play and seriousness, so that the idea of play becomes too restricted for him and he has to say: 'We doubt whether the play of children is only play' and 'The play of art is not only play'

3 F. J. J. Buytendijk, *Wesen und Sinn des Spiels*, 1933

4 This obvious point must be made against those who seek to criticise the truth of Heidegger's statements on the basis of his etymological practice

5 Cf J. Trier, *Beiträge zur Geschichte der deutschen Sprache und Literatur* 67, 1947

6 J. Huizinga (*Homo ludens, Vom Ursprung der Kultur im Spiel*, p 43) points out the following linguistic facts: 'One can certainly say in German *ein Spiel treiben* ('to play a game') and in Dutch *een spelletje doen* (the same), but the appropriate verb is really *spielen* ('to play') itself. *Man spielt ein Spiel* ('one plays a game'). In other words, in order to express the kind of activity, the idea contained in the noun must be repeated in the verb. That means, it seems, that the action is of such a particular and independent kind that it is different from the usual kinds of activity. Playing is not an activity in the usual sense'. Similarly, the phrase *ein spielchen machen* (to take a hand) describes a use of one's time that is by no means play

7 Huizinga, *loc cit*, p 32

8 Rilke writes in the fifth Duino Elegy: 'wo sich das reine Zuwenig unbegreiflich verwandelt – umspringt in jenes leere Zuviel' ('where the sheer dearth is incomprehensibly transformed – switches into that void excess')

9 Friedrich Schlegel, *Gespräch über die Poesie* (*Friedrich Schlegels* Jugendschriften, ed J. Minor, 1882, II, p 364)

10 F. G. Junger, *Die Spiele*

11 Huizinga, *loc cit*, p 17

12 In numerous writings Adolf Portmann has made this criticism and given a new basis to the legitimacy of the morphological approach

13 Cf Rudolf Kassner, *Zahl und Gesicht*, p 161 f. Kassner states that 'the extraordinary unity and duality of child and doll' is connected with the fact that the fourth 'open wall of the audience' (as in a religious rite) is missing. I am arguing the other way round that it is precisely this fourth wall of the audience that closes the play world of the *world of art*

14 Cf note 13

15 I am making use here of the classical distinction in which Aristotle (*Eth Eud* B1; *Eth Nic* VI, 5, 1140 a 20) separates the *poesis* from the *praxis*

16 Plato, *Phileb*, 50b

17 Cf the recent research by Koller, *Mimesis*, 1954, which proves the original connection between *mimesis* and dance

18 Aristotle, *Poet* 4 esp 1448 b 16: 'inferring what class each object belongs to; for example that this individual is a so-and-so' (Else trans)

19 *loc cit* 1448 b 10

20 Kant, *Critique of Judgement*, § 48

21 Plato, *Phaed* 73 ff

22 Plato, *Republic* x

23 Aristotle, *Poet*, 9, 1451 b 6

24 Anna Tumarkin has been able to show very clearly in the aesthetics of the eighteenth century the transition from 'imitation' to 'expression' (*Festschrift für Samuel Singer*, 1930)

25 It is a problem of a particular kind whether the formative process itself should not be seen also as an aesthetic reflection on the work. It is undeniable that when he considers the idea of his work the creator can ponder and critically compare and judge various possibilities of carrying it out. But this sober awareness which is part of creation itself seems to me to be something very different from aesthetic reflection and aesthetic criticism, which is able to be stimulated by the work itself. It may be that what was the object of the creator's reflection, ie the possibilities of form, can also be the occasion of aesthetic criticism. But even in the case of this kind of agreement in content between creative and critical reflection the criterion is different. Aesthetic criticism is based on the disturbance of unified understanding, whereas the aesthetic reflection of the creator is directed towards establishment of the unity of the work itself. We shall see later the hermeneutical consequences of this point. It still seems to me a remnant of the false psychologism that stems from taste and genius aesthetics if one makes the processes of production and of reproduction coincide in the idea. This is to fail to appreciate the event of the success of a work, which goes beyond the subjectivity both of the creator and of the spectator or listener

26 Although I think his analyses on the 'schematism' of the literary work of art have been too little noted, I cannot agree when R. Ingarden (in his 'Bemerkungen zum Problem des ästhetischen Werturteils', *Rivista di Estetica*, 1959) sees in the process of the concretisation of an 'aesthetic object' the area of the aesthetic evaluation of the work of art. The aesthetic object is not constituted in the aesthetic experience of grasping it, but the work of art itself is experi-

enced in its aesthetic quality through the process of its concretisation and creation. In this I agree fully with L. Pareyson's aesthetics of *formativita*

27 This is not limited to the interpretative arts, but includes any work of art, in fact any meaningful structure, that is raised to a new understanding, as we shall see later

28 Hans Sedlmayr, *Kunst und Wahrheit*, 1958, p 140 ff

29 For the following, compare the fine analyses by R. and G. Koebner, *Vom Schönen und seiner Wahrheit*, 1957, which I came across only when my own work was completed. Cf the review in the *Philosophische Rundschau* 7, p 79

30 Walter F. Otto and Karl Kerényi have noted the importance of the festival for the history of religions and anthropology (cf Karl Kerényi, *Vom Wesen des Festes*, Paideuma, 1938)

31 Aristotle refers to the characteristic mode of being of the *apeiron*; for instance in his discussion of the mode of being of the day, the games, and hence the festival – a discussion that does not forget Anaximander. (Physics III, 6, 206 a 20). Had Anaximander already sought to define the fact that the *apeiron* never came to an end in relation to such pure time phenomena? Did he perhaps intend more than can be conceived in the Aristotelian ideas of becoming and being? For the image of the day recurs in another connection with a special function: in Plato's *Parmenides* (131b) Socrates seeks to demonstrate the relation of the idea to things in terms of the presence of the day, which exists for all. Here by means of the nature of the day, there is demonstrated not what exists only as it passes away, but the unsharable presence and *parousia* of something that remains the same, despite the fact that the day is everywhere different. When the early thinkers thought of being, ie presence, did that which was presence for them appear in the light of a sacral communion in which the divine shows itself? The *parousia* of the divine is still for Aristotle the most real being, *energeia* (Met XIII, 7) which is limited by no *dunamei*. The character of this time cannot be grasped in terms of the usual experience of succession. The dimensions of time and the experience of these dimensions cause us to see the return of the festival only as something historical: the one and the same thing changes from time to time. But in fact a festival is not one and the same thing; it exists by being always something different. An entity that exists only in always being something else is temporal in a radical sense: it has its being in becoming. Cf on the ontological character of the 'while' (*Weile*) M. Heidegger, *Holzwege*, p 322 ff

32 Cf my essay 'Zur Vorgeschichte der Metaphysik' on the relationship between '*Zein*' and '*Denken*' in Parmenides (*Anteile*, 1949)

33 Cf what was said above [*not reproduced here*] about culture, formation (*Bildung*)

34 Cf Gerhard Krüger, *Einsicht und Leidenschaft. Das Wesen des platonischen Denkens*, first edition (1940). The Introduction in particular contains important insights. Since then a published lecture by Krüger (*Grundfragen der Philosophie*, 1958) has made his systematic intentions even clearer. Perhaps we may make a few observations on what he says. His criticism of modern thinking and its emancipation from all connections with 'ontic truth' seems to me without foundation. That modern science, however constructively it may proceed, has never abandoned and never can abandon its fundamental connection with experiment, modern philosophy has never been able to forget. One only has to think of Kant's question of how a pure natural science is possible. But one is also very unfair to speculative idealism if one understands it in the onesided way that Krüger does. Its construction of the totality of all determinants of thought is by no means the thinking out of some random view of the world, but desires to bring into thinking the absolute *a posteriori* character of experiment. This is the exact sense of transcendental reflection. The example of Hegel can teach us that even the renewal of classical conceptual realism can be attempted by its aid. Krüger's view of modern thought is based entirely on the desperate extremism of Nietzsche. However, the perspectivism of the latter's 'will-to-power' is not in agreement with idealistic philosophy but, on the contrary, has grown up on the soil which nineteenth century historicism had prepared after the collapse of idealist philosophy. Hence I am not able to give the same value as Krüger to Dilthey's theory of knowledge in the human sciences. Rather, the important thing, in my view, is to correct the philosophical interpretation of the modern human sciences, which even in Dilthey proves to be too dominated by the onesided methodological thinking of the exact natural sciences. I certainly agree with Krüger when he appeals to the experience of life and the experience of the artist. But the continuing validity of these for our thinking seems to me to show that the contrast between classical thought and modern thought, in Krüger's oversimplified formulation, is itself a modern construction.

If we are reflecting on the experience of art – as opposed to the subjectivisation of philosophical aesthetics – we are not concerned simply with a question of aesthetics, but with an adequate self-interpretation of modern thought in general, which has more in it than the modern concept of method recognises

35 E. Fink has tried to clarify the meaning of man's being outside himself in enthusiasm by making a distinction which is obviously inspired by Plato's *Phaedrus*. But whereas there the counter-ideal of pure rationality makes the distinction that between good and bad madness, Fink lacks a corresponding

criterion when he contrasts 'purely human rapture' with that enthusiasm by which man is in God. For ultimately 'purely human rapture' is also a being away from oneself and an involvement with something else which man is not able to achieve of himself, but which comes over him, and thus seems indistinguishable from enthusiasm. That there is a kind of rapture which it is in man's power to induce and that enthusiasm is the experience of a superior power which simply overwhelms us: these distinctions of control over oneself and of being overwhelmed are themselves conceived in terms of power and therefore do not do justice to the interrelation of being outside oneself and being involved with something, which is the case in every form of rapture and enthusiasm. The forms of 'purely human rapture' described by Fink are themselves, if only they are not narcissistically and psychologically misinterpreted, modes of 'finite self-transcendence of finiteness' (cf Eugen Fink, *Vom Wesen des Enthusiasmus*, esp pp 22–25)

36 Kierkegaard, *Philosophical Fragments*, ch 4, and elsewhere

37 Richard Hamann, *Asthetik*, p 97: 'Hence the tragic has nothing to do with aesthetics', Max Scheler, *Vom Umsturz der Werte*, 'Zum Phänomen des Tragischen': 'It is even doubtful whether the tragic is an essentially "aesthetic" phenomenon'. For the meaning of the word 'tragedy' see E. Staiger, *Die Kunst der Interpretation*, p 132 ff

38 Aristotle, *Poetics*, 13, 1453 a 29. Kierkegaard, *Either–Or* I

39 Max Kommerell (*Lessing und Aristoteles*) has described this history of pity, but not distinguished sufficiently from it the original sense of *eleos*. Cf also W. Schadewaldt, "Furcht und Mitleid?", *Hermes* 83, 1955, p 129 ff and the supplementary article by H. Flashar, *Hermes* 1956, pp 12–48

40 Aristotle, *Rhet*, II, 13, 1389 b 32

41 Cf M. Kommerell, who gives an account of the older interpretations: *loc cit*, pp 262–272. There have also been those who defend the objective genitive, eg K. H. Volkmann-Schluck in 'Varia Variorum' (*Festschrift für Karl Reinhardt*, 1952)

42 Kierkegaard, *Either–Or*, I

43 *ibid*

44 Aristotle, *Poetics*, 4, 1448 b 18: '... but by virtue of its workmanship or its finish or some other cause of that kind'. (Else trans)

21

Metaphor and the Problem of Hermeneutics

Paul Ricoeur

5 What is a Text? Explanation and Understanding

This essay will be devoted primarily to the debate between two fundamental attitudes which may be adopted in regard to a text. These two attitudes were summed up, in the period of Wilhelm Dilthey at the end of the last century, by the two words 'explanation' and 'interpretation'. For Dilthey, 'explanation' referred to the model of intelligibility borrowed from the natural sciences and applied to the historical disciplines by positivist schools; 'interpretation', on the other hand, was a derivative form of understanding, which Dilthey regarded as the fundamental attitude of the human sciences and as that which could alone preserve the fundamental difference between these sciences and the sciences of nature. Here I propose to examine the fate of this opposition in the light of conflicts between contemporary schools. For the notion of explanation has since been displaced, so that it derives no longer from the natural sciences but from properly linguistic models. As regards the concept of interpretation, it has undergone profound transformations which distance it from the psychological notion of understanding, in Dilthey's sense of the word. It is this new position of the problem, perhaps less contradictory and more fecund, which I should like to explore. But before unfolding the new concepts of explanation and understanding, I should like to pause at a preliminary question which in fact dominates the whole of our investigation. The question is this: what is a text?

I What is a text?

Let us say that a text is any discourse fixed by writing. According to this definition, fixation by writing is constitutive of the text itself. But what is fixed by writing? We have said: any discourse. Is this to say that discourse had to be pronounced initially in a physical or mental form? that all writing was initially, at least in a potential way, speaking? In short, what is the relation of the text to speech?

To begin with, we are tempted to say that all writing is added to some anterior speech. For if by speech [*parole*] we understand, with Ferdinand de Saussure, the realisation of language [*langue*] in an event of discourse, the production of an individual utterance by an individual speaker, then each text is in the same position as speech with respect to language. Moreover, writing as an institution is subsequent to speech, and seems merely to fix in linear script all the articulations which have already appeared orally. The attention given almost exclusively to phonetic writings seems to confirm that writing adds nothing to the phenomenon of speech other than the fixation which enables it to be conserved. Whence the conviction that writing is fixed speech, that inscription, whether it be graphics or recording, is inscription of speech – an inscription which, thanks to the subsisting character of the engraving, guarantees the persistence of speech.

The psychological and sociological priority of speech over writing is not in question. It may be asked, however, whether the late appearance of writing has not provoked a radical change in our relation to the very statements of our discourse. For let us return to our definition: the text is a discourse fixed by writing. What is fixed by writing is thus a discourse which could be said, of course, but which is written precisely because it is not said. Fixation by writing takes the very place of speech, occurring at the site where speech could have emerged. This suggests that a text is really a text only when it is not restricted to transcribing an anterior speech, when instead it inscribes directly in written letters what the discourse means.

This idea of a direct relation between the meaning of the statement and writing can be supported by reflecting on the function of reading in relation to writing. Writing calls for reading in a way which will enable us shortly to introduce the concept of interpretation. For the moment, let us say that the reader takes the place of the interlocutor, just as writing takes the place of speaking and the speaker. The writing–reading relation is thus not a particular case of the speaking–answering relation. It is not a relation of interlocution, not an instance of dialogue. It does not suffice to say that reading is a dialogue with the author through his work, for the relation of the reader to the book is of a completely different nature. Dialogue is an exchange of questions and answers; there is no exchange of this sort between the writer and the reader. The writer does not respond to the reader. Rather, the book divides the act of writing and the act of reading into two sides, between which there is no communication. The reader is absent from the act of writing; the writer is absent from the act of reading. The text thus produces a double eclipse of the reader and the writer. It thereby replaces the relation of dialogue, which directly connects the voice of one to the hearing of the other.

The substitution of reading for a dialogue which has not occurred is so manifest that when we happen to encounter an author and to speak to him (about his book, for example), we experience a profound disruption of the peculiar relation that we have with the author in and through his work. Sometimes I like to say that to read a book is to consider its author as already dead and the book as posthumous. For it is when the author is dead that the relation to the book becomes complete and, as it were, intact. The author can no longer respond; it only remains to read his work.

The difference between the act of reading and the act of dialogue confirms our hypothesis that writing is a realisation comparable and parallel to speech, a realisation which takes the place of it and, as it were, intercepts it. Hence we could say that what comes to writing is discourse as intention-to-say and that writing is a direct inscription of this intention, even if, historically and psychologically, writing began with the graphic transcription of the signs of speech. This emancipation of writing, which places the latter at the site of speech, is the birth of the text.

Now, what happens to the statement itself when it is directly inscribed instead of being pronounced? The most striking characteristic has always been emphasised: writing preserves discourse and makes it an archive available for individual and collective memory. It may be added that the linearisation of symbols permits an analytic and distinctive translation of all the successive and discrete features of language and thereby increases its efficacy. Is that all? Preservation and increased efficacy still only characterise the transcription of oral language in graphic signs. The emancipation of the text from the oral situation entails a veritable upheaval in the relations between language and the world, as well as in the relation between language and the various subjectivities concerned (that of the author and that of the reader). We glimpsed something of this second upheaval in distinguishing reading from dialogue; we shall have to go still further, but this time beginning from the upheaval which the referential relation of language to the world undergoes when the text takes the place of speech.

What do we understand by the referential relation or referential function? In addressing himself to another speaker, the subject of discourse says something about something; that about which he speaks is the referent of his discourse. As is well known, this referential function is supported by the sentence, which is the first and the simplest unit of discourse. It is the sentence which intends to say something true or something real, at least in declarative discourse. The referential function is so important that it compensates, as it were, for another characteristic of language, namely the separation of signs from things. By means of the referential function, language 'pours back into the universe' (according to an expression of Gustave Guillaume) those signs which the symbolic function, at its birth, divorced from things. All discourse is, to some extent, thereby reconnected to the world. For if we did not speak of the world, of what should we speak?

When the text takes the place of speech, something important occurs. In speech, the interlocutors are present not only to one another, but also to the situation, the surroundings and the circumstantial milieu of discourse. It is in relation to this circumstantial milieu that discourse is fully meaningful; the return to reality is ultimately a return to this reality, which can be indicated 'around' the speakers, 'around', if we may say so, the instance of discourse itself. Language is, moreover, well equipped to secure this anchorage. Demonstratives, adverbs of time and place, personal pronouns, verbal tenses, and in general all the 'deictic' and 'ostensive' indicators serve to anchor discourse in the circumstantial reality which surrounds the instance of discourse. Thus, in living speech, the *ideal* sense of what is said turns towards the *real* reference, towards that 'about which' we speak. At the limit, this real reference tends to merge with an ostensive designation where speech rejoins the gesture of pointing. Sense fades into reference and the latter into the act of showing.

This is no longer the case when the text takes the place of speech. The movement of reference towards the act of showing is intercepted, at the same time as dialogue is interrupted by the text. I say intercepted and not suppressed; it is in this respect that I shall distance myself from what may be called henceforth the ideology of the absolute text. On the basis of the sound remarks which we have just made, this ideology proceeds, by an unwarranted hypostasis, through a course that is ultimately surreptitious. As we shall see, the text is not without reference; the task of reading, *qua* interpretation, will be precisely to fulfil the reference. The suspense which defers the reference merely leaves the text, as it were, 'in the air', outside or without a world. In virtue of this obliteration of the relation to the world, each text is free to enter into relation with all the other texts which come to take the place of the circumstantial reality referred to by living speech. This relation of text to text, within the effacement of the world about which we speak, engenders the quasi-world of texts or *literature*.

Such is the upheaval which affects discourse itself, when the movement of reference towards the act of showing is intercepted by the text. Words cease to efface themselves in front of things; written words become words for themselves.

The eclipse of the circumstantial world by the quasi-world of texts can be so complete that, in a civilisation of writing, the world itself is no longer what can be shown in speaking but is reduced to a kind of 'aura' which written works unfold. Thus we speak of the Greek world or the Byzantine world. This world can be called 'imaginary', in the sense that it is *represented* by writing in lieu of the world *presented* by speech; but this imaginary world is itself a creation of literature.

The upheaval in the relation between the text and its world is the key to the other upheaval of which we have already spoken, that which affects the relation of the text to the subjectivities of the author and the reader. We think that we know what the author of a text is because we derive the notion of the author from that of the speaker. The subject of speech, according to Benveniste, is what designates itself in saying 'I'. When the text takes the place of speech, there is no longer a speaker, at least in the sense of an immediate and direct self-designation of the one who speaks in the instance of discourse. This proximity of the speaking subject to his own speech is replaced by a complex relation of the author to the text, a relation which enables us to say that the author is instituted by the text, that he stands in the space of meaning traced and inscribed by writing. The text is the very place where the author appears. But does the author appear otherwise than as first reader? The distancing of the text from its author is already a phenomenon of the first reading which, in one move, poses the whole series of problems that we are now going to confront concerning the relations between explanation and interpretation. These relations arise at the time of reading.

II Explanation or understanding?

As we shall see, the two attitudes which we have initially placed under the double title of explanation and interpretation will confront one another in the act of reading. This duality is first encountered in the work of Dilthey. For him, these distinctions constituted an alternative wherein one term necessarily excluded the other: either you 'explain' in the manner of the natural scientist, or you 'interpret' in the manner of the historian. This exclusive alternative will provide the point of departure for the discussion which follows. I propose to show that the concept of the text, such as we have formulated it in the first part of this essay, demands a renewal of the two notions of explanation and interpretation and, in virtue of this renewal, a less contradictory conception of their interrelation. Let us say straightaway that the discussion will be deliberately oriented towards the search for a strict complementarity and reciprocity between explanation and interpretation.

The initial opposition in Dilthey's work is not exactly between explanation and interpretation, but between explanation and understanding, interpretation being a particular province of understanding. We must therefore begin from the opposition between explanation and understanding. Now if this opposition is exclusive, it is because, in Dilthey's work, the two terms designate two spheres of reality which they serve to separate. These two spheres are those of the natural sciences and the human sciences. Nature is the region of objects offered to scientific observation, a region subsumed since Galileo to the enterprise of mathematisation and since John Stuart Mill to the canons of inductive logic. Mind is the region of psychological individualities, into which each mental life is capable of transposing itself. Understanding is such a transference into another mental life. To ask whether the human sciences can exist is thus to ask whether a scientific knowledge of individuals is possible, whether this understanding of the singular can be objective in its own way, whether it is susceptible of universal validity. Dilthey answered affirmatively, because inner life is given in external signs which can be perceived and understood as signs of another mental life: 'Understanding', he says in the famous article on 'The development of hermeneutics', 'is the process by which we come to know something of mental life through the perceptible signs which manifest it.'[1] This is the understanding of which interpretation is a particular province. Among the signs of another mental life, we have the 'manifestations fixed in a durable way', the 'human testimonies preserved by writing', the 'written monuments'. Interpretation is the art of understanding applied to such manifestations, to such testimonies, to such monuments, of which writing is the distinctive characteristic. Understanding, as the knowledge through signs of another mental life, thus provides the basis in the pair understanding–interpretation; the latter element supplies the degree of objectification, in virtue of the fixation and preservation which writing confers upon signs.

Although this distinction between explanation and understanding seems clear at first, it becomes increasingly obscure as soon as we ask ourselves about the conditions of scientificity of interpretation. Explanation has been expelled from the field of the human sciences; but the conflict reappears at the very heart of the concept of interpretation between, on the one hand, the intuitive and unverifiable character of the psychologising concept of understanding to which interpretation is subordinated, and on the other hand the demand for objectivity which belongs to the very notion of human science. The splitting of hermeneutics between its psychologising tendency and its search for a logic of interpretation ultimately calls into question the relation between understanding and interpretation. Is not interpretation a species of understanding which explodes the genre? Is not the specific difference, namely fixation by writing, more important here than the feature common to all signs, that of presenting inner life in an external form? What is more important: the inclusion of hermeneutics in the sphere of understanding or its difference therefrom? Schleiermacher, before Dilthey, had witnessed this internal splitting of the hermeneutical project and had overcome it through a happy marriage of *romantic genius* and *philological virtuosity*. With Dilthey, the epistemological demands are more pressing. Several generations separate him from the scholar of Romanticism, several generations well versed in epistemological reflection; the contradiction now explodes in full daylight. Listen to Dilthey commenting upon Schleiermacher: 'The ultimate aim of hermeneutics is to understand the author better than he understands himself.' So much for the psychology of understanding. Now for the logic of interpretation: 'The function of hermeneutics is to establish theoretically, against the constant intrusion of romantic whim and sceptical subjectivism into the domain of history, the universal validity of interpretation, upon which all certitude in history rests.'[2] Thus hermeneutics fulfils the aim of understanding only by extricating itself from the immediacy of understanding others – from, let us say, dialogical values. Understanding seeks to coincide with the inner life of the author, to liken itself to him (*sich gleichsetzen*), to reproduce (*nachbilden*) the creative processes which engendered the work. But the signs of this intention, of this creation, are to be found nowhere else than in what Schleiermacher called the 'exterior' and 'interior form' of the work, or again, the 'interconnection' (*Zusammenhang*) which makes it an organised whole. The last writings of Dilthey ('The construction of the historical world in the human sciences') further aggravated the tension. On the one hand, the objective side of the work was accentuated under the influence of Husserl's

Logical Investigations (for Husserl, as we know, the 'meaning' of a statement constitutes an 'ideality' which exists neither in mundane reality nor in psychic reality: it is a pure unity of meaning without a real localisation). Hermeneutics similarly proceeds from the objectification of the creative energies of life in works which come in between the author and us; it is mental life itself, its creative dynamism, which calls for the mediation by 'meanings', 'values' or 'goals'. The scientific demand thus presses towards an ever greater de-psychologisation of interpretation, of understanding itself and perhaps even of introspection, if it is true that memory itself follows the thread of meanings which are not themselves mental phenomena. The exteriorisation of life implies a more indirect and mediate characterisation of the interpretation of self and others. But it is a self and another, posed in psychological terms, that interpretation pursues; interpretation always aims at a reproduction, a *Nachbildung*, of lived experiences.

This intolerable tension, which the later Dilthey bears witness to, leads us to raise two questions which guide the following discussion: Must we not abandon once and for all the reference of interpretation to understanding and cease to make the interpretation of written monuments a particular case of understanding the external signs of an inner mental life? But if interpretation no longer seeks its norm of intelligibility in understanding others, then does not its relation to explanation, which we have set aside hitherto, now demand to be reconsidered?

III The text and structural explanation

Let us begin again from our analysis of the text and from the autonomous status which we have granted it with respect to speech. What we have called the eclipse of the surrounding world by the quasi-world of texts engenders two possibilities. We can, as readers, remain in the suspense of the text, treating it as a wordless and authorless object; in this case, we explain the text in terms of its internal relations, its structure. On the other hand, we can lift the suspense and fulfil the text in speech, restoring it to living communication; in this case, we interpret the text. These two possibilities both belong to reading, and reading is the dialectic of these two attitudes.

Let us consider them separately, before exploring their articulation. We can undertake a first type of reading which formally records, as it

were, the text's interception of all the relations to a world that can be pointed out and to subjectivities that can converse. This transference into the 'place' – a place which is a non-place – constitutes a special project with respect to the text, that of prolonging the suspense concerning the referential relation to the world and to the speaking subject. By means of this special project, the reader decides to situate himself in the 'place of the text' and in the 'closure' of this place. On the basis of this choice, the text has no outside but only an inside; it has no transcendent aim, unlike a speech which is addressed to someone about something.

This project is not only possible but legitimate. For the constitution of the text as text and of the body of texts as literature justifies the interception of the double transcendence of discourse, towards the world and towards someone. Thus arises the possibility of an explanatory attitude in regard to the text.

In contrast to what Dilthey thought, this explanatory attitude is not borrowed from a field of knowledge and an epistemological model other than that of language itself. It is not a naturalistic model subsequently extended to the human sciences. The nature–mind opposition plays no role here at all. If there is some form of borrowing, it occurs within the same field, that of signs. For it is possible to treat the text according to the explanatory rules that linguistics successfully applies to the simple system of signs which constitute language [*langue*] as opposed to speech [*parole*]. As is well known, the language–speech distinction is the fundamental distinction which gives linguistics an homogenous object; speech belongs to physiology, psychology and sociology, whereas language, as rules of the game of which speech is the execution, belongs only to linguistics. As is equally well known, linguistics considers only systems of units devoid of proper meaning, each of which is defined only in terms of its difference from all of the others. These units, whether they be purely distinctive like those of phonological articulation or significant like those of lexical articulation, are oppositive units. The interplay of oppositions and their combinations within an inventory of discrete units is what defines the notion of structure in linguistics. This structural model furnishes the type of explanatory attitude which we are now going to see applied to the text.

Even before embarking upon this enterprise, it may be objected that the laws which are valid only for language as distinct from speech could not be applied to the text. Although the text is not speech, is it not, as it were, on the same side as speech in relation to language? Must not discourse, as a series of statements and ultimately of sentences, be opposed in an overall way to language? In comparison to the language–discourse distinction, is not the speaking–writing distinction secondary, such that speaking and writing occur together on the side of discourse? These remarks are perfectly legitimate and justify us in thinking that the structural model of explanation does not exhaust the field of possible attitudes which may be adopted in regard to a text. But before specifying the limits of this explanatory model, it is necessary to grasp its fruitfulness. The working hypothesis of any structural analysis of texts is this: in spite of the fact that writing is on the same side as speech in relation to language – namely, on the side of discourse – the specificity of writing in relation to speech is based on structural features which can be treated as analogues of language in discourse. This working hypothesis is perfectly legitimate; it amounts to saying that under certain conditions the larger units of language [*langage*], that is, the units of a higher order than the sentence, display organisations comparable to those of the smaller units of language, that is, the units which are of a lower order than the sentence and which belong to the domain of linguistics.

In *Structural Anthropology*, Claude Lévi-Strauss formulates this working hypothesis for one category of texts, the category of myths:

Like every linguistic entity, myth is made up of constitutive units. These units imply the presence of those which normally enter into the structure of language, namely the phonemes, the morphemes and the semantemes. The constituent units of myth are in the same relation to semantemes as the latter are to morphemes, and as the latter in turn are to phonemes. Each form differs from that which precedes it by a higher degree of complexity. For this reason, we shall call the elements which properly pertain to myth (and which are the most complex of all): large constitutive units.[3]

By means of this working hypothesis, the large units which are minimally the size of the sentence, and which placed together constitute the narrative proper to the myth, can be treated according to the same rules that are applied to the smaller units familiar to linguistics. To indicate this analogy, Lévi-Strauss speaks of 'mythemes' in the same way that one speaks of phonemes, morphemes and semantemes. But in order to remain within the limits of the analogy between mythemes and the linguistic units of a lower level, the analysis of texts will have to proceed to the same sort of abstraction as that practised by the phonologist. For the latter, the phoneme is not a concrete sound, to be taken absolutely in its sonorous substance; it is a function defined by the commutative method and its oppositive value is determined by the relation to all other phonemes. In this sense it is not, as Saussure would say, a 'substance' but a 'form', an interplay of relations. Similarly, a mytheme is not one of the sentences of the myth but an oppositive value which is shared by several particular sentences, constituting, in the language of Lévi-Strauss, a 'bundle of relations'. 'Only in the form of combinations of such bundles do the constituent units acquire a signifying function.'[4] What is called here the 'signifying function' is not at all what the myth means, its philosophical or existential import, but rather the arrangement or disposition of mythemes, in short, the structure of the myth.

I should like to recall briefly the analysis which, according to this method, Lévi-Strauss offers of the Oedipus myth. He divides the sentences of the myth into four columns. In the first column he places all the sentences which speak of overrated blood relations (for example, Oedipus marries Jocasta, his mother; Antigone buries Polynices, her brother, in spite of the order forbidding it). In the second column, we find the same relation, but modified by the inverse sign: underrated or devalued blood relations (Oedipus kills his father, Laios; Eteocles kills his brother, Polynices). The third column concerns monsters and their destruction; the fourth groups together all those proper names whose meaning suggests a difficulty in walking straight (lame, clumsy, swollen foot). The comparison of the four columns reveals a correlation. Between the first and second columns we have blood relations overrated or underrated in turn; between the third and fourth we have an affirmation and then a negation of the autochthony of man. 'It follows that the fourth column is related to the third column as the first is to the second . . .; the overrating of blood relations is to their underrating as the attempt to escape from autochthony is to the impossibility of succeeding in it.' The myth thus appears as a kind of logical instrument which brings together contradictions in order to overcome them: 'the impossibility of connecting the groups of relations is overcome (or, more exactly, replaced) by the assertion that two contradictory relations are identical, insofar as each is, like the other, self-contradictory'.[5] We shall return shortly to this conclusion; let us restrict ourselves here to stating it.

We can indeed say that we have thereby explained the myth, but not that we have interpreted it. We have brought out, by means of structural analysis, the logic of the operations which interconnect the packets of relations; this logic constitutes 'the structural law of the myth concerned'.[6] We shall not fail to notice that this law is, *par excellence*, the object of reading and not at all of speech, in the sense of a recitation whereby the power of the myth would be reactivated in a particular situation. Here the text is only a text and the reading inhabits it only as such, while its meaning for us remains in suspense, together with any realisation in present speech.

I have just taken an example from the domain of myths; I could take another from a nearby domain, that of folklore. This domain has been explored by the Russian formalists of the school of Propp and by the French specialists in the structural analysis of narratives, Roland Barthes and A.J. Greimas. In the work of these authors, we find the same postulates as those employed by Lévi-Strauss: the units above the sentence have the same composition as the units below the sentence; the sense of the narrative consists in the very arrangement of the elements, in the power of the whole to integrate the sub-units; and conversely, the sense of an element is its capacity to enter in relation with other elements and with the whole of the work. These postulates together define the closure of the narrative. The task of structural analysis will be to carry out the segmentation of the work (horizontal aspect), then to establish the various levels of integration of the parts in the whole (hierarchical aspect). Thus the units of action isolated by the analyst will not be psychological units capable of being experienced, nor will they be units of behaviour which could be subsumed to a behaviourist psychology. The extremities of these sequences are only the switching points of the narrative, such that if one element is changed, all the rest is different. Here we recognise the transposition of the method of commutation from the phonological level to the level of narrative units. The logic of action thus consists in an interconnected series of action kernels which together constitute the structural continuity of the narrative. The application

of this technique ends up by 'dechronologising' the narrative, in a way that brings out the logic underlying narrative time. Ultimately the narrative would be reduced to a combination [*combinatoire*] of a few dramatic units (promising, betraying, hindering, aiding, etc.) which would be the paradigms of action. A sequence is thus a succession of nodes of action, each closing off an alternative opened up by the preceding one. Just as the elementary units are linked together, so too they fit into larger units; for example, an encounter is comprised of elementary actions like approaching, calling out, greeting, etc. To explain a narrative is to grasp this entanglement, this fleeting structure of interlaced actions.

Corresponding to the nexus of actions are relations of a similar nature between the 'actants' of the narrative. By that we understand, not at all the characters as psychological subjects endowed with their own existence, but rather the roles correlated with formalised actions. Actants are defined entirely by the predicates of action, by the semantic axes of the sentence and the narrative: the actant is the one by whom, to whom, with whom,...the action is done; it is the one who promises, who receives the promise, the giver, the receiver, etc. Structural analysis thus brings out a hierarchy of *actants* correlative to the hierarchy of *actions*.

The narrative remains to be assembled as a whole and put back into narrative communication. It is then a discourse which a narrator addresses to an audience. For structural analysis, however, the two interlocutors must be sought only in the text. The narrator is designated by the signs of narrativity, which belong to the very constitution of the narrative. Beyond the three levels of actions, actants and narration, there is nothing else that falls within the scope of the science of semiology. There is only the world of narrative users, which can eventually be dealt with by other semiological disciplines (those analysing social, economic and ideological systems); but these disciplines are no longer linguistic in nature. This transposition of a linguistic model to the theory of the narrative fully confirms our initial remark: today, explanation is no longer a concept borrowed from the natural sciences and transferred to the alien domain of written artefacts; rather, it stems from the very sphere of language, by analogical transference from the small units of language (phonemes and lexemes) to the units larger than the sentence, such as narratives, folklore and myth. Henceforth, interpretation – if it is still possible to give a sense to this notion – will no longer be confronted by a model external to the human sciences. It will, instead, be confronted by a model of intelligibility which belongs, from birth so to speak, to the domain of the human sciences, and indeed to a leading science in this domain: linguistics. Thus it will be upon the same terrain, within the same sphere of language [*langage*], that explanation and interpretation will enter into debate.

IV Towards a new concept of interpretation

Let us consider now the other attitude that can be adopted in regard to the text, the attitude which we have called interpretation. We can introduce this attitude by initially opposing it to the preceding one, in a manner still close to that of Dilthey. But as we shall see, it will be necessary to proceed gradually to a more complementary and reciprocal relation between explanation and interpretation.

Let us begin once again from reading. Two ways of reading, we said, are offered to us. By reading we can prolong and reinforce the suspense which affects the text's reference to a surrounding world and to the audience of speaking subjects: that is the explanatory attitude. But we can also lift the suspense and fulfil the text in present speech. It is this second attitude which is the real aim of reading. For this attitude reveals the true nature of the suspense which intercepts the movement of the text towards meaning. The other attitude would not even be possible if it were not first apparent that the text, as writing, awaits and calls for a reading. If reading is possible, it is indeed because the text is not closed in on itself but opens out onto other things. To read is, on any hypothesis, to conjoin a new discourse to the discourse of the text. This conjunction of discourses reveals, in the very constitution of the text, an original capacity for renewal which is its open character. Interpretation is the concrete outcome of conjunction and renewal.

In the first instance, we shall be led to formulate the concept of interpretation in opposition to that of explanation. This will not distance us appreciably from Dilthey's position, except that the opposing concept of explanation has already gained strength by being derived from linguistics and semiology rather than being borrowed from the natural sciences.

According to this first sense, interpretation retains the feature of appropriation which was recognised by Schleiermacher, Dilthey and Bult-

mann. In fact, this sense will not be abandoned; it will only be mediated by explanation, instead of being opposed to it in an immediate and even naive way. By 'appropriation', I understand this: that the interpretation of a text culminates in the self-interpretation of a subject who thenceforth understands himself better, understands himself differently, or simply begins to understand himself. This culmination of the understanding of a text in self-understanding is characteristic of the kind of reflective philosophy which, on various occasions, I have called 'concrete reflection'. Here hermeneutics and reflective philosophy are correlative and reciprocal. On the one hand, self-understanding passes through the detour of understanding the cultural signs in which the self documents and forms itself; it mediates the relation to himself of a subject who, in the short circuit of immediate reflection, does not find the meaning of his own life. Thus it must be said, with equal force, that reflection is nothing without the mediation of signs and works, and that explanation is nothing if it is not incorporated as an intermediary stage in the process of self-understanding. In short, in hermeneutical reflection – or in reflective hermeneutics – the constitution of the *self* is contemporaneous with the constitution of *meaning*.

The term 'appropriation' underlines two additional features. One of the aims of all hermeneutics is to struggle against cultural distance. This struggle can be understood in purely temporal terms as a struggle against secular estrangement, or in more genuinely hermeneutical terms as a struggle against the estrangement from meaning itself, that is, from the system of values upon which the text is based. In this sense, interpretation 'brings together', 'equalises', renders 'contemporary and similar', thus genuinely making one's *own* what was initially *alien*.

Above all, the characterisation of interpretation as appropriation is meant to underline the 'present' character of interpretation. Reading is like the execution of a musical score; it marks the realisation, the enactment, of the semantic possibilities of the text. This final feature is the most important because it is the condition of the other two (that is, of overcoming cultural distance and of fusing textual interpretation with self-interpretation). Indeed, the feature of realisation discloses a decisive aspect of reading, namely that it fulfils the discourse of the text in a dimension similar to that of speech. What is retained here from the notion of speech is not the fact that it is uttered but that it is an event, an instance of discourse, as Benveniste says. The sentences of a text signify *here and now*. The 'actualised' text finds a surrounding and an audience; it resumes the referential movement – intercepted and suspended – towards a world and towards subjects. This world is that of the reader, this subject is the reader himself. In interpretation, we shall say, reading becomes like speech. I do not say 'becomes speech', for reading is never equivalent to a spoken exchange, a dialogue. But reading culminates in a concrete act which is related to the text as speech is related to discourse, namely as event and instance of discourse. Initially the text had only a sense, that is, internal relations or a structure; now it has a meaning, that is, a realisation in the discourse of the reading subject. By virtue of its sense, the text had only a semiological dimension; now it has, by virtue of its meaning, a semantic dimension.

Let us pause here. Our discussion has reached a critical point where interpretation, understood as appropriation, still remains external to explanation in the sense of structural analysis. We continue to oppose them as if they were two attitudes between which it is necessary to choose. I should like now to go beyond this antithetical opposition and to bring out the articulation which would render structural analysis and hermeneutics complementary. For this it is important to show how each of the two attitudes which we have juxtaposed refers back, by means of its own peculiar features, to the other.

Consider again the examples of structural analysis which we have borrowed from the theory of myth and narrative. We tried to adhere to a notion of sense which would be strictly equivalent to the arrangement of the elements of a text, to the integration of the segments of action and the actants within the narrative treated as a whole closed in upon itself. In fact, no one stops at so formal a conception of sense. For example, what Lévi-Strauss calls a 'mytheme' – in his eyes, the constitutive unit of myth – is expressed in a sentence which has a specific meaning: Oedipus kills his father, Oedipus marries his mother, etc. Can it be said that structural explanation neutralises the specific meaning of sentences, retaining only their position in the myth? But the bundle of relations to which Lévi-Strauss reduces the mytheme is still of the order of the sentence; and the interplay of oppositions which is instituted at this very abstract level is equally of the order of the sentence and of meaning. If one speaks of 'overrated' or 'underrated blood relations', of the 'autochthony' or 'non-

autochtony' of man, these relations can still be written in the form of a sentence: the blood relation is the highest of all, or the blood relation is not as high as the social relation, for example in the prohibition of incest, etc. Finally, the contradiction which the myth attempts to resolve, according to Lévi-Strauss, is itself stated in terms of meaningful relations. Lévi-Strauss admits this, in spite of himself, when he writes: 'The reason for these choices becomes clear if we recognise that mythical thought proceeds from the consciousness of certain oppositions and tends towards their progressive mediation';[7] and again, 'the myth is a kind of logical tool intended to effect a mediation between life and death'.[8] In the background of the myth there is a question which is highly significant, a question about life and death: 'Are we born from one or from two?' Even in its formalised version, 'Is the same born from the same or from the other?', this question expresses the anguish of origins: whence comes man? Is he born from the earth or from his parents? There would be no contradiction, nor any attempt to resolve contradiction, if there were not significant questions, meaningful propositions about the origin and the end of man. It is this function of myth as a narrative of origins that structural analysis seeks to place in parentheses. But such analysis does not succeed in eluding this function: it merely postpones it. Myth is not a logical operator between any propositions whatsoever, but involves propositions which point towards limit situations, towards the origin and the end, towards death, suffering and sexuality.

Far from dissolving this radical questioning, structural analysis reinstates it at a more radical level. Would not the function of structural analysis then be to impugn the surface semantics of the recounted myth in order to unveil a depth semantics which is, if I may say so, the living semantics of the myth? If that were not the function of structural analysis, then it would, in my opinion, be reduced to a sterile game, to a derisory combination [*combinatoire*] of elements, and myth would be deprived of the function which Lévi-Strauss himself recognises when he asserts that mythical thought arises from the awareness of certain oppositions and tends towards their progressive mediation. This awareness is a recognition of the *aporias* of human existence around which mythical thought gravitates. To eliminate this meaningful intention would be to reduce the theory of myth to a necrology of the meaningless discourses of mankind. If, on the contrary, we regard structural analysis as a stage – and a necessary one – between a naive and a critical interpretation, between a surface and a depth interpretation, then it seems possible to situate explanation and interpretation along a unique *hermeneutical arc* and to integrate the opposed attitudes of explanation and understanding within an overall conception of reading as the recovery of meaning.

We shall take another step in the direction of this reconciliation between explanation and interpretation if we now turn towards the second term of the initial contradiction. So far we have worked with a concept of interpretation which remains very subjective. To interpret, we said, is to appropriate *here and now* the intention of the text. In saying that, we remain enclosed within Dilthey's concept of understanding. Now what we have just said about the depth semantics unveiled by the structural analysis of the text invites us to say that the intended meaning of the text is not essentially the presumed intention of the author, the lived experience of the writer, but rather what the text means for whoever complies with its injunction. The text seeks to place us in its meaning, that is – according to another acceptation of the word *sens* – in the same direction. So if the intention is that of the text, and if this intention is the direction which it opens up for thought, then depth semantics must be understood in a fundamentally dynamic way. I shall therefore say: to explain is to bring out the structure, that is, the internal relations of dependence which constitute the statics of the text; to interpret is to follow the path of thought opened up by the text, to place oneself *en route* towards the *orient* of the text. We are invited by this remark to correct our initial concept of interpretation and to search – beyond a subjective process of interpretation as an act *on* the text – for an objective process of interpretation which would be the act *of* the text.

I shall borrow an example from a recent study which I made of the exegesis of the sacerdotal story of creation in Genesis 1–2, 4a.[9] This exegesis reveals, in the interior of the text, the interplay of two narratives: a *Tatbericht* in which creation is expressed as a narrative of action ('God made . . .'), and a *Wortbericht*, that is, a narrative of speech ('God said, and there was . . .'). The first narrative could be said to play the role of tradition and the second of interpretation. What is interesting here is that interpretation, before being the act of the exegete, is the act of the text. The relation between tradition and interpretation is a relation internal to the text; for the exegete, to interpret is to place himself in the meaning indicated by the relation of interpretation which the text itself supports.

This objective and, as it were, intra-textual concept of interpretation is by no means unusual. Indeed, it has a long history rivalling that of the concept of subjective interpretation which is linked, it will be recalled, to the problem of understanding others through the signs that others give of their conscious life. I would willingly connect this new concept of interpretation to that referred to in the title of Aristotle's treatise *On Interpretation*. Aristotle's *hermenetia*, in contrast to the hermeneutical technique of seers and oracles, is the very action of language on things. Interpretation, for Aristotle, is not what one does in a second language with regard to a first; rather, it is what the first language already does, by mediating through signs our relation to things. Hence interpretation is, according to the commentary of Boethius, the work of the *vox significativa per se ipsam aliquid significans, sive complexa, sive incomplexa* [significative voice signifying something through itself, whether comprehensible or incomprehensible]. Thus it is the noun, the verb, discourse in general, which interprets in the very process of signifying.

It is true that interpretation in Aristotle's sense does not exactly prepare the way for understanding the dynamic relation between several layers of meaning in the same text. For it presupposes a theory of speech and not a theory of the text: 'The sounds articulated by the voice are symbols of states of the soul, and written words are symbols of words uttered in speech' (*On Interpretation*, para. 1). Hence interpretation is confused with the semantic dimension of speech: interpretation is discourse itself, it is any discourse. Nevertheless, I retain from Aristotle the idea that interpretation is interpretation *by* language before being interpretation *of* language.

I would look in the work of Charles Sanders Peirce for a concept of interpretation which is closer to that required by an exegesis which relates interpretation to tradition in the very interior of a text. According to Peirce, the relation of a 'sign' to an 'object' is such that another relation, that between 'interpretant' and 'sign', can be grafted onto the first. What is important for us is that this relation between interpretant and sign is an open relation, in the sense that there is always another interpretant capable of mediating the first relation. G.-G. Granger explains this very well in his *Essai d'une philosophie du style*:

The interpretant which the sign evokes in the mind could not be the result of a pure and simple deduction which would extract from the sign something already contained therein ... The interpretant is a commentary, a definition, a gloss on the sign in its relation to the object. The interpretant is itself symbolic expression. The sign–interpretant association, realised by whatever psychological processes, is rendered possible only by the community, more or less imperfect, of an experience between speaker and hearer ... It is always an experience which can never be perfectly reduced to the idea or object of the sign of which, as we said, it is the structure. Whence the indefinite character of Peirce's series of interpretants.[10]

We must, of course, exercise a great deal of care in applying Peirce's concept of interpretant to the interpretation of texts. His interpretant is an interpretant of signs, whereas our interpretant is an interpretant of statements. But our use of the interpretant, transposed from small to large units, is neither more nor less analogical than the structuralist transfer of the laws of organisation from units of levels below the sentence to units of an order above or equal to the sentence. In the case of structuralism, it is the phonological structure of language which serves as the coding model of structures of higher articulation. In our case, it is a feature of lexical units which is transposed onto the plane of statements and texts. So if we are perfectly aware of the analogical character of the transposition, then we can say that the open series of interpretants, which is grafted onto the relation of a sign to an object, brings to light a triangular relation of object–sign–interpretant; and that the latter relation can serve as a model for another triangle which is constituted at the level of the text. In the new triangle, the object is the text itself; the sign is the depth semantics disclosed by structural analysis; and the series of interpretants is the chain of interpretations produced by the interpreting community and incorporated into the dynamics of the text, as the work of meaning upon itself. Within this chain, the first interpretants serve as tradition for the final interpretants, which are the interpretation in the true sense of the term.

Thus informed by the Aristotelian concept of interpretation and above all by Peirce's concept, we are in a position to 'depsychologise' as far as possible our notion of interpretation, and to connect it with the process which is at work in the text. Henceforth, for the exegete, to interpret is to place himself within the sense indicated by the relation of interpretation supported by the text.

The idea of interpretation as appropriation is not, for all that, eliminated; it is simply postponed until the termination of the process. It lies at the extremity of what we called above the *hermeneutical arc*: it is the final brace of the bridge, the anchorage of the arch in the ground of lived experience. But the entire theory of hermeneutics consists in mediating this interpretation-appropriation by the series of interpretants which belong to the work of the text upon itself. Appropriation loses its arbitrariness insofar as it is the recovery of that which is at work, in labour, within the text. What the interpreter says is a re-saying which reactivates what is said by the text.

At the end of our investigation, it seems that reading is the concrete act in which the destiny of the text is fulfilled. It is at the very heart of reading that explanation and interpretation are indefinitely opposed and reconciled.

6 Metaphor and the Central Problem of Hermeneutics

It will be assumed here that the central problem of hermeneutics is that of interpretation. Not interpretation in any sense of the word, but interpretation determined in two ways: the first concerning its field of application, the second its epistemological specificity. As regards the first point, I shall say that there is a problem of interpretation because there are texts, written texts, the autonomy of which creates specific difficulties. By 'autonomy' I understand the independence of the text with respect to the intention of the author, the situation of the work and the original reader. The relevant problems are resolved in oral discourse by the kind of exchange or intercourse which we call dialogue or conversation. With written texts, discourse must speak by itself. Let us say, therefore, that there are problems of interpretation because the writing–reading relation is not a particular case of the speaking–hearing relation which we experience in the dialogical situation. Such is the most general feature of interpretation as regards its field of application.

Second, the concept of interpretation seems, at the epistemological level, to be opposed to the concept of explanation. Taken together, these concepts form a contrasting pair which has given rise to a great many disputes since the time of Schleiemacher and Dilthey. According to the tradition to which the latter authors belong, interpretation has certain subjective connotations, such as the implication of the reader in the processes of understanding and the reciprocity between interpretation of the text and self-interpretation. This reciprocity is known by the name of the hermeneutical circle; it entails a sharp opposition to the sort of objectivity and non-implication which is supposed to characterise the scientific explanation of things. Later I shall say to what extent we may be able to amend, indeed to reconstruct on a new basis, the opposition between interpretation and explanation. Whatever the outcome of the subsequent discussion may be, this schematic description of the concept of interpretation suffices for a provisional circumscription of the central problem of hermeneutics: the status of written texts *versus* spoken language, the status of interpretation *versus* explanation.

Now for the metaphor! The aim of this essay is to link up the problems raised in hermeneutics by the interpretation of texts and the problems raised in rhetoric, semantics, stylistics – or whatever the discipline concerned may be – by metaphor.

I The text and metaphor as discourse

Our first task will be to find a common ground for the theory of the text and the theory of metaphor. This common ground has already received a name – discourse; it has yet to be given a status.

One thing is striking: the two sorts of entities that we are considering are of different lengths. In this respect, they can be compared to the sentence, which is the basic unit of discourse. A text can undoubtedly be reduced to a single sentence, as in proverbs or aphorisms; but texts have a maximum length which can extend from a paragraph to a chapter, a book, a collection of 'selected works' or even the corpus of the 'complete works' of an author. Let us use the term 'work' to describe the closed sequence of discourse which can be considered as a text. Whereas texts can be identified on the basis of their maximal length, metaphors can be identified on the basis of their minimal length, that of the word. Even if the rest of this discussion seeks to show that there is no metaphor – in the sense of a word taken metaphorically – in the absence of certain contexts, and consequently even if we are constrained by what

follows to replace the notion of metaphor by that of the metaphorical statement which implies at least the length of the sentence, nevertheless the 'metaphorical twist' (to speak like Monroe Beardsley) is something which happens to the word. The change of meaning, which requires the full contribution of the context, affects the word. We can describe the word as having a 'metaphorical use' or a 'non-literal meaning'; the word is always the bearer of the 'emergent meaning' which specific contexts confer upon it. In this sense, Aristotle's definition of metaphor as the transposition of an unusual name (or word) is not invalidated by a theory emphasising the contextual action which creates the shift of meaning in the word. The word remains the 'focus', even if the focus requires the 'frame' of the sentence, to use the vocabulary of Max Black.

This first, altogether formal remark concerning the difference in length between the text and the metaphor, or better between the *work* and the *word*, is going to help us to elaborate our initial problem in a more precise way: to what extent can we treat the metaphor as a *work in miniature*? The answer to this question will then help us to pose the second: to what extent can the hermeneutical problems raised by the interpretation of texts be considered as a large-scale extension of the problems condensed in the explanation of a local metaphor in a given text?

Is a metaphor a work in miniature? Can a work, say a poem, be considered as a sustained or extended metaphor? The answer to this first question requires a prior elaboration of the general properties of discourse, if it is true that text and metaphor, work and word, fall within the same category of discourse. I shall not elaborate in detail the concept of discourse, restricting my analysis to the features which are necessary for the comparison between text and metaphor. It is remarkable that all of these features present themselves in the form of paradoxes, that is, apparent contradictions.

To begin with, all discourse is produced as an event; as such, it is the counterpart of language understood as code or system. Discourse *qua* event has a fleeting existence: it appears and disappears. But at the same time – and herein lies the paradox – it can be identified and reidentified as the same. This 'sameness' is what we call, in a broad sense, its meaning. All discourse, we shall say, is realised as event but understood as meaning. Soon we shall see in what sense the metaphor concentrates this double character of event and meaning.

The second pair of contrasting features stems from the fact that meaning is supported by a specific structure, that of the proposition, which envelops an internal opposition between a pole of singular identification (this man, this table, Monsieur Dupont, Paris) and a pole of general predication (humanity as a class, brightness as a property, equality as a relation, running as an action). Metaphor, we shall also see, rests upon this 'attribution' of characteristics to the 'principal subject' of a sentence.

The third pair of opposing features is the polarity, which discourse primarily in sentential form implies, between sense and reference. That is, discourse implies the possibility of distinguishing between *what* is said by the sentence as a whole and by the words which compose it on the one hand, and *that about which* something is said on the other. To speak is to say something about something. This polarity will play a decisive role in the second and third parts of this essay, where I shall try to connect the problem of explanation to the dimension of 'sense' or the immanent pattern of discourse, and the problems of interpretation to the dimension of 'reference', understood as the power of discourse to apply itself to an extra-linguistic reality about which it says what it says.

Fourth, discourse as an act can be considered from the viewpoint of the 'contents' of the propositional act (it predicates a certain characteristic of a certain subject), or from the viewpoint of what Austin called the 'force' of the complete act of discourse (the *speech-act* in his terminology). What is said of the subject is one thing; what I 'do' *in* saying it is another: I can make a mere description, or give an order, or formulate a wish, or give a warning, etc. Hence the polarity between the locutionary act (the act *of* saying) and the illocutionary act (what I do *in* saying). This polarity may seem less useful than the preceding ones, at least at the structural level of the metaphorical statement. Nevertheless, it will play a decisive role when we have to place the metaphor back in the concrete setting of, for example, a poem, an essay, or a work of fiction.

Before developing the dichotomy of sense and reference as the basis of the opposition between explanation and interpretation, let us introduce a final polarity which will play a decisive role in hermeneutical theory. Discourse has not merely one sort of reference but two: it is related to an extralinguistic reality, to the world or a world; and

it refers equally to its own speaker, by means of specific procedures which function only in the sentence and hence in discourse – personal pronouns, verbal tenses, demonstratives, etc. In this way, language has both a reference to reality and a self-reference. It is the same entity – the sentence – which supports this double reference: intentional and reflexive, turned towards the thing and towards the self. In fact, we should speak of a triple reference, for discourse refers as much to the one to whom it is addressed as to its own speaker. The structure of personal pronouns similarly designates, as Benveniste taught, the triple reference: 'it' designates the reference to the thing, 'you' the reference to the one to whom the discourse is addressed, and 'I' the reference to the one who speaks. As we shall see later, this connection between the two and even the three directions of reference will provide us with the key to the hermeneutical circle and the basis for our reinterpretation of this circle.

I shall list the basic polarities of discourse in the following condensed fashion: event and meaning, singular identification and general predication, propositional act and illocutionary act, sense and reference, reference to reality and reference to interlocutors. In what sense can we now say that the text and metaphor both rest upon the sort of entity which we have just called discourse?

It is easy to show that all texts are discourses, since they stem from the smallest unit of discourse, the sentence. A text is at least a series of sentences. We shall see that it must be something more in order to be a work; but it is at least a set of sentences, and consequently a discourse. The connection between metaphor and discourse requires a special justification, precisely because the definition of metaphor as a transposition affecting names or words seems to place it in a category of entities smaller than the sentence. But the semantics of the word demonstrates very clearly that words acquire an actual meaning only in a sentence and that lexical entities – the words of the dictionary – have merely potential meanings in virtue of their potential uses in typical contexts. In this respect, the theory of polysemy is a good preparation for the theory of metaphor. At the lexical level, words (if indeed they can already be called that) have more than one meaning; it is only by a specific contextual action of sifting that they realise, in a given sentence, a part of their potential semantics and acquire what we call a determinate meaning. The contextual action which enables univocal discourse to be produced with polysemic words is the model for that other contextual action whereby we draw genuinely novel metaphorical effects from words whose meaning is already codified in the vocabulary. We are thus prepared to allow that even if the meaningful effect which we call metaphor is inscribed in the word, nevertheless the origin of this effect lies in a contextual action which places the semantic fields of several words in interaction.

As regards the metaphor itself, semantics shows with the same force that the metaphorical meaning of a word is nothing which can be found in the dictionary. In this sense, we can continue to oppose metaphorical meaning to literal meaning, if by the latter we understand *any* of the meanings that can be found among the partial meanings codified by the vocabulary. By literal meaning, therefore, we do not understand the supposedly original, fundamental, primitive or proper meaning of a word on the lexical plane; rather, literal meaning is the totality of the semantic field, the set of possible contextual uses which constitutes the polysemy of a word. So even if metaphorical meaning is something more and other than the actualisation of one of the possible meanings of a polysemic word (and all of the words in natural languages are polysemic), nevertheless this metaphorical use must be solely contextual, that is, a meaning which emerges as the unique and fleeting result of a certain contextual action. We are thus led to oppose contextual changes of meaning to the lexical changes which concern the diachronic aspect of language as code or system. Metaphor is one such contextual change of meaning.

In this respect, I am partially in agreement with the modern theory of metaphor, as elaborated in English by I.A. Richards, Max Black, Monroe Beardsley, Douglas Berggren, etc.[11] More precisely, I agree with these authors on the fundamental point: a word receives a metaphorical meaning in specific contexts, within which it is opposed to other words taken literally. The shift in meaning results primarily from a clash between literal meanings, which excludes the literal use of the word in question and provides clues for finding a new meaning capable of according with the context of the sentence and rendering the sentence meaningful therein. Consequently, I retain the following points from this recent history of the problem of metaphor: the replacement of the rhetorical theory of substitution by a properly semantic theory of the interaction between seman-

tic fields; the decisive role of semantic clash leading to logical absurdity; the issuance of a particle of meaning which renders the sentence as a whole meaningful. We shall now see how this properly semantic theory – or the interaction theory – satisfies the principal characteristics which we have recognised in discourse.

To begin with, let us return to the contrast between event and meaning. In the metaphorical statement (we shall speak of metaphor as a sentence and no longer as a word), contextual action creates a new meaning which is indeed an event, since it exists only in this particular context; but at the same time, it can be repeated and hence identified as the same. Thus the innovation of an 'emergent meaning' (Beardsley) may be regarded as a linguistic creation; but if it is adopted by an influential part of the language community, it may become an everyday meaning and add to the polysemy of lexical entities, contributing thereby to the history of language as code or system. At this final stage, when the meaningful effect that we call metaphor has rejoined the change of meaning which augments polysemy, the metaphor is no longer living but dead. Only authentic, living metaphors are at the same time 'event' *and* 'meaning'.

Contextual action similarly requires our second polarity, that between singular identification and general predication. A metaphor is said of a 'principal subject'; as 'modifier' of this subject, it works like a kind of 'attribution'. All of the theories to which I have referred above rest upon this predicative structure, whether they oppose 'vehicle' to 'tenor' (Richards), 'frame' to 'focus' (Max Black), or 'modifier' to 'principal subject' (Beardsley).

To show that metaphor requires the polarity between sense and reference, we shall need a whole section of this essay; the same thing must be said of the polarity between reference to reality and reference to self. Later it will become clear why, at this stage, I am not in a position to say more about these polarities. We shall require the mediation of the theory of the text in order to discern the oppositions which do not appear so clearly within the narrow limits of a simple metaphorical statement.

Having thus delimited the field of comparison, we are ready to reply to the second question: to what extent can the explanation and interpretation of texts on the one hand, and the explanation and interpretation of metaphors on the other, be regarded as similar processes which are merely applied to two different strategic levels of discourse, the level of the work and that of the word?

II From metaphor to the text: explanation

I propose to explore a working hypothesis which, to begin with, I shall simply state. From one point of view, the understanding of metaphor can serve as a guide to the understanding of longer texts, such as a literary work. This point of view is that of explanation; it concerns only that aspect of meaning which we have called the 'sense', that is, the immanent pattern of discourse. From another point of view, the understanding of a work taken as a whole gives the key to metaphor. This other point of view is that of interpretation proper; it develops the aspect of meaning which we have called 'reference', that is, the intentional orientation towards a world and the reflexive orientation towards a self. So if we apply explanation to 'sense', as the immanent pattern of the work, then we can reserve interpretation for the sort of inquiry concerned with the *power of a work* to project a world of its own and to set in motion the hermeneutical circle, which encompasses in its spiral both the apprehension of projected worlds and the advance of self-understanding in the presence of these new worlds. Our working hypothesis thus invites us to proceed from metaphor to text at the level of 'sense' and the explanation of 'sense', then from text to metaphor at the level of the reference of a work to a world and to a self, that is, at the level of interpretation proper.

What aspects of the explanation of metaphor can serve as a paradigm for the explanation of a text? These aspects are features of the explanatory process which could not appear so long as trivial examples of metaphor were considered, such as man is a wolf, a fox, a lion (if we read the best authors on metaphor, we observe interesting variations within the bestiary which provides them with examples!). With these examples, we elude the major difficulty, that of *identifying a meaning* which is *new*. The only way of achieving this identification is to construct a meaning which alone enables us to make sense of the sentence as a whole. For what do trivial metaphors rest upon? Max Black and Monroe Beardsley note that the meaning of a word does not depend merely on the semantic and syntactic rules which govern its literal use, but also on other rules (which are nevertheless rules) to which the members of a language community are 'committed' and which determine

what Black calls the 'system of associated commonplaces' and Beardsley the 'potential range of connotations'. In the statement, 'man is a wolf' (the example favoured by Black!), the principal subject is qualified by one of the features of animal life which belongs to 'the lupine system of associated commonplaces'. The system of implications operates like a filter or screen; it does not merely select, but also accentuates new aspects of the principal subject.

What are we to think of this explanation in relation to our description of metaphor as a new meaning appearing in a new context? As I said above, I entirely agree with the 'interaction view' implied by this explanation; metaphor is more than a simple substitution whereby one word would replace a literal word, which an exhaustive paraphrase could restore to the same place. The algebraic sum of these two operations – substitution by the speaker and restoration by the author or reader – is equal to zero. No new meaning emerges and we learn nothing. As Black says, ' "interaction-metaphors" are not expendable...This use of a "subsidiary subject" to foster insight into a "principal subject" is a distinctive intellectual operation.' Hence interaction metaphors cannot be translated into direct language without 'a loss in cognitive content'.[12]

Although this account describes very well the meaningful effect of metaphor, we must ask whether, by simply adding the 'system of associated commonplaces' and cultural rules to the semantic polysemy of the word and semantic rules, this account does justice to the power of metaphor 'to inform and enlighten'. Is not the 'system of associated commonplaces' something dead or at least something already established? Of course, this system must intervene in some way or another, in order that contextual action may be regulated and that the construction of new meaning may obey some prescription. Black's theory reserves the possibility that 'metaphors can be supported by specially constructed systems of implications, as well as by accepted commonplaces'.[13] The problem is precisely that of these 'specially constructed systems of implications'. We must therefore pursue our investigation into the process of interaction itself, if we are to explain the case of new metaphors in new contexts.

Beardsley's theory of metaphor leads us a stage further in this direction. If, following him, we emphasise the role of logical absurdity or the clash between literal meanings within the same context, then we are ready to recognise the genuinely creative character of metaphorical meaning: 'In poetry, the principal tactic for obtaining this result is logical absurdity.'[14] Logical absurdity creates a situation in which we have the choice of either preserving the literal meaning of the subject and the modifier and hence concluding that the entire sentence is absurd, or attributing a new meaning to the modifier so that the sentence as a whole makes sense. We are now faced not only with 'self-contradictory' attribution, but with a 'meaningful self-contradictory' attribution. If I say 'man is a fox' (the fox has chased away the wolf!), I must slide from a literal to a metaphorical attribution if I want to save the sentence. But from where do we draw this new meaning?

As long as we ask this type of question – 'from where do we draw ...?' – we return to the same type of ineffectual answer. The 'potential range of connotations' says nothing more than the 'system of associated commonplaces'. Of course, we expand the notion of meaning by including 'secondary meanings', as connotations, within the perimeter of full meaning; but we continue to bind the creative process of metaphor to a non-creative aspect of language.

Is it sufficient to supplement this 'potential range of connotations', as Beardsley does in the 'revised verbal-opposition theory',[15] with the properties which do not yet belong to the range of connotations of my language? At first sight, this supplementation ameliorates the theory; as Beardsley forcefully says, 'metaphor transforms a *property* (actual or attributed) into a *sense*'.[16] This change is important, since it must now be said that metaphors do not merely actualise a potential connotation, but establish it 'as a staple one'; and further, 'some of [the object's] relevant properties can be given a new status as elements of verbal meaning'.[17]

However, to speak of properties of *things* (or *objects*), which are supposed not yet to have been signified, is to admit that the new, emergent meaning is not drawn from anywhere, at least not from anywhere in language (the property is an implication of things, not of words). To say that a metaphor is not drawn from anywhere is to recognise it for what it is: namely, a momentary creation of language, a semantic innovation which does not have a status in the language as something already established, whether as a designation or as a connotation.

It may be asked how we can speak of a semantic innovation, a semantic event, as a meaning capable of being identified and reidentified (that was the first criterion of discourse stated above). Only one answer remains possible: it is necessary to take the viewpoint of the hearer or the reader and to treat the novelty of the emergent meaning as the counterpart, on the author's side, of a construction on the side of the reader. Thus the process of explanation is the only access to the process of creation.

If we do not take this path, we do not really free ourselves from the theory of substitution; instead of substituting a literal meaning restored by paraphrase for the metaphorical expression, we substitute the system of connotations and commonplaces. This task must remain a preparatory one, enabling literary criticism to be reconnected to psychology and sociology. The decisive moment of explanation is the construction of a network of interactions which constitutes the context as actual and unique. In so doing, we direct our attention towards the semantic event which is produced at the point of intersection between several semantic fields. This construction is the means by which all of the words taken together make sense. Then and only then, the 'metaphorical twist' is both an event and a meaning, a meaningful event and an emergent meaning in language.

Such is the fundamental feature of explanation which makes metaphor a paradigm for the explanation of a literary work. We construct the meaning of a text in a manner similar to the way in which we make sense of all the terms of a metaphorical statement.

Why must we 'construct' the meaning of a text? First, because it is written: in the asymmetrical relation between the text and the reader, one of the partners speaks for both. Bringing a text to language is always something other than hearing someone and listening to his speech. Reading resembles instead the performance of a musical piece regulated by the written notations of the score. For the text is an autonomous space of meaning which is no longer animated by the intention of its author; the autonomy of the text, deprived of this essential support, hands writing over to the sole interpretation of the reader.

A second reason is that the text is not only something written but is a work, that is, a singular totality. As a totality, the literary work cannot be reduced to a sequence of sentences which are individually intelligible; rather, it is an architecture of themes and purposes which can be constructed in several ways. The relation of part to whole is ineluctably circular. The presupposition of a certain whole precedes the discernment of a determinate arrangement of parts; and it is by constructing the details that we build up the whole. Moreover, as the notion of singular totality suggests, a text is a kind of individual, like an animal or a work of art. Its singularity can be regained, therefore, only by progressively rectifying generic concepts which concern the class of texts, the literary genre and the various structures which intersect in this singular text. In short, understanding a work involves the sort of judgement which Kant explored in the third *Critique*.

What, then, can we say about this construction and this judgement? Here understanding a text, at the level of its articulation of sense, is strictly homologous to understanding a metaphorical statement. In both cases, it is a question of 'making sense', of producing the best overall intelligibility from an apparently discordant diversity. In both cases, the construction takes the form of a wager or guess. As Hirsch says in *Validity in Interpretation*, there are no rules for making good guesses, but there are methods for validating our guesses.[18] This dialectic between guessing and validating is the realisation at the textual level of the micro-dialectic at work in the resolution of the local enigmas of a text. In both cases, the procedures of validation have more affinity with a logic of probability than with a logic of empirical verification – more affinity, let us say, with a logic of uncertainty and qualitative probability. Validation, in this sense, is the concern of an argumentative discipline akin to the juridical procedures of legal interpretation.

We can now summarise the corresponding features which underlie the analogy between the explanation of metaphorical statements and that of a literary work as a whole. In both cases, the construction rests upon 'clues' contained in the text itself. A clue serves as a guide for a specific construction, in that it contains at once a permission and a prohibition; it excludes unsuitable constructions and allows those which give more meaning to the same words. Second, in both cases, one construction can be said to be more probable than another, but not more truthful. The more probable is that which, on the one hand, takes account of the greatest number of facts furnished by the text, including its potential connotations, and on the other hand, offers a qualitatively better convergence between the features which it takes into account. A mediocre explanation can be called narrow or forced.

Here I agree with Beardsley when he says that a good explanation satisfies two principles: the principle of congruence and that of plenitude. Until now, we have in fact spoken about the principle of congruence. The principle of plenitude will provide us with a transition to the third part of the essay. This principle may be stated as follows: 'All of the connotations which are suitable must be attributed; the poem means all that it can mean.' This principle leads us further than a mere concern with 'sense'; it already says something about reference, since it takes as a measure of plenitude the requirements stemming from an experience which demands to be said and to be equalled by the semantic density of the text. I shall say that the principle of plenitude is the corollary, at the level of meaning, of a principle of full expression which draws our investigation in a quite different direction.

A quotation from Humboldt will lead us to the threshold of this new field of investigation: 'Language as discourse (*Rede*) lies on the boundary between the expressible and the inexpressible. Its aim and its goal is to push back still further this boundary.' Interpretation, in its proper sense, similarly lies on this frontier.

III From the text to metaphor: interpretation

At the level of interpretation proper, understanding the text provides the key to understanding metaphor. Why? Because certain features of discourse begin to play an explicit role only when discourse takes the form of a literary *work*. These features are the very ones which we have placed under the heading of reference and self-reference. It will be recalled that I opposed reference to sense, saying that sense is the 'what' and reference the 'about what' of discourse. Of course, these two features can be recognised in the smallest units of language as discourse, namely in sentences. The sentence is about a situation which it expresses, and it refers back to its speaker by means of the specific procedures that we have enumerated. But reference and self-reference do not give rise to perplexing problems so long as discourse has not become a text and has not taken the form of a work. What are these problems?

Let us begin once again from the difference between written and spoken languages. In spoken language, that to which a dialogue ultimately refers is the situation common to the interlocutors, that is, the aspects of reality which can be shown or pointed to; we then say that the reference is 'ostensive'. In written language, the reference is no longer ostensive; poems, essays, works of fiction speak of things, events, states of affairs and characters which are evoked but which are not there. And yet literary texts are about something. About what? I do not hesitate to say: about a world, which is the world of the work. Far from saying that the text is without a world, I shall say that only now does man have a world and not merely a situation, a *Welt* and not merely an *Umwelt*. In the same way that the text frees its meaning from the tutelage of mental intention, so too it frees its reference from the limits of ostensive reference. For us, the world is the totality of references opened up by texts. Thus we speak of the 'world' of Greece, not to indicate what the situations were for those who experienced them, but to designate the non-situational references which outlast the effacement of the first and which then offer themselves as possible modes of being, as possible symbolic dimensions of our being-in-the-world.

The nature of reference in the context of literary works has an important consequence for the concept of interpretation. It implies that the meaning of a text lies not behind the text but in front of it. The meaning is not something hidden but something disclosed. What gives rise to understanding is that which points towards a possible world, by means of the non-ostensive references of the text. Texts speak of possible worlds and of possible ways of orientating oneself in these worlds. In this way, disclosure plays the equivalent role for written texts as ostensive reference plays in spoken language. Interpretation thus becomes the apprehension of the proposed worlds which are opened up by the non-ostensive references of the text.

This concept of interpretation expresses a decisive shift of emphasis with respect to the Romantic tradition of hermeneutics. In that tradition, the emphasis was placed on the ability of the hearer or reader to transfer himself into the spiritual life of a speaker or writer. The emphasis, from now on, is less on the other as a spiritual entity than on the world which the work unfolds. To understand is to follow the dynamic of the work, its movement from what it says to that about which it speaks. Beyond my situation as reader, beyond the situation of the author, I offer myself to the possible mode of being-in-the-world which the text opens up and discloses to me. That is what Gadamer calls the 'fusion of horizons' (*Horizontverschmelzung*) in historical knowledge.

The shift of emphasis from understanding the other to understanding the world of his work entails a corresponding shift in the conception of the 'hermeneutical circle'. For the thinkers of Romanticism, the latter term meant that the understanding of a text cannot be an objective procedure, in the sense of scientific objectivity, but that it necessarily implies a pre-understanding, expressing the way in which the reader already understands himself and his work. Hence a sort of circularity is produced between understanding the text and self-understanding. Such is, in condensed terms, the principle of the hermeneutical circle. It is easy to see how thinkers trained in the tradition of logical empiricism could only reject, as utterly scandalous, the mere idea of a hermeneutical circle and consider it to be an outrageous violation of all the canons of verifiability.

For my part, I do not wish to conceal the fact that the hermeneutical circle remains an unavoidable structure of interpretation. An interpretation is not authentic unless it culminates in some form of appropriation (*Aneignung*), if by that term we understand the process by which one makes one's own (*eigen*) what was initially other or alien (*fremd*). But I believe that the hermeneutical circle is not correctly understood when it is presented, first, as a circle between two subjectivities, that of the reader and that of the author; and second, as the projection of the subjectivity of the reader into the reading itself.

Let us correct each of these assumptions in turn. What we make our own, what we appropriate for ourselves, is not an alien experience or a distant intention, but the horizon of a world towards which a work directs itself. The appropriation of the reference is no longer modelled on the fusion of consciousnesses, on empathy or sympathy. The emergence of the sense and the reference of a text in language is the coming to language of a world and not the recognition of another person. The second correction of the Romantic concept of interpretation results from the first. If appropriation is the counterpart of disclosure, then the role of subjectivity must not be described in terms of projection. I should prefer to say that the reader understands himself in front of the text, in front of the world of the work. To understand oneself in front of a text is quite the contrary of projecting oneself and one's own beliefs and prejudices; it is to let the work and its world enlarge the horizon of the understanding which I have of myself. [...] Thus the hermeneutical circle is not repudiated but displaced from a subjectivistic level to an ontological plane. The circle is between my mode of being – beyond the knowledge which I may have of it – and the mode opened up and disclosed by the text as the world of the work.

Such is the model of interpretation which I now propose to transfer from texts, as long sequences of discourse, to the metaphor, understood as 'a poem in miniature' (Beardsley). Of course, the metaphor is too short a discourse to unfold this dialectic between the disclosure of a world and the disclosure of oneself in front of that world. Nevertheless, this dialectic points to some features of metaphor which the modern theories cited so far do not seem to take into consideration, but which were not absent from the classical theory of metaphor.

Let us return to the theory of metaphor in Aristotle's *Poetics*. Metaphor is only one of the 'parts' (*mere*) of what Aristotle calls 'diction' (*lexis*). As such, it belongs to a group of discursive procedures – using unusual words, coining new words, abbreviating or extending words – which all depart from the common (*kurion*) use of words. Now what constitutes the unity of *lexis*? Only its function in poetry. *Lexis*, in turn, is one of the 'parts' (*mere*) of tragedy, taken as the paradigm of the poetic work. In the context of the *Poetics*, tragedy represents the level of the literary work as a whole. Tragedy, in the form of a poem, has sense and reference. In Aristotle's language, the 'sense' of tragedy is secured by what he calls the 'fable' (*mythos*). We can understand the latter as the sense of tragedy because Aristotle constantly emphasises its structural characteristics. The *mythos* must have unity and coherence; it must make of the represented actions something 'whole and complete'. The *mythos* is thus the principal 'part' of tragedy, its 'essence'. All the other parts of tragedy – the 'characters', the 'thoughts', the 'delivery', the 'production' – are linked to the myth as means or conditions, or as the performance of tragedy *qua* myth. We must draw the consequence that it is only in relation to the *mythos* of tragedy that its *lexis*, and hence metaphor, make sense. There is no local meaning of metaphor outside of the regional meaning secured by the *mythos* of tragedy.

If metaphor is linked to the 'sense' of tragedy by means of its *mythos*, it is also linked to the 'reference' of tragedy in virtue of its general aim, which Aristotle calls *mimesis*.

Why do poets write tragedies, elaborate fables, use 'unusual' words such as metaphors? Because tragedy itself is connected to a more fundamental human project, that of *imitating* human actions in a *poetic* way. With these two keywords – *mimesis* and *poiesis* – we reach the level which I have called the referential world of the work. Indeed we may say that the Aristotelian concept of *mimesis* already encompasses all of the paradoxes of reference. On the one hand, it expresses a world of human actions which is already there; tragedy is destined to express human reality, to express the tragedy of life. But on the other hand, *mimesis* does not mean the duplication of reality; *mimesis* is not a copy: *mimesis* is *poiesis*, that is, construction, creation. Aristotle gives at least two indications of this creative dimension of *mimesis*. First, the fable is an original, coherent construction which attests to the creative genius of the artist. Second, tragedy is an imitation of human actions which makes them appear better, higher, more noble than they are in reality. Could we not say that *mimesis* is the Greek term for what we have called the non-ostensive reference of the literary work, or in other words, the Greek term for the disclosure of a world?

If this is right, we are now in a position to say something about the *power* of metaphor. I speak now of power and no longer of structure or even of process. The power of metaphor stems from its connection, internal to the poetic work, with three features: first, with the other procedures of the *lexis*; second, with the *fable*, which is the essence of the work, its immanent sense; and third, with the intentionality of the work as a whole, that is, with its intention to represent human actions as higher than they are in reality – and therein lies the *mimesis*. In this sense, the power of the metaphor arises from the power of the poem as a totality.

Let us apply these remarks, borrowed from Aristotle's *Poetics*, to our own description of metaphor. Could we say that the feature of metaphor which we have placed above all others – its nascent or emergent character – is linked to the function of poetry as the creative imitation of reality? Why should we invent new meanings, meanings which exist only in the instant of discourse, if it were not to serve the *poiesis* in the *mimesis*? If it is true that the poem creates a world, then it requires a language which preserves and expresses its creative power in specific contexts. By taking the *poiesis* of the poem together with metaphor as emergent meaning, we shall give sense to both at the same time, to poetry and to metaphor.

Thus the theory of interpretation paves the way for an ultimate approximation to the power of the metaphor. The priority given to the interpretation of the text in this final stage of the analysis does not mean that the relation between the two is not reciprocal. The explanation of metaphor, as a local event in the text, contributes to the interpretation of the work as a whole. We could even say that if the interpretation of local metaphors is illuminated by the interpretation of the text as a whole and by the clarification of the kind of world which the work projects, then in turn the interpretation of the poem as a whole is controlled by the explanation of the metaphor as a local phenomenon of the text.

As an example of this reciprocal relation between the regional and local aspects of the text, I shall venture to mention a possible connection, implicit in Aristotle's *Poetics*, between what he says about *mimesis* on the one hand and metaphor on the other. *Mimesis*, as we have seen, makes human actions appear higher than they are in reality; and the function of metaphor is to transpose the meanings of ordinary language by way of unusual uses. Is there not a mutual and profound affinity between the project of making human actions appear better than they are and the special procedure of metaphor which raises language above itself?

Let us express this relation in more general terms. Why should we draw new meanings from our language if we have nothing new to say, no new world to project? The creations of language would be devoid of sense unless they served the general project of letting new worlds emerge by means of poetry . . .

Allow me to conclude in a way which would be consistent with a theory of interpretation which places the emphasis on 'opening up a world'. Our conclusion should also 'open up' some new perspectives, but on what? Perhaps on the old problem of the imagination which I have carefully put aside. Are we not ready to recognise in the power of imagination, no longer the faculty of deriving 'images' from our sensory experience, but the capacity for letting new worlds shape our understanding of ourselves? This power would not be conveyed by images, but by the emergent meanings in our language. Imagination would thus be treated as a dimension of language. In this way, a new link would appear between imagination and metaphor. We shall, for the time being, refrain from entering this half-open door.

Notes

1   W. Dilthey, 'Origine et développement de l'herméneutique' (1900) in *Le Monde de l'Esprit* I (Paris: Aubier, 1947), p. 320 [English translation: 'The development of hermeneutics' in *Selected Writings*, edited and translated by H.P. Rickman (Cambridge: Cambridge University Press, 1976), p. 248].

2   Ibid., p. 333 [pp. 259–60].

3   Claude Lévi-Strauss, *Anthropologie structurale* (Paris: Plon, 1958) p. 233 [English translation: *Structural Anthropology*, translated by Claire Jacobson and Brooke Grundfest Schoepf (Harmondsworth: Penguin Books, 1968), pp. 210–11].

4   Ibid., p. 234 [p. 211].

5   Ibid., p. 239 [p. 216].

6   Ibid., p. 241 [p. 217].

7   Ibid., p. 248 [p. 224].

8   Ibid., p. 243 [p. 220].

9   See Paul Ricoeur, 'Sur l'exégèse de Genèse 1, 1–2, 4a' in Roland Barthes et al., *Exégèse et herméneutique* (Paris: Seuil, 1971), pp. 67–84.

10 G.-G. Granger, *Essai d'une philosophie du style* (Paris: A. Colin, 1968), p. 115.

11 On this subject, see: I.A. Richards, *The Philosophy of Rhetoric* (New York: Oxford University Press, 1936); Max Black, *Models and Metaphors* (Ithaca: Cornell University Press, 1962); Monroe Beardsley, *Aesthetics* (New York: Harcourt, Brace and World, 1958), and 'The metaphorical twist', *Philosophy and Phenomenological Research*, 20 (1962), pp. 293–307; Douglas Berggren, 'The use and abuse of metaphor, I and II', *Review of Metaphysics*, 16 (1962), pp. 237–58, and 16 (1963), pp. 450–72.

12 *Models and Metaphors*, p. 46.

13 Ibid., p. 43; see condition 4 in his summary, p. 44.

14 *Aesthetics*, p. 138.

15 Cf. 'The metaphorical twist'.

16 Ibid., p. 302.

17 Ibid.

18 Cf. Eric D. Hirsch, Jr, *Validity in Interpretation* (New Haven: Yale University Press, 1967), chapter 5.

Part III

Postmodernism

Introduction

The term "postmodern" first became popular in architectural and literary theory in the sixties, but it was with the publication of *The Postmodern Condition* by Jean-François Lyotard in 1978 that the term assumed the status of a properly philosophical notion. Lyotard defined postmodernism as an "incredulity towards metanarratives" – in particular those of Western metaphysics, Christian messianism, Enlightenment Reason, and Marxist-Hegelian dialectics. In lieu of such totalizing worldviews, postmodernism endorses the modest proliferation of "little narratives," a bricolage of stories and images celebrating difference, plurality, and paradox. If modernity's proud pretension to ineluctable progress has been shattered by the horrors of Auschwitz, Hiroshima, and the Gulag, an alternative postmodern paradigm appears to be emerging from its ashes. Though, Lyotard stresses, the "post-" should be read here not as some chronological sequel to modernity but rather as an invitation to rework its nascent, hidden, or forgotten stories. For Lyotard, as for many other practictioners of the postmodern, some of the most powerful testimonies to this re-creation are to be found in art.

Under the postmodern dispensation, art and aesthetics cease to occupy the elite confines of an exclusively high culture and descend into the byways of popular entertainment culture – an expanded space of inquiry which in turn solicits its own kind of academic response: that specific crossing of disciplines which has come to be known as "cultural studies." Roland Barthes has proved to be one of the most influential avatars of this postmodern turn with his dramatic announcement of the "death of the author." Extrapolating the structuralist thesis that in texts "no one speaks," Barthes claims that the demise of the illusory bourgeois subject, controlling and dominating the discourse of his or her text, marks the birth of multiple readers and readings, each one as legitimate as the next. Barthes resolves to explode the old notions of knowledge and truth, replacing them with the excesses of textual play and pleasure. And there is no better place for such subversive activity, he insists, than the free realm of aesthetic experimentation.

Where Barthes's chosen examples are primarily literary, Foucault turns the structuralist prism on the art of painting. Analysing René Magritte's celebrated tableau of a pipe, bearing the title *This Is Not a Pipe*, Foucault sees it as a harbinger of the postmodern separation of images from meanings, signalling the loss of given identity. Images which were traditionally thought to "resemble" reality are converted into mere copies of copies with no fixed origin or end – a tendency borne out, for Foucault, in Andy Warhol's multi-series of Coca-Cola and Campbell soup advertisements.

Hélène Cixous's landmark essay, "The Laugh of the Medusa," published in 1975, extended the structuralist and post-structuralist celebration of the plural text to the specific question of "women's writing." Woman must learn to write herself into literature, from which she has been traditionally exiled, Cixous argues. And such a writing will open a new mode of "invention" where the "signifier" is emancipated from the patriarchal authority of the "signified." This deeply poetic text reads as a manifesto for a new postmodern feminism, extending beyond the limits of norm and theory toward a limitless play of differences. Together with Luce Irigaray and Julia Kristeva, Cixous represents a highly challenging turn in continental feminism.

Umberto Eco opens yet another front on the postmodern civilization of signs and images. Though originally known for his writings on Thomist aesthetics, this Italian polymath soon struck out in new directions, authoring a number of best-selling postmodern novels – notably *The Name of the Rose* – and applying contemporary semiotic methods to readings of popular culture. The extract in this volume, "Travels in Hyperreality," details Eco's critical and comic exploration of some of the most excessive images of our postmodern entertainment industry, from holographic voyeurism and comic-strip fetishes to kitsch museums and hyperrealist replicas. All of these pseudo-images serve, for Eco, to illustrate the postmodern motto: "We are giving you the reproduction so you will no longer feel any need for the original."

Jean Baudrillard's essay may be read as something of a companion piece to Eco's, in that it provides a more theoretical and historical account of the genesis and emergence of the postmodern phenomenon of "simulation." Tracing the genealogy of the fake image from the classical paradigm of "counterfeit" and the modern schema of industrial "production," Baudrillard concludes his analysis with a startling description of cybernetic and digital simulations, where the old contrasts between true and false, real and imaginary, are abolished. The postmodern era of the simulacrum is one where models replace originals. "For opinions as for material goods: production is dead, long live reproduction." Baudrillard offers several concrete descriptions of this phenomena, including the Twin Trade Towers in New York and the larger-than-life simulations of Disneyland.

Though he repudiates the term itself, Derrida is no doubt one of the most cited exponents of a postmodern approach to art and literature. Curiously, the figures that Derrida comments on most are avant-garde modernists like James Joyce,

Stéphane Mallarmé, Vincent Van Gogh, or Jean Genet, rather than postmodernists *per se*. But this does not diminish the postmodern implications of Derrida's deconstructive readings. Indeed one might say that the deconstruction of modernism is itself a postmodernist gesture. The text selected for this anthology, "Economimesis", features a detailed deconstructive analysis of some of the key categories of Kant's aesthetic theory – genius, taste, production, fine art, imagination, play, and, above all, "imitation." Derrida points out that while Kant appears to be enunciating the romantic-idealist liberation of productive imagination from nature, he is in fact reinscribing aesthetic creation ever more firmly in the economy of imitation and repetition. So that Kant, the founder of modern aesthetics, turns out to be, in spite of himself, a crypto-postmodernist *avant la lettre*.

Derrida's deconstruction of the canons of modern aesthetics is deeply indebted to the pioneering work of Maurice Blanchot. Of special importance to Derrida, and indeed the movement of postmodern criticism as a whole, is Blanchot's distinction between the "book" as a closed masterpiece or narrative totality, and the "text" as a work of infinite unworking (*désoeuvrement*) – as an exigency of "writing" that exceeds every law opening us to a radical exteriority of meaning. Whereas the book was essentially theological – "God only remains God in so far as he speaks through the book" – postmodern writing exposes us to the disaster and risk of an "insane game." Our extract here from Blanchot's highly influential work, *The Absence of the Book*, provides a characteristic sample of his provocative thinking.

We conclude our anthology with an extract from Kristeva's *Black Sun*, entitled "The Malady of Grief." This close textual study of several contemporary novels and films by Marguerite Duras displays Kristeva's original deployment of several postmodern methods – from semiotics and deconstruction to post-Lacanian psychoanalysis and neo-feminist critique. Her culminating reflections on the apocalyptic character of our postmodern culture, dominated by the "artifice of seeming" and "distraction of parody," sound a note of defiance against the reign of "mirror games."

22

Note on the Meaning of the Word "Post" and Answering the Question "What is Postmodernism?"

Jean-François Lyotard

Note on the Meaning of "Post-"

I would like to pass on to you a few thoughts that are merely intended to raise certain problems concerning the term "postmodern," without wanting to resolve them. By doing this, I do not want to close the debate but rather to situate it, in order to avoid confusion and ambiguity. I have just three points to make.

First, the opposition between postmodernism and modernism, or the modern movement (1910–45) in architecture. According to Portoghesi, the rupture of postmodernism consists in an abrogation of the hegemony of Euclidean geometry (its sublimation in the plastic poetics of "de Stijl," for example). To follow Gregotti, the difference between modernism and postmodernism would be better characterized by the following feature: the disappearance of the close bond that once linked the project of modern architecture to an ideal of the progressive realization of social and individual emancipation encompassing all humanity. Postmodern architecture finds itself condemned to undertake a series of minor modifications in a space inherited from modernity, condemned to abandon a global reconstruction of the space of human habitation. The perspective then opens onto a vast landscape, in the sense that there is no longer any horizon of universality, universalization, or general emancipation to greet the eye of postmodern man, least of all the eye of the architect. The disappearance of the Idea that rationality and freedom are progressing would explain a "tone," style, or mode specific to postmodern

architecture. I would say it is a sort of "bricolage": the multiple quotation of elements taken from earlier styles or periods, classical and modern; disregard for the environment; and so on.

One point about this perspective is that the "post-" of postmodernism has the sense of a simple succession, a diachronic sequence of periods in which each one is clearly identifiable. The "post-" indicates something like a conversion: a new direction from the previous one.

Now this idea of a linear chronology is itself perfectly "modern." It is at once part of Christianity, Cartesianism, and Jacobinism: since we are inaugurating something completely new, the hands of the clock should be put back to zero. The very idea of modernity is closely correlated with the principle that it is both possible and necessary to break with tradition and institute absolutely new ways of living and thinking.

We now suspect that this "rupture" is in fact a way of forgetting or repressing the past, that is, repeating it and not surpassing it.

I would say that, in the "new" architecture, the quotation of motifs taken from earlier architectures relies on a procedure analogous to the way dream work uses diurnal residues left over from life past, as outlined by Freud in *The Interpretation of Dreams* (*Traumdeutung*). This destiny of repetition and quotation – whether it is taken up ironically, cynically, or naively – is in any event obvious if we think of the tendencies that at present dominate painting, under the names of transavantgardism, neoexpressionism, and so forth. I will return to this a bit later.

This departure from architectural "postmodernism" leads me to a second connotation of the term "postmodern" (and I have to admit that I am no stranger to its misunderstanding).

The general idea is a trivial one. We can observe and establish a kind of decline in the confidence that, for two centuries, the West invested in the principle of a general progress in humanity. This idea of a possible, probable, or necessary progress is rooted in the belief that developments made in the arts, technology, knowledge, and freedoms would benefit humanity as a whole. It is true that ascertaining the identity of the subject who suffered most from a lack of development – the poor, the worker, or the illiterate – continued to be an issue throughout the nineteenth and twentieth centuries. As you know, there was controversy and even war between liberals, conservatives, and "leftists" over the true name to be given to the subject whose emancipation required assistance. Yet all these tendencies were united in the belief that initiatives, discoveries, and institutions only had legitimacy insofar as they contributed to the emancipation of humanity.

After two centuries we have become more alert to signs that would indicate an opposing movement. Neither liberalism (economic and political) nor the various Marxisms have emerged from these bloodstained centuries without attracting accusations of having perpetrated crimes against humanity. We could make a list of proper names – places, people, dates – capable of illustrating or substantiating our suspicions. Following Theodor Adorno, I have used the name "Auschwitz" to signify just how impoverished recent Western history seems from the point of view of the "modern" project of the emancipation of humanity. What kind of thought is capable of "relieving" Auschwitz – relieving (relever) in the sense of aufheben – capable of situating it in a general, empirical, or even speculative process directed toward universal emancipation? There is a sort of grief in the Zeitgeist. It can find expression in reactive, even reactionary, attitudes or in utopias – but not in a positive orientation that would open up a new perspective.

Technoscientific development has become a means of deepening the malaise rather than allaying it. It is no longer possible to call development progress. It seems to proceed of its own accord, with a force, an autonomous motoricity that is independent of us. It does not answer to demands issuing from human needs. On the contrary,

human entities – whether social or individual – always seem destabilized by the results and implications of development. I am thinking of its intellectual and mental results as well as its material results. We could say that humanity's condition has become one of chasing after the process of the accumulation of new objects (both of practice and of thought).

As you might imagine, understanding the reason for this process of complexification is an important question for me – an obscure question. We could say there exists a sort of destiny, or involuntary destination toward a condition that is increasingly complex. The needs for security, identity, and happiness springing from our immediate condition as living beings, as social beings, now seem irrelevant next to this sort of constraint to complexify, mediatize, quantify, synthesize, and modify the size of each and every object. We are like Gullivers in the world of technoscience: sometimes too big, sometimes too small, but never the right size. From this perspective, the insistence on simplicity generally seems today like a pledge to barbarism.

On this same point, the following issue also has to be elaborated. Humanity is divided into two parts. One faces the challenge of complexity, the other that ancient and terrible challenge of its own survival. This is perhaps the most important aspect of the failure of the modern project – a project that, need I remind you, once applied in principle to the whole of humanity.

I will give my third point – the most complex – the shortest treatment. The question of postmodernity is also, or first of all, a question of expressions of thought: in art, literature, philosophy, politics.

We know that in the domain of art, for example, or more precisely in the visual and plastic arts, the dominant view today is that the great movement of the avant-gardes is over and done with. It has, as it were, become the done thing to indulge or deride the avant-gardes – to regard them as the expression of an outdated modernity.

I do not like the term avant-garde, with its military connotations, any more than anyone else. But I do observe that the true process of avant-gardism was in reality a kind of work, a long, obstinate, and highly responsible work concerned with investigating the assumptions implicit in modernity. I mean that for a proper understanding of the work of modern painters, from, say, Manet to Duchamp or Barnett Newman, we would have to compare their work with anamnesis, in the sense of a psychoanalytic therapy. Just as patients try to elaborate their current problems by freely associating apparently inconsequential details with past situations – allowing them to uncover hidden meanings in their lives and their behavior – so we can think of the work of Cézanne, Picasso, Delaunay, Kandinsky, Klee, Mondrian, Malevich, and finally Duchamp as a working through (*durcharbeiten*) performed by modernity on its own meaning.

If we abandon that responsibility, we will surely be condemned to repeat, without any displacement, the West's "modern neurosis" – its schizophrenia, paranoia, and so on, the source of the misfortunes we have known for two centuries.

You can see that when it is understood in this way, the "post-" of "postmodern" does not signify a movement of *comeback*, *flashback*, or *feedback*, that is, not a movement of repetition but a procedure in "ana-": a procedure of analysis, anamnesis, anagogy, and anamorphosis that elaborates an "initial forgetting."

[. . .]

Answering the Question: What Is Postmodernism?

A Demand

This is a period of slackening – I refer to the color of the times. From every direction we are being urged to put an end to experimentation, in the arts and elsewhere. I have read an art historian who extols realism and is militant for the advent of a new subjectivity. I have read an art critic who packages and sells "Transavantgardism" in the marketplace of painting. I have read that under the name of postmodernism, architects are getting rid of the Bauhaus project, throwing out the baby of experimentation with the bathwater of functionalism. I have read that a new philosopher is discovering what he drolly calls Judaeo-Christianism, and intends by it to put an end to the impiety which we are supposed to have spread. I have read in a French weekly that some are displeased with *Mille Plateaux* [by Deleuze and Guattari] because they expect, especially when reading a work of philosophy, to be gratified with a little sense. I have read from the pen of a reputable historian that writers and thinkers of the 1960 and 1970 avant-gardes spread a reign of terror in the use of language, and that the conditions for a

fruitful exchange must be restored by imposing on the intellectuals a common way of speaking, that of the historians. I have been reading a young philosopher of language who complains that Continental thinking, under the challenge of speaking machines, has surrendered to the machines the concern for reality, that it has substituted for the referential paradigm that of "adlinguisticity" (one speaks about speech, writes about writing, intertextuality), and who thinks that the time has now come to restore a solid anchorage of language in the referent. I have read a talented theatrologist for whom postmodernism, with its games and fantasies, carries very little weight in front of political authority, especially when a worried public opinion encourages authority to a politics of totalitarian surveillance in the face of nuclear warfare threats.

I have read a thinker of repute who defends modernity against those he calls the neoconservatives. Under the banner of postmodernism, the latter would like, he believes, to get rid of the uncompleted project of modernism, that of the Enlightenment. Even the last advocates of *Aufklärung*, such as Popper or Adorno, were only able, according to him, to defend the project in a few particular spheres of life – that of politics for the author of *The Open Society*, and that of art for the author of *Ästhetische Theorie*. Jürgen Habermas (everyone had recognized him) thinks that if modernity has failed, it is in allowing the totality of life to be splintered into independent specialities which are left to the narrow competence of experts, while the concrete individual experiences "desublimated meaning" and "destructured form," not as a liberation but in the mode of that immense *ennui* which Baudelaire described over a century ago.

Following a prescription of Albrecht Wellmer, Habermas considers that the remedy for this splintering of culture and its separation from life can only come from "changing the status of aesthetic experience when it is no longer primarily expressed in judgments of taste," but when it is "used to explore a living historical situation," that is, when "it is put in relation with problems of existence." For this experience then "becomes a part of a language game which is no longer that of aesthetic criticism"; it takes part "in cognitive processes and normative expectations"; "it alters the manner in which those different moments *refer* to one another." What Habermas requires from the arts and the experiences they provide is, in short, to bridge the gap between cognitive, ethical, and political discourses, thus opening the way to a unity of experience.

My question is to determine what sort of unity Habermas has in mind. Is the aim of the project of modernity the constitution of sociocultural unity within which all the elements of daily life and of thought would take their places as in an organic whole? Or does the passage that has to be charted between heterogeneous language games – those of cognition, of ethics, of politics – belong to a different order from that? And if so, would it be capable of effecting a real synthesis between them?

The first hypothesis, of a Hegelian inspiration, does not challenge the notion of a dialectically totalizing *experience*; the second is closer to the spirit of Kant's *Critique of Judgment*; but must be submitted, like the *Critique*, to that severe re-examination which postmodernity imposes on the thought of the Enlightenment, on the idea of a unitary end of history and of a subject. It is this critique which not only Wittgenstein and Adorno have initiated, but also a few other thinkers (French or other) who do not have the honor to be read by Professor Habermas – which at least saves them from getting a poor grade for their neoconservatism.

Realism

The demands I began by citing are not all equivalent. They can even be contradictory. Some are made in the name of postmodernism, others in order to combat it. It is not necessarily the same thing to formulate a demand for some referent (and objective reality), for some sense (and credible transcendence), for an addressee (and audience), or an addressor (and subjective expressiveness) or for some communicational consensus (and a general code of exchanges, such as the genre of historical discourse). But in the diverse invitations to suspend artistic experimentation, there is an identical call for order, a desire for unity, for identity, for security, or popularity (in the sense of *Öffentlichkeit*, of "finding a public"). Artists and writers must be brought back into the bosom of the community, or at least, if the latter is considered to be ill, they must be assigned the task of healing it.

There is an irrefutable sign of this common disposition: it is that for all those writers nothing is more urgent than to liquidate the heritage of the avant-gardes. Such is the case, in particular, of the so-called transavantgardism. The answers given by

Achille Bonito Oliva to the questions asked by Bernard Lamarche-Vadel and Michel Enric leave no room for doubt about this. By putting the avant-gardes through a mixing process, the artist and critic feel more confident that they can suppress them than by launching a frontal attack. For they can pass off the most cynical eclecticism as a way of going beyond the fragmentary character of the preceding experiments; whereas if they openly turned their backs on them, they would run the risk of appearing ridiculously neoacademic. The *Salons* and the *Académies*, at the time when the bourgeoisie was establishing itself in history, were able to function as purgation and to grant awards for good plastic and literary conduct under the cover of realism. But capitalism inherently possesses the power to derealize familiar objects, social roles, and institutions to such a degree that the so-called realistic representations can no longer evoke reality except as nostalgia or mockery, as an occasion for suffering rather than for satisfaction. Classicism seems to be ruled out in a world in which reality is so destabilized that it offers no occasion for experience but one for ratings and experimentation.

This theme is familiar to all readers of Walter Benjamin. But it is necessary to assess its exact reach. Photography did not appear as a challenge to painting from the outside, any more than industrial cinema did to narrative literature. The former was only putting the final touch to the program of ordering the visible elaborated by the quattrocento; while the latter was the last step in rounding off diachronies as organic wholes, which had been the ideal of the great novels of education since the eighteenth century. That the mechanical and the industrial should appear as substitutes for hand or craft was not in itself a disaster – except if one believes that art is in its essence the expression of an individuality of genius assisted by an elite craftsmanship.

The challenge lay essentially in that photographic and cinematographic processes can accomplish better, faster, and with a circulation a hundred thousand times larger than narrative or pictorial realism, the task which academicism had assigned to realism: to preserve various consciousnesses from doubt. Industrial photography and cinema will be superior to painting and the novel whenever the objective is to stabilize the referent, to arrange it according to a point of view which endows it with a recognizable meaning, to reproduce the syntax and vocabulary which enable the addressee to decipher images and sequences quickly, and so to arrive easily at the consciousness of his own identity as well as the approval which he thereby receives from others – since such structures of images and sequences constitute a communication code among all of them. This is the way the effects of reality, or if one prefers, the fantasies of realism, multiply.

If they too do not wish to become supporters (of minor importance at that) of what exists, the painter and novelist must refuse to lend themselves to such therapeutic uses. They must question the rules of the art of painting or of narrative as they have learned and received them from their predecessors. Soon those rules must appear to them as a means to deceive, to seduce, and to reassure, which makes it impossible for them to be "true." Under the common name of painting and literature, an unprecedented split is taking place. Those who refuse to reexamine the rules of art pursue successful careers in mass conformism by communicating, by means of the "correct rules," the endemic desire for reality with objects and situations capable of gratifying it. Pornography is the use of photography and film to such an end. It is becoming a general model for the visual or narrative arts which have not met the challenge of the mass media.

As for the artists and writers who question the rules of plastic and narrative arts and possibly share their suspicions by circulating their work, they are destined to have little credibility in the eyes of those concerned with "reality" and "identity"; they have no guarantee of an audience. Thus it is possible to ascribe the dialectics of the avant-gardes to the challenge posed by the realisms of industry and mass communication to painting and the narrative arts. Duchamp's "ready made" does nothing but actively and parodistically signify this constant process of dispossession of the craft of painting or even of being an artist. As Thierry de Duve penetratingly observes, the modern aesthetic question is not "What is beautiful?" but "What can be said to be art (and literature)?"

Realism, whose only definition is that it intends to avoid the question of reality implicated in that of art, always stands somewhere between academicism and kitsch. When power assumes the name of a party, realism and its neoclassical complement triumph over the experimental avant-garde by slandering and banning it – that is, provided the "correct" images, the "correct" narratives, the "correct" forms which the party requests, selects,

and propagates can find a public to desire them as the appropriate remedy for the anxiety and depression that public experiences. The demand for reality – that is, for unity, simplicity, communicability, etc. – did not have the same intensity nor the same continuity in German society between the two world wars and in Russian society after the Revolution: this provides a basis for a distinction between Nazi and Stalinist realism.

What is clear, however, is that when it is launched by the political apparatus, the attack on artistic experimentation is specifically reactionary: aesthetic judgment would only be required to decide whether such or such work is in conformity with the established rules of the beautiful. Instead of the work of art having to investigate what makes it an art object and whether it will be able to find an audience, political academicism possesses and imposes a priori criteria of the beautiful, which designate some works and a public at a stroke and forever. The use of categories in aesthetic judgment would thus be of the same nature as in cognitive judgment. To speak like Kant, both would be determining judgments: the expression is "well formed" first in the understanding, then the only cases retained in experience are those which can be subsumed under this expression.

When power is that of capital and not that of a party, the "transavantgardist" or "postmodern" (in Jencks's sense) solution proves to be better adapted than the antimodern solution. Eclecticism is the degree zero of contemporary general culture: one listens to reggae, watches a western, eats McDonald's food for lunch and local cuisine for dinner, wears Paris perfume in Tokyo and "retro" clothes in Hong Kong; knowledge is a matter for TV games. It is easy to find a public for eclectic works. By becoming kitsch, art panders to the confusion which reigns in the "taste" of the patrons. Artists, gallery owners, critics, and public wallow together in the "anything goes," and the epoch is one of slackening. But this realism of the "anything goes" is in fact that of money; in the absence of aesthetic criteria, it remains possible and useful to assess the value of works of art according to the profits they yield. Such realism accommodates all tendencies, just as capital accommodates all "needs," providing that the tendencies and needs have purchasing power. As for taste, there is no need to be delicate when one speculates or entertains oneself.

Artistic and literary research is doubly threatened, once by the "cultural policy" and once by the art and book market. What is advised, sometimes through one channel, sometimes through the other, is to offer works which, first, are relative to subjects which exist in the eyes of the public they address, and second, works so made ("well made") that the public will recognize what they are about, will understand what is signified, will be able to give or refuse its approval knowingly, and if possible, even to derive from such work a certain amount of comfort.

The interpretation which has just been given of the contact between the industrial and mechanical arts, and literature and the fine arts is correct in its outline, but it remains narrowly sociologizing and historicizing – in other words, one-sided. Stepping over Benjamin's and Adorno's reticences, it must be recalled that science and industry are no more free of the suspicion which concerns reality than are art and writing. To believe otherwise would be to entertain an excessively humanistic notion of the mephistophelian functionalism of sciences and technologies. There is no denying the dominant existence today of techno-science, that is, the massive subordination of cognitive statements to the finality of the best possible performance, which is the technological criterion. But the mechanical and the industrial, especially when they enter fields traditionally reserved for artists, are carrying with them much more than power effects. The objects and the thoughts which originate in scientific knowledge and the capitalist economy convey with them one of the rules which supports their possibility: the rule that there is no reality unless testified by a consensus between partners over a certain knowledge and certain commitments.

This rule is of no little consequence. It is the imprint left on the politics of the scientist and the trustee of capital by a kind of flight of reality out of the metaphysical, religious, and political certainties that the mind believed it held. This withdrawal is absolutely necessary to the emergence of science and capitalism. No industry is possible without a suspicion of the Aristotelian theory of motion, no industry without a refutation of corporatism, of mercantilism, and of physiocracy. Modernity, in whatever age it appears, cannot exist without a shattering of belief and without discovery of the "lack of reality" of reality, together with the invention of other realities.

What does this "lack of reality" signify if one tries to free it from a narrowly historicized inter-

pretation? The phrase is of course akin to what Nietzsche calls nihilism. But I see a much earlier modulation of Nietzschean perspectivism in the Kantian theme of the sublime. I think in particular that it is in the aesthetic of the sublime that modern art (including literature) finds its impetus and the logic of avant-gardes finds its axioms.

The sublime sentiment, which is also the sentiment of the sublime, is, according to Kant, a strong and equivocal emotion: it carries with it both pleasure and pain. Better still, in it pleasure derives from pain. Within the tradition of the subject, which comes from Augustine and Descartes and which Kant does not radically challenge, this contradiction, which some would call neurosis or masochism, develops as a conflict between the faculties of a subject, the faculty to conceive of something and the faculty to "present" something. Knowledge exists if, first, the statement is intelligible, and second, if "cases" can be derived from the experience which "corresponds" to it. Beauty exists if a certain "case" (the work of art), given first by the sensibility without any conceptual determination, the sentiment of pleasure independent of any interest the work may elicit, appeals to the principle of a universal consensus (which may never be attained).

Taste, therefore, testifies that between the capacity to conceive and the capacity to present an object corresponding to the concept, an undetermined agreement, without rules, giving rise to a judgment which Kant calls reflective, may be experienced as pleasure. The sublime is a different sentiment. It takes place, on the contrary, when the imagination fails to present an object which might, if only in principle, come to match a concept. We have the Idea of the world (the totality of what is), but we do not have the capacity to show an example of it. We have the Idea of the simple (that which cannot be broken down, decomposed), but we cannot illustrate it with a sensible object which would be a "case" of it. We can conceive the infinitely great, the infinitely powerful, but every presentation of an object destined to "make visible" this absolute greatness or power appears to us painfully inadequate. Those are Ideas of which no presentation is possible. Therefore, they impart no knowledge about reality (experience); they also prevent the free union of the faculties which gives rise to the sentiment of the beautiful; and they prevent the formation and the stabilization of taste. They can be said to be unpresentable.

I shall call modern the art which devotes its "little technical expertise" (*son "petit technique"*), as Diderot used to say, to present the fact that the unpresentable exists. To make visible that there is something which can be conceived and which can neither be seen nor made visible: this is what is at stake in modern painting. But how to make visible that there is something which cannot be seen? Kant himself shows the way when he names "formlessness, the absence of form," as a possible index to the unpresentable. He also says of the empty "abstraction" which the imagination experiences when in search for a presentation of the infinite (another unpresentable): this abstraction itself is like a presentation of the infinite, its "negative presentation." He cites the commandment, "Thou shalt not make graven images" (*Exodus*), as the most sublime passage in the Bible in that it forbids all presentation of the Absolute. Little needs to be added to those observations to outline an aesthetic of sublime paintings. As painting, it will of course "present" something though negatively; it will therefore avoid figuration or representation. It will be "white" like one of Malevitch's squares; it will enable us to see only by making it impossible to see; it will please only by causing pain. One recognizes in those instructions the axioms of avant-gardes in painting, inasmuch as they devote themselves to making an allusion to the unpresentable by means of visible presentations. The systems in the name of which, or with which, this task has been able to support or to justify itself deserve the greatest attention; but they can originate only in the vocation of the sublime in order to legitimize it, that is, to conceal it. They remain inexplicable without the incommensurability of reality to concept which is implied in the Kantian philosophy of the sublime.

It is not my intention to analyze here in detail the manner in which the various avant-gardes have, so to speak, humbled and disqualified reality by examining the pictorial techniques which are so many devices to make us believe in it. Local tone, drawing, the mixing of colors, linear perspective, the nature of the support and that of the instrument, the treatment, the display, the museum: the avant-gardes are perpetually flushing out artifices of presentation which make it possible to subordinate thought to the gaze and to turn it away from the unpresentable. If Habermas, like Marcuse, understands this task of derealization as an aspect of the (repressive) "desublimation" which characterizes the avant-garde, it is because he confuses the Kantian sublime with Freudian sublimation, and because aesthetics has remained for him that of the beautiful.

The Postmodern

What, then, is the postmodern? What place does it or does it not occupy in the vertiginous work of the questions hurled at the rules of image and narration? It is undoubtedly a part of the modern. All that has been received, if only yesterday (*modo, modo*, Petronius used to say), must be suspected. What space does Cézanne challenge? The Impressionists'. What object do Picasso and Braque attack? Cézanne's. What presupposition does Duchamp break with in 1912? That which says one must make a painting, be it cubist. And Buren questions that other presupposition which he believes had survived untouched by the work of Duchamp: the place of presentation of the work. In an amazing acceleration, the generations precipitate themselves. A work can become modern only if it is first postmodern. Postmodernism thus understood is not modernism at its end but in the nascent state, and this state is constant.

Yet I would like not to remain with this slightly mechanistic meaning of the word. If it is true that modernity takes place in the withdrawal of the real and according to the sublime relation between the presentable and the conceivable, it is possible, within this relation, to distinguish two modes (to use the musician's language). The emphasis can be placed on the powerlessness of the faculty of presentation, on the nostalgia for presence felt by the human subject, on the obscure and futile will which inhabits him in spite of everything. The emphasis can be placed, rather, on the power of the faculty to conceive, on its "inhumanity" so to speak (it was the quality Apollinaire demanded of modern artists), since it is not the business of our understanding whether or not human sensibility or imagination can match what it conceives. The emphasis can also be placed on the increase of being and the jubilation which result from the invention of new rules of the game, be it pictorial, artistic, or any other. What I have in mind will become clear if we dispose very schematically a few names on the chessboard of the history of avant-gardes: on the side of melancholia, the German Expressionists, and on the side of *novatio*, Braque and Picasso, on the former Malevitch and on the latter Lissitsky, on the one Chirico and on the other Duchamp. The nuance which distinguishes these two modes may be infinitesimal; they often coexist in the same piece, are almost indistinguishable; and yet they testify to a difference (*un différend*) on which the fate of thought depends and will depend for a long time, between regret and assay.

The work of Proust and that of Joyce both allude to something which does not allow itself to be made present. Allusion, to which Paolo Fabbri recently called my attention, is perhaps a form of expression indispensable to the works which belong to an aesthetic of the sublime. In Proust, what is being eluded as the price to pay for this allusion is the identity of consciousness, a victim to the excess of time (*au trop de temps*). But in Joyce, it is the identity of writing which is the victim of an excess of the book (*au trop de livre*) or of literature.

Proust calls forth the unpresentable by means of a language unaltered in its syntax and vocabulary and of a writing which in many of its operators still belongs to the genre of novelistic narration. The literary institution, as Proust inherits it from Balzac and Flaubert, is admittedly subverted in that the hero is no longer a character but the inner consciousness of time, and in that the diegetic diachrony, already damaged by Flaubert, is here put in question because of the narrative voice. Nevertheless, the unity of the book, the odyssey of that consciousness, even if it is deferred from chapter to chapter, is not seriously challenged: the identity of the writing with itself throughout the labyrinth of the interminable narration is enough to connote such unity, which has been compared to that of *The Phenomenology of Mind*.

Joyce allows the unpresentable to become perceptible in his writing itself, in the signifier. The whole range of available narrative and even stylistic operators is put into play without concern for the unity of the whole, and new operators are tried. The grammar and vocabulary of literary language are no longer accepted as given; rather, they appear as academic forms, as rituals originating in piety (as Nietzsche said) which prevent the unpresentable from being put forward.

Here, then, lies the difference: modern aesthetics is an aesthetic of the sublime, though a nostalgic one. It allows the unpresentable to be put forward only as the missing contents; but the form, because of its recognizable consistency, continues to offer to the reader or viewer matter for solace and pleasure. Yet these sentiments do not constitute the real sublime sentiment, which is in an intrinsic combination of pleasure and pain: the pleasure that reason should exceed all presentation, the pain that imagination or sensibility should not be equal to the concept.

The postmodern would be that which, in the modern, puts forward the unpresentable in presentation itself; that which denies itself the solace of good forms, the consensus of a taste which would make it possible to share collectively the nostalgia for the unattainable; that which searches for new presentations, not in order to enjoy them but in order to impart a stronger sense of the unpresentable. A postmodern artist or writer is in the position of a philosopher: the text he writes, the work he produces are not in principle governed by preestablished rules, and they cannot be judged according to a determining judgment, by applying familiar categories to the text or to the work. Those rules and categories are what the work of art itself is looking for. The artist and the writer, then, are working without rules in order to formulate the rules of what *will have been done*. Hence the fact that work and text have the characters of an *event*; hence also, they always come too late for their author, or, what amounts to the same thing, their being put into work, their realization (*mise en oeuvre*) always begin too soon. *Post modern* would have to be understood according to the paradox of the future (*post*) anterior (*modo*).

It seems to me that the essay (Montaigne) is postmodern, while the fragment (*The Athaeneum*) is modern.

Finally, it must be clear that it is our business not to supply reality but to invent allusions to the conceivable which cannot be presented. And it is not to be expected that this task will effect the last reconciliation between language games (which, under the name of faculties, Kant knew to be separated by a chasm), and that only the transcendental illusion (that of Hegel) can hope to totalize them into a real unity. But Kant also knew that the price to pay for such an illusion is terror. The nineteenth and twentieth centuries have given us as much terror as we can take. We have paid a high enough price for the nostalgia of the whole and the one, for the reconciliation of the concept and the sensible, of the transparent and the communicable experience. Under the general demand for slackening and for appeasement, we can hear the mutterings of the desire for a return of terror, for the realization of the fantasy to seize reality. The answer is: Let us wage a war on totality; let us be witnesses to the unpresentable; let us activate the differences and save the honor of the name.

23

The Death of the Author

Roland Barthes

In his story *Sarrasine* Balzac, describing a castrato disguised as a woman, writes the following sentence: '*This was woman herself, with her sudden fears, her irrational whims, her instinctive worries, her impetuous boldness, her fussings, and her delicious sensibility.*' Who is speaking thus? Is it the hero of the story bent on remaining ignorant of the castrato hidden beneath the woman? Is it Balzac the individual, furnished by his personal experience with a philosophy of Woman? Is it Balzac the author professing 'literary' ideas on femininity? Is it universal wisdom? Romantic psychology? We shall never know, for the good reason that writing is the destruction of every voice, of every point of origin. Writing is that neutral, composite, oblique space where our subject slips away, the negative where all identity is lost, starting with the very identity of the body writing.

No doubt it has always been that way. As soon as a fact is *narrated* no longer with a view to acting directly on reality but intransitively, that is to say, finally outside of any function other than that of the very practice of the symbol itself, this disconnection occurs, the voice loses its origin, the author enters into his own death, writing begins. The sense of this phenomenon, however, has varied; in ethnographic societies the responsibility for a narrative is never assumed by a person but by a mediator, shaman or relator whose 'performance' – the mastery of the narrative code – may possibly be admired but never his 'genius'. The author is a modern figure, a product of our society insofar as, emerging from the Middle Ages with English empiricism, French rationalism and the personal faith of the Reforma-

tion, it discovered the prestige of the individual, of, as it is more nobly put, the 'human person'. It is thus logical that in literature it should be this positivism, the epitome and culmination of capitalist ideology, which has attached the greatest importance to the 'person' of the author. The *author* still reigns in histories of literature, biographies of writers, interviews, magazines, as in the very consciousness of men of letters anxious to unite their person and their work through diaries and memoirs. The image of literature to be found in ordinary culture is tyrannically centred on the author, his person, his life, his tastes, his passions, while criticism still consists for the most part in saying that Baudelaire's work is the failure of Baudelaire the man, Van Gogh's his madness, Tchaikovsky's his vice. The *explanation* of a work is always sought in the man or woman who produced it, as if it were always in the end, through the more or less transparent allegory of the fiction, the voice of a single person, the *author* 'confiding' in us.

Though the sway of the Author remains powerful (the new criticism has often done no more than consolidate it), it goes without saying that certain writers have long since attempted to loosen it. In France, Mallarmé was doubtless the first to see and to foresee in its full extent the necessity to substitute language itself for the person who until then had been supposed to be its owner. For him, for us too, it is language which speaks, not the author; to write is, through a prerequisite impersonality (not at all to be confused with the castrating objectivity of the realist novelist), to reach that point where only language acts, 'performs', and not 'me'.

Mallarmé's entire poetics consists in suppressing the author in the interests of writing (which is, as will be seen, to restore the place of the reader). Valéry, encumbered by a psychology of the Ego, considerably diluted Mallarmé's theory but, his taste for classicism leading him to turn to the lessons of rhetoric, he never stopped calling into question and deriding the Author; he stressed the linguistic and, as it were, 'hazardous' nature of his activity, and throughout his prose works he militated in favour of the essentially verbal condition of literature, in the face of which all recourse to the writer's interiority seemed to him pure superstition. Proust himself, despite the apparently psychological character of what are called his *analyses*, was visibly concerned with the task of inexorably blurring, by an extreme subtilization, the relation between the writer and his characters; by making of the narrator not he who has seen and felt nor even he who is writing, but he who *is going to write* (the young man in the novel – but, in fact, how old is he and who is he? – wants to write but cannot; the novel ends when writing at last becomes possible), Proust gave modern writing its epic. By a radical reversal, instead of putting his life into his novel, as is so often maintained, he made of his very life a work for which his own book was the model; so that it is clear to us that Charlus does not imitate Montesquiou but that Montesquiou – in his anecdotal, historical reality – is no more than a secondary fragment, derived from Charlus. Lastly, to go no further than this prehistory of modernity, Surrealism, though unable to accord language a supreme place (language being system and the aim of the movement being, romantically, a direct subversion of codes – itself moreover illusory: a code cannot be destroyed, only 'played off'), contributed to the desacrilization of the image of the Author by ceaselessly recommending the abrupt disappointment of expectations of meaning (the famous surrealist 'jolt'), by entrusting the hand with the task of writing as quickly as possible what the head itself is unaware of (automatic writing), by accepting the principle and the experience of several people writing together. Leaving aside literature itself (such distinctions really becoming invalid), linguistics has recently provided the destruction of the Author with a valuable analytical tool by showing that the whole of the enunciation is an empty process, functioning perfectly without there being any need for it to be filled with the person of the interlocutors. Linguistically, the author is never more than the instance writing, just as *I* is nothing other than the instance saying *I*: language knows a 'subject', not a 'person', and this subject, empty outside of the very enunciation which defines it, suffices to make language 'hold together', suffices, that is to say, to exhaust it.

The removal of the Author (one could talk here with Brecht of a veritable 'distancing', the Author diminishing like a figurine at the far end of the literary stage) is not merely an historical fact or an act of writing; it utterly transforms the modern text (or – which is the same thing – the text is henceforth made and read in such a way that at all its levels the author is absent). The temporality is different. The Author, when believed in, is always conceived of as the past of his own book: book and author stand automatically on a single line divided into a *before* and an *after*. The Author is thought to *nourish* the book, which is to say that he exists before it, thinks, suffers, lives for it, is in the same relation of antecedence to his work as a father to his child. In complete contrast, the modern scriptor is born simultaneously with the text, is in no way equipped with a being preceding or exceeding the writing, is not the subject with the book as predicate; there is no other time than that of the enunciation and every text is eternally written *here and now*. The fact is (or, it follows) that *writing* can no longer designate an operation of recording, notation, representation, 'depiction' (as the Classics would say); rather, it designates exactly what linguists, referring to Oxford philosophy, call a performative, a rare verbal form (exclusively given in the first person and in the present tense) in which the enunciation has no other content (contains no other proposition) than the act by which it is uttered – something like the *I declare* of kings or the *I sing* of very ancient poets. Having buried the Author, the modern scriptor can thus no longer believe, as according to the pathetic view of his predecessors, that this hand is too slow for his thought or passion and that consequently, making a law of necessity, he must emphasize this delay and indefinitely 'polish' his form. For him, on the contrary, the hand, cut off from any voice, borne by a pure gesture of inscription (and not of expression), traces a field without origin – or which, at least, has no other origin than language itself, language which ceaselessly calls into question all origins.

We know now that a text is not a line of words releasing a single 'theological' meaning (the 'message' of the Author-God) but a multi-dimensional space in which a variety of writings, none of them original, blend and clash. The text is a tissue of quotations drawn from the innumerable centres of culture. Similar to Bouvard and Pécuchet, those eternal copyists, at once sublime and comic and whose profound ridiculousness indicates precisely the truth of writing, the writer can only imitate a gesture that is always anterior, never original. His only power is to mix writings, to counter the ones with the others, in such a way as never to rest on any one of them. Did he wish to *express himself*, he ought at least to know that the inner 'thing' he thinks to 'translate' is itself only a ready-formed dictionary, its words only explainable through other words, and so on indefinitely; something experienced in exemplary fashion by the young Thomas de Quincey, he who was so good at Greek that in order to translate absolutely modern ideas and images into that dead language, he had, so Baudelaire tells us (in *Paradis Artificiels*), 'created for himself an unfailing dictionary, vastly more extensive and complex than those resulting from the ordinary patience of purely literary themes'. Succeeding the Author, the scriptor no longer bears within him passions, humours, feelings, impressions, but rather this immense dictionary from which he draws a writing that can know no halt: life never does more than imitate the book, and the book itself is only a tissue of signs, an imitation that is lost, infinitely deferred.

Once the Author is removed, the claim to decipher a text becomes quite futile. To give a text an Author is to impose a limit on that text, to furnish it with a final signified, to close the writing. Such a conception suits criticism very well, the latter then allotting itself the important task of discovering the Author (or its hypostases: society, history, psyche, liberty) beneath the work: when the Author has been found, the text is 'explained' – victory to the critic. Hence there is no surprise in the fact that, historically, the reign of the Author has also been that of the Critic, nor again in the fact that criticism (be it new) is today undermined along with the Author. In the multiplicity of writing, everything is to be *disentangled*, nothing *deciphered*; the structure can be followed, 'run' (like the thread of a stocking) at every point and at every level, but there is nothing beneath: the space of writing is to be ranged over, not pierced; writing ceaselessly posits meaning ceaselessly to evaporate it, carrying out a systematic exemption of meaning. In precisely this way literature (it would be better from now on to say *writing*), by refusing to assign a 'secret', an ultimate meaning, to the text (and to the world as text), liberates what may be called an anti-theological activity, an activity that is truly revolutionary since to refuse to fix meaning is, in the end, to refuse God and his hypostases – reason, science, law.

Let us come back to the Balzac sentence. No one, no 'person', says it: its source, its voice, is not the true place of the writing, which is reading. Another – very precise – example will help to make this clear: recent research (J.-P. Vernant[1]) has demonstrated the constitutively ambiguous nature of Greek tragedy, its texts being woven from words with double meanings that each character understands unilaterally (this perpetual misunderstanding is exactly the 'tragic'); there is, however, someone who understands each word in its duplicity and who, in addition, hears the very deafness of the characters speaking in front of him – this someone being precisely the reader (or here, the listener). Thus is revealed the total existence of writing: a text is made of multiple writings, drawn from many cultures and entering into mutual relations of dialogue, parody, contestation, but there is one place where this multiplicity is focused and that place is the reader, not, as was hitherto said, the author. The reader is the space on which all the quotations that make up a writing are inscribed without any of them being lost; a text's unity lies not in its origin but in its destination. Yet this destination cannot any longer be personal: the reader is without history, biography, psychology; he is simply that *someone* who holds together in a single field all the traces by which the written text is constituted. Which is why it is derisory to condemn the new writing in the name of a humanism hypocritically turned champion of the reader's rights. Classic criticism has never paid any attention to the reader; for it, the writer is the only person in literature. We are now beginning to let ourselves be fooled no longer by the arrogant antiphrastical recriminations of good society in favour of the very thing it sets aside, ignores, smothers, or destroys; we know that to give writing its future, it is necessary to overthrow the myth: the birth of the reader must be at the cost of the death of the Author.

Note

1   Cf. Jean-Pierre Vernant (with Pierre Vidal-Naquet), *Mythe et tragédie en Grèce ancienne*, Paris 1972, esp. pp. 19–40, 99–131.]

24

This Is Not a Pipe

Michel Foucault

1
Two Pipes

The first version, that of 1926 I believe: a carefully drawn pipe, and underneath it (handwritten in a steady, painstaking, artificial script, a script from the convent, like that found heading the notebooks of schoolboys, or on a blackboard after an object lesson[1]), this note: "This is not a pipe."

The other version – the last, I assume – can be found in *Aube à l'Antipodes.*[2] The same pipe, same statement, same handwriting. But instead of being juxtaposed in a neutral, limitless, unspecified space, the text and the figure are set within a frame. The frame itself is placed upon an easel, and the latter in turn upon the clearly visible slats of the floor. Above everything, a pipe exactly like the one in the picture, but much larger.

The first version disconcerts us by its very simplicity. The second multiplies intentional ambiguities before our eyes. Standing upright against the easel and resting on wooden pegs, the frame indicates that this is an artist's painting: a finished work, exhibited and bearing for an eventual viewer the statement that comments upon or explains it. And yet this naive handwriting, neither precisely the work's title nor one of its pictorial elements; the absence of any other trace of the artist's presence; the roughness of the ensemble; the wide slats of the floor – everything suggests a blackboard in a classroom. Perhaps a swipe of the rag will soon erase the drawing and the text. Perhaps it will erase only one or the other, in order to correct the "error" (drawing something that will truly not be a pipe, or else writing a sentence affirming that this indeed is a pipe). A temporary slip (a "mis-writing" suggesting a misunderstanding) that one gesture will dissipate in white dust?

But this is still only the least of the ambiguities; here are some others. There are two pipes. Or rather must we not say, two drawings of the same pipe? Or yet a pipe and the drawing of that pipe, or yet again two drawings each representing a different pipe? Or two drawings, one representing a pipe and the other not, or two more drawings yet, of which neither the one nor the other are or represent pipes? Or yet again, a drawing representing not a pipe at all but another drawing, itself representing a pipe so well that I must ask myself: To what does the sentence written in the painting relate? "See these lines assembled on the blackboard – vainly do they resemble, without the least digression or infidelity, what is displayed above them. Make no mistake; the pipe is overhead, not in this childish scrawl."

Yet perhaps the sentence refers precisely to the disproportionate, floating, ideal pipe – simple notion or fantasy of a pipe. Then we should have to read, "Do not look overhead for a true pipe. That is a pipe dream. It is the drawing within the painting, firmly and rigorously outlined, that must be accepted as a manifest truth."

But it still strikes me that the pipe represented in the drawing – blackboard or canvas, little matter – this "lower" pipe is wedged solidly in a space of visible reference points: width (the written text, the upper and lower borders of the frame); height (the sides of the frame, the easel's mounts); and depth (the grooves of the floor). A stable prison. On the other hand, the higher pipe lacks coordinates. Its enormous proportions render uncertain its location (an opposite effect to that found in *Tombeau des lutteurs*,[3] where the gigantic is caught inside the most precise space). Is the disproportionate pipe drawn in front of the painting, which itself rests far in back? Or indeed is it suspended just above the easel like an emanation, a mist just detaching itself from the painting – pipe smoke taking the form and roundness of a pipe, thus opposing and resembling the pipe (according to the same play of analogy and contrast found between the vaporous and the solid in the series *La Bataille de l'Argonne*[4])? Or might we not suppose, in the end, that the pipe floats behind the painting and the easel, more gigantic than it appears? In that case it would be its uprooted depth, the inner dimension rupturing the canvas (or panel) and slowly, in a space henceforth without reference point, expanding to infinity?

About even this ambiguity, however, I am ambiguous. Or rather what appears to me very dubious is the simple opposition between the higher pipe's dislocated buoyancy and the stability of the lower one. Looking a bit more closely, we easily discern that the feet of the easel, supporting the frame where the canvas is held and where the drawing is lodged – these feet, resting upon a floor made safe and visible by its own coarseness, are in fact beveled. They touch only by three tiny points, robbing the ensemble, itself somewhat ponderous, of all stability. An impending fall? The collapse of easel, frame, canvas or panel, drawing, text? Splintered wood, fragmented shapes, letters scattered one from another until words can perhaps no longer be reconstituted? All this litter on the ground, while above, the large pipe without measure or reference point will linger in its inaccessible, balloon-like immobility?

2
The Unraveled Calligram

Magritte's drawing (for the moment I speak only of the first version) is as simple as a page borrowed from a botanical manual: a figure and the text that names it. Nothing is easier to recognize than a pipe, drawn thus; nothing is easier to say – our language knows it well in our place – than the "name of a pipe."[5] Now, what lends the figure its strangeness is not the "contradiction" between the image and the text. For a good reason: Contradiction could exist only between two statements, or within one and the same statement. Here there is clearly but one, and it cannot be contradictory because the subject of the proposition is a simple demonstrative. False, then, because its "referent" – obviously a pipe – does not verify it? But who would seriously contend that the collection of intersecting lines above the text *is* a pipe? Must we say: My God, how simpleminded! The statement is perfectly true, since it is quite apparent that the drawing representing the pipe is not the pipe itself. And yet there is a convention of language: What is this drawing? Why, it is a calf, a square, a flower. An old custom not without basis, because the entire function of so scholarly, so academic a drawing is to elicit recognition, to allow the object it represents to appear without hesitation or equivocation. No matter that it is the material deposit, on a sheet of paper or a blackboard, of a little graphite or a thin dust of chalk. It does not "aim" like an arrow or a pointer toward a particular pipe in the distance or elsewhere. It *is* a pipe.

What misleads us is the inevitability of connecting the text to the drawing (as the demonstrative pronoun, the meaning of the word *pipe*, and the likeness of the image all invite us to do here) – and the impossibility of defining a perspective that would let us say that the assertion is true, false, or contradictory.

I cannot dismiss the notion that the sorcery here lies in an operation rendered invisible by the simplicity of its result, but which alone can explain the vague uneasiness provoked. The operation is a calligram[6] that Magritte has secretly constructed, then carefully unraveled. Each element of the figure, their reciprocal position and their relationship derive from this process, annulled as soon as it has been accomplished. Behind this drawing and these words, before anyone has written anything at all, before the formation of the picture (and within it the drawing of the pipe), before the large, floating pipe has appeared – we must assume, I believe, that a calligram has formed, then unraveled. There we have evidence of failure and its ironic remains.

In its millennial tradition, the calligram has a triple role: to augment the alphabet, to repeat something without the aid of rhetoric, to trap things in a double cipher. First it brings a text and a shape as close together as possible. It is composed of lines delimiting the form of an object while also arranging the sequence of letters. It lodges statements in the space of a shape, and makes the text *say* what the drawing *represents*. On the one hand, it alphabetizes the ideogram, populates it with discontinuous letters, and thus interrogates the silence of uninterrupted lines.[7] But on the other hand, it distributes writing in a space no longer possessing the neutrality, openness, and inert blankness of paper. It forces the ideogram to arrange itself according to the laws of a simultaneous form. For the blink of an eye, it reduces phoneticism to a mere grey noise completing the contours of the shape; but it renders outline as a thin skin that must be pierced in order to follow, word for word, the outpouring of its internal text.

The calligram is thus tautological. But in opposition to rhetoric. The latter toys with the fullness of language. It uses the possibility of repeating the same thing in different words, and profits from the extra richness of language that allows us to say different things with a single word. The essence of rhetoric is in allegory. The calligram uses that capacity of letters to signify both as linear elements that can be arranged in space and as signs that must unroll according to a unique chain of sound. As a sign, the letter permits us to fix words; as line, it lets us give shape to things. Thus the calligram aspires playfully to efface the oldest oppositions of our alphabetical civilization: to show and to name; to shape and to say; to reproduce and to articulate; to imitate and to signify; to look and to read.

Pursuing its quarry by two paths, the calligram sets the most perfect trap. By its double function, it guarantees capture, as neither discourse alone nor a pure drawing could do. It banishes the invincible absence that defeats words, imposing upon them, by the ruses of a writing at play in space, the visible form of their referent. Cleverly arranged on a sheet of paper, signs invoke the very thing of which they speak – from outside, by the margin they outline, by the emergence of their mass on the blank space of the page. And in return, visible form is excavated, furrowed by words that work at it from within, and which, dismissing the immobile, ambiguous, nameless presence, spin forth the web of significations that christen it, determine it, fix it in the universe of discourse. A double trap, unavoidable snare: How henceforth would escape the flight of birds, the transitory form of flowers, the falling rain?

And now Magritte's drawings. Let us begin with the first and simplest. It seems to be created from the fragments of an unraveled calligram. Under the guise of reverting to a previous arrangement, it recovers its three functions – but in order to pervert them, thereby disturbing all the traditional bonds of language and the image.

After having invaded the figure in order to reconstitute the old ideogram, the text has now resumed its place. It has returned to its natural site – below the image, where it serves to support it, name it, explain it, decompose it, insert it in the series of texts and in the pages of the book. Once more it becomes a "legend." Form itself reascends to the ethereal realm from which the complicity of letters with space had forced it for an instant to descend. Free from all discursive attachment, it can float anew in its natural silence. We return to the page, and to its old principle of distribution – but only apparently. Because the words we now can read underneath the drawing are themselves drawn – images of words the painter has set apart from the pipe, but within the general (yet still undefinable) perimeter of the picture. I must read them superimposed upon themselves. They are words drawing words; at the surface of the image, they form the reflection of a sentence saying that this is not a pipe. The image of a text. But conversely, the represented pipe is drawn by the same hand and with the same pen as the letters of the text: it extends the writing more than it illustrates it or fills its void. We might imagine it brimming with small, chaotic letters, graphic signs reduced to fragments and dispersed over the entire surface of the image. A figure in the shape of writing. The invisible, preliminary calligraphic operation intertwined the writing and the drawing: and when Magritte restored things to their own places, he took care that the shape would preserve the patience of writing and that the text remain always only a drawing of a representation.

The same for tautology. From calligraphic doubling, Magritte seemingly returns to the simple correspondence of the image with its legend. Without saying anything, a mute and adequately recognizable figure displays the object in its essence; from the image, a name written below receives its "meaning" or rule for usage. Now, compared to the traditional function of the legend, Magritte's text is doubly paradoxical. It sets out to name something that evidently does not need to be named (the form is too well known, the label too familiar). And at the moment when he should reveal the name, Magritte does so by denying that the object is what it is. Whence comes this strange game, if not from the calligram? From the calligram that says things twice (when once would doubtless do); from the calligram that shuffles what it says over what it shows to hide them from each other. For the text to shape itself, for all its juxtaposed signs to form a dove, a flower, or a rainstorm, the gaze must refrain from any possible reading. Letters must remain points, sentences lines, paragraphs surfaces or masses – wings, stalks, or petals. The text must say nothing to this gazing subject who is a viewer, not a reader. As soon as he begins to read, in fact, shape dissipates. All around the recognized word and the comprehended sentence, the other graphisms take flight, carrying with them the visible plenitude of shape and leaving only the linear, successive unfurling of meaning – not one drop of rain falling after another, much less a feather or a torn-off leaf. Despite appearances, in forming a bird, a flower, or rain, the calligram does not say: These things *are* a dove, a flower, a downpour. As soon as it begins to do so, to speak and convey meaning, the bird has already flown, the rain has evaporated. For whoever sees it, the calligram *does not say*, *cannot yet say*: This is a flower, this is a bird. It is still too much trapped within shape, too much subject to representation by resemblance, to formulate such a proposition. And when we read it, the deciphered sentence ("this is a dove," "this is a rainstorm") *is not* a bird, is no longer a shower. By ruse or impotence, small matter – the calligram never speaks and represents at the same moment. The very thing that is both seen and read is hushed in the vision, hidden in the reading.

Magritte redistributed the text and the image in space. Each regains its place, but not without keeping some of the evasiveness proper to the calligram. The drawn form of the pipe is so easily recognized that it excludes any explanatory or descriptive text. Its academic schematicism says very explicitly, "You see me so clearly that it would be ridiculous for me to arrange myself so as to write: This is a pipe. To be sure, words would draw me less adequately than I represent myself." And in this sketch representing handwriting, the text in turn prescribes: "Take me for what I manifestly am – letters placed beside one another, arranged and shaped so as to facilitate reading, assure recognition, and open themselves even to the most stammering schoolboy. I do not claim to swell, then stretch, becoming first the

bowl, then the stem of the pipe. I am no more than the words you are now reading." Against one another in the calligram are pitted a "not yet to say" and a "no longer to represent." In Magritte's *Pipe*, the birthplace of these negations is wholly different from the point where they are applied. The "not yet to say" returns not exactly in an affirmation, but in a double position. On the one hand, overhead, the polished, silent, visible shape, on whose proud and disdainful evidence the text is allowed to say whatever it pleases. On the other hand, below, the text, displayed according to its intrinsic law, affirms its own autonomy in regard to what it names. The calligram's redundance rested on a relation of exclusion. In Magritte, the separation of the two elements, the absence of letters in the drawing, the negation expressed in the text – all of these positively manifest two distinct positions.

But I have neglected, I fear, what is perhaps essential to Magritte's *Pipe*. I have proceeded as if the text said, "I (the ensemble of words you are now reading) am not a pipe." I have gone on as if there were two simultaneously and clearly differentiated positions within the same space: the figure's and the text's. But I have omitted that from one position to the other a subtle and instable dependency, at once insistent and unsure, is indicated. And it is indicated by the word "this." We must therefore admit between the figure and the text a whole series of intersections – or rather attacks launched by one against the other, arrows shot at the enemy target, enterprises of subversion and destruction, lance blows and wounds, a battle. For example, "this" (the drawing, whose form you doubtless recognize and whose calligraphic heritage I have just traced) "is not" (is not substantially bound to..., is not constituted by..., does not cover the same material as...) "a pipe" (that is, this word from your language, made up of pronounceable sounds that translate the letters you are reading). Therefore, *This is not a pipe* can be read thus:

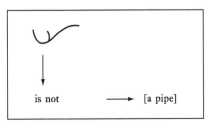

377

But at the same time, the text states an entirely different proposition: "This" (the statement arranging itself beneath your eyes in a line of discontinuous elements, of which *this* is both the signifier and the first word) "is not" (could neither equal nor substitute for..., could not adequately represent...) "a pipe" (one of the objects whose possible rendering can be seen above the text – interchangeable, anonymous, inaccessible to any name). Then we must read:

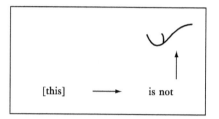

Now, on the whole it easily seems that Magritte's statement is negated by the immediate and reciprocal dependency between the drawing of the pipe and the text by which the pipe can be named. Designation and design do not overlap one another, save in the calligraphic play hovering in the ensemble's background and conjured away simultaneously by the text, the drawing, and their current separation. Hence the third function of the statement: "This" (this ensemble constituted by a written pipe and a drawn text) "is not" (is incompatible with) "a pipe" (this mixed element springing at once from discourse and the image, whose ambiguous being the verbal and visual play of the calligram wants to evoke).

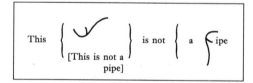

Magritte reopened the trap the calligram had sprung on the thing it described. But in the act, the object itself escaped. On the page of an illustrated book, we seldom pay attention to the small space running above the words and below the drawings, forever serving them as a common frontier. It is there, on these few millimeters of white, the calm sand of the page, that are established all the relations of designation, nomination, description, classification. The calligram absorbed that

interstice; but once opened, it does not restore it. The trap shattered on emptiness: image and text fall each to its own side, of their own weight. No longer do they have a common ground nor a place where they can meet, where words are capable of taking shape and images of entering into lexical order. The slender, colorless, neutral strip, which in Magritte's drawing separates the text and the figure, must be seen as a crevasse – an uncertain, foggy region now dividing the pipe floating in its imagistic heaven from the mundane tramp of words marching in their successive line. Still it is too much to claim that there is a blank or lacuna: instead, it is an absence of space, an effacement of the "common place" between the signs of writing and the lines of the image. The "pipe" that was at one with both the statement naming it and the drawing representing it – this shadow pipe knitting the lineaments of form with the fiber of words – has utterly vanished. A disappearance that from the other side of this shallow stream[8] the text confirms with amusement: This is not a pipe. In vain the now solitary drawing imitates as closely as possible the shape ordinarily designated by the word *pipe*; in vain the text unfurls below the drawing with all the attentive fidelity of a label in a scholarly book. No longer can anything pass between them save the decree of divorce, the statement at once contesting the name of the drawing and the reference of the text.

Nowhere is there a pipe.

On this basis, we can understand Magritte's second version of *This Is Not a Pipe*. In placing the drawing of the pipe and the statement serving as its legend on the very clearly defined surface of a picture (insofar as it is a painting, the letters are but the image of letters; insofar as it is a blackboard, the figure is only the didactic continuation of a discourse), in placing the picture on a thick, solid wood tripod, Magritte does everything necessary to reconstruct (either by the permanence of a work of art or else by the truth of an object lesson) the space common to language and the image.

Everything is solidly anchored within a pedagogic space. A painting "shows" a drawing that "shows" the form of a pipe; a text written by a zealous instructor "shows" that a pipe is really what is meant. We do not see the teacher's pointer, but it rules throughout – precisely like his voice, in the act of articulating very clearly, "This is a pipe." From painting to image, from image to text, from text to voice, a sort of imaginary pointer indicates, shows, fixes, locates, imposes a system of references, tries to stabilize a unique space. But why have we introduced the teacher's voice? Because scarcely has he stated, "This is a pipe," before he must correct himself and stutter, "This is not a pipe, but a drawing of a pipe," "This is not a pipe but a sentence saying that this is not a pipe," "The sentence 'this is not a pipe' is not a pipe," "In the sentence 'this is not a pipe,' *this* is not a pipe: the painting, written sentence, drawing of a pipe – all this is not a pipe."

Negations multiply themselves, the voice is confused and choked. The baffled master lowers his extended pointer, turns his back to the board, regards the uproarious students, and does not realize that they laugh so loudly because above the blackboard and his stammered denials, a vapor has just risen, little by little taking shape and now creating, precisely and without doubt, a pipe. "A pipe, a pipe," cry the students, stamping away while the teacher, his voice sinking ever lower, murmurs always with the same obstinacy though no one is listening, "And yet it is not a pipe." He is not mistaken; because the pipe floating so obviously overhead (like the object the blackboard drawing refers to, and in whose name the text can justifiably say that the drawing is truly not a pipe) is itself merely a drawing. It is *not* a pipe. No more on the board than above it, the drawing of the pipe and the text presumed to name it find nowhere to meet and be superimposed, as the calligrapher so presumptuously had attempted to bring about.

So, on its beveled and clearly rickety mounts, the easel has but to tilt, the frame to loosen, the painting to tumble down, the words to be scattered. The "pipe" can "break": The common place[9] – banal work of art or everyday lesson – has disappeared.

3
Klee, Kandinsky, Magritte

Two principles, I believe, ruled Western painting from the fifteenth to the twentieth century. The first asserts the separation between plastic representation (which implies resemblance) and linguistic reference (which excludes it). By resemblance we demonstrate and speak across difference: The two systems can neither merge nor intersect. In one way or another, subordination is required. Either the text is ruled by the image (as in those paintings where a book, an inscription, a letter, or the name of a person are represented); or else the image is ruled

by the text (as in books where a drawing completes, as if it were merely taking a short cut, the message that words are charged to represent). True, the subordination remains stable only very rarely. What happens to the text of the book is that it becomes merely a commentary on the image, and the linear channel, through words, of its simultaneous forms; and what happens to the picture is that it is dominated by a text, all of whose significations it figuratively illustrates. But no matter the meaning of the subordination or the manner in which it prolongs, multiplies, and reverses itself. What is essential is that verbal signs and visual representations are never given at once. An order always hierarchizes them, running from the figure to discourse or from discourse to the figure.

This is the principle whose sovereignty Klee abolished, by showing the juxtaposition of shapes and the syntax of lines in an uncertain, reversible, floating space (simultaneously page and canvas, plane and volume, map and chronicle). Boats, houses, persons are at the same time recognizable figures and elements of writing. They are placed and travel upon roads or canals that are also lines to be read. Trees of the forest file over musical staves. The gaze encounters words as if they had strayed to the heart of things, words indicating the way to go and naming the landscape being crossed. And at the nexus of these figures and signs, the arrow that crops up so often (the arrow, sign bearing a primal resemblance, like a graphic onomatopoeia, and shape that formulates an order) – the arrow indicates the direction in which the boat is traveling, shows that the sun is setting, prescribes the direction that the gaze must follow, or rather the line along which it must imaginatively shift the figure provisionally and a bit arbitrarily placed here. It is not, in fact, a question of those calligrams that by turns bring into play the subordination of sign to form (a cloud of words and letters taking the shape they designate), then of form to sign (the figure dissecting itself into alphabetical elements). Nor is it any longer a question of those collages or reproductions that capture the cut out form of letters in fragments of objects; but rather a question of the intersection, within the same medium, of representation by resemblance and of representation by signs. Which presupposes that they meet in quite another space than that of the painting.

The second principle that long ruled painting posits an equivalence between the fact of resemblance and the affirmation of a representative bond. Let a figure resemble an object (or some other figure), and that alone is enough for there to slip into the pure play of the painting a statement – obvious, banal, repeated a thousand times yet almost always silent. (It is like an infinite murmur – haunting, enclosing the silence of figures, investing it, mastering it, extricating the silence from itself, and finally reversing it within the domain of things that can be named.) "What you see is *that*." No matter, again, in what sense the representative relation is posed – whether the painting is referred to the visible world around it, or whether it independently establishes an invisible world that resembles itself.

The essential point is that resemblance and affirmation cannot be dissociated. The rupture of this principle can be ascribed to Kandinsky: a double effacement simultaneously of resemblance and of the representative bond, by the increasingly insistent affirmation of the lines, the colors that Kandinsky called "things," neither more nor less objects than the church, the bridge, or the knight with his bow. Kandinsky's is a naked affirmation clutching at no resemblance, and which, when asked "what it is," can reply only by referring itself to the gesture that formed it: an "improvisation," a "composition"; or to what is found there: "a red shape," "triangles," "purple orange"; or to tensions or internal relations: "a determinant pink," "upwards," "a yellow milieu," "a rosy balance." No one, apparently, is further from Klee and Kandinsky than Magritte. More than any other, his painting seems wedded to exact resemblances, to the point where they willfully multiply as if to assert themselves. It is not enough that the drawing of the pipe so closely resembles a pipe. Nor is it enough that the tree so closely resembles the tree, and the leaf the leaf. Rather the leaf of the tree will take on the shape of the tree itself, and the latter will take the form of the leaf (*L'Incendie*[10]). The ship at sea will not resemble merely a ship, but also the sea itself, even to its hull and sails being composed of waves (*Le Séducteur*[11]). And the exact representation of a pair of shoes moreover will try to resemble the bare feet the shoes ought to cover.[12]

An art more committed than any other to the careful and cruel separation of graphic and plastic elements. If they happen to be superimposed within the painting like a legend and its image, it is on condition that the statement contest the obvious identity of the figure, and the name we are prepared to give it. Something exactly like an egg is called *l'acacia* – a shoe *la lune*, a bowler hat *la niege*, a candle *la plafond*.[13] And yet Magritte's art is not foreign to the enterprise of Klee and Kandinsky. Rather it constitutes, facing them and on the basis of a system common to them all, a figure at once opposed and complementary.

4
Burrowing Words[14]

The exteriority of written and figurative elements, so obvious in Magritte, is symbolized by the non-relation – or in any case by the very complex and problematic relation – between the painting and its title. This gulf, which prevents us from being both the reader and the viewer at the same time, brings the image into abrupt relief above the horizontal line of words. "The titles are chosen in such a way as to keep anyone from assigning my paintings to the familiar region that habitual thought appeals to in order to escape perplexity." A little like the anonymous hand that designated the pipe by the statement, "This is not a pipe," Magritte names his paintings in order to focus attention upon the very act of naming. And yet in this split and drifting space, strange bonds are knit, there occur intrusions, brusque and destructive invasions, avalanches of images into the milieu of words, and verbal lightning flashes that streak and shatter the drawings. Patiently, Klee constructed a space without name or geometry, tangling the chain of signs with the fiber of figures. Magritte secretly mines a space he seems to maintain in the old arrangement. But he excavates it with words: And the old pyramid of perspective is no more than a molehill about to cave in.

In any reasonable drawing, a subscript such as "This is not a pipe" is enough immediately to divorce the figure from itself, to isolate it from its space, and to set it floating – whether near or apart from itself, whether similar to or unlike itself, no one knows. Against *Ceci n'est pas une pipe*, there is *L'Art de la conversation*:[15] In a landscape of battling giants or of the beginning of the world, two tiny persons are speaking – an inaudible discourse, a murmur instantly reabsorbed into the silence of the stones, into the silence of a wall whose enormous blocks overhang the two garrulous mutes. Jumbled together, the blocks form at their base a group of letters where it is easy to make out the word: REVE[16] (which can, if we look a bit more closely, be completed as TREVE[17] or CREVE[18] – as if all these airy, fragile words had been given the power to organize the chaos of stones. Or as if, on the contrary, behind the alert but immediately lost chatter of men, things could in their silence and sleep compose a word – a permanent word no one could efface; yet this word now designates the most fleeting of images. But this is not all: Because it is in dream that men, at last reduced to silence, commune with the signification of things and allow themselves to be touched by enigmatic, insistent words that come from elsewhere. *Ceci n'est pas une pipe* exemplifies the penetration of discourse into the form of things; it reveals discourse's ambiguous power to deny and to redouble. *L'Art de la conversation* marks the anonymous attraction of things that form their own words in the face of men's indifference, insinuating themselves, without men even being aware of it, into their daily chatter.

Between the two extremes, Magritte's work deploys the play of words and images. Often invented after the fact and by other people, the titles intrude into the figures where their applicability was if not indicated at least authorized in advance, and where they play an ambiguous role: supporting pegs and yet termites that gnaw and weaken. The countenance of an absolutely serious man, unsmiling, unblinking, "breaks up" with a laughter that comes from nowhere.[19] *Le Soir qui tombe*[20] cannot fall without shattering a windowpane whose fragments (still retaining, on their sharp edges and glass shards, the sun's reflections) are scattered on the floor and sill. Referring to the sun's disappearance as a "fall," the words have swept along, with the image they evoke, not only the windowpane but the other sun, the twin sun perfectly outlined on the smooth and transparent glass. Like a clapper in a bell, the key stands vertically "in the keyhole": it rings forth the familiar expression[21] until it becomes absurd.

Moreover, listen to Magritte: "Between words and objects one can create new relations and specify characteristics of language and objects generally ignored in everyday life." Or again: "Sometimes the name of an object takes the place of an image. A word can take the place of an object in reality. An image can take the place of a word in a proposition." And the following statement, conveying no contradiction but referring to the inextricable tangle of words and images and to the absence of a common ground to sustain them: "In a painting, words are of the same cloth as images. Rather one sees images and words differently in a painting."[22]

Of these substitutions, these transubstantiations, there are many examples in Magritte's work. In *Personnage marchant vers l'horizon*,[23] there is the famous fellow seen from behind, with dark hat and coat, hands in his pockets. He is situated near five colored blobs. Three of them rest on the ground and bear the italicized words *fusil, fauteuil, cheval*; another, overhead, is called *nuage*; finally, at the terminus of earth and sky, another vaguely triangular blob is called *horizon*.[24] We are a long way from Klee and his *regard-lecture*.[25] This is by no means a matter of weaving signs and spatial figures into a unique and absolutely novel form. Words are not bound directly to other pictorial elements. They are merely inscriptions on blobs and shapes: Their distribution above and below, right and left, is true to the traditional layout of the painting. The horizon is indeed in the background, the cloud overhead, the sun situated vertically and to the left. But within this familiar context, words do not replace missing objects. They occupy no empty or hollow spaces, because the inscription-bearing blobs are thick, voluminous masses, stones or menhirs whose shadows stretch forth on the ground beside that of the man. These "word-bearers" are thicker, more substantial than the objects themselves. They are barely-formed things (a vague triangle for the horizon, a rectangle for the horse, a perpendicular for the gun) with neither shape nor identity. The sort of things that cannot be named and that in fact "name" themselves bear an exact and familiar name. The painting is the converse of a rebus, that chain of shapes so easily recognized as to be immediately identifiable, its mere formulation enjoining the articulation of a sentence whose meaning has nothing to do with the figures actually seen there. Here, shapes are so vague as to be unnameable if they did not identify themselves. And on the real painting as seen – blobs, shadows, silhouettes – there is superimposed the invisible possibility of another painting at once familiar because of the figures presented and yet bizarre because of the juxtaposition of horse and armchair. An object in a painting is a volume organized and tinted so that its shape is immediately recognizable and need not be named. In form, the indispensable mass is absorbed, the useless name dismissed. Magritte elides the object's form and superimposes the name directly upon the mass. The substantive link of the object itself is no longer represented except by its two extreme points, the mass that casts a shadow and the name that designates it.

L'Alphabet des révélations[26] contrasts rather precisely with *Personnage marchant vers l'horizon*: a great wooden frame divided into panels; on the right, some simple, perfectly recognizable forms: a pipe, a key, a leaf, a glass. At the bottom of the right panel, the configuration of a rip shows that the shapes are no more than cut outs in a sheet of thin paper. On the other panel, a kind of twisted, tangled string depicts no recognizable shape (save perhaps, and this is very doubtful: LA, LE[27]). No mass, no name, form without volume, an empty cut out, this is the object – the object that had vanished from the preceding painting.

Make no mistake: In a space where every element seems to obey the sole principle of resemblance and plastic representation, linguistic signs (which had an excluded aura, which prowled far around the image, which the title's arbitrariness seemed to have banished forever) have surreptitiously reapproached. Into the solidity of the image, into its meticulous resemblance, they have introduced a disorder – an order pertaining to the eyes alone. They have routed the object, revealing its filmy thinness.

In order to deploy his plastic signs, Klee wove a new space. Magritte allows the old space of representation to rule, but only at the surface, no more than a polished stone, bearing words and shapes: beneath, nothing. It is a gravestone: The incisions that drew figures and those that marked letters communicate only by void, the non-place hidden beneath marble solidity. I will note that this absence reascends to the surface and impinges upon the painting itself. When Magritte offers his version of *Madame Récamier* or *Le Balcon*,[28] he replaces the traditional paintings' characters with coffins. Invisibly contained between waxen oak planks, emptiness undoes the space composed by the volume of living bodies, the arrangement of clothing, the direction of the gaze and all the faces that are about to speak. The "non-place" emerges "in person" – in place of persons and where no one is present any longer.[29]

And when the word assumes the solidity of an object, I think about that corner of the floor on which is written, in white paint, the word "*sirene*" – written with a huge upraised finger, piercing the floor vertically at the *i* and directed toward the small bell that serves to dot it. Word and object do not tend to constitute a single figure; on the contrary they are deployed in two different dimensions. The finger that traverses the script rises above it, imitating and obscuring the *i*; the finger

that represents the word's pointing function and takes somewhat the shape of those towers upon which sirens were placed – the finger points only toward the ubiquitous bell.[30]

5
Seven Seals of Affirmation

With a sovereign and unique gesture, Kandinsky dismissed the old equivalence between resemblance and affirmation, freeing painting from both. Magritte proceeds by dissociating the two: disrupting their bonds, establishing their inequality, bringing one into play without the other, maintaining that which stems from painting, and excluding that which is closest to discourse – pursuing as closely as possible the indefinite continuation of the similar, but excising from it any affirmation that would attempt to say what is resembled. An art of the "Same," liberated from the "as if." We are farthest from *trompe-l'oeil*.[31] The latter seeks to support the weightiest burden of affirmation by the ruse of a convincing resemblance: "What you see on the wall's surface is not an aggregate of lines and colors. It is depth, sky, clouds that have shaded your house, a real column around which you could walk, a stairway that continues the steps you have begun to climb (already you start toward it, despite yourself), a stone balustrade over which lean the attentive faces of ladies and courtiers, wearing clothes identical to your own, to the very ribbons, smiling at your astonishment and your own smiles, gesturing to you in a fashion that is mysterious because they have answered you without even waiting for your own gestures to them."

To me it appears that Magritte dissociated similitude from resemblance, and brought the former into play against the latter. Resemblance has a "model," an original[32] element that orders and hierarchizes the increasingly less faithful copies that can be struck from it. Resemblance presupposes a primary reference that prescribes and classes. The similar develops in series that have neither beginning nor end, that can be followed in one direction as easily as in another, that obey no hierarchy, but propagate themselves from small differences among small differences. Resemblance serves representation, which rules over it; similitude serves repetition, which ranges across it. Resemblance predicates itself upon a model it must return to and reveal; similitude circulates the simulacrum as an indefinite and reversible relation of the similar to the similar.

Take *Représentation* (1962): an exact representation of a portion of a ball game, seen from a kind of terrace fenced by a low wall. On the left, the wall is topped by a balustrade, and in the juncture thus formed can be seen exactly the same scene, but on a smaller scale (about one-half). Must we suppose, unfolding on the left, a series of smaller and smaller other "representations," always identical? Perhaps. But it is unnecessary. In the same painting, two images bound thus laterally by a relation of similitude are enough for exterior reference to a model – through resemblance – to be disturbed, rendered floating and uncertain. What "represents" what? Even as the exactness of the image functioned as a finger pointing to a model, to a sovereign, unique, and exterior "pattern," the series of similitudes (and two are enough to establish a series) abolishes this simultaneously real and ideal monarchy. Henceforth the simulacrum, in a sense always reversible, ranges across the surface.

In *Décalcomanie* (1966):[33] Occupying two thirds of the painting, a red curtain with large pleats obscures a landscape of sky, sea, and sand. Beside the curtain, turning his back as usual to the viewer, the man with the bowler hat looks out to sea.

Now, we find that the curtain has been cut out in exactly the shape of the man: as if he himself (although of another color, texture, and width) were merely a section of curtain snipped away by scissors. Within the large opening the beach is visible. What are we to make of this? Is it that the man, in changing places, having departed the curtain, exposes what he was looking at when he was still enfolded within it? Or is it that the painter, in moving the man a few centimeters, has set against the curtain that fragment of sky, water, and sand that the man's silhouette hid from the viewer – so that thanks to the cooperation of the artist, we can see what is contemplated by the silhouette that blocks our view? Or must we admit that at the moment the man turns to look at it, the fragment of landscape immediately before him has leapt aside, avoiding his gaze so that before his eyes it became his shadow, the black smudge of his body? Transference? Doubtless. But from what to what? From where to where? The thick black silhouette of the man seems to have been shifted from right to left, from the curtain onto the landscape he now obscures; the fold he makes in the curtain displays his prior position. But in the shape of a man's silhouette, the landscape has also been cut loose

and transferred from left to right. The scrap of red curtain that remains bizarrely attached to the shoulder of this human landscape, and that corresponds to the small part of curtain hidden by the black silhouette, in itself demonstrates the origin and the location from which the sky and water were cut. A displacement and exchange of similar elements, but by no means mimetic reproduction.

And thanks to *Décalcomanie* the advantage of similitude over resemblance can be grasped. The latter reveals the clearly visible; similitude reveals what recognizable objects, familiar silhouettes hide, prevent from being seen, render invisible. ("Body" = "curtain," says mimetic representation. "Right is left, left is right; the hidden here is visible there; the sunken is in relief; flatness extends into depth," say the similitudes of *Décalcomanie*.) Resemblance makes a unique assertion, always the same: This thing, that thing, yet another thing is something else. Similitude multiplies different affirmations, which dance together, tilting and tumbling over one another.

Hounded from the space of the painting, excluded from the relation between things that refer to one another, resemblance vanishes. But is it not in order to reign elsewhere, freed from the indefinite play of similitude? Is it not the role of resemblance to be the sovereign that makes things appear? Is not resemblance, a property of objects, also the property of thought as well? "Only thought," says Magritte, "can resemble. It resembles by being what it sees, hears, or knows; it becomes what the world offers it." Thought resembles without similitude, becoming those things whose mutual similitude excludes resemblance. Magritte's painting doubtless rests here, where thought in the mode of resemblance and things in relations of similitude have just vertically intersected.[34]

Let us reconsider the drawing of a pipe that bears so strong a resemblance to a real pipe; the written text that bears so strong a resemblance to the drawing of a written text. In fact, whether conflicting or just juxtaposed, these elements annul the intrinsic resemblance they seem to bear within themselves, and gradually sketch an open network of similitudes. Open – not onto the "real" pipe, absent from all these words and drawings,[35] but onto all the other similar elements (including all "real" pipes of clay, meerschaum, wood, etc.) that, once drawn into the network, would take the place and function of the simulacrum. Each element of "this is not a pipe" could hold an apparently negative discourse – because it denies, along with resemblance, the assertion of reality resemblance conveys – but one that is basically affirmative: the affirmation of the simulacrum, affirmation of the element within the network of the similar.

Let us establish the series of these affirmations, which reject the assertion of resemblance and are found concentrated in the proposition: This is not a pipe. To do so it is sufficient to pose the question: Who speaks in the statement? Or rather it suffices to interrogate in turn the elements deployed by Magritte; because at bottom all of them can say either of themselves or of their neighbors: This is not a pipe.

First the pipe itself: "What you see here, the lines I form or that form me, is not a pipe as you doubtless believe; but a drawing in a relation of vertical similitude to the other pipe (real or not, true or false, I do not know) that you see over there – just above the painting where I am, a simple and solitary similitude." To which the higher pipe responds in the same words: "What you see floating before your eyes, beyond space and without fixed foundation, this mist that settles neither on canvas nor on a page, how could it really be a pipe? Don't be misled: I am mere similarity – not something similar to a pipe, but the cloudy similitude that, referring to nothing, traverses and brings together texts such as the one you can read and drawings such as the one below." But the statement, already articulated twice by different voices, in turn comes forward to speak for itself. "The letters that form me and that you see – the moment you try to read them as naming the pipe, how can they say that they are a pipe, these things so divorced from what they name? This is a graphism that resembles only itself, and that could never replace what it describes."

But there is more. Two by two the voices mingle to say a third element is not a pipe. Bound together by the frame of the painting enclosing them, the text and the lower pipe enter into complicity: The designating power of words and the illustrative power of drawing denounce the higher pipe, and refuse the abstract apparition the right to call itself a pipe, because its unanchored existence renders it mute and invisible. Bound together by their reciprocal similitude, the two pipes contest the written statement's right to call itself a pipe, for it is composed of signs with no resemblance to the thing they designate. Bound together by the fact that they each come from elsewhere, that one

is a discourse capable of conveying truth while the other is like the ghost of a thing-in-itself, the text and the higher pipe join to assert that the pipe in the painting is not a pipe. And perhaps we must also assume that from beyond these three alliances, a dislocated voice (that of the painting or the blackboard, possibly) speaks of both the pipe in the painting and the one above it: "None of these is a pipe, but rather a text that simulates a pipe; a drawing of a pipe that simulates a drawing of a pipe; a pipe (drawn other than as a drawing) that is the simulacrum of a pipe (drawn after a pipe that itself would be other than a drawing)." Seven discourses in a single statement – more than enough to demolish the fortress where similitude was held prisoner to the assertion of resemblance.

Henceforth similitude is restored to itself – unfolding from itself and folding back upon itself. It is no longer the finger pointing out from the canvas in order to refer to something else. It inaugurates a play of transferences that run, proliferate, propagate, and correspond within the layout of the painting, affirming and representing nothing. Thus in Magritte's art we find infinite games of purified similitude that never overflow the painting. They establish metamorphoses: but in what sense? Is it the plant whose leaves take flight and become birds, or the birds that drown and slowly botanize themselves, sinking into the ground with a final quiver of greenery (*Les Grâces naturelles*, *La Saveur des larmes*[36])? Is it a woman who "takes to the bottle" or the bottle that feminizes itself by becoming a "nude study"[37] (here composing a disturbance of plastic elements because of the latent insertion of verbal signs and the play of an analogy that, affirming nothing, is doubly activated by the playfulness of the statement)? Instead of blending identities, it happens that similitude also has the power to destroy them: a woman's torso is sectioned into three parts (increasingly larger as we move from top to bottom). While holding back all affirmation of identity, the shared proportions guarantee analogy: three segments lacking a fourth in just the same fashion, though the fourth element is incalculable. The head (final element = x) is missing: *Folie des grandeurs*,[38] says the title.

Another way similitude is freed from its old complicity with representative affirmation: perfidiously mixing (and by a ruse that seems to indicate just the opposite of what it means) the painting and what it represents. Evidently this is a way of affirming that the painting is indeed its own model. But in fact such an affirmation would imply an interior distance, a divergence, a disjuncture between the canvas and what it is supposed to mimic. For Magritte, on the contrary, there exists from the painting to the model a perfect continuity of scene, a linearity, a continuous overflowing of one into the other. Either by gliding from left to right (as in *La Condition humaine*, where the sea's horizon follows the horizon on the canvas without a break); or by the inversion of distances (as in *La Cascade*,[39] where the model invades the canvas, envelops it on all sides, and gives it the appearance of being behind what ought to be on its far side). Opposed to this analogy that denies representation by erasing duality and distance, there is the contrary one that evades or mocks it by means of the snare of doubling. In *Le Soir qui tombe*, the windowpane bears a red sun analogous to the one hung in the sky (against Descartes and the way in which he resolved the two suns of appearance within the unity of representation). This is the converse of *La Lunette d'approche*:[40] through the transparence of a window can be seen the passing of clouds and the sparkle of a blue sea; but the window opens onto black void, showing this to be a reflection of nothing.

In *Les Liaisons dangereuses*,[41] a nude woman holds before her a mirror that almost completely hides her. She has her eyes nearly shut, she lowers and turns her head to the left, as if she did not want to be seen and to see that she is seen. Now the mirror, which is in the same plane as the painting and facing the viewer, reflects the image of the same woman who is trying to hide. The mirror's reflecting face shows the segment of her body (from shoulders to thighs) that the blind face conceals. The mirror functions a little like a fluoroscope, but with a whole play of differences. The woman is seen in profile, turned to the right, body bent slightly forward, arm not outstretched to hold the heavy mirror but rather tucked beneath her breasts. The long hair that ought to extend behind the mirror on the right streams down, in the mirror image, on the left, slightly interrupted by the frame at the point of the acute angle. The image is noticeably smaller than the woman herself, indicating a certain distance between the glass and the reflected object that contests or is contested by the posture of the woman who presses the mirror against her body the better to hide. The small gap behind the mirror is shown again by the extreme proximity of a large grey wall. On it can be clearly seen the shadows cast by the woman's

head and thighs and by the mirror. From the shadow one part is missing – that of the left hand that holds the mirror. Normally it should be seen on the right of the painting; here it is missing, as if in the shadow the mirror was supported by no one.

Behind the wall and the mirror, the hidden body is elided; in the thin space separating the mirror's polished, reflection-capturing surface and the opaque surface of the wall that catches only shadows, there is nothing. Through all these scenes glide similitudes that no reference point can situate: translations with neither point of departure nor support.

6
Nonaffirmative Painting[42]

Separation between linguistic signs and plastic elements; equivalence of resemblance and affirmation. These two principles constituted the tension in classical painting, because the second reintroduced discourse (affirmation exists only where there is speech) into an art from which the linguistic element was rigorously excluded. Hence the fact that classical painting spoke – and spoke constantly – while constituting itself entirely outside language; hence the fact that it rested silently in a discursive space; hence the fact that it provided, beneath itself, a kind of common ground where it could restore the bonds of signs and the image.

Magritte knits verbal signs and plastic elements together, but without referring them to a prior isotopism. He skirts the base of affirmative discourse on which resemblance calmly reposes, and he brings pure similitudes and nonaffirmative verbal statements into play within the instability of a disoriented volume and an unmapped space. A process whose formulation is in some sense given by *Ceci n'est pas une pipe*.

1 To employ a calligram where are found, simultaneously present and visible, image, text, resemblance, affirmation, and their common ground.
2 Then suddenly to open it up, so that the calligram immediately decomposes and disappears, leaving as a trace only its own absence.
3 To allow discourse to collapse of its own weight and to acquire the visible shape of letters. Letters which, insofar as they are drawn, enter into an uncertain, indefinite relation, confused with

the drawing itself – but minus any area to serve as a common ground.

4 To allow similitudes, on the other hand, to multiply of themselves, to be born from their own vapor and to rise endlessly into an ether where they refer to nothing more than themselves.

5 To verify clearly, at the end of the operation, that the precipitate has changed color, that it has gone from black to white, that the "This is a pipe" silently hidden in mimetic representation has become the "This is not a pipe" of circulating similitudes.

A day will come when, by means of similitude relayed indefinitely along the length of a series, the image itself, along with the name it bears, will lose its identity. Campbell, Campbell, Campbell, Campbell.[43]

Notes

1 *Leçon de choses*, literally "lesson of things." An allusion to the title of a 1947 Magritte canvas, as well as a 1960 film about Magritte made by Luc de Heusch. Magritte also wrote an essay to which he gave the title.

2 "Dawn at the Ends of the Earth," the title of a book with illustrations by Magritte. Actually, Magritte's pipe and its wry subscript appear in a whole series of paintings and drawings. There is also a pun on the word *aube*, which can mean either "dawn" or "float."

3 "The Wrestlers' Tomb."

4 "The Battle of the Argonne."

5 An untranslatable pun. Le *"nom d'une pipe"* is a mild or euphemistic oath on the order of "for Pete's sake" when substituted for "for God's sake." In the preceding remark, Foucault's point is that the slang expression has entered speech so integrally as to become idiomatic, with speakers using it without consciously attending its literal meaning.

6 A poem whose words are arranged in such fashion as to form a picture of its "topic," the calligram is associated closely with Apollinaire – who was, in fact, one of Magritte's favorite writers. In *The Shock of the New*, Robert Hughes speculates that Magritte's pipe was painted as a "riposte" to Le Corbusier, who had in 1923 held up the image of a pipe as an image of pure functionalism. Foucault also treats Magritte's canvas as a riposte, but aimed at an entirely different target [...]. Perhaps the most paradoxical riposte imaginable is the recent cover drawing of the avant-garde journal *Tel Quel*: there, the tiny letters composing a calligraphic depiction of a bull turn out, on closer inspection, to be Chinese ideograms – "picture-words" whose calligraphic shape in turn denotes a purely linguistic vulgarism.

7 Literally, "makes speak the silence of uninterrupted lines."

8 I am indebted to Dr. Sally Lawall for pointing out that in Mallarmé's poem on Verlaine, *ce peu profond ruisseau* ("this shallow stream") is an image of death. See "Tombeau," the funeral sonnet for Paul Ver-laine, in *Oeuvres complètes de Stéphane Mallarmé*, ed. Henri Mondor et G. Jean-Aubry (Paris: Gallimard [Éditions de la Pléiade], 1956).

9 A complex pun that works oddly well in English. *Lieu commun*, "common place," signifies the common ground or shared conceptual site of language and drawing, visual and verbal representation; it also signifies the *commonplace*, that is, the ordinary. Foucault's point is that by effacing the former, Magritte also undermines the latter, enabling him to use quotidian objects to evoke mystery.

10 "The Conflagration."

11 "The Seducer."

12 Foucault is referring to *La Philosophie dans le boudoir*, "Philosophy in the Bedroom," and similar variations. [...]

13 In order, "acacia," "moon," "snow," and "ceiling."

14 TRANSLATOR'S NOTE: The original title of this chapter is "Le Sourd travail des mots," literally, "The Subterranean Work of Words." The connotation is of weakening or subversion through undercutting.

15 "The Art of Conversation."

16 "Dream."

17 "Peace."

18 "Death."

19 Foucault refers to a sketch that illustrated the French edition of *Ceci n'est pas une pipe*. In it, a man's face is splintering, while on a rock at the left is inscribed, *homme éclatant avec rire*, "man breaking up with laughter." The visual pun is on the phrase "breaking up," which in French as well as English is slang for an abrupt seizure with merriment.

20 "The evening that falls," or "night fall."

21 That is, the expression by which evening's arrival is designated a "fall."

22 AUTHOR'S NOTE: I cite all these quotations from P. Waldberg's *Magritte*. They illustrated a series of drawings in the twelfth issue of *Revolution surrealiste*.

23 "Person walking toward the horizon."

24 In order, "gun," "armchair," "horse," "cloud," and "horizon."

25 Literally, "reading-gaze." The neologism remains less confusing in French than in English.

26 "The Alphabet of Revelations."

27 LA and LE could represent the feminine and masculine forms of "the."

28 "The Balcony." A Magritte painting reinterpreting a famous work by Manet. [...]

29 Foucault seems to be contrasting the "non-place" of mystery with the "commonplace" of ordinariness. See [...] Foucault's reference to "the non-place of language" in the preface to *Les Mots et les choses* [...].

30 In various sizes, a round bell of the sort Americans call a "jingle bell" is a frequently encountered figure in Magritte's work.

31 Regarding *trompe-l'oeil*, Magritte wrote in 1946: " ... if the images are precise, in formal terms, the more precise they are, the more perfect the *trompe-l'oeil*, THE GREATER THE DECEPTION ..." In 1963 he added, "*Trompe-l'oeil* (if indeed there is such a thing) does not belong to the realm of painting. It is rather a 'playful physics'?"

32 "Original" in its most transitive sense, that is, not only "first" but also "generative."

33 "Decalcomania." The title embodies a complex play of ideas. *Décalcomanie* means transference, transferency, or decal; it is also a painterly technique (often mentioned by Breton) in which pigment is transferred from one side of a painted surface to another by folding over the canvas. Finally, *décalcomanie* refers to a species of *madness* bound up with the idea of shifting identities.

34 AUTHOR'S NOTE: The reader should examine René Passeron's *René Magritte*, particularly the last chapter.

35 Another echo of Mallarmé: Flowers "absent from all bouquets" are mentioned in the essay "*Crise de vers*" and in Mallarmé's preface to René Ghil's "*Traite du Verbe*." Both are included in the Pleiade edition of *Oeuvres complètes*.

36 "The Natural Graces," "The Flavor of Tears."

37 A bizarre pun. Literally *corps nu*, "naked body." Spoken aloud, the phrase sounds like *cornu*, "horned" – slang for cuckoldry, or more generally any sexual betrayal.

38 "Delusions of Grandeur."

39 "The Waterfall."

40 "The Field Glass."

41 "Dangerous Liaisons."

42 TRANSLATOR'S NOTE: The original title of this chapter is "Peindre n'est pas affirmer," literally, "To Paint Is Not to Affirm."

43 Foucault's reference is not to Magritte but to Andy Warhol, whose various series of soup cans, celebrity portraits, and so on Foucault apparently sees as undermining any sense of the unique, indivisible identity of their "models." See Foucault's comments on Warhol in the important essay "Theatricum Philosophicum," reprinted in *Language, Counter Memory, Practice* (Ithaca, New York: Cornell University Press, 1977).

25

The Laugh of the Medusa

Hélène Cixous

I shall speak about women's writing: about *what it will do*. Woman must write her self: must write about women and bring women to writing, from which they have been driven away as violently as from their bodies – for the same reasons, by the same law, with the same fatal goal. Woman must put herself into the text – as into the world and into history – by her own movement.

The future must no longer be determined by the past. I do not deny that the effects of the past are still with us. But I refuse to strengthen them by repeating them, to confer upon them an irremovability the equivalent of destiny, to confuse the biological and the cultural. Anticipation is imperative.

Since these reflections are taking shape in an area just on the point of being discovered, they necessarily bear the mark of our time – a time during which the new breaks away from the old, and, more precisely, the (feminine) new from the old (*la nouvelle de l'ancien*). Thus, as there are no grounds for establishing a discourse, but rather an arid millennial ground to break, what I say has at least two sides and two aims: to break up, to destroy; and to foresee the unforeseeable, to project.

I write this as a woman, toward women. When I say "woman," I'm speaking of woman in her inevitable struggle against conventional man; and of a universal woman subject who must bring women to their senses and to their meaning in history. But first it must be said that in spite of the enormity of the repression that has kept them in the "dark" – that dark which people have been trying to make

them accept as their attribute – there is, at this time, no general woman, no one typical woman. What they have *in common* I will say. But what strikes me is the infinite richness of their individual constitutions: you can't talk about *a* female sexuality, uniform, homogeneous, classifiable into codes – any more than you can talk about one unconscious resembling another. Women's imaginary is inexhaustible, like music, painting, writing: their stream of phantasms is incredible.

I have been amazed more than once by a description a woman gave me of a world all her own which she had been secretly haunting since early childhood. A world of searching, the elaboration of a knowledge, on the basis of a systematic experimentation with the bodily functions, a passionate and precise interrogation of her erotogeneity. This practice, extraordinarily rich and inventive, in particular as concerns masturbation, is prolonged or accompanied by a production of forms, a veritable aesthetic activity, each stage of rapture inscribing a resonant vision, a composition, something beautiful. Beauty will no longer be forbidden.

I wished that that woman would write and proclaim this unique empire so that other women, other unacknowledged sovereigns, might exclaim: I, too, overflow; my desires have invented new desires, my body knows unheard-of songs. Time and again I, too, have felt so full of luminous torrents that I could burst – burst with forms much more beautiful than those which are put up in frames and sold for a stinking fortune. And I, too, said nothing, showed nothing; I didn't open my mouth, I didn't repaint my half of the world. I was ashamed. I was afraid, and I swallowed my shame and my fear. I said to myself: You are mad! What's the meaning of these waves, these floods, these outbursts? Where is the ebullient, infinite woman who, immersed as she was in her naiveté, kept in the dark about herself, led into self-disdain by the great arm of parental-conjugal phallocentrism, hasn't been ashamed of her strength? Who, surprised and horrified by the fantastic tumult of her drives (for she was made to believe that a well-adjusted normal woman has a . . . divine composure), hasn't accused herself of being a monster? Who, feeling a funny desire stirring inside her (to sing, to write, to dare to speak, in short, to bring out something new), hasn't thought she was sick? Well, her shameful sickness is that she resists death, that she makes trouble.

And why don't you write? Write! Writing is for you, you are for you; your body is yours, take it. I know why you haven't written. (And why I didn't write before the age of twenty-seven.) Because writing is at once too high, too great for you, it's reserved for the great – that is for "great men"; and it's "silly." Besides, you've written a little, but in secret. And it wasn't good, because it was in secret, and because you punished yourself for writing, because you didn't go all the way, or because you wrote, irresistibly, as when we would masturbate in secret, not to go further, but to attenuate the tension a bit, just enough to take the edge off. And then as soon as we come, we go and make ourselves feel guilty – so as to be forgiven; or to forget, to bury it until the next time.

Write, let no one hold you back, let nothing stop you: not man; not the imbecilic capitalist machinery, in which publishing houses are the crafty, obsequious relayers of imperatives handed down by an economy that works against us and off our backs; and not *yourself*. Smug-faced readers, managing editors, and big bosses don't like the true texts of women – female-sexed tests. That kind scares them.

I write woman: woman must write woman. And man, man. So only an oblique consideration will be found here of man; it's up to him to say where his masculinity and femininity are at: this will concern us once men have opened their eyes and seen themselves clearly.[1]

Now women return from afar, from always: from "without," from the heath where witches are kept alive; from below, from beyond "culture"; from their childhood which men have been trying desperately to make them forget, condemning it to "eternal rest." The little girls and their "ill-mannered" bodies immured, well-preserved, intact unto themselves, in the mirror. Frigidified. But are they ever seething underneath! What an effort it takes – there's no end to it – for the sex cops to bar their threatening return. Such a display of forces on both sides that the struggle has for centuries been immobilized in the trembling equilibrium of a deadlock.

Here they are, returning, arriving over and again, because the unconscious is impregnable. They have wandered around in circles, confined to the narrow room in which they've been given a deadly brainwashing. You can incarcerate them, slow them down, get away with the old Apartheid routine, but for a time only. As soon as they begin to speak, at the same time as they're taught their name, they can be taught that their territory is black: because you are Africa, you are black. Your continent is dark. Dark is dangerous. You can't see anything in the dark, you're afraid. Don't move, you might fall. Most of all, don't go into the forest. And so we have internalized this horror of the dark.

Men have committed the greatest crime against women. Insidiously, violently, they have led them to hate women, to be their own enemies, to mobilize their immense strength against themselves, to be the executants of their virile needs. They have made for women an antinarcissism! A narcissism which loves itself only to be loved for what women haven't got! They have constructed the infamous logic of antilove.

We the precocious, we the repressed of culture, our lovely mouths gagged with pollen, our wind knocked out of us, we the labyrinths, the ladders, the trampled spaces, the bevies – we are black and we are beautiful.

We're stormy, and that which is ours breaks loose from us without our fearing any debilitation. Our glances, our smiles, are spent; laughs exude from all our mouths; our blood flows and we extend ourselves without ever reaching an end; we never hold back our thoughts, our signs, our writing; and we're not afraid of lacking.

What happiness for us who are omitted, brushed aside at the scene of inheritances; we inspire ourselves and we expire without running out of breath, we are everywhere!

From now on, who, if we say so, can say no to us? We've come back from always.

It is time to liberate the New Woman from the Old by coming to know her – by loving her for getting by, for getting beyond the Old without delay, by going out ahead of what the New Woman will be, as an arrow quits the bow with a movement that gathers and separates the vibrations musically, in order to be more than her self.

I say that we must, for, with a few rare exceptions, there has not yet been any writing that inscribes femininity; exceptions so rare, in fact, that, after plowing through literature across languages, cultures, and ages,[2] one can only be startled at this vain scouting mission. It is well known that the number of women writers (while having increased very slightly from the nineteenth century on) has always been ridiculously small. This is a useless and deceptive fact unless from their species of female writers we do not first deduct the immense majority whose workmanship is in no way different from male writing, and which either obscures women or reproduces the classic representations of women (as sensitive – intuitive – dreamy, etc.).[3]

Let me insert here a parenthetical remark. I mean it when I speak of male writing. I maintain unequivocally that there is such a thing as *marked* writing; that, until now, far more extensively and repressively than is ever suspected or admitted, writing has been run by a libidinal and cultural – hence political, typically masculine – economy; that this is a locus where the repression of women has been perpetuated, over and over, more or less consciously, and in a manner that's frightening since it's often hidden or adorned with the mystifying charms of fiction; that this locus has grossly exaggerated all the signs of sexual opposition (and not sexual difference), where woman has never *her* turn to speak – this being all the more serious and unpardonable in that writing is precisely *the very possibility of change*, the space that can serve as a springboard for subversive thought, the precursory movement of a transformation of social and cultural structures.

Nearly the entire history of writing is confounded with the history of reason, of which it is at once the effect, the support, and one of the privileged alibis. It has been one with the phallocentric tradition. It is indeed that same self-admiring, self-stimulating, self-congratulatory phallocentrism.

With some exceptions, for there have been failures – and if it weren't for them, I wouldn't be writing (I-woman, escapee) – in that enormous machine that has been operating and turning out its "truth" for centuries. There have been poets who would go to any lengths to slip something by at odds with tradition – men capable of loving love and hence capable of loving others and of wanting them, of imagining the woman who would hold out against oppression and constitute herself as a superb, equal, hence "impossible" subject, untenable in a real social framework. Such a woman the poet could desire only by breaking the codes that negate her. Her appearance would necessarily bring on, if not revolution – for the bastion was supposed to be immutable – at least harrowing explosions. At times it is in the fissure caused by an earthquake, through that radical mutation of things brought on by a material upheaval when every structure is for a moment thrown off balance and an ephemeral wildness sweeps order away, that the poet slips something by, for a brief span, of woman. Thus did Kleist expend himself in his yearning for the existence of sister-lovers, maternal daughters, mother-sisters, who never hung their heads in shame. Once the palace of magistrates is restored, it's time to pay: immediate bloody death to the uncontrollable elements.

But only the poets – not the novelists, allies of representationalism. Because poetry involves gaining strength through the unconscious and because the unconscious, that other limitless country, is the place where the repressed manage to survive: women, or as Hoffmann would say, fairies.

She must write her self, because this is the invention of a *new insurgent* writing which, when the moment of her liberation has come, will allow her to carry out the indispensable ruptures and transformations in her history, first at two levels that cannot be separated.

a) Individually. By writing her self, woman will return to the body which has been more than confiscated from her, which has been turned into the uncanny stranger on display – the ailing or dead figure, which so often turns out to be the nasty companion, the cause and location of inhibitions. Censor the body and you censor breath and speech at the same time.

Write your self. Your body must be heard. Only then will the immense resources of the unconscious spring forth. Our naphtha will spread, throughout the world, without dollars – black or gold – nonassessed values that will change the rules of the old game.

To write. An act which will not only "realize" the decensored relation of woman to her sexuality, to her womanly being, giving her access to her native strength; it will give her back her goods, her pleasures, her organs, her immense bodily territories which have been kept under seal; it will tear her away from the superegoized structure in which she has always occupied the place reserved for the guilty (guilty of everything, guilty at every turn: for having desires, for not having any; for being frigid, for being "too hot"; for not being both at once; for being too motherly and not enough; for having children and for not having any; for nursing and for not nursing...) – tear her away by means of this research, this job of analysis and illumination, this emancipation of the marvelous text of her self that she must urgently learn to speak. A woman without a body, dumb, blind, can't possibly be a good fighter. She is reduced to being the servant of the militant male, his shadow. We must kill the false woman who is preventing the live one from breathing. Inscribe the breath of the whole woman.

b) An act that will also be marked by woman's *seizing* the occasion to *speak*, hence her shattering entry into history, which has always been based *on her suppression*. To write and thus to forge for herself the antilogos weapon. To become *at will* the taker and initiator, for her own right, in every symbolic system, in every political process.

It is time for women to start scoring their feats in written and oral language.

Every woman has known the torment of getting up to speak. Her heart racing, at times entirely lost for words, ground and language slipping away – that's how daring a feat, how great a transgression it is for a woman to speak – even just open her mouth – in public. A double distress, for even if she transgresses, her words fall almost always upon the deaf male ear, which hears in language only that which speaks in the masculine.

It is by writing, from and toward women, and by taking up the challenge of speech which has been governed by the phallus, that women will confirm women in a place other than that which is reserved in and by the symbolic, that is, in a place other than silence. Women should break out of the snare of silence. They shouldn't be conned into accepting a domain which is the margin or the harem.

Listen to a woman speak at a public gathering (if she hasn't painfully lost her wind). She doesn't "speak," she throws her trembling body forward; she lets go of herself, she flies; all of her passes into her voice, and it's with her body that she vitally supports the "logic" of her speech. Her

flesh speaks true. She lays herself bare. In fact, she physically materializes what she's thinking; she signifies it with her body. In a certain way she *inscribes* what she's saying, because she doesn't deny her drives the intractable and impassioned part they have in speaking. Her speech, even when "theoretical" or political, is never simple or linear or "objectified," generalized: she draws her story into history.

There is not that scission, that division made by the common man between the logic of oral speech and the logic of the text, bound as he is by his antiquated relation – servile, calculating – to mastery. From which proceeds the niggardly lip service which engages only the tiniest part of the body, plus the mask.

In women's speech, as in their writing, that element which never stops resonating, which, once we've been permeated by it, profoundly and imperceptibly touched by it, retains the power of moving us – that element is the song: first music from the first voice of love which is alive in every woman. Why this privileged relationship with the voice? Because no woman stockpiles as many defenses for countering the drives as does a man. You don't build walls around yourself, you don't forego pleasure as "wisely" as he. Even if phallic mystification has generally contaminated good relationships, a woman is never far from "mother" (I mean outside her role functions: the "mother" as nonname and as source of goods). There is always within her at least a little of that good mother's milk. She writes in white ink.

Woman for women – There always remains in woman that force which produces/is produced by the other – in particular, the other woman. *In* her, matrix, cradler; herself giver as her mother and child; she is her own sister-daughter. You might object, "What about she who is the hysterical offspring of a bad mother?" Everything will be changed once woman gives woman to the other woman. There is hidden and always ready in woman the source; the locus for the other. The mother, too, is a metaphor. It is necessary and sufficient that the best of herself be given to woman by another woman for her to be able to love herself and return in love the body that was "born" to her. Touch me, caress me, you the living no-name, give me my self as myself. The relation to the "mother," in terms of intense pleasure and violence, is curtailed no more than the relation to childhood (the child that she was, that she is, that she makes, remakes, undoes, there at the point where, the same, she mothers herself). Text: my body – shot through with streams of song; I don't mean the overbearing, clutchy "mother" but, rather, what touches you, the equi-voice that affects you, fills your breast with an urge to come to language and launches your force; the rhythm that laughs you: the intimate recipient who makes all metaphors possible and desirable; body (body? bodies?), no more describable than god, the soul, or the Other; that part of you that leaves a space between yourself and urges you to inscribe in language your woman's style. In women there is always more or less of the mother who makes everything all right, who nourishes, and who stands up against separation; a force that will not be cut off but will knock the wind out of the codes. We will rethink womankind beginning with every form and every period of her body. The Americans remind us, "We are all Lesbians": that is, don't denigrate woman, don't make of her what men have made of you.

Because the "economy" of her drives is prodi-gious, she cannot fail, in seizing the occasion to speak, to transform directly and indirectly *all* sys-tems of exchange based on masculine thrift. Her libido will produce far more radical effects of polit-ical and social change than some might like to think.

Because she arrives, vibrant, over and again, we are at the beginning of a new history, or rather of a process of becoming in which several histories intersect with one another. As subject for history, woman always occurs simultaneously in several places. Woman un-thinks[4] the unifying, regulating history that homogenizes and channels forces, herding contradictions into a single battlefield. In woman, personal history blends together with the history of all women, as well as national and world history. As a militant, she is an integral part of all liberations. She must be farsighted, not limited to a blow-by-blow interaction. She foresees that her liberation will do more than modify power rela-tions or toss the ball over to the other camp; she will bring about a mutation in human relations, in thought, in all praxis: hers is not simply a class struggle, which she carries forward into a much vaster movement. Not that in order to be a woman-in-struggle(s) you have to leave the class struggle or repudiate it; but you have to split it open, spread it out, push it forward, fill it with the fundamental struggle so as to prevent the class struggle, or any other struggle for the liberation of a class or people, from operating as a form of repression, pretext for postponing the inevitable,

the staggering alteration in power relations and in the production of individualities. This alteration is already upon us – in the United States, for ex-ample, where millions of night crawlers are in the process of undermining the family and disintegrat-ing the whole of American sociality.

The new history is coming; it's not a dream, though it does extend beyond men's imagination, and for good reason. It's going to deprive them of their conceptual orthopedics, beginning with the destruction of their enticement machine.

It is impossible to *define* a feminine practice of writing, and this is an impossibility that will remain, for this practice can never be theorized, enclosed, coded – which doesn't mean that it doesn't exist. But it will always surpass the dis-course that regulates the phallocentric system; it does and will take place in areas other than those subordinated to philosophico-theoretical domin-ation. It will be conceived of only by subjects who are breakers of automatisms, by peripheral figures that no authority can ever subjugate.

Hence the necessity to affirm the flourishes of this writing, to give form to its movement, its near and distant byways. Bear in mind to begin with (1) that sexual opposition, which has always worked for man's profit to the point of reducing writing, too, to his laws, is only a historico-cultural limit. There is, there will be more and more rapidly pervasive now, a fiction that produces irreducible effects of femininity. (2) That it is through ignorance that most readers, critics, and writers of both sexes hesitate to admit or deny outright the possibility or the pertinence of a distinction between feminine and masculine writing. It will usually be said, thus disposing of sexual difference: either that all writ-ing, to the extent that it materializes, is feminine; or, inversely – but it comes to the same thing – that the act of writing is equivalent to masculine masturbation (and so the woman who writes cuts herself out a paper penis); or that writing is bisex-ual, hence neuter, which again does away with differentiation. To admit that writing is precisely working (in) the in-between, inspecting the pro-cess of the same and of the other without which nothing can live, undoing the work of death – to admit this is first to want the two, as well as both, the ensemble of the one and the other, not fixed in sequences of struggle and expulsion or some other form of death but infinitely dynamized by an incessant process of exchange from one subject to another. A process of different subjects knowing one another and beginning one another anew only from the living boundaries of the other: a multiple and inexhaustible course with millions of encounters and transformations of the same into the other and into the in-between, from which woman takes her forms (and man, in his turn; but that's his other history).

In saying "bisexual, hence neuter," I am referring to the classic conception of bisexuality, which, squashed under the emblem of castration fear and along with the fantasy of a "total" being (though composed of two halves), would do away with the difference experienced as an operation incurring loss, as the mark of dreaded sectility.

To this self-effacing, merger-type bisexuality, which would conjure away castration (the writer who puts up his sign: "bisexual written here, come and see," when the odds are good that it's neither one nor the other), I oppose the *other bisexuality* on which every subject not enclosed in the false theater of phallocentric representationalism has founded his/her erotic universe. Bisexuality: that is, each one's location in self (*repérage en soi*) of the presence – variously manifest and insistent according to each person, male or female – of both sexes, nonexclusion either of the difference or of one sex, and, from this "self-permission," multiplication of the effects of the inscription of desire, over all parts of my body and the other body.

Now it happens that at present, for historico-cultural reasons, it is women who are opening up to and benefiting from this vatic bisexuality which doesn't annul differences but stirs them up, pursues them, increases their number. In a certain way, "woman is bisexual"; man – it's a secret to no one – being poised to keep glorious phallic monosexuality in view. By virtue of affirming the primacy of the phallus and of bringing it into play, phallocratic ideology has claimed more than one victim. As a woman, I've been clouded over by the great shadow of the scepter and been told: idolize it, that which you cannot brandish. But at the same time, man has been handed that grotesque and scarcely enviable destiny (just imagine) of being reduced to a single idol with clay balls. And consumed, as Freud and his followers note, by a fear of being a woman! For, if psychoanalysis was constituted from woman, to repress femininity (and not so successful a repression at that – men have made it clear), its account of masculine sexuality is now hardly refutable; as with all the "human" sciences, it reproduces the masculine view, of which it is one of the effects.

Here we encounter the inevitable man-with-rock, standing erect in his old Freudian realm, in the way that, to take the figure back to the point where linguistics is conceptualizing it "anew," Lacan preserves it in the sanctuary of the phallos (ϕ) "sheltered" from *castration's lack*! Their "symbolic" exists, it holds power – we, the sowers of disorder, know it only too well. But we are in no way obliged to deposit our lives in their banks of lack, to consider the constitution of the subject in terms of a drama manglingly restaged, to reinstate again and again the religion of the father. Because we don't want that. We don't fawn around the supreme hole. We have no womanly reason to pledge allegiance to the negative. The feminine (as the poets suspected) affirms: "...And yes," says Molly, carrying *Ulysses* off beyond any book and toward the new writing; "I said yes, I will Yes."

The Dark Continent is neither dark nor unexplorable. – It is still unexplored only because we've been made to believe that it was too dark to be explorable. And because they want to make us believe that what interests us is the white continent, with its monuments to Lack. And we believed. They riveted us between two horrifying myths: between the Medusa and the abyss. That would be enough to set half the world laughing, except that it's still going on. For the phallologocentric sublation[5] is with us, and it's militant, regenerating the old patterns, anchored in the dogma of castration. They haven't changed a thing: they've theorized their desire for reality! Let the priests tremble, we're going to show them our sexts!

Too bad for them if they fall apart upon discovering that women aren't men, or that the mother doesn't have one. But isn't this fear convenient for them? Wouldn't the worst be, isn't the worst, in truth, that women aren't castrated, that they have only to stop listening to the Sirens (for the Sirens were men) for history to change its meaning? You only have to look at the Medusa straight on to see her. And she's not deadly. She's beautiful and she's laughing.

Men say that there are two unrepresentable things: death and the feminine sex. That's because they need femininity to be associated with death; it's the jitters that give them a hard-on! for themselves! They need to be afraid of us. Look at the trembling Perseuses moving backward toward us, clad in apotropes. What lovely backs! Not another minute to lose. Let's get out of here.

Let's hurry: the continent is not impenetrably dark. I've been there often. I was overjoyed one day to run into Jean Genet. It was in *Pompes funèbres*.[6] He had come there led by his Jean. There are some men (all too few) who aren't afraid of femininity.

Almost everything is yet to be written by women about femininity: about their sexuality, that is, its infinite and mobile complexity, about their eroticization, sudden turn-ons of a certain minuscule-immense area of their bodies; not about destiny, but about the adventure of such and such a drive, about trips, crossings, trudges, abrupt and gradual awakenings, discoveries of a zone at one time timorous and soon to be forthright. A woman's body, with its thousand and one thresholds of ardor – once, by smashing yokes and censors, she lets it articulate the profusion of meanings that run through it in every direction – will make the old single-grooved mother tongue reverberate with more than one language.

We've been turned away from our bodies, shamefully taught to ignore them, to strike them with that stupid sexual modesty; we've been made victims of the old fool's game: each one will love the other sex. I'll give you your body and you'll give me mine. But who are the men who give women the body that women blindly yield to them? Why so few texts? Because so few women have as yet won back their body. Women must write through their bodies, they must invent the impregnable language that will wreck partitions, classes, and rhetorics, regulations and codes, they must submerge, cut through, get beyond the ultimate reserve-discourse, including the one that laughs at the very idea of pronouncing the word "silence," the one that, aiming for the impossible, stops short before the word "impossible" and writes it as "the end."

Such is the strength of women that, sweeping away syntax, breaking that famous thread (just a tiny little thread, they say) which acts for men as a surrogate umbilical cord, assuring them – otherwise they couldn't come – that the old lady is always right behind them, watching them make phallus, women will go right up to the impossible.

When the "repressed" of their culture and their society returns, it's an explosive, *utterly* destructive, staggering return, with a force never yet unleashed and equal to the most forbidding of suppressions. For when the Phallic period comes to an end, women will have been either annihilated or borne up to the highest and most violent incandescence. Muffled throughout their history, they have lived in dreams, in bodies (though muted), in silences, in aphonic revolts.

And with such force in their fragility; a fragility, a vulnerability, equal to their incomparable intensity. Fortunately, they haven't sublimated; they've saved their skin, their energy. They haven't worked at liquidating the impasse of lives without futures. They have furiously inhabited these sumptuous bodies: admirable hysterics who made Freud succumb to many voluptuous moments impossible to confess, bombarding his Mosaic statue with their carnal and passionate body words, haunting him with their inaudible and thundering denunciations, dazzling, more than naked underneath the seven veils of modesty. Those who, with a single word of the body, have inscribed the vertiginous immensity of a history which is sprung like an arrow from the whole history of men and from biblico-capitalist society, are the women, the supplicants of yesterday, who come as forebears of the new women, after whom no intersubjective relation will ever be the same. You, Dora, you the indomitable, the poetic body, you are the true "mistress" of the Signifier. Before long your efficacity will be seen at work when your speech is no longer suppressed, its point turned in against your breast, but written out over against the other.

In body. – More so than men who are coaxed toward social success, toward sublimation, women are body. More body, hence more writing. For a long time it has been in body that women have responded to persecution, to the familial-conjugal enterprise of domestication, to the repeated attempts at castrating them. Those who have turned their tongues 10,000 times seven times before not speaking are either dead from it or more familiar with their tongues and their mouths than anyone else. Now, I-woman am going to blow up the Law: an explosion henceforth possible and ineluctable; let it be done, right now, *in* language.

Let us not be trapped by an analysis still encumbered with the old automatisms. It's not to be feared that language conceals an invincible adversary, because it's the language of men and their grammar. We mustn't leave them a single place that's any more theirs alone than we are.

If woman has always functioned "within" the discourse of man, a signifier that has always referred back to the opposite signifier which annihilates its specific energy and diminishes or stifles its very different sounds, it is time for her to dislocate this "within," to explode it, turn it around, and seize it; to make it hers, containing it, taking it in her own mouth, biting that tongue with her very own teeth to invent for herself a language to get inside of. And you'll see with what ease she will spring forth from that "within" – the "within" where once she so drowsily crouched – to overflow at the lips she will cover the foam.

Nor is the point to appropriate their instruments, their concepts, their places, or to begrudge them their position of mastery. Just because there's a risk of identification doesn't mean that we'll succumb. Let's leave it to the worriers, to masculine anxiety and its obsession with how to dominate the way things work – knowing "how it works" in order to "make it work." For us the point is not to take possession in order to internalize or manipulate, but rather to dash through and to "fly."[7]

Flying is woman's gesture – flying in language and making it fly. We have all learned the art of flying and its numerous techniques; for centuries we've been able to possess anything only by flying; we've lived in flight, stealing away, finding, when desired, narrow passageways, hidden crossovers. It's no accident that *voler* has a double meaning, that it plays on each of them and thus throws off the agents of sense. It's no accident: women take after birds and robbers just as robbers take after women and birds. They (*illes*)[8] go by, fly the coop, take pleasure in jumbling the order of space, in disorienting it, in changing around the furniture, dislocating things and values, breaking them all up, emptying structures, and turning propriety upside down.

What woman hasn't flown/stolen? Who hasn't felt, dreamt, performed the gesture that jams sociality? Who hasn't crumbled, held up to ridicule, the bar of separation? Who hasn't inscribed with her body the differential, punctured the system of couples and opposition? Who, by some act of transgression, hasn't overthrown successiveness, connection, the wall of circumfusion?

A feminine text cannot fail to be more than subversive. It is volcanic; as it is written it brings about an upheaval of the old property crust, carrier of masculine investments; there's no other way. There's no room for her if she's not a he. If she's a her-she, it's in order to smash everything, to shatter the framework of institutions, to blow up the law, to break up the "truth" with laughter.

For once she blazes *her* trail in the symbolic, she cannot fail to make of it the chaosmos of the "personal" – in her pronouns, her nouns, and her clique of referents. And for good reason. There will have been the long history of gynocide. This is known by the colonized peoples of yesterday, the workers, the nations, the species off whose backs the history of men has made its gold: those who have known the ignominy of persecution derive from it an obstinate future desire for grandeur; those who are locked up know better than their jailers the taste of free air. Thanks to their history, women today know (how to do and want) what men will be able to conceive of only much later. I say woman overturns the "personal," for if, by means of laws, lies, blackmail, and marriage, her right to herself has been extorted at the same time as her name, she has been able, through the very movement of mortal alienation, to see more closely the inanity of "propriety," the reductive stinginess of the masculine-conjugal subjective economy, which she doubly resists. On the one hand she has constituted herself necessarily as that "person" capable of losing a part of herself without losing her integrity. But secretly, silently, deep down inside, she grows and multiplies, for, on the other hand, she knows far more about living and about the relation between the economy of the drives and the management of the ego than any man. Unlike man, who holds so dearly to his title and his titles, his pouches of value, his cap, crown, and everything connected with his head, woman couldn't care less about the fear of decapitation (or castration), adventuring, without the masculine temerity, into anonymity, which she can merge with, without annihilating herself: because she's a giver.

I shall have a great deal to say about the whole deceptive problematic of the gift. Woman is obviously not that woman Nietzsche dreamed of who gives only in order to.[9] Who could ever think of the gift as a gift-that-takes? Who else but man, precisely the one who would like to take everything?

If there is a "propriety of woman," it is paradoxically her capacity to depropriate unselfishly, body without end, without appendage, without principal "parts." If she is a whole, it's a whole composed of parts that are wholes, not simple partial objects but a moving, limitlessly changing ensemble, a cosmos tirelessly traversed by Eros, an immense astral space not organized around any one sun that's any more of a star than the others.

This doesn't mean that she's an undifferentiated magma, but that she doesn't lord it over her body or her desire. Though masculine sexuality gravitates around the penis, engendering that centralized body (in political anatomy) under the dictatorship of its parts, woman does not bring about the same regionalization which serves the couple head/genitals and which is inscribed only within boundaries. Her libido is cosmic, just as her unconscious is worldwide. Her writing can only keep going, without ever inscribing or discerning contours, daring to make these vertiginous crossings of the other(s) ephemeral and passionate sojourns in him, her, them, whom she inhabits long enough to look at from the point closest to their unconscious from the moment they awaken, to love them at the point closest to their drives; and then further, impregnated through and through with these brief, identificatory embraces, she goes and passes into infinity. She alone dares and wishes to know from within, where she, the outcast, has never ceased to hear the resonance of fore-language. She lets the other language speak – the language of 1,000 tongues which knows neither enclosure nor death. To life she refuses nothing. Her language does not contain, it carries; it does not hold back, it makes possible. When id is ambiguously uttered – the wonder of being several – she doesn't defend herself against these unknown women whom she's surprised at becoming, but derives pleasure from this gift of alterability. I am spacious, singing flesh, on which is grafted no one knows which I, more or less human, but alive because of transformation.

Write! and your self-seeking text will know itself better than flesh and blood, rising, insurrectionary dough kneading itself, with sonorous, perfumed ingredients, a lively combination of flying colors, leaves, and rivers plunging into the sea we feed. "Ah, there's her sea," he will say as he holds out to me a basin full of water from the little phallic mother from whom he's inseparable. But look, our seas are what we make of them, full of fish or not, opaque or transparent, red or black, high or smooth, narrow or bankless; and we are ourselves sea, sand, coral, seaweed, beaches, tides, swimmers, children, waves... More or less wavily sea, earth, sky – what matter would rebuff us? We know how to speak them all.

Heterogeneous, yes. For her joyous benefits she is erogenous; she is the erotogeneity of the heterogeneous: airborne swimmer, in flight, she does not cling to herself; she is dispersible, prodigious, stunning, desirous and capable of others, of the other woman that she will be, of the other woman she isn't, of him, of you.

Woman be unafraid of any other place, of any same, or any other. My eyes, my tongue, my ears, my nose, my skin, my mouth, my body-for-(the)-other – not that I long for it in order to fill up a hole, to provide against some defect of mine, or because, as fate would have it, I'm spurred on by feminine "jealousy"; not because I've been dragged into the whole chain of substitutions that brings that which is substituted back to its ultimate object. That sort of thing you would expect to come straight out of "Tom Thumb," out of the *Penisneid* whispered to us by old grandmother ogresses, servants to their father-sons. If they believe, in order to muster up some self-importance, if they really need to believe that we're dying of desire, that we are this hole fringed with desire for their penis – that's their immemorial business. Undeniably (we verify it at our own expense – but also to our amusement), it's their business to let us know they're getting a hard-on, so that we'll assure them (we the maternal mistresses of their little pocket signifier) that they still can, that it's still there – that men structure themselves only by being fitted with a feather. In the child it's not the penis that the woman desires, it's not that famous bit of skin around which every man gravitates. Pregnancy cannot be traced back, except within the historical limits of the ancients, to some form of fate, to those mechanical substitutions brought about by the unconscious of some eternal "jealous woman"; not to penis envies; and not to narcissism or to some sort of homosexuality linked to the ever-present mother! Begetting a child doesn't mean that the woman or the man must fall ineluctably into patterns or must recharge the circuit of reproduction. If there's a risk there's not an inevitable trap: may women be spared the pressure, under the guise of consciousness-raising, of a supplement of interdictions. Either you want a kid or you don't – *that's your business*. Let nobody threaten you; in satisfying your desire, let not the fear of becoming the accomplice to a sociality succeed the old-time fear of being "taken." And man, are you still going to bank on everyone's blindness and passivity, afraid lest the child make a father and, consequently, that in having a kid the woman land herself more than one bad deal by engendering all at once child – mother – father – family? No; it's up to you to break the old circuits. It will be up to man and woman to render obsolete the former relationship and all its consequences, to consider the launching of a brand-new subject, alive, with defamilialization. Let us dematerpaternalize rather than deny woman, in an effort to avoid the cooptation of procreation, a thrilling era of the body. Let us defetishize. Let's get away from the dialectic which has it that the only good father is a dead one, or that the child is the death of his parents. The child is the other, but the other without violence, bypassing loss, struggle. We're fed up with the reuniting of bonds forever to be severed, with the litany of castration that's handed down and genealogized. We won't advance backward anymore; we're not going to repress something so simple as the desire for life. Oral drive, anal drive, vocal drive – all these drives are our strengths, and among them is the gestation drive – just like the desire to write: a desire to live self from within, a desire for the swollen belly, for language, for blood. We are not going to refuse, if it should happen to strike our fancy, the unsurpassed pleasures of pregnancy which have actually been always exaggerated or conjured away – or cursed – in the classic texts. For if there's one thing that's been repressed, here's just the place to find it: in the taboo of the pregnant woman. This says a lot about the power she seems invested with at the time, because it has always been suspected, that, when pregnant, the woman not only doubles her market value, but – what's more important – takes on intrinsic value as a woman in her own eyes and, undeniably, acquires body and sex.

There are thousands of ways of living one's pregnancy; to have or not to have with that still invisible other a relationship of another intensity. And if you don't have that particular yearning, it doesn't mean that you're in any way lacking. Each body distributes in its own special way, without model or norm, the nonfinite and changing totality of its desires. Decide for yourself on your position in the arena of contradictions, where pleasure and reality embrace. Bring the other to life. Women know how to live detachment; giving birth is neither losing nor increasing. It's adding to life an other. Am I dreaming? Am I misrecognizing? You, the defenders of "theory," the sacrosanct yes-men of Concept, enthroners of the phallus (but not of the penis):

Once more you'll say that all this smacks of "idealism," or what's worse, you'll splutter that I'm a "mystic."

And what about the libido? Haven't I read the "Signification of the Phallus"? And what about separation, what about that bit of self for which,

to be born, you undergo an ablation – an ablation, so they say, to be forever commemorated by your desire?

Besides, isn't it evident that the penis gets around in my texts, that I give it a place and appeal? Of course I do. I want all. I want all of me with all of him. Why should I deprive myself of a part of us? I want all of us. Woman of course has a desire for a "loving desire" and not a jealous one. But not because she is gelded; not because she's deprived and needs to be filled out, like some wounded person who wants to console herself or seek vengeance. I don't want a penis to decorate my body with. But I do desire the other for the other, whole and entire, male or female; because living means wanting everything that is, everything that lives, and wanting it alive. Castration? Let others toy with it. What's desire originating from a lack? A pretty meager desire.

The woman who still allows herself to be threatened by the big dick, who's still impressed by the commotion of the phallic stance, who still leads a loyal master to the beat of the drum: that's the woman of yesterday. They still exist, easy and numerous victims of the oldest of farces: either they're cast in the original silent versions in which, as titanesses lying under the mountains they make with their quivering, they never see erected that theoretic monument to the golden phallus looming, in the old manner, over their bodies. Or, coming today out of their *infans* period and into the second, "enlightened" version of their virtuous debasement, they see themselves suddenly assaulted by the builders of the analytic empire and, as soon as they've begun to formulate the new desire, naked, nameless, so happy at making an appearance, they're taken in their bath by the new old men, and then, whoops! Luring them with flashy signifiers, the demon of interpretation – oblique, decked out in modernity – sells them the same old handcuffs, baubles, and chains. Which castration do you prefer? Whose degrading do you like better, the father's or the mother's? Oh, what pwetty eyes, you pwetty little girl. Here, buy my glasses and you'll see the Truth-Me-Myself tell you everything you should know. Put them on your nose and take a fetishist's look (you are me, the other analyst – that's what I'm telling you) at your body and the body of the other. You see? No? Wait, you'll have everything explained to you, and you'll know at last which sort of neurosis you're related to. Hold still, we're going to do your portrait, so that you can begin looking like it right away.

Yes, the naives to the first and second degree are still legion. If the New Women, arriving now, dare to create outside the theoretical, they're called in by the cops of the signifier, fingerprinted, remonstrated, and brought into the line of order that they are supposed to know; assigned by force of trickery to a precise place in the chain that's always formed for the benefit of a privileged signifier. We are pieced back to the string which leads back, if not to the Name-of-the-Father, then, for a new twist, to the place of the phallic-mother.

Beware, my friend, of the signifier that would take you back to the authority of a signified! Beware of diagnoses that would reduce your generative powers. "Common" nouns are also proper nouns that disparage your singularity by classifying it into species. Break out of the circles; don't remain within the psychoanalytic closure. Take a look around, then cut through!

And if we are legion, it's because the war of liberation has only made as yet a tiny breakthrough. But women are thronging to it. I've seen them, those who will be neither dupe nor domestic, those who will not fear the risk of being a woman; will not fear any risk, any desire, any space still unexplored in themselves, among themselves and others or anywhere else. They do not fetishize, they do not deny, they do not hate. They observe, they approach, they try to see the other woman, the child, the lover – not to strengthen their own narcissism or verify the solidity or weakness of the master, but to make love better, to invent.

Other love. – In the beginning are our differences. The new love dares for the other, wants the other, makes dizzying, precipitous flights between knowledge and invention. The woman arriving over and over again does not stand still; she's everywhere, she exchanges, she is the desire-that-gives. (Not enclosed in the paradox of the gift that takes nor under the illusion of unitary fusion. We're past that.) She comes in, comes-in-between herself me and you, between the other me where one is always infinitely more than one and more than me, without the fear of ever reaching a limit;

she thrills in our becoming. And we'll keep on becoming! She cuts through defensive loves, motherages, and devourations: beyond selfish narcissism, in the moving, open, transitional space, she runs her risks. Beyond the struggle-to-the-death that's been removed to the bed, beyond the love-battle that claims to represent exchange, she scorns at an Eros dynamic that would be fed by hatred. Hatred: a heritage, again, a reminder, a duping subservience to the phallus. To love, to watch-think-seek the other in the other, to despecularize, to unhoard. Does this seem difficult? It's not impossible, and this is what nourishes life – a love that has no commerce with the apprehensive desire that provides against the lack and stultifies the strange; a love that rejoices in the exchange that multiplies. Wherever history still unfolds as the history of death, she does not tread. Opposition, hierarchizing exchange, the struggle for mastery which can end only in at least one death (one master – one slave, or two nonmasters $\neq$ two dead) – all that comes from a period in time governed by phallocentric values. The fact that this period extends into the present doesn't prevent woman from starting the history of life somewhere else. Elsewhere, she gives. She doesn't "know" what she's giving, she doesn't measure it; she gives, though, neither a counterfeit impression nor something she hasn't got. She gives more, with no assurance that she'll get back even some unexpected profit from what she puts out. She gives that there may be life, thought, transformation. This is an "economy" that can no longer be put in economic terms. Wherever she loves, all the old concepts of management are left behind. At the end of a more or less conscious computation, she finds not her sum but her differences. I am for you what you want me to be at the moment you look at me in a way you've never seen me before: at every instant. When I write, it's everything that we don't know we can be that is written out of me, without exclusions, without stipulation, and everything we will be calls us to the unflagging, intoxicating, unappeasable search for love. In one another we will never be lacking.

Notes

"The Laugh of the Medusa" in *Signs*, Summer 1976. This is a revised version of "Le rire de la méduse," which appeared in *L'arc* (1975), pp. 39–54.

1 Men still have everything to say about their sexuality, and everything to write. For what they have said so far, for the most part, stems from the opposition activity/passivity from the power relation between a fantasized obligatory virility meant to invade, to colonize, and the consequential phantasm of woman as a "dark continent" to penetrate and to "pacify." (We know what "pacify" means in terms of scotomizing the other and misrecognizing the self.) Conquering her, they've made haste to depart from her borders, to get out of sight, out of body. The way man has of getting out of himself and into her whom he takes not for the other but for his own, deprives him, he knows, of his own bodily territory. One can understand how man, confusing himself with his penis and rushing in for the attack, might feel resentment and fear of being "taken" by the woman, of being lost in her, absorbed or alone.

2 I am speaking here only of the place "reserved" for women by the Western world.

3 Which works, then, might be called feminine? I'll just point out some examples: one would have to give them full readings to bring out what is pervasively feminine in their significance. Which I shall do elsewhere. In France (have you noted our infinite poverty in this field? – the Anglo-Saxon countries have shown resources of distinctly greater consequence), leafing through what's come out of the twentieth century – and it's not much – the only inscriptions of femininity that I have seen were by Colette, Marguerite Duras, . . . and Jean Genet.

4 *Dé-pense*, a neologism formed on the verb *penser*, hence "unthinks," but also "spends" (from *dépenser*). – Tr.

5 Standard English term for the Hegelian *Aufhebung*, the French *la relève*.

6 Jean Genet, *Pompes funèbres* (Paris, 1948), p. 185 [privately published].

7 Also, "to steal." Both meanings of the verb *voler* are played on, as the text itself explains in the following paragraph. – Tr.

8 *Illes* is a fusion of the masculine pronoun *ils*, which refers back to birds and robbers, with the feminine pronoun *elles*, which refers to women. – Tr.

9 Reread Derrida's text, "Le style de la femme," in *Nietzsche aujourd'hui* (Union Générale d'Editions, Coll. 10/18), where the philosopher can be seen operating an *Aufhebung* of all philosophy in its systematic reducing of woman to the place of seduction: she appears as the one who is taken for; the bait in person, all veils unfurled, the one who doesn't give but who gives only in order to (take).

26

Travels in Hyperreality

Umberto Eco

The Fortresses of Solitude

Two very beautiful naked girls are crouched facing each other. They touch each other sensually, they kiss each other's breasts lightly, with the tip of the tongue. They are enclosed in a kind of cylinder of transparent plastic. Even someone who is not a professional voyeur is tempted to circle the cylinder in order to see the girls from behind, in profile, from the other side. The next temptation is to approach the cylinder, which stands on a little column and is only a few inches in diameter, in order to look down from above: But the girls are no longer there. This was one of the many works displayed in New York by the School of Holography.

Holography, the latest technical miracle of laser rays, was invented back in the '50's by Dennis Gabor; it achieves a full-color photographic representation that is more than three-dimensional. You look into a magic box and a miniature train or horse appears; as you shift your gaze you can see those parts of the object that you were prevented from glimpsing by the laws of perspective. If the box is circular you can see the object from all sides. If the object was filmed, thanks to various devices, in motion, then it moves before your eyes, or else you move, and as you change position, you can see the girl wink or the fisherman drain the can of beer in his hand. It isn't cinema, but rather a kind of virtual object in three dimensions that exists even where you don't see it, and if you move you can see it there, too.

Holography isn't a toy: NASA has studied it and employed it in space exploration. It is used in medicine to achieve realistic depictions of anatomical changes; it has applications in aerial cartography, and in many industries for the study of physical processes. But it is now being taken up by artists who formerly might have been photorealists, and it satisfies the most ambitious ambitions of photorealism. In San Francisco, at the door of the Museum of Witchcraft, the biggest hologram ever made is on display: of the Devil, with a very beautiful witch.

Holography could prosper only in America, a country obsessed with realism, where, if a reconstruction is to be credible, it must be absolutely iconic, a perfect likeness, a "real" copy of the reality being represented.

[...]

The most amazing Fortress of Solitude was erected in Austin, Texas, by President Lyndon Johnson, during his own lifetime, as monument, pyramid, personal mausoleum. [...]

Constructing a full-scale model of the Oval Office (using the same materials, the same colors, but with everything obviously more polished, shinier, protected against deterioration) means that for historical information to be absorbed, it has to assume the aspect of a reincarnation. To speak of things that one wants to connote as real, these things must seem real. The "completely real" becomes identified with the "completely fake." Absolute unreality is offered as real presence. The aim of the reconstructed Oval Office is to supply a "sign" that will then be forgotten as such: The sign aims to be the thing, to abolish the distinction of the reference, the mechanism of replacement. Not the image of the thing, but its plaster cast. Its double, in other words.

Is this the taste of America? Certainly it is not the taste of Frank Lloyd Wright, of the Seagram Building, the skyscrapers of Mies van der Rohe. Nor is it the taste of the New York School, or of Jackson Pollock. It isn't even that of the photorealists, who produce a reality so real that it proclaims its artificiality from the rooftops. We must understand, however, from what depth of popular sensibility and craftsmanship today's photorealists draw their inspiration and why they feel called upon to force this tendency to the point of exacerbation. There is, then, an America of furious hyperreality, which is not that of Pop art, of Mickey Mouse, or of Hollywood movies. There is another, more secret America (or rather, just as public, but snubbed by the European visitor and also by the American intellectual); and it creates somehow a network of references and influences that finally spread also to the products of high culture and the entertainment industry. It has to be discovered.

And so we set out on a journey, holding on to the Ariadne-thread, an open-sesame that will allow us to identify the object of this pilgrimage no matter what form it may assume. We can identify it through two typical slogans that pervade American advertising. The first, widely used by Coca-Cola but also frequent as a hyperbolic formula in everyday speech, is "the real thing"; the second, found in print and heard on TV, is "more" – in the sense of "extra." The announcer doesn't say, for example, "The program will continue" but rather that there is "More to come." In America you don't say, "Give me another coffee"; you ask for "More coffee"; you don't say that cigarette A is longer than cigarette B, but that there's "more" of it, more than you're used to having, more than you might want, leaving a surplus to throw away – that's prosperity.

This is the reason for this journey into hyperreality, in search of instances where the American imagination demands the real thing and, to attain it, must fabricate the absolute fake; where the boundaries between game and illusion are blurred, the art museum is contaminated by the freak show, and falsehood is enjoyed in a situation of "fullness," of *horror vacui*.

The masterpiece of the reconstructive mania (and of giving more, and better) is found when this industry of absolute iconism has to deal with the problem of art.

Between San Francisco and Los Angeles I was able to visit seven wax versions of Leonardo's *Last Supper*. Some are crude and unwittingly caricatural; others are more accurate though no less unhappy in their violent colors, their chilling demolition of what had been Leonardo's vibrance. Each is displayed next to a version of the original. And you would naturally – but naïvely – suppose that this reference image, given the development of color photo reproduction, would be a copy of the original. Wrong: because, if compared to the original, the three-dimensional creation might come off second-best. So, in one museum after the other, the waxwork scene is compared to a reduced reproduction carved in wood, a nineteenth-century engraving, a modern tapestry, or a bronze, as the commenting voice insistently urges us to note the resemblance of the waxwork, and against such insufficient models, the waxwork, of course, wins. The falsehood has a certain justification, since the criterion of likeness, amply described and analyzed, never applies to the formal execution, but rather to the subject: "Observe how Judas is in the same position, and how Saint Matthew..." etc., etc.

[...]

Enchanted Castles

Winding down the curves of the Pacific coast between San Francisco, Tortilla Flat, and Los Padres National Park, along shores that recall Capri and Amalfi, as the Pacific Highway descends toward Santa Barbara, you see the castle of William Randolph Hearst rise, on the gentle Mediterranean hill of San Simeon. The traveler's heart leaps, because this is the Xanadu of *Citizen Kane*, where Orson Welles brought to life his protagonist, explicitly modeled on the great newspaper magnate, ancestor of the unfortunate Symbionese Patricia.

Having reached the peak of wealth and power, Hearst built here his own Fortress of Solitude, which a biographer has described as a combination of palace and museum such as had not been seen since the days of the Medicis. Like someone in a René Clair movie (but here reality far outstrips fiction), Hearst bought, in bits or whole, palaces, abbeys, and convents in Europe, had them dismantled brick by numbered brick, packaged and shipped across the ocean, to be reconstructed on the enchanted hill, in the midst of free-ranging wild animals. Since he wanted not a museum but a Renaissance house, he complemented the original pieces with bold imitations, not bothering to distinguish the genuine from the copy. An incontinent collectionism, the bad taste of the *nouveau riche*, and a thirst for prestige led him to bring the past down to the level of today's life; but he conceived of today as worth living only if guaranteed to be "just like the past."

Amid Roman sarcophagi, and genuine exotic plants, and remade baroque stairways, you pass Neptune's Pool, a fantasy Greco-Roman temple peopled with classical statues including (as the guidebook points out with fearless candor) the famous Venus rising from the water, sculpted in 1930 by the Italian sculptor Cassou, and you reach the Great House, a Spanish–Mexican-style cathedral with two towers (equipped with a thirty-six-bell carillon), whose portal frames an iron gate brought from a sixteenth-century Spanish convent, surmounted by a Gothic tympanum with the Virgin and Child. The floor of the vestibule encloses a mosaic found in Pompeii, there are Gobelins on the walls, the door into the Meeting Hall is by Sansovino, the great hall is fake Renaissance presented as Italo-French. A series of choir stalls comes from an Italian convent (Hearst's agents sought the scattered pieces through various European dealers), the tapestries are seventeenth-century Flemish, the objects – real or fake – date from various periods, four medallions are by Thorvaldsen. The Refectory has an Italian ceiling "four hundred years old," on the walls are banners "of an old Sienese family." The bedroom contains the authentic bed of Richelieu, the billiard room has a Gothic tapestry, the projection room (where every night Hearst forced his guests to watch the films he produced, while he sat in the front row with a handy telephone linking him with the whole world) is all fake Egyptian with some Empire touches; the Library has another Italian ceiling, the study imitates a Gothic crypt, and the fireplaces of the various rooms are (real) Gothic, whereas the indoor pool invents a hybrid of the Alhambra, the Paris Métro, and a Caliph's urinal, but with greater majesty.

The striking aspect of the whole is not the quantity of antique pieces plundered from half of Europe, or the nonchalance with which the artificial tissue seamlessly connects fake and genuine, but rather the sense of fullness, the obsessive determination not to leave a single space that doesn't suggest something, and hence the master-piece of bricolage, haunted by *horror vacui*, that is here achieved. The insane abundance makes the place unlivable, just as it is hard to eat those dishes that many classy American restaurants, all darkness and wood paneling, dotted with soft red lights and invaded by nonstop music, offer the customer as evidence of his own situation of "affluence": steaks four inches thick with lobster (and baked potato, and sour cream and melted butter, and grilled tomato and horseradish sauce) so that the customer will have "more and more," and can wish nothing further.

An incomparable collection of genuine pieces, too, the Castle of Citizen Kane achieves a psychedelic effect and a kitsch result not because the Past is not distinguished from the Present (because after all this was how the great lords of the past amassed rare objects, and the same continuum of styles can be found in many Romanesque churches where the nave is now baroque and perhaps the campanile is eighteenth century), but because what offends is the voracity of the selection, and what distresses is the fear of being caught up by this jungle of venerable beauties, which unquestionably has its own wild flavor, its own pathetic sadness, barbarian grandeur, and sensual perversity, redolent of contamination, blasphemy, the Black Mass. It is like making love in a confessional with a prostitute dressed in a prelate's liturgical robes reciting Baudelaire while ten electronic organs reproduce the *Well-Tempered Clavier* played by Scriabin.

[...]

This craving for opulence, which goads the millionaire as it does the middle-class tourist, seems to us a trademark of American behavior, but it is much less widespread on the Atlantic coast, and not because there are fewer millionaires. We could say that the Atlantic millionaire finds no difficulty in expressing himself through the means of essential modernity, by building in glass and reinforced concrete, or by restoring an old house in New England. But the house is already there. In other words, the Atlantic coast yearns less for Hearstian architectural expression because it has its own architecture, the historical architecture of the eighteenth century and the modern, business-district architecture. Baroque rhetoric, eclectic frenzy, and compulsive imitation prevail where wealth has no history. And thus in the great expanses that were colonized late, where the post-urban civilization represented by Los Angeles is being born, in a metropolis made up of seventy-six different cities where alleyways are ten-lane free-ways and man considers his right foot a limb designed for pressing the accelerator, and the left an atrophied appendix, because cars no longer have a clutch – eyes are something to focus, at steady driving speed, on visual-mechanical wonders, signs, constructions that must impress the mind in the space of a few seconds. [. . .]

The Monasteries of Salvation

The art patronage of California and Florida has shown that to be D'Annunzio (and to outstrip him) you don't have to be a crowned poet; you only have to have a lot of money, plus a sincere worship of all-consuming syncretism. And yet you can't help wondering whether, when America patronizes the past, it always does so in a spirit of gluttony and bricolage. So we had to run other checks, but our trip was undertaken in the name of the Absolute Fake, and thus we had to exclude examples of correct, philological art collections, where famous works are shown without any manipulation. Extreme instances had to be found, examples of the conjunction of archeology and falsification. And California in this respect is still the land of gold mines.

Eyes (and nerves) saturated with wax museums, Citizen Kane castles, and Madonna Inns, we approach the J. Paul Getty Museum in Malibu, on the Pacific coast below Santa Monica, in a spirit of profound mistrust. The beautiful and sensitive curator (wife of a university colleague in Los Angeles) who introduces me to the mysteries of the museum, sparing me the use of the earpiece and personal cassette supplied to visitors, is very reticent. She knows why I have come to the Getty Museum and where I have been recently; she is afraid of my sarcasm, as she shows me rooms filled with works by Raphael, Titian, Paolo Uccello, Veronese, Magnasco, Georges de la Tour, Poussin, even Alma-Tadema; and she is amazed at my bored manner as, after days of fake Last Suppers and Venuses de Milo, I cast absent glances on these drearily authentic pictures. She leads me through the wondrous collection of sculpture, Greek, Hellenistic, Roman, and takes me to the restoration workshop, where with scientific skill and philological scruple they chip away from the latest acquisitions even noses added in the eighteenth century, because the Museum's philosophy is stern, learned, fiercely German; and J. Paul

Getty has proved in fact a cultivated patron, who wants to show the California public only works of unquestionable worth and authenticity. But my Beatrice is shy and apologizes because to reach the inner rooms we have to cross two large gardens and the airy peristyle. We cross the Villa of the Papyruses of Herculaneum, totally reconstructed, with its colonnades, the Pompeiian wall-paintings, intact and dazzling, the snowy marble, the statue-population of the garden where only plants that flourish along the bay of Naples are growing. We have crossed something that is more than the Villa of the Papyruses, because the Villa of the Papyruses is incomplete, still buried, the supposition of an ancient Roman villa, whereas the Malibu one is all there. J. Paul Getty's archeologists worked from drawings, models of other Roman villas, learned conjectures, and archeological syllogisms, and they have reconstructed the building as it was or at least as it ought to have been. My guide is bewildered, because she knows that the most modern notions of museography insist that the container should be modern and aseptic, and the number-one model is Wright's Guggenheim Museum. She senses that the public, flung from the realer-than-real reconstruction to the authentic, could lose its bearings and consider the exterior real and the interior a great assemblage of modern copies. In the decorative arts section, the Versailles rooms contain only real and precious pieces, but here, too, the reconstruction is total, even if the guidebook specifies what is antique and what is reconstruction, and the Régence Period Room is sheathed in the paneling from the Hôtel Herlaut, but the plaster cornice and the rosette are reconstructed and the parquet, though also eighteenth-century, was not part of the original room. The period commodes also come from other residences, and are too numerous. And so on. To be sure, in this reconstruction the visitor gets an idea of the architecture of French rococo interiors far better than if he saw the items displayed in separate cases, but the curators of the Getty Museum are European-trained and fear that their work may be contaminated by the suspicion and confusion generated by experiments like the Hearst Castle.

For the rest, J. Paul Getty's declarations, quoted in the guide, are perceptive and coherent. If there is error, it is lucid error; there is nothing makeshift or ingenuous, but a precise philosophy of how the European past can be reexperienced on the coast of a California torn between memories of the pioneers and Disneyland, and hence a country with much future but no historical reminiscence.

How can a rich man, a lover of the arts, recall the emotions he felt one day in Herculaneum or in Versailles? And how can he help his compatriots understand what Europe is? It is easy to say: Put your objects all in a row with explanatory labels in a neutral setting. In Europe the neutral setting is called the Louvre, Castello Sforzesco, Uffizi, Tate Gallery (just a short walk from Westminster Abbey). It is easy to give a neutral setting to visitors who can breathe in the Past a few steps away, who reach the neutral setting after having walked, with emotion, among venerable stones. But in California, between the Pacific on one hand and Los Angeles on the other, with restaurants shaped like hats and hamburgers, and four-level freeways with ten thousand ramps, what do you do? You reconstruct the Villa of the Papyruses. You put yourself in the hands of the German archeologist, taking care he doesn't overdo; you place your busts of Hercules in a construction that reproduces a Roman temple; and if you have the money, you make sure that your marble comes from the original places of the model, that the workers are all from Naples, Carrara, Venice, and you also announce this. Kitsch? Perhaps. [...]

The Getty Museum, on the contrary, is the work of one man and his collaborators who tried in their way to reconstruct a credible and "objective" past. If the Greek statues are not Greek, they are at least good Roman copies, and presented as such; if the tapestries based on authentic Raphael cartoons were woven today, they were studied so as to put the picture in a setting not unlike the one for which it was designed. The Cybele from the Mattei collection in Rome is placed in a temple of Cybele whose freshness, whose air of being just completed, upsets us, accustomed as we are to ancient, half-ruined temples; but the museum archeologists have made sure that it would look the way a little Roman temple must have looked when just finished; and for that matter we know very well that many classical statues, which fascinate us with their whiteness, were originally polychrome, and in the eyes, now blank, there was a painted pupil. The Getty Museum leaves the statues white (and in this sense is perhaps guilty of European-style archeological fetishism); but it supplies polychrome marbles for the walls of the temple, presented as a hypothetical model. We are tempted to think that Getty is more faithful to the

past when he reconstructs the temple than when he displays the statue in its chill incompleteness and the unnatural isolation of the "correct" restoration.

In other words the Getty Museum, after the first reaction of mockery or puzzlement, raises a question: Who is right? How do you regain contact with the past? Archeological respect is only one of the possible solutions; other periods resolved the problem differently. Does the J. Paul Getty solution belong to the contemporary period? We try to think how a Roman patrician lived and what he was thinking when he built himself one of the villas that the Getty Museum reconstructs, in its need to reconstruct at home the grandeur of Greek civilization. The Roman yearned for impossible parthenons; from Hellenistic artists he ordered copies of the great statues of the Periclean age. He was a greedy shark who, after having helped bring down Greece, guaranteed its survival in the form of copies. Between the Roman patrician and the Greece of the fifth century there were, we might say, from five to seven hundred years. Between the Getty Museum and the remade Rome there are, roughly speaking, two thousand. The temporal gap is bridged by archeological knowledge; we can rely on the Getty team, their reconstruction is more faithful to Herculaneum than the Herculaneum reproduction was faithful to the Greek tradition. But the fact is that our journey into the Absolute Fake, begun in the spirit of irony and sophisticated repulsion, is now exposing us to some dramatic questions.

[...]

The condition for the amalgamation of fake and authentic is that there must have been a historic catastrophe, of the sort that has made the divine Acropolis of Athens as venerable as Pompeii, city of brothels and bakeries. And this brings us to the theme of the Last Beach, the apocalyptic philosophy that more or less explicitly rules these reconstructions: Europe is declining into barbarism and something has to be saved. This may not have been the reasoning of the Roman patrician, but it was that of the medieval art lover who accumulated classical reminiscences with incredible philological nonchalance and (see Gerbert d'Aurillac) mistook a manuscript of Statius for an armillary sphere, but could also have done the opposite (Huizinga says that the medieval man's sensitivity to works of art is the same that we would expect today from an astonished bourgeois). And we don't feel like waxing ironic on the piety mixed with accumulative instinct that led the Ringlings to purchase the entire theater of Asolo (wooden frame, stage, boxes, and gallery), which was housed in the villa of Caterina Cornaro from 1798 (and welcomed Eleonora Duse) but which was dismantled in 1930 and sold to a dealer in order to make room for a "more modern" hall. Now the theater is not far from the fake Venetian palazzo and houses artistic events of considerable distinction.

But to understand the Last Beach theme we must go back to California and to the Forest Lawn–Glendale cemetery. The founder's idea was that Forest Lawn, at its various sites, should be a place not of grief but of serenity, and there is nothing like Nature and Art for conveying this feeling. So Mr. Eaton, inventor of the new philosophy, peopled Forest Lawn with copies of the great masterpieces of the past, David and Moses, the St. George of Donatello, a marble reproduction of Raphael's Sistine Madonna, complementing it all with authentic declarations from Italian Government fine arts authorities, certifying that the Forest Lawn founders really did visit all the Italian museums to commission "authentic" copies of the real masterpieces of the Renaissance.

To see the Last Supper, admitted at fixed times as if for a theater performance, you have to take your seat, facing a curtain, with the Pietà on your left and the Medici Tombs sculptures on your right. Before the curtain rises, you have to hear a long speech that explains how in fact this crypt is the new Westminster Abbey and contains the graves of Gutzon Borglum, Jan Styka, Carrie Jacobs Bond, and Robert Andrews Millikan. Apart from mentioning the fact that the last-named won a Nobel Prize in physics, I won't even try to say who the others are (but Mrs. Bond is the composer of "I Love You Truly"). If it hadn't been for Westminster Abbey, many characters we consider historic today would have remained insignificant barons: In the construction of Immortal Fame you need first of all a cosmic shamelessness.

Very well. Before revealing to the dewy eyes of the audience the stained-glass reproduction of the Last Supper, the Voice tells us what happened to Mr. Eaton when he went to Santa Maria delle Grazie and realized that the joint action of time and human wickedness (it was before the Second World War) would one day destroy Leonardo's masterpiece. Gripped by a sacred fever of preservation, Mr. Eaton contacts Signora Rosa Caselli-Moretti, descended of an ancient family of Perugian artisans, and commissions her to make a *glass* reproduction of Leonardo's masterpiece. Not the way it looks now in Santa Maria delle Grazie, but the way we suppose it must have looked when Leonardo painted it, or rather – better – the way Leonardo ought to have painted it if he had been less shiftless, spending three years and never managing to complete the picture. At this point the curtain rises. And I must say that, compared with the wax reproductions scattered all over California, this work by Signora Caselli-Moretti is a piece of honest craftsmanship and would not look out of place in a nineteenth-century European church. The artist also had the good sense to leave the face of Christ vague, sharing Leonardo's own fear in dealing with the icon of the Divine; and, from behind the glass, the cemetery management shines various lights that render every nuance of the sun (dawn, noon, dusk) in such a way as to demonstrate the mobility of the face of Jesus in the play of atmospheric variations.

All this machinery to reproduce the Past at Forest Lawn is exploited for profit. But the ideology proclaimed by Forest Lawn is the same as that of the Getty Museum, which charges no admission. It is the ideology of preservation, in the New World, of the treasures that the folly and negligence of the Old World are causing to disappear into the void. Naturally this ideology conceals something – the desire for profit, in the case of the cemetery; and in the case of Getty, the fact that it is the entrepreneurial colonization by the New World (of which J. Paul Getty's oil empire is part) that makes the Old World's condition critical. Just like the crocodile tears of the Roman patrician who reproduced the grandeurs of the very Greece that his country had humiliated and reduced to a colony. And so the Last Beach ideology develops its thirst for preservation of art from an imperialistic efficiency, but at the same time it is the bad conscience of this imperialistic efficiency, just as cultural anthropology is the bad conscience of the white man who thus pays his debt to the destroyed primitive cultures.

But, having said this, we must in fairness employ this American reality as a critical reagent for an examination of conscience regarding European taste. Can we be sure that the European tourist's pilgrimage to the *Pietà* of St. Peter's is less fetishistic than the American tourist's pilgrimage to the Pietà of Forest Lawn (here more accessible, tangible at close range)? Actually, in these museums the idea of the "multiple" is perfected.

The Goethe Institut recently remade in Cologne Man Ray's spiked flatiron and his metronome with an eye; and since Duchamp's bicycle wheel survives only in a photograph, they reconstructed an identical one. In fact, once the fetishistic desire for the original is forgotten, these copies are perfect. And at this point isn't the enemy of the rights of art the engraver who defaces the plate to keep low the number of prints?

This is not an attempt to absolve the shrines of the Fake, but to call the European sanctuaries of the Genuine to assume their share of guilt.

[...]

But once the "total fake" is admitted, in order to be enjoyed it must seem totally real. So the Polynesian restaurant will have, in addition to a fairly authentic menu, Tahitian waitresses in costume, appropriate vegetation, rock walls with little cascades, and once you are inside nothing must lead you to suspect that outside there is anything but Polynesia. If, between two trees, there appears a stretch of river that belongs to another sector, Adventureland, then that section of stream is so designed that it would not be unrealistic to see in Tahiti, beyond the garden hedge, a river like this. And if in the wax museums wax is not flesh, in Disneyland, when rocks are involved, they are rock, and water is water, and a baobab a baobab. When there is a fake – hippopotamus, dinosaur, sea serpent – it is not so much because it wouldn't be possible to have the real equivalent but because the public is meant to admire the perfection of the fake and its obedience to the program. In this sense Disneyland not only produces illusion, but – in confessing it – stimulates the desire for it: A real crocodile can be found in the zoo, and as a rule it is dozing or hiding, but Disneyland tells us that faked nature corresponds much more to our daydream demands. When, in the space of twenty-four hours, you go (as I did deliberately) from the fake New Orleans of Disneyland to the real one, and from the wild river of Adventureland to a trip on the Mississippi, where the captain of the paddle-wheel steamer says it is possible to see alligators on the banks of the river, and then you don't see any, you risk feeling homesick for Disneyland, where the wild animals don't have to be coaxed. Disneyland tells us that technology can give us more reality than nature can.

[...]

An allegory of the consumer society, a place of absolute iconism, Disneyland is also a place of total passivity. Its visitors must agree to behave like its robots. Access to each attraction is regulated by a maze of metal railings which discourages any individual initiative. The number of visitors obviously sets the pace of the line; the officials of the dream, properly dressed in the uniforms suited to each specific attraction, not only admit the visitor to the threshold of the chosen sector, but, in successive phases, regulate his every move ("Now wait here please, go up now, sit down please, wait before standing up," always in a polite tone, impersonal, imperious, over the microphone). If the visitor pays this price, he can have not only "the real thing" but the abundance of the reconstructed truth. Like the Hearst Castle, Disneyland also has no transitional spaces; there is always something to see, the great voids of modern architecture and city planning are unknown here. If America is the country of the Guggenheim Museum or the new skyscrapers of Manhattan, then Disneyland is a curious exception and American intellectuals are quite right to refuse to go there. But if America is what we have seen in the course of our trip, then Disneyland is its Sistine Chapel, and the hyperrealists of the art galleries are only the timid voyeurs of an immense and continuous "found object."

Ecology 1984 and Coca-Cola Made Flesh

Spongeorama, Sea World, Scripps Aquarium, Wild Animal Park, Jungle Gardens, Alligator Farm, Marineland: the coasts of California and Florida are rich in marine cities and artificial jungles where you can see free-ranging animals, trained dolphins, bicycling parrots, otters that drink martinis with an olive and take showers, elephants and camels that carry small visitors on their backs among the palm trees. The theme of hyperrealistic reproduction involves not only Art and History, but also Nature.

The zoo, to begin with. In San Diego each enclosure is the reconstruction, on a vast scale, of an original environment. The dominant theme of the San Diego zoo is the preservation of endangered species, and from this standpoint it is a superb achievement. The visitor has to walk for hours and hours so that bison or birds can always move in a space created to their measure. Of all existing zoos, this is unquestionably the one where the animal is most respected. But it is not clear whether this respect is meant to convince the animal or the human. The human being adapts to any sacrifice, even to not seeing the animals, if he knows that they are alive and in an authentic environment. This is the case with the extremely rare Australian koala, the zoo's symbol, who can live only in a wood entirely of eucalyptus, and so here he has his eucalyptus wood, where he happily hides amid the foliage as the visitors seek desperately to catch a glimpse of him through their binoculars. The invisible koala suggests a freedom that is easily granted to big animals, more visible and more conditioned. Since the temperature around him is artificially kept below zero, the polar bear gives the same impression of freedom; and since the rocks are dark and the water in which he is immersed is rather dirty, the fearsome grizzly also seems to feel at his ease. But ease can be demonstrated only through sociability and so the grizzly, whose name is Chester, waits for the microbus to come by at three-minute intervals and for the girl attendant to shout for Chester to say hello to the people. Then Chester stands up, waves his hand (which is a terrifying huge paw) to say hi. The girl throws him a cookie and we're off again, while Chester waits for the next bus.

This docility arouses some suspicions. Where does the truth of ecology lie? We could say that the suspicions are unfair, because of all possible zoos the San Diego is the most human, or rather, the most animal. But the San Diego zoo contains, *in nuce*, the philosophy that is rampant in such ecological preserves as Wild World or – the one we would choose as an example – Marine World Africa–USA in Redwood City, outside San Francisco. Here we can speak more legitimately of an Industry of the Fake because we find a Disneyland for animals, a corner of Africa made up of sandbars, native huts, palm trees, and rivers plied by rafts and *African Queens*, from which you can admire free-ranging zebras and rhinoceroses on the opposite shore; while in the central nucleus there is a cluster of amphitheaters, underground aquaria, submarine caves inhabited by sharks, glass cases with fierce and terribly poisonous snakes. The symbolic center of Marine World is the Ecology Theater, where you sit in a comfortable amphitheater (and if you don't sit, the polite but implacable hostess will make you, because everything must proceed in a smooth and orderly fashion, and you can't sit where you choose, but if possible next to the latest to be seated, so that the line can move properly and everybody takes his place without pointless search), you face a natural area arranged like a stage. Here there are three girls, with long blond hair and a hippie appearance; one plays very sweet folk songs on the guitar, the other two show us, in succession, a lion cub, a little leopard, and a Bengal tiger only six months old. The animals are on leashes, but even if they weren't they wouldn't seem dangerous because of their tender age and also because, thanks perhaps to a few poppy seeds in their food, they are somewhat sleepy. One of the girls explains that the animals, traditionally ferocious, are actually quite good when they are in a pleasant and friendly environment, and she invites the children in the audience to come up on stage and pet them. The emotion of petting a Bengal tiger isn't an everyday occurrence and the public is spurting ecological goodness from every pore. From the pedagogical point of view, the thing has a certain effect on the young people, and surely it will teach them not to kill fierce animals, assuming that in their later life they happen to encounter any. But to achieve this "natural peace" (as an indirect allegory of social peace) great efforts had to be made: the training of the animals, the construction of an artificial environment that seems natural, the preparation of the hostesses who educate the public. So the final essence of this apologue on the goodness of nature is Universal Taming.

The oscillation between a promise of uncontaminated nature and a guarantee of negotiated tranquillity is constant: In the marine amphitheater where the trained whales perform, these animals are billed as "killer whales," and probably they are very dangerous when they're hungry. Once we are convinced that they are dangerous, it is very satisfying to see them so obedient to orders, diving, racing, leaping into the air, until they actually snatch the fish from the trainer's hand and reply, with almost human moans, to the questions they are asked. The same thing happens in another amphitheater with elephants and apes, and even if this is a normal part of any circus repertory, I must say I have never seen elephants so docile and intelligent. So with its killer whales and its dolphins, its strokable tigers and its elephants that gently sit on the belly of the blond trainer without hurting her, Marine World presents itself as a reduced-scale model of the Golden Age, where the struggle for survival no longer exists, and men and animals interact without conflict. Only, if the Golden Age is to be achieved, animals have to be willing to respect a contract: In return they will be given food, which will relieve them from having to hunt, and humans will love them and defend them against civilization. Marine World seems to be saying that if there is food for all then savage revolt is no longer necessary. But to have food we must accept the *pax* offered by the conqueror. Which, when you think about it, is yet another variation on the theme of the "white man's burden." As in the African stories of Edgar Wallace, it will be Commissioner Sanders who establishes peace along the great river, provided Bozambo doesn't think of organizing an illicit powwow with the other chiefs. In which case the chief will be deposed and hanged.

Strangely, in this ecological theater the visitor isn't on the side of the human master, but on the side of the animals; like them, he has to follow the established routes, sit down at the given moment, buy the straw hats, the lollipops, and the slides that celebrate wild and harmless freedom. The animals earn happiness by being humanized, the visitors by being animalized.

In the humanization of animals is concealed one of the most clever resources of the Absolute Fake industry, and for this reason the Marinelands must be compared with the wax museums that reconstruct the last day of Marie Antoinette. In the latter all is sign but aspires to seem reality. In the Marinelands all is reality but aspires to appear sign. The killer whales perform a square dance and answer the trainers' questions not because they have acquired linguistic ability, but because they have been trained through conditioned reflexes, and we interpret the stimulus–response relationship as a relationship of meaning. Thus in the entertainment industry when there is a sign it seems there isn't one, and when there isn't one we believe that there is. The condition of pleasure is that something be faked. And the Marinelands are more disturbing than other amusement places because here Nature has almost been regained, and yet it is erased by artifice precisely so that it can be presented as uncontaminated nature.

This said, it would be secondhand Frankfurt-school moralism to prolong the criticism. These places are enjoyable. If they existed in our Italian civilization of bird killers, they would represent praiseworthy didactic occasions; love of nature is a constant of the most industrialized nation in the world, like a remorse, just as the love of European art is a passion perennially frustrated. I would like to say that the first, most immediate level of communication that these Wild Worlds achieve is positive; what disturbs us is the allegorical level superimposed on the literal one, the implied promise of a *1984* already achieved at the animal level.

What disturbs us is not an evil plan; there is none. It is a symbolic threat. We know that the Good Savage, if he still exists in the equatorial forests, kills crocodiles and hippopotamuses, and if they want to survive the hippopotamuses and the crocodiles must submit to the falsification industry: This leaves us upset. And without alternatives.

The trip through the Wild Worlds has revealed subtle links between the worship of Nature and the worship of Art and History. We have seen that to understand the past, even locally, we must have before our eyes something that resembles as closely as possible the original model. There can be no discussion of the White House or Cape Kennedy unless we have in front of us a reconstruction of the White House or a scale-model of the Cape Kennedy rockets. Knowledge can only be iconic, and iconism can only be absolute. The same thing happens with nature; not only far-off Africa but even the Mississippi must be re-experienced, at Disneyland, as a reconstruction of the Mississippi. It is as if in Rome there were a park that reproduced in smaller scale the hills of the Chianti region. But the parallel is unfair. For the distance between Los Angeles and New Orleans is equal to that between Rome and Khartoum, and it is the spatial, as well as the temporal, distance that drives this country to construct not only imitations of the past and of exotic lands but also imitations of itself.

The problem now, however, is something else. Accustomed to realizing the Distant (in space and in time) through almost "carnal" reproduction, how will the average American realize the relationship with the supernatural?

If you follow the Sunday morning religious programs on TV you come to understand that God can be experienced only as nature, flesh, energy, tangible image. And since no preacher dares show us God in the form of a bearded dummy, or as a Disneyland robot, God can only be found in the form of natural force, joy, healing, youth, health, economic increment (which, let Max Weber teach us, is at once the essence of the Protestant ethic and of the spirit of capitalism).

Oral Roberts is a prophet who looks like a boxer; in the heart of Oklahoma he has created Oral Roberts University, a science-fiction city with computerized teaching equipment, where a "prayer tower" looking something like a TV transmitter sends out through the starry spaces the requests for divine aid that arrive there, accompanied by cash offerings, from all over the world, via Telex, as in the grand hotels. Oral Roberts has the healthy appearance of a retired boxer who isn't above putting on the gloves and trading a few punches every morning, followed by a brisk shower and a Scotch. His broadcast is presented like a religious music hall (Broadway in Heavenly Jerusalem) with interracial singers praising the Lord as they come tap dancing down the stairs, one hand stretched forward, the other behind, singing "ba ba doop" to the tune of "Joshua Fit the Battle of Jericho," or words like "The Lord is my comfort." Oral Roberts sits on the staircase (the reference is to Ziegfeld and not to Odessa) and converses with Mrs. Roberts while reading the letters of distressed faithful. Their problems don't involve matters of conscience (divorce, embezzlement of workers' wages, Pentagon contracts) but rather matters of digestion, of incurable diseases. Oral Roberts is famous because he possesses healing power, the touch that cures. He can't touch over TV, but he constantly suggests an idea of the divine as energy (his usual metaphor is "electric charge"), he orders the devil to take his hands off the postulant, he clenches his fists to convey an idea of vitality and power. God must be perceived in a tactile way, as health and optimism. Oral Roberts sees heaven not as the Mystic Rose but as Marineland. God is a good hippopotamus. A rhinoceros fighting his Armageddon. Go 'way, devil, or God will have you by the balls.

We switch channels. Now a middle-aged Dark Lady is holding forth, on a program about miracles. Believing in miracles means as a rule believing in the cancer that vanishes after the doctors have given up all hope. The miracle is not the Transubstantiation, it is the disappearance of something natural but bad. The Dark Lady, heavily made up and smiling like the wife of a CIA director visiting General Pinochet, interviews four doctors with an array of very convincing degrees and titles. Seated in her garden scented with roses, they try desperately to save their professional dignity. "Dr. Gzrgnibtz, I'm not here to defend God, who doesn't need my help, but tell me: Haven't you ever seen a person who seemed doomed to die and then suddenly recovered?" The doctor is evasive. "Medicine can't explain everything. Sometimes there are psychosomatic factors. Every doctor has seen people with advanced cancers, and two months later they were riding a bicycle." "What did I tell you? It's a remission that can only come from God!" The doctor ventures a last defense of reason: "Science doesn't have all the answers. It can't explain everything. We don't

know everything. . . . " The Dark Lady rocks with almost sensual laughter. "What did I tell you? That's the Truth! You've said something very profound, Doctor! We can't know everything! There's your demonstration of the power of God, the supernatural power of God! The supernatural power of God doesn't need any defending. I know! I know! Thank you, dear friends, our time is up!" The Dark Lady didn't even try, as a Catholic bishop would have done, to discover if the healed person had prayed, nor does she wonder why God exercised his power on that man and not on his unfortunate neighbor in the next bed. In the Technicolor rose garden something that "seems" a miracle has taken place, as a wax face seems physically a historic character. Through a play of mirrors and background music, once again the fake seems real. The doctor performs the same function as the certificate from the Italian fine arts authorities in the museums of copies: The copy is authentic.

But if the supernatural can assume only physical forms, such is also the inescapable fate of the Survival of the Soul. This is what the California museums say. Forest Lawn is a concentration of historical memories, Michelangelo reproductions, *Wunderkammern* where you can admire the reproduction of the British crown jewels, the life-size doors of the Florentine Baptistery, the Thinker of Rodin, the Foot of Pasquino, and other assorted bijouterie, all served up with music by Strauss (Johann). The various Forest Lawn cemeteries avoid the individual cenotaph; the art masterpieces of all time belong to the collective heritage. The graves at the Hollywood Forest Lawn are hidden beneath discreet bronze plaques in the grass of the lawns; and in Glendale the crypts are very restrained, with nonstop Muzak and reproductions of nineteenth-century statues of nude girls: Hebes, Venuses, Disarmed Virgins, Pauline Borgheses, a few Sacred Hearts. Forest Lawn's philosophy is described by its founder, Mr. Eaton, on great carved plaques that appear in every cemetery. The idea is very simple: Death is a new life, cemeteries mustn't be places of sadness or a disorganized jumble of funerary statues. They must contain reproductions of the most beautiful artworks of all time, reminders of history (great mosaics of American history, mementoes – fake – of the Revolutionary War), and they must be a place with trees and peaceful little churches where lovers can come and stroll hand in hand (and they do, dammit), where couples can marry (a large sign at the entrance to Forest Lawn–Glendale announces the availability of marriage ceremonies), where the devout can meditate, reassured of the continuity of life. So the great California cemeteries (undeniably more pleasant than ours in Italy) are immense imitations of a natural and aesthetic life that continues after death. Eternity is guaranteed by the presence (in copies) of Michelangelo and Donatello. The eternity of art becomes a metaphor for the eternity of the soul, the vitality of trees and flowers becomes a metonymy of the vitality of the body that is victoriously consumed underground to give new lymph to life. The industry of the Absolute Fake gives a semblance of truth to the myth of immortality through the play of imitations and copies, and it achieves the presence of the divine in the presence of the natural – but the natural is "cultivated" as in the Marinelands.

Immediately outside these enclosures, the amusement industry deals with a new theme: the Beyond as terror, diabolical presence, and nature as the Enemy. While the cemeteries and the wax museums sing of the eternity of Artistic Grace, and the Marinelands raise a paean to the Goodness of the Wild Animal, popular movies, in the vein of *The Exorcist*, tell of a supernatural that is ferocious, diabolical, and hostile. The number-one hit movie, *Jaws*, was about a fierce and insatiable monster animal that devours adults and children after having torn them apart. The shark in *Jaws* is a hyperrealistic model in plastic, "real" and controllable like the audioanimatronic robots of Disneyland. But he is an ideal relative of the killer whales in Marineland. For their part, the devils that invade films like *The Exorcist* are evil relatives of the healing divinity of Oral Roberts; and they reveal themselves through physical means, such as greenish vomit and hoarse voices. And the earthquakes or tidal waves of the disaster movies are the brothers of that Nature that in the California

cemeteries seems reconciled with life and death in the form of privet, freshly mown lawns, pines stirring in a gentle breeze. But as Good Nature must be perceived physically also in the form of string music, Evil Nature must be felt in the form of physical jolts through the synesthetic participation of "Sensurround," which shakes the audience in their seats. Everything must be tactile for this widespread and secondary America that has no notion of the Museum of Modern Art and the rebellion of Edward Kienholz, who remakes wax museums but puts on his dummies disturbing heads in the form of clocks or surrealist diving helmets. This is the America of Linus, for whom happiness must assume the form of a warm puppy or a security blanket, the America of Schroeder, who brings Beethoven to life not so much through a simplified score played on a toy piano as through the realistic bust in marble (or rubber). Where Good, Art, Fairytale, and History, unable to become flesh, must at least become Plastic.

The ideology of this America wants to establish reassurance through Imitation. But profit defeats ideology, because the consumers want to be thrilled not only by the guarantee of the Good but also by the shudder of the Bad. And so at Disneyland, along with Mickey Mouse and the kindly Bears, there must also be, in tactile evidence, Metaphysical Evil (the Haunted Mansion) and Historical Evil (the Pirates), and in the waxwork museums, alongside the Venuses de Milo, we must find the graverobbers, Dracula, Frankenstein, the Wolf Man, Jack the Ripper, the Phantom of the Opera. Alongside the Good Whale there is the restless, plastic form of the Bad Shark. Both at the same level of credibility, both at the same level of fakery. Thus, on entering his cathedrals of iconic reassurance, the visitor will remain uncertain whether his final destiny is hell or heaven, and so will consume new promises.

27

Simulations

Jean Baudrillard

Three orders of appearance, parallel to the mutations of the law of value, have followed one another since the Renaissance:

- *Counterfeit* is the dominant scheme of the "classical" period, from the Renaissance to the industrial revolution;
- *Production* is the dominant scheme of the industrial era;
- *Simulation* is the reigning scheme of the current phase that is controlled by the code.

The first order of simulacrum is based on the natural law of value, that of the second order on the commercial law of value, that of the third order on the structural law of value.

The Stucco Angel

Counterfeit (and fashion at the same time) is born with the Renaissance, with the destructuring of the feudal order by the bourgeois order and the emergence of open competition on the level of the distinctive signs. There is no such thing as fashion in a society of cast and rank, since one is assigned a place irrevocably, and so class mobility is non-existent. An interdiction protects the signs and assures them a total clarity; each sign then refers unequivocally to a status. Likewise no counterfeit is possible with the ceremony – unless as black magic and sacrilege, and it is thus that any confusion of signs is punished: as grave infraction of the order of things. If we are starting to dream again, today especially, of a world of sure signs, of a strong "symbolic order," make no mistake about it: this order has existed and it was that of a ferocious hierarchy, since transparency and cruelty for signs go together. In caste societies, feudal or archaic, *cruel* societies, the signs are limited in number, and are not widely diffused, each one functions with its full value as interdiction, each is a reciprocal obligation between castes, clans or persons. The signs therefore are anything but arbitrary. The arbitrary sign begins when, instead of linking two persons in an unbreakable reciprocity, the signifier starts referring back to the disenchanted universe of the signified, common denominator of the real world toward which no one has any obligation.

End of the *obliged* sign, reign of the emancipated sign, that all classes will partake equally of. Competitive democracy succeeds the endogomy of signs proper to statutory order. At the same time we pass, with the transfer of values/signs of prestige from one class to another, necessarily into *counterfeit*. For we have passed from a limited order of signs, which prohibits "free production," to a proliferation of signs according to demand. But the sign multiplied no longer resembles in the slightest the obliged sign of limited diffusion: it is its counterfeit, not by corruption of an "original," but by extension of a material whose very clarity depended on the restriction by which it was bound. No longer discriminating (it is no more than competitive), unburdened of all restraint, universally available, the modern sign still simulates necessity in taking itself as tied somehow to the world. The modern sign dreams of the signs of the past and would well appreciate finding again, in its reference to the real, an *obligation*: but what it finds again is only a *reason*: this referential reason, this real, this "natural" off which it is going to live. But this bond of designation is only the simulacrum of symbolic obligation: it produces neutral values only, that can be exchanged in an objective world. The sign here suffers the same destiny as work. The "free" worker is free only to produce equivalents – the "free and emancipated" sign is free only to produce the signs of equivalence.

It is therefore in the simulacrum of a "nature" that the modern sign finds its value. Problematic of the "natural," metaphysics of reality and appearance: that is the history of the bourgeoisie since the Renaissance, mirror of the bourgeois sign, mirror of the classical sign. And still today the nostalgia for a natural referent of the sign is still alive, in spite of the revolutions that have come to break up this configuration, including one in production, where the signs refer no longer to any nature, but only to the law of exchange, and come under the commercial law of value.

It is in the Renaissance that the false is born along with the natural. From the fake shirt in front to the use of the fork as artificial prosthesis, to the stucco interiors and the great baroque theatrical machinery. The entire classical era belongs *par excellence* to the theatre. Theatre is the form which takes over social life and all of architecture from the Renaissance on. It's there, in the prowesses of stucco and baroque art, that you read the metaphysic of the counterfeit and the new ambitions of Renaissance man – those of a *worldly demiurge*, a transubstantiation of all of nature into a unique substance, theatrical like social life unified under the sign of bourgeois values, beyond all differences in blood, rank, or of caste. Stucco means democracy triumphant over all artificial signs, the apotheosis of theatre and fashion, and it betrays the new classes' infinite capabilities, its power to do anything once it has been able to break through the exclusiveness of signs. The way lies open to unheard-of combinations, to all the games, all the counterfeits – the Promethean verve of the bourgeoisie first plunged into the *imitation of nature* before throwing itself into *production*. In the churches and palaces stucco is wed to all forms, imitates everything – velvet curtains, wooden corniches, charnel swelling of the flesh. Stucco exorcizes the unlikely confusion of matter into a single new substance, a sort of general equivalent of all

the others, and is prestigious theatrically because [it] is itself a representative substance, a mirror of all the others.

But simulacra are not only a game played with signs; they imply social rapports and social power. Stucco can come off as the exaltation of a rising science and technology; it is also connected to the baroque – which in turn is tied to the enterprise of the Counter Reformation and the hegemony over the political and mental world that the Jesuits – who were the first to act according to modern conceptions of power – attempted to establish.

There is a strict correlation between the mental obedience of the Jesuits ("*perinde ac cadaver*") and the demiurgic ambition to exorcize the natural substance of a thing in order to substitute a synthetic one. Just like a man submitting his will to his organization, things take on the ideal functionality of the cadaver. All technology, all technocracy are incipiently there: the presumption of an ideal counterfeit of the world, expressed in the invention of a universal substance and of a universal amalgam of substances. Reunify the scattered world (after the Reformation) under the aegis of a homogenous doctrine, universalize the world under a single word (from New Spain to Japan: the Missions), constitute a political elite *of the state*, with an identically centralized strategy: these are the objectives of the Jesuits. In order to accomplish this, you need to create effective simulacra: the apparatus of the organization is one, but [so] also is clerkly magnificence and the theatre (the great theatre of the cardinals and grey eminences). And training and education are other simulacra that aimed, for the first time ever in a systematic manner, at remodeling an ideal nature from a child. That architectural sauce of stucco and baroque is a great apparatus of the same kind. All of the above precedes the productivist rationality of capital, but everything testifies already – not in production, but in counterfeit to the same project of control and universal hegemony – to a social scheme where the internal coherence of a system is already at work.

Once there lived in the Ardennes an old cook, to whom the molding of buildings out of cakes and the science of plastic patisserie had given the ambition to take up the creation of the world where God had left it, in its natural phase, so as to eliminate its organic spontaneity and substitute for it a single, unique and polymorphous matter: Reinforced Concrete: concrete furniture, chairs, drawers, concrete sewing machines, and outside in the courtyard, an entire orchestra, including violins, of concrete – all concrete! Concrete trees with real leaves printed into them, a hog made out of reinforced concrete, but with a real hog's skull inside, concrete sheep covered with real wool. Camille Renault had finally found the original substance, the paste from which different things can only be distinguished by "realistic" nuance: the hog's skull, leaves of the tree – but this was doubtless only a concession of the demiurge to his visitors...for it was with an adorable smile that this 80-year-old god received visitors to his creation: He sought no argument with divine creation; he was remaking it only to render it more intelligible. Nothing here of a Luciferan revolt, or a will-to-parody, or of a desire to espouse the cause of naive art. The Ardennes cook reigned simply over a unified mental substance (for concrete is a *mental* substance; it allows, just like a concept, phenomena to be organized and divided up at will). His project was not so far from that of the builders in stucco of baroque art, nor very different from the projection on the terrain of an urban community in the current great ensembles. The counterfeit is working, so far, only on substance and form, not yet on relations and structures. But it is aiming already, on this level, at the control of a pacified society, ground up into a synthetic, deathless substance: an indestructible artifact that will guarantee an eternity of power. Is it not man's miracle to have invented, with plastic, a non-degradable material, interrupting thus the cycle which, by corruption and death, turns all the earth's substances ceaselessly one into another? A substance out-of-the-cycle; even fire leaves an indestructible residue. There is something incredible about it, this simulacrum where you can see in a condensed form the ambition of a universal semiotic. This has nothing to do with the "progress" of technology or with a rational goal for science. It is a project of political and cultural hegemony, the fantasy of a closed mental substance – like those angels of baroque stucco whose extremities meet in a curved mirror.

The Automation of the Robot

A whole world separates these two artificial beings. One is a theatrical counterfeit, a mechanical and clock-like man; technique submits entirely to *analogy* and to the effect of semblance. The other is dominated by the technical principle; the machine overrides all, and with the machine *equivalence* comes too. The automaton plays the part of courtier and good company; it participates in the pre-Revolutionary French theatrical and social games. The robot, on the other hand, as his name indicates, is a worker: the theatre is over and done with, the reign of mechanical man commences. The automaton is the *analogy* of man and remains his interlocutor (they play chess together!). The machine is man's *equivalent* and annexes him to itself in the unity of its operational process. This is the difference between a simulacrum of the first order and one of the second.

We shouldn't make any mistakes on this matter for reasons of "figurative" resemblance between robot and automaton. The latter is an interrogation upon nature, the mystery of the existence or non-existence of the soul, the dilemma of appearance and being. It is like God: what's underneath it all, what's inside, what's in the back of it? Only the counterfeit men allow these problems to be posed. The entire metaphysics of man as protagonist of the *natural theatre* of the creation is incarnated in the automaton, before disappearing with the Revolution. And the automaton has no other destiny than to be ceaselessly compared to living man – so as to be more natural than him, of which he is the ideal figure. A perfect double for man, right up to the suppleness of his movements, the functioning of his organs and intelligence – right up to touching upon the anguish there would be in becoming aware that there is no difference, that the soul is over with and now it is an ideally naturalized body which absorbs its energy. Sacrilege. This difference is then always maintained, as in the case of that perfect automaton that the impersonator's jerky movements on stage imitate; so that at least, even if the roles were reversed, no confusion would be possible. In this way the interrogation of the automaton remains an open one, which makes it out to be a kind of mechanical optimist, even if the counterfeit always connotes something diabolical.[1]

No such thing with the robot. The robot no longer interrogates appearance; its only truth is in its mechanical efficacy. It is no longer turned towards a resemblance with man, to whom furthermore it no longer bears comparison. That infinitesimal metaphysical difference, which made all the charm and mystery of the automaton, no longer exists; the robot has absorbed it for its own benefit. Being and appearance are melted into a common substance of production and work. The first-order simulacrum never abolished difference. It supposes an always detectable alteration between semblance and reality (a particularly subtle game with trompe-l'oeil painting, but art lives entirely off of this gap). The second-order simulacrum simplifies the problem by the absorption of the appearances, or by the liquidation of the real, whichever. It establishes in any case a reality, image, echo, appearance; such is certainly work, the machine, the system of industrial production in its entirety, in that it is radically opposed to the principle of theatrical illusion. No more resemblance or lack of resemblance, of God, or human being, but an immanent logic of the operational principle.

From then on, men and machines can proliferate. It is even their law to do so – which the automatons never have done, being instead sublime and singular mechanisms. Men themselves only started their own proliferation when they achieved the status of machines, with the industrial revolution. Freed from all resemblance, freed even from their own double, they expand like the system of production, of which they are only the miniaturized equivalent. The revenge of the simulacrum that feeds the myth of the sorcerer's apprentice doesn't happen with the automaton. It is, on the other hand, the very law of the second type; and from that law proceeds still the hegemony of the robot, of the machine, and of dead work over living labor. This hegemony is necessary for the cycle of production and reproduction. It is with this reversal that we leave behind the counterfeit to enter (re)production. We leave natural law and the play of its forms to enter the realm of the mercantile law of value and its calculations of force.

The Industrial Simulacrum

It is a new generation of signs and objects which comes with the industrial revolution. Signs without the tradition of caste, ones that will never have known any binding restrictions. They will no longer have to be *counterfeited*, since they are going to be produced all at once on a gigantic scale. The problem of their uniqueness, or their origin, is no longer a matter of concern; their origin is technique, and the only sense they possess is in the dimension of the industrial simulacrum.

Which is to say the series, and even the possibility of two or of *n* identical objects. The relation

between them is no longer that of an original to its counterfeit – neither analogy nor reflection – but equivalence, indifference. In a series, objects become undefined simulacra one of the other. And so, along with the objects, do the men that produce them. Only the obliteration of the original reference allows for the generalized law of equivalence, that is to say the *very possibility of production*.

The entire analysis of production changes according to whether you no longer see in it an original process, or even one that is at the core of all the others, but on the contrary a process of absorption of all original being and of introduction to a series of identical beings. Until now we have considered production and work as potential, as force, as historical process, as generic activity; the energetic-economic myth proper to modernity. We must now ask if production does not interfere *in the order of signs*, as a *particular* phase – if it is not basically only an episode in the line of simulacra: that precisely when, thanks to technique, potentially identical beings are produced in an indefinite series.

The immense energies that are at work in technique, industry, and the economy should not hide the fact that it is basically only a matter of attaining to that indefinite reproductibility. That is the challenge certainly to the "natural" order, but finally is only a second-order simulacrum, and rather inadequate as an imaginary solution to the problem of mastering the world. By comparison to the era of the counterfeit (the time of the double and the mirror, of theatre and the games of mask and appearance), the serial and technical era of reproduction is all-in-all a time of lesser scope (the era that follows – that of models of simulation and of third-order simulacra – is of more considerable dimension).

It is Walter Benjamin who, in *The Work of Art in the Age of Mechanical Reproduction*, first elicited the implications essential in this principle of reproduction. He shows that reproduction absorbs the process of production, changing its finalities and altering the status of product and producer. He demonstrates this mutation on the terrain of art, cinema and photography, because it is there that open up, in the 20th century, new territories without a tradition of classical productivity, and that are placed immediately under the sign of reproduction. But we know that today all material production enters into this sphere. We know that now it is on the level of reproduction (fashion, media, publicity, information and communication networks), on the level of what Marx negligently called the nonessential sectors of capital (we can hereby take stock of the irony of history), that is to say in the sphere of simulacra and of the code, that the global process of capital is founded. Benjamin first (and later McLuhan) understood technique not as a "productive force" (wherein marxist analysis is locked) but as medium, as form and principle of a whole new generation of sense. The fact alone that anything might be simply reproduced, as such, in two copies, is already a revolution; you only have to consider the shock of the African native seeing, for the very first time, two identical books. That these two products of technique should be *equivalent* under the sign of socially necessary work is less important in the long run than the *serial* repetition of the same object (which is also that of individuals as force-of-work). Technique as medium dominates not only the "message" of the product (its use-value) but also the force-of-work that Marx wished to make the revolutionary message of production. Benjamin and McLuhan saw this matter more clearly than Marx; they saw the true message: *the true ultimatum was in reproduction itself.* And that production no longer has any sense; its social finality is lost in the series. The simulacra win out over history.

Furthermore, this stage of serial reproduction (that of the industrial mechanism, of the factory belt, of expanded reproduction) is ephemeral. As soon as dead work wins out over living work – that is, as soon as the era of primitive accumulation is over – serial production yields to generation by means of models. And here it is a question of a reversal of origin and finality, for all the forms change once they are not so much mechanically reproduced but even *conceived from the point-of-view of their very reproductibility*, diffracted from a generating nucleus we call the model. Here we are in the third-order simulacra; no longer that of the counterfeit of an original as in the first order, nor that of the pure series as in the second. Here are the models from which proceed all forms according to the modulation of their differences. Only affiliation to the model makes sense, and nothing flows any longer according to its end, but proceeds from the model, the "signifier of reference," which is a kind of anterior finality and the only resemblance there is. We are in simulation in the modern sense of the word, of which industrialization is but the final manifestation. Finally, it is not serial reproductibility which is fundamental, but the modulation. Not quantitative equivalences, but

distinctive oppositions. No longer the law of capital, but the structural law of value. And not only shouldn't we look to technique or the economy for the secrets of the code; it is, on the contrary, the very possibility of industrial production that we should look for in the genesis of the code and the simulacra. Each order submits to the order following. Just like the order of the counterfeit was abolished by that of serial production (we can see how art has passed entirely into the realm of the "mechanical"), so in the same way the entire order of production is in the process of tumbling into operational simulation.

The analyses of Benjamin and McLuhan are situated on these limits of reproduction and simulation, at the point where referential reason disappears, and where production is no longer sure of itself. In this sense they mark a decisive progress compared to the analyses of Veblen and Goblot. These latter, describing for example the signs of fashion, still refer to the classical configuration: the signs constitute a distinct material, have a finality and use for prestige, status, social differentiation. They manifest a strategy contemporaneous to that of profit and merchandise with Marx, at a time when you could still talk about the use-value of a sign or of force-of-work, when purely and simply, one could still talk about an economy because there was still a Reason of the sign, and a Reason of production.

The Metaphysic of the Code

Leibniz, that mathematical spirit, saw in the mystic elegance of the binary system that counts only the zero and the one, the very image of creation. The unity of the supreme Being, operating by binary function in nothingness, would have sufficed to bring out of it all the beings.

McLuhan

The great simulacra constructed by man pass from a universe of natural laws to a universe of force and tensions of force, today to a universe of structures and binary oppositions. After the metaphysic of being and appearance, after that of energy and determination, comes that of indeterminacy and the code. Cybernetic control, generation from model, differential modulation, feed-back, question/answer, etc.: such is the new *operational* configuration (industrial simulacra are only *operational*). Digitality is its metaphysical principle (the God of Leibniz), and DNA its prophet. It is in effect in the genetic code that the "genesis of simulacra" today finds its most accomplished form. At the limit of an always more extensive abolition of references and finalities, of the loss of resemblance and designation, we find the digital program-sign, whose value is purely tactical, at the intersection of the other signals (corpuscles of information/test) and whose structure is that of a macro-molecular code of command and control.

At this level the question of signs, of their rational destination, their real or imaginary, their repression, their deviation, the illusion they create or that which they conceal, or their parallel meanings – all of that is erased. We have already seen signs of the first order, complex signs and rich in illusion, change, with the machines, into crude signs, dull, industrial, repetitive, echoless, operational and efficacious. What a mutation, even more radical still, with signals of the code, illegible, with no gloss possible, buried like programmatic matrices light-years away in the depths of the "biological" body – black boxes where all the commandments, all the answers ferment! End of the theatre of representation, the space of signs, their conflict, their silence; only the black box of the code, the molecular emitter of signals from which we have been irradiated, crossed by answers/questions like signifying radiations, tested continuously by our own program inscribed in the cells. Jail cells, electronic cells, party cells, microbiological cells: always the search for the smallest indivisible element, whose organic synthesis would be made according to the givens of the code. But the code itself is but a genetic cell, a generator where myriads of intersections produce all the questions and possible solutions, so that choices (by whom?) can be made. No finality involved with these "questions" (informational and signifying impulsions) but the answer, genetically unchangeable or inflected by minute and aleatory differences. Space is no longer even linear or one-dimensional: *cellular* space, indefinite generation of the same signals, like the tics of a prisoner gone crazy with solitude and repetition. Such is the genetic code: an erased record, unchangeable, of which we are no more than cells-for-reading. All aura of sign, of significance itself is resolved in this determination; all is resolved in the inscription and decodage.

Such is the third-order simulacrum, our own. Such is the "mystic elegance of the binary system, of the zero and the one," from which all being

proceeds. Such is the status of the sign that is also the end of signification: DNA or operational simulation.

All of this is perfectly well summed up by Sebeok ("Genetics and Semiotics", in *Versus*):

Numerous observations confirm the hypothesis that the internal organic world descends in a straight line from the primordial forms of life. The most remarkable fact is the omnipresence of the DNA molecule. The genetic material of all organisms known on earth is in great measure made up of the nucleonic acids DNA and RNA that contain in their information structure, transmitted by reproduction from one generation to another and furthermore gifted with the capacity of self-reproduction and imitation. Briefly, the genetic code is universal, or almost. Its deciphering was an immense discovery, in the sense that it showed that "the two languages of the great polymers, the language of nucleonic acid and that of protein, are tightly correlated" [...]. The Soviet mathematician Liapounov demonstrated in 1963 that all living systems transmit by prescribed canals with precision a small quantity of energy or of matter containing a great volume of information, which is responsible for the ulterior control of a great quantity of energy and matter. In this perspective numerous phenomena, biological as well as cultural (stockage, feed-back, canalization of messages and others) can be seen as aspects of the treatment of information. In the last analysis information appears in great part as the repetition of information, or even as another sort of information, a sort of control that seems to be a universal property of terrestrial life, independent of form or substance.

Five years ago I drew attention to the convergence of genetics and linguistics – autonomous disciplines, but parallel in the larger field of communication science (of which animal semiotics also is a part). The terminology of genetics is full of expressions taken from linguistics and communication theory [...], which also underlined either the major resemblances or the important differences of structure and of function between genetic and verbal codes ... It is obvious today that the genetic code must be considered the most fundamental of all the semiotic networks, and therefore a prototype of all the other systems of signaling that animals use, man included. From this point of view, molecules which are systems of quanta and behave like stable vehicles of physical information, systems of animal semiotics and cultural systems, including language, constitute a continuous chain of stages, with always more complex energy levels, in the framework of a universal unique evolution. It is therefore possible to describe either language or living systems from a unified cybernetic point-of-view. For the present, this is only a useful analogy or a prediction. A reciprocal rapprochement between animal communication and linguistics can lead to a complete knowledge of the dynamics of semiotics, and such a knowledge can be revealed, in the last analysis, to be nothing less than the very definition of life.

And so the current strategic model is designed that everywhere is replacing the great ideological model which constituted political economy in its time.

You will find it under the rigorous sign of "science" in the *Chance and Necessity* of Jacques Monod. The end of dialectical evolution, it is the discontinuous indeterminism of the genetic code that now controls life – the teleological principle. Finality no longer belongs to the term; there is no longer a term, nor a determination. Finality is there beforehand, inscribed in the code. We see that nothing has changed – simply the order of ends yields to the play of molecules, and the order of signifieds to the play of infinitesimal signifiers, reduced to their aleatory commutation. All the transcendant finalities reduced to a dashboard full of instruments. There is still, however, recourse to a nature, to an inscription in "biological" nature – in actuality, a nature distorted by fantasy like she always was, metaphysical sanctuary no longer of origin and substance, but this time of the code; the code must have an "objective" basis. What could be better for that purpose than the molecule and genetics? Monod is the strict theologian of this molecular transcendence, Edgar Morin the rapt disciple (A.D.N.* + Adonai!). But for one as well as the other, the fantasy of the code, which is equivalent to the reality of power, is merged with molecular idealism.

Thus we find once more in history that delirious illusion of uniting the world under the aegis of a single principle – that of a homogenous substance with the Jesuits of the Counter Reformation; that

of the genetic code with the technocrats of biological science (but also linguistics as well), with Leibniz and his binary divinity as precursor. For the program here aimed at has nothing genetic about it, it is a social and historical program. That which is hypostatized in biochemistry is the ideal of a social order ruled by a sort of genetic code of macromolecular calculation, of P.P.B.S. (Planned Programming Budgeting System), irradiating the social body with its operational circuits. The technical cybernetic finds its "natural philosophy" here, as Monod says. The fascination of the biological, of the biomedical dates from the very beginnings of science. It was at work in Spencerian organicism (sociobiology) on the level of second- and third-order structures (Jacob's classification in *The Logic of Life*, it is active today in modern biochemistry, on the level of structures of the fourth order).

Coded similarities and dissimilarities: that is certainly the image of cyberneticized social exchange. You only have to add "stereospecific complex" in order to re-inject intracellular communication; that Morin will come to transfigure into molecular Eros.

Practically and historically, this signified the substitution of social control by the *end* (and by a more or less dialectical *providence* which surveys the accomplishment of this *end*) for social control by anticipation, simulation and programming, and indeterminate mutation directed by the code. Instead of a process which is finalized according to its ideal development, we generalize from a *model*. Instead of a right to a prophecy, we have the right of *registration*. There is no really radical difference between the two, only the schemes of control have become fantastically perfected. From a capitalist-productivist society to a neo-capitalist cybernetic order that aims now at total control. This is the mutation for which the biological theorization of the code prepares the ground. There is nothing of an accident in this mutation. It is the end of a history in which, successively, God, Man, Progress, and History itself die to profit the code, in which transcendence dies to profit immanence, the latter corresponding to a much more advanced phase in the vertiginous manipulation of social rapports.

In its indefinite reproduction, the system puts an end to the myth of its origin and to all the referential values it has itself secreted along the

* D.N.A.

way. Putting an end to its myth of beginning, it ends its internal contradictions (no more real or referential to be confronted with), and it puts an end also to the myth of its own end: the revolution itself. What was profiled with revolution was the victory of human and generic reference, of the original potential of man. But if capital erases from the map generic man himself (for the sake of genetic man?) the Golden Age of the revolution was that of capital, where the myths of origin and end still circulated. Once shortcircuited the myths (and the only danger capital confronted historically came to it from this *mythical* exigency of rationality that accompanied it from the very beginning) in an operationality of fact and without discourse, once capital itself has become its own myth, or rather an interminable machine, aleatory, something like a *social genetic code*, it no longer leaves any room for a planned reversal; and this is its true violence. It remains to be seen if this operationality is not itself a myth, if DNA is not also a *myth*.

Once and for all there is posed, in effect, the problem of science as discourse. A good occasion to pose it here, where this discourse is absolutized with such candor. "Plato, Heraclitus, Hegel, Marx: these ideological edifices, presented as *a priori*, were really *a posteriori* constructions, destined to justify a preconceived ethico-political theory ... The only *a priori* for science is the postulate of objectivity, that forbids itself any part in this debate." (Monod). But this postulate results itself from a never innocent decision for objectification of the world and of the "real." In fact it is the coherence of a certain *discourse*, and all scientific movement is nothing but the space of this discourse, never revealing itself as such, and the "objective" simulacrum of which hides the political, strategic word. A little farther on, furthermore, Monod very well expresses the arbitrary nature of this phenomenon: "We might wonder if all the invariance, conservations and symmetries that constitute the scheme of scientific discourse are only fictions substituted for reality so as to offer an operational image ... A logic founded on a purely abstract principle of identity possibly conventional. Convention, however, that human reason seems incapable of doing without." You couldn't say it better: that science has selected itself as generating formula, a model discourse, upon the faith of a conventional order (not just any, however; that of total reduction). But Monod slides rapidly into this dangerous hypothesis of a "conventional" identity principle. It would be bet-

ter to base science, more crudely, upon an "object-ive" reality. Physics is there to witness that identity is only a postulate – it is *within things*, since there is "absolute identity of two atoms in the same quantitative state." Well then? Convention, or objective reality? The truth is that science is organized, like any other discourse, on the basis of a conventional logic, but it demands for its justification, like any other ideological discourse, a real "objective" reference, in a process of substance. If the principle of identity is somehow "true," even at the infinitesimal level of two atoms, then the entire conventional edifice of science that derives its inspiration from that level is also "true." The hypothesis of the genetic code, DNA, is also true and unsurpassable. So it goes with metaphysics. Science accounts for things previously encircled and formalized so as to be sure to obey it. "Objectivity" is nothing else than that, and the ethic which comes to sanction this object-ive knowledge is nothing less than a system of defense and imposed ignorance, whose goal is to preserve this vicious circle intact.[2]

"Down with all hypotheses that have allowed the belief in a true world," said Nietzsche.

The Tactile and the Digital

This regulation on the model of the genetic code is not at all limited to laboratory effects or to the exalted visions of theoreticians. Banal, everyday life is invested by these models. Digitality is with us. It is that which haunts all the messages, all the signs of our societies. The most concrete form you see it in is that of the test, of the question/answer, of the stimulus/response. All content is neutralized by a continual procedure of directed interrogation, of verdicts and ultimatums to decode, which no longer arise this time from the depths of the genetic code but that have the same tactical indeterminacy – the cycle of sense being infinitely shortened into that of question/answer, of bit or minute quantity of energy/information coming back to its beginning, the cycle only describing the perpetual reactualization of the same models. The equivalent of the total neutralization of the signified by the code is the instantaneousness of the verdict of fashion, or of any advertising or media message. Any place where the offer swallows up the demand, where the question assimilates the answer, or absorbs and regurgitates it in a decodable form, or invents and anticipates it in a predictible form. Everywhere the same "scenario," the scenario of "trial and error" (guinea pigs in laboratory experiments), the scenario of the breadth of choice offered everywhere ("the personality test") – everywhere the test functions as a fundamental form of control, by means of the infinite divisibility of practices and responses.

We live by the mode of *referendum* precisely because there is no longer any *referential*. Every sign, every message (objects of "functional" use as well as any item of fashion or televised news, poll or electoral consultation) is presented to us as question/answer. The entire system of communication has passed from that of a syntactically complex language structure to a binary sign system of question/answer – of perpetual *test*. Now tests and referenda are, we know, perfect forms of simulation: the answer is called forth by the question, it is designated in advance. *The referendum is always an ultimatum*: the unilateral nature of the question, that is no longer exactly an interrogation, but the immediate imposition of a sense whereby the cycle is suddenly completed. Every message is a verdict, just like the one that comes from polling statistics. The simulacrum of distance (or even of contradiction between the two poles) is only – like the effect of the real the sign seems to emit – a tactical hallucination.

Benjamin analyzes concretely, on the level of the technical instrument, this operation of the test:

The performance of the movie actor is transmitted to the public by means of an array of technical instruments, with a twofold consequence. The camera that presents the performance of the film actor to the public need not respect the performance as an integral whole. Guided by the cameraman, the camera continually changes its position with respect to the performance. The sequence of positional views which the editor composes from the material supplied him constitutes the completed film...Hence, the performance of the actor is subjected to a series of optical tests. This is the first consequence of the fact that the actor's performance is presented by means of the camera. Also, the film actor lacks the opportunity of the stage actor to adjust to the audience during the performance, since he does not present his performance to the audience in person. This permits the audience to take the position of the critic, without experiencing any personal contact with the actor. The audience's identification with the actor is really an identification with the camera. Consequently the audience takes the position of the camera; its approach is that of testing.

Note: The expansion of the field of the testable which mechanical equipment brings about for the actor corresponds to the extraordinary expansion of the field of the testable brought about for the individual through economic conditions. Thus, vocational aptitude tests become constantly more important. What matters in these tests [is] segmental performances of the individual. The film short and the vocational aptitude test are taken before a committee of experts. The camera director in the studio occupies a place identical with that of the examiner during aptitude tests. (Translated by H. Zohn in *Illuminations*, from *The Work of Art in the Age of Mechanical Reproduction*.)

"The work of art with the dadaists becomes a projectile. It plunges in on the spectator, it takes on a tactile quality. The diverging element in film is also first-and-foremost a tactile element, based effectually on the constant change of place and camera angles that stimulate the spectator."

No contemplation is possible. The images fragment perception into successive sequences, into stimuli toward which there can be only instantaneous response, yes or no – the limit of an abbreviated reaction. Film no longer allows you to question. It questions you, and directly. It is in this sense that the modern media call for, according to McLuhan,[3] a greater degree of immediate participation, an incessant response, a total plasticity (Benjamin compares the work of the cameraman to that of the surgeon: tactility and manipulation). The role of the message is no longer information, but testing and polling, and finally control ("contra-role," in the sense that all your answers are already inscribed in the "role," on the anticipated registers of the code). Montage and codification demand, in effect, that the receiver construe and decode by observing the same procedure whereby the work was assembled. The reading of the message is then only a perpetual examination of the code.

Every image, every media message, but also any functional environmental object, is a test – that is to say, in the full rigor of the term, liberating response mechanisms according to stereotypes and analytic models. Today, the object is no longer "functional" in the traditional meaning of the word; it no longer serves you, it *tests* you. It has nothing to do with the object of yesteryear, no more than does media news with a "reality" of facts. Both objects and information result already from a selection, a montage, from a point-of-view. They have already tested "reality," and have asked only questions that "answered back" to them. They have broken down reality into simple elements that they have reassembled into scenarios of regulated oppositions, exactly in the same way that the photographer imposes his contrasts, lights, angles on his subject (any photographer will tell you: you can do anything, all you have to do is approach the original from the right angle, at that right moment or mood that will render it the *correct answer* to the instantaneous test of the instrument and its code). It is exactly like the test or the referendum when they translate a conflict or problem into a game of question/answer. And reality, thus tested, tests you according to the same grill; you decode it according to the same code, inscribed within each message and object like a miniaturized genetic code.

All is presented today in a spread-out series, or as part of a line of products, and this fact alone tests you already, because you are obliged to make decisions. This approximates our general attitude toward the world around us to that of a *reading*, and to a selective deciphering. We live less like users than readers and selectors, reading cells. But nevertheless: by the same token you also are constantly selected and tested by the medium itself. Just like cutting out a sample for the ends of the survey, the media frame and excise their message bundles, which are in fact bundles of selected questions, samples of their audience. By a circular operation of experimental modification, of incessant interference, like a nervous input, tactile and retractile, that explores an object by means of brief perceptive sequences, until it has been localized and controlled. What the media thereby localize and control are no real and autonomous groups, but samples, samples modelled socially and mentally by a barrage of messages. "Public opinion" is evidently the prettiest of these samples – not an unreal political substance, but one that is hyperreal – a fantastic hyperreality that lives only off of montage and test-manipulation.

The eruption of the binary scheme question/answer is of an incalculable importance. It renders inarticulate every discourse. It short-circuits all that was, in a golden age come again, the dialectic of signifier and signified, of a representing and a

represented. It is the end of objects whose meaning would be function, and of opinions that "representative" representatives would be able to vote for. It is the end of the real interrogation to which it was possible to answer (the end especially to unanswerable questions). This process has been entirely overthrown. The contradictory process of true and false, of real and the imaginary, is abolished in this hyperreal logic of montage. Michel Tort, in his book *Intelligence Quotient*, analyzes this quite well: "What is going to determine the answer to the question is not the question as such in the form in which it was posed, it is also the idea that the interrogated subject forms about the most appropriate tactic to adopt in function of the concept he has formed about the expectations of the interrogator." And further: "The artifact is something else entirely than a controlled transformation of the object for the ends of knowledge: it is a rude interference with reality, at the end of which it is impossible to say what in reality can be objectively known and what is the result of technical intervention (medium). The I.Q. is an artifact." No more true or false, because no more distinguishable hiatus between question and response. In the light of the tests, intelligence, like opinion – and more generally the entire process of meaning – is reduced to the "ability to produce contrasting reactions to a growing series of adequate stimuli."

This entire analysis sends us back to McLuhan's formula: "The Medium is the Message." It is in effect the medium – the very style of montage, of decoupage, of interpellation, solicitation, summation, by the medium – which controls the process of meaning. And you understand why McLuhan saw in the era of the great electronic media an era of *tactile* communication. We are closer here in effect to the tactile than to the visual universe, where the distancing is greater and reflection is always possible. At the same time as touch loses its sensorial, sensual value for us ("touching is an interaction of the senses rather than a simple contact of an object with the skin"), it is possible that it returns as the strategy of a universe of communication – but as the field of *tactile* and *tactical* simulation, where the message becomes "massage," tentacular solicitation, test. Everywhere you're tested, palpated, the method is "tactical," the sphere of communication is "tactile." Without even speaking of the ideology of "contact," that is being pushed in all its forms as a substitute for social rapport, there is an entire social configuration that orbits around the test (the question/

answer cell) as around the commandments of the molecular code.

The political sphere entirely loses its specificity when it enters into the game of the media and public opinion polls, that is to say into the sphere of the integrated circuit of question/answer. The electoral sphere is in any case the first great institution where social exchange is reduced to obtaining an answer. It is due to this sign-simplification that it is the first one to become universal. Universal suffrage is the first of the mass-media. All through the 19th and 20th centuries political and economic practice merge increasingly into the same type of discourse. Propaganda and advertising fuse in the same marketing and merchandising of objects and ideologies. This convergence of language between the economic and the political is furthermore what marks a society such as ours, where "political economy" is fully realized. It is also by the same token its end, since the two spheres are abolished in an entirely separate reality, or hyperreality, which is that of the media. There, too, there is an elevation of each term to a greater power, that of the third-order simulacra.

"That many regret the 'corruption' of politics by the media, deploring that TV and public opinion polls have replaced so quickly the formation of opinion, shows only that they understand nothing about politics."

What is characteristic of this phase of political hyperrealism is the necessary conjunction between the bipartite system and the entry into the play of the polls as mirror of this alternating equivalence of the political game.

The polls are located in a dimension beyond all social *production*. They refer only to a simulacrum of public opinion. A mirror of opinion analogous in its way to that of the Gross National Product: imaginary mirror of the productive forces, without regard to their social ends or lack thereof. What is essential is only that "it" reproduces itself. The same as for public opinion: what is essential is that it shadow itself incessantly in its own image. Therein lies the secret of mass representation. It is no longer necessary that anyone *produce* an opinion, all that is needed is that all *reproduce* public opinion, in the sense that all opinions get caught up in this kind of general equivalent, and once more proceed from it (reproduce it, whatever they make of it, on the level of individual choice). For opinions as for material goods: production is dead, long live reproduction.

If McLuhan's formula makes any sense it is certainly in this connection.[4] Public opinion is *par excellence* at the same time medium and message. And the polls that inform it are the incessant imposition of the medium as message. In this sense they are of the same nature as TV and the electronic media, which we have seen are also only a perpetual game of question/answer, an instrument of perpetual polling.

The polls manipulate *that which cannot be decided*. Do they really affect the vote? True, false? Do they give an exact picture of reality, or simple tendencies, or the refraction of this reality in a hyperspace of simulation whose curve even is unknown? True, false, undecidable. Their most sophisticated analyses leave room always for the reversibility of the hypotheses. Statistics is only casuistry. This undecidable quality is proper to any process of simulation (see above, the crisis of indecision). The internal logic of these procedures (statistics, probability, operational cybernetics) is certainly rigorous and "scientific"; somehow though it does not stick, it is a fabulous fiction whose index of refraction in any reality (true or false) is nil. This is even what gives these *models* their forcefulness. But also it is this which only leaves them, as truth, the paranoid projection tests of a case, or of a group which dreams of a miraculous correspondence of the real to their models, and therefore of an absolute manipulation.

What is true of the statistics scenario is also true of the regulated partition of the political sphere: the alternation of the forces in power, majority/minority, substitutive, etc. On this limit of pure representation, "that" no longer represents anything. Politics die of the too-well-regulated game of distinctive oppositions. The political sphere (and that of power in general) becomes empty. This is somehow the payment for the accomplishing of the political class's desire: that of a perfect manipulation of social representation. Surreptitiously and silently, all social substance has left this machine in the very moment of its perfect reproduction.

The same thing holds true for the polls. The only ones who believe in them finally are the members of the political class, just as the only ones who really believe in advertising and market studies are the marketeers and advertisers. This is not because they are particularly stupid (though that we can't exclude either) but because the polls are homogenous with the current functioning of politics. They take on a "real" tactical value, they come into play as a factor in the regulation of the political class according to its own rules of the game. It therefore has reason to believe in them, and it believes. But who else does, really? It is the political class's burlesque spectacle, hyperrepresentative of nothing at all, that people taste by way of the polls and media. There is a jubilation proper to spectacular nullity, and the last form it takes is that of *statistical contemplation*. This is accompanied always, we know, by a profound disappointment – the kind of disillusion that the polls provoke in absorbing so utterly the public's voice, in short-circuiting all process of expression. The fascination they exercise is in accordance with this neutralization by emptiness, with this trance they create by anticipation of the image over all possible reality.

The problem of the polls is not at all that of their objective influence. Just as for propaganda or publicity, their influence is negated by individual or collective inertia or resistance. The problem is the operational simulation that they institute over the entire spectrum of social practices: that of the progressive *leukemiazation* of all social substance, that is the substitution for blood of the white lymph of media.

The question/answer cycle finds extension in all domains. You slowly find that the entire realm of inquiries, polls, and statistics needs to be looked at again in relation to this radical suspicion which falls upon their methods. But the selfsame suspicion falls on ethnology. Unless you admit that the natives are perfect naturals, incapable of simulation, the problem is the same as here: the impossibility of obtaining for a *directed* question any answer other than *simulated* (other than reproducing the question). It isn't even certain that you can interrogate plants, animals, nor even inert matter in the exact sciences with any chance of "objective" response. As to the response of the polled to the poll-takers, the natives to the ethnologist, the analyzed to the analyst, you can be sure that the circularity is total: the ones questioned always pretend to be as the question imagines and solicits them to be. Even psychoanalytic transference and countertransference fall today under the sway of this stimulated, simulated-anticipated response, which is none other than the very model of the self-fulfilling prophecy.[5] We come then upon a strange paradox: the word of the polled, the analyzed, the natives, is irremediably short-circuited and lost, and it is on the basis of this foreclosure that these respective disciplines – ethnology, psychoanalysis, sociology

– are going to be able to experience such marvelous growth. But they become puffed-up on mere wind, for it is in that respect that the circular response of the polled, the analyzed, the natives is all the same a challenge and a triumphant revenge. It is that they place the spotlight back on the question itself, isolate it in offering it the mirror of the answer it was awaiting, and show it helpless to ever quit the vicious circle which in fact is that of power. Just as in the electoral system, in which the representatives no longer represent anything because they control so well the responses of the electoral body. But everything has, somehow, eluded the ruling class's grasp. This is why the dominated answer of the natives is all the same a real response, a desperate vengeance: that of letting power bury power.

The "advanced democratic" systems are stabilized on the formula of bipartite alternation. The monopoly in fact remains that of a homogenous political class, from left to right, but it must not be exercised as such. The one-party totalitarian regime is an unstable form – it defuses the political scene, it no longer assures the feed-back of public opinion, the minimal flux in the integrated circuit which constitutes the transistorized political machine. Alternation, on the other hand, is the end of the end of representation, so solicitation is maximal, by dint of simple formal constraint, when you are approaching most nearly a perfect competitive equation between the two parties. This is logical. Democracy realizes the law of equivalence in the political order. This law is accomplished in the back-and-forth movement of the two terms which reactivates their equivalence but allows, by the minute difference, a public consensus to be formed and the cycle of representation to be closed. Operational theatre, where the only play staged anymore is the fulginous [*sic*] reflection of political Reason. The "free choice" of individuals, which is the credo of democracy, leads in fact precisely to the opposite: the vote becomes functionally *obligatory*: if it is not legally, it is by statistical constraint, the structure of alternation, reinforced by the polls.[6] The vote becomes functionally *aleatory*: when democracy attains an advanced formal stage, it distributes itself around equal quotients (50/50). The vote comes to resemble a Brownian movement of particles or the calculation of probabilities. It is as if everyone voted by chance, or monkeys voted.

At this point it makes no difference at all what the parties in power are expressing historically and socially. It is *necessary* even that they represent nothing: the fascination of the game, the polls, the formal and statistical compulsion of the game is all the greater.

"Classical" universal suffrage already implies a certain neutralization of the political field, if only by the consensus on the rules of the game. But you can still distinguish therein the representatives from the represented, on the basis of a real social antagonism of opinion. It is the neutralization of this contradictory referent, under the sign of a public opinion from now on equal unto itself, mediated and homogenized by anticipation (the polls) that will make alternation possible "at the top": simulation of opposition between two parties, absorption of their respective objectives, reversibility of the entire discourse one into the other. It is, beyond the representing and the represented, the pure form of representation – just as simulation characterizes, beyond the signifier and the signified, the pure form of the political economy of the sign – exactly as the floating of currency and its countable relations characterizes, beyond use and exchange value, beyond all substance of production, the pure form of value.

It might appear that the historical movement of capital carries it from one open competition towards oligopoly, then towards monopoly – that the democratic movement goes from multiple parties toward bipartism, then toward the single party. Nothing of the sort: oligopoly, or the current duopoly results from a *tactical doubling of monopoly*. In all domains duopoly is the final stage of monopoly. It is not the public will (state intervention, anti-trust laws, etc.) which breaks up the monopoly of the market – it is the fact that any unitary system, if it wishes to survive, must acquire a *binary regulation*. This changes nothing as far as monopoly is concerned. On the contrary, power is absolute only if it is capable of diffraction into various equivalents, if it knows how to take off so as to put more on. This goes for brands of soap-suds as well as peaceful coexistence. You need two superpowers to keep the universe under control: a single empire would crumble of itself. And the equilibrium of terror alone can allow a regulated opposition to be established, for the strategy is structural, never atomic. This regulated opposition can furthermore be ramified into a more complex scenario. The matrix remains binary. It will never again be a matter of a duel or open competitive struggle, but of couples of simultaneous opposition.

From the smallest disjunctive unity (question/answer particle) up to the great alternating systems that control the economy, politics, world coexistence, the matrix does not change: it is always the 0/1, the binary scansion that is affirmed as the metastable or homeostatic form of the current systems. This is the nucleus of the simulation processes which dominate us. It can be organized as a play of unstable variations, from polyvalence to tautology, without threatening the strategic bipolar form: it is the divine form of simulation.[7]

Why are there *two* towers at New York's World Trade Center? All of Manhattan's great buildings were always happy enough to affront each other in a competitive verticality, the result of which is an architectural panorama in the image of the capitalist system: a pyramidal jungle, all the buildings attacking each other. The system profiled itself in a celebrated image that you had of New York when you arrived there by boat. This image has completely changed in the last few years. The effigy of the capitalist system has passed from the pyramid to the perforated card. Buildings are no longer obelisks, but lean one upon the other, no longer suspicious one of the other, like columns in a statistical graph. This new architecture incarnates a system that is no longer competitive, but compatible, and where competition has disappeared for the benefit of the correlations. (New York is the world's only city therefore that retraces all along its history, and with a prodigious fidelity and in all its scope, the actual form of the capitalistic system – it changes instantly in function of the latter. No European city does so.) This architectural graphism is that of the monopoly; the two W.T.C. towers, perfect parallelepipeds a $\frac{1}{4}$-mile high on a square base, perfectly balanced and blind communicating vessels. The fact that there are two of them *signifies* the end of all competition, the end of all original reference. Paradoxically, if there were only one, the monopoly would not be incarnated, because we have seen how it stabilizes on a dual form. For the sign to be pure, it has to duplicate itself: it is the duplication of the sign which destroys its meaning. This is what Andy Warhol demonstrates also: the multiple replicas of Marilyn's face are there to show at the same time the death of the original and the end of representation. The two towers of the W.T.C. are the visible sign of the closure of the system in a vertigo of duplication, while the other skyscrapers are each of them the original moment of a system constantly transcending itself in a perpetual crisis and self-challenge.

There is a particular fascination in this reduplication. As high as they are, higher than all the others, the two towers signify nevertheless the end of verticality. They ignore the other buildings, they are not of the same race, they no longer challenge them, nor compare themselves to them, they look one into the other as into a mirror and culminate in this prestige of similitude. What they project is the idea of the model that they are one for the other, and their twin altitude presents no longer any value of transcendence. They signify only that the strategy of models and commutations wins out in the very heart of the system itself – and New York is really the heart of it – over the traditional strategy of competition. The buildings of Rockefeller Center still direct their gaze one at the other into their glass or steel facades, in the city's infinite specularity. The towers, on the other hand, are blind, and no longer have a facade. All referential of habitat, of the facade as face, of interior and exterior, that you still find in the Chase Manhattan or in the boldest mirror-buildings of the 60's, is erased. At the same time as the rhetoric of verticality, the rhetoric of the mirror has disappeared. There remains only a series closed on the number two, just as if architecture, in the image of the system, proceeded only from an unchangeable genetic code, a definitive model.

The Hyperrealism of Simulation

All of this defines a digital space, a magnetic field for the code, with polarizations, diffractions, gravitations of the models and always, always, the flux of the smallest disjunctive unities (the question/answer cell, that is like the cybernetic atom of meaning). We should compare this kind of control with the traditional repressive space, the police-space that still corresponded to a *signifying* violence. Space of reactionary conditioning that took its inspiration from the total Pavlovian disposition of programmed, repetitive aggressions, and which you find again multiplied in scale in "hard sell" advertising and in the political propaganda of the 1930's. Raw industrial violence, aiming to induce behaviors of terror and of animal obeisance. All of that no longer has any meaning. The totalitarian, bureaucratic concentration is a scheme which dates from the era of the mercantile law of value. The system of equivalences imposes in effect the form of a general equivalent, and therefore the centralization of a global process. Archaic rationality

compared to that of simulation; there is no longer a single general equivalent, but a diffraction of models that plays a regulatory role. No longer the form of the general equivalent, but that of distinctive opposition. From injunction you pass to disjunction by the code, from the ultimatum you pass to the solicitation, from the required passivity to models constructed all at once on the basis of the "active response" of the subject, on its implication, its "ludic" participation, etc., towards a total environmental model made out of incessant spontaneous responses of joyous feed-back and irradiating contact. This is the "concretization of the general atmosphere," according to Nicolas Schöffer, the great festival of Participation, made out of myriads of stimuli, miniaturized tests, infinitely divisible question/answers, all magnetized by a few great models in the luminous field of the code.

Here comes the time of the great Culture of tactile communication, under the sign of the technico-luminous cinematic space of total spatio-dynamic theatre.

This is a completely imaginary contact-world of sensorial mimetics and tactile mysticism; it is essentially an entire ecology that is grafted on this universe of operational simulation, multistimulation and multiresponse. We naturalize this incessant test of successful adaptation in assimilating it into animal mimesis. "The adaptation of animals to the colors and forms of their milieu is a valid phenomenon for man" (Nicolas Schöffer), and the same for Indians, with their "innate sense of ecology"! Tropisms, mimetics, empathy: the complete ecological Evangel of open systems, with positive or negative feedback, is going to rush into this breach, with an ideology of regulation by information which is only the avatar, according to a more flexible rationality, of Pavlov's reflex. So it is that we graduate from electro-shock therapy to bodily expression as a means of conditioning mental health. Everywhere the disposition of force and forcing yield to dispositions of ambiance, with operationalization of the notions of need, perception, desire, etc. Generalized ecology, mystique of the "niche" and of the context, milieu-simulation right up to "Centers of Esthetic and Cultural Re-Animation" foreseen in the VIIth Plan (why not?) and Center of Sexual Leisure, constructed in the form of a breast, that will offer a "superior euphoria due to a pulsating ambiance.... The workers from all classes will be able to penetrate into these stimulating centers." Spatiodynamic fascination, like this "total theatre" established "according to a hyperbolic circular disposition turning around a cylindrical cone": no more scene, cut-off point, or "regard": end of the spectacle as well as of the spectacular, towards the total environmental, fused together, tactile, esthesia and no longer esthetics, etc. We can think of the total theatre of Artaud only with black humor, his Theatre of Cruelty, of which this spatiodynamic simulation is only an abject caricature. Here cruelty is replaced by "minimal and maximal stimulus thresholds," by the invention of "perceptive codes calculated on the basis of saturation thresholds." Even the good old "catharsis" of the classical theatre of the passions has become today homeopathy by simulation. So goes creativity.

This also means the collapse of reality into hyperrealism, in the minute duplication of the real, preferably on the basis of another reproductive medium – advertising, photo, etc. From medium to medium the real is volatilized; it becomes an allegory of death, but it is reinforced by its very destruction; it becomes the real for the real, fetish of the lost object – no longer object of representation, but ecstasy of denegation and of its own ritual extermination: the hyperreal.

Realism had already begun this tendency. The rhetoric of the real already meant that the status of the latter had been gravely menaced (the golden age is that of language's innocence, where it doesn't have to add an "effect of reality" to what is said). Surrealism is still solidary with the realism it contests, but augments its intensity by setting it off against the imaginary. The hyperreal represents a much more advanced phase, in the sense that even this contradiction between the real and the imaginary is effaced. The unreal is no longer that of dream or of fantasy, of a beyond or a within, it is that of a *hallucinatory resemblance of the real with itself*. To exit from the crisis of representation, you have to lock the real up in pure repetition. Before emerging in pop art and pictorial neo-realism, this tendency is at work already in the new novel. The project is already there to empty out the real, extirpate all psychology, all subjectivity, to move the real back to pure objectivity. In fact this objectivity is only that of the pure look – objectivity at last liberated from the object, that is nothing more than the blind relay station of the look which sweeps over it. Circular seduction where you can detect easily the unconscious desire of no longer being visible at all.

This is certainly the impression that the new novel leaves: this rage for eliding sense in a minute and blind reality. Syntax and semantics have disappeared – there is no longer apparition, but instead subpoena of the object, severe interrogation of its scattered fragments – neither metaphor nor metonymy: successive immanence under the policing structure of the look. This "objective" minuteness arouses a vertigo of reality, a vertigo of death on the limits of representation-for-the-sake-of-representation. End of the old illusions of relief, perspective and depth (spatial and psychological) bound to the perception of the object: it is the entire optic, the view become operational on the surface of things, it is the look become molecular code of the object.

Several modalities of this vertigo of realistic simulation are possible:

I. The deconstruction of the real into details – closed paradigmatic declension of the object – flattening, linearity and seriality of the partial objects.

II. The endlessly reflected vision: all the games of duplication and reduplication of the object in detail. This multiplication is presented as a deepening, that is for a critical metalanguage, and it was doubtless true in a reflexive configuration of the sign, in a dialectic of the mirror. From now on, though, this indefinite refraction is only another type of seriality. The real is no longer reflected, instead it feeds off itself till the point of emaciation.

III. The properly serial form (Andy Warhol). Here not only the syntagmatic dimension is abolished, but the paradigmatic as well. Since there no longer is any formal flection or even internal reflection, but contiguity of the same – flection and reflection zero. Like those two twin sisters in a dirty picture: the charnel reality of their bodies is erased by the resemblance. How to invest your energies in one, when her beauty is immediately duplicated by the other? The regard can go only from one to the other, all vision is locked into this coming-and-going. Subtle way of murdering the original, but also singular seduction, where all attention to the object is intercepted by its infinite diffraction into itself (inverted scenario of the Platonic myth of the reunion of the separated halves of the symbol – here the sign multiplies like protozoans). This seduction is possibly that of death, in the sense that for sexual beings, death is possibly not nothingness, but simply the mode of reproduction anterior to the sexual. This generation by model along an endless chain that in effect recalls the protozoans and is opposed to a sexual mode that we tend, inaccurately, to confuse with life itself.

IV. But this pure mechanization is doubtless only a paradoxical limit: the true generating formula, that which englobes all the others, and which is somehow the stabilized form of the code, is that of binarity, of digitality. Not pure repetition, but the minimal separation, the least amount of inflection between the two terms, that is to say the "very smallest common paradigm" that the fiction of sense could possibly support. Combination of differentiation internal to the pictorial object and to the object of consummation, this simulation retreats in contemporary art to be no more than the minute difference that still separates the hyperreal from hyperpainting. The latter pretends to extend right up to a sacrificial effacement before the real, but you know how all these prestigious elements in painting resuscitate in this minute difference: all of painting takes refuge in the border that separates the painted surface and the wall. And in the signature: metaphysical sign of painting and of the whole metaphysic of representation, at the limit where it takes itself for model (the "pure look") and turns back upon itself in the compulsive repetition of the code.

The very definition of the real becomes: *that of which it is possible to give an equivalent reproduction.* This is contemporaneous with a science that postulates that a process can be perfectly reproduced in a set of given conditions, and also with the industrial rationality that postulates a universal system of equivalency (classical representation is not equivalence, it is transcription, interpretation, commentary). At the limit of this process of reproductibility, the real is not only what can be reproduced, but *that which is always already reproduced.* The hyperreal.

And so: end of the real, and end of art, by total absorption one into the other? No: hyperrealism is the limit of art, and of the real, by respective exchange, on the level of the simulacrum, of the privileges and the prejudices which are their basis. The hyperreal transcends representation (cf. J.F. Lyotard, *L'Art Vivant*, number on hyperrealism) only because it is entirely in simulation. The tourniquet of representation tightens madly, but of an implosive madness, that, far from eccentric (marginal) inclines towards the center to its own infinite repetition. Analogous to the distancing characteristic of the dream, that makes us say that we are only dreaming; but this is only the game of censure and of perpetuation of the dream. Hyperrealism is made an integral part of a coded reality that it perpetuates, and for which it changes nothing.

In fact, we should turn our definition of hyperrealism inside out: *It is reality itself today that is hyperrealist.* Surrealism's secret already was that the most banal reality could become surreal, but only in certain privileged moments that nevertheless are still connected with art and the imaginary. Today it is quotidian reality in its entirety – political, social, historical and economic – that from now on incorporates the simulatory dimension of hyperrealism. We live everywhere already in an "esthetic" hallucination of reality. The old slogan "truth is stranger than fiction," that still corresponded to the surrealist phase of this estheticization of life, is obsolete. There is no more fiction that life could possibly confront, even victoriously – it is reality itself that disappears utterly in the game of reality – radical disenchantment, the cool and cybernetic phase following the hot stage of fantasy.

It is thus that for guilt, anguish and death there can be substituted the total joy of the signs of guilt, despair, violence and death. It is the very euphoria of simulation, that sees itself as the abolition of cause and effect, the beginning and the end, for all of which it substitutes reduplication. In this manner all closed systems protect themselves at the same time from the referential – as well as from all metalanguage that the system forestalls in playing at its own metalanguage; that is to say in duplicating itself in its own critique of itself. In simulation, the metalinguistic illusion duplicates and completes the referential illusion (pathetic hallucination of the sign and pathetic hallucination of the real).

"It's a circus," "It's theatre," "It's a movie," old adages, old naturalistic denunciation. These sayings are now obsolete. The problem now is that of the *satellization of the real*, the putting into orbit of an indefinable reality without common measure to the fantasies that once used to ornament it. This satellization we find further naturalized in the two-rooms–kitchen–shower that they have launched into orbit – to the powers of space, you could say – with the last lunar module. The banality of the earthly habitat lifted to the rank of cosmic value, of absolute decor – hypostatized in space – this is the end of metaphysics, the era of hyperreality that begins.[8] But the spatial transcendence of the banality of the two-rooms, like its cool and mechanical figuration of hyperrealism,[9] says only one thing: that this module, such as it is, participates in a hyperspace of representation – where each is already technically in possession of the instantaneous reproduction of his own life, where the pilots of the Tupolev that crashed at Bourget could see themselves die live on their own camera. This is nothing else than the short-circuit of the response by the question in the test, instantaneous process of re-conduction whereby reality is immediately contaminated by its simulacrum.

There used to be, before, a specific class of allegorical and slightly diabolical objects: mirrors, images, works of art (concepts?) – simulacra, but transparent and manifest (you didn't confuse the counterfeit with the original), that had their characteristic style and savoir-faire. And pleasure consisted then rather in discovering the "natural" in what was artificial and counterfeit. Today, when the real and the imaginary are confused in the same operational totality, the esthetic fascination is everywhere. It is a subliminal perception (a sort of sixth sense) of deception, montage, scenario – of the overexposed reality in the light of the models – no longer a production space, but a reading strip, strip of coding and decoding, magnetized by the signs – esthetic reality – no longer by the premeditation and the distance of art, but by its elevation to the second level, to the second power, by the anticipation and the immanence of the code. A kind of non-intentional parody hovers over everything, of technical simulation, of indefinable fame to which is attached an esthetic pleasure, that very one of reading and of the rules of the game. Travelling of signs, the media, of fashion and the models, of the blind and brilliant ambiance of the simulacra.

A long time ago art prefigured this turning which is that today of daily life. Very quickly the work turns back on itself as the manipulation of the signs of art: over-signification of art, "academism of the signifier," as Lévi-Strauss would say, who interprets it really as the form-sign. It is then that art enters into its indefinite *reproduction*: all that reduplicates itself, even if it be the everyday and banal reality, falls by the token under the sign of art, and becomes esthetic. It's the same thing for production, which you could say is entering today this esthetic reduplication, this phase when, expelling all content and finality, it becomes somehow abstract and non-figurative. It expresses then the pure form of production, it takes upon itself, as art, the value of a finality without purpose. Art and industry can then

exchange their signs. Art can become a reproducing machine (Andy Warhol), without ceasing to be art, since the machine is only a sign. And production can lose all social finality so as to be verified and exalted finally in the prestigious, hyperbolic signs that are the great industrial combines, the $\frac{1}{4}$-mile-high towers or the number mysteries of the GNP.

And so art is everywhere, since artifice is at the very heart of reality. And so art is dead, not only because its critical transcendence is gone, but because reality itself, entirely impregnated by an aesthetic which is inseparable from its own structure, has been confused with its own image. Reality no longer has the time to take on the appearance of reality. It no longer even surpasses fiction: it captures every dream even before it takes on the appearance of a dream. Schizophrenic vertigo of these serial signs, for which no counterfeit, no sublimation is possible, immanent in their repetition – who could say what the reality is that these signs simulate? They no longer even repress anything (which is why, if you will, simulation pushes us close to the sphere of psychosis). Even the primary processes are abolished in them. The cool universe of digitality has absorbed the world of metaphor and metonymy. The principle of simulation wins out over the reality principle just as over the principle of pleasure.

[. . .]

Hyperreal and Imaginary

Disneyland is a perfect model of all the entangled orders of simulation. To begin with it is a play of illusions and phantasms: Pirates, the Frontier, Future World, etc. This imaginary world is supposed to be what makes the operation successful. But what draws the crowds is undoubtedly much more the social microcosm, the miniaturised and *religious* revelling in real America, in its delights and drawbacks. You park outside, queue up inside, and are totally abandoned at the exit. In this imaginary world the only phantasmagoria is in the inherent warmth and affection of the crowd, and in that sufficiently excessive number of gadgets used there to specifically maintain the multitudinous affect. The contrast with the absolute solitude of the parking lot – a veritable concentration camp – is total. Or rather: inside, a whole range of gadgets magnetise the crowd into direct flows – outside, solitude is directed onto a single gadget:

the automobile. By an extraordinary coincidence (one that undoubtedly belongs to the peculiar enchantment of this universe), this deep-frozen infantile world happens to have been conceived and realised by a man who is himself now cryogenised: Walt Disney, who awaits his resurrection at minus 180 degrees centigrade.

The objective profile of America, then, may be traced throughout Disneyland, even down to the morphology of individuals and the crowd. All its values are exalted here, in miniature and comic strip form. Embalmed and pacified. Whence the possibility of an ideological analysis of Disneyland (L. Marin does it well in *Utopies, jeux d'espaces*): digest of the American way of life, panegyric to American values, idealised transposition of a contradictory reality. To be sure. But this conceals something else, and that "ideological" blanket exactly serves to cover over a *third-order simulation*: Disneyland is there to conceal the fact that it is the "real" country, all of "real" America, which *is* Disneyland (just as prisons are there to conceal the fact that it is the social in its entirety, in its banal omnipresence, which is carceral). Disneyland is presented as imaginary in order to make us believe that the rest is real, when in fact all of Los Angeles and the America surrounding it are no longer real, but of the order of the hyperreal and of simulation. It is no longer a question of a false representation of reality (ideology), but of concealing the fact that the real is no longer real, and thus of saving the reality principle.

The Disneyland imaginary is neither true nor false; it is a deterrence machine set up in order to rejuvenate in reverse the fiction of the real. Whence the debility, the infantile degeneration of this imaginary. It is meant to be an infantile world, in order to make us believe that the adults are elsewhere, in the "real" world, and to conceal the fact that real childishness is everywhere, particularly amongst those adults who go there to act the child in order to foster illusions as to their real childishness.

Moreover, Disneyland is not the only one. Enchanted Village, Magic Mountain, Marine World: Los Angeles is encircled by these "imaginary stations" which feed reality, reality-energy, to a town whose mystery is precisely that it is nothing more than a network of endless, unreal circulation – a town of fabulous proportions, but without space or dimensions. As much as electrical and nuclear power stations, as much as film studios, this town, which is nothing more than an immense script and a perpetual motion picture, needs this old imaginary made up of childhood signals and faked phantasms for its sympathetic nervous system.

Notes

1 Counterfeit and reproduction imply always an anguish, a disquieting foreignness: the uneasiness before the photograph, considered like a witch's trick – and more generally before any technical apparatus, which is always an apparatus of reproduction, is related by Benjamin to the uneasiness before the mirror-image. There is already sorcery at work in the mirror. But how much more so when this image can be detached from the mirror and be transported, stocked, reproduced at will (cf. *The Student of Prague*, where the devil detaches the image of the student from the mirror and harasses him to death by the intermediary of this image). All reproduction implies therefore a kind of black magic, from the fact of being seduced by one's own image in the water, like Narcissus, to being haunted by the double and, who knows, to the mortal turning back of this vast technical apparatus secreted today by man as his own image (the narcissistic mirage of technique, McLuhan) and that returns to him, cancelled and distorted – endless reproduction of himself and his power to the limits of the world. Reproduction is diabolical in its very essence; it makes something fundamental vacillate. This has hardly changed for us: simulation (that we describe here as the operation of the code) is still and always the place of a gigantic enterprise of manipulation, of control and of death, just like the imitative object (primitive statuette, image of photo) always had as objective an operation of black image.

2 There is furthermore in Monod's book a flagrant contradiction, which reflects the ambiguity of all current science. His discourse concerns the code, that is the third-order simulacra, but it does so still according to "scientific" schemes of the second order – objectiveness, "scientific" ethic of knowledge, science's principle of truth and transcendence. All things incompatible with the indeterminable models of the third order.

3 "It's the feeble 'definition' of TV which condemns its spectator to rearranging the few points retained into a kind of *abstract work*. He participates suddenly in the creation of a reality that was only just presented to

him in dots: the television watcher is in the position of an individual who is asked to project his own fantasies on inkblots that are not supposed to represent anything." TV as perpetual Rorshach test. And furthermore: "The TV image requires each instant that we 'close' the spaces in the mesh by a convulsive sensuous participation that is profoundly kinetic and tactile."

4   "The Medium is the Message" is the very slogan of the political economy of the sign, when it enters into the third-order simulation – the distinction between the medium and the message characterizes instead signification of the second order.

5   The entire current "psychological" situation is characterized by this short-circuit.

Doesn't emancipation of children and teenagers, once the initial phase of revolt is passed and once there has been established the *principle* of the *right* to emancipation, seem like the *real* emancipation of parents. And the young (students, high-schoolers, adolescents) seem to sense it in their always more insistent demand (though still as paradoxical) for the presence and advice of parents or of teachers. Alone at last, free and responsible, it seemed to them suddenly that other people possibly have absconded with their true liberty. Therefore, there is no question of "leaving them be." They're going to hassle them, not with any emotional or material spontaneous demand, but with an exigency that has been premeditated and corrected by an implicit oedipal knowledge. Hyperdependence (much greater than before) distorted by irony and refusal, *parody of libidinous original mechanisms*. Demand without content, without referent, unjustified, but for all that all the more severe – naked demand with no possible answer. The contents of knowledge (teaching) or of affective relations, the pedagogical or familial referent having been eliminated in the act of emancipation, there remains only a demand linked to the empty form of the institution – perverse demand, and for that reason all the more obstinate. "Transferable" desire (that is to say nonreferential, un-referential), desire that has been fed by lack, by the place left vacant, "liberated," desire captured in its own vertiginous image, desire of desire, as pure form, hyperreal. Deprived of symbolic substance, it doubles back upon itself, draws its energy from its own reflection and its disappointment with itself. This is literally today the "demand," and it is obvious that unlike the "classical" objective or transferable relations this one here is insoluble and interminable.

Simulated Oedipus.

Francois Richard: "Students asked to be seduced either bodily or verbally. But also they are aware of this and they play the game, ironically. 'Give us your knowledge, your presence, you have the word, speak, you are there for that.' Contestation certainly, but not only: the more authority is contested, vilified, the greater the need for authority as such. They play at Oedipus also, to deny it all the more vehemently. The 'teach', he's Daddy, they say; it's fun, you play at incest, malaise, the untouchable, at being a tease – in order to de-sexualize finally." Like one under analysis who asks for Oedipus back again, who tells the "oedipal" stories, who has the "analytical" dreams to satisfy the supposed request of the analyst, or to resist him? In the same way the student goes through his oedipal number, his seduction number, gets chummy, close, approaches, dominates – but this isn't desire, it's simulation. Oedipal psychodrama of simulation (neither less real nor less dramatic for all that). Very different from the real libidinal stakes of knowledge and power or even of a real mourning for the absence of same (as could have happened after '68 in the universities) Now we've reached the phase of desperate reproduction, and where the stakes are nil, the simulacrum is maximal – exacerbated and parodied simulation at one and the same time – as interminable as psychoanalysis and for the same reasons.

The interminable psychoanalysis.

There is a whole chapter to add to the history of transference and countertransference: that of their liquidation by simulation, of the impossible psychoanalysis because it is itself, from now on, that produces and reproduces the unconscious as its institutional substance. Psychoanalysis dies also of the exchange of the *signs* of the unconscious. Just as revolution dies of the exchange of the critical signs of political economy. This short-circuit was well known to Freud in the form of the gift of the analytic dream, or with the "uninformed" patients, in the form of the gift of their analytic knowledge. But this was still interpreted as resistance, as detour, and did not put fundamentally into question either the process of analysis or the principle of transference. It is another thing entirely when the unconscious itself, the discourse of the unconscious becomes unfindable – according to the same scenario of simulative anticipation that we have seen at work on all levels with the machines of the third order. The analysis then can no longer end, it becomes logically and historically interminable, since it stabilizes on a puppet-substance of reproduction, an unconscious programmed on demand – an impossible-to-break-through point around which the whole analysis is rearranged. The messages of the unconscious have been short-circuited by the psychoanalysis "medium." This is libidinal hyperrealism. To the famous categories of the real, the symbolic and the imaginary, it is going to be necessary to add the hyperreal, which captures and obstructs the functioning of the three orders.

6   Athenian democracy, much more advanced than our own, had reached the point where the vote was considered as payment for a service, after all other repressive solutions had been tried and found wanting in order to insure a quorum.

7 In this sense we should radically criticize the projection that Lévi-Strauss makes of binary structures as "anthropological" mental structures and of dual organization as the basic structure of primitive society. The dualist form that Lévi-Strauss would so love to apply to primitive society is never anything less than *our* own structural logic. Our very own code, that selfsame one that we use to dominate the "archaic" societies. Lévi-Strauss has the kindness to slip this to them under the guise of mental structures that are common to the whole human race. They will thereby be better prepared to receive the baptism of the Occident.

8 The coefficient of reality is proportional to the imaginary in reverse which gives it its specific density. This is true of geographical and spatial exploration also. When there is no more territory virgin and therefore available for the imaginary, when the map covers the whole territory, then something like a principle of reality disappears. The conquest of space constitutes in this sense an irreversible threshold in the direction of the loss of the earthly referential. This is precisely the hemorrhage of reality as internal coherence of a limited universe when its limits retreat infinitely. The conquest of space follows that of the planet as the same fantastic enterprise of extending the jurisdiction of the real – to carry for example the flag, the technique, and the two-rooms-and-kitchen to the moon – same tentative to substantiate the concepts or to territorialize the unconscious – the latter equals making the human race unreal, or [...] reversing it into a hyperreality of simulation.

9 Or that of the metal-plated caravan or supermarket dear to hyperrealists, or Campbell's Soup dear to Andy Warhol, or the Mona Lisa, since she too has been satellized around the planet, as absolute model of earthly art, no longer a work of art but a planetary simulacrum where everyone comes to witness himself (really his own death) in the gaze of the future.

28

Economimesis

Jacques Derrida

Under the cover of a controlled indeterminacy, pure morality and empirical culturalism are allied in the Kantian critique of pure judgments of taste. [...] A politics, therefore, although it never occupies the center of the stage, acts upon this discourse. It ought to be possible to read it. Politics and political economy, to be sure, are implicated in every discourse on art and on the beautiful. But how does one discern the most pointed specificity of such an implication? Certain of its motifs belong to a long sequence, to a powerful traditional chain going back to Plato and to Aristotle. Very tightly interlaced with these, though at first indistinguishable, are other narrower sequences that would be inadmissible within an Aristotelian or Platonic politics of art. But sorting out and measuring lengths will not suffice. Folded into a new system, the long sequences are displaced; their sense and their function change. Once inserted into another network, the "same" philosopheme is no longer the same, and besides it never had an identity external to its functioning. Simultaneously, "unique and original" ["*inédits*"] philosophemes, if there are any, as soon as they enter into articulated composition with inherited philosophemes, are affected by that composition over the whole of their surface and under every angle. We are nowhere near disposing of rigorous criteria for judging philosophical specificity, the precise limits framing a corpus or what properly belongs [*le propre*] to a system. The very project of such a delimitation itself already belongs to a set of conditions [*un ensemble*] that remains to be thought. In turn, even the concept of belonging [to a set] is open to elaboration, that is dislocation, by the structure of the *parergon* [Cf. "Le parergon," *La verité en peinture* (Paris: Champs Flammarion, 1978].

Production as Mimesis

That is what prompts us once again to feign a point of departure in examples, in any case in very particular locations, following a procedure which for reasons already recognized can be neither empirical nor metaempirical.

These locations, here and now, are two; their choice is motivated by the concept of *economimesis*. It would appear that *mimesis* and *oikonomia* could have nothing to do with one another. The point is to demonstrate the contrary, to exhibit the systematic link between the two; but not between some particular political economy and *mimesis*, for the latter can accommodate itself to political systems that are different, even opposed to one another. And we are not yet defining economy as an economy of circulation (a restricted economy) or a general economy, for the whole difficulty is narrowed down here as soon as – that is the hypothesis – there is no possible *opposition* between these two economies. Their relation must be one neither of identity nor of contradiction but must be other.

The two particular locations are signaled by statements that are economic in the current sense. Each time it is a question of *salary*. Remarks of this kind are rare in the third *Critique*. That is not a reason, quite the contrary, to consider them insignificant. Is it merely an accident of construction, a chance of composition that the whole Kantian theory of *mimesis* is set forth between these two remarks on salary?

One of these remarks is found in section 43 (*On art in general*): it is the definition of free (or liberal: *freie*) art by opposition to mercenary art [*Lohnkunst*]. The other one is in paragraph 51, in a parenthesis, where it is declared that in the Fine-Arts the mind must occupy itself, excite and satisfy itself without having any end [*but*] in view and independently of any salary.

The first remark intervenes in the course of a definition of art in general – a definition that comes rather late in the book. Up to this point, the subject has been beauty and pure judgments of taste, and if examples have been drawn from art, natural beauty might just as well have furnished them for a theory of judgments of taste. In the preceding paragraph, the superiority of natural beauty had been justified from a moral point of view and by recourse to an analogy between judgments of taste and moral judgments. On the basis of this analogy one can read the "ciphered language" [*Chiffreschrift*] that nature "speaks to us figurally [*figürlich*] through its beautiful forms," its real signatures which make us consider it, nature, as art production. Nature lets itself be admired as art, not by accident but according to well-ordered laws. If on this point Hegel seems to say the contrary – that there is nothing beautiful but what is art – the analogy between art and nature here as always provides a principle of reconciliation.

What is art? Kant seems to begin by replying: art is not nature, thus subscribing to the inherited, ossified, simplified opposition between *tekhnè* and *physis*. On the side of nature is mechanical necessity; on the side of art, the play of freedom. In between them is a whole series of secondary determinations. But analogy annuls this opposition. It places under Nature's dictate what is most wildly free in the production of art. Genius is the locus of such a dictation – the means by which art receives its rules from nature. All propositions of an anti-mimetic cast, all condemnations leveled against imitation are undermined at this point. One must not imitate nature; but nature, assigning its rules to genius, folds itself, returns to itself, reflects itself through art. This specular flexion provides both the principle of reflexive judgments – nature

guaranteeing legality in a movement that proceeds from the particular – and the secret resource of *mimesis* – understood not, in the first place, as an imitation of nature by art, but as a flexion of the *physis*, nature's relation to itself. There is no longer here any opposition between *physis* and *mimesis*, nor consequently between *physis* and *tekhnè*; or that, at least, is what now needs to be verified.

Section 43 begins: "Art is distinguished from nature as doing (*Thun*) (*facere*) is distinguished from acting (*Handeln*) or working (*Wirken*) generally (*agere*), and as the product (*Produkt*) or result of the former is distinguished as work (*Werk*) (*opus*) from the working (*Wirkung*) (*effectus*) of the latter." [*Critique of Judgment*, trans. J. H. Bernard (New York: Hafner Press, 1974)]

These proportional analogies are constructed on a certain number of apparently irreducible oppositions. How are they finally, as they always do, going to dissolve? And to the advantage of what political economy?

In order to dissolve, as they always do, the oppositions must be produced, must be propagated and multiplied. The process is one that has to be followed.

Within art in general (one of the two terms of the preceding opposition) another split engenders a series of distinctions. Their logical structure is not insignificant: there is no symmetry between the terms, but rather a regular hierarchy such that any attempt to distinguish between the two is also to classify one as being more and the other less. The attempt is to define two distinct sorts of art, but in order to display two phenomena of which one is more properly "art" than the other.

Immediately after having distinguished art from nature, Kant specifies that the only thing one ought to call "art" is the production of freedom by means of *freedom* [*Hervorbringung durch Freiheit*]. Art properly speaking puts free-will (*Wilkür*) to work and places reason at the root of its acts. There is therefore no art, in a strict sense, except that of a being who is free and *logon ekon* [has speech]: the product of bees ["cells of wax regularly constructed"] is not a work of art. What can be glimpsed in this inexhaustible reiteration of the humanist theme, of the ontology bound up with it as well, in this obscurantist buzzing that always treats animality *in general*, under the purview of one or two scholastic examples, as if there were only a single "animal" structure that could be opposed to the human (inalienably endowed with reason, freedom, sociality, laughter, language, law, the symbolic, with consciousness, or an unconscious, etc.), is that the concept of art is also constructed with just such a guarantee in view. It is there to raise man up [*ériger l'homme*], that is, always, to erect a man-god, to avoid contamination from "below," and to mark an incontrovertible limit of anthropological domesticity. The whole of economimesis (Aristotle: only man is capable of *mimesis*) is represented in this gesture. Its ruse and its naiveté – the logic of man – lie in the necessity, in order to save the absolute privilege of emergence (art, freedom, language, etc.), of grounding it in an absolute naturalism and in an absolute indifferentialism; somewhere human production has to be renaturalized, and differentiation must get effaced into opposition.

Thus bees have no art. And if one were to name their production a "work of art," it would be "only by analogy" [*nur wegen der Analogie*]. The work of art is always that of man [*ein Werk der Menschen*].

A power, aptitude, property, destiny of man [*Geschicklichkeit des Menschen*], art is distinguished in its turn from science. Scientific knowledge is a power [*un pouvoir*]; art is what it does not suffice to know, in order to know how to do it [*savoir faire*], in order to be able to do it [*pouvoir faire*]. In the region that Kant comes from, the common man is rarely wrong. Solving the problem of the egg of Columbus, that is science: it suffices to know in order to know how. The same may be said of prestidigitation. As for high-wire dancing, that is something else: you have to do it [*faut le faire*] and it does not suffice to know about it (there is a very brief passage of a tight-rope walker in a confidential note, "*In meinen Gegenden...*" For anyone who would like to take the plunge and put in something of himself: Kant, Nietzsche, Genet).

Distinct from science, art in general (the question of the Fine-Arts has not yet arisen) cannot be reduced to craft [*Handwerk*]. The latter exchanges the value of its work against a salary; it is a mercenary art [*Lohnkunst*]. Art, strictly speaking, is liberal or free [*freie*], its production must not enter into the economic circle of commerce, of offer and demand; it must not be exchanged. Liberal art and mercenary art therefore do not form a couple of opposite terms. One is higher than the other, more "art" than the other; it has more value for not having any economic value. If art, in the literal sense, is "production of freedom," liberal art better conforms to its essence. Mercenary art belongs to art only by analogy. And if one follows this play of analogy, mercenary productivity also

resembles that of bees: lack of freedom, a determined purpose or finality, utility, finitude of the code, fixity of the program without reason and without the play of the imagination. The craftsman, the worker, like the bee, does not play. And indeed, the hierarchical opposition of liberal art and mercenary art is that of play and work. "We regard the first as if it could only prove purposive as play, i.e. as occupation that is pleasant in itself. But the second is regarded as work, i.e. as occupation which is unpleasant (a trouble) in itself and which is only attractive on account of its effect (for example salary) and which can consequently only be imposed on us by constraint (*zwangmässig*)." [§ 43].

Let us follow the law of analogy:

1. If art is the distinguishing property of man as freedom, free art is more human than remunerated work, just as it is more human than the so-called instinctual activity of bees. The free man, the artist in this sense, is not *homo oeconomicus*.

2. Just as everything in nature prescribes the utilization of animal organization by man [§ 63], in the same way free man should be able to utilize, were it by constraint, the work of man insofar as it is not free. Liberal art ought thus to be able to use mercenary art (without touching it, that is without implicating itself); an economy must be able to utilize (render useful) the economy of work.

3. The value of play defines pure productivity. With the beautiful and art both proceeding from the imagination, it was still necessary to distinguish between the reproductive imagination and the productive imagination that is spontaneous, free, and playful: "If we seek the result of the preceding analysis, we find that everything runs up into this concept of taste – that it is a faculty for judging an object in reference to the imagination's *free conformity to law*. Now, if in the judgment of taste the imagination must be considered in its freedom, it is in the first place not regarded as reproductive [*reproductiv*], as subject to the laws of association, but as productive [*productiv*] and spontaneous [*selbstthätig*] (as the author of arbitrary forms of possible intuitions); and although in the apprehension of a given object of sense it is tied [*gebunden*] to a definite form of this object and so far has no free play [*freies Spiel*] (such as that of poetry), yet it may be readily conceived that the object can furnish it with such a form containing a collection of the manifold as the imagination itself, if it were let free, would project [*entwerfen*], in accordance with the *conformity to law of the*

understanding in general." [*General Remark on the First Section of the Analytic*].

Poetry, the summit of fine art considered as a species of art, carries the freedom of play announced in the productive imagination to its extreme, to the top of the hierarchy. *Mimesis* intervenes, however, not only as one would expect in reproductive operations, but in the free and pure productivity of the imagination as well. The latter deploys the brute power of its invention only by *listening* to nature, to its dictation, its edict. And the concept of nature here itself functions in the service of that onto-theological humanism, of that obscurantism of the economy one could call liberal in its era of *Aufklärung*. Genius, as an instance of the Fine-Arts ("Fine-Arts must necessarily be considered arts of *genius*", § 46), carries freedom of play and the pure productivity of the imagination to its highest point. It gives rules or at least examples but it has its own rules dictated to it by nature: so that the whole distinction between liberal and mercenary art, with the whole machinery of hierarchical subordination that it commands, reproduces nature in its production, breaks with *mimesis*, understood as imitation of what is, only to identify itself with the free unfolding-refolding of the *physis*.

One ought to analyze closely the paragraph that exploits the false opposition between liberal art and craft. Liberal art is an occupation that is agreeable in itself. The liberal artist – the one who does not work for a salary – enjoys and gives enjoyment. Immediately. The mercenary, insofar as he is practicing his art, does not enjoy. But since we are dealing here with a hierarchy inside of a general organization governed by the universal law of nature, the non-enjoyment of the mercenary artist (his work) serves the cause of liberal enjoyment. And what imposes mercenary art by force, in the last analysis, is nature, which commands genius and which, through all sorts of mediations, commands everything. Speaking immediately after of a "hierarchy" [*Rangliste*] in the grade of the professions, Kant asks whether we ought to consider an occupation such as watchmaking a (free) art or a (mercenary) handicraft. A difficult question that is immediately put aside: it would require "another point of view", that of the "proportion of talents." The rigorous criterion is lacking. Similarly, Kant "does not want to discuss here" the question whether, among the seven liberal arts, some could be classed as sciences and others as handicrafts. The liberal arts taught in the arts faculties

of the Middle Ages (*trivium*: grammar, dialectic, rhetoric; *quadrivium*: arithmetic, geometry, astronomy, music) are the disciplines that depend the most on the mind's work – by contrast with the mechanical arts, which above all require manual labor. And yet in the exercise of a liberal art (of the free spirit) a certain constraint must be at work. Something compulsory ("*zwangmässiges*" is also the word used to designate the constraint imposed on handicraft) must intervene as a "mechanism" [*Mechanismus*]. Without this coercive constriction, this tight corset [*corsage*], the spirit which must be free in art "would have no body and would evaporate altogether." The body, constraint, or mechanism, for example, of poetry, the highest of the liberal arts, would be lexical accuracy or richness [*Sprachrichtigkeit, Sprachreichtum*], prosody or metrics. The freedom of a liberal art relates to the system of coercions or constraints, to its own mechanism, as the spirit does to the body or the living body to its corset, which as always, as its name indicates, gives body to things. Attention is required here to seize the organic linchpin of the system: the two arts (liberal and mercenary) are not two totalities independent of or indifferent to one another. Liberal art relates to mercenary art as the mind does to the body, and it cannot produce itself, in its freedom, without the very thing that it subordinates to itself, without the force of mechanical structure which in every sense of the word it *supposes* – the mechanical agency, mercenary, laborious, deprived of pleasure. Hence we hear already the well-known reaction against any non-directive pedagogy: "many modern educators believe that the best way to produce a free art is to remove it from all constraint [*Zwang*] and thus to change it from work into mere play." [Ibid]

It was just said that the free play of liberal art, unlike mercenary art, offers enjoyment [*donne à jouir*]. This is still vague. One needs to distinguish pleasure [*plaisir*] from enjoyment [*jouissance*]. In this context and in a slightly conventional fashion, in order to mark two different concepts, Kant opposes *Lust* and *Genuss*. And that precisely at the moment when he defines the Fine-Arts [*Beaux-Arts*], fine art [*schöne Kunst*]. Once again, this definition does not proceed by symmetrical opposition, by classification of gender and species. Fine-Arts are free arts certainly, but they do not all belong to the liberal arts. Certain among these belong to the Fine-Arts, others to the Sciences.

What then characterizes the "Fine-Arts"?[1]

This locution, despite being so familiar, is not self-evident. Is there a reason for terming "fine" or "beautiful" an art that produces the beautiful? The beautiful is the object, the *opus*, the form produced. Why then would art be fine or beautiful? Kant never asks this question. It seems called for by his critique. If one transfers to art a predicate which, in all rigor, seems to belong to its product, it is because the relation to the product cannot, structurally, be cut off from the relation to a productive subjectivity, however indeterminate, even anonymous it may be: we have here the implication of signature which should not be confused with the extrinsic demands of some empiricism (whether psychological, sociological, historical, etc.). The beautiful would always be the work [*l'oeuvre*] (as much the act as the object), the art whose signature remains marked at the limit of the work, neither in nor out, out and in, in the parergonal thickness of the frame. If the beautiful is never ascribed simply to the product *or* to the producing act, but to a certain passage to the limit between them, then it depends, provided with another elaboration, on some parergonal effect: the Fine-Arts are always of the frame and the signature. Kant doubtless would not endorse these propositions which nevertheless do not appear to be entirely incompatible with his problematic of aesthetic subjectivity.

When one says that an art is fine or beautiful, one is not referring to a singularity, to some productive act or to some unique production. The generality (music is a fine art, the art of some composer) implies, within the totality of the operation's subjective powers, a repetition, a possibility of beginning again. This iterability belongs to the very concept of the "Fine-Arts."

The repetition is of a pleasure. Whence the answer to the question: can a science be beautiful? No, says Kant. "A beautiful science" would be an absurdity, a non-sense, a nonentity [*Unding*]: nothing. One can certainly find beautiful things around scientific activity; an artist can also put scientific knowledge to work. But as such, an act or an object of science, for example a scientific statement, could not be called beautiful – any more than one could speak of the scientific value of an art. That would just be idle talk [*bavardage*]. The beauty of a scientific statement would be of the order of the *Bonmot*: "tasteful witticisms" [*geschmacksvolle Ausspruche (Bonmots)*].

If *Witz* as such can have no scientific value, science must do without it in order to be what it is. It must therefore do without art, without beauty, and indissolubly, without pleasure. It must not proceed from (in view of) pleasure, must neither take nor give any.

A remark in passing, in the *Introduction*, nevertheless recognizes pleasure at the distant origin of knowledge: "but this pleasure has certainly been present at one time, and it is only because the commonest experience would be impossible without it that it is gradually confounded with mere cognition and no longer arrests particular attention."

If in an immemorial time, which cannot be a time of consciousness, pleasure does not allow itself to be separated from knowledge, one can no longer exclude science from all relation to beauty, to *Witz*, as well as to the whole economy of pleasure (return to the self-same, reduction of the heterogeneous, recognition of the law, etc.). [Cf. "Le parergon" (II) (*Le sans de la coupure pure*), p. 27.] Moreover, one has to admit that in the *bon mot*, the force of *Witz* leads back into the buried or repressed origin of science, that is to the science of science, to the point where all the distinctions, oppositions, limits remarked by the Kantian critique lose their pertinence. It is important to take note of the sweeping consequences [*enjeu*] of this problem in the place where the Kantian text itself allows the effacement of that pertinence to be announced.

Let us return to the point where the limits are firmly inscribed, even if this inscription remains derived. The Fine-Arts are not at all scientific, sciences are not at all beautiful or artistic. The Fine-Arts proceed from and give pleasure, not enjoyment [*jouissance*], science, neither pleasure or enjoyment; fine art, pleasure without enjoyment. Nevertheless, not every art procures pleasure. A new series of distinctions intervenes.

An art that conforms to the knowledge of a possible object, which executes the operations necessary to bring it into being, which knows in advance that it must produce and consequently does produce it, such a *mechanical art* neither seeks nor gives pleasure. One knows how to print a book, build a machine, one avails oneself of a model and a purpose. To mechanical art Kant opposes aesthetic art. The latter has its immediate end in pleasure.

But aesthetic art in turn splits into two hierarchic species. Not every aesthetic art is a fine or beautiful art. There is thus aesthetic art that has no relation to the beautiful. Among aesthetic arts,

Jacques Derrida

certain of them, the agreeable arts, have enjoyment [*jouissance, Genuss*] as their aim. The Fine-Arts seek pleasure [*Lust*] without enjoyment. Kant defines them first in two stringent lines without parentheses after having leisurely described the art of enjoyment (fourteen lines including a long parenthesis), the art of conversation, jest, laughter, gaiety, simple-minded entertainment, irresponsible gossip around the table, the art of serving, the management of music during the meal, party games, etc. All these are directed to enjoyment. "On the other hand, fine or beautiful art is a mode of representation which is purposive for itself and which, although devoid of purposes [*ohne Zweck*], yet furthers the culture of the mental powers in reference to social communication." [§ 44]

Sociality, universal communicability: that can only be pleasure, not enjoyment. The latter involves an empirical sensibility, includes a kernel of incommunicable sensation. Pure pleasure, without empirical enjoyment, therefore belongs to judgment and reflection. But the pleasure of judgment and reflection must be *without* concept, for the reasons already recognized.

This pleasure dispenses with [*faire son deuil de*] both concept and enjoyment. It can only be given in reflective judgment. And according to the order of a certain *socius*, of a certain reflective intersubjectivity.

So what is the relation with *economimesis*? To be able to take pleasure in a reflective pronouncement [*prédication*] without enjoying and without conceiving, belongs, of course, to the essence [*le propre*] of man, of free man – capable of pure, that is non-exchangeable productivity. Non-exchangeable in terms of sensible objects or signs of sensible objects (money for example), non-exchangeable in terms of enjoyment – neither as a use value nor as exchange value.

And nevertheless this pure productivity of the inexchangeable liberates a sort of immaculate commerce. Being a reflective exchange, universal communicability between free subjects opens up space for the play of the Fine-Arts. There is in this a sort of pure economy in which the *oikos*, what belongs essentially to the definition [*le propre*] of man, is reflected in his pure freedom and his pure productivity.

Why then *mimesis* here? The productions of the Fine-Arts are not productions of nature; that, as Kant repeatedly recalls, goes without saying. *Facere* and not *agere*. But a certain *quasi*, a certain *als ob* re-establishes analogical *mimesis* at the point

where it appears detached. The works of the Fine-Arts must have the appearance of nature and precisely in so far as they are productions (fashionings) of freedom. They must resemble *effects* of natural *action* at the very moment when they, most purely, are works [*opera*] of artistic confection. "In a product of the Fine-Arts, we must become conscious that it is art and not nature; but yet the purposiveness in its form must seem [*scheinen*] to be as free from all constraint [*Zwang*] of arbitrary rules as if [*als ob*] it were a product of pure nature. On this feeling of freedom in the play of our cognitive faculties, which must at the same time be purposive, rests that pleasure [*Lust*] which alone is universally communicable, without being based on concepts." [§ 45].

What is the scope of the *as if*?

Pure and free productivity must resemble that of nature. And it does so precisely because, free and pure, it does not depend on natural laws. The less it depends on nature, the more it resembles nature. *Mimesis* here is not the representation of one thing by another, the relation of resemblance or of identification between two beings, the reproduction of a product of nature by a product of art. It is not the relation of two products but of two productions. And of two freedoms. The artist does not imitate things in nature, or, if you will, in *natura naturata*, but the acts of *natura naturans*, the operations of the *physis*. But since an analogy has already made *natura naturans* the art of an author-subject, and, one could even say, of an artist-god, *mimesis* displays the identification of human action with divine action – of one freedom with another. The communicability of pure judgments of taste, the (universal, infinite, limitless) exchange between subjects who have free hands in the exercise or the appreciation of fine art, all that presupposes a commerce between the divine artist and the human one. And indeed this commerce is a *mimesis*, in the strict sense, a play, a mask, an identification with the other on stage, and not the imitation of an object by its copy. "True" *mimesis* is between two producing subjects and not between two produced things. Implied by the whole third *Critique*, even though the explicit theme, even less the word itself, never appears, this kind of *mimesis* inevitably entails the condemnation of imitation, which is always characterized as being servile.

As the first effect of this anthropo-theological *mimesis*, a divine teleology secures the political economy of the Fine-Arts, the hierarchical opposition of free art and mercenary art. *Economimesis* puts everything in its place, starting with the instinctual work of animals without language and ending with God, passing by way of the mechanical arts, mercenary art, liberal arts, aesthetic arts and the Fine-Arts.

We are now at the point where the structure of *mimesis* effaces the opposition between nature and art, *agere* and *facere*. And perhaps we rediscover here the root of that pleasure which, before having been reserved for art and for the beautiful, used to belong to knowledge. As for Aristotle, *mimesis* is that which belongs to the essential definition [*le propre*] of man. Kant speaks of imitation as "aping" (*singerie*) [§ 49]; the ape knows how to imitate, but he does not know how to mime in the sense in which only the freedom of a subject mimes itself. The ape is not a subject and has no relation – not even that of subjection – to the other as such. And the *Poetics* places *mimesis* at the conjoined origin of knowledge and pleasure: "Poetry does seem to owe its origin to two causes, and two natural causes [*physikai*]. To imitate [*mimeisthai*] is natural [*symphyton*: innate, congenital] for men and shows itself from infancy – man differs from other animals in that he is very apt at imitation [*mimetikôtaton*] and it is by means of this that he acquires his first knowledge [*mathesis protas*], and secondly in that all men take pleasure in imitations [*khairein tois mimemasi pantas*]" [1448 b].

It must still be explained, in order to carry the analysis of a traditional link as far as possible, why the Poetics associates pleasure and knowledge while, in the same space of *mimesis*, the third *Critique* appears to disassociate them. In the first place it is because here, as we have seen, the unity of pleasure and knowledge was not excluded but merely re-assigned to the unconsciousness of some immemorial time. And in the second, because nature, the object of knowledge, will turn out to have been an art, an object of pleasure; and natural beauty will have been the production of a natural art. A strange imperfect tense signals it, referring either to an "above-in-the-text" or to some originary production. Following an *als ob*: "On this feeling of freedom in the play of our faculties of knowledge, which must at the same time be purposive, rests that pleasure which alone is universally communicable, without however being based on concepts. Nature was beautiful when it simultaneously was seen as art [*Die Natur war schön, wenn sie zugleich als Kunst aussah*] and art cannot be called beautiful unless we are conscious that it is art while yet it is seen, by us, as nature." [§ 45]

The only beauty therefore remains that of productive nature. Art is beautiful to the degree that it is productive *like* productive nature, that it reproduces the production and not the product of nature, to the degree that nature may once have been (was), before the critical disassociation and before a still to be determined forgetfulness, beautiful. The analogy leads back to this precritical time, anterior to all the disassociations, oppositions, and delimitations of critical discourse, "older" even than the time of the transcendental aesthetic.

The beautiful brings productive nature back to itself, it qualifies a spectacle that artist-nature has given itself. God has given himself to be seen in a spectacle, just as if he had masked – had shown – himself: a theomime, a physiomime, for the pleasure of God – an immense liberality which however can only give itself to itself to be consumed.

If *economimesis* institutes a specular relation between two liberties, readable in reflective judgment and in *gustus reflectans*, how can man's freedom be said to resemble the freedom of God? Do we know what freedom is, what *freedom* means before having conceived of *physis* as *mimesis*? Before the fold God gives himself in a miroir? How can man's freedom (in a liberal economy) resemble God's freedom which resembles itself and reassembles itself in it? It resembles it precisely by not imitating it, the only way one freedom can resemble another.

The passage of *mimesis* cannot proceed by concepts but only – between freedoms – by exemplars with reflective value, quasi-natural productions which will institute the non-conceptual rules of art.

The original agency here is the figure of genius. It capitalizes freedom but in the same gesture naturalizes the whole of *economimesis*. "Fine art is the art of genius" [§ 46]. *Ingenium* is natural, it is a natural talent, a gift of Nature [*Naturgabe*]. A productive and donative instance, genius is itself produced and given by nature. Without this gift of nature, without this present of a productive freedom, there would not be any fine art. Nature produces what produces, it produces freedom [for] itself [*elle se produit la liberté*] and gives it to itself. In giving non-conceptual rules to art (rules "abstracted from the act, that is from the product"), in producing "exemplars," genius does nothing more than reflect nature, represent it: both as its legacy or its delegate and as its faithful image. "Genius is the innate disposition of the spirit [*ingenium*], *by which* nature gives rules to art." [§ 46.]

The non-conceptual role, readable in the act and off the exemplar, does not derive from imitation (genius is incompatible with "the spirit of imitation"). Genius is not learned. "To learn is nothing other than to imitate." Beyond the fact that with this last proposition (§ 47), one returns to the language of the *Poetics*, the affinity is confirmed by the fact that the originality of genius and the exemplarity of its products must incite a certain imitation. A good imitation: one which is not a servile repetition, which does not reproduce, which avoids counterfeiting and plagiarism. This free imitation of a freedom (that of genius) which freely imitates divine freedom is a point that is "difficult to explain." The ideas "awaken," stir up, excite "similar ideas," neighboring, related, analogical [*ähnliche*] ones. The difficult nuance which relates good to bad imitation, good to bad repetition, is fixed briefly in the opposition between *imitation* and *copy* [*contrefaçon*], between *Nachahmung* and *Nachtmachung*. The indiscernibility of that distinction, which nevertheless pervades everything, is repeated, imitated, counterfeited in the signifier: a perfect anagrammatical inversion, except for a single letter.

Once nature has detached genius in order to represent it and to give its rules to art, everything turns out to be naturalized, immediately or not, everything is interpreted as a structure of naturality: the content of empirical culturalism, the political economy of art, its very particular propositions, going from the verse of Frederick the Great to assertions about salary scales.

The second remark on salary belongs to the chapter "On the Divisions of the Fine-Arts" [§ 51]: "Everything which is studied and painful must therefore be avoided [in the Fine-Arts]; for fine art must be free art in a double sense: it is not, of course, in the form of some salaried activity [*Lohngeschäft*], work whose quantity can be evaluated according to a determined measure, which can be imposed [*erzwingen*] or paid for [*bezahlen*]; but at the same time the mind must feel itself occupied, although appeased and excited without looking to any other purpose (independent, that is, of any salary).

"The orator therefore gives something that he does not promise, namely an attractive play of the imagination; but he also cheats a little on what he promises and on what he announces as being properly his business, namely the purposive occupation of the understanding. The poet conversely promises little and announces a mere play with ideas, but he supplies something which has the value of a serious occupation, because he provides in this play food for the understanding and gives life to his concepts by the aid of the imagination: on the whole, the poet thus gives more, and the orator less than he promises."

At the summit is the poet, analogous (and that precisely by a return of *logos*) to God: he gives more than he promises, he submits to no exchange contract, his overabundance generously breaks the circular economy. The hierarchy of the Fine-Arts therefore signifies that some power supersedes the (circular) economy, governs and places itself above (restricted) political economy. The naturalisation of political economy subordinates the production and the commerce of art to a transeconomy.

Economimesis is not impaired by it, on the contrary. It unfolds itself there to infinity. It suffers that transeconomy in order to pass to infinity as "Kantism" passes into "Hegelianism." An infinite circle plays [with] itself and uses human play to reappropriate the gift for itself. The poet or genius receives from nature what he gives, of course, but first he receives from nature (from God), besides the given, the giving, the power to produce and to give more than he promises to men. The poetic gift, content and power, wealth and action, is an add-on [*un en-plus*] given as a [power] to give [*un donner*] by God to the poet, who transmits it in order to permit this supplementary surplus value to make its return to the infinite source – this source which can never be lost (by definition, if one can say that of the infinite). All that must pass through the voice. The genius poet is the voice of God who gives him voice, who gives himself and by giving gives to himself, gives himself what he gives, gives himself the [power] to give (*Gabe* and *es gibt*), plays freely with himself, only breaks the finite circle or contractual exchange in order to strike an infinite accord with himself. As soon as the infinite gives itself (to be thought), the *opposition* tends to be effaced between restricted and general economy, circulation and expendiary productivity. That is even, if we can still use such terms, the *function* of the passage to the infinite: the passage *of* the infinity between gift and debt.

Being what he is, the poet gives more than he promises. More than anyone asks of him. And this more belongs to the understanding: it announces a game and it gives something conceptual. Doubtless it is a plus-law [a more/no-more law] [*un plus-de-loi*], but one produced by a faculty whose essential character is *spontaneity*. Giving more than he promises or than is asked of him, the genius poet is paid for this more by no one, at least within the political economy of man. But God supports him. He supports him with speech and in return for gratitude. He furnishes him his capital, produces and reproduces his labor force, gives him surplus value and the means of giving surplus-value.

This is a poetic commerce, because God is a poet. There is a relation of hierarchical analogy between the poetic action of the speaking art, at the summit, and the action of God who dictates *Dichtung* to the poet.

This structure of *economimesis* necessarily has its *analogon* in the city. The poet, when he is neither writing nor singing, is just a man among men, must also eat. He must sustain the (mechanical) labor force which poetry, Kant shows, *cannot* forego. So that he may not forget that his essential wealth comes to him from on high, and that his true commerce links him to the loftiness of free, not mercenary art, he receives subsidies from the sun-king or from the enlightened-and-enlightening monarch, from the king-poet, the analogue of the poet-god: from Frederick the Great, a sort of national fund for letters which serves to lessen the rigors of supply and demand in a liberal economy. But this powerful scheme does not necessarily carry over into another organization of the restricted economy. *Economimesis* itself can still find a way to make a profit [*peut s'y retrouver dans ses comptes*].

Frederick the Great, the "great king", is almost the only poet quoted by the third *Critique* – a sign of the servile precaution and bad taste on the part of the philosopher, it is often ironically noted. But these poetic lines, like the commentary that surrounds them, very rigorously describe the generous overabundance of a solar source. God, King, Sun, Poet, Genius, etc. give of themselves without counting. And if the relation of alterity between a restricted economy and a general economy is above all not a relation of opposition, then the various helio-poetics – Platonic, Kantian, Hegelian, Nietzschean (up to and including Bataille's) – form an apparently *analogical* chain. No oppositional logic seems fitted to disassociate its *themes*.

"When the great king in one of his poems expresses himself as follows:

Oui, finissons sans trouble et mourons sans
    regret,
En laissant l'univers comblé de nos bienfaits.
Ainsi l'astre du jour au bout de sa carrière,
Répand sur l'horizon une douce lumière,

Et les derniers rayons qu'il darde dans les airs
Sont les derniers soupirs qu'il donne à l'univers,

("Yes, let us finish without disquiet and die
    without regret
Leaving the universe overflowing with our
    benefactions.
Thus the star of day at the end of its career,
Spreads over the horizon a soft light,
And the last rays that it shoots in the air
Are the last sighs that it gives to the universe.")

he quickens his rational idea of a cosmopolitan disposition at the end of life by an attribute of the imagination." [§ 49]. Inversely, Kant specifies, an intellectual concept can serve as an attribute for a sensible representation and thus animate it ("the sun arose/as calm from virtue springs", "*Die Sonne quoll hervor, wie Ruh aus Tugend quillt*") on the condition that there be recourse to the perceptible awareness of the suprasensible. [Ibid.] And in a note: "Perhaps nothing more sublime was ever said and no sublimer thought ever expressed than the famous inscription on the Temple of Isis (Mother Nature): 'I am all that is and that was and that shall be, and no mortal hath lifted my veil.'" Between the quotation about the springing sun and the note on the veil of Mother Nature comes the analysis of Kant: "The consciousness of virtue, if we substitute it in our thoughts for a virtuous man, diffuses in the mind a multitude of sublime and restful feelings, and a boundless prospect of a joyful future, to which no expression that is measured by a definite concept completely attains."

Examplorality

Perhaps we are approaching the embouchure [the mouth or outlet], if not the sea.

What is it in an embouchure that could open onto *economimesis*?

We have recognized the fold of *mimesis* at the origin of pure productivity, a sort of gift for itself [*pour soi*] of God who makes a present of himself to himself, even prior to the re-productive or imitative structure (that is foreign and inferior to the Fine-Arts): genius imitates nothing, it identifies itself with the productive freedom of God who identifies himself in himself, at the origin of the origin, with the production of production. Is the very concept of production marked by it everywhere and *in general*? Does it belong, by an irreducible semantic invariant, to this logic of economimesis? Let us allow the question to ferment.

The analogy between the free productivity of nature and the free productivity of genius, between God and the Poet, is not only a relation of proportionality or a relation between two – two subjects, two origins, two productions. The analogical process is also a refluence towards the *logos*. The origin is the *logos*. The origin of analogy, that from which analogy proceeds and towards which it returns, is the *logos*, reason and word, the source as a mouth and as an outlet [*embouchure*].

Now it must be demonstrated.

Nature furnishes rules to the art of genius. Not concepts, not descriptive laws, but rules precisely, singular norms which are also orders, imperative statements. When Hegel reproaches the third *Critique* for staying at the level of the "you must," he very well evinces the moral order which sustains the aesthetic order. That order proceeds from one freedom to another, it gives itself from one to the other: and as discourse, it does so through a signifying element. Every time we encounter in this text something that resembles a discursive metaphor (nature says, dictates, prescribes, etc.), these are not just any metaphors but analogies of analogy, whose message is that the literal meaning is analogical: nature is properly [*proprement*] logos towards which one must always return [*remonter*]. Analogy is always language.

For example, one reads (at the end of § 46) that "nature, by the medium of genius, does not prescribe [*vorschreibe*] rules to science but to art . . . " Genius transcribes the prescription and its *Vorschreiben* is written under the dictation of nature whose secretary it freely agrees to be. At the moment it writes, it allows itself literally to be inspired by nature which dictates to it, which tells it in the form of poetic commands what it must write and in turn prescribe; and without genius really understanding what it writes. It does not understand the prescriptions that it transmits; in any case it has neither concept nor knowledge of them. "The author of a product for which he is indebted to his genius does not know himself how he has come by his ideas; and he has not the power to devise the like at pleasure or in accordance with a plan, and to communicate it to others in precepts [*Vorschriften*] that will enable them to produce [*hervorbringen*] similar products [*Producte*]." Genius prescribes, but in the form of

non-conceptual rules which forbid repetition, imitative reproduction.

At the moment it freely gives orders to man through the voice of genius, nature is already, itself, a product, the production of the divine genius. At the moment it dictates, it is already in a situation analogous to that of human genius which, furthermore, itself produces a second nature. Productive imagination has the power to create "as it were" [*gleichsam*] "another nature" [*Schaffung einer andern Natur*] [§ 49]. There is an analogy therefore between genius which creates a second nature (for example by prescribing rules to other artists), the first nature which dictates its precepts to genius, and God who creates the first nature and produces the archetype which will serve as example and rule. Such hierarchical analogy forms a society of the *logos*, a sociology of genius, a logoarchy. In any case, at each step of the analogy, it (id) speaks [*ça parle*]: God commands, nature speaks in order to transmit to genius; the highest genius is the speaking one, the poet.

Analogy is the rule. What does that mean [*veut dire*]? It means that it means and that it says that it means that it wants [*ça veut*] and that it wants what it wants, for example. [*ça veut dire que ça veut dire et que ça dit que ça veut dire que ça veut et que ça veut ce que ça veut par exemple.*]

For example. It is by example that it means that it means and that it says that it means that it wants and that it wants what it wants by example. [*C'est par exemple que ça veut dire que ça veut dire et que ça dit que ça veut dire que ça veut et que ça veut ce que ça veut par exemple.*]

For example, analogy is the rule, that means that the analogy between the rule of art (of fine art) and the moral rule, between the aesthetic order and the moral order, that analogy is the rule. It consists in a rule. There is an "analogy" [*Analogie*] between the pure judgment of taste which, independent of any interest, provokes a *Wohlgefallen* suitable *a priori* to humanity, and the moral judgment that does the same thing by means of concepts [§ 42, *Of the intellectual interest in the beautiful*]. This analogy confers an equal and immediate interest upon the two judgments. The articulated play of this analogy (*Wohl/Gut*) is itself subject to a law of supplementarity: we admire nature "which displays itself in its beautiful products as art" and "as it were designedly" (ibid.), but in aesthetic experience the purpose or end of this purposiveness does not appear to us.

It is the purpose-lessness [*le sans-fin*] which leads us back inside ourselves. Because the outside appears purposeless, we seek purpose within. There is something like a movement of interiorizing suppliance [*suppleance interiorisante*], a sort of slurping [*suçotement*] by which, cut off from what we seek outside, from a purpose suspended outside, we seek and give within, in an autonomous fashion, not by licking our chops, or smacking our lips or whetting our palate, but rather (what is not entirely something else) by giving ourselves orders, categorical imperatives, by chatting with ourselves through universal schemas once they no longer come from the outside.

Kant describes this movement of idealizing interiorisation: "To this is to be added our admiration for nature, which displays itself in its beautiful products as art, not merely by chance, but as it were designedly, in accordance with a regular arrangement and as purposiveness without purpose. This latter, as we never meet with it outside ourselves, we naturally seek in ourselves and, in fact, in that which constitutes the ultimate purpose of our being [*Dasein*], viz. our moral destination [*moralischen Bestimmung*]. (Of this question as to the ground of possibility of such natural purposiveness we shall first speak in the teleology.)" [§ 42.]

Not finding in aesthetic experience, which here is primary, the determined purpose or end from which we are cut off and which is found too far away, invisible or inaccessible, over there, we fold ourselves back towards the purpose of our *Da-sein*. This interior purpose is at our disposal, it is ours, ourselves, it calls us and determines us from within, we are *there* [*da*] so as to respond to a *Bestimmung*, to a vocation of autonomy. The *Da* of our *Dasein* is first determined by this purpose which is present to us, and which we present to ourselves as our own and by which we are present to ourselves as what we are: a free existence or presence [*Dasein*], autonomous, that is to say moral.

That is what our *Da* is called and it passes through the mouth. The *Da* of the *Sein* gives itself what it cannot consume outside, while not-to-consume forms the condition of possibility of taste understood as what relates us to purpose-lessness.

Moreover it is in this chapter that "analogies" multiply concerning the language of nature. It is a matter of explaining why we ought to take a moral interest in the beautiful in nature, a moral interest in this disinterested experience. It must be that

nature harbors in itself a principle of harmony [*Ubereinstimmung*] between its productions [*Producte*] and our disinterested pleasure. Although the latter is purely subjective and remains cut off from all determined purpose or end, a certain agreement must nevertheless reign between the purposiveness of nature and our *Wohlgefallen*. The *Wohl* would not be explicable but for this harmony. As this agreement cannot be shown nor demonstrated by concepts, it must be announced otherwise.

How is it announced? How does one announce, in other words, the adherence between adherence and non-adherence?

By means of signs. Here we recognize the proper site, the primary place of *signification* in the third *Critique*. All subsequent signification will depend on it. Nature, then, announces to us by signs and traces (not to be distinguished for the moment) that there must be a harmonious agreement [*un accord*], a correspondence, concert, reciprocal understanding [*Übereinstimmung*], between the purposiveness of its own productions and our disinterested *Wohlgefallen* precisely as it appears cut off from any purpose. "But it also interests reason that the ideas (for which in moral feeling it arouses an immediate interest) should have objective reality, i.e. that nature should at least show a trace [*Spur*] or give an indication [*Wink*: a sign that one rather makes silently, a signal or wink, a brief and discreet hint instead of a discourse] that it contains in itself a ground for assuming a regular agreement [*Übereinstimmung*] of its products with our entirely disinterested satisfaction (which we recognize *a priori* as a law for everyone, without being able to found it on proofs). Hence reason must take an interest in every expression [*Ausserung*] on the part of nature of an agreement of this kind. Consequently the mind cannot ponder upon the beauty of nature without finding itself at the same time interested therein. But this interest is akin to a moral interest [*der Verwandschaft nach moralisch*]."

Meditation on a disinterested pleasure therefore provokes a moral interest in the beautiful. It is a strange motivation, this interest taken in disinterestedness, the interest of the interestlessness [*le sans-intérêt*], a moral revenue drawn from a natural production that is without interest for us, from which one takes wealth without interest, the singular moral surplus value of the *without* [*le sans*] of pure detachment – all that maintains a necessary relation with the trace [*Spur*] and the sign [*Wink*] of nature. The latter leaves us signs so that we might still feel assured, in the *without* of pure detachment, of banking on our own account, of satisfying our purpose, of seeing our stocks and our values on the moral rise.

And in order to respond to those who might find this argument subtle, specious, and studied [*studiert*], Kant specifies the nature of the analogy between judgment of taste and moral judgment: "It will be said that this account [*Deutung*] of aesthetical judgments, as akin to the moral feeling, seems far too studied to be regarded as the true interpretation [*Auslegung*] of that cipher [*Chiffres-chrift*] through which nature speaks to us [*uns spricht*] figuratively [*figürlich*] in her beautiful forms. However . . ." [§ 42.]

Beautiful forms, which signify nothing and have no determined purpose, are therefore *also, and by that very fact*, encrypted signs, a figural writing set down in nature's production. The *without* of pure detachment is in truth a language that nature speaks to us – she who loves to encrypt herself and record her signature on things. Try to improvise an epistemic framework for this proposition which is common to Heraclites, to the field of the *signatura rerum* and to the configuration of the third *Critique*, and you will observe that it does not fit all by itself and that it causes the *parergon* to strain.

Thus the in-significant non-language of forms which have no purpose or end and make no sense, this silence is a language between nature and man.

It is not only beautiful forms, purely formal beauties which seem to converse, it is also the adornments and charms that too often, mistakenly, says Kant, we confuse with beautiful forms. He is referring, for example, to colors and sounds. It all seems as if these charms had some "higher sense" [*ein höhern Sinn*], as if these changes in meaning [*Modificationen der Sinne*] had a more elevated sense and possessed "as it were a language" [*gleich-sam eine Sprache*]. The white color of lilies seems to "dispose" [*stimmen*] the mind to ideas of innocence; the seven colors, in order from red to violet, seem respectively to suggest the ideas of sublimity (red then), intrepidity, candor, friendliness, modesty, constancy, tenderness.

These meanings are not posited as objective truths. The moral interest that we take in beauty, moreover, presupposes that the trace and the wink of nature do not have to be objectively regulated by conceptual science. We interpret colors like a natural language and it is this hermeneutic *interest*

that matters: it is not a matter of knowing whether nature speaks to us and means to tell us this or that, but rather of our interest in its doing so, in involving it necessarily, and of the intervention of this *moral* interest in aesthetic disinterestedness. It belongs to the structure of this interest that we believe in the sincerity, the loyalty, the authenticity of the ciphered language, even if it remains impossible to control objectively. And Kant will say the same thing later about poetry: it is not what it is in the absence of loyalty and sincerity. That which speaks through the mouth of the poet as through the mouth of nature, that which, having been dictated by their voice, is written in their hand, must be veridical and authentic. For example, when the voice of the poet celebrates and glorifies the song of the nightingale, in a lonely copse, on a still summer evening by the soft light of the moon, the mouth to mouth or beak to beak of the two songs must be authentic. If a trickster simulated the song of the nightingale, "by means of a reed or tube in his mouth," no one would find it tolerable as soon as we realized that it was a cheat. If the contrary were the case, if you should happen to like that sort of thing, it must be that your feelings are coarse and ignoble. In order to characterize those who are deprived of any "*feeling for beautiful nature*," Kant again has recourse to an oral example. – And it is a certain exemplorality that is being treated here. – We judge to be coarse and ignoble the "mental attitude" of those who have no feeling for beautiful nature and who "confine themselves to eating and drinking – to the mere enjoyments of sense." In the first exemplorality, in the exemplary orality, it is a question of singing and hearing, of unconsummated voice or ideal consummation, of a heightened or interiorized sensibility; in the second case that of a consuming orality which as such, as an interested taste or as actual tasting, can have nothing to do with pure taste. What is already announced here is a certain allergy in the mouth, between pure taste and actual tasting [*dégustation*]. We still have before us the question of where to inscribe disgust. Would not disgust, by turning itself back against actual tasting, also be the origin of pure taste, in the wake of a sort of catastrophe?

The mouth in any case no longer merely occupies one place among others. It can no longer be situated *in* a typology of the body but seeks to organize all the sites and to localize all the organs. Is the *os* of the system, the place of tasting or of consumption but also the emitting production of the *logos*, still a term in an analogy? Could one, by a figure, compare the mouth to this or that, to some other orifice, lower or higher? Is it not itself the analogy, towards which everything returns as towards the logos itself? The *os* for example is no longer a term that can be substituted for the anus, but is determined, hierarchically, as the absolute of every analogon. And the split between all the values that at one moment or another are opposed will pass through the mouth: what it finds good or what it finds bad, according to what is sensible or ideal, as between two means of entering and two means of leaving the mouth, where one would be expressive and emissive (of the poem in the best case), the other vomitive or emetic.

To show this we need to make a detour, through the division of the Fine-Arts [§ 51]. Before this chapter, by an effect of framing that we keep on following, Kant had situated taste as a fourth term which serves to unify the three faculties, imagination, understanding, spirit, that are required by the Fine-Arts: "The first three faculties only arrive at their *unification* by means of the fourth."

The chapter on the division of the Fine-Arts will interest us for three of its major motifs. 1. It puts into operation the category of *expression*. 2. It allows itself to be guided by the expressive organization of the human body. 3. For these two reasons it organizes the description of the arts as a hierarchy. These three motifs are inseparable.

Forceful interventions are required, a violent framing activity of which Kant's rhetoric bears the marks. Take the first sentence: "We may describe beauty in general (whether natural or artificial) as the *expression* of aesthetical ideas." In the Fine-Arts the concept of the object pre-exists expression: that is not necessary in nature, but the absence of the concept does not prevent us from considering natural beauty as the expression of an idea.

Then why *expression*? Why "we may describe" that as expression? Who, we? By what right? And why as an expression of ideas?

Kant does not say. It goes without saying. He says only what he says, namely that it expresses, and, as it will shortly be confirmed, that the highest form of expression is the spoken, that it says what it expresses and that it passes through the mouth, a mouth that is self-affecting, since it takes nothing from the outside and takes pleasure in what it puts out.

From this dictate which posits as an axiom that the beautiful is expression (even if it signifies

nothing), there naturally follows a division of the Fine-Arts with reference to the so-called expressive organs of expression in man. It has been recognized in effect that the Fine-Arts could only be arts of man. In explaining that he is going to classify the arts as a function of the organs of expression in man, Kant clearly senses that the forcing is a little obvious. The signs of his embarrassment multiply: "If, then, we wish to make a division of the Fine-Arts, we cannot choose a more convenient principle, at least tentatively, than the analogy of art with the mode of expression of which men avail themselves in speech [*Sprechen*], in order to communicate to one another as perfectly as possible not merely their concepts but also their sensations." This calls for a note which marks the embarrassment: "The reader is not to judge this scheme for a possible division of the Fine-Arts as a deliberate theory. It is only one of various attempts which we may and ought to devise." Another note is added, on the following page, saying exactly the same thing.

The principle therefore is analogy and a very particular analogy: the analogy with *Sprechen*, with language and with its modes. Everything moves back to language; analogy is produced by language which therefore puts everything in relation to itself, as both the reason for the relation and the ultimate term of the relation.

Language having been decomposed, we find *word*, *gesture*, and *tone*. There will therefore only be three kinds of Fine-Arts: speech [*redende*], the formative [*figuratif, bildende*] and the art of the *"play of sensations"* [*Spiel der Empfindungen*] as external sensible impressions.

Discursive arts in turn are reduced to rhetoric [*éloquence, Beredsamkeit*] and poetry [*Dichtkunst*], a concept whose very great generality explains why there is no question of any other literary art. But also a very pure concept: through complex combinations we will obtain poetic genres like *tragedy, didactic poem, oratorio,* etc. (§ 52). The orator and the poet meet one another and exchange their masks, masks of an *as if*. Both pretend, but the *as if* of one is more and better than the *as if* of the other. In the service of truth, of loyalty, of sincerity, of productive freedom is the *as if* of the poet, who therefore *expresses* more and better. The orator's *as if* deceives and machinates. It is precisely a machine or rather a "deceitful art" which manipulates men "like machines" [§ 53]. The orator announces serious business and treats it as if it were a simple play of ideas. The poet merely proposes an entertaining play of the imagination and proceeds as if he were handling the business of the understanding. The orator certainly gives what he had not promised, the play of the imagination, but he also withholds what he had promised to give or to do: namely, to occupy the understanding in a fitting manner. The poet does just the contrary; he announces a play and does serious work [*eines Geschäftes würdig*]. The orator promises understanding and gives imagination; the poet promises to play with the imagination while he nurtures the understanding and gives life to concepts. These nursing metaphors are not imposed on Kant by me. It is food [*Nahrung*] that the poet brings by playing at understanding, and what he does thereby is give life [*Leben zu geben*] to concepts: conception occurs through the imagination and the ear, while nutrition passes from mouth to mouth and from mouth to ear, overflowing the finite contract by giving more than it promises.

At the summit of the highest of the speaking arts is poetry. It is at the summit [*den obersten Rang*] because it emanates almost entirely from genius. It stands therefore in the greatest proximity, by virtue of its "origin," to that free productivity which rivals that of nature. It is the art which *imitates* the least, and which therefore *resembles* most closely divine productivity. It produces more by liberating the imagination; it is more playful because the forms of external sensible nature no longer serve to limit it. Unleashing the productive imagination, poetry blows up the finite limits of the other arts. "It expands the mind by setting the imagination at liberty and by offering [*darbietet*], within the limits of a given concept, amid the unbounded variety of possible forms accordant therewith, that which unites [*verknüpft*] the presentation [*Darstellung*] of this concept with a wealth of thought [*Gedankenfülle*] to which no verbal expression [*Sprachausdruck*] is fully adequate [*völlig adäquat*] and so rising [*sich erhabt*] aesthetically to ideas. It strengthens the mind by making it feel its faculty – free, spontaneous, and independent of natural determination." [§ 53.]

The criteria here are those of *presentation (darbieten, darstellen)*. Poetry, more and better, presents – the plenitude of thought [*Gedankenfülle*]. It binds presentation (on the side of expression) to a fullness of thought. It better "binds" the presenting to the presented in its plenitude. Poetry, more and better, presents the fullness, the fullness of conceptual thought or the fullness of the idea, in so far as it frees us from the limits of external

sensible nature. By remaining an art, a fine art, it certainly still belongs to the imagination. And like all language, it is still inadequate to the absolute plenitude of the supra-sensible. And Kant immediately speaks of the "schema" of the supra-sensible. Imagination of course is the locus of schematism and the name of that art which is concealed in the depths of the soul, but here we can better understand why this art should be "speech" and why it is "poetic" *par excellence*.

Why does the poetic have this privilege? Beyond what poetry shares with the speaking arts in general and which has to do with the structure (mouth to ear) of hearing oneself speak, what is it that raises it above eloquence?

The answer is its relation to truth, more precisely its authenticity, its sincerity and its loyalty, its faithful adequation to *itself*, to its interior content if not *ad rem* – to what it is that assures in presentation the fullness of meaning, full of presented thought. These values are not narrowly or immediately moral. The moral agency itself derives from or depends on the value of full presence or full speech. When the poet gives more than he promises, he does of course give a present, an authentic gift: a gift of truth and the truth of the gift. He does not deceive since he presents a fullness of thought [*Gedankenfülle*] but also because he declares his exercise to be merely playing with imagination and with inadequate schemes: "Poetry plays with illusion, which it produces [*bewirkt*] at pleasure, but without deceiving by it; for it declares its exercise to be mere play, which however can be purposively used by the understanding." [§ 53.] Poetry manages not to deceive by saying that it plays, and what is more its play, auto-affection elaborating appearances without external limitation, "at pleasure" [*à volonté*], maintains itself seriously in the service of truth. The value of full presence guarantees both the truth and the morality of the poetic. The plenitude can only be achieved within the interiority of hearing oneself-speak [*du s'entendre-parler*] and poetic formalisation favors the process of interiorization by doing without the aid of any external sensible content.

Rhetoric on the contrary defines an art of deceiving, of frustrating with beautiful appearances, with artifices of sensible presentation [*sinnliche Darstellung*], with machines of persuasion [*Maschinen der Überredung*]. The classical condemnation of the machine signifies exactly that discourse produces effects on others in the absence of intention, that no intentions intervene to animate and fill up the speech. Hence, the false life and the empty symbolism of these sophistical *tekhnai*.

If art is expressive, if speech expresses more than other modes of expression, poetic speech in turn is the most telling [*la plus parlante*]; interiority is produced there and is better preserved there in its plenitude. And it produces not only the most moral and the truest disinterested pleasure, which is therefore the most present and the highest, but also the most positive pleasure. A priceless pleasure. By breaking with the exchange of values, by giving more than is asked and more than it promises, poetic speech is both out of circulation, at least outside any finite commerce, without any determinate value, and yet of infinite value. It is the origin of value. Everything is measured on a scale on which poetry occupies the absolutely highest level. It is the universal analogical equivalent, and the value of values. It is in poetry that the work of mourning, transforming hetero-affection into auto-affection, produces the maximum of disinterested pleasure.

What relation does this exemplorality maintain with the structure of *gustus* (relation between the palate, lip, tongue, teeth, throat, opposition between *gustus reflectus* and *gustus reflectens*, etc.) on the one hand, and with the structure of hearing-oneself-speak on the other? And what is the place of the negative, singularly of "negative pleasure" in this process?

Hearing holds a certain privilege among the five senses. The classification of the *Anthropology* places it among the *objective* senses (touch, sight, and hearing) which gives a *mediate* perception of the object (sight and hearing). Objective senses put us in relation to an outside – which is not what taste and smell do. Here the sensible gets mixed in, with saliva for example, and penetrates the organ without preserving its objective subsistence. Mediate objective perception is reserved for sight and hearing which require the mediation of light or air. As for touch, it is objective and immediate.

There are thus two mediate objective senses, hearing and sight. In what respect does hearing prevail over sight? By virtue of its relation to air, that is to vocal production which can cause it to vibrate. A look is incapable of that. "It is precisely by this element, moved by the organ of voice, the mouth, that men, more easily and more completely, enter with others in a community of thought and sensations, especially if the sounds that each gives the other to hear are articulated and if, linked

together by understanding according to laws, they constitute a language. The form of an object is not given by hearing, and linguistic sounds [*Sprachlaute*] do not immediately lead to the representation of the object, but by that very fact and because they signify nothing in themselves, at least no object, only, at most, interior feelings, they are the most appropriate means for characterizing concepts, and those who are born deaf, who consequently must also remain mute (without language) can never accede to anything more than an *analogon* of reason" [*Anthropology*, § 18].

"More easily and more completely": no exterior means is necessary, nothing exterior poses an obstacle. Communication here is closer to freedom and spontaneity. It is also more complete, since interiority expresses itself here directly. It is more universal for all these reasons. Speaking now of tone and modulation, the third *Critique* discovers in hearing a sort of "universal tongue." And once sounds no longer have any relation of natural representation with external sensible things, they are more easily linked to the spontaneity of the understanding. Articulated, they furnish a language in agreement with its laws. Here indeed we have the arbitrary nature of the vocal signifier. It belongs to the element of freedom and can only have interior or ideal signifieds, that is, conceptual ones. Between the concept and the system of hearing-oneself-speak, between the intelligible and speech, the link is privileged. One must use the term hearing-oneself-speak [*le s'entendre-parler*] because this structure is auto-affective; in it the mouth and the ear cannot be disassociated. And the proof of it, at the juncture of the empirical and the metempirical, is that the deaf are dumb. They have no access to the *logos itself*. With other senses and other organs they can *imitate* the *logos*, establish with it a sort of empty or purely external relation. They can only become *analogons* of that which regulates all analogy and which itself is not analogical, since it forms the ground of analogy, the *logos* of analogy towards which everything flows back but which itself remains without system, outside of the system that it orients as its end and its origin, its embouchure and its source. That is why the mouth may have analogues in the body at each of the orifices higher or lower than itself, but is not simply exchangeable with them. If there is a vicariousness of all the senses it is *less true* of the sense of hearing; that is, of hearing-oneself-speak. The latter has a unique place in the system of the senses. It is not the "noblest" of senses. The greatest nobility accrues to sight which achieves the greatest remove from touch, allows itself to be less affected by the object. In this sense, the beautiful has an essential relation with vision in so far as it consumes less. Mourning presupposes sight. *Pulchritudo vaga* gives itself above all to be seen: and, by suspending consumption on behalf of the *theorein*, it forms an object of pure taste in nature. Poetry, as a fine art, presupposes a preliminary concept and occasions a more adherent beauty on a more immediately present horizon of morality.

But if hearing is not the most noble of the senses, it takes its absolute privilege from its status as the least replaceable. It tolerates substitution badly and almost succeeds in resisting all vicariousness.

Is there anything *vicarious in the senses* [*Vicariat der Sinne*], that is, can one sense be used as a substitute for another? There may be. One can evoke by gesture the usual speech from a deaf person, granted that he has once been able to hear. In this, the eyes serve/in place of ears/. The same thing may happen through observing the movements of his teacher's lips, indeed by his own speech muscles. But he will never attain real concepts [*wirklichen Begriffen*], since the signs necessary to him are not capable of universality, seeing the movements of another's organs of speech must convert the sounds, which his teacher has coaxed from him, into a feeling of the movement of his own speech muscles. But he will never attain real concepts [*wirklichen Begriffen*], since the signs necessary to him are not capable of universality. (...) Which deficiency [*Mangel*] or loss of sense is more serious, that of hearing or sight? When it is inborn, deficiency of hearing is the least reparable [*ersetzlich*]. [Ibid. § 22.]

Hence hearing, by its unique position, by its allergy to prosthesis, by the auto-affective structure that distinguishes it from sight, by its proximity to the inside and to the concept, by the constitutive process of hearing-oneself-speak is not merely one of the senses among others. It is not even, in spite of the conventional classifications, an external sense. It has a relation of evident affinity with what Kant calls internal sense. Now the latter is unique and its element, its "form" is time. Like hearing-oneself-speak. It does not properly belong, as the other senses do, to anthropology but to psychology. Thus hearing-oneself-speak, in

its singular relation to the unique internal sense and by the eminent place it occupies in the third *Critique*, tears the problematic away from its anthropological space in order to make it pass, with all the consequences that can entail, into a psychological space.

§ 24. The inner sense is not pure apperception, a consciousness of what man does (for the latter belongs to the power of thought) but of what man *feels*, to the extent he is affected by his own play of thought. Inner intuition, and consequently the relation between representations in time (whether simultaneous or successive), is at the basis of this consciousness. Its perceptions, and the (true or apparent) inner experience resulting from the combination of the perceptions does not simply belong to anthropology, in which one neglects the question of knowing whether or not man has a soul (as a special incorporal substance), but to psychology in which we believe that we perceive such a sense within ourselves, and in which the mind, represented in its quality as a pure faculty of feeling and thinking, is considered as a substance especially inhabiting man. – As a result there is but one inner sense, for there are not various organs by which man receives an inner sensation of himself... [Ibid. § 24].

If hearing-oneself-speak, in so far as it also passes through a certain mouth, transforms everything into auto–affection, assimilates everything to itself by idealizing it within interiority, masters everything by mourning its passing, refusing to touch it, to digest it naturally, but digests it ideally, consumes what it does not consume and *vice versa*, produces disinterestedness in the possibility of pronouncing judgments, if that mouth governs a space of analogy into which it does not let itself be drawn, if it is from the irreplaceable place of this enormous "phantasm" (but one does not know what a phantasm is prior to the system of *these* effects) that it orders pleasure, what is the border or the absolute overboard [*le bord ou le débord absolu*] of this problematic? What is the (internal and external) border which traces its limit and the frame of its *parergon*? In other words, what is it that does not enter into this theory thus framed, hierarchised, regulated? What is excluded from it and what, proceeding from this exclusion, gives it form, limit, and contour? And what about this over-board with respect to what one calls the mouth? Since the mouth orders a pleasure dependant on assimilation, to ideal auto-affection, what is it that does not allow itself to be transformed into oral auto-affection, taking the *os* for a *telos*? What is it that does not let itself be regulated by exemplorality?

There is no answer to such a question. One cannot say, it is this or that, this or that thing. We will see why. And the impossibility of finding examples in this case, Kant's inability to furnish any at a certain moment, will be very noticeable. In the same way that we have often had to treat examples preceding the law in a reflective manner, we are now about to discover a sort of law without example; and first of all we shall state our answer in a tautological form, as the inverted duplication of the question.

What this logo–phonocentric system excludes is not even a negative. The negative is its business and its work. What it excludes, what this very work excludes, is what does not allow itself to be digested, or represented, or stated – does not allow itself to be transformed into auto-affection by exemplorality. It is an irreducible heterogeneity which cannot be eaten either sensibly or ideally and which – this is the tautology – by never letting itself be swallowed must therefore *cause itself to be vomited.*

Vomit lends its form to this whole system, beginning with its specific parergonal overflow. It must therefore be shown that the scheme of vomiting, as the experience of disgust, is not merely one excluded term among others.

What then is the relation between disgust and vomit? It is indeed vomit that interests us rather than the act or process of vomiting, which are less disgusting than vomit in so far as they imply an activity, some initiative whereby the subject can at least still mimic mastery or dream it in auto-affection, believing that he *makes himself vomit*. Here, hetero-affection no longer even allows itself to be pre-digested in an act of making-oneself-vomit.

Why vomit then, as a parergon of the third *Critique* considered as a general synthesis of transcendental idealism?

I start from the place of the negative. Kant admits the possibility and the concept of *negative pleasure*. For example the feeling of the sublime. While "the beautiful directly brings with it a feeling of the furtherance of life, and thus is compatible with charms and with the play of the imagination, the other [the feeling of the sublime] is a pleasure that arises [*entspringt*] only indirectly; viz. it is produced by the feeling of a momentary

checking [*inhibition*] (*Hemmung*: an arrest, a retention) of the vital powers and a consequent stronger outflow [*Ergiessung*: pouring out] of them [the corporal scheme here, since there is *Wohlgefallen* and pleasure, is rather that of ejaculation than vomiting which this outflow might at first resemble] so that it seems to be regarded," continues Kant, "as emotion – not play, but earnest in the exercise of the imagination. Hence it is not incompatible with charm; and as the mind is not merely attracted by the object but is ever being alternately repelled, the *Wohlgefallen* in the sublime does not so much involve a positive pleasure as admiration or respect, which rather deserves to be called negative pleasure." (§ 23)

Although repulsive on one of its faces, the sublime is not the absolute other of the beautiful. It still provokes a certain pleasure. Its negativity does indeed provoke a disagreement between the faculties and disorder in the unity of the subject. But it is still productive of pleasure and the system of reason can account for it. A still internal negativity does not reduce to silence; it lets itself be spoken. The sublime itself can dawn in art. The silence it imposes by taking the breath away and by preventing speech is less than ever heterogeneous to spirit and freedom. The movement of reappropriation on the contrary is even more active. That which in this silence works against our senses or in opposition to the interest of sense (*hindrance* and *sacrifice*, says Kant) keeps the extension of a domain and of power in view. *Sacrifice* [*Aufopferung*] and *spoliation* [*Beraubung*], through the experience of a negative *Wohlgefallen*, thus allows for the acquisition of an extension and a power [*Macht*] greater than what is sacrificed to them. (*General Remark upon the Exposition of the Aesthetical Reflective Judgment*) Economic calculation allows the sublime to be swallowed. The same is the case for all sorts of "negative pleasures," of pleasures that displease whoever feels them in the present: for example the needy but well-meaning man at becoming the heir of an affectionate but avaricious father; or the widow at the death of her husband (in this latter case her grief is satisfying while the pleasure of the orphan, in the former example, causes him grief.) [§ 54] In all these cases, whether or not they amount to the same thing, there is negative pleasure or a negative of pleasure but still pleasure, and the work of mourning is consequently not absolutely blocked, impossible, excluded.

In the same way, the Fine-Arts can give beauty to ugly or displeasing things and therein lies their superiority. [§ 48.] The ugly, the evil, the false, the monstrous, the negative in general can be assimilated by art. An old *topos*: furies, diseases, the ravages of war, etc. can all furnish beautiful descriptions and "even be represented in paintings." The ugly, the evil, the horrible, the negative in general are therefore not unassimilable to the system.

A single "thing" is unassimilable. It will therefore form the transcendental of the transcendental, the non-transcendentalisable, the non-idealisable, and that is the *disgusting*. It presents itself, in the Kantian discourse, as a "species" (*Art*) of the hideous or of the hateful, but one quickly observes that it is not a species that would peacefully belong to its genus. "There is only one kind of ugliness [*Hasslichkeit*] which cannot be represented in accordance with nature without destroying [send to ground: *zu Grunde zu richten*] all aesthetical satisfaction, and consequently artificial beauty, viz. that which excites *disgust* (*Eckel*)." [§ 48.]

Thus it is no longer a question here of one of those negative values, one of those ugly or harmful things that art can represent and thereby idealize. The absolute excluded [*l'exclu absolu*] does not allow itself even to be granted the status of an object of negative pleasure or of ugliness redeemed by representation. It is unrepresentable. And at the same time it is unnameable in its singularity. If one could name it or represent it, it would begin to enter into the auto-affective circle of mastery or reappropriation. An economy would be possible. The disgusting X cannot even announce itself as a *sensible* object without immediately being caught up in a teleological hierarchy. It is therefore in-sensible and un-intelligible, irrepresentable and unnameable, the absolute other of the system.

Nevertheless Kant does speak of a certain representation regarding it: "For in this singular [*sonderbaren*] sensation, which rests on mere imagination [therefore there is none], the object is represented as it were [*der Gegenstand gleichsam ... vorgestellt wird*] obtruding itself for our enjoyment [*als ob er sich zum Genuss aufdränge*: the disgusting, vomit is represented in advance as forcing pleasure, and that is why it disgusts] while we strive against it with all our might [*wider den wir doch mit Gewalt streben*]. And the artistic representation of the object is no longer distinguished from the nature of the object itself in our sensation, and thus it is impossible that it can be regarded as beautiful."

Vomit is related to enjoyment [*jouissance*], if not to pleasure. It even *represents* the very thing that forces us to enjoy – in spite of ourselves [*notre corps défendant*]. But this representation annuls itself, and that is why vomit remains unrepresentable. [A representation of the irrepresentable, a presentation of the unpresentable, is also the structure of the *colossal*, as it is described, or circumvented, in § 26. Cf. "Le colossal," in *La verité en peinture*, p. 136.] By limitlessly violating our enjoyment, without granting it any determining limit, it abolishes representative distance – beauty too – and prevents mourning. It irresistibly forces one to consume, but without allowing any chance for idealisation. If it remains unrepresentable or unspeakable – absolutely heterogeneous – it is not because it is this or that. Quite the contrary. By forcing enjoyment, it suspends the suspense of non-consummation, which accompanies pleasure that is bound up with representation [*Vorstellung*], pleasure bound to discourse, to the poetic in its highest form. It can be neither beautiful, nor ugly, nor sublime, give rise neither to positive nor negative, neither to interested nor disinterested pleasure. It gives too much enjoyment [*trop à jouir*] for that and it burns up all work as mourning work.

Let it be understood in all senses that what the word *disgusting* de-nominates is what one cannot resign oneself to mourn [*faire son deuil*].

And if the work of mourning always consists in biting off the bit,[2] the disgusting can only be vomited.

It will be objected that all that is tautological. It is quite normal that the other of the system of taste [*goût*] should be distaste. And if taste metaphorizes exemplorality, then disgust should have the same form, but inverted; nothing has been learned. Certainly. Unless we learn to question this tautological necessity in another way; and to wonder whether the tautological structure is not itself the very form of what the exclusion [of dis-gust] serves to construct.

If it can be confirmed that everything can be said (assimilated, represented, interiorized, idealized) by this logocentric system except vomit, it is only because the oral relation taste/disgust constitutes, other than as a metaphor, this whole discourse on discourse, this whole tautology of the *logos* as self-same-identity [*le même*]. And to confirm it, it must be ascertained that the word disgust [*Eckel*] does not designate the repugnant or the negative in general. It refers precisely to what makes one desire to vomit. But how can anyone desire to vomit? [That is a question (the question precisely of *Eckel*) on which Zarathoustra (in the third passage) endlessly ruminates.]

Moreover, once fixed in its "literal sense" by the *Anthropology*, the word *disgust* can be seen to be caught up in an analogical derivation. There is worse than the literally disgusting. And if there is worse, it is because the literally disgusting is maintained, as security, in place of the worse. If not of something worse, at least in place of an "in place," in place of the replacement that has no proper place, no proper trajectory, no circular and economical return. In place of prosthesis.

All that can no longer take place between "objective" senses (hearing, sight, touch) but only between subjective "senses"; and that no longer depends on mechanics but on chemistry:

§ 20 The senses of taste and smell are both more subjective than objective. The sense of *taste* is activated when the *organ of the tongue*, the *gullet*, and the *palate* come into touch with an external object. The sense of smell is activated by drawing in air which is mixed with alien vapors; the body itself from which the vapors emanate may be distant from the sensory organ. Both senses are closely related, and he who is deficient in the sense of smell is likewise weak in taste. Neither of the two senses can lead by itself to the cognition of the object without the help of one of the other senses; for example, one can say that both are affected by *salts* (stable and volatile) of which one must be broken up by liquefaction in the mouth, the other by air which has to penetrate the organ, in order to allow its specific sensation to reach it.

§ 21 We may divide the sensations of the external senses into those of mechanical and those of chemical operation. To the mechanical belong the three higher senses, to the chemical the two lower senses. The first three senses are those of *perception* (of the surface), while the other two are senses of pleasure (*Genusses*) (of innermost sensation). Therefore it happens that nausea (*Eckel*), a stimulus to rid oneself [*entledigen*] [by vomiting: *sich zu erbrechen*] of food [*that which has been enjoyed: genossenen*] by the quickest way through the gullet, is given to man as such a strong vital sensation, since such an internal feeling can be dangerous to the animal.

However, there is also a pleasure of the intellect [*Geistesgenuss*] consisting in the communication of thought. But when it is forced upon us

[*uns aufgedrungen*], the mind finds it repugnant and it ceases to be nutritive as food for the intellect. (A good example of this is the constant repetition of amusing or witty [*witzig*] quips, which can become indigestible through sameness.) Thus the natural instinct to be free of it is by analogy called nausea, although it belongs to the inner sense.

Smell is, so to speak, taste at a distance, and other people are forced to share in the pleasure [*mit zu geniessen*] whether they want to or not. Hence, by interfering with individual freedom, smell is less sociable than taste; when confronted with many dishes and bottles, one can choose that which suits his pleasure without forcing others to participate in that pleasure. Filth seems to awaken nausea less through what is repulsive to eye and tongue than through the stench associated with it. Internal penetration (into the lungs) through smell is even more intimate than through the absorptive vessels of mouth or gullet.

There is then something more disgusting than the disgusting, than what disgusts taste. The chemistry of smell exceeds the tautology taste/disgust. Disgust is not the symmetrical inverse of taste, the negative key to the system, except in so far as some interest sustains its excellence, like that of the mouth itself – the chemistry of the word –, and prohibits the substitution of any non-oral analogue. The system therefore is interested in determining the other as *its* other, that is, as literally disgusting.

What is absolutely foreclosed is not vomit, but the possibility of a vicariousness of vomit, of its replacement by anything else – by some other unrepresentable, unnameable, unintelligible, insensible, unassimilable, obscene other which forces enjoyment and whose irrepressible violence would undo the hierarchizing authority of logocentric analogy – its power of *identification*.

Vicariousness would in turn be reassuring only if it substituted an identifiable term for an unrepresentable one, if it allowed one to step aside from the abyss in the direction of another place, if it were interested in some other go-around [*interessé à quelque manège*]. But for that it would have to be *itself* and represent itself as such. Whereas it is starting from that impossibility that economimesis is constrained in its processes.

This impossibility cannot be said to be something, something sensible or intelligible, that could fall under one or the other senses or under some concept. One cannot name it within the logocentric system – within the name – which in turn can only vomit it and vomit itself in it. One cannot even say: what is it? That would be to begin to eat it, or – what is no longer absolutely different – to vomit it. The question *what is?* already parleys [*arraisonne*] like a *parergon*, it constructs a framework which captures the energy of what is completely inassimilable and absolutely repressed. Any philosophical question already determines, concerning this other, a paregoric *parergon*. A paregoric remedy softens with speech; it consoles, it exhorts with the word. As its name indicates.

The word *vomit* arrests the vicariousness of disgust; it puts the thing in the mouth; it substitutes, but only for example, oral for anal. It is determined by the system of the beautiful, "the symbol of morality," as *its* other; it is then for philosophy, still, an elixir, even in the very quintessence of its bad taste.

Notes

1 *Fine-Arts* has been used throughout to translate *Beaux-Arts*, which translates *Schöne Kunst*.

2 *le mors*: the bit of a bridle, what is bitten or bitten off (*un mor-ceau*), a remainder, a corpse (*un mort*). In Freud, mourning reconciles one to the loss of a beloved object by cannibalizing – incorporating, internalizing, hence idealizing – the dead. [RK]

29

Literature One More Time

Maurice Blanchot

"We should try one more time to grasp, perhaps not the traits proper to what literature is understood to be, but those that have ceased to belong to it.

– At the risk of being a bit crude.

– Necessarily so. But a simple inventory might suffice: for example, the idea of the masterpiece has disappeared. When we speak of a masterpiece it is always out of convenience, facility, or respect for the past. Literature, in its obscure self-assertion, excludes the promotion of the work of art called a *chef d'oeuvre*.

– Perhaps because it also excludes the idea of a work, an *oeuvre*.

– At least a certain idea of the work. Thus we know that the work counts less than the experience of the search for it, and that an artist is always ready to sacrifice the work's accomplishment to the truth of the movement that leads to it.

– Or that prohibits attaining it. Then what counts? The artist, the writer?

– The artist as a creative personality, the literary figure as an exceptional existence, the poet as genius – the hero – these fortunately no longer have a place even in our myths. Vanity, of course, remains; the literary 'I' continues to be in evidence. We still speak of great writers and artists. Yet no one attaches any importance to this; these old echoes are beginning to die out. Consider what the theme of immortality signified for so many centuries – the hope of posterity's acclaim and the word glory (already degraded in the desire to be known by all and for all time). Who today would dare to feel justified by the good fortune of having his ashes tomorrow in the Pantheon?

– Yes, who would? Many perhaps: but let's disregard them. The idea of immortality has become devalued, while at the same time the belief in a beyond is wearing away. I grant that we are indifferent to the idea of survival. One who is conscious of what is at stake in becoming will be happy to disappear; Nietzsche already attempted to teach us this. Are we then, by way of compensation, to exalt the idea of actuality (as has been done), that is, seek the meaning of literature and art in the exigency of the present?

– *One must be absolutely modern.* Rimbaud's and Baudelaire's summons, which inaugurated a new age or corresponded to a mutation in the arts by putting them in relation with the secret essence of something that would be the 'modern,' certainly had great meaning; but even if the new retains its prestige, even if the provocative seeking of what lies ahead can still play a critical role for us, it represents nothing binding. The thought of being modern seems to us almost as strange as the idea of becoming classical or of falling in with a secure tradition. Why? We could try to find out, were it worth the trouble.

– Some words no longer suffice to convey what they are a sign of. 'The modern era' presupposes relations that have been maintained between the present, the past, and the future, be these relations of opposition or of contrast. But let us imagine changes such that these relations would no longer have a directing force. We will now no longer be conscious of belonging to modern times, nor of opposing ourselves to an age that is past; the modern will in its turn be outmoded as a mode of becoming. When history turns, this movement of turning that implies even the suspension of history (in the name of a utopian truth) also revokes 'the tradition of the new.'

– A rupture such that this interruption would constitute an event uninscribable in the continuity of a memory, and would signify the interruption of the memorable, if not the birth of a new memory. And one would have to think of literature as being bound up with this interruption, yet necessarily almost ungraspable by means of the categories that continue to be ours. So literature could no longer be content with simply being modern, even in the sense Baudelaire and Rimbaud intended, and even considering the gain that comes to us from what we call modern art.

– We therefore also have to renounce the exigency of the alternative: 'Literature will be modern or it will not be.'

– But by the same movement, renounce seeking to base our efforts on some tradition, and on the hope – always secretly entertained, even by the most innovative – of forming a happy synthesis between what was and what will be. Being classical insofar as one is modern is a seed that will no longer germinate.

– One could perhaps say more precisely that by the secret constituting it, literature remains distinct from culture. To make a poetic work is not to make a cultural work, and the writer does not write to enrich the cultural patrimony. Culture can doubtless lay claim to literary acts; it absorbs them by introducing them into the ever more unified cultural universe that is its own, and where works exist as spiritual, transmissible, durable, comparable things that are in relation with the other products of culture. Here the work seems to have found its certainty and consistency; books are added to books in order to constitute that beautiful Alexandria no flame will ever reach, that always finished, always unfinished Babel that is the world of literature and literature as world. Let us recognize that the immense work of culture, which makes a whole of literature and makes literature an element within a larger whole, constantly furnishes us with an alibi. The consolidation of culture allows all writers and artists, in the current of ordinary life, to feel themselves still of use amidst the values they uphold by putting them in question. But let's maintain the idea that Kafka does not write to make a cultural work (nor does he write to check culture), any more than did Homer, any more

than would the last writer that we all for a moment suppose ourselves to be.

– To write to ... or not to write to ... is not sufficiently determining. Let us put it better by saying that, on the one hand, literature belongs to culture (since it can be studied as a fact of culture) but, on the other hand, what is affirmed on the basis of literature not only contests culture in what it values, but also escapes it and deceives it – if what literature communicates to culture with regard to its substantial contents is only an empty becoming, or if what culture succeeds in extracting from literature in order to study it immediately becomes substantialized, and thereby falls outside literature.

– Let us try to put this still more precisely. Literature is a language. Every language (as we formulate it today) is constituted by a signifier, a signified, and the relation of the one to the other. It is not sufficient to say, as Paul Valéry for a long time affirmed, that form has more importance in literary language than in ordinary languages; it must first be said that in literary language the relation between signifier and signified, or between what one calls form and (erroneously) content, becomes infinite.

– Which means?

– Which means many things, too many for us to delimit them. It means essentially that this relation is not a relation that unifies: form and content are in relation in such a way that all comprehension, all efforts to identify them, to relate them one to the other, or to a common measure in accordance with a regularly valid order or with a natural legality, alters them and necessarily fails. From which follow consequences so difficult to ascertain that we could never discover them all. Here is one of them: the signified can never be taken as being a response to the signifier, or as its end, but rather as that which indefinitely restores to the signifier its power to give meaning and to constitute a question (the reality of the 'content' is there only to recharge form, to reestablish it as form, a form that, in its turn, is exceeded by a 'meaning' that conceals itself and cannot fill it). Here is another: this infinite relation – bearing the exigency of an infinite distortion – will accomplish itself all the more as the terms between which it is produced give themselves as more distant, entailing from one to the other the strongest element of disjunction so that the relation between them does not have the effect of unifying them, but on the contrary prohibits all synthesis, thus affirming through the strangeness of this relation only the improbable becoming of signification in its infinite – that is to say, infinitely empty – plurality. Hence one is able to conceive why this relation of strangeness seems to precede and to deceive every significa- tion, and, at the same time, seems to signify infin- itely and signify itself as infinite, and why the innermost meaning of every literary work is always 'literature' signifying itself.

– As though, in literary language, the signifier's emptiness functioned as positive and the content's 'reality' as negative, so that the greater the differ- ence of potential between the two conductors and the stronger the resistance – to the point of tending to the infinite – the closer the work would come to signifying itself as literature. Let us suppose this, although there is much here to object to. But it seems to me that in limiting ourselves to this we have forgotten our point of departure, which was to establish why culture is able to lay claim to literature while the literary experience, at the limit, falls outside the field or the jurisdiction of culture.

– Perhaps we have not forgotten it. Perhaps now we are better able to say something about this difficult problem. For culture tends to conceive of and to establish as relations of unity relations that, on the basis of literature, give themselves as infin- ite, that is, irreducible to any unifying process. Culture works for the whole. This is its task, and it is a good one. Having the whole as its horizon, it retains all that contributes to the movement of the whole. A cumulative process. It therefore privil- eges results. For culture, a work's signification is its content, and what is set down and deposited in literary works, their positive side, is the represen- tation or reproduction of an exterior or an interior reality. Literature communicates society, human beings, and objects to us in a manner that is proper to it. It is a volume in the encyclopedia. The ideal of culture is to bring off pictures of the whole, panoramic reconstitutions that situate in the same view Schönberg, Einstein, Picasso, Joyce – throw- ing Marx into the bargain, if possible, or better yet, Marx and Heidegger. Then the man of culture is happy; he has lost nothing, he has gathered up all the crumbs of the feast.

– Well, now we have kept our promise of being crude. I shall add this remark. A while back we evoked masterpieces; it is culture that loves and perhaps invents them; it needs them to simplify and facilitate reception of the contributions of the centuries. A masterpiece is a kind of concept,

gathering together and resuming the reality of the numerous works for which it stands; and it is from the perspective of culture that certain books rise above the others to become at this altitude the visible sign of a whole. And yet, at the same time, culture aims to destroy the notion of the work: what interests culture is, properly speaking, what does not belong to the work of art.

– Because these two tendencies go hand in hand. Whoever wants masterpieces has never dis- cerned what is at stake in the idea of the work – its secret difference, what constitutes it as always unperceived, non-produced, not set into work; the strangeness of its unworking.

– Let us then conclude that literature is not simply a manifestation of culture, which only holds onto results, and above all those that corres- pond to an established state of the world – some would say its most alienated part. But perhaps we might have avoided this lengthy detour simply by remarking that what is proper to the literary work is being creative, whereas what is proper to culture is to receive what has been created. The first gives; the second has to do only with what is already given, its work being to constitute in a kind of new natural reality the initiatives and the begin- nings that, procured by the arts, tend to modify the state of things.

– So that when one speaks of culture one would do better to speak of nature. Still, the idea of creation, though compelling, remains problematic. What does it mean to create? Why would the artist or the poet be the creator par excellence? Creating belongs to the old theology, and we are content to transfer the most common divine attribute to a privileged individual. To create something from nothing is the sign of power. To create a work: in so doing, not only to imitate the demiurgy of divinity, but also to prolong and reestablish the creative forces that once made the world, thus to take over for God. All these myths are indistinctly implied by the word creation when, as though by rights, we apply it to the labor of the artist. To which is added, mixed in with this word, the idea of natural growth, the power of unfolding and springing forth that belongs to nature. To create, to grow, to increase; to participate in the divine secret that created nature, or in the secret of nature that creates itself in the play of metamorphoses – I wonder why we accept, almost without question, such an inheritance of imposing ideas.

– Imposing, and perhaps excessively so. Upon further reflection, it might well come out that we use the term 'creator' or 'creation' only as a com-monplace. In the romantic period the artist takes his place at the summit and as though outside any social role: for what at this moment counts in the work of art is neither the work, nor art, but the artist and, in the artist, his brilliance and genius. The creator can even create nothing. He is the divine and absolute self that in itself bears the highest sovereignty, and this sovereignty need be neither socially recognized nor humanly productive. But just as the prestige attributed to inspired subjectivity has worn away, so has the idea of the creator become less distinct and with it, perhaps, the idea of creation as what properly characterizes art.

– Or it has been modified. What does it mean to create? We don't know, or no longer know, how this term would apply to literature. We might say that it seems too strong to us, too charged with received and poorly defined ideas, and also too laden with pretension – in a word, too positive. We have become very modest.

– That is to say, very mistrustful. Because the more the values of this world impose themselves upon us by their natural appearance and their look of positivity, the more we mistrust them; we mis-trust their very power to posit, let alone create, processes by which something more is added to a reality that does not satisfy us. Whoever creates risks doing no more than conserving what is by enriching it, and even though he is admired, he already attracts our suspicion. Consequently, the interest we bring today to literature goes, if it goes anywhere, to its critical force, let us say more precisely: to its mysteriously negative forces. Nietzsche, for whom the word creator retained all its attraction, already said that the true creator has the face of the destroyer and the malice of the criminal.

– Is this not to suggest that literature – foreign to culture, repugnant to the order of established values, revoking the criteria of tradition and even that of the modern, refusing to be creative in a world in which creating has no admissible signifi-cation – dangerously opens itself to a nihilist per-spective, as certain important contemporary literary movements have shown?

– We could say so, if in speaking of nihilism we had the sense that we knew of what we were speaking. But nihilism is precisely one of those words that no longer suffices to convey what it points to. Perhaps what hides beneath this word and escapes every direct hold has its essence in this very movement of slipping away.

– Which amounts to sensing that nihilism, indistinguishable from its masks and nothing other than the false appearance of its false appear-ances, threatens us precisely when it reassures us, and never poses the most dangerous threat when the threat is most manifest. When, for example, nihilism joined forces with what was called nazism or fascism, it was doubtless not due to what in this movement had an openly negative signification (it never wanted to be seen as destructive; the destroy-ers were the others, the decadent, the Jews, the atheist Marxists), but rather through the positive values it advanced and that roused other values that are opposed, but related (the values of race, nation-alism, force, the value of humanism, and, on both sides, the value of the West); at the same time, this movement claimed kinship with Nietzsche, not the Nietzsche who knew nihilism profoundly, but the Nietzsche who wanted to go beyond it, and precisely by caricaturing such possibilities of going beyond (the overman, the will to power).

– So it would be a matter of coming to maintain ourselves face to face, through an always more direct search, with what only assails us indirectly: as though Orpheus, as long as he did not turn around, thus accepting the infernal law of detour, had done nothing other than let himself be seduced by the nihilist illusion, incarnate, as is fitting, in his art and in its pretension to triumph over nothing-ness, that is to say, to assure the triumph of noth-ingness by carrying along in its wake all the forces of dispersion of hell. But he had the courage to look face-on at the fascinating and fascinated thing, and he saw it was nothing, that the nothing was nothing: at which moment hell was really vanquished. An interpretation of the myth so reassuring and so tempting that I would be ready to see in it the very temptation to which Orpheus succumbed. Nihilism has always sought to lure us into challen-ging it immediately and to suggest we would come more openly to the end of it if we were to dare notice, looking straight-on at the Medusa's head, that she herself is no more than a beautiful face with empty, already petrified eyes.

– Hence you would be inclined to conclude that at this moment nihilism itself is speaking through us.

– When two partners in speech, renouncing all controversy, and through the play of redoubling and alternance, attempt to bring even the unknown to resound, one of them perhaps necessarily assumes the role of nihilism. Only which of the two enters into this game? The one who admits it? The one who does not? Where is the other when two men come to speak, speaking in accord with what they cannot say directly? One of the two is the other, which is neither the one nor the other. As for nihilism, this dry and in any case Latin word, I think it has ceased to reecho in the direction of what it cannot reach. So let us renounce employing it to situate what might come to us from literature – that is, if what came from literature did not itself always in some sense hold itself back in it, and did not hold literature itself back and as though in retreat. At bottom, if to say plainly of literature that it is creative seems to us to be an indiscreet claim, to say that it is nihilist, or in league with some force of nothingness, is no less pretentious and indiscreet. To state it is sufficient to realize this.

– There is still too much positivity in nothingness. The enormity of this word, like the enormity of the word being, has made both of them collapse beneath their ruins (ruins moreover still too easily turned to advantage). These are terms one would do well to be wary of. Literature, we discern, holds itself at a distance from any determination that is too strong: hence it is averse to masterpieces, and even withdraws from the idea of the work to the point of making the latter a form of worklessness. Literature is perhaps creative, but what it creates is always recessed in relation to what is, while this receding only renders what is more slippery, less sure of being what it is, and because of this as though attracted to another measure: that of its unreality where in the play of infinite difference what is affirms itself, though all the while stealing away under cover of the no. Thus not really 'creative,' but also not destructive through the violence of a decisive negation, for the absence literature produces is a kind of overfullness with regard to the 'real,' and this effacement that comes from it, which is also within it as the movement that would efface it – its own infinite questioning – does not really succeed in making it disappear, but rather affirms it through this disappearance, leading it back toward the strangeness of that which gives origination and, at times, perhaps always, allows it in turn to become a thing, a thing full of itself, a self-imposing reality that claims to be of value in consolidating the reign of values.

– When I hear the word origin pronounced, a word the habits of time push toward us, I wonder why we so willingly call it to assist us when, concerning art, speech, and thought, we have some enigma in view. Is it because it is itself enigmatic? Is it because it would hold within itself the word of the enigma – its answer?

– If it holds it, it does not hand it over. Note that as regards the notions we have stirred up so as to seize this possibility that is literature, we have each time sensed that it was ready to rouse itself in the background. Were it a matter of the tradition, we could have said with a certain philosopher: tradition is the forgetting of the origin. Or we could have called it a forgetting of the modern, and then we could have said with another: to live in the modern world is to detach the real from its origin. Or again, were it a matter of the idea of creation, we would have rediscovered behind this idea, before any theological reminiscence and justifying its prestige, the relation with the origin. And it is not merely this power of destruction or effacement at work in literary speech that would lay claim to this obscure origin: not only because, in relation to every thing established, an originary perturbation ruins and prevents any subsistence, but because the origin itself, excluding in its unrecoverable anteriority all that is born of it, is, not being, but rather what turns away from it – the harsh breach of the void out of which everything arises and into which everything sinks and gives way, the very play of the indifferent difference between Arising and Giving-way.

– So when we pronounce the word *origin*, we do no more than gather into a privileged word all the traits that constitute the enigma in our research.

– All these traits perhaps converge, in fact, toward this word, which is in turn the center of all divergence – or, to state this more precisely: divergence itself as the center of every relation.

– A center that in this case is the absence of any center, since it is there that the thrust of all unity comes to be shattered: in some sense the non-center of non-unity. This amounts to maintaining the origin itself under the harsh interrogation of the absence of origin, which, as soon as the origin poses as the cause, the reason, and the word for the enigma, immediately deposes it and speaks as a more profound enigma: the Arising that, as such, sinks down, is engulfed and swallowed up.

– Which amounts therefore to rejecting this reference to the origin to which we had hoped to limit ourselves. I cannot help but remark that we have overturned and effaced, one after another, and in a rather disappointing movement, all the traits we have evoked in order to grasp what is at play in literature.

– Perhaps because literature is essentially made to disappoint, being in some sense always wanting in relation to itself. And, it is true, the word masterpiece, then the words work, posterity, glory, and culture, the words creation and being, destruction and nothingness, and finally the word origin have each in turn offered themselves and retired – but perhaps each time not being entirely erased, leaving in this movement of withdrawal a trace and an almost ineffaceable trait. Thus the masterpiece disappeared, leaving in its place the work understood as its own self-elevation; and in its turn the work disappeared, leaving in its place the affirmation of the work as non-produced, idle, the experience of worklessness; in the place of the idea of the modern there was left the idea of a more profound rupture signifying the suspension of anything memorable; as for culture, it has helped us to conceive of literature as the language in which the relation between form and content becomes infinite (that is to say, the most rigorous and the most aleatory, the affirmation of a rigor and an arbitrariness); finally, the idea of creation and destruction has led us to the idea of origin, which has seemed almost by itself to efface itself, leaving us, as a sign, the idea of difference, of divergence as a first center. This is little, I admit. Nonetheless, it seems to me that an indication remains, an Ariadne's thread that, at each turn of the labyrinth, has allowed us not to lose ourselves definitively. This idea, so many times proposed and always displaced, is that there would be at play in literature some affirmation irreducible to every unifying process, not permitting itself to be unified and itself not unifying, not provoking unity. This is why we can grasp it only indirectly through a series of negations, for it is always in terms of unity that thought, at a certain level, composes its positive references. This is also why literature, if it is made to disappoint all identity and to deceive comprehension as a power of identification, is not really identifiable. That beside all the forms of language in which the whole constructs and speaks itself – speech of the universe, speech of knowledge, of labor and of salvation – one shall always sense an entirely different speech, liberating thought from being always only a thought in view of unity – this is perhaps what would still remain for us at the bottom of the crucible.

– At least momentarily."

The Malady of Grief: Duras

Julia Kristeva

Grief is one of the most important things in my life.
                                                           Grief

I told him that during my childhood my mother's misfortune took up the space of dreams.
                                                      The Lover

The Blank Rhetoric of the Apocalypse

We, as civilizations, we now know not only that we are mortal, as Paul Valéry asserted after the war of 1914;[1] we also know that we can inflict death upon ourselves. Auschwitz and Hiroshima have revealed that the "malady of death," as Marguerite Duras might say, informs our most concealed inner recesses. If military and economic realms, as well as political and social bonds, are governed by passion for death, the latter has been revealed to rule even the once noble kingdom of the spirit. A tremendous crisis of thought and speech, a crisis of representation, has indeed emerged; one may look for analogues in past centuries (the fall of the Roman empire and the dawning of Christianity, the years of devastating medieval plagues and wars) or for its causes in economic, political, and juridical bankruptcies. Nonetheless, never has the power of destructive forces appeared as unquestionable and unavoidable as now, within and without society and the individual. The despoliation of nature, lives, and property is accompanied by an upsurge, or simply a more obvious display, of disorders whose diagnoses are being refined by psychiatry – psychosis, depression, manic-depressive states, borderline states, false selves, etc.

While political and military cataclysms are dreadful and challenge the mind through the monstrosity of their violence (that of a concentration camp or of an atomic bomb), the shattering of psychic identity, whose intensity is no less violent, remains hard to perceive. That fact already struck Valéry as he compared the disaster affecting the spirit (following on the First World War but also, earlier, on the nihilism stemming from the "death of God") to what a physicist observes "in a kiln heated to incandescence: if our eyes endured, they would see *nothing*. No luminous disparity would remain, nothing would distinguish one point in space from another. This tremendous, trapped energy would end up in invisibility, in *imperceptible equality*. An equality of that sort is nothing else than *a perfect state of disorder*."[2]

One of the major stakes of literature and art is henceforth located in that invisibility of the crisis affecting the identity of persons, morals, religion, or politics. Both religious and political, the crisis finds its radical rendering in the crisis of signification. From now on, the difficulty in naming no longer opens onto "music in literature" (Mallarmé and Joyce were believers and aesthetes) but onto illogicality and silence. After Surrealism's rather playful and yet always politically committed interlude, the actuality of the Second World War brutalized consciousness through an outburst of death and madness that no barrier, be it ideological or aesthetic, seemed able to contain any longer. This was a pressure that had found its intimate,

457

unavoidable repercussion at the heart of psychic grief. It was experienced as an inescapable emergency, without for that matter ceasing to be invisible, nonrepresentable – but in what sense?

If it is still possible to speak of "nothing" when attempting to chart the minute meanderings of psychic grief and death, are we still in the presence of nothing when confronting the gas chambers, the atomic bomb, or the gulag? Neither the spectacular aspect of death's eruption in the universe of the Second World War nor the falling apart of conscious identity and rational behavior ending in institutional aspects of psychosis, often equally spectacular, are at stake. What those monstrous and painful sights do damage to are our systems of perception and representation. As if overtaxed or destroyed by too powerful a breaker, our symbolic means find themselves hollowed out, nearly wiped out, paralyzed. On the edge of silence the word "nothing" emerges, a discreet defense in the face of so much disorder, both internal and external, incommensurable. Never has a cataclysm been more apocalyptically outrageous; never has its representation been assumed by so few symbolic means.

Within some religious movements there was a feeling that in the presence of so much horror silence alone was appropriate; death should be removed from living speech and be called to mind only in indirect fashion in the rifts and unspoken bits of a concern bordering on contrition. A fascination with Judaism – one would rather not call it a flirtation – was conspicuous along those lines, revealing the guilt of an entire generation of intellectuals in the presence of anti-semitism and the collaboration [with the Germans] that existed during the early years of the war.

A new rhetoric of apocalypse (etymologically, *apocalypso* means de-monstration, dis-covering through sight, and contrasts with *aletheia*, the philosophical disclosure of truth) seemed necessary for a vision of this nevertheless monstrous nothing to emerge – a monstrosity that blinds and compels one to be silent. Such a new apocalyptic rhetoric was carried out in two seemingly opposite, extreme fashions that complement each other: a wealth of images and a holding back of words.

On the one hand, the art of imagery excels in the raw display of monstrosity. Films remain the supreme art of the apocalypse, no matter what the refinements, because the image has such an ability to "have us walk into fear," as Augustine had already seen.[3] On the other hand, verbal and

pictorial arts have turned to the "uneasy, infinite quest of [their] source."[4] Beginning with Heidegger and Blanchot respectively evoking Hölderlin and Mallarmé, and including the Surrealists, commentators have noticed that poets – doubtless diminished in the modern world by the ascendancy of politics – turn back to language, which is their own mansion, and they unfold its resources rather than tackle innocently the representation of an external object. Melancholia becomes the secret mainspring of a new rhetoric: what is involved this time is to follow ill-being step by step, almost in clinical fashion, without ever getting the better of it.

Within this image/words dichotomy, it falls to films to spread out the coarseness of horror or the external outlines of pleasure, while literature becomes internalized and withdraws from the world in the wake of the crisis in thought. Inverted into its own formalism, thereby more lucid than the existentialists' enthusiastic commitment and libertarian/adolescent eroticism, contemporary postwar literature sets out nevertheless on a difficult course. Its quest of the invisible, perhaps metaphysically motivated by the ambition to remain faithful to the intensity of horror down to the ultimate exactness of words, becomes imperceptible and progressively antisocial, nondemonstrative, and also, by dint of being antispectacular, uninteresting. Mass communication arts on the one hand, the experience of the *nouveau roman* on the other, exemplify the two alternatives.

An Aesthetics of Awkwardness

The practice of Marguerite Duras seems less that of "working toward the origin of the work," as Blanchot had hoped, than a confrontation with Valéry's "nothing" – a "nothing" that is thrust upon a perturbed consciousness by the horror of the Second World War and independently but in similar fashion by the individual's psychic unease due to the secret impacts of biology, the family, the others.

Duras' writing does not analyze itself by seeking its sources in the music that lies under the words nor in the defeat of the narrative's logic. If there be a formal search, it is subordinate to confrontation with the silence of horror in oneself and in the world. Such a confrontation leads her to an aesthetics of *awkwardness* on the one hand, to a *non-cathartic literature* on the other.[5]

The affected rhetoric of literature and even the common rhetoric of everyday speech always seem somewhat festive. How can one speak the truth of pain, if not by holding in check the rhetorical celebration, warping it, making it grate, strain, and limp?

There is some appeal, however, to her drawn-out sentences, lacking in acoustic charm, and whose verb seems to have forgotten its subject ("Her elegance, both when resting and when in motion, Tatiana tells, was worrisome"),[6] or come to a sudden end, having run out of breath, out of grammatical object or qualifier ("Then, while remaining very quiet, she again began asking for food, that the window be opened, for rest"[7] and, "Such are the last obvious pertaining facts [of her recent history]").[8]

Often one comes up against last-minute additions piled up into a clause that has made no allowance for them, but to which it brings its full meaning, a surprise ("his fond desire for girls who are not quite grown-up, sad, immodest, *and speechless*";[9] "Their union is based on insensitivity that is of a general nature and which they momentarily dread; *all predilection is excluded.*").[10] One also meets with words that are too learned and superlative, or on the contrary too ordinary and hackneyed, conveying a stilted, artificial, and sickly grandiloquence: "I don't know. I know something concerning only the *stillness of life*. Therefore, when it is shattered, I know it."[11] "When you cried, it was over yourself alone and not the *wonderful impossibility* of reuniting with her through the difference that separates you."[12]

We are not dealing with spoken discourse but with a speech that is overrated by dint of being underrated, as one can be without makeup or undressed without being slovenly but because one is compelled by some unconquerable disease that is nevertheless filled with a pleasure that enthralls and challenges. Meanwhile, and perhaps for that very reason, the distorted speech sounds strange, unexpected, and above all painful. A difficult seduction drags one into the characters' or the narrator's weaknesses, into that nothing, into what is nonsignifiable in an illness with neither tragic crisis nor beauty, a pain from which only tension remains. Stylistic awkwardness would be the discourse of dulled pain.

For such silent or precious exaggeration of speech, for its weakness tensed as if on a tightrope above suffering, films come as a substitute. Having recourse to theatrical representation, and especially to the film image, necessarily leads to an uncontrollable wealth of associations, of semantic and sentimental richness or poverty according to the viewer. If it be true that images do not make up for verbal stylistic awkwardness, they do nevertheless plunge it into the inexpressible – the "nothing" becomes undecidable and silence inspires one to muse. As a collective art, even when the scriptwriter manages to control it, the cinema adds something to the Spartan indications of the author (who ceaselessly protects a sickly secret at the heart of a more and more elusive plot); what it adds are the inevitably spectacular volumes and aggregates of bodies, gestures, actors' voices, setting, lighting, producers and all those whose task is to show. If Duras uses the screen in order to burn out its spectacular strength down to the glare of the invisible by engulfing it in elliptical words and allusive sounds, she also uses it for its excess of fascination, which compensates for verbal constriction. As the characters' seductive power is thus increased, their invisible malady becomes less infectious on the screen because it can be performed: filmed depression appears to be an alien artifice.

We now understand why Duras' books should not be put into the hands of oversensitive readers. Let them go see the films and the plays; they will encounter the same malady of distress but subdued, wrapped up in a dreamy charm that softens it and also makes it more feigned and made up – a convention. Her books, on the contrary, bring us to the verge of madness. They do not point to it from afar, they neither observe it nor analyze it for the sake of experiencing it at a distance in the hope of a solution, like it or not, some day or other ... To the contrary, the texts domesticate the malady of death, they fuse with it, are on the same level with it, without either distance or perspective. There is no purification in store for us at the conclusion of those novels written on the brink of illness, no improvement, no promise of a beyond, not even the enchanting beauty of style or irony that might provide a bonus of pleasure in addition to the revealed evil.

Without Catharsis

Lacking recovery or God, having neither value nor beauty other than illness itself seized at the place of its essential rupture, never has art had so little cathartic potential. Undoubtedly and for that very reason it falls more within the province of sorcery and bewitchment than within that of grace and forgiveness traditionally associated with artistic genius. A complicity with illness emanates from Duras' texts, a complicity that is somber and at the same time light because absentminded. It leads us to X-ray our madness, the dangerous rims where identities of meaning, personality, and life collapse. "The mystery in full daylight" is how Maurice Barrès described Claude Lorrain's paintings. With Duras what we have is madness in full daylight: "I went mad in the full light of reason."[13] We are in the presence of the nothing of meaning and feelings as lucidity accompanies them to their dying out, and we bear witness to the neutralization of our own distress, with neither tragedy nor enthusiasms, with clarity, in the frigid insignificance of a psychic numbness, both the minimal and also ultimate sign of grief and ravishment.

Clarice Lispector (1924–1977), too, offered a revelation of suffering and death that does not share in the aesthetics of forgiveness. Her *A maçã no escuro* (*The Apple in the Dark*)[14] seems opposed to Dostoyevsky. Lispector's hero has murdered a woman, as Raskolnikov has (but here she happens to be his own wife), and then meets two others, a voluptuous one and a platonic one. While they free him of the murder – as Sonia does for the prisoner in *Crime and Punishment* – they neither save nor forgive him. Worse yet, they turn him over to the police. Nevertheless, such an outcome is neither the reverse of forgiveness nor a punishment. The inescapable stillness of destiny closes in on the protagonists and bounds the novel with an implacable, perhaps feminine, gentleness, not unlike Duras' disenchanted tone, a truthful mirror of the sorrow that permeates the subject. While Lispector's universe, in contrast to Dostoyevsky's, is not one of forgiveness, it still exudes complicity among protagonists; their bonds outlast their separation and, once the novel is ended, weave a friendly, invisible environment.[15] One might add that beyond a sinister display of evil, so much humor runs through the writer's fierce novellas that it acquires a purifying value and shields the reader from the crisis.

There is nothing like that in Duras. Death and pain are the spider's web of the text, and woe to the conniving readers who yield to its spell: they might remain there for good. The "crisis in literature" that Paul Valéry, Roger Caillois, or Maurice Blanchot discussed reaches here a kind of apotheosis. Literature is neither self-criticism, nor criticism, nor a generalized ambivalence cleverly blending man and woman, real and imaginary, true and false, within the disillusioned celebration of the seeming, dancing on the volcano of an impossible object or lost time. . . . Here, the crisis leads writing to remain on the near side of any warping of meaning, confining itself to baring the malady. Lacking catharsis, such a literature encounters, recognizes, but also spreads the pain that summons it. It is the reverse of clinical discourse – very close to it, but as it enjoys the illness' secondary benefits cultivates and tames it without ever exhausting it. Considering such faithfulness to discomfort, it is understandable that an option may be found in films' neoromanticism or in the concern for sending ideological or metaphysical messages and meditations. Between *Détruire, dit-elle* (1969; *Destroy, She Said*, 1986) and *La Maladie de la mort* (1982; *The Malady of Death*, 1986), which brings to the utmost degree of condensation the death–love theme, there extend thirteen years of films, plays, explanations.[16]

The exotic eroticism of *L'Amant* (1984; *The Lover*, 1985) then takes over from those beings and words that have been prostrated by tacit death. It displays the same painful, deadly passion (a constant with Duras), conscious of itself and held back ("She might answer that she doesn't love him. She says nothing. Suddenly she knows, right here, at that moment, knows he doesn't understand her, knows he never will, knows he hasn't the means to understand so much perversity").[17] But geographic and social realism, the journalistic account of colonial destitution and of the discomforts of the Occupation, the naturalistic presentation of the mother's failures and hatreds – all that shrouds the smooth, sickly pleasure of the prostituted child who gives herself over to the tearful sensuality of a wealthy Chinese grownup, sadly and yet with the perseverance of a professional narrator. While it remains an impossible dream, feminine jouissance becomes rooted in local color and in a story, a distant one to be sure, but one that the Third World's irruption, on the one hand, and the realism of family carnage on the other, make henceforth plausible and strangely close, intimate. With *L'Amant* suffering gains a social and historical neoromantic congruity that has insured its place among bestsellers.

The whole of Duras' work does perhaps not correspond to the aescetic faithfulness to madness that precedes *L'Amant*. A few texts, however, among others, will allow us to observe the high points of that madness.

Hiroshima of Love

Because of what took place in history, there can be no artifice involving Hiroshima. Neither tragical nor pacifist artifice facing the atomic explosion, nor rhetorical artifice facing the mutilation of feelings. "All one can do is to speak of the impossibility of speaking of Hiroshima. The knowledge of Hiroshima is something that must be set down, a priori, as being an exemplary delusion of the mind."[18] Hiroshima itself, and not its repercussions, is the sacrilege, the death-bearing event. The text sets out to "be done with description of horror through horror, for that has been done by the Japanese themselves" and to "have the horror rise from its ashes by having it inscribed into a love that will inevitably be distinctive and 'wonder-filling.'"[19] The nuclear explosion therefore permeates love itself, and its devastating violence makes love both impossible and gorgeously erotic, condemned and magically alluring – as is the nurse, portrayed by Emmanuelle Riva, at one of the high points of passion. The text and the film open not with the image of the nuclear mushroom as initially planned, but with parts of clasping bodies belonging to a couple of lovers who might be a couple of dying people. "In their place and stead mutilated bodies are seen – at the level of the head and hips – moving – preys either to love or to the pangs of death – successively covered with ashes, dew, atomic death – and the sweat of love fulfilled."[20] Love stronger than death? Perhaps. "Always their personal history, brief as it might be, will prevail over Hiroshima." But perhaps not. For, if He comes from Hiroshima, She comes from Nevers where "she has been mad with meanness." Her first lover was German, he was killed during the Liberation, her hair was shorn. A first love destroyed by the "utterness and dreadfulness of stupidity." On the other hand, the horror of Hiroshima somehow liberated her from her French tragedy. The recourse to the atomic weapon seems to prove that horror is not limited to one side; it knows neither place nor party but can rage absolutely. Such a transcendence of horror frees the loving woman of mistaken guilt. The young woman henceforth wanders with her "purposeless love" all the way to Hiroshima. Beyond their wedding, which they term a happy one, the new love of the two protagonists – although powerful and strikingly authentic – will also be "strangled": sheltering a disaster on either side, Nevers here, Hiroshima there. However intense it may be in its unnameable silence, love is henceforth in suspense, pulverized, atomized.

To love, from her point of view, is to love a dead person. The body of her new lover merges with the corpse of her first love, which she had covered with her own body, a day and a night, and whose blood she savored. Furthermore, passion is intensified by a taste for the impossible forced on her by the Japanese lover. In spite of his "international" appearance and Western face as per the scriptwriter's directions, he remains if not exotic at least other, from an other world, a beyond, to the extent of merging with the image of the German who was loved and who died in Nevers. But the very dynamic Japanese engineer is also marked by death because he necessarily bears the moral scars of the atomic death of which his countrymen were the first victims.

A love crippled by death or a love of death? A love that was made impossible or a necrophilic passion for death? *My love is a Hiroshima*, or else, *I love Hiroshima for its suffering is my Eros*? *Hiroshima mon amour* preserves that ambiguity, which is, perhaps, the postwar version of love. Unless that historical version of love reveals the profound ambiguity of love with respect to death, the death-bearing halo of all passion . . . "His being dead does not keep her from desiring him. She can no longer help herself wanting him, dead as he might be. Her body is drained, breathless. Her mouth is moist. Her posture is that of a desiring woman, shameless to the point of crudeness. More shameless than anywhere else. Disgusting. She desires a dead man."[21] "The purpose of love is to die more comfortably into life."[22]

The implosion of love into death and of death into love reaches its highest expression in the unbearable grief of madness. "They pretended I was dead . . . I went mad. With meanness. I would spit, so I was told, in my mother's face."[23] Such a madness, bruised and deadly, might be no more than the absorption, on Her part, of His death. "One might think her dead, so fully is she dying of his own death."[24] The identification of the protagonists with each other as they fuse their borders, their words, their being, is a standing metaphor with Duras. While she does not die as he does, while she outlasts their dead love, she nevertheless becomes *like* a dead woman – severed from others and from time, she has the endless, animal stare of cats, she is mad – "Having died of love in Nevers." "... I couldn't manage to find the slightest difference between that dead body and mine... Between that body and mine I could find only similarities... such that I could scream, do you understand?"[25] Frequent, even permanent, identification with the object of mourning is nonetheless absolute and inescapable. Because of that very fact, mourning becomes impossible and changes the heroine into a crypt inhabited by a living corpse...

Private and Public

Duras' entire work is perhaps contained in the 1960 text that sets the plot of Resnais' film in the year 1957, fourteen years after the atomic explosion. Everything is there – suffering, death, love, and their explosive mixture within a woman's mad melancholia; but above all the combination of sociohistorical *realism* adumbrated in *Un Barrage contre le Pacifique* (1950; *The Sea Wall*, 1986), which resurfaced in *L'Amant*, with the *X-ray of depression* that was inaugurated in *Moderato cantabile* (1958; Eng. tr. 1960) and would become the favorite ground, the exclusive area of the subsequent intimist texts.

While history is unobtrusive and later disappears, it is here cause and setting. This drama of love and madness appears to be independent of the political drama as the power of passion outstrips political events, atrocious as they may be. What is more, this mad, impossible love seems to triumph over the events – if one may speak of triumph when eroticized suffering or love in suspense hold sway.

Nevertheless, Duras' melancholia is *also* like an explosion in history. Private suffering absorbs political horror into the subject's psychic microcosm. The French woman in Hiroshima might have come out of Stendhal; perhaps she is even eternal and yet she nonetheless exists because of the war, the Nazis, the bomb...

Because of its integration into private life, however, political life loses the autonomy that our consciousness persists in setting aside for it, religiously. The different participants in the global conflict do not disappear, for all that, through a global condemnation that would amount to a remission of the crime in the name of love. The young German is an enemy, the Resistance's

severity has its logic, and nothing is said that could justify the Japanese intervention on the side of the Nazis any more than the violence of the belated American counterattack. Political events having been acknowledged by an implicit political consciousness that belongs to the left (the Japanese man should unquestionably appear as a leftist), the aesthetic stake just the same remains that of love and death. It therefore sets public events in the light of madness.

Today's milestone is human madness. Politics is part of it, particularly in its lethal outbursts. Politics is not, as it was for Hannah Arendt, the field where human freedom is unfurled. The modern world, the world of world wars, the Third World, the underground world of death that acts upon us, do not have the civilized splendor of the Greek city state. The modern political domain is massively, in totalitarian fashion, social, leveling, exhausting. Hence madness is a space of antisocial, apolitical, and paradoxically free individuation. Confronting it, political events, outrageous and monstrous as they might be – the Nazi invasion, the atomic explosion – are assimilated to the extent of being measured only by the human suffering they cause. Up to a point, considering moral suffering, there is no common ground between a shorn lover in France and a Japanese woman scorched by the atom. In the view of an ethic and an aesthetic concerned with suffering, the mocked private domain gains a solemn dignity that depreciates the public domain while allocating to history the imposing responsibility for having triggered the malady of death. As a result, public life becomes seriously severed from reality whereas private life, on the other hand, is emphasized to the point of filling the whole of the real and invalidating any other concern. The new world, necessarily political, is unreal. We are living the reality of a new suffering world.

Starting with that imperative of fundamental uneasiness, the various political commitments appear identical and disclose their strategies for flight and mendacious weakness: "Collaborators, the Fernandezes. And myself, two years after the war, a member of the communist party. An absolute, final equivalence. It's the same thing, the same call for help, the same judgment deficiency, let's say the same superstition, which consists in believing there is a political solution to a personal problem."[26]

One might, on that basis, defer the examination of political matters and scrutinize only the spectrum of suffering. We are survivors, living dead, corpses on furlough, sheltering personal Hiroshimas in the bosom of our private worlds.

It is possible to imagine a form of art that, while acknowledging the weight of contemporary suffering, would drown suffering in the conquerors' triumph, or in metaphysical sarcasms and enthusiasms, or yet in the fondness of erotic pleasure. Is it not also true, is it not especially true, that contemporary man succeeds, better than ever, in defeating the grave, that life prevails in the experience of the living, and that, from a military and political standpoint, the destructive forces of the Second World War appear to have been arrested? Duras chooses or yields to the appeal of another path – the conniving, voluptuous, bewitching contemplation of death within us, of the wound's constancy.

The publication of *La Douleur* in 1985 – a strange secret diary kept during the war and whose main narrative relates the return of Robert L. from Dachau – reveals one of the essential biographical and historical roots of such suffering. The struggle of man against death in the face of the Nazi-imposed extermination. The survivor's struggle in the midst of normal life to recapture for what is close to a corpse the elemental forces of life. The narrator – both witness and fighter in this life-and-death venture – explains it as if from within, from within her love for the renascent dying man.

The struggle with death began very soon. One had to deal softly with it, with delicacy, tact, diplomacy. It surrounded him on all sides. But there was still one way of reaching him, there was an opening, it was not too wide, through which one could communicate, but life was yet in him, hardly a splinter, but a splinter just the same. Death would launch an attack – a temperature of 103 the first day. Then 104. Then 106. Death was out of breath – 106: the heart quivered like a violin string. Still 106, but it quivers. The heart, we thought, the heart is going to stop. Still 106. Death strikes, as with a battering ram, but the heart is deaf. It isn't possible, the heart is going to stop.[27]

The narrator is meticulously fastened to the minute, essential details of the body's struggle against death, of death's against the body; she scrutinizes the "distraught but sublime" head, the bones, the skin, the intestines, even the "in-

human" or "human" shit...At the heart of her love, her dying love for this man, she yet regains, through and thanks to suffering, her passion for the singular, unique, hence loved forever, being – Robert L., the survivor. Death rekindles dead love.

At the mere mention of that name, Robert L., I weep. I weep again. I shall weep all my life... during his mortal agony...I had known this man, Robert L., best...I had registered forever what made him himself, and himself alone, and nothing or no one else in the world, and I spoke of the distinctive gracefulness of Robert L.[28]

Would suffering enamored of death be the supreme individuation?

What was perhaps necessary was the strange experience of having been uprooted, a childhood on the Asian continent, the stress of a difficult existence next to her courageous, harsh mother (who was a teacher), the precocious encounter with her brother's mental illness and the prevailing poverty – all of which may have led her personal sensitivity to suffering to espouse with such eagerness the drama of our times, a drama that imprints the malady of death at the heart of the psychic experience of most of us. Add a childhood where love, already scorched by the fire of restrained hatred, and hope were displayed only in the depths of misfortune. "I am going to spit in his face. She opened the door and the spittle weighed in her mouth. It wasn't worth it. It was bad luck, Mister Jo was bad luck, like the sea walls, the horse that kicked the bucket, it was nobody's fault, just bad luck."[29] Such a childhood of hatred and fear became the source and blazon of a vision of contemporary history. "We are a family of stone, petrified in a mass that affords no access. Every day we try to kill ourselves, to kill. We not only don't speak with one another, we don't look at one another...Because of what was done to our mother, who was so kind, so trusting, we hate life, we hate one another."[30] "The remembrance is that of a crucial fear."[31] "I believe I am already able to admit it, I vaguely feel I would like to die."[32] "...I am immersed in a sadness that I expected and comes from me alone. I have always been sad."[33]

With a thirst for suffering to the point of madness Duras reveals the mercy that comes with our most persistent despondencies, those that are most resistant to faith, the most contemporary.

Woman as Sadness

"By what means does one take a woman? the vice-consul asks. The manager laughs... I would use sadness with her, the vice-consul says, if I were allowed to do so."[34]

Sadness would be the basic illness, if it were not, for Duras, women's sickly core: Anne-Marie Stretter (*The Vice-Consul*), for instance, Lol V. Stein (*The Ravishing of Lol V. Stein*), or Alissa (*Destroy, She Said*), to mention only three. It is a nondramatic, wilted, unnameable sadness. A mere nothing that produces discreet tears and elliptical words. Suffering and rapture flow together somewhat discreetly. "I have heard it said... her heaven is made of tears," the vice-consul notes with respect to Anne-Marie Stretter. The peculiar ambassadress to Calcutta seems to wander about with a kind of death buried in her pale, thin body. "Death in the course of life, the vice-consul finally said, but which would never catch up with you? That's it."[35] She wanders about the world, and beyond her shattered loves, bearing the melancholy charm of the Venice of her childhood and a musician's unfulfilled destiny. She is the walking metaphor of a glaucous green Venice, an end-of-the-world city, while for others the city of the Doges remains a source of excitement. Anne-Marie Stretter, however, is the embodied suffering of any ordinary woman "from Dijon, Milan, Brest, Dublin," vaguely English perhaps, or rather no, she is universal: "In other words, it is rather simplistic to think one comes only from Venice; it is also possible to come from other places one has gone through along the way, it seems to me."[36]

Suffering is her sex, the high point of her eroticism. When she brings together her set of lovers, on the sly at the *Blue Moon* or at her secret home, what do they do?

They look at her. She is thin in her black dressing gown, her eyelids are taut, her beauty has vanished. What is her unbearable well-being?

And suddenly what Charles Rossett didn't know he was expecting happened. Is it really so? Yes. There are tears. They come out of her eyes and roll down her cheeks, they are very small, they sparkle.[37]

... They look at her. Her broad eyelids tremble, the tears do not flow... I weep without any reason that I could explain to you, it is like a sorrow that goes through me, someone has to weep, it's as if it were me.

She knows they are there, very close, without a doubt, the men of Calcutta, she doesn't move at all, if she did... no... she gives one the impression that she is now trapped in a pain that is too old still to cause tears.[38]

Such a suffering expresses an impossible pleasure; it is the heartrending sign of frigidity. Holding back a passion that could not flow, suffering is nevertheless and more profoundly so the prison where mourning is locked in; it is the impossible mourning for an old love entirely made up of sensations and *autosensations* that is inalienable, inseparable, and for that very reason, unnameable. The unfulfilled mourning of the autosensual pre-object determines feminine frigidity. Hence the pain that goes with it grips a woman unknown to the one who lives on the surface – a stranger. To a narcissism deprived of melancholy appearances, suffering opposes and adds deep narcissism, the archaic autosensuality of wounded affects. One therefore discovers an unacceptable renunciation at the source of such suffering. That is why suffering is revealed through the interplay of reduplications where one's own body recognizes itself in the image of another provided it is the replica of his own.

"Not I" or Abandonment

Abandonment represents the insuperable trauma inflicted by the discovery – doubtless a precocious one and for that very reason impossible to work out – of the existence of a *not-I*.[39] Indeed, abandonment structures the remains of history in Duras' texts: the woman is deserted by her lover, the German lover of the Nevers Frenchwoman dies (*Hiroshima Mon Amour*, 1960); Michael Richardson openly abandons Lol V. Stein (*The Ravishing of Lol V. Stein*, 1964); again Michael Richardson, an impossible lover, articulates a series of disasters in the life of Anne-Marie Stretter (*The Vice-Consul*, 1965); Elizabeth Alione has lost her stillborn child, and beforehand there was the young doctor's love for her, the doctor who attempts to kill himself when she shows his letter to her husband (*Destroy, She Said*, 1969); as to the man and the young woman in *The Malady of Death* (1982), they seem possessed of an inherent mourning that makes their physical passion morbid, distant, always already dismissed; finally, the young French girl and her Chinese lover are from the start convinced of the impossibility and condemnation of their affair, and as a result the girl convinces herself that she does not love him and allows herself to be disturbed by an echo of her neglected passion only by a Chopin melody on the ship that takes her to France (*The Lover*).

The feeling of unavoidable abandonment that reveals the separation or the actual death of the lovers also seems immanent and as if predestined. It is formed about the maternal figure. The mother of the young woman of Nevers was separated from her husband...or else (the narrator hesitates) she was Jewish, and left for the unoccupied area. As for Lol V. Stein, the night of the fateful dance when Michael Richardson abandoned her, she noticed the arrival of Anne-Marie Stretter accompanied by her daughter. That woman, who thus introduces the theme of the mother, had a graceful, bony figure, and she bore "the emblems of a vague denial of nature."[40] Her thinness was elegant, mortuary, and inaccessible, and she turned out to be Lol's successful rival. More dramatically, the mad bonzian woman in *The Vice-Consul* who, pregnant and gangrened, unconsciously travels from Indochina to India, struggles against death but above all against her mother who had driven her out of her native house. "She says a few words of Cambodian: hello, good night. To the child, she would speak. And now, to whom? To her old mother in Tonle-Sap, the source, the cause of all evils, of her crooked destiny, her pure-hearted love."[41]

Like an archetype of the madwomen who fill Duras' universe, the madness of the girl's mother, in *The Lover*, towers with dismal Gothic force. "I see that my mother is clearly mad...From birth. It's in the blood. She wasn't ill with it, she lived with it as if it were healthy."[42] Hatred grips daughter and mother in a passion-driven vise that turns out to be the source of the mysterious silence that striates writing: "she should be locked up, beaten, killed."[43] "...I believe I have spoken of the love we bore our mother but I don't know if I spoke of the hatred we also bore...She is the place on the threshold of which silence begins. What happens there is precisely silence, that slow labor for my entire life: I am still there, before these possessed children, at the same distance from mystery. I have never written, although I thought I did, I have never loved, although I thought I loved,

I have never done anything except wait before the closed door."[44] Fear of maternal madness leads the novelist to have the mother disappear, to free herself from her through a violence no less deadly than that of the mother herself as she beat her prostitute daughter. Destroy, the narrating daughter in *The Lover* seems to say, but in erasing the mother's image she simultaneously takes her place. The daughter acts as a substitute for maternal madness; rather than killing her mother she continues her through the negative hallucination of an always faithfully loving identification. "Suddenly there was, next to me, someone sitting in my mother's place, she wasn't my mother...the identity that could not be replaced with any other had disappeared, and I had no means to make her come back, to have her begin to come back. Nothing offered itself that might fill the figure. I became mad in full possession of my senses."[45]

While pointing out that the bond to the mother constitutes the previous history of suffering, the text names it neither as cause nor as origin. Suffering is sufficient unto itself; it transcends effects as well as causes and sweeps away all entities, that of the subject as well as of the object. Would suffering be the ultimate threshold of our objectless states? It does not lend itself to description, but it is accessible through inspirations, tears, blank spaces between words. "I get carried away over suffering in India. It happens to all of us, more or less, right? One cannot speak of that suffering unless one insures that it breathes within us..."[46] Both massive and exterior, suffering merges with indifference or some deep splitting of the female being; such a splitting is experienced as the *emptiness of a boredom* that would be insuperable if it emerged at the very site of subjective division:

She spoke merely to say that it was impossible for her to express how boring and time-consuming it was being Lol V. Stein. They asked her to make an effort. She didn't understand why, she would say. The difficulty she encountered when searching just for one word appeared insurmountable. She appeared to expect nothing more.

Was she thinking of something, of herself? they would ask. She didn't understand the question. One might have said that she took herself for granted, and the infinite weariness of not being able to relinquish such an attitude need not even come to mind; she had become a desert into which a nomadic power had propelled her in a never-ending quest for what? One didn't know. She didn't answer.[47]

On Ravishment: Lacking Pleasure

One should doubtless not assume that the women in Duras' fiction represent *all* there is in woman. Nevertheless, a few common features of feminine sexuality show up. One is led to postulate, in such a being racked by sadness, not a *repression* but an *exhaustion of erotic drives*. Appropriated by the object of love – by the lover or, behind him, the mother whose mourning remains impossible – the drives are blank, so to speak, emptied of their ability to provide a bond of sexual pleasure or of symbolic complicity. To be sure, the lost Thing has left its mark on its disused affects and on a discourse relieved of its meaning – but this is the mark of an absence, of a *basic disconnection*. It can cause ravishment – but not pleasure. If one were to identify that woman and her love one would have to look for her in the secret cellar where there is no one, except for the sparkling eyes of Nevers' cats and the catastrophic anguish of the young woman who merges with them. "Shall I come back and go with her? No. Is it tears that deprive one of a person?"[48]

Would such a ravishment, hidden and anerotic (in the sense of being deprived of bonds, detached from the other, and turning only toward the hollow of one's own proper body that nevertheless at once is disappropriated of jouissance and sinks into the fondness of death for one's self), would it be if not the secret at least one aspect of feminine jouissance? That is what *The Malady of Death* gives us to understand. The man savors the young woman's open body like a blissful discovery of the otherwise inaccessible sexual difference, but which nevertheless appears to him as death-bearing, engulfing, dangerous. He defends himself against the pleasure of lying in his partner's moist sex by imagining that he kills her. "You discover that it is there, within her, that the malady of death is aroused, that it's this figure arrayed before you that decrees the malady of death."[49] On the other hand, she is on friendly terms with death. Aloof, unconcerned about sex and yet loving love and compliant to pleasure, she is fond of the death she believes she bears within herself. Even more so, such a complicity with death gives her the feeling that she is beyond death; a woman neither gives nor under-

goes death because *she is part of it* and because she imposes it. He is the one who *catches* the malady of death; she *is* part of it, therefore she moves on, elsewhere: "she looks at you through the green filter of her eyes. She says, you herald the realm of death. One cannot love death if it is imposed on you from outside. You think you are weeping on account of not loving. You weep because you cannot impose death."[50] She goes away, inaccessible, deified by the narrator because she brings death to others through a love that is an "admirable impossibility" for herself as for him. A certain truth of feminine experience involving the jouissance of suffering verges, with Duras, on the mythification of the inaccessible feminine.

Nonetheless, the no man's land of aching affects and devalued words that comes close to being the height of mystery, dead as it may be, is not lacking expression. It has its own language – it is called *reduplication*. It creates echoes, doubles, kindred beings who display a passion or a destruction such as the aching woman is not up to putting into words and suffers for being deprived of.

Couples and Doubles: A Reduplication

Reduplication is a jammed repetition. While what is repeated is rippled out in time, reduplication lies outside time. It is a reverberation in space, a play of mirrors lacking perspective or duration. A double may hold, for a while, the instability of the same, giving it a temporary identity, but it mainly explores the same in depth, opening up an unsuspected, unfathomable substance. The double is the unconscious substance of the same, that which threatens it and could engulf it.

Produced by the mirror, reduplication precedes the specular identification specific to the "mirror stage." It refers to the outposts of our unstable identities, blurred by a drive that nothing could defer, deny, or signify.

The unnameable power of such a gaze in addition to sight asserts itself as a privileged universe, unfathomable as to desire: "He merely looked at Suzanne with blurred eyes, he looked at her again, he heightened his gaze with additional sight, as one usually does when choked by passion."[51] On the far or near side of sight, hypnotic passion sees doubles.

Anne Desbaresdes and Chauvin in *Moderato cantabile* construct their love story as a reflection of what they imagine to be the story of the passionate couple where the woman wanted to be killed by the man. Would the two protagonists exist without the imaginary reference to the masochistic jouis-sance of the couple who preceded them? The framework is laid for another reduplication to be played out, "moderato cantabile," that of the mother and her son. Mother and child carry out the crisis of the imaginary thought process in which the identity of a woman is buried in the love for her young. If mother and daughter can be rivals and enemies (*The Lover*), the mother and her small boy appear in *Moderato cantabile* as pure devouring love. Like wine, and even before she drinks, her son engrosses Anne Desbaresdes; she accepts herself, lenient and delighted, only through him; he is the hinge that substitutes for implied amorous disappointments and reveals her insanity. The son is the visible form of a disap-pointed mother's madness. Without him, perhaps, she would be dead. With him, she is caught in the whirlwind of love, of practical and educational concerns, but also of solitudes; she is forever exiled from others and from herself. As daily, banal replica of the woman who, at the beginning of the novel, desired to be killed by her lover, Anne Desbaresdes as mother lives her ecstatic death in the love for her son. While revealing the masochis-tic chasms of desire, this complex figure (mother–son/male lover–female lover/passionate dead woman–passionate killer) shows by what narcis-sistic and autosensuous delights feminine suffering is supported. The son of course is his mother's resurrection, but, conversely, her own deaths sur-vive in him – her humiliations, her nameless wounds that are now living flesh. The more motherly love hovers over a woman's suffering, the more the child is painfully and subtly affec-tionate…

The Japanese and the German in *Hiroshima Mon Amour* are also doubles. In the amorous experience of the young woman from Nevers, the Japanese man revives the memory of her dead lover, but the two male images fuse into a hallucin-atory jigsaw puzzle that suggests that the love for the German is present without any possibility of being forgotten and, conversely, the love for the Japanese man is destined to die. Reduplication and exchange of complements. Through that strange osmosis, the vitality of a survivor of the Hiroshima catastrophe comes to be dimmed by a gruesome fate, while the other's definitive death lives on, translucently, in the young woman's bruised pas-sion. Such a reverberation of her objects of love

shatters the heroine's identity: she belongs to no time period but to the space of the contamination of entities where her own being wavers, dejected and delighted.

The Criminal Secret

The technique of reduplication reaches its height in *The Vice-Consul*. Anne-Marie Stretter's deca-dent melancholia corresponds to the expressionis-tic madness of the Savannakhet bonzian woman – who takes up again the theme of the Asian woman with a diseased foot in *The Sea Wall*.[52] Facing the heartrending poverty and rotting flesh of the Asian woman, Anne-Marie Stretter's Venetian tears seem a luxurious, unbearable caprice. Neverthe-less, the contrast between the two fades away when suffering intervenes. Against a backdrop of illness the images of the two women merge, and Anne-Marie Stretter's ethereal universe aquires a meas-ure of madness that would not be as strong without the imprint of the other wanderer. Two musicians – the pianist, the raving singer; two exiles – one from Europe, the other from Asia; two wounded women – one with an invisible wound, the other gangrened by social, family, human violen-ce… The duet becomes a threesome with the addition of another replica, this time a masculine one: the Vice-Consul from Lahore. He is a strange figure, supposedly bearing a never acknowledged archaic distress; all that is known of him are his sadistic acts – stinkbombs in school, shooting human beings in Lahore… Is it true, is it false? The Vice-Consul, whom every one fears, becomes Anne-Marie Stretter's accomplice and a lover con-demned to suffer her coldness alone, for even the tears of this charmer are intended for others. Could the Vice-Consul be a corrupted, possible metamorphosis of the melancholy ambassadress, her masculine replica, her sadistic variant, the expression of taking action – something she pre-cisely does not do, not even through intercourse? He may be homosexual, loving with an impossible love a woman who, in her sexual distress, haunted by a desire without satisfaction, would very much have liked to be like him – beyond the law, beyond reach. The unbalanced threesome – the bonzian woman, the Vice-Consul, the depressed ambassa-dress – weave a world that is beyond the other characters in the novel, even when they are most attached to the ambassadress. They provide the narrator with a rich soil for her psychological search – uncovering the insane, criminal secret that lies beneath the surface of our diplomatic behavior, of which the sadness of a number of women bears discreet witness.

The act of love is often the occasion for such a reduplication, as each partner becomes the other's double. Thus, in *The Malady of Death*, the man's death-bearing obsession merges with his mistress' deathful thoughts. The tears of the man, as he joys in the woman's "abominable frailty," correspond to her languid, detached silence and reveal its meaning: suffering. What she believes to be the falseness of his discourse, which would not fit the subtle reality of things, becomes abreacted in her own flight when, indifferent to his passion, she leaves the room of their love-making. As a result, the two characters end up appearing as two voices, two waves "between the whiteness of the sheets and that of the sea."[53]

A suffering that has faded (as a color does) fills these men and women, doubles and replicas, and, gratifying them, deprives them of any other psychology. Those carbon copies are henceforth individuated only through their *names* – black, matchless diamonds, unfathomable, that harden over the expanse of suffering. Anne Desbaresdes, Lol V. Stein, Elisabeth Alione, Michael Richardson, Max Thor, Stein... The names seem to condense and retain a story of which their bearers are perhaps as much unaware as the reader, a story that almost ends up revealing itself to our own unconscious uncanniness by becoming suddenly incomprehensible but in a familiar fashion.

Event and Hatred: Among Women

As an echo to death-bearing symbiosis with the mothers, passion between two women represents one of the most intense images of doubling. When Lol V. Stein becomes deprived of her fiancé by Anne-Marie Stretter (who does not, however, benefit, and whose inconsolable sadness will become known to us in *The Vice-Consul*), she confines herself in a bored and inaccessible isolation: "To know nothing about Lol was already to know her."[54] Nevertheless, years later, while everyone thinks she is healed and peaceably married, she watches the love-making of her former friend Tatiana Karl with Jacques Hold. She is in love with the couple, especially with Tatiana – she would like to take her place, in the same sheets, in the same bed. Such an absorption of the other

woman's passion – Tatiana being here the substitute for the first rival, Anne-Marie Stretter, and, in the last instance, for the mother – also works the other way. Tatiana, who until then has been careless and playful, begins to suffer. The two women are henceforth carbon copies of each other, replicas in the script of suffering, which, in Lol V. Stein's delighted eyes, controls the world's merry-go-round:

> things are becoming clearer around her and she suddenly sees their sharp edges, the remains that lie around all over the world, revolving, there is a scrap already half-eaten by rats, it is Tatiana's suffering, she sees it, she is ill-at-ease, always those feelings, one slips on that grease. She believed that time was possible, a time that was alternately filled and emptied, that fills and drains, and then is yet, always, ready for use, she still believes it, she believes it always, never will she be cured.[55]

Doubles are multiplied in the mirror of *Destroy, She Said* and drift over the theme of destruction, which, once it is named in the body of the text, rises to the surface to clarify the title and make one understand all the relations that the novel presents. Elisabeth Alione, who is depressed following an unhappy love affair and the stillbirth of her baby girl, is resting in a bleak hotel, full of sick people. There she meets Stein and his double, Max Thor, two Jews ceaselessly about to become writers: "How strongly it compels one sometimes not to write it down."[56] Two men bound by an inexpressible passion that one assumes is homosexual, and which precisely does not succeed in inscribing itself, except through the medium of two women. He loves/they love Alissa and are fascinated by Elisa. Alissa Thor discovers that her husband is happy to know Elisa, who captivates Stein; therefore she herself allows the same Stein to get close to her and love her (the reader is free to make up dyads within that suggestive web). She is amazed to discover that Max Thor is happy here in the kaleidoscopic world of doubles – with Stein, possibly on account of Elisa? But he also asserts that it is due to Alissa herself – " 'Destroy,' she says."[57] As fully obsessed as she is by that destruction, Alissa gazes at herself in Elisa and reveals, through the ambiguity of identification and decomposition, a true madness under the appearance of a fresh-looking young woman. "I am someone who is afraid, Alissa goes on, afraid of being deserted, afraid of the future, afraid to love, afraid of violence, of crowds, afraid of the unknown, of hunger, of poverty, of truth."[58]

Which truth? Hers or Elisa's? "Destroy, she said." The two women, however, get along. Alissa is Elisa's mouth-piece. She repeats her words, she bears witness to her past and prophesies about her future, in which, moreover, she sees only repetitions and doubles, the more so as the uncanniness of each one to him or herself causes each to become, in time, his/her own double and his/her own other.

> Elisabeth doesn't answer.
> "We knew each other when we were kids, she says. Our families were on good terms."
> Alissa repeats in a very low voice:
> "We knew each other when we were kids. Our families were on good terms."
> Silence.
> "If you loved him, if you had loved him, just once, only once, in your life, you would have loved the others," Alissa says, "Stein and Max Thor."
> "I don't understand..." Elisabeth says, "but..."
> "That will happen some other time," Alissa says, "later. But it will be neither you nor them. Don't pay any attention to what I am saying."
> "Stein says that you are mad," Elisabeth says.
> "Stein says it all."[59]

The two women echo each other; one finishes the other's sentences and the other denies them while knowing that those words speak a portion of their common truth, their complicity.

Does such a duality stem from their being women, from partaking in a same, so-called hysterical malleability, each being quick to take her own image for the other's ("She experiences what the other experiences")?[60] Or does it stem from loving the same man, who is double? From not having a stable object of love, dissecting that object into a shimmering of elusive reflections, since no support is able to hold and assuage an endemic passion, perhaps a maternal one?

Indeed, the man dreams of her – of them. Max Thor is in love with his wife Alissa, but since he has not forgotten that he is Stein's double he calls her Elisa in his dreams, while Stein himself dreams and speaks Alissa's name...Elisa/Alissa...The fact remains that they "both find themselves caught in a mirror."

> "We resemble each other," Alissa says. "We would love Stein if it were possible to love."...
> "How beautiful you are," Elisabeth says.
> "We are women," Alissa says. "Look."...
> "I love you and I desire you," Alissa says.[61]

Homonymy notwithstanding, it is nevertheless not an identification that takes place between them. Beyond the fleeting moment of specular, hypnoidal recognition, the impossibility of being the other opens up in breathtaking fashion. Hypnosis (whose motto might be, *the one is the other*) is accompanied by the pain of seeing that the merging of their bodies is an impossibility, they will never become the mother and her inseparable daughter – Elisabeth's daughter is dead, the daughter is destroyed at birth. That is enough to unbalance each protagonist and hollow out even more her unsettled identity.

What are the ingredients of such a mixture of hypnosis and utopic passion?

Jealousy, suppressed hatred, fascination, sexual desire of the rival and her man: the entire gamut creeps into the behavior and the words of those temperamental beings who live through "a tremendous grief" and complain without saying so but "as if they were singing."[62]

The violence of drives that cannot be reduced to words is subdued particularly by behavioral restraints; it is as if behavior were already mastered in itself thanks to the effort of giving it shape, as in a preexistent writing. The scream of hatred therefore is not sounded in its wild brutality. It is changed into music, which (reminding one of the smile of the Virgin or Mona Lisa) bares the knowledge of a secret that is itself invisible, underground, uterine, and conveys to civilization a suffering that is civilized, delighted but always unquenched, and for which words are too much. It is a music both neutral and destructive – "smashing trees, bringing down walls," weakening wrath into "sublime gentleness" and "absolute laughter."[63]

Would feminine melancholia be appeased by reunion with the other woman, as soon as the latter could be imagined as man's privileged partner? Or else would it be revived, or perhaps even caused, by the impossibility of meeting – of satisfying – the other woman? Among women, at any rate, the hatred that has been harnessed, swallowed, where the archaic rival lies confined, becomes exhausted. When depression expresses itself, it becomes eroticized as destruction – unleashed violence with the mother, graceful tearing down with the friend.

The domineering, tattered, mad mother establishes herself powerfully in *The Sea Wall* and determines her children's sexuality. "She is desperate of hope itself."[64] "The doctor diagnosed the source of her attacks as being the sea wall's collapse. Perhaps he was wrong. So much resentment, year after year, day after day. There was more than one cause. There were a thousand, including the dams' collapse, injustice in the world, the sight of her children bathing in the river...to die of that, to die of misfortune."[65] Exhausted by "bad luck," exasperated by her daughter's wanton sexuality, the mother is subject to fits. "She was still hitting her, as if under the pressure of an unrelenting necessity. Suzanne, at her feet, half naked in her torn dress, was crying...What if I want to kill her? If it suits me to kill her?"[66] That is what she says concerning her daughter. Under the influence of that passion, Suzanne gives herself without loving anyone. Except, perhaps, her brother Joseph. And that incestuous desire that the brother shares in and carries out in his own furious and nearly delinquent fashion ("...I slept with a sister when I slept with her")[67] sets up the favored theme of the novels that followed – the impossibility of a love defined by doubles...

After the implosion of the mother's hatred in the mad bonzian woman (*The Vice-Consul*), the mother/daughter destruction in *The Lover* compels us to realize that the mother's outburst of fury against the daughter is the "event" that the hateful, loving daughter watches for, experiences, and restores with wonder: "In her fits my mother rushes at me, locks me up in the room, beats me with her fists, slaps me, undresses me, comes close to me, smells my body, my underwear, she says she recognizes the scent of the Chinese man..."[68]

Thus the elusive double reveals the staying power of an archaic object of love, one that is uncontrollable, imaginary, and which puts me to death on account of its domination and its evasions, its sisterly or motherly closeness, but also on account of its impregnable and thus malevolent, detestable exteriority. All the figures of love converge on this autosensual, harrowing object, even if they are constantly revived by the mainspring of a masculine presence. Often at the center, the man's desire is nevertheless always outflanked and carried away by the ruffled but deceitfully powerful passivity of women.

All those men are aliens – the Chinese in *The Lover*, the Japanese in *Hiroshima Mon Amour*, and the whole series of Jews or uprooted diplomats ...Both sensuous and abstract, they are undermined by a fear that their passion never succeeds in overcoming. That passionate fear is like a mountain crest, an axis, or revival of mirror-playing among women who spread out of the flesh of suffering, of which men are the skeleton.

Beyond the Looking Glass

An unfillable lack of satisfaction, delighted nevertheless, opens up in the space that has thus been set up and which separates two women. It might be called, clumsily, feminine homosexuality. With Duras, however, we are dealing more with an ever nostalgic quest for the same as other, for the other as same, within the array of narcissistic mirage or a hypnosis that the narrator finds inevitable. She relates the psychic substratum previous to our conquests of the other sex, and which still underlies the eventual, perilous encounters between men and women. One is accustomed to pay no attention to that nearly uterine space.

And one is not wrong. For in that crypt full of reflections, identities, bonds, and feelings destroy one another. "Destroy, she said." And yet the society of women is neither necessarily wild nor simply destructive. Out of the weakness or impossibility of the inevitably erotic bonds, it erects an imaginary aura of complicity that can prove to be slightly painful and necessarily plunged into mourning because it has sunk all sexual objects, all sublime ideals into its narcissistic flow. Values do not hold in the face of that "irony of the community" (as Hegel called women), whose destructiveness, however, is not necessarily amusing.

Suffering unfurls its microcosm through the reverberation of characters. They are articulated as doubles, as in mirrors that magnify their melancholia to the point of violence and delirium. That display of reduplication recalls the child's unstable identity when, in the mirror, it finds the image of its mother only as a (soothing or terrifying) replica or echo of itself. Like an alter ego that has been frozen within the gamut of drive intensities that disturb it, detached in front of it, but never steady and on the brink of invading it through a hostile return, like a boomerang. Identity, in the sense of a stable and solid image of the self where the autonomy of the subject will be established, emerges only at the end of this process when narcissistic shimmering draws to a close in a jubilatory assumption that is the work of the Third Party.

Even the soundest among us know just the same that a firm identity remains a fiction. Suffering, in Duras' work, in a mannered way and with empty words evokes that impossible mourning, which, if its process had been completed, would have removed our morbid lining and set us up as independent, unified subjects. Thus it takes hold of us and carries us to the dangerous, furthermost bounds of our psychic life.

Modern and Postmodern

As the literature of our illness, Duras' fiction accompanies the distress that has certainly been triggered and increased by the contemporary world but proves to be essential and transhistorical.

It is a literature of limits because it also displays the limits of the nameable. The characters' elliptical speech, the obsessive conjuring up of a "nothing" that might epitomize the malady of suffering, point to a disaster of words in the face of the unnameable affect. Such a silence, as I mentioned earlier, recalls the "nothing" that Valéry's eye saw in an incandescent oven at the heart of a gruesome confusion. Duras does not orchestrate it in the fashion of Mallarmé, who sought for the music in words, nor in the manner of Beckett who refines a syntax that marks time or moves ahead by fits and starts, warding off the narrative's flight forward. The reverberation among characters as well as the silence inscribed as such, the emphasis on the "nothing" to be spoken as ultimate expression of suffering, leads Duras to a blankness of meaning. Coupled with rhetorical awkwardness, they make up a world of unsettling, infectious ill-being.

Historically and psychologically contemporary, this writing is today confronted with the postmodern challenge. The point now is to see in "the malady of grief" only one moment of the *narrative synthesis* capable of sweeping along in its complex whirlwind philosophical meditations as well as erotic protections or entertaining pleasures. The postmodern is closer to the human comedy than to the abyssal discontent. Has not hell as such, thoroughly investigated in postwar literature, lost its infernal inaccessibility and become our everyday, transparent, almost humdrum lot – a "nothing" – like our "truths" henceforth made visible, televised, in short not so secret as all that...? The desire for comedy shows up today to conceal – without for that matter being unaware of it – the concern for such a truth without tragedy, melancholia without purgatory. Shades of Marivaux and Crébillon.

A new amatory world comes to the surface within the eternal return of historical and intellectual cycles. Following the winter of discontent comes the artifice of seeming; following the whiteness of boredom, the heartrending distraction of parody. And vice versa. Truth, in short, makes its way amid the shimmering of artificial amenities as well as asserting itself in painful mirror games. Does not the wonderment of psychic life after all stem from those alternations of protections and downfalls, smiles and tears, sunshine and melancholia?

Notes

1 Paul Valéry, "La Crise de l'esprit," *Variété*, in *Oeuvres*, Bibliothèque de la Pléiade (Paris: Gallimard, 1957), 1:988.

2 *Ibid.*, 1:991. Emphasis added.

3 "Even though man worries to no avail, nevertheless he proceeds within the image" (Augustine, "Images," *On the Trinity*, XIV, IV, 6).

4 See Maurice Blanchot, "Où va la littérature?," in *Le Livre à venir* (Paris: Gallimard, 1959), p. 289.

5 Roger Caillois recommends, in literature, "techniques permitting the exploration of the unconscious": "accounts, with or without comments, of *depressions, confusion, anxiety*, and personal emotional experiences," in "Crise de littérature," *Cahiers du Sud* (Marseille, 1935). Emphasis added.

6 Marguerite Duras, *Le Ravissement de Lol V. Stein* (Paris: Gallimard, 1964), p. 14 [All quotations in this chapter are from the French editions of Duras' novels [...]]

7 *Ibid.*, p. 25.

8 *Ibid.*, p. 26.

9 *Ibid.*, p. 31.

10 *Ibid.*, p. 69.

11 *Ibid.*, p. 151.

12 Duras, *La Maladie de la mort* (Paris; Minuit, 1982), p. 56.

13 Duras, *L'Amant* (Paris: Minuit, 1984), pp. 105–6.

14 Clarice Lispector, *An Apple in the Dark*, trans. from the Brazilian edition by Gregory Rabassa (New York: Knopf, 1967).

15 "They both avoided looking at one another, overwrought with themselves, as if they finally had become part of that greater thing which sometimes manages to express itself in tragedy . . . as if they had just again realized the miracle of forgiveness; embarrassed by that miserable scene, they avoided looking at each other, uneasy, there are so many unaesthetic things to forgive. But, even covered with ridicule and rags, the mimicry of the resurrection had been done. Those things which seem not to happen, but do happen" (*An Apple in the Dark*, pp. 353–54).

16 Duras has written nineteen film scripts and fifteen plays, three of which are adaptations.

17 Duras, *L'Amant*, p. 48.

18 Duras, *Hiroshima mon amour, synopsis* (Paris: Gallimard, 1960), p. 10.

19 *Ibid.*, p. 11.

20 *Ibid.*, pp. 9–10.

21 *Ibid.*, pp. 136–37.

22 *Ibid.*, p. 132.

23 *Ibid.*, p. 149.

24 *Ibid.*, p. 125.

25 *Ibid.*, p. 100.

26 Duras, *L'Amant*, p. 85.

27 Duras, *La Douleur* (Paris: POL, 1985), p. 57.

28 *Ibid.*, p. 80.

29 Duras, *Un Barrage contre le Pacifique* (Paris: Gallimard, 1950), pp. 73–74.

30 Duras, *L'Amant*, p. 69.

31 *Ibid.*, p. 104

32 *Ibid.*, p. 146.

33 *Ibid.*, p. 57.

34 Duras, *Le Vice-consul* (Paris: Gallimard, 1966), p. 80.

35 *Ibid.*, p. 174.

36 *Ibid.*, p. 111.

37 *Ibid.*, pp. 195–96.

38 *Ibid.*, p. 198.

39 Marguerite Duras' asset is that she dares to write in between the "seduction that would work by setting free" and the "suicidal shock" of a death drive where what one calls sublimation would originate." See Marcelle Marini and Marguerite Duras, *Territoires du féminin* (Paris; Minuit, 1977), p. 56.

40 Duras, *Le Ravissement de Lol V. Stein*, p. 14.

41 Duras, *Le Vice-consul*, p. 67.

42 Duras, *L'Amant*, p. 40.

43 *Ibid.*, p. 32.

44 *Ibid.*, pp. 34–35.

45 *Ibid.*, p. 105.

46 Duras, *Le Vice-consul*, p. 157.

47 Duras, *Le Ravissement de Lol V. Stein*, p. 24.

48 Duras, *Le Vice-consul*, p. 201.

49 Duras, *La Maladie de la mort*, p. 38.

50 *Ibid.*, p. 48.

51 Duras, *Un Barrage contre le Pacifique*, p. 69.

52 *Ibid.*, p. 119.

53 Duras, *La Maladie de la mort*, p. 61.

54 Duras, *Le Ravissement de Lol V. Stein*, p. 81.

55 *Ibid.*, p. 159.

56 Duras, *Détruire, dit-elle* (Paris; Minuit, 1969), p. 46.

57 *Ibid.*, p. 34.

58 *Ibid.*, p. 72.

59 *Ibid.*, pp. 102–3.

60 *Ibid.*, p. 131.

61 *Ibid.*, pp. 99–100.

62 *Ibid.*, p. 126.

63 *Ibid.*, pp. 135–37.

64 Duras, *Un Barrage contre le Pacifique*, p. 142.

65 *Ibid.*, p. 22.

66 *Ibid.*, p. 137.

67 *Ibid.*, p. 257.

68 Duras, *L'Amant*, p. 73.

Index

Index

Cervantes, Miguel de 83, 122, 131, 133, 258–9, 266
Cezanne, Paul 289–90, 293, 298–9, 364, 369
charm 14, 29, 32, 66, 332, 447, 459, 464
chorus 148–53, 228, 256
Christianity 84, 363, 457
cinema 301, 366, 414, 459–61
color 62, 276, 278, 291, 294, 299–300, 322, 424, 442, 468
comedy 150, 157–8, 238, 326, 471
contemplation 23, 31, 54, 64, 67, 143, 148, 175, 240, 281, 285, 419
critics 283–5, 373
Critique of Judgement 132, 249–50, 354, 366, 431–50
cubism 247, 299, 369

Dadaism 175, 419
dance 153, 245
Dante 62, 123, 133, 272, 273, 308
death 393, 425, 457–8, 460–1, 463, 466
deconstruction 308–10, 425
delight 5–6, 8, 10, 24, 32, 212
Descartes, René 139, 293–8, 368
design 15, 294, 378
Dilthey, Wilhelm 308, 339, 341–3, 346, 348, 350
disgust 37, 66, 212, 447, 449
Disneyland 404, 406–10, 427–8
dithyramb 144–50, 152
Dostoevsky, Fyodor 230, 260, 265, 460
drama 71, 87, 237, 325, 327, 330–1, 333, 393
dream 143, 147, 247, 406, 411, 426
Duchamp, Marcel 301, 364–9, 406

emotion 14, 29, 212
enthusiasm, drunken 147
Eros 237, 239–40, 395, 417, 461
Euripides 90, 145, 155, 157–9, 333

film 167–70, 171–6, 458–9 *see also* cinema
freedom 43, 107, 432–4, 436
Freud, Sigmund 248–67, 363, 393–4

genius 35–41, 54–9, 61, 80, 87, 93, 96, 102, 105–6, 121, 128–9, 139, 144–7, 166, 285, 366, 371, 432, 434, 437–40, 451
  Apolline 148
  Greek 73
  invention of 335
  lyric 146
  and madness 57–8
  related to taste 36–8, 272
  Romantic 342
God 234, 280, 282, 295, 297, 302, 373, 408–9, 412–14, 417, 437, 453, 457, 459
Goethe 56–7, 76, 83, 88, 100–2, 105–6, 124, 133, 149, 153, 177, 222, 265

Hamlet 90, 96
Hamlet 65, 83, 89, 150
handicraft 33, 433–4

Hegel, G. W. F. 224, 244–7, 252, 278, 307, 370, 418, 440, 470
Heidegger, Martin 223–4, 226, 229–30, 233, 307–8, 330, 453, 458
hermeneutics 321–35, 342–3, 346–50, 442
hero 224, 272, 451
history 86, 224, 232, 285, 289, 296, 331, 342, 365, 388, 391, 406, 408, 410, 417, 452, 461–2, 464
Homer 36, 76, 83, 84, 88, 106, 123, 133, 143–5, 153, 176, 227, 230, 246, 327, 452
human condition 223–5, 228–9, 280, 282

idealism 248, 288, 327, 397, 417
Ideas 46–57, 60–6, 68–70, 72–3, 79–80, 89, 91, 102–3, 134, 368
ideology 225–7, 236, 341, 405, 410, 421, 428
  art as 235
  phallocratic 393
image 279, 291, 376–8, 414, 419
imagination 5, 12, 24, 41, 55, 99, 142, 235–6, 273, 335, 358, 401, 433–4, 438, 444
imitation 314, 327–30, 357, 410, 416, 424, 431–4, 436–9, 445
inspiration 105–6, 292
intention 223, 314
  authorial 256, 340, 348–9, 354
interpretation 329–30, 339–53, 355–6

Joyce, James 222–4, 228, 234, 377, 453, 457
judgment 5, 14, 31, 44, 272, 431

Kafka, Franz 224, 229–30, 233–4, 452
Kant, Immanuel 46, 48, 65, 113, 132, 246, 249–51, 321, 327, 329, 354, 367, 369, 370, 433–7, 439–44, 446–9
Kierkegaard, Søren 226, 247, 333
Klee, Paul 292, 299–301, 303, 365, 379–82
knowledge 50, 326, 364, 368, 435, 437, 456

language 148, 237, 261, 271, 277, 291, 307–18, 322, 327, 335, 339–47, 350, 355, 365–8, 371, 376, 378, 385, 388, 391–3, 421, 432, 437, 440–5, 452, 456
  common 254–5
  destruction of 281
  distinguished from speech 343
  literary 254–69, 370, 453
  painting as 274, 296
Last Supper, The 401, 405
lentils 113
Leonardo da Vinci 216–19, 247, 274, 300, 302, 401, 405
Lévi-Strauss, Claude 344–5, 347, 427
light 62–3, 70, 292–3, 297, 322
literary criticism 308, 310–12, 317–18 *see also* deconstruction
literature 276–87, 304, 313, 327–9, 341, 364, 366–8, 370, 371–3, 451–6
Los Angeles 175, 401–4, 408, 428

magic 170, 216, 243, 252, 291, 293–4, 411